Development Through Life

A Psychosocial Approach

Seventh Edition

Development Through Life

A Psychosocial Approach

SEVENTH EDITION

Barbara M. Newman

Philip R. Newman

The Ohio State University

Brooks/Cole • Wadsworth

I**T**P® An International Thomson Publishing Company

Belmont · Albany · Bonn · Boston · Cincinnati · Detroit · Johannesburg
London · Madrid · Melbourne · Mexico City · New York · Pacific Grove ·
Paris · Singapore · Tokyo · Toronto · Washington

Sponsoring Editor: Jim Brace-Thompson, Stacey Purviance
Project Development Editor: Jim Strandberg
Marketing Manager: Lauren Harp
Editorial Assistant: Bryon Granmo
Advertising Communications: Margaret Parks
Production Coordinator: Kirk Bomont
Production: Graphic World Inc.
Manuscript Editor: Sarah Aldridge
Permissions Editor: Mary Kay Hancharick
Interior Design: Jeanne Wolfgeher

Cover Design: Roy R. Neuhaus
Cover Art: Pablo Picasso, "Colombe Bleue avec Fleurs" 1957
Le Visage de la Paix by Pablo Picasso (1881–1973)
Private Collection/Bridgeman Art Library, London/New York
© 1999 Estate of Pablo Picasso/Artist Rights Society (ARS), New York
Art Editor: Graphic World Publishing Services
Photo Researcher: Sue Howard
Typesetting: Graphic World Inc.
Printing and Binding: The Courier Co., Inc./Kendallville
Cover Printing: Phoenix Color Corporation

Wadsworth Publishing Company
A division of International Thomson Publishing Inc.
I(T)P The ITP logo is a registered trademark under license.
Copyright © 1999, 1995, 1991, 1987, 1984, 1979, 1975 by Barbara M. Newman and Philip R. Newman

For more information, contact:

WADSWORTH PUBLISHING COMPANY
10 Davis Drive
Belmont, CA 94002
USA

International Thomson Publishing Europe
Berkshire House 168-173
High Holborn
London WC1V 7AA
England

Thomas Nelson Australia
102 Dodds Street
South Melbourne, 3205
Victoria, Australia

Nelson Canada
1120 Birchmount Road
Scarborough, Ontario
Canada M1K 5G4

International Thomson Editores
Seneca 53
Col. Polanco
11560 México, D. F., México

International Thomson Publishing GmbH
Königswinterer Strasse 418
53227 Bonn
Germany

International Thomson Publishing Asia
60 Albert Street #15-01
Albert Complex
Singapore 189969

International Thomson Publishing Japan
Hirakawacho Kyowa Building, 3F
2-2-1 Hirakawacho
Chiyoda-ku, Tokyo 102
Japan

Printed in the United States of America

10 9 8 7 6 5 4 3

Library of Congress Cataloging-in-Publication Data
Newman, Barbara M.
  Development through life : a psychosocial approach / Barbara M.
Newman, Philip R. Newman.—7th ed.
    p. cm.
  Includes bibliographical references and index.
  ISBN 0-534-35798-9
  1. Developmental psychology I. Newman, Philip R. II. Title.
BF713.N48 1998
155—dc21   98-42025
                              CIP

THIS BOOK IS PRINTED ON ACID-FREE RECYCLED PAPER

To Erik H. Erikson and Robert J. Havighurst

Brief Contents

Contents

3   *Major Theories for Understanding Human Development*   62

4 *The Period of Pregnancy and Prenatal Development* 90

5   *Infancy (First 24 Months)*   136

6   *Toddlerhood (Ages 2 and 3)*   *182*

7 *Early School Age (4–6 Years)* 224

8   *Middle Childhood (6–12 Years)* 262

9 *Early Adolescence (12–18 Years)* 302

I2   *Middle Adulthood (34–60 Years)*   430

I3   *Later Adulthood (60–75 Years)*   468

14   *Very Old Age (75 Until Death)*   504

Preface

When we wrote the first edition of *Development Through Life,* we had just completed graduate study and were in the midst of our early adulthood. Now, at the publication of the seventh edition, our oldest child has just been married, and we are entering a new transition as middle adulthood comes to a close. The psychosocial, lifespan perspective has been a valuable orienting framework for our scholarly work, as well as our personal lives, through the birth and parenting of our three children, the death of our parents, the successes, disappointments, and transitions of our work lives, and the conflicts and delights of our relationship as husband and wife. The themes of this book have allowed us to anticipate and cope with many of the normative challenges of adult life, as well as to maintain a hopeful outlook in the face of unanticipated crises. We hope that the ideas presented in this text will provide these same benefits for you.

In addition to enhancing self-understanding, the lifespan perspective is a means of understanding the challenges, conflicts, and achievements that are central to people living through stages other than our own. In this respect, it challenges our egocentrism. It assumes an interconnectedness among people at various periods of life and helps guide one's interactions with others so that they are optimally sensitive, supportive, and facilitative to the forces for growth at each life stage.

PERSPECTIVE

Development Through Life is a general introduction to the study of human development from conception through very old age. The text treats physical, intellectual, social, and emotional growth in each of 11 stages, emphasizing that development results from the interdependence of these areas at every stage. The text gives special attention to the conditions that promote optimal development throughout life. Psychosocial theory provides a conceptual framework for the text, highlighting the continuous interaction of individual competencies with the demands and resources of culture. Development is viewed as a product of genetic, maturational, societal, and self-directed factors.

Applying this integrating perspective to an analysis of human development has several advantages. First, although the subject matter is potentially overwhelming, the psychosocial framework helps to identify and highlight themes and directions of growth across the life span. Second, the framework helps readers to assess the influence of experiences during earlier life stages on later development, as well as the impact of later development on the course of earlier stages. It clarifies how one's past, present, and expectations about the future are systematically connected to the lives of those older and younger. Third, the framework offers a hopeful outlook on the total life course. The promise of continuous growth validates many of the struggles of childhood, adolescence, and early and middle adulthood.

FEATURES TO GUIDE STUDY

Several features have been added to the seventh edition that we expect will contribute to the learning process. Each chapter begins with an outline and a brief list of objectives. These can be used to guide the reader to the main topics and help summarize basic ideas of the chapter. Glossary terms are presented in boldface to help focus the review of new concepts. Boxed material within each chapter provides an extended discussion on a topic of special interest, illustrating how research helps to clarify a particular developmental topic. Each chapter ends with a case study and related questions. Our hope is that these cases will stimulate analytic thinking. They suggest new directions for thought about how developmental themes are revealed in individual lives. The cases can be a focus for self-study, or used in groups to foster discussion regarding the application of main ideas in the chapter.

The text is accompanied by a Student Study Guide. The guide is designed to improve mastery of the subject matter and to encourage students to take an active role in extending their learning through additional readings and observations. Each chapter of the Study Guide includes a pre- and post-test, matching terms and definitions, focusing questions, and suggestions for further study. Multiple choice questions from the Student Study Guide are also included in the Instructor's Manual Test Bank.

ORGANIZATION

Chapter 1 establishes the orientation and assumptions of the text and introduces the scientific process through which a systematic study of development becomes possible. Chapter 2 presents a detailed discussion of the basic concepts of psychosocial theory, including an analysis of its strengths and weaknesses. Proponents of psychosocial theory argue that human development can be conceptualized as a sequence of stages from conception through very old age. At each stage, several major tasks require new kinds of learning. Further, at each stage there arises a major developmental conflict, or psychosocial crisis. This conflict results from a discrepancy between one's competencies upon entering a particular stage and the demands of one's environment—including family, school, work, and community. Development occurs in an ever-changing social context; successfully resolving conflicts and accomplishing tasks at one stage of life allows us to cope with new demands our culture and members of our immediate social groups impose at the next stage. At each stage, we redefine ourselves and our relationships with others. Continuity and change, whether in response to internal pressures and environmental demands or as a result of our own choices and commitments, are both products of development.

Chapter 3 outlines significant ideas about change and growth from other theoretical perspectives. In this edition, the presentation of each theory has been shortened to highlight basic features. Each theory is followed by a section linking it to psychosocial theory, thereby providing greater understanding of how different theoretical perspectives contribute to the broad conceptualization of development. The range of theoretical concepts provides the intellectual structure for later discussions of physical, cognitive, social, and emotional development. These theories help readers analyze apparent conflicts among the maturational, societal, and individual forces toward growth. In presenting a variety of theoretical perspectives, we also offer a multidimensional source of information about individual behaviors and patterns of change.

In Chapter 4, fetal development is studied in relation to the pregnant woman and her social environment. Continued discoveries in the field of behavioral genetics have been included in this revision. We have emphasized research on the risks to fetal development associated with a pregnant woman's exposure to a wide range of substances, especially nicotine, alcohol, caffeine, other drugs, and environmental toxins. Poverty is highlighted as a context that increases risk factors for optimal fetal development. The topic of abortion is also examined in this chapter, and, in this edition, the characteristics of women who experience abortion and their emotional reactions are presented in new detail.

Chapters 5 through 14 trace basic patterns of normal growth and development in the remaining stages of human life: infancy, toddlerhood, early school age, middle childhood, early adolescence, later adolescence, early adulthood, middle adulthood, later adulthood, and very old age. In these chapters we consider how individuals organize and interpret their experience, noting changes both in their behavior and in the environmental demands they face. Each chapter begins with an examination of four or five of the critical developmental tasks of the stage. These tasks reflect global aspects of development, including physical growth and sensory and motor competence, cognitive maturation, social relationships, and self-understanding. We consider the psychosocial crisis of each stage in some detail. We also show how successfully resolving a crisis helps individuals develop a prime adaptive ego quality and how unsuccessful resolution leads to a core pathology. Although most people grow developmentally—albeit with pain and struggle—others do not. People who acquire core pathologies lead withdrawn, guarded lives; for the most part, they become psychologically unhealthy and, often, physically unhealthy as well.

We conclude each chapter by applying research and theory to a topic of societal importance at the given life stage. These applied topics provide an opportunity for students to link the research and theory about normative developmental processes to the analysis of pressing social concerns. Table 2.7 contains an overview of the basic tasks, crises, and applied topics for each stage of life.

THE SEVENTH EDITION

Changes in the seventh edition do not affect the basic structure of the book. We hope that many new sections bring greater clarity, elaboration, or a fresh way of thinking to a topic. Many new references from 1995–1998 have been included, updating census data and integrating new studies in the narrative. References, citations, and credits have been moved to the back of the book.

We have continued to increase the focus on information about development in cultures outside the United States and expanded the picture of how the ethnic subcultures in the United States influence the processes and directions of development. The notion that development is a product of the continuous interaction between individuals' genetically guided characteristics and cultural resources, beliefs, and values is illustrated time and again in the discussion of cultural and subcultural comparisons. This edition introduces numerous examples of the ways that poverty, discrimination, and various forms of societal oppression affect individual development. These revisions help to raise questions about which aspects of development are universal and which are shaped by society. They help us appreciate the wide range of contexts in which development takes place and the remarkable capacities for growth and adaptation that are evidenced at every period of life.

We continue to emphasize the theme of genetic and environmental interaction. Research in human development reveals the dynamic interplay between genetically based human capacities and the sociocultural context in which they are nurtured and expanded. We have tried to reflect this in many of the developmental tasks discussed, including language, self-regulation, emotional development, motor development, the elaboration of cognitive skills, orientation toward parenting, the formation of intimate relationships, the development of capacities necessary to carry out productive work, and the ability to cope with the physical changes of aging.

The work of Erik Erikson and Robert Havighurst have guided and inspired our own intellectual development. The combined contributions of these scholars have shaped the basic direction of psychosocial theory and have guided an enormous amount of research in human development. They directed us to look at the process of growth and change across the life span. They recognized the intimate interweaving of the individual's life story with the sociohistorical context, emphasizing societal pressures that call for new levels of functioning at each life stage. In their writing, they communicated an underlying optimism about each person's resilience, adaptability, and immense capacity for growth. At the same time, they wrote with a moral passion of our responsibility as teachers, therapists, parents, scholars, and citizens to create a caring society. We celebrate these ideas and continue their expression in the seventh edition of *Development Through Life*.

ACKNOWLEDGMENTS

We express our appreciation to many students, colleagues, and friends who shared their ideas with us. Brenda Lohman and Mary Myers played a key role in helping us meet production deadlines. Our children, Sam, Abe, and Rachel, made constructive comments about the content, appearance, and tone of the book. For this edition, Rachel served as a technical assistant. To each new edition, our children bring new talents and perspectives that enrich our efforts. The seventh edition was produced under the guidance of wonderful editors, Jim Brace-Thompson, Vicki Knight, and Stacey Purviance. Others who helped bring this edition to life include Kirk Bomont, Roy Neuhaus, and Jim Strandberg at Brooks/Cole, photo researcher Sue Howard, and staff at Graphic World, especially Anne Gassett. We were very lucky to have had the benefit of their creative energy. Finally, we acknowledge the thoughtful, constructive comments and suggestions of the following reviewers: Robert Bornstein, Miami University Oxford; Linda Breytspraak, University of Missouri-Kansas City; Sheldon S. Brown, North Shore Community College; Llewellyn Cornelius, University of Maryland at Baltimore; Lena Ericksen, Western Washington University; JoAnn Farver, University of Southern California; Tina Feiger, Santa Monica College; Elaine Haglund, California State University Long Beach; Vivian Harper, San Joaquin Delta College; Terry Isbell, Northwestern State University; Tim Loboschefski, Sweetbriar College; Lyla S. Maynard, Des Moines Area Community College; Nancy Billings Meyer, Northeast Iowa Community College; Jeffrey Nagelbush, Ferris State University; John O'Donnell, Rose State College; Joan Rafter, Hudson County Community College; Paul Silverman, University of Montana; Sharron Singleton-Bowie, Barry University; Amy Stivelman, Molloy College; Ilga Svechs, Case Western Reserve University; Daniel Tovar, Portland State University; David Yarbrough, University of Southwestern Louisiana; and Elizabeth Yost-Hammer, Belmont University.

Barbara M. Newman
Philip R. Newman

Development Through Life

A Psychosocial Approach

Seventh Edition

Chapter I

*T*he study of human development reflects the interdependence of people at all ages. Children become adults; adults guide and nurture children. Issues of childhood are revisited in every major adult transition; and issues of adulthood are foreshadowed in each stage of childhood.

The Development Through Life Perspective

Chapter Objectives

- To introduce the basic assumptions that underlie the organization and focus of the text.
- To introduce the psychosocial approach, including the interrelationships among the biological, psychological, and societal systems.
- To define the scientific process and review basic research principles for the study of human development.
- To consider the ethical guidelines that should be used in conducting research with human subjects.
- To note historical changes in life expectancy and examine the implications of these changes for the study of development over the life span.

Patrick Jonathan Carmichael was born the son of a freeman, who earned his way out of slavery in North Carolina before moving to Alabama and the Rump plantation. Carmichael attended Snowhill Institute, which was modeled after Booker T. Washington's Tuskegee Institute. It was here that the dream for his own school began. After graduating from high school, he taught for five years, then founded Purdue Hill Industrial High.

"The state put up just seventy-five dollars a year for expenses," Carmichael says. "Students paid tuition of twenty-five cents a year and paid in chickens or cans of syrup if they didn't have the money. You couldn't get a dime out of a state to build a Negro school back then. I'd write letters to people all over the country who I thought had a little charity about them to help us. I'd be the last man to put his light out because I'd be writing letters."

"He got twenty-five dollars a month," Carmichael's son adds. "He fed us kids by farming, getting up before dawn to work the fields, raise chickens and cattle and pigs. He had a big garden. All his earning went back into the school. At night he'd write those letters to wealthy people in Boston or New York, trying to get a little money for the school. He was persistent. A little at a time. People in the area built the school. It started out as a one-room school with one teacher and eleven students and grew to a twelve-room school with two hundred and fifty students and ten teachers."

. . . Patrick Jonathan Carmichael is now living with his son and daughter-in-law. He is 101 but has been with them for only the past few years. After retiring from his career in education in 1958, he lived alone on his farm until he broke his hip after going out to feed his cattle. He was 97.

"I didn't get along with my father when I was younger," says his son. "He was such a hard-working, disciplined man. Now it's different. It's like we're getting another chance. I have to take care of him, do

things for him like shave him. He needs me and we're developing more of a buddy relationship." (Heynan, 1990, p. 9. Patrick Jonathan Carmichael, born 1886, interviewed in 1987.)

Think for a moment about Patrick Jonathan Carmichael: his hopes, determination, sacrifices, family, accomplishments, disappointments, and the new challenges he must have faced as he retired from education, lived alone, and formed new, interdependent relationships with his son and daughter-in-law. Think of living 100 years—so many changes and so much to learn; so many losses and so many victories. What do we know of development through life? How can we conceptualize the dynamic development of individuals within the contexts of their societies, the period of history in which they grew up and entered adulthood, their families, their values and goals, and the obstacles they faced? How can we preserve the intriguing uniqueness of individual lives and still begin to detect patterns of change and growth? These are some of the challenges facing the broad discipline of human development.

The study of human development is puzzling and relatively unexplored. If we are to understand it, we must study how maturation and experience shape beliefs and expectations at each stage of development. Our goal is to gain a more accurate picture of how individuals make sense of their experiences, adapt to their environments, cope with challenges, and continue to develop from one period of life to the next. This process is as individual as each person's life story and is influenced heavily by such factors as gender, ethnicity, socioeconomic status, geography, sexual orientation, and physical abilities and disabilities. Yet common patterns of organization and meaning allow us to know and care for one another, and contribute to one another's well-being.

This chapter provides a brief introduction to four topics that are central to the study of the life span. First, we outline our assumptions about human de-

velopment that guide the orientation of the text. Second, we introduce the broad concept of a psychosocial approach to development. Third, we highlight basic principles of the scientific process from which much of our knowledge about development is derived. Finally, we introduce data about life expectancy in order to start you thinking in a concrete way about the course of your own life and the decisions you make that may directly impact your own life story. ❖

Each life story is one of continuity and change. The family is shown during two widely separated periods of time, consists of the same people, recognizable yet changed. Maturation and experience interact to produce a continually modified family group, but the sense of affection and closeness remains.

ASSUMPTIONS OF THE TEXT

Our perspective on development through life embraces the following four assumptions that are critical to the organization and focus of this book:

1. *Growth occurs at every period of life, from conception through very old age.* At each period, new capacities emerge, new roles are undertaken, new challenges must be faced, and, as a result, a new orientation toward self and society unfolds.
2. *Individual lives show continuity and change as they progress through time.* An awareness of the processes that contribute to both continuity and change is central to an understanding of human development.
3. *We need to understand the whole person, because we function in an integrated manner.* To achieve such an understanding we need to study the major developments in physical, social, emotional, and cognitive capacities and their interrelationships. We also need to study actions, the many forms of observable behavior.
4. *Every person's behavior must be analyzed in the context of relevant settings and personal relationships.* Human beings are highly skilled in adapting to their environment. The meaning of a given behavior pattern or change must be interpreted in light of the significant physical and social environments in which it occurs.

A PSYCHOSOCIAL APPROACH: THE INTERACTION OF THE BIOLOGICAL, PSYCHOLOGICAL, AND SOCIETAL SYSTEMS

Erik Erikson (1963, p. 37) wrote that human life as the individual experiences it is produced by the interaction and modification of three major systems: the biological system, the psychological system, and the societal system.

The Biological System

The **biological system** includes all those processes necessary for the physical functioning of the organism (Figure 1.1). Sensory capacities, motor responses, and the workings of the respiratory, endocrine, and circulatory systems are all biological processes. They develop and change as a consequence of genetically guided maturation, environmental resources such as nutrition and sunlight, exposure to environmental toxins, encounters with accidents and diseases, and life habits related to daily exercise, eating, sleeping, and the use of drugs.

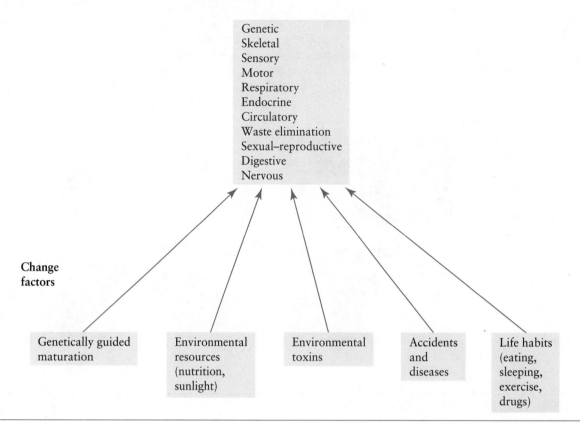

FIGURE 1.1
The biological system

The Psychological System

The **psychological system** includes those mental processes central to the person's ability to make meaning of experiences and take action (Figure 1.2). Emotion; memory and perception; problem solving, language, and symbolic abilities; and our orientation to the future—all require the use of psychological processes. The psychological system provides the resources for processing information and navigating reality. Like the biological processes, the psychological processes develop and change over one's life span. Change is guided in part by genetic information. The capacity for intellectual functioning and the direction of cognitive maturation are genetically guided. A number of genetically transmitted diseases result in intellectual impairment and a reduced capacity for learning. Change also results from the accumulation of experiences and from encounters with various educational settings. The psychological processes are further enhanced by numerous other life experiences, such as sports, camping, travel, reading, and talking with people. Finally, change can be self-directed. A person can decide to pursue a new interest, to learn another language, or to adopt a new set of ideas. Through self-insight or perhaps psychotherapy, one can begin to think about oneself and others in a new light.

The Societal System

The **societal system** includes those processes through which a person becomes integrated into society (Figure 1.3). Societal influences include social roles, rituals, cultural myths, social expectations, leadership styles, communication patterns, family organization, ethnic and subcultural influences, political and religious ideologies, patterns of economic prosperity or poverty and war or peace, and exposure to racism, sexism, and other forms of discrimination, intolerance, or intergroup hostility. The impact of the societal system on psychosocial development results largely from interpersonal relationships, often relationships with significant others.

Societal processes change over one's life span. One of the most striking instances of such change occurs when a person moves from one culture to another. In this case,

FIGURE 1.2
The psychological system

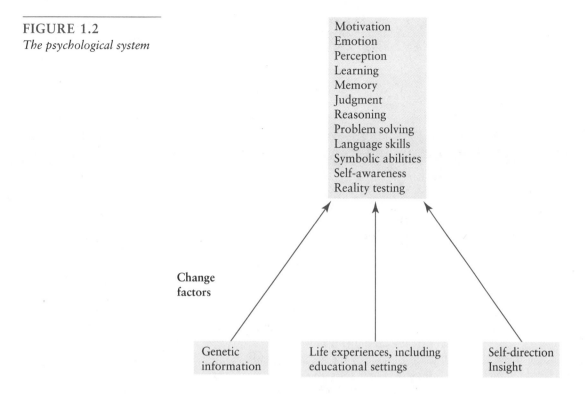

Motivation
Emotion
Perception
Learning
Memory
Judgment
Reasoning
Problem solving
Language skills
Symbolic abilities
Self-awareness
Reality testing

Change
factors

Genetic
information

Life experiences, including
educational settings

Self-direction
Insight

FIGURE 1.3
The societal system

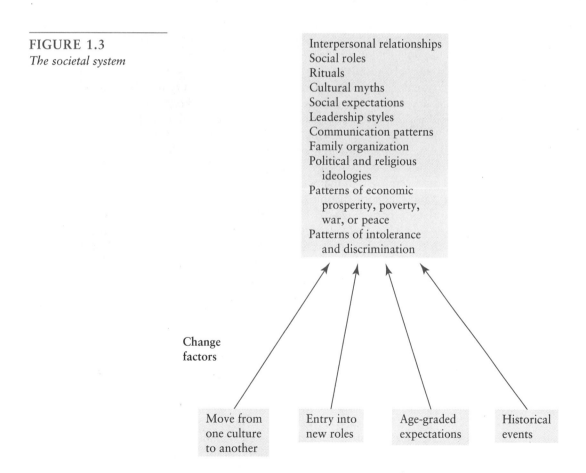

Interpersonal relationships
Social roles
Rituals
Cultural myths
Social expectations
Leadership styles
Communication patterns
Family organization
Political and religious
   ideologies
Patterns of economic
   prosperity, poverty,
   war, or peace
Patterns of intolerance
   and discrimination

Change
factors

Move from
one culture
to another

Entry into
new roles

Age-graded
expectations

Historical
events

Poverty represents a powerful characteristic of the societal system. Children growing up in poverty are exposed to stressors and risks that can severely restrict development. What factors might help reduce the negative impact of poverty?

many of one's fundamental assumptions about oneself and one's social relationships are modified. Historical events—conditions of war or peace, being the victor or the vanquished, living in prosperity or poverty—influence how people in a given culture perceive themselves. For example, the conditions of World War II—forced military service, decreases in the availability of resources and the resulting system of rationing, the increased involvement of women in the labor market, the bombing of European cities, the unveiling of unprecedented human atrocities, the explosion of the first nuclear bomb over Japan—had a lasting impact on the values and ideology of the people who lived through that period. In recent times, the AIDS epidemic has had a significant influence on numerous domains of personal and family life, including changing sexual practices, new approaches to sex education among youth, greater visibility of the gay and lesbian communities, modifications in health care practices and workplace practices, increased attention to the care-giving relationship within families, and new concerns about privacy, to name a few.

The influence of society on an individual changes over the life course. Entry into new roles brings new demands and behaviors. Most societies have expectations about competence and participation of members in settings and roles that change for each stage of life. These expectations may be in harmony or in conflict with the maturation of the biological and psychological processes.

The Psychosocial Impact of Poverty

In thinking about the impact of societal factors on development, we want to highlight the context of poverty as a major obstacle to optimal development. Racism, sexism, ageism, homophobia, and discrimination against individuals with physical, intellectual, and emotional disabilities are other examples. However, under conditions of poverty, individuals have fewer options and less opportunity to escape or avoid these other societal deterrents. Poverty has potentially powerful and pervasive effects on the biological and psychological systems across the life span. In and of itself, poverty does not place inevitable limits on development. There are many instances, both famous and less well-known, of children who grew up in poverty and achieved eminence. We need only think of the case of Patrick Jonathan Carmichael, introduced at the beginning of this chapter, to recognize that many children flourish under conditions of meager family resources, and that some people choose to live very modest material lives in order to achieve other important goals. However, it is well documented that poverty increases the risks individuals face, including risks associated with malnourishment, poor quality health care, living in a hazardous physical environment, living in a dangerous neighborhood, and participating in an ineffective school system. Poverty is linked with reduced access to the basic resources associated with survival (Duncan et al., 1994). Because of the complex and pervasive impact of poverty on development, we introduce it here as a fundamental societal theme (Box 1.1). Issues related to the impact of poverty on patterns of development and family life will be addressed in more detail in subsequent chapters.

Overview of the Psychosocial Approach

The **psychosocial approach** highlights the continuous interaction of the individual and the social environment. At each period of life, people spend much of their time mastering a unique group of psychological tasks that are essential for social adaptation within their society. Each life stage brings a normative crisis, which can be viewed as a tension between one's competencies and the new demands of society. The resolution of each crisis provides a new set of social abilities that influences the person's general orientation to the succeeding stages.

BOX 1.1 POVERTY

Conditions Leading to Poverty

In the first half of this century, most poverty was a result of nonemployment, unemployment, or work involving low or temporary wages (Hernandez, 1993). Since the 1960s, however, three major factors have contributed to the increase in the numbers of families living in poverty: the decline in well-paying, blue-collar jobs; large increases in single-mother households due to increases in births to adolescent mothers and increases in the divorce rate; and the decline in the value of federal benefits such as Aid to Families with Dependent Children (Huston, et al., 1994).

Poverty is transitory for some families, as when a wage earner becomes unemployed and then finds new work, but persistent over the life course for others. For unmarried women who become mothers in adolescence, poverty is often a result of interrupted education, the inability to work full time (usually because of time needed to care for their children), and the low-paying jobs that are available to those who have limited educational attainment. In addition, many of these women are growing up in families that are already poor.

Divorce places many women and their children into poverty. In many instances, the family was already encountering financial strain, which is known to be one of the primary factors associated with divorce. However, following divorce, 27% of divorced women and their children fall below the poverty line (Chase-Landsdale, 1993). The level of poverty experienced by newly divorced women is aggravated by the failure of many fathers to pay child support. Poverty for these families is often temporary, since many divorced women remarry or are able to find adequate employment after a year or two. However, the negative impact of poverty on children coupled with the stresses associated with experiencing parental divorce are likely to affect a child's adjustment (Demo & Ganong, 1994).

African-American, Hispanic, and Native American families are overrepresented among the poor, and their experiences of poverty are likely to be more long lasting. For individuals in these ethnic groups, the stresses associated with racism and cultural alienation are likely to be combined with the emotional distress associated with persistent poverty, producing even greater challenges for accomplishing the developmental tasks of each life stage (McLoyd, 1990; Duncan et al., 1994; Corcoran & Chaudry, 1997).

Factors that Mediate the Impact of Poverty

Like every other environmental factor, poverty has a differential impact on children and families. Although we are still a long way from fully understanding how some children escape its negative effects, we do know that many children who live in poverty continue to develop optimally. Some scholars have emphasized the notion of **resilience** as a characteristic of children. Resilient children appear to have inner strengths that permit them to get the resources they need, to define their situation in a positive way, and to transcend their lives' challenges (Garmezy, 1991). These children are characterized by an easy, sociable temperament. They are active, seeking out stimulation and evoking responses from others. They are bright and able to solve problems readily. They usually have at least one supportive, loving relationship with a family member and they have access to supportive contacts outside the family.

In addition to the resilience of children, there are other resources that help parents buffer the impact of poverty. Among low-income, single African-American mothers, for example, a higher level of education, the presence of an emotionally supportive social network, and strong religious beliefs all help reduce the negative effects of poverty (Kelley et al., 1992; McLoyd, 1990; Jayakovy et al., 1993). Other studies of factors that mediate the negative effects of poverty on children have identified aspects of the mother's mental health, especially low levels of depression and active behavioral coping as important additions to the resources mentioned above (Duncan et al., 1994). Persistent poverty in a small child's life is a strong predictor of a wide variety of physical and mental health problems. In contrast, parents who are able to see their poverty as transitory and to take steps to move out of poverty may also differ with respect to their supportiveness and responsiveness to their children.

Throughout life, personal relationships occupy our attention. Some of these relationships are more important than others, but their quality and diversity provide a basis for the study of one's psychosocial development. As we progress through the stages of life, most of us develop an increasing capacity to initiate new relationships and to innovate in our thoughts and actions so as to direct the course of our lives.

We strive to make sense of our experiences. The meaning we derive depends on our beliefs about ourselves, our relationships with others, and the world as our society defines it. This meaning changes over the course of life as a result of the maturation of the biological and psychological systems and as participation in the societal system changes. Think about the concept of love as an example. In infancy, love is almost entirely physical. It is the pervasive sense of comfort and security that we feel in the presence of our caregivers. By adolescence, the idea of love includes loyalty, emotional closeness, and sexuality. In adulthood, the concept of love may expand to include a new emphasis on companionship and open communication. The need to be loved and to give love remain important throughout life, but the self we bring to a loving rela-

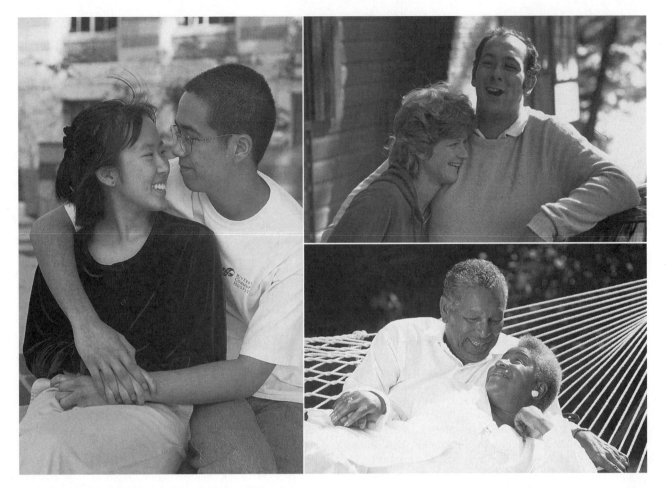

The desire to experience a loving relationship remains strong throughout life. However, the self one brings to a loving relationship changes at each stage. How might experiences of love change from adolescence to early adulthood to later adulthood?

tionship, the context within which the relationship is established, and the signs we look for as evidence of love change with age.

Humans struggle to define themselves—to achieve a sense of identity—through a sense of connectedness with certain other people and groups and through feelings of distinctiveness from others. We establish categories that define whom we are connected to, whom we care about, and which of our own qualities we admire. We also establish categories that define those to whom we are not connected, those whom we do not care about, and those qualities of our own that we reject or deny. These categories provide us with an orientation toward certain kinds of people and away from others, toward certain life choices and away from others.

The psychosocial approach seeks to understand the internal experiences that are the products of interactions among the biological, psychological, and societal processes. Changes in one of the three systems—biological, psychological, or societal—generally bring about changes in the others. During the 20th century, remarkable progress has been made in bringing together observations, theories, and research to build a scientific knowledge base for the study of development across the life span. In the next section, we describe the fundamental elements of the scientific process that lead to the gradual building of a systematic understanding of development.

THE SCIENTIFIC PROCESS

The **scientific process** allows us to create a body of knowledge. Essentially it is a method for developing information that contains within it procedures for ensuring that the information will be correct. In this section, we describe the process through which scientific knowledge is achieved (Figure 1.4) and then discuss the fundamental components of research design, including selecting a sample, a method, and an approach to data collection; evaluating the existing research; and conducting research according to ethical principles.

Scientific thinking usually begins when one attempts to reason systematically about a puzzling idea or observation. The observer tries to figure out how the observation may be explained and thinks about what leads to what and which things cause other things to happen. As a result, one develops a set of interrelated ideas to account for the observation. These ideas, often referred to as **assumptions, hypotheses,** and **predictions,** constitute a theory. The theory is not an end in itself, but a way to get going.

The next step of the scientific process is to test the theory through experimentation and observation. A good theory contains specific predictions about cause and effect. After the predictions are stated, one must figure out how to test whether they are accurate.

One must **operationalize** the concepts of a theory in order to test them. That is, one must translate an abstract concept into something that can be observed and measured. Consider the concept of personal attraction. One who decided to measure personal attraction, for example, could think about the various ways in which people show they are attracted to each other. One might observe that people who are mutually attracted tend to look into each other's eyes rather than off to the side. The amount of eye contact is a way of defining the concept of attraction so that it can be observed and measured. Eye contact thus becomes an **operational definition** of personal attraction.

Often the theory is not tested by the same person who develops it because this person may therefore have some personal investment in demonstrating that the theory is correct. The scientific process usually involves the ideas of more than one person. Sometimes people with different points of view engage in a debate as they try to refute positions they find flawed. At other times two or more people work on different phases of theory building, experimentation, and evaluation.

If a theory is fruitful, many researchers working in independent groups will devise ways of extending and clarifying it. Working in this way, as a community of scholars, helps to ensure that a theory will not be confirmed simply because of the theorist's per-

FIGURE 1.4
The scientific process

Puzzling observation

Constructing a theory
(assumptions, hypotheses, and predictions)

Operationalizing the theory
(making concepts measurable)

Testing the theory
(systematic observation and experimentation)

Evaluating the results
(statistical analysis)

Accept the theory
Revise the theory
Reject the theory
Develop a new theory

sonal biases. For example, Erik Erikson was not the person who tested his psychosocial theory. Researchers such as James Marcia, Ruthellen Josselson, Alan Waterman, and Jacob Orlofsky pursued some of Erikson's hypotheses about identity development and devised strategies for operationalizing Erikson's concepts, especially the psychosocial crisis of personal identity versus identity confusion. Their work clarified Erikson's concepts and supported many of his views about the relation of personal identity to subsequent development. You will read more about this in Chapter 10.

The final phase of the scientific process involves an evaluation of the observations. Statistical techniques help determine the likelihood that observations could have happened by chance or not. Observations that appear to be a result of chance do not confirm the theory. If the observations have a low probability of having occurred by chance, one says that they are **statistically significant.** If statistically significant results support the theory's predictions, one is likely to accept them as providing evidence for the theory. Nevertheless, scientists may continue to examine the propositions of the theory, involving new participants or new methods.

What if the results do not fit the theory's predictions? One approach is to reexamine the methods and design of the study. Perhaps the key concepts were not measured appropriately or the sample was biased in some way. When results of research are inconclusive or contrary to the predictions, scholars may try another research approach before revising the theory. But when several different studies fail to support the hypotheses, we tend to lose confidence in the entire structure of the theory. We may revise or discard the theory and begin to develop an alternative explanation for our observations.

In summary, the scientific process consists of creating a theory, testing it through research, and modifying, rejecting, or accepting it. To the extent that it is confirmed by the scientific process, a theory helps us interpret many observations about reality.

The sections that follow provide an overview of the basic principles of the research process as it is applied to the study of human development. In reviewing these principles, you will begin to grasp the challenge of trying to arrive at a systematic body of knowledge about the patterns of continuity and change in the human life course. At the same time you will encounter concepts that will improve your ability to ask critical, analytic questions about the research discussed in subsequent chapters and elsewhere.

Scientific Observation

Scientific observation is characterized by three essential qualities: it must be objective, repeatable, and systematic (Creswell, 1994). These qualities may or may not be characteristic of the way you make observations in your personal life.

Objective observations accurately reflect the events that are taking place. They are not unduly influenced by what the observer expects or hopes to see. Suppose, for example, that you want an objective assessment of your child's talent for playing the guitar. You are unlikely to get objective feedback from friends or relatives. Because they know you, and presumably would not like to insult you, they may be inclined to slant their answers to please you.

A more objective approach might be to include an audio tape of your child's guitar playing with tapes of ten other children. You would then ask another person to give the tapes to ten people who do not know you or your child and ask each of them to rate the quality of musical ability demonstrated on each tape. You may or may not like the outcome, but at least your method would be more objective. It would reveal what other people think of your child's musical ability without being biased by any feelings about you or your child.

Social science research is always vulnerable to the theoretical biases and value orientations of the researchers. Certain practices of research design, sampling, and methodology are used to help overcome biases and build a higher level of objectivity into the process. However, many will argue that it is impossible to be entirely objective. One's orientation toward framing research questions and interpreting the results are always influenced to some degree by one's cultural and historical contexts that influence values, beliefs, and assumptions that guide the research process. That is why it is so important for the research carried out by one investigator to be repeatable.

If research is **repeatable,** then others could carry out a similar investigation and observe the same results as the original investigator. In order for this to occur, the original investigator must carefully define all the procedures and equipment used in the study, describe all the essential characteristics of the participants (such as age, sex, and social class background), and describe the setting or situation where the observations were made. Since there are so many ways that one group of participants might differ from another, and so many different ways that observations can be made, repeatability is an important part of building a body of social science knowledge.

Usually a problem or process is investigated by an individual or research team, taking great care to make sure that observations are unbiased, orderly, carefully collected and recorded, and comprehensive. In order to insure that the results of a study are accurate, the original researchers encourage other investigators to repeat the study to see if the same results are observed.

A **systematic** approach ensures that research is done in a careful, orderly way. Scientists have a framework of essential questions that they strive to answer based on what is already known and what certain theories predict. They approach research by having clear objectives, carefully defining the purpose of the research and the specific methods they will use to reach those objectives. Although sometimes discoveries are made by accident, scientific research typically does not poke here and there at unrelated events.

Research Design

Research investigations are designed just as cars, bridges, and buildings are designed. In formal, scientific work, research design is often conducted in meetings where small groups of scholars try to think up the most appropriate, objective, and systematic approach for answering their questions. Scientists know that the information they gain from conducting research will be heavily influenced by the characteristics of the participants who are involved in their study, the kinds of data that are gathered, and the conditions under which the data are gathered. The principles of research design focus on the sample that is selected to participate in the study, the method that is used to gather information, the approach to studying change, and the statistical techniques that are used to analyze the data (Miller, 1991). In this chapter, we focus on the first three: sampling, methods, and designs for studying change.

Selecting a Sample

Sampling is the approach for choosing participants who will be included in the study. The nature of the questions that are being addressed usually has implications for the best way to identify the sample. If the study is about some universal principle of development, it should apply to individuals from a wide variety of family and social backgrounds. For example, studies of normal language development should include children from various ethnic, racial, social class, and cultural backgrounds. One cannot argue for universal principles if the research has shown the process or pattern to be true only for a homogeneous group of children.

Every sample is taken from a population. The **population** is the large group to which the findings of the research are intended to apply. There is no single, predetermined population; the relevant population depends on the purpose and scope of the research. The **sample** is a smaller subgroup of the larger population that will participate in the study. For example, the population of interest might be adolescents in the United States who graduate from high school but do not go on to college. In 1994, roughly 2 million adolescents aged 18 and 19 had graduated from high school but were not enrolled in any postsecondary school (U.S. Dept. of Education, 1995). No research study is going to include all of those adolescents. So a sample is drawn that is expected to be representative of the population. Under ideal conditions, the participants in any study of this population ought to have the same general characteristics (such as family income; race; gender; urban, suburban, or rural environment; and high school academic background) as the population from which the sample was selected. The sample and the population from which the sample is taken determine what generalizations may be made from the research findings. We must be careful not to assume that research findings based on one sample are generalizable for all ages, both sexes, all racial and ethnic groups, all social classes, or individuals from other cultures.

The generalizability of research depends heavily on the sampling process. Studies that focus on older adults often require interviewers who can meet face to face with participants in a variety of settings. What factors might limit the researcher's ability to sample older adults?

Four approaches to sampling are common in the research literature. Each one has somewhat different implications for the generalizability of the findings.

Random Samples

In a random sample, each person in a given population has an equal chance of being included. The researcher may ensure equal opportunity by putting each person's name on a slip of paper and then choosing some of the slips blindly, or by selecting names from a list at random by using numbers produced by a random number generator.

Stratified Samples

Participants are deliberately selected from a variety of levels (strata) or subgroups within the population. For example, the males and females in the sample might be selected to correspond to the proportion of males and females who attend a certain college or who are employed in a certain industry. Within each group, however, the participants are selected at random.

Matched Groups

The researcher selects two or more groups of subjects who are similar on many dimensions. In most studies using matched groups, participants in one group receive some type of treatment or participate in some type of experimental intervention that the participants in the other group do not receive. In this way, effects of the treatment can be observed since the participants are thought to be very similar in all other respects.

Volunteer Samples

Participants are solicited by advertisements, notes to teachers or parents asking for participants, or requests to professionals or groups of potential participants. Those who are included in the study are selected from among those who volunteer.

Strengths and Weaknesses of Approaches to Sampling

What are some of the strengths and weaknesses of these approaches to sampling? Random sampling and stratified sampling are most likely to ensure that a sample is representative of the population from which it is drawn. If each person in the population had an equal chance of being included in the study, then the outcome ought to be equally likely to apply to those who did not participate as to those who did. The method that places the greatest limits on generalization is volunteer sampling. One never knows what type of person will volunteer to participate in social science research. Can you think of how reliance on volunteers may produce special problems? For example, people who volunteer to participate in research may be especially in need of money, have more time on their hands, or be hoping to find some kind of help as a result of participating in the research.

Regardless of these difficulties, volunteer samples are widely used. Frequently the only way to study a certain question is to ask for volunteers. Some of the research findings discussed in the text are based upon **clinical studies.** This usually means that the participants have been involved in some type of treatment program or are on the waiting list to receive clinical treatment. These studies are especially important for understanding the causes of clinical conditions, the developmental paths or patterns these conditions exhibit, the impact of certain interventions, and the long-term consequences of these conditions. Without this voluntary participation, there would be no way to begin to document the effectiveness of treatment. At the same time, one must be cautious not to generalize findings from clinical studies to the population as a whole.

Clinical samples often focus on children or adults who are undergoing a special, experimental treatment or who have undergone some unusual trauma. Without their participation, we could not learn about the potential benefits of new forms of treatment or intervention.

Research Methods

A variety of methods has been used to study development. Each one has its strengths and weaknesses, allowing the investigator to focus on one set of behaviors at the expense of others. The choice of method must fit the problem under study. Six general categories of developmental research are described here: observation, case study, interviews, surveys, tests, and experimentation. These methods have all contributed to the discovery of knowledge, and as you read further in the text you will find examples of each method. Some techniques, especially observation, case study, and interview, are more commonly used in the exploratory phase of research when investigators are trying to uncover basic themes or dimensions of a problem. Other methods, especially observation using a predetermined coding scheme, experimentation, and surveys and tests, tend to be used in the hypothesis testing phase of the research process.

Observation

Direct **observation** of children in their home and school environments is one of the oldest methods for studying development (Kessen, 1965). Researchers have used mothers' diaries and observation logs to gather information about behavior in intimate settings that could not be known in any other way. Jean Piaget was guided by the observations of his own children in the formulation of his theory of cognition. Today, some researchers conduct observations in the homes, schools, and day-care centers where children typically spend their time. Others bring children and their families or friends into "homelike" laboratory settings where they can watch children's behaviors under somewhat more constant and controlled physical conditions (Kochanska, Kuczynski et al., 1989).

Naturalistic observation, in which behavior in a setting is carefully observed without any other kinds of manipulation, provides insight about how things occur in the real world. In some instances, researchers go into a setting to observe the full range of interactions and behavior patterns. Based on their field notes, they begin to develop hypotheses or tentative explanations about the meaning of the behaviors. Then, they may test these hypotheses through more focused observation or through more controlled experimentation.

In other instances, researchers use observation to examine a specific behavior or relationship. They may be looking for different forms of peer aggression, patterns of social cooperation, or conditions that promote cross-gender interactions. In these cases, the observers limit the scope of their observations to behaviors that are relevant to their concerns.

The technology of videotaping has expanded the use of observational techniques for developmental research. A videotaped record can be reviewed over and over again. Several observers can watch a tape, stop it, and discuss what they saw. The same events can be observed from several points of view. For example, researchers interested in children's play might videotape a child's free play in three or four different settings such as day care, a park, at home, and with friends. Several observers might review the tapes, each one rating different aspects of the behavior. Videotaped records can also be slowed to frame-by-frame viewing, allowing for very detailed microanalysis of behavior. Facial expressions and motor sequences have been examined using this approach.

Observational studies lend themselves to an examination of correlation rather than causation. **Correlation** refers to a statistical analysis of the strength and direction of the relationships among variables. It reflects the degree to which knowing the value of one variable, such as age, allows one to predict the level of another variable, such as helpfulness. In observational research, many correlational questions can be addressed. Do children who often play alone show more creativity in their play? Do younger children use fewer words to describe an object than older children? Do children who are most aggressive with their peers at day care also act aggressively at home?

The **correlation coefficient** is a numeric index of the strength of relationship between variables that can range from values of $+1.0$ to -1.0. Let us take, as an example, the correlation between popularity with peers and aggressiveness. If higher levels of aggressiveness are associated with higher popularity, the correlation is positive (toward $+1.0$). If higher levels of aggressiveness are associated with lower popularity, the correlation is negative (toward -1.0). If there is no systematic relationship between aggressiveness and popularity, the correlation is close to 0 (Figure 1.5). A correlation of .40 suggests that there is a positive relationship between aggressiveness and popularity, but that popularity cannot be predicted entirely or even predominantly by knowing about one's level of aggressiveness. Research that actually focuses on the relationship between popularity with peers and aggressiveness is discussed in the chapters on early and middle childhood.

A strong correlation between two variables only shows that there is an association between them. It does not provide information about causation. Knowing that aggression is negatively correlated with popularity does not necessarily mean that being aggressive causes children to be rejected by peers. It could be that some other factor, such as mistrust of others, accounts for both aggression and peer rejection.

In a naturalistic setting, observers can capture the flow of ongoing behavior and note the interactions among participants. Here, the observer watches as teacher and children engage in a reading lesson. Her presence does not appear to interfere with the children's interest and attention. What kinds of behaviors might be the focus of this observational study?

Note: Each point represents one person measured on both variables.

FIGURE 1.5
Patterns reflecting positive, zero, and negative correlations

Strengths and Limitations of the Observation Method. One strength of naturalistic observation is the ability to capture naturally occurring responses as they take place. Another strength is the ability to allow children's behaviors to guide the researcher's conceptualization. Rather than setting up a specific task or group of questions and having children respond, the observer examines the full range of relevant behaviors and builds an interpretation of the meaning of the events from the patterns that have been observed.

Observational research also has weaknesses. It is often difficult to establish agreement among observers about exactly what occurred. Think about the times that you and a friend have been in the same situation but have entirely different reactions to what is happening or describe it very differently to a third party. Typically two or more observers' codings of the same situation are compared to determine whether different observers rated the same event in the same way. This is called **interobserver reliability.** When interobserver reliability is high, one has confidence that all the observers are describing or coding the events in the same way. When interobserver reliability is low, the researchers must determine why and correct the differences in observation techniques. This may result in changing the category scheme so that it is easier to link each behavior with a category, or it may result in more training so the observers know more precisely how to code each behavior.

Another difficulty with the observational method results when so much activity is taking place that it is difficult to select specific behaviors or to code fast enough to keep up with the pace of activity in the setting. Finally, some research focuses on a particular kind of behavior or behavioral sequence such as helping behavior, peer rejection, or conflict. In naturalistic observation, one cannot be assured that the behavior of interest will take place during the observational period.

Case Study

A **case study** is an in-depth description of a single person, family, or social group. The purpose of a case study is to describe the behavior of only that person or group. Case studies are often carried out to illustrate a general principle by providing specific details, to examine a phenomenon that does not conform to theoretical predictions, or to stimulate theory development in an area that has not been investigated. Case studies have been used to examine the sequence of life events that have led up to a certain crisis or major turning point. They have been used to document the course of mental disorder or to illustrate the process of treatment (Runyan, 1982). Case studies can be based on a variety of sources of information including interviews, therapy sessions, prolonged observation, diaries or journals, letters, historical documents, and talks with people who know the subject of study.

Some case studies document the lives of great individuals. In *Gandhi's Truth (1969),* Erikson provided a psychosocial analysis of the life of Mahatma Gandhi. Erikson considered Gandhi's childhood, adolescence, and young adulthood as they contributed to his personality, his moral philosophy, and to the contradictions between his personal social relationships and his role as a powerful social leader.

Case studies can also focus on social groups, families, and organizations. One of Anna Freud's most famous cases described the attachments that developed among a group of orphans who had lived together in a concentration camp during World War II (Freud & Dann, 1951). The study focused on the strong feelings the children had for

Senator John Glenn has volunteered to participate in a case study of the effects of space on the aging process. Because of his unique background, long-term medical records are available that can be used to trace his physical health over a 50-year span.

one another and their strategies for maintaining their sense of connectedness once they were placed in a more normal social environment. The case illustrated a unique phenomenon, the intense emotional attachment of young children to each other, that had not been documented before.

Strengths and Limitations of the Case Study Method. Case studies have the advantage of illustrating the complexity and uniqueness of individual lives. Studies carried out with large samples often identify general principles. Case studies provide concrete examples of how these principles play themselves out in the lives of specific individuals. Some cases give the details of an experience that is rare and might not be captured in a large-scale study. Sometimes the case study brings a problem to the attention of researchers who then pursue it through other methods (Yin, 1994).

Case studies have been criticized as unscientific. In the first place, they are obviously not representative of large groups of individuals. One must be cautious about generalizing the conclusions drawn from a case study to other individuals or groups. Moreover, if the information that provides the basis of the case study is gathered in a biased or subjective way, then the results or conclusions of the study will be of little worth. Of course, this criticism applies to any type of research. Finally, critics argue that there is no reliability in case studies. If different people were writing a case study on the same individual, they might come up with very different views of the events and their significance.

These limitations suggest that one must have a very clear idea of the purpose and a systematic approach to gathering information in order to conduct case studies that would meet the standards of scientific observation. At the same time, vividly written, compelling case material has had a consistent impact in stimulating theory and research in the field of child development.

Interviews

Many case studies are based largely on face-to-face **interviews**. This method can also be used to gather data from large numbers of individuals and from people in clinical settings.

Interviews can be highly structured, almost like a verbal survey, or very open-ended, allowing the participant to respond freely to a series of general questions. The success of the interview method depends heavily on the skill of the interviewer (Holstein & Gubrium, 1995). Interviewers are trained to be nonjudgmental as they listen to a participant's responses. They try to create **rapport** with the participant by conveying a feeling of trustworthiness and acceptance. In unstructured interviews, the interviewer must make use of this rapport to encourage the participant to say more about a question and to share thoughts that may be private or personal. Matching the race and gender of the interviewer and the participant being interviewed have been found to help foster rapport and improve the quality of the data that is produced.

The interview method has traditionally been associated with clinical research, and it is becoming a major method in the study of cognition and language as well. Piaget's structured interview technique (Piaget, 1929) provides a model for the investigation of conceptual development (Box 1.2). The researcher who uses this technique asks a child a question (e.g., "Are clouds living or dead?"), and then follows up on the answer with questions about how the child arrived at his or her conclusion. In other studies, Piaget asked children to solve a problem, and then asked them to explain how they arrived at

BOX 1.2 PIAGET'S INTERVIEW METHOD

Piaget's use of the interview method to elicit a young child's cognitive reasoning can be seen in two excerpts from his works. In the first, Piaget (1929) was exploring a 5-year-old child's understanding of dreams:

Where does the dream come from?—I think you sleep so well that you dream.—*Does it come from us or from outside?*—From outside.—*What do we dream with?*—I don't know.—*With the hands? . . . With nothing?*—Yes, with nothing.—*When you are in bed and you dream, where is the dream?*—In my bed, under the blanket. I don't really know. If it was in my stomach(!) the bones would be in the way and I shouldn't see it.—*Is the dream in your head?*—It is I that am in the dream: it isn't in my head(!) When you dream, you don't know you are in the bed. You know you are walking. You are in the dream. You are in bed, but you don't know you are (pp. 97–98).

Here Piaget (1963) was describing a 7-year-old child's understanding of class inclusion:

You present the child with an open box that contains wooden beads. The child knows they are all wooden because he handles them, touching each and finding that it is made of wood. Most of these beads are brown, but a few are white. The problem we pose is simply this: Are there more brown beads or more wooden beads? Let us call A the brown beads, B the wooden beads: Then the problem is simply that of the inclusion of A in B. This is a very difficult problem before the age of 7 years. The child states that all the beads are wooden, and that most of them are brown and a few are white, but if you ask him if there are more brown beads or more wooden beads he immediately answers, "There are more brown ones because there are only two or three white ones."

So you say, "Listen, this is not what I am asking. I don't want to know whether there are more brown beads or more white beads, I want to know whether there are more brown beads or more wooden beads." And, in order to make it easier, I take an empty box and place it next to the one with the beads and I ask, "If I were to put the wooden beads into that box would any remain in this one?" The child answers, "No, none would be left because they are all wooden." Then I say, "If I were to take the brown beads and put them into that box, would any be left in this one?" The child replies, "Of course, two or three white ones would remain." Apparently he has now understood the situation, the fact that all the beads are wooden and that some are not brown. So I ask him once more, "Are there more brown beads or more wooden beads?" Now it is evident that the child begins to understand the problem, sees that there is indeed a problem, that matters are not as simple as they seemed at first. As we watch him we observe that he is thinking very hard. Finally he concludes, "But there are still more brown beads; if you take the brown ones away, only two or three white beads remain."

In studies using a Piagetian-style interview, children explain how they reached an answer and why they think their answer is correct. This provides insight into the reasoning behind correct and incorrect responses.

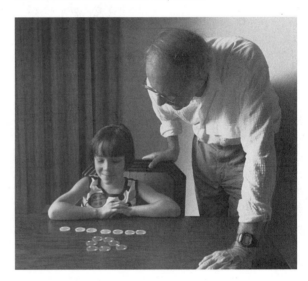

In this Piagetian interview about conservation of number, a child is asked to explain how he arrived at his answers and why he believes that the answer is correct.

the solution. The child becomes an informant about his or her own conceptual capacities. This approach has been adapted in the study of moral development, interpersonal development, and positive, helping behavior.

Strengths and Limitations of the Interview Method. The interview method has the advantage of allowing individuals to contribute their own views on the topic being studied. They can tell the interviewer what is important to them, why they might choose one alternative over another, or what they think is wrong with the investigator's view of the situation. Participants may also, of course, present themselves in the way they want the interviewer to see them; when they do, they are said to be exhibiting a **self-presentation bias.**

Research suggests that young children's responses are especially vulnerable to influence by the interviewer. By smiling, nodding, frowning, or looking away, the interviewer can deliberately or inadvertently communicate approval or disapproval. There is a fine line between establishing rapport and influencing responses.

Surveys and Tests

Survey research is a means of collecting specific information from a large number of participants. If people are to respond directly to surveys, they must be able to read and write, unless the survey questions are read to them. The survey method is, therefore, most commonly used with participants in middle childhood, adolescence, and adulthood. However, survey information about infants and toddlers is often collected from parents, child-care workers, physicians, nurses, and others who are responsible for meeting the needs of young children. Thus, surveys have contributed a great deal to our knowledge about the way adults perceive the behaviors and needs of young children.

Survey methods can be used to collect information about attitudes (Do you believe teachers should be permitted to use corporal punishment with their students?), about current behaviors and practices (How many hours per day do you watch television?), about aspirations (What do you hope to do when you graduate from high school?), and about perceptions (How well does your mother/father or son/daughter understand your views?).

Survey questions are prepared in a standard form, and the responses are usually coded according to a prearranged set of categories. In well-designed surveys the questions are stated clearly and offer response choices that are not ambiguous or overlapping. In the most powerful surveys, the sample of subjects is carefully selected to be representative of the population under study. Surveys may be conducted by telephone, through the mail, in classrooms, at work, or in the participants' homes (Fowler, 1993).

Tests are often similar in form to surveys. They consist of groups of questions or problems the child is expected to answer. Usually tests are designed to measure a specific ability or characteristic. You are no doubt familiar with the kinds of tests typically given in school. You are presented with a group of items and asked to produce the correct answer or to select the correct answer from among several choices. Intelligence tests and achievement tests are of this nature. A researcher might give these tests along with some other measures in order to learn how intelligence relates to social life, emotions, or self-understanding.

Other tests are designed to measure a variety of psychological constructs, such as creativity, conformity, depression, and extroversion. Some tests are administered to assess whether a person has some form of mental illness, learning disorder, or developmental or physical disability.

Psychological tests must be reliable and valid to be useful. Tests are **reliable** when they provide approximately the same score or the same diagnosis each time a person takes the test. This is not to say that the test should not indicate change when change has occurred. But a person who takes a reliable test on two consecutive days should get approximately the same score on both days unless some deliberate training or intervention has been introduced between them. There ought to be a positive correlation (toward $+1.0$) between the two scores.

Tests are **valid** when they measure what they claim to measure. The people who design the tests have to define what it is they are trying to measure. They also have to provide evidence that their test really measures this construct (Messick, 1989). Consider the various tests that have been designed to measure intelligence in infants and very young children. The results of these tests are not very closely related to the results of tests of intelligence given in adolescence and adulthood (Bayley, 1970). In other words, correlations between intelligence tests given to infants and those given to the same subjects when they are older tend to be low (nearer to 0.0 than to -1.0 or $+1.0$). Perhaps the underlying components of intelligence differ in babies and in adolescents and adults. Or perhaps intelligence evolves in so many ways that the intelligence of the adult bears little relation to that of the infant. Or perhaps these infant tests are not really tests of broad, adaptive intelligence, but are measures of sensory processing and central nervous system coordination.

Strengths and Limitations of Surveys and Tests. Surveys and tests have certain advantages that make them widely used in developmental research. They allow us to compare the responses of large groups of respondents. Surveys and tests have been designed to address a wide variety of topics. With a prearranged coding or scoring system, many tests can be administered and evaluated without difficulty.

This method also has limitations. Some surveys create attitudes where none existed before. For example, you might ask sixth-grade children questions about their satisfaction with their school curriculum. The students may answer a lot of questions on this topic, but they may not have given much thought to the issue before. Another problem is the gap between answers to survey questions or scores on tests and actual behavior. Adults may say they believe strongly in First Amendment rights, but they object when certain groups petition for the right to hold a rally in their town. Similarly, parents may say that they allow their children to participate in family decisions, but when it comes to real family decisions, they may not give their children much voice.

The use of tests to determine school admissions and placement has come under serious attack (Weinberg, 1989). Some tests have been criticized for putting unfair emphasis on knowledge derived from a white, middle-class, Eurocentric cultural perspective. Some tests have been criticized for putting at a disadvantage children whose first language is not English or for being insensitive to different learning styles and modes of synthesizing information.

Intelligence tests in particular have been criticized because they are used to decide children's educational placement, but they do not encompass the full array of psychological factors associated with social competence and adaptive behavior. Psychological tests continue to be used in research to explore the relationship among developmental domains. However, their use in settings such as schools and treatment facilities is becoming increasingly controversial for the many reasons mentioned above.

Experimentation

Experimentation is a method best suited for examining causal relationships. In an experiment, some variable or group of variables is systematically manipulated to examine the effect on an outcome. For example, one might study the effect of different types of instructions on student performance, or different learning environments on a student's ability to recall information. The variable that is manipulated by the experimenter is called the **independent variable.** The variable defined by the participant's responses or reactions is the **dependent variable** (Davis, 1995). The research is carried out to determine whether the independent variable or some combination of independent variables can produce a change in the dependent variable.

In some experiments, one group of participants has a certain set of experiences or receives information (usually referred to as a **treatment**) that is not provided to another group. The group that experiences the experimenter's manipulation is called the **experimental group.** The group that does not experience the treatment or manipulation is called the **control group.** Differences in behavior between the two groups are then attributed to the treatment. For example, in a study of academic performance in human development courses, students enrolled in a course would be randomly assigned to the experimental group, in which they are linked as a study group through e-mail so they can contact one another, discuss questions from the course, and share their ideas. The other students, who are in the control group, do not receive this Internet support. Differences in course grades between the experimental and the control groups would be attributed to the Internet intervention.

In other experiments, the behavior of a single group of participants is compared before and after the treatment or across several treatments. Once again, systematic differences in behavior before and after the treatment are attributed to the experimental manipulation. In this case each participant serves as his or her own control.

Control is the key to successful experimentation. The experimenter must exercise control in selecting the children or families who participate in a study. The participants must be able to bring equivalent competencies to the situation. If this condition is not met, one cannot assume that differences in behavior between groups are due to the treatment.

Experimenters control the way a task is presented to the participants so that such factors as the ability to understand the instructions, the order of events, and the degree

The experimental method has been used widely to learn more about infants' visual and auditory abilities and their capacity to remember stimuli from one presentation to the next. As a parent, what would you want to know before deciding to give permission for your child to participate in experimental research?

of comfort and familiarity with the setting do not interfere with the participants' behavior. Control ensures that changes in behaviors do in fact result from the experimental manipulation.

Many studies in human development are **quasiexperimental.** This means that the treatment was not controlled by the experimenter but was a result of some pattern of life events (Wilson, 1995). Suppose we are interested in the impact of unemployment on conflict between married couples. We cannot (nor do we want to) cause some adults to lose their jobs while others remain employed. We can, however, compare couples of about the same age and social class who have experienced unemployment with those who have not.

In these studies, assignment to a "treatment" occurs as a result of real-world events. One would select participants for the study who are as much alike as possible in other respects except for their encounters with unemployment. It is the task of the scientist to compare some of the consequences of this treatment—the experience of unemployment—and to deal with the limitations that are imposed on the results by the way the individuals arrived in one treatment group or the other to begin with.

Strengths and Limitations of the Experimental Method. The experimental method has the advantage of providing conclusions about causal relationships. If we can show that the participants' behavior changes only when something about the experimental situation changes, we can conclude that the manipulation has caused the changes in behavior. This is a very powerful statement, particularly as we search for explanations for how conditions that occur early in development might influence later outcomes.

Experiments also have limitations. We cannot be certain about how applicable a controlled laboratory situation is to the real world. Would the behaviors that are observed in the laboratory also be observed at home, at school, or at work? For example, through studies of attachment (which is discussed in Chapter 5) we have learned that infants and young children do not behave the same way in the presence of their mothers as they do when their mothers are absent. Thus, experimental research conducted with children that does not allow mothers to be present may produce behavior that differs in quantity, quality, and sequence from the behavior that would be observed under more normal conditions, when the mothers are present.

Experimental studies tend to suggest that event *A* causes response *B*. In many domains of development, however, a multifaceted, reciprocal process promotes change. Just think a moment about the development of friendship. A friendship depends on so many domains and the fit or lack of fit along each domain for the two people. Friendships may be influenced by physical appearance, abilities, temperaments, intelligence, family background, whether others support the friendship or ridicule it, and so on. Friendships are sustained and promoted by continuous feedback and interaction among the friends rather than by one or two factors that could be said to promote or inhibit friendship. We want to avoid imposing a unidirectional, causal explanation on behaviors that are more accurately described using an interactional model.

Advantages and disadvantages of the five research methods are summarized in Table 1.1.

Designs for Studying Development

The primary concern of developmental research is to describe and account for patterns of continuity and change. Four major research approaches have been created for examining development: retrospective studies, cross-sectional studies, longitudinal studies, and cohort sequential studies.

Retrospective Studies

A researcher engaged in a **retrospective study** asks the participants to report on experiences from an earlier time in their lives. Many early studies of child-rearing used parents' recollections of their parenting techniques to evaluate their patterns of child care. Researchers who studied the effects of stress during pregnancy often asked women to recall their emotional state before, during, and after their child was born. Investigators of personality development use retrospective data by asking adolescent or adult subjects to recall important events of their childhood.

This approach produces a record of what a person has retained of past events. We cannot be certain that these events really occurred as they are remembered. For that matter, we cannot be certain that they occurred at all. Piaget (1951) described a vivid memory from his second year of life:

> I was sitting in my pram, which my nurse was pushing in the Champs Elysées, when a man tried to kidnap me. I was held in by the strap fastened around me while my nurse bravely tried to stand between me and the thief. She received various scratches, and I can still see vaguely those on her face. (p. 188)

Thirteen years later, when Piaget was 15, the nurse joined a religious order. She wrote to his parents and returned a watch they had given her for protecting Jean from the

TABLE 1.1   Advantages and Disadvantages of Methods of Developmental Research

Method	Definition	Advantages	Disadvantages
Observation	Systematic description of behavior	Documents the variety of ongoing behavior; captures what happens naturally, without experimental intervention	Time-consuming; requires careful training of observers; observer may interfere with what would normally occur
Case studies	In-depth description of a single person, family, or group	Focuses on complexity and unique experiences of individual; permits analysis of unusual cases	Lacks generalizability; conclusions may refelect bias of investigator; hard to replicate
Interviews	Face-to-face interaction in which each person can give a full account of his or her views	Provides complex first-person account	Vulnerable to investigator bias
Surveys and tests	Standard questions administered to large groups	Permits data collection from large samples; requires little training; very flexible	Wording and way of presenting questions may influence responses; response may not be closely related to behavior; tests may not be appropriate for use in schools or clinical settings
Experimentation	Analysis of cause-effect relations by manipulation of some conditions while others are held constant	Permits testing of causal hypotheses; permits control and isolation of specific variables	Laboratory findings may not be applicable to other settings; focuses on a unidirectional model of causality

kidnapper. She confessed that she had made up the story even to the point of scratching her own face. Piaget believed he had created the visual memory from the story his parents had told him about the incident.

The passage of time may change the significance of certain past events in a person's memory. As we gain new levels of cognitive complexity or change our attitudes, we reorganize our memories of the past so as to bring them into line with our current level of understanding (Kotre, 1995). Sometimes, people claim to have recovered memories of past events that have been long forgotten or "repressed." It is extremely difficult to determine the accuracy of these memories (Loftus, 1993). They may be entangled with current experiences or with ideas taken from books, movies, or conversations with others. They may be altered by the suggestion that something happened that actually did not, or by the suggestion that something did not happen that actually did. Because memory is so easily modified by suggestion, its usefulness in uncovering systematic data about the past is limited. However, retrospective data are of value for understanding how people make sense of their past, and what role they perceive past experiences to have had in their present way of thinking. Studies that use the technique of **life review** provide insight into the way adults organize and structure key periods and events from their life history (McAdams et al., 1997).

Cross-Sectional Studies

Studies that compare people of different ages or of different social backgrounds or from different school or community settings are called **cross-sectional studies.** Such studies are quite commonly used in research on child development. Investigators may compare children of different levels of biological maturity or of different chronological ages to learn how a particular developmental domain changes with age.

One such study explored differences in how children aged 7, 9, and 12 were able to reason about problems to which there was more than one solution (Horobin & Acredolo, 1989). Even though the younger children were aware that there were multiple solutions, they were more likely than the older children to settle on one solution and insist that it was correct.

The limitation of the cross-sectional method is that it blurs the pattern of individual development. With respect to the study on reasoning, the cross-sectional approach tells us that most 12-year-olds are more flexible in their reasoning than most 7-year-olds. It does not tell us how the children who were the most flexible at age 7 would have performed at age 12 in comparison with those who were the least flexible.

Longitudinal Studies

A **longitudinal study** involves repeated observations of the same subjects at different times. The time between observations may be brief, as from immediately after birth to two or three days after birth. Or observations may be repeated over the entire life course, as in Leo Terman's longitudinal study of gifted children (Holahan et al., 1995; Sears & Barbee, 1978; Terman et al., 1947, 1959).

Longitudinal studies have the advantage of allowing us to consider the course of development of a particular group of individuals. We can discover how certain characteristics of children in infancy or toddlerhood relate to those same characteristics when the individuals reach adolescence or adulthood. We can also learn whether certain qualities of childhood, such as intelligence or outgoingness, are related to overall social adjustment or life satisfaction in later years. Longitudinal studies permit us to trace individual patterns within a group over time, rather than comparing typical patterns across age groups (Schaie, 1994).

Longitudinal studies may be very difficult to complete, especially if they are intended to cover a significant age period, such as the years from childhood into adulthood. Over this span of time, participants may drop out of the study, the investigators may lose funding or interest in the project, and the methods may become outdated. Questions that once seemed important may no longer be seen as vital. One of the greatest limitations of these studies is that they focus on only one generation of subjects. Historical and social factors that may influence the course of this group's development will be inextricably intertwined in the observations. One cannot tell if all people growing up at all times in history would exhibit the pattern of changes that characterize this particular group.

Cohort Sequential Studies

A **cohort sequential design** combines the cross-sectional and the longitudinal approaches into one method of study (Schaie, 1965, 1992). Groups of participants, called **cohorts,** are selected because they are a certain number of years apart in age. For example, we might begin with a group of adolescents who are 11, 14, and 17. Every three years, this group would be interviewed until the 11-year-olds have turned 17. In addition, every three years, a new group of 11-year-olds would be added to the study. This combination of a longitudinal and a cross-sectional design is a powerful developmental research method. It produces immediate cross-sectional data, longitudinal data after three and six years, and a comparison of children who were the same age (11, 14, or 17) at three different times. This third comparison permits us to identify social and historical factors that may influence age-related differences. The elements of a cohort sequential design are seen in Figure 1.6.

Evaluating Existing Research

In addition to collecting new data, social scientists give considerable scholarly effort to reviewing and evaluating the existing research. Statistical techniques allow us to compare the findings of a variety of studies in order to identify patterns of results. As a student, you may be asked to review research findings on a topic of interest to you. Most researchers use this method to keep well informed on the research being reported in their subject area. They analyze the work of others to generate new questions and to formulate well-founded conclusions about issues in their specialization. The study, analysis, and evaluation of current research literature constitute special skills in their own right.

Ethics

In conducting research with living beings, and especially with children, social scientists continually confront ethical questions. **Ethics** refers to principles of conduct that are founded on a society's moral code. As part of their professional socialization, researchers are obligated to maintain humane, morally acceptable treatment of all living subjects (American Psychological Association, 1992).

The ethical guidelines for research with human subjects encompass a variety of considerations. Because we are concerned about subjects' right to privacy, the identities of individual subjects must be kept confidential. The subjects must not be coerced into participating in a research project, and a refusal to participate should have no negative consequences. If children in a classroom, for example, decide that they do not want to participate in a research project, or if their parents do not give permission for them to

FIGURE 1.6
The cohort sequential design

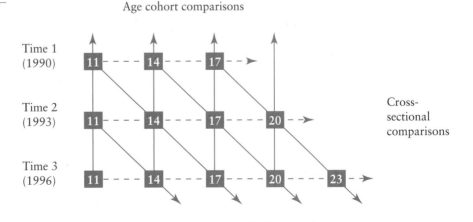

Age cohort comparisons

Time 1 (1990)

Time 2 (1993)

Cross-sectional comparisons

Time 3 (1996)

Longitudinal comparisons

In the famous Milgram experiment, participants were deceived into believing that they were causing physical harm to another person. One aspect of the deception was to involve research participants in connecting electrodes to the "learner." The distress they experienced in the experimental procedure led to important revisions in the code of ethical conduct in social science research.

participate, they should not be shamed, given an undesirable alternate assignment, or given a lower grade.

Researchers must protect subjects from unnecessary painful physical and emotional experiences, including shame, failure, and social rejection. Researchers must weigh the benefits of the new information they may discover in a particular study against the potential risks or harm to the subjects. Two questions must guide the researcher's decisions:

1. How would you feel if you, or one of your family members, were a subject in this study?
2. Can the problem be studied in ways that do not involve pain, deception, or emotional or physical stress?

The American Psychological Association has published a guide for researchers titled *Ethical Principles in the Conduct of Research with Human Participants* (1982). This guide requires that human subjects be told about all aspects of the research that may influence their decision to participate. They must be free to withdraw from the study at any time. They are entitled to a full explanation of the study once it has been completed. When the subjects are children, their parents must be given this information and must approve their children's participation. Most schools, day-care centers, hospitals, nursing homes, and other treatment centers also have their own review procedures for determining whether they will permit research to be carried out with the people in their programs.

THE LIFE SPAN

The task of mapping one's future depends on how long one expects to live. Naturally, we can make only rough predictions. We know that our lives may be cut short by a disaster, an accident, or an illness. However, our best guess about how long we will live is based on the average **life expectancy** of others in our group.

Table 1.2 presents data on the average **life span** of people in the United States during eight time periods. Look first at the top row of the table, labeled "At birth." The average life expectancy of people born at the turn of the 19th century was about 49 years. For people born at the time of the stock market crash and the beginning of the

TABLE 1.2   Average Remaining Lifetime at Various Ages, 1900-1994

Age	1994	1989	1978	1968	1954	1939-1941	1929-1931	1900-1902
At birth	75.7	75.3	73.3	70.2	69.6	63.6	59.3	49.2
65 years	17.4	17.2	16.3	14.6	14.4	12.8	12.3	11.9
75 years	11.0	10.9	10.4	9.1	9.0	7.6	7.3	7.1
80 years	8.3	8.3	8.1	6.8	6.9	5.7	5.4	5.3

SOURCE: U.S. Bureau of the Census, 1984, 1992, 1997.

Great Depression, the average life expectancy was about 59 years. The average life expectancy of people born at the beginning of World War II was around 64. The average life expectancy of people born in 1978 was approximately 73 years and rose to 75 years for those born in 1989. As of 1994, this figure was 75.7 (U.S. Bureau of the Census, 1997). As we look across these generations, it is quite clear that the length of life has been increasing for more and more people.

The next few lines in Table 1.2 show something else. People who had reached advanced ages (65, 75, and 80) in each of the time periods (1900–1902, 1929–1931, 1939–1941, 1954, 1968, 1978, 1989, and 1994) had a longer life expectancy than people who were born in those time periods. Thus, someone who was 65 at the turn of the century (born in 1835) was expected to live to be 76.9; someone who was 75 at that time (born in 1825) was expected to live to be 82.1; and someone who was 80 years old during that period (born in 1820) was expected to live to be 85.3. These figures suggest that hazards during the early and middle years of life shorten the average life expectancy at birth. Infant mortality was a major factor in limiting life expectancy at the turn of the century. In addition, many women died in childbirth, and respiratory diseases and heart disease were serious threats to life during the middle adult years. If one survived these common killers, one's chance for a long later life increased.

Using these kinds of statistics to estimate the life span, we are able to compute projections of changes in its length. The average person born in 1994 can expect to live 26.5 years longer than one who was born in 1900. At the later end of the life span, however, we find much less dramatic increases in life expectancy today as compared to 1900. On the average, people who were 65 in 1994 (born in 1929) can expect to live to be about 82.4; people who were 75 in 1994 (born in 1919) can expect to live to be 86; and people who were 80 in 1994 (born in 1914) can expect to live to be 88.3.

The Social Security Administration makes *projections* of life expectations that are quite reliable. These data, showing the life expectations of men and women separately, are seen in Table 1.3. Overall, men do not live as long as women. They die younger around the world as well as in various regions of the United States. The gap in life expectancy for U.S. males and females has been declining from 1980 to the present, and is expected to continue to decline at least through 2010, but is expected to increase again by the year 2050. What might account for this widening of the gender difference in the middle of the next century?

In the Appendix, you will find data on national patterns of life expectancy by race and sex as well as regional patterns within the United States and international comparisons. Here you will note significant racial differences in life expectancy, differences that show an advantage for whites in the early years of life, but an advantage for blacks in the later years after 65. The observation of racial differences in life expectancy at advanced ages has not been fully explained. One speculation is that African-Americans who survive the stresses and hardships of childhood, adolescence, and adult life may be especially hardy and resistant to the effects of biological aging in later life. These data provide very concrete evidence of the impact of the societal system on the biological system. Medical advances, knowledge about

Sex	1980	1990	2000	2005	2010
Male	70.0	72.1	73.0	73.5	74.1
Female	77.4	79.0	79.7	80.2	80.6
Difference	7.4	6.9	6.7	6.7	6.5

TABLE 1.3   Projections of Life Expectation at Birth for 1980, 1990, 2000, 2005, and 2010 by Sex

SOURCE: U.S. Bureau of the Census, 1991, 1997.

the impact of lifestyle choices, access to health care services, and success in coping with life stresses or protection from life stresses can all contribute to a longer and healthier adulthood.

According to government projections presented in Table 1.3, the life span of both men and women is expected to increase from now until the year 2010. The question arises whether this increase can continue or whether there is an upper limit to the length of the life span. There are theories supporting both sides. Bernice Neugarten (1981), a noted human development scholar, argued that, if the rates of advance in such fields as medicine and nutrition proceed for the next 40 years at the rate at which they have progressed for the last 60, by 2020 many people may be living to be 120 years old. Others suggest that the primary killers of infants, adults, and aging persons have already been brought under control and that there is little room left for expansion in the human life span, which they view as genetically limited. They have argued that the best we can hope for is a healthier, rather than a longer, period of life (Olshansky et al., 1990).

When you try to estimate your own life expectancy, you must consider projections for people in your country, region, and state, and in your age, educational, racial, and sex groups. In addition, research with identical twins suggests that some component of longevity is genetically guided. People with long-lived ancestors are likely to be long-lived themselves. Individual lifestyle factors are also associated with longevity. In an article entitled "How to Live to 100," *Newsweek* magazine prepared a grid that allows one to calculate one's projected age based on health, lifestyle, family, and ancestry (Cowley, 1997) (Table 1.4). These factors mirror longitudinal studies of adults born between 1895 and 1919 who were studied in 1965 and again in 1984 (Guralnick & Kaplan, 1989). A variety of demographic, health, and lifestyle factors were associated with a high level of functioning when the group

Lifestyle decisions that are made in early and middle adulthood can have a significant impact on longevity. Participation in regular aerobic exercise has a beneficial impact on the cardiovascular system, and on maintaining a high level of intellectual functioning in later life. What other kinds of lifestyle choices might have a positive impact on longevity?

TABLE 1.4 Factors Associated with Longevity

This chart will give you a rough idea of how your life expectancy varies from the norm. To estimate how long you'll live, begin by using the table at right to find the median life expectancy of your age group. Then add or subtract years based on the risk factors listed below (you should adjust your risk-factor score by the percentages at right if you're over 60).

Age	Male	Female	Scoring: Risk Factors
20–59	73	80	Use table as shown
60–69	76	81	Reduce loss or gain by 20%
70–79	78	82	Reduce loss or gain by 50%
80 +	add five years to current age		Reduce loss or gain by 75%

	Gain in Life Expectancy			No Change	Loss in Life Expectancy			
Health	+3 Years	+2 Years	+1 Year		−1 Year	−2 Years	−3 Years	Tally
Blood Pressure	Between 90/65 and 120/81	Less than 90/65 without heart disease	Between 121/82 and 129/85	130/86	Between 131/87 and 140/90	Between 141/91 and 150/95	More than 151/96	
Diabetes	–	–	–	None	Type II (adult onset)	–	Type I (juvenile onset)	
Total cholesterol	–	–	Less than 160	161–200	201–240	241–280	More than 280	
HDL cholesterol	–	–	More than 55	45–54	40–44	Less than 40	–	
Compared with that of others my age, my health is:	–	–	Excellent	Very good or fair	–	Poor	Extremely poor	

Lifestyle	+3 Years	+2 Years	+1 Year		−1 Year	−2 Years	−3 Years	Tally
Cigarette smoking	None	Ex-smoker, no cigarettes for more than 5 yrs.	Ex-smoker, no cigarettes for 3–5 yrs.	Ex-smoker, no cigarettes for 1–3 yrs.	Ex-smoker, no cigarettes for 5 mos.–1 yr.	Smoker, 0–20 pack-years*	Smoker, more than 20 pack-years	
Secondhand-smoke exposure	–	–	–	None	0–1 hour per day	1–3 hours per day	More than 3 hours per day	
Exercise average (give yourself most positive category)	More than 90 min. per day of exercise (e.g., walking) for more than 3 yrs.	More than 60 min. per day for more than 3 yrs.	More than 20 min. per day for more than 3 yrs.	More than 10 min. per day for more than 3 yrs.	More than 5 min. per day for more than 3 yrs.	Less than 5 min. per day	None	
Saturated fat in diet	–	Less than 20%	20%–30%	31%–40%	–	More than 40%	–	
Fruits and vegetables	–	–	5 servings per day	–	None	–	–	

Family	+3 Years	+2 Years	+1 Year		−1 Year	−2 Years	−3 Years	Tally
Marital status	–	Happily married man	Happily married woman	Single woman, widowed man	Divorced man, widowed woman	Divorced woman	Single man	
Disruptive events in the past year†	–	–	–	–	One	Two	Three	
Social groups, friends seen more than once/month**	–	Three	Two	One	–	None	–	
Parents' age of death	–	–	Both lived past 75	One lived past 75	–	–	Neither lived past 75	

Your estimated life expectancy ▶ [   ]

*A pack-year is one pack per day for a year. †Deaths of family members, job changes, moves, lawsuits, financial insecurity, etc.

**People who offer support through disruptive events (applicable only in case of two or more such events). Source: Michael F. Roizen, M.D., using data abstracted from the real age and age-reduction-planning programs of medical informatics.

Source: *Newsweek*, June 30, 1997, p. 65.

Age, as well as time, are relative. As the lifespan increases, the way we calculate our sense of maturity and aging changes. How old do you feel you are? In what way does your sense of being old depend on the situation?

ranged in age from 65 to 89. These factors included having a fairly high family income; having no hypertension, arthritis, or back pain; being a nonsmoker; having normal weight; and consuming a moderate amount of alcohol. The last three factors in particular are influenced largely by personal decisions, and even hypertension and back pain are linked in part to lifestyle factors that are under a person's control. A growing body of research emphasizes the potential benefits of reduced fat in the diet combined with the strategic use of vitamin and mineral supplements to slow the cellular damage associated with aging (Carper, 1995; Rusting, 1992; Walford, 1990).

Many of our most important life decisions are made with either an implicit or an explicit assumption about how long we expect to live. For example, Colleen expects to live to be about 80 years old. She reasons that there is no rush about getting married since even if she waits until she is 40, she will still have 40 years of married life and that is a long time to get along with one partner. Our perception of our life expectancy has an impact on our behavior, self-concept, attitudes, and outlook on the future.

The way we feel about ourselves, our activities, and our relationships are often guided by underlying assumptions about the point we have reached in life. Consider an African-American male born in 1995; he can expect to live to age 68. A European-American female born in 1995 can expect to live to age 80. The African-American male will grow up looking at the years after about age 55 or 60 as old age. In fact, many young African-American males express doubt about whether they will live to be 25. The European-American female will probably not consider herself old until she reaches about age 70. Differences in outlook, coupled with actual differences in health and resources, will affect the way these two people regard themselves and go about their daily activities in middle and later life. As we think about stages of life and themes of development it is important to keep these demographic realities in mind. Our thinking about adulthood and aging has changed over this century to reflect dramatic changes in life expectancy. The field of social gerontology has emerged in part as a result of the large numbers of individuals who are living to advanced ages. At the same time, subgroup differences associated with race, family ancestry, and social class require us to take a flexible outlook on models of the life span.

Chapter Summary

Psychosocial theory emphasizes interaction among the biological, psychological, and societal systems. As a result of maturation and change in each of these systems, individuals' beliefs about themselves and their relationships are modified. Although each life story is unique, we can identify important common patterns, allowing us to anticipate the future and to understand one another.

The scientific process results in a body of knowledge that informs our understanding of human development. Scientific observation must be objective, repeatable, and systematic. Five principal research methods are: observation, case studies, interviews, surveys and tests, and experimentation. Each has its advantages and disadvantages, but all provide insights into continuity and change over the life span. Research design is also important in the study of change. Four significant designs are: retrospective studies, cross-sectional studies, longitudinal studies, and cohort sequential designs. The method and design of research have a powerful effect on how the findings may be interpreted.

Demographic information about the life span stimulates thought about one's own life expectancy. In the United States, the average life expectancy has increased by almost 50% in this century. This dramatic change affects how each of us views our own future. We need to study human development within a constantly changing context. We can never be satisfied that the information from earlier periods will hold true for future generations.

$\mathscr{E}$*nd of Chapter Case*

Rose is a 60-year-old woman who has been having serious attacks of dizziness and shortness of breath as Thanksgiving approaches. Rose is normally active and energetic. In the past, she looked forward to entertaining her family, which included three married daughters, one married son, and their children. However, her son has recently been divorced. Feelings between him and his ex-wife are bitter. Any attempts on Rose's part to communicate with her former daughter-in-law or her granddaughter are met with outbursts of hostility from her son. Even though Rose is very fond of her daughter-in-law and her granddaughter, she knows that she cannot invite them to the family gathering without stirring up intense conflict with her son.

Rose's daughters suggest having the dinner at one of their homes in order to prevent further conflict. They hope this solution will take some of the pressure off their mother and ease the attacks. Rose agrees, but her attacks continue.

The biological, psychological, and societal systems are involved in Rose's situation. The conflict is being expressed in the biological system through the symptoms of dizziness and shortness of breath. Psychological and societal demands may elicit responses from the biological system, as they commonly do in people under stress. Although the solution to the problem must be found in the psychological system, the biological system often alerts the person to the severity of the problem through the development of physical symptoms.

Rose's psychological system is involved in interpreting her son's behavior, which she views as forcing her to choose between him and her daughter-in-law and granddaughter. She might also use psychological processes to try to arrive at a solution to the conflict. So far, Rose has not identified any satisfactory solution. Although she can avoid the conflict most of the time, the impending Thanksgiving dinner is forcing her to confront it directly.

The psychological system includes Rose's self-concept as well as her emotional state. Through memory, Rose retains a sense of her family at earlier periods, when they enjoyed greater closeness. Having to face a Thanksgiving dinner at which she will feel angry at her son or guilty about excluding her daughter-in-law and her granddaughter places her in a fundamental conflict. The Thanksgiving meal is also a symbolic event, representing Rose's idea of family unity, which she cannot achieve.

The societal system influences the situation at several levels. First, there are the societal expectations regarding the mother role: Mother is nurturing, loving, and protecting. But Rose cannot be nurturing without sending messages of rejection either to her son or to her daughter-in-law and granddaughter. Second, norms for relating to various family members after a divorce are unclear. How should Rose behave toward her son's former spouse? How should she relate to her grandchild if her son is no longer the child's custodial parent? Rose is confused about what to do.

Third, the Thanksgiving celebration has social, religious, and cultural significance. This family ritual was performed in Rose's home when she was a child, and she has carried it through in her own home as an adult. Now, however, she is being forced to pass the responsibility for this gathering to her daughter before she is ready to do so and, as a result, Rose is likely to feel a special sense of loss. She will also lose the sense of family unity that she has tried to preserve.

Thought Questions

1. How does this case illustrate the interconnections among the biological, psychological, and societal systems?
2. Given what you know about the assumptions of psychosocial theory, how might Rose's stage of development influence her perceptions of this situation and her approach to coping with this conflict?
3. How might you frame a research question based on the information raised in this case study? (For example, how likely is it that parents experience health problems following their child's divorce?)
4. What research method(s) would you use to pursue this research question?

Chapter 2

*P*sychosocial theory focuses on the ongoing interaction of the person and the social environment from infancy through very old age. Society makes its first impact through the family as infants, children, adolescents, and adults protect, nurture, and teach one another.

Psychosocial Theory

*C*hapter Objectives

- To define the concept of theory and explain how one makes use of theory to increase understanding.
- To define the six basic concepts of psychosocial theory.
- To demonstrate how the concepts of psychosocial theory contribute to an analysis of basic processes that foster or inhibit development over the life span.
- To evaluate psychosocial theory, pointing out its strengths and weaknesses.

*I*n this chapter, we will define the concept of theory and introduce the basic concepts of psychosocial theory, which provides the integrating framework for our analysis of human development. In Chapter 3 we will discuss other theories that also account for growth and change. Some of those theories provided the foundational concepts upon which psychosocial theory was based. Others complement psychosocial theory by offering insight into dynamic processes through which physical, intellectual, emotional, social, and self-development take place. ❖

WHAT IS A THEORY?

A **theory** is a logical system of general concepts that underlies the organization and understanding of observations. The sciences have their formal theories, and we all have our informal, intuitive theories about our social lives. A formal scientific theory is a set of interconnected statements, including assumptions, definitions, axioms, postulates, hypothetical constructs, intervening variables, laws, and hypotheses. The function of this set of interconnected statements is to describe unobservable structures, mechanisms, or processes and to relate them to one another and to observable events. For example, in learning, the information that has been learned is not observable. However, according to certain principles of learning theory, we infer that new learning has taken place when some responses or behaviors become more likely and others become less likely under particular conditions.

A formal theory should meet certain requirements. It should be logical and internally consistent with no contradictory statements. The theory should be testable; that is, its hypothetical constructs should be translatable into testable hypotheses. The theory should be parsimonious, relying on as few assumptions, constructs, and propositions as possible. Finally, a theory should integrate previous research, and it should deal with a relatively large area of science (Miller, 1993). Most current developmental theories do not meet all of these requirements of formal, scientific theories. However, they offer a language of constructs and hypotheses that guide systematic inquiry and compare observations in order to build a body of knowledge. In order to evaluate a theory, we must ask three questions:

1. *Which phenomena is the theory trying to explain?* A theory of intellectual development may include hypotheses about the evolution of the brain, the growth of logical thinking, or the capacity to use symbolism. Such a theory is less likely to explain fears, motives, or friendship. As an example, Jean Piaget offered a developmental theory of the origins of logical thought. In his view, every organism strives to attain equilibrium with its environment, and equilibrium among the cognitive elements within itself. He hypothesized that (a) thought is organized in order to achieve equilibrium; (b) development takes place in a predictable sequence of naturally occurring stages, each with unique strategies for making

meaning out of experiences; and (c) children are active agents in constructing knowledge. His theory has been useful in helping to understand how children differ from adults and how they interpret and explain events. Piaget's theory does not, for example, direct attention to how children learn and remember specific facts, why certain fears persist, or how children and parents achieve a sense of attachment.

Understanding the focus of the theory helps to identify its **range of applicability.** Although principles from one theory may have relevance to another area of knowledge, a theory is evaluated in terms of the behavior it was originally intended to explain.

2. *What assumptions does the theory make?* **Assumptions** are the guiding premises underlying the logic of a theory. In order to evaluate a theory, you must first understand what its assumptions are. Charles Darwin assumed that lower life forms "progress" to higher forms in the process of evolution. Freud assumed that all behavior is motivated and that the unconscious is a "storehouse" of motives and wishes.

The assumptions of any theory may or may not be correct. Assumptions may be influenced by the cultural context that dominates the theorist's period of history, by the sample of observations from which the theorist has drawn inferences, by the current knowledge base of the field, and by the intellectual capacities of the theorist.

3. *What does the theory predict?* Theories add new levels of understanding by suggesting causal relationships, by unifying diverse observations, and by identifying the importance of events that may have gone unnoticed. Theories of human development offer explanations regarding the origins and functions of human behavior and the changes that can be expected in it from one period of life to the next.

We expect a theory of human development to provide explanations about four questions:

1. What are the mechanisms that account for growth from conception through old age, and to what extent do these mechanisms vary across the life span?
2. What factors underlie stability and change across the life span?
3. How do physical, cognitive, emotional, and social functions interact? How do these interactions account for mixtures of thoughts, feelings, health states, and social relationships?
4. How does the social context affect individual development?

THE RATIONALE FOR EMPHASIZING PSYCHOSOCIAL THEORY

We have selected psychosocial theory as an organizing framework for the text because it allows us to identify and integrate information from a wide range of disciplines covering a diversity of topics. Psychosocial theory is not the only or the most widely accepted framework for studying human development, however, it combines three features that are not as clearly articulated or integrated in other theories.

First, psychosocial theory addresses growth across the life span, identifying and differentiating central issues from infancy through old age. This perspective allows one to trace themes from infancy and childhood into adulthood and later life. It also suggests that experiences of adolescence or adulthood can lead to a review and reinterpretation of early periods.

Second, psychosocial theory assumes that individuals have the capacity to contribute to their psychological development at each stage of life. People have the ability to integrate, organize, and conceptualize their experiences in order to protect themselves, cope with challenges, and direct the course of their lives. Therefore, the direction of development is shaped by self-regulation as well as by the ongoing interaction of biological and societal influences.

At the Quinciniera, a 15-year-old Mexican-American girl celebrates mass with her family. This ceremony illustrates one way that culture imparts new demands and expectations at critical developmental transitions. What might be the personal and social meaning of this rite of passage?

Third, the theory takes into consideration the active contribution of culture to individual growth. At each life stage, cultural goals and aspirations, social expectations and requirements, and the opportunities that the culture provides make demands that draw forth reactions. These reactions influence which of a person's capabilities will be developed further. This vital link between the individual and the world is a key mechanism of development. In order to preserve and protect its culture, each society encourages patterns of parenting, provides unique opportunities for education, and communicates values and attitudes toward basic domains of behavior, including sexuality, intimacy, and work. Each society has its own view of the qualities that enter into maturity, qualities that are infused into the lives of individuals and help determine the direction of human growth within the society.

One of the great theorists who identified and developed psychosocial theory was Erik H. Erikson. Erikson initially was trained as a psychoanalyst (see the case at the end of this chapter). His theory was influenced by the work of many others, including Sigmund and Anna Freud, Peter Blos, Robert White, Jean Piaget, and Robert Havighurst, whose ideas you will encounter throughout this book. His wife, Joan, was an important intellectual influence as well. Erik and Joan collaborated on the formulation of the first presentation of the psychosocial theory and its eight stages of development in 1950 (J. Erikson, 1988). This theory has provided a rich body of ideas that have been elaborated in our own writings, as well as in the work of many other students of human development.

BASIC CONCEPTS OF PSYCHOSOCIAL THEORY

Psychosocial theory represents human development as a product of the interaction between individual *(psycho)* needs and abilities, and societal *(social)* expectations and demands. The theory accounts for the patterns of individual development that emerge from the more global process of psychosocial evolution.

Psychosocial theory is linked to an earlier use of the construct offered by Julian Huxley (1941, 1942) who introduced the term **psychosocial evolution** to refer to those human abilities that have allowed us to gather knowledge from our ancestors and transmit it to our descendants. Child-rearing practices, education, and modes of communication transmit information and ways of thinking from one generation to the next. At the same time, people learn how to develop new information, new ways of thinking, and new ways of teaching their discoveries to others. Through this process, according to Huxley, psychosocial evolution has proceeded at a rapid pace, bringing with it changes in technology and ideology that have allowed us to create and modify our physical and social environments.

The theory of psychosocial development offers an organizational framework for considering individual development within the larger perspective of psychosocial evolution. The transmission of values and knowledge across generations requires the maturation of individuals who are capable of internalizing knowledge, symbolizing it, adapting it, and transferring it to others. People change and grow systematically, enhancing their potential for carrying their own and succeeding generations forward.

Psychosocial theory is based on six organizing concepts: (1) stages of development, (2) developmental tasks, (3) psychosocial crises, (4) a central process for resolving the crisis of each stage, (5) a radiating network of significant relationships, and (6) coping—the new behavior people generate to meet new challenges. Figure 2.1 shows development as a building process that incorporates these six constructs. The structure grows larger as the radius of significant relationships expands and as the achievements of earlier stages are integrated into the behavior of the next stage of development.

Stages of Development

A **developmental stage** is a period of life that is characterized by a specific underlying organization. A wide variety of behaviors can be viewed as expressing the underlying structure of each stage. At every stage, some characteristics differentiate it from the preceding and succeeding stages. Stage theories propose a specific direction for development, and each new stage incorporates the gains made during earlier stages. At each stage, the accomplishments from the previous stages provide resources for mastering the new challenges. The interplay of the developmental tasks, psychosocial crisis, central process, and significant relationships provides the experiential base for new psy-

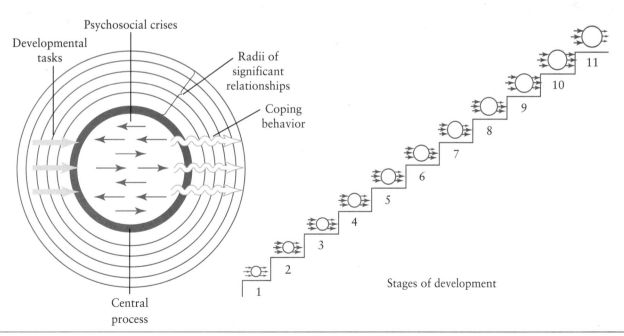

FIGURE 2.1
Six basic concepts of psychosocial theory

chosocial learning, and therefore for development. Each stage is unique and leads to the acquisition of new skills related to new capabilities (Davison et al., 1980; Flavell, 1982; Fischer & Silvern, 1985; Levin, 1986; Miller, 1993).

The stage concept suggests areas of emerging competence or conflict that may explain a range of behaviors. To some extent, you can verify the stage concept through reflection on your own past. You can probably recall earlier periods when you were very preoccupied by efforts first to gain your parents' approval, then to win acceptance by your peers, and later to understand yourself. Each of these concerns may have appeared all-encompassing at the time, but eventually it gave way to a new preoccupation. At each stage, you were confronted with a unique problem that required the integration of your personal needs and skills with the social demands of your culture. The end product was a new orienting mode and a new set of capabilities for engaging in interactions with others.

Erikson (1950/1963) proposed eight stages of psychosocial development. The conception of these stages can be traced in part to the stages of psychosexual development proposed by Freud and in part to Erikson's own observations and rich mode of thinking.

Figure 2.2 is the chart Erikson produced in *Childhood and Society* to describe the stages of psychosocial development. The boxes identify the main psychosocial ego conflicts of the various stages. These ego conflicts produce new ego skills. In Erikson's original model, you will note that the periods of life are given names, such as oral sensory

	1	2	3	4	5	6	7	8
8. Maturity								Ego integrity vs. Despair
7. Adulthood							Generativity vs. Stagnation	
6. Young adulthood						Intimacy vs. Isolation		
5. Puberty and adolescence					Identity vs. Role confusion			
4. Latency				Industry vs. Inferiority				
3. Locomotor-genital			Initiative vs. Guilt					
2. Muscular-anal		Autonomy vs. Shame, doubt						
1. Oral-sensory	Basic trust vs. Mistrust							

FIGURE 2.2

Erikson's model of the psychosocial stages of development
SOURCE: *Erikson, 1963.*

or puberty and adolescence, but no ages. This approach reflected Erikson's emphasis on an individual timetable for development, guided by both biological maturation and cultural expectations.

The concept of the psychosocial stages of development is very good as far as it goes, but Erikson's road map seems incomplete. If the idea of psychosocial evolution has validity—and we believe it does—new stages can be expected to develop as a culture evolves. We have identified 11 stages of psychosocial development, each associated with an approximate age range: (1) prenatal, from conception to birth; (2) infancy, from birth to 2 years; (3) toddlerhood, 2 and 3 years; (4) early school age, 4 to 6 years; (5) middle childhood, 6 to 12 years; (6) early adolescence, 12 to 18 years; (7) later adolescence, 18 to 22 years; (8) early adulthood, 22 to 34 years; (9) middle adulthood, 34 to 60 years; (10) later adulthood, 60 to 75 years; and (11) very old age, 75 until death.

By discussing a prenatal stage, a second stage of adolescent development, and very old age, we are adding three stages to the ones Erikson proposed. This revision is a product of our analysis of the research literature, our observations through research and practice, discussions with colleagues, and suggestions from other stage theorists. The addition of these three new stages provides a good demonstration of the process of theory construction. Theories of human development emerge and change within a cultural and historical context. Patterns of biological evolution and psychosocial evolution occur within a cultural frame of reference. The extension of the adolescent period, for example, is a product of changes in the timing of onset of puberty in modern society, the expanding need for education and training before entry into the world of work, related changes in the structure of the educational system, and the variety of the available life choices in work, marriage, parenting, and ideology.

Figure 2.3 shows the 11 stages of psychosocial development. The age range given for each stage is only an approximation. Each person has his or her own timetable for growth. In addition, differences associated with poverty, health, cultural group (e.g., differing rates of longevity) and exposure to environmental risks lead to different timetables. The lengths of the stages vary, from the nine months of the prenatal period to the roughly 26 years of middle adulthood.

Erikson (1950/1963) proposed that the stages of development follow the **epigenetic principle;** that is, a biological plan for growth allows each function to emerge systematically until the fully functioning organism has developed. An assumption of this and other stage theories is that the psychological development that takes place at each stage will have a significant effect on all subsequent stages. The stages are viewed as a sequence. Although one can anticipate challenges that will occur at a later stage, one passes through the stages in an orderly pattern of growth. In the logic of psychosocial theory, the entire life span is required for all the functions of psychosocial development to appear and become integrated. There is no going back to an earlier stage because experience makes retreat impossible. In contrast to other stage theories, however, Erikson suggested that one can review and reinterpret previous stages in the light of new insight and/or new experiences. In addition, the themes of earlier stages may re-emerge at any point, bringing a new meaning or a new resolution to an earlier conflict. Joan Erikson reflects on the fluidity and hopefulness in this perspective:

> This sequential growth . . . is now known to be more influenced by the social milieu than was in previous years considered possible. . . . Where a strength is not adequately developed according to the given sequence for its scheduled period of critical resolution, the supports of the environment may bring it into appropriate balance at a later period. Hope remains constant throughout life that more sturdy resolutions of the basic confrontation may be realized. (J. Erikson, 1988, p. 74–75)

The concept of life stages permits us to consider the various aspects of development at a given period of life and to speculate about their interrelation. It also encourages a

FIGURE 2.3
Eleven stages of the life span

Prenatal	Conception to birth
Infancy	Birth to 2 years
Toddlerhood	2 and 3 years
Early school age	4 to 6 years
Middle childhood	6 to 12 years
Early adolescence	12 to 18 years
Later adolescence	18 to 24 years
Early adulthood	24 to 34 years
Middle adulthood	34 to 60 years
Later adulthood	60 to 75 years
Very old age	75 until death

focus on the experiences that are unique to each life period—experiences that deserve to be understood both in their own right and in terms of their contribution to subsequent development. When programs and services are designed to address critical needs in such areas as education, health care, housing, and social welfare, the developmental stage approach allows the designers to focus on the needs and resources of the particular population to be served.

Despite the usefulness of a stage approach, one must avoid thinking of stages as pigeonholes. Just because a person is described as being at a given stage does not mean that he or she cannot function at other levels. It is not unusual for people to anticipate later challenges before they become dominant. Many children of toddler and preschool age, for example, play "house," envisioning having a husband or a wife and children. You might say that, in this play, they are anticipating the issues of intimacy and generativity that lie ahead. While some elements of the central psychosocial skills can be observed at all ages, the intensity with which they are expressed at certain times marks their importance in the definition of a developmental stage. Erikson et al. (1986) put it this way:

The epigenetic chart also rightly suggests that the individual is never struggling only with the tension that is focal at the time. Rather, at every successive developmental stage, the individual is also increasingly engaged in the anticipation of tensions that have yet to become focal and in reexperiencing those tensions that were inadequately integrated when they were focal; similarly engaged are those whose age-appropriate integration was then, but is no longer, adequate. (p. 39)

The epigenetic principle assumes that it takes the entire life span, from the prenatal period through very old age, for all facets of human capacity to emerge. In later adulthood and very old age, grandparents transmit the wisdom of their generation to their grandchildren by teaching them stories, songs, customs, and beliefs.

As one leaves a stage, the achievements of that stage are neither lost nor irrelevant to later stages. Erikson (1950/1963) warns us not to become too structural in our thinking. Although the theory suggests that important ego strengths emerge from the successful resolution of conflicts at every stage, one should not assume that these strengths, once established, are never challenged or shaken. Events may take place later in life that call into question the essential beliefs established in an earlier period.

For example, the psychosocial conflict during early school age is initiative versus guilt. Its positive outcome, a sense of initiative, is a joy in innovation and experimentation and a willingness to take risks in order to learn more about the world. Once achieved, the sense of initiative provides a positive platform for the formation of social relationships as well as for further creative intellectual inquiry and discovery. However, experiences in a highly authoritarian school environment or in a very judgmental, shaming personal relationship may cause one to inhibit this sense of initiative or to mask it with a facade of indifference.

The idea of life stages should be used to highlight the changing orientations toward oneself and others that dominate periods of the life span. The essential idea is that the way one perceives and experiences life varies qualitatively from stage to stage. Movement from one stage to the next is the result of changes in several major systems at approximately the same time. The new mixture of needs, capabilities, and expectations is what produces the new orientation toward experience at each stage.

Developmental Tasks

Developmental tasks, the second organizing concept of psychosocial theory, consist of a set of skills and competencies that contribute to increased mastery over one's environment. These developmental tasks reflect areas of accomplishment in physical, cognitive, social, and emotional development, as well as development of the self-concept. The tasks define what is healthy, normal development at each age in a particular society. The tasks form a sequence: Success in learning the tasks of one stage leads to development and a greater chance of success in learning the tasks of later stages. Failure at the tasks of one stage leads to greater difficulty with later tasks or may even make later tasks impossible to master.

Robert J. Havighurst, who first introduced the concept of developmental tasks, believed that human development is a process in which people attempt to learn the tasks required of them by the society to which they are adapting. These tasks change with age because each society has age-graded expectations for behavior. "Living in a modern society is a long series of tasks to learn" (Havighurst, 1972, p. 2). The person who learns well receives satisfaction and reward; the person who does not suffers unhappiness and social disapproval.

Although Havighurst's view of development emphasizes the guiding role of society in determining which skills need to be acquired at a certain age, it does not totally ignore the role of physical maturation. Havighurst believed that there are **sensitive periods** for learning developmental tasks—that is, times when the person is most ready to acquire a new ability. Havighurst called these periods **teachable moments.** Most people learn developmental tasks at the time and in the sequence appropriate in their society. If a particular task is not learned during the sensitive period, learning it may be much more difficult later on.

Learning that occurs during a sensitive period may enhance learning and performance in this task later in life. Initially, skills are learned in the sensitive period, when much is happening both internally and externally to stimulate that area of growth. Once the sensitive period has passed, however, learning may still continue. Language skills, for example, do not cease to develop after toddlerhood. New and more complex ways of using language are learned throughout life. Much of the elementary and high school curriculum focuses on developing language, including expanding one's vocabulary, developing skills in oral and written communication, and learning new languages. Gerontologists have found that motivation plays a great role in increasing the linguistic skills of elderly people who wish to learn a new language before taking a trip to Europe.

The basic tasks we identify differ from those outlined in Havighurst's writings. Our choice of tasks is based on broad areas of accomplishment that have been identified by researchers as critical to psychological and social growth at each stage of life in a modern, technological culture. We recognize that the demands for growth may differ according to the orientation and complexity of a particular society. The tasks we present as central to successful adaptation in a highly technical, information-age society such as that of the United States are not necessarily the appropriate standards for maturation and growth in a developing country or in a traditional, tribal culture.

We believe that a relatively small number of major psychosocial tasks dominate a person's problem-solving efforts and learning during a given stage. As these tasks are mastered, new competencies enhance the person's ability to engage in more complex social relationships. We assume that successful cultures must stimulate behavior that helps its members learn what they need to know for both their own survival and that of the group.

The tasks may reflect gains in physical skills, cognitive skills, social skills, emotional skills, and elaboration of the self-concept. One of the developmental tasks of infancy, for example, is the formation of a bond of attachment to the caregiver. A person's ability to form close friendships in childhood and intimate relationships in adolescence and adult life builds on the capacity for attachment that is established with a caregiver during infancy.

The birth of a child is often considered a teachable moment, when parents are especially eager to learn what they can in order to protect, nurture, and ensure the optimal development of their infant. What are other examples of teachable moments?

Keep in mind that one is changing on several major levels during each period of life. Tasks involving physical, emotional, intellectual, and social growth, as well as growth in the self-concept, all contribute to one's resources for coping with the challenges of life. Table 2.1 shows the developmental tasks we have identified as having major effects on the

TABLE 2.1	Developmental Tasks Associated with the Life Stages
Life Stage*	**Developmental Tasks**
Infancy (birth to 2 years)	Maturation of sensory, perceptual, and motor functions
	Social attachment
	Sensorimotor intelligence and early causal schemes
	Understanding the nature of objects and creating categories
	Emotional development
Toddlerhood (2 and 3)	Elaboration of locomotion
	Fantasy play
	Language development
	Self-control
Early school age (4 to 6)	Gender identification
	Early moral development
	Self-theory
	Group play
Middle (childhood 6 to 12)	Friendship
	Concrete operations
	Skill learning
	Self-evaluation
	Team play
Early adolescence (12 to 18)	Physical maturation
	Formal operations
	Emotional development
	Membership in the peer group
	Sexual relationships
Later adolescence (18 to 24)	Autonomy from parents
	Gender identity
	Internalized morality
	Career choice
Early adulthood (24 to 34)	Exploring intimate relationships
	Childbearing
	Work
	Lifestyle
Middle adulthood (34 to 60)	Managing a career
	Nurturing the marital or other intimate relationship
	Expanding caring relationships
	Managing the household
Later adulthood (60 to 75)	Promoting intellectual vigor
	Redirecting energy toward new roles and activities
	Accepting one's life
	Developing a point of view about death
Very old age (75 until death)	Coping with physical changes of aging
	Developing a psychohistorical perspective
	Traveling through uncharted terrain

*We do not consider the concept of development tasks appropriate to the prenatal stage.

life experiences of most people in modern society and the stages during which each set of tasks is of primary learning value. There are 42 developmental tasks in the list. Whereas the infant is learning orientations and skills related to the first five, the young adult in the early adulthood stage has already acquired skills related to 27 tasks from the previous stages. New learning may continue in these areas as well as in the four new developmental tasks faced by the young adult. The very old person has all the areas of previous learning to draw from while working on three tasks and the crisis of the final stage.

Mastery of the developmental tasks is influenced by the resolution of the psychosocial crisis of the previous stage, and it is this resolution that leads to the development of new social capabilities. These capabilities orient the person toward new experiences, a new aptitude for relationships, and new feelings of personal worth as he or she confronts the challenges of the developmental tasks of the next

Drawing on a full life of experience and competence, President Jimmy Carter, now in his late 70s, applies his wisdom, talent, and physical energy to support the efforts of Habitat for Humanity.

stage. In turn, the skills learned during a particular stage as a result of work on its developmental tasks provide the tools for the resolution of the psychosocial crisis of that stage. Task accomplishment and crisis resolution interact to produce individual life stories.

Psychosocial Crisis

A **psychosocial crisis,** the third organizing concept of psychosocial theory (Erikson, 1950/1963), arises when one must make psychological efforts to adjust to the demands of one's social environment at each stage of development. The word *crisis* in this context refers to a normal set of stresses and strains rather than to an extraordinary set of events.

Societal demands vary from stage to stage. The individual experiences these demands as mild but persistent guidelines for and expectations of behavior. They may be demands for greater self-control, a further development of skills, or a stronger commitment to goals. Before the end of each stage of development, the individual tries to achieve a resolution, to adjust to society's demands, and at the same time to translate those demands into personal terms. This process produces a *state of tension* that the individual must reduce in order to proceed to the next stage. It is this tension state that produces the psychosocial crisis.

A Typical Psychosocial Crisis

The psychosocial crisis with which you are probably most familiar is identity versus identity confusion, which is associated with later adolescence. An **identity crisis** is a sudden disintegration or deterioration of the framework of values and goals that a person relies on to give meaning and purpose to daily life. An identity crisis usually involves strong feelings of anxiety and depression. The anxiety occurs because the person fears that without the structure of a clear value system, unacceptable impulses will break through and he or she will behave in ways that may be harmful or immoral. The depression occurs because the person suddenly feels worthless. When our previously established goals come to seem meaningless, we are likely to be overwhelmed by a feeling that our actions have no purpose or value.

A college student's identity crisis may be intensified under two conditions, both of which demand a rapid, intense examination of one's values. First, the identity crisis may be heightened when students attend a college where the value orientation departs significantly from their own and where they interact frequently with faculty members. These students believe they should admire and respect adults, especially their professors, and they suddenly feel at a loss when significant adults challenge their values. They may respond by desperately clinging to their old value system in order to maintain a sense of control or by abandoning all sense of confidence in their values and adopting a stance of complete indifference.

The identity crisis may also be heightened when external demands force students to make a value commitment while they are still uncertain or confused. For some students, the need to decide on a major, to make a commitment to a love relationship, or to take a stand on a campus controversy will reveal that they do indeed know what they want, and they will be reassured that their values are more fully shaped than they had realized. Students who make this happy discovery will move in the direction of identity achievement. Other students, however, who are uncertain about which values and goals are best, may feel overwhelmed when sudden demands for commitment send their existing tentative value structure into disorganization.

At the end of the chapter you will read Erikson's account of his own identity crisis. Erikson never went to college. In his case, conflict about identity was a product of early childhood confusion about his family origins as well as emerging feelings of alienation from family values. His circumstances, coupled with the complexity of his creative intellect, produced an intense crisis.

Psychosocial Crises of the Life Stages

Table 2.2 lists the psychosocial crisis at each stage of development from infancy through very old age. This scheme, derived from Erikson's model shown in Figure 2.2, expresses the crises as polarities—for example, trust versus mistrust, and autonomy versus shame and doubt. These contrasting conditions suggest the underlying dimensions along which each psychosocial crisis is resolved. According to psychosocial theory, most people experience both ends of the continuum. The inevitable discrepancy between one's level of development at the beginning of a stage and society's push for a new level of functioning by the end of it creates at least a mild degree of the negative condition. Even within a loving, caring social environment that promotes trust, an infant will experience some moments of frustration or disappointment that result in mistrust. Even the most industrious, skillful child of middle childhood will encounter some tasks that are too difficult or some feelings of inferiority in comparison with a more talented peer. The outcome of the crisis at each stage is a balance or integration of the two opposing forces. For each person, the relative frequency and significance of positive and negative experiences will contribute to a resolution of the crisis that lies at some point along a continuum from extremely positive to extremely negative.

The likelihood of a completely positive or a completely negative resolution is small. Most individuals resolve the crisis in a generally positive direction, supported

---

TABLE 2.2　The Psychosocial Crises

Life Stage*	Psychosocial crisis
Infancy (birth to 2 years)	Trust versus mistrust
Toddlerhood (2 and 3)	Autonomy versus shame and doubt
Early school age (4 to 6)	Initiative versus guilt
Middle childhood (6 to 12)	Industry versus Inferiority
Early adolescence (12 to 18)	Group identity versus alienation
Later adolescence (18 to 24)	Individual identity versus identity confusion
Early adulthood (24 to 34)	Intimacy versus isolation
Middle adulthood (34 to 60)	Generativity versus stagnation
Later adulthood (60 to 75)	Integrity versus despair
Very old age (75 until death)	Immortality versus extinction

*We do not consider the concept of psychosocial crisis appropriate to the prenatal stage.

In threatening or dangerous situations, such as the conditions of combat, some degree of mistrust and vigilance are adaptive.

by a combination of positive experiences combined with natural maturational tendencies. At each successive stage, however, the likelihood of a negative resolution increases as the developmental tasks become more complex and the chances of encountering societal barriers to development rise. A positive resolution of each crisis provides new ego strengths that help the person meet the demands of the next stage.

To understand the process of growth at each life stage, we have to consider the negative as well as the positive pole of each crisis. The dynamic tension between the positive and negative forces respects and reflects the struggles we all encounter to restrain unbridled impulses, to overcome fears and doubts, and to look past our own needs to consider the needs of others. The negative poles offer an insight into basic areas of human vulnerability. Experienced in moderation, the negative forces result in a clarification of ego positions, individuation, and moral integrity. While a steady diet of mistrust is undesirable, for example, it is important that a trusting person be able to evaluate situations and people for their trustworthiness and to discern cues about safety or danger in any encounter. Recognizing those who may not be concerned about one's needs or welfare is certainly advantageous. However, mistrusting others and being overly careful in all relationships may lead to hopelessness. In every psychosocial crisis, the experiences at both the positive and the negative poles contribute to the total range of a person's adaptive capacities.

Why conceptualize life in terms of crises? Does this idea adequately portray the experience of the individual, or does it overemphasize conflict and abnormality? The term **crisis** implies that normal development does not proceed smoothly. The theory hypothesizes that tension and conflict are necessary elements in the developmental process; crisis and its resolution are basic, biologically based components of life experience at every stage. In fact, they are what drive the ego system to develop new capacities. "Growing pains" occur at every stage of life. Those who expect their problems to be over after adolescence will be sorely disappointed.

The term *psychosocial* draws our attention to the fact that these developmental crises are, in part, the result of cultural pressures and expectations. In the process of normal development, individuals will experience tension regardless of their culture because of the culture's need to socialize and integrate its members. The concept acknowledges the dynamic conflicts between individuality and group membership at each period of life. Although the tension itself is not a result of personal inadequacies, failure to resolve it can seriously limit future growth. To some extent, psychosocial theory attempts to account for failures in development that appear at every stage in life. The concept of crisis implies that at any stage something can interfere with growth and reduce one's opportunities to experience personal fulfillment.

The exact nature of the conflict is not the same at all stages. Few cultural limits are placed on infants. The outcome of the infancy stage depends greatly on the skill of the caregiver. At early school age, the culture stands in fairly direct opposition to the child's initiative in some matters and offers abundant encouragement to initiative in others. In

Floods, earthquakes, and hurricanes produce unforeseen crises in which homes and communities are destroyed. At different developmental stages, people adapt in unique ways to these crises. Children may experience a loss of confidence in their parents' ability to protect them. Older adults may grieve for the loss of a lifetime of treasure or be inspired by the miracle of their survival.

young adulthood, the dominant cultural push is toward the establishment of intimate relationships; yet an individual may be unable to attain intimacy because of cultural norms against certain expressions of intimacy or restrictions against certain types of unions.

Psychosocial theory suggests that crises are a predictable part of growth. At every life stage, we can anticipate that there will be some discrepancy between the skills that have been developed before it begins and the expectations for growth during the stage. As reflected in the epigenetic principle, the succession of crises occurs in a predictable sequence over the life course. Although Erikson did not specify the exact ages for each crisis, the theory hypothesizes an age-related progression in which each crisis has its time of special ascendancy. The combination of biological, psychological, and societal forces that operate to bring about change has a degree of regularity that places each psychosocial crisis at a particular period of life.

In addition to these predictable crises, any number of unforeseen stresses may arise. Parents' divorce, the death of a sibling, victimization by violence, the loss of a job, and widowhood are examples of unforseen life crises. The need to cope with them may overwhelm a person, particularly if several occur at the same time. The picture of predictable developmental stress that is emphasized in psychosocial theory must be expanded to include the possibility of unanticipated crises. Although these chance events may foster growth and new competencies, they may also result in defensiveness, regression, or dread. The impact of an unpredictable crisis will depend in part on whether the person is in a state of psychosocial crisis at the time (Cummings, Greene & Karraker, 1991; Larson & Ham, 1993).

The combination of predictable crises, unpredictable crises, and unique historical pressures may bring to light prior crises that require reorganization. For example, during early adulthood, when issues of intimacy versus isolation are salient, it is common to find a reworking of industry versus inferiority as well (Whitbourne et al., 1992). Young adults encounter the very concrete challenges of establishing themselves in the labor market and achieving self-sufficiency through paid employment. The intensity of this additional crisis will depend in part on historical factors, such as the economic and materialistic orientation of the society as a specific age group enters early adulthood. It will also depend on individual factors, especially whether the young adult has developed a clear commitment to occupational values during the earlier period of identity versus identity confusion. Thus, the crises are not resolved and put to rest once and for all: Each crisis is played and replayed both during ongoing developmental changes and when life events challenge the balance that was achieved earlier.

The Central Process for Resolving the Psychosocial Crisis

Every psychosocial crisis reflects some discrepancy between the person's developmental competencies at the beginning of the stage and societal pressures for more effective, integrated functioning. How is the discrepancy resolved? What experiences or processes underlay the person's efforts to cope with the challenges of de-

Paulo, Picasso's son, is shown in deep concentration as he sketches at his desk. Through imitation, a child takes ownership of actions and skills that he or she has observed among adults. It is little wonder that Paulo, surrounded by his fathers' ongoing artistic activity, would be drawn to imitate it.

velopment at each stage? We have offered an extension of psychosocial theory by identifying a central process through which each psychosocial crisis is resolved. The **central process,** the fourth organizing concept of psychosocial theory, links the individual's needs with the requirements of the culture at each life stage. Significant relationships and relevant competencies change at every life stage. Specific modes of psychological work and of social interaction must occur if a person is to continue to grow.

For example, imitation is viewed as the central process for psychosocial growth during toddlerhood (ages 2 and 3), when children expand their range of skills by imitating adults, siblings, television models, playmates, and even animals. Imitation provides toddlers with enormous satisfaction. As they increase the similarity between themselves and admired members of their social groups through imitation, they begin to experience the world as other people and animals experience it. They exercise some control over potentially frightening or confusing events by imitating elements of those occurrences in their play.

The movement toward a sense of autonomy in toddlerhood is facilitated by the child's readiness to imitate and by the variety of models available for observation. Imitation expands children's range of behavior, and through persistent imitative activity, children expand their sense of self-initiated behavior and control over their actions. Repetitive experiences of this kind lead to the development of a sense of personal autonomy.

Imitation is more dominant in the behavioral repertoire during toddlerhood than at any other time in life, although it is often used as a learning and social strategy at other stages. Also, the society—in this case, through the significant relationship with the parents—tells the child, "That's good, Robbie. Now watch Daddy, and do it just the way he does." Not only are this child's tendencies toward imitation internally motivated, but his society is telling him, "Imitate! It will help you learn."

Table 2.3 shows the central processes that lead to the acquisition of new skills, the resolution of the psychosocial crisis, and successful coping at each life stage. Each of

TABLE 2.3 The Central Process for Resolving Each Psychosocial Crisis

Life Stage*	Central Process
Infancy (birth to 2 years)	Mutuality with caregiver
Toddlerhood (2 and 3)	Imitation
Early school age (4 to 6)	Identification
Middle childhood (6 to 12)	Education
Early adolescence (12 to 18)	Peer pressure
Later adolescence (18 to 24)	Role experimentation
Early adulthood (24 to 34)	Mutuality among peers
Middle adulthood (34 to 60)	Person-environment fit and creativity
Later adulthood (60 to 75)	Introspection
Very old age (75 until death)	Social support

*We do not consider the concept of central process appropriate to the prenatal stage.

these processes appears to take on heightened significance during a particular stage, and each can be encouraged through the organization of significant social relationships.

The central process for coping with the challenges of each life stage provides both personal and societal mechanisms for taking in new information and reorganizing existing information. It also suggests the means that are most likely to lead to a revision of the psychological system so that the crisis of the particular stage may be resolved. Each central process results in an intensive reworking of the psychological system, including a reorganization of boundaries, values, and images of oneself and others.

Radius of Significant Relationships

The fifth organizing principle of psychosocial theory is the **radius of significant relationships** (Erikson, 1982, p. 31) (Figure 2.4). Our society is organized in such a way that age-related demands on individuals are communicated through their significant social relationships. For example, the law requires that all 6-year-olds go to school, but it is parents who actually send them there. The law requires that people remain in school until they are 16, but it is peers, teachers, parents, and adolescents' own aspirations that encourage their continued attendance.

The demands exerted on a person by all elements of the social world make up the **societal system.** A person's ego includes a social processing system that is sensitive to social expectations, which serve as natural stimulators of one's social processing mechanisms. Initially, a person focuses on a small number of relationships. During childhood, adolescence, and early adulthood, the number of relationships expands and takes on greater variety in depth and in intensity. In middle and later adulthood, the person often returns to a small number of extremely important relationships that provide opportunities for great depth and intimacy. Most of the demands made on a person are made by people in these significant relationships.

According to Erikson's formulation, readiness to engage in this ever-changing network is a result of the epigenetic plan. At each stage of life, this network determines the demands that will be made on the person, the way he or she will be taken care of, and the meaning that the person will derive from the relationships. The relationship network varies from person to person, but each person has a network of significant relationships and an increasing readiness to enter into more complex social life (Vanzetti & Duck, 1996). The quality of these relationships and the norms for interaction are influenced by the nature of the specific social context.

Contexts of Development

One way of thinking about the impact of the societal system is to consider individuals as embedded in a kaleidoscope of changing, interconnected systems. Children are members of families. Parents and other relatives are members of other important work and community groups that can influence families. Children, as they

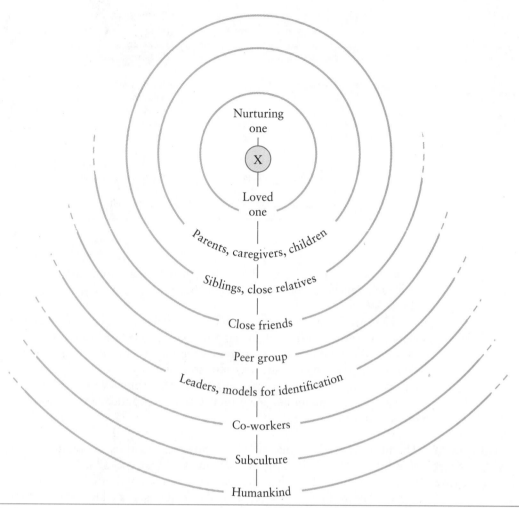

FIGURE 2.4
The radius of significant relationships

grow, may become members of other institutions such as day-care programs, schools, religious groups, community clubs, or athletic teams. Communities are nested in cities, counties, states, and national governments. An understanding of development requires insight into each level of social organization as well as across the culture as a whole. These organizations influence what is expected of each person, the roles they play, the activities they engage in, the resources available to meet these expectations, and the risks they may encounter. In addition, the contexts of development embody social, economic, and historic factors. Events such as war, political revolution, famine, or economic collapse may temporarily alter the prevailing child-rearing values, opportunities for education or employment, and the availability of resources. In addition, these events may increase exposure to violence and separation of family members, or provide exposure to other unpredictable stressors that may disrupt the course of development. Family, culture, and ethnic group are three of the major contexts through which the radius of significant relationships is organized.

Families. All over the world, children are raised by small groups or families. **Family** is the universal primary social context of childhood. The family continues to be a meaningful context throughout life, especially as we think of the relationship of adults with their aging parents, the formation of new families in adulthood, and the lifelong connections among siblings. Historically, the term *family* has referred to a group of people, usually related by blood, marriage, or adoption. In contemporary U.S. society,

Families are a fundamental component of the radius of significant relations. Family reunions bring generations of a family in contact and preserve the sense of identification with one's ancestry, personal family history, and family values.

however, people who view themselves as members of a family may have no legal relationship or shared ancestral bond. The psychosocial meaning of family continues to be defined as individuals who share a common destiny and who experience a sense of emotional intimacy. People in a family care about one another and take care of one another.

Culture. **Culture** refers to the socially standardized ways of thinking, feeling, and acting that a person acquires as a member of a society. Culture includes the concepts, habits, skills, arts, technology, religion, and government of a people. It encompasses the tools and symbol systems that give structure and meaning to experience. Often, a culture exerts influence directly through families as well as through other social organizations such as churches and schools. The United States, like other nations, has a culture that has a strong, unifying impact on its citizens. Within the United States, there are also noticeable regional cultural patterns marked by unique vocabulary and dialect, mannerisms, and styles of social interaction. Throughout this book, we will note the great differences in what life, including family life, is like in different cultures, and how the integration of person and culture produces distinctive personal experiences for individuals in various cultures.

Ethnic Groups. Despite the common threads of culture that affect everyone who grows up or lives for a long time in the United States, there are also persistent subcultural forces that shape the daily lives of children and adults. The United States is a complex society that is made up of people from a vast array of cultures throughout the world. We call these groups **ethnic subcultures** or **ethnic groups**. People who belong to ethnic groups share socially standardized ways of thinking, feeling, and acting with other members of their group. The subculture may or may not be in conflict with the mainstream culture of the United States. Much of the literature on human development in this country is based on observations of white middle class participants of European ancestry. However, increasing attention is being given to the lifestyles, parenting practices, and family values of various other ethnic groups, and we will try to give special attention to studies that highlight ethnic group comparisons where possible.

Coping Behavior   Coping behavior, the sixth organizing concept of psychosocial theory, consists of active efforts to resolve stress and create new solutions to the challenges of each developmental stage. Robert White (1974) identified three components of the coping process: (1) the ability to gain and process new information, (2) the ability to maintain

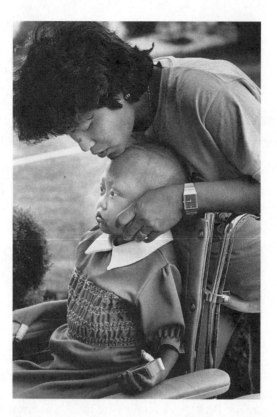

After a terrible accident, this child and her mother struggle to preserve the child's optimal level of functioning, find hope in small signs of improvement, and create innovative ways of solving innumerable social, financial, and medical problems. What are the coping resources that make it possible for this mother and child to remain proactive and optimistic?

control over one's emotional state, and (3) the ability to move freely within one's environment.

Coping behavior is an important concept in psychosocial theory because it explains how new, original, creative, unique, and inventive behavior occurs. In addition, it lets us predict that individuals will behave in original, spontaneous, and successful ways in their active social lives. In the face of threat, coping behavior allows for the individual to develop and grow, rather than merely maintain equilibrium or become disorganized.

White illustrated the coping process by describing high school seniors' strategies for coping with the challenge of college. Those who go to the campus, talk to the students there, start reading for courses they will take, or take summer jobs in which they will be interacting with college students are doing more than maintaining their current level of functioning or equilibrium. They are devising coping strategies that will lead to increased information about their future setting and increased competence in it.

In coping with life challenges, individuals create their own strategies, which reflect their talents and motives. Think of the first day of kindergarten for a group of 5-year-olds. Some children are just sitting, shyly watching the teacher and the other children. Others are climbing all over the equipment and eagerly exploring the new toys. Still others are talking to the teacher or the other children, finding out names, making friends, or telling about the bus ride to school. Each of these strategies can be understood as a way of gathering information while preserving a degree of autonomy and integrity in a new and potentially threatening environment. No one way is right or even best, except as it serves the person by allowing access to information, freedom of movement, and some control over the emotions evoked by the new challenge.

An individual's characteristic style of coping appears to be influenced by a variety of factors, including gender, the available resources, the nature of interpersonal relationships, and the accumulation of life experiences. Some people face chronic stressors associated with poverty, illness, or some form of disability. In the face of these demands, one's capacity for coping may become exhausted or one may need to seek help in order to learn new coping strategies.

Prime Adaptive Ego Qualities

Erikson (1978) postulated **prime adaptive ego qualities** that develop from the positive resolution of the psychosocial crisis of a given stage and provide resources for coping with the next. He described these qualities as mental states that form a basic orientation toward the interpretation of life experiences. A sense of competence, for example, permits a person to feel free to exercise his or her wits to solve problems without being weighed down by a sense of inferiority.

The prime adaptive ego qualities and their definitions are listed in Table 2.4. These ego qualities contribute to the person's dominant worldview, which is continuously reformulated to accommodate new ego qualities. The importance of many of the

TABLE 2.4   Prime Adaptive Ego Qualities

Life Stage	Ego Quality	Definition
Infancy	Hope	An enduring belief that one can attain one's deep and essential wishes
Toddlerhood	Will	A determination to exercise free choice and self-control
Early school age	Purpose	The courage to imagine and pursue valued goals
Middle childhood	Competence	The free exercise of skill and intelligence in the completion of tasks
Early adolescence	Fidelity (I)	The ability freely to pledge and sustain loyalty to others
Later adolescence	Fidelity (II)	The ability freely to pledge and sustain loyalty to values and ideologies
Early adulthood	Love	A capacity for mutuality that transcends childhood dependency
Middle adulthood	Care	A commitment to concern about what has been generated
Later adulthood	Wisdom	A detached yet active concern with life itself in the face of death
Very old age	Confidence	A conscious trust in oneself and assurance about the meaningfulness of life

Source: Based on Erikson, 1978.

prime adaptive ego qualities has been verified by research. For example, hope has been identified as a significant factor in allowing people to cope with adversity as well as to organize their actions to achieve difficult goals (Snyder, 1994). People with a hopeful attitude have a better chance of maintaining their spirits and strength in the face of crisis than people who are pessimistic. In interviews with people in very old age, Erikson and his colleagues found that those who maintained a sense of hope about their own future as well as that of their children were more intellectually vigorous and psychologically resilient than those not characterized by this orientation (Erikson et al., 1986).

Core Pathologies

Although most people develop the prime adaptive ego qualities, a potential **core pathology** or destructive force may also develop as a result of ineffective, negatively balanced crisis resolution at each stage (Erikson, 1982) (Table 2.5). The core pathologies also serve as guiding orientations for behavior. These pathologies move people away from others, tend to prevent further exploration of interpersonal relations, and obstruct the resolution of subsequent psychosocial crises. The energy that would normally be directed toward mastering the developmental tasks of a stage is directed instead toward resisting or avoiding change. The core pathologies are not simply passive limitations or barriers to growth. They are energized worldviews leading to strategies that protect people from further unwanted association with the social system and its persistent, tension-producing demands.

TABLE 2.5   Core Pathologies

Life Stage	Core Pathology	Definition
Infancy	Withdrawal	Social and emotional detachment
Toddlerhood	Compulsion	Repetitive behaviors motivated by impulse or by restrictions against the expression of impulse
Early school age	Inhibition	A psychological restraint that prevents freedom of thought, expression, and activity
Middle childhood	Inertia	A paralysis of action and thought that prevents productive work
Early adolescence	Dissociation	An inability to connect with others
Later adolescence	Repudiation	Rejection of roles and values that are viewed as alien to oneself
Early adulthood	Exclusivity	An elitist shutting out of others
Middle adulthood	Rejectivity	Unwillingness to include certain others or groups of others in one's generative concern
Later adulthood	Disdain	A feeling of scorn for the weakness and frailty of oneself and others
Very old age	Diffidence	An inability to act because of overwhelming self-doubt

Source: Based on Erikson, 1982.

EVALUATION OF PSYCHOSOCIAL THEORY

Although we believe that psychosocial theory provides a useful theoretical framework for organizing the vast array of observations in the field of human development, we recognize that it has weaknesses as well as strengths. We want you to be aware of its strengths and its weaknesses so that you can form your own independent judgment of its usefulness and to be alert to how the theory may influence your thinking. The strengths and weaknesses of psychosocial theory that are discussed below are listed in Table 2.6.

Strengths   Psychosocial theory provides a broad context within which to study development. The theory links the process of child development to the later stages of adult life, to the needs of society, and to the ability of societies to interact. Although many scholars agree that such a broad perspective is necessary, few other theories attempt to address the dynamic interplay between individual development and society.

The emphasis of psychosocial theory on ego development and ego processes provides insight into the directions of healthy development throughout life. Concepts central to the theory such as trust, autonomy, identity achievement, generativity, coping, well-being, social support, and intergenerational interdependence have become thoroughly integrated into contemporary human development scholarship (e.g., Snyder, 1994; Ryff, 1995; Zimmerman et al., 1995). At the same time, the theory identifies tensions that may disrupt development at each life stage, providing a useful framework for approaching psychotherapy and counseling.

The concept of normative psychosocial crises is a creative contribution that identifies predictable tensions between socialization and maturation throughout life. Societies, with their structures, laws, roles, rituals, and sanctions, are organized to guide individual growth toward a particular ideal of mature adulthood. If individuals grew in that direction naturally, as a result of an unfolding, genetically guided plan, presumably there would be no need for these elaborate social structures. But every society faces problems when it attempts to balance the needs of the individual with the needs of the group. All individuals face problems when they attempt to experience their individuality while still maintaining the support of their group. Psychosocial theory gives us concepts for exploring these natural tensions.

Weaknesses   One weakness of psychosocial theory is that its basic concepts are presented in language that is abstract and difficult to examine empirically (Crain, 1985; Miller, 1993). Such

---

TABLE 2.6   Strengths and Weaknesses of Psychosocial Theory

Strengths	Weaknesses
The theory provides a broad context, linking development in various stages of life to the resources and demands of society.	The basic concepts of the theory are abstract and difficult to operationalize.
It emphasizes ego development and directions for healthy development across the life span.	Explanations of the mechanisms for resolving crisis and moving from one stage to the next are not well developed.
It provides a useful framework for psychotherapy.	The specific number of stages and their link to a genetic plan for development have not been adequately demonstrated, especially in adulthood.
It emphasizes the dynamic interplay between a genetic plan and the forces of culture and society in guiding individual development.	The theory and research have been dominated by a male, Eurocentric perspective that gives too much emphasis to the emergence of individuality and not enough to social needs and competence in other cultural contexts.
The concept of normative psychosocial crises provides an effective set of constructs for examining the tension between the individual and society.	The specific way in which culture encourages or inhibits development at each life stage is not clearly elaborated.

All of these young people are in the stage of later adolescence. Some have reached the point of identity achievement; others have not. What determines whether a person moves from one developmental stage to the next?

terms as *initiative, personal identity, intimacy, generativity,* and *integrity*—concepts included in the psychosocial crises—are hard to define and even more difficult to translate into objective measures. Nonetheless, efforts have been made along this line. James Marcia, Alan Waterman, Anne Constantinople, and others have contributed to an extensive literature that examines the construct of personal identity. Other researchers have tackled the concept of intimacy, and still others have tried to operationalize the concepts of generativity and integrity. Questionnaire measures based on Erikson's psychosocial theory, including the Inventory of Psychosocial Development and Measures of Psychosocial Development (MPD) have been used to trace the emergence of psychosocial crises and their resolution in samples varying in age from adolescence to later adulthood (Constantinople, 1969; Waterman & Whitbourne, 1981; Hawley, 1988; Whitbourne et al., 1992). In addition to studies meant to test psychosocial theory, many others have a bearing on its constructs. In each of the stages of life that we will be examining, you will find an analysis of research that has a clear link to the constructs of psychosocial theory.

Another weakness of the theory is that explanations of the mechanisms for resolving crises and moving from one stage to the next are not well developed. Erikson has not offered a universal mechanism for crisis resolution, nor has he detailed the kinds of experiences that are necessary at each stage if one is to cope successfully with the crisis of that stage. We have addressed this weakness by introducing the concepts of developmental tasks and a central process for each stage. The developmental tasks suggest some of the major achievements that permit a person to meet the social expectations of each stage. The central process identifies the primary social context within which the crisis is resolved. Using these two mechanisms, one can begin to clarify the process of movement from one stage to the next.

The specific number of stages and their link to a biologically based plan for development have been criticized, most notably in discussions of the stages of adulthood (Crain, 1985). Other human development theorists, such as Robert Peck, Robert Gould, Daniel Levinson, and Marjorie Lowenthal, have taken a more differentiated view of the stages of adulthood and later life. We have responded to these criticisms by treating adolescence as two distinct stages and by adding a fourth stage of adulthood: very old age. You will also read about the important developmental issues of the prenatal period, a stage that Erikson's theory does not consider, but one that clearly plays a central role in setting the stage for a lifetime of vulnerabilities and competences. In our view, these revisions demonstrate the natural evolution of a theoretical framework as it continues to encounter new observations. Nevertheless, the increasing life expectancy, accompanied by a longer period of healthy later life and the elaboration of lifestyles, make it difficult to chart a normative life course from early adulthood into very old age.

Finally, the theory and related research have been criticized as being dominated by a male, Eurocentric, individualistic perspective (Gilligan, 1982). The themes of autonomy, initiative, industry, and personal identity all emphasize the process of individuation. In this and other theories of development, ego development, separateness from family, autonomy, and self-directed goal attainment have been equated with psychological maturity. Relatively little attention has been given to themes that have been identified as central to the developmental experiences of girls and young women—themes of interpersonal competence, connection, and affiliation (Josselson, 1987). These themes also seem to be emerging within more collectively oriented ethnic groups, cultures in which maturity is equated with one's ability to support and sustain the success of the family or the extended-family group rather than with one's own achievement of status, wealth, or recognition.

Within the framework of psychosocial theory, the theme of connection is addressed directly through the first psychosocial crisis of trust versus mistrust in infancy, but then the thread is lost until early adolescence and early and middle adulthood, when group identity, intimacy, and generativity direct the focus back to the critical links that individuals build with others. The concept of the radius of significant relationships is present at every phase of life, suggesting that how one defines oneself is always intimately linked to one's meaningful social connections. This construct helps to maintain the perspective of the person interwoven in a tapestry of relationships, focusing especially on family and friends in childhood; the family, peer group, love relationships, and close friends in early and later adolescence; and intimate partners, family, friends, and co-workers in various phases of adult life.

To extend the theme of connection, the text elaborates on developing capabilities for social interaction and differences in socialization practices and outcomes for males and females in our society. A variety of social abilities, including empathy, prosocial behavior, interaction skills, and components of social cognition are traced as they emerge in the context of family relationships, friendship, peer groups, and work. The text considers ethnic groups as well as broader social influences on development and the importance of a collective orientation toward responsibility in caring for children and creating a sense of community.

FIGURE 2.5
*The mechanism for
positive and negative
psychosocial development*

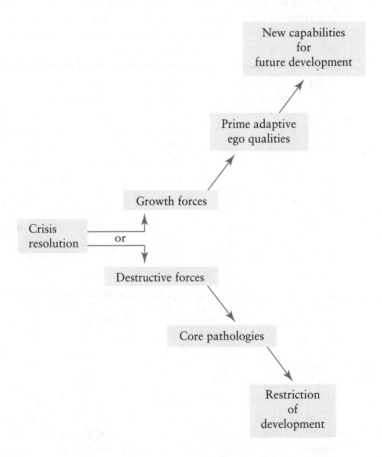

A Recap of Psychosocial Theory

At the beginning of this chapter we discussed the three questions you must ask in order to evaluate a theory. Let us now answer these questions with respect to psychosocial theory:

1. *Which phenomena is the theory trying to explain?* The theory attempts to explain human development across the life span, especially patterned changes in self-understanding, social relationships, and worldview.
2. *What assumptions does the theory make?* Human development is a product of three factors: biological evolution, the interaction between individuals and social groups, and the contributions that individuals make to their own psychological growth.
3. *What does the theory predict?* There are 11 distinct stages of development. Developmental tasks are dictated by the interaction of the biological, psychological, and societal systems during each stage. A normal crisis arises at each stage of development, and a central process operates to resolve it. Each person is part of an expanding network of significant relationships that convey society's expectations and demands. These relationships also provide encouragement in the face of challenges. New behaviors continue to be possible throughout life.

Development will be optimal if a person can create new behavior and relationships as a result of skill acquisition and successful crisis resolution during each stage of growth. Lack of development and core pathologies result from tendencies that restrict behavior in general and new behavior in particular (especially social behavior). The mechanism for positive and negative development is diagrammed in Figure 2.5.

Chapter Summary

Psychosocial theory offers a life-span view of development, which is a product of the interactions between individuals and their social environments. The needs and goals of both the individual and society must be considered in conceptualizing human development. Predictability is found in the sequence of psychosocial stages, in the central process involved in the resolution of the crisis at each stage, and in the radius of significant relationships. Individuality is expressed in the achievement of the developmental tasks, the balance of the positive and negative poles of each psychosocial crisis and the resulting worldview, and in the style and resources for coping that a person brings to each new life challenge.

The basic concepts of psychosocial theory provide the framework for analyzing development across 11 life stages. Each chapter from 4 through 14 is devoted to one life stage. With the exception of Chapter 4, on pregnancy and prenatal development, each starts with a discussion of the developmental tasks of that life stage. By tracing developments in physical growth, emotional growth, intellectual skills, social relationships, and self-understanding, you can begin to recognize the interrelationship among all of these dimensions during each period of life.

In the second section of each chapter, we describe the psychosocial crisis of the stage under discussion, accounting for the tension by examining the individual's needs and personal resources in light of the dominant societal expectations. In addition to defining the crisis, we conceptualize the central process by which it is resolved. The resolution of the crisis at each stage develops either new ego strengths or new core pathologies.

At the end of each chapter, we use the material we have discussed to analyze a selected topic that is of persistent concern to our society. These topics are controversial, and they may generate sentiment as they deepen understanding. We intend these sections to stimulate the application of developmental principles to other real-world concerns.

Take a moment to study Table 2.7. You can use this table as a guide to the major themes of the text. It may help you to see the connections among the topics within a chapter, or to trace threads of continuity over several periods of life. You may also use this table in constructing a life map for yourself, which will reveal the levels of tension and the major psychosocial factors that are currently affecting your self-concept and your relationships with others.

TABLE 2.7   The Organization of the Text

Life Stage	Developmental Tasks	Psychosocial Crisis
Prenatal (conception to (birth)		
Infancy (birth to 2 years)	Maturation of sensory, perceptual, and motor functions Social attachment Sensorimotor intelligence and early causal schemes Understanding the nature of objects and creating categories Emotional development	Basic trust versus basic mistrust
Toddlerhood (2 and 3)	Elaboration of locomotion Fantasy play Language development Self-control	Autonomy versus shame and doubt
Early school age (4 to 6)	Gender identification Early moral development Self-theory Group play	Initiative versus guilt
Middle childhood (6 to 12)	Friendship Concrete operations Skill learning Self-evaluation Team play	Industry versus inferiority
Early adolescence (12 to 18)	Physical maturation Formal operations Emotional development Membership in the peer group Sexual relationships	Group identity versus alienation
Later adolescence (18 to 24)	Autonomy from parents Gender identity Internalized morality Career choice	Individual identity versus identity confusion
Early adulthood (24 to 34)	Exploring intimate relationships Childbearing Work Lifestyle	Intimacy versus isolation
Middle adulthood (34 to 60)	Managing a career Nurturing the marital or other intimate relationship Expanding caring relationships Managing the household	Generativity versus stagnation
Later adulthood (60 to 75)	Promoting intellectual vigor Redirecting energy toward new roles Accepting one's life Developing a point of view about death	Integrity versus despair
Very old age (75 until death)	Coping with the physical changes of aging Developing a psychohistorical perspective Traveling through uncharted terrain	Immortality versus extinction

Central Process	Prime Adaptive Ego Quality	Care Pathology	Applied Topic
			Abortion
Mutuality with caregiver	Hope	Withdrawal	The role of the parents
Imitation	Will	Compulsion	Day care
Identification	Purpose	Inhibition	School readiness
Education	Competence	Inertia	Violence in the lives of children
Peer pressure	Fidelity (I)	Dissociation	Adolescent alcohol and drug use
Role experimentation	Fidelity (II)	Repudiation	Challenges of social life
Mutuality among peers	Love	Exclusivity	Divorce
Person-environment fit and creativity	Care	Rejectivity	Discrimination in the workplace
Introspection	Wisdom	Disdain	Retirement
Social support	Confidence	Diffidence	Meeting the needs of the frail elderly

End of Chapter Case

Erik Erikson illustrates the psychosocial perspective by describing the personal, family, and societal factors that contributed to his own identity crisis. (Erik H. Erikson 1902–1994)

Before I continue my account of psychoanalytic training as I experienced it, I must come to the question of how a wandering artist and teacher came to find in it an occupational identity and a field for the use of his given capacities. Here it must be said first that in the Europe of my youth, the choice of the occupational identity of "artist" meant, for many, a way of life rather than a specific occupation—or, indeed, a way of making a living—and, as today, it could mean primarily an anti-establishment way of life. Yet, the European establishment had created a well-institutionalized social niche for such idiosyncratic needs. A certain adolescent and neurotic shiftlessness could be contained in the custom of Wanderschaft; and if the individual had some gifts into the bargain, he could convince himself and others that he should have a chance to demonstrate that he might have a touch of genius.

. . . There is first of all the question of origin, which often looms large in individuals who are driven to be original. I grew up in Karlsruhe in southern Germany as the son of a pediatrician, Dr. Theodor Homburger, and his wife Karla, née Abrahamsen, a native of Copenhagen Denmark. All through my earlier childhood, they kept secret from me the fact that my mother had been married previously; and that I was the son of a Dane who had abandoned her before my birth. They apparently thought that such secretiveness was not only workable (because children then were not held to know what they had not been told) but also advisable, so that I would feel thoroughly at home in their home. As children will do, I played in with this and more or less forgot the period before the age of three, when mother and I had lived alone. Then her friends had been artists working in the folk style of Hans Thoma of the Black Forest. They, I believe, provided my first male imprinting before I had to come to terms with that intruder, the bearded doctor, with his healing love and mysterious instruments. Later, I enjoyed going back and forth between the painters' studios and our house, the first floor of which, in the afternoons, was filled with tense and trusting

Erik H. Erikson, the father of psychosocial theory

mothers and children. My sense of being "different" took refuge (as it is apt to do even in children without such acute life problems) in fantasies of how I, the son of much better parents, had been altogether a foundling. In the meantime, however, my adoptive father was anything but the proverbial stepfather. He had given me his last name (which I have retained as a middle name) and expected me to become a doctor like himself.

Identity problems sharpen with that turn in puberty when images of future roles become inescapable. My stepfather was the only professional man (and a highly respected one) in an intensely Jewish small bourgeois family, while I (coming from a racially mixed Scandinavian background) was blond and blue-eyed, and grew flagrantly tall. Before long, then, I was referred to as "goy" in my stepfather's temple; while to my schoolmates I was a "Jew." Although during World War I, I tried desperately to be a good German chauvinist, I became a "Dane" when Denmark remained neutral.

. . . At the time, like other youths with artistic or literary aspirations, I became intensely alienated from everything my bourgeois family stood for. At that point, I *set out* to be different. After graduation from the type of high school called a humanistic *Gymnasium*, . . . I went to art school, but always again took to wandering. . . . And in those days every self-respecting stranger in his own (northern) culture drifted sooner or later to Italy, where endless time was spent soaking up the southern sun and the ubiquitous sights with their grand blend of artifact and nature. I was a "Bohemian" then.

Source: Erikson, 1975.

Thought Questions

As you think about this autobiographical case, consider the following questions:

1. Why did Erikson feel like a "stranger in his own culture"?

2. What are the biological, psychological, and societal factors that contributed to Erikson's identity crisis?

3. What factors from childhood appear to be influencing his experiences as an adolescent?

4. What factors might have contributed to Erikson's ability to cope with the challenges of this period of his life, eventually finding a direction and meaning to which he could commit his talent and energy?

5. Based on what Erikson tells about his childhood and adolescence, how might his own life experiences have influenced the nature and focus of his psychosocial theory?

Chapter 3

*C*ubism is like theoretical painting. It moves beyond the surface to reveal the elements of which the subject is composed. Theories provide ways of understanding behavior by introducing structures and processes that are not immediately observable.

Major Theories for Understanding Human Development

*C*hapter Objectives

- To review the basic concepts of seven major theories that have guided research in the study of human development. These theories include: evolutionary theory, psychosexual theory, cognitive developmental theory, theories of learning, cultural theory, social role theory, and systems theory.
- To examine the implications of each theory for the study of human development.
- To clarify the links between each theory and psychosocial theory.

*I*magine that you are taking a long road trip across the country. In order to plan your route and find your way, you might want a map of the United States, which gives you major highways and the location of urban centers and major scenic areas. However, you will probably want to get more detailed maps of the states you will visit. Once you arrive at a city, or a state or national park, you will need tourist maps showing the historic sites, shopping areas, hotels, and walking trails of the specific location so that you can enjoy each spot to its fullest.

With respect to this book, psychosocial theory is like the map of the United States. It provides the broad, conceptual umbrella for our approach to the study of human development. However, we need other theories to explain behavior at different levels of analysis. The theories presented in this chapter are like the maps of the states, cities, and special scenic areas. They guide research and thinking in a variety of specific aspects of human development.

First, we present the parent theory, evolution, to provide a sense of the large picture of species change over long time periods. Evolutionary theory places the study of individual development in the broad context of the history of the species. Next,

psychosexual theory will be discussed. A forerunner of psychosocial theory, psychosexual theory explains the relationship of mental activity to changing needs, wishes, and drives with a particular focus on the role of sexual and aggressive needs. Another developmental perspective, cognitive theory, describes the maturation of capacities for logical thought. Learning theory, cultural theory, social role theory, and systems theory each introduce mechanisms that explain how the environment makes its unique impact on the person and guides the content as well as the direction of growth. These theories attempt to account for individual differences in life stories by offering various processes of adaptation to the social environment.

The use of a family of theoretical perspectives helps to maintain flexibility in interpreting behavior and facilitates our understanding of the integration of individuals and social systems. With each theory, a brief explanation of the focus of the theory and a few major constructs are presented, along with an analysis of the contributions of the theory to the study of development and links to psychosocial theory. In subsequent chapters, additional ideas from many of the theories will be presented as they relate to specific topics. ❖

THE THEORY OF EVOLUTION

The theory of evolution explains how diverse and increasingly more complex life forms come to exist. Evolutionary theory assumes that the natural laws that apply to plant and animal life also apply to humans. The **law of natural selection** explains how, over generations, species gradually change to respond to changing environmental conditions (Darwin, 1859/1979). The law of natural selection claims that behavior is adapted to the environment in which it occurs. Natural selection operates at the level of genes that are passed, via an individual organism's reproductive success, from one generation to the next. Reproductive success, sometimes called **fitness,** varies among members of a species (Archer, 1991).

Every species produces more offspring than can survive to reproduce because of limitations of the food supply and natural dangers. Darwin observed that there was quite

The value of variability in the species is illustrated in the fate of the silvery and black peppered moths. As their environment became increasingly polluted, the silver peppered moths were more readily seen and eaten, but the dark peppered moths survived.

a bit of **variability** among members of the same species in any given location. The variability he observed was due to genetic differences. As a result of varying patterns of genetic makeup, some individuals were better suited than others to their immediate environment and were more likely to survive, mate, and produce offspring. These offspring were also more likely to have characteristics appropriate for that location. Overall, the species would change to become more successful, or it would evolve into a new species. If the environment changed (in climate, for example), only certain variations of organisms would survive, and again species would evolve. Forms of life that failed to adapt would become extinct. It is important to understand that it is the variability within a species that ensures the species' continuation or its development into new forms.

Two subspecialties that have emerged from evolutionary theory are ethology and sociobiology. **Ethology** is an extension of evolutionary theory into the realm of animal and human behavior. It focuses on describing the unique adaptive behaviors of specific species, such as mating, caregiving, or strategies for obtaining resources. Through comparisons among species, this type of study helps clarify the contributions of each generation to the long-term survival of the species (Charlesworth, 1992).

Sociobiology is the scientific study of the biological basis of social behavior. It focuses on practices within populations that increase the likelihood of certain genes surviving in subsequent generations of offspring (Wilson, 1978). It, too, takes a comparative approach, looking at the potential role of genes in guiding the nature and quality of such practices as the subordination of females, polygamy, homosexuality, and altruism within populations and across species.

Implications for Human Development

Evolutionary theory assumes that human beings arrived at their current forms through a long process of natural selection. Thus, one must conclude that the basic biological mechanisms underlying human behavior, such as the development of the brain, the capacity for coordinated movement, the nature of infant instincts, and the sensory and perceptual systems, are a result of their adaptive advantage (Gray, 1996). With its focus on reproductive success, evolutionary theory highlights three phases of the life history: healthy growth and development leading up to the reproductive period; success in mating and the conception of offspring; and the ability to parent offspring so they can reach reproductive age and bear offspring of their own (Charlesworth, 1992).

An organism is most vulnerable during childhood; children require care if they are to survive to reproductive age. It is important to understand that biological capacities and the environments in which they can be expressed operate together to produce behavior. A genetic plan, shaped through hundreds of generations, guides infants' predispositions, capacities, and sensitivities. Evolutionary theory points out that infants come into the world with a range of innate capacities and potentials. They have competence that permits them to establish social contact, to organize information, and to recognize and communicate their needs. At the same time, these innate capacities are expressed within specific contexts. The quality of parenting, adequacy of resources, and competition for resources with other siblings are examples of environmental factors to which infants must adapt. Childhood experiences shape the future of the human species by providing the context for the establishment of attachments, meaningful

From an evolutionary perspective, the attachment behavioral system is central to the offspring's survival. Adults have strategies for monitoring and protecting their young, and infants have capacities for alerting their caregivers when they are frightened or upset. What behaviors in human infant-mother pairs help them stay connected in times of distress?

social competence, and problem-solving capacities, all of which have a bearing on an individual's behavior in adulthood, particularly the ability to form intimate relationships and to parent offspring. In adolescence and adulthood, the evolutionary focus shifts to emerging reproductive capacities—the ability to find a mate, reproduce, and rear one's young so that they can reach their own reproductive age. The adaptive success of one generation is based largely on its ability to pass its genetic information on to future generations.

The evolutionary perspective draws attention to the interconnection between an individual's life history and the long-range history of the species. Principles of natural selection operate slowly over generations. However, the reproductive success of individuals over the course of their own life span will determine whether their genetic material continues to be represented in the larger population. Many general areas of human behavior are functionally relevant to the successful survival and fitness of individuals and groups (Charlesworth, 1992). They include:

Reproductive strategies, such as having few or many sex partners; or early or later entry into sexual activity.
Infant immaturity requiring prolonged care.
Infant-caregiver attachment.
Parent-child conflicts and sibling rivalry.
Peer group formation and functions, especially cooperation, competition, dominance, and submission.
Pair bonding and mate selection.
Helping behavior and altruism.
Learning as adaptive behavior.
Individual creation and modification of the environment.
Social evolution and the elaboration of rites, rituals, and religions.

The evolutionary perspective directs attention to the importance of variability for a species' survival. Although theories of development typically focus on general patterns of continuity and change across individuals, evolutionary theory prompts one to attend to individual differences as a given in the study of development. They are not a factor to ignore or exclude as a source of error, but a factor to attend to in order to understand the capacity of the human species to adapt successfully to a wide variety of environmental conditions.

Links to Psychosocial Theory

Evolutionary theory is the larger framework within which broad issues of individual adaptation, species adaptation, and species survival are considered. Erikson drew heavily upon concepts first introduced in Huxley's (1942) theory of **psychosocial evolution.** Huxley studied the processes through which human beings influenced their own adaptation. He focused on the creation of new information and the invention of strategies for communicating that information from one generation to the next. Psychosocial theory translates the idea of species adaptation to the individual level through the concepts of the psychosocial crisis and coping. Each individual encounters a necessary developmental struggle in which individuals repeatedly experience tension between their own traits and capacities and the requirements and demands of the environment.

Each generation within a society faces similar challenges to cycle critical resources to the young, to nurture competence and a capacity for caring in the new generation of adults, and to inspire younger generations with hope and anticipation about the prospects of growing old. Within cultural groups, rites and rituals serve to protect and preserve resources, direct the rearing of children, and assist individuals through key transitions. Groups that adapt successfully are those that effectively cycle resources, help new members, and pass along information that will help individuals cope with future challenges.

One unique aspect of the human species is our ability to modify the environment in significant ways. We not only adapt to the environment but also alter it to suit our needs. Many of these modifications of the environment increase the chances that individuals within the group will survive; however, some modifications introduce grave risks. Psychosocial theory indicates a direction of individual growth in which the adults of a society use their competence and power to ensure the safety and well-being of future generations.

PSYCHOSEXUAL THEORY

Freud's (1933/1964) psychosexual theory focuses on the development of an individual's emotional and social life. Although much of this theory has been revised, refuted, or repressed, many contributions of psychosexual theory continue to influence contemporary personality theories and the study of development. Freud focused on the impact of sexual and aggressive drives on the individual's psychological functioning. He distinguished between the impact of sexual drives on mental activity and their effect on reproductive functions. Based largely on material from therapeutic sessions with his patients, Freud recognized the profound influence of sexuality on mental activity. In addition, he came to believe that very young children had strong sexual drives. He argued that although children are incapable of reproduction, their sexual drives operate to direct aspects of their fantasies, problem solving, and social interactions.

The most enduring contribution of psychosexual theory is the identification of domains of consciousness, referred to as the **conscious**, the **preconscious**, and the **unconscious**. Many explanations for seemingly irrational behavior can be found by analyzing the conflicting sexual and aggressive needs, fears, and wishes that are housed in the unconscious.

Psychosexual theory describes three basic structures of the personality: the **id** (the sexual and aggressive impulses), the **ego** (reality-oriented functions), and the **superego** (the moral, ethical principles). As ego develops, the child becomes increasingly adept

Freud's patients visited him in his office in Vienna, surrounded by cultural artifacts that were sources of stimulation to his own thinking. Central to the office was the famous couch. Freud invented the technique of free association as a way to gain insight into the unconscious.

In each of us, the id is the source of instincts and impulses. At age 22, Picasso drew this devilish caricature of himself, suggesting his impulsive, primate nature.

at satisfying id impulses in ways that are socially acceptable and do not offend the moral and ethical content of the superego.

Frequently, id impulses become so strong that they threaten to overwhelm the ego. For example, a man may find himself extremely jealous of the time his wife is spending with their infant. He may have strong, hostile feelings toward the infant or his wife—feelings he believes are unacceptable. Under these conditions, Freud argued, defense mechanisms come into play to protect the ego from guilt and anxiety. **Defense mechanisms** include a variety of mental "tricks" that recast or distort the feelings so that they are more acceptable, or bury them so that they are removed from consciousness. Repression is a global defense in which the feelings and thoughts are simply pushed into the unconscious. Denial, claiming that the feelings or the experience never happened, and projection, placing the blame for the feelings onto someone else, are two of the more common, primitive defense mechanisms. At moments of heightened emotionality or threat, everyone uses some form of defense to help them preserve some semblance of control. However, the use of defense mechanisms to manage anxiety over a long time can be destructive to reality testing and to forward movement in adapting to the new, altered reality.

Psychosexual theory describes five stages of development: the oral, anal, phallic, latent, and genital stages. At each stage, the focus of conflict around the expression of sexual and aggressive impulses changes. The stages reflect shifts in the body areas where pleasure is experienced, and shifts in the orientation to self and social relationships.

In adolescence, a resurgence of sexual and aggressive energy challenges many of the ego's earlier coping strategies. The ego must find new ways to express and modify impulses. An essential aspect of this process is thought to be the separation of ego from earlier figures of attachment and investment of energy in the self as well as in new social relationships.

Implications for Human Development

Psychosexual theory emphasizes the importance of the tension between interpersonal demands and intrapsychic demands in the shaping of personality. The ego develops skills for dealing with the realities of the interpersonal world. It also develops skills for satisfying personal needs and for imposing personal standards and aspirations on the way these needs are satisfied. The expectations of others, particularly parents, are internalized and given personal meaning in the formation of the superego. By developing this idea, Freud was able to show how a child translated the demands of the interpersonal world into his or her own personal way of functioning. At the same time, new demands and experiences continue to play a role in the development of personality. Freud focused on the effects of sexual impulses on personal and interpersonal life throughout adulthood.

One of the major early contributions of psychoanalytic theory was the identification of the influence of childhood experiences on adult behavior. Freud argued that the basic dynamics of personality are established by the age of 6 or 7. Psychoanalytic theory was unique in its focus on stages of development, family interactions, and unresolved family conflicts as explanations for ongoing adult behavior. The emphasis Freud gave to the importance of parenting practices and their implications for psychosexual development provides one of the few theoretical frameworks for examining parent-child relationships. Many of the early empirical studies in developmental psychology focused on issues that derived from his theory, such as child-rearing and discipline practices, moral development, and childhood aggression.

The psychoanalytic approach recognizes the importance of motives, emotions, and fantasies that guide behavior. Within this framework, human behavior springs at least as much from emotional needs as from reason. The theory suggests that underlying motives and wishes explain behaviors that otherwise might not make sense. Psychoanalytic theory recognizes domains of thought that may not appear to be logical to the observer, but that make sense from the point of view of the person. Many domains of mental activity, including fantasies, dreams, primary process thoughts and symbols, and defense mechanisms, influence how individuals make meaning from their experiences. Through the construct of the unconscious, Freud provided a means for conceptualizing explanations for thoughts and behaviors that appear irrational, self-destructive, or contradictory. The idea that development involves efforts to find acceptable outlets for strong, often socially unacceptable impulses still guides therapeutic intervention with children, adolescents, and adults.

Another critical point is Freud's open recognition of the role of sexual impulses during childhood. Freud believed that a sexual relationship with a loving partner is important for healthy adult functioning. He concluded that sexual impulses have a direct outlet in behavior during adult life. Freud recognized that children have sensual needs for stimulation and satisfaction, but they seemed to have no acceptable means to satisfy those needs. Today we are more aware of a child's need for hugging, snuggling, and physical warmth with loving caregivers, but most adults in our society still find it difficult to acknowledge that young children have sexualized impulses. Childhood wishes and needs, bottled up in the unconscious by defense mechanisms, guide behavior indirectly through symbolic expression, dreams, or, in some cases, the symptoms of mental disorders. We need only look at a daily newspaper to recognize that the acceptance and expression of sexual impulses continue to be points of conflict in modern society. Controversies over sexual dysfunction, sexual abuse, rape by strangers and acquaintances, sexual harassment in the workplace, sexually transmitted diseases, contraception, abortion, infidelity, and homophobia reveal the difficulties Americans have in dealing with the expression of sexual impulses.

Links to Psychosocial Theory

Both psychosexual theory and psychosocial theory are stage theories that address basic, qualitative changes in self-understanding and social orientation. Erikson, having been trained in psychoanalysis under Anna Freud and having been mentored by Freud and other members of the Analytic Institute, readily acknowledged his intellectual ties to Freud's psychosexual theory. Freud and Erikson both posited five stages from infancy through adolescence. Psychosexual theory deals with conflicts the child experiences in satisfying basic needs and impulses, especially sexual and aggressive impulses, within socially acceptable boundaries. Psychosocial theory expands this view by considering the broad range of social demands and social expectations that confront children at each point in development as well as the wide variety of competencies and social resources children have for meeting those demands.

Of particular note is the difference between how Freud and Erikson conceptualized the period of middle childhood. Freud referred to this time as **latency,** and argued that it was a time of relative quiet with respect to sexual and aggressive drives when no new personality characteristics were emerging. Erikson gave emphasis to these years as a time of critical focus on ego skills and mastery, highlighting the social expectations for children during the period from ages 6 to 12 to begin developing competence in skills and knowledge that are valued by the culture.

Both psychosocial theory and psychosexual theory describe characteristics and functions of the ego system. However, psychosocial theory goes beyond childhood and adolescence, suggesting the direction for ego development in early, middle, and later adulthood. Psychosocial theory gives a greater role to the individual in guiding and shaping the direction of development through the introduction of coping strategies that may redefine conflicts and identify new resources.

Sexual impulses and needs are central to the psychosexual analysis. In the psychosocial framework, sexual behavior is considered within the complex network of

Freud emphasized the role of sexual impulses in directing and shaping personality and social life.

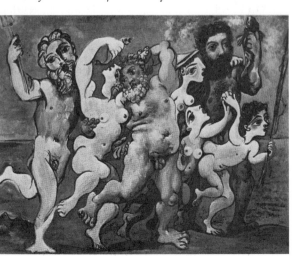

social relations. Sex-role development, sexual relationships, sex-role identity, intimacy, marriage, and nurturing the marriage relationship are all elements of psychosocial development that are addressed as the product of a complex synthesis of thoughts, wishes, behaviors, and social expectations at various stages of life.

Psychosexual theory suggests that basic issues of personal development are in place by adolescence. The results of this development are played out for the remainder of adult life in a person's defensive style, fixations, typical sexual behavior and sexual fantasies, and the strategies for sublimating sexual and aggressive impulses. In contrast, psychosocial theory assumes that development goes on throughout life. The skills resulting from accomplishing new developmental tasks are learned and new social abilities are achieved. The radius of significant relationships expands, bringing new expectations and new sources of social support. As new conflicts arise, they stimulate new growth, and new ego qualities emerge as a result of successfully coping with each new challenge.

COGNITIVE DEVELOPMENTAL THEORY

Cognition is the process of organizing and making meaning of experience. Interpreting a statement, solving a problem, synthesizing information, critically analyzing a complex task—all are cognitive activities. Perhaps the most widely known and influential of the modern cognitive theorists is Jean Piaget. His concepts provide the initial focus of this section. Recent interest in the social framework within which cognition develops has been stimulated by the work of L. S. Vygotsky. Several of his important contributions, introduced toward the end of this section, complement and expand the developmental perspective on how cognition emerges and changes over the life course.

Basic Concepts in Piaget's Theory

According to Piaget, every organism strives to achieve equilibrium. **Equilibrium** is a balance of organized structures, whether motor, sensory, or cognitive. When structures are in equilibrium, they provide effective ways of interacting with the environment. Whenever changes in the organism or in the environment require a revision of the basic structures, they are thrown into disequilibrium (Piaget, 1978/1985). Piaget focused both on equilibrium with the environment, achieved through the formation of **schemes** (the structure or organization of action in thought) and **operations** (the mental manipulation of schemes and concepts) that form systematic, logical structures for comprehending and analyzing experience, and on equilibrium within the schemes and operations themselves.

Equilibrium is achieved through **adaptation,** a process of gradually modifying existing schemes and operations in order to take into account change or discrepancies between what is known and what is being experienced (Figure 3.1). Adaptation is a two-part process in which the continuity of existing schemes and the possibility of altering schemes interact. One part of adaptation is **assimilation,** the tendency to interpret new experiences in terms of an existing scheme. Assimilation contributes to the continuity of knowing. The second part of adaptation is **accommodation,** the tendency to modify familiar schemes in order to account for new dimensions of the object or event that are revealed through experience.

Piaget hypothesized that cognitive development occurs in four stages, each characterized by a unique capacity for organizing and interpreting information. At each new stage, competences of the earlier stages are not lost but are integrated into a qualitatively new approach to thinking and knowing. The essential features of the stages are introduced here. They will be discussed in greater detail in subsequent chapters.

The first stage, **sensorimotor intelligence,** begins at birth and lasts until approximately 18 months of age. This stage is characterized by the formation of increasingly complex sensory and motor schemes that allow infants to organize and exercise some control over their environment.

The second stage, **preoperational thought,** begins when the child learns a language and ends about age 5 or 6. During this stage, children develop the tools for representing schemes symbolically through language, imitation, imagery, symbolic play, and symbolic drawing. Their knowledge is still very much tied to their own perceptions.

FIGURE 3.1
Adaptation = assimilation and accommodation

The third stage, **concrete operational thought,** begins about age 6 or 7 and ends in early adolescence, around age 11 or 12. During this stage, children begin to appreciate the logical necessity of certain causal relationships. They can manipulate categories, classification systems, and hierarchies in groups. They are more successful at solving problems that are clearly tied to physical reality than at generating hypotheses about purely philosophical or abstract concepts.

The final stage of cognitive development, **formal operational thought,** begins in adolescence and persists through adulthood. This level of thinking permits a person to conceptualize about many simultaneously interacting variables. It allows for the creation of a system of laws or rules that can be used for problem solving. Formal operational thought reflects the quality of intelligence on which science and philosophy are built.

At the start of each new stage, the child experiences a type of egocentrism or imitation in point of view. With experience, children gain new objectivity about their perspective and are able to step back from the situation and see it more flexibly. Each of the stages will be described in some detail in subsequent chapters.

Implications for Human Development

Piaget's theory has had an enormous influence on research in the study of cognition. At the risk of oversimplifying, let us give a few of the implications of the theory for the study of child development. First, the theory suggests that cognition has its base in the biological capacities of the human infant—knowledge is derived from action. For example, infants learn about the features of objects by grasping and sucking on them. Second, discrepancies between existing schemes or concepts and contemporary experiences promote cognitive development. Encounters with all types of novelty, especially experiences that are moderately distinct rather than widely different from what is already known, are important for advancing new ideas and new ways of organizing thought. Extending this idea, encounters with differences in opinions through discussion and reading are just as important in adolescence and adulthood as encounters with different types of sensory materials in infancy and toddlerhood.

Third, infants do have the capacity for thinking and problem solving. Although infants do not make use of symbolic strategies, they are able to establish certain logical connections between means and ends that guide their problem-solving efforts. Fourth, infants, toddlers, and school age children think in different ways, and the ways they think are different from the ways adults think. This does not mean that their thinking is unorganized or illogical, but the same principles of logic that typically govern adult thought do not govern the thinking of young children. Fifth, beginning with the period of concrete operations children can approach problems using many of the principles that are fundamental to scientific reasoning. They can also begin to reason about their reasoning—introducing the importance of **metacognition** or the many strategies that are involved in guiding the way we organize and prepare ourselves in order to think more clearly and effectively. Sixth, thinking about the social world is regulated by many of the same principles as thinking about objects in the physical world. As we learn about the principles that govern objects and physical relationships, we are also learning about ourselves and others.

Vygotsky's Concepts of Cognitive Development

Piaget's focus on cognitive development emphasizes a process in which individuals investigate, explore, discover, and rediscover meaning in their world. Although Piaget acknowledged the significance of social factors, especially parents and peers, in the cognitive process, his theory focuses on individuals in interaction with their environment. In contrast, Vygotsky, often referred to as a **contextualist,** argued that development can only be understood within a social framework. Vygotsky (1962, 1978) proposed that the study of cognitive development must take as its unit of analysis *the person in activity in a setting.* The person and the culture are intricately interwoven through the process of social interaction. New levels of understanding begin at an interpersonal level as two individuals, initially an infant and an adult, coordinate their interactions. Eventually interpersonal collaboration becomes internalized to make up the child's internal mental framework. Through continuous interaction with others, especially adults and older children, a child revises and advances his or her levels of understanding.

"New understanding, gained through collaboration, is a product of the child's original understanding, the partner's different understanding, the child's difficulties with the task and the ways they are expressed in the course of their interaction, the partner's response to those difficulties, and so on. Since this process evolves over time, and each person's responses depend on what the other has previously done or said, the outcome is one that cannot be attributed to either one or the other. The unit of analysis extends beyond the individual." (Tudge & Winterhoff, 1993, p. 76).

Three of the central concepts in Vygotsky's theory are introduced here: culture as a mediator of cognitive structuring, movement from the intermental to the intramental, and the zone of proximal development.

Vygotsky argues that cognitive development can only be understood in the context of

Experimentation with a string is an example of sensorimotor exploration. This infant is discovering the properties of the string through tactile, visual, and motor strategies. What are some examples of sensorimotor exploration that you continue to use as an adult?

culture. Think for a moment about the many ways that culture shapes the content of thought and the processes through which ideas are developed. A simple conversation between a mother and a child or a situation in which a grandparent is trying to instruct a young child include layers of cultural beliefs and strategies— beliefs about what children think about, the skills they are encouraged to attain, the sources of information that are available to them, the ways that information is shared, the kinds of activities that children, adolescents, and adults are permitted to engage in, and the limits that are placed on participation in certain settings or certain forms of interaction (Miller, 1993).

Of the many elements of culture that shape cognition, one that was of special interest to Vygotsky was the idea of tools and signs as human inventions that shape thought. Technical *tools* like plows, cars, and weapons and *signs,* sometimes referred to as psychological tools, like symbolic systems, counting systems, and strategies for remembering, modify the person's relationship to the environment.

Vygotsky's theory emphasizes the social context of cognitive development. Children often learn by interacting with older, more competent peers or adults who can answer their questions and show them how to solve problems.

Through the use of tools, humans change the way they organize and think about the world. Vygotsky viewed tools as a means through which the human mind is shaped and modified over the course of history.

Perhaps contrary to common sense, Vygotsky argued that high-level mental functions begin in external activity that is gradually reconstructed and internalized. He gave the example of pointing. Vygotsky claimed that initially an infant will reach toward an object that is out of reach, stretching the hand in the direction of the object and making grasping motions with the fingers. This is a movement directed to the object. But as soon as the caregiver recognizes that the child wants the object and is able to satisfy the child's request, the child begins to modify the reaching and grasping motion into a socially meaningful gesture—pointing. The caregiver's understanding of the gesture and **intermental** coordination between caregiver and infant result in an **intramental** process for the infant, an understanding of the special relationship in this case between the desired goal, the caregiver as mediator, and the pointing as a meaningful sign.

Taking the idea of internalization a step further, Vygotsky offered the concept of the **zone of proximal development** as the immediate framework through which learning and development converge. The zone is "the distance between the actual developmental level as determined by independent problem solving and the level of potential development as determined through problem solving under adult guidance or in collaboration with more capable peers" (Vygotsky, 1978, p.86).

We have all experienced a situation in which we were able to solve a task only with the assistance and advice of someone else. The typical efforts of parents to help a child put together a jigsaw puzzle by suggesting strategies, like selecting all the straight-edged pieces first to make the border, or sorting the many pieces into those with a similar color, is an example of how learning takes place within the zone. Vygotsky suggests that the level of functioning a person can reach when taking advantage of the guidance of others reflects the functions that are in the process of maturation, as compared to those that have already matured. Learning within the zone of proximal development sets into motion the reorganization and internalization of existing developmental competence, which then become synthesized at a new, higher intramental level.

Implications for Human Development

Vygotsky's theory suggests that the boundaries between the individual and the environment are much less clear than one might infer from most other theories of human development. In fact, he directs attention to the guiding role of social interaction and culture in shaping and orienting cognition, thus bringing the study of cognitive development into much greater harmony with many of the concepts of psychosocial theory than might be seen in Piaget's framework.

Several specific implications of Vygotsky's work can be inferred (Davydov, 1995). First, the mental structures and functioning of people raised in a specific culture will be different from those raised in other cultures, just as the thinking of a toddler is different from the thinking of an adult. Second, because of the way that intermental experiences and networks structure intramental events, one's family and others who influence and control the structure of early learning and problem-solving experiences will have a strong influence on the structure of one's thinking. Third, individuals can promote their own cognitive development by seeking interactions with others who can help draw them to higher levels of functioning within their zone of proximal development.

Links to Psychosocial Theory

Both cognitive developmental theory and psychosocial theory focus on development as a product of ongoing interactions between the individual and the environment. For both theories, psychological development is a product of some discrepancies, referred to as disequilibrium in cognitive developmental theory and as psychosocial crises in psychosocial theory. Piaget's theory, like psychosocial theory, proposes a set of stages of development, with each stage growing from and integrating achievements of earlier stages. Piaget considered development in four stages that covered the period from infancy through adolescence. Erikson described these same years in five stages, drawing a greater distinction in functioning between early and middle childhood than did Piaget. Although contemporary scholars are addressing issues of changes in cognitive functioning in adulthood, Piaget's theory does not offer any hypotheses about the qualitative changes that might follow the period of formal operational reasoning, whereas psychosocial theory makes clear predictions about the direction of ego development in early, middle, and later adulthood.

Perhaps the most significant distinction between the theories is their focus or range of applicability. Piaget's focus, as well as that of Vygotsky, is on the cognitive domain, especially the process of knowledge acquisition and logical reasoning. The meaning a person makes of a situation depends largely upon the stage of mental development attained. Feelings, social relationship, and self-understanding are viewed as cognitive schemes that are constructed with the same logic that the person applies to the understanding of objects. Psychosocial theory considers the emotional domain as a pervasive filter through which a person organizes and interprets experience. The nature of the resolution of each psychosocial crisis guides a person's ability to adapt and mature within society. As a psychotherapist, Erikson was aware of the many instances in which one's reasoning abilities and problem-solving skills were disrupted by strong emotional conflicts, unconscious wishes and fears, and conflicting social demands. He draws attention to the broad array of outlooks and coping strategies—such as trust and mistrust, hope and withdrawal—that determine the direction of psychological development from one period of life to the next. For example, feelings of hope or hopelessness will influence a person's willingness to engage in new learning situations with interest and enthusiasm or with caution and apprehension. The nature of one's cognition during a period of life will be influenced by one's psychosocial orientation.

Vygotsky's theory provides an important link between Piaget's emphasis on the maturation of logical reasoning, and psychosocial theory's emphasis on the maturation of self in society by emphasizing the interpersonal nature of cognition. The idea of a zone of proximal development relates closely to the construct of the radius of significant relationships, highlighting the unique interpersonal and cultural context of all aspects of knowing, whether it is knowing about the logic of the physical world or about the logic of relationships.

THEORIES OF LEARNING

Learning theorists have proposed mechanisms to account for the relatively permanent changes in behavior that occur as a result of experience. The reason that humans have such an extensive capacity to adapt to changes in the environment is that they are so well equipped to learn. Four theories of learning that have made significant contributions to the study of human development are reviewed below: (1) classical conditioning, (2) operant conditioning, (3) social learning, and (4) cognitive behaviorism.

Classical Conditioning   The principles of classical conditioning, sometimes referred to as Pavlovian conditioning, were developed by Ivan Pavlov (1927/1960). **Classical conditioning** highlights the types of learning that occur when events take place close together in time and thereby acquire similar meaning. In much of his work, Pavlov used the salivary reflex as the response system. He carried out an extensive body of research in an effort to understand the conditions under which stimuli in the environment other than food would elicit or inhibit salivation.

The model for classical conditioning is seen in Figure 3.2. The four basic elements in a classical conditioning experiment are the neutral stimulus (NS), the unconditioned stimulus (UC), the unconditioned response (UR), and the conditioned response (CR). Before conditioning, the bell is a **neutral stimulus** (NS). It elicits a response of interest or attention, but nothing more. The sight and smell of food are **unconditioned stimuli** (US) that elicit salivation, the **unconditioned response** (UR). No learning is required for the smell of food to evoke salivation. During conditioning trials, the bell is rung shortly before the food appears. The dog is said to have been conditioned when it salivates to the sound of the bell, even before the food is presented. The bell, therefore, comes to control the salivation response. It becomes a **conditioned stimulus.** The bell is no longer neutral; it has come to have meaning as a signal for food. Salivation that occurs in response to the bell alone is called the **conditioned response** (CR). You might be able to relate to this form of learning by thinking of your own reaction when you look at your watch or the clock and realize that it is approaching dinner time. Often, just knowing that it is nearing the time when you usually eat is a stimulus for feeling hunger pangs.

Conditioning does not take place randomly between any two events linked in time. A conditioned response is established to the degree that there is a "meaningful" relationship between the NS and the US. Usually they must occur together many times before conditioning is established. Furthermore, the NS itself is not totally neutral. A visual stimulus such as a colored light will prompt visual orienting, for instance, whereas an auditory stimulus may simply increase attention or arousal. In a conditioning experiment, the learner builds many associations simultaneously. Although the focus of a particular experiment may be on establishing a link between one NS and one US, the learner will build links among many elements of the environment—its visual, auditory, and olfactory components, including the US. Pavlovian conditioning provides a model for understanding how multiple associations, sometimes stored at the unconscious level, can be established and triggered in the process of concept formation, memory, and problem solving (McClelland & Rumelhart, 1986; Rumelhart & McClelland, 1986).

Implications for Human Development

Classical conditioning can account for a great deal of the associational learning that occurs throughout life. When a specific symbol is paired with an image, emotional reaction, or object, that symbol takes on new meaning. The associations that are made through classical conditioning may involve labels and concepts, but they do not necessarily require language skills. During infancy and toddlerhood, a variety of positive and negative emotional reactions are conditioned to people, objects, and environments as the child develops attachments. Your reactions to the taste of a certain type of food or the feel of a particular material may be the result of conditioned learning that has persisted until adulthood. Similarly, fears can be the results of classical conditioning. Many people recall at least one frightening experience from childhood, such as nearly drowning, being beaten, or falling from the top of a slide. The association of fear or pain with a specific target may lead to systematic avoidance of that object for the rest of one's life.

Operant Conditioning

Operant conditioning emphasizes the role of repetition and the consequences of behavior in learning. In this type of learning process, behaviors are strengthened when they are followed by positive consequences and weakened when they are followed by negative consequences. One of the best-known American learning theorists, B. F. Skinner, developed many of the principles of operant conditioning. Skinner's (1938) work focused on the modification of voluntary behaviors as a result of the consequences of those behaviors. In the traditional operant conditioning experiment, the researcher selects a response in advance and then waits until the subject makes the desired response (or at least a partial response). Then the experimenter presents a reinforcement. **Reinforcement** is operationally defined as any stimulus that makes a repetition of the response more likely.

There are two kinds of reinforcers. Some, such as food and smiles, increase the rate of response when they are present. These are called positive reinforcers. Others, such as electric shock, increase the rate of response when they are removed. These are called negative reinforcers. Suppose a mother gets upset whenever she hears her baby cry. She may try a number of things to stop the crying—rocking, feeding, talking, or changing the baby's diapers. If one of these behaviors leads to an end to the noise, it

FIGURE 3.2
Classical conditioning

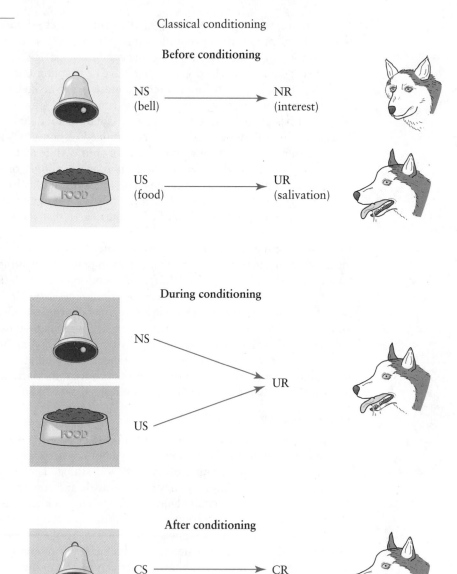

Classical conditioning

Before conditioning

NS (bell) ——→ NR (interest)

US (food) ——→ UR (salivation)

During conditioning

NS ⟍
        UR
US ⟋

After conditioning

CS ——→ CR

NS = Neutral stimulus   UR = Unconditioned response
NR = Neutral response   CS = Conditioned stimulus
US = Unconditioned stimulus   CR = Conditioned response

Before conditioning, the bell is a neutral stimulus that evokes interest but no other response. With several pairings of the bell and food, the bell becomes a conditioned stimulus that evokes the conditioned salivation response.

is reinforced. The mother is more likely to try that behavior the next time. The baby's cry is a negative reinforcer because when it stops, the specific caregiving response is strengthened.

In many instances, the behavior to be learned is one that has never been performed before. How can you be reinforced for making a complex response if you have never done it? One means of developing a new complex response is **shaping**. (Davey & Cullen, 1988). The response is broken down into its major components. At first a response that is only an approximation of one element of the behavior is reinforced. Gradually new elements of the behavior are added, and a reinforcement is given only

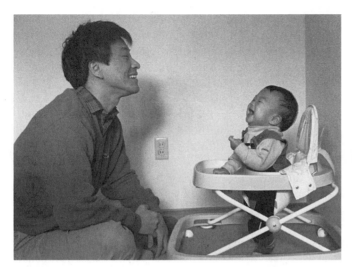

Smiling is an important positive reinforcement. The dad's smile encourages the child, and the child's laughter keeps the dad engaged in the dialogue. What are some other examples of how social behavior serves as a positive reinforcement?

when two or three components of the response are linked together. Once the person makes a complete response, earlier approximations are no longer reinforced. Parents often use the shaping process to teach their young children such complicated behaviors as using the toilet, table manners, and caring for their belongings.

Within the field of operant conditioning, research has been devoted to understanding which conditions of learning result in the strongest, longest-lasting habits. **Schedules of reinforcement** refers to the frequency and regularity with which reinforcements are given. A new response is conditioned rapidly if reinforcement is given on every learning trial. This schedule is called **continuous** reinforcement. Responses that are established under conditions of continuous reinforcement are very vulnerable to **extinction**—that is, if the reinforcement is removed for several trials, performance deteriorates rapidly.

Some schedules vary the amount of time or the number of trials between reinforcements. This procedure is called **intermittent reinforcement.** The learner responds on many occasions when no reinforcement is provided but does receive reinforcement every once in a while. Such schedules result in the most durable learning. Intermittent reinforcement lengthens the time an operant behavior remains in the learner's repertoire after reinforcement has been permanently discontinued (Ferster & Culbertson, 1982).

An intermittent reinforcement schedule is probably most like real life. It would be very difficult for anyone to learn a behavior if every instance of it had to be reinforced. A child often exhibits a new response when no observers are present, when teachers are attending to other matters, or in the context of other behaviors that are followed by a negative consequence. Research on operant conditioning demonstrates that conditions of intermittent reinforcement are precisely those under which the longest-lasting habits are formed.

Implications for Human Development

The principles of operant conditioning apply whenever the environment sets up priorities for behavior and conditional rewards or punishments for approximating a desired behavior. People change whenever their operant behaviors adapt to changes in environmental contingencies. The environment controls the process of adaptation through the role it plays in establishing and modifying contingencies (Skinner, 1987). Behavior can be modified in the desired direction as long as the person who is guiding the conditioning has control over the distribution of valued rewards. These principles are especially applicable to the learning that takes place during toddlerhood (ages 2 and 3) and early school age (4 to 6). Children of these ages are unlikely to be able to consider the existing framework of reinforcement. Once individuals analyze a reinforcement schedule, they may choose to adapt to it, resist it, or redefine the environment in order to discover new sources of reinforcement.

The operant conditioning process occurs throughout life. Although one typically thinks of adults establishing the reinforcement schedules that shape the behavior of children, it is clear that a child's behavior is often a reinforcement for an adult. A child's smile or laugh, or enthusiasm or attention, are the rewards that modify a parent's or a teacher's behavior. Negative reinforcement is a process that is often used to account for moral behavior. In a well-socialized person, anxiety and guilt build up in anticipation of performing some socially unacceptable behavior. By resisting the temptation to perform the misbehavior, the anxiety and guilt are reduced. Thus, restraint or social control is negatively reinforced.

Social Learning

The concept of **social learning** evolved from an awareness that much learning takes place as a result of observing and imitating other people's behavior (Bandura & Walters, 1963). Changes in behavior can occur without being linked to a specific pattern

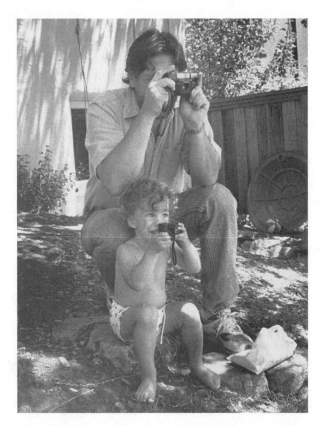

Social learning theory emphasizes the role of observation and imitation as means of learning new behaviors. Can you think of a new response that you recently learned through imitation?

of positive or negative reinforcement. They can also occur without numerous opportunities for trial-and-error practice. A person can watch someone perform a task or say a new expression and imitate that behavior accurately on the first try.

The role of **imitation** is emphasized as the central process in resolving the crisis of autonomy versus shame and doubt in toddlerhood. At that age, imitation provides a mechanism for the rapid acquisition of new behaviors. Think about all the things a child of 4 can say or do. It would be impossible for parents to deliberately teach a child every single behavior—they would have no time left to eat, sleep, or work. Children must acquire much of their knowledge by observing and imitating others. Adults provide the **models** for many activities. They express feelings, voice attitudes, perform tasks, and enact their moral values. By observing and imitating many of these behaviors, children become socialized into their family's and community's way of life.

Early research in social learning theory was devoted to identifying conditions that determine whether or not a child will imitate a model (Bandura, 1971, 1977, 1986). Children have been found to imitate aggressive, altruistic, helping, and stingy models. They are most likely to imitate models who are prestigious, who control resources, or who themselves are rewarded. Bandura and Walters (1963) suggested that children not only observe the behaviors carried out by a model, but they also watch what happens to the model. When the model's behavior is rewarded, the behavior is more likely to be imitated; when the model's behavior is punished, the behavior is more likely to be avoided. When naughty behaviors go unpunished they too are likely to be imitated. This process is called **vicarious reinforcement.** Through observational learning, a child can learn a behavior and also acquire the motivation to perform the behavior or resist performing that behavior depending on what is learned about the consequences linked to the behavior. Thus, observational learning can hold the key to self-regulation and the internalization of standards for resisting certain behaviors as well as for enacting behaviors (Grusec, 1992).

Recent directions in social learning theory have taken an increasingly cognitive orientation, sometimes referred to as social cognition (Bandura, 1989, 1991). Through observational learning, the child becomes acquainted with the general concepts of the situation as well as the specific behaviors. Direct reinforcement or nonreinforcement provides one type of information about how to behave in a certain situation. In addition, people watch others, learn about the consequences of their actions, and remember what others have told or shown them and what they have read or learned about the situation. Over time, one forms a symbolic representation for the situation, the required behaviors, and the expected outcomes. A worker may learn that with one type of supervisor, it is appropriate to ask lots of questions and offer suggestions for ways of solving problems, while with another supervisor, it is better to remain quiet and try not to be noticed. The rules for behavior in each setting are abstracted from what has been observed in watching others, what happened following one's own behavior in the past, and what one understands about the demands in the immediate situation.

Implications for Human Development

The principles of social learning theory are assumed to operate in the same way throughout life. The concept of social learning highlights the relevance of models' behavior in guiding the behavior of others. These models may be parents, older siblings, peers, entertainment stars, or sports heroes. Since new role models may be encountered at any life stage, new learning through the process of observational learning is always possible. Exposure to a certain array of models and a certain pattern of rewards or punishments results in the encouragement to imitate some behaviors and to inhibit the performance of others. The similarity in behavior among people of the same ages reflects their exposure to a common history of models, rewards, and punishments. Recognition of the potential impact one has as a model for others, especially in the role of parent, teacher, clinician, counselor, or supervisor ought to impart a certain level of self-conscious monitoring about the behaviors one exhibits and the strategies one employs in the presence of those who are likely to perceive one as a model for new learning.

Cognitive Behaviorism

One objection that has been raised frequently against classical and operant conditioning as theories of learning is that they have no language or concepts to describe events that occur in the learner's mind. **Cognitive behaviorists** study the many internal mental activities that influence behavior. Edward Tolman (1932/1967, 1948) discussed the notion of an intervening set of responses that influence learning. He said that the learner develops a **cognitive map,** an internal mental representation of the learning environment. Individuals who perform a specific task in a certain environment attend primarily to that task, but they also form a representation of the rest of the setting. The map includes expectations about the reward system in operation, the existing spatial relationships, and the behaviors accorded highest priority. An individual's performance in a situation represents only part of the learning that has occurred. The fact that people respond to changes in the environment indicates that a complex mental map actually develops in this situation.

According to Walter Mischel (1973, 1979), at least six cognitive factors must be taken into account if a person's behavior is to be understood: cognitive competencies, self-encoding, expectancies, values, goals and plans, and self-control strategies (Figure 3.3). **Cognitive competencies** consist of knowledge, skills, and abilities. **Self-encoding** is the evaluation and conceptualization of information about the self. An interesting finding in this area is that depressed people tend to evaluate themselves more realistically than those who are not depressed. Mischel (1979) argued that "to feel good about ourselves we may have to judge ourselves more kindly than we are judged" (p. 752). In other words, most people who are not chronically depressed may bias their evaluations of themselves in a self-enhancing way.

Expectancies refer to expectations about one's ability to perform, the consequences of one's behavior, and the meaning of events in one's environment. **Values** consist of the relative importance one places on the outcomes of situations. One person may value high levels of task performance, while another may value success in social situa-

FIGURE 3.3

Six cognitive dimensions that influence behavior

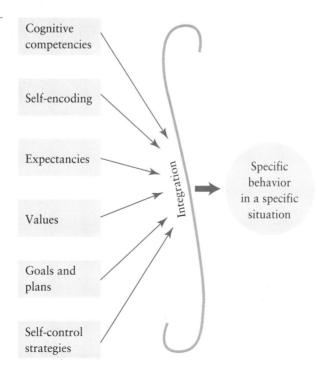

tions. One's behavior in a situation is influenced by how one values its possible outcomes. *Goals and plans* are personal standards of performance and the strategies one develops for achieving them. Obviously individuals differ in their goals and plans; these differences will lead to considerable variation in behavior. **Self-control strategies** are the techniques an individual develops for regulating his or her own behavior. Self-control helps us to understand how we can leave the realm of stimulus control in order to gain control over our behavior. The more aware we are of the effects of stimuli on our behavior, the more effectively we may overcome, channel, or eliminate their influence. Of these six areas, the one that has received considerable attention among those interested in learning and performance is the area of expectancies.

Implications for Human Development

Cognitive behaviorism suggests that through the full range of learning processes including classical conditioning, operant conditioning, and observational learning, the learner acquires cognitive structures that influence subsequent learning and performance. The learner acquires an outlook on the learning situation. This outlook influences the learner's feeling of familiarity with the task, motivation to undertake the task, optimism about performing the task successfully, and strategies for approaching the task. In addition to everything a parent, teacher, or supervisor might do to structure a learning environment, one must always take into account the outlook the learner brings to the task. Differences in expectancies, self-control strategies, values, and goals all influence the way individuals approach a learning situation.

Summary of the Learning Theories

All four of the learning theories contribute insights into human behavior (Table 3.1). Classical conditioning can account for the extensive network of associations that are formed between symbols and stimuli, enduring emotional reactions to one's environment, and the organization of learning associated with reflexive patterns. Operant conditioning emphasizes the acquisition of behavioral patterns on the basis of their consequences. Social learning theory adds the important element of imitation. People learn new behaviors by watching others. Through social learning, individuals develop an understanding of the social consequences of behavior leading to new patterns of behavioral expression and self-regulation. Finally, cognitive behaviorism suggests that a complex set of expectations, goals, and values can be treated as behavior and can influence performance. Although information or skills can be learned, they will not be expressed in behavior unless expectations about the self and the environment justify their enactment. This perspective highlights the person's capacity to guide the performance of new learning.

Links to Psychosocial Theory

The learning theories and psychosocial theory operate on different levels of abstraction. The learning theories provide insight into the laws that govern many of the basic mechanisms of adaptation. Psychosocial theory assumes that growth and change continue throughout the life span; however, the theory does not attempt to account for the exact processes by which new behaviors, new coping strategies, or new ego strengths are acquired. The learning theories provide explanations for the ways that the patterns of daily events might shape the direction of adaptation and growth. They offer insight into the processes through which society's rules, norms, and customs become internalized and

---

TABLE 3.1   Four Learning Processes

Classical Conditioning	Operant Conditioning	Social Learning	Cognitive Behaviorism
When two events occur very close together in time, they acquire similar meanings and produce similar responses.	Responses that are under voluntary control can be strengthened or eliminated, depending on the consequences associated with them.	New responses can be acquired through the observation and imitation of models.	In addition to new responses, the learner acquires a mental representation of the situation, including expectations about rewards and punishments, the kinds of responses that are appropriate, and the physical and social settings in which they occur.

translated into habits, preferences, and expectations. The learning theories emphasize the significance of the immediate environment in directing the course of growth. They speak less to the epigenetic process to which Erikson referred as he described a predictable pattern in the nature and direction of development over the life span.

CULTURAL THEORY

The concept of **culture,** although defined in a wide variety of ways by anthropologists, sociologists, psychologists, and political scientists, is meant here to refer to the learned systems of meanings and patterns of behaviors that are shared by a group of people and transmitted from one generation to the next. **Physical culture** encompasses the objects, technologies, structures, tools, and other artifacts of a culture. **Social culture** encompasses the norms, roles, beliefs, values, rites, and customs (Herkovits, 1948; Triandis et al., 1980; Rohner, 1984; Betancourt & Lopez, 1993).

On a general level, culture has been described as a **worldview,** a way of making meaning of the relationships, situations, and objects encountered in daily life. Basic ideas such as whether people are considered to be in control of nature or a part of nature, who is included in the definition of family, what characteristics are considered signs of mental health or mental illness, which acts are construed as hostile and which as nurturing, which aspects of the environment are considered dangerous and which are valued—all these and many other mental constructions are shaped by the culture into which one is born (Kagitcibasi, 1990). Culture guides development, not only through encounters with certain objects, roles, and settings, but through the meanings linked to actions as well.

The principle of **cultural determinism,** created by Ruth Benedict (1934/1950), suggests that the individual's psychological experiences are shaped by the expectations, resources, and challenges posed by one's specific cultural group. The extent to which development is viewed as distinct stages of life depends on the degree to which socialization within a culture is characterized by continuity or discontinuity.

Continuity is found when a child is given information and responsibilities that apply directly to his or her adult behavior. For example, Margaret Mead (1928/1950) observed that in Samoan society, girls of 6 or 7 years of age commonly took care of their younger siblings. As they grew older, their involvement in the caregiving role increased; however, the behaviors that were expected of them were not substantially changed.

Discontinuity is found when a child is either barred from activities that are open only to adults or forced to "unlearn" information or behaviors that are accepted in children but considered inappropriate for adults. The change from expectations of virginity before marriage to expectations of sexual responsiveness after marriage is an example of discontinuity. In some societies, sexuality and sex play are viewed as inappropriate behavior for children but appropriate for adults.

Cultures that have discrete, age-graded expectations for individuals at different periods in the life span produce a pattern of development in which age groups have distinct characteristics and appear to function at different skill levels. These societies are marked by public ceremonies, graduations, and other rites of passage from one stage to the next. Cultures that are permissive, open, and recognize few distinctions between the responsibilities of children and those of adults do not produce age-graded stages of development. In those societies, development is a much more gradual, fluid transformation in which adult competencies are built directly on childhood accomplishments.

Implications for Human Development

According to the concept of cultural determinism, the events of the various stages of development will be experienced as stressful or calm depending on how they are noted by the culture. This contrast is seen in the ways in which different cultures mark an adolescent girl's first menstruation (Mead, 1949/1955). In some societies people fear menstruation, and treat the girl as if she were dangerous to others. In other societies she is viewed as having powerful magic that will affect her own future and that of the tribe. In still others, the perceived shamefulness of sex requires that the menstruation be kept as secret as possible. The culture thus determines how a biological change is marked and how the transition will be perceived.

This painting of two brothers illustrates the concept of cultural continuity. The older brother assumes responsibility for the protection and care of his younger sibling. When he is an adult, we can imagine that he will draw on these experiences for the love and care of his own children.

Societies vary in the extent to which they expect people to make significant life decisions during each period and in the range of choices they make available. American adolescents are asked to make decisions regarding sex, work, politics, religion, marriage, and education. In each of these areas, the alternatives are complex and varied. As a result, adolescence is prolonged and the risk of leaving this period without having found a solution to these problems is great. In cultures that offer fewer choices and provide a clearer path from childhood to adulthood, adolescence may be brief and relatively free of psychological stress.

The study of development must be approached with appreciation for the cultural context. Cultural expectations for the timing of certain life events, such as schooling, work, marriage, childbearing, and political and religious leadership, influence the tempo and tone of one's life history. Cultures also vary in the personal qualities they admire and those they consider inappropriate or shameful. A society's standards of beauty, leadership, and talent determine how easily an individual can achieve status within it.

One of the criticisms of scientific knowledge about development is that it lacks the diversity of cultural contexts. If we accept the idea of cultural determinism, we must agree that development can only be fully understood by taking into consideration the particular ecological and cultural context in which it occurs. Much of what we know about development is based on a very small sample of the peoples of the world. In particular, advances in the social sciences in the United States, Canada, Japan, Australia, and Europe have not been matched by the study of development in the less economically developed nations within Africa, Latin American, and Asia. Thus, attempts to identify and establish universal principles of development must always be tempered by the realization that our scientific observations do not reflect the variations in cultural environments that guide the socialization process and the paths to maturity and aging (Nsamenang, 1992).

A life story is influenced by identification with **ethnic group** norms and values, as well as by the overarching norms and values of the dominant culture. The relative contribution of ethnic group influences to a person's development depends on the intensity of the family's loyalty to the group, the balance of time spent with members of one's own ethnic group and with members of other cultural groups, and the way the group is viewed or treated within the larger society (Phinney, 1996). In studying patterns and processes of development, we must keep in mind that people of various ethnic groups may have unique views on such issues as the definition of appropriate child behavior and successful maturity, the nature of gender roles, and the proper balance between individual achievement and responsibility to family and community.

Links to Psychosocial Theory

Psychosocial theory is based on the assumption that culture makes a fundamental contribution in shaping an individual's development. In fact, Erikson argued that basic cultural values could be interpreted from infant caregiving practices. By observing how adults respond to infants' needs one could understand key cultural values regarding generosity, self-control, independence, or cooperation. Just as evolutionary theory asserts that adaptation is a product of the interaction between the organism and the physical environment, psychosocial theory assumes that individual development is a product of continuous interaction between the developing child and the demands and resources of the cultural environment.

In contrast to Ruth Benedict's view that the degree to which development appears stagelike depends on the continuity or discontinuity of the society, psychosocial theory argues for stages of development. However, the stages themselves are derived from the

Kwanza was created to strengthen the cultural identity of the African-American ethnic group. Family members participate in rituals that highlight a common ancestry and shared cultural values.

view that all cultures must be able to adapt to changes in economic, environmental, and intercultural conditions. Stages of individual development are interwoven with the ability of the society to adapt and continue. Psychosocial theory suggests, for example, that the way trust is established will differ from one culture to the next, but that all societies have mechanisms for building levels of trust and mistrust during the period of infancy. The psychosocial stages emerge as the mechanisms of socialization within each culture call them forth.

SOCIAL ROLE THEORY

The social role of "healer" can be found in most cultures. Although the costumes and the techniques may differ, healers typically have access to knowledge not known by most of the people in the society. What are some of the role expectations associated with healers in our society?

Another approach to conceptualizing the effect of the environment on development is suggested by such social psychologists as Orville Brim (1966) and such sociologists as Talcott Parsons (Parsons & Bales, 1955). They trace the process of socialization and personality development through the person's participation in increasingly diverse and complex social roles. A **role** is any set of behaviors that has a socially agreed-upon function and an accepted code of norms (Biddle, 1979; Biddle & Thomas, 1966; Brown, 1965). The term role was taken from the context of the theater. In a play, actors' behaviors are distinct and predictable because each actor has a part to play and follows a script. You will recall this metaphor from Shakespeare's analysis in *As You Like It,* "All the world's a stage, and all the men and women merely players; They have their exits and their entrances; And one man in his time plays many parts" (Act 2, scene 7).

BOX 3.1   ROLE STRAIN AND PARENTHOOD

A recurring theme in the literature on parenthood is the experience of role strain. **Role strain** can be defined as a sense of overload that results when too many expectations are associated with a role (Biddle, 1986). Each of the four dimensions of social roles may contribute to strain in the role of parent. When parenting is added to other adult roles, especially those of worker and spouse, the demands of the new role may seem overwhelming. Because the parent role has great intensity, the sense of involvement in all the behaviors associated with the role intensifies, and so does anxiety about failure to meet the expectations of the role. First-time parents especially may have little confidence in their ability to fulfill their roles, and the level of worry associated with the role rises accordingly.

The parent role does indeed take a lot of time. Most first-time parents underestimate how much time infants and toddlers require. When new parents, especially mothers, reflect on the time they spend in a variety of social roles, they point to the parent role as more time-consuming than any other role, now or in the past.

Role strain linked with parenting is related to the structure of the role. Some adults have a very clear set of ideas about how they should enact their parent role, but many are unsure. Husbands and wives are likely to differ in their views on child-rearing techniques. These differences require time to resolve. Because of the hardships or distress they recall from their own childhoods, many adults do not want to raise their children the way they were raised. They have to learn a new script for this role.

There are at least four ways to minimize the role strain associated with the parent role (Cowan & Cowan, 1988; Nickols, 1994; Bornstein, 1995):

1. When the rewards for role enactment are frequent, the demands of the role seem less onerous. Adults who have a lot of encouragement from family, friends, and community for their active involvement in parenting will probably feel less stressed about the amount of time and effort they invest in it.
2. The ability to delegate role responsibilities can reduce role strain. Adults who can hire others to help with some of the parenting responsibilities or who can turn to family members for help will experience less role strain than those who are solely responsible for the parenting role. Couples who can flexibly alter and share household responsibilities in response to the demands of parenting will experience more satisfaction and less strain.
3. The ability to integrate several aspects of the role in one activity can reduce role strain. Some parents become quite inventive about ways to maintain contact with their infant and still carry out their household chores and other work and also have time with each other.
4. Role strain is reduced when marriage partners reach consensus about their parent roles. New parents who have resolved their differences regarding child-rearing philosophy, child-care activities, and the division of household responsibilities experience less role strain and a higher level of marital satisfaction than those who continue to have opposing views on these issues.

Role theory applies this same framework to social life (Biddle, 1986). The three elements of concern to role theory are the patterned characteristics of social behavior (**role enactment**), the parts or identities a person assumes (**social roles**), and the scripts or shared expectations for behavior that are linked to each part (**role expectations**).

Social roles serve as a bridge between the individual and the society. Every society has a range of roles, and individuals learn about the expectations associated with them. As people enter new roles, they modify their behavior to conform to these role expectations. Each role is usually linked to one or more related, or **reciprocal,** roles. The student and the teacher, the parent and the child, and the salesperson and the customer are in reciprocal roles. Each role is partly defined by the other roles that support it. The function of the role is determined by its relation to the surrounding role groups to which it is allied.

Four dimensions are used to analyze the impact of social roles on development: the number of roles a person occupies, the intensity of role involvement or how deeply identified the person is with the role, the amount of time the role demands, and the extent to which the expectations associated with each role are highly structured or flexible and open to improvisation.

Implications for Human Development

All cultures offer new roles that await individuals as they move from one stage of life to another. These roles may be directly associated with age, such as the role of a high school student. Other roles may be accessible only to those of a certain age who demonstrate other relevant skills, traits, or personal preferences. In many elementary schools, for example, the fifth-grade students become eligible to serve in the role of crossing guard to help the younger children get across the streets near the school. Families, organizations, and the larger community have implicit theories of development that determine what role positions open up for individuals in each age group.

Some of the most important life roles persist across several stages, including child, parent, and sibling. The expectations for role performance remain the same in some respects, but change in others. We can begin to see how social roles provide consistency to life experiences and how they prompt new learning.

Links to Psychosocial Theory

Role relationships provide a central mechanism through which the socialization process takes place. In psychosocial theory, one might think of the radius of significant relationships as an interconnected web of reciprocal roles and role relationships through which the expectations and demands of society make themselves known. The idea of reciprocity in roles is closely linked to the concept of interdependence of people in different psychosocial stages. The capacity of adults to resolve the crises of their life stages and to achieve new ego strengths is intricately linked to the ability of children and youth to flourish and grow (Box 3.1). Social role theory helps clarify why this is so important since children and adults occupy many reciprocal roles.

In the following chapters, we describe a number of life roles especially related to family, school, and work. As the number of roles that individuals fill simultaneously increases, they must learn some of the skills of role playing, role differentiation, and role integration. The developmental crisis of later adolescence (individual identity versus identity confusion) emphasizes the significance of being able to integrate several diverse roles so that one may maintain a sense of personal continuity. With each new role, one's self-definition changes and the potential for influencing the world increases.

SYSTEMS THEORY

Systems theories attempt to describe and account for the characteristics of systems and view individuals as interconnected elements (Sameroff, 1982). To a large degree, these theories highlight *differences in perspective*. Systems theories take the position that the whole is more than the sum of its parts. Any **system,** whether it is a cell, an organ, an individual, a family, or a corporation, is composed of *interdependent elements* that share some common goals, interrelated functions, boundaries, and an identity. The system cannot be wholly understood by identifying each of the component parts. The processes and relationships of those parts make for a larger coherent entity. The language system, for example, is more than the capacity to make vocal utterances, to use grammar, and to acquire vocabulary. It is the coordination of these elements in a useful way within a context of shared meaning. Similarly, a family system is more than the sum of the characteristics and competence of the individual family members.

A system cannot violate laws that govern the functioning of the parts, but at the same time it cannot be explained solely by those laws. Biological functioning cannot violate the laws of physics and chemistry, but the laws of physics and chemistry cannot fully explain biological functioning. Similarly, children's capacities for cognitive growth cannot violate the laws of biological functioning, but biological growth does not fully explain quality of thought.

Individuals, families, communities, schools, and societies are all examples of **open systems.** Ludwig von Bertalanffy (1950, 1968) defined open systems as structures that maintain their organization even though their parts constantly change. Just as the water in a river is constantly changing while the river itself retains its boundaries and course, so the molecules of human cells are constantly changing while the various biological systems retain their coordinated functions.

Systems move in the direction of adjusting to or incorporating more and more of the environment into themselves in order to prevent disorganization as a result of environmental fluctuations (Sameroff, 1982). Adaptation, whether the concept is articulated by Darwin, Piaget, Skinner, or Bandura, seems to be a fundamental process. Ervin Laszlo (1972) described this property of an open system as **adaptive self-regulation.** A system uses **feedback mechanisms** to identify and respond to environmental changes. The more information about the environment the system is capable of detecting, the more complex these feedback mechanisms must be. When the oxygen level of the environment is reduced, for example, you tend to grow sleepy. While you sleep, your breathing slows and you use less oxygen. Some of these adjustments are managed unconsciously by the organization of biological systems. Others are managed more deliberately by efforts to minimize the effects of environmental changes. Most systems have a capacity for storing or saving resources so that temporary shortages do not disrupt their operations.

When open systems are confronted by new, or changing environmental conditions, they have the capacity for **adaptive self-organization.** The system retains its essential identity by creating new substructures, by revising the relationships among components, or by creating new, higher levels of organization that coordinate existing substructures.

From the systems perspective, the components and the whole are always in tension. What one understands and observes depends on where one stands in this complex set of interrelationships. All living entities are parts and wholes. A person is a part of a family, a classroom or workgroup, a friendship group, and a society. A person is also a whole—a coordinated complex system composed of physical, cognitive, emotional, social, and self subsystems. Part of the story of human development is told in an analysis of the adaptive regulation and organization of those subsystems. Simultaneously, the story is told in the way larger systems fluctuate and impinge on individuals, forcing adaptive regulation and reorganization as a means of achieving stability at higher levels of system organization.

In an effort to elaborate and clarify the interlocking system of systems in which human behavior takes place, Urie Bronfenbrenner (1979) offered the following topography of the environmental structure (Figure 3.4):

> A **microsystem** is a pattern of activities, roles, and interpersonal relations experienced by the developing person in a given setting with particular physical and material characteristics.
> A **mesosystem** comprises the interrelations among two or more settings in which the developing person actively participates (such as, for a child, the relations among home, school, and neighborhood peer group; for an adult, among family, work, and social life).
> An **exosystem** refers to one or more settings that do not involve the developing person as an active participant, but in which events occur that affect, or are affected by, what happens in the setting containing the developing person.
> The **macrosystem** refers to consistencies in the form and content of lower-order systems (micro-, meso-, and exo-) that exist, or could exist, at the level of the subculture or the culture as a whole, along with any belief systems of ideology underlying such consistencies. (Bronfenbrenner, 1979, pp. 22, 25, 26)

Bronfenbrenner argues that development is influenced directly by the interactions that take place within a single microsystem, such as the family, and by the similarities and differences in patterns of interaction that occur across the various systems in which the person functions (the mesosytem). In addition, events in other adjoining systems, such as decisions in the workplace that affect the parent's work schedule, or decisions in city government that affect resources for the local schools, have an impact on development even though the child does not participate directly in these settings. Further, the roles, norms, and resources within settings as well as the interrelationships among systems have a unique pattern of organization and reflect an underlying set of beliefs and values that differ from one culture or ethnic group to the next. These cultural characteristics are transmitted to the developing person.

Implications for Human Development

The relevance of systems theory for human development can be most readily appreciated in its application to families. Family system theories focus on how families establish and maintain stable patterns of functioning. Families are viewed as emotional units identifiable by certain **boundaries** and **rules** (Broderick, 1993). The boundaries of the family determine who is considered to be a family member and who is an outsider. They influence the way information, support, and validation of the family unit are sought and the way new members are admitted into the family. Some families have very strict rules that maintain a narrow boundary around the family. Few sources of information or contact are admitted. Other families extend the sense of belonging to a wide range of people who bring ideas and resources to the family system.

Family systems are maintained by patterns of communication. Positive and negative feedback loops operate to stabilize, diminish, or increase certain types of interactions.

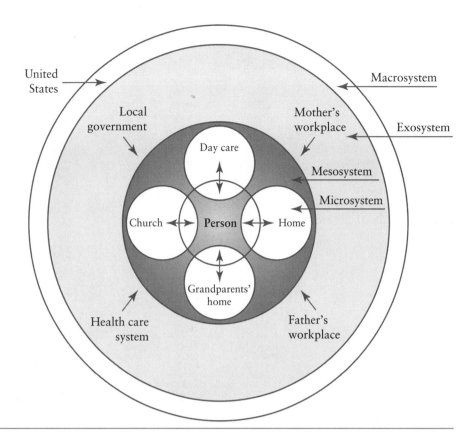

Specific examples of microsystems and systems in the exosystem are given, but many other systems could be shown. Arrows in the mesosystem show a two-way, or bidirectional influence; arrows in the exosystem are undirectional, since the developing person does not participate in those settings.

FIGURE 3.4

A topography of the relationship among systems
SOURCE: *Adapted from Bronfenbrenner, 1979.*

A feedback loop is positive when a child offers a suggestion and a parent recognizes and compliments the child on that suggestion. In such a pattern, the child is encouraged to continue to offer suggestions, and the parent comes to view the child as someone who has valuable suggestions to offer. A feedback loop is negative if a parent ignores the child's suggestion or scolds the child for making it. The child is less likely to make further suggestions, and the parent is likely to view the child as someone who has no valuable ideas to offer. Many positive and negative feedback loops operate in all families to sustain certain underlying qualities of the system, such as the power hierarchy, the level of conflict, and the balance between autonomy and dependency among the members.

One of the most commonly noted characteristics of family systems is the interdependence of the family members. Changes in one family member are accompanied by changes in the others. Imagine for a moment that family members are standing in a circle and holding a rope. Each person is trying to exert enough tension on the rope to keep it tight and preserve the circular shape. The amount of tension each person must exert depends on what every other person is doing. Now imagine that one member of the family lets go of the rope and steps away. In order to retain the shape and tension of the rope, everyone else has to adjust his or her grip. Letting go of the rope is an analogy for many kinds of changes that can occur in a family—a parent becomes ill, a child goes off to college, or a parent takes on a demanding job outside of the home. The system adjusts by redefining relationships, modifying patterns of communication, and adjusting its boundaries. The members and their interdependencies change. Similar adjustments must be made if a member is added to the family system, or when the system undergoes some other major transition.

The systems theory perspective offers an especially productive approach to clinical problems. A person who has been identified as dysfunctional is treated not as a lone individual but as part of a family system. From a systems theory perspective, the assumption is that the person's problems occur as a result of the way the person—

Systems theory emphasizes the interconnection of systems. Children adapt their play to their neighborhood microsystem. The hand-made swing hanging from a tree in a grassy field and the metal swings on the asphalt playground create two distinct ecologies in which to observe coordinated peer interaction. How might the quality of play differ in these two settings?

whether a child, a parent, or a grandparent—is treated by other family members. The only way to bring about changes in the person's functioning is to alter the functioning of the other members of the system as well. If the person is "underfunctioning"—that is, acting irresponsibly, not communicating, not performing at his or her level of capability, withdrawing, or acting impulsively—one assumes that others in the family are "overfunctioning"—that is, assuming many of the person's roles and responsibilities in order to "take up the slack." The dysfunctional behavior is maintained because it is a component of an emotional unit. In other words, the dysfunction belongs neither to the person nor to the other family members but to the particular interdependence among the family members that appears to be necessary to preserve the viability of the family system as a whole (Bowen, 1978).

By definition, family systems are also interdependent with adjacent systems. Thus, the understanding of families requires an analysis of the resources and demands of other social systems that impinge on families, and the opportunities families have for influencing adjoining systems. A woman who is experiencing an extremely demanding, stressful, and sexist work environment, for example, may be constantly tired, tense, and irritable in her behavior toward her family members. She may bring home the resentments from work in the way she treats and expects to be treated by males and females in her family. If the job is important to her and to her family, no one may be willing to acknowledge the disruptive impact the work setting is having on family life. Family violence, the effects of unemployment on families, participation of mothers in the labor force, day care, and the role of parents in their children's schooling are all being examined from a systems perspective.

Links to Psychosocial Theory   Psychosocial theory embraces the basic assumption of systems theory, that an understanding of development requires an analysis of the child embedded in a number of interrelated systems. Systems theory, however, is not really a developmental theory. Systems are expected to change through adaptive self-regulation and adaptive self-organization. The direction of this change is not necessarily patterned except that it is expected to move in the direction of creating new, higher levels of organization to coordinate newly developed substructures. According to psychosocial theory, however, change is developmental. With expanding cognitive capacities and the resolution of each new psychosocial crisis, a child is propelled into increasingly complex social systems and encounters new stimulation for growth through participation in a greater variety of social relationships. At each new stage, children develop new coping skills and devise strategies for new levels of participation in the social system. Eventually, they create innovative approaches for modifying the social system itself.

Chapter Summary

The seven theoretical perspectives we have reviewed take distinct approaches to continuity and change across the life span. Evolutionary theory provides an overall temporal framework within which to understand individual development. Although a life span of 85 or 90 years may seem long, it is but a flicker in the 1 to 2 million years of human biological adaptation. Evolutionary theory highlights the genetically governed aspects of growth and development. The environment provides the specific conditions that require adaptation. However, adaptive change can occur only if it is supported by the genetically based characteristics of the organism. The basic mechanism that accounts for species change over many generations is natural selection.

Ethology, the study of evolutionarily significant behaviors, provides a systematic approach to analyzing reproductive practices, care-giving behaviors, strategies for obtaining resources, and other behaviors that contribute to individual and species survival.

According to psychosexual theory, development is seen as following a biologically determined path along which changing patterns of social relationships follow the unfolding of sexual impulses and the sexualization of body zones. Culture plays a major role in establishing the taboos and acceptable patterns of sexual gratification that lead to conflicts, fixations, and strategies for sublimation. Sexual impulses, wishes, and fears, many of which are unconscious, guide behavior and give it meaning. Psychosexual theory emphasizes the years of infancy and childhood as those in which basic personality patterns are established. It also identifies the family, especially the parent-child relationship, as the primary context within which conflicts related to the socialization of sexual impulses are resolved.

Psychosexual theory describes three basic structures of the personality: id, ego, and superego. Defense mechanisms are strategies the ego uses to protect itself from being overwhelmed by id impulses or the punishing influences of the superego. As ego develops, the child becomes increasingly adept at satisfying id impulses in ways that are socially acceptable. In adolescence, a resurgence of id energy challenges many of the ego's earlier coping strategies. Ego must find new ways to express and modify impulses. An essential aspect of this process is thought to be the separation of ego from earlier objects of attachment and investment of energy in the self as well as in new social relationships.

Cognitive developmental theories focus on the etiology of rational thought and the capacity for scientific reasoning. Piaget's cognitive theory, like psychosexual theory, views development as a product of a biologically guided plan for growth and change. The elements that make cognitive growth possible are all present in the genetic information that governs the growth of the brain and nervous system. However, the process of intellectual growth requires interaction with a diverse and responsive environment. Cognitive development is fostered by recognition of discrepancies between existing schemes and new experiences. Through the reciprocal processes of assimilation and accommodation, schemes are modified and integrated to form the basis for organizing and explaining experience.

Vygotsky's contribution places the development of higher mental processes in a dynamic social context. Although thinking and reasoning are dependent upon biologically based capacities, the way mental activity is organized reflects unique characteristics of the social context, especially as culture is transmitted through language, tools, and social relationships.

Learning theories focus on the mechanisms that permit individuals to respond to their diverse environments and the permanent changes in thought and behavior that accompany changes in the environment. Behavior can be shaped and modified by systematic changes in environmental conditions. According to learning theorists, human beings have an especially flexible behavioral system. No assumptions are made about universal stages of growth. As conditions in the environment change, response patterns also change. Similarity among individuals at a particular period of life is explained by the fact that they are exposed to similar environmental conditions, patterns of reinforcement, and models.

Cultural theory, like learning theories, emphasizes the role of the environment in directing the course of development. Within this framework, the significance of biological maturation depends on the interaction between the individual and the social context. The possibilities for cultural variation are enormous. What we define as the normal or natural pattern and tempo of change in competence, roles, and status depends largely on the way a society recognizes and treats individuals of different ages, gender, and degree of kinship.

Instead of looking at the environment at the microscopic level of the learning theories, considering every unique stimulus and its corresponding response, social role theory suggests that learning is organized around key social functions called roles. As people attempt to enact roles, they integrate their behavior into meaningful units. Meaning is provided by the definition of the role and the expectations of those in reciprocal roles. Development is a product of entry into an increasing number of complex roles over the life span. As children acquire and lose roles, they change their self-definitions and their relationships with social groups. Most societies define roles that are linked with gender, age, marital status, and kinship. These roles provide patterning to the life course. However, the patterns are understood to be products of the structures and functions of the society rather than of genetic information.

Systems theory takes a unique scientific perspective. Rather than seeking to analyze causal relationships, systems theory emphasizes the multidimensional sources of influence on individuals, and the simultaneous influence of individuals on the systems of which they are a part. Each person is at once a component of one or more larger systems and a system unto itself. One must approach the study of child development from many angles, identifying the critical resources, the flow of resources, and the transformation of resources that underlie an adaptive process of reorganization and growth.

*E*nd of Chapter Case

Robert Meyer, a single parent, and his adopted daughter, Juliet.

Our family came to be as a sort of dream. I was a single man, working in a well-paying position as the executive director of a fund-raising agency for a residential treatment facility for chemically dependent kids. I am a substance abuser, that is, a chemically dependent person recovering from addiction to alcohol and drugs. I had just purchased my home and was wanting to give something back to society. At the time, I was considering becoming a foster parent. I approached the social service department of the county where I live and was directed to the "fostadopt" program.

To make a long story short, while I was doing a home study for the program, a friend of mine who noticed what I was doing asked me if I might be interested in a newborn child. She had a friend who was pregnant and wanting to give up her child for adoption, but hadn't chosen a family or parent yet. We met, both had good feelings about the other, and entered a contract. . . . Also, it should be mentioned that the birth mother was chronically alcoholic, 39 years old, homeless, and without much prenatal care. She continued to drink throughout her pregnancy. . . .

Juliet was born premature, weighing three pounds thirteen ounces. I was there for the delivery, which was not normal, as planned. Juliet was in the intensive care nursery for five days, and came home with me after she reached four pounds. She was born very small because of the alcoholism and prematurity and she's still not on the charts. At 2 years of age she weighs eighteen pounds, but developmentally she's beyond the charts in her intelligence. . . .

The difference between the way I was raised and the way I raise Juliet are far apart and the same in many ways. I sleep with Juliet a lot and, for the first six months of life together, we shared the same bed. This was something that never existed in the home I grew up in. Also, Juliet stays up a lot longer than I did as a child because it is our only time together after a long day of work and day care. I was raised at home by my mother, who took care of me and the household while my father worked all day. Today I have to find the best substitute for the job of child care, and it is away from the house. We wake before the sun, get dressed, and drive 20 miles to the day care. I go to work for nine hours and pick her up and drive home in traffic. We return home after sunset. Lots of our meals are bought at restaurants as a means of saving time.

Juliet is a part of me. We go almost everywhere together, not only for her entertainment but to my social events and affairs. I take Juliet along to as many things as possible, much to the displeasure of others who don't want to hear from an infant. I spoil my child with all sorts of extras, and I work an additional part-time job to afford this luxury. I feel as if I spend more time with Juliet than my parents did with me. I'm not sure how accurate this is, since I don't remember much from my twos and threes. But, as a single parent, I am the sole person responsible to feed, change, doctor, pick up, drop off, etc.

Juliet and I have created a bonding with each other that is stronger than any I ever had with either of my parents, as well as a friendship. The type of parenting that I practice is that of learning by experiment and experience. I try to be as direct as you can with an infant. I try to listen and answer, not yell and shut down with anger and frustration.

. . . I see my role as parent as a great job. I'm both a parent and a friend. We both teach each other about life and how it works. Sometimes I'm more amazed with what Juliet knows than with what I can teach her. Watching the process of growing and learning from the beginning is a wonderful experience that fulfills my life greatly.

Source: Nestor, 1991.

Thought Questions

As you think about this case of a single-parent dad raising a high-risk, infant daughter, consider the ways that each of the theories presented in this chapter might be applied.

1. How might psychosocial inventions such as foster parenting and adoptive parenting serve an evolutionarily adaptive role?

2. What ideas does evolutionary theory offer about men as primary caregivers?

3. How might psychosexual theory interpret the issues of drug and alcohol addiction raised in this case?

4. According to psychosexual theory, what experiences in Juliet's infancy might have enduring effects on her personality development?

5. Robert Meyer says that he parents by experiment and experience. How does this strategy relate to Piaget's view of the process of cognitive development?

6. How do Robert and Juliet function in what Vygotsky calls the "zone of proximal development" for one another?

7. How might principles of the learning theories relate to the patterns of adaptation that are revealed in this case? Consider evidence for the following concepts: associational learning; positive and negative reinforcement; shaping; observational learning, expectancies; goals and plans; self-control strategies.

8. What aspects of this case might support the principles of cultural determinism? What aspects challenge this concept?

9. How are ideas such as role enactment, role expectations, reciprocal roles, and role strain related to the case? What is the impact of role learning for Robert?

10. What various microsystems make up Juliet's mesosystem? Robert's mesosystem? How do factors in the exosystem influence the process of foster child placement and adoption? What are aspects of the macrosystem that might influence the ease or difficulty with which Robert enacts his role as an adoptive father?

Chapter 4

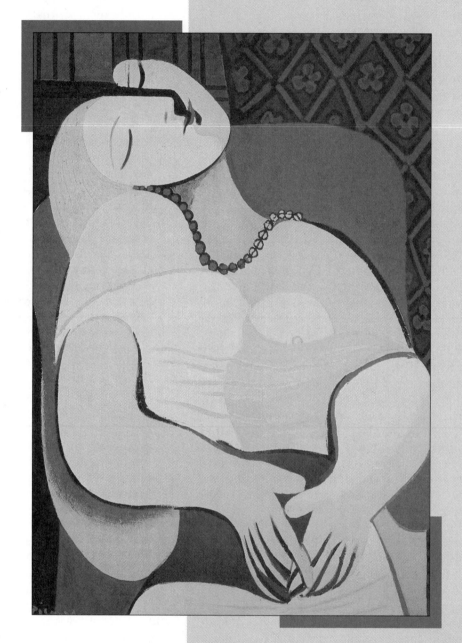

The period of pregnancy involves the most intricate of interactions between the developing fetus and the pregnant woman. The pattern of fetal development is guided largely by genetic factors, but the pregnant woman's health, social support, and emotional well-being can have substantial impact on fetal growth.

The Period of Pregnancy and Prenatal Development

Chapter Objectives

- To describe the biochemical basis of genetic information and the process through which it is transmitted from one generation to the next.
- To identify the contributions of genetic factors to individuality through their role in controlling the rate of development, their contributions to individual traits, and the genetic sources of abnormalities.
- To trace fetal development through three trimesters of pregnancy, including an understanding of critical periods when normal fetal development can be disrupted.
- To describe the birth process and factors that contribute to infant mortality.
- To analyze the reciprocity between the pregnant woman and the developing fetus, focusing on ways that pregnancy affects a childbearing woman and expectant father, as well as basic influences on fetal growth such as maternal age, drug use, nutrition, and environmental toxins.
- To examine the impact of culture on pregnancy and childbirth.
- To analyze abortion from a psychosocial perspective, including the legal context, its social and emotional impact on women, and men's views.

The fetus develops within the context of the pregnant woman's body, her family, and her culture. During the prenatal period, the pattern of development is guided largely by genetic information, but the outcome of the pregnancy and the robustness or vulnerability of the newborn are also influenced by the kind of environment the pregnant woman provides. In this chapter, we take the perspective of both the developing fetus and the expectant parents. For the parents, their role begins at the decision to have children, the experiences of pregnancy, and the events of childbirth. For the child, the process of growth begins at the moment of fertilization.

During the prenatal period, genetic factors guide the tempo of growth and the emergence of individual characteristics. As the human fetus grows, sensory and motor competencies emerge. The psychosocial environment provides resources for and challenges to healthy development. Cultural attitudes toward pregnancy and childbirth, poverty and the associated stressors, support from the child's father and other significant family members, maternal nutrition, and the use of obstetric drugs are among the factors that affect fetal growth. ❖

GENETICS AND DEVELOPMENT

From the time of fertilization, genetic information provides a set of guidelines for the individual's development. Given one's genetic potential, a wide range of individual variation is possible, depending on the quality of the environment and one's interaction with it.

Genes and Chromosomes as Sources of Genetic Information

When we talk about inherited characteristics, we are really referring to two different kinds of heredity. The first includes all the genetic information that comes to us as members of the human species. We inherit genetic information that is shared by all human beings, such as patterns of motor behavior (walking upright, for instance), brain size, and body structure, including the proportional size of the head, torso, and limbs. Two of the most relevant of these species-related characteristics are the readiness to learn and the inclination to participate in social interaction. All humans share these attributes.

The second kind of heredity consists of characteristics that have been transmitted through a specific **gene pool**. Such traits as hair color, skin color, blood group, and height result from the genetic information passed on from one generation to the next. The principles of genetics that we describe here refer primarily to the products of a specific gene pool (Thompson et al., 1991). Genetic information links each new person to the human species in general and also to a specific genetic ancestry.

Chromosomes—long, thin strands of genetic material located in the cell nucleus— are formed from chains of DNA molecules (Figure 4.1). **A gene** is a portion of DNA that codes for one hereditary characteristic and occupies a specific place on a chromosome. Human beings have about 100,000 functional genes distributed along the 23 pairs of chromosomes (Figure 4.2). Genetic mapping involves identifying the specific location of each gene on a specific chromosome, which is an enormous task: The smallest human chromosome bands that can be recognized under the microscope contain from 2 to 5 million base pairs of DNA and many genes (Patterson, 1987; NIH/CEPH Collaborative Mapping Group, 1992).

The biochemical basis of genetic information is the DNA *(deoxyribonucleic acid)* molecule, which is in the shape of a double helix and looks something like a twisted rope ladder. The sides of this genetic ladder are composed of alternating units of sugar

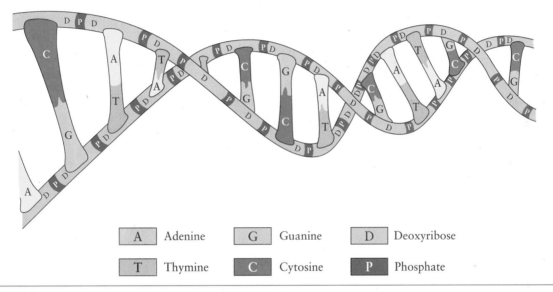

| A | Adenine | G | Guanine | D | Deoxyribose |
| T | Thymine | C | Cytosine | P | Phosphate |

FIGURE 4.1
Diagram of a small part of a DNA molecule

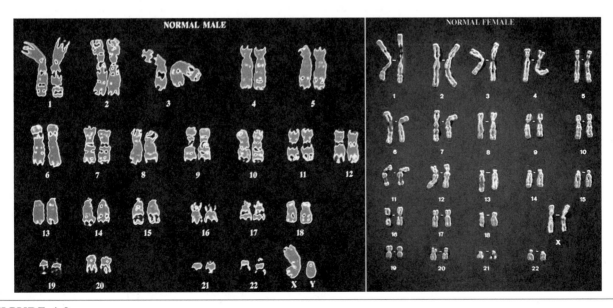

FIGURE 4.2
The 23 pairs of chromosomes in a normal human male (left) and female (right)

(deoxyribose) and phosphate, and the rungs are made up of pairs of nitrogen bases. Nitrogen bases are so named because they include the element nitrogen as well as the elements hydrogen and carbon. Four nitrogen bases are involved: *adenine (A), guanine (G), cytosine (C),* and *thymine (T).* These bases are often referred to by their initial letters, and A, G, C, and T are called the genetic alphabet.

In each chromosome pair, one chromosome comes from the father and one from the mother. The chromosome pairs differ in size, some containing over 1000 genes and others containing 2000. In 22 pairs of chromosomes, both members are similar in shape and size. They also contain the same kinds of genes. The 23rd pair of chromosomes is a different story: Females have two X chromosomes, and males have one X and one Y chromosome. The X and Y notation is used because these chromosomes differ in shape and size (the X chromosome is longer than the Y chromosome; see the last pair in Figure 4.2). There are very few similarities in the genes present on the X and Y chromosomes.

The same group of chromosomes does not appear in each **gamete** (egg or sperm cell). When the cells divide, the chromosomes separate independently. There are 2^{23} possible combinations of chromosome separation in any individual's gametes. When one considers the fertilization process and the chance meeting of one sperm and one egg cell, the number of different individuals that might be produced by two adults is $2^{23} \times 2^{23}$, or 64 trillion.

Additional variability in the pattern of genetic information results from **crossing over.** When the cells divide during **meiosis,** some of the material from the paternal and maternal chromosome strands may cross over and exchange places on the strand. The resulting sequence of specific genetic information on a chromosome is unlike that in either the original maternal or paternal code. Through crossing over, new arrangements of genetic information may be passed on to offspring. This variation in the patterning of genetic information adds to the diversity of offspring possible for any single couple.

The Laws of Heredity

The laws that govern the process by which genetic information is transmitted from parent to offspring were discovered by Gregor Mendel (1866), a monk who studied the inherited characteristics of plants, particularly garden peas. His laws were formulated long before the discovery of the biochemical materials that compose genes and chromosomes.

Alleles

In the 22 pairs of identical chromosomes, each gene has at least two states or conditions, one on each chromosome strand in the pair. These alternative states are called **alleles.** Whatever the allelic state of the gene from one parent, the other parent's allele for that gene may be either the same or different. If both alleles are the same, the gene is said to be **homozygous.** If the alleles are different, the gene is **heterozygous.**

Genotype and Phenotype

The genetic information about a trait is called the **genotype** (for example, the genetic information that guides skin color). The observed characteristic (for example, one's actual skin color) is called the **phenotype.** Genotype influences phenotype in three different ways. First, the differences in the allelic states of a gene sometimes result in a **cumulative relation,** in which more than one pair of genes influences the trait. An example of this kind of relation is the genetic contribution to height. A person who receives mostly "tall" genes will be tall; a person who receives mostly "short" genes will be short. Most people receive a mix of "tall" and "short" genes and are of average height.

Second, the differences between alleles may result in **codominance,** a state in which both genes are expressed in the new cell. An example of codominance is the AB blood type, which results from the joining of an A blood-type allele and a B blood-type allele. This blood type is not a mixture of A and B, nor is A subordinate to B or B to A; instead, a new blood type, AB, is formed.

Two dark-haired parents can have a blond child if both parents are heterozygous for blond hair color.

Third, the differences in the allele states of a gene may result in a dominance relation. **Dominance** means that, if one allele is present, its characteristic is always observed whether or not the other allele of the allelic pair is the same. The allele that dominates is called the **dominant gene.** The other allele that is present, but whose characteristic is masked by the dominant gene, is called the **recessive gene.** Eye color is the result of a dominance relation. The gene for brown eyes (B) is dominant over the gene for blue eyes (b). The probability that the recessive trait of blue eyes will emerge in the offspring of two heterozygous parents is illustrated in Figure 4.3. The possible combinations of the gene related to brown or blue eye color are BB, Bb, bB, and bb. Only if both parents carry the b allele and it is present in each of the gametes that form the offspring will the child have blue eyes. As the figure shows, on the average only 25% of the offspring of heterozygous parents have blue eyes.

In the case of a dominance relation, genetic information is not always observed in some outward characteristic. For example, people with alleles BB and Bb may both have brown eyes, even though they have different genetic information. For brown and blue eye color, there are two phenotypes (brown and blue) but three genotypes—two dominant alleles (BB), two recessive alleles (bb), or one dominant and one recessive allele (Bb or bB).

Sex-Linked Characteristics

Certain genetic information is said to be **sex-linked** because the gene for the specific characteristic is found on the sex chromosomes. The female ova carry only X chromosomes. Half of the male sperm carry Y chromosomes, and half carry X chromosomes. Male children can be produced only when a sperm carrying a Y chromosome fertilizes an egg, and the result is an XY combination in the 23rd chromosome pair. All sperm carrying X chromosomes will produce female children.

Sex-linked traits are more likely to be observed in males, even though they are present in the genotype of females. You will understand this more readily if you visualize the XY chromosome pair. When a trait is carried on the Y chromosome, it will be inherited and transmitted only by males, since only males have the Y chromosome.

FIGURE 4.3

Probability of heterozygous parents producing a blue-eyed offspring

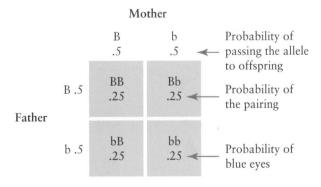

Note: Whenever B allele is present, eyes will be brown.

Interestingly, the Y chromosome is quite small, and very few exclusively Y-linked traits have been identified. One of the key genes that has been identified on the Y chromosome is referred to as **testis-determining factor** (TDF). This gene (or genes) is responsible for setting into motion the differentiation of the testes during embryonic development. Once the testes are formed, they begin to produce hormones that account for the further differentiation of the male reproductive system.

In addition to the Y-linked genes, sex-linked traits that are carried on the X chromosome are more likely to be observed in males than in females, because males do not have a second X chromosome with which to offset the effects of an X-linked trait. Currently, a map of the human X chromosome is being constructed through a coordinated, international research effort. The X chromosome comprises about 160 million base pairs. Genes associated with 26 inherited diseases have already been reproduced, and the location of genes associated with 50 others has been identified (Mandel et al., 1992).

Hemophilia is an example of a sex-linked trait. **Hemophiliacs** lack a specific blood protein that causes blood to clot after a wound (Lawn & Vehar, 1986). The allele for hemophilia is carried on the X chromosome. If the allele is either heterozygous or homozygous for the dominant characteristic (normal clotting), a female child will have normal blood-clotting capability. Only if she is homozygous for the recessive characteristic (a very rare occurrence) will she be hemophilic. The male, on the other hand, has only one allele for the blood-clotting gene, which he inherits from his mother. If that allele is dominant, his blood will clot normally; if it is recessive, he will be hemophilic (Figure 4.4).

There are other genes that are expressed exclusively in one sex but are not found on the sex chromosomes per se. For example, the genes for male beard development and female breast development are not located on the sex chromosomes. However, these characteristics will emerge only in the presence of the appropriate hormonal environment, which *is* directed by the sex chromosomes.

Genetic Sources of Individuality

The study of genetics reveals that individual variability is due to more than the many variations in environment and experience that confront a growing person. Variability is built into the mechanisms of heredity. Each adult couple has the potential for producing a great variety of genetically distinct children. Three areas in which genetic determinants contribute to individual variability are rate of development, individual traits, and abnormal development.

FIGURE 4.4

Sex-linked inheritance of hemophilia. Sex-linked inheritance of hemophilia results from the location of the factor VIII gene on the X chromosome. A male carrying a mutant factor VIII gene lacks normal factor VIII and is hemophilic. A female carrier is protected by the normal gene on her second X chromosome, but half of her daughters will be carriers and half of her sons will be hemophilic. When a father is hemophilic (not shown), his sons will not be hemophilic, because they receive his Y (not his X) chromosome, but his daughters will be carriers. SOURCE: *Lawn & Vehar, 1986.*

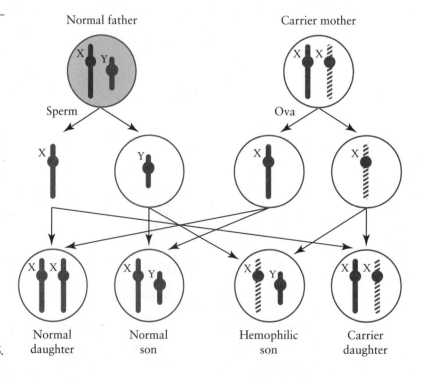

Normal father   Carrier mother

Sperm   Ova

Normal daughter   Normal son   Hemophilic son   Carrier daughter

Genetic Determinants of Rate of Development

Genes regulate the rate and sequence of maturation. The concept of an epigenetic plan for growth and development is based on the assumption that a genetically guided system promotes or restricts the growth of cells over the life span. Genetic factors have been found to play a role in behavioral development, including the onset of various levels of reasoning, language, and social orientation.

Considerable evidence of the role of genetics in guiding the rate and sequence of development has been provided by studies of identical twins (who have the same genetic structure). The rates at which identical twins develop are highly correlated, even when those twins are reared apart. A number of characteristics, including the timing of the acquisition of motor skills, personality development, changes in intellectual capacity among aged twins, and the timing of physical maturation, show a strong genetic influence (Holden, 1987).

Genes can be viewed as internal regulators that set the pace for maturation. They signal the onset of significant developmental changes throughout life, such as growth spurts, the eruption of teeth, puberty, and menopause. They also appear to set the limits of the life span. A small number of genes influences how many times the cells of a specific organism can divide and replicate (Marx, 1988). Research on three different animal species—fruit flies, worms, and mice—shows that when the most long-lived of a species are bred, the offspring have a longer life than average (Barinaga, 1991).

Differences in the rate of development contribute to our understanding of psychosocial growth. These differences bring different children into contact with new aspects of their environments and provide them with changing capacities at different chronological ages. Thus, the genetic processes that regulate readiness for certain kinds of growth and vulnerabilities to particular kinds of stress contribute to systematic differences among individuals. For example, adult expectations for the accomplishment of such specific tasks as toilet training, getting dressed without help, and learning to write interact with the child's developmental level. Disappointment may be conveyed to developmentally "late" children, and pride and approval may be conveyed to developmentally "accelerated" children.

Genetic Determinants of Individual Traits

Genes contain specific information about a wide range of human characteristics, from eye color and height to the ability to taste a particular substance called **phenylthio-carbamide** (which to tasters is bitter, but to nontasters has no taste at all). Some characteristics are controlled by a single gene. However, most significant characteristics, such as height, weight, blood group, skin color, and intelligence, are controlled by the combined action of several genes. When multiple genes are involved in the regulation of a single trait, the possibilities for individual differences in that trait increase. Since many characteristics are regulated by multiple genes, the variety of human genotypes is enormous.

Genetic factors also play a substantial role in individual differences in personality (Plomin, 1990, 1994; Loehlin, 1992; Holden, 1987). Traits such as sociability (a tendency to be outgoing), inhibition (a tendency to be cautious and socially shy or withdrawn), and neuroticism (a tendency to be anxious and emotionally sensitive) are pervasive dimensions of personality that appear to have strong genetic components. Research on the biological basis of sexual orientation suggests that genes may influence the development of the part of the brain that guides sexual behavior (LeVay, 1991). Identical twins are more likely to have the same sexual orientation than are fraternal twins or adoptive siblings (Bailey & Pillard, 1991; 1994). Even in rather specific areas of personality, such as political attitudes, aesthetic preferences, and sense of humor, identical twins show greater similarity than fraternal twins, even when the identical twins are reared apart from each other.

Extending the analysis of the impact of genetics on individual differences, Sandra Scarr (1992) suggested at least three ways in which genetic factors influence the environments of individuals, thus increasing the impact of genetics on the expression and

The many possible combinations of genetic information can produce tremendous individual variation. In this painting, Picasso shows how basic geometric shapes can be combined in a variety of ways to produce human-like figures, similar and yet each unique.

elaboration of individual differences. First, most children are raised by their parents in environments created by their parents. Thus, children receive both their genes and their environment from a common genetic source—their parents. As an example, a parent who is temperamentally sociable is more likely than a withdrawn or timid parent to have lots of people at the house, to enjoy the companionship of others, and therefore to expose his or her children to more companionate adults. Second, people draw out responses from others that are related to their own personality characteristics. Thus, broad, genetically based aspects of one's individuality will affect the kinds of social responses one receives from others, including one's parents. Third, as people mature and become increasingly assertive in selecting certain experiences and rejecting others, their own temperaments, talents, intelligence, and level of sociability will guide the kinds of environments they select and will strengthen certain genetic predispositions, while dampening others.

Genetic Determinants of Abnormal Development

In addition to characteristics such as physical appearance, temperament, talent, and intellectual capacity, a wide variety of abnormalities, or **anomalies,** have a genetic cause. The most dramatic anomalies result in a spontaneous abortion of the fetus early in the pregnancy. It is estimated that a majority of the spontaneous abortions that occur early in pregnancy are due to results of chromosomal abnormalities in the fertilized zygotes (the developing organism formed from the father's sperm and the mother's egg) (Clayman, 1989).

Of those infants who survive the neonatal period, an estimated 3–5% of newborns have one or more major recognizable anomalies (Cunningham et al., 1997). The incidence of anomalies increases to 6 or 7% as some disorders are diagnosed later in childhood. Some birth defects are linked to a specific chromosome or a single gene. Other birth defects are linked solely to environmental factors, such as drugs, medications, and fetal and maternal infections. The majority of malformations, however, result from the interaction of genetic vulnerabilities in the presence of environmental hazards or are of unknown origin (Moore, 1993).

Some examples of genetic and chromosomal disorders are listed in Table 4.1. The disorders are presented in two broad categories: those associated with specific genes and those associated with chromosomal abnormalities. Within those categories, some disorders are found on 1 of the 22 pairs of autosomal chromosomes (chromosomes other than the sex chromosomes), and others are on one of the sex chromosomes. Among the genetic disorders that result from a dominant gene, about 300 have been identified; among those that result from a recessive gene, about 250 have been identified. Molecular biologists have begun to identify the chromosomal site of a number of genetic disorders. This work will lead to a clearer understanding of the molecular mechanisms that account for these disorders and, eventually, to the development of gene therapies for many genetically caused abnormalities (Anderson, 1992; Crystal, 1995).

Certain genetic diseases are linked directly to our ancestry; therefore, the incidence of some genetic diseases is higher in certain populations than in others (Thompson et al., 1991; Emery & Mueller, 1992). For example, Tay-Sachs disease is present in 1 out of 3900 infants born to Ashkenazi Jews (Jews who settled in eastern Europe) but only

TABLE 4.1	**Examples of Genetic and Chromosomal Disorders**

I. Genetic disorders
  A. Autosomal dominant gene
    1. *Huntington's chorea:* rapid jerky, involuntary movements; deterioration of muscle coordination and mental functioning. Symptoms usually do not appear until age 35–50. Caused by genetic defect on chromosome 4.
    2. *Marfan's syndrome:* Elongated fingers; deformed chest and spine; abnormal heart. Tendons, ligaments, and joint capsules are weak.
  B. Autosomal recessive gene
    1. *Albinism:* Hair, skin, and eyes lack the pigment melanin. Often accompanied by visual problems and a susceptibility to skin cancer.
    2. *Cystic fibrosis:* Certain glands do not function properly. The glands in the lining of the bronchial tubes produce excessive amounts of thick mucus, which lead to chronic lung infections. Failure of the pancreas to produce enzymes necessary for the breakdown of fats and their absorption from the intestines leads to malnutrition. Sweat glands are also affected. Often fatal by age 30. Caused by missing base pairs on chromosome 7.
    3. *Sickle-cell anemia:* Malformation of red blood cells reduces the amount of oxygen they can carry. Results in fatigue, headaches, shortness of breath on exertion, pallor, jaundice, pain, and damage to kidneys, lungs, intestine, and brain.
    4. *Tay-Sachs disease:* Absence of a certain enzyme results in the buildup of harmful chemicals in the brain. Results in death before age 3.
  C. X-linked recessive
    1. *Color blindness:* Defect of light-sensitive pigment in one or more classes of cone cells in the retina of the eye and/or an abnormality in or reduced number of cone cells themselves. The two common types are reduced discrimination of light wavelengths within the middle (green) and long (red) parts of the visible spectrum.
    2. *Hemophilia:* Absence of a blood protein (factor VIII) reduces effectiveness of blood clotting. Severity of disorder varies. Bleeding episodes likely to begin in toddlerhood.
II. Chromosomal disorders
  A. Autosomal abnormality
    1. *Down syndrome:* Additional 21st chromosome; also called trisomy 21. The excess chromosome results in physical and intellectual abnormalities, including IQ in the range of 30–80; distinctive facial features, heart defects, intestinal problems, hearing defects; susceptibility to repeated ear infections. Tendency to develop narrowing of the arteries in adulthood, with attendant increase in risk of heart disease.
  B. Sex-chromosome abnormalities
    1. *Turner's syndrome:* Usually caused by a lack of one X chromosome in a girl; sometimes one of two X chromosomes is defective; occasionally some cells are missing on an X chromosome. These abnormalities result in defective sexual development and infertility, short stature, absence or retarded development of secondary sex characteristics, absence of menstruation, narrowing of the aorta, and a degree of mental retardation.
    2. *Klinefelter's syndrome:* One or more extra X chromosomes in a boy. This abnormality results in defective sexual development, including enlarged breasts and small testes, infertility, and often mental retardation.

SOURCE: Based on information provided in Clayman, 1989.

1 in 112,000 other U. S. infants. Thalassemia, a disease involving faulty production of hemoglobin (which carries oxygen in the blood), is found most often in people of Mediterranean, Middle Eastern, and Southeast Asian origins. The variety of genetic abnormalities serves to broaden the range of individual variability. Many of the irregularities pose a challenge both to the adaptive capacities of the affected person and to the care-giving capacities of the adults involved.

Genetic Technology and Psychosocial Evolution

Psychosocial evolution has typically been differentiated from biological evolution in that change is accomplished by social mechanisms rather than incorporated in the genetic structure. As a result of scientific knowledge, however, we are entering an era when it is possible to intervene to influence the genotype. One such intervention is **genetic counseling.** Individuals and couples with a family history of a genetic disease, or who for some other reason worry about the possibility of transmitting a genetic disease to their children, can have a blood test to identify genes that may result in the inherited disorder. The location of the genes that account for such abnormalities as Tay-Sachs disease, sickle-cell anemia, Duchenne muscular dystrophy, and cystic fibrosis have been identified. Recent discoveries make it possible to identify genes responsible for certain forms of prostate, breast, and colon cancers. Couples who have reason to believe that they may carry genes for one of these diseases can be advised about the probability of having children who may be afflicted (Somerson, 1997). If significant numbers of the carriers of genetic diseases decided not to reproduce, the incidence of these diseases in the population would decline over time. Thus, a psychosocial intervention would modify the gene pool.

Mapping the Genome

In the future, genetic technology promises to take us even further in the direct modification of the genetic structure of an individual. A project to map the **human genome**—to identify and list in order all of the genome's approximately 3 billion base pairs—was

Cloning of animals for research and medical purposes has raised new questions about the ethics of genetic research, especially its applicability to humans. What are some of the ethical considerations that come to mind as you think of cloning human beings?

initiated in January 1989 by the National Institutes of Health (NIH). The project, expected to be completed between 2002 and 2005, will permit specialists to predict an individual's susceptibility to genetic diseases, to treat genetically caused diseases, and possibly to "enhance" a person's genetic potential through the introduction of gene modifications (NIH/CEPH Collaborative Mapping Group, 1992; Beardsley, 1996). As an example, the gene that is defective in patients with *cystic fibrosis,* a condition that occurs in children and young adults in which a thick, sticky mucus obstructs the airways and increases vulnerability to infection, has recently been identified (Collins, 1992). Cystic fibrosis is the most common and potentially lethal of the autosomal recessive diseases among Caucasians. Now that the biochemical process associated with the defective gene has been analyzed, a wide variety of therapeutic techniques are being developed, including both drug and gene therapy.

Ethical Considerations

Gene transfer, the patenting of new life forms created through genetic engineering; genetic fingerprinting, which is used to help identify criminal suspects; and, most recently, cloning from an adult mammal are topics that are raising new ethical concerns. There is a general consensus that gene therapy used to treat serious diseases such as cystic fibrosis or cancer is ethical. However, there is less agreement about the use of intervention to alter the genetic code at the level of the zygote or to attempt to introduce genes intended to enhance aspects of normal development in humans. Some people are finding that even the advances in identifying genetic markers for specific diseases can lead to ethical dilemmas. Individuals are turning down the opportunity to be tested for possible genetic diseases for fear that they will be denied health insurance, life insurance, or employment (Beardsley, 1996).

The possibility of reproducing genetically identical clones from adult human tissue has stirred the conscience of the religious, political, and medical communities. Is it ethical to clone human genes so that great scholars, scientists, and artists can walk the earth again? Should cloning become an approved technology for coping with infertility? Of course, based on what we know of the dynamic interaction between genetics and environment, the similarity of an adult human clone to its genetic parent may not be as great as that of an adult cloned sheep or calf to its genetic parent. Through discussion, debate, research, observation of events, and court cases, a set of ethics is being hammered out that not only deals with specific issues but also sets the tone for the way life itself is conceptualized (Kluger, 1997; Woodward, 1997).

Evaluating the Impact of Heredity on Behavior

One way to summarize the influences of genetics on behavior is to view the genotype as establishing a **reaction range**—that is, a range of possible responses to environmental conditions, the limits of which are determined by one's genotype. Under similar environmental conditions, genetic differences are most likely to be expressed; however, when environmental conditions vary, the advantages of one genotype over another may be masked by the adversities or opportunities of the situation. Figure 4.5 shows the hypothetical reaction ranges of three children with respect to intelligence. Child A has greater genetic potential for intelligence than Child B, who has greater potential than Child C. When all three children are in unstimulating environments, their IQs develop at the lower end of their potential range. When all three children are in stimulating environments, their IQs develop toward the upper end of their potential range. If the three children are in different environments, the differences in genetic potential

FIGURE 4.5

Hypothetical reaction ranges of intelligence for three genotypes

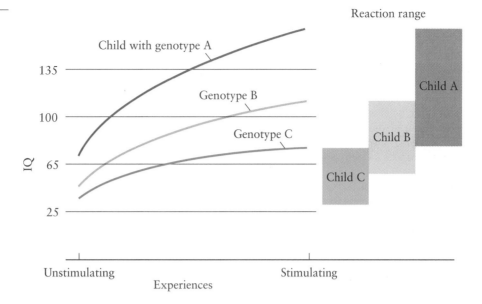

may be masked by the way the environments act on this potential. If Child B and Child C are in stimulating environments and Child A is in an unstimulating environment, Child B may have the highest measured IQ, and the IQs of Children C and A may be lower and very similar. Each child's intellectual ability can be expressed as a range that is a product of the interaction of genetic potential and environment (Box 4.1).

The concept of the reaction range can be seen clearly in the outlook for children with **Down syndrome** (Patterson, 1987). This condition, which occurs in 1 of every 700 live births, is the most common genetic cause of mental retardation in the United States. In the early part of this century, children born with Down syndrome had a life expectancy of 9 years. Today, the life expectancy of a child with Down syndrome is 30 years, and 25% live to age 50. Medical care, early and constant educational intervention, physical therapy, and a nurturing home environment have significant, positive results for children with Down syndrome. Under optimal conditions, individuals with Down syndrome are able to achieve a moderate degree of independence and to participate actively in the life of their schools, communities, and families.

The concept of reaction range is illustrated in the high level of functioning evidenced by this girl with Down Syndrome. With optimal home and school support, she can enjoy interacting with peers and learn many skills required for self-sufficiency.

BOX 4.1   HEREDITARY INFLUENCES ON INTELLIGENCE

What are the relative contributions of genetic and environmental factors to intelligence? Intelligent behavior requires the successful integration of both (Plomin, 1990). It relies on the structure of the central nervous system and the sense receptors, which are products of genetically guided information. However, the healthy functioning of these systems requires adequate nutrition, rest, and freedom from disease, conditions that vary with the environment. Intelligent behavior builds upon experiences with diverse stimuli, social interactions, and schooling—all elements of the physical and social environment.

The influence of genetic factors on intelligence may be observed in two ways. First, specific genetic irregularities can cause degrees of mental retardation. Two examples are Down syndrome and Turner's syndrome (See Table 4.1). These and many other genetic diseases play an indisputable role in restricting intellectual potential.

A second approach to understanding the influence of genetics on intelligence is through the study of family relationships. Family members may be related closely or distantly. The closer the relatives, the more similar their genetic makeup. If intelligence is influenced by genetics, close relatives should be more similar in intelligence than distant relatives.

Figure 4.6 shows the degree of similarity found in more than 100 studies of intelligence in siblings of four degrees of relationship. Similarity in intelligence increases with the degree of genetic relatedness. The similarity in intelligence of identical, or monozygotic (MZ), twins gives striking evidence of the contribution of genetics to intelligence. Fraternal, or dizygotic (DZ), twins who share the same prenatal, home, and child-rearing environments show much less similarity than do identical twins and not much more than "ordinary" siblings. An overview of studies that have attempted to evaluate the contribution of genetic factors to cognitive

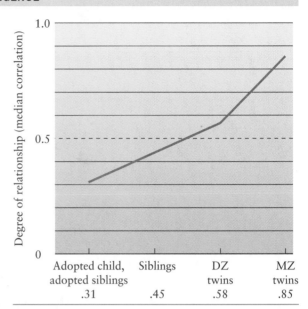

FIGURE 4.6
Similarity in intelligence among siblings of four levels of relationship

ability suggests that genetics accounts for 50% of the variance, shared environmental factors account for 33% of the variance, nonshared environmental factors account for 17% of the variance, and measurement error accounts for 10% of the variance (Gottesman, 1997). Thus, while genetics is central, in shaping the capacity for complex thinking and the level of cognitive performance, so are environmental factors.

Identical twins have the exact same genotype and have shared the same fetal environment. Fraternal twins are no more alike genetically than siblings, but they also share the same fetal environment.

NORMAL FETAL DEVELOPMENT

Let us now explore the physical process through which genetic information is actually transmitted and see how the early phases of development unfold.

Fertilization

One normal ejaculation contains several hundred million sperm. This large number is necessary to ensure fertilization, because most sperm die on the way through the vagina and the uterus. Each microscopic sperm is composed of a pointed head and a tail. The head contains the genetic material necessary for reproduction. The tail moves like a whip as the sperm swims through the cervix and uterus and into the fallopian tubes. Swimming at a rate of an inch in 8 minutes, sperm may reach the egg in as little as 30 minutes, but the journey usually takes about 6 hours; sperm can stay alive in the uterus for up to 5 days.

During most of the menstrual cycle, the plug of mucus in the cervix is thick and difficult to penetrate. At the middle of the cycle, when an ovum is about ready to be released, the mucus thins out, allowing more sperm to pass through the cervix and travel farther into the uterus in search of an ovum. The change in the mucus also lessens the vagina's natural acidity, making it a more hospitable environment for sperm cells.

In contrast to the male, who produces billions of sperm in a lifetime, the female ordinarily releases just one ovum, or egg, each month, midway through the menstrual cycle. In a lifetime of approximately 40 fertile years, during which she can be expected to have two children, the average woman releases approximately 450 eggs. Each female is born with her complete supply of eggs.

Like the sperm, the ovum is a single cell that contains genetic material. In comparison with body cells, the egg cell is quite large (0.12 millimeters), about the size of the period at the end of this sentence. When the ovum is mature, it is encased in a sac of fluid and floats to the surface of the ovary. The sac ruptures and releases the ovum into one of the two fallopian tubes. Millions of feathery hairlike structures in the fallopian tube sweep around the ovum and gently move it toward the uterus.

The ovum may be fertilized at any point as it moves through the fallopian tube, but it usually occurs in the outer third of the tube, close to the uterus. Only one sperm can enter the egg. As the first sperm passes through the cell membrane, a rapid change in the membrane's chemistry effectively locks out other sperm. If the ovum is not fertilized within the first 24 hours of its maturity, it begins to disintegrate and is shed along with the lining of the uterus in the next menstrual period.

Once inside the egg cell, the sperm loses its tail, and the head becomes a normal cell nucleus. The egg cell also goes through a final change in preparation for fertilization. The two nuclei meet in the egg cytoplasm, lose their nuclear membranes, and integrate their separate chromosomal material into a single set of 23 pairs of chromosomes. At

When the sperm breaks through the lining of the egg, a biochemical reaction takes place that prevents other sperm from entering the cell.

this moment, all the information necessary to activate growth and produce a new, unique individual is contained in a single cell.

Twins

The cell produced when the sperm fertilizes the egg is referred to as a **zygote.** The zygote travels down the fallopian tube and divides as it travels toward the uterus without growing larger. After about a week, this mass of cells implants in the uterus. Occasionally, a zygote divides in two and separates, forming two individuals with the same chromosomal composition. These individuals are referred to as **monozygotic (MZ) twins** because they come from a single zygote. They are always of the same sex, and they are strikingly similar in physical appearance, a characteristic leading to the term *identical twins.* Much research has been done on identical twins who have been raised together and those who have been raised apart to reveal the relative contributions of heredity and environment to intellectual, emotional, social, and physical development.

Fraternal twins occur as a result of multiple ovulations in the same cycle. Each egg develops separately in the ovary, is shed and fertilized individually, and develops separately in the uterus. The result is **dizygotic (DZ) twins**—that is, two-egg twins. Actually, they are litter mates and may be of different sexes. Genetically, they bear no more resemblance to one another than other children of the same parents. However, they do share the same prenatal environment and a more common parenting environment than do most siblings who are born one or more years apart. Approximately 1 in 90 pregnancies results in twins, most commonly dizygotic twins (Clayman, 1989).

Infertility and Alternative Means of Reproduction

Infertility, or the inability to conceive, can result from problems in the reproductive system of either the man or the woman, or both. The limited research literature on the emotional impact of infertility suggests that it is a major source of stress. The discovery of infertility forces a couple to reassess the meaning and purpose of their marriage. It raises doubts in the couple about their self-worth, it often disrupts their satisfaction with their sexual relationship, and it often isolates them because of the difficulty of discussing this personal family problem with others (Sabatelli et al., 1988; Jarboe, 1986).

A woman who had tried unsuccessfully to conceive for eight years said,

> I can tell you that everyone who faces this is extremely vulnerable and will pretty much try anything . . . because we're desperate. . . . I felt like the fact that I couldn't do the very thing that my body was designed to do—to conceive and carry a child—must mean that I wasn't fully a woman. And all my other accomplishments seemed to fade into the background in the face of this failure. (Sperling, 1989, p. 1D)

Although many couples seek treatment for infertility (Box 4.2), others choose adoption. For many, the pain, disappointment, loss of control, invasiveness, and uncertainty associated with infertility treatments are more stressful than the infertility itself.

> Throughout the months of treatment, I frayed Joe's nerves with my fretting over each test and procedure. What if I messed up again on the twice-daily urine tests, designed to pinpoint ovulation, each of which required an hour of vigilance as I transferred the specimen between three vials at precise intervals? What if my luteinizing hormone surged before we received the results of Joe's latest sperm tests? Would the doctor still proceed with the intrauterine insemination? Timing, of course, was of the essence; miss the narrow window of opportunity and I would be sentenced to weeks of worrying about whether I could handle another rocky cycle of skeptical hope and certain despair. (Smolowe, 1997, p. 46)

In addition to the emotional costs of treatment, there are tremendous financial costs, ranging from $10,000 to $100,000, most of which is not covered by insurance. What is more, many procedures are unsuccessful. Over the course of one year of unprotected sexual relations, 90% of healthy couples get pregnant. In 1993, from the 267 U. S. clinics reporting to the American Society for Reproductive Medicine, it was found that of 41,000 assisted procedures, only 21% resulted in live births (Begley, 1995).

Ethical Considerations. All these alternatives have raised legal and ethical questions (Elmer-Dewitt, 1991; Lemonick, 1997). The husband of a woman who is planning to

BOX 4.2 REPRODUCTIVE TECHNOLOGIES

Roughly 2.3 million couples seek help for infertility in the U.S. each year (Begley, 1995). Problems of infertility increased 25% from 1988 to 1995, stimulating new and expanding research into reproductive technologies (Lemonick, 1997). Some remarkable alternatives have been developed for couples who are unable to conceive. With each of these procedures comes new challenges in the ways to define families and in the meanings given to men's and women's reproductive functions.

The following list describes practices in use today. However, newer strategies are evolving that will permit DNA and cytoplasm from older eggs to be swapped with or transferred to new eggs to improve chances of embryonic maturation.

Fertility Drugs The administration of fertility drugs usually results in the release of multiple eggs at a cycle, increasing the chances that one egg will be fertilized. In about 20% of cases, multiple births result. The birth of the McCaughey septuplets in 1997 was a result of the use of the fertility drug, Metrodin.

Artificial insemination Sperm, which have been donated and frozen are injected into a woman's vagina monthly at the time of her ovulation. Some sperm banks keep the donors' characteristics on file, which enables the woman to select the sperm of a donor whose features she desires in her offspring. Other banks blend sperm so that the recipient cannot trace the donor's identity. In one recent case, a woman froze her husband's sperm and was able to conceive his child using artificial insemination after his death. Success rate: 10%.

In vitro fertilization (fertilization in an artificial environment) Eggs are removed from the ovary and placed in a petri dish inside an incubator. Then a few drops of sperm are added to the dish. If the eggs are fertilized and the cells begin to divide, they are replanted in the uterus for subsequent development. Typically two or three embryos are transferred at once in the hopes that at least one will implant and mature. Success rate: 18.6%.

Sperm injection A modification of in vitro fertilization in which the sperm is injected directly into the egg. Embryos produced from in vitro fertilization can be frozen for future use, if the pregnancy does not go full term. Success rate: 24%.

Gamete intrafallopian transfer (GIFT) Eggs and sperm are transferred into a woman's fallopian tubes. Fertilization takes place as it normally would, within the woman's reproductive system. These eggs and sperm may come from the couple or from other donors. Thus, the fetus may be genetically related to the man and/or the woman in the couple, or to neither. Success rate: 28%.

In vivo fertilization (fertilization in a living body) Partners involve another woman in the conception. The second woman, who has demonstrated her fertility, is artificially inseminated with the man's sperm. Once an embryo has formed, it is transferred to the first woman's uterus, which becomes the gestational environment. The child is therefore genetically related to the man but not to the woman.

Surrogate mother Sperm from an infertile woman's husband are injected into the surrogate mother during the time of her monthly ovulation. The surrogate mother bears the child and returns it to the couple at birth. About 100 babies per year are born to surrogate mothers (Byrne, 1988). In one remarkable case, a woman agreed to be the surrogate mother for her own daughter who wanted a child but was born without a uterus. At age 42, this mother gave birth to twin grandchildren (Elmer-Dewitt, 1991).

be artificially inseminated must consent to the procedure and agree to assume legal guardianship of the offspring. The lack of official guidelines for screening donors raises the issue of who should be responsible if a child resulting from artificial insemination has a severe genetic anomaly. Another concern being raised is what the sperm donor's rights are to a relationship with his offspring. In 1983, a California man was granted weekly visitation rights to a child who had been conceived with his sperm.

In the widely publicized case of Baby M., William and Elizabeth Stern paid Mary Beth Whitehead $10,000 to be a surrogate mother. Baby M. was conceived with Ms. Whitehead's egg and Mr. Stern's sperm. After the birth, Ms. Whitehead decided that she wanted to keep the baby. In ensuing court battles, the New Jersey Supreme Court decided that the contract between the couple and Ms. Whitehead was void and that it was illegal to pay a woman to bear a child for someone else. Nonetheless, the court granted custody of the child to the Sterns, arguing that they could provide the child a more stable home environment. The court rejected the right of Elizabeth Stern to adopt the baby and supported Ms. Whitehead's right of continued visitation as the genetic as well as gestational mother (Lacayo, 1988; Silverman, 1989). In order to avoid the problems in the Stern/Whitehead case, John and Luanne Buzzanca paid Pamela Snell to be a surrogate mother for a baby conceived through in vitro fertilization from anonymous donors. Before the baby was born, John divorced Luanne. When Luanne later filed for child support, the judge ruled that John was in no legal sense the father and Luanne was not the legal mother although she is raising Baby J (Foote, 1998).

As a result of fertility intervention, a 63-year-old post-menopausal woman recently gave birth. She is reported to be the oldest birth mother on record (Kalb, 1997). Ethical considerations have been raised about the use of medical technology to keep the birth window open at this advanced age. Although some people seem to respond with a note of awe, possibly admiration, at the news that an older man has fathered a child, the idea that an older woman has had a child is raising questions about the appropriateness of this type of medical intervention. Concerns focus on the medical complications associated with pregnancy in older women and speculations about the ability of older men and women to sustain effective parenting as their children move into adolescence and they enter later adulthood.

Finally, what limits should be placed on the production and use of embryos in vitro? Should we permit scientists to produce embryos from frozen sperm and egg cells for purposes other than implantation? Thousands of frozen embryos are held in various medical and laboratory facilities in the United States. State laws governing their use as well as their rights are often conflicting and confusing. Ethical and legal questions are being raised about the rights of parents to determine the fate of these embryos, the embryos' rights to protection and inheritance, and the responsibility of institutes and laboratories to ensure the proper use of the embryos. A disturbing element here is the obvious detachment of the embryo from its parental origins, which tends to encourage a view of embryos as products rather than as emerging beings to be nurtured within a family unit.

On a more encouraging note, one of the first studies has been completed that reports on the quality of parenting and developmental outcome for children conceived through artificial insemination and in vitro fertilization (Golombok et al., 1995). In this study conducted in the United Kingdom, 86 families with children conceived through alternative reproductive technologies were compared with families with naturally conceived and adopted children. In general, parents of children conceived through both types of assisted reproduction showed more warmth and involvement with their children, higher levels of interaction, and lower levels of stress than the parents of children who were conceived naturally. Parents of adopted children typically scored in between the levels of the other two groups. There were no significant differences among the groups of children with respect to social and emotional development; all were well within the norms for their age groups.

Development in the First Trimester

The period of pregnancy, typically 40 weeks after the last menstrual period or 38 weeks from ovulation, is often conceptualized in three 3-month periods called **trimesters.** Perhaps because development is so rapid and dramatic during the first trimester, it is divided further into the Germinal Period, the Embryonic Period, and the Fetal Period. Each trimester brings changes in the status of the developing fetus and its supporting systems. These changes are summarized briefly in Table 4.2 (Moore, 1993). The pregnant woman also experiences changes during the trimesters. In the first

---

TABLE 4.2   Major Developments in Fetal Growth During the Three Trimesters

First Trimester	Second Trimester	Third Trimester
Fertilization	Sucking and swallowing	Nervous system matures
Growth of the amniotic sac	Preference for sweet taste	Coordination of sucking and swallowing
Growth of the placenta	Skin ridges on fingers and toes	Mechanisms for regulating body temperature
Emergence of body parts	Hair on scalp, eyebrows, back, arms, legs	More efficient digestion and excretion
Differentiation of sex organs	Sensitivity to touch, taste, light	Degeneration of the placenta toward the end of
Initial formation of central nervous system	Sucks thumb	the ninth month
Movement	6-month average size: 10 inches, 2 pounds	9-month average size: 20 inches, 7 to 7 1/2
Grasp reflex		pounds
Babinski reflex		
Heartbeat		
3-month average size: 3 inches, about 2/5 ounce		

The fertilized egg begins to divide as it travels along the fallopian tube toward the uterus.

By the sixth day after fertilization, the zygote implants in the thickened uterine wall.

trimester, many women are not certain that they are pregnant. By the last trimester, though, the woman is usually certain, and so is everyone else!

The Germinal Period

After fertilization, the egg begins to divide. The first series of cell divisions does not increase the mass of the cells, nor do the cells take on specialized functions; rather, the cell material is redistributed among several parts. When implantation is successful, by the sixth day after fertilization the egg makes contact with the lining of the uterus and begins to attach itself there. Sometimes the egg does not reach the uterus but attaches itself to the fallopian tube or even some area of the intestine. The embryo may grow in these locations until the organ ruptures.

The Embryonic Period

The three weeks following implantation are devoted primarily to elaboration of the supportive elements that will house the embryo. An **amniotic sac** surrounds the embryo and fills with a clear, watery fluid. This fluid acts as a cushion that buffers the embryo and permits it to move about and change position.

At this point—about three weeks after implantation, when the woman's menstrual period is about two weeks overdue—the first reliable tests can determine if she is pregnant. Once the embryo is firmly implanted in the uterus, special cells in the placenta produce a hormone that maintains the uterine lining. This hormone is excreted through the kidneys, so a urine sample can be evaluated to determine its presence. A large number of pregnancies are spontaneously aborted in these early weeks, usually as a result of some major abnormalities of the embryo (Winston & Handyside, 1993).

The **placenta** is an organ that is newly formed with each pregnancy and is expelled at birth. The nutrients necessary for the embryo's growth pass through the placenta, as does the embryo's waste, which then passes into the mother's blood. Thus, the placenta is an exchange station at which adult material is synthesized for the embryo's use, and foreign materials harmful to the embryo's development can be screened out. However, the screening is imperfect. Even though the mother's blood and the embryo's blood are separated by independent systems, the placenta permits the two systems to come close enough so that oxygen and nutrients from the mother's blood can enter the fetal system, and waste products from the fetal system can be removed. In the process, certain substances in the mother's system may affect the fetal system. Agents that can produce malformations in the fetus while the tissues and organs are forming are referred to as **teratogens.** Teratogens have a wide variety of forms, such as viruses; medicines, alcohol, and other drugs that a pregnant woman takes; and environmental toxins. During the first trimester—especially weeks 3 through 9—the embryo is particularly sensitive to the disruptive influences of teratogens (Figure 4.7).

In the third and fourth weeks, the embryo's cells differentiate rapidly, taking on the specialized structures that will permit them to carry out unique functions in the body. Similar cells are grouped into tissues that gradually emerge as body organs. The first essential changes include the establishment of the body form as an elongated cylinder and the formation of precursors of the brain and the heart. The **neural tube,** which is the structural basis of the central nervous system, begins to take shape at the end of the third week after conception. Cells in the neural tube are produced at a miraculous rate of 250,000 a minute over the first five weeks as the tube is differentiated into five bulges that are the forerunners of the major subdivisions of the brain. The central nervous system begins to develop early in the prenatal period and continues to develop throughout childhood and adolescence. Most of the neurons that make up the cerebral cortex are produced by the end of the second trimester. By birth, the infant's brain contains roughly 100 billion neurons, ready to be linked and organized into networks as the infant responds to environmental stimulation and patterned experience (Nash, 1997; Aoki & Siekevitz, 1988).

By the end of the fourth week, the head, the upper trunk, and the lower trunk are visible, as are limb buds and forerunners of the forebrain, midbrain, hindbrain, eyes, and ears. The embryo will have increased 50 times in length and 40,000 times in weight since the moment of fertilization.

By the end of the second month, the embryo looks quite human. It weighs about 2.25 grams and is about 28 millimeters (1 inch) long. Almost all the internal organs are formed, as well as the external features of the face, limbs, fingers, and toes. At eight weeks, the embryo will respond to mild stimulation. The embryonic period ends at about ten weeks after the last menstrual period—most of the essential structures are formed by this time. The term **fetus** is used from this point until birth.

The Fetal Period

In the third month, the fetus grows to 3 inches and its weight increases to 14 grams. The head is about one-third of the total body length.

At 5 ½ weeks, cell differentiation has resulted in an embryo that is about 0.4 inch (1 cm) long. Emerging shapes of the head, arm, and fingers are visible. Many women are not even sure about their pregnancy at this point in fetal development.

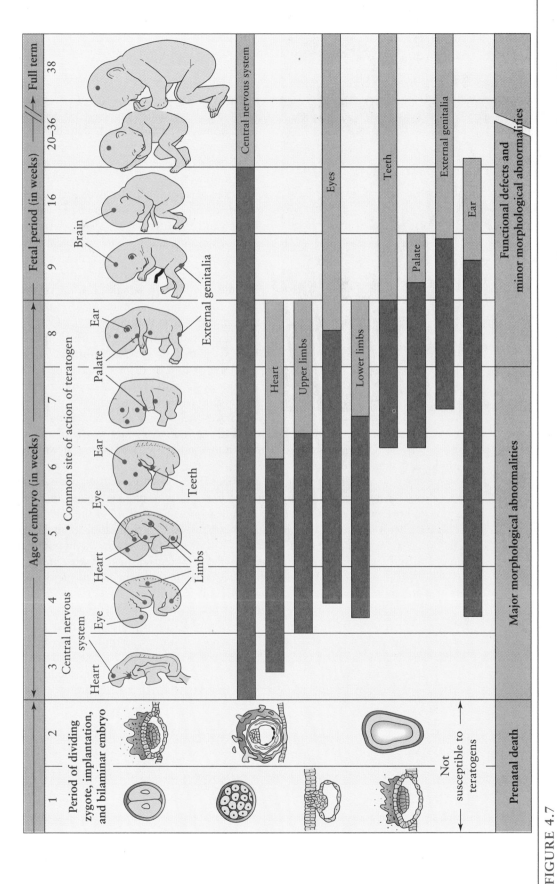

FIGURE 4.7

Critical periods in prenatal development. During the first two weeks of development, the embryo is usually not susceptible to teratogens. During these predifferentiation stages, a substance either damages all or most of the cells of the embryo, resulting in its death, or damages only a few cells, allowing the embryo to recover without developing defects. Dark denotes highly sensitive periods; light indicates stages that are less sensitive to teratogens. Severe mental retardation may result from the exposure of the embryo/fetus to certain teratogenic agents, such as high levels of radiation, from the 8th to 16th weeks. SOURCE: *Moore, 1988.*

At 8 weeks, the fingers are clearly differentiated and the hand is distinct from the forearm. Reflexes sometimes guide the hand toward the face. The fetus is encased in the amniotic sac.

During this month, the fetus assumes the "fetal position," arms curled up toward the face and knees bent in to the stomach. The eyelids are fused.

A dramatic change takes place in the sex organs during this period. All embryos go through a bisexual stage during which no sex-linked characteristics can be discerned. Both females and males have a surface mass that becomes the testes in males and eventually deteriorates in females, and new sex cells grow to form the ovaries. Both males and females have two sets of sex ducts. In males, the sperm ducts develop and the female ducts dissolve. In females, the fallopian tubes, the uterus, and the vagina develop, and the other ducts degenerate. Finally, both males and females have a conical area that is the outlet for the bladder duct. When the male testes develop, this area forms into the penis and scrotum. In females it remains to form the clitoris, which is surrounded by the genital swellings of the labia majora.

Differentiation of the male and female genitalia is guided by genetic information. In the presence of the "maleness" gene, or testes-determining factor (TDF), the undifferentiated embryonic tissue is transformed into the testes. The testes then produce hormones that facilitate the further elaboration of male genitalia and internal reproductive structures. Genes carried on the X chromosome are thought to guide the formation of the ovaries (Crooks & Bauer, 1996).

The genetic factors that produce the differentiation of the fetus as male or female appear to influence more than the formation of the reproductive organs and the production of hormones. Research on the organization and structure of the brain suggests that during fetal and early postnatal development, sex hormones direct male and female brains along slightly different paths. Three areas of the brain, the hypothalamus, amygdala, and hippocampus, have been studied as potential sites for sex differences in structure that may relate to some of the functional areas in which men's and women's problem-solving and cognitive skills differ (Kimura, 1992).

The 3-month-old fetus moves spontaneously and has both a grasp reflex and a Babinski reflex, in which the toes extend and fan out in response to a mild stroke on the sole of the foot. When an amplified stethoscope, called a **Doppler,** is placed on the mother's abdomen, the fetal heartbeat can be heard through the uterine wall by the expectant parents as well as the physician and nurse. When we were expectant parents, we were unbelievably thrilled to hear those first faint heartbeats of a life still strangely remote!

Development in the Second Trimester

During the second trimester, the average fetus grows to 10 inches and increases in weight to almost 2 pounds. The fetus continues to grow at the rate of about an inch every ten days from the fifth month until the end of the pregnancy. During this trimester, the uterus itself begins to stretch and grow. It rises into the mother's abdominal cavity and expands until, by the end of the ninth month, it is pushing against the ribs and diaphragm. The reality of a growing life becomes more evident to the pregnant woman during this trimester as she observes the changes in her body and experiences the early fetal movements called **quickening.** These movements first feel like light bubbles or twitches; later, they can be identified as the foot, elbow, or fist of the restless resident.

At 16 weeks, the fetus is about 6.4 inches (16 cm) long and is clearly recognizable as a human child. The fetus has assumed what is known as the "fetal position"—arms curled up near the head and legs bent in toward the stomach—a position that remains part of the human behavioral repertoire throughout life.

During the fourth month, the fetus begins to suck and swallow. Whenever the fetus opens its mouth, amniotic fluid enters and cycles through the system. This fluid provides some nutrients in addition to those absorbed through the placenta. The 4-month-old fetus shows some preference for a sweet taste: If sugar is introduced into the amniotic fluid, it will swallow the fluid at a faster rate.

In the fifth month, the skin begins to thicken, and a cheesy coating of dead cells and oil, the vernix caseosa, covers the skin. The individuality of the fetus is marked by the pattern of skin ridges on the fingers and toes. Hair covers the scalp, eyebrows, back, arms, and legs.

The sensory receptors of the fetus are well established by the end of the sixth month. The fetus is sensitive to touch and may react to it with a muscle movement. It will also stick out its tongue in response to a bitter taste. Throughout the sixth month, the nostrils are plugged by skin cells. When these cells dissolve, the nose fills with amniotic fluid; thus, the sense of smell is probably not functional until birth.

The external ear canal is filled with fluid, and the fetus does not tend to respond to sound until the eighth or ninth month; however, the semicircular canals of the inner ear are sensitive to stimulation. The nerve fibers that connect the retina to the brain are developed by six months, and infants born prematurely at this time respond to light.

At 25 weeks, the fetus functions well within its uterine environment. It swallows, digests, excretes, moves about, sucks its thumb, rests, and grows. However, the nervous system, which begins to develop at 3 weeks, is still not mature enough to coordinate the many systems that must function simultaneously to ensure survival. With advances in medical technology, a 25-week-old fetus weighing roughly 1000 grams has about a 70% chance of survival if it is placed in an intensive-care neonatal nursery. By 30 weeks, survival outside the uterus is almost certain (Usher, 1987). Box 4.3 provides information on strategies that are used to evaluate the health and maturity of the developing fetus.

Development in the Third Trimester

In the last trimester, the average fetus grows from 10 to 20 inches and increases in weight from 2 to 7 or 7½ pounds. These increases in body size and weight are paralleled by a maturation of the central nervous system. Studies of infants' responses to maternal speech suggest that a fetus experiences its mother's speech sounds during the third trimester and becomes familiar with the sound of her voice (DeCasper & Spence, 1986; Spence & DeCasper, 1987).

The advantages that a full-term fetus has over a premature 28-week-old fetus include: (1) the ability to begin and maintain regular breathing, (2) a stronger sucking re-

BOX 4.3   LOOKING IN ON THE FETUS

Most expectant parents worry about whether their baby is developing normally. Today, many of these worries can be minimized through technologies that allow the evaluation of fetal development during the early months of pregnancy. Several of these techniques are associated with some risk and should not be used without ample justification. However, especially in high-risk pregnancies, monitoring fetal development may lead to interventions that will save lives when problems do exist, and that will reduce the stress associated with unfounded worry. Four monitoring strategies are described here (Cunningham et al., 1997).

Electronic fetal heart rate monitoring: Rather than listen to the fetal heart rate periodically by stethoscope, birth attendants can monitor it continuously with electronic equipment that is painlessly attached to the pregnant woman's abdomen. This technique is especially useful in detecting any disruption in the fetal oxygen supply during labor.

Ultrasound: Based on submarine sonar technology from World War II, ultrasound uses reflected sound waves to produce a visual image of the fetus. Ultrasound can be used to date the pregnancy more precisely, to diagnose multiple pregnancies, and to detect certain structural defects in the fetus.

Amniocentesis: In this procedure, about 20 cubic centimeters of amniotic fluid are withdrawn from the uterus, as illustrated in the figure. This procedure is sometimes performed in the 16th week of pregnancy to evaluate fetal cells for chromosomal or enzyme disorders. Later in pregnancy, fetal cells can be evaluated for the maturation of the lungs. Thus, serious respiratory disorders can be prevented when cesarean deliveries are delayed until the lungs are adequately developed.

Fetoscopy: The fetus can be examined directly and its blood sampled through a fiber optic lens inserted into the uterus. This technique permits the diagnosis of genetic disorders, especially blood diseases that cannot be detected in amniotic fluid, which in some cases can be treated surgically and medically before birth.

Amniocentesis

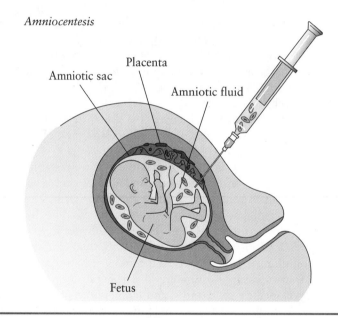

sponse, (3) well-coordinated swallowing movements, (4) stronger peristalsis and therefore more efficient digestion and waste excretion, and (5) a more fully balanced control of body temperature.

The full-term fetus has been able to take advantage of minerals in the mother's diet for the formation of tooth enamel. As the placenta begins to degenerate in the last month of pregnancy, antibodies against various diseases that have been formed in the mother's blood pass into the fetal bloodstream. They provide the fetus with immunity to many diseases during the first few months of life.

The uterus cannot serve indefinitely as the home of the fetus. Several factors necessitate the eventual termination of the fetal-uterine relationship. First, as the placenta degenerates, antibodies that form in both the mother's and the fetus's blood would destroy the blood of the other. Second, because the placenta does not grow much larger than 2 pounds, the fetus, as it reaches its maximum size, cannot obtain enough nutrients to sustain life. Third, the fetal head cannot grow much larger than the pelvic opening without endangering the brain in the birth process. Even though soft connecting membranes per-

At 23 weeks, the fetus is about 12 inches (30 cm.) long, still small enough to have room to swim about in the expanding uterus. As any pregnant woman will tell you, the fetus is active at this stage, kicking, grasping, waving its arms, and turning over.

These are the birth footprints of a baby born prematurely at 23 weeks, and one born at a full 40-week gestational age.

mit the skull plates to overlap, head size is a factor that limits fetal growth. Current research suggests that late in pregnancy, the fetal brain begins to produce hormones that increase the production of estrogen in the placenta. This in turn, leads to a shift from mild to strong uterine contractions, which result in dilatation of the cervix, rupture of the amniotic sac, and delivery (Nathanielsz, 1996). The approximate time from conception to birth is 38 weeks. However, there is a great deal of variability in the duration of pregnancies and in the size of full-term infants, even infants born to the same mother.

THE BIRTH PROCESS

Birth is initiated by involuntary contractions of the uterine muscles, commonly referred to as **labor.** The length of time from the beginning of labor to the birth of the infant is highly variable. The average time is 14 hours for women undergoing their first labor (primiparas) and 8 hours for women undergoing later labors (multiparas).

The uterine contractions serve two central functions: effacement and dilation. **Effacement** (or thinning) is the shortening of the cervical canal. **Dilation** is the gradual enlargement of the cervix from an opening only millimeters wide to one of about 10 centimeters—large enough for the baby to pass through. Effacement and dilation occur without deliberate effort by the mother. Once the cervix is fully enlarged, the mother can assist in the birth by exerting pressure on the abdominal walls of the uterus. The baby, too, helps in the birth process by squirming, turning its head, and pushing against the birth canal.

Stages of Labor   The medical profession describes three stages of labor, two of which are illustrated in Figure 4.8. The first stage begins with the onset of uterine contractions and ends with

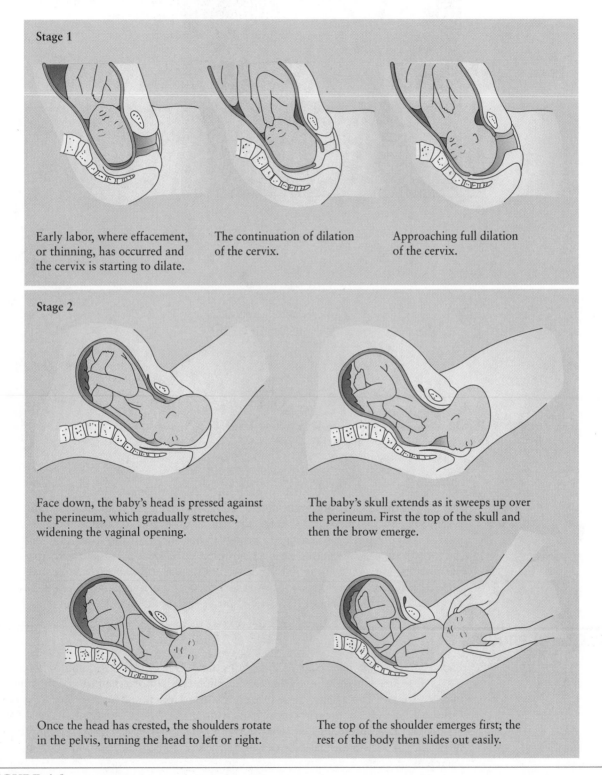

Stage 1

Early labor, where effacement, or thinning, has occurred and the cervix is starting to dilate.

The continuation of dilation of the cervix.

Approaching full dilation of the cervix.

Stage 2

Face down, the baby's head is pressed against the perineum, which gradually stretches, widening the vaginal opening.

The baby's skull extends as it sweeps up over the perineum. First the top of the skull and then the brow emerge.

Once the head has crested, the shoulders rotate in the pelvis, turning the head to left or right.

The top of the shoulder emerges first; the rest of the body then slides out easily.

FIGURE 4.8
The first two stages of labor and delivery

In the U.S. birth culture, childbirth usually takes place in a sterile, hospital delivery room where doctors and nurses have access to a wide range of technology to support the mother and newborn. Increasingly, a supportive person, often the father, is present as well.

the full dilation of the cervix; this is the longest stage. The second stage involves the expulsion of the fetus. It begins at full dilation and ends with the delivery of the baby. The third stage begins with delivery and ends with the expulsion of the placenta. This stage usually lasts five to ten minutes.

These three stages of labor do not precisely parallel the personal experience of childbirth. For example, while the expulsion of the placenta is considered a unique stage of labor in the medical model, it is rarely mentioned in women's accounts of their birth experiences. On the other hand, many of the signs of impending labor that occur in the last weeks of pregnancy may well be viewed as the experiential beginning of labor.

In terms of the psychological adaptation to the birth process, labor can be viewed as having five phases: (1) early signs that labor is approaching; (2) strong, regular uterine contractions signaling that labor has begun and generally accompanied by a move from the home to the hospital or birthing center; (3) the transition phase, during which contractions are strong, rest times between contractions are short, and women experience the greatest difficulty or discomfort; (4) the birth process, which allows the mother's active participation in the delivery and is generally accompanied by a move from the labor area to the more sterile delivery room; and (5) the postpartum period, which involves the initial interactions with the newborn, physiological changes that mark a return to the prepregnant state, and a return home. The significant events of these phases are summarized in Table 4.3.

Cesarean Delivery

Sometimes a normal, spontaneous vaginal delivery is dangerous to the mother or the newborn (Cunningham et al., 1997). One alternative is to remove the baby surgically through an incision in the uterine wall. The procedure, called a **cesarean section,** is named after the Roman emperor Julius Caesar, who, legend has, was delivered this way. The likelihood that he was actually delivered surgically is questionable, since until as late as the 17th century the operation was usually fatal to mothers.

The incidence of cesarean deliveries in the United States increased from 5.5% of births in 1970 to 23% in 1993 (U.S. Bureau of the Census, 1995). The procedure may be used if labor is severely prolonged and the fetus appears to be at risk for lack of oxygen. It may also be used when the infant is in the breech position (feet or buttocks first rather than head first) or if the mother's pelvis is too small for the infant's head to pass through. The rate of cesarean deliveries is higher for mothers age 30 and older than for younger mothers.

It is still standard procedure to deliver a baby by cesarean if the mother has had such an operation before. However, this practice may vary by region. With the physician's approval, some women do have vaginal deliveries after they have had a cesarean delivery.

TABLE 4.3   **Significant Events of Five Stages of Labor**

Phase 1: Early signs that labor is approaching

1. Lightening (about 10 to 14 days before delivery). The baby's head drops into the pelvic area.
2. Release of the plug that has kept the cervix closed.
3. Discharge of amniotic fluid.
4. False labor: irregular uterine contractions.

Phase 2: Onset of labor

1. Transition from home to hospital or birthing center.
2. Strong, regular contractions 3–5 minutes apart.

Phase 3: Transition

1. Accelerated labor, with contractions lasting up to 90 seconds and coming 2 or 3 minutes apart.
2. Some sense of disorientation, heightened arousal, or loss of control.

Phase 4: Birth

1. The baby's head presses down on the bottom of the birth canal.
2. The mother experiences a strong, reflexive urge to push to expel the baby.
3. The mother typically is moved from a labor area to a more sterile delivery room.

Phase 5: Postpartum period

1. Mother and infant have initial contact.
2. Placenta is expelled.
3. Rapid alteration of the hormone system to stimulate lactation and shrink the uterus.
4. Mother and infant engage in early learning behaviors; infant attempts to nurse; mother explores infant and begins to interpret his or her needs.
5. Return to the home and introduction of the newborn into the family setting.

The cesarean delivery makes childbirth a surgical procedure, requiring anesthetics, intravenous feeding of the mother, and a prolonged recovery period. Although the procedure undoubtedly saves many infants and mothers who would not survive vaginal childbirth, there is concern that it is being misused for the convenience of health professionals or of busy mothers who want to be able to schedule deliveries and thus avoid waiting for the unpredictable onset of labor. The U.S. Public Health Service goal statement *Healthy People 2000* (1990) calls for a reduction of the national cesarean rate to 15%—a goal implying that a substantial number of the current cesarean procedures are not required.

Some researchers have begun to examine the impact of the cesarean delivery on both the newborn and the parents. At this point, it appears that in the short run, that is, within five minutes after birth, babies delivered by cesarean section are more likely to show signs of risk than babies delivered vaginally. This difference holds for babies who are delivered by repeat cesarean section, and who therefore are not at risk in other ways (Burt et al., 1988). However, long-term follow-ups of babies delivered by cesarean section find no effects on the child's IQ or standardized math and verbal test scores (Entwisle & Alexander, 1987).

The effects of cesarean delivery on parents can be seen in the findings of two studies. In one, mothers whose children had been delivered by cesarean section expressed greater dissatisfaction with the childbirth experience itself than mothers whose children had been born vaginally. However, they did not show more problems in postpartum adjustment. Their levels of anxiety, depression, and perceptions of their competence as mothers were about the same as those of mothers who had a more normal delivery. Both the mothers and fathers of babies delivered by cesarean section tended to be more involved in the parental role. They viewed their children in a more positive light and had higher expectations of their children's school success than did other parents (Padawer et al., 1988).

The other study showed that parents' expectations concerning a child's academic ability and school success appear to be a long-term outcome of the birth experience and have a significant influence on the child's own expectations of school performance in the first and second grades (Entwisle & Alexander, 1987). One explanation suggested for these findings is that the special difficulties associated with childbirth increase the commitment the parents make to their child. Care must be taken not to overgeneralize the results of the research, but the implication that involvement in parenting is related to difficulties associated with childbirth deserves further study.

Infant Mortality

The **infant mortality rate** is the number of infants who die during the first year of life per 1000 live births during that year. In 1994, the U.S. rate was estimated at 8.0 deaths per 1000 live births, a mortality rate that was equaled only by the rates of those 55 and older. Although the infant mortality rate has declined for both whites and blacks, the rate for black babies in the United States in 1994—15.8 deaths per 1000 live births—was higher than the rates in countries such as Chile, Croatia, Cuba, and Poland, which are considered economically emergent nations (U.S. Bureau of the Census, 1997). Roughly two-thirds of infant deaths occur during the first month after birth. Most of these deaths result from severe birth defects, premature birth, or *sudden infant death syndrome* (SIDS), in which apparently healthy babies are put to bed and are later found dead with no clear explanation, even after autopsy (Clayman, 1989).

Infant mortality rates are influenced by many factors, including: (1) the frequency of birth complications; (2) the robustness of the infants who are being born, which is influenced by their prenatal nutrition and degree of exposure to viruses or bacteria, damaging X rays, drugs, and other teratogens; (3) the mother's age; and (4) the facilities that are available for prenatal and newborn care. One-fourth of infant deaths result from complications associated with low birth weight. If the conditions leading to prematurity could be altered, the U.S. infant mortality rate would be significantly improved (Wilcox & Skjoerven, 1992).

Infant mortality rates vary from one country and region of the world to another. In 1995, the infant mortality rate in Japan was 4.3, but in that same year, the infant mortality rate in 20 other countries of the world was over 100. The United States, with all its resources and advanced technology, in fact, ranks behind 17 other industrialized countries, including Australia, Austria, Canada, Denmark, France, Italy, Spain, Hong Kong, and Japan. Within the United States, regional infant mortality rates range from a low of 5.0 per 1000 in Rhode Island to a high of 17.8 per 1000 in the District of Columbia (U.S. Bureau of the Census, 1997).

The density of low-income populations, the availability of educational materials on the impact of diet and drugs on the developing fetus, and the adequacy of the medical facilities for high-risk newborns all contribute to the regional variations in infant death rates among populations of different incomes. Children conceived in poverty are at the greatest risk of infant mortality. Their mothers receive poorer quality prenatal care, and as we will see in the sections to follow, they are exposed to more dangerous environmental and health factors during the prenatal period that jeopardize their survival than are children conceived in more advantaged families. The chances that any one infant will survive the stresses of birth depend on the convergence of biological, environmental, cultural, and economic influences on his or her intrauterine growth, delivery, and postnatal care (Polednak, 1991).

THE MOTHER, THE FETUS, AND THE PSYCHOSOCIAL ENVIRONMENT

The course and pattern of prenatal development are directly guided by genetic information. Yet we cannot ignore the psychosocial environment of pregnant women. A woman's attitudes toward pregnancy and childbirth, her lifestyle, the resources available to her during her pregnancy, and the behavior demanded of her by her culture all influence her sense of well-being. Many of these same factors may directly affect the health and growth of the fetus.

The Impact of the Fetus on the Pregnant Woman

Consider some of the ways in which a fetus influences a pregnant woman. Pregnancy alters a woman's body image and her sense of well-being. Some women feel especially vigorous and energetic during much of their pregnancy; others experience distressing symptoms such as nausea, backache, swelling, headache, and irritability. In some cases, pregnancy is accompanied by serious illnesses that threaten the mother's health.

Changes in Roles and Social Status

Women who become pregnant may be treated in new ways by their significant partners. Usually, fathers become more concerned for and supportive of their pregnant partners, and pregnant women may also be viewed in a new light by their peers. In some communities, adolescent girls who become pregnant feel ashamed or guilty. In others, becoming pregnant during adolescence is viewed by the peer group as an accomplishment, a sign of maturity. At work, women who become pregnant may be given fewer responsibilities or may be passed over for promotions. In business settings, pregnancy may be viewed as an annoyance, something that is likely to interfere with productivity and is, at best, to be tolerated.

Within the family, a pregnant woman is likely to be treated with new levels of concern and care. Her pregnancy affects her partner, her parents, and siblings, previous children, and her partner's family. By giving birth to a first child, a woman transforms her mother and father into grandparents and her brothers and sisters into uncles and aunts. In addition, pregnancy may strengthen the gender identity of the baby's mother and/or father: Becoming pregnant may be viewed as confirmation of a woman's femininity and also of a man's virility in impregnating her (Heitlinger, 1989).

In some societies, pregnancy and childbirth confer special status on a woman. In Japan, for example, traditional values place motherhood above all other women's roles. "Only after giving birth to a child did a woman become a fully tenured person in the family" (Bankart, 1989). When they become mothers, Japanese women begin to have an impact on government, community, and public life as the people who are specially responsible for molding and shaping the next generation. For Mexican-American women, childbearing is likely to be viewed within a broad religious context. "It is considered the privilege and essential obligation of a married woman to bear children, but children come 'when God is willing'" (Hahn & Muecke, 1987).

Changes in the Mother's Emotional State

Women have emotional as well as physical reactions to pregnancy, which is listed as the 12th most stressful life change in a list of 43 life events in the Social Readjustment Rating Scale (Holmes & Rahe, 1967). The woman's attitude toward her unborn child may be pride, acceptance, rejection, or, as is usually the case, ambivalence. In most normal pregnancies, women experience anxiety and depression as well as positive feelings of excitement and hopefulness. The normal physical changes during the gestational period include symptoms that are often associated with depression, such as fatigue, sleeplessness, slowed physical movement, preoccupation with one's physical state, and moodiness (Kaplan, 1986). In addition, throughout the pregnancy, the expectant woman has recurring worries about whether the baby will be healthy and the delivery will go smoothly. One study reported that at the seventh month of pregnancy and again during the fourth month after birth, most women organized their thoughts about themselves as mothers around the theme of fear, including fears for their babies' well-being or for their own ability to provide for their infants' needs (Vizziello et al., 1993).

Certain psychosocial factors are associated with increased anxiety and depression during pregnancy. Women who are having marital difficulties, who do not have adequate social support during pregnancy, and who have conflict about their own personal identity are likely to experience greater emotional stress (Fleming et al., 1988). It is possible that strong emotional reactions, such as prolonged anxiety or depression, may influence the fetal environment directly through the secretion of maternal hormones that cross the placental barrier. However, evidence in this regard is mixed (Sameroff & Chandler, 1975/1992; Vaughn et al., 1987). The evidence is much clearer that the

Sometimes being pregnant brings out a woman's special sense of humor. It looks as if Florence just couldn't wait to get a glimpse of baby Theo, so she improvised.

mother's emotional state during pregnancy is related to her experiences during labor and to her subsequent parenting behaviors.

A woman's feelings about her femininity, her attitudes toward the unborn child, and her psychological stability are associated with difficulties experienced during pregnancy and labor. Women who have more stable personalities and a positive orientation toward pregnancy react more favorably to the stresses of labor than do anxious, irritable women, who are more likely to have longer labors and more complications during labor and delivery. During delivery, women who are anxious tend to request and receive more medication, which may influence the responsiveness of their newborn infants (Yang et al., 1976; Standley et al., 1979).

The contribution of maternal anxiety to complications during labor and delivery was studied with a group of Guatemalan women (Sosa et al., 1980). The hospital normally did not permit any visitors to remain with an expectant woman on the maternity ward. Each woman in this study, however, was assigned a companion who stayed with her until delivery, talking to the woman, holding her hand, rubbing her back, and providing emotional support during labor. These mothers had fewer complications during labor than a group of women who had no companion, and their babies showed fewer signs of fetal distress. The mean length of labor was more than ten hours shorter for those women who had a companion than for those who were alone during labor.

The mother's emotional state during pregnancy has an impact beyond the events of childbirth. Women who experience notable depression during pregnancy are more likely to continue feeling depressed in the months after giving birth. Studies of these mothers show that they have difficulty feeling attached to their babies, are more likely to feel out of control or incompetent in their parenting, and exhibit fewer affectionate behaviors toward their infants (Fleming et al., 1988; Field et al., 1985).

In interactions with depressed mothers, infants are less playful, show less activity, and express fewer signs of contentment, fewer face-to-face interactions, and less imitation of their mothers than do babies of nondepressed mothers (Field et al., 1985). At 3 months, infants of depressed mothers show similar characteristics even in interaction with nondepressed adults, a finding suggesting that a "depressed" temperamental social style has developed (Field et al., 1990). This research still leaves the question of causality unanswered. Is the impact of maternal depression on the infant the result of genetic influences, the presence of hormones associated with the mother's depression in the prenatal environment, the style of mothering characteristic of depressed women, or some cumulative effect of these factors?

Fathers' Involvement During Pregnancy and Childbirth

During the second trimester, a father is able to make contact with his unborn child as he places his hand on his partner's abdomen and feels the life and movement within. For many fathers, this is a time of great joy as the prospect of fatherhood becomes more than abstract empathy with his partner's experiences. Investment in the new life begins to increase as the reality of the fetus becomes more concrete. These times can provide the basis for a new kind of intimacy for the expectant couple as they begin to talk about their plans and hopes for the child, share their feelings about the pregnancy and upcoming birth, and explore their feelings related to assuming responsibility for the care and protection of their new child.

Sometimes, however, the first movements of the fetus stimulate a negative reaction in the father. This may, in turn, have a negative effect on the mother, leaving her depressed and aware that she is without the support she was expecting. Some men are not comfortable with the physical events of pregnancy, and they try to deny them by turning away from the mother. They do not want to feel the fetus's movements and are extremely uneasy or embarrassed by pressure to understand the details of the female anatomy. Some men think that the fetus and then the baby threaten their own position with the mother, and they feel resentful and competitive toward the woman and the unborn infant. In some families, this resentment may lead to violence. For example, one study of low-income, urban women found that 38% had experienced violence from their male partner during their pregnancy (O'Campo et al., 1995).

Some men worry about the economic ramifications of the impending birth. If they are unemployed or underemployed, they may long for more income, have low confidence, feel they are not worth much, or be fearful that the mother's income will decrease. Some of these men may become more distant from the mother. In these cases, both the mother and father experience increased feelings of isolation rather than intimacy. Emotions associated with isolation including feeling more anxious and depressed can have a negative impact on the fetus as well as the mother. As we discussed in earlier sections, these emotions can increase the difficulties of pregnancy, the birth itself, and the early months of parenting—difficulties that can have strong negative effects on establishing a healthy parent-child relationship (Field et al., 1985; Field et al., 1990).

The many different types of relationships that are possible between the mother and her partner have implications for both the emotional state of the mother during pregnancy and the psychosocial development of the child.

Research supports the idea of continuity between the quality of the relationship between the partners during the prenatal period and the quality of their parenting in the early years of childhood. This in turn has implications for the child's growth and development. Partners who show high levels of negative interaction or detachment during the prenatal period have trouble providing an emotionally secure environment for their newborn. "Couples characterized by positive mutuality, partner autonomy, and the ability to confront problems and regulate negative affect are responsive to the needs of their infants, promote their autonomy, and have more secure and autonomous children, as seen throughout the first four years of life" (Heinicke, 1995).

Trends in the United States have shifted dramatically toward greater involvement of the father during labor and delivery. Expectant fathers often attend childbirth classes to learn to assist their partners during the delivery. The father's presence during labor and delivery is clearly a great comfort to the pregnant woman. When the father is present, women tend to have shorter labors, report experiencing less pain, use less medication, and feel more positive about themselves and their childbirth experience (Grossman et al., 1980). Fathers also describe their participation in the birth as a peak experience. However, research does not permit us to conclude that fathers who participate in the birth experience have a more intimate relationship with their children than fathers who do not (Palkovitz, 1985; Palm & Palkovitz, 1988).

Fathers are becoming increasingly involved in supporting their partner's pregnancy and delivery. This support is both an important aspect of identification with the father role, and a great emotional comfort to the mother.

The Impact of the Pregnant Woman on the Fetus

Among the factors that influence the fetus's development are the mother's age, use of drugs during pregnancy and delivery, exposure to environmental toxins, and diet. The quality of a pregnant woman's physical and emotional health before and during pregnancy is linked to her own knowledge about and preparation for pregnancy, as well as to her culture's attitudes and practices associated with childbearing. One of the most harmful influences of the psychosocial environment on fetal development is poverty. Embedded in the conditions of poverty are many of the individual factors associated with suboptimal prenatal development.

The Impact of Poverty

Perhaps the most powerful psychosocial factor that influences the life chances of the developing fetus is poverty. Poor women are likely to experience the cumulative effects of many of the factors associated with infant mortality and developmental vulnerabilities (Swyer, 1987). Poverty is directly linked to poor prenatal care. Poor women are likely to begin having babies at an earlier age and to have repeated pregnancies into their later adult years—practices that are associated with low-birth-weight infants. Women who have had little education are less likely to be aware of the risks of smoking, alcohol, and drug use for their babies and are more likely to use or abuse these substances. In addition, poor women are less likely to have been vaccinated against some of the infectious diseases, such as rubella, that can harm the developing fetus. Poverty is linked with maternal malnutrition, higher instances of infection, and higher rates of diabetes and cardiovascular disease, which are all linked to the infant's low birth weight and physical vulnerability (Cassady & Strange, 1987).

Many of the risks that face infants born to poor women are preventable. A well-organized, accessible system of regional medical care facilities combined with an effective educational program on pregnancy and nutritional support can improve significantly the health and vigor of babies born to poor women (Swyer, 1987). A systematic evaluation of a program of coordinated maternity care for women on Medicaid in North Carolina demonstrated that a comprehensive prenatal care program improves birth outcomes, even in a high-risk population (Buescher et al., 1991). This kind of coordination involves more than prenatal visits alone. It includes nonmedical support services, such as making sure the woman has access to food stamps, is part of the Women, Infants, and Children (WIC) food program, has the transportation needed for prenatal and postnatal health appointments, and receives housing assistance or job training when necessary. In addition, resources must be provided to care for, educate, and support children whose intellectual, physical, and emotional capabilities have been restricted before birth by their mothers' poverty. The life chances and quality of survival of infants born in poverty are a reflection of the value that a society places on social justice.

Mother's Age

The capacity for childbearing begins about 1 to 1½ years after menarche (the beginning of regular menstrual periods) and normally ends at the climacteric, or menopause (the ending of regular menstrual periods). Thus, a woman is potentially fertile for about 35 years of her life. Pregnancy and childbirth can occur at various times during this period. The effects of childbirth on the physical and psychological well-being of a mother vary with her age and emotional commitment to the mother role. Similarly, these factors also contribute significantly to the survival and well-being of her infant.

Women between the ages of 16 and 35 tend to provide a better uterine environment for the developing fetus and to give birth with fewer complications than do women under 16 or over 35. Particularly when it is their first pregnancy, women over 35 are likely to have a longer labor than younger women, and labor is more likely to result in the death of either the infant or the mother. As expected, the two groups with the highest probability of giving birth to premature babies are women over 35 and those under 16 (Schuster, 1986).

Premature children of teenage mothers are more likely than those of older mothers to have neurological defects that will influence their coping capacities. Also, mothers under 16 tend to receive less adequate prenatal care and to be less biologically mature. Consequently, adolescent mothers are more likely to experience complications during pregnancy that may endanger their infants and themselves. Evidence suggests that good medical care, nutrition, and social support improve the childbirth experiences of adolescent mothers who are *over* 16. However, the physical immaturity of those under 16 puts the mother and the infant at greater risk (Roosa, 1984).

A primary risk for infants of mothers who are over 40 is Down syndrome (Moore, 1993). It is hypothesized that the relatively high incidence of Down syndrome in babies born to older women is the result, in part, of deteriorating ova. However, older women are also likely to have male partners who are their age or older. Even though new sperm are produced daily, some evidence suggests that among older men, the rate of genetically defective sperm increases. Thus, aging in one or both partners may contribute to the increased incidence of Down syndrome in babies born to older women. These explanations are not entirely satisfactory, however, since older women who have had multiple births are not as likely to have a baby with Down syndrome as are women who have their first child at an older age. What is more, many babies with Down syndrome are born to women who are under 35. It is likely that in some cases, Down syndrome is a result of errors that occur during cell division, and that in others it is a result of a genetically transmitted condition.

Table 4.4 shows the rate of live births to women in the age range 10–44 from 1960 through 1994. In every age range except the youngest, fewer women are having babies today than was the case in the 1960s. Two other observations about the data presented in the table are relevant to our understanding of the timing and role of childbearing in adult life. First, since 1960 the trend has shifted from a higher birthrate at the ages 20–24 to a more equal rate during the full decade of the 20s. Second, although far fewer children were born to women 30 years and older in 1994 than in 1960, the current trend seems to be a spreading out of childbearing for women during their 30s.

In later chapters, we will discuss the psychosocial consequences of childbearing for adolescents and adults. Here we want to emphasize the pattern of fetal development, the quality of prenatal care, and the degree of risk during childbirth that are associated with the age of the mother during pregnancy.

Maternal Drug Use

The range of drugs used by pregnant women is enormous. Iron, diuretics, antibiotics, hormones, tranquilizers, appetite suppressants, and other drugs are being either prescribed for or taken voluntarily by pregnant women. In addition, women influence the fetal environment through their voluntary use of such drugs as alcohol, nicotine, caffeine, marijuana, cocaine, and other narcotics (Chasnoff, 1988). Studies of the effects of specific drugs on fetal growth suggest that many drugs ingested by pregnant women are in fact metabolized in the placenta and transmitted to the fetus. What is more, although the impact of a specific dosage of a drug on the pregnant woman may be minimal, the impact on the fetus may be quite dramatic.

In reviewing the following sections on the impact of drugs on fetal development, two principles must be considered. First, evidence suggests that genetic predisposition may make some developing fetuses more vulnerable than others to the negative effects of certain drugs or toxins. Data on this genetic variability were derived from animal studies because animals are more likely to have large litters of offspring, some of which show greater resilience to the presence of prenatal teratogens than others (Vorhees & Mollnow, 1987). Second, especially most teratogens do not have an all-or-none impact

TABLE 4.4	Live Birthrates by Age of Mother, 1960–1994 (Births per 1000 women in each age group)						
	Age						
Year	10–14	15–19	20–24	25–29	30–34	35–39	40–44
1960	0.8	89.1	258.1	197.4	112.7	56.2	15.5
1970	1.2	68.3	167.8	145.1	73.3	31.7	8.1
1980	1.1	53.0	115.1	112.9	61.9	19.8	3.9
1994	1.4	58.9	111.1	113.9	81.5	33.7	6.4

Source: U.S. Bureau of the Census, 1986, 1989, 1992, 1997.

on the central nervous system. The consequence to the fetus of exposure to teratogens varies by the dosage, the duration, and the timing.

Nicotine. Babies born to mothers who smoke during pregnancy weigh less than those born to nonsmoking mothers. A review of 45 studies on this relationship reported that babies born to smokers weighed an average of 200 grams less than babies born to nonsmokers (U.S. Department of Heath, Education, and Welfare, 1979). Women who smoke are at greater risk for miscarriages and stillbirths (Streissguth et al., 1989; Armstrong et al., 1992). In addition, neurological examinations of babies exposed to nicotine during the prenatal period showed decreased levels of arousal and responsiveness at 9 and 30 days after birth (Fried et al., 1987).

Alcohol. The evidence is conclusive that alcohol is a teratogen. Prenatal exposure to alcohol can disrupt brain development, interfering with cell development and organization, and modifying the production of neurotransmitters, which are critical to the maturation of the central nervous system (West, 1986). The complex impact of alcohol on fetal development has been given the name **fetal alcohol syndrome** (Abel, 1984). Fetal alcohol syndrome is associated with disorders of the central nervous system, low birth weight, and malformations of the face, eyes, ears, and mouth. The risk of fetal alcohol syndrome for infants born to women who drink heavily—that is, about 1.5 ounces or more of alcohol a day—is 30–50%. Even moderate daily alcohol use can produce some of these symptoms, especially if it is combined with malnutrition. At a rate of 1 to 3 infants affected per 1000 live births, fetal alcohol syndrome is the greatest source of environmentally caused developmental disruption in the prenatal central nervous system (Voorhees & Mollnow, 1987).

In a longitudinal study of the effects of prenatal exposure to alcohol, children born to mothers who consumed 1.5 ounces of alcohol (one average-strength drink) daily during pregnancy showed significantly lower IQ scores at age 4 than did children whose mothers used little or no alcohol (Streissguth et al., 1989). Alcohol use was a significant predictor of reduced IQ scores, even when many other factors—the mother's educational level, the child's birth order, the family's socioeconomic level, the child's involvement in preschool, and the quality of the mother-child interaction—were taken into account. In other words, the many environmental variables that are known to have a positive effect on a young child's intellectual functioning did not compensate for the disruption in development in the central nervous system associated with exposure to alcohol during pregnancy. We emphasize the risks associated with prenatal exposure to alcohol because it is so widely used in American society, and because what many adults consider to be a "safe" or socially acceptable amount of alcohol during pregnancy can have a negative effect on the fetus.

Caffeine. Caffeine freely crosses the placenta. It is commonly consumed in coffee, certain sodas, and tea. Heavy caffeine consumption—defined in one study as more than 300 milligrams, or roughly three cups of coffee per day or more—is associated with an increased risk of low birth weight, and there is a modest relationship to prematurity. Infants born to women who reduced the amount of caffeine they drank after the sixth week of pregnancy showed no ill effects associated with early caffeine consumption (Fenster et al., 1991; McDonald et al., 1992).

This premature, cocaine-addicted infant will struggle to survive the negative effects of the prenatal environment.

Narcotics. The use of narcotics, especially heroin and cocaine as well as methadone (a drug used in the treatment of heroin addiction), has been linked to increased risks of birth defects and low birth weight and also to higher rates of infant mortality (Dinges et al., 1980; Zuckerman et al., 1989). Infants who have been exposed prenatally to opiates, cocaine, and methadone show a pattern of extreme irritability, high-pitched crying that is evidence of neurological disorganization, fever, sleep disturbances, feeding problems, muscle spasms, and tremors (Hans, 1987). These babies are at high risk for sudden infant death syndrome. Longer-range studies found that children who were exposed to addictive drugs in the prenatal period continued to show problems with fine-motor co-ordination, had difficulty focusing and sustaining their attention, and, perhaps as a re-sult, had more school adjustment problems. Of course, it is difficult to separate the direct prenatal effects of these drugs on the nervous system from effects after birth as-sociated with being parented by a drug-using mother or the effects on parenting of the social and educational environment in which the mother herself may have developed.

In the 1980s, the widespread use of crack, an inexpensive, smokable form of co-caine, dramatically increased the number of cases of cocaine-exposed babies, especially in major cities such as New York, Los Angeles, Detroit, and Washington, D.C. In a sur-vey, 18 large hospitals in 15 large cities reported increases in the numbers of cocaine-exposed babies during the second half of the 1980s. Estimates ranged from 30,000 to 100,000 crack-exposed babies born annually (Gittler & McPherson, 1991).

Because of the widespread abuse of cocaine, some law-enforcement officials are ar-resting and charging women who have exposed their unborn infants to these harmful and illegal substances. In 1997, a woman in South Carolina was charged with murder by child abuse when it was determined that smoking crack cocaine was responsible for the death of her unborn child (*New York Times,* 1997). State laws have been passed that allow criminal charges to be filed against women who give birth to babies who have illegal substances in their blood. Several states have tried taking babies away from these mothers, but this action poses an extremely difficult ethical dilemma. Those who oppose such actions argue that alcohol use, smoking, and other forms of maternal be-havior also have known negative effects on the developing fetus. Should women who use these substances also be charged with child abuse? What is more, can society en-sure that the babies taken from these mothers and placed in foster care will do better than they would have done in the care of their birth mothers? On the other hand, some argue that the state has the responsibility to protect the well-being of the unborn child, especially during the third trimester when the fetus has reached a point of viability. Ac-cording to this view, actions that result in harm or death to the fetus ought to be con-sidered child abuse and prosecuted as such (Willwerth, 1991; Feinman, 1992).

Prescription Drugs. Other drugs are administered to women during pregnancy as part of the treatment for a medical condition. The tragic outcome of the use of thalidomide for the treatment of morning sickness in the 1960s alerted society to the potential dan-ger of certain chemicals to the fetus, particularly during the period of fetal differentia-tion and growth in the first trimester. Thalidomide taken during the 21st to 36th days after conception can cause gross deformities of the baby's limbs.

Some drugs are administered to help sustain the pregnancy. In one case, a group of boys whose mothers had been treated during pregnancy with the female hormones es-trogen and progesterone were studied when they were 6 and 16 years old. At both ages, the boys showed lower ratings in aggressiveness and athletic ability than a matched sample of boys whose mothers had not been treated with these female hor-mones (Yalom, et al., 1973). In another case, a sample of 119 women were treated with prednisone, first to alleviate infertility and then to maintain their pregnancies. Their babies' birth weights were significantly lower than that of the babies in the control group. Both male and female children who are exposed to testosterone-type hormones prenatally show more masculine behavior and respond in a more masculine way on tests of personality, gender role, and work and family values (Reinisch & Karow, 1977; Reinisch & Sanders, 1984). The effects of some kinds of drugs may persist for a long time after birth, either by directly altering the central nervous system or by influencing the pattern of caregiver-infant interactions.

Obstetric Anesthetics. The study of the effects on the newborn of drugs used during de-livery provides further evidence of the infant's dependence on the immediate environ-ment. Initially, pain-relieving drugs were used for the benefit and convenience of pregnant women and their physicians, and their effects on the newborn were not no-ticed. However, evidence suggests that the type, amount, and timing of anesthetic use in delivery are all factors that may induce neonatal depression and affect the coping ca-pacities of newborns. The use of anesthetic drugs during delivery has been found to in-terfere with the infant's ability to habituate to a stimulus (that is, to stop responding after repeated presentations of the stimulus); to reduce the infant's smiling and cuddliness; and to reduce alert responses to new stimuli. Furthermore, the relationship between drug use and some infant behavior has been observed to last as long as 28 days (Stechler & Halton, 1982; Naulty, 1987).

AIDS

One concern associated with intravenous drug use is the spread of the human immunodeficiency virus (HIV) and the acquired immunodeficiency syndrome (AIDS) from pregnant women to their unborn children. About 70% of women who test positive for HIV infection have been infected through their own drug use or that of a sex partner. The relationship among cocaine use, prostitution, and sexually transmitted diseases, including AIDS, is posing a growing health risk to unborn children, especially among poor urban minorities (Judson, 1989; Darney et al., 1989). Increasing numbers of young adults are being diagnosed with HIV, probably as a result of early sexual activity during adolescence. Adolescent females, especially low-income African-American females, experience a high risk of contracting HIV. Additionally, the number of HIV-infected women is expected to increase substantially in the coming decade (Demi et al., 1997). These patterns, coupled with the high rates of adolescent childbearing, lead to risks of prenatal exposure to AIDS (Paikoff et al., 1997). Children born to untreated HIV positive mothers have about a 25% chance of developing the disease. However, the use of drugs such as azidothymidine (AZT) can reduce the transmission rate to as low as 8%. The problem with administering these strong drugs to pregnant women is the harm that adult dosage levels might have on the immature fetus (Gorman, 1997).

Environmental Toxins

As an increasing number of women enter the work force and assume nontraditional work roles, concern about the hazards of work settings for fetal development continues to grow. In an Allied Chemical plant, fear that fluorocarbon 22 might cause fetal damage led to the layoff of five women workers. Two of those women chose to be sterilized in order to hold their jobs (Bronson, 1979). Wives of men who are employed in hazardous environments may also experience higher rates of miscarriage, sterility, and birth defects in their babies. In one study, fathers' exposure to specific solvents and chemicals at work was linked to higher rates of spontaneous abortions among their wives (Lindbohm et al., 1991). Recent research links men's workplace exposure to lead to reduced sperm count, sperm motility, and sperm concentration, resulting in negative consequences for fertility. Paternal exposure to lead is also associated with low-birthweight babies (Alexander et al., 1996; Min et al., 1996).

The workplace is not the only setting in which pregnant women may be exposed to environmental toxins. Women who regularly ate a large amount of polluted fish from Lake Michigan for six years before they became pregnant had infants who showed certain memory deficits at 7 months of age (Jacobson et al., 1985). Although the level of these toxins—industrial waste products found in air, water, and soil—had no measurable effects on the mothers, it was high enough to influence central nervous system functioning in the fetuses. This finding makes it clear that all communities must be sensitive to the quality of their water, air, and soil. Each new generation depends on its predecessors for protection from these environmental hazards.

Mother's Diet

The notion that no matter what the pregnant woman eats, the fetus will get what it needs for growth is simply not true. Providing adequate nutrition for fetal development requires both a balanced diet for the mother and the capacity to transform nutrients into a form that the fetus can ingest (which the placenta takes care of) (Lindblad, 1987).

Experimental research on the effects of maternal malnutrition on fetal development has been conducted primarily with rats. Fetal rats exposed to a low-protein diet had lower body and brain weights, fewer cerebral cells, and less cerebral protein than rats whose mothers received a normal diet. In most of these experimental studies, few of the offspring survived birth or lived to adulthood, and the reproductive behavior of those that did survive was greatly reduced. Thus, the experimental evidence suggests that severe malnutrition interferes with normal fetal and postnatal development (Coursin, 1974).

The effects of maternal malnutrition on the developing human fetus remain a topic of scientific controversy. Some experts suggest that birth weight is affected only when the mother experiences starvation or dramatically inadequate nutrition during the last trimester of pregnancy (Cassady & Strange, 1987). Others argue that malnutrition during the phase of cell division in the first trimester of fetal development results in smaller organ size, which cannot be reversed by later dietary supplements (Brazelton, 1987).

Most of the data on the effects of malnutrition on human fetal growth have come from studying the impact of disasters and crises, such as famines, wars, and extreme poverty, on pregnant women. Malnutrition is inferred from the baby's low birth weight in comparison with his or her **gestational age** (the age of the fetus from the time of conception until birth). Babies who are small for their gestational age have a higher mortality rate, more complications during post-delivery care, and a higher risk of mental or motor impairment than do babies who are of average weight for their gestational age (Cassady & Strange, 1987). The relative contribution of malnutrition to these outcomes is difficult to assess. Women who experience these conditions encounter other stresses, such as anxiety and increased exposure to disease and environmental toxins, that may also affect fetal growth.

A child may be malnourished during pregnancy, after birth, or both. Although some degree of growth retardation is hypothesized to occur if a fetus is malnourished, the most severe impact on growth occurs when resources are inadequate both before and after the child is born. This is the case in many poverty-stricken areas of the world. When prenatal malnutrition is followed by postnatal malnutrition and disease, it is impossible to study the effects of prenatal malnutrition alone.

Studies that have been designed to intervene by supplementing the mother's diet during pregnancy have provided mixed evidence that a pregnant woman's diet can be successfully modified to increase the newborn's weight. When Guatemalan mothers consumed 20,000 additional calories during the nine months of pregnancy, their babies were an average of 0.2 kilograms (7 ounces) heavier than the babies born to mothers whose diets had not been supplemented (Habicht et al., 1974). The rate of infant mortality declined 69% for the babies born to the Guatemalan women who were given a protein-enriched supplement (Brown & Pollitt, 1996).

In order for prenatal intervention to have the greatest impact, it must be coupled with efforts to reduce the continued effects of poverty after birth. Children who are at risk for malnutrition are likely to experience more illness, lethargy and withdrawal, delayed physical growth, and, as a result, delayed intellectual growth. On the other hand, some of the negative effects of malnutrition can be offset after the baby's birth. Studies of infants' growth potentials show that those who are adequately fed can make up for their slowed prenatal growth (Tanner, 1990). These infants showed increased activity, made greater demands on the environment, and prompted more active care-giving responses (Brazelton, 1987). This pattern of interaction may offset the initial deficits resulting from an inadequate prenatal nutritional environment.

THE IMPACT OF CULTURE

In order to appreciate the events surrounding the birth of a child, one must understand some of the idiosyncrasies in a culture's approach to birth. The beliefs, values, and guidelines for behavior regarding pregnancy and childbirth have been referred to as the **birth culture** (Jordan, 1983; Hahn & Muecke, 1987). The decision to have a child, the social and physical experiences of pregnancy, the particular style of help that is available for the delivery of the child, and the care and attitudes toward both mother and baby after delivery are all components of the birth culture. One cannot assume that everyone in a cultural group adheres to the full script of the birth culture, but at the very least, these guidelines are part of the mythology or lore that surfaces as a woman and her partner experience the events of pregnancy.

Data on the approaches to pregnancy and childbirth in traditional cultures are drawn primarily from the Human Relations Areas Files (Murdock & White, 1969) and from Ford's (1945) comparison of reproductive behavior in 64 cultures. In most traditional societies, men and nontribal women are not allowed to observe delivery. Further, many of the events related to conception and delivery are considered too personal or private to discuss with outsiders. Thus, the data on childbearing practices are not complete. Comparisons across cultures serve only to place the American system in a cultural context.

Reactions to Pregnancy

Many cultures share a strong assumption that the behavior of expectant parents will influence the developing fetus and the ease or difficulty of childbirth. Of the 64 cultures studied by Ford (1945), 42 prescribed certain behaviors for expectant parents and prohibited others (Box 4.4). Many such restrictions were dietary.

> Among the Pomeroon Arawaks, though the killing and eating of a snake during the woman's pregnancy is forbidden to both father and mother, the husband is allowed to kill and eat any other animal. The cause assigned for the taboo of the snake is that the little infant might be similar, that is, able neither to talk nor to walk. (Roth, 1953, p. 122)

In many Asian, Mediterranean, and Central and South American cultures, pregnancy is believed to be affected by the balance of what are considered "hot" and "cold" foods in a woman's diet. Pregnant women are advised to avoid both very "hot" foods, such as chili peppers and salty or fatty foods, and very "cold" foods, such as acidic, sour, or cold fresh foods (Hahn & Muecke, 1987).

Attitudes toward pregnant women can be characterized along two dimensions: (1) solicitude versus shame and (2) adequacy versus vulnerability (Mead & Newton, 1967).

Solicitude Versus Shame

Solicitude toward the pregnant woman is shown in the care, interest, and help of others. For example, it is said among Jordon villagers that "as people are careful of a chicken in the egg, all the more so should they be of a child in its mother's womb" (Grandquist, 1950). As the Chagga in Africa say, "Pay attention to the pregnant woman! There is no one more important than she" (Guttmann, 1932).

At the other end of this spectrum are the cultures that keep pregnancy a secret as long as possible. This custom may stem from a fear that damage will come to the fetus through supernatural demons, or from shyness about the sexual implications of pregnancy.

Societies that demonstrate solicitude increase the care given to the pregnant woman and fetus. These attitudes emphasize the importance of birth as a mechanism for replenishing the group, and additional resources are likely to be provided to the pregnant woman. By keeping the pregnancy a secret, cultures that instill a sense of shame in the woman do not promote the health of the mother or the fetus and may not encourage other couples to have children.

BOX 4.4 COUVADE

Some cultures observe the formal practice of **couvade,** in which the expectant father takes to his bed and observes very specific taboos during the period shortly before birth. Among the Arapesh of New Guinea, childbearing is believed to place as heavy a burden and drain of energy on the father as on the mother. Some cultures believe that by following the ritual of couvade, the fathers distract the attention of evil spirits so that the mother and baby can go through the childbirth transition more safely (Helman, 1990).

Even in groups that do not practice the ritual of couvade, it is common to find men experiencing some couvade symptoms, such as general fatigue, stomach cramps, nausea, dizziness, or backache. Trethowan (1972), one of the first to document the nature and extent of couvade symptoms in the normal population, suggested that these physical symptoms are a product of a man's emotional ambivalence toward his wife. The expectant father may experience empathy and identify with his wife's pregnant state. At the same time, he may experience some jealousy of his wife, resentment of the loss or potential loss of intimacy in their relationship, repulsion by his wife's physical appearance, or some envy of his wife's ability to bear a child. These psychological conflicts, many of which are probably unconscious or unexpressed, are amplified by an expectant father's conscious worries about the health and well-being of his wife and their baby. The combination of these stresses may produce the couvade syndrome.

Adequacy Versus Vulnerability

In many societies, pregnancy is a sign of sexual prowess and a means of entrance into social status. Some cultures do not arrange a wedding until after the woman has become pregnant. In a **polygynous** family, one in which a man has more than one wife, the pregnant wife receives the bulk of her husband's attention and may prevent her husband from taking an additional wife (Grandquist, 1950). In some cultures, women are considered more attractive after they have borne children, "Thus, the Aymara widow of South America with many children is regarded as a desirable bride" (Tichauer, 1963); "Lepcha men consider that copulation with women who have borne more than one child is more enjoyable and less exhausting than with other adult women" (Gorer, 1938).

The other end of this continuum is the view that child-making is exhausting, that pregnant women are vulnerable, and that women grow more frail with each pregnancy. Among the Arapesh of New Guinea (Mead, 1935), pregnancy is tiring for both men and women! Once menstruation stops, the husband and the wife believe that they must copulate repeatedly in order to provide the building materials for the fetus's semen and blood.

Many cultures teach that during pregnancy the woman and the fetus are more readily exposed to evil spirits. In several cultures, the forces of life and death are thought to be engaged in a particularly intense competition for the mother and the fetus around the time of delivery.

One can think of solicitude and shame, and adequacy and vulnerability, as two dimensions that create a matrix within which the birth culture of any society or subculture can be located. One might describe the U.S. medical birth culture, for example, as being characterized by solicitude and vulnerability. Pregnant women are usually treated with increased concern and care, and they are often placed within a medical system that increases their sense of dependency. Attitudes in the workplace also contribute to the sense of vulnerability because pregnancy is often viewed as incompatible with serious dedication to the job.

Within this framework, pregnancy may be viewed as a time of great rejoicing or extreme shame, and of feeling sexually powerful or extremely vulnerable. One may expect that the culture's view of pregnancy determines the kinds and severity of the symptoms associated with it, the types of treatment or medical assistance sought during pregnancy, and the degree to which it is responded to as a life stressor. A culture's attitudes toward pregnancy and birth also influence parenting attitudes and behavior. For example, in attitudes of solicitude or shame, one finds notions of the value of children and fears about whether the child will be a good or evil force in the family or community. In attitudes of adequacy versus vulnerability, one finds ideas about whether children bring resources or drain the family of them, and whether children are an extension of the family's power or a new source of vulnerability and risk.

Reactions to Childbirth Childbirth is an important event in traditional cultures. The delivery is usually attended by two or more assistants with specific assigned roles. Traditional birth attendants are found in all areas of the world. They are usually women who have had children themselves and who are respected members of their community. In Jamaica, the **nana,** or midwife, is one of the key figures in the village. She is called on to assist in many family crises. During pregnancy and childbirth, the nana provides assistance in the many rituals and taboos that mark the rebirth of the woman as a mother, and she usually cares for the mother and the infant until the ninth day after birth (Kitzinger, 1982).

In most traditional cultures, childbirth takes place in a familiar setting, either at home or in a nearby birthing hut. If the birth takes place at home, a woman may be separated from others by a curtain for privacy, but she knows that her family members are close at hand. Women typically give birth standing, squatting, or sitting and reclining against something or someone. The Western custom of lying on one's back with one's feet propped up in the air has no counterpart in traditional birth cultures (Helman, 1990), nor are women expected to be moved from one setting or room to another during the phases of labor. That appears to be a ritual reserved for women in modern, industrialized societies.

Views about the birth itself range from an extreme negative pole, at which birth is seen as dirty and defiling, to an extreme positive pole, at which it is seen as a personal achievement. The view of childbirth as a normal physical event is the midpoint on this continuum.

When birth is viewed as dirty, as it is by the Arapesh of New Guinea and the Kadu Gollas of India, the woman must go to an area away from the village to deliver her child. Many cultures, such as that of the ancient Hebrews, require extensive purification rituals after childbirth. Vietnamese villagers believe that mothers should not bathe or shampoo their hair for a month after giving birth so that the baby will not "fall apart," and that the new mother must not have sexual intercourse for 100 days (Stringfellow, 1978). A slightly more positive orientation toward childbirth is to identify it as a sickness. This view causes a pregnant Cuna Indian woman to visit her medicine man for daily medication. The midpoint of this spectrum—what we might most appropriately describe as "natural childbirth"—is a setting in which the mother delivers her baby in the presence of many members of the community, without much expression of pain and little magic or obstetrical mechanics. Clark and Howland (1978) described childbirth for Samoan women as follows:

> The process of labor is viewed by Samoan women as a necessary part of their role and a part of the life experience. Since the baby she is producing is highly valued by her culture, the mother's delivery is also commendable and therefore ego-satisfying. Pain relief for labor may well present the patient with a conflict. She obviously experiences pain as demonstrated by skeletal muscle response, tossing and turning, and fixed body positions, but her culture tells her that she does not need medication. It is the "spoiled" palagi [Caucasian] woman who needs pain-relieving drugs. Moreover, the culture clearly dictates that control is expected of a Samoan woman, and no overt expressions of pain are permissible. (p. 166)

At the most positive end of the scale, birth is seen as a proud achievement. Among the Ila of Northern Zimbabwe, women attending childbirth were observed to shout praises of the woman who had a baby. They all thanked her, saying, "I give thanks to you today that you have given birth to a child" (Mead & Newton, 1967, p. 174).

A similar sentiment is expressed in Marjorie Karmel's (1983) description of the Lamaze method of childbirth,

> From the moment I began to push, the atmosphere of the delivery room underwent a radical transformation. Where previously everyone had spoken in soft and moderate tones in deference to my state of concentration, now there was a wild encouraging cheering section, dedicated to spurring me on. I felt like a football star, headed for a touchdown. (pp. 93–94)

The American view of childbirth seems to be evolving toward an emphasis on safety for mother and child, and toward building a sense of competence in the mother and the father as they approach the care of their newborn (Sameroff, 1987). In comparison with the medical practices of the 1940s and 1950s, there is now less use of obstetrical medication during childbirth, greater involvement of fathers or other birth coaches during labor and delivery, and more immediate contact between infants and their parents. There are more opportunities for the baby to spend much of the day with the mother and for siblings to visit. Hospital stays are typically shorter.

At the same time, women are taught that the best way to promote the healthy development and safe delivery of their child is to make early and regular visits to their obstetrician during the prenatal period and to observe restrictions in diet, use of drugs, and exposure to certain environmental hazards that may harm the fetus. In some instances, a woman may feel that she is an active member of a team that will participate in the delivery of her baby, but often she does not know the physicians, nurses, or other medical professionals who are actually present when the baby is born. Midwifery and birthing centers have been slow to develop in the United States, and most physicians continue to strongly urge their patients to deliver their children in a hospital. What is more, the steady increase in the use of cesarean deliveries contradicts the view of childbirth as a natural event that is largely within the control of mothers and their family support systems.

It is reasonable to speculate that events at the time of the birth influence the mother's feelings about herself and her parenting ability. Efforts by the community, especially family members, close friends, and health care professionals, to foster a woman's competence in and control of parenting, as well as to express care and support for her, seem to promote a woman's positive orientation toward herself and her mothering role. On the other hand, messages of social rejection, doubts about a woman's competence, and attempts to take away control or to isolate the mother from her infant or her social support system may undermine the woman's self-esteem and interfere with her effectiveness as she approaches the demanding and exhausting task at hand.

The population of the United States is increasingly diverse, and attention must be given to understanding the variety of cultural norms of the pregnant woman and her family support system. In addition, efforts are needed to interpret the key elements of the U.S. birth culture for women who are not familiar with it, so that they may understand and possibly reinterpret those aspects that may appear disrespectful or threatening (Hahn & Muecke, 1987).

Applied Topic   ABORTION

Abortion is the termination of pregnancy before the fetus is able to live outside the uterus. Each year, thousands of pregnancies are terminated through spontaneous abortion, usually referred to as **miscarriage.** However, the focus of this section is on the voluntary termination of pregnancy. In obstetrical practice, abortions are induced differently before and after 12 weeks of gestation. Before 12 weeks, the pregnancy is aborted by dilating the cervix and then either removing the contents of the uterus by suction with a vacuum aspirator or scraping out the uterus. After 12 weeks, abortion can be induced by the injection of a saline solution or prostaglandin, which stimulates labor. The fetus may be removed surgically by a procedure similar to a cesarean section (Cunningham et al., 1997).

Researchers in France have developed the drug, RU 486, that interrupts pregnancy by interfering with the synthesis and circulation of progesterone (Baulieu, 1989). It is most effective if it is taken within the first seven to nine weeks after the last menstrual period. It causes the uterine lining to slough off, so there is no need for vacuum aspiration or surgical intervention. The application of RU 486 typically requires several clinic visits. If a complete expulsion has not occurred by the third visit, a surgical abortion is required. Studies find that 1 woman out of 100 is still pregnant at 12 days and 2 to 4 have had incomplete abortions (*U.S News & World Report,* 1997). At present, the drug is being evaluated in the United States. Many physicians who would not perform abortions on moral grounds say that they would be willing to prescribe and monitor the use of RU 486 to women who requested it (Rosenblatt et al., 1995).

In 1920, after the Russian Revolution, the USSR was one of the first countries to permit abortion at the mother's request. Although the legalization of abortion is a modern phenomenon, abortion as a means of birth control has been practiced, along with infanticide, throughout history and across cultures (Krannich, 1980). Both the Aranda of central Australia and the Hopi of Arizona, for example, have been known to induce abortions by tying a belt very tightly around the mother's abdomen (Murdock, 1934). In modern China, official policy permits each married couple to have only one child. Many pregnant women who already have a child are forced to have an abortion.

The Legal Context of Abortion in the United States

At the heart of the abortion controversy in the United States is the conflict between society's responsibility to protect the rights of a woman and to protect the rights of an unborn child. On one side are those who insist that a woman has a right to privacy and to choose or reject motherhood. On the other side are those who seek to protect the rights of the unborn fetus, which is incapable of protecting its own interests.

A main point requiring definition in the abortion controversy is the developmental age at which the embryo is considered an individual and is entitled to protection by the state. In 1973, in the case of *Roe v. Wade,* the U.S. Supreme Court proposed a developmental model to address that issue. The Court supported the division of pregnancy into three trimesters and considered abortion a woman's right in the first trimester, guarded by the Constitution's protection of privacy. The Court said that, in the second trimester, some restrictions could be placed on access to abortion because of its risk to

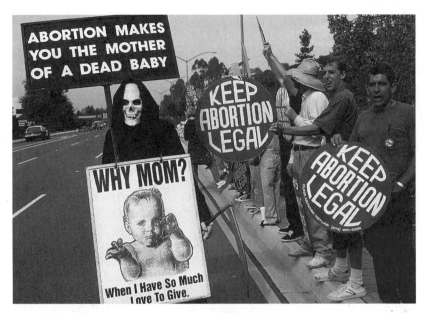

The abortion controversy continues to highlight the social, political, religious, and cultural significance of the prenatal period. What do you see as the eventual resolution of this controversy in the United States?

the mother; however, the fetus's rights were still not an issue during this period. In the final trimester, when the fetus was regarded as having a good chance of surviving outside the uterus, states could choose not to permit abortion. This ruling endorsed a woman's right to full control over the abortion decision until the fetus reaches a point of **developmental viability.** At that point, the Court ruled, the society's responsibility to the unborn child outweighs the woman's right to freedom and privacy.

For some years since that decision, the Supreme Court has ruled unconstitutional the state laws that tried to regulate abortions. In a decision reached in June 1992, the Supreme Court reviewed a set of laws passed by the Pennsylvania legislature. In its decision, it confirmed that *Roe v. Wade* "established a rule of law and component of liberty we cannot renounce" (Greenhouse, 1992). The Court argued that state laws ought not to impose an *undue burden* on a woman by placing major obstacles in her way if she seeks an abortion before the fetus has reached viability. However, of five sections of the Pennsylvania law, the Court considered four acceptable and agreed that they did not represent an undue burden. These restrictions were:

1. Requiring a woman to wait for 24 hours after hearing a presentation at the physician's office intended to persuade her to change her mind.
2. Requiring teenagers to have the consent of one parent or a judge before having an abortion.
3. Requiring the physician to specify any medical emergency that would justify waiving requirements 1 or 2.
4. Requiring the physician or clinic to make regular reports to the state.

A fifth provision, requiring a married woman to tell her husband of her intention to have an abortion, was rejected.

States are defining in their own ways the degree to which they will make resources available for abortions and the extent to which they will try to direct the abortion-making decision through the presentation of certain types of information and the exclusion of others. Currently, the abortion debate focuses on the legality of certain procedures used in third trimester or late-term abortions when fetal viability is much more clearly in competition with the mother's health.

The Incidence of Legal Abortions

The number of reported legal abortions increased dramatically after the *Roe v. Wade* decision, from 745,000 in 1973 to 1,609,000 in 1990. However, in the early 1990s, the trend has been a decline in abortions, with 1.3 million reported in 1993 (*U.S. News & World Report,* 1996). This decline is attributed to the interaction of a number of factors, including changes in attitudes toward abortion, decline in access to abortion clinics, more effective contraceptive use, and a resulting decline in the number of unwanted pregnancies.

Some of the characteristics of U.S. women who had legal abortions in 1991 are summarized in Table 4.5. The data suggest that women who have had abortions came from a great diversity of socioeconomic, family, and cultural contexts and that they had different reasons for having an abortion. The **abortion ratio**—that is, the number of abortions per 1000 combined abortions and live births—increased from 193 in 1973 to 300 in 1980 and declined to 275 in 1991. The age group 20–24 years old had the highest rate of abortions (34% of all abortions), followed by those 25–29 (22% of all abortions), and 15–19 (20% of all abortions). White women had slightly more than 60% of all legal abortions. Most of the abortions were performed on unmarried women, the majority of whom had had no prior births or abortions.

The Psychosocial Impact of Abortion

What do we know about the impact of abortions on women? Are abortions medically risky? How do women cope emotionally with the experience of abortion?

In 1965, 20% of all deaths associated with pregnancy and childbirth were linked to abortion. Since the legalization of abortion, related deaths have decreased by over 50%. In 1989, maternal deaths associated with legal abortions were 0.8 per 100,000; maternal deaths associated with pregnancy and childbirth were 8 per 100,000 (U.S. Bureau of the Census, 1992). Legal abortion, especially before 12 weeks, was ten times safer physically than carrying a pregnancy to term.

In 1987, President Reagan asked Surgeon General C. Everett Koop to evaluate the impact of abortion on women's physical and mental health. If abortions were found to be associated with increased rates of physical or mental illnesses, this could provide a scientific basis for framing public health policies limiting access to abortions. After an extensive evaluation of roughly 250 studies, Surgeon General Koop reported that, "the scientific studies do not provide conclusive data about the health effects of abortion on women" (Holden, 1989, p. 730). Of the studies included in Koop's review that focused on the psychological impact of abortion, most were so seriously flawed methodologically that their results could not be used to support either side of the abortion debate (Wilmoth, 1992).

The typical psychological experience of women who have abortions is relief (Lemkau, 1988; Elias, 1998). In a study of over 400 women two years after they had

TABLE 4.5   Legal Abortions in the U.S.: Selected Characteristics, 1991

Total legal abortions 1.557.000
Abortion ratio (number of abortions per 1000 abortions and live births) 275

Age of women (%)

Under 15 = 1	15–19 = 20	20–24 = 34
25–29 = 22	30–34 = 14	35–39 = 7
40 and over = 2		

Race (%)

White = 63	Black and other = 37

Marital status (%)

Married = 17	Unmarried = 83

Number of prior live births (%)

None = 46	1 = 26	2 = 18	3 = 7	4 or more = 3

Number of prior induced abortions (%)

None = 54	1 = 28	2 or more = 18

Weeks of gestation (%)

Less than 9 weeks = 52	9–10 weeks = 26	11–12 weeks = 12
13 weeks or more = 11		

Source: U.S Bureau of the Census, 1996.

an abortion, 70% felt they had made the right decision. Especially when the pregnancy is unwanted and the abortion is performed within the first 12 weeks, women generally resolve any negative feelings and thoughts they may have had soon after the abortion (Adler et al., 1990). However, roughly 30% of women do experience some ambivalence and/or regret as they look back on their decision.

Several factors are associated with a positive abortion outcome (Alter, 1984; Miller, 1992). Women who have an androgynous gender identity—that is, a flexible view of both masculine and feminine characteristics—report less sense of loss, less anxiety, fewer physical symptoms, and fewer thoughts about death than other women (androgyny is discussed further in Chapter 10). These women tend to have a less traditional gender-role orientation and expect to find a variety of sources of satisfaction in their lives in addition to or instead of child-rearing.

Another factor related to post-abortion adjustment is a woman's views about the acceptability of abortion. Not surprisingly, women who believe that abortion is an acceptable solution to an unwanted pregnancy and that abortion is also acceptable to their friends, family, and partner are less likely to experience strong feelings of regret or emotional upset following an abortion (Miller, 1992).

For women whose support systems do not sanction abortion, the decision to have an abortion is likely to be associated with strong negative emotions. Lemkau (1988) reviewed clinical cases in which abortion produced strong, unresolved negative emotions. Sometimes, when a genetic anomaly is discovered in the fetus, abortion is performed late in pregnancy. A woman who has already become attached to the fetus grieves for her loss. In other second trimester abortions, the ambivalence that caused the delay in the decision to have an abortion is exaggerated by the physical discomfort associated with a later abortion. Finally, some women discover that they are unable to conceive after an abortion, and guilt, anger, and regret surface. Women who are divorced, separated, or widowed at the time of an abortion appear to be more vulnerable to strong negative emotional reactions (Speckhard & Rue, 1992). Even though abortions can be associated with positive feelings of having taken control of one's destiny, one must not overlook the emotional reactions some women face.

Women and their unborn babies are not the only persons affected by the abortion decision. In 1976, the Supreme Court ruled that a woman did not need the consent of her husband or the child's father to have an abortion, overruling a previous requirement of the father's consent that had been legislated in 12 states (Etzioni, 1976). This opinion was reconfirmed in the 1992 Pennsylvania ruling cited above. The Supreme Court has supported a woman's independence from her husband or a child's father with regard to reproductive decision-making. However, questions about the legal rights of fathers to determine the fate of their unborn children are still being raised, and the laws will probably continue to be challenged as fathers become increasingly committed to participation in parenting.

Not much is known about men's reactions to their partners' abortions. Shostak and McLouth (1985) interviewed 1000 men who had accompanied women to abortion clinics across the United States. Of these men, 93% said they would alter their birth-control methods as a result of the experience; 83% believed that abortion was a desirable way of resolving the pregnancy problem. Many of these men expressed anxiety, frustration, and guilt in relation to the unwanted pregnancy and the abortion. More research is needed to learn how fathers' reactions to and attitudes about abortion contribute to the abortion decision and how abortion affects a man's future sexual and psychosocial adjustment.

The debate surrounding the legalization and availability of abortion services is an excellent example of a psychosocial controversy. Embedded in this controversy are key human development issues: When does human life begin? When is a fetus viable—that is, capable of life outside the uterus? What is the impact of an abortion on a woman's physical health and psychological well-being? What is the impact of bearing and rearing an unwanted child on a woman's physical health and psychological well-being? What is the impact of being an unwanted child? What are the rights of fathers with respect to a woman's decision to have an abortion? What are the rights and responsibilities of parents in regard to an adolescent's abortion? In much the same way that the society is struggling to define death and to resolve the ethical issues surrounding the technological interventions that prolong the lives of people who have been severely brain damaged or who are terminally ill, the society is struggling to define the beginnings of life and to resolve the ethical issues surrounding society's responsibilities to adult women and their unborn children.

Chapter Summary

A fetus develops in a psychosocial context—genetic inheritance links each new infant to both a specific ancestry and the evolutionary history of the species. Genetic factors contribute to the rate of development as well as to the pattern of individual characteristics. Many personal competencies and abnormalities have their origins in the pattern of genetic information provided at fertilization. Our understanding of the biochemical basis of genetics is leading to the development of new technologies that may one day result in the ability to correct genetic abnormalities or to modify the genotype. These advances pose new psychosocial dilemmas and require that the public become better educated in such areas as science, human development, and ethics.

The nine months of fetal development involve a rapid differentiation of body organs and a gradual integration of survival functions, especially the ability to suck and swallow, the regulation of breathing and body temperature, and the maturation of the digestive system. Sense receptors are prepared to respond to stimulation long before they are put into use. The central nervous system, which begins to take shape in the third and fourth weeks after conception, continues to develop and change throughout the prenatal period and into childhood and adolescence.

The birth process itself has five phases. The early signs that birth is approaching orient the parents and ready the birth canal for the baby's passage. Labor and delivery involve involuntary uterine contractions. The length of labor is variable, although it is usually shorter for women who have already had a child. The most difficult phase of delivery is the transition to full labor, when the contractions are the strongest and last the longest.

During pregnancy, the mother and the fetus are interdependent. Pregnancy affects a woman's social roles and social status, and influences how people treat her and what resources become available to her. A woman's physical well-being and emotional state, along with her attitude toward her pregnancy and her developing attachment to her unborn child, set the stage for the quality of her parenting after the child is born.

Characteristics of the mother, her lifestyle, and her physical and cultural environment all influence fetal development. Of special concern are the mother's age, any drugs she takes during her pregnancy, her exposure to certain diseases and environmental toxins, the use of anesthetic drugs during delivery, and her diet. A specific social concern is the impact of poverty on fetal development: infants conceived by very poor women are exposed to the cumulative effects of many of the environmental hazards that are known to result in low birth weight and congenital abnormalities.

The experiences of pregnancy and childbirth are embedded in a cultural context. The birth culture provides a set of guidelines for behavior and attitudes toward and beliefs about restrictions on the woman's activities, the availability of resources, and the treatment of a pregnant woman by others. A matrix of orientations toward pregnancy reflects solicitude versus shame, and adequacy versus vulnerability. Most birth cultures can be located within this matrix.

Several factors involved in the prenatal period converge in the issue of abortion. The decision to abort reflects the mother's attitude toward childbirth; her criteria for a healthy, normal child; her age and economic resources; and her access to a safe means of ending the pregnancy. The decision about abortion also reflects the culture's attitudes about the moral implications of ending a life after conception and the legal principles about when the fetus itself has a right to society's protection. Finally, the decision to abort is related to its safety, accessibility, and expense.

The stage is now set to consider the remaining life stages in a psychosocial context. We have discussed the emergence of a child into an existing family, community, and cultural network. The challenges to growth at every life stage reflect the balance between the unique talents and resources that a person offers and the barriers, expectations, and resources that he or she confronts in the environment.

End of Chapter Case

Karen and Don cope with the decision about giving birth to an infant with severe genetic anomalies.

A young couple, whom we will call Karen and Don, wanted to start a family but were troubled by a puzzling coincidence. A few years before, Don's sister had given birth to a daughter with abnormalities that matched a pattern in Don's younger brother: a heart defect, a double thumb, a club foot, and severe mental retardation. One child like this in the family could be attributed to "accident" or "fate," thought the couple, but two could not.

Karen and Don went to a human genetics clinic and began a process of discovery. With the help of a counselor, they constructed a family tree, ... identified potential carriers of the disorder in Don's family, and persuaded them to get a blood test. Don's test confirmed the young couple's worst fear: he was a carrier and potential children were at risk. . . .

The impact of these discoveries on Don's family was profound. When blood testing revealed that his mother was not a carrier, she was relieved of a burden of guilt she had secretly carried for years. She had always thought that she was the cause of her son's and her granddaughter's abnormalities. The same information implicated Don's father; his reaction to it can be gauged by his refusal to have a blood test. Don's sister, who had just given birth to a normal child, had a tubal ligation. Don himself fell into guilty silence. Not only was he the carrier of a genetic defect; he was disappointing his wife, who desperately wanted to have a baby. He thought of artificial insemination, rejected the idea, and came close to abandoning altogether the idea of having children. Then, suddenly and surprisingly, after beginning to look into adoption, Karen discovered she was pregnant. . . .

Now the process of discovery was extended one generation down, as Karen underwent amniocentesis to determine the status of her unborn fetus. . . . Karen's mother . . . would not tolerate abortion. "She kept saying, 'There is no way that you will terminate your pregnancy if you get bad news. There is just no way.' She didn't tell anyone I was pregnant." . . .

A process of intervention began for Karen and Don when amniocentesis revealed that theirs was to be a child with severe abnormalities. "Maybe I should go ahead and have the child," she remembered thinking, "because it could be the only one I'll ever have." But they had already decided under what conditions they would terminate their pregnancy. "If the fetus had been a carrier, then we were going to go ahead and go full term and have the child. Be we did not want to have a child that we knew would have physical deformities and be mentally retarded." They had to inform their families of their intentions, and that included Karen's mother. "When we called and said, 'It's bad news and I'm terminating the pregnancy,' she just couldn't believe it."

Karen's abortion was no easy matter for her. "It's not like I just lost the baby, I had a miscarriage. I willfully went in and terminated a pregnancy, and it was hard for people to deal with it. Some people think it was the kind of thing . . . you go in and you're knocked out and you wake up and you're not pregnant anymore. And that's not the way it was at all. They induced labor, and I was in labor for ten hours, and I delivered a child. I was awake. My mother called to find out how I was doing afterward, but then dropped the subject. When I went back to work, everyone acted like things should be normal, like nothing had ever happened, and I was definitely mourning.

Source: Kotre, J., & Kotre, K. B.

Thought Questions

1. What do you think are the major conflicts in this case?
2. Put yourself in the roles of the main characters in this case: Karen, Don, Karen's mother, Don's mother, Don's father. How might you react?
3. How does technology enter into the case?
4. How are the biological, psychological, and societal systems involved in understanding the issues faced by Karen and Don?
5. How might Karen and Don's relationship be influenced by these experiences?
6. What are the ethical considerations in this case?
7. In what ways do cultural issues related to pregnancy, childbirth, and abortion come into play in this case? How might a couple living in a different cultural context approach this situation differently?

Chapter 5

*T*hrough a process of mutual adaptation,
mother and infant establish a pattern of
meaningful interactions and build the
foundation for trust.

Infancy (First 24 Months)

Chapter Objectives

- To identify important milestones in the maturation of the sensory and motor systems, and to describe the interactions among these systems during the first two years of life.
- To define social attachment as the process through which infants develop strong emotional bonds with others, and to describe the dynamics of attachment formation during infancy.
- To describe the development of sensorimotor intelligence, including an analysis of how infants organize experiences and conceptualize causality.
- To examine how infants understand the properties of objects, including the sense that objects are permanent, that they have unique properties and functions, and that they can be categorized.
- To examine the nature of emotional development, including emotional differentiation, the interpretation of emotions, and emotional regulation.
- To analyze the factors that contribute to the resolution of the psychosocial crisis of trust versus mistrust, including the achievement of mutuality with the caregiver and the attainment of a sense of hope or withdrawal.
- To evaluate the critical role of parents/caregivers during infancy with special attention to issues of safety in the physical environment; optimizing cognitive, social, and emotional development; and the role of parents/caregivers as advocates for their infants with other agencies and systems.

Infancy is a stage of strikingly rapid development. During the first year of life, the infant's birth weight almost triples. (Imagine if your weight tripled within one year at any other time in life!) The baby seems to grow before one's very eyes. Parents will remark that they go to work in the morning, and their baby seems to have changed by the time they return in the evening. Along with this extraordinary rate of physical growth comes a remarkable process of increased control and purposefulness, leading to the integration of simple responses into coordinated, patterned behavior. By the age of 2, the fundamentals of movement, language, and concept formation can be observed. Most infants are marvelously flexible, capable of adapting to any of the varied social environments into which they may be born.

As American families have become smaller, we have seen a change in the emphasis society places on infancy. Each child is taken much more seriously. The medical community is devising complex technologies for saving the lives of babies born weighing 1000 grams (32 oz.) or less. The psychological community is giving attention to infant temperament and the early origins of personality, focusing on individual differences among infants from the very first weeks of life. A growing "baby industry" offers special equipment, foods, toys, books, and other paraphernalia intended to enrich the infant's sensory

and motor development and to support the parent-infant bond. In addition, parents take classes, read books and magazines, and join support groups so that they can "get it right the first time."

The story of development during infancy requires that one keep in mind a strong, genetically guided pattern of growth and development in continuous interaction with a complex and changing social and physical environment (Plomin, 1990, 1994). The mother's personality, the father's involvement in child care, cultural beliefs surrounding child-rearing practices, and poverty or economic strain that influence the parents' psychological well-being are all factors that influence a child's vulnerability or resilience (Plomin & McClearn, 1993). As the infant's capacities change, they bring him or her into interaction with new facets of the environment, and as new experiences take place, they shape and channel the infant's genetic potential into patterns of thought and behavior.

From the perspective of psychosocial development, five major developmental tasks are especially critical during infancy:

- establishment and coordination of the perceptual, motor, and sensory systems
- formation of an attachment to at least one person

- *elaboration of the sensorimotor intellectual system*
- *initial understanding of the nature of objects and creation of categories for organizing the physical and social world*
- *differentiation of the emotional system*

In each of these tasks, one finds evidence of the complex interaction of genetics and environment shaping the direction of growth. This chapter begins *with a description of the physical status of the newborn, and then discusses each of the five developmental tasks listed above. The psychosocial crisis of infancy—trust versus mistrust—is explored as a way of conceptualizing the foundational orientation toward self and society. The chapter closes with an examination of the key roles of parents/caregivers in providing the environmental supports that promote optimal development in the infant and lay the foundation for future growth.* ❖

NEWBORNS

In the United States, the average full-term baby weighs 3300 grams (7 to 7.5 pounds) and is 51 centimeters (20 inches) long. Boys are slightly heavier and longer than girls. At birth, girls' nervous systems and bones are about two weeks more mature than boys'.

In the first minute after birth, and then again at five minutes, the newborn's life signs are evaluated using the **Apgar Scoring Method,** named for its originator, Virginia Apgar (Table 5.1.) Five life signs are scored on a scale from 0 to 2: heart rate, respiratory effort, muscle tone, reflex irritability, and body color. A score of 7 to 10 means the infant is in good condition. Scores of 4 to 6 mean fair condition and indicate the need for the administration of supplemental oxygen. Scores of 0 to 3 suggest extremely poor condition and the need for resuscitation. Even among the highest group of infants who score 7 to 10, those with scores of 7 or 8 show less efficient attention and less habituation to stimuli than the higher-scoring infants. The most important use of the Apgar Method is for evaluating the need for immediate intervention rather than as a means of assessing subsequent development (Francis, Self, & Horowitz, 1987).

Babies differ in their physical maturity and appearance at birth. Differences in physical maturity have distinct consequences for the capacity to regulate survival functions such as breathing, digesting, waking, and sleeping. Infants who weigh less than 2500 grams (about 5 pounds, 8 ounces) are called **low-birth-weight babies.** Low birth weight may result from prematurity, being born before the full period of gestation. It may also result from the mother's inadequate diet, smoking, or use of drugs, as discussed in Chapter 4. These factors tend to lower the fetus's weight for a given gestational age. Babies who are small for their gestational age (SGA) are at greater risk for health problems than those who are born prematurely but are of average weight for their gestational age (Cassady & Strange, 1987). Box 5.1 discusses some of the available information on the development of very small babies.

TABLE 5.1 The Apgar Scoring Method

Sign	Score		
	0	1	2
Heart Rate	Absent	Slow (less than 100 beats/minutes)	Over 100 beats/minute
Respiratory Effort	Absent	Slow or irregular breathing	Good crying, strong breathing
Muscle Tone	Flaccid or limp	Weak; some flexion of extremities	Active motion, strong flexion of extremities
Reflex Irritability	No response	Weak cry, grimace, cough, or sneeze	Vigorous cry, grimace, cough, or sneeze
Color	Blue, pale	Body pink, extremities blue	Completely pink

Source: Apgar, 1953.

BOX 5.1 VERY SMALL BABIES

Many babies are born before they are fully developed. Modern technology has pushed back the boundary of fetal viability to about 24 weeks of gestational age, or a weight of about 500 grams (slightly over 1 pound). These tiny babies, not much bigger than the palm of your hand, receive weeks of round-the-clock care in their struggle to survive.

What do we know about the developmental progress of these very small babies? How is the quality of the relationship with their parents modified by prolonged hospitalization and their obvious vulnerability? How do parents cope with the anxieties and frustrations of caring for a very tiny baby? What are the anticipated outcomes of the child's cognitive capacities and later intellectual development? Because this is a very new population, a group that has survived in appreciable numbers only in recent decades, many of these questions are still being addressed. But researchers are beginning to provide a better picture of the psychosocial development of very small babies.

Very-low-birth-weight babies are clearly different from full-term babies. They are less physically attractive; they have higher-pitched, unpleasant cries; they are more easily overstimulated and more difficult to soothe; and they are less able to establish rhythmic patterns of social interaction. What is more, during the first weeks and months of life, parental contact takes place in the intimidating environment of the hospital, where the babies are usually hooked up to monitors, have one or more tubes in their bodies, and are going through periodic physical crises in the struggle for survival.

In this context, the process of attachment formation appears to face significant challenges. Parents find it hard to synchronize their parenting activities with the activities of their babies. They perceive their babies as difficult and find that they receive few cues of satisfaction or responsiveness from them. In other words, the establishment of a sense of reciprocity between parent and infant is more difficult to establish in the early months of life (Levy-Shiff et al., 1989).

Depending on the health and robustness of the infants, and with the appropriate parental responsiveness, approximately 65% of parents and low-birth-weight babies are able to establish a framework of secure, trusting interactions by the end of the child's infancy, just as do parents and full-term infants (Goldberg & DiVitto, 1995). However, in a study of very low-birth-weight babies (average weight 955 grams), significantly fewer preterm babies had secure attachments at 19 months than the comparison group of full-term babies. In fact, the percentage of very small babies who showed a secure attachment *declined* from 14 to 19 months. One explanation for this decline is that the disruptive effects of prematurity accumulate during the second year of life, introducing more anxiety among caregivers and greater difficulty in achieving mutuality in the infant-caregiver relationship (Mangelsdorf et al., 1996).

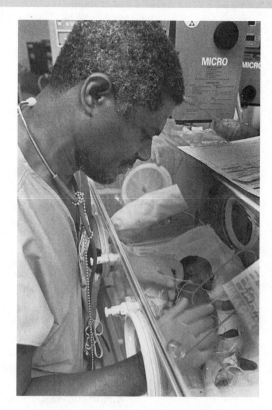

Hours of intensive care combined with new medical technologies increase the life chances for very tiny babies. Yet, many of them are at high risk for developmental disabilities associated with their extremely low birth weight and related physical immaturity.

Extreme low-birth-weight infants are at risk for problems in subsequent cognitive development. Infants who are born weighing less than 1500 grams are likely to suffer serious brain hemorrhages. In addition, their undeveloped lungs cannot deliver an adequate supply of oxygen to the brain. Chronic lung disease, frequently associated with prematurity, results in breathing problems, feeding difficulties, lung infections, and disrupted flow of oxygen (Singer et al., 1996). These insults to the nervous system have an impact on a variety of information-processing skills that can be measured in newborns. High-risk preterm infants show deficits in measures of regulation of arousal and attention, visual recognition of familiar stimuli, and reactivity to novel stimuli (DiPietro et al., 1992; Rose et al., 1992). Severe respiratory distress experienced during the early months of life is associated with cognitive deficits observed in the first year of life, and with learning and language deficits during the preschool years and into the early school years (Brooks-Gunn et al., 1993; Rose et al., 1992). Those at greatest risk for cognitive delays are the babies born before 30 weeks to parents with very limited educational and financial resources.

Many interventions have been devised to improve the care of very small babies. Management of their breathing, temperature regulation, monitoring of heart rate, creation of appropriate stimulation and nurturant care in the hospital all contribute to improving the chances for survival. Nonetheless, the continuing high risk for developmental disabilities among these small babies suggests that renewed efforts need to be placed on determining the causes and preventing as many preterm births as possible (Holzman & Paneth, 1998).

DEVELOPMENTAL TASKS

The Development of Sensory/ Perceptual and Motor Functions

During the first months of life the sensory/perceptual system—vision, hearing, taste, smell, touch, motion sensitivity, and responsiveness to internal cues (proprioception)— is developing rapidly and appears to function at a more advanced level than the motor system. Since most muscle movements are not yet under the infant's voluntary control in the early days and months of life, researchers have had to apply considerable ingenuity to study infants' sensory/perceptual competencies. They cannot simply ask an infant to point to a circle or press a button to respond to a certain change in color or taste. Currently, behaviors such as gazing time, changes in heart rate, the strength and/or frequency of sucking, facial action, and head turning are used as indicators of infants' interest or change in response to stimuli (Box 5.2). Using these strategies, researchers can document the nature of infants' sensory capacities.

The genetic plan that has been carried out during the gestation period provides most newborn infants with intact sensory organs and a well-formed brain at birth. The infant's brain contains about 100 billion neurons, or nerve cells, which are already connected in pathways that are designed to execute definite functions. The fundamental organization of the brain does not change after birth, but details of its structure demonstrate **plasticity** for some time (Singer, 1995; Nash, 1997). Each sensory capacity is associated with an area of the cortex that links sensations with memories of similar sensations and, over time, an emerging meaning of the sensory array. As a result of early experience, sights, smells, sounds, tastes, touches, and posture activate and, over time, strengthen specific neural pathways, while others fall into disuse. Thus, the infant's interaction with the immediate stimulus environment begins to shape the organization of neural connections, creating very early patterns of familiarity and meaning (Brierley, 1993).

Sensory/Perceptual Development

It would be difficult to review the full range and detail of sensory capacities that emerge and develop during infancy. Maturation in these domains is breathtaking. Our discussion focuses primarily on those abilities that permit infants to participate in and adapt to their social environment. From birth, sensory/perceptual capacities are vital resources that help infants establish emotional links with their caregivers, gather information about their environment, and cope with sources of stress.

Hearing. You may be surprised to learn that hearing rather than vision is the sense that provides the very earliest link between the newborn and the mother. Research has confirmed that the fetus is sensitive to auditory stimulation in utero (DeCasper & Spence, 1986; Aslin, 1987). Before birth, the fetus hears the mother's heartbeat. This sound continues to be soothing to the infant in the days and weeks after birth. Newborns show a preference for the sound of their mother's voice over the voice of an unfamiliar female (DeCasper & Fifer, 1980). They also show a preference for the sound of melodies their mother sang during the pregnancy and even for the sound of prose passages she read during the prenatal period. One must assume that an infant's indication of preference for these auditory stimuli is based on familiarity with the sounds from exposure in utero.

Young infants can distinguish changes in loudness, pitch, duration, and location of sounds (Kuhl, 1987). Many of these capacities are present among newborns but become increasingly sensitive by 6 months. Infants can use sounds to locate objects in

BOX 5.2   LOOKING IN ON THE NEWBORN

One of the adaptive mechanisms that applies to all sense modalities is the infant's capacity to habituate to any particular repetitive stimulation. **Habituation** means that the infant's response decreases after each presentation of an identical stimulus (Rovee-Collier, 1987). Habituation allows the infant to shift attention to new aspects of the environment as certain elements become familiar. When a new stimulus is presented, such as a new level of loudness or the same tone presented to a different ear, the infant shows an increase in alert responsiveness. Habituation is one of the most primitive forms of learning and is observed in many other mammalian species.

Habituation is often used as a means of determining whether an infant can discriminate between two different stimuli. The researcher first habituates the infant to one stimulus, then a second stimulus is presented. If the infant shows signs of renewed interest or alertness, measured by changes in heart rate, gazing time, or eye movements, this is taken as evidence that the infant has detected a difference between the two stimuli. If the infant shows no new signs of interest or responsiveness, this is taken as evidence that the differences between the two stimuli were too slight to be perceived.

Habituation depends in part on the nature of the stimulus. For example, newborns did not habituate to the sound of a door buzzer after 15 presentations. However, they did habituate to a blue light that stayed lit for 20 seconds after 6 presentations. Some babies are fast habituators; others are slow. Some infants quickly decrease their attentiveness to repeated stimuli, while others continue to respond to each presentation. Differences in speed of habituation may be related to the maturity of the infant at birth, to the amount of anesthetic used during delivery, or to innate differences in intellectual competence.

An infant's ability to differentiate among complex stimuli can be evaluated by observing the patterns of habituation and dishabituation. For example, four-month-old infants were habituated to a three-element mobile. Then the babies were allowed to gaze at an identical mobile or some variation of the mobile for one-half hour each day at home for three weeks. At the end of the three weeks, the babies were observed in response to the original mobile. Looking time was longest when there was a moderate difference between the original and the home mobiles. Identical stimuli or extremely discrepant stimuli did not appear to be as interesting as stimuli that were somewhat different from the original (Super et al., 1972). Similar findings have been observed in infants' responses to patterns of musical notes, phonetic sounds, and complex shapes. These studies support the notion that young infants are capable of forming and retaining a scheme for sensory experiences against which they can compare new events (Bornstein, 1992).

---

space. In one study, babies ages 6 to 8 months were placed in a darkened room. Objects that made sounds were located within reach and out of reach, and off to the right or left of midline. The babies made reaching motions in the correct direction of the sounds and made more efforts to reach objects that sounded as if they were within reach than to objects that sounded out of reach (Clifton et al., 1991).

The human voice is one of the earliest stimuli to evoke an infant's smile; infants appear to be particularly sensitive to language sounds. Very young babies are able to differentiate basic sound distinctions used in human speech throughout the world. Infants from all language environments are able to perceive and distinguish among speech sounds that could be used in one or more of the world's languages. By 6 months of age, however, infants prefer to listen to sequences of words spoken in the mother's language rather than in a foreign language, especially if the two languages differ in their overall tone, pauses, and rhythm (Sansavini et al., 1997). During the second 6 months of life, after exposure to a native language, the infant's ability to make some sound distinctions declines. Speech perception becomes more tied to the native language as infants begin to attach meaning to certain sound combinations, indicating a reorganization of sensory capabilities as the child learns to listen to people speaking a particular language (Werker, 1989; Bornstein, 1995). This is an example of the plasticity referred to earlier, a fine-tuning of the neural network as a result of experience.

Vision. Infants respond to a variety of visual dimensions, including movement, color, brightness, complexity, light/dark contrast, contours, depth, and distance (Hickey & Peduzzi, 1987; Banks & Dannemiller, 1987). The vast majority of research on sensory development in infancy has concentrated on assessing the acuity or sensitivity of vision and on analyzing the ways infants use it to understand their environment as well as to coordinate exploratory behaviors. Visual behaviors have also served as one of the primary windows for research into the infant's sensory and cognitive capacities. For instance, the time an infant takes to scan an object and the length of time spent fixating on a novel object appear to be indications of infant intelligence. Shorter fixation time is apparently a result of greater speed and efficiency in visual processing (Jacobson et al., 1992; Colombo et al., 1991).

Visual acuity improves rapidly during the first 4 months. Pattern perception and movement perception mature as well. By 2 months, infants form an expectation of a visual sequence. As they watch a pattern of events, they show evidence of anticipating the next event in the sequence (Canfield & Haith, 1991; Aslin, 1987). Three-month-old infants respond to wavelengths of light as though they perceive distinct hues of blue, green, yellow, and red (Bornstein et al., 1976; Teller & Bornstein, 1987; Aslin, 1987). Four-month-old babies perceive objects as adults would, although they do not have the same set of cognitive associations with them that imply specific functions or categories. They recognize shapes and detect complex patterns of motion such as human walking. A great deal of infant learning occurs through listening and watching (Bornstein, 1995).

Faceness. The human face and "faceness" in general appear to have special appeal for newborns. Infants also show preference for facelike stimuli. In the early weeks following birth, infants have optimal focus on objects that are about 20 cm away, approximately the distance between the mother's face and her baby cradled in her arms. Newborns can shift focus to scan and keep track of a moving target, but not as easily and smoothly as older babies. Young infants appear to focus their attention on the contours or external borders of objects rather than on the internal details. Thus, if you were holding a young baby, the child might appear to be staring at your hairline or your chin rather than at your mouth. Faces have many of the properties that infants prefer. The hairline is a type of contour; the eyes provide a dark-light contrast; and the facial expressions provide a changing, moving stimulus.

In addition to the form, shape, and movement of the human face, certain facial expressions appear to have meaning to very young babies. One- and two-day-old babies are able to discriminate and imitate the happy, sad, and surprised expressions of a live model (Field et al., 1982). This very early capacity for imitation wanes and is replaced between the ages of 1 and 2 months with a voluntary capacity for imitation of facial expressions when the model is not present. Some time between 4 and 7 months, infants are able to recognize and classify some expressions such as happiness and anger (Caron et al., 1988; Nelson, 1987; Ludemann, 1991).

Lack of motion in an adult face appears to have a disturbing effect on infants. When adults pose with a still face, babies stop looking at the adult and, in some cases, begin grimacing or showing other signs of discomfort. This reaction suggests that infants anticipate a certain normal sequence of facial movements in a human interaction. Thus, the absence of facial movements is noted as not simply novel but distressing (Stack & Muir, 1992; Segal et al., 1995).

Pattern perception, visual tracking, anticipation of sequences of movement, color, shape and motion perception all come into play as this baby watches the fish in the aquarium.

Some 2-day-old infants discriminate between a mother's face and the face of a stranger (Field et al., 1984). By 3 months, almost all infants can distinguish a parent's face from that of a stranger (Zucker, 1985). These visual perceptual skills illustrate the highly developed capacities for orienting toward social stimuli, which permit infants to participate so readily in the social context upon which their survival depends.

Taste and Smell. The sense of taste at least partially functions in utero (Mistretta & Bradley, 1977). Newborns can differentiate sweet, sour, bitter, and salty tastes. Facial responses to salty, sour, and bitter solutions share the same negative upper- and mid-face response

This sequence of facial expressions in a newborn was elicited by a sweet solution. The initial negative grimace is followed by relaxation and sucking.

but differ in the accompanying lower-face actions: the lips purse in response to a sour taste, the mouth gapes in response to a bitter taste, and no distinctive lower facial reaction is seen in response to a salty taste. Two hours after birth, an infant's facial responses to a sweet taste (sucrose) are characterized primarily by relaxation and sucking. Sucrose has an especially calming effect on newborns and appears to reduce pain. In one experiment, newborns 1 to 3 days old who were undergoing circumcision or having their heel pricked for a blood test for phenylketonuria cried much less when they were given a small sucrose solution to suck (Blass & Hoffmeyer, 1991). The calming effect of sweet-tasting substances has been observed in both preterm and full-term infants (Smith & Blass, 1996). It is likely that the normal taste of milk, which includes this sweet flavor, has the combined effect of releasing natural opioids, thereby raising the pain threshold, and reducing heart rate and activity level, thereby conserving energy.

Breast-fed babies are particularly sensitive to their mothers' body odors (Cernoch & Porter, 1985). One study found that 7-day-old babies could use the sense of smell to distinguish their own mothers' nursing pads from those of other mothers (MacFarlane, 1975). The mother's odor may play an important role in stimulating early mother-infant interactions (Porter et al., 1988).

Touch. The skin is the largest sensory organ and the earliest to develop in utero. A variety of evidence from animal and human research suggests that touch plays a central role in development. Gentle handling, including rocking, stroking, and cuddling, all have soothing effects on a baby. **Swaddling,** the practice of wrapping a baby snugly in a soft blanket, is a common technique for soothing a newborn in many cultures. One of the effective techniques for caring for low-birth-weight babies is to introduce regular gentle stroking, rocking, and other forms of soothing touch.

Touch is an active as well as a passive sense; babies use it to explore objects, people, and their own bodies. Sucking is one of the earliest coping strategies infants use to calm themselves (Blass & Ciaramitaro, 1994). Sucking and mouthing also comprise an early form of exploratory touch. Babies can recognize qualities of objects from the way they feel in their mouths—nubby or smooth, chewy and flexible, or rigid (Rose & Ruff, 1987). For older infants, most tactile information comes through touching with the hands and bringing objects to the face in order to take a closer look or to explore with the mouth. By 5 or 6 months of age, infants can use their hands for controlled examination of objects, fingering the surface to explore small details and transferring the object from one hand to the other hand to detect corners, shapes, and the flexibility of surfaces as well as its the overall size (Gibson, 1962; Ruff, 1984).

The Interconnected Nature of Sensory/Perceptual Capacities. The sensory/perceptual capacities function as an interconnected system to provide a variety of sources of information about the environment at the same time. Consider the situation when an infant is being nursed. At first, the mother guides the baby toward her breast, but the baby makes use of visual, tactile, olfactory, and kinesthetic cues to find and grab hold of the nipple. If the baby is very hungry, she may close her eyes in order to concentrate exclusively on bursts of sucking behavior, coordinating sucking and swallowing as efficiently as possible. But as the initial swallows of milk satisfy the strong hunger pangs, the baby pauses to take in other aspects of the situation. She may gaze at the contours of her mother's face, playfully lick the milk dripping from her mother's breast, smell the milk's fragrance and taste its special sweet taste, and listen to the sound of her mother's

Close, physical contact during nursing provides infants with a combination of sensory stimuli, sight, sound, smell, and touch that contribute to the formation of an early scheme for their mother.

voice offering comfort or inviting conversation. She may reach up to explore her mother's skin or relax in the comfort of her mother's gentle embrace. All the sensory information becomes integrated to create familiarity with this scenario, including a growing recognition of the mother and a rich mixture of sensory impressions associated with this special situation in which hunger is satisfied.

Motor Development

Organization and Progression of Motor and Movement Skills. At birth, an infant's voluntary muscle responses are poorly coordinated. Most early motor responses appear to be reflexive, meaning that a specific stimulus will evoke a particular motor response without any voluntary control or direction. Many of these built-in responses help infants survive and lead them to developing more complicated sequences of voluntary behavior. The sucking reflex is a good example. At birth, inserting something in an infant's mouth produces a sucking reflex. This helps infants gain nourishment relatively easily before sucking behavior is under their control. Before long, infants become skillful at controlling the strength and sensitivity of sucking behavior. They use sucking and mouthing as strategies for tactile exploration. Infants have been shown to use their mouths to explore objects that they can then identify visually, thus transferring information from the tactile sense to the visual sense (Meltzoff & Borton, 1979; Gibson & Walker, 1984).

Table 5.2 describes a number of common infant reflexes, the evoking stimulus, and the response. Infant reflexes include sucking, grasping, rooting (turning the head in the direction of the cheek that is stroked), coughing, and stepping. With time, many of these behaviors make a *transition from an involuntary to a voluntary behavior.* In the process, infants may lose a response before they regain control over simple movements. Then they blend several of these new voluntary movements into increasingly coordinated and complex patterns of behavior (Fentress & McLeod, 1986). For example,

TABLE 5.2 Some Reflexes of the Human Infant

Reflex	Evoking Stimulus	Response
Reflexes That Facilitate Adaptation and Survival		
Sucking reflex	Pressure on lips and tongue	Suction produced by movement of lips and tongue
Pupillary reflex	Weak or bright light	Dilation or constriction of pupil
Rooting reflex	Light touch to cheek	Head movement in direction of touch
Startle reflex	Loud noise	Similar to Moro reflex (below), with elbows flexed and fingers closed
Swimming reflex	Neonate placed prone in water	Arm and leg movement
Reflexes Linked to Competences of Related Species		
Creeping reflex	Feet pushed against a surface	Arms and legs drawn under, head lifted
Flexion reflex	Pressure on sole of foot	Involuntary bending of leg
Grasp reflex	Pressure on fingers or palm	Closing and tightening of fingers
Moro reflex	Infant lying on back with head raised—rapidly release head	Extension of arms, head thrown back, spreading of fingers, crossing arms across body
Springing reflex	Infant held upright and slightly forward	Arms extended forward and legs drawn up
Stepping reflex	Infant supported under the arms above a flat surface	Rhythmical stepping movement
Abdominal reflex	Tactile stimulation	Involuntary contraction of abdominal muscles
Reflexes of Unknown Function		
Achilles tendon reflex	Blow to Achilles tendon	Contraction of calf muscles and downward bending of foot
Babinski reflex	Mild stroke on sole of foot	Fanning and extension of toes
Tonic neck reflex	Infant on back with head turned to one side	Arm and leg on side toward which head is facing are extended, other arm and leg flexed

very young infants can support their full weight through the strength of their grasping reflex. When propped in an infant seat, they will reach and grasp reflexively at an object, reaching their target about 40% of the time. At 4 weeks of age, this reflexive reaching behavior seems to disappear, but by 5 months it is replaced by voluntary reaching, accurate grasping, clutching, and releasing (Bower, 1987).

The transition from involuntary to voluntary reaching and grasping results from genetically guided maturation coupled with repeated discovery, exploration, and practice of controlled, coordinated muscle movements, which are guided by visual and auditory cues, particularly cues about size, distance, and direction. In the following example, a 2-month-old girl gains control of her hands and fingers:

> She has discovered her hands, stares at them many times a day for three or four minutes at a time, watches them as she wiggles fingers, extends and flexes them, rotates wrists. She also clasps her hands together and stares at them out in front of her at arm's length. (Church, 1966, p. 7)

Voluntary reaching begins as the child tries to make contact with objects on the same side of the body as the outstretched hand. By 4 months, babies will reach for objects placed on the same side, the opposite side, or in the middle of the body. By this age, babies have also become skilled in using both hands to hold an object, so they are more able to keep the object close enough to investigate. They may shift from exploring with their fingers to sucking and biting to find out more about the object (Rochat, 1989). Between 5 and 7 months, babies become increasingly accurate at reaching and grasping a moving object, alternating hands to intercept an object by anticipating the direction of its movement (Robin et al., 1996). By 12 months, babies have mastered the pincer grasp, using their index finger and thumb to pick up tiny things, such as string and thread, pieces of dry cereal, and spaghetti noodles. With this advance, they can also manipulate things by lifting latches, turning knobs, and placing small things inside bigger things and trying to get them out again. These activities give the baby new information about how objects work and how they relate to one another. At the same time, they cause new conflicts between the baby and caregiver, who knows that tiny things that shouldn't are going to go into the mouth and objects that need to be left alone are going to be touched, moved, and manipulated.

Motor skills also develop as a result of physical growth and maturation of bones, muscles, and the nervous system. Figure 5.1 shows the normal sequence of development of motor and movement skills during the first year of life, however, babies vary in the sequence and rate at which they acquire these skills. Individual children grow in spurts, interspersed with times of slow growth and some periods of regression (Fischer & Rose, 1994). Usually, however, during the first 12 months babies begin to hold their heads up and roll over by themselves; they learn to reach for things and grasp them; they sit, crawl, stand, and walk. Parental expectations seem to influence the timing of the onset for some of the milestones (Hopkins & Westra, 1990). During the second year, walking becomes increasingly steady; crawling may be used for play but is no longer the preferred method for locomotion. Babies explore stairs, climbing up and down using a variety of strategies. They start to slide or jump down from modest heights. Each of these accomplishments requires practice, refinement, struggle, and, finally, mastery.

FIGURE 5.1

A typical sequence of motor development and locomotion in infancy

0 months	2½ months	3 months
Fetal posture	Chest up	Roll over
3½ months	5½ months	6 months
Sit with support	Sit alone	Stand holding furniture
9 months	11½ months	12 months
Walk when led	Stand alone	Walk alone

Although the normative pattern of motor development suggests a pre-programmed sequence of stages that is heavily guided by genetics and neural structures, recent research on the process of motor development challenges this assumption. Researchers now regard the regularities in motor behavior as the result of a dynamic process of exploration in which infants coordinate their physical actions with the demands and opportunities of the situation.

Perception and action work hand in hand, giving the infant information about the physical properties of the situation and feedback about the consequences of a specific motor strategy. Over time and with practice in similar situations, the infant discovers the combination of action, intensity, direction, and speed that will create the desired outcome. With additional practice, this pattern then becomes most likely and increasingly efficient (Thelen, 1995).

Consider Brad's efforts to crawl. He is placed face down in the middle of a brightly colored blanket. His mother kneels at the edge of the blanket and dangles a favorite stuffed bear. She smiles and says encouragingly, "Come on, Brad, come get Teddy." Brad looks intently, reaches toward the bear and by kicking and squirming, manages to move forward. This snakelike movement is Brad's first accomplishment en route to well-organized crawling. Before he masters crawling, however, he must learn to raise himself on his knees, coordinate hand and leg movements, and propel himself forward rather than backward. Most babies reach a point when they rock in a stationary position on all fours before they can crawl. In repeated observations of 15 infants as they made the transition to crawling, a key precursor was found to be the establishment of a strong hand preference. When infants fell from a seated position onto their hands, they tended to fall onto their nonpreferred hand so that the preferred hand was available to reach out and begin crawling. Confidence in being able to maintain one's body weight on one arm and two legs while reaching out with the preferred hand is part of the motor sequence necessary for forward crawling (Goldfield, 1989). The crawling behavior that tends to be regarded as natural and easily performed in infancy is in fact achieved by long and patient effort in the coordination of head and shoulder movement, reaching, and kicking.

The Contributions of Nature and Nurture in Motor Development. Motor development provides an excellent illustration of the interaction between the genetically guided plan for growth and the contributions of experience. The unfolding of motor capacities is guided by genetics, beginning as it does with the presence of a wide range of reflexive responses that are "hard wired" so to speak into the infant's neurological system. At the same time, within this plan, one observes both individual and group differences. Differences in motor behavior have been assessed along dimensions such as activity level, soothability, reactivity to stimuli, calm and fluid movement or spastic and jerky movement, and cuddliness (Brazelton et al., 1987). Not only are babies different from one another at birth, but they also show different rates of motor advancement.

Along with these individual differences are cultural differences in child-rearing practices that encourage certain types of motor behavior and restrict others. The following cross-cultural example illustrates this point. Among the Zinacantecos of southeastern Mexico, the newborn infant is draped in a long skirt held in place by a belt or wrap, as described here:

> Then the newborn is wrapped in additional layers of blankets to protect him from "losing parts of his soul." This swaddling acts as a constant suppressant to motor activity...Infants' faces are covered except during feedings, especially during the first three months, to ward off illness and the effects of the "evil eye." (Brazelton, 1977, p. 155)

Among the Zinacantecos, babies are rarely on the floor. Rather, they are held in the mother's lap, in her arms, or carried on her back. Mothers use breast-feeding as a frequent quieting strategy. They respond to any signs of restlessness or crying by offering the breast. In comparison to many U.S. parents, the Zinacanteco mothers rarely urged their babies to perform new motor behaviors and showed no special recognition or excitement when a new behavior was accomplished.

The Zinacanteco babies are quieter and less demanding than typical U.S. babies. Most of those evaluated in this study lagged behind U.S. babies by one month in motor development. Despite a very restrictive environment for motor development, they all showed about the same pattern of motor skill acquisition over the first year as did the U.S. infants.

This example suggests that motor behavior, like language, is shaped by the socialization context. Nurture plays a role in offering various opportunities for exploration and movement, and in modulating the pace and perhaps the style with which motor behaviors are expressed. The social context can either subdue and temper or evoke and encourage the way babies maneuver through their environment.

Temperament

Temperament is a theoretical construct that refers to relatively stable characteristics of response to the environment that can be observed during the first months of life (Thomas & Chess, 1980; Hubert et al., 1982; Lerner & Lerner, 1983). In early work on this construct, Escalona (1968) focused on individual differences among infants in the permeability of the boundary between the self and the stimulus environment, and the differential sensitivity of the infant to various sense modalities. Thomas, Chess, and Birch (1970) rated newborn infants on nine temperamental qualities: activity level, rhythmicity, approach/withdrawal, adaptability, intensity of reaction, threshold of responsiveness, quality of mood, distractibility, and attention span and persistence. These dimensions of temperament are closely linked to the sensory/motor system and to the adaptive mechanisms that infants have for orienting to and withdrawing from stimulation. Based on their research, Thomas, Chess, and Birch were able to classify infants into three temperamental groupings: Easy, Slow to Warm Up, and Difficult. Table 5.3 summarizes the characteristics of each of these temperaments and the percentages of the sample that could be clearly identified as one of the three categories. Roughly 35% of the sample could not be classified.

Several aspects of temperament, including activity level, sociability, and emotionality, are largely influenced by genetic factors (Thomas & Chess, 1977, 1986; Buss & Plomin, 1984, 1986; Goldsmith et al., 1987; Goldsmith & Campos, 1986; Wilson & Matheny, 1986; Braungart et al., 1992). In addition, dimensions of temperament, especially emotionality and activity level, show modest stability over adjacent periods of infancy and toddlerhood (Bates, 1987; Calkins & Fox, 1992).

A child's temperament influences the tone of interactions, the frequency with which interactions take place, the way others react to the child, and the way the child reacts to the reactions of others. Highly active, social children are likely to initiate interactions and to respond positively to the attentions of others. More passive, inhibited children will be less likely to initiate interactions and may withdraw when other children or adults direct attention to them. Many studies emphasize the relevance of the fit or match between the parent's temperament and that of the child (Plomin, 1990).

As an example, Aletha is an active, socially outgoing woman who has eagerly looked forward to motherhood. She has prepared her baby's room with brightly colored wallpaper. She likes to sing and listen to music, and she has even bought a cas-

TABLE 5.3	Three Types of Infant Temperament	
Type	Description	% of Total Sample
Easy	Positive mood, regular body functions, low or moderate intensity of reaction, adaptability, positive approach rather than withdrawal from new situations	40
Slow to Warm up	Low activity level, tendency to withdraw on first exposure to new stimuli, slow to adapt, somewhat negative in mood, low intensity of reaction to situations	15
Difficult	Irregular body functions, unusually intense reactions, tendency to withdraw from new situations, slow to adapt to change, generally negative mood	10

sette player so she and her baby can listen to music together. Her infant, Patrice, is very sensitive to stimulation and does not react well to novelty. Aletha is disappointed and frustrated that Patrice is so irritable. Patrice seems to cry every time Aletha turns on the tape player. The baby does not like to be bounced or jiggled, and she seems to withdraw whenever her mother tries to show her a new toy, tickle her, or try to evoke a response. As time goes along, Aletha simply lets Patrice lie in the bassinet for longer periods of the day. Aletha questions her ability to be a good mother and wonders if Patrice is abnormal.

One ought not overestimate the stability of infant temperament, however. Measures of temperament in infancy do not correlate all that highly with measures in the early and middle school years. In all likelihood, temperamental characteristics are modified as they come into contact with socialization pressures at home and at school, as well as with new internal capacities to regulate behavior. Thomas and Chess (1977, 1986) found that when parents were calm and allowed their difficult children to adapt to novelty at a leisurely pace, the children grew more comfortable and had an easier time adapting to new routines. However, if parents were impatient and demanding, then their difficult children remained difficult and had a hard time adjusting to new situations as they grew older. More research in this area is needed, especially studies that include assessments of parental values and beliefs, socioeconomic conditions, and subcultural context. These factors may influence a parent's perceptions of his or her child as easy or difficult as well as subsequent parenting practices (Bates, 1987).

Attachment

Have you ever wondered how feelings of love and connectedness form between babies and their caregivers? At birth, an infant could be taken home from the hospital by any adult and be perfectly content. The newborn baby has not yet clearly differentiated his or her parents from others. Yet, by the end of the first year of life, babies not only know their caregivers but also have very strong emotional preferences for these adults over all others. **Attachment** is the process through which people develop specific, positive emotional bonds with others. John Bowlby proposed the notion of the attachment behavior system as an organized pattern of infant signals and adult responses that lead to a protective, trusting relationship during the very earliest stage of development. The nurturing responses of the caregiver comprise a corresponding behavioral system that is often referred to as **parenting** or **care giving** (Bowlby, 1988; Ainsworth, 1985).

The construct of attachment introduced a perspective for understanding infant-caregiver interactions that was quite different from Freud's description of the oral stage. Freud emphasized a more dependent view of infants, using the symbol of nursing to highlight the infant's role as a passive recipient of nurturance and care. The oral stage is characterized by an initial fusion between the infant and the caregiver that is gradually differentiated through experiences of delay of gratification. In contrast, attachment highlights the active, social orientation of the infant in a behavioral system that is designed to protect the infant from harm. Many of the sensory and motor competencies described earlier in this chapter contribute to an infant's ability to establish a vivid mental scheme of the caregiver and to stimulate care-giving behaviors.

Certain patterns of caregiver-infant interaction in the first months of life contribute to the formation of attachment. One of the most significant of these is **synchrony** of interaction (Isabella & Belsky, 1991). Parent-infant pairs that show positive attachment relations at one year are characterized in the early months by interactions that are rhythmic, well timed, and mutually rewarding. When the caregiver is unresponsive to the infant's signals of distress, overly intrusive when the infant is calm, or underinvolved, a less positive attachment is formed. In addition to the quality of interactions, the quantity of interaction also plays a key role in establishing the infant's confidence about the caregiver's capacity to protect and comfort (Cox et al., 1992).

Evidence that an attachment has been formed is seen in at least three behaviors. First, infants try to maintain contact with the object of attachment (Ainsworth, 1973). Second, infants show distress when the object of attachment is absent (Schaffer & Emerson, 1964). Third, infants are more relaxed and comfortable with the object of attachment and more fretful with others (Bronson, 1973).

The Development of Attachment

Five Sequential Stages. Ainsworth (1973, 1985) described a series of five stages in the development of attachment (Table 5.4). In the first stage, during the first three months of life, infants engage in a variety of behaviors, including sucking, rooting, grasping, smiling, gazing, cuddling, and visual tracking, which serve to maintain closeness with a caregiver or bring the caregiver to the infant. However, these behaviors do not appear to be aimed at a specific person. Through these contacts, babies learn about the unique features of their caregivers.

In the second stage, from about 3 to 6 months, an infant's attachment is expressed through preferential responsiveness to a few familiar figures. Infants smile more at the familiar person than at a stranger, show more excitement at that person's arrival, and appear to be upset when he or she leaves.

In the third stage, from about 6 to 9 months, babies seek physical proximity with the objects of attachment. The ability to crawl and to coordinate reaching and grasping contribute to greater control over the outcomes of their actions.

In the fourth stage, from about 9 to 12 months, babies form the first internal representation of their caregivers. This internal representation provides the first robust working model of an attachment relationship. Specific characteristics of a caregiver and patterns of expectations about how a caregiver will respond to the infant's actions are organized into a complex attachment scheme—the internal, mental representations of the anticipated responses of a caregiver.

In the fifth stage, in toddlerhood and later, young children use a variety of behaviors to influence the behavior of their parents and other objects of attachment in order to satisfy their own needs for closeness. Children may ask to be read to, cuddled at bedtime, and taken along on errands. These are strategies that they develop to produce caregiver behaviors that will satisfy their continuing needs for physical contact, closeness, and love.

As children mature, they begin to conceptualize new risks and threats to their security. They may initiate new strategies for maintaining closeness to the objects of their attachment. Especially when they are undergoing unusual stress, as in times of illness, divorce, or rejection, children of any age who have a secure attachment may try to activate the attachment system by sending signals that will result in comforting and closeness.

Stranger Anxiety. During the second half of the first year, two signs of the child's growing attachment to a specific person are observed: stranger anxiety and separation anxiety. **Stranger anxiety** is the baby's discomfort or tension in the presence of unfamiliar adults. Babies vary in how they express their protest to strangers and in how intensely they react. They may cling to their parents, refuse to be held, stiffen at the stranger's touch, or merely avert their eyes from the stranger's face.

The baby's response to a stranger will depend on some very specific dimensions of the situation, including how close the mother is, how the stranger approaches the baby, and how the mother responds to the stranger (Keltenbach et al., 1980). For example, if a mother speaks in a positive tone of voice to her baby about a stranger, the baby's

---

TABLE 5.4   Five Sequential Stages in the Development of Attachment

Stage	Age	Characteristics
1	Birth to 3 months	Infant uses sucking, rooting, grasping, smiling, gazing, cuddling, and visual tracking to maintain closeness with caregivers.
2	3 to 6 months	Infant is more responsive to familiar figures than to strangers.
3	6 to 9 months	Infant seeks physical proximity and contact with object(s) of attachment.
4	9 to 12 months	Infant forms internal mental representation of object of attachment, including expectations about the caregiver's typical responses to signals of distress.
5	12 months and older	Child uses a variety of behaviors to influence the behavior of the objects of attachment in ways that will satisfy needs for safety and closeness.

With her mother close by, this baby is cautiously exploring a stranger's face. The baby's reaction to the stranger is influenced by her mother's reassuring manner.

response to the stranger is likely to be positive (Feinman & Lewis, 1983). The baby's response will also be influenced by the amount of prior experience with unfamiliar adults. Normally, wariness of strangers is taken as a positive sign—that is, babies are able to detect the differences between their parents and adults they do not know. Of course, wariness of strangers continues to be expressed throughout life. In fact, one often sees more distinct expressions of suspiciousness or fear among adults encountering strangers than among babies.

Separation Anxiety. At about 9 months, infants give another indication of the intensity of their attachment to their parents by expressing rage and despair when their parents leave. This reaction is called **separation anxiety.** Separation can evoke two different kinds of behavior. Under some conditions, separation from the caregiver will stimulate attachment behaviors, especially efforts to find the caregiver and regain physical contact (Ainsworth et al., 1971). Separation can also evoke protest, despair, or detachment, depending on the length of the separation (Bowlby, 1960; Robertson & Robertson, 1989).

Separation from the mother for periods of 30 minutes has been identified as a distinct source of stress for babies 9 months of age and older. Neurological and biochemical evidence of stress, including increases in adrenocortical activity and concentrations of cortisol in the saliva, were associated with 30 minutes of separation from the mother in a laboratory situation (Larson et al., 1991; Gunnar et al., 1992). The impact of stressful separations can be seen in the disruption of basic physical patterns, especially sleep disturbances. The effects of prolonged periods of maternal separation, as when a mother goes away to attend a conference or for a brief vacation, can also be observed in the childcare setting in regression to more immature forms of play behavior, aimless wandering, and altered interactions with peers and teachers (Field, 1991).

The baby's response to separation depends on the conditions. Infants are less distressed when mothers leave them alone in a room at home than when they do so in a laboratory (Ross et al., 1975). They are less likely to protest if the mother leaves the door to the room open than if she closes the door as she leaves. The protest response to separation seems to be tied to the baby's strong desire to maintain contact with the object of attachment. The importance of contact may be to (1) meet physical needs, (2) help the child overcome physical barriers, (3) provide protection or comfort, or (4) provide novel and stimulating interactions (Hay, 1980). When there are high levels of responsiveness and warmth in the parent-infant relationship, the infant has many reasons to want to maintain access to the caregiver.

Babies' responses to separation may also be related to their temperament (Gunnar et al., 1992; Gunnar et al., 1989; and Izard et al., 1991). Babies who have a strong negative reaction to uncertainty, those who are especially distressed when they are confined or prevented from attaining a goal, and those who are upset by novelty or who tend to withdraw from it may find the experience of separation more stressful than others. Unique strategies of care-giving might be needed to buffer these babies from the stressful impact of separation.

We expect babies to become more flexible over time about parents' temporary departures. Young children learn to tolerate brief separations. At 2 years of age, children are able to use a photograph of their mother to help sustain their adaptation to a new setting in the mother's absence (Passman & Longeway, 1982). By the age of 3, children may even look forward to a night with a baby-sitter or an afternoon at grandfather's house. Once the attachment is fully established, children can comfort themselves by creating mental images of their parents and by remembering their parents' love for them. During infancy, however, the parents' physical presence remains a focal point of attention and concern.

Formation of Attachments with Mother, Father, and Others

An infant may establish an attachment with any person who is performing a large portion of the child-care activities. Most commonly, the first object of attachment is the mother, but fathers, siblings, grandparents, and childcare professionals also become objects of attachment. Infants are likely to have the same type of attachment with their fathers and their mothers, but these relationships are established independently and depend on the time spent together and the quality of interactions (Fox et al., 1991). Early studies found that babies tended to have playful interactions with their fathers—smiling, laughing, and looking—and comforting, stress-reducing interactions with their mothers. When only one parent was present, the babies showed evidence of attachment to that parent. However, when both parents were present, babies demonstrated a different pattern of interaction with each (Lamb, 1976). In a more recent study of 126 firstborn sons, 60% were found to have secure attachments with their fathers at 13 months of age (Belsky, 1996).

In Israel, kibbutz-reared infants showed great similarity between their attachment to their fathers and to their specially trained caregiver (called metapelet). However, there was no consistent pattern of similarity in the quality of their attachments to mother and father and to mother and metapelet (Sagi et al., 1985). In subsequent research, when these kibbutz-reared children had reached the age of 5, the quality of their infant attachment to the metapelet was a significant predictor of their socioemotional development as observed in school and at free play in their dormitory (Oppenheim et al., 1988). This research suggests that infants are able to have a variety of attachment relationships. Exactly how the infant synthesizes the internal representations of various attachments is not well-understood. Possibly the distinct relationships have relevance for different interpersonal domains or become central as individuals assume a variety of social roles (Bretherton, 1985; Bridges et al., 1988).

Patterns of Attachment

The quality of attachment varies from family to family and from one parent-child pair to another. The adults' acceptance of the infant and their ability to respond to his or her varying communications are important to a secure attachment. The parents' patterns of expressing affection and rejection will influence how well babies can meet their strong needs for reassurance and comfort (Tracy & Ainsworth, 1981).

The Strange Situation. Differences in the quality of attachment have been highlighted by observations of babies and their caregivers in a standard laboratory procedure called the **Strange Situation** (Ainsworth et al., 1978; Bretherton, 1990). During an approximately 20-minute period, the child is exposed to a sequence of events that are likely to stimulate the attachment system (Table 5.5). The infant and caregiver enter an unfamiliar laboratory environment, a stranger enters, the caregiver leaves briefly, and the caregiver and infant experience opportunities for reunion. During this situation, researchers have the opportunity to make systematic observations of the child's behaviors, the caregiver's behaviors, and characteristics of their interactions, as well as to compare these behaviors across varying segments of the situation.

Four Patterns of Quality of Attachment. Four patterns of attachment behavior have been distinguished using the Strange Situation methodology: (1) secure attachment, (2) anxious-avoidant, (3) anxious-resistant, and (4) disorganized attachment. In American samples, about two-thirds of the children tested have been characterized as securely attached. Of the remainder, more children fall into the anxious-avoidant category than into the anxious-resistant category (Ainsworth et al., 1978). Only a small percentage of infants show the disorganized pattern (van Ijzendoorn et al., 1992; Carlson et al., 1989; Radke-Yarrow et al., 1985). More research is needed in order to identify subsequent developmental outcomes linked to this attachment pattern, but it is likely that this highly disorganized attachment will be shown to be associated with very serious mental health problems in later childhood and beyond.

Infants who have a **secure attachment** actively explore their environment and interact with strangers while their mothers are present. After separation, the babies actively greet their mothers or seek interaction. If the babies were distressed during separation,

TABLE 5.5   The Strange Situation Laboratory Procedure

Episode	Duration	Participants*	Events
1	30 sec.	M, B, O	O shows M and B into the room. Instructs M on where to put B down and where to sit; O leaves.
2	3 min.	M, B	M puts B down close to her chair, at a distance from the toys. She responds to B's social bids but does not initiate interaction. B is free to explore. If B does not move after 2 minutes, M may take B to the toy area.
3	3 min.	M, B, S	This episode has three parts. S enters, greets M and B, and sits down opposite M without talking for 1 minute. During the 2nd minute, S engages M in conversation. S then joins B on the floor, attempting to engage B in play for 1 minute. At the end of this episode, M leaves "unobtrusively" (B usually notices).
4	3 min.	B, S	S sits on her chair. She responds to B's social bids but does not initiate social interaction. If B becomes distressed, S attempts to comfort B. If this is not effective, M returns before 3 minutes are up.
5	3 min.	M, B	M calls B's name outside the door and enters (S leaves unobtrusively). If B is distressed, M comforts B and tries to reengage B in play. If B is not distressed, M goes to sit on her chair, taking a responsive, noninitiating role. At the end of the episode, M leaves, saying, "Bye-bye; I'll be back."
6	3 min.	B	B remains alone. If B becomes distressed, the episode is curtailed and S enters.
7	3 min.	B, S	S enters, comforting B if required. If she cannot comfort B, the episode is curtailed. If B calms down or is not distressed, S sits on her chair, taking a responsive role as before.
8	3 min.	M, B	M returns (S leaves unobtrusively). M behaves as in episode 5.

*O = observer; M = mother; B = baby; S = stranger.
SOURCE: Bretherton, 1990.

the mothers' return reduces their distress and the babies return to exploration of the environment. Infants who show an **anxious-avoidant attachment** avoid contact with their mothers after separation or ignore their efforts to interact. They show less distress at being alone than other babies. Infants who show an **anxious-resistant attachment** are very cautious in the presence of the stranger. Their exploratory behavior is noticeably disrupted by the caregiver's departure. When the caregiver returns, the infants appear to want to be close to the caregiver, but they are also angry, so that they are very hard to soothe or comfort. In the **disorganized attachment**, babies' responses are particularly notable in the reunion sequence. In the other three attachment patterns, infants appear to use a coherent strategy for managing the stress of the situation. The disorganized babies have no consistent strategy. They behave in contradictory, unpredictable ways that seem to convey feelings of extreme fear or utter confusion (Belsky et al., 1996).

Within the home environment, babies who have a secure attachment are observed to cry less than other babies (Tracy & Ainsworth, 1981; Ainsworth, 1985). They greet their mothers more positively upon reunion after everyday separations, and appear to respond more cooperatively to their mothers' requests. One can sense that securely attached babies have a working model of attachment in which they expect their caregiver to be accessible and responsive.

Mothers of babies who were characterized as anxious-avoidant seem to reject their babies. It is almost as if they were angry at their babies. They spend less time holding and cuddling their babies than other mothers, and more of their interactions appear to be unpleasant or even hurtful. At home these babies cry a lot, they are not readily soothed by contact with the caregiver, and yet they appear to be quite distressed by separations.

Infants who are characterized as anxious-resistant have mothers who are inconsistent in their responsiveness. Sometimes these mothers ignore clear signals of distress. At other times they interfere with their infants in order to make contact. Although these mothers appear to be able to enjoy close physical contact with their babies, they do not necessarily do so in ways appropriate to the baby's needs. The result is the formation of an internal representation of attachment that is highly unpredictable. These babies try to maintain proximity and to avoid unfamiliar situations that increase uncertainty about accessibility to their caregiver.

More research is needed to characterize the home environment behaviors of children who have been identified as having a disorganized-insecure attachment. This categorization is overrepresented among mothers who have serious deficits in maternal behaviors and may be linked to a variety of psychological problems in the mother, including abusive tendencies, depression, and other mental illnesses. These mothers are likely to be psychologically unavailable and unpredictable (van Ijzendoorn et al., 1992).

Parental Sensitivity and the Quality of Attachment

How can we account for differences in the quality of the attachment? Early work on the formation of a secure attachment argued that a cornerstone in this process was maternal sensitivity (Ainsworth et al., 1978). **Sensitivity** is generally defined as attentiveness to the infant's state, accurate interpretation of the infant's signals, and well-timed responses that promote mutually rewarding interactions (Isabella et al., 1989). Mothers who are psychologically available, responsive, consistent, and warm in their interactions with their babies, especially during the first 6 months of the baby's life, are found to be most successful in establishing a secure attachment relationship that can be measured by the time the baby is 12 months old.

Four general factors come into play in producing the kind of sensitivity that underlies secure attachments (Figure 5.2). First, cultural and subcultural differences are integrated into one's mental representation of a parental or care-giving person. The culture's beliefs about infants, including how fragile or vulnerable they are, how best to respond to their signals of distress, and what skills or temperamental qualities are most valued, are likely to shape a caregiver's practices (Coll, 1990). The study of attachment-related responses across American ethnic subgroups is grossly incomplete. However, some examples suggest how a cultural worldview influences the pattern of

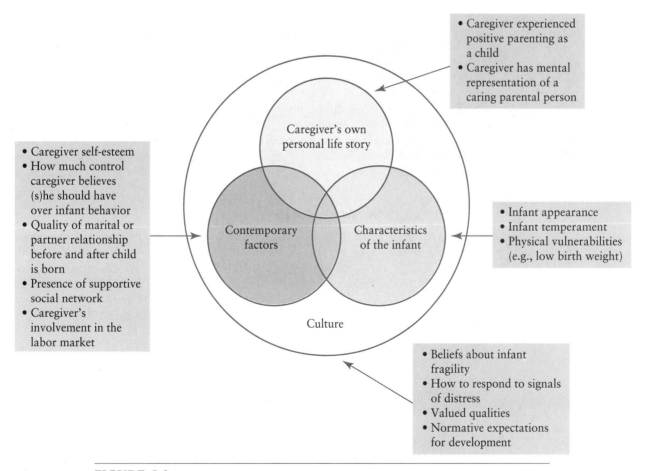

FIGURE 5.2
Factors affecting caregiver's sensitivity to infant's needs

parental responsiveness and sensitivity. In a comparison of working-class African-American, Chicano, and Anglo parents, the African-American and Chicano parents valued moving beyond the dependency of infancy as soon as possible (Bartz & Levine, 1978). Thus, they expected their children to show earlier autonomy and responsibility for their behavior than the Anglo group. This difference translated into earlier weaning and toileting, as well as the expectation of earlier walking and gaining control over the expression of feelings. Another study compared Anglo, African-American, and Cuban-American mothers' perceptions of infant crying and related responses (Zeskind, 1983). The African-American mothers were least likely to perceive their babies' cries as urgent or distressing, and in line with this perception, they were least likely to cuddle their babies. The Cuban-American mothers were most likely to soothe their babies with a pacifier and by cuddling and responding quickly to their babies' cries. These comparisons suggest distinct normative patterns of care giving across ethnic groups.

Second, aspects of the caregiver's own personal life story contribute to being able to serve as a secure base for a child. Adults who recall their own parents as accepting, responsive, and available are more likely to be able to transmit those qualities as they enact the caregiver role. Adults who have experienced early loss or disruption of an attachment relationship themselves have more difficulty providing a secure base for their offspring (Fonagy et al., 1991; Belsky, 1996).

Third, contemporary factors can influence the ability of an adult to provide a secure base for attachment. Among them are the caregiver's self-esteem, the degree of control the caregiver believes he or she should have over the infant's behavior, the quality of the relationship with the intimate partner or spouse both before and after the child is born, the presence of a supportive social network that validates the person's care giving efforts, and the person's involvement in the labor market (Chase-Lansdale & Owen, 1987; Donovan & Leavitt, 1989; Howes & Markman, 1989; Jacobson & Frye, 1991). All these factors can influence the caregiver's sensitivity to the infant's signals.

Fourth, the quality of the attachment can be influenced by characteristics of the infants. Certain aspects of the infant's temperament, especially fearfulness, sociability, and the intensity of negative emotions, may influence the way the attachment relationship is established (Izard et al., 1991). Most studies have shown, however, that temperament per se does not determine whether or not a secure attachment can be established. Rather, it influences the kinds of caregiver responses that are most likely to create an internal sense of security for the infant (Thompson et al., 1988; Vaughn et al., 1989).

The Relevance of Attachment to Later Development

Long-term benefits of a secure attachment have been documented. Secure attachments in infancy have been associated with positive adaptive capacities when the child is 3 to 5 years old. Securely attached infants become preschoolers who show greater resilience, self-control, and curiosity (Vaughn et al., 1979). In contrast, infants who have a disorganized attachment are very hostile, aggressive preschoolers. A new clinical diagnosis—reactive attachment disorder—has been linked to serious disturbances in infant attachment. Two expressions of this disorder have been described: inhibited type, in which the person is very withdrawn, hypervigilant in social contacts, and resistant to comfort; and uninhibited type, in which the person shows a lack of discrimination, being overly friendly and attaching to any new person (DeAngelis, 1997).

From a life-span perspective, the quality of the attachment formed in infancy influences the formation of later relationships (Ainsworth, 1989). Children who have formed secure attachments are likely to find more enjoyment in close peer friendships during their preschool years (Park & Waters, 1989). Consequently, children who have secure maternal attachments are more likely to attribute positive intentions to peers, whereas children with anxious attachments are more likely to view peers with wariness.

The attachment construct continues to be evident in adult, loving relationships. This mother and daughter enjoy physical closeness, comfort each other, and look to each other for reassurance in times of stress.

Furthermore, it makes sense that the cognitive representation one forms of an attachment relationship influences one's expectations of an intimate partner. Adult love relationships can be characterized along many of the same dimensions as infant attachments, including the desire to maintain physical contact with the loved one, increased disclosure and responsiveness to the loved one, the effectiveness of the loved one in providing comfort and reassurance that reduce distress, and an element of exclusiveness or preferential response to the loved one.

The parenting relationship can also be understood as an elaboration of the attachment representation. Adults who have experienced a secure attachment in their own infancy are more likely to be able to comfort and respond to their children. Adults whose childhood attachments were unpredictable or even hostile are more likely to have difficulty coping successfully with young infants' needs (Ricks, 1985).

It would be a mistake to assume that the quality of adult love relationships or parental behavior is determined solely by the quality of childhood attachments. Many experiences and concepts intervene to modify the attachment representation and to expand one's capacity to love another person after infancy. However, a growing body of work links the quality of early attachments with a person's orientation to and capacity for social relationships within the context of friendships, intimate relationships, and parent-child relations.

Sensorimotor Intelligence and Early Causal Schemes

Think for a moment of a familiar experience such as tying your shoelaces. The pattern of tying the shoelace unfolds with little, if any, language involved. In fact, the task of explaining to a young child how to tie a shoelace is particularly difficult because very few words or concepts are part of the process. This kind of motor routine is an example of **sensorimotor intelligence.** When infants begin to adapt their sucking reflex to make it more effective, or when they use different techniques of sucking for the breast and the bottle, they are demonstrating sensorimotor intelligence. The familiar scheme for sucking is modified so that it takes into account the special properties of the breast and the bottle, depending on the situation.

How Do Infants Organize Their Experiences?

According to Piaget's (1970) theory of cognitive development, the chief mechanism governing the growth of intelligence during infancy is **sensorimotor adaptation.** From the very earliest days of life, infants use their reflexes to explore their world. At the same time, they gradually alter their reflexive responses to take into account the unique properties of objects around them. Infants do not make use of the conventional symbolic system of language to organize experience. Rather, they form concepts through perception and direct investigation of the environment. The notion of sensorimotor intelligence, then, encompasses the elaboration of patterns of movement and sensory experiences that the child comes to recognize in association with specific environmental events.

According to an emerging view, sometimes referred to as the Theory theory, infants form theories about how their world operates and modify them as new information is gathered. The infant starts out with some basic sensory, motor, and cognitive organizational structures. With each new challenge, a process of adaptation results in the revision of basic schemes to better predict and interpret experience (Gopnick &

Meltzoff, 1997). For example, Ruby, who is 12 months old, may be surprised and upset when her grandmother scolds her as she reaches for a shiny glass bowl on the table. Grandmother knows that the bowl will break if Ruby pushes it off the table. By 16 months, Ruby warily watches her grandmother's face as she reaches for the bowl, and may withdraw her hand if she sees Grandma frown or hears the sharp "NO!" that has come to be associated with "Don't touch." Ruby has developed a theory that she should not touch the bowl, which she cautiously tests by reaching and watching for the response.

One of the most important components of sensorimotor intelligence is the capacity to anticipate that certain actions will have specific effects on objects in the environment. Infants develop an understanding of **causality** based largely on sensory and motor experience. Babies discover that if they cry, Mama will come to them; if they kick a chair, it will move; and if they let go of a spoon, it will fall to the floor. These predictable sequences are learned through repetition and experimentation. The predictability of the events depends on the consistency with which objects in the world respond as well as on the child's initiation of the action. Babies learn to associate specific actions with regularly occurring outcomes. They also experiment with their own actions to determine the variety of events that a single behavior may cause (Keil, 1975; Rovee & Rovee, 1969). Eventually they are able to work backward: They can select a desirable outcome and then perform the behavior that will produce it.

The Development of Causal Schemes

The achievement of complex, purposeful causal behaviors develops gradually during the first two years of life. This achievement requires that infants have an understanding of the properties of objects in their environment and a variety of strategies for manipulating those objects. They must be able to select the most effective strategies for coordinating actions to achieve specific goals. The dynamics of this process are illustrated in a study of the emergence of the use of a spoon as a tool for eating (Connolly & Dalgleish, 1989). The infants were observed once a month for six months in their home during a meal time. At first, actions involving the spoon appeared to focus on exploration of the spoon itself. The infants banged the spoon, sucked it, or rubbed it in their hair. Then the babies showed an understanding of the purpose of the spoon as a tool by repeating the action sequence of dipping the spoon in the dish and bringing it to the mouth. However, no food was on the spoon. In the third phase, babies began to integrate the function and the action by loading the spoon with food and then bringing it to the mouth. During this phase, they made so many errors that very little food actually got to the mouth via the spoon. Finally, babies were able to coordinate the action and the function by using the other hand to steady the bowl, altering the angle of the spoon, picking up food they had dropped, and devising other strategies to enhance the function, depending on the type of food involved. Here we see a demonstration of how one rather complex motor behavior becomes part of a problem-solving action sequence during the sensorimotor period of development.

Piaget and Inhelder (1966/1969) described six phases in the development of causal schemes (Table 5.6). Subsequent research and related theoretical revisions confirm these levels of cognitive development (Fischer & Silvern, 1985). In phase one, *reflexes,* cause and effect are linked through the involuntary reflexive responses. The built-in stimulus-response systems of key reflexes are viewed as the genetic origin of intelligence. Babies suck, grasp, and root in response to specific types of stimulation. Piaget viewed the reflexes as adaptive learning systems. In detailed observations of

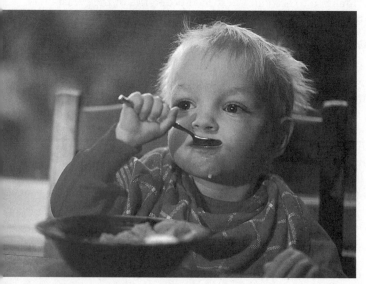

Spoon use illustrates the gradual coordination of actions and outcomes in the development of purposeful behavior.

Phase	Approximate age	Characteristic	Example
1. Reflexes	From birth	Reflexive responses to specific stimuli	Grasp reflex
2. First habits	From 2nd week	Use of reflexive responses to explore new stimuli	Grasp rattle
3. Circular reactions	From 4th month	Use of familiar actions to achieve new goals	Grasp rattle and make banging noise on table
4. Coordination of means and ends	From 8th month	Deliberate use of actions to achieve new goals	Grasp rattle and shake to play with dog
5. Experimentation with new means	From 11th month	Modification of actions to reach goals	Use rattle to bang a drum
6. Insight	From 18 months	Mental recombination of means and ends	Use rattle and string to make a new toy

TABLE 5.6
Six phases in the development of sensorimotor causality
SOURCE: Adapted from Piaget & B. Inhelder, 1969.

his youngest child, Laurent, he noted day-to-day changes in sucking behavior during the first month of life. Laurent became increasingly directed in groping for the breast and also appeared to form very early associations between those situations in which he would be fed and those in which he would not (Gratch & Schatz, 1987; Piaget, 1936/1952).

In the second phase, *first habits,* the reflexive responses are used to explore a wider range of stimuli. Babies explore toys, fingers, parents' noses, and blankets by sucking on them. Gradually, they discover the unique properties of objects and modify their responses according to the demands of those objects. The fact that a baby can satisfy his or her own need to suck by bringing an object to the mouth is a very early form of purposive causal behavior.

The third and fourth phases involve coordination of means and ends, at first with familiar situations and then with new ones. In the third phase, *circular reactions,* babies connect an action with an expected outcome (Wentworth & Haith, 1992). They shake a rattle and expect to hear a noise; they drop a spoon and expect to hear a noise when it hits the floor; they pull Daddy's beard and expect to hear an "ouch." They do not yet understand why the specific action leads to the expected outcome, but they will signal surprise when the expected outcome does not follow.

In the fourth phase, *coordination of means and ends,* infants use familiar actions or means to achieve new outcomes. They may shake a rattle to startle Mommy or pull Daddy's beard to force him to look away from the television set. The means and the outcomes have become quite distinct. There can be no question about the purposiveness of behavior at this point.

Coordination of means and ends are likely to be very closely tied to a specific context at this stage. For example, a baby may know how to make certain kicking motions to move a mobile or to get a toy to jiggle in the crib. But in another room with the same toy, the baby may not make the same connection. This may explain why babies might perform less competently in the laboratory environment than they do at home. Many of the causal strategies that become part of a baby's daily repertoire are supported by the context of a familiar environment (Rovee-Collier, et al., 1992).

The fifth phase, *experimentation with new means,* begins as children experiment with familiar means to achieve new goals. When familiar strategies do not work, children will modify them in light of the situation. One can think of this stage as sensorimotor problem solving. Children will try to reach a drawer by standing on a box, to fix a broken toy with a string, or to make a gift by wrapping a toy in a piece of tissue.

The last phase in the development of sensorimotor causality, *insight,* involves mental manipulation of means-end relationships. Instead of actually going through a variety of physical manipulations, children carry out trial-and-error problem-solving activities and planning in their minds, anticipating outcomes. They can sort out possible solutions and reject some without actually having to try them out. The result is insight. Mental experimentation brings the child to the best solution, which is the only one necessary to enact.

The capacity to perceive oneself as a causal agent and to predict the outcome of one's actions is essential to all subsequent experiences of mastery. This capacity is the cornerstone of the development of a sense of competence. It involves investigation of the environment, directed problem solving, and persistence toward a goal (Yarrow et al., 1983; MacTurk et al., 1987). Furthermore, adults' abilities to formulate a plan, execute it, and evaluate its outcome depend on this skill.

Understanding the Nature of Objects and Creating Categories

Rather than being passive spectators, babies are active explorers of their environment (Rochat, 1989). From birth they try to make direct sensory contact with objects. They reach for, grasp, and mouth objects. They track objects visually, altering their gaze to maintain contact with them. Although not all manipulative behavior is exploratory, certain combinations of mouthing, looking, and manipulating objects have been categorized as a type of examining behavior that provides infants as young as five months of age with a scheme for gathering information about novel objects (Ruff et al., 1992). As products of this active engagement with the object world, two related but independent aspects of infant intelligence develop: an understanding of the nature of objects and the ability to categorize similar ones.

The Nature of Objects

Through looking, manipulating, and examining, infants establish that objects have basic properties. In the discussion of vision on p. 143, we pointed out that very young babies recognize the contours of objects and that by 4 months they seem to perceive objects just as adults would. That is, babies see objects as separate from each other, defined by boundaries, taking up space, having depth, and having certain attributes of weight, color, malleability, texture, and the capacity to contain something else or not. All of these properties influence the types of actions infants use to explore the objects and the ways they are eventually woven into other actions (Sera et al., 1988; MacLean & Schuler, 1989; Palmer, 1989; Spelke et al., 1989).

Object Permanence. One of the most carefully documented of these properties is **object permanence** (Wellman et al., 1986). Piaget (1954) argued that understanding the properties of objects was one of the foundations of logical thought. He discussed the scheme for object permanence as a gradual process through which infants develop the concept that objects in the environment are permanent and do not cease to exist when they are out of reach or out of view. A permanent object retains its physical properties even when it cannot be seen.

Piaget suggested that initially the infant is aware of only those objects that are in the immediate perceptual field. If a 6-month-old girl is playing with a rattle, it exists for her. If the rattle drops out of her hand or is taken away, she may show some immediate distress but will not pursue the object. In a very real sense, out of sight is out of mind. The attainment of the concept of the permanent object frees children from total reliance on what they can see. The ability to hold the image of an object in the mind is the first step in the emergence of complex representational thinking.

To understand object permanence, we might remove a rattle from a baby's grasp and hide it under a cushion. If the baby makes no effort to pursue the rattle, we can assume that he or she has no sense of its continued existence. However, if the baby pursues the rattle and looks for it under the cushion, we take our experiment one step further. Again, we take the rattle from the baby and place it under the cushion. Then we remove it from beneath that cushion and place it under a second one. This transition from cushion one to cushion two takes place in the child's full view. The normal adult would go directly to the second cushion to retrieve the rattle. The child who has developed a sense of object permanence will also do this. Some children, however, will look for the rattle beneath the first cushion and, not finding it, cease their search. Slightly older children will trace the movement of the rattle exactly by looking first under cushion one and then under cushion two. The last two groups of children have learned some of the steps in pursuing an object but have not yet attained the concept of object permanence.

Progress in developing the concept of object permanence can be traced through the child's reactions when objects are removed from the perceptual field or displaced from one location to another (Harris, 1975; Bertenthal & Fischer, 1983; Sophian & Yengo, 1985). Babies as young as 9 months can understand that an object has been moved from one location to another. If they are permitted to search for an object immediately after it is hidden, they are effective in finding it. However, if the babies have to wait for 5 or 10 seconds before they can search, or if the object has been moved from one container to another similar container, they may become confused. By the age of about 17 months, infants can solve complex object permanence tasks in which objects are moved from one hiding place to the next in such a way that the infant cannot follow the path of the object (Gopnik & Meltzoff, 1987). However, even 2-year-olds can get confused if the object is displaced more than two or three times.

Certain experiences help build the scheme for object permanence. Babies who are adept at crawling or who have mobility through the use of an infant walker seem to be more effective in their search strategies when objects are hidden from view (Benson & Uzgiris, 1985; Kermoian & Campos, 1988). As babies gain greater control over their movement through the environment, they are better able to use landmarks other than their own body to locate objects. They can also experiment with the notion of leaving and retrieving objects, and discovering familiar objects in novel locations.

Precursors of Object Permanence. There is some controversy among scholars about the age at which infants understand that objects continue to exist when they are hidden from view. Piaget suggested that the capacity to understand that objects continue to exist requires a level of representational or symbolic thinking, which would permit an infant to hold the idea of the object in mind while it was hidden. It also requires a combination of sensory motor capacities that permit the infant to become actively engaged in reaching, tracking, and uncovering hidden objects and learning about the spatial properties of objects in the environment. Thus, according to Piaget, the first real evidence that infants have the ability to pursue a hidden object could not really be observed much before 8 or 9 months of age, when babies begin to crawl. And the full confidence in an object's permanence could probably not emerge much before 16 to 18 months, when infants have access to representational thinking. By this age, infants can imagine various movements and displacements of objects without actually viewing them.

In a series of experiments, Renee Baillargeon has tried to determine how infants evaluate objects that are hidden from view. One of the features of her experiments is that she has deleted the motor search component. Most of her experiments use infant looking time as the evidence of habituation in pretest conditions and reaction in the test conditions. Even at very early ages, before infants can search for and retrieve objects, they appear to have a memory of the locations of objects and can anticipate that they take up space (Baillargeon, 1987; Baillargeon & Graber, 1988). In more recent experiments, infants as young as 4 months were able to retain the image of an object as it disappeared behind a screen and showed surprise when the object emerged from the screen when it ought to have been blocked (Baillargeon & DeVos, 1991). (Figure 5.3 describes the experiment).

The question remains whether an infant's visual response to hidden objects is evidence that object permanence exists long before Piaget expected. Baillargeon argues that her evidence supports the view that infants as young as 3.5 to 4 months can represent the continued existence of objects when they are out of view. Others suggest that Baillargeon's visual task highlights an important perceptual precursor of the more complex scheme for the permanent object. They consider the infant's ability to anticipate an object's trajec-

HABITUATION EVENT

TEST EVENTS
Possible event

Impossible event

Prior to the experiment, the infant explores the toy care and the mouse. The infant sits on a parent's lap facing the apparatus. In the *Familiarization* Phase, the infant sees the mouse sitting on the track or behind the track with the screen raised. In the *Habituation* Phase, the screen is lifted and then lowered, then the car is pushed down the ramp at the left, rolling across the apparatus behind the screen, and continuing out the right side. These trials continued until habituation was achieved. In the *Impossible* test, the mouse was placed on top of the track, the screen was raised so the baby could see the mouse, then the screen was lowered, the car was propelled down the track, and emerged at the other side of the screen rolling off to the right. The *Possible* test was the same as the *Impossible* test except that the mouse was placed about 10 cm behind the track so that it would not impede the rolling car.

FIGURE 5.3
Habituation and test events in a study of object permanence
SOURCE: Baillargeon & DeVos, 1991.

tory behind a screen as an early step in a sequence of abilities that will eventually produce the complex search process that Piaget described (Fischer & Bidell, 1992).

Object Permanence and Attachment. The process through which infants establish a scheme for objects as permanent and subject to all the laws of nature is closely linked to their understanding of themselves and their relationships with others. Each step taken to analyze and organize the object world provides insight about self as well as about others.

The scheme for the permanent object applies to both humans and inanimate objects. One reason babies experience separation anxiety is that they do not have the certainty that a person to whom they are attached will continue to exist when that person is out of sight or inaccessible. Once the infant has a clear understanding of object permanence, the fear that a loved caregiver may vanish when he or she leaves the house is reduced. Interestingly, some qualities of maternal care are associated with the emergence of object permanence during the first seven months of life. The babies of mothers who communicate with them frequently, who express positive feelings toward them, and who actively stimulate their achievements are more likely to apply the scheme of permanence to people as well as things (Chazan, 1981). The growth of attachment and the achievement of object permanence are mutually enhancing.

The Categorization of Objects

Objects have properties and functions. As infants explore and experiment with them, they begin to devise schemes for grouping objects together. They modify these schemes to add new items to the category and to differentiate one category from another. Categories can consist of the physical properties of objects, such as "smooth" and "rough," or they can consist of the functions of objects, as in "something to sit on" and "something to dig with."

The classification of objects and events into categories is one method infants have of coping with the vast array of new experiences that they encounter. **Categorization** is a fundamental element of information processing. By treating certain individual objects as similar because they belong to the same basic grouping, like two individual red blocks or two wiggly goldfish, the potential amount of information to process is reduced (Younger, 1992; Rosch, 1978). If an item is classified as a member of a category, then all the information that has been accumulated regarding that category can automatically be applied to the specific object. This process aids in the storage and recall processes of memory, in reasoning and problem solving, and in the acquisition of new information. Classification of objects into categories is a cognitive capacity that becomes increasingly sophisticated over the childhood years.

One of the most robust categories that appears early in infancy is the distinction between people and inanimate objects (Ellsworth et al., 1993). Infants have been observed to smile, vocalize, and become more active when interacting with people as compared to things. By 3 months of age, infants already show their ability to categorize stimuli as people or things by smiling almost exclusively at people. Infants may look with equal interest at inanimate objects, especially novel ones, but their smiles are reserved for people. This distinction between the social and the nonsocial realm can be considered a *foundational category*. It provides a basis for our emphasis on the unique role of social relationships in the process of adaptation and growth. From this basic distinction between a person and a thing, many further subdivisions of categories emerge that begin to differentiate the infant's social world.

Research on infant categorization skills typically involves sorting objects into categories. By 15 months, babies will touch all the objects that belong to one category and then touch all the objects in another category. By 18 months of age, children can perform multidimensional categorization tasks, for example, sorting eight objects, such as four brightly colored yellow rectangles and four human-shaped plastic figures, into two distinct groups (Gopnik & Meltzoff, 1987; 1992). This kind of sorting does not require the ability to give names to the objects. However, shortly after children demonstrate the capacity to manage two-group sorting, they often show a rapid acceleration in the acquisition of names for objects (Gopnick & Meltzoff, 1992). Thus, categorizing and naming appear to be closely linked. By the close of the second year of life, babies know that objects have certain stable properties, that some objects "belong" with others, and that objects have names. With these achievements, infants impose a new degree of order and predictability on their daily experiences.

Emotional Development

Emotional development during infancy can be understood along four dimensions. First, new emotions emerge and they are differentiated along dimensions of intensity. Second, with cognitive maturation, a child interprets events differently. New emotions may become attached to familiar situations. An experience that may once have caused wariness, such as a new toy or a loud noise, becomes a source of excitement or joy as the child gains mastery over the situation. Third, children develop strategies for regulating their emotions so that they are not overwhelmed by emotional intensity. Fourth, emotions serve as a channel for adult-infant communication.

Emotional Differentiation

Emotions gradually become differentiated during the first two years of life. Peter Wolff (1966) described seven states of arousal in newborn infants. Each is characterized by a distinctive pattern or respiration, muscle tone, motor activity, and alertness (Table 5.7). In these states, one observes the earliest differentiation among distress (crying), interest (alert inactivity), and excitement (waking activity). A newborn's state of arousal will influence his or her capacity to respond to the environment. Changes in arousal state also serve to cue responses from caregivers. Crying usually brings some effort to comfort or soothe. Visual alertness is likely to prompt social interactions. Parents try to interact with their infants, achieve eye contact, and initiate nonverbal exchanges during the alert phases (Tronick et al., 1979).

Crying is an especially important emotional expression that contributes to the infant's survival. Until about 6 or 7 months of age, the infant's mobility is quite limited. The cry is one of the primary signals available that will bring the caregiver into proximity to the infant. Infant cries vary in pitch as well as in tempo and duration.

Studies from laboratory and natural field settings as well as across cultures suggest that higher-pitched cries are considered more upsetting to the caregiver and are treated as a signal of a more urgent nature than are low-pitched cries. In addition, information is contained in the pauses within and between cries. Cries that involve shorter pauses between crying sounds are perceived by adults as more arousing and unpleasant (Zeskind et al., 1992).

A broader pallet of emotions emerges gradually from the basic states of arousal and distress. The differentiation of emotions follows a regular pattern, as Table 5.8 suggests. This table describes age-related changes for three dimensions of emotion: *pleasure-joy, wariness-fear,* and *rage-anger.* Emotional responses during the first month are closely tied to the infant's internal state. Physical discomfort, arousal, pain, and

TABLE 5.7	States of Arousal in Newborns
Regular sleep (RS)	Full rest; low muscle tonus, low motor activity; eyelids firmly closed and still; even, regular respiratory rhythm, about 36 breaths per minute.
Irregular sleep (IS)	Slightly greater muscle tonus; gentle motor activity; frequent facial grimaces and smiles; occasional rapid eye movement; irregular respiration, about 48 breaths per minute.
Periodic sleep (PS)	Intermediate between RS and IS; bursts of rapid, shallow breathing alternate with bursts of deep, slow breathing.
Drowsiness (D)	More active than RS but less active than IS or PS; eyes open and close; eyes, when open, are dull and glazed and may roll upward; respiration variable but of higher frequency than during RS.
Alert inactivity (AI)	Slight activity; face relaxed; eyes open and "bright"; respiration constant and more rapid than in RS.
Waking activity (WA)	Frequent, diffuse motor activity; vocalizations; skin flushed when active; irregular respiration.
Crying (C)	Vigorous, diffuse motor activity; facial grimaces; skin red; eyes open or partially closed; crying vocalization.

Source: Adapted from Wolff, 1966.

At 10 weeks of age, the expression of emotion through cooing and crying provides distinct, easily interpreted messages that cue caregivers to the baby's inner state.

changing tension in the central nervous system are the major sources of emotions. During the period from 1 to 6 months, emotions begin to be tied more to a separation of self and environment. Babies smile at familiar faces; they show interest in and curiosity about novel stimuli. They express rage when nursing is disrupted or when they are prevented from viewing an activity they have been intently watching.

The period from 6 to 12 months reflects a greater awareness of the context of events. Emotions of joy, anger, and fear are tied to a baby's ability to recall previous experiences and to compare them with an ongoing event. These emotions also reflect a baby's ability to exercise some control over the environment and frustration when goals are blocked. At this age, the distinctions among some of the negative emotions such as anger, fear, and sadness may be blurred and difficult to detect by someone who is not familiar with the child (Camras et al., 1991).

Emotions that are observed during the second year of life—especially anxiety, pride, defiance, and shame—suggest an emerging sense of self. Infants recognize that they can operate as causal agents. They also begin to respond to the emotions of others. They can give love to others through hugs, kisses, and tender pats. They can share toys, comfort another distressed infant, and imitate another person's excitement. In becoming a more distinct being, an infant achieves a new level of awareness of the capacity to give and receive pleasure as well as the vulnerability of self and others.

The dimension of wariness-fear becomes more differentiated during the second year. The theme of anxiety was introduced in the discussion of attachment, pointing out the emergence of stranger anxiety at about 6 months and separation anxiety at about 9 months. Anxiety of a more nonspecific form begins to be observed during the second

TABLE 5.8   Age-Related Changes in Three Dimensions of Emotion

Month	Pleasure-Joy	Weakness-Fear	Rage-Anger
0–3	Endogenous smile; turning torward	Startle/pain; obligatory attention	Distress due to covering the face, physical restraint, extreme discomfort Rage (disappointment)
3	Pleasure		
4–5	Delight; active laughter	Wariness	
7	Joy		
9		Fear (stranger aversion)	Anger
12	Elation	Anxiety; immediate fear	Angry mood, petulance
18	Positive valuation of self	Shame	Defiance
24	Affection		Intentional hurting
36	Pride, love		Guilt

Note: The age specified is that of neither the first appearance of the affect in question nor its peak occurrence; it is the age at which the literature suggests the reaction is common.

Periodic visits to the doctor's office provide a chance to observe babies' developing emotional repertoires. In this photo, it's hard to know who is evaluating whom.

year. Babies begin to anticipate negative experiences and express fear of objects or events that have been associated with negative experiences in the past. The construct of anxiety is included as a major dynamic in describing patterns of attachment, especially in relationships characterized by potentially rejecting or unpredictable caregivers.

Emotions as a Key to Understanding Meaning

An infant's emotional reactions provide a channel for determining the meaning the child is giving to a specific situation. Often, these reactions are studied by systematic coding of facial expressions. One example of how emotions provide a window on meaning comes from a study of infants in an operant conditioning experiment. Infants aged 2, 4, and 6 months were observed while they learned an operant arm-pulling task. A string was attached to the infant's wrist. When the string was pulled, it activated a switch that turned on a color slide of an infant smiling accompanied by the sound of children singing the "Sesame Street" theme song. During the Learning Phase, pulling the string produced the visual and auditory stimulus. During the Extinction Phase, nothing happened when the string was pulled.

Even as young as 2 months old, the babies' expressions changed from interest and enjoyment during the Learning Phase to anger and sadness during the Extinction Phase. The findings were interpreted to illustrate that infants' anger is associated with violation of expectations and that expressions of interest and enjoyment are associated with learning and increased control. What is more, individual differences in emotional response to the task showed stability over the two-month period, particularly if one looks at the expressions of interest during learning and anger during extinction (Sullivan et al., 1992). The discussion of infant smiling in Box 5.3 provides further evidence of the link between emotional expression and meaning.

The Ability to Regulate Emotions

Infants develop strategies for coping with intense emotions, both positive and negative. Most research in this area has focused on the ways infants deal with distress (Dodge, 1989). Even newborns have some strategies for reducing the intensity of distress such as turning the head away, sucking on the hands or lips, or closing the eyes. As infants gain new motor coordination and control, they can move away, distract themselves with other objects, or soothe themselves by rocking, stroking, or thumb-sucking (Kopp, 1989). However, one surely has observed many instances when infants are not able to regulate the intensity of their emotions. Researchers who work with infant subjects about this topic will tell you of the number of babies who had to be eliminated from their study because they simply could not be calmed enough in the experimental procedure to attend to the task.

BOX 5.3   THE MEANING OF AN INFANT'S SMILE

The infant's smile is a social treasure. Parents and grandparents may go to great lengths to bring out this sweet expression. Yet, researchers have discovered that an infant's smile can have a wide variety of meanings and can be produced in response to many stimuli.

The very earliest smiles, observed during the first month of life, may occur spontaneously during sleep or in response to a high-pitched human voice. Gentle tactile stimulation—touching, tickling, and rocking—can produce these early smiles. A baby's first smiles are not a true form of social communication, although they are likely to produce positive feelings in the adult caregiver (Wolff, 1963, 1987).

Social smiles begin to be observed at about 5 weeks of age. These smiles are first produced in response to a wide range of stimuli: familiar faces and voices (especially the mother's), strangers, and nonhuman objects. After about 20 weeks, the smiling response becomes differentiated. Infants continue to smile broadly and frequently at people, especially familiar people, but they no longer smile readily at strangers or objects. The social smile conveys both a recognition of familiarity and an invitation to further communication or interaction (Ambrose, 1963; Sroufe et al., 1984).

The *cognitive smile* seems to develop alongside the social smile. Infants smile in response to their own behaviors, as if they were expressing satisfaction with their accomplishments (Papousek & Bernstein, 1969; Watson, 1970). At 3 months, babies smile in response to events that are moderately familiar, as if expressing pleasure in understanding the situation (Kagan, 1984). Infants also smile elaborately when they are able to make something happen, as when they wiggle a mobile or hear a bell jangle when they kick their feet (Cicchetti & Schneider-Rosen, 1984). These "mastery" smiles do not appear to have a social intention. By 8 months, infants smile when they are able to grasp a new concept (Kagan, 1984). In the second year of life, smiling is associated with a primitive form of humor. Babies smile when they recognize an incongruity, such as seeing their mother drinking from a baby bottle or crawling on her hands and knees. These smiles suggest that the baby appreciates something about the discrepancy between what is being presented and what is normally observed (Cicchetti & Schneider-Rosen, 1984).

Babies smile in a variety of contexts. The conditions that evoke smiles change as the baby matures. Thus smiles, like other emotional expressions, should be interpreted in relation to the infants' existing schemes and goals.

Boy, these cubes are slippery.

The mastery smile!

One of the most important elements in the development of **emotional regulation** is the way caregivers assist infants to manage their strong feelings (Kopp, 1989; Tronick, 1989). Caregivers can provide direct support when they observe that a child is distressed, They may cuddle, hug, rock, or swaddle a baby. They may offer food or a pacifier to the baby, or nurse her as a means of comfort. Through words and actions, the caregiver may help a child interpret the source of the stress or suggest ways to reduce the stress.

Concern has been focused especially on babies who are characterized as showing negative emotionality early in infancy. Babies who show high levels of motor activity and who cry a lot at 4 months of age have been found to show high levels of wariness, fearfulness, and shyness at later ages (Park et al., 1997). These babies tend to be at risk for subsequent behavior problems. Studies have been directed toward analyzing continuity and discontinuity in negative emotionality and the family characteristics that might be associated with changes in negativity over the first year of life. In one such study involving 148 babies and their parents, characteristics of the mothers and the fathers were examined separately to learn what might lead to increased negativity in the infants from 3 months to 9 months of age. In addition to the direct quality of interactions between the mother-infant and father-infant pairs, researchers found that high levels of marital dissatisfaction on the part of the mother or the father and the father's emotional insensitivity were associated with increases in the infant's negativity during the period. This is quite significant since it suggests that the emotional climate of the parental system is communicated along channels that the infant can perceive as early as 3 to 9 months of age (Belsky et al., 1991).

Caregivers' approaches to the issue of emotional regulation vary with the culture. In some cultures, caregivers regulate emotions by preventing a child from being exposed to certain arousing situations. Japanese mothers, for example, try hard to prevent their children from being exposed to anger by avoiding frustrating them. In addition, parents rarely express anger to their young children, especially in public. Thus, Japanese parents try to regulate anger by minimizing the child's experiences with it (Miyake et al., 1986). Cultural values influence how mothers respond to infants' distress and what they teach their babies about how to regulate feelings of wariness, fear, and anxiety.

Emotional regulation can also be achieved by observing emotional reactions of others (Campos et al., 1989). Children observe anger, pride, shame, or sadness in others, often in response to their own emotional expressions. For example, Connie stumbles and falls in trying to take a step on her own. She looks up at her mother. If her mother looks upset and frightened, Connie may begin to cry. On the other hand, if her mother laughs or speaks to her in a comforting tone, Connie may get up and try again. Children can be distracted from their sadness by seeing laughter and joy in someone else. Through empathy, they can reduce their angry feelings toward someone else by seeing how sad or frightened the other person is.

As children understand the consequences or implications of a situation, they have new motives for regulating or failing to regulate their emotions. Children may extend or expand their signals of distress if they think they will help them achieve their goals, such as special attention or nurturing. Children may try to disguise their distress if they think it will provoke additional pain. Emotional regulation, like emotional signaling, takes place within an interpersonal context.

Emotions as a Channel for Adult-Infant Communication

Emotions provide a two-way channel through which infants and their caregivers can establish **intersubjectivity**. An infant has the capacity to produce a range of emotional expressions, including fear, distress, disgust, surprise, excitement, interest, joy, anger, and sadness. Parents and other caregivers rely on facial, vocal, and behavioral cues related to these emotions as ways of determining an infant's inner states and goals and responding to them (Malatesta & Izard, 1984). Babies in turn can also detect and differentiate the affective expressions of others. Young infants can differentiate facial expressions of fear, anger, happiness, sadness, and surprise (Walker-Andrews, 1986; Hornik et al., 1987; Caron et al., 1988; Ludemann & Nelson, 1988). Similarly, adults can detect and differentiate the affective expressions of infants. The most readily recognized facial expressions are those of joy, interest, surprise, and distress (Oster et al., 1992). In cycles of interaction, responsive caregivers monitor changes in a baby's affect as a way of determining whether their interventions are effective.

Think of a 6-month-old baby who wants a toy that is out of reach. The baby waves her arms in the direction of the toy, makes fussy noises, and looks distressed. As her father tries to figure out what the baby wants, he watches her expressions in order to discover whether he is on the right track. Parents who are attuned to this form of communication are more likely to help babies achieve their goals, and babies are more likely to persist in attempts to communicate because they have experienced success in such interactions. Through a shared repertoire of emotions, babies and their caregivers are able to understand one another and to create shared meanings. Thus, emotional expression becomes a building block of trust.

Social Referencing.   One of the most notable ways that infants and adults have of co-constructing their reality is the mechanism of **social referencing**. Under certain cir-

Emotions provide a channel of communication before speech and language. The exchange of playful laughing and smiling is an early form of conversation.

cumstances, infants make use of the emotional responses of another person to guide their own behavior. They often use their mothers as a *social reference,* but other adults can serve this function as well (Klinnert et al., 1986; Hornik & Gunnar, 1988; Walden & Ogan, 1988). As infants approach an unfamiliar adult, an ambiguous situation, or a novel object, they look to their mother and use her facial expression and/or verbal expressions as a source of information about the situation. If the mother expresses wariness or a negative emotion, the infant is more likely to withdraw or to explore with caution. On the other hand, if the mother expresses a positive emotion, the infant is more likely to approach the situation or the unfamiliar person with confidence. By 12 months of age, infants consistently use this mechanism to try to appraise an ambiguous situation (Rosen et al., 1992).

Social referencing illustrates how members of a cultural group begin to build a shared view of reality during infancy. Infants actively request information by looking to their mothers or other adults present. The adult's expression, either positive or negative, cues the infant about whether to approach or withdraw. Infants reduce their uncertainty and begin to appraise their world in the context of the emotional responses of their caregivers. You can probably imagine the wide range of objects and situations that can be evaluated through this mechanism. Foods, toys, people, animals, sounds, plants, objects of all sorts can be discerned as positive and approachable or negative and a cause for wariness. Depending on the cultural outlook, infants in different societies will begin to categorize their experiences differently based in part on these early appraisals derived from social referencing.

THE PSYCHOSOCIAL CRISIS: TRUST VERSUS MISTRUST

The term *psychosocial crisis* refers to a state of tension that occurs as a result of the developmental needs of the individual and the social expectations of the culture. At each stage of life, the crisis is expressed as a struggle between the positive and the negative poles of a critical dimension. In infancy, the specific nature of the crisis—trust versus mistrust—focuses on the fundamental nature of an infant's sense of connection to the social world.

Trust   In adult relationships, **trust** refers to an appraisal of the predictability, dependability, and genuineness of another person (Rempel et al., 1985). Trust emerges in the course of a relationship as one person discovers those traits in another person. As the level of trust grows, the partners may take some risks by disclosing information or feelings that may lead to rejection. Relationships that endure through periods of risk grow in feelings of trust. However, trust is more than a summary of the past: it is a faith that the relationship will survive the uncertainties of an unpredictable future. This faith begins in infancy. A trusting relationship links confidence about the past with faith about the future.

For infants, trust is an emotion, an experiential state of confidence that their needs will be met and that they are valued. Trust is inferred from the infant's increasing capacity to delay gratification and from the warmth and delight that are evident in interactions with family members. The sense of trust expands from immediate figures in the social environment to the supportiveness and responsiveness of the broader social and physical world. Infants also learn to trust their sensory systems in processing stimulation from the environment. In this function, the sense of trust extends to learning to trust oneself.

The sense of basic trust is related to but not identical to Bowlby's concept of attachment. Attachment refers to the behavioral system that ensures safety and security for the infant. Over time, the internal representation of the attachment relationship generalizes to other dyadic (paired) relationships, especially where issues of intimacy and protection are relevant. Trust is a broader construct. Within the framework of trust, infants not only establish an assessment of the central social figures in their world as trustable or untrustable, but they also achieve a sense of their own value and trustworthiness. Over time, a basic sense of trust expands to a global optimism about how one expects to be treated by others and about one's ability to cope with life's challenges. Trust is an integrating force that helps synthesize emotions, cognitions, and actions under conditions of uncertainty, allowing the person to pursue goals with a belief that things will work out well.

Mistrust   During infancy, experiences of **mistrust** can arise from at least three sources: infant wariness, lack of confidence in the caregiver, and doubt in one's own lovableness. Wariness, one of the earliest infant emotions, is linked initially to at least two infant reflexes, the "startle" response in reaction to loud noises and the Moro reflex in response to sudden loss of support. All infants are prewired neurologically to be alert to certain environmental dangers. One of the functions of the caregiver is to minimize the infant's exposure to stimuli that evoke these reflexes, and, over time, to comfort and reassure the infant after exposure to threatening stimuli.

Second, babies can lack confidence in the good intentions of others. If the caregiver is unable to differentiate the infant's needs and respond appropriately to them or is unusually harsh while meeting the infant's needs, seeds of doubt about the trustworthiness of the environment may be planted within the infant. Third, babies experience the

---

BOX 5.4   IS THERE A CRITICAL PERIOD FOR ATTACHMENT?

A **critical period** is a time of maximal sensitivity or readiness for the development of certain skills or behavior patterns. The particular skill or behavior pattern is not likely to emerge before the onset of the critical period, and it is extremely difficult, if not impossible, to establish once the critical period has passed. The successful emergence of any behavior that has a critical period for development depends on the coordination of the biological readiness of the organism and environmental supports (Scott, 1987).

Konrad Lorenz (1935, 1937/1961) was one of the first ethologists to compare the critical periods in physical development and those in behavioral development. Lorenz described a process of social attachment among birds that he called **imprinting.** In this process, the young bird establishes a comparatively permanent bond with its mother. In her absence, however, the young bird will imprint on other available targets, including a model of its mother or a human being. For birds, the onset of the critical period coincides with the time at which they are able to walk and ends when they begin to fear strangers. After this point, no new model or species can be substituted as a target for imprinting.

Soon after a baby's birth, the parent's attachment to the baby becomes quite specific, that is, the parents would not be willing to replace his or her own baby with any other baby of similar age. Is there a time when infants are most likely to form such an attachment to the primary caregiver?

Is there a point after which such attachments cannot be formed? The most direct way to examine this question would be to separate an infant from his or her mother and observe the consequences in the infant's ability to establish a bond with a new caregiver. Since such experimentation would be unethical, however, evidence to address these questions has been drawn from real-life situations in which the mother-infant relationship has been disrupted.

Leon Yarrow (1963, 1964, 1970) observed 100 infants who were shifted from foster mothers to adoptive mothers. The infants who were separated from their foster mothers at 6 months or earlier showed minimal distress. They did not express prolonged anger or depression over separation if their physical and emotional needs continued to be met. In contrast, all the infants who were transferred from foster mothers to adoptive mothers at 8 months or older showed strong negative reactions, including angry protest and withdrawal. These infants found the disruption of their earlier relationships very stressful.

Later research by John Bowlby (1980) focused on adolescents who had moved repeatedly from one foster home or institution to another. These children never had an opportunity to form an enduring, loving relationship with a caring adult. As adolescents, they were described as *affectionless,* and unable to form close relationships with others. Recent studies confirm that children who spend their infancy in institutions where the turnover in caregivers power of their own rage. They can doubt their own lovableness as they encounter the violence of their own capacity for anger.

Most parents also contribute to experiences of mistrust because they inevitably make some mistakes in responding to their infant's signs of distress, particularly when the baby is young. They may first try the bottle and, if the crying continues, they may change the diaper, give water, move the baby to another room, or put the baby to bed, trying a variety of things until something "works." Over time, however, sensitive caregivers learn to interpret their child's signals correctly and to respond appropriately, thereby fostering the infant's sense of trust in the environment (Kropp & Haynes, 1987).

Feelings of doubt or anxiety about the bond of trust are more common than may have been expected. About one-third of American infant-mother pairs who have been systematically observed show evidence of an insecure attachment. Cross-cultural research provides further evidence that a significant proportion of infants have difficulty deriving emotional comfort or security from their caregivers (van Ijzendoorn & Kroonenberg, 1988; Posada et al., 1995).

In addition to the mistrust that emerges within the context of inconsistent or unresponsive caregiving, there are many cases in which the mother-infant relationship is disrupted (Box 5.4). In extreme cases, parents and caregivers grossly neglect their infants and leave the baby alone without anyone to care for his or her needs. They refuse to change or bathe the baby. They do not treat the baby's wounds or protect the child from danger. And they may consistently express hostility to the infant, or provide almost no communication at all (Lyons-Ruth et al., 1987). Under these circumstances, infants discover that their parents are physically and psychologically unavailable (Egeland & Sroufe, 1981). The resulting growth of mistrust in the infant stems from an inability to gain physical or psychological comfort from caregivers.

Mistrust may manifest itself in the infant by withdrawal from interaction and by symptoms of depression and grief, which include sobbing, lack of emotion, lethargy,

is high show disruptions in social functioning including indiscriminate friendship formation, difficulty in forming close relationships, and difficulty in finding emotional support from peers (Rutter, 1995).

From these real-world examples of disruption in the mother-infant relationship, we can say that the onset of a critical period for attachment must begin at about 6 months of age.

When might this period be over? The quality of the attachment relationship is established well before 24 months. Longitudinal studies have reported consistency in the quality of attachment from 12 to 18 months, from 12 to 20 months, and from 12 months to 6 years (Main et al., 1985). Is there really a closing-off point, a time after which a secure attachment can no longer be established? If there is no opportunity to form a consistent relationship with a loving adult, as in the case of the adolescents Bowlby studied, no attachment will be formed. In a study of children who spent their first years of life in an institution where the quality of care was good but staff turnover was high, children who were adopted at age 2 were able to form secure attachments to their adoptive parents. However, at later observations at ages 8 and 16, they showed evidence of difficulty in peer relations similar to the children who remained in the institution (Hodges & Tizard, 1989). Lack of continuity in caregiving during infancy, such as might occur in institutional care or in shifts from one foster home to the next, is likely to produce long-lasting disruptions in relationship formation, even if a secure attachment with a caregiver is formed at a later time.

Konrad Lorenz inadvertently became the target of imprinting for these geese. They followed him as if he were their mother.

and loss of appetite (Field et al., 1988). It may also be revealed later on in development in the expressions of interpersonal distress observed in the angry, anxious, and resistant behaviors of children with insecure attachments or in the inability to form close, satisfying relationships with others as adolescents and adults. Finally, mistrust may provide a foundation for the emergence of a negative scheme about the self—a scheme that is elaborated over time by defining the self with a cluster of closely related, negative attributes such as cautiousness, nervousness, or introversion (Malle & Horowitz, 1995).

All infants experience some aspects of mistrust, either as a result of mismatches between their needs and the caregiving strategies they receive or as a product of their own difficulties in modulating strong feelings of fear or anger. Thus, the resolution of the crisis in the direction of trust reflects a real psychological achievement in which infants are able to minimize their wariness of the environment and to regulate their own inner passions.

Over the life span, the sense of trust is transformed and matures into an inner paradigm for understanding life. Among older adults who have a strong sense of trust, many of life's disappointments and complexities are minimized by a growing religious faith. Their basic sense of trust evolves into a powerful belief in a great source of goodness and love in the universe, a force that can transcend the pain of daily tragedies and give integrity and meaning to their dying as well as to their living (Erikson et al., 1986).

THE CENTRAL PROCESS FOR RESOLVING THE CRISIS: MUTUALITY WITH THE CAREGIVER

To resolve the crisis of trust versus mistrust, an infant must establish a feeling of **mutuality** with a caregiver. Initially this mutuality is built on the consistency with which the caregiver responds appropriately to the infant's needs. When a baby cries because of thirst, the caregiver is able to interpret that cry and gives the baby water rather than changing the child's diaper. The caregiver comes to appreciate the variety of an infant's needs, and the infant learns to expect that personal needs will be met.

An infant influences the responses of a caregiver in many ways. Infants' irritability and soothability contribute to the kinds of responses that adults make. Infants can reject or end an interaction by fussing, becoming tense, crying, or falling asleep. They can maintain an interaction by smiling, cooing, snuggling comfortably, or maintaining eye contact. Techniques of comforting do not call forth the same responses from all babies (Campos, 1989). A pacifier helps comfort some babies, while others respond to being wrapped snugly in a warm blanket.

An infant and a caregiver learn to regulate the amount of time that passes between the expression of a need and its satisfaction. In a study of mother-infant interactions, Bell and Ainsworth (1972) observed mothers' responses to infant crying during the first year of life. Over the course of the year, the infants' crying decreased and mothers tended to respond more quickly to their cries. This finding suggests a process of mutual adaptation by mothers and infants. Some mothers came quickly and ignored few cries. Other mothers waited a long time and ignored much of the crying. A striking finding was that the longer mothers delayed in responding to their infants' cries, the more crying the infants did in later months. Babies whose mothers responded promptly in the first six months of life cried less often in the second six months.

Coordination, Mismatch, and Repair of Interactions

The study of mutuality with the caregiver has focused in some detail on patterns and rhythms of social interaction, especially coordination, matching, and synchrony (Brazelton et al., 1974; Tronik & Cohn, 1989). **Coordination** refers to two related characteristics of interaction: matching and synchrony. **Matching** means that the infant and the caregiver are involved in similar behaviors or states at the same time. They may be playing together with an object, cooing and smiling at each other, or fussing and angry at each other. **Synchrony** means that the infant and the caregiver move from one state to the next in a fluid pattern. When infants are paying attention to their caregivers, the caregivers attempt to stimulate them. As they withdraw attention, the caregivers learn to reduce stimulation and wait until the infants are ready to engage again.

In the normal pattern of development, mother-infant interactions become increasingly coordinated (Tronick & Cohn, 1989; Isabella & Belsky, 1991). This does not mean that most of the interactions are coordinated. In fact, especially when babies are very young, matched interactions appear to become mismatched rather quickly. A mother and infant may be engaged in a period of cooing and laughing. The mother makes a funny noise, the baby reacts by cooing and laughing, then the mother makes the noise again and the baby laughs. On the third try, the mother cannot get the baby to make eye contact. She may try shifting the baby to another position or making the noise at a different pitch, but the baby looks away and squirms. The game is over; the connection is temporarily broken. The explanation for these frequent failures in coordination may lie partly in the infant's inability to sustain coordinated communication, partly in a rapid shift of need states, and partly in the inability of adults to sustain nonverbal communication for lengthy periods. In normal mother-infant pairs, however, periods of mismatch are usually followed by **communication repairs,** so that infants and mothers cycle again through points of coordination in their interactions.

At a theoretical level, this process of coordination, mismatch, and repair can be viewed as a fundamental building block for mutuality. Infants and caregivers gain confidence in their ability to communicate. Infants have many opportunities to experience the satisfaction of shared communication and the sense of being embedded in a responsive social environment. They also experience frequent recovery from a mismatched state to a state of effective communication, so that they can be hopeful about the ability to make these repairs in the future.

Establishing a Functional Rhythm in the Family

The match or mismatch between an infant's rhythms and the family's rhythms is an important factor in the overall adjustment of a family to a new baby (Sprunger et al., 1985). Some babies are quite predictable; the timing of their sleeping, eating, playtime, and even fussy periods follows a clear pattern. Other babies are much less regular. All babies are changing rapidly during the first 24 months of life, so daily patterns are bound to change and families must make frequent adjustments in order to continue to meet the infant's needs.

In American culture, by the end of the first year of life babies are typically expected to modify their schedule of needs so that they sleep when the rest of the family sleeps, play when the rest of the family is awake, and eat three or at most four times a day, generally when the other family members eat. During the second year of life, the demands of parenting change. Toddlers become more mobile and have new capacities to initiate activities. Their attention span increases, they have new requirements for stimulation, and they have new areas of wariness and resistance—things they don't want to do (like take a nap) or people they don't want to be with (like a certain babysitter). These and other changes require adaptation on the part of parents in order to sustain the mutuality that had been achieved or to rectify problems in attachment and trust that may now be evident (Heinicke & Guthrie, 1992).

Parents with Psychological Problems

The importance of reciprocal interactions in building trust and hope during infancy is highlighted by studies of parents with psychological problems. Sensitivity to an infant's emotional states, the ability to respond appropriately to an infant's needs, and the quality of common, daily interactions can all be impaired by **family risk factors.** Studies of parents who are experiencing marital discord, who have been victims of child abuse or neglect, who are depressed, or who are mentally ill suggest that the interactional cycles of these parents and their children lack synchrony (Rutter, 1990). For example, in a comparison of mothers who had been maltreated as children and those who had not, the maltreated mothers were less involved with their children during play, made use of fewer strategies to direct their children's activities, and used a more negative tone with their children (Alessandri, 1992).

The results of an early intervention study with mother-infant pairs assessed as having anxious attachments help clarify those aspects of mutuality that may be most

When mothers are depressed, they are less psychologically available for reciprocal interactions. This baby is trying to get her mother's attention, but her mom, although physically present, seems to be in a world of her own.

amenable to repair. The study involved 100 Spanish-speaking mothers who had recently emigrated from Mexico or Central America to the United States and their 12-month-old babies (Lieberman et al., 1991). These families were considered to be at risk for attachment disturbances because the combination of poverty, unemployment, and sudden cultural transition increased both anxiety and depression among the mothers. The mother-infant dyads were assessed using a home visit and observation in the Strange Situation. Of those who could be clearly classified, 34 anxious dyads were placed in the experimental intervention program, 25 anxious dyads were placed in the anxious control group, and 34 secure dyads were placed in a second, secure control group. The intervention involved weekly home visits with a trained intervenor over the second year of life.

The intervenors' efforts focused on two themes. First, they tried to encourage the mother's ability to express her own feelings including her longings for security, concerns for protection and safety when she was a child and in the present, and negative feelings of self-doubt and anger toward others including the child and the intervenor. Second, they tried to provide developmentally relevant information about the child, including observations about the child's temperament, observations about age-appropriate opportunities to foster exploration, and strategies for negotiating mother-infant conflicts that would help restore synchrony.

The impact of the intervention was assessed at 24 months using videotapes of a 1 1/2-hour laboratory session. The session included free play with mother and baby, play with a female stranger while the mother was present, child-directed play while the adults were unavailable, separation from the mother while the stranger remained in the room, reunion with the mother when the stranger left the room, and snack with mother, child, and observer.

Mothers in the experimental anxious attachment group showed significantly greater levels of empathy toward their children during this laboratory session than did the anxious controls. These mothers also initiated more interactions with their babies. The children showed fewer angry, avoidant, and resistant behaviors than did the anxious controls. Upon reunion after the brief separation, the mothers and children in the experimental group showed more evidence of eagerness and readiness to resume interaction than did the anxious controls. There were no significant differences between the intervention group and the securely attached controls on any of the behavioral measures at 24 months, suggesting that the intervention was effective in repairing the attachment system to the point that the initially anxious group was behaving very much like the secure group in the laboratory situation.

The results of this study suggest that interventions that engage the mother and support her emotional involvement in the parenting process can have a beneficial impact on the emotional development of the child. The intervention contributes to the mother's greater self-acceptance and reduced frustration, as well as her increased empathy for the child's needs and developmental level. These changes lead to the child's improved capacity to regulate his or her behavior in harmony with a more predictable, responsive partner.

THE PRIME ADAPTIVE EGO QUALITY AND THE CORE PATHOLOGY

Hope Erikson (1982) has argued that the positive resolution of the psychosocial crisis of trust versus mistrust leads to the adaptive ego quality of hope. As you will recall from Chapter 2, the prime adaptive ego qualities shape a person's outlook on life in the direction of greater openness to experience and information, greater capacity to identify a variety of pathways to achieve one's goals, more willingness to assert the self and to ex-

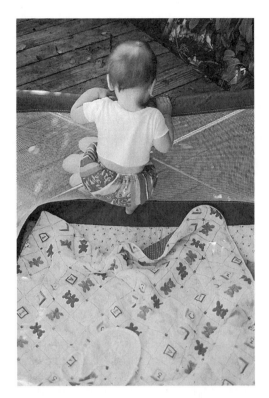

Using all her problem-solving skills and motor coordination, this baby is surging forward toward independence by clambering out of her playpen. Hopefulness allows babies to set new goals and take new risks.

press one's wishes and views, and a positive approach to the formation of close relationships. Even in the face of difficulties and stressful life events, these qualities contribute to higher levels of functioning and of well-being.

As the first of the prime adaptive ego qualities, **hope** pervades the entire life story. It is a global cognitive orientation that one's goals and dreams can be attained and that events will turn out for the best. As Erikson described it, "Hope bestows on the anticipated future a sense of leeway inviting expectant leaps, either in preparatory imagination or in small initiating actions. And such daring must count on basic trust in the sense of a trustfulness that must be, literally and figuratively, nourished by maternal care and—when endangered by all-too-desperate discomfort—must be restored by competent consolation" (1982, p. 60).

The construct of hope has had very little attention in the developmental research literature. This is of concern, especially since research with adults shows that people who have a hopeful, optimistic outlook about the future have different achievement beliefs and emotional reactions in response to actual achievement than do people who have a pessimistic outlook (Norem & Cantor, 1988; Dweck, 1992). People who have higher levels of hopefulness undertake a larger number of goals across life areas and select tasks that are more difficult. Hopefulness is generally associated with higher goals, higher levels of confidence that the goal will be reached, and greater persistence in the face of barriers to goal attainment, thus leading to higher overall levels of performance (Snyder et al., 1991).

Within the psychosocial framework, hope can be seen as the platform from which very young children take certain "leaps of faith." When you see an infant overcome doubts and hesitancy in taking a first independent step, you see the dividend of hope. When you watch a toddler clamber over the bars of her crib and let herself drop several inches to the floor, you see the dividend of hope. And as a parent, when you give your adolescent the keys to the car and watch as he or she drives off alone, you see the dividend of hope. Without hope, neither the individual nor the society could bear the weight of uncertainty of our changing world.

Withdrawal

As a core pathology, **withdrawal** refers to a general orientation of wariness toward people and objects. This is especially disturbing since during infancy healthy development is a pattern of outward motion, extension, and increasing engagement with the social and physical worlds. Infants typically reach and grasp, crawl, stand, and walk. They explore through gazing, mouthing, and manipulating objects. Their behavior is typically characterized by interest in novelty, joy in learning, and frustration at encountering barriers to goal achievement. Over the first year, babies become increasingly connected to significant figures in their social world, following them about, devising strategies to engage them in interaction, and looking to them for consolation when they are distressed.

Infants who are characterized by withdrawal may show evidence of passivity, lethargy, and neutral or negative affect. They are not readily engaged in social interaction and do not show the signs of self-directed exploration typical of most healthy infants. Withdrawal may have some of its roots in genetically determined temperamental characteristics. Some babies have a very low threshold for pain. They are highly sensitive to sensory stimulation and recoil from the kinds of handling that other babies find comforting or pleasurable. Some babies are more passive than others, requiring little in the way of stimulation and showing less evidence of exploratory behavior than active babies.

One of the earliest descriptions of withdrawal in infancy was provided by Rene Spitz's (1945, 1946) analysis of children who had been institutionalized before one year of age. The babies who suffered the most had been placed in a Foundling Home in which eight babies were cared for by one nurse. These babies went through a phase of initial rage followed by a period of physical and emotional withdrawal. They lay passively in their cribs, showing limited motor exploration and little emotionality. In addition, they rarely smiled or showed excitement. The babies' babbling and language were extremely delayed. They deteriorated physically. Their measured developmental level dropped substantially over a year's time. These babies suffered from a combination of a loss of their attachment figure, a lack of meaningful social interaction, and an absence of appropriate sensory stimulation—all of which produced what Spitz called **anaclitic depression.**

Applied Topic   THE ROLE OF PARENTS

Parents have an enormous responsibility for maintaining and promoting the psychological growth of their children. We have portrayed infants as active, adaptive, and eager to master the environment. At the same time, the immaturity of human infants at birth necessitates a long period of dependence on adults. The few instinctive behaviors of human infants in comparison with the infants of other species is compensated for by an enormous capacity to learn. For this potential to be realized, infants must rely on their parents to maintain their health, provide stimulation, and protect them from danger. During the long period of dependence, infants become entwined in complex social systems and develop strong emotional bonds to their caregivers. The quality of these early relationships provides infants with a mental representation that guides their later development of friendships, intimacy, and relationships with their own children.

Safety in the Physical Environment

One of the central responsibilities that parents face is to ensure infants' survival by protecting them from environmental dangers. The ecology of home and neighborhood, including the society's degree of modernization, influences the kinds of dangers to which infants are exposed and the kinds of practices families and cultures invent to protect their offspring. In addition to physical risks, some dangers are linked to superstitions, religious beliefs, and matters of the spirit world.

The presence of dangers or risks in the environment usually elicits some effort to restrict a child's movement through swaddling, carrying the baby in a sling, or placing the baby in a playpen. Because of concern about dangers, caregivers also invoke certain prohibitions, such as telling the child, "No, don't touch that," or pulling the child away from something dangerous. As infants become more mobile in the second half of the first year, the need to introduce prohibitions and to monitor exploratory activities increases. Depending on the cultural values concerning independent exploration, caregivers may heighten their restrictions and prohibitions or may try to modify the environment to permit safe, unrestricted exploration.

Certain child-rearing practices arise from a desire to protect young children from known dangers. For example, Robert LeVine (1977) described the practice of many African cultures of carrying infants 18 months and older on the back, even though they were able to walk around. He learned that this practice was used to prevent toddlers from getting burned on the open cooking fires at an age when they were mobile enough to walk or stumble into the fire and yet not old enough to know how to inhibit their movements. Other hazards in the neighborhood, such as falling off steep cliffs or into lakes, rivers, or wells, prompted this same carrying behavior.

In societies with high infant mortality rates, infants are more likely to be carried for long periods of the day and for a longer part of their infancy (Goldberg, 1977). This custom promotes continuous monitoring of the infant's needs and protection from harmful agents in the home or environment. However, practices such as swaddling and carrying may severely limit a child's exploratory behavior. They discourage activities in which infants act as causal agents, discovering the multiple consequences of their actions. Very close, prolonged swaddling actually places infants at high risk of developing serious respiratory infections (Yurdakok et al., 1990). However, if a caregiver's primary concern is the baby's survival, that goal will dominate the caregiver's orientation.

In industrialized countries, infants face different types of hazards, such as electrical outlets, steep stairs, and open containers of insecticides, cleaning agents, and other poisons. Many American families protect babies from these dangers by putting up gates at a doorway or at the top of a stairway, or by placing an infant in a crib or playpen to restrict her or his exploration. In other homes, the strategy is to baby proof the home by removing as many known dangers as possible so that the baby has maximum freedom for exploration. These two different strategies reflect two different values concerning child-rearing, both with the same goal of providing maximum safety and protection from danger. In the former case, parents try to preserve their adult environment. Children must modify their behavior in order to fit into the home. In the latter case, parents modify their adult environment to accommodate the baby's developmental needs.

Fostering Emotional and Cognitive Development

Another component of the parents' role during infancy is their ability to promote emotional and cognitive development. Much of the behavior that appears to be important in the development of strong emotional bonds between infants and parents is also central to the fostering of intellectual growth.

If you have ever observed a child and a parent in a novel environment, such as a doctor's office, you may have seen an example of this dual function. The parent serves as an island of safety and reassurance from which the child can explore (Ainsworth, 1979; Bowlby, 1988). The child first moves out into the environment and returns to the parent. The next time, the child may wander a bit farther, exploring magazines, couches, or other children before once again returning to the parent. One may even see the child leave the room and wander into the hallway or into an empty examining room, eventually returning (if not first retrieved by a watchful nurse) to the parent's side. Parents can see the trust and confidence they have built with their infants to encourage exploration, to introduce their infants to new and unfamiliar objects, and to support the infants' efforts to master difficult motor tasks. The image comes to mind of a smiling mother with outstretched arms bending toward her child and saying, "Walk to Mommy." Trust in a human relationship serves to generate trust in the broader environment. Once children trust the bond between themselves and their parents, the parents can use that confidence to encourage an open, exploring attitude toward the unfamiliar (Zahn-Waxler et al., 1977; Heckhausen, 1987).

Another way that parents foster both emotional and intellectual growth is by structuring the stimulus environment to suit the infant's developmental level (Bornstein, 1985; Stevens & Bakeman, 1985; Bradley et al., 1988). Parents need to recognize the infant's perspective in providing toys, sounds, and visual stimulation. Part of the parents' function is to initiate interactions and not just to respond to their infants' demands for attention. Parents need to create what they perceive to be a suitable environment: one that allows a variety of experiences, a reasonable amount of challenge, and adequate opportunities to experience success. Furthermore, parents should be attuned to their infants developing skills and alter the environment appropriately. As their children mature, parents must provide more complex stimuli, more opportunities for autonomy, and more encouragement for tolerating frustration.

In one study that demonstrated this process, mothers and fathers were videotaped as they played with their 7-, 10-, and 13-month-old babies. Their toy play changed with the developmental competencies of the infants. The parents of the younger babies were likely to demonstrate or direct their infants' play. The parents of the older babies were more likely to encourage turn taking, pretend play, and play involving the coordination of several toys. Parents of older babies were more likely to use words rather than actions in guiding the play. Their babies showed greater competence in exploring the toys, and the parents demonstrated developmentally appropriate strategies as play companions (Power, 1985).

Fathers' and Mothers' Parental Behavior

Do fathers and mothers differ in how they enact the parent role with infants? As we noted earlier, babies form strong attachments to their fathers as well as to their mothers. Fathers may be just as involved in and sensitive to their babies' needs as mothers. However, the daily interactions between mothers and babies and those between fathers and babies are distinct (Belsky et al., 1984; Power, 1985). A greater proportion of the time mothers spend with their babies is devoted to care-giving. Fathers, who spend less time overall with their babies, tend to focus more on play, especially physical play.

Dads tend to enjoy rough and tumble play with their babies. And babies usually love this form of exciting physical contact in which risk or surprise is alternated with comfort and reassurance.

When mothers play with their babies, the play tends to be with words or with toys, as opposed to rough-and-tumble activity (Power, 1985).

Mothers more frequently respond to their babies, express affection, and follow up on behavior their babies initiate. They are also likely to be more accepting of their child's behavior and to emphasize and value emotional expressiveness. Fathers are more likely to disregard babies' cues and to direct their attention to new targets. They are more likely to emphasize control and discipline (Rosen & Rothbaum, 1993). At home, fathers are likely to continue their leisure activity, such as reading or watching television, in the presence of their babies, whereas mothers are likely to interact with their babies.

Fathers and mothers probably view their parental roles differently. American mothers tend to emphasize the *process* of development: They use parenting techniques that focus on enhancing their children's comfort, trust, and curiosity. American fathers tend to emphasize *product*: They use parenting techniques to strengthen their children's bodies and to direct their behavior toward correct solutions to problems.

Evidence also suggests that mothers and fathers view their infants differently. Fathers tend to consider infants less cognitively and socially competent than mothers do. The more involved a father is in infant care, however, the less difference there is between his and the mother's conception of the infant's competence (Ninio & Rinott, 1988). These differences in perception may help explain why fathers pay less attention to infants, engage them in rough-and-tumble play, and disregard babies' cues in playful interchanges. This style of play may underestimate the infant's need for and capability of engaging in more demanding and stimulating activities. Fathers become more effective parents the more they understand the complexity and sophistication of infant competencies.

Parents as Advocates

In addition to providing care themselves, more and more parents are responsible for arranging alternative care for their infants. As a result, parents become **advocates** for their child. Parents must review the alternatives available to them and select a setting that will meet their infant's needs as well as accommodate their work requirements and economic resources. Family day care, in-home baby-sitting, and day care at a center are three common alternatives for the single-parent or two-earner family.

To function as advocates for their children, parents may have to engage in an unfamiliar kind of thinking. They may even feel unqualified to make the kinds of judgments required. For example, parents must evaluate the competence and motivation of the adults who will care for their child. They must estimate how successful these caregivers will be in meeting their child's needs for security and stimulation. And they must consider the degree to which alternative caregivers reflect their own parental values, beliefs, and strategies.

Even when pressures to continue a care-giving arrangement are very strong, parents must be able to assess its impact on their children. They must try to judge whether their children are in the kind of responsive, stimulating environment that will enhance development. In the best situations, alternative care settings actually complement a parent-infant relationship. In the worst settings, infants may be neglected and abused. It is essential for parents to maintain communication with the alternative caregivers, to assess the quality of the care, and to intervene promptly when necessary to ensure their infant's well-being.

The Importance of Social Support

A variety of contextual factors play their part in parents' ability to promote their child's optimal development. Adults who had difficult experiences with their own care-givers come to the parental role with special challenges. They may not have experienced the comfort, responsiveness, or appropriate stimulation that are essential for effective parenting. Some factors, however, help to make up for these deficits. The quality of one's marriage and the emotional support one receives from one's spouse are important in sustaining positive parent-child relationships (Cox et al., 1989; Dickstein & Parke, 1988; Egeland et al., 1988; Simons et al., 1993). Couples who experience mutuality and trust in their own relationship are better able to create a predictable, supportive, and caring family environment for their children.

Sources of social support beyond the marriage partner may also enhance one's effectiveness as a parent. This support may come from the child's grandparents and other family members, friends, and health and mental health professionals (Levitt et al., 1986; Stevens, 1988). The effective use of a social support network ensures that adults will not be isolated as parents, and that other people will be available to help the parents identify and interpret child-rearing problems. Often, the help is very direct—for example, child care or sharing of clothes, playthings, and furniture. Support may also take the form of companionship and validation of the importance of the parenting role. However, evidence suggests that social support cannot fully compensate for the lack of spousal support or for the stresses on parenting caused by economic pressures that prevent parents from meeting basic life needs (Simons et al., 1993).

In reviewing this chapter, you can begin to appreciate the demanding nature of the parents' role in promoting optimal development during their baby's infancy. The elements of effective parenting that we have identified or implied are listed in Table 5.9. As a parent, one must rely heavily on one's own psychological well-being and on the loving support of caring friends and family to sustain the ego strengths and emotional resources necessary to the task.

How parents conceive of their role has a major influence on the direction and rate of their infants' development. Parenting also allows adults opportunities for creative problem solving, empathy, physical closeness, and self-insight. The role of a parent

---

TABLE 5.9   Optimizing an Infant's Develpment

Spend time with the child; be available when the child needs you.

Provide warmth and affection; express positive feelings toward the baby in many ways—verbally, through touching and hugging, and through playful interactions.

Communicate often, directly with the child; engage the child in verbal interaction.

Provide stimulation.

Encourage the child's active engagement in and exploration of the environment.

Help the child understand that he or she causes things to happen.

Help the child engage in directed problem solving.

Encourage the child to persist in efforts to reach a goal.

Keep things predictable, especially when the infant is very young.

Guide language development by using words to name, sort, and categorize objects and events.

Accept the child's efforts to achieve closeness.

Be sensitive to the child's state; learn to interpret the child's signals accurately; time your responses appropriately.

Find effective ways to soothe and comfort the child in times of distress.

Help the child interpret sources of distress and find ways to regulate distress.

Minimize the child's exposure to intensely negative, hostile, and frightening events.

Be aware of the visual and auditory cues you send when you interact with the child.

Pay attention to how the child is changing over time.

Monitor the child's emotional expressions to evaluate the success of specific actions and interventions.

makes considerable cognitive and emotional demands, but attachment to a child also promotes the parent's own psychological development. These contributions to adult development are described further in Chapters 11 and 12.

Chapter Summary

Although the genetic plan plays a major role in guiding physical and sensory/perceptual maturation during infancy, there is considerable evidence for plasticity in neurological development as an infant's sensory/motor system interacts with the social and physical environment. During infancy, a child rapidly develops sensory and motor skills, social relationships, and conceptual skills. Babies are born with the capacity to perceive their environment and to evoke responses from their caregivers. In this sense, they are not helpless. During the first year, voluntary motor functions mature rapidly. A social attachment forms between the infant and the primary caregiver, creating the basic mental representation for subsequent intimate relationships. Sensorimotor intelligence begins with the use of motor and sensory capacities to explore and understand the environment. Of the many schemes that are established during this period, the emergence of an increasingly complex sense of causal relationships, the establishment of the concept of object permanence, and the formation of categories of objects are achievements that impose order and predictability on experience. Emotions are an early and continuous means of achieving intersubjectivity between infants and their caregivers.

The establishment of trust between the infant and the caregiver is significant in both intellectual and social development. Through repeated interaction with the caregiver, the infant develops a concept of the adult as both separate and permanent. Parental sensitivity is an underlying factor in determining the quality of attachment. The three factors that appear to influence sensitivity are the adult's past experiences, including the way he or she was cared for as a young child; contemporary factors that influence the caregiver's well-being, self-esteem, and emotional availability; and characteristics of the infant. Once established, the trusting relationship between the infant and the caregiver becomes a source of security for the infant's further explorations of the environment.

Infants are skilled in adapting to their environment, but they cannot bring about major changes in it. Parents and other caregivers are ultimately responsible for structuring the environment so that it is maximally suited to the infant. These adults are also the sources of the responsiveness, sensitivity, acceptance, and warmth that create an atmosphere conducive to the establishment of trust.

End of Chapter Case

The Cotton Family. Nancy and Paul Cotton are a professional couple who gave birth to their first child Anna after they had been married for 7½ years.

Nancy says, "We wanted a baby but couldn't decide when to have one. Finally we realized that we could not control everything, or time things perfectly. No one can predict the future. So we finally decided to go ahead and have a child as soon as possible. . . . We were both privileged, lucky, and had lived well. By the time we had Anna, I was thirty-three, and our marriage and careers were established. We felt secure.

Being an optimistic person, I guess I expected nirvana. Anna was difficult to deliver, and breast-feeding was a nightmare. Every time she nursed, it hurt. But I didn't want to miss the op-

portunity. I was so determined. I used a stopwatch to make sure Anna got enough milk, and I gave her a pacifier for recreation. When she was five weeks old, I went off to our summer house on Martha's Vineyard. I wondered if it was the right decision because there was less in the way of family and friends for support. But we worked things out together that summer. She was energetic from the first, and I was constantly sleep-deprived, but we were oh! so close. I found ways to make it easier for us. I found a babysitter to give me an afternoon break; I used the Swyngo-matic so that I could eat a warm supper every once in a while, and I learned to give Anna pacifiers or bottles to soothe herself. . . . ."

Paul interjected: "She was like a miracle to me. She was fabulous! Miraculous! She even looked like me. I did as much for her as Nancy did, not out of guilt, but because I couldn't keep my hands off her. I took her with me everywhere when I was off work. At the Stop-and-Shop, all the ladies crowded around me, 'How do you do it? You're so good with her!'" As he talked of Anna, his cheeks flushed, his whole body actively described the dramatic and exciting time they had together. "I learned all about babies from her. I can bathe a kid faster than anyone in the world."

"I went back to work when Anna was three months," said Nancy. "I found full-time help. That way, I could enjoy her when I was home and get away when I needed to. I am a high activity person, so I could understand a high-activity child like Anna. We could cycle together. I've never felt a bit of anxiety or ambivalence about her. I feel as if I've known her from the very first.

"Anna fit," said Nancy. "From the time she was born, we'd pick her up and just go. As you can see, going is pretty important in our family, and Anna thrived on it. We were not the only ones who enjoyed her; my own mother thought she was fabulous. She took care of her part-time after I went back to work. I had a chance to see my mother be loving and kind, a good mother to Anna. It was like reliving my own childhood—another kind of miracle. You see, I'd had a sister, Ginny, who had died. Anna gave my mother an opportunity to heal the pain of Ginny's death.

This was true for me, too. We called her Anna Virginia after this sister. Ginny had a devastating mental illness. Ginny's spirit, intelligence, and humor seemed to live again in Anna, but without the shadow of vulnerability."

SOURCE: Brazelton, T. B., 1987.

Thought Questions

1. How would you describe Anna's temperament? What problems might the Cotton family have faced if Anna had been a more passive, reserved, and inhibited child?

2. In what ways was Anna being expected to adapt to the Cotton family lifestyle?

3. What are some of the challenges Nancy and Paul faced as new parents? How did they cope with these challenges?

4. How would you describe Paul's enactment of the father role? What factors might influence how involved men become in parenting?

5. How would you describe Nancy's enactment of the mother role? What factors might influence how involved women become in parenting?

6. Anna seems to be influencing the well-being of her mother, father, and her grandmother. What impact does Anna have on each of these family members? What are some other examples of how infants influence, and even enhance, the lives of their family members?

Chapter 6

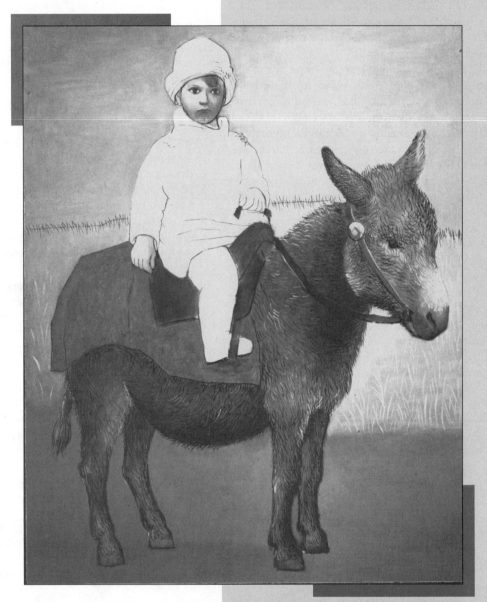

*B*uilding on a foundation of trust, toddlerhood is a period of tackling new challenges and achieving new levels of autonomy. Picasso captures the initial timidity of his son, Paulo, as he takes the reins of the donkey for the first time and asserts himself.

Toddlerhood (Ages 2 and 3)

Chapter Objectives

- To describe the expansion of locomotor skills during toddlerhood, indicating their importance for the child's expanding capacity to explore the environment and experience opportunities for mastery.
- To examine the development of fantasy play and its importance for cognitive and social development.
- To document accomplishments in language development and describe the major influence of interactive experiences and the language environment for the process of language acquisition.
- To examine the development of self-control, especially impulse management and goal attainment, highlighting strategies young children use to help them regulate their actions.
- To analyze the psychosocial crisis of autonomy versus shame and doubt, to clarify the central process of imitation, and to describe the prime adaptive ego strength of will and the core pathology of compulsion.
- To apply a psychosocial analysis to the topic of day care, emphasizing the impact of the social environment on patterns of development during toddlerhood.

Toddlers seem to bubble with unpredictable, startling thoughts and actions that keep adults in a state of puzzled amazement. Toddlers are extremely busy—talking, moving, fantasizing, and planning all the time. Their outpouring of physical activity—its vigor, constancy, and complexity—is remarkable. Equally impressive is the flood of cognitive accomplishments, especially language production and unique forms of playful fantasy.

Building on a foundation of trust and optimism formed during infancy, toddlerhood brings a flowering of the sense of personal autonomy, an enjoyment and confidence in doing things for oneself and expressing one's will. The successful blending of these two basic capacities for trust and autonomy provides a strong, protective shield for the young child's ego system. From this basis, children are able to venture into satisfying and meaningful social relationships, engage in playful problem solving, and face their future with an outlook of hopefulness and assertiveness.

The chances for such a positive conclusion to the period of toddlerhood rest largely on the quality of the home environment. Toddlers, with their high energy level, improbable ideas, impish willfulness, and needs for mastery, run headlong into the full range of limits in their physical and social environment. Parenting during toddlerhood is like paddling a ca-

noe through the rapids. It requires vigilance, good communication between the bow and the stern, flexibility, and a certain joie de vivre that keeps the whole trip fun. A child's cognitive and social development during this period of life can be facilitated by the parents' own ego development, their style of parenting in dealing with the challenges of toddlerhood, and the quality of their relationship (Miller et al., 1993). The degree to which discord and conflict introduce stress into the lives of parents, brings special risk for some toddlers.

The developmental tasks of toddlerhood—expanded locomotion, fantasy play, language and communication skills, and self-control—all contribute to the child's emerging independence within the boundaries of the social group. Some theorists refer to this as the first individuation process (Mahler et al., 1975; Blos, 1979). Obviously, 3-year-olds are not ready to set out for life alone in the big city. But they are ready to express independent thoughts, exercise some control in making choices, and try doing things independently. The psychosocial crisis during this period of life—autonomy versus shame and doubt—is a struggle to establish a sense of separateness without disrupting the bonds of affection and protection that are critical to a young child's physical survival and emotional connection to the family. ❖

DEVELOPMENTAL TASKS

Elaboration of Locomotion

The use of the word *toddler* to describe development for 2- and 3-year-olds is in itself a clue to the important part that locomotion plays. In fact, it is only during the first year of this stage that the child actually toddles. By age 3, the child's walk has changed from the precarious, determined, half-humorous waddle known as the toddle to a more graceful, continuous, effective stride. Removal of diapers probably plays an important role in the progress of the child's walk. When toddlers no longer have a large wad of padding between their legs, they quickly make the transition from ugly duckling to swan. Of course, physical development, including changes in the shape and strength of leg muscles, contributes significantly to this transformation (Clark & Phillips, 1993).

Locomotion plays a central role in the toddler's psychosocial development, facilitating the transformation of ideas into action and prompting new types of interactions with the social and physical environment. As locomotor skills develop, the child has new ways of remaining close to the object of attachment, new avenues for investigating the environment, and new strategies for coping with stressful situations. Locomotor skills also figure prominently in the elaboration of play during this period. To the extent that coping involves the ability to maintain freedom of movement under conditions of threat, the locomotor skills acquired during toddlerhood provide a fundamental arsenal of lifelong strategies for "fight" or "flight."

Advanced locomotor skills may also increase conflicts with caregivers, introducing new struggles of willfulness and new parental constraints (Biringen et al., 1995). When Ellen was about 2½ years old, she enjoyed watching her older brother climbing up a tree in the neighbor's yard. She would beg her brother to lift her up so she could get into the tree with him. One afternoon, Ellen's brother lifted her into the tree and then ran off to play with a friend. Ellen tried to get down from the tree, but she got her foot stuck in a crack between the branches. She cried and yelled until her mom came to get her. Ellen's mom scolded her for being in the tree and warned her never to go up there again. But the next afternoon, Ellen was back trying to figure out how to climb into the tree on her own. From this example one can see that when locomotor skills occur early in a developmental period, before the maturation of verbal and cognitive competence, toddlers may find themselves at odds with caregivers who must limit locomotion to protect the child's safety and to secure the safety of other people and objects in the environment.

Difficulties encountered by engineers and inventors in trying to duplicate human locomotor skills with robots have demonstrated just how intricate and exquisite are the toddler's accomplishments (Pick, 1989). The possibility that lifelong movement patterns are acquired during these two years extends our appreciation of toddlers' locomotor accomplishments. Renewed interest in motor development suggests that qualitative changes in locomotive behavior are not simply a result of maturation of the cerebral cortex (Kalverboer et al., 1993). Changes in body weight and muscle mass combined with new capacities to coordinate feedback from the limbs and to judge the amount of effort needed to achieve a motoric goal are all components in what appears to be a regular progression in motor behavior (Getchell & Roberton, 1989). Some landmarks of motor development that are reached from ages 2 to 6— walking and running, jumping, hopping, throwing and catching, peddling and steering—are described in Table 6.1.

Toddlerhood brings tremendous advances in locomotion as children enjoy walking, running, jumping, and hopping. Leaping from steps, walls, chairs, and benches is almost like flying!

TABLE 6.1   Changes in Gross Motor Skills During Toddlerhood and Early School Age

Age	Walking and Running	Jumping	Hopping	Throwing and Catching	Peddling and Steering
2–3 years	Walks more rhythmically; widely spaced legs, feet narrow; opposite arm–leg swing appears. Hurried walk changes to true run.	Jumps down from step. Jumps several inches off floor with both feet, no arm action.	Hops 1 to 3 times on same foot with stiff upper body and non-hopping leg held still.	Throws balls with forearm extension only; feet remain stationary. Awaits thrown ball with rigid arms outstretched.	Pushes riding toy with feet; does little steering.
3–4 years	Walks up stairs, alternating feet. Walks downstairs, leading with one foot. Walks in a straight line.	Jumps off floor with coordinated arm action. Broad jumps about 1 foot.	Hops 4 to 6 times on same foot, flexing upper body and swinging non-hopping leg.	Throws ball with slight body rotation but little or no transfer of weight with feet. Flexes elbows in preparation for catching; traps ball against chest.	Pedals and steers tricycle.
4–5 years	Walks downstairs, alternating feet. Walks circular line. Walks awkwardly on balance beam. Runs more smoothly. Gallops and skips with one foot.	Improved upward and forward jumps. Travels greater distance.	Hops 7 to 9 times on same foot. Improved speed of hopping.	Throws ball with increased body rotation and some transfer of weight forward. Catches ball with hands; if unsuccessful, may still trap ball against chest.	Rides tricycle rapidly, steers smoothly.
5–6 years	Walks securely on balance beam. Increased speed of run. Gallops more smoothly. True skipping appears.	Jumps off floor about 1 foot. Broad jumps 3 feet.	Hops 50 feet on same foot in 10 seconds. Hops with rhythmical alternation (2 hops on one foot and 2 on the other).	Has mature throwing and catching pattern. Moves arm more and steps forward during throw. Awaits thrown ball with relaxed posture, adjusting body to path and size of ball.	Rides bicycle with training wheels.

Source: Reprinted by permission from *Infants, Children, and Adolescents*, Third Edition, by L. E. Berk, Table 8.1, p. 312. Copyright ©1999 Allyn & Bacon. Based on material from: Cratty, B. J. (1986). *Perceptual and motor development in infants and children* (3rd ed.). Englewood Cliffs, NJ: Prentice-Hall; Getchell N., and Roberton, M. A. (1989). Whole body stiffness as a function of developmental level in children's hopping. *Developmental Psychology, 25*, 920–928; Newborg, J., Stock, J. R., and Wnek, L. (1984). Battelle Developmental Inventory. Allen, TX: LINC Associates; Roberton, M. A. (1984). Changing motor patterns during childhood. In J. R. Thomas (Ed.), *Motor development during childhood and adolescence* (pp. 48–90). Minneapolis, MN: Burgess.

The development and perfecting of these skills depends on opportunity and encouragement, as well as on the maturation of the cognitive and motor systems.

As walking becomes a more comfortable form of locomotion, new skills are added to the child's repertoire. Running and jumping are the first to emerge. By the age of 4, children are likely to leap from stairways, porches, or ladders. They have begun to imagine what it might be like to fly. Jumping is their closest approximation to flying. Evidence suggests that the underlying structure of the jumping pattern remains stable throughout childhood and into adulthood (Clark et al., 1989). The child's delight in exploring jumping behavior may be the result of the acquisition of a fundamental movement pattern that fills the child with a basic sense of mastery as well as a sense of lifelong possibilities.

Children's running abilities become more elaborated all through toddlerhood. In films used to study the emergence of running, it appears that for toddlers, running and walking

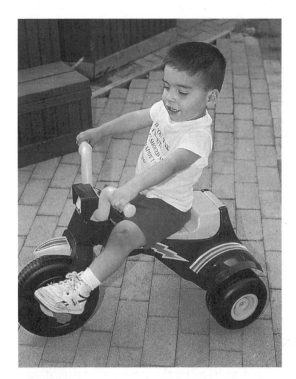

Locomotion is expanded with access to pedal toys. Once they figure out how to pedal, children can move faster, go farther, stop and start, reverse, and screech to a grinding halt.

are very much alike with little increase in velocity and little or no "flight" (the time when both feet are off the ground) in running. At the beginning, toddlers appear to be running because they are moving a bit faster, but their action is not similar to adult running. Over time, however, the movements smooth out as flight time and velocity increase (Whitall & Getchell, 1995).

At first, youngsters may run for the sake of running. They practice the art over and over again. Later in toddlerhood, running changes from a kind of game in itself to a valuable component of many other games. The absolute speed of toddlers is limited by somewhat precarious balance and short legs. This does not discourage them, however, from devoting a great deal of time and energy to running. The goals of mastery and getting to new places for exploration are too strong to dampen their enthusiasm.

Toddlers are often exposed to a wide variety of other forms of locomotion such as swimming, skiing, skating, sledding, and dancing. Children seem eager to use their bodies in a variety of ways, and they learn quickly (Ridenour, 1978). As their physical coordination improves, children engage in a new repertoire of large-muscle activities: climbing, sliding, swinging, pounding, digging, and rough-and-tumble play. These forms of physical activity provide an important source of information about the physical self. They offer a key avenue to experiencing mastery, and they are also the basis for a lot of fun. Toddlers enjoy their bodies and are generally joyful when in the midst of physical play. Thus, physical activity contributes in an essential way to the toddler's self-concept. Children who lack muscle strength or coordination experience strong feelings of frustration as they struggle to keep their balance, throw or catch a ball, or use their hands and feet to perform new tasks.

One of the vehicles of locomotion that has special meaning for the American toddler is the tricycle. It provides enormous pleasure because of its potential speed, reversibility, turning capacity, and horn. It is also an object through which the toddler can identify with other children and adults. The connection among tricycle, bicycle, and car is quickly and easily made by the toddler. The tricycle combines the joys of physical movement, the thrill of danger and independence, and the social significance of mechanized transportation. A tricycle (or comparable pedal toy) usually has great value for the child for the fun it provides and for the opportunities it offers to experience new levels of mastery. It also has symbolic significance for the parent who recognizes it as the first in a chain of objects that will foster the child's increased independence from the family and heightened identification with the peer group.

Fantasy Play The worlds of make-believe, poetry, fairy tales, and folklore, the domains we often associate with childhood, open up to the toddler as the ability for symbolization expands. Pretense play is not possible without semiotic thinking; it underlies the capacity for imagination, for allowing objects and people to take on new identities and new meaning.

Semiotic Thinking

Jean Piaget (1970) described the years from about 2 to 5 or 6 as the stage of **preoperational thought.** This is a transitional period during which the schemes that were developed during infancy are represented internally. The most significant achievement of this new stage of cognitive development is the capacity for **semiotic** thinking, the understanding that one thing can stand for another (Miller, 1993). In semiotic thinking, children learn to recognize and use symbols and signs. **Symbols** are usually related in some way to the object for which they stand. The cross, for example, is a symbol of Christianity. In pretend play, a scarf or a blanket may be a symbol for a pillow or a dress. **Signs** stand for things in a more abstract, arbitrary way. Words are signs; there is no direct relation between the word *dog* and the animal to which the word refers, yet the word stands for the object. For adults, it seems natural to use match sticks or little squares of cardboard to represent people or buildings, but for children, the idea that a stick may be a car or a horse is a dramatic change in thinking that emerges gradually during the preoperational period.

Symbolization brings enormous flexibility to human thought. The symbol embodies an idea of something separate from the thing itself. With the elaboration of various types of symbols, children can begin to recount events apart from the situation in which they occurred. They can invent worlds that never existed.

Children acquire five representational skills that allow them to manipulate objects mentally rather than by actual behavior: imitation in the absence of the model, mental images, symbolic drawing, symbolic play, and language. Each of these skills frees children from real events. Children can express relationships they may have known in the past by imitating them, drawing them, or acting them out in fantasy. They can also portray events and relationships that they wish would occur or that they wish to alter.

The Nature of Pretend Play

During infancy, play often consists of the repetition of a motor activity. Infants delight in sucking their toes or dropping a spoon from the high chair. These are typical **sensorimotor play** activities. Toward the end of infancy, sensorimotor play includes the deliberate imitation of parental acts. Children who see their mothers washing the dishes may enjoy climbing up on a chair and getting their hands wet, too. At first, these imitations occur only when they are stimulated by the sight of the parent's activity. As children enter toddlerhood, they begin to imitate parental activities when they are alone. A vivid mental image of an action permits them to copy what they recall instead of what they see. This is the beginning of **symbolic play.** Before the period of preoperational thought, children do not really pretend because they cannot let one thing stand for something else. Once the capacity for symbolic thought emerges, children become increasingly flexible in allowing an object to take on a wide variety of pretend identities.

Two-year-olds appear to be able to understand the context of a pretend situation. Using pretend props, they can pretend to feed a hungry animal or give a drink to a thirsty animal. They can assign a pretend function to a substitute prop, treating a wooden block as if it were a banana or a piece of cake. And they can follow through with the consequences of a pretend situation, like pretending to wipe up pretend spilled tea with a towel (Harris & Kavanaugh, 1993). These young children can construct a make-believe world in which objects are assigned a pretend meaning (toy blocks can be bananas) and words are used in pretend ways ("feed the monkey a banana" is acted out by putting a toy block up to the mouth of a toy monkey).

The Capacity for Pretense

Pretense, whether through symbolic play, symbolic drawing, or telling make-believe stories, requires that children understand the difference between pretend and real. Sometimes, adults wonder whether children can in fact distinguish between the two. The line between make-believe and reality may become blurred for all of us. At times, adults can encounter such confusion when watching television. Which televised images are pretend and which are real? Are the images and messages used to advertise products real or pretend? Is a television news story real or pretend? Are dramatic reenactments of historical events real or pretend?

In simplified situations, children as young as 2 can tell when someone is pretending and can follow the transformations in a pretend sequence (Walker-Andrews & Harris, 1993). For example, an investigator might tell a child that she is going to fill two bowls with cereal, and then pretend to fill the bowls. Then the investigator pretends to eat all of the cereal in her bowl, saying something at the end to indicate that all the cereal is gone. She then asks the child to feed a doll its cereal. Many 2-year-olds and most 3-year-olds can follow this type of scenario, selecting the bowl that is still full of pretend cereal and feeding it to the doll.

Toddlers know the difference between what an object really is and what someone is pretending that it is (Flavell et al., 1987). For example, 3-year-olds understand that a sponge is really a sponge, but they can pretend it is a boat floating in the water or a car driving along the road. Three-year-olds also understand the difference between knowing something and pretending something. If they see a rabbit, they know it is real, but they also know that they do not have to have seen a rabbit in order to imagine one. However, compared with older children, 3-year-olds are more convinced that imagination reflects reality. For example, if they imagine something, like a fire-breathing dragon or a horse with wings, they think it may actually exist. In contrast, 4-year-olds understand that something that is imagined may not have a counterpart in reality (Woolley & Wellman, 1993).

Fantasy play and language are contrasting forms of representation. In acquiring language, children learn to translate their thoughts into a commonly shared system of signs and rules. For language to be effective, children must use the same words and grammar as the older members of the family, discovering how to translate their thoughts into existing words and categories. Fantasy serves almost the opposite function. In fantasy, children create characters and situations that may have a very private meaning. There is no need to make the fantasy comprehensible to an audience. There are probably many times when children have strong feelings but lack the words to express them. They may be frustrated by their helplessness or angry at being overlooked. They can express and soothe these feelings in the world of imagination, even though the feelings may never become part of a shared conversation (Erikson, 1972).

Changes in Fantasy Play During Toddlerhood

Toddlers can direct their play in response to mental images that they have generated by themselves. At first, their symbolic play is characterized by the simple repetition of familiar activities. Pretending to sweep the floor, to be asleep, to be a dog or cat, and to drive a car are some of the early play activities of toddlers. Fantasy play changes in four ways during toddlerhood (Lucariello, 1987):

1. The action component becomes more complex as children integrate a sequence of actions.
2. Children's focus shifts from the self to fantasies that involve others and the creation of multiple roles.
3. The play involves the use of substitute objects, including objects children only pretend to have, and eventually the invention of complex characters and situations.
4. The play becomes more organized and planned, and play leaders emerge.

First, children combine a number of actions in a play sequence. From pretending to sweep the floor or take a nap, they devise strings of activities that are part of a complex play sequence. While playing firefighter, children may pretend to be the fire truck, the hose, the ladder, the engine, the siren, the people being rescued, and the firefighters. All the elements of the situation are brought under the children's control through this fantasy enactment.

One of the favorite forms of social pretense is "doctor." With the use of a few props, friends can explore the fascinating realm of illness, healing, comforting, and advising. Patient-doctor play allows children to gain mastery over an area of great concern and uncertainty.

Second, children become increasingly able to include others in their play and to shift the focus of the play from the self to the others (Howes, 1987; Howes et al., 1989). One can see a distinction here between solitary pretense, social play, and social pretend play. Children engaged in **solitary pretense** are involved in their own fantasy activities, such as pretending that they are driving a car or giving a baby a bath. Children engaged in **social play** join with other children in some activity. They may dig together in the sand, build with blocks, or imitate each other's silly noises. In **social pretend play**, children have to coordinate their pretense. They establish a fantasy structure, take roles, agree on the make-believe meaning of props, and solve pretend problems. That 2- and 3-year-olds can participate in this type of coordinated fantasy play is remarkable, especially given their very limited use of language to establish and sustain coordination.

Third, fantasy play changes as children become more flexible in their use of substitute objects in their play. Fantasy play begins in the areas closest to children's daily experience. They use real objects or play versions of those objects as props in their pretense. For example, they pick up a toy telephone and pretend to call Grandma or to have a picnic with toy cups and plates and plastic foods. But as they develop their fantasy skills, these props are no longer essential. Children can invent objects, create novel uses for common objects, and sometimes pretend to have an object when they have nothing (Boyatzis & Watson, 1993).

Play moves away from common daily experiences to invented worlds based on stories, television programs, or purely imagined characters and situations. Children may take the roles of characters with extraordinary powers. They may pretend to fly, become invisible, or transform themselves into other shapes with the aid of a few secret words or gestures. Their identification with a particular fantasy hero or heroine may last for days or even weeks as they involve the characters of the story in a variety of fantasy situations.

Fourth, fantasy play becomes more planned and organized. The planning emerges as children try to coordinate their pretend play with other players. It is also a product of a new realization of what makes pretend play most fun, and of the desire to make sure that those components are included in the play. In a preschool or day-care group, certain children are likely to take the lead in organizing the direction of fantasy play. They may set the play in motion or give it direction by suggesting the use of certain props, assigning roles, or working out the context of the play. In this example, a child demonstrates this kind of leadership:

> **Stuart** (climbing up on a tractor tire): This will be our shark ship, OK? Get on quick, Jeremy! The sharks will eat you!
>
> **Jeremy:** No! This is my police helicopter!
>
> **Stuart:** Well, OK. We're police. But we need to chase the sharks, OK? I see the sharks way down there! Come on!
>
> **Jeremy:** OK. Let's get 'em! (They both make helicopter noises and swat at make-believe sharks with plastic garden tools.) (Trawick-Smith, 1988, p. 53)

Some theorists distinguish symbolic role playing from games with rules, implying that the latter are guided by a formal set of mental operations that constrain play, while the former is open and flexible. However, it is clear that pretend play operates within a rule-bound structure (Vygotsky, 1978; Harris & Kavanaugh, 1993). In order to coordinate symbolic play with a partner, children have to come to some mutual understanding about the situation, props, characters, and plot. The players have to limit their behavior in ways that conform to the unspoken or latent rules of the pretense. For example, if the children decide that certain leaves are the pretend food, then no one can use the leaves as bricks to build a house or as hats. If one player is supposed to be the mommy, that player has to act like the mommy and not like the baby. In games with rules, the rules are more readily spelled out, but in both types of play, part of what makes it fun is to function within the boundaries of certain kinds of constraints.

Dramatic role playing, in which a child takes on the role of another person or creates a fantasy situation, increases steadily from the ages of 3 through 5. By the age of 6, however, children become involved in games with rules. They may use their fantasy skills during play by making up new games or new rules rather than by engaging in pretend play. If one is looking for the experts in diversified, elaborated fantasy, observe 4- and 5-year-olds (Cole & La Voie, 1985).

The Contributions of Fantasy Play to Development

Fantasy play is not simply a diversion. Children use fantasy to experiment with and understand their social and physical environments and to expand their thinking (Piers

& Landau, 1980; Hutt et al., 1988). Views of the importance and value of fantasy play vary widely. Piaget (1962) emphasized the assimilative value of play. He believed that through fantasy and symbolic play, children are able to make meaning of experiences and events that are beyond their full comprehension. Fantasy play is a private world to which the rules of social convention and the logic of the physical world do not necessarily apply. From this perspective, fantasy play frees the child from the immediacy of reality, permitting mental manipulations and modifications of objects and events.

> Vygotsky (1978) saw fantasy play quite differently. He argued that: play creates a zone of proximal development of the child. In play a child always behaves beyond his average age, above his daily behavior; in play it is as though he were a head taller than himself. As in the focus of a magnifying glass, play contains all developmental tendencies in a condensed form and is itself a major source of development. (p. 102)

When Vygotsky used the term **zone of proximal development,** he was referring to a range of potential performance. When trying to assess a child's developmental level, it is important to understand not only what the child already knows and can already perform, but also the domains that are "in progress" so to speak, the areas that are emerging as new fields of mastery. He argued that normally adults, especially parents and teachers, and more advanced peers promote development by engaging children in activities and problem-solving tasks that draw children into their zone of proximal development, the new directions along which their capacities are moving. However, in play, Vygotsky saw a cognitive process that in and of itself captures a foreshadowing of the child's next higher level of functioning. In pretend play, children address areas where they do not yet feel competent in their lives and try to act as if they were competent. They set certain rules for their performance, and commit themselves to function according to them. So if a child is pretending to be a good mother, she brings forward all the ideas she has about how to be a good mother and applies them to the pretend situation. Similarly, if a child is pretending to be a superhero, she imposes all the rules of power, goodness, and helpfulness that she knows of and tries to limit her actions to those rules. Vygotsky regarded fantasy play as a window into the areas of competence that the child is striving to master but are still out of reach.

Erikson (1972) considered play vital in promoting personality and social development. He valued play as a mechanism for dramatizing the psychological conflicts that children are struggling with, such as angry feelings toward their siblings or parents or jealousy over a friend's new toys. According to Erikson, the play often not only represents the problem but also offers a solution so that children experience some new sense of resolution and a reduction in the tension associated with the conflict. Symbolic play provides a certain flexibility or leeway in structuring the situation and, at the same time, imposes some limits so that children may experience a new mastery of issues that are perplexing or overwhelming in real life.

Pretend play actually fosters cognitive and social development (Rubin, 1980; Saltz & Saltz, 1986). Children who have well-developed pretending skills tend to be well-liked by their peers and to be viewed as leaders (Ladd et al., 1988). This is a result of their advanced communication skills, their greater ability to take the point of view of others, and their ability to reason about social situations. Children who have been encouraged in a playful, imaginative approach to the manipulation and exploration of materials and objects through fantasy show more complex language use and more flexible approaches to problem solving (Burke, 1987). Clearly, the importance of fantasy play in the full social, intellectual, and emotional development of young children cannot be underestimated. Some parents and teachers want to define a young child's cognitive growth in terms of the acquisition of words and concepts that seem relevant to the "real world." They emphasize the importance of learning numbers and letters, memorizing facts, and learning to read. However, research on cognitive development suggests that gains in the capacity for symbolic thought provide the essential underpinnings of subsequent intellectual abilities, such as abstract reasoning and inventive problem solving.

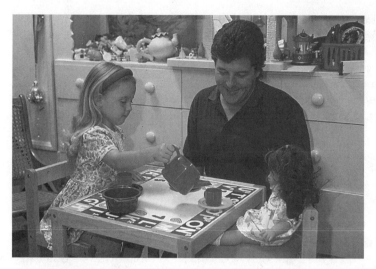

As a play companion, Dad can extend the play, draw the conversation in new directions, introduce new possible fantasies, and, of course, laugh and have fun.

The Role of Play Companions

Cognitive developmental theory emphasizes the normal emergence of representational thought and symbolic play as the natural outcome of cognitive maturation during toddlerhood. However, the quality of that play as well as its content depends in part on the behavior of a child's play companions. Consider the following incident. In a university preschool where college students were having their first supervised experience as teachers of young children, a child of 3 made a bid for some pretend play with a student teacher. The child picked up the toy telephone and made ringing noises. The student teacher picked up another phone and said, "Hello." The child asked, "Is Milly there?" The student teacher said, "No," and hung up the phone. Rather than extending the pretense into a more elaborate social pretend situation by saying something like "Who is calling?" or pretending to put Milly on the phone, the student teacher brought the scenario to a close.

As play companions, parents, siblings, peers, and child-care professionals can significantly enrich a child's fantasy play. Play companions can elaborate a child's capacity for fantasy, legitimize fantasy play, and help the child to explore new domains of fantasy. Research has shown that when mothers are available as play companions, the symbolic play of their 2-year-old children is more complex and lasts for a longer time (Slade, 1987). When adults are trained to engage in and encourage pretend play with toddlers, the toddlers show a higher level of ability to coordinate their responses with those of the adults. From the ages of 16–32 months, toddlers become increasingly skillful in directing an adult's behavior and negotiating changes in kinds of play (Eckerman & Didow, 1989). Early and frequent opportunities to pretend with older siblings as well as with parents contribute to a young child's ability to understand other people's feelings and beliefs. As toddlers experiment with various pretend roles, help construct fantasy situations, and manipulate objects with a play companion, they are forced to establish new channels of shared meaning, thus fostering a new degree of awareness about others (Youngblade & Dunn, 1995).

In child-care settings, the availability of a stable group of age-mates results in more complex, coordinated play. In contrast, children who have had many changes in their child-care arrangements are less likely to engage in complex social pretend play with other children (Howes & Stewart, 1987). Since toddlers rely so heavily on imitation and nonverbal signals to initiate and develop their social pretend play, the more time they have together, the more complex their fantasy play will be (Eckerman & Didow, 1996).

Imaginary Companions

Probably the most sophisticated form of symbolic play is the creation of an imaginary friend (Singer, 1975). An imaginary friend, which may be an animal, a child, or some other creature, springs, complete in concept, from the mind of the child. It occupies space. It has its own personality, which is consistent from day to day. It has its own likes and dislikes, which are not necessarily the same as those of its creator. Although not all children who have imaginary companions disclose this information to adults, some studies have shown that as many as 65% of toddlers have imaginary companions, and some children have more than one (Singer & Singer, 1990).

In one study, investigators invited children who had imaginary companions to come to the laboratory and play with their companions (Taylor et al., 1993). The children seemed willing to talk about their companions, and they thought the investigators would be able to see and touch their companions just as they could. For most of the children, the companions remained consistent for six months and retained an active role in the child's fantasy life.

Several functions are served by an imaginary friend: It takes the place of other children when there are none around; it serves as a play companion for pretend play; it serves as a confidant for children's private expression; and it is often involved in their efforts to differentiate between right and wrong. Sometimes, toddlers do things they know are wrong because they cannot stop themselves, and they find it difficult to accept responsibility for their misdeeds. They did not wish to be bad; they do not want to displease their parents; and the imaginary friend becomes a convenient scapegoat. Toddlers report that, although they tried very hard to stop their friend, it went right ahead and did the "bad" thing anyway. When children use an excuse of this kind, they are communicating that they understand the difference between right and wrong but are unwilling or unable to assume total responsibility for their misconduct. In general, imaginary friends can be seen as evidence of toddlers' ability to differentiate themselves from others and of their attempts to gain control over their impulses.

Language Development

In the process of language development, children acquire **communicative competence:** they become adept at using all the aspects of language that permit effective participation in the language environment of their culture (Harris, 1992). This includes learning to produce the sounds of the language, understanding the system of meanings, the rules of word formation, and the rules of sentence formation; developing a rich vocabulary; making adjustments to the social setting that are necessary to produce and interpret communication (pragmatics) and acquiring the ability to express thoughts in written as well as oral form. Through the achievement of communicative competence, children become increasingly integrated into their culture. They learn the expressions, tone of voice, and gestures that link them intimately to the language environment of their home and community. They learn when to speak and when to remain silent, and how to approach communication with peers, parents, and authority figures. They learn the terms applied to kin, close friends, acquaintances, and strangers; the words that are used to disparage or devalue, and those used to recognize and praise. If nurturing is the primary vehicle for cultural socialization in infancy, communication is the primary vehicle in toddlerhood.

Communicative competence begins during infancy and develops across the entire life span. Vocabulary, grammar, and pragmatics continue to be expanded and refined as one engages in formal schooling, and enters a wider range of social settings where specific words, expressions, and styles of interaction are in use. But toddlerhood appears to be the time of a dramatic expansion in verbal competence when remarkable achievements are made in an exceptionally brief period. The discussion of language and communication that follows is divided into two major segments: language milestones and the language environment. The first segment outlines the pattern of communication accomplishments of infancy and toddlerhood, including the expanded use of words with meaning, the formation of two-word sentences, more complex sentence formation, and grammar. Important physiological structures support this emerging competence (Box 6.1). The second segment identifies factors in the social environment that help facilitate and optimize communicative competence.

The discussion that follows provides a picture of patterns of accomplishment in language and communication from infancy through about age 4. At the outset, however, it is important to recognize the wide variability in the development of communicative skills. Certain sequences of ability appear to be quite common among children from many language environments. For example, communicative gestures precede the production of spoken words, and the production of a substantial vocabulary of spoken words precedes the linking of words into two-word sentences. But the timing of the onset of various abilities and their rate of growth varies from child to child. For example, in a large national study of infant-toddler language, word production for 12-month-old infants ranged from the 90th percentile who used 26 words or more to the 10th percentile who produced no words. By 16 months of age, those in the 90th percentile were using 180 words, and those in the bottom 10th percentile produced 10 words or less (Fenson et al., 1994). (Figure 6.1). All these children were healthy, normal children with no known history of developmental delay, prematurity, or genetic disease. As you

FIGURE 6.1
Word production from 8 to 16 months
SOURCE: Fenson et al., 1994.

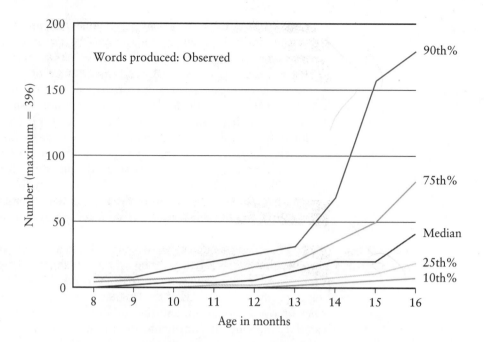

read about modal or typical patterns, try to remember that these patterns disguise important variations.

Communication Accomplishments in Infancy

Thought and language seem to travel independent courses that intersect during the second year of life (Molfese et al., 1982). Before that time, one can observe vocalization without meaning; that is, cooing (mostly vowel sounds noticeable at 1 to 2 months) and babbling (consonant-vowel sounds repeated over and over, which begin at about 4 months). One also observes thoughtful action patterns without verbal labels—reaching and grasping, or learning to use a spoon. (This type of behavior is discussed as sensorimotor intelligence in Chapter 5.)

Language Perception. Infants are able to recognize sounds and differentiate between sound combinations before they understand their meanings (Bates et al., 1987). This capacity to recognize language sounds, including the phonetic combinations of letters and words and the intonation of sentences, is called **language perception.** Young infants are able to hear and distinguish among all the major language sounds used in natural language. By the age of 4.5 months, infants recognize the sound of their own name (Mandel et al., 1995).

BOX 6.1   LOOKING IN ON THE BRAIN: HOW THE BRAIN PROCESSES LANGUAGE

Research evidence confirms that linguistic competence, especially the ability to produce and understand verbal material, is based in the left hemisphere of the brain. Further, with the use of positron emission tomography (PET) one can observe different areas of activity in the brain related to varying language activities including speaking, seeing, and hearing words. Verbal communication is distinct from other cognitive functions such as symbolization or associative memory. Studies involving deaf users of sign language, as well as hearing subjects who use spoken language, provide evidence that injury to the left hemisphere can result in a form of language aphasia. For the deaf, this injury does not interrupt the capacity to make other types of gestures, con-

firming that language functions are differentiated from other symbolic and motor functions that might be involved in the communicative process (Corina et al., 1992). Using pictorial information, studies have suggested that the right hemisphere applies conventional rules for determining meaning, whereas the left hemisphere is better suited for detecting deviations from standard meaning and for assigning meaning when the stimuli are unfamiliar (Cronin-Golomb, 1995). One would expect that, in time, researchers will be able to observe substantial changes in organization and activity in this area of the left hemisphere during the period of toddlerhood when many new stimuli are encountered and few rules are already established.

Gestures, such as pointing, are forms of preverbal communication. Ellie wants her dad to look at something, even though he is trying to get the shirt off the baby.

Babbling. Babbling, initially characterized by sounds used in many languages, begins to reflect the sounds and intonation infants are most likely to hear. Sounds they do not hear drop out of their babbling and, at about this same time, the capacity to differentiate among language sounds not found in their native language diminishes (Bates et al., 1987). This environmental shaping of language competence provides another example of plasticity of brain functions, discussed in Chapter 5, in which some networks grow and become strengthened by experience while others wither and are absorbed into the neural mass.

Babbling begins to take on a special character, connecting consonants and vowels and repeating these combinations when the baby is around 6–10 months. Although parents may eagerly receive this type of babbling as evidence of first words (i.e., *baba, mama, dada*), research suggests that these repetitions of babbling sounds do not have a symbolic value.

Communication with Gestures. By 8 months, infants also use sounds like grunting and whining in combination with gestures to achieve a goal. Thus, sounds combined with gestures and looks in a certain direction become part of purposeful communication—trying to get the caregiver to reach a cookie or get a certain toy off the shelf. A common first gesture is to raise the arms up toward the caregiver in a desire to be picked up (Fenson et al., 1994). Sounds may also be used to express emotion or to get someone's attention (Garton, 1992; Bates et al., 1987). Two other major communicative strategies among infants emerge at about 9–11 months. Infants begin to seek adult interest and attention by *showing* them objects and thereby initiating an interaction. Soon after showing, the infant begins *giving* objects. Adults who are willing to engage in this type of exchange will find the baby bringing them a whole variety of toys, utensils, and pieces of dirt or dust for inspection. Following giving, a common next key gesture is *pointing*. There is some debate about whether pointing is a form of reaching or a way of getting an adult's attention to notice an object. In either case, it is an example of an infant's initial ability to establish a shared reference point with respect to some object in the environment. (In our family, our first child, Sam, used pointing combined with a "whasziss?" sound to ask for the names of things at about 10 months.)

First Words. Around the age of 8 months, infants understand the meanings of some individual words and phrases (Harris, 1992; Fenson et al., 1994). This ability to understand words, called **receptive language,** precedes the ability to produce spoken words and phrases. You can direct a baby's glance by saying, "Look at the flowers," or "Do you want some candy?" At this age babies can go through their paces in the ever delightful game of "point to your nose, eyes, ears, etc." The number of words infants understand increases rapidly after 12 months. According to one analysis, 16-month-old infants have a receptive vocabulary of between 92 and 321 words (Fenson et al., 1994).

One of the first significant events in the development of **language production** is the naming of objects. With repetition, a sound or word becomes associated with a specific object or a set of related objects. For example, a child may say *ba* whenever she sees her bottle. If she is thirsty and wants her bottle, she may try saying *ba* in order to influence her caregiver to produce the bottle. Gestures, actions, and facial expressions often accompany the baby's word and help establish its meaning in the caregiver's mind. If the baby's word has meaning to the caregiver and serves to satisfy the baby's needs, it will probably be retained as a meaningful sign. The word *ba* may come to mean "bottle" and other liquids the child wishes to drink, such as juice, water, or milk.

The important characteristic of first words is their shared meaning. Even though *ba* is not a real word, it functions in the same way that any noun does: it names a person, place, or thing. These single-word utterances accompanied by gestures, actions, vocal intonation, and emotion are called **holophrases.** They convey the meaning of an entire sentence. For example, saying "ba, ba" in a pleading tone while pointing to the refrigerator and bouncing up and down conveys the meaning "I need a bottle," or "Get me the bottle." Gradually, the child discovers that every object, action, and relationship has a name.

Young children first talk about what they know and what they are interested in. Common first words include important people (*Mama, Dada,* names of siblings), foods, pets, toys, body parts *(eye, nose)* clothes *(shoe, sock),* vehicles *(car),* favorite objects *(bottle, blanket),* other objects in the environment *(keys, trees),* actions *(up, bye-bye), yes, no, please, down, more,* pronouns *(you, me),* and states *(hot, hungry).* Lois Bloom (1993) has suggested that what she calls a "Principle of Relevance" guides the early acquisition of new words. Babies pay special attention to words and expressions that are most closely linked with what they are doing and thinking about at the time. For that reason, the actual vocabulary that is acquired during infancy is quite idiosyncratic, reflecting the themes and experiences of each child's everyday life.

Communicative Competence in Toddlerhood

Language development in toddlerhood brings rapid acquisition of a wide-ranging vocabulary and the initial use of a primitive grammar that is quickly transformed into the grammar of the spoken language.

Vocabulary. During the period from 12 to 16 months, infants make significant progress in learning the names of objects and applying them to pictures or real examples. There is a rapid expansion of vocabulary during these four months from few or no spoken words to about 26. Sometime around 18 months, the child acquires a large number of new words and vocabulary continues to expand at a rapid rate throughout the toddler and early school years (Rice, 1989). The average toddler of 30 months has a spoken vocabulary of about 570 words. In order to accomplish this feat, children seem to **fast-map** new meanings as they experience words in conversation. To fast-map is to quickly form an initial partial understanding of a word's meaning. It is an information processing technique in which children relate the new word to the known vocabulary by linking it to the known-word storage space and to concepts that are already well understood (Carey, 1978). The child has to hear the new word only a few times in a context that makes its meaning clear. Thus, without direct word-by-word tutoring, children accumulate numerous samples of their culture's language from the speech they hear and attach a minimally satisfactory definition to each word or phrase.

The early phase of vocabulary development seems to focus on broad semantic categories—animals, cars, fruits, clothes, etc. New words, particularly nouns, are treated like the name of a category of things rather than only one specific object or a part of it. For example, when a child learns the word *cup,* it is used to refer to all objects that have the general shape and function of a cup (Golinkoff et al, 1992; Smith et al., 1992; Jones et al., 1991).

A much slower process of vocabulary development occurs as children and adults learn the distinctions among words within categories (Miller & Gildea, 1987). You may have a very good idea about the distinction between annual and perennial flowering plants, but you may not know the difference between the many types of each group and how to recognize them. In fact, building a vocabulary of subcategories may become an entire field of study, such as botany or zoology, in which the types and subtypes of a larger category are identified, classified, and named.

Two-Word Sentences. At 16 months of age, few children use two-word sentences, but by 30 months almost all children make them (Fenson et al., 1994). These two-word sentences are referred to as **telegraphic speech.** Children link two words that are essential to communicate what they intend to say. Just as in a telegram, however, other words—verbs, articles, prepositions, pronouns, conjunctions—are left out. A child will say, "big ball," "more juice," and "Daddy gone." Before this point, children tend to utter single words accompanied by gestures and actions. By stringing two words together, they convey more meaning through verbal communication and rely less heavily on gestures and actions. The acquisition of telegraphic speech allows a child to make fuller use of the symbolism inherent in language to communicate meaning.

Children are quite innovative in using two-word sentences. They continue to understand more than they are able to say, but they appear to use their limited number of words and the newfound ability to combine them to get their point across. Children may convey different meanings with the same sentence. "Daddy go," for example, may be used to tell someone that Daddy has left, or it may be used to tell Daddy to leave. Children often indicate their meanings by tone of voice or by the words they stress. The use of two-word sentences is characteristic of toddler-age language learners in many cultures (Slobin, 1985).

Braine (1976) analyzed the first word combinations spoken by children in English, Samoan, Finnish, Hebrew, and Swedish. His goal was to identify the kinds of rules or patterns that governed these early combinations. Ten patterns of word combination were embedded in those early language samples:

1. Making reference to something: See + X (see mother)
2. Describing something: Hot + X (hot stove)
3. Possession: X has a Y (Billy has a bottle)
4. Plurality: Two + X (two dogs)
5. Repetition or other examples: More + X (more up)
6. Disappearance: All gone + X (all gone milk)
7. Negation: No + X (no sleep)
8. Actor-action relations : Person + X (Daddy sleep)
9. Location: X + here (Grandma here)
10. Requests: Have + X (Have it, ball)

Braine found that although he could identify some common patterns of word combinations, they were not guided by the grammatical categories of the spoken language but by the meanings that the child wished to express and by the variety of objects, people, and interactions in the immediate environment. The patterns of word combinations used by some children did not overlap at all with those used by other children in the same culture.

Early language appears to be closely tied to the representation of sensorimotor schemes—the kinds of activities that dominate the child's life such as eating, sleeping, playing games with mommy or daddy or the siblings, going places, coming back home, and so on. It expresses the properties and relationships of objects and people that are important in a child's life. Language use emerges within a larger communication system and reflects a child's cognitive capacities. At the same time, it reflects the perceptual and functional characteristics of the environment. The kinds of objects and relationships that are central to daily life influence the content and complexity of a child's early language (Nelson, 1981).

Grammatical Transformations. By combining words according to the set of rules of grammar for a given language, a person can produce a limitless number of messages that can be understood by another person. Remarkably, by the age of 4, children appear to be able to structure their sentences using most of these rules without any direct instruction. The **grammar** of a particular language provides a set of rules that permit the complexity and variety of one person's thinking to be readily understood by someone else. Consider the difference in meaning between "The boy hit the ball" and "The ball hit the boy." The simple matter of word order in a sentence is critical for preserving meaning. The basic format of an English sentence—noun phrase followed by verb phrase—is a central part of its grammar. In order to ask a question or produce a negative sentence, the speaker transforms this word order according to a specific set of rules. (e.g., "You are going" versus "Are you going?") The addition of certain inflections and modifiers conveys information about time, possession, number, and relation. As children learn the grammatical transformations of their language, they become much more effective in conveying exactly what they have in mind.

When Brown (1973) analyzed the development of grammar in three children, he found that although the rate of acquiring inflections varied among the children, the order was surprisingly constant. The typical order in which children learn basic grammatical inflections is listed in Table 6.2.

TABLE 6.2	Basic Sequence in Adding Grammatical Inflections
Inflection	**Example**
-ing	Puppy is run*ing*.
in	*in* the pot.
on	I am *on* the bed.
Plural: -s	Apples.
Past irregular	*Fell, hit, ran.*
Possessive: -s	Baby's toy.
Use of *to be* as main verb without contraction	The boys *are* home.
Articles	I want *a* bottle.
Past regular	You walk*ed* too fast.
Third person regular	He walks.
Third person irregular	She *has*, he *does*.
Uncontractible progressive auxiliary	This *is* going fast.
Use of *to be* as a main verb with contraction	That's Bill.
Contractible progressive auxiliary	I'*m* talk*ing*.

A surprising observation is that children use correct transformations for the past tenses of irregular verbs (went, gave, run) before they use correct inflections of regular verbs (talked, walked, jumped). It appears that children first learn the past tenses of irregular verbs through rote memory. Once they learn the rule for expressing the past tense by adding -ed, they occasionally **overregularize** this rule and begin making errors in the past tense. Thus, a 2-year-old is likely to say "I ran fast," but a 3-year-old may say "I runned fast." According to a model proposed by Gary Marcus, children recognize and have a symbolic category for words that are verbs. They establish a default rule: "to form the past tense, add -*ed* to any word that can be categorized as a verb." They also memorize the past forms of the irregular verbs as they encounter them. When an irregular verb is required, its irregular past tense form is always used if the child can recall it. However, if the child cannot recall the past tense, or if the word is novel, the default rule is called into play. In a study of preschoolers, the rate of overregularization was 4.5%. This fell to 2.5% for first graders and 1% for fourth graders, suggesting that as a child's vocabulary grows, the need to apply the default rule to unfamiliar verbs declines (Marcus, 1996).

The grammatical errors young children make alert us to the fact that they are working to figure out a system of rules with which to communicate meaning. It is unlikely, however, that these errors result from imitation of adult speech. Children say such things as, "What dat feeled like?" or "Dose are mines." They have certainly not copied those expressions from adults; rather, these errors suggest the beginning of a grammar that becomes more specialized and accurate as children acquire the opportunity to match their speech to that of others (Schatz, 1983).

The milestones in language development during the first four years of life are summarized in Table 6.3. During the first year of life, babies are highly sensitive to spoken language. They use vocalization in a playful way as a source of sensory stimulation. Gradually, babies produce vocalizations that imitate spoken language. In the second year, babies understand words and phrases. They develop a vocabulary and begin to form two-word phrases. During the third year, language is definitely used to communicate ideas, observations, and needs. Com-

Toddlers love to talk on the phone. They recognize this as an adult behavior, and may carry on elaborate conversations whether there is someone on the other end or not.

TABLE 6.3   Milestones in Language Development

At the Completion of:	Vocalization and Language Characteristics
12 weeks	Markedly less crying than at 8 weeks; when talked to and nodded at, smiles, followed by squealing-gurgling sounds usually called cooing, that is, vowel-like in character and pitch-modulating; sustains cooing for 15–20 seconds.
16 weeks	Responds to human sounds more definitely; turns head; eyes seem to search for speaker; occasionally some chuckling sounds. Recognizes the sound of his/her name.
20 weeks	The vowel-like cooing sounds begin to be interspersed with consonantal sounds; acoustically, all vocalizations are very different from the sounds of the mature language of the environment.
6 months	Cooing changing into babbling resembling one-syllable utterances, neither vowels nor consonants have very fixed recurrences; most common utterances sound somewhat like *ma, mu, da,* or *di.*
8 months	Reduplication (or more continuous repetition) becomes frequent; intonation patterns become distinct; utterances can signal emphasis and emotions. Produces meaningful gestures like wanting to be picked up, showing, or giving. Understands some words and phrases.
10 months	Vocalizations are mixed with sound play such as gurgling or bubble blowing; appears to wish to imitate sounds, but the imitations are never quite successful; expansion in comprehension of words.
12 months	Identical sound sequences are replicated with higher relative frequency of occurrence and early word production (*mama* or *dada*); understands about 50 words and simple commands (i.e., "Show me your eyes.").
16 months	Has a definite repertoire of about 40 words (the top 90th percentile has 180 word vocabulary); still much babbling but now of several syllables with intricate intonation pattern; no pattern; words may include items such as *thank you* and *come here,* but there is little ability to join items into spontaneous two-word phrases; understanding is progressing rapidly.
24 months	Vocabulary of more than 300 items (some children seem to be able to name everything in the environment); begin spontaneously to join vocabulary items into two-word phrases; all phrases appear to be own creations; definite increase in communicative behavior and interest in language.
30 months	Continuing increase in vocabulary with over 550 words; many new additions every day; no babbling at all; utterances have communicative intent; frustrated if not understood by others; utterances consist of at least two words, many have three or even five words; use of linguistic suffixes for possession, plural, and past tense; frequent use of irregular plural noun (foot/feet) and irregular verbs; intelligibility is not very good yet by those unfamiliar with the child's speech.
3 years	Vocabulary of some 1,000 words; about 80% of utterances are intelligible even to strangers; grammatical complexity of utterances is roughly that of colloquial adult language, although mistakes still occur.
4 years	Language is well established; deviations from the adult norm tend to be more in style than in grammar.

SOURCE: Adapted from Lenneberg, 1967 and Fenson et al., 1994.

prehension of spoken language seems almost complete. Some of their speech may not be easily understood by people outside the family, partly because they are unable to produce clear phonetic sounds and also because their knowledge of adult grammar is limited. During the fourth year, most children acquire an extensive vocabulary. They can create sentences that reflect most of the basic rules of grammar. Their language is a vehicle for communicating complex thoughts that are usually understood by children and adults outside the family.

Language Development Beyond Toddlerhood

Although the fundamentals of language are well established by age 4, there are still some things that toddlers cannot achieve with language. For example, Mary may raise a fuss about wanting the biggest piece of cake. If you allow her to make a choice, she selects a piece with lots of frosting. Clearly, the word *biggest* is not being used correctly. Even though Mary is able to memorize and repeat the words *big, bigger,* and *biggest,* she does not yet fully understand the concept to which they refer. Other observations suggest that 2- and 3-year-olds have difficulty using verbal instructions to control or guide their behavior (Tinsley & Waters, 1982). They may be able to tell themselves to "stop" or "go slow," but these commands are not effective in slowing them down. Both of these examples demonstrate that toddlers' language development can be some-what misleading. One may assume that children fully understand the more abstract meaning of the words they use, but in fact their language continues to be very idio-syncratic throughout toddlerhood.

As the process of fast-mapping implies, children may add a word to their vocabu-lary without understanding the several meanings this word has in different contexts. During the periods of early and middle childhood, considerable time and attention is devoted to exploring vocabulary, correcting some meanings that were incorrectly learned, and expanding the full range of meanings and underlying concepts that are linked to the many words that were acquired so rapidly during toddlerhood. One esti-mate is that the reading vocabulary or comprehension of dictionary entries of a ten-year-old child is close to 40,000 words, with perhaps another 40,000 proper names, places, and expressions unique to the child's own family, neighborhood, and cultural group (Anglin, 1993).

Important language functions develop more fully during early and middle child-hood. These older children can use language to plan a problem-solving strategy, guide a complex series of motor activities, or identify the relationships among objects. Vo-cabulary expands, and words are used more frequently in the ways they are used in adult speech. Sentences become more complex, including conditional and descriptive clauses. The irregular verbs and nouns are learned and used correctly. As children at-tend school, they learn to conceptualize the grammatical structure of their language. Beyond the formal elements of vocabulary, grammar, reading, and writing, language becomes a vehicle for creative expression. Children write poems, essays, and stories. They begin to use sarcasm, puns, and metaphors to elaborate their speech. They cre-ate secret codes with their special friends. Children make up riddles and jokes, put on plays and puppet shows, work on school newspapers, and leave enigmatic or corny messages in their friends' yearbooks. Language plays a critical role in subsequent psy-chosocial crises, especially the establishment of group identity, intimacy, and genera-tivity. It is primarily through the quality of one's spoken language that one achieves the levels of disclosure that sustain significant personal relationships. Language also serves as a mechanism for resolving conflicts and for building a sense of cohesiveness within groups, whether of friends, co-workers, or family members.

The Language Environment

Language is a cultural tool, a means for socializing and educating young children. It is one of many inventions for creating a sense of group identity and for passing the mythology, wisdom, and values of the culture from one generation to the next. Lan-guage is a part of the psychosocial environment. Competence in the use of language so-lidifies the young child's membership in the immediate family and in the larger cultural group (Rogoff & Morelli, 1989). Although there is strong evidence for genetically based origins of the capacity for language learning, the specific content and tone of a child's communication is strongly influenced by the language environment. In this sec-tion, we focus primarily on the nature of the in-teraction between toddlers and their caregivers, with some attention to the issue of bilingualism and the relationship of the language environment at home and school.

As language skills develop, children and adults can share their perceptions, talk about how they are feeling, figure out how to solve problems, and learn from one another.

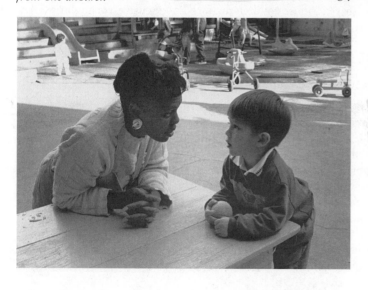

Interaction and Language Development. Probably the most important factor that caregivers contribute to cognitive growth is the opportunity for inter-actions. An interactive human being can respond to a child's questions, provide information, react in unexpected ways and surprise the child, ex-plain plans or strategies, and offer praise or crit-icism. With the achievement of language skills, children and their caregivers begin to explore a vast array of topics through spoken language. They explore their needs—hunger, thirst, sleepi-ness, and companionship. They travel along the paths of emotions such as anger, sadness, delight, pride, and shame. They talk playfully with one another, examining new objects, discussing kinship relations, and creating fantasies. In addition, adults and children talk about philosophical and moral questions like lying, helping, "what ifs," and the question "how would you feel if it happened to you?" As children speak from their own inner world revealing their own point of view, parents begin to know and appreciate their children's concerns and needs in a new way. Similarly, children begin to hear and understand their family's talk in a new way. They can question what they do not understand, and expand what they know through family talk.

Burton White compared the child-rearing practices of mothers whose children were judged to be socially and intellectually competent with those of mothers whose children were judged to be below average (White et al., 1979). The mothers of the competent children spent more time in interaction with them than did the mothers of the below-average children. This was true at every age period from 12 to 33 months. "The amount of live language directed to a child was perhaps the strongest single indicator of later intellectual and linguistic and social achievement" (White et al., 1979). This does not mean that it is necessary to be with a child continuously, but it is clear that children benefit from frequent opportunities for interaction.

The causal relationship between child competence and frequency of parent-child interaction is still a matter of some controversy. Consider these three different explanations:

1. Parents and their offspring may share a genetic predisposition for verbal competence, which is evident in the frequency of parent-child interaction and in the early acquisition of verbal skills.
2. Parents who interact frequently with their children provide a rich array of verbal stimuli and thereby promote high levels of verbal comprehension and production.
3. Children who are more verbally competent stimulate more interaction from their caregivers, which then establishes a more active and diverse verbal environment. Over time, research will no doubt clarify the nature of these relationships.

Certain characteristics of a language partner have been shown to facilitate a child's language acquisition and communication skills (Snow, 1984). When talking to toddlers, adults tend to modify their speech so that they are more likely to be understood. They use simplified, redundant speech that corresponds to the child's level of comprehension and interest. A caregiver will speak to an infant in long, complex sentences, but as soon as the baby begins to speak, the caregiver's speech becomes exaggerated and simplified. When speaking to toddlers, adults and older children adjust their spoken language in the following ways (Rice, 1989):

1. They simplify utterances to correspond with the toddler's interests and comprehension level.
2. They emphasize the here and now.
3. They use a more restricted vocabulary.
4. They do a lot of paraphrasing.
5. They use simple, well-formed sentences.
6. They use frequent repetitions.
7. They use a slow rate of speech with pauses between utterances and after the major content words.

These characteristics of caregiver speech are not universal. They seem to reflect cultural norms for addressing toddlers (Pye, 1986). They are most typically observed in white, middle-class Western societies. In one cross-cultural analysis, for example, it was observed that African-American adults in the rural South did not simplify or censor their speech for young children (Heath, 1989). They frequently did not address children directly, but expected the children to hear what they said and to interrupt if they had something to add. Adults and children directed one another's behavior with specific commands. It was just as acceptable for a toddler to command an adult as the other way around. Adults tease children, especially in the presence of others, in order to give the children a chance to show off their quick wit and to practice assertiveness.

Within this language environment, children have the opportunity to hear a variety of opinions, gather information that extends their direct experience, and observe shifts in language tone and style that accompany changes in the topic or purpose of the conversations.

This example illustrates the wide variation in parenting styles that characterize American families, producing substantial differences in the language-learning environments of the home. In one longitudinal study, 40 families (15 black and 25 white) were observed once per month over 2½ years (Hart & Risley, 1992). The observations covered the period shortly before, during, and after the child was learning to talk. The number of words spoken to a child in an hour varied from 232 to 3,606; the percentage of time that parents were in the same room as the child during the observation ranged from 38 to 99%; and the average number of times that parents and children took turns in an interaction ranged from 1.8 to 17.4.

One question raised in this observational study was whether parenting style during the period of toddlerhood was related to the child's measured IQ at 37 months. Three dimensions or factors of parenting style were identified (Table 6.4) The first and third factors, Parental Activity and Quality of a Parent's Speech Toward the Child, were positively related to the child's IQ. The second factor, Performance as a Social Partner, was not correlated with the child's IQ. Both the first and third factors were correlated with the family's socioeconomic status, whereas the second factor was not. Children in lower socioeconomic families experienced less time with their parents, fewer moments of joint play, and exposure to fewer words. They were less likely to have their speech repeated or paraphrased by their parents, less likely to be asked questions, and more likely to experience prohibitions placed on their behavior. Those parents who were most likely to place prohibitions on their child's activities during this age period were less likely to listen intently to their child's speech, repeat what the child had said, or ask the child questions.

Scaffolding and Other Strategies for Enhancing Language Development. The process of language learning involves a pattern of mutual regulations and upward "scaffolding." Children try to match the verbal expressions used by adults, both in pronunciation and in selection of words (Nelson, 1973). Sometimes a child may be misunderstood because the child's pronunciation is so discrepant from the real word (*ambiance* for *ambulance, tommick cake* for *stomach ache*). At the same time, adults may use simplification or some other strategy to make sure they are being understood. Through frequent interactions, adults encourage language development by establishing a good balance between modifying their speech somewhat and modeling more complex, accurate speech for their children.

Adults make use of several strategies to clarify a child's meaning when the speech is unclear. One is **expansion**, or the elaboration of the child's expressions:

Child: Doggie wag.
Parent: Yes, the dog is wagging her tail.

TABLE 6.4   Parenting Factors During Language Learning

Parental Activity:	The percentage of time the parent was present in the same room with the child.
	The percentage of time the parent joined the child in play.
	The number of words directed to the child.
	The number of **different** words directed to the child.
Performance as a Social Partner:	The likelihood that a parent will respond to a child's initiation.
	The length of a social interaction as measured by the number of turns the parent takes.
	The relative length of a parent's phrases in comparison to the child's phrases.
The Quality of a Parent's Speech Toward the Child:	The likelihood that parents will ask their child questions.
	The likelihood that parents will repeat or paraphrase their child's speech.
	The frequency with which the parent imposes prohibitions on the child's behavior.

Source: Adapted from Hart & Risley, 1992.

The reading activities that parents and toddlers share are an important part of literacy. By reading aloud and talking about pictures, parents create the environment within which their children eventually think of themselves as readers.

Another strategy is **prompting,** often in the form of a question. Here the parent urges the child to say more:

| *Child:* | More crackel. |
| *Parent:* | You want more what? |

In both of these interactions, the adult is helping the child to communicate more effectively by expanding on or asking the child to elaborate on something of interest to him. In addition, the kinds of sentences parents use help children to see how they can produce new sentences that are more grammatically correct and therefore more meaningful to others.

Reading and Language Games. Socially interactive rituals such as telling stories, playing word games, verbal joking and teasing, and reading books together also seem to enhance language development, especially by building vocabulary and preparing children to use language comfortably in social situations. Reading aloud has been identified as an especially important language activity, not only for the preparation for literacy, but also for expanding a child's language skills (Crain-Thoreson & Dale, 1992; Valdez-Menchaca & Whitehurst, 1992). During toddlerhood, an adult may start out by reading picture books and asking the child questions about the pictures. The adult may try to relate the picture to some event in the child's life or ask children to tell something they notice about the pictures. Over time, the child becomes more and more of the storyteller, while the adult listens, encourages, and expands the tale. Some books are read aloud so often that the toddler begins to "read" them from memory or retell the story in their own words from the pictures.

As children enter early school age, this type of ritualized reading activity provides a framework for the child's concept of what it means to be a reader, including the ideas that printed letters make up words; that stories usually have a beginning, middle, and end; and that printed words and spoken words are similar in some ways. Depending on the context in which children read, they may also discover that you can learn things from printed words that you can't always know from the pictures, and that reading is a way to learn about the world beyond what you can know through direct experiences (Schickedanz, 1986).

Children and parents often engage in language games that expand the child's use of words and phrases. These games are usually part of ongoing family life. They are introduced not as a separate activity but as an extension of a related activity. Hoffman (1985) described one of her 3½-year-old son David's spontaneous games that began to build the bridge from speech to literacy. As the game developed, the object was for David to point to road signs as he rode with his mother to nursery school and for her to read as many of the signs as possible while they were driving along. David had created this game, and his mother played along willingly:

On the way to nursery school, David said, "Let's talk about signs! What does that sign say?" I answered, "Right turn signal."
David proceeded with, "And what does that yellow and red shell say?"
I answered him, "It says 'Shell'—that's a gasoline station."
He asked, "Does it have seashells in it?"
I answered, "No."
We proceeded to read signs. I read the majority as he requested. However, David read "Speed Limit 35," "Bike Route," and "No Parking Any Time." When we came to "No Parking This Side of Street," he thought it was "No Parking Any Time."

These were the signs that I was able to read as he requested while I was driving. They were not the only ones on the route.

SPEED LIMIT 40
SPEED LIMIT 35 (12 times)
NO PARKING ANY TIME (20 times)
SCHOOL SPEED LIMIT (2 times)
NO PARKING ON THIS SIDE OF
STREET (7 times)
Source: Hoffman, 1985.

NO TURN ON RED (3 times)
WATCH CHILDREN
SIGNAL AHEAD (3 times)
NO LITTERING
DRIVEWAY
BIKE ROUTE (2 times)

Families and ethnic groups vary not only in the language or dialect they speak but in their reliance on verbal as opposed to nonverbal expression, their typical patterns of communication, and the importance they place on language as a means to help children achieve competence in various domains. One area that has received special attention in recent years is the role of family conversation about feelings and its relation to a child's ability to express feelings and to identify feelings in others. Children's use of words to refer to feelings and to describe emotions increases notably at 3 and 4 years of age. At this same time, children become more skilled at recognizing feelings in others and in understanding how a person might feel in a certain situation (Brown & Dunn, 1992). Toddlers who have frequent experiences of talking with their mothers when they are in distress or conflict appear to be more effective at the age of 6 in understanding the point of view of others and in anticipating others' needs (Dunn et al., 1991). Children who grow up in families that are open to identifying and talking about emotions are more likely to show sensitivity to others in relationships outside the family.

Language at Home and at School. Currently, the United States faces critical challenges with respect to the education of young children. Many of these challenges are related to the quality of the young child's language environment, its correspondence with the language environment of the schools, and the relevance of the school's approach to language learning for the requirements of the workplace. Language proficiency has at least two components (Snow, 1987). One is the use of language in face-to-face interactions—language used specifically for social situations. The other is language removed from any specific context—language knowledge as it is usually measured by tests of vocabulary, verbal reasoning, and writing. Proficiency in one area may not predict proficiency in the other.

Consider **bilingualism**. Bilingualism is a social as well as a linguistic characteristic. Children who are proficient in two or more languages are also embedded in a complex sociocultural environment (Hakuta & Garcia, 1989). In some countries in Europe, in many provinces in Canada, and in areas of the United States, bilingualism is the norm. People who cannot speak more than one language are left out of important transactions in a major segment of their community. Research has found that the learning of two languages generally does not hamper children's cognitive development, especially if being a native speaker of one language rather than another has no stigmatizing consequences (Diaz, 1983). It appears that young bilingual children are adept at switching from one language to another as the conversational situation demands. In one study of bilingual Hispanic children in Miami, Florida, the children had access to a non-overlapping vocabulary in Spanish and English. In this instance, knowing the two languages actually expanded their access to concepts in comparison to children who spoke English or Spanish only (Umbel et al., 1992). In addition to the potential advantage in language performance, bilingual children may use their two languages as a way to impose boundaries on social interactions or to add a degree of clarity to social relationships.

Self-Control

Self-control is the ability to comply with a request, modify behavior according to the situation, postpone action, and behave in a socially acceptable way without having to be guided or directed by someone else (Kopp, 1982). These abilities reflect a growing sense of selfhood. They also reflect the cognitive ability to assess a situation and to compare it with previously learned guidelines on how to behave. Finally, they reflect the ability to express or inhibit impulses in order to reduce their intensity.

Early in infancy, self-control is usually understood as the infant's ability to prevent disorganization brought on by overstimulation and to recover from emotional distress. In addition to the many strategies that caregivers use to try to arouse infants when they are not paying attention and to soothe or calm infants when they are overaroused, babies have their own internal regulating strategies (Kopp, 1982). For example, by sucking or rocking, babies can soothe themselves. They can also resist overstimulation by turning away, crying, or going to sleep. Further maturation in the ability to override negative emotions and to regulate or reduce the intensity of emotional responses is noted at about 9–10 months. These gains have been linked to maturation of the frontal cortex and to an increased interconnection of the right and left frontal lobes. In the face of emotionally arousing situations, these advances in cerebral maturation permit infants to override habitual responses with a more reasoned, problem-solving orientation. In addition, the left frontal lobe may play a role in modifying the intensity of negative emotional reactions in the right frontal lobe (Fox & Davidson, 1984, 1987; Thompson, 1990).

Control of Impulses

During toddlerhood, self-control develops in two directions: control of impulses and self-regulated goal attainment, which is discussed later in this chapter. First, children improve their ability to modify and control their impulses. The case of Colin described below illustrates how toddlers may fall prey to their impulses. Sometimes, they simply cannot interrupt an ongoing action, even one they know is inappropriate.

> Colin, aged 2 years, 9 months, is just starting nursery school:
> In his relations with children, Colin progressed quickly from a quiet, friendly, watching relationship on the first few days to actively hugging the other children. The hugging seemed to be in an excess of friendliness and was only mildly aggressive. Having started hugging, he didn't know how to stop, and usually just held on until he pulled the child down to the floor. This was followed very closely by hair pulling. He didn't pull viciously, but still held on long enough to get a good resistance from the child. He grabbed toys from others. When stopped by an adult from any of these acts, he was very responsive to reason, would say, smiling, "I won't do it any more," would tear around the room in disorganized activity, and then return to hugging or pulling hair. (Murphy, 1956, pp. 11–12)

It takes a lot of self-control for Anna to cope with the baby's screaming. She holds her ears, grits her teeth, and shakes her leg rather than give the baby a wallop.

From the ages 2 to 3, children are increasingly able to modify and control their impulses and withstand delays in the gratification. They also become more willing to modify their behavior because they do not wish to cause distress to others. The ability to regulate or restrain behavior is a product of changing cognitive, social, and emotional competencies. Children become increasingly sensitive to the negative consequences of impulsive acts. At the same time, they develop new strategies to help them manage feelings of frustration such as distracting themselves and redirecting their attention to some alternative activity or toy, creating a pretend scenario in which they soothe themselves through a fantasy character, using some physical soothing/comforting strategy like thumb-sucking or cuddling with a blanket, and seeking comfort or distraction from a parent or play companion (Grolnick et al., 1996; Zahn-Waxler, Radke-Yarrow et al., 1992).

Increasing Sensitivity to the Distress of Others. Toddlers can observe and empathize with distress expressed in others, both children and adults. In addition, they begin to understand when they have been the cause of someone else's distress (Zahn-Waxler, Radke-Yarrow et al., 1992; Zahn-Waxler, Robinson et al., 1992). Often, the socialization environment helps focus toddlers' attention on these instances when parents or teachers point out their actions and the consequences. The following observation from a study of family interaction shows how a conversation

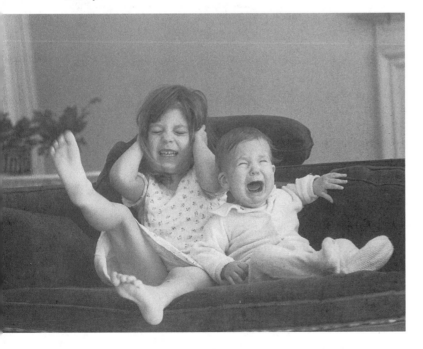

about negative consequences and a child's concern over his mother's distress contributed to the self-regulation of impulses:

> Danny is 33 months old. He and his mother are at the sink washing dishes. Danny blows a handful of suds at his mother and some gets in her eyes. Danny is laughing at this new game.
> M: No! Nuh uh, Danny. Danny you got it in my eye. (mild negative affect)
> Danny stops laughing.
> M: Don't do that in my eye, OK? It hurts to get soap in your eye.
> D: (very serious) I won't. (Brown & Dunn, 1992, pp. 347—348)

A New Sense of Time. During toddlerhood, children gain in self-control as they begin to develop a rudimentary sense of time, including some appreciation of the future. Toddlers repeatedly discover and then learn to trust that, although what they want is not available to them at the moment, it will often be available after a brief delay. As they become aware that after a period of delay their needs will very likely be met, the delay itself becomes less frustrating. This sequence depends heavily on the caregivers' responsiveness and on their ability at the appropriate moment to provide the gratifications that they have asked the children to delay. As children learn that they can trust their caregivers to keep promises, it becomes easier to wait.

Discipline Strategies and Impulse Control. In toddlerhood, the immediate aim of discipline is to achieve compliance (Kochanska et al., 1995). A parent typically wants children to stop doing something ("Don't touch those figurines; they might break.") or to do something ("Help me put the toys away now, it's time to go to bed."). If the child complies, a parent might respond positively by smiling, patting the child or giving a hug, or complimenting the child for being good, helpful, or obedient. If the child does not comply, a parent may try some form of distraction or offer some choice ("You can help clean up now or in five minutes"). But if compliance is not forthcoming, some type of discipline is likely to ensue.

Discipline practices have been described in three general categories (Hoffman, 1977):

1. **Power assertion:** Physical punishment, shouting, attempts to physically move a child or inhibit behavior, taking away privileges or resources, or threatening any of these things.
2. **Love withdrawal:** Expressing anger, disappointment, or disapproval; refusing to communicate; walking out or turning away.
3. **Inductions:** Explaining why the behavior was wrong; pointing out the consequences of behavior to others; redirecting behavior by appealing to the child's sense of mastery, fair play, or love of another person.

In addition to these three general categories of discipline techniques, parental modeling and reinforcement of acceptable behaviors are significant in the development of internal control (Maccoby, 1992). In order to correct their behavior, children must know what acts are considered appropriate, as well as how to inhibit their inappropriate acts. Modeling and reinforcement aid children in directing their behavior; discipline serves to inhibit or redirect it.

The manner in which the discipline is carried out over time is associated with child outcomes, especially increases in compliance, prosocial behavior, and the eventual internalization of moral standards; or increases in noncompliance, aggressiveness, and low levels of moral reasoning. Three features of the approach to discipline appear to be important (O'Leary, 1995):

1. The discipline should be immediate or as close in time to the situation as possible. Laxness in discipline, such as laughing at an undesirable behavior, waiting too long to respond, reprimanding the child sometimes but not others for the same misconduct, or inadvertently rewarding a child for misconduct are all practices that are likely to increase rather than decrease the undesired behavior.
2. The discipline should be appropriately firm, but not overreactive. Practices that are intensely harsh, abusive, or cruel, whether they involve physical or emotional in-

tensity, are associated with increases in problem behaviors. The infrequent use of power assertive punishment within an overall context of a warm, nurturing relationship may prove effective in fostering compliance. However, intense and frequent harsh punishment is associated with a variety of maladaptive consequences for children (Weiss et al., 1992).

3. The discipline for a toddler should be brief. It is important to make sure the toddler understands what the misbehavior was and why it was wrong, but the explanation should be concise and presented at the toddler's level of understanding. Punishment involving love withdrawal is especially likely to be carried on too long. The parent should make sure the toddler knows when she or he is back in the parent's "good graces," and not let the child spend hours thinking the parent is still angry.

Language and Fantasy as Strategies for Controlling Impulses. Language and fantasy are children's most useful tools for managing impulses. Talking about feelings and needs enables adults to help children understand more about their emotions and to help them devise strategies for self-regulation. Thompson (1990) identified four ways that caregivers use talking about emotions to help young children gain control. First, parents articulate the family or cultural rules of emotional expression: "Don't get so excited; calm down!" or "Stop that fussing; big boys don't whine and cry!" These lessons give young children an idea about the acceptable levels of impulses or emotional intensity and about the types of emotions that need to be regulated.

Second, adults help modify the intensity of emotions through reassuring or distracting talk. They may try to distract a child who is worried about getting an injection, or try to convince the child that the shot won't hurt or that it will be just a little sting. They may try to comfort a sobbing child by talking about some happy event that will distract the child from his or her troubles.

Third, adults may give children ideas for ways to manage their impulses. They might help by suggesting that the child think of pleasant times from the past or by singing a cheerful song. Adults teach children superstitions, rituals, and stories about how people handle their strong feelings (Box 6.2).

Fourth, children listen to adults talking about their own strong emotions and impulses.

The development of symbolic imagery allows children to create imaginary situations in which disturbing problems can be expressed and resolved. Through fantasy play, toddlers can control situations that are far beyond their real-world capacities (Singer & Singer, 1990). They can punish and forgive, harm and heal, fear and conquer fear—all within the boundaries of their own imagination. When children are asked to resist temptation, they use a variety of verbal strategies, including talking quietly to themselves and singing songs to distract themselves (Mischel et al., 1989). Toddlers who can talk to themselves may be able to control their fears, modify their anger, and soften their disappointments. They may repeat their parents' comforting words, or they may develop their own verbal strategies for reducing pain and suffering. When a boy who feels bad about something says, "Superheroes don't cry," he is making use of fantasy and language to control his emotional state.

Individual Differences in the Ability to Control Impulses

The ability to delay gratification varies with the individual. At least three factors are associated with differences in the ease or difficulty children have in controlling their impulses (Figure 6.2). First, toddlers differ in their capacity to empathize with the distress of others. Empathy itself appears to have a genetic as well as an environmental basis. In a study of monozygotic and dizygotic twins who were 2 years old, the monozygotic twins showed greater similarity in their emotional concern about and response to others' distress than did the dizygotic twins. In addition, mothers who showed a stronger concern for others in their child-rearing strategies had children whose empathy was more fully developed. Further, girls were observed to be more empathic than boys (Zahn-Waxler, Robinson et al., 1992). Individual differences in sensitivity to the distress of others lead to differences in how upset a child might be by

BOX 6.2   THE CONTROL OF ANGRY FEELINGS

The expression of anger, which is important to the child's development of a sense of autonomy, typically generates tension between parents and children (Wenar, 1982). Toddlers get angry for many reasons, including inability to perform a task, parental restrictions on behavior, and peer or sibling rivalry. As toddlers become increasingly involved in directing the outcomes of their activities, they get angry when someone interrupts them or offers unrequested assistance (Bullock & Lutkenhaus, 1988). In addition, it appears that some children are temperamentally more aggressive than others.

Children rely heavily on their parents as models for learning how to express and control anger. The times when parents are angry are very important. Children learn as much or more about the expression of anger from watching their parents when they are angry as they do from verbal explanations or punishment (Bandura, 1977). Children are sensitive to anger between their parents, even when it is not directed at them. Parents' hostility to each other, expressed through quarrels, sarcasm, and physical abuse, increases children's sensitivity to anger and is closely related to disturbances in development (J. S. Cummings et al., 1989).

In an ethnographic study of the socialization of anger and aggression, three 2½-year-old girls and their mothers from a working-class neighborhood of Baltimore were studied in detail. The mothers of these girls considered assertiveness and self-defense essential to survival in their neighborhood. Along with socialization strategies that focused on controlling aggression when it was inappropriate, the mothers found many ways to model aggressiveness as they talked to others in the girls' presence and to reward certain displays of toughness and assertiveness in the girls' behavior (Miller & Sperry, 1987).

The child who can express anger and not lose control makes tremendous gains in the development of autonomy. Anger at and conflict with parents give toddlers evidence that they are indeed very separate from their parents, and that the separateness, although painful, is legitimate. Children who are severely punished or ridiculed for their anger are left in a state of doubt. They see models for the ex-

Sometimes children are overwhelmed by their angry feelings and have temper tantrums. Although inpleasant, these moments provide evidence to parents and children of their legitimately separate wills.

pression of anger in the way their parents respond to them and yet are told that anger is not appropriate for them.

Several strategies that help young children manage or reduce the intensity of their anger (Berkowitz, 1973; Thompson, 1990) are:

- ignoring aggression
- providing brief "time-out" periods in a nearby quiet area until the emotion has subsided
- arousing feelings that are incompatible with the anger, especially empathy for the victim
- minimizing exposure to stimuli that arouse aggressive impulses
- explaining the consequences of aggressive actions for the other person
- explaining the circumstances that may have led to the initial feelings of anger or frustration

For the sake of the child's emerging self-concept, angry feelings must be allowed some form of legitimate expression. In the process of expressing angry feelings, children learn to control themselves and to channel these emotions into constructive rather than destructive activity. Between ages 2 and 5, the frequency of angry, aggressive behaviors declines as children develop effective strategies for self-control (Cummings et al., 1989).

finding that his or her behavior had caused someone suffering and in how willing the child may be to curb that behavior in the future.

Second, differences in temperament affect self-control. Children who are more aggressive, active, or socially outgoing may experience more situations in which their actions are viewed as disruptive or in need of control. On the other hand, children who are more socially inhibited, withdrawn, or passive may encounter fewer expectations to curb or restrict their behavior (Kochanska & Radke-Yarrow, 1992). The temperamental characteristic described as **inhibitory control** shows stability from the toddler period to early school age. It reflects an ability to slow down one's actions upon request, suppress a movement in response to instructions, and override the tendency to respond to a global display and pay close attention to the details in a stimulus (Kochanska et al., 1997). Inhibitory control in toddlerhood provides a basis for the formation of conscience and moral development in the early school age period. It allows the young child to respond more easily to parental requests and to interrupt or suppress undesirable behavior.

FIGURE 6.2

Factors associated with the ability to control impulses

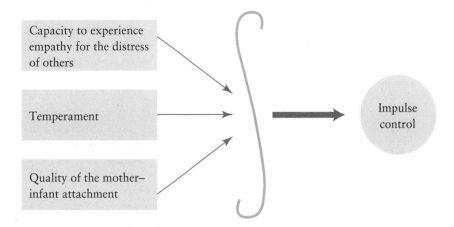

Third, the capacity for self-regulation may depend on the quality of the mother-infant attachment. Children who lack attachment security are more likely to exhibit irritability, avoidance, resistance, and aggressiveness as preschoolers (Teti et al., 1991). They will have more difficulty calming themselves and reducing the intensity of their impulses. In contrast, sensitive caregiving in which the mother and toddler are able to coordinate their interactions to sustain longer periods of mutually responsive interaction, is associated with enhanced capacity for self-regulation. Toddlers who experience this rhythmic coregulation are better able to distract themselves and deliberately guide their attention away from tempting objects that they are not allowed to touch (Raver, 1996).

Since the early 1960s, Walter Mischel and his colleagues have investigated the process by which children delay gratification. At age 4, children who tend to delay gratification longer tend to be more intelligent, more likely to resist temptation, demonstrate greater social responsibility, and have higher achievement strivings (Mischel et al., 1989). According to Mischel's research, a 4-year-old's ability to use self-regulatory strategies to delay gratification seems to have enduring effects. More than 10 years later, children who had waited longer in the experimental situation that required self-imposed delay of gratification at age 4 were described by their parents as socially and academically more competent than their peers. Their parents rated these children as more verbally fluent and able to express ideas, as using and responding to reason, and as being more competent and skillful. These children were more attentive and able to concentrate, plan, and think ahead, and they were also seen as better able to cope with frustration and resist temptation.

Self-Regulated Goal Attainment

The second sense in which self-control develops has to do with toddlers' feelings that they can direct their behavior and the behavior of others to achieve intended outcomes (Messer et al., 1987). During infancy, children become increasingly aware of themselves as causal agents. They make things happen. In toddlerhood, children become much more assertive about their desire to initiate actions, persist in activities, and determine when these activities should stop. Their sense of **agency**—their view of themselves as the originators of action—expands to include a broad array of behaviors. Children want to participate in decisions about bedtime, the clothes they wear, the kinds of foods they eat, and family activities. They want to do things they see their parents and their older siblings doing. Their confidence in their own ability to handle very difficult tasks is not modified by a realistic assessment of their own skills. According to toddlers, "Anything you can do, I can do better." When they have opportunities to do some of these new and complex things and they succeed, they gain confidence in themselves and their abilities. Toddlers feel themselves to be valuable members of the family as they contribute to routine household tasks. Their feelings of confidence and value

In toddlerhood, children begin to develop self-reliance. Maria can wash her hands by herself, just one of many areas where she is gaining confidence about guiding her own behavior.

are matched by the acquisition of a wide variety of complex, coordinated skills.

However, a number of abilities must come together before the toddler (referred to as the "actor" in this example) can engage in these self-regulated, goal-directed behaviors (Bullock & Lutkenhaus, 1988, p. 664):

- The actor must be able to anticipate a not-yet-attained goal state and understand that it can be reached through some specific activity.
- The actor must represent the means-end relation between activities and their outcomes.
- The actor must keep the anticipated goal in mind, and monitor progress toward the goal.
- The actor must remain task-oriented, waiting for appropriate opportunities to act, resisting distractions, overcoming obstacles, correcting actions, and stopping when a goal is reached.

Speech and Goal Attainment. Vygotsky (1978) argued that speech plays a central role in self-directed goal attainment and practical problem-solving. Summarizing his own research observations and those of others, he described the problem-solving behaviors of toddlers as involving both speech and action. Toddlers use what was described by Piaget (1952) as "egocentric speech" to control and direct their behavior. The speech is considered egocentric because it is not intended to communicate with anyone else and often doesn't make sense to anyone else. Vygotsky (1978) suggested that egocentric speech, or speech turned toward the self, and actions are part of the same problem-solving function. The more difficult the problem, the more speech is necessary for the child to find a solution. "Children solve practical tasks with the help of their speech, as well as their eyes and hands" (p. 26).

Speech gives children a new degree of freedom, flexibility, and control in approaching tasks and working toward a goal. They can use words to call to mind tools that are not visible. They can plan steps toward a goal and repeat them to guide their actions. They can use words like *slowly, be careful,* or *hold tight* to control their behavior as they work on a task.

The kind of speech that guides problem-solving emerges from the social speech that characterizes children's interactions with adults. Often, when young children try to figure out how to work something or how to get something that is out of reach, they turn to adults for help. Vygotsky suggested that the kinds of talk that adults use as they guide young children is then used by the children themselves to support and guide their own behavior. He referred to this process as the "internalization of social speech" and suggested that through this mechanism children's social environment shapes their thinking, planning, and problem-solving. In a sense, a child's capacity for self-directed goal attainment depends largely on what he or she has taken in of the spoken, practical advice and guidance given by adults and older peers who have tried to help the child solve problems in the past.

We have considered two rather different phenomena under the developmental task of self-control. Children's ability to control their impulses is closely linked to the psychoanalytic concept of delay of gratification, as Freud (1905/1953) used it to describe development during the oral and anal stages. Self-directed goal attainment, sometimes referred to as agency, is a general motivation that accounts for children's efforts to increase their competence through persistent investigation and skillful problem-solving (White, 1960; Harter, 1982). Both abilities foster toddlers' growing awareness of themselves. To function effectively as family members, toddlers must feel confident in their ability to control the inner world of their feelings and the outer world of decisions and tasks. As toddlers discover that they can tolerate stress, express or withhold their anger as appropriate, and approach difficult tasks and succeed at them, they also lay claim to a growing definition of selfhood. Toddlerhood is an important time in the development of a person's sense of self-efficacy—the conviction that one can perform the behaviors demanded by a specific situation (Bandura, 1989). The more toddlers can do by themselves, the more confidence they will have in their ability to control the outcomes of their actions and to achieve their goals.

THE PSYCHOSOCIAL CRISIS: AUTONOMY VERSUS SHAME AND DOUBT

During toddlerhood, children become aware of their separateness. Through a variety of experiences, they discover that their parents do not always know what they want and do not always understand their feelings. In early toddlerhood, children use rather primitive devices to explore their independence. They may say "no" to everything offered to them whether they want it or not. This is the period that people often refer to as the **terrible twos.** Toddlers seem very demanding and insist on having things done their own way.

Autonomy

The positive pole of the psychosocial crisis of toddlerhood is **autonomy.** During this period of life, autonomy refers to the ability to behave independently, to perform actions on one's own. In most cultures, expectations for autonomy are expressed as encouragement for children to perform daily tasks such as dressing and feeding themselves, playing alone or with peers, and sleeping apart from parents. The exact list of expectations and the age at which these behaviors are to be accomplished varies from one society to the next. Within U. S. society, pressures for autonomy are often expressed in early expectations for skill acquisition and verbal expressiveness. Children do not just prefer to do most things on their own, they *insist* on it. Once children begin to work on a task, such as putting on pajamas or tying shoelaces, they will struggle along time after time until they have mastered it. They may adamantly reject help and insist that they can manage on their own. They will allow someone else to help them only when they are sure that they can progress no further by themselves. In other cultures, expectations for autonomy may emphasize the ability to demand less of the mother, become sensitive to the needs of others, and function cooperatively with peers (Edwards et al., in press).

The establishment of a sense of autonomy requires not only tremendous effort by the child but also extreme patience and support from the parents. Toddlers' demands for autonomy are often exasperating. They challenge their parents' good sense, goodwill, and good intentions. Parents must learn to teach, cajole, absorb insults, wait, and praise. Sometimes, they must allow their children to try things that the children may not be able to do. By encouraging their children to engage in new tasks, parents hope to promote their sense of competence.

In the development of autonomy, toddlers shift from a somewhat rigid nay-saying, ritualized, unreasonable style to an independent, energetic, persistent one (Erikson, 1963). The behavior of older toddlers is characterized by the phrase "I can do it myself." They are less concerned about doing things their own way and more concerned with doing them on their own. Toddlers demonstrate an increasing variety of skills. Each new accomplishment gives them great pride. When doing things independently leads to positive results, the sense of autonomy grows. Toddlers begin to create an image of themselves as people who can manage situations competently and who can satisfy many of their own needs. Children who have been allowed to experience autonomy should, by the end of toddlerhood, have a strong foundation of self-confidence and feelings of delight in behaving independently.

Shame and Doubt

Some children fail to emerge from toddlerhood with a sense of mastery. Because of their failure at most attempted tasks or continual discouragement and criticism from parents, or most likely because of both, some children develop an overwhelming sense of shame and self-doubt. This is the negative resolution of the psychosocial crisis of toddlerhood (Erikson, 1963). **Shame** is an intense emotion that can result from two different types of experiences (Morrison, 1989).

One source of shame is social ridicule or criticism. You can probably recall feelings of shame for having spilled your milk or having lost your jacket. One of the earliest experiences of shaming is typically linked to toilet training, which is discussed in Box 6.3. Shame generally originates in an interpersonal interaction in which you feel that you have violated a valued social standard or in which you have been embarrassed or ridiculed for behaving in a stupid, thoughtless, or clumsy way (Tangney et al., 1992). When you are shamed, you feel small, ridiculed, and humiliated. Some cultures rely heavily on public humiliation as a means of social control. Adults in these cultures grow up with a strong concern about "saving face." One of their greatest fears is to be publicly accused of immoral or dishonorable actions. Sometimes such shame can lead to suicide.

Internal conflict is another source of shame. As children construct an idea of what it means to be a good, decent, capable person, they build a mental image of an ideal person, the **ego ideal.** Children feel shame when their behavior does not meet the standards of their ideal, even though they have not broken a rule or done anything naughty.

BOX 6.3   TOILET TRAINING

Within Freud's psychoanalytic theory, the classic psychological conflict between individual autonomy and social demands for conformity is toilet training. As Robert White (1960) pointed out, in this particular conflict children are destined to lose. They must subordinate their autonomy to expectations for a specific routine regarding elimination. Toddlers must master a number of skills in order to succeed at toilet training. They must have some word or signal to use to communicate their need to go to the bathroom. They must be able to get to the bathroom, either by finding their own way or by finding someone to direct them. They must be able to delay elimination until they have arrived at the bathroom and removed their clothes.

Children cannot control elimination until their musculature is sufficiently developed. This is an obvious but extremely important point. On average, the sphincter muscles, which control the ability to hold and let go of fecal material, do not become fully mature and workable until the child is between 1½ and 2 years old. Before the sphincters have attained this maturation, children will be unable to control their bowel movements.

For the child to experience a sense of competence during the toilet-training period, a number of things must occur: (1) the body must be ready; (2) the child must be able to give a signal when it is time to go; and (3) the child must be able to respond to an internal cue and anticipate the necessary action. There is some evidence that girls achieve bladder control earlier than boys. Problems with bed-wetting are somewhat more common for boys than for girls. This difference in bladder control is probably due to a difference in muscle development rather than a difference in motivation, frustration, or activity level.

If parents wait to begin toilet training until their children show signs of readiness in all areas, the children are likely to see this task as a source of pride and accomplishment rather than as a struggle of wills. They will be happy to be able to accomplish something that is so important to their parents. Their success will increase their self-confidence.

Although toilet training is an interesting paradigm that highlights the issues of willfulness, body control, and paren-

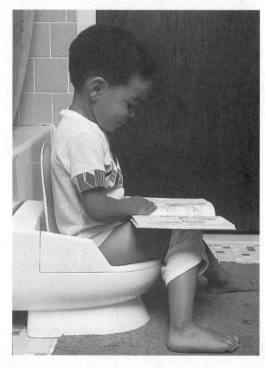

Spencer is able to relax on a potty just his size, taking advantage of a few quiet moments for reading as he develops his toilet habits.

tal authority, the concept of autonomy encompasses a much broader spectrum of behavior. The historical emphasis on toilet training in the development of personality seems to have been too narrow and restrictive. Bowel control is only one of a variety of skills that are mastered during a healthy toddlerhood and that are channeled into the development of autonomy and competence.

Shame is extremely unpleasant. In order to avoid it, children may refrain from all kinds of new activities. Children who feel shame lack confidence in their abilities and expect to fail at what they do. The acquisition of new skills becomes slow and painful when feelings of self-confidence and worth are replaced by constant doubt. Children who have a pervasive sense of **doubt** feel comfortable only in highly structured and familiar situations in which the risk of failure is minimal. As college students, young people who have high levels of shame were also characterized by high levels of resentment, irritability, anger, suspiciousness, and a tendency to blame others (Lewis, 1987; Kaufman, 1989).

All children experience some failures amid their many successes. In the process of achieving a new level of separateness, children may discover that they have harmed a loved one, broken a treasured toy, or wandered too far away and become separated from the caregiver at a crowded store or an unfamiliar park. Toddlers often exhibit periods of ambivalent dependency alternating with what appears to be unrealistic self-assurance as they try to establish a comfortable level of individuation from the loved one. The successful outcome to this process requires flexibility and warmth on the part of caregivers who accept and welcome the emerging selfhood of their child while building support for appropriate levels of self-control (Edwards, 1995).

THE CENTRAL PROCESS: IMITATION

The primary mechanism by which toddlers emerge as autonomous individuals is **imitation.** Although imitation requires the presence of active models, its outcome is a shift of the action from the model to the imitator. In other words, once toddlers succeed in imitating a certain skill, that skill belongs to them and they can use it for any purpose they like. Toddlers seem driven to imitate almost everything they observe, including their parents' positions at the toilet. Toddlers' vocabularies expand markedly through their imitation of the words they hear in adult conversations, on television, and in stories. Their interest in dancing, music, and other activities stems from imitation of parents and peers. When one child in a play group makes a funny noise or performs a daring act, other children appear to be compelled to re-create this novel behavior.

The imitative behavior of toddlers is different from the socially induced conformity observed in older children. Toddlers are not aware of a great many social norms and therefore feel little pressure to conform to them. Their imitative behavior is really a vehicle for learning. Every act becomes their own, even if it has been inspired by others. The primary motivation for imitation during toddlerhood is the drive for mastery and competence.

In studies of imitation in the home environment, toddlers show an impressive pattern of imitating their parents' household, self-care, and caretaking activities. They show increasing interest in imitating behaviors that are socially meaningful and valued. These observations have led researchers to suggest that imitation is critical in satisfying toddlers' need for social competence (Kuczynski et al., 1987). Through imitation, they may also derive pleasure from the similarity they perceive between themselves and their model. This perceived similarity is a secondary benefit of the imitative process (Kagan, 1958).

Imitation is also a means of participating in and sustaining social interactions (Grusec & Abramovitch, 1982). Within a peer setting, imitation emerges as a dominant strategy whereby children coordinate their behaviors with those of other toddlers. Before verbal communication becomes a truly useful tool for establishing or maintaining social contact, toddlers imitate one another. Through imitation, toddlers can feel connected to one another and begin to invent coordinated games (Eckerman et al., 1989). With increasing cognitive maturity, children select for imitation behaviors that have relevance to their own needs for mastery, nurturance, and social interaction.

The emphasis on imitation highlights the central role of culture at this period of life. In many cultures, adults orient young children toward important tasks and expect them to watch and learn in a process of imitation and shared problem solving (Rogoff et al., 1993). Children are surrounded by daily events that provide models for imitation, which reflect the culture of their families and communities. Toddlers rapidly accumulate the vocabulary of speech and action that belongs to their cultural group. How visitors are greeted when they arrive at the home; how adults groom themselves, dress, and speak to one another; how household tasks and chores are performed; how older children amuse themselves; how young people and older people treat each other—the thousands of words, gestures, and rituals of daily life make up the culture absorbed by watchful toddlers as they arm themselves with the resources to press toward autonomy.

THE PRIME ADAPTIVE EGO QUALITY AND THE CORE PATHOLOGY

Will   Erikson et al. (1986) identified the prime adaptive ego quality that emerges through the successful resolution of the psychosocial crisis of toddlerhood as **will**. Will is the capacity of the mind to direct and control action. It is directly linked to the idea of self-directed goal attainment. Will is the inner voice, focusing attention, encouraging, and urging one on, especially in the face of obstacles. It provides the psychological energy that allows people to press harder in competition, work to surpass previous achievements, and reach for new goals. In the face of disability, it is the force that urges the person to make peace with the loss and focus on alternate goals. In the face of crisis, people often refer to their will to survive or their will to live as the fundamental strength that kept them looking for new solutions or that prevented them from giving up hope. In older people who experience potentially spirit-crushing painful losses or disabilities, it is the force that provides buoyancy as they learn to accept their decline, look for areas of continued mastery, and reflect nostalgically upon past achievements.

Will reflects an inner determination to persist toward a goal. Cody shows his will as he drags the beach equipment out to the family spot.

Sometimes, we think of will in a negative way as associated with stubbornness or overbearing dominance, i.e., "bending to someone's will." But the meaning of will in the psychosocial context refers to the sense of inner determination and purpose that permits a person to set goals freely and make persistent efforts to achieve them. Will leads to a positive belief in oneself as someone who can make things happen. When you see a child struggling to carry a heavy box or drag a wagon filled with toys up a steep hill, you see *will* in action. When you watch an older child chew and twist a pencil trying to figure out a tough math problem, you see *will* in action. And when you go to the high school swimming pool at 6 in the morning and see students working out and swimming laps to get ready for the upcoming meet, you see *will* in action.

Compulsion   Will provides a voluntary energy and focus to action. In contrast, **compulsions** are repetitive behaviors that are motivated by impulse or restrictions on the expression of it. They are nonspontaneous and unchanging. Compulsions are a close relative to the ritualization that is developed in toddlerhood. Children in this stage typically devise some well-ordered rituals, especially around important transitions such as going to bed, getting dressed, and leaving the house (Albert et al., 1977). They insist that these rituals be followed precisely and threaten to become extremely angry if the rituals are violated. Rituals represent efforts to bring control and order to the environment. They also help provide feelings of sameness and continuity during changes in setting or state that may threaten toddler's feelings of selfhood. Toddlers' rituals usually do not repeat adult ways of doing things, thus they are not mere imitations of adult rituals. Their rituals, however, like those of adults, serve an important psychological function of bringing order and a sense of mastery to the unknown or the unpredictable. This in turn provides a feeling of security as toddlers pursue well-learned behaviors that work and may also have private symbolic meaning. In comparison to adaptive rituals that actually provide a sense of comfort and relief from uncertainty, compulsions must be carried out again and again, never adequately resolving the anxiety that motivates them.

Obsessions are persistent, repetitive *thoughts* that serve as mechanisms for binding anxiety. **Compulsions** are repetitive, ritualized *actions* that serve the same function. The idea of binding anxiety means that the person feels that the thoughts or behaviors reduce some other source of distress. For instance, a person with a compulsive neurosis may become committed to repeated hand washing to rid the self of uncleanness. The compulsive handwasher "scrubs his hands in tortured solitude, until they become raw, and yet he never feels clean" (Erikson, 1977, p. 78). Over time, a neurosis may become very disruptive to daily life since it takes a lot of time, makes it hard to concentrate on tasks, and the person feels a loss of control.

In a sense, people who suffer from obsessions and compulsions have a damaged will. Their ability to willfully direct their thoughts and actions toward a goal is impaired. Rather, they feel that their thoughts and actions are being controlled by some powerful force outside their voluntary control. It is not the same as an hallucination. People with compulsions or obsessions do not think that someone from outer space or some voice from the spirit world is telling them what to do. They recognize the directive as coming from their mind, but not from their will.

Compulsions represent the ego's attempts to provide some structure to reality, but they do not work to promote further development because they are not meaningful (Erikson, 1986). The experience of the doubt-filled, shame-ridden person tends to be continuously unpleasant, uncertain, and sometimes tortuous. Life is enacted around carefully orchestrated patterns of meaningless, compulsive behaviors.

THE IMPACT OF POVERTY ON PSYCHOSOCIAL DEVELOPMENT IN TODDLERHOOD

Poverty is often associated with parental behaviors that are disruptive to optimal development. Economic hardship produces emotional distress among parents, which is likely to result in parent-child interactions that are not supportive of the child's intellectual or emotional development (McLoyd, 1990). Poor mothers are more likely than more affluent mothers to use power-assertion and physical punishment as a form of discipline. One national study of poverty, parenting practices, and children's mental health, found that the amount of spanking parents do was directly related to their current level of poverty. This pattern was the same for Black, Hispanic, and non-Hispanic white families. In addition, the more likely parents were to use spanking and harsh discipline, the more likely their children were to show signs of emotional distress (depression, fearfulness, and crying) as well as externally directed behaviors such as arguing, disobedience, destructiveness, and impulsiveness (McLeod & Shanahan, 1993).

Parents living in poverty emphasize obedience and are less likely to use reasons and explanations in their discipline practices. They are less likely to reward their children through praise and encouragement, and less likely to ask their children for their ideas and opinions. In general, parents living in poverty have been characterized as less sensitive to their child's needs and less emotionally supportive. This approach to parenting may be due in large part to the emotional distress created by conditions of poverty. Frustration and anger at being poor may give way to feelings of weakness, victimization, and loss of control. These factors are often associated with both physical and mental health problems that can be expressed in pessimism, loss of hope, depression, drug and alcohol abuse, and psychosomatic ailments (McLoyd, 1990).

Poverty exposes children to high levels of risk and stress in day-to-day life.

Another explanation for the use of harsh parenting that emphasizes obedience is the fact that poor families are more likely to live in high-risk neighborhoods where children are likely to be exposed to violence. As a result, parents in poverty worry more about their children's safety and may be more emotionally reactive when children defy their authority.

From a psychosocial perspective, one might ask how poverty influences the developmental tasks of toddlerhood—the elaboration of locomotion, the experiences of fantasy and play, learning language, and the development of self-control. How do the conditions of poverty affect the expression of autonomy or the experiences of shame and doubt?

Current literature does not address these questions directly. Despite wide social interest and extensive policy debates regarding the needs of poor children, little research focuses on the consequences of poverty for specific developmental tasks. We hypothesize that toddlers are not directly aware of their poverty status. In comparison to older children who might understand from watching television, reading the newspaper, or interacting with other children in school that they are in a relatively impoverished situation, toddlers are not likely to have any comparative perspective. They assume that what they experience from day to day is what most everyone experiences. Toddlers probably do not feel shame about being poor, nor define themselves in this way. Poverty probably does not produce the same level of frustration and anger for toddlers that it does for adolescents or adults.

However, toddlers suffer direct effects of poverty. Two major consequences of poverty are poor health and inadequate nutrition. A national study found that children from families with incomes below $10,000 were three times more likely to be in poor health than were children from families with incomes above $35,000. Many children from low-income families have not been immunized for measles and other infectious diseases. Repeated bouts of illness combined with poor nutrition detract from a child's energy. The combination of malnutrition and illness have multiple consequences including the possibility of structural brain damage, especially when coupled with prenatal malnutrition, lethargy, delayed physical growth, and, as a result, minimal exploration of the environment. All these factors taken together produce what has been observed as delayed psychomotor and cognitive development in toddlerhood (Brown & Pollitt, 1996; Pollitt, 1994).

We can speculate that other aspects of poverty may interfere with the achievement of developmental tasks. Living in especially crowded conditions with many other children and adults may result in limited exploration; in addition, many poor neighborhoods lack safe play spaces in or near the home (Bradley et al., 1994). Lack of access to a variety of play materials may have a negative impact on language development as well as symbolic play. Crowding may also make it difficult for toddlers to have the private, uninterrupted space or permission for fantasy. On the other hand, some children may make use of fantasy to block out some of the more negative or troubling aspects of their environment or use it to create an inner space where their situation is less stark. Language development may be deterred if parents or caregivers do not interact much with their toddlers, if they tell their children what to do rather than involve them in discussion, or if they consistently tell their children to be quiet and not to speak. Self-regulation may be achieved early, especially if parenting is harsh and the costs of impulsive action are high. However, if parenting is chaotic and unpredictable, or if the levels of anger and aggression in the home are high, children may find it difficult to organize or direct their behavior in any systematic way.

Applied Topic DAY CARE

What happens during the waking hours and in the transitions from naps to waking or from waking to sleep is what toddler care is all about. Toddlers seek out time to elaborate their locomotion, engage in fantasy play, interact verbally so as to developed effective language skills, and learn self-control. Psychosocial development will occur to the extent that the mix of the child's time includes opportunities to engage in and continuously extend these abilities with supportive adults and other children as well as during time alone. There must be numerous opportunities for toddlers to explore their individuality and self-directed action, as well as experiences of reassurance, connection, and support.

In the United States, child-care arrangements constitute a highly diverse "market," especially when compared with kindergarten through 12th grade public education (Holloway & Fuller, 1992). Child care in America is covered by minimal federal and state regulation. Thus, children are in the care of a wide range of caregivers with varying types of education and training, from no specific background and training at all to bachelor's and master's degrees. Table 6.5 summarizes the child-care arrangements for children under 6 who have not yet entered kindergarten. Overall, 60% of children are

TABLE 6.5 Patterns of Child Care in the United States

Characteristic	Children		Type of Nonparental Arrangement				
	Number (1,000)	Percent distribution	Total[1]	In relative care	In nonrelative care	In center-based program[2]	No nonparental arrangement
Total	21,421	100	60	21	18	31	40
Race-ethnicity:							
White, non-Hispanic	13,996	65	62	18	21	33	38
Black, non-Hispanic	3,344	16	66	31	12	33	34
Hispanic	2,838	13	46	23	12	17	54
Other	1,243	6	58	25	13	28	42
Mother's employment status:[3]							
35 or more hours per week	7,101	34	88	33	32	39	12
Less than 35 hours per week	4,034	19	75	30	26	35	25
Looking for work	1,635	8	42	16	4	25	58
Not in labor force	8,354	40	32	7	6	22	68
Household income:							
Less than $10,001	4,502	21	50	22	10	25	50
$10,001 to $20,000	2,909	14	54	27	12	24	46
$20,001 to $30,000	3,385	16	53	22	14	25	47
$30,001 to $40,000	3,047	14	60	23	20	27	40
$40,001 to $50,000	2,304	11	63	19	22	32	37
$50,001 to $75,000	3,063	14	74	20	26	40	26
$75,001 or more	2,211	10	77	14	30	49	23

[In percent, except as indicated. Estimates are based on children under 6 years old who have yet to enter kindergarten. Based on 14,064 interviews from a sample survey of the civilian, noninstitutional population in households with telephones; see source for details.

[1]Columns do not add to total because some children participated in more than one type of nonparental arrangement.

[2]Center-based programs include day care centers, Head Start programs, preschool, prekindergartens, and other early childhood programs.

[3]Children without mothers are not included.

Source: U.S. National Center for Education Statistics. *Statistics in Brief,* October 1995 (NCES 95-824).

involved in some type of nonparental care. The largest group, 31%, is in center-based care, which includes day-care centers, Head Start programs, preschool, pre-kindergarten, and other early childhood programs (U. S. Bureau of the Census, 1996). Arrangements vary by race-ethnicity, mother's employment status, and household income. Households with the higher incomes are more likely to make some kind of non-parental arrangements for their children and most likely to use center-based programs. Hispanic families are less likely to make nonparental arrangements than other racial/ethnic groups. Even among mothers who are not in the labor force, 32% have some type of non-parental care for their children.

Child care arrangements reflect a variety of philosophies about the care of young children, wide differences in curriculum, and a wide range of physical settings. The laissez-faire approach to the care of toddlers seems to reflect a cultural belief that the nurturance and socialization of young children is primarily the responsibility of the family, while the schooling of children over the age of 5 is a public concern.

Because of the growing national need for child care and a wide choice of child-care arrangements, parents, educators, and policy makers are asking such critical questions as: How does day care influence the development of young children? What is our obligation to ensure quality day care for the children of working parents? What is our obligation as a society to meet the health, nutrition, and safety needs of the children of poor parents?

The Impact of Day Care

Assessments of day care's effects on young children generally focus on intellectual abilities, socioemotional development, and peer relations. Research has tended to emphasize the impact of day care on the children of poor families, those who are at a higher risk for school failure, illiteracy, and subsequent minimal employment or unemployment. Many studies focus on Head Start, a federally funded early childhood program that has a complex mission, including education, health, mental health, and family support. However, Head Start has typically been structured as a preschool enrichment program rather than full day care. Not all day care programs have the same educational emphasis or developmental curriculum as Head Start. Many studies that investigate the impact of day care do not systematically control for the differences in program focus, services, and hours of service that exist among public and private day care and preschool programs.

Intelligence and Academic Achievement

Increasingly, researchers agree that the effect of quality day care on toddlers is positive, but modest (Azar, 1997). The research literature is still developing, and many questions are still unanswered, but data from model programs show that quality day care contributes to intellectual achievement, as reflected in higher IQ scores, both during the preschool years and during the first grade (Burchinal et al., 1989).

The National Institute of Child Health and Human Development (NICHD) is carrying out a longitudinal study of the effects of early child care (Owen, 1997). In this study, 1300 children under one month of age and their families were identified as participants from 10 sites across the United States. The study, initiated in 1991, will continue until the children reach age 7. Families varied by race, income, family structure, mother's education and employment status, and the number of hours children spent in nonparental care. The kinds of care included that given by grandparents and other relatives, by a nonrelative in the home, in a home-based setting, and in a center. The quality of care was measured with a focus on caregiver interactions expected to promote positive emotions, social competence, and cognitive and language skills.

Current findings from this research suggest that family variables including income, mother's vocabulary, home environment, and the way mothers stimulate their babies to promote cognitive growth were more important predictors of the child's cognitive development than the quality of child care. However, after all these family factors were taken into account, the quality of language stimulation directed to the child in the child-care setting made a significant additional contribution to children's language and cognitive competence measured at ages 2 and 3. Children in higher

The resources and curriculum of high quality day care make a significant contribution to cognitive development among 2- and 3-year-old children

quality care had higher scores on measures of infant development and school readiness.

In addition to test score benefits, children who have participated in model programs and Head Start are less likely to be placed in special education classrooms and to be held back a grade. These advantages are of significance in thinking about the trade-off in costs and benefits of providing early educational experiences to children at risk of school failure (Haskins, 1989). The Perry Preschool Project, a model program that has carried out extensive longitudinal research on its participants, has seen a number of indications of academic success. At age 19, children who had attended a quality child-care program had higher grades, fewer failing grades, a more positive attitude toward school, and a higher literacy rate than a comparable group of poor young adults who had not participated in a quality child-care program (Schweinhart & Weikart, 1988).

In studies of the impact of day care on intelligence and school achievement, researchers in the United States have tended to study how quality child care modifies the negative effects of poverty. This focus leaves open the question of whether early day care is enriching for the children of middle-class parents, whose resources and educational backgrounds are likely to be more supportive of a child's intellectual achievement. A study of Swedish child care showed positive effects of early day care (beginning sometime after age 6 or 7 months) on the cognitive performance and teacher ratings of children of both low- and middle-income parents with varying educational backgrounds (Andersson, 1989). The children who entered day care during their first year of life were described as "more persistent and independent and more verbally facile than other children, and they were less anxious and more socially confident" (Andersson, 1992, p. 20). Advantages of early day care that transcended the family's socioeconomic status continued to be observed when the children were 13 years old. Similar research is needed in the United States to understand the relative benefits of early-childhood education for children in middle- and upper-middle-class families as well as those in poor families.

Social Competence

Quality day care is also associated with higher levels of social competence, self-esteem, and empathy. Children who interact positively with adults in their day-care settings are more likely to continue to interact positively and comfortably with their teachers and classmates in the elementary grades (Vandell et al., 1988). Some studies have found that children with day-care experience are less compliant with their parents' wishes than children who have not been in day care (Clarke-Stewart & Fein, 1983). The recent study conducted by NICHD (Owen, 1997) helps explain these findings. The more time children spent in nonmaternal care, the less responsive mothers were to their children at age 15 and 36 months, and the less affectionate the child was to the mother at 24 and 36 months. These findings were strongest for children who were in poor quality care for the longest time periods. One might infer that mothers who are separated from their children for long periods each day become less attuned to their children's cues and less effective in establishing an effective communicative rhythm. At the same time, children who are exposed to poor quality alternative care do not have the support for effective self-control and communicative competence that are experienced in higher quality settings.

Few of the evaluations of model programs or Head Start have reported on long-term social consequences. However, results from the Perry Preschool Project showed that, by age 19, fewer of the children studied had committed delinquent acts or had been processed by the courts, fewer had been on welfare, and more had been employed (Berrueta-Clement et al., 1984; Haskins, 1989). Comparable data to indicate this type of long-term social benefit from Head Start are not available.

Peer Relations

Quality day care also has an impact on peer relations. Children benefit from opportunities to interact with a variety of peers in settings where adults are readily available to help them make choices and resolve differences. The quality and complexity of social play are especially enhanced when children remain in the same child-care setting rather than moving from one arrangement to another. In stable conditions, toddlers, whose verbal skills are limited, expand their strategies for coordinating their play with others and for exploring shared fantasies (Clarke-Stewart, 1989; Howes & Stewart, 1987). By the time they reached age 8, children who had experienced quality care at age 4 were more likely to engage in friendly interactions with their age-mates, were less likely to play alone, and were less likely to be described as shy than children who had low-quality day-care experiences (Vandell et al., 1988). At age 19, students who had been in the Perry Preschool Project were more likely to report that they provided help to their friends and family than were comparison subjects, but they were less likely to volunteer without pay for community service.

Since Head Start is a more comprehensive program, it is worthwhile to consider its additional benefits for children. In 30 studies that reported on the health impact of Head Start, the data show that participating children are more likely to get a wide variety of examinations and assessments covering medical and dental health, speech and hearing, vision, and nutrition. All of these opportunities allow a direct response to young children's physical needs when their parents may not be aware of emerging problems or are unsure how to address them. Because Head Start provides meals, young children in the program have a much higher daily nutritional intake than similar children who are not in the program. Thus, Head Start succeeds in bringing to young children essential benefits that they are not receiving through their families.

As an additional benefit, Head Start has had a positive impact on families and communities. An estimated 30,000 parents and community members have been involved in

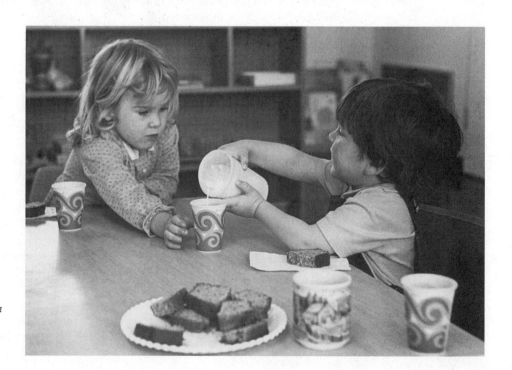

Social competence is enhanced in quality day care through experiences in taking turns, helping, sharing, and coordination of pretend play.

some form of training and career development. Head Start has created an estimated 76,000 jobs, the majority of which are held by minority members in the communities where the programs are located. These benefits empower adults to influence the quality of education in their communities and broaden their understanding of the educational process (Holloway & Fuller, 1992; Haskins, 1989).

Directions for the Future

The United States faces a critical gap between the demand for *affordable, quality* day care and its availability. Although the number of child-care settings appears to be ample, those that meet the standards of high quality are comparatively scarce. In addition, services for certain groups, including children with disabilities, those whose parents have evening work schedules, children who are ill, and those who need year-round programs, are in short supply (National Commission on Children, 1993).

Concern about the need for affordable, quality day care is expressed by parents who are in the labor market as well as by those who would like to be in the labor market. The U.S. now has a national parental leave policy, so that parents can take time off to care for their newborns without risking the loss of their jobs. But concerns about child care continue throughout toddlerhood and well into the elementary school years, when children need adult supervision before and after school hours.

Corporations are recognizing the need to address their employees' child-care needs. Worries about their children and the difficulty of making adequate child-care arrangements result in parental anxiety, missed workdays, and decreased productivity. Companies are addressing this issue in the following ways (Quinn, 1988):

- Emergency care: The company provides temporary care on those days when an employee's regular arrangement fails.
- *Discounts:* The company arranges for a 10% discount with a national child-care chain or picks up 10% of the fee.
- *Vouchers:* The company makes payments toward whatever child-care arrangement a parent selects. One company gives special assistance to all employees who earn less than $30,000 a year. Another provides a subsidy during a child's first year of life.
- *Referral services:* The company identifies and lists quality day-care centers it can recommend to its employees.
- *On-site day care:* Day-care centers are created at the workplace. For examples, the U.S. Senate and House of Representatives provide on-site day care for their members and employees.
- *Flexible benefits:* Employees arrange to have the money they pay for child care deducted from their salaries; this money does not count as taxable income.

Changes in national welfare policies place new pressures on the need for affordable, quality child-care services. In the past, for example, Head Start programs, which have been an important resource to children in low-income families, have not offered full day care. However, if mothers of young children who were previously receiving welfare benefits are required to enter the labor market, they will need to find full day care for their children.

As policies are developed for the education of children from poor families, it is critical to sustain the gains made during the preschool Head Start years (Zigler, 1993). Most poor children are not only poor when they are toddlers. They remain poor throughout their elementary- and middle-school years. Research has shown that, beginning in the early elementary grades, poor children lose ground during the summers in comparison to their more affluent peers, who are exposed to new experiences and resources when school is out (Entwistle & Alexander, 1990). Poor children may require access to additional educational and cultural experiences throughout the elementary- and middle-school years in order to keep pace with their wealthier age-mates. Extra involvement in intellectually stimulating activities, whether through summer activities, after-school programs, weekend workshops, or talent clubs, may be necessary to sustain academic motivation and bring more poor children into the work force with the required skills and a positive orientation toward learning and problem solving.

Chapter Summary

The developmental tasks of toddlerhood improve children's ability to find order and consistency in their world and to express the self. Locomotive skills heighten toddlers' sense of mastery and expand their boundaries of experience. The emergence of fantasy provides them with an internal, personal form of symbolic representation. In areas in which control is very difficult or impossible, fantasy allows a pseudomastery in which barriers are overcome and limitations of reality are of less importance—conflicts can be acted out and pretend solutions can be found. Fantasy may be enhanced by language, but it thrives even in the absence of words. Language is both a tool for the expression of feelings and concepts and a primary mechanism of socialization. Toddlers' use of language gives us clues to their cognitive development and their needs. Through language, children influence others, gain access to worlds of information, and learn new strategies for the control and expression of their impulses. Efforts at self-control, both impulse regulation and self-directed goal attainment, begin in toddlerhood and continue through life.

The psychosocial crisis of autonomy versus shame and doubt reflects the child's needs for self-expression and mastery. Young children develop individuality by exercising the skills that develop during toddlerhood. Self-doubts result from repeated ridicule, shame, and failure. The adaptive ego quality of will, directly linked to self-directed goal attainment, emerges in a positive resolution of this crisis. In the context of shame and doubt, the child is likely to rely more and more on compulsive, ritualized behaviors.

Autonomy and individuation ordinarily emerge in the context of the parent-child relationship. Toddlers are avid observers, imitating and incorporating parental behaviors and values into their own routines. Parental interaction, acceptance, and discipline all contribute to a child's emerging sense of individuality. However, living in poverty increases the likelihood that parents will be psychologically unavailable or will use harsh, restrictive disciplinary strategies that produce shame or unexpressed rage in their young children.

Increasing numbers of young children are being cared for in group settings. The impact of day care depends heavily on the quality of the personnel, the nature of the program, and an appropriate physical environment. Many studies suggest that quality child care contributes to the toddler's optimal development. A major concern, however, is the availability of affordable, quality care to all those families that need it.

End of Chapter Case

It is unusual to find first person recollections of the period of toddlerhood. In this selection, Alice Walker, Pulitzer Prize winning novelist and poet, shares an early memory.

It is a bright summer day in 1947. My father, a fat, funny man with beautiful eyes and a subversive wit, is trying to decide which of his eight children he will take with him to the county fair. My mother, of course, will not go. She is knocked out from getting most of us ready: I hold my neck stiff against the pressure of her knuckles as she hastily completes the braiding and then the beribboning of my hair.

My father is the driver for the rich old white lady up the road. Her name is Miss Mey. She owns all the land for miles around, as well as the house in which we live. All I remember about her is that she once offered to pay my mother thirty-five cents for cleaning her house, raking up piles of her magnolia leaves, and washing her family's clothes, and that my mother—she of no money, eight children, and a chronic earache—refused it. But I do not think of this in 1947. I am two and a half years old. I want to go everywhere my daddy goes. I am excited at the prospect of riding in a car. Someone has told me fairs are fun. That there is room in the car for only three of us doesn't faze me at all. Whirling happily in my starchy frock, showing off my biscuit-polished patent-leather shoes and lavender socks, tossing my head in a way that makes my ribbons bounce, I stand, hands on hips, before my father. "Take me, Daddy," I say with assurance; "I'm the prettiest!"

Later, it does not surprise me to find myself in Miss Mey's shiny black car, sharing the back seat with the other lucky ones. Does not surprise me that I thoroughly enjoy the fair. At home that night I tell the unlucky ones all I can remember about the merry-go-round, the man who eats live chickens, and the teddy bears, until they say: that's enough baby Alice. Shut up now, and go to sleep.

SOURCE: Walker, A., 1991.

Thought Questions

1. What aspects of the developmental tasks of toddlerhood are captured in this narrative?
2. In what ways might you describe Alice as egocentric?
3. What images of her mother and father are being established at this age?
4. From what you have read, what aspects of Alice's self-concept might be forming during this period of her life?
5. How do the themes of autonomy, shame and doubt, will and compulsion relate to this narrative?

Chapter 7

*S*tarting school brings an expansion of the child's social world—encounters with new adults and peers, new social norms, higher expectations, and new information. Each of these changes has an effect on the child's self-concept.

Early School Age (4 to 6 years)

*C*hapter Objectives

- To describe the process of gender identification during early school age and its importance for the way a child interprets his or her experiences.
- To describe the process of early moral development, drawing from research and theories to explain how knowledge, emotion, and action combine to produce internalized morality.
- To analyze changes in the self-theory, with special focus on self-evaluation and self-esteem during the early-school-age years.
- To explore the transition to more complex group play and the process of friendship development in the early-school-age years.
- To explain the psychosocial crisis of initiative versus guilt, the central process of identification, the prime adaptive ego function of purpose, and the core pathology of inhibition.
- To consider social expectations for school readiness, its relation to the developmental tasks of early school age, and the obstacles that may prevent children from being able to adapt and learn in the school environment.

*F*rom a psychosocial perspective, the early school age brings with it increasingly complex social influences. By the age of 6, virtually all American children are enrolled in school. Children today are encountering school or school-like experiences at earlier ages than they have in the past. In 1994, 49% of 3- and 4-year-olds were enrolled in school, an increase from 20% in 1970 (U.S. Bureau of the Census, 1997). School brings external evaluation, new opportunities for success and failure, settings for peer-group formation and social evaluation, and the initiation of a set of experiences that may lead to advancement of socioeconomic status in adulthood. At a more immediate level, school is a new source of influence on the child beyond the family.

Beliefs and practices followed at home will come under scrutiny and may be challenged by community norms and values. Parents' personal hopes and aspirations for their children may be tempered by the reality of the children's school performance. In addition to family and school, the peer group, neighborhood, and television all influence children's self-concept during early school age.

Most early-school-age children exhibit wide-ranging curiosity about all facets of life. Once they become aware of alternatives to their own families' philosophies and lifestyles, they begin to question familiar notions. The independence of action seen in the toddler is replaced by independence of thought in the early-school-age child. ❖

DEVELOPMENTAL TASKS

In this chapter, four developmental tasks are discussed that contribute to the child's capacity to resolve the psychosocial crisis of initiative versus guilt. The topic of **gender identification** includes a discussion of the physical, cognitive, emotional, and social domains as they become integrated into an early scheme for thinking of oneself as male or female. Issues of right and wrong surface constantly as a result of the child's newly acquired abilities for independent thought and exposure to a much wider range of social influences. These experiences provide the basis for early **moral development.** Understanding and experiencing the self expands markedly during early school age. This developmental task centers around the acquisition of a personal **self-theory** that becomes increasingly complex because it is being stimulated by expanding social influences. Accompanying the development of the self-theory is the development of a set of complex feelings about the self called self-esteem. A fourth area for new development involves new levels of participation in **group play.** Through the process of learning the rules and playing cooperatively with others, children begin to form meaningful friendships and mental representations of ways of participating in groups.

Gender Identification

Every human society has patterns of organization based partially on gender. Males and females are often assigned different roles, engage in different tasks, have access to different resources, and are viewed as having different powers and attributes. The specific content of these gender roles varies widely from one culture to another.

Individual Differences versus Constructivism

The current debate about gender is not whether gender differences exist but rather how to explain them (Bohan, 1993; Thompson, 1993). The *individual-differences* perspective suggests that gender differences reside within the individual as persistent, internal attributes. Whether the differences are a result of biological evolution, socialization, or an interaction between the two, this perspective suggests that differences between males and females are stable characteristics that individuals bring to various situations.

The **constructivist** perspective suggests that gender differences are a product of particular interactions that have a certain socially agreed-upon, gender-related meaning. In this view, the specific behaviors that are described as masculine or feminine depend largely on the situation, including expectations that people will behave in gender-appropriate ways. For example, in a study of social interaction between pairs of toddlers (Jacklin & Maccoby, 1978; Maccoby, 1990), one variable measured was the amount of time one partner stood watching while the other child played with the toys, a behavior called *passive*. No sex differences were observed overall in the frequency of passive behavior. In same-sex pairs, girls were rarely passive, but in mixed-sex pairs, the girl frequently stood watching while the boy played with the toys. This kind of finding is replicated at older ages, showing that girls and boys, men and women, interact in stereotypically gender-defined ways, particularly when they are observed in public settings and in mixed-sex groups.

We cannot resolve this debate. Our goal in the discussion that follows is to understand how children begin to conceptualize gender as a dimension of their self-concept, an organizing principle of social life, and a guide to their behavior. We do not expect a lifetime's work on gender identity to have been completed by the end of early school age. During this period, however, significant conceptual and emotional changes give the sex role greater clarity and highlight the relevance of one's sex in the overall self-concept.

Understanding Gender

Understanding one's gender involves four components that emerge in a developmental sequence from toddlerhood through early school age (Kohlberg, 1966): using the correct gender label, understanding that gender is stable, understanding gender constancy, and understanding the genital basis of gender (Figure 7.1).

The correct use of the appropriate gender label is the earliest component of gender identification to be achieved. The categorization of people as male and female is a natural category, much like the distinction between the familiar object and the stranger or between people and inanimate objects, as discussed in Chapter 5. Even before the abstract categories *male* and *female* are understood, children learn to refer to themselves as boys or girls by imitating their parents. From infancy, parents make continual reference to a child's gender in such statements as "That's a good boy" or "That's a good girl."

The women of the Hopi, a Native American tribe of the southwestern United States, enjoy comparatively high status, because the land, house, and household furnishings belong to the wife and are passed from mother to daughter. Even though men function as village chiefs, the title of chief follows the female's ancestry. In traditional Hopi culture, the woman initiated a marriage proposal, and either the husband or wife could initiate a divorce. To divorce her husband, a woman could simply pack up his belongings and leave them outside the door to the pueblo.

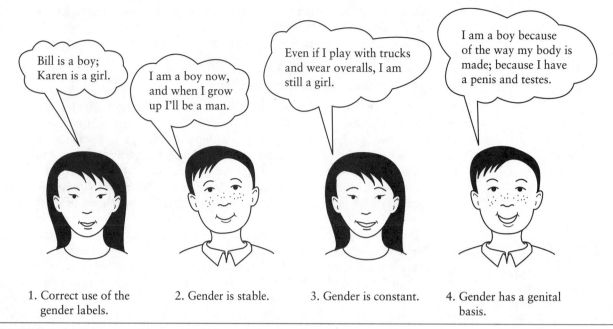

FIGURE 7.1
Four components of the concept of gender

By the age of 2½, children can accurately label other children as boys or girls, and by the age of 3, they can accurately sort photographs of boys and girls. They can also apply gender labels such as *Mommy* and *Daddy*, *brother* and *sister*, and *boy* and *girl* accurately (Thompson, 1975; Leinbach & Fagot, 1986). Once they know these sex-related labels, children seek out cues that will help them make these distinctions correctly. Their attention is directed to the differences between males and females.

Understanding gender constancy appears to emerge somewhat later, usually between ages 4 and 7 (Serbin et al., 1993). Understanding the genital basis of gender provides a fundamental context for understanding that gender is constant. In research involving 3-, 4-, and 5-year-olds, the majority of children who understood the genital differences between the sexes could also tell that a child's sex did not change simply because the child was dressed up to look like a member of the opposite sex. These young children understood that sex is a constant feature of a person, no matter how the person is dressed or whether the hair is long or short. In contrast, the majority of the children who had no knowledge of genital differences were unable to respond correctly to questions about constancy (Bem, 1989).

Sex-Role Standards

Sex-role standards are cultural expectations about appropriate behavior for boys and girls, and for men and women. What are the sex-role standards in American culture? In research on sex-role standards, children are asked to identify whether certain activities, occupations, or traits are more frequently associated with males, females, or both. For example, in the Sex-Role Learning Index, children are shown drawings of 20 objects traditionally associated with sex roles, 10 for the male sex role (such as a hammer, a shovel, and a fire helmet) and 10 for the female sex role (such as an iron, a stove, and dishes). By age 7, most children make a perfect score on this type of test, illustrating that they know how their society links gender and activities or occupations (Beere, 1990; Serbin et al., 1993). Knowledge of sex-typed personality traits, such as gentle and affectionate or adventurous and self-confident, emerges somewhat later. In one study of over 550 children, sixth-graders answered about 90% of these types of questions correctly (Serbin et al., 1993).

The significance of an early-school-age child's knowledge about sex-role standards is the implication that they will shape the child's preferences and behaviors. For example, once children identify certain toys as more appropriate for girls and others as more appropriate for boys, then their own toy preferences are guided by these standards. Conversely, when they like a toy that is not obviously sex-stereotyped, they are inclined to think that other children of their same sex would like that toy as well (Martin et al., 1995). One consequence of this sex-typed thinking is that it limits a child's willingness to play with certain toys and games, and therefore reduces the child's opportunities to learn from a variety of play experiences.

Accompanying sex-role standards are conditional rewards, incentives, and sanctions. Adults not only expect things of a child in relation to the child's gender but also do things in order to produce compliance with these expectations. The nature of parental influences on children's sex-role stereotyping is very complex (Turner and Gervai, 1995). Some parents believe that boys should be assertive and fight for their rights. Others believe that boys should think carefully about what is right and wrong and guide their actions by reason rather than impulsive aggression. Each of these sets of parents has a conception of male attributes that is communicated to their sons by a variety of means over a long period. The toys parents give their children, the experiences to which they expose them, and the activities in which they encourage their children's participation all reflect some dimensions of the parents' sex-role standards. By the time children reach school age, they have been encouraged to adopt those standards and disciplined for what their parents have viewed as gender-inappropriate behavior. Young girls may be shamed for their assertiveness by being told that they are acting "bossy," and young boys may be warned to "stop acting like a sissy."

Recent work on gender-role development suggests that, as the cognitive underpinnings related to the concept of gender mature, children form **gender schemes,** or personal theories about cultural expectations and stereotypes related to gender. Children tend to organize their perceptions, focus their attention, and interpret information in such a way as to be consistent with their gender scheme (Levy & Carter, 1989; Bem, 1981; Martin & Halverson, 1987). For boys, gender schemes play a role in the recollection of behavior from as early as age 2 (Bauer, 1993). By the kindergarten years, both boys and girls recall information that is consistent with their gender stereotypes better than information that is counter to the stereotype or that is more relevant to the opposite sex (Liben & Signorella, 1993). Among children aged 5–12, the greater their knowledge of sex-role standards, the greater their preference for same-sex peers and for sex-typed adult activities and occupations (Serbin et al., 1993).

Not all children are equally rigid in applying sex-role standards to themselves or to others. Flexibility in the application of sex-role standards to oneself and others appears to be influenced by both cognitive factors and socialization. Children appear to learn the stereotypes and expectations related to their own gender before learning the expectations for the opposite gender (Martin, C.L., Wood et al., 1990). Preschool-age children are more likely to see gender-role transgressions (e.g., boys playing with dolls or girls pretending to be firefighters) as more permissible than are older children, aged 6 and 7 (Smetana, 1986; Lobel & Menashri, 1993). In particular, young children who have more advanced abilities to differentiate between moral norms (like telling the truth) and social norms (like saying "please" and "thank you") are also less stereotyped in their play activities and toy choices (Lobel & Menashri, 1993). Among 5- to 10-year-olds, training in multiple-classification

Although early school age children are familiar with gender stereotypes, they are also likely to be flexible in their gender-role play. Here we have a rancher, a fire chief, and a construction worker all joining together to make a pretend meal.

skills (sorting objects into more than one category) is associated with more egalitarian, less stereotyped responses to gender-related tasks (Bigler & Liben, 1992).

Variations in family environment and socialization influence children's thinking about sex-role norms. Girls are generally more flexible about sex roles than boys. Young boys whose fathers live in the home typically have an earlier knowledge of sex-typed roles. However, if these fathers participate in nontraditional activities in the home, the boys' sex-role knowledge is delayed. Children whose mothers do nontraditional tasks develop a more flexible attitude, seeing more activities and occupations as appropriate for both males and females, and they themselves are more flexible in their preferences for activities, occupations, and friends (Serbin et al., 1993).

Identification with Parents

The third component of gender identification involves parental identification. **Identification** is the process through which one person incorporates the values and beliefs of another. To identify with someone is not to become exactly identical to that person, but to increase one's sense of allegiance and closeness to him or her. Through the process of identification, ideals, values, and standards of the family and community are internalized so that they become a part of the individual's own belief system. During early school age, most children admire and emulate their parents. They begin to internalize their parents' values, attitudes, and world views. (We emphasize identification as a major mechanism of socialization in childhood, but it can occur at any point in the life span.) There appear to be four substantially different theories about the motives for identification (Table 7.1).

The **fear of loss of love** is founded on a child's initial realization of dependence on the parents. A child behaves like a parent in order to ensure a continued positive relationship. Eventually, the child incorporates aspects of the loved one's personality into his or her own self-concept. The child can then feel close to the loved person even when they are not physically together (Jacobson, 1964). If a child can be like a loved parent, the parent's continuous presence is not required to reassure the child about that parent's love.

Identification with the aggressor is aroused when children experience some degree of fear of their parents. In order to protect themselves from harm, they perform behaviors that are similar to those they fear. This kind of identification may give children a magical feeling of power as well as decrease the parents' tendency to aggress against them. Parents who see a great deal of similarity between themselves and their children are less likely to threaten or harm them (Freud, 1936).

A third motive for identification is the need for *status and power* (Bandura, 1977, 1986). Studies of modeling show that children are more likely to imitate the behavior of a model who controls resources than they are the behavior of a model who is rewarded. The imitative behavior is motivated by a vicarious feeling of power experienced when they behave in the same way as the powerful model. Within a family, children are likely to have personality characteristics similar to those of the more dominant parent (Hetherington, 1967).

TABLE 7.1   Four Motives for Parental Identification

Motive	Definition
Fear of loss of love	A child behaves like a parent in order to ensure a continued positive love relationship.
Identification with the aggressor	A child behaves like a parent in order to protect himself or herself from the parent's anger.
Identification to satisfy needs for power	A child behaves like a parent in order to achieve a vicarious sense of the power associated with the parent.
Identification to increase perceived similarity	A child behaves like a parent to increase his or her perceived similarity to the parent and thereby to share in the parent's positive attributes.

Children often hear people say, "You look just like your mom." These comments increase the child's sense of perceived similarity and strengthen motivation for parental identification.

A fourth motive for identification results from the children's need to increase the *perceived similarity* with their parents (Kagan, 1958). Children attribute a number of valued characteristics to their parents, including physical size, good looks, special competencies, power, success, and respect. Children more readily share these positive attributes when they perceive a similarity between themselves and their parents. They experience this sense of similarity in three principal ways: (1) by perceiving actual physical and psychological similarities, (2) by adopting parental behaviors, and (3) by being told about similarities by others. Increasing perceptions of similarity promote stronger identifications.

These motives apply to the process of identification at all ages and regardless of the sex of the identifier or the model. How do these motives influence the specific task of developing gender identification? For a particular child, one of these motives may dominate the dynamics of gender identification, but all four motives are involved in the process.

Individual differences in sex-typed preferences in toys and play activities as well as in sex-role knowledge are linked to parental attitudes and behaviors. Parents who have more traditional sex-typed attitudes tend to have children who are more sex-typed in their play preferences and whose knowledge of sex-typed stereotypes develops at a younger age (Fagot & Leinbach, 1989; Weinraub et al., 1984). When mothers work outside the home, their children tend to form more flexible cognitions and less sex-typed preferences for activities and adult occupations. Evidence related to specific efforts to reduce gender-related stereotypes and to increase nontraditional preferences suggests that vicarious reinforcement of nontraditional or countertraditional behaviors may be effective with children, especially in the age range of 4–10 (Katz & Walsh, 1991). Thus, parents can make deliberate efforts to encourage more flexibility in gender-role conceptualization and preferences by deliberately modeling atypical activities or by reading or devising stories that involve counterstereotypical situations.

Gender Preference

The fourth component of gender identification is the development of a personal preference for the kinds of activities and attitudes associated with the masculine or feminine sex role. Preferences for sex-typed play activities and same-sex play companions have been observed among preschoolers as well as older children (Caldera et al., 1989; Maccoby, 1988). The attainment of these preferences is a more complex accomplishment than might be imagined. In fact, one's gender-role preference may fluctuate considerably throughout life.

Gender preference depends primarily on three factors. First, the more closely one's own strengths and competencies approximate the sex-role standards, the more one will prefer being a member of that sex. Second, the more one likes the same-sex parent, the more one will prefer being a member of that sex. These two factors begin to have a significant impact on a child's gender preference as his or her self-concept becomes more clearly differentiated. As children enter school and are exposed to the process of evaluation, they begin to have a more realistic sense of their unique qualities. As they acquire this self-reflective ability, they can appreciate the similarities and discrepancies between (1) self and the sex-role standard and (2) self and the same-sex parent. Box 7.1 addresses the process of gender preference for children whose parents are gays or lesbians.

The third determinant of gender preference consists of environmental cues as to the value of one sex or the other. The cues may emanate from the family, ethnic and religious groups, the media, social institutions (such as the schools), and other culture carriers. Many cultures have traditionally valued males more than females and have given

BOX 7.1   CHILDREN RAISED BY GAY OR LESBIAN PARENTS

A growing number of gay and lesbian couples are rearing children. In most cases, the children were conceived in heterosexual marriages, but then one parent established a lesbian or gay relationship and continued to raise the child. In addition, some lesbian couples have children conceived through artificial insemination, and both lesbian and gay couples have assumed the parent role through adoption (Flaks et al., 1995; Bailey et al., 1995). The emergence of this unique family structure provides an opportunity to better understand the process of gender-role socialization and the development of sexual orientation. Many questions about child-rearing environments and child outcomes can be posed. Do parents who have a homosexual orientation differ from heterosexual parents in their parenting strategies or parental role behaviors? How relevant is a parent's sexual orientation in shaping a child's gender role identification?

Research has just begun to address some of these issues. Several studies have reported that when compared to heterosexual couples, lesbian couples exhibit more sensitive parenting and more egalitarian role relationships. Open disclosure of the lesbian relationship, the ability to maintain ties with the rest of the child's family, and a perception that the partners share equally in the tasks associated with household and childcare all contribute to the child's emotional well-being (Patterson, 1995). In general, studies of the well-being, and cognitive and emotional adjustment of children growing up with lesbian mothers find no differences between these children and those growing up in heterosexual families. The children have gender-role preferences that are very similar to those of children growing up in heterosexual families (Patterson, 1992; Flaks et al., 1995).

One study of the sexual orientation of young men who were raised by gay fathers found that about 90% of the sons whose sexual orientation could be determined were heterosexual (Bailey et al., 1995). This rate suggests that the process of identification with the father does not typically lead to an internalization of the father's sexual orientation. The authors argue that this finding, confirmed by data from other studies, is more supportive of a genetic than an environmental or socialization explanation for sexual orientation among males.

Research in this area is relatively new, and one must approach any conclusions with caution. The published studies are limited to small volunteer samples recruited through public advertisements. Participants are typically white, middle- or upper middle-class couples who are comfortable enough about their children's sexual orientation to be willing to discuss it with researchers. In addition, few studies include comparison groups, which would permit a more systematic assessment of the rate of gay or lesbian sexual orientation among children raised by heterosexual parents (Bailey et al., 1995; Baumrind, 1995). Future research with larger, more diverse samples will undoubtedly continue to clarify the genetic, environmental, and personal contributions to gender identification and sexual orientation.

males higher status (Huber, 1990). To the extent that such culturally determined values are communicated to children, males are likely to establish a firmer preference for their sex group, and females are likely to experience some ambivalence toward, if not rejection of, their sex group. In other words, it is easier to be happy and content with oneself if one feels highly valued than if one feels less valued.

Some families develop a strong preference regarding the sex of an expected child. In a longitudinal study of Swedish children from birth to age 25, the parents' prenatal preferences for a son or daughter were related to perceived problems in the mother-child and father-child relationships (Stattin & Klackenberg-Larsson, 1991). Mothers' perceptions of problems in the parent-child relationship, especially the relationship between fathers and their nonpreferred daughters, were significantly related to the fathers' disappointed hopes for a son. Looking back on their relationship with their parents at age 25, nonpreferred daughters were especially likely to note problems, saying that their mothers did not have time for them, their fathers were stricter with them and had less time for them, and their relationships with their fathers were, in general, worse than the relationships described by preferred daughters.

Thus, it is possible to know what sex one is and what behaviors are expected of members of that sex and yet wish one were a member of the opposite sex. In our own experience, if groups of men and women are asked whether they ever wished to be of the opposite sex, many more women than men will admit to having wished to be of the opposite sex. This finding may reflect some perceived advantages of the male role in our culture or the more serious sanctions against men who value or exhibit behaviors defined as feminine. It may reflect the greater flexibility that girls and women exhibit in their gender schemes, which permits them access to a wider range of behaviors as desirable and possible.

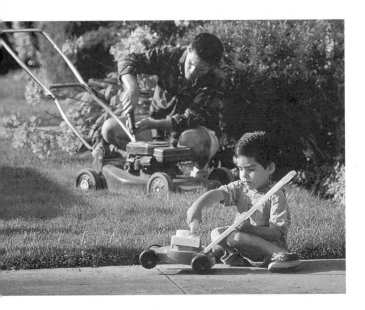

A child's gender identity becomes a guiding scheme that shapes his or her interests, expectations, and beliefs about self and others. Raymond sees 'mower repair' as part of his domain, just like his dad.

Table 7.2 summarizes the four components of the acquisition of gender identification: (1) developing an understanding of gender, (2) learning sex-role standards, (3) identifying with parents, and (4) establishing a gender preference. What was once viewed as a predominantly biological process of sex-role differentiation is now viewed as a product of the interaction of biological, cognitive, and social factors. The outcome of the process for an individual child depends greatly on the characteristics of his or her parents and their approach to sex-role socialization, the child's personal capacities and preferences, and the cultural and familial values that create gender-linked expectations for behavior.

A child's gender identity becomes a basic cognitive scheme that influences the interpretation of experiences (Bem, 1981; Martin, 1989). Children learn that people are grouped into two sexes—males and females. In our society, this dichotomy tends to impose itself on a wide array of social situations including work, play, and politics, where one's genital sex is not especially relevant. Once children have this powerful category, they go about the business of figuring out how to apply it. They recognize people as men and women, boys and girls, and they identify themselves as members of one of these two groups. They form expectations based on this categorization that certain toys, interests, and behaviors are appropriate for boys and others are appropriate for girls; certain activities, dispositions, and occupations are appropriate for men and women. These expectations are generally reinforced by the beliefs of the older children and adults with whom the children interact. Thus, the gender schemes that are conceived during childhood play a significant role in shaping the direction of a child's daily activities and in formulating a preliminary vision of the future.

Early Moral Development

Early moral development involves a process called **internalization,** which means taking parental standards and values as one's own. During toddlerhood, a child's attention is focused on limits of and standards for behavior. Children feel that demands for proper behavior do not come from within themselves but emanate from the external world. During early school age, standards and limits become part of a child's self-concept. Specific values are acquired from parents, but they become integrated elements of the child's world view.

For example, a 3-year-old boy may take great delight in hitting his dog with a stick. In the midst of one of these attacks, his mother scolds him. She insists that he stop and explains that it is cruel to hurt the dog. She may have to remind the boy on several other occasions that hitting the dog is not permitted. As the boy internalizes this standard, he begins to experience internal control over his own behavior. He may see the

TABLE 7.2	**Dimensions of Gender Identification**
	Dimensions of Gender-Role Identification
Dimension	**Gender-Role Outcome**
Developing an understanding of gender	I am a boy; I will grow up to be a man.
	I am a girl; I will grow up to be woman.
Acquiring sex-role standards	Boys are independent; they play with trucks.
	Girls are interpersonal; they play with dolls.
Identifying with the same-sex parent	I am a lot like Daddy. I want to be like him when I grow up.
	I am a lot like Mommy. I want to be like her when I grow up.
Establishing a gender-role preference	I like being a boy. I'd rather be a boy than a girl.
	I like being a girl. I'd rather be a girl than a boy.

dog lying calmly in the sun and, with a gleam in his eye, begin to pick up a stick. At that moment, his behavior is interrupted by a feeling of tension, which is accompanied by the thought that it is wrong to hit the dog. If the standard has been successfully internalized, the emotional tension and the thought will be sufficient to inhibit the boy from hitting the dog. For early school-age children, achievements in moral development include changes in three interrelated domains:

1. Knowledge. Learning the moral code of one's community and making judgments about whether something is good or bad, right or wrong.
2. Emotions. Experiencing the array of emotions that foster caring about others and that produce anxiety, guilt, and remorse when a moral standard has been violated.
3. Action. Taking appropriate actions to inhibit negative impulses or to act in a caring, helpful manner, depending on the situation.

A variety of theories explain how these domains of knowledge, emotion, and action evolve to produce the internalized moral behavior considered appropriate for the early-school-age child.

Learning Theory

Behavioral learning theory provides explanations for shaping moral behavior. Within this theoretical perspective, moral behavior and the process of internalization are viewed as a response to environmental reinforcements and punishments (Aronfreed, 1969). Moral behaviors, like other operant responses, can be shaped by the consequences that follow them. A positive, prosocial behavior, like offering to help put the toys away or comforting another child who is distressed, is likely to be repeated if it is rewarded. In contrast, if a behavior is ignored or punished, it is less likely to occur. If a child performs a misdeed or defies an authority and suffers negative consequences, this ought to reduce the likelihood that such behavior will recur. If a child is in an unpleasant or painful environment and performs a behavior that reduces or eliminates the unpleasantness, he or she is more likely to perform this same behavior again in similar situations. For example, if a child says, "I'm sorry. I'll try to do better next time," and this apology reduces the parent's anger or irritability, this behavior is likely to be repeated at other times when the parent is angry at the child. Internalization may result, therefore, as the behaviors that lead to a more comfortable, less unpleasant or threatening environment become more common and the behaviors that produce parental anger or conflict disappear.

The special case of **avoidance conditioning** is often viewed as a paradigm for understanding internalization in behavioral terms. Having been disciplined in the past for wrongdoings, a child contemplating a misdeed should feel tension. Avoiding or inhibiting the impulse to misbehave reduces the tension and is therefore reinforcing. This process may occur even when the person who has been involved in administering the discipline is absent. In other words, the scenario of thinking about a wrong or naughty action, feeling the anxiety that is associated with past discipline, and reducing that anxiety by exercising restraint may take place mentally, without any observable behavior. Over time, the reinforcement of tension reduction that is linked to controlling a wrongful impulse strengthens the tendency to inhibit it, and the child's behavior becomes increasingly less impulsive.

Social learning theory offers another source of moral learning: the observation of models. By observing and imitating helpful models, children can learn prosocial behavior. By observing the negative consequences that follow the misdeeds of models, they can also learn to inhibit their own misbehavior. Their moral behavior is not limited to the actions they have performed—it may be based on expectations formulated from observations of how the conduct of relevant models has been rewarded or punished (Bandura, 1977). Children may even formulate abstract rules, concepts, and sets of propositions about moral behavior by extracting meaningful elements from several incidents of observational learning. In the process, children form a mental representation by selecting and organizing observed responses and use this mental model to guide, compare, and modify their own moral behavior (Bandura, 1991).

When Camilla gets a scolding for breaking a plate, she learns that intentions are not as important as consequences. She reasons that she was naughty because the plate got broken and her mother got angry.

Finally, cognitive learning theory describes how moral behavior is influenced by the interaction of situational factors and expectations, values, and goals that have been derived from earlier learning (Mischel, 1973). For example, some people place great value on success in athletics and may be more tempted to violate norms in order to succeed in such a milieu than in an academic setting. The expectation that a misdeed will be observed and punished leads to greater resistance to temptation than does the expectation that a misdeed will go unnoticed. Similarly, the belief that positive, prosocial behaviors are expected and will be noticed influences a child's generosity and helpfulness (Froming et al., 1985). Although enduring moral qualities may be developed through the consistent reinforcement of empathetic, sensitive, and just responses, the specific situation will also influence the extent to which moral behavior is displayed (Carroll & Rest, 1982). The formation of moral character is built upon the accumulation of many experiences across different situations day after day.

Cognitive-Developmental Theory

Cognitive-developmental theorists have focused on the orderly sequence of development of the child's thoughts about moral issues. Piaget (1932/1948) described the major transition in moral judgment as a shift from heteronomous to autonomous morality. In **heteronomous morality**, rules are understood as fixed, unchangeable aspects of social reality. Children's moral judgments reflect a sense of subordination to authority figures. An act is judged as right or wrong depending on the letter of the law, the amount of damage that was done, and whether or not the act was punished. In **autonomous morality**, children see rules as products of cooperative agreements. Moral judgments reflect a child's participation in a variety of social roles and in egalitarian relationships with friends. Give-and-take with peers highlights mutual respect and mutual benefit as rewards for holding to the terms of agreement or abiding by the law.

Expanding on this view, cognitive-developmental theorists have described a sequence of stages of moral thought (Kohlberg, 1976; Gibbs, 1979; Damon, 1980). As children become increasingly skillful in evaluating the abstract and logical components of a moral dilemma, their moral judgments change. At the core of this change is the mechanism called **equilibration**. Stage changes in moral reasoning are associated with efforts to reconcile new perspectives and ideas about basic moral concepts, such as justice, intentionality, and social responsibility, with existing views about what is right and wrong. Children's reasoning may be thrown into disequilibrium by external sources, such as their parents' use of explanations and inductions regarding a moral dilemma or encounters with friends who reason differently about a moral conflict. In addition, children's own cognitive maturation, especially the ability to think abstractly and hypothetically about interrelated variables, determines how their reasoning about moral dilemmas will be structured (Piaget, 1975/1985; Walker, 1988).

Kohlberg (1969, 1976) described three levels of moral thought, each characterized by two stages of moral judgment (Table 7.3). At Level I, **preconventional morality**, Stage 1 judgments of justice are based on whether a behavior is rewarded or punished. Stage 2 judgments are based on an instrumental view of whether the consequences will be good for "me and my family." The first, and to some degree the second, stages of Level I characterize children of early school age. Level II, **conventional morality**, is concerned with maintaining the approval of authorities at Stage 3 and with upholding the social order at Stage 4. Level III, **postconventional morality**, brings an acceptance of moral principles that are viewed as part of a person's own ideology rather than simply being imposed by the social order. At Stage 5, justice and morality are determined by a democratically derived social contract. At Stage 6, a person develops a sense of universal ethical principles that apply across history and cultural contexts.

TABLE 7.3   Stages in the Development of Moral Judgment

Level I: Preconventional

Stage 1	Judgments are based on whether behavior is rewarded or punished.
Stage 2	Judgments are based on whether the consequences result in benefits for self or loved ones.

Level II: Conventional

Stage 3	Judgments are based on whether authorities approve or disapprove.
Stage 4	Judgments are based on whether the behavior upholds or violates the laws of society.

Level III: Postconventional

Stage 5	Judgments are based on preserving social contracts based on cooperative collaboration.
Stage 6	Judgments are based on ethical principles that apply across time and cultures.

SOURCE: Based on Kohlberg, 1969, 1976.

This view of moral development leads one to expect the moral reasoning of early-school-age children to be at Level I, preconventional morality, which is dominated by concerns about the consequences of their behavior. At Stage 1, children's judgments of good and bad, right and wrong, are based on whether a behavior has been rewarded or punished. At Stage 2, children's moral judgments are based on whether the behavior will bring about benefits for them or for other people they care about. Thus, young children's moral outlook has a utilitarian orientation (Kohlberg, 1976). Kohlberg's theory of moral development, which was based on interviews with male participants, has been criticized for its emphasis on justice and abstract ideological principles. The theory tends to ignore critical interpersonal values that guide moral reasoning in most social contexts (Gilligan and Attanucci, 1988). In Chapter 10, in the discussion of Internalized Morality in later adolescence, alternative views about the direction of change in moral reasoning are explored. However, research with first-graders confirms that this preconventional outlook is quite common, whether children are discussing hypothetical or real-life moral dilemmas (Walker, 1989).

The preoccupation with consequences highlights the significance of the home and school environments in establishing and supporting young children's moral code. To build a basis for making moral judgments, children need to understand the consequences of their behaviors for others. Thus, we can appreciate clearly why inductions—explanations that emphasize the effects of one's actions on others—are such a key disciplinary method for young children. In addition, the moral climate of home and school provide the early structure for the content of the moral code. Behaviors that are linked to moral principles, such as telling the truth, being generous, respecting the feelings of others, and being respectful of authority figures, become woven into children's concepts of right and wrong. The clarity of this moral code depends on the consistency with which positive examples lead to positive outcomes and negative examples lead to negative outcomes (Garrod, 1993).

Moral Transgressions versus Social Convention Transgressions. Not all rules or prohibitions have to do with moral concerns. There is a difference between morality, which usually involves the rights, dignity, and welfare of others, and **social convention,** which involves socially accepted norms and regulations (Turiel, 1983). For example, in the preschool context, stealing another child's toy would be a moral transgression; a transgression of social convention would be getting up and wandering away during large-group time. Preschool-age children are consistently able to differentiate between moral and social-convention transgressions. They understand that moral transgressions are wrong because they affect the welfare of others and that social-convention transgressions are wrong because they are disruptive or create disorder (Smetana, 1985). Social-convention transgressions depend on the situation. At home, it may be permissible to get up from the table during dinnertime before everyone has finished and go somewhere to play, whereas it is not permissible to get up from the snack table at preschool until the teacher says everyone may leave. Moral transgressions apply more consistently across settings: It is morally wrong to steal at home, at preschool, or at a friend's house. It is significant that children as young as 3 and 4 make this distinction when they evaluate transgressions. In addition, in contrast to social-convention transgressions, young children tend to judge moral transgressions to be more serious, deserving of greater punishment, and independent of the rules or authority in a situation (Smetana et al., 1993).

Psychoanalytic Theory

The psychoanalytic theorists suggest that a moral sense develops as a result of strong parental identification. Its focus is on the internalization of values and the factors that sustain impulse control under conditions of temptation. The earlier discussion of identification with parents provides the basis for understanding the psychoanalytic treatment of moral development. Classical psychoanalytic theory views a child's conscience, or **superego,** as an internalization of parental values and moral standards. It holds that the superego is formed during the phallic stage, between the ages of about 4 and 7, as a result of the conflict between internal sexual and aggressive impulses and the ways in which the parents deal with the behavioral manifestations of those impulses.

According to psychoanalytic theory, the more severely a parent forces a child to inhibit her or his impulses, the stronger the child's superego will be. Freud (1925/1961) assumed that males would develop more highly differentiated and punitive superegos than females because he believed that males' impulses are more intense. He also believed that because of the greater impulsive energy demonstrated by males, boys are treated more harshly by their parents than are girls. Finally, Freud suggested that males identify with their fathers for two reasons: fear of losing the father's love and fear of the father as an aggressor. This identification with the father is intense, and typically leads to a fully incorporated set of moral standards. According to Freud, a female identifies with her mother for a single reason: fear of loss of love. Since Freud considered this motivation for identification less intense than that of the male, he believed that the female's superego would be correspondingly weaker.

The ability to control one's impulses and resist temptation are key elements of early morality. Randy is struggling here. Would anybody miss just one cookie?

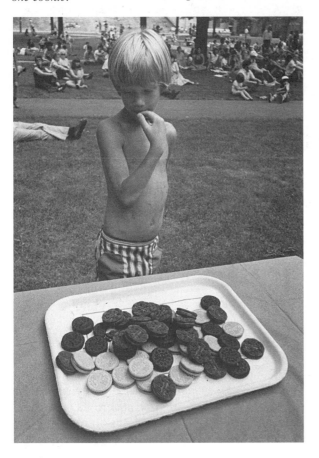

Research on the Development of Conscience. Research on the development of conscience has failed to support Freud's hypotheses. Studies that have investigated the ability to resist temptation or to confess after wrongdoing have found that young girls are better able to resist temptation than boys and show a pattern of decreasing moral transgressions over the toddlerhood and early school years (Mischel et al., 1989). Studies that have attempted to assess the relative contributions of mothers and fathers to children's moral behavior have found that mothers' values and attitudes are strongly related to the moral behavior of their children, whereas the values and attitudes of fathers have little relationship to such behavior (Hoffman, 1970). Finally, research has found that the children of parents who use harsh physical punishment do not have higher levels of internalization. They are likely to inhibit impulsive behaviors in the presence of their parents, but when they are observed with their peers away from home, they tend to be physically aggressive and do not control their behavior well (Hart et al., 1990; Pettit et al., 1988). Parental warmth, de-emphasis on power assertion, democratic decision making, and modeling of resistance to temptation appear to contribute to high levels of prosocial behavior and social responsibility (Maccoby, 1992).

Neopsychoanalytic Theory. These findings raise doubts about Freud's views on the formation of conscience and the relative strength of the superego in males and females. In fact, psychoanalytic theory now tends to view the critical time for moral development as coming earlier in life, in infancy (Mahler, 1963; Kohut, 1971). Infants develop an awareness of three domains: the body and its physical experiences and needs; the existence of others; and the relations between the self and others (Beit-Hallahmi, 1987). All subsequent psychological growth must be assimilated into these three domains. Thus, according to this view, the origins of moral reasoning and behavior have links to early feelings about the self and its needs, especially the feelings of pleasure and pain. Morality has a basis in a young child's awareness of others who are valued, and behaviors that strengthen or threaten the bonds between the self and these others. This view suggests that one basis of early morality lies in the child's own sense of self-love, a wish to enhance and not harm or violate the self. Another basis is the extension of this self-love to the other and the wish to preserve feelings of connection, trust, and security that have been established in the early parent-infant relationship. The moral aspect of the self is built on close, affectionate bonds with the caregiver, including positive feelings of empathy and connection that emerge in this early relationship and the internalization of early prohibitions that are accompanied by emotional signals such as anger and disapproval (Emde et al., 1987; Emde et al., 1991).

Freud's work remains a significant contribution to the area of moral development because he drew attention to the powerful role of the superego and the ego ideal in motivating and inhibiting behavior. He also created interest in the origins of moral beliefs in early childhood. However, his description of the process by which parental values are incorporated into a child's moral code appears to be faulty. Most likely, Freud underestimated the power of the need to reassure oneself about parental love. The strong affectional bonds between a parent and child are the most effective forces in promoting positive moral behavior.

Research on Empathy and Perspective Taking

Moral judgment and moral action rely on the ability to assess another person's discomfort and to think about another person's point of view.

Empathy. Empathy has been defined as sharing the perceived emotion of another—"feeling with another" (Eisenberg & Strayer, 1987, p. 5). This definition emphasizes one's emotional reaction to the observation of another person's emotional condition. By merely observing the facial expressions, body attitudes, and vocalizations of another person, a child can identify that person's emotion and feel it personally. The range of emotions with which one can empathize depends on the clarity of the cues the other person sends and on one's own prior experiences.

The capacity for empathy changes with development. Hoffman (1987) described four levels of empathy, especially in reference to the perception of another person's distress:

- **Global empathy:** You experience and express distress as a result of witnessing someone else in distress. Example: A baby cries upon hearing the cries of other infants.
- **Egocentric empathy:** You recognize distress in another person and respond to it in the same way you would respond if the distress were your own. Example: A toddler offers his own cuddle blanket to another child who is crying.
- **Empathy for another's feelings:** You show empathy for a wide range of feelings and anticipate the kinds of reactions that might really comfort someone else. Example: A child sees another child crying because his favorite toy is broken. She offers to help fix the toy.
- **Empathy for another's life conditions:** You experience empathy when you understand the life conditions or personal circumstances of a person or group. Example: A child learns of children in another town who have become homeless after a flood. The child asks his mother if he can send some of his clothes to those children.

The capacity for empathy begins in infancy and evolves as children achieve new levels of understanding about the self and others, as well as a greater capacity to use language to describe their emotions. Young children appear to be able to recognize and interpret auditory and facial cues that suggest emotional expressions in others. In the newborn nursery, when one infant starts to wail, the other infants begin to cry

(Martin & Clark, 1982; Sagi & Hoffman, 1976). Three- and 4-year-olds can recognize the emotional reactions of other children to specific problems. Both American and Chinese children were able to recognize "happy" and "unhappy" reactions by age 3. The differentiation among "afraid," "sad," and "angry" developed slightly later. The specific cues for these feelings were linked to cultural patterns of expressing emotions. Nevertheless, it was clear that the youngest children in both cultural groups could recognize emotional states in another person (Borke, 1973).

In addition to being able to correctly recognize another's emotions, early-school-age children can usually identify the circumstances that may have produced another child's emotional response, especially anger and distress, and can understand and empathize with another child's feelings. Children are most likely to think that external events produce emotional reactions: "The teacher made her put her toys away," or "He tripped over the blocks." But they can also think about internal states that may produce strong emotions: "He's mad because he didn't get a turn," or "She's sad because her stomach hurts" (Hoffner & Badzinski, 1989; Fabes et al., 1988, 1991).

The ability to identify pleasurable and unpleasurable emotions in others and to empathize with them makes the child receptive to moral teachings. Empathy can serve a proactive function by enlisting a child's efforts to help another person. It can also serve a reactive function by generating remorse for having caused an emotional state in another person. In the case of social attitude formation, empathy has been engaged in efforts to help children develop more compassion and acceptance of stigmatized groups (Batson et al., 1997).

Perspective Taking. **Perspective taking** refers to a person's ability to consider a situation from the point of view of another person. This faculty requires a recognition that someone else's point of view may differ from one's own. It also requires the ability to analyze the factors that may account for these differences. When children can assess these factors, they can begin to transcend the personal perspective and attempt to look at a situation from another person's point of view.

Imagine a child who wants to play with another child's toy. If the first child thinks, "If I had that toy, I would be happy, and if I am happy, everyone is happy," then she or he may take the toy without anticipating that the other child will be disappointed. Although empathy provides an emotional bridge that enables children to discover the similarities between self and others, it does not teach them about differences. Learning

Young children can be very caring and supportive in comforting others, especially if they understand the reason behind another child's distress.

about differences requires perspective taking. In fact, several psychologists have argued that the capacity to take another person's perspective is achieved only gradually through peer interaction and conflict (Flavell, 1974; Piaget, 1932/1948; Selman, 1971).

Children aged 4 and 5 frequently exhibit prosocial behaviors that evidence an understanding of others' needs. The most common of these behaviors are sharing, cooperating, and helping. Two examples illustrate the nature of this kind of social perspective taking:

> The path of a child with an armload of play dough was blocked by two chairs. Another child stopped her ongoing activity and moved the chair before the approaching child reached it.
> A boy saw another child spill a puzzle on the floor and assisted him in picking it up. (Iannotti, 1985, p. 53)

Interestingly, the young children who score highest in formal measures of perspective taking do not necessarily exhibit high levels of prosocial behavior in preschool settings. At this early age, an important determinant of whether children will spontaneously offer help is whether they can pinpoint others' emotional states in real-life situations.

Robert Selman (1980) studied the process of social perspective taking by analyzing children's responses to a structured interview. Children watched audiovisual filmstrips that depict interpersonal conflicts. They were then asked to describe the motivation of each actor and the relationships among the various performers. Four levels of social perspective taking were described. At Level 1, the youngest children (4–6 years old) recognized different emotions in the various actors, but they assumed that all the actors viewed the situation much as they did. The children at Level 4 (about 10–12 years old) realized that two people were able to take each other's perspective into account before deciding how to act. Furthermore, they realized that each of those people may have viewed the situation differently from the way they did.

Many moral dilemmas require that children subordinate their personal needs for someone else's sake. To resolve such situations, children must be able to separate their personal wants from the other person's. Selman's research suggests that children under 10 can rarely approach interpersonal conflicts with this kind of objectivity (Selman, 1994).

Evidence of the gradual change in perspective-taking abilities can be seen in a study of how young children evaluated the emotional reactions of children who were categorized as victims and victimizers (Arsenio & Kramer, 1992). Children aged 4, 6, and 8 were shown pictures and told the accompanying story:

> Two children were at their coat lockers in school, and one child showed the other child some candies that he or she (two sets of drawings with female and male characters depending on sex of child) had received. The child who had been shown the candies saw that the locker room was empty, and that child (the victimizer) took the candies out of the victim's coat and put them into his or her own pocket. (p. 917)

After seeing the pictures and hearing the story, the children were asked to tell and then rate how the two children felt at the end of the story. The responses were categorized by whether the children described the victim or the victimizer first. All the children identified the victim as having strong negative feelings, regardless of whether they described the victim first or second. Most of the children at each age level evaluated the victimizer as having happy or good feelings. Only the oldest children attributed some mixed emotions to the victimizer, and then only when they described the victim first. These older children could see that there might be some negative emotional consequence to victimizing someone, although the predominant view, based on the positive consequences of the actions, was to assume that the victimizer would be basically happy. The results of this research suggest that the young child's ability to understand the negative emotions of the victim do not necessarily outweigh the anticipated positive emotions of being the victimizer.

Research on Parental Discipline

The last contribution to a theory of moral development that we will consider comes from the research on parental discipline, which was introduced in Chapter 6 in relation to self-control. When disciplining a child, the parent emphasizes that certain behaviors are wrong and should be inhibited while other behaviors are positive and should be repeated. This distinction between good and bad behaviors and the accompanying parental approval or disapproval begins to form the content of the child's moral code.

In addition, the parent uses some specific techniques of discipline. Four elements seem to be important in determining the impact of these techniques on the child's future behavior:

1. The discipline should help the child interrupt or inhibit the forbidden action.
2. The discipline should point out a more acceptable form of behavior so that the child will know what is right in a future instance.
3. The discipline should provide some reason, understandable to the child, why one action is inappropriate and the other more desirable.
4. The discipline should stimulate the child's ability to empathize with the victim of his or her misdeeds. In other words, children are asked to put themselves in their victim's place and to see how much they dislike the feelings they caused in the other person.

In considering discipline as a mechanism for teaching morality, one becomes aware of the many interacting and interrelated components of a moral act. The discipline techniques that are most effective in teaching morality to children are those that help them control their own behavior, understand the meaning of their behavior for others, and expand their feelings of empathy. Discipline techniques that do not include these characteristics may succeed in inhibiting undesired behavior but may fail to achieve the long-term goal of incorporating moral values into future behavior.

Kochanska (1997) has provided evidence to support the notion that the child's temperament is often overlooked in determining the likely effectiveness of certain disciplinary techniques. In particular, children who are temperamentally fearful, inhibited in response to novel stimuli, and choose to retain close proximity to their mothers during toddlerhood are especially sensitive to messages of disapproval. For these children, a small dose of parental criticism is adequate to promote moral internalization, and too much power assertion appears to be counterproductive. In contrast, children who are highly active and who are insensitive to messages of disapproval appear to require much more focused and directive discipline, especially a consistent program of recognizing and rewarding good behaviors while minimizing the situations and stimuli that may provoke impulsive or aggressive actions.

In addition to using approval or disapproval, parents guide moral development by modeling positive, prosocial behaviors and by talking with their children about moral issues. In Chapter 6, we discussed the use of scaffolding to promote more effective communicative competence. In much the same way, parents can scaffold their child's moral reasoning by raising questions about moral decisions their children are facing and introducing new arguments or alternative points of view as their children think about moral conflicts (Walker & Taylor, 1991a).

The Impact of Television on Moral Development

Moral influences extend beyond the family to include schools, religious institutions, and the community. One of the societal influences that has been of great concern over the past 25 years is the impact of the media, especially television (Herbert, 1996). The dominant focus of research on the socioemotional impact of television viewing has been on the role of televised *violence* on the beliefs and behaviors of young children. Concern about television violence is particularly meaningful within the context of the child's growing moral consciousness. More than 20 years of laboratory experiments, field experiments, and analyses of naturally occurring behaviors have led to the conclusion that televised violence has definite negative consequences for young children's behaviors and beliefs.

Studies of children in the United States and in other countries provide evidence that at least three processes are at work that may increase the level of aggressiveness in children who watch televised violence (Table 7.4) (Comstock & Paik, 1991; Huston et al., 1992; Huesmann & Eron, 1986; Huesmann & Malamuth, 1986; Josephson, 1987; Liebert & Sprafkin, 1988). First, children observe televised role models who perform aggressive actions. Especially when the hero is provoked and retaliates with aggression, the child is likely to imitate the aggressive actions. Thus, the viewing of televised violence adds new violent behaviors to the child's repertoire. In addition, when the hero is rewarded or viewed as successful because of his or her violent actions, children's tendencies to express aggression are increased (Bandura, 1973).

The second process linked to the impact of televised violence is a heightening of arousal. The fast action that usually accompanies televised violence captures the viewer's attention. The violent incident raises the child's level of emotionality, bringing to the fore other aggressive feelings, thoughts, memories, and action tendencies. The more frequently this network of elements is activated, the stronger will be their association. Thus, children who have seen a lot of televised violence and are temperamentally aggressive are likely to engage in overt acts of aggression because of the strength of arousal prompted by the televised stimulus (Berkowitz, 1984, 1986).

Finally, exposure to televised violence affects a young child's beliefs and values. Children who are exposed to frequent episodes of televised violence are more likely to be-

TABLE 7.4	Three Processes that May Increase the Level of Aggressiveness in Children Who Watch Televised Violence
Process	**Possible Consequence**
Observing role models who engage in aggressive actions.	Imitation of violent action likely when: 1. Hero is provoked and retaliates with aggression. 2. Hero is rewarded for violent actions. New violent behaviors added to repertoire.
Viewing aggressive actions leads to heightened level of arousal.	Brings network of aggressive thoughts, feelings, memories, and action tendencies into consciousness. Repeated stimulation strengthens this network. Stimulation interacts with aggressive temperament to increase the likelihood of aggressive action.
Viewing aggression affects beliefs and values.	Aggressive behavior is seen as an acceptable way to resolve conflicts. Viewers are hardened to use of aggression in peer interactions. Aggression is used as a response to frustration. Viewers expect others to be aggressive toward them. Viewers worry about being victims of aggression. Viewers see the world as a dangerous place.

lieve that aggressive behavior is an acceptable way to resolve conflicts, and they become hardened to the use of aggression in peer interactions. They are also more accepting of the use of aggression as a response to frustration. In addition, children (and adults) who are exposed to televised violence are more likely to expect that others will be aggressive toward them, to worry about being victims of aggression, and to see the world as a dangerous place (Bryant et al., 1981; Gerbner et al., 1980; Thomas & Drabman, 1977).

Researchers have barely begun to scratch the surface of television's uses to promote prosocial development. There is clear evidence that children who are exposed to prosocial programming are influenced toward more positive social behavior (Hearold, 1986). Many programs, some developed for children and others intended for a broader viewing audience, convey positive ethical messages about the value of family life, the need to work hard and sacrifice in order to achieve important goals, the value of friendship, the importance of loyalty and commitment in relationships, and many other cultural values. A number of contemporary programs include characters of many races and ethnic backgrounds. Many feature women in positions of authority or performing acts of heroism. Increasingly, programs include characters with physical disabilities who play important roles. Through exposure to these programs, children learn to challenge social stereotypes and develop positive images of people from many ethnic groups (Liebert & Sprafkin, 1988).

Public controversies over the impact of violence on children's moral development and mental health have led to some changes. The Children's Television Act, passed in 1990, requires television stations to meet the "educational and informational needs of children" in order to renew their license. This bill has been credited with an increase in the amount of educational television directed to children from about 1 hour to about 3 hours

Exposure to many hours of televised violence increases young children's repertoire of violent behavior and increases the prevalence of angry feelings, thoughts, and actions. These children are caught up in the violent fantasy, taking part in the televised situation while they watch.

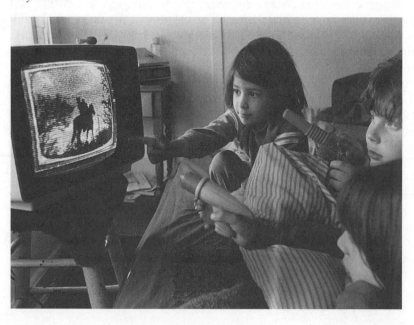

per week. In addition, new cable stations that are aimed directly toward children have entered the television market. At the same time, those who monitor contemporary television estimate that a typical child, watching an average of 27 hours of TV a week, will view "8,000 murders and 100,000 acts of violence from age 3 to age 12" (Silver, 1995). Parental concerns about the impact of observing too much televised violence will have to be translated into internalized norms about what types of televised programming is acceptable.

Review

The child of early school age is in the process of developing an initial moral code. The approaches to this issue are summarized in Table 7.5. Each highlights an essential element of the larger, more complex phenomenon. *Learning theory* points out that an external reward structure inhibits or reinforces behavior. *Cognitive theory* suggests that conceptual immaturity characterizes this early phase of moral development. *Psychoanalytic theory* is especially concerned with the relationship between parental identification and the development of conscience. The work on *empathy and perspective taking* shows that moral behavior requires an emotional and cognitive understanding of the needs of others. These prosocial skills help children to appreciate how other children or adults may be experiencing reality. With this insight, children can modify their own actions to benefit others. Theory and *research on parental discipline* suggest that parents promote moral development when they try to increase children's understand-

TABLE 7.5   Contributions to the Study of Moral Development

Conceptual Source	Significant Contributions	Consequences for a Particular Aspect of Moral Development
Learning theory	Relevance of an external system of rewards and punishments Imitation of models Formation of expectations about the reward structure	Moral behavior Internalization of a moral code
Cognitive theory	Conceptual development of notions of intentionality, rules, justice, and authority Stages of moral judgment	Moral judgments Distinction between moral transgressions and social-convention transgressions
Psychoanalytic theory	Parental identification Formation of the superego	Internalization of parental values Experience of guilt
Research on empathy and perspective taking	Ability to experience another's feelings begins very early and changes with age Ability to recognize differences in point of view emerges slowly during early-school-age and middle childhood years Peer conflict, peer interactions, and specific role-taking training all increase perspective taking skills	Empathy heightens concern for others and helps inhibit actions that might cause distress Perspective taking can foster helping and altruism
Research on parental discipline	Parents define moral content Parents point out the implications of a child's behavior for others Creation of a reward structure Differential impact of power, love withdrawal, warmth, and inductions	Moral behavior Moral reasoning Internalization of moral values Empathy and guilt
Research on watching televised violence	Observing aggressive role models Arousal of aggressive emotions, memories, and action tendencies Formation of beliefs and values	New repertoire of aggressive behavior Lower threshold for aggressive action Expectation of aggression from others Desensitization to acts of violence

ing of the effects of their behavior on others. *Research on television violence* shows that although television programming can reinforce prosocial values, children who are exposed to many hours of violent programming are more likely to accept violence as a method for resolving conflicts, and are more likely to interpret the behavior of others as having an aggressive intention.

Self-Theory

The self-concept is viewed as a theory that links the child's understanding of the nature of the world, the nature of the self, and the meaning of interactions between the two (Epstein, 1973, 1991; Epstein et al., 1993). The function of the **self-theory** is to make transactions between the self and the world turn out as positively and beneficially as possible. One's theory about oneself draws on such inner phenomena as dreams, emotions, thoughts, fantasies, and feelings of pleasure or pain. It is also based on the consequences of interactions with the environment. As with any set of concepts, the complexity and logic of the self-theory depend on the maturation of cognitive functions. Further, since the self-theory is based on personal experiences and observations, one would expect it to be modified over the life course by changing physical and socioemotional competencies as well as by participation in new roles.

One of the earliest psychological analyses of self-theory was provided by William James (1892/1961). He described two elements of the self, the "me" and the "I." The "me" is the self as object—the self one can describe—including physical characteristics, personality traits, social roles and relationships, thoughts, and feelings. The "I" is more subjective. It is the self as one who is aware of one's own actions. It can be characterized by four fundamental features: a sense of agency or initiation of behaviors, a sense of uniqueness, a sense of continuity from moment to moment and day to day, and an awareness of one's own awareness—metacognition (Damon & Hart, 1988).

James thought of the "I" as the essential domain through which one experiences a vivid, compelling sense of self-sameness and meaning from day to day. Yet, he thought of it as largely unmeasurable. However, building on these ideas and more contemporary research and theory, Damon and Hart (1988) devised a model of self-understanding that includes both the "me" (self-as-object) and the "I" (self-as-subject) (Figure 7.2). Along the front face of the cube, the self-as-object, Damon and Hart identified four domains of the "me": physical self, active self, social self, and psychological self. Along the side face of the cube, self-as-subject, they identified three domains of the "I": continuity, distinctiveness, and agency. Development, shown by the vertical changes in each of these seven domains, is traced from early childhood through late adolescence. According to Damon and Hart, one can recognize evidence of self-understanding in each domain even in early childhood. Rather than seeing development as movement from an awareness of physical properties and behaviors at an early age to an awareness of social relationships and psychological traits at a later age, the domains provided evidence that what changes is the general organizing principle around which all aspects of the "me" and the "I" are synthesized.

Developmental Changes in the Self-Theory

At each stage, the self-theory is the result of a person's cognitive capacities and dominant motives as he or she comes in contact with the stage-related expectations of the culture (Stipek et al., 1992). In infancy, the self consists primarily of an awareness of one's independent existence. The infant discovers body boundaries, learns to identify recurring need states, and feels the comfort of loving contact with caregivers. During the second year of life, self-recognition and the evolving sense of the self as a causal agent add new dimensions to the self-theory. Gradually, these experiences are integrated into a sense of the self as a permanent being who has an impact on the environment, existing in the context of a group of other permanent beings who either do or do not respond adequately to the infant's internal states.

In toddlerhood, the self-theory grows through an active process of self-differentiation. Children explore the limits of their capacities and the nature of their impact on others. Because of toddlers' inability to entertain abstract concepts and their tendency toward egocentrism (the perception of oneself as the center of the world), their self-

Developmental Level	General organizing principle	Domains of the "Me"				Domains of the "I"		
		The self-as-object				The self-as-subject		
		Physical self	Active self	Social self	Psychological self	Continuity	Distinctiveness	Agency
4. Late adolescence	Systematic beliefs and plans	Physical attributes reflecting volitional choices or personal and moral standards	Active attributes that reflect choices, personal or moral standards	Moral or personal choices concerning social relations or social-personality characteristics	Belief systems, personal philosophy, self's own thought processes	Relations between past, present, and future selves	Unique subjective and experiential interpretations of events	Personal and moral evaluations self influence self
3. Early adolescence	Interpersonal implications	Physical attributes that influence social appeal and social interactions	Active attributes that influence social appeal and social interactions	Social-personality characteristics	Social sensitivity, communicative competence, and other psychologically related social skills	Ongoing of recognition self by others	Unique of combinational psychological and physical attributes	Communication and reciprocal interaction self influence self
2. Middle and late childhood	Comparative assessments	Capability-related physical attributes	Abilities relative to others, self, or normative standards	Abilities or acts considered in light of others' reactions	Knowledge, cognitive abilities, or ability-related emotions	Permanent, and cognitive capable active capabilities and immutable self-characteristics	Comparisons self between self and other along and other isolated dimensions	Efforts and talents self influence self
1. Early childhood	Categorical identifications	Bodily properties or material possessions	Typical behavior	Fact of membership in particular social relations or groups	Momentary moods, feelings, preferences, and aversions	Categorical identifications	Categorical identifications	External, uncontrollable factors determine self

FIGURE 7.2
A developmental model of self-understanding

theories are likely to depend on being competent and loved. There is little recognition of social comparisons (being better or worse than someone else), but an increasing sensitivity to the positive and negative reactions of others. By the age of 3 1/2 or 4, children seem to understand the idea of competition in a game, and they seem to take pleasure in winning and experience some disappointment in losing. However, it is unclear to what extent they actually reflect on the self, making judgments of their strengths and weaknesses or distinguishing their various arenas of competence (Emde & Buchsbaum, 1990).

During early school age, the self-theory becomes more differentiated. Children can distinguish between the real self (how one actually is) and the ideal self (how one would like to be). They can recognize some discrepancies between how they describe themselves and how their parents or friends may describe them (Oosterwegel & Oppenheimer, 1993). And they can differentiate among various areas of activities like math, reading, and music, indicating perceptions of strength in certain areas and weakness in others (Eccles et al., 1993).

According to Damon and Hart (1988), in early childhood, the self is understood as an accumulation of **categorical identifications.** No additional linkage or significance is taken from these categorical statements, simply a recognition that they exist.

> Examples: What kind of person are you? *I have blue eyes.* Why is that important? *It just is.* What kind of a person are you? *I'm Catholic.* What does that say about you? *I'm Catholic, and my mother is, and my father is, and my grandmother, and my grandfather, and I'm Catholic too.* (pp. 59–60)

In middle childhood, the organizing principle shifts to **comparative assessments.** Self-understanding relies on comparisons of oneself with social norms and standards or with specific other people.

> Examples: What are you like? *I'm bigger than most kids.* Why is that important? *I can run faster than everybody.*
>
> What are you like? *I'm not as smart as most kids.* Why is that important? *It takes me longer to do my homework.* (pp. 62–63)

From ages 4 to 6, children become more aware that people have different points of view. An understanding of logical relations contributes to an appreciation of the concept of cultural norms: If one is in a certain role, one is expected to act in a certain way. Sex-role standards are especially important in this regard. Children are very sensitive to any implication that they are not living up to the expectations of how a boy or girl ought to act. Children are also aware of moral imperatives that define good and evil. All these cognitive gains make a child more sensitive to social pressure, more likely to experience feelings of guilt or failure, and more preoccupied with issues of social comparison, self-criticism, and self-evaluation. At the same time, the child remains largely dependent on adults for material and emotional resources and is therefore highly attuned to positive and negative parental feedback. For these reasons, the issue of self-esteem becomes especially salient during early- and middle-childhood.

Self-Esteem

For every component of the self—the physical self, the self as reflected in others' behavior, and the array of personal aspirations and goals—a person makes an evaluation of worthiness. This self-evaluation, or **self-esteem,** is based on three essential sources: (1) messages of love, support, and approval from others; (2) specific attributes and competencies; and (3) the way one regards these specific aspects of the self, both in comparison with others and in relation to one's ideal self (Pelham & Swann, 1989).

Feelings of being loved, valued, admired, and successful contribute to a sense of worth. Feelings of being ignored, rejected, scorned, and inadequate contribute to a sense of worthlessness. These early affective experiences contribute to a general sense of pride or shame, worthiness

Experiences of success build confidence and contribute to positive self-esteem. Abby is thrilled to be able to ride her big two-wheeler without the training wheels. She feels competent, proud of her accomplishment, and happy to be riding so well. What other kinds of accomplishments are likely to contribute to self-esteem at this age?

or worthlessness, that is captured in the global statements children make about themselves even as early as age 3 or 4 (Eder, 1989; Eder et al., 1987).

Information about specific aspects of the self is accumulated through experiences of success and failure in daily tasks or when particular aspects of one's competence are challenged. A young child may develop a positive sense of self in athletics, problem solving, or social skills through the encouraging reactions of others as well as through the pleasure associated with succeeding in each of these areas (Harter, 1985).

With experience in a variety of roles and settings, each specific ability takes on a certain level of importance for a person. Not all abilities are equally valued at home, at school, and by friends. People may believe they have abilities in some areas but not in those they consider highly important. Others may believe they have only one or two areas of strength, but they may highly value those areas and believe them to be critically important to overall success. Self-esteem is influenced by the value one assigns to specific competencies in relation to one's overall life goals and personal ideals. Thus, it is possible to be a success in the eyes of others and still feel a nagging sense of worthlessness. Similarly, it is possible to feel proud and confident even though others may not value the activities and traits in which one takes great satisfaction (Box 7.2).

Feelings of positive self-worth provide a protective shield. If a person has a positive, optimistic self-evaluation, then messages that are negative and incongruent with it will be deflected. People with high self-esteem will explain a failure by examining the task, the amount of time needed for its completion, the other people involved, or the criteria for evaluating success and failure. They use a variety of strategies to minimize the importance of negative feedback. They do not permit a failure to increase doubt about their basic worth. By contrast, people with low self-esteem will see any failure as new evidence of their lack of worth (Brown & Mankowski, 1993; Brown & Gallagher, 1992).

Low self-esteem appears to be associated with a lack of clarity about one's essential characteristics. For example, a person with low self-esteem may endorse contradictory pairs of descriptive terms, seeing the self as both timid and bold or flexible and rigid. This confusion is linked to inconsistency, instability, and a lack of confidence in one's essential nature. Because of this confusion, people with low self-esteem are likely to have difficulty deciding in what social situations to participate. They are likely to place themselves in situations where they receive contradictory or negative social messages about their worth, exposing themselves to even greater confusion (Brockner, 1984;

BOX 7.2 CONTEXTUAL DISSONANCE

Children are influenced by the social groups that immediately surround them. During early school age, children emerge from the continuity of their families and neighborhoods into the more diverse context of school. This new context may complement or contrast with the major social characteristics of the family, specifically religion, race, and social class. Morris Rosenberg (1979) defined **contextual dissonance** as the difference between characteristics of the primary child-rearing and home environment, and other environments in which the child participates. He studied the impact of contextual dissonance on self-esteem, citing evidence of the negative effects of a dissonant environment in all three areas. Catholics who had been raised in a non-Catholic neighborhood were likely to have lower self-esteem than those raised in a Catholic one. Similar findings were observed among Protestants and Jews raised in dissonant neighborhoods. Racial dissonance and economic dissonance have also been found to be related to low self-esteem. For example, black preschool-age children in an all-black Mississippi rural town reportedly had higher self-esteem than did those in a racially mixed Michigan urban area (McAdoo, 1985). The implication of these studies is that self-esteem is bolstered by a feeling of continuity and belonging. Conversely, experiences of dissonance and lack of fit between one's personal values or qualities and those valued by the community may result in lowered self-esteem.

Many people are thrust into situations that undermine their basically positive self-esteem (Setterlund & Niedenthal, 1993). Circumstances that may lead to disruption in a basic sense of self-worth include adolescents' moving to a new high school where peers' values are discrepant from their home and personal values, immigrants who are viewed as outsiders by the members of their new community, or individuals hired to perform an important leadership role in an organization where the other employees have a different background and training. Being the only female in a classroom of male students or the only male in an office of female workers may have similar undermining effects on self-esteem.

Swann, 1990). Over time, lack of certainty about oneself is likely to be related to problems with identity achievement and greater vulnerability to negative feedback that increases confusion and produces negative emotions (Campbell, 1990; Baumgardner, 1990; Setterlund & Niedenthal, 1993).

Some scholars have speculated about the possible negative consequences of an unrealistically positive self-esteem. For example, people with high self-esteem seem to deflect failure messages in one area by exaggerating their abilities in another area (Brown & Smart, 1991). This strategy may be viewed as producing an inappropriately grandiose assessment of the self that is not validated by the views of others. Others suggest that parents and teachers may be so intent on providing self-enhancing strategies for their children, focusing on building up the "me," that the children become indifferent to the plight of others and lose sight of the kinds of positive feelings associated with helping others (Burr & Christensen, 1992). We speculate that it may be very important to develop strategies to enhance self-esteem in children who have low self-esteem or whose self-esteem has declined because of current experiences of failure or loss. This type of intervention may help prevent serious episodes of depression (Pelham, 1991). However, it is not clear whether it is advisable to take active steps toward self-esteem enhancement for children who already have a healthy, positive sense of self-worth.

Self-Esteem and the Early-School-Age Child.   At each life stage, as individuals set new goals for themselves or as discrepancies in competence become apparent, temporary periods of lowered self-esteem may be anticipated. Research on self-esteem suggests that early-school-age children may be especially vulnerable to fluctuations in feelings of self-worth (Kegan, 1982). Preschool- and kindergarten-age children assess their own competence to be significantly higher than do children in grades 1–4. In addition, young girls are more critical of their abilities than are boys and have lower expectations of success (Frey & Ruble, 1987; Butler, 1990).

Toddlers have been described as highly egocentric. In general, they feel good about themselves and do not differentiate between competence and social approval; rather, they respond to all positive experiences as evidence of their ultimate importance and value. They are much more likely to react to positive feedback after a success than to react to negative feedback after a failure (Stipek et al., 1992). They also use imitation to build a greater sense of their own mastery (Butler, 1989).

Early-school-age children, by comparison, are increasingly aware of the discrepancy between their own competencies and what they recognize as the skills expected of them by their teachers and parents or exhibited by older children. They are able to view themselves as objects of the evaluations of others. They are also aware of the importance of acceptance by adults and peers outside the family, especially their teachers and classmates (Weinstein et al., 1987). These newly valued others may not be as proud of their skills or as understanding about their limitations as are their family members. In peer competition, they begin to feel anxious about their performance and about how their abilities will be evaluated in comparison with those of others (Butler, 1989). At school, for example, young children often make critical comments about one another's work. Criticisms tend to outnumber compliments, and boys tend to be more critical than girls of their peers' work (Frey & Ruble, 1987). The combination of open peer criticism and a heightened emphasis on peer competition may make the school an environment in which one's self-esteem is frequently challenged.

Finally, early-school-age children are beginning to achieve a degree of internalization of social norms, including ideals to be attained as well as prohibitions, which they apply in a rather strict, rule-bound way. They are highly

By the age of 5 or 6, children are trying hard to gain acceptance from adults and peers. Even mild criticism from a teacher is often enough to arouse feelings of guilt or remorse. What kind of teacher criticism do you imagine might be taking place in this photo?

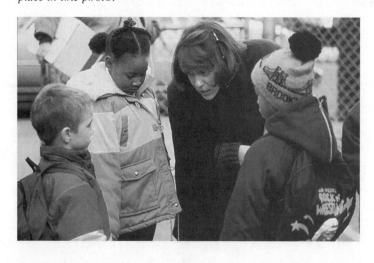

critical of rule violations, whether committed by themselves or others. Intentions, motives, and special circumstances are less salient to early-school-age children than the overt consequences of behavior. Thus, their newly formed capacity for guilt may lead to a heightened anxiety over failure to live up to their own moral code.

For all these reasons, early-school-age children are likely to experience feelings of depression and worthlessness. This decrease in self-esteem may be seen as a temporary fluctuation. Young children need frequent reassurance from adults that they are competent and loved. They need numerous opportunities to discover that their unique talents and abilities are useful and important, and that they can have a positive impact on others. As competencies increase, as thought becomes more flexible, and as the child makes meaningful friendships, self-esteem is expected to increase.

Group Play

Although experiences in the family provide the primary information that guides a young child's construction of the social world, interactions with peers contribute important opportunities for physical, cognitive, social, and emotional development. The quality of play expands during the early-school-age period, introducing more complex games with larger numbers of participants. In addition, children form friendship groups that allow them to sustain more elaborate fantasy play, experience group conflict and group problem solving, and encounter varying ideas about the topics discussed previously: gender, morality, and the self.

Group Games

The early-school-age child continues to use vivid fantasies in play. During this period, a new form of play emerges. Children show interest in group games that are more structured and somewhat more oriented to reality than play that is based primarily on imagination. Ring-around-the-rosie, London Bridge, and farmer-in-the-dell are examples of early group play. Hide-and-seek and statue-maker are more complex games of early school age. They involve more cognitive complexity, physical skill, and ritual. These games combine fantasy with an emphasis on peer cooperation. Group play is a transitional form between the fantasy play of the toddler and the team sports and other games with rules of middle childhood (Erikson, 1977).

Group games usually include a few rules that are simple enough so that a child can use them effectively to begin a game and determine a winner without the help of an adult. Usually, no team concept is involved. A game is played repeatedly, so that many children have an opportunity to win. The particular pleasure that children derive from these games seems to result more from peer cooperation and interaction than from the possibility of being a winner (Garvey, 1977).

Many of these games permit children to shift roles. A child is the hider and then the seeker, the catcher and then the thrower, the statue-maker and then the statue. Through group play, children experience the reciprocal nature of role relationships. Whereas many of their social roles are fixed—son or daughter, sibling, student—in play with peers, children have opportunities to experience a variety of perspectives (Lee, 1975; Sutton-Smith, 1972).

Friendship Groups

Friendship relations in early school age are based on the exchange of concrete goods and the mutual enjoyment of activities. Friendships are maintained through acts of affection, sharing, or collaboration in fantasy or constructive play. By the age of 4 or 5, children who have stable friendships become skilled in coordinating their interactions with their friends, creating elaborate pretend games, and being willing to modify their play preferences so that both members in the friendship have a chance to enjoy the kinds of play they like best (Park et al., 1993). Children build a snow fort together, play space adventure with one another, or sleep over at one another's homes. Friendships may be broken by the taking of a toy, hitting, or name-calling. The opportunity to form friendships benefits young children by enhancing their interpersonal sensitivity, social-reasoning skills, and conflict-resolution skills (Volling et al., 1997).

Conflicts Among Friends. Young children tend to evaluate situations on the basis of outcomes rather than intentions. Therefore, they are often harsh in assigning blame in the case of negative outcomes. For example, children were asked how much they should be blamed for another child's getting hurt. The "injury" took place in six different hypothetical situations. In the case of lowest level of responsibility, the child was accidentally hurt by someone's toy, but the owner did not actually cause the injury. At this level, 6-year-olds were more likely than older children or adults to blame themselves for the outcome (Fincham & Jaspars, 1979). Because of this rigid approach to social responsibility, peer play is frequently disrupted by quarrels, "tattling" on others, and hard feelings about injustices.

Even though children appear to be drawn into the active world of peer friendships, it is an uneven, difficult, and often extremely frustrating terrain for many early-school-age children. For example, many 5- and 6-year-olds participate in play fighting. In a study of children's perceptions of play fighting, Italian and British children of ages 5, 8, and 11 were surveyed about the differences between real fighting and play fighting (Smith et al., 1992). About half the children liked play fighting, a somewhat larger number of boys than girls. But about 80% thought that there was a risk that play fighting could lead to a serious, "real" fight. This might happen if there was an accidental injury, if the play fighting got carried away into mean name-calling, or if, when one child accidentally hurt the other, the second child mistook the injury as purposeful and hurt the first child back. Five-year-olds said that if play fighting turned into real fighting they would tell an adult. No matter whether the other child was a friend or not, they believed that such a transgression had to be handled with a serious intervention by a grown-up. The older children were more likely to forget about it, especially if the other person was a friend.

Sex-Segregation Among Friends. One of the most noticeable characteristics of young children's friendship groups is that they are likely to be segregated by sex. When boys and girls are free to choose play companions, they tend to choose others of their own sex. This pattern of same-sex social groupings among children is found not only in the United States but also in most other cultures (Edwards & Whiting, 1988). In one longitudinal study, children aged 4 1/2 were found playing with same-sex friends about three times more often than with opposite-sex friends. By age 6 1/2, they were *11* times more likely to be playing with same-sex friends (Maccoby & Jacklin, 1987).

By early-school-age, boys and girls tend to interact in same-sex friendship groups. Here, girls are playing together with stuffed animals, while the boys are playing together at the computer.

The significance of the formation of same-sex social groups is that boys and girls grow up in distinct peer environments (Maccoby, 1988, 1990). They tend to use different strategies to achieve dominance or leadership in their groups. Boys are more likely to use physical assertiveness and direct demands; girls are more likely to use verbal persuasiveness and polite suggestions. The verbal exchanges in all-boy groups are apt to include frequent boasts, commands, interruptions, heckling, and generally playful teasing. Boys try to top one another's stories and to establish dominance through verbal threats. The interactions in all-girl groups, on the other hand, tend to include agreeing with and acknowledging the others' comments, listening carefully to one another's statements, and talking about things that bind the group together in a shared sentiment or experience. In mixed-sex groups, girls discover that the leadership and interpersonal skills they have developed in their all-girl groups are not very effective in controlling the behaviors of boys. As a result, their negative views of boys are reinforced and their tendency to seek all-girl peer interactions increases.

Of course, many young children do form friendships with children of the opposite sex. These friendships may begin as early as infancy or toddlerhood between children who live in the same neighborhood or attend the same day-care center. They seem to be sustained by a compatibility of interests and play preferences and may survive the trend toward seeking same-sex friendships, even during early and middle childhood (Howes & Phillipsen, 1992). However, the general tendency to form same-sex friendship groups is an important aspect of social development that is established during the early childhood years and continues into adolescence (Bukowski et al., 1993). Even though a boy and a girl grow up in the same culture, in the same neighborhood, and even in the same family, the tendency to establish separate play and friendship groups fosters the development of distinctive gender-linked communication strategies and makes the achievement of mutual understanding between boys and girls difficult.

Groups and Dyads. In addition to the preference for same-sex friends, boys and girls tend to prefer to interact in different-size groups. Early-school-age girls seem to enjoy dyadic (two-person groups) interactions over larger groups, whereas boys seem to enjoy larger groups (Benenson, 1993). This is not to say that boys and girls cannot function effectively in both dyadic and larger peer-group situations, but when given their choice, boys tend to prefer the group and girls the dyad. These two configurations, the group and the dyad, provide different opportunities for intimacy, different needs to exercise dominance and control, and different problems in the coordination of action. They provide models for different forms of adult social relationships—the dyad being associated with intimacy between partners or in parent-child relationships, and the peer group being associated with sports teams, work groups, and families.

THE PSYCHOSOCIAL CRISIS: INITIATIVE VERSUS GUILT

As children resolve positively the toddlerhood crisis of autonomy versus shame and doubt, they emerge from that stage with a very strong sense of themselves as unique individuals. During early school age, children shift their attention toward investigation of the external environment. They attempt to discover the same kind of stability, strength, and regularity in the external world that they have discovered within themselves.

Initiative   Initiative is an expression of agency, an outgrowth of early experiences of the self as a causal agent that continues to find expression as children impose themselves and their ideas and questions onto their social world. It is an expression of the "I," the executive branch of the self (Damon & Hart, 1988). Initiative is the active, conceptual investigation of the world in much the same sense that autonomy is the active, physical manipulation of it (Erikson, 1963). The child's motivation for and skill in investigation depends on the successful development of a strong sense of autonomy. When children have acquired self-control and confidence in themselves, they can perform a variety of actions and observe the consequences. They discover, for example, what makes parents or teachers angry and what pleases them. They may deliberately perform a hostile act in order to evoke a hostile response. Children's curiosity about the order of the universe ranges from the physical to the metaphysical. They may ask questions about the color of the sky, the purpose of hair, the nature of God, the origin of babies, or the speed at which fingernails grow. They take things apart, explore the alleys and dark corners of their neighborhood, and invent toys and games out of odds and ends.

One expression of initiative is children's playful exploration of their own bodies and sometimes of their friends'. It is not uncommon to find 5- and 6-year-olds intently involved in a game of "doctor" in which both "doctor" and "patient" have their pants off. Boys of this age may occasionally be observed in a game that is won by the individual who can achieve the longest urine trajectory. Girls report occasions on which they have attempted to urinate from a standing position "in the same way a boy does." Both boys and girls engage in some form of masturbation. These behaviors are evidence of children's growing curiosity about and pleasure in their bodies and their physical functioning.

Children may express initiative while they are alone, by attempting to discover how things work and by building or inventing novel devices. They may also express initiative in social situations by asking questions, asserting their presence, and taking leadership. In one study of social competence, children described the strategies they used to enter a peer play group (Dodge et al., 1986). Two children were playing a game (they were referred to as the hosts), and a third child was asked to enter the room and try to initiate play with the others. The entry episode was videotaped and coded. In addition, both the child who tried to initiate play and the two hosts were interviewed about the episode and asked to evaluate how successful the entry child had been. Three strategies for initiating interaction were judged to be effective and were associated with other evidence of social competence:

1. Children established common ground by giving meaningful information in response to questions.
2. Children engaged in a positive, friendly interchange with the others.
3. Children did not show evidence of negative, irritable behaviors. The children who were least successful in initiating entry into the play "were disruptive, . . . made nagging, weak demands, . . engaged in incoherent behaviors, or . . . disagreed with hosts without citing a rule or reason" (Dodge et al., 1986, p. 25).

Children who experience a positive sense of initiative can apply this orientation to investigation of the physical as well as the social world. They innovate through the creation of "magic potions" mixed together with soap, perfume, pine cones, leaves, and other powerful ingredients. They create plays, stories, puppet shows, dances, and ceremonies. They dress up in costumes, entertain company by standing on their heads, engage in daring acts by hanging from tree limbs or walking on the tops of high ledges, and impose themselves in any and all curious and private discussions. They spend time trying to figure out ways to catch a glimpse of Santa Claus on Christmas Eve or the Tooth Fairy when she comes at night to collect her treasures. These are the "Little Rascal" years when a sense of initiative is associated with a naive, exuberant, entrepreneurial spirit, and a desire to discover, direct, and dominate. All manner of investigation and inquiry is fair game.

Guilt   **Guilt** is an emotion that accompanies the sense that one has been responsible for an unacceptable thought, fantasy, or action (Izard, 1977). It is recognized as a fundamental negative emotion that usually is accompanied by remorse and a desire to make reparation for real or imagined wrongdoing. It has the adaptive function of promoting social harmony because it disrupts or inhibits aggressive actions and leads people to ask for forgiveness or to try to compensate for wrongs they may have done.

Three theories offer different explanations for the dynamics that underlie feelings of guilt (Zahn-Waxler & Kochanska, 1990). The first, the psychoanalytic perspective, views guilt as an emotional reaction to one's unacceptable sexual and aggressive impulses. These impulses are especially threatening during the phallic stage, when hostility and feelings of sexuality toward one's parents become a focus of the child's wishes and must be repressed.

Second, research on empathy suggests that guilt may be awakened at a very early age through emotional arousal and sensitivity to another person's emotional distress. This view of guilt based on empathy is not defensive; it is closely linked to prosocial feelings and the basic emotional ties between infants and their caregivers (Hoffman, 1982).

The third, cognitive perspective suggests that guilt occurs when one fails to act in accord with one's own personal standards and beliefs. This view supposes a more advanced level of self-reflection and the ability to compare one's behaviors against personal standards. In this theory, guilt begins to be experienced in early and middle childhood as children begin to be more comparative in their organization and evaluation of self.

Every culture imposes some limits on legitimate experimentation and investigation. Some questions may not be asked; some acts may not be performed. Adults' reactions determine whether the child will learn to view specific behaviors, such as aggressiveness, sexual play, or masturbation, as wrong or acceptable. Children gradually internalize cultural prohibitions and learn to inhibit their curiosity in the taboo areas. One taboo shared by most cultures is the prohibition of incest. Most children learn that any

Saniosa made her sister cry by calling her a bad name. Now she is in her room, thinking things over. For most children, occasional feelings of guilt lead to wanting to set things right and regain positive feelings with their family or friends.

behavior that suggests sexual intimacy between family members is absolutely forbidden. Even the thought of such a relationship comes to generate feelings of anxiety and guilt. The child's curiosity in other domains is limited to the extent that the family and the school impose restrictions on certain areas of inquiry or action. The psychosocial crisis of initiative versus guilt is resolved positively when children develop the sense that an active, questioning investigation of the environment is informative and pleasurable. Inquiry is tempered by a respect for personal privacy and cultural values. However, the preponderant psychological state of mind is curiosity and experimentation. The child learns that, even though certain areas are off limits, efforts to understand most aspects of the world are appropriate.

Guilt, like other negative poles of the psychosocial crises, can have an adaptive function. As children grow in their sense of empathy and ability to take responsibility for their actions, they are able to acknowledge when their actions or words may have caused harm to someone else. Normal levels of guilt have been associated with positive levels of prosocial behavior and high levels of empathy (Tangney, 1991). Feelings of guilt generally lead to remorse and some attempt to set things right again, to restore the positive feelings in a relationship.

Girls and boys may show different patterns in the experience of guilt, based upon different patterns of socialization and relationships (Maccoby, 1990). Girls tend to have higher levels of empathy and boys higher levels of aggression. Girls are socialized to be concerned about others and to pay attention to preserving connections with them. Thus, they are more likely to experience guilt when they have lied or been inconsiderate to others. They are also more likely to experience guilt when they blame themselves for unhappiness or conflict among others. In contrast, boys are socialized to be assertive and control the expression of their emotions. They are more likely to experience guilt over overt actions like fighting, victimizing other children or animals, or damaging property (Williams & Bybee, 1994).

Some children suffer from overwhelming guilt. They feel that each of their questions or doubts about the world is inappropriate. They frequently experience guilt about their own impulses and fantasies, even when they have taken no actions and no negative consequences have resulted. In addition, these children begin to believe that their thoughts and actions are responsible for much of the misfortune or unhappiness of others. For example, young children of depressed mothers express unusually high levels of distress, concern, and feelings of responsibility for others' unhappiness. Mothers who are consistently sad set an example of blaming themselves for most of the bad things that happen. In addition, depressed mothers are likely to withdraw love when the child has misbehaved, a discipline technique associated with high levels of guilt and anxiety (Zahn-Waxler et al., 1990). In this kind of environment, a child learns to restrict new behaviors out of fear that they may cause harm or unhappiness to someone else. In effect, the child comes to feel that curiosity itself is taboo and feels guilty whenever it is aroused. The child who resolves the initiative vs. guilt crisis in the direction of guilt is left to rely almost totally on his or her parents or on other authorities for directions on how to operate in the world.

The psychosocial crisis of initiative versus guilt highlights the intimate relationship between intellectual curiosity and emotional development. During this stage, the parents and the school transmit the cultural attitudes toward experimentation, curiosity, and investigation. They also make demands that direct the child's curiosity away from familial, subgroup, and cultural areas of taboo. Children are expected to develop the ability to control their own questions and behavior. Whereas violations may bring disapproval and punishment, successful self-control may attract no notice whatsoever. Children must develop a strong internal moral code that will help them avoid discipline. They must also develop the ability to reward themselves for correct behavior.

The more areas of restriction that are imposed on children's thinking, the more difficult it will be for children to distinguish between legitimate and inappropriate areas of investigation. The only way that children have of coping with this problem is to develop a rigid moral code that restricts many aspects of thought and action.

THE CENTRAL PROCESS: IDENTIFICATION

The discussion of the developmental tasks during early school age points directly to identification as the central process in the resolution of the conflict between initiative and guilt. Children at this age actively strive to enhance their self-concepts by incorporating into their own behavior some of the valued characteristics of their parents. Identification is one mechanism that children use to maintain connection with their parents. Children identify even with parents who are extremely brutal. Since most of the behaviors that these children incorporate are aggressive, they often tend to be aggressive toward others. Parental identification allows children to feel that their parents are with them even when they are not physically present. This feeling of connection with parents provides an underlying sense of security for children in a wide variety of situations.

Viewed from another perspective, identification allows children a growing sense of independence from their parents (Jacobson, 1964). Children who know how their parents would respond in a given situation no longer need the parents' physical presence to direct their behavior. Children who can praise or punish themselves for their actions are less dependent on their parents to perform these functions.

Parental identification affects children's development in two rather different ways. On the one hand, the closeness with parents provides the basis for the incorporation of parental sanctions and prohibitions. Once children have integrated these guidelines for behavior, they are bound to feel guilty whenever they anticipate abandoning them. On the other hand, the security that results from strong parental identification allows children increased freedom when they are away from their parents. The child whose parental identification is strong is more likely to question the environment, take risks, and initiate action.

Identification with parents results in a strengthening of the child's personality. An important outcome of early-school-age identification is the formation of an ideal self-image, which psychoanalytic theorists sometimes refer to as the **ego ideal** (Freud, 1929/1955; Sandler et al., 1963). The conscience not only punishes misdeeds but also rewards actions that bring children closer to some aspect of their ideal self-image. The ideal self is a complex view of the self as it may be in the future, including skills, profession, values, and personal relationships. It is a fantasy, a goal that is unlikely to be attained even in adulthood. Nonetheless, the discrepancy between the real self and the ideal self is a strong motivator. As children strive to achieve their ideal, they attempt new activities, set goals that strain the limits of their abilities, take risks, and resist temptations that might interfere with their desired goals.

The ego ideal is more unrealistic during early school age than it is at later stages. Children fantasize anything they wish about themselves in the future. They take their parents' values literally and use them to project an ideal person of mythic proportions. The ideal self may include the strength of Hercules, the wealth of Queen Elizabeth II, the wisdom of Confucius, and the compassion of Jesus. The lack of realistic constraints on the ego ideal allows children to investigate and experience vicariously certain human qualities that may always be beyond their reach. As people grow older, it is important that the fantasy of the ideal self-image becomes increasingly attainable, although still beyond

In this moment of prayer before a bountiful meal, parents demonstrate a value system with which children can identify. Identification with parents strengthens the child's self-system and provides a moral content to guide future behavior.

what has been attained. People who find it difficult to modify their ideal self-images become vulnerable to personal frustration and psychological despair because they are unable to be what they wish. Many 6-year-old children may wish to become President of the United States. This largely unrealistic fantasy is exciting and, for some, ennobling. However, few people actually achieve this position. By the time one reaches early adulthood, it is important to have developed an occupational ideal that is closer to what is actually attainable.

Identification with parents is the process by which the ideal self-image and moral prescriptions are blended into the child's personality. When children are unable to control their behavior so that it corresponds to the sanctions and ideals that they have internalized, they will experience guilt. In contrast, when children's behavior approaches their ideals and conforms to internalized sanctions, they will experience feelings of self-confidence that allow them to take initiative. The balance between guilt and self-confidence determines the eventual resolution of the psychosocial crisis of initiative versus guilt.

The crisis of initiative versus guilt captures the child's need to question existing norms and the emerging feelings of moral concern when these norms are violated. This crisis does not focus specifically on intellectual development; however, one must assume that the level of questioning that takes place during this stage is possible only because of an increase in cognitive complexity. The process of positive parental identification promotes the incorporation of cultural norms and strengthens the child's sense of competence. Socialization during this stage may either foster a creative openness or an anxious dread of novelty.

THE PRIME ADAPTIVE EGO QUALITY AND THE CORE PATHOLOGY

As a result of efforts to resolve the crisis of initiative versus guilt, children emerge from the period of early school age with the benefit of the prime adaptive ego quality of purpose or the core pathology of inhibition. These predispositions suggest an orientation that leaves a child with coping resources that will support directed, action-oriented problem solving or a more passive, self-protective approach to stress in which the child is more likely to allow others to guide the course of his or her behavior.

Purpose

Purpose is thought or behavior with direction, and therefore, with meaning. "Purposefulness is the courage playfully to imagine and energetically to pursue valued goals." (Erikson, 1978, p. 29) It is a cognitively more complex extension of the will gained in

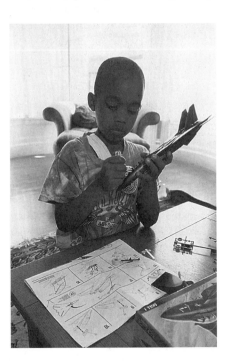

The sense of purpose is illustrated as Cedric follows the instructions to complete this model plane. He is following a plan to reach a goal. He is intent, focused, and serious about getting the plane just right.

toddlerhood in that it combines a sense of agency with a plan. In contrast to the toddler who exercises his or her will through the mere delight in action, the early-school-age child imposes intention and goals on action. This is the difference, for example, between running around the yard, laughing and shouting—typical behavior for toddlers—and saying to a friend, "Let's play tag," which is more likely for early-school-age children. Toddlers may enjoy stacking blocks or splashing in water, while early-school-age children want to turn materials and toys into a story or a project. Their actions are going in a direction; their play has a plan. Behind the process of planning is a complex sense of the situation, the creation of a goal, strategies to achieve it, and monitoring success in realizing the goal (Scholnick, 1995). The sense of purpose, expressed in planning and enacting plans, reflects a significant expansion of the ego into the realm of the present and the future.

A sense of purpose suggests that not only does the action have meaning but also that the person initiating it has meaning. Ricky enters a play situation and says, "I have an idea. Let's play trains." This kind of suggestion reflects Ricky's sense of a goal-directed plan, and a sense of confidence about introducing his idea into the ongoing activities of the group.

Inhibition

Inhibition can be thought of as the restraint or suppression of behavior. In a psychological context, one might define inhibition as a conscious or unconscious blocking of unacceptable wishes and behaviors. Often inhibition results when a child experiences guilt associated with certain wishes or fear about having been disciplined for the expression of those wishes in the past. Inhibition is assumed to emerge when parents or caregivers use high levels of love withdrawal and guilt-inducing interactions with their children. These kinds of interactions suggest to the child that the parent's love, affection, and approval are conditional upon the child matching certain specific parental standards. In order to adapt in this kind of environment and avoid risking loss of love, the child becomes self-conscious and restrained in action. In contrast to the sense of confidence and agency implied in the notion of purpose, a child who is inhibited does not want to take the risks associated with imposing a plan or suggesting a direction for fear that his or her suggestions will result in parental disapproval.

Lois Murphy (1972) proposed that inhibition has even earlier origins in the mother-infant relationship. She suggested that in "healthy" mother-infant interactions, mothers take care to provide meaningful feedback and consequences for their babies' actions. When mothers are very depressed or psychologically unavailable, they may be unable to engage in the kinds of consistent, rhythmic behaviors that produce early experiences of cause-effect. Babies who have never internalized the schemes for these kinds of behaviors cannot impose them on external circumstances. As a result of the lack of early, structured cause-effect interactions in the mothering relationship, some early-school-age children have a very passive orientation toward play and social interactions. According to Murphy, their inhibition is not so much a product of guilt but a lack of basic early structures or schemes for the positive process of initiation. These children do not impose organization on toys or integrate sensory and motor play into a more complex scenario. They remain focused on the sensory activity itself, like digging in the sand, or on the imitation of basic behaviors like feeding the baby.

These children are likely to emerge as shy, withdrawn, and often lonely during the subsequent period of middle childhood. Without some form of social intervention, they become increasingly withdrawn and inhibited, not knowing how to impose their ideas into the ongoing activities of the group, and not experiencing the confidence-building effects of making suggestions and having them accepted. Consequently, by the end of the early-school-age period, their inhibition produces new deficits in social skill development.

Applied Topic SCHOOL READINESS

In 1989, President Bush and the state governors created an educational agenda for the United States. The first goal was that by the year 2000, all children in America would start school ready to learn. This goal identified the importance of the first years of schooling as critical in setting the long-term course for school achievement and entry into adulthood as an educated person ready to undertake the roles and responsibilities of adult life. The goal, which seems positive and appropriate on the face of it, has resulted in important dialogue about what is meant by readiness, how to measure it, what obstacles stand in its way, and who should be responsible for achieving it (Lewit & Baker, 1995).

Readiness

The concept of **readiness** is a familiar idea in the study of development. Typically, the term is used to refer to a time when the child's physical, cognitive, social, and emotional maturation are at a level to undertake new learning or to engage in a more complex, demanding type of activity or relationship. It is also called a sensitive period or a teachable moment. The idea of readiness in relation to attachment relationships and walking was discussed in Chapter 5, language use and toilet training was discussed in Chapter 6, and gender-role identification was discussed in a previous section of this chapter. Vygotsky's concept of a zone of proximal development is another way of conceptualizing readiness; it is the next higher level of performance one can achieve with the help of more competent teachers. When thinking about the goal stated above, however, the concept of readiness becomes somewhat more complicated. Does it refer to readiness to learn or readiness to start school? One might argue that all children, except perhaps those with very severe neurological damage, are ready to learn. However, not all children have the combination of physical, cognitive, emotional, and social skills that allow them to adapt to the demands of the kindergarten classroom environment or to succeed at the academic challenges of its curriculum (Kagan, 1990).

How to Measure Kindergarten Readiness?

In the past, kindergarten readiness was established largely by chronological age. School districts typically established a birthday cut-off. For example, if a child was 5 by December 1st of a given year, he or she could start kindergarten in September of that year. Those who missed the December 1st date had to wait until the following year. In the 1980s, concern about the quality of education in the United States led to an upgrading of the elementary school curriculum. As part of this school reform, academic demands for school performance were raised, and children were exposed to a more challenging curriculum in earlier grades. Many skills that had been introduced in first grade are now part of the kindergarten curriculum, and more children are having trouble meeting the expectations for school performance. In efforts to prevent early school failure, some states began to administer school readiness tests. However, there is no agreement or universal acceptance of a measure of kindergarten readiness, and some educators dispute whether any test given to 5-year-olds can accurately predict a child's ability to learn in the school environment (American Academy of Pediatrics, 1995).

In the midst of these changes in the school environment, parents began to make their own decisions about whether or not their child was ready for kindergarten. In a 1993 National Household Education Survey, slightly over 8% of children who were eligible by age to attend kindergarten were being held back (National Center for Education Statistics, 1994). An increasingly large group of parents have begun to think that it is better to wait a year and give their child a developmental advantage than to have their child compete with older children who will outperform their child. Although there may be some advantage for the older children in kindergarten, especially in the area of language skills, no special advantage is seen for delayed kindergartners over on-time kindergartners by the third grade (Shepard & Smith, 1986).

School readiness is reflected as this kindergarten class participates in a "workout" session. The children are interacting in a positive way, showing enthusiasm, following instructions, and having fun without being disruptive to others.

Given the lack of an objective, accepted measure or screening test, what do parents and teachers think are essential markers of school readiness? How can a parent judge if a child is ready or should wait a year before beginning kindergarten? In two separate national surveys, parents and teachers were asked what characteristics a child needs to be ready to start school. Figure 7.3 shows the responses. Some items from the teacher survey were not on the parent survey. Teachers emphasized that children need to be physically healthy, well-rested, and well-nourished as the most important aspects of readiness. Beyond that, they emphasized the ability to communicate effectively, demonstrate enthusiasm and curiosity, follow directions, not be disruptive, and show sensitivity to the feelings of other children as important indicators. Parents, on the other hand, tended to emphasize the importance of specific skills, such as using a pencil or scissors, knowing the alphabet, or counting to 20, more frequently than the teachers (Lewit & Baker, 1995). Typically, the teachers' opinions about kindergarten readiness place a somewhat greater emphasis on social and emotional competence than on skills and knowledge. Children need to be ready to separate comfortably from their parents, interact in a positive way with other children, and engage in the "appropri-

Percentage of preschoolers' parents and kindergarten teachers who rate specific characteristics as either "essential" or "very important" to being ready to start kindergarten, 1993

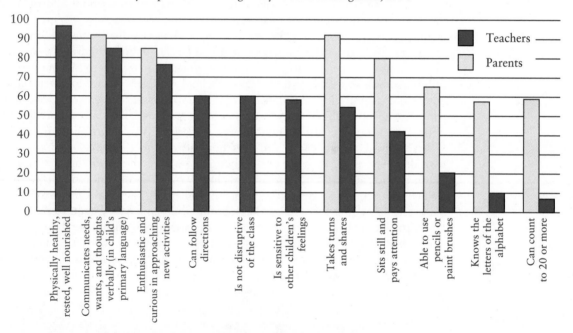

Parents and teachers are arguably the most important forces in a child's early school experiences. This graph, which uses parent responses from the 1993 National Household Education Survey (NHES) and teacher responses from the 1993 kindergarten Teacher Survey on Student Readiness (KTSSR), presents the characteristics that parents and teachers believe are important for being ready to begin kindergarten. For some characteristics, such as physical health and following directions, data are available only for teacher responses from the KTSSR because no parallel question was asked of parents in the NHES.

• Teachers were more likely to rate good health as essential or very important than any other characteristic.

• Parents and teachers agree that both the ability to communicate needs, wants, and thoughts verbally in a child's primary language and the qualities of being enthusiastic and curious in approaching new activities are very important aspects of school readiness.

• Substantially more parents than teachers believe that the more academic items, such as counting to 20 or knowing the letters of the alphabet, are important for school readiness.

FIGURE 7.3

Parents' and teachers' responses about important indicators of school readiness ate" behaviors associated with the student role: following directions, being quiet when asked, and asking and answering questions.

What Obstacles Stand in the Way of School Readiness?

Success in kindergarten is based on a combination of intellectual and social skills and the motivation to succeed. Most children are excited about going to kindergarten and do well. However, certain demographic characteristics are associated with the likelihood of poor school adjustment, even in kindergarten. These include: poverty; limited English language proficiency; and having a physical, cognitive, or emotional disability (National Commission on Children, 1993). Poverty is perhaps the most serious factor. Children growing up in poor families are likely to suffer from malnutrition, many have not been immunized against infectious diseases, and many are exposed to parental distress that affects their overall sense of confidence and self-worth. Many of the children have no access to health or dental services. Children growing up in poor, urban neighborhoods are exposed to violence in their streets and even in their schoolyards; and their parents may not have the educational background or the financial resources to supplement or complement the activities of the school in order to meet their specific needs (Stallings, 1995). By the age of 9 (roughly the fourth grade), the effects of poverty can be seen in the lower reading scores of children from disadvantaged urban communities as compared to children from other kinds of communities (U. S. Department of Education, 1995).

Supporting Children with Disabilities

A significant number of young children enter the early-school-age period with moderate to severe disabilities. About 47% of the 3-to-5 year-olds receiving educational service for the the disabled are in regular classrooms in public schools (U. S. Department of Education, 1995). By definition, these children are performing at or below the 50th percentile of their age-mates in one or more domains, including motor skills, speech and language, social and emotional competence, and learning and memory (Siegel, 1996). The term *disability* can refer to a wide variety of possible functional challenges. Preschool and kindergarten programs that include children with disabilities face a significant task—to ensure that the inclusion benefits the child both socially and academically. Many children with disabilities are mainstreamed in a classroom without any provision for encouraging social interaction with the other children. Effective inclusion requires strategies for promoting contact between nondisabled and disabled students. In addition, the interventions must be tailored to address the unique areas of deficit. An autistic child, for example, may need to be taught how to imitate a model and may have difficulty cooperating with peers, but might be able to play successfully with puzzles or listen to the teacher read a story. A moderately mentally retarded child may have difficulty with tasks that require fast reaction time, such as competitive games among students, but could perform well if speed of response is not a concern. Teachers need to find ways to build upon each child's level of performance so that the child is not stigmatized for his or her disability and continues to make progress toward an appropriate academic standard.

Who is Responsible for Meeting the Goal for School Readiness?

One of the questions raised by establishing a national goal for children to start school ready to learn is, "Whose responsibility is it to meet this goal?" Do we need to place more responsibility on families to provide the early experiences that will foster health, confidence, motivation, and cognitive and social development during the first 4 years of life? Do we need to place more responsibility on schools to work with children where they are by providing the environment, services, curriculum, and methods of instruction that will facilitate learning for an increasingly diverse group of students? Do we need to place more responsibility on local, state, and federal government to sustain and expand programs such as Head Start so that more children can participate in early educational experiences that can help offset the negative effects of poverty?

A psychosocial perspective would call for action on all three fronts. The child's chances of success in school can be improved if all interacting systems support one another and keep the goal of academic success for the widest range of students in focus. Schools, businesses, and families must come together to identify the children who are at greatest risk for school failure in their community and make plans for integrated, multiyear, multiservice programs (Madden et al., 1993; Stallings, 1995).

One such model, described as the CoZi schools, integrates the philosophies of James Comer, a psychiatrist, and Edward Zigler, a developmental psychologist (Zigler et al., 1996; Hornblower, 1996). In these schools, the staff reach out to families as early as the last trimester of pregnancy. They visit the homes of families, encourage interest in books and educational activities, and talk with parents about child development and child-rearing. The schools involve parents in school-based activities that meet their own needs (e.g. exercise classes, adult education classes) as well as the needs of their children. The schools serve as a site for day care, before and after-school care, and summer programming. Individual staff members take the responsibility of mentoring specific children who suffer from neglect or are going through unusual family disorganization. These schools have redefined their role as a community resource in which the goal of each child's educational success is reached by addressing the child's and the family's broader social, emotional, and physical needs at the earliest possible moment (Dryfoos, 1994).

Chapter Summary

Early school age marks the beginning of work on developmental tasks that will persist well into adulthood. The four tasks of early school age are closely interrelated. The complex process of gender identification has cognitive, affective, physical, and interpersonal elements. As young children clarify the content of their gender identity, they create a set of beliefs about the self including their self-worth, relationships with other children, and the kinds of activities and interests that are appropriate for them, not only in the present but also in the future. The gender identity of the early-school-age child will be revised and reintegrated as it becomes a core element of personal identity in adolescence.

The development of conscience, with its capacity to reward and punish, brings an internalization of moral standards. Moral development is accompanied by a heightened sensitivity to violating basic cultural standards, many of which relate to interpersonal behavior, especially toward adults and peers. The child's experiences with transgressions, guilt, or praise for prosocial behavior have implications for the elaboration of the self-theory and particularly for the establishment of self-esteem.

Although the self-theory is continuously revised with entry into new roles and cognitive capacities, the establishment of a positive sense of worth in early school age brings an important tone of optimism as the child faces new challenges. Competence and social acceptance are the essential antecedents of self-esteem. The increased involvement with peers during play brings about an appreciation of others' perspectives, social acceptance, and delight in the intimacy of friends.

The psychosocial crisis of initiative versus guilt has direct implications for such essential personality characteristics as self-esteem, creativity, curiosity, and risk taking. The child who resolves this crisis positively will be fortified with an active, exploratory approach to the environment. Guilt plays an important role in orienting children toward the implications of their actions for others. In moderation, it appears to be an essential ingredient in preserving social bonds. In the extreme, however, excessive guilt restricts creative thought and limits action.

The applied topic of school readiness illustrates the potential conflict between development and socialization. The society has determined that 5-year-old children will attend school. At the same time, 5-year-olds are at a wide array of developmental levels, bringing them to the door of the school with substantial differences in physical, cognitive, social, and emotional competence. Factors such as disabilities, poverty, and a non-English-speaking home environment may all complicate the child's ability to adapt to the school environment. How does the caring community cope with this reality?

End of Chapter Case

Lee, a mother of six children, recalls with warmth and humor her early childhood years growing up in New Mexico in the 1920s and 30s.

I was born in the southern part of New Mexico in Ruidoso. The town was up in the pines in the mountains and was mostly just a main street that followed the river. There was a meadow on one side of the river with a lot of Indian arrowheads and shards and the biggest grasshoppers in the world. I used to go catch grasshoppers and find arrowheads, and my cousin Bob and I would wander around by ourselves.

. . . . My father was a carpenter and my mother had planned to be a nurse until she stopped and got married. I think my father must have really wanted a son because I was quite a tomboy and grew up as his only son. I helped him dig and move rocks instead of learning how to cook and sew. We had a large family, uncles and aunts and a grandmother and great aunt, with houses right next to each other and big, traditional holiday dinners with everybody there.

My cousin Bob was two years younger than I was and we were inseparable. . . . He was a rough, tough little kid. He ran around without coats in the winter and hardly ever got sick, and he and I grew up together. It was almost like two boys because we used to go to the river and fish with our hands and churn the fish over a little fire and try to eat it. We just grew up like little wild things. My parents expected me to be on the premises by nightfall, but that was about it. We played cowboys and Indians with the other kids in the neighborhood, and we never played with girls at all; they were really something to be scorned. But he was allowed to cuss and have good tantrums that I wasn't allowed to have.

. . . My mother always provided books and she would tell stories about Huckleberry Finn. The river in our town was much too small for a raft; it was rocky and was just a stream, but we'd pretend rafts and imagine running away. One time I got tied up on an Indian raid and left there, and I was too stubborn to call for help, so I was there past supper time and my mother found me and brought me in.

I was always tearing up my clothes, and my mother was always tearning me up about that. I think she would have liked to have a daughter. It wasn't until my sister Barbara was born that she had a daughter. Barbara had long curls and was pretty feminine. That way mother had the daughter to play with and daddy had the son and everything was all right.

SOURCE: Buss, F.L., 1985.

Thought Questions

1. What aspects of the developmental tasks of the early-school-age period are captured in this narrative?

2. What images of mother and father are being established at this age?

3. From what you have read, and drawing on your own experiences, how might Lee's gender identification at this period of her life influence later relationships with male and female peers, and her capacity to form intimate relationships in later adolescence or early adulthood?

4. What role might the rural, small town environment play in Lee's experiences of early childhood?

5. How do the themes of initiative, doubt, purpose, and inhibition relate to this narrative?

6. To what extent do you think this narrative is cohort specific? Might children growing up today have these same experiences, or are they limited to childhood in the early part of this century?

Chapter 8

*C*hildren struggle to increase their competence in the shadow of a culture, teacher, or mother who urges, instructs, compliments, and criticizes.

Middle Childhood (6–12 Years)

Chapter Objectives

- To clarify the role of friendship in helping children to learn to take the point of view of others, be sensitive to the norms and pressures of the peer group, and experience closeness in relationships as well as to clarify negative consequences that result from social rejection and loneliness.
- To describe the development of concrete operational thought, including conservation, classification skills, combinatorial skills, and the child's ability to understand and monitor his or her own knowledge and understanding.
- To explore skill learning, including the presentation of a model for the process of acquisition of complex skills such as reading and the examination of societal factors that provide the context within which skill learning occurs.
- To analyze the development of self-evaluation skills, including self-efficacy, and ways that social expectations of parents, teachers, and peers contribute to a child's self-evaluation.
- To describe a new level of complexity in play as children become involved in team sports and athletic competition.
- To explain the psychosocial crisis of industry versus inferiority, the central process through which the crisis is resolved—education—the prime adaptive ego quality of competence, and the core pathology of inertia.
- To explore the impact of exposure to violence on development during middle childhood.

*H*istorically, middle childhood, which covers the ages from about 6 to 12, was not considered of major importance to an understanding of development. Freud's psychoanalytic theory treated the years following the resolution of the Oedipal conflict as a time when sexual and aggressive impulses are repressed and active only in the unconscious. He called this period the **latency stage,** a term that suggests that no significant contributions to personality formation can be traced to it. For a long time, psychologists tended not to study the psychological development of middle childhood.

Interest in the theories of Erik Erikson and Jean Piaget stimulated developmental research focusing on children who are between the ages of 6 and 12. These theories emphasize intellectual growth, competence, and a growing investment in work. During this time, children are learning the fundamental skills of their culture. They spend a great deal of their time every day learning the skills that are valued by their society, whether they be reading, writing, and arithmetic or hunting, fishing, and weaving. As children gain confidence in their abilities, they begin to have more realistic images of their potential contributions to the larger community.

The competence that develops during middle childhood applies to social as well as work-related domains. This is a time when parent-child relationships, peer friendships, and participation in meaningful interpersonal communication provide children with the social skills they will need if they are to cope with the upcoming challenges of adolescence. Children's cognitive accomplishments appear to develop in conjunction with their achievements in the social and emotional domains.

For many children, this is a joyful, vigorous time. The fears and vulnerabilities of their early school days are behind them. Energized by ego qualities of hope, will, and purpose, most children are able to enjoy many of the resources and opportunities of their communities. Even as the presence of their family members continues to be a comfort to them, they begin to explore more complex social relationships with their peers and other significant adults.

In some parts of the world, however, the lives of children aged 6–12 are marked by extreme disorganization and exploitation. Slavers travel through impoverished areas kidnapping, buying, or luring children into forms of slavelike labor where they are often beaten, sexually abused, and degraded. Children as young as 6 are being sold or given away by poor families as slaves or bonded laborers: "In Haiti, more than 100,000 children, sold or given away by poor families, toil as domestic servants . . . in Pakistan as many as 20 million people, 7.5 million of them children, are working as bonded laborers in factories, on farms and on construction projects, unable to pay off employer advances" (Time, 1993). These hardships are not *limited to economically developing countries. In New Orleans, at the corner of Congress and Law streets, walls of the buildings are covered with bullet holes. In 1994, there were 3 or more killings per month in the streets surrounding the St. Philip Social Service Center located there. Preschoolers attending school in the center have "shooting drills," when they are instructed to drop to the floor until an all-clear siren is sounded. In a study of African-American mothers and children aged 9 to 12 living in a similar violent section of New Orleans, 51% of the children reported being victims of violence and 91% of the children reported having witnessed some type of street violence (Lacayo, 1996; Osofsky, 1995).*

In such circumstances, the opportunity for young children to work on the developmental tasks of friendship formation, concrete operational reasoning, skill learning, self-evaluation, and team play may be viewed as a great luxury. Having time, resources, and security to promote areas of cognitive, social, and emotional development is only possible within the context of communities that are economically and politically stable and ideologically committed to the intellectual and interpersonal future of its children. ❖

DEVELOPMENTAL TASKS

New tasks for development are highlighted as children become focused on friendship formation, concrete mental operations, skill learning, self-evaluation, and team play. This mix of tasks coupled with new capacities for complex social, emotional, and intellectual activity produce a remarkable synergy. While play dominates the behavior of early-school-age children, middle childhood is characterized by more purposeful, industrious behavior. This is not to say that play is lost. New thrills and excitement are generated by the capacity to engage in more complex forms of play and the desire to take new risks—riding one's bike further from home, jumping and then diving from the high board, and riding on the big, fast roller coasters without a parent.

Friendship   Can you remember some things about a friend you had when you were 10 years old? Friendships of middle childhood are not likely to be as enduring as the attachment relationships of infancy. Yet, some of these friendships are quite memorable; they have many of the elements of a close affectional bond. At this age, children describe close friends as people who like the same activities, share common interests, enjoy each other's company, and can count on each other for help (Youniss, 1980; Ainsworth, 1989).

Friendships may not be as essential to survival as attachment relations, but they clearly provide social and developmental advantages (Ainsworth, 1989; Hartup, 1989). According to ethological theory, being a member of a group has protective advantages. Group cooperation gives a selective advantage to many social species, especially in tracking and hunting for food. Therefore, the skills of cooperation and sociability may advance the species as a whole as well as the individual. On an individual level, children who are able to participate in positive peer friendships are embedded in an intellectually and socially stimulating environment.

Family Influences on Social Competence

Not all children enter middle childhood with the same capacity to make friends and enjoy the benefits of close peer relations. Early family experiences contribute to a child's sociability and social competence; the process of becoming ready for friendship may begin in infancy. Children who have secure attachments in infancy are more popular in preschool and engage more freely in social interactions. They are perceived as more helpful and better able to consider the needs of others (Sroufe & Fleeson, 1986; Park & Waters, 1989).

A mother's discipline techniques, the way she speaks to her child, and her parenting values are all linked to a child's social competence and popularity. Children whose mothers interact with them in positive, agreeable ways and openly express their feelings are likely to have more positive friendship relations. These patterns are observable as early as preschool and continue to be found in the elementary grades (Youngblade & Belsky, 1992). In contrast, mothers who use power-assertive discipline techniques and who believe that aggression is an acceptable way of resolving conflicts have children who expect to get their way by asserting power in peer conflicts (Dishion et al., 1991; Haskett & Kistner, 1991). In observations of the social relationships of 8- to 12-year-old children who had been physically abused, they had lower ratings of social status among their peers, were described by their peers as being aggressive and uncooperative, and their teachers described them as showing noticeable behavior problems (Salzinger et al., 1993).

The family environment influences a child's social competence in at least three ways. First, children may directly imitate their parents' positive or aggressive behaviors. If parents ask a lot of questions and invite their child's opinions, for example, the child may be more likely to show interest in other's ideas and opinions. Second, a parent's disciplinary technique may influence what a child expects in a social interaction. Children who have been exposed to aggressive parental techniques believe that these same strategies will work with their peers. As a result, these children are more likely to experience social rejection. Third, parents who are highly restrictive and who try to control their children's behavior are less likely to permit their young children to have many peer social interactions. These children arrive at the middle childhood years with less experience in peer play (Putallaz, 1987; Pettit et al., 1988; Hart et al., 1990).

Three Contributions of Friendship to Social Development

Children learn at least three lessons from daily interactions with their peers. The first lesson is an increasing appreciation of the many points of view that are represented in the peer group. As children play together, they discover that there may be several versions of the same song, differing sets of rules for the same game, and different customs for the same holiday. The second lesson teaches children to be increasingly sensitive to the social norms and pressures of their peer group. The third lesson is closeness to a same-sex peer.

Perspective Taking and Cognitive Flexibility. As children interact with peers who see the world differently than they do, they begin to understand the limits of their own points of view. Piaget (1932/1948) suggested that peers have an important influence in diminishing one another's self-centered outlook precisely because they interact as equals. Children are not forced to accept one another's ideas in quite the same way as they are with adults. They argue, bargain, and eventually compromise in order to maintain friendships. The opportunity to function in social peer groups for problem solving and for play leads children away from the egocentrism of early childhood and closer to the eventual flexibility of adult thought. The benefit of these interactions is most likely to occur when peers have differences in perspective that result in conflicts that must be resolved. The benefits are especially positive for children who interact with slightly more competent peers who can introduce more advanced or flexible approaches to problem solving (Tudge, 1992).

The behavior of well-adjusted, competent children is maintained in part by a number of social-cognitive abilities, including social perspective taking, interpersonal problem solving, and information processing (Dodge et al., 1986; Elias et al., 1989; Downey & Walker, 1989; Carlo et al., 1991). These cognitive

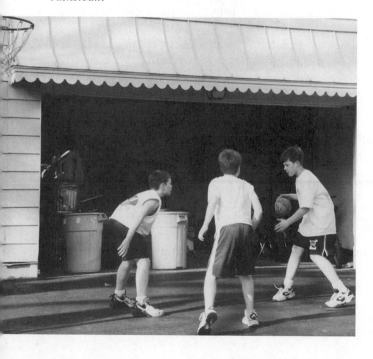

By figuring out the rules to informal games, friends exchange points of view and learn to work out their differences. What might these boys have to decide in order to play an informal game of basketball?

abilities foster a child's entry into successful peer interactions. At the same time, active participation with peers promotes the development of these social-cognitive abilities.

Perspective-taking ability relates to other social skills that contribute to the quality of a child's social relationships. Such skills include the ability to analyze social problems, empathize with the emotional state of another person, understand that others may construe a situation differently because of their own information or beliefs, and a willingness to accept individual differences in personality or abilities (Chalmers & Townsend, 1990; Wellman, 1990; Pillow, 1991; Montgomery, 1993). Children who are sensitive to the variety of perspectives that coexist in a social situation are also likely to be more positively evaluated by their peers (Pellegrini, 1985). Rejected and withdrawn children often lack the social skills that would win them acceptance by their age-mates (Patterson, 1982; French, 1988).

An interactive process is thus set in motion. Children who have opportunities to participate in peer friendships make progress in achieving new levels of interpersonal understanding. As interpersonal understanding grows, children acquire the skills and sensitivity with which to be more effective—and usually more valued by—their peers. Rejected children come to expect negative behaviors from others. A vicious cycle develops between the rejected child and her or his peers, each having negative expectations of the other. As this cycle continues, the rejected child's reputation becomes increasingly negative, and the child has little opportunity to develop positive relationship skills (Waas, 1988).

Social Norms and Peer Group Pressure. The peer group evolves **norms** for acceptance and rejection. As children become aware of these norms, they begin to experience pressures to conform to the peer group. Adults, particularly teachers, then lose some of their power to influence children's behavior. In the classroom, the early-school-age child focuses primarily on the teacher as a source of approval and acceptance. By ages 9 or 10, children perceive the peer group as an equally significant audience. Children often play to the class instead of responding to the teacher. The roles of class joker, class snob, and class hero or heroine emerge during middle childhood and serve as ways of gaining approval from the peer group.

The need for peer approval becomes a powerful force toward conformity. Children learn to dress, talk, and joke in ways that are acceptable to their peers. From Grades 3 through 9, they become increasingly willing to conform to peer behaviors that might be considered antisocial. For example, it has been reported that ninth-graders are more willing than third-graders to go along with peer cheating, stealing, and trespassing (Berndt, 1979). Heterosexual antagonism, which is common at this stage, is perpetuated by pressures toward conformity. If all the fifth-grade boys hate girls, Johnny is not very likely to admit openly that he likes to play with Mary. There are indications that perceived pressures to conform are stronger in the fifth and sixth grades than at later times, even though the importance of specific peer groups has not yet peaked (Gavin & Furman, 1989).

Loneliness

With the increased emphasis on peer acceptance and conformity comes the risk of peer rejection and feelings of loneliness. In a study of over 500 children between the ages of 8 and 11, more than 10% expressed feelings of loneliness and social dissatisfaction (Asher et al., 1984). A significant proportion of the children had trouble making friends (17%), felt left out (18%), and agreed that they felt alone (14%). Not surprisingly, children who were infrequently mentioned as a best friend by others were more lonely than those who were mentioned as a best friend by three or more other children.

Four social characteristics combine to increase a child's experiences of loneliness. First, children who are withdrawn and tend to be alone or prefer to be involved in isolated activities even when other children are present tend to form a negative view of themselves as socially incompetent. Second, children who have trouble forming any kind of close friendship that provides emotional closeness and support are more likely to feel lonely. Third, peer rejection is especially powerful in producing feelings of loneliness. Children who experience a generally positive level of peer acceptance feel less alone than those who are rejected by their peers (Crick & Ladd, 1993). Finally, children who tend to blame themselves for their lack of social acceptance feel more lonely and are possibly less likely to believe that they can do anything to improve their situation (Renshaw & Brown, 1993; Cassidy & Asher, 1992; Rubin et al., 1990).

Rejection. Research has identified three paths to peer rejection. Some children who are rejected are disruptive and aggressive with their peers; others are socially withdrawn but do not exhibit aggressive tendencies; a third group has been described as both aggressive and withdrawn (French, 1988, 1990; Hymel et al., 1993). All these groups tend to have multiple problems. **Aggressive-rejected** children, often referred to as bullies, are more likely than nonaggressive children to attribute hostile intentions to others (Box 8.1). They tend to see peer interactions as threatening, and they also say they would be likely to use aggressive strategies in response to negative peer behaviors (Quiggle et al., 1992; Waldman, 1996). The aggressive-rejected children tend to have a somewhat exaggerated idea of their competence and social status. They are less ac-

---

BOX 8.1 BULLYING

Bullying is a common and long-standing problem for children in many different cultures. A child is considered to be bullied when he or she is repeatedly exposed to negative actions by peers including physical contact, harsh and degrading words and gestures, exploitation, and exclusion. Dan Olweus (1995), who has been studying aggression and bullying since the 1970s, has estimated that roughly 9% of children aged 7 through 16 have been victims of bullying and 7% of school-age children have bullied others. This suggests that as many as 5 million children in the United States are involved in problems of bullying or peer intimidation each year.

What are the characteristics of bullies and their victims? Bullies typically are physically stronger than their peers. They have strong needs for power and enjoy being in control. They have been reared in a family environment characterized by indifference, low involvement, and lack of warmth. This context results in little sense of personal empathy and a high degree of hostility toward others. Bullies are often aggressive toward teachers and other authority figures as well as toward peers. Finally, bullies often find some reward or reinforcement for their behavior, especially when they coerce their victims into giving them money, taking things of value, and being treated with respect by other peers.

Victims of bullying, on the other hand, commonly have low self-esteem. They are anxious, cautious, and fit into the withdrawn category of rejected children. By comparison to the bullies, the victims, especially boys, are physically weaker. When attacked, they do not retaliate. As a result, the abuse continues and often escalates.

In designing a school-based intervention program to reduce bullying and prevent children from feeling harassed and degraded at school, Olweus (1993) focused on five basic principles:

1. Create an environment in which children experience warmth, interest, and frequent involvement with adults.
2. Set clear, firm limits about unacceptable behavior that are endorsed at school and home.
3. When rules and limits are violated, sanctions should be nonhostile and nonviolent, but consistently enforced.

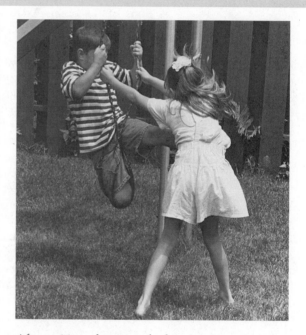

After waiting a long time for his turn, Lenny finally gets the swing. Then Linda grabs the swing and tries to get him off. Linda is tall and strong for her age; she often asserts herself to get what she wants without concern for others. Even though she is only 7, Linda is getting a reputation as a bully.

4. Student activities during and after school must be monitored through the presence of adult supervision at recess and lunch times, and regular meetings with parents during PTA meetings and parent conferences.
5. Students need to meet regularly with teachers to discuss problems associated with the social environment of the school and to work on ways of improving the school climate.

curate in reading their own social status among their classmates, although they are just as accurate as other children in reading the social status of others (Zakriski & Coie, 1996).

However, aggressiveness is not always associated with rejection. One study looked at the relationship of antisocial and prosocial characteristics of young children and their social standing in the classroom (Farmer & Rodkin, 1996). Children in four different types of classroom groups were compared: academically gifted, emotionally and behaviorally disordered, general education, and learning disabled. Across all four types of classrooms, the most popular and socially central children were more athletic, cooperative, and studious, and were rated as having more leadership skills than the less popular children. Aggressive, disruptive characteristics were strongly associated with peer rejection or isolation for girls. For boys in the general education classes, however, aggressive behavior was positively associated with popularity. Thus, one is led to consider person-environment fit in evaluating the relationship between aggressiveness and peer rejection. In some classroom contexts, aggressiveness, particularly among boys, may be a viable path toward bonding with other boys and asserting one's visibility, especially for boys who cannot achieve notice through their academic performance.

Children in the **withdrawn** group tend to be inhibited, anxious, and interpersonally reserved. They have a negative self-concept and tend to interpret negative peer reactions as resulting from their own personal failings (Hymel et al., 1993). They have difficulty dealing with stress. These children also exhibit inappropriate emotions and display various unusual behavioral mannerisms that are likely to draw ridicule from their peers (French, 1988). Some withdrawn children report close relationships with a favorite sibling. However, having this kind of sibling support does not appear to protect these children entirely from the negative consequences of peer rejection (East & Rook, 1992). The withdrawn-rejected children are more likely to experience high levels of loneliness and to worry about the quality of their relationships with peers (Parkhurst & Asher, 1992).

Children in the **aggressive-withdrawn** group tend to be the least well liked of all three types of rejected children. They exhibit anxiety, poor self-control, and social withdrawal in addition to aggressive behavior. They are rated by other children as incompetent in school ability; unattractive; showing the poorest skills in leadership, cooperation, or sense of humor; and the most likely to behave inappropriately in school. Despite high levels of peer rejection, however, they do not have the same low self-concept and negative view of their abilities as the withdrawn children.

Rejected children tend to retain this status throughout elementary school. They are likely to have future adjustment problems and often require psychiatric treatment in adolescence or adulthood (Coie & Krehbiel, 1984; Hymel et al., 1990).

Close Friends

The opportunity for peer-group interaction usually leads to the formation of dyadic, same-sex friendships that may become quite intimate (Berndt, 1981). These are the years in which children have "best friends." In the course of these friendships, children share private jokes, develop secret codes, tell family secrets, set out on "dangerous" adventures, and help each other in times of trouble. They also fight, threaten, break up, and reunite. Sullivan (1949) pointed out the significance of these early same-sex friendships as building blocks for adult relationships. It is significant that the child experiences love for and closeness to a peer rather than an adult. The relationship is more likely to allow for mutuality of power, status, and access to resources (French, 1984). Conflicts in a relationship may be worked out in terms that the children control rather than escalating into dimensions having adult significance. One child cannot take away another child's allowance or send the other child out of the room when a conflict arises. The children must resolve their differences within the framework of their commitment to each other.

The stability of close friendships is quite variable, with some children remaining friends over several years, despite changes in classrooms and schools, while other children seem to be in different friendship relationships every few months (Kindermann,

1996). The structure of a school or classroom influences friendship formation and stability. Close friends often see each other during the school day in classes and extracurricular activities. In schools that tend to promote stable classroom groupings, where children remain in the same homeroom or class group from one grade to the next, friendship groups also remain more stable (Neckerman, 1996).

Close friendships are influenced by attractiveness, intelligence, classroom social status, and satisfaction with and commitment to the best friend (Clark & Ayers, 1988). In a study of over 800 children in Grades 3–5, 78% had at least one reciprocating best friend (one child named another as one of his or her three best friends, and that other child named the first child on his or her list as well), and 55% had a *very* best friend. More girls than boys had best friends, and the quality of their best friendships was somewhat different. Girls and boys described their best friend relationships quite similarly with respect to having low levels of conflict or betrayal and high levels of companionship and shared recreational activities. However, girls described their best friend relationships as having higher levels of caring and personal validation ("makes me feel good about my ideas"), intimacy ("we always tell each other our problems"), help and guidance ("help each other with schoolwork a lot"), and conflict resolution ("we make up easily when we have a fight") (Parker & Asher, 1993).

Children's need for the friendship of peers brings them into an increasingly complex social system. They learn that approval is conditional on conformity to certain norms, that other children do not necessarily share their view of the world, and that there are opportunities for unique emotional experiences that cannot be duplicated in the home. The friendship group is a transitional allegiance between commitment to the family and to the larger social community.

Concrete Operations

Our discussion of infant intelligence focused on the establishment of sensory and motor patterns used to explore the environment and gain specific ends. During toddlerhood, children develop a variety of representational skills. These skills free them from complete reliance on their immediate physical environment. Toddlers create novel situations and solve problems by using thought, fantasy, and language. Piaget (Piaget & Inhelder, 1969) suggested that at about age 6 or 7 a qualitatively new form of thinking develops. He described this new stage of intellectual development as **concrete operational thought.**

The word **operation** refers to an action that is performed on an object or a set of objects. A mental operation is a transformation that is carried out in thought rather than in action. Piaget argued that such transformations are built on some physical relationship that the younger child can perform but cannot articulate. For example, a toddler can arrange a graduated set of circles on a stick so that the largest circle is at the bottom of the stick and the smallest circle is at the top. The child does not have a verbal label for the ordering operation but can perform it. With the emergence of concrete operations, children begin to appreciate a large group of actions that can be performed on objects and can do so mentally without having to do them physically. Thus, a mental operation is an internal representation of an alteration in the relationships among objects.

Piaget (1972a) used the term *concrete* to contrast this quality of thinking to the more hypothetical reasoning of adolescents and adults. The child reasons about objects and relations among them but has difficulty entertaining hypothetical statements or propositions. Thinking is typically focused on relationships among adjoining or related terms rather than among any two or more terms. For example, children can reason about problems involving grouping trees into different categories and identifying the features of these categories. It would be much more difficult, however, for them to identify variables that relate trees to other life forms such as bacteria, insects, and mammals.

During the stage of concrete operations, the three conceptual skills that have received the most attention are: (1) conservation, (2) classification, and (3) combinatorial skills. Over the period of middle childhood, children apply these skills to achieve a clearer understanding of the logic, order, and predictability of the physical world. As

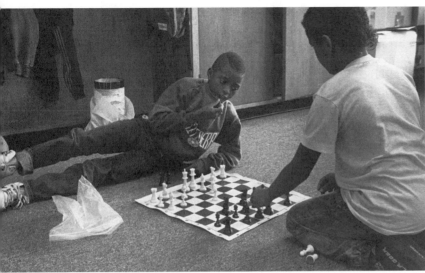

children take a new approach to problem solving through the use of the logical principles associated with concrete operational thought, they generalize these principles to their thinking about friendships, team play and other games with rules, and their own self-evaluation. As the order of the physical world becomes more apparent, children begin to seek logic and order in the social and personal domains as well. Sometimes, this search for order is frustrated by the unpredictability of the social world. At other times, children find that they can use their enhanced capacities for reasoning to solve interpersonal problems and to arrange their daily life so that it better meets their interests and needs.

Mental operations are critical to the game of chess. In order to play well, you have to be able to manipulate relationships in your mind, coordinate related pieces, and anticipate your opponent's responses to your moves. These third graders are just beginning to show some finesse in their play.

Conservation

The basic meaning of **conservation** is that physical matter does not magically appear or disappear despite changes in form or container. The concept of conservation can be applied to a variety of dimensions, including mass, weight, number, length, and volume. The child who "conserves" is able to resist perceptual cues that alter the form of an object, insisting that the quantity remains the same despite the change in form. One of the most common problems of this type that Piaget investigated involves conservation of mass. The child is presented with two clay balls and asked to tell whether or not they are equal. Once the child is satisfied that the balls are equal, one of them is flattened out into a pancake. The child is then asked, "Which has more—this one [the pancake] or this one [the ball]?" Sometimes, the child is also asked whether the clay pieces are still the same. The child who does not conserve might say the pancake has more clay because it is a lot wider than the ball. This child is still in the preoperational stage of thought. He or she is using personal perceptions to make judgments. In contrast, the child who conserves knows that the two pieces of clay are still identical in mass and can explain why.

Children eventually use three concepts to ascertain that equality in any physical dimension has not been altered (Figure 8.1). First, the child may explain that the pancake has the same amount of clay as the ball; no clay has been added or taken away. This is an example of the concept of **identity:** The pancake is still the *same* clay, and nothing has been changed except its shape. Second, the child may point out that the experimenter can turn the pancake back into a ball. This is an example of the concept of **reversibility.** The child becomes aware that operations can be reversed, so that their effects are nullified. Third, the child may notice that, although the pancake has a larger

Identity:
It's the same clay.

Reversibility:
You can roll it back into a ball.

Reciprocity:
The ball is small and thick; the pancake is large and thin.

FIGURE 8.1

Three concepts that contribute to conservation

circumference, the ball is much thicker. When the child can simultaneously manipulate two dimensions, such as circumference and thickness, we observe the concept of **reciprocity**. In the clay ball example, change in one dimension is compensated for by change in another; the total mass remains the same. With consolidation of the concepts of identity, reversibility, and reciprocity, the child is able to conserve in any physical dimension. There appears to be a developmental sequence in the capacity to conserve. Children generally conserve mass and number earliest, weight later, and volume last.

Conservation does not generalize across all of the physical modes. For example, children who are unable to conserve quantity in an unfamiliar object, such as poker chips, can do so with a more familiar one, such as M & M's (Gulko et al., 1988). In another study, girls were able to perform a conservation of liquid task when it was presented in the standard manner of comparing the experimenter's glass and their own. However, when the task was embedded in a story where juice had to be divided between two dolls, their performance declined. Evidence of a lack of generalizability of knowledge from in-school to out-of-school contexts is found in other areas of reasoning, especially mathematical codes and scientific principles (Perret-Clermont et al., Bell, 1991).

Extensions of Piaget's Ideas about Conservation. Researchers have raised questions about the meaning of conservation tasks, the timing of the emergence of conservation, and the possibility of teaching children to conserve. The way the task is presented and the kinds of questions asked may influence a child's responses. For example, the task may emphasize identity or equivalence. In an identity task, the child is asked to judge whether a single clay ball has the same amount of clay after it has been rolled into a sausage. In an equivalence task, there are two balls of clay. The child is asked to judge whether the ball that is rolled into a sausage has the same amount of clay as the standard, comparison ball. Some studies have shown that children can perform the identity task earlier than the equivalence task; others have shown the opposite; and still others have argued that identity and equivalence are achieved at the same time (Silverstein et al., 1982). In a study of 5- to 7-year-olds, children were asked to tell how the materials looked, and then to tell how they really were. Giving the child this distinction between appearance and reality resulted in more correct answers than the standard procedure, in which this distinction was not made (Bijstra et al., 1989).

It is possible to train young children of preschool age to conserve (Brainerd, 1977). These training studies have both theoretical and practical implications. Theoretically, Piaget's view of development suggests that there is a period of maturational readiness for the application of logical operations to physical objects. Thus, explanations of rules and relationships should not be relevant to a child who is not cognitively ready to understand them. The training studies suggest that it is possible to introduce such concepts as identity and reversibility so that children as young as 4 can achieve conservation. Further, they transfer conservation from the tasks involved in training to other materials and dimensions (Field, 1981; May & Norton, 1981). Apparently, the most important element in modifying a child's approach to conservation is being confronted by someone else's reasoning that contradicts one's own. For this contradiction to be effective, however, the child must be approaching a level of readiness to reorganize his or her thinking, and the gap between the current level of reasoning and the new ideas must not be too great. The implication here is that entry into a new stage of thought may emerge earlier and may be more readily influenced by the social environment than Piaget's cognitive developmental theory predicts.

Contemporary work on cognition emphasizes the idea of the *social construction of meaning*. This notion, extended from Vygotsky's theory, emphasizes that, in most learning situations, the child is trying to understand not only the logical or symbolic features of the problem but also the social meaning of the situation. For example, in one study of 6- to 10-year-olds, the children were given a task with incomplete instructions. The focus of the study was on how children would handle the task and the extent to which they would ask for information from the experimenter to fill in the gaps in the instructions. Most of the children tried to complete the task on their own, without asking any questions to clarify the instructions. Even older children who were clearly aware that the instructions were inadequate did not ask for clarification. Most of the questions that were asked seemed to be directed toward confirming that they were doing the right thing—that is, the questions were directed toward gaining social approval from the experimenter rather than revealing more about the logic of the task. The idea is that learning is embedded in the social norms for interactions between adult authority figures and children. Transactions such as question asking, which adults may construe as a means of gaining information, are often constructed by children as a means of reassuring themselves that they are behaving appropriately and meeting the adults' expectations (Perret-Clermont et al., 1991).

Practically speaking, the implication is that preschool- and kindergarten-age children can integrate and apply more abstract concepts than educators once believed they could. For example, studies of children as young as 3 and 4 have shown that they understand the idea that materials are made of tiny particles that retain their properties even when they are invisible. They can use this notion of particles to explain how a substance, such as sugar, continues to exist in a solution and retains its sweetness even when it is invisible (Au et al., 1993; Rosen & Rozin, 1993). Early-childhood educators have found that, through a planned program of exploring, experimenting, and describing the transformation of materials, young children can be guided to conceptualize the physical world in a systematic, logical manner.

Classification Skills

Classification was first discussed in Chapter 5, describing basic categorization skills. **Classification** is the ability to identify properties of categories, to relate categories or classes to one another, and to use categorical information to solve problems. One of the adaptive benefits of categorization is that one can assume that whatever holds true for one member of a category is likely to hold true for other members as well. For example, if water and juice are both liquids, then if you can pour water, you can pour juice. Other substances classified as liquids should also have this property, even substances one has never seen. From the ages 6 to 12, children's knowledge of categories and of the information associated with them expands dramatically. What is more, children have a broad range of categories available into which to incorporate a novel observation. The value of classification skills is not purely to organize objects or experiences into classes, but to take advantage of what is known about these categories to make inferences about the characteristics and dynamics of members of the same categories, members of hierarchically related categories, and objects that are not members of a specific category (Kalish & Gelman, 1992; Lopez et al., 1992; Farrar et al., 1992).

One component of classification skills is the ability to group objects according to some dimension that they share. The other component is the ability to order subgroups hierarchically, so that each new grouping will include all previous subgroups. Vygotsky (1932/1962) suggested a method for studying classification in young children. Children are presented with a variety of wooden blocks that differ in shape, size, and color. Under each block is a nonsense syllable. The children are instructed to select, one at a time, all the blocks that have the same syllable. The youngest children, who would be characterized as preoperational in Piaget's stage theory, tend to select blocks by their color. Their technique for grouping is highly associative. They choose each new block to match some characteristic of the previous selection, but they do not hold in mind a single concept that guides their choices.

Children who have entered the stage of concrete operations tend to focus on one dimension at first, perhaps shape, and continue to select blocks until they discover that they have made an incorrect choice. They use this discovery to change their hypothesis about which characteristics of the blocks are associated with the nonsense syllable. This clas-

After many family trips to the beach, Randy has accumulated quite a collection of shells. Now he is learning to categorize them and to group them by species.

sification task demonstrates the child's ability to hold a concept in mind and to make a series of decisions based on it. It also demonstrates that during the stage of concrete operations, children can use mistakes to reorient their problem-solving strategy.

Piaget studied reasoning about class hierarchies or inclusion by asking questions about whether a group of objects included more members of one subtype than of the group as a whole (Piaget, 1941/1952; Chapman & McBride, 1992). Thus, when a set of pictures shows three ducks, six sparrows, and two robins, one might ask, "Are there more sparrows or more birds in these pictures?" This is an unusual kind of question, one that children are probably rarely asked. By the age of 8 or 9, however, many children can respond correctly because they recognize the distinction between classes and subclasses. In order to handle such problems, children have to inhibit their tendency to reinterpret the question in line with a more common comparison, such as, "Are there more sparrows than ducks?"

In one study of class inclusion reasoning, an intriguing pattern was found. Children aged 3 and 4, who could not repeat the question and who clearly had not learned any rules about classes, were more likely to answer correctly than children of 5 and 6. Children aged 7 and 8 performed better than any of the younger children. The 5- and 6-year-olds, who answered quickly and confidently, were consistently incorrect. They seemed unable to inhibit the more obvious comparison in order to consider the actual question (McCabe et al., 1982).

The capacity for classifying and categorizing has been explored in relation to specific domains such as health and illness concepts or concepts of the family. For example, children were told about 21 different human groupings and asked to say whether these groupings were a family: "Here are Mr. Mead and his son, Tom. They live together, just the two of them. Are they a family?" The youngest subjects (4- to 6-year-olds) had trouble accepting examples involving single parents or biologically related people who do not live in the same home as instances of a family. Principles of biological relatedness and shared physical residence were both important to these children's view of a family. By middle childhood, the children were able to accept a wider variety of groups as meeting certain essential criteria of a family, usually biological relatedness and emotional closeness. Emotional closeness was endorsed by 80% of the subjects as a defining feature of a family and was used repeatedly as a basis for judging whether a specific instance of a grouping could be considered a family or not (Newman et al., 1993).

Combinatorial Skills

A third characteristic of concrete operational thought is the development of **combinatorial skills.** Once they have acquired the scheme for conservation of number, children understand that certain physical transformations will not alter the number of units in a set. If 10 poker chips are lined up in a row, the number remains constant whether they are spread out, squeezed tightly together, or stacked. Children can use counting to answer a "how many" question sometime between the ages of 3 and 4. For example, they can assign one number to each item in a set of four poker chips and tell you that there are four chips in all. However, young children have more difficulty selecting a set of six chips from a larger pile, or establishing that two sets of chips are equal in number. They also have trouble solving verbal story problems when no concrete objects are present (Jordan et al., 1992; Sophian, 1988). Conservation of number is achieved around age 6 or 7 (Halford & Boyle, 1985). Addition, subtraction, multiplication, and division are all learned at this stage. Children learn to apply the same operations no matter what specific objects or quantities are involved. Piaget claimed that it is no coincidence that schools begin to instruct children in the basic skills of arithmetic at age 6. It is probably a strength of our schools that they meet an important aspect of intellectual readiness at the appropriate time.

The stage we have identified as early school age marks the beginnings of concrete operational thought. At this age, children's performance on tests of cognitive maturity is likely to be inconsistent. For example, children can conserve quantity but may make errors in conservation of weight, volume, or space. They may be able to perform a classification task correctly when they sort by one dimension, such as color, but may make errors when asked to sort objects that have more than one dimension in common. The process of classifying objects and the logic of conservation are not fully integrated until sometime during middle childhood and may not reach peak performance until adolescence or adulthood (Flavell, 1982).

As concrete operational intelligence develops, the child gains insight into the regularities of the physical world and the principles that govern relationships among objects. Table 8.1 summarizes the components of concrete operational thought. Perceptions of reality become less convincing than a logical understanding of how the world is organized. For example, even though it looks as if the sun sinks into the water, we know that what we see is a result of the earth's rotation on its axis.

Metacognition

As Piaget began his method of inquiry into concrete operational thought, he pointed the way to the study of metacognition. Rather than being concerned with the exact answers children gave to the questions he asked, he was concerned about how they explained their answers. How do children know what they know? What reasons can they give to justify or support their answers? **Metacognition** refers to a whole range of processes and strategies used to assess and monitor knowledge. It includes the "feeling of knowing" that accompanies problem solving, the ability to distinguish those answers about which we are confident from those we doubt (Butterfield et al., 1988). One element of this "feeling of knowing" is understanding the source of one's beliefs. For example, we can be told about something, we can see it for ourselves, or we can feel and touch it. All three of these sources of information may coincide to create a single belief, or we may discover that there are inconsistencies between what someone says is true and what we perceive through sight or touch. By the ages of 4 and 5, children are able to understand how all three sources of information have contributed to their understanding of an experience (O'Neill & Gopnik, 1991).

Metacognition includes the ability to review various strategies for approaching a problem in order to choose the one that is most likely to result in a solution (Carr et al., 1989). It includes the ability to monitor one's comprehension of the material one has just read and to select strategies for increasing one's comprehension (Cross & Paris, 1988).

Metacognition develops in parallel with other cognitive capacities. As children develop in their ability to attend to more variables in their approach to problems, they simultaneously increase their capacity to take an "executive" posture in relation to cognitive tasks. They can detect uncertainty and introduce strategies to reduce it. They can learn study techniques that will enhance their ability to organize and recall information. These capacities continue to develop as the child becomes a more sophisticated learner. They are also quite amenable to training, both at home and at school. Metacognition appears to be a natural component of cognitive development. However, just like first-level cognitive capacities, it is constructed in a social context. Interactions between children and adults or peers nurture and stimulate metacognition by helping children to identify sources of information, talk about and recognize the differences between feelings of certainty and uncertainty in their knowledge, and devise effective strategies for increasing their "feelings of knowing."

TABLE 8.1   Components of Concrete Operational Thought

Component	New Abilities
Conservation	Ability to perceive identity Ability to perceive reversibility Ability to manipulate two dimensions simultaneously in reciprocity
Classification	Ability to group objects according to some common dimension Ability to order subgroups in a hierarchy
Combinatorial skills	Ability to manipulate numbers in addition, subtraction, multiplication, and division

Skill Learning   One area of impressive growth during middle childhood is the acquisition of skills. Skills are the basis of intellectual competence. They combine knowledge (knowing about) and practice (know how) directed toward identifying and solving significant, meaningful problems (Gardner, 1983; Kuhn et al., 1995). Typically, a person moves through a developmental progression within a skill area, starting off as a novice, becoming more proficient, and then, depending upon a combination of aptitude, training, and practice, becoming an expert. Cultures differ on the value placed on various skills; in some societies like ours, symbolic skills focusing on reading, mathematics, and abstract reasoning are highly valued. In other cultures, reading and mathematics are of less use and value than agricultural skills, hunting, or food preparation. In the United States, one observes the emergence of a wide range of valued skills during middle childhood, including:

mathematics	science
writing	computer operation
sports	mechanics
music	dance
theater	art
cooking	sewing
crafts	reading

Based on research on how skilled reading develops, four principles have been identified for understanding how complex behavioral skills are achieved.

Features of Skilled Learning

Laura is just beginning to use her family's laptop for school projects. Try to think of the sensory, motor, perceptual, cognitive, emotional, linguistic, and social processes that will be involved as Laura moves from a novice to a skilled computer user.

First, the development of skill depends on a combination of sensory, motor, perceptual, cognitive, linguistic, emotional, and social processes. In sports, for example, a child must learn to coordinate specific sensory information and motor activities, understand the rules of the game, be able to communicate with the coach and the other players, gain control over emotions such as fear or anger that might interfere with performance, and sustain motivation to keep trying despite errors or defeat.

Second, skills are attained through the simultaneous integration of many levels of the component behaviors. They are not acquired in strict sequence from simple to complex. Instead, children work on the simple and more complex components of the skill at the same time. For example, in art, children may experiment with mixing paints to achieve new colors at the same time as they are experimenting with line drawing, perspective, and shading.

Third, limits of the human system place constraints on an individual's capacity to perform skilled behavior. With practice, lower-level processes begin to function automatically, so a person can attend to higher-order processes. In writing, for example, young children struggle with the physical act of printing and writing, concentrating largely on the motor skills necessary to make each letter, word, and sentence. A skilled writer can write with little effort, focusing attention on the meaning of the writing, the plot, or the character development rather than on the physical aspects of the task.

Fourth, skilled behavior requires the use of strategies. Skillful people operate with purpose and continuously monitor their performance. They perceive breakdowns in performance, are selective in focusing attention on various aspects of what they are working on, and refine higher-order processes as they perform the skill. This model of skill development focuses on the elements that are necessary in order to move from what might be considered a novice level to a more advanced level in skill performance.

One must keep in mind that children vary widely in their rate of intellectual development and in their capacities to perform

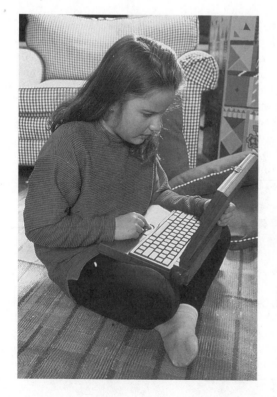

skills. For example, by the first or second grade, children have been identified as mathematically gifted, normal, or mathematically "disabled" (Geary et al., 1991; Geary & Brown, 1991). These designations relate to children's abilities to perform relatively simple mathematical operations such as addition. Differences in early mathematical ability relate to children's capacity for using a variety of counting strategies as well as to their ability to retain and recall math facts from memory. In each distinct area of skill development, a combination of maturational factors, aptitude or talent, opportunities for exposure and training, and the value placed on the skill by the family, school, or larger society all play a role in how rapidly and how well a skill will be developed.

In the sections that follow, we look at reading as a specific case of skill development, then more broadly at a model of the developing mind, and finally at the social and cultural contexts within which skill learning occurs.

Reading

In some ways, reading is the most significant intellectual skill that develops during middle childhood because it opens the door to all the others. Reading provides access to new information, new uses of language, and new forms of thinking. Children are limited in their ability to learn mathematics, social studies, and science if they cannot read. However, once they can read fluently, the possibilities for independent inquiry expand significantly.

Children probably begin to read in a variety of ways. As David and his mother drove from home to preschool every day, they used a game with street signs along the road to build the bridge from language to literacy. At first, David would ask his mother to tell him what every sign said. After a while, David began to "read" the signs by memorizing words and phrases that were linked to certain shapes and patterns in the signs. Other children begin to read by learning letters and the sounds linked to them, and by experimenting with sounding out the letters when they are strung together. At first, most children are bewildered and confused by these experiences. This is a time when they require a good deal of support and encouragement for their efforts. Gradually, through a process of trial, feedback, and repetition, children learn to read simple words and sentences (Knight & Fischer, 1992).

Early in the process of learning to read, children understand and communicate orally a great deal more than they can read by themselves. Their task is to learn how to use these oral communication skills in the comprehension of written language (Carroll, 1986). At some point, a child begins to articulate the concept "I can read" or "I am a reader." Once this idea is part of the self-concept, efforts to read increase and are energized by a confidence in one's potential for success.

Reading is a complex skill that involves the acquisition and integration of many new techniques (Hall, 1989). Children do not have to score extremely high in intelligence tests to make substantial progress in learning to read (Share et al., 1989). Most children, unfortunately, spend little or no time reading books outside school; over time, those who do some book reading show the greatest gains in reading achievement between the second and fifth grades (Anderson et al., 1988).

Parents' influence on children's reading achievement has been consistently documented. Parents affect their children's reading in at least five ways: in the value they place on literacy, the emphasis they place on academic achievement, the reading materials they make available at home, the time they spend reading with their children, and the opportunities they provide for verbal interaction in the home (Hess & Holloway, 1984; Schickedanz, 1986). Parents who value the ability to read, urge their children to do well in school, provide resources for reading, read with their children, and talk with them produce children who are more skilled readers (Bus et al., 1995).

Parents also have an indirect effect on how well a child will learn to read by influencing the child's placement in a school reading group (Goldenberg, 1989). Ability grouping for reading instruction is practically universal in elementary schools (Slavin, 1987). Teachers depend on their perceptions of a child's ability, work habits, and behavior when they assign students to reading groups (Haller & Waterman, 1985). The higher the level of the children's reading group, the better they learn how to read. Parents may help a child understand his or her school's reading curriculum (schools differ in their approaches to teaching reading), and encourage good work habits and appropriate classroom behavior. Parents who do these things may influence a teacher's perception of their child and, as a result, the child's assignment to a reading-level group.

A Model of the Developing Mind

Think about the skill development that takes place in so many domains from about age 6 to about age 12. During this time, children reach high levels of functioning in such diverse areas as sports, reading, writing and story making, mathematical problem solving, art, and science. One is led to marvel at the complexity of the expansion of human thought processes needed to support such advanced functioning. Demetriou, Efklides, and Platsidou (1993) presented a general model of the developing mind that brings some of this complexity to light (Figure 8.2). In their model, intellectual development is a product of the ongoing interactions among three structural systems: the processing system, the hypercognitive system, and the specialized structural systems (SSSs). The **processing system** (the inner circle in Figure 8.2) is composed of the elements of thinking that enter into every form of intellectual endeavor. It includes the speed of processing information, the control of processing information, and the storage and retrieval of information. According to the model, these processing systems respond to whatever task activates them, whether the stimuli are musical, verbal, or mathematical symbols.

The **hypercognitive system** (the circle surrounding the processing system in Figure 8.2) is composed of all the functions that make meaning of something. In this model, the hypercognitive system tries to interpret a particular task or problem, evaluating what is required to solve it, and then assigning the problem to the one or more specialized systems that are best equipped to solve it. As new skill areas are established, more alternative strategies are available to approach the solution of particular tasks or problems.

The **specialized structural systems** (areas labeled *SSS* in the outer circle of Figure 8.2) are viewed as modular rather than generally available across all cognitive domains. In their model, Demetriou et al. (1993) identified five SSSs, each of them best suited to a particular family of problems and associated with a unique profile of mental abilities. They include: qualitative-analytic (skills related to categorizing and systematically organizing information such as are required in fields like geology or botany); quantitative-relational (skills related to counting, measuring, and comparing information such as are required in fields like mathematics, statistics, or accounting); causal-experimental (skills related to hypothesis raising and hypothesis testing such as are required in any experimental science like psychology, physics, or chemistry); verbal-propositional (skills related to the organization and meaning of language and other symbol systems such as are required in the study of grammar, logic, and law); and spatial-imaginal (skills related to mental imagery and visual and spatial reasoning such as are required in the visual arts, weaving and pottery, or architecture).

In this model, each of the five SSSs can be brought into action to apply its own unique set of concepts or schemes, operations, or strategies to the task at hand. The more familiar the task and the more fully developed the SSS, the less likely it is that any other SSS will be recruited to aid in the problem-solving process.

According to this model, development can occur in all three components. The processing system can become more efficient, attention can be

Michelle's assignment was to give a speech in which she takes a position on a controversial topic and tries to convince her classmates to support her view. She is developing the specialized structural system of verbal propositional reasoning. She is trying to use logic and evidence to argue for her position.

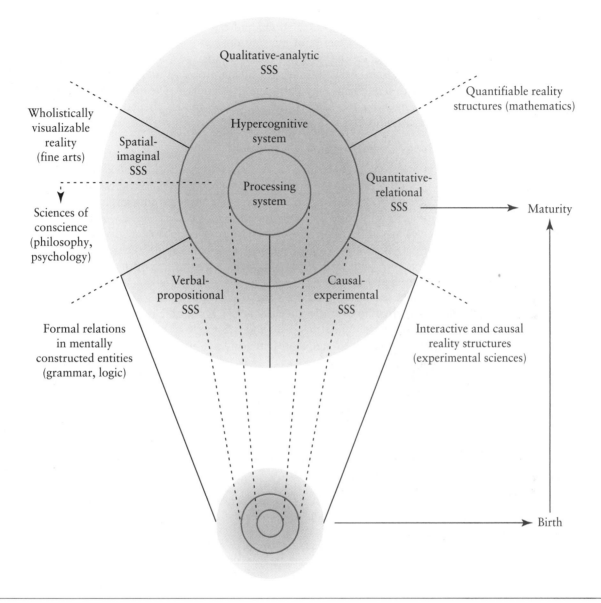

FIGURE 8.2
The general model of the developing mind
SOURCE: Demetriou, A., Efklides, A., & Platsidou, M., 1993.

improved to control the input of information, and storage and retrieval can become more effective. The hypercognitive system can develop as metacognitive capacities mature, allowing the person to make finer and more accurate assessments of the nature of problems being encountered and the kinds of skills that are most appropriate to their solution. Within each SSS, new subcapacities may be acquired. For example, in the causal-experimental domain, the achievement of schemes for conservation are elaborated into the more formal scientific hypothesis-raising and hypothesis-testing strategies of scientific research. Developmental changes may result from the maturation of the central nervous system and the perceptual-motor capacities. They may also arise from a child's motivation to increase his or her skill level in a particular SSS. And they may arise from external sources such as participation in peer interactions that model new approaches to problem solving or from direct instruction or intervention, both at the hypercognitive level (teaching new approaches to recognizing and analyzing problems) and at the SSS level (teaching new techniques for representing and solving specific kinds of problems). Over time, and especially from about the ages of 10 to 12, there is a fantastic synergy of maturation, motivation, and external stimulation that seems to accelerate the growth process so that 11- and 12-year-olds appear qualitatively different in their approach to solving problems and enormously more skillful in their day-to-day functioning than younger children. The question of how to conceptualize intelligence and what is meant when someone is labeled as "smart" are discussed in more detail in Box 8.2.

The Social Context of Skill Development

Recent attention has been given to the social and cultural context in which many skills, especially school-related abilities, emerge (Eccles, 1993). Progress in skill development is influenced by parental and school expectations regarding levels of performance. It is also influenced by a child's motivation to want to achieve new levels of ability and to direct her or his attention and energy to practice, problem solving, and the formulation of new strategies within a particular domain. Skill development may be enriched by interactions with skillful peers as well as by the appropriate intervention of teachers, coaches, and guides.

Consider the ongoing concern regarding mathematics ability among U.S. students, especially in comparison to their Japanese and Chinese counterparts. In 1980, comparative studies showed that 1st- and 5th-grade children in Minneapolis were substantially behind their age-mates in Sendai, Japan, and Taipei, Taiwan in tests of mathematics achievement. In a 10-year follow-up, U.S. children still lagged behind, and by the 11th grade, the gap in achievement had widened (Stevenson, 1992; Stevenson et al., 1993). Even the top 10% of the Minneapolis students scored at about the average level of the Taipei and Sendai students. It is difficult to account for these cross-

---

BOX 8.2   WHAT IS INTELLIGENCE?

The model of the mind presented in Figure 8.2 is not the only approach to conceptualizing intelligence. The term **intelligence** is used in many contexts, with a variety of meanings. At a conceptual level, it may refer to the ability to solve important problems or to adapt to environmental conditions. At a psychometric level, it may refer to the score on a standardized test comprised of one type of item (such as Peabody's Picture Vocabulary Test) or many kinds of items (such as the Stanford-Binet Intelligence Test). Some theorists emphasize a general underlying factor, *g*, that reflects what many different types of items have in common (Spearman, 1927). Other models of intelligence offer different ideas about the number and content of distinct areas of specialization.

Jean Piaget (1972b) analyzed intelligence from a developmental perspective. He described four basic types of intelligence, each emerging at a different period of childhood: (1) sensorimotor intelligence (the ability to know through direct observation and manipulation of objects); (2) representational intelligence (the ability to distinguish between the real and the pretend; to think about and represent objects and events that are not present); (3) concrete operational intelligence (the ability to detect the

logical relationships among objects; to place objects in sequences; and to comprehend and manipulate numbers); and (4) formal operational intelligence (the ability to use experimental techniques and hypothetical reasoning to solve problems, to generalize observations from one situation to another, and to relate cause and effect in complex, multidimensional problems). These kinds of intelligence reflect different processes or approaches to solving problems.

Howard Gardner's (1983) theory of multiple intelligences identifies at least eight distinct intelligences, each with its own content and unique contribution to solving important, meaningful problems. These include linguistic intelligence, musical intelligence, logical-mathematical intelligence, spatial intelligence, naturalist intelligence, bodily-kinesthetic intelligence, and two forms of personal intelligence, one directed toward understanding one's own internal feelings (intrapersonal intelligence) and the other directed toward identifying and differentiating among the characteristics of others (interpersonal intelligence). This theory recognizes domains of human functioning that show evidence of high levels of achievement that are not necessarily related to the scientific reasoning of specific concern national comparisons on the basis of ability. All three countries have practically universal enrollment of school-age children. What is more, when children were compared in their knowledge of general information of the type not included in the school curriculum, the U.S. children in 1st and 5th grades scored higher than the Japanese and Chinese children.

At least four sociocultural factors interact to contribute to the advantage that Japanese and Chinese children show in mathematical skill development. First, there is a difference in parents' views about what they should expect of their children. U.S. parents appear to be satisfied with their children's level of mathematics performance and do not expect their children to do better. In contrast, Japanese and Chinese parents have high expectations for their children's performance. Second, there is a difference in how parents evaluate their children's schools. U.S. parents are generally satisfied with the school curriculum and think that the schools are doing a good job. Far fewer Japanese and Chinese parents view the schools as good or excellent. The public pressure in these cultures is for greater improvement in the quality of education. They are more critical of their schools, and even though Japanese and Chinese children spend more time on homework than do U.S. children, their parents are more likely to encourage them to spend even more time on homework.

Third, there are cultural differences in the emphasis given to ability as compared to effort. U.S. parents and teachers highlight the importance of natural ability as a major factor in accounting for individual differences in mathematical ability. Japanese and Chinese parents and teachers are more likely to see outstanding performance as being a result of studying hard. On the one hand, if you believe that skill depends on natural ability, you might conclude that not much can be done to improve performance. On the other hand, if you believe that skill depends on effort, you may be more inclined to devote additional time and focused application to reach a new level of performance.

Finally, in contrast to what might be expected, by 11th grade U.S. children are more stressed by school than Chinese or Japanese children. U.S. students in the 11th grade reported frequent experiences of stress, anxiety about school, and aggression. They

to Piaget or to the broader areas of intellectual and scientific thinking discussed by Demetriou et al. (Gardner et al., 1996).

Another view is presented by Robert Sternberg's (1985) idea of three kinds of intelligence—analytic, creative, and practical. According to Sternberg, only the first is systematically measured by tests of intelligence, but the latter two are often required in job performance or adaptation to the demands of daily life. Cultures differ in what kinds of abilities are valued as evidence of intelligence. Many parents consider social skills (knowing how to behave appropriately with peers and teachers), practical skills necessary for adjustment to school (completing one's homework), and motivation (working hard to understand a problem) as more important indications of intelligence than cognitive accomplishments (Okagaki & Sternberg, 1993; Neisser et al., 1996). The debate about intelligence is especially relevant in middle childhood since this is when intelligence tests are administered and school placement decisions are made. As children discover the results of these tests, they make personal attributions about their ability or potential. Thus, IQ tests have a direct impact on the kind of educational experiences children encounter and on their sense of academic self-efficacy.

Practical intelligence is knowing the skills and strategies necessary to get along as an independent person in your culture. Here, an Amish father is teaching his son to make a cinder-block building.

were less clear about the central role of school achievement in their lives. They had more competing demands on their time from after-school jobs, sports, and dating than did the Japanese or Chinese adolescents. One interpretation of this difference is that U.S. families and children set a greater value on freedom of choice and individuality than the Japanese or Chinese families. As a result, there is less consistency in the priority that U.S. schoolchildren, their parents, and their teachers place on academic achievement in relation to the many other activities that claim time and attention.

The emphasis on skill building and the energy that children ages 6 to 12 bring to the acquisition of new skills suggest a strong parallel to toddlerhood. At both stages, children's motives for competence and mastery are directed outward to the environment. At both stages, children appear to be delighted by the potential for learning that almost every new encounter offers. However, as a result of their cognitive capacities and their awareness of social expectations, skill learning at middle childhood is embedded in a much more complex framework of continuous monitoring and self-assessment. In addition, children's beliefs and attitudes about which skills are important, what they should expect of themselves, what others expect of them, and what kinds of competing demands should influence their dedication to skill development all contribute to the levels of performance they are likely to achieve.

Self-Evaluation   During middle childhood, the emphasis on skill building is accompanied by a new focus on self-evaluation. Children strive to match their achievements to internalized goals and external standards. Simultaneously, they receive feedback from others about the quality of their performance. Some children may be asked to sit at one table to receive "special" help, while others may be told to go down the hall for tutoring. Some children are designated as peer tutors who assist their classmates. These and many other signs are sources of social evaluation that children incorporate into their own self-evaluations.

During middle childhood, the process of self-evaluation is further complicated because the peer group joins the adult world as a source of social comparison, criticism, and approval. Toddlers and early-school-age children are likely to observe and imitate their peers in order to learn new strategies for approaching a task or out of curiosity to see how their peers are doing a particular project. But in middle childhood, pressures toward conformity, competition, and the need for approval feed into the self-evaluation process. At this age, children begin to pay attention to the work of others in order to assess their own abilities (Butler & Ruzany, 1993). Their athletic skills, intellectual abilities, and artistic talents are no longer matters to which only teachers and parents respond. Peers also identify others' skills and begin to generate profiles of one another: "Oh, Rafael is good in math, but he runs like a girl"; "Jane is kind of fat, but she writes great stories"; "I like Rashidah best because she's good at everything." Depending on their resolution of the crises of toddlerhood and early school age, children approach the process of self-evaluation from a framework of either self-confidence or self-doubt. They may expect to find tasks easy to accomplish and approach them vigorously, or they may anticipate failure and approach tasks with hesitation.

In research involving children in the age range 8–13, Susan Harter (1985, 1993) devised a method for assessing children's perceptions of competence in five specific domains: scholastic competence, athletic competence, likability by peers, physical appearance, and behavioral conduct. In addition, she measured general or global self-esteem. Her research was guided by the idea that by the age of 8 children not only would be able to differentiate specific areas of competence, but would view certain areas as more important than others. She found that self-esteem is highest in those children who view themselves as competent in domains that they judge to be important. Competence in relatively unimportant domains is not especially strongly related to overall self-esteem. In the sections that follow, we focus on two different paths toward self-evaluation: self-efficacy, which reflects a child's personal judgment of ability, and social expectations, which reflect the impact of the expectations of others on a child's performance.

Self-Efficacy

How do children assess their competence in a specific ability area? Albert Bandura (1982) theorized that judgments of self-efficacy are crucial to understanding this process. **Self-efficacy** is defined as the person's sense of confidence that he or she can perform the behaviors demanded in a specific situation. Expectations of efficacy vary with the specific ability. In other words, a child may view efficacy in one way in a situation requiring mathematical ability and in another way when the situation requires physical strength.

Bandura has suggested that four sources of information contribute to judgments of self-efficacy (Figure 8.3). The first source is **enactive attainments,** or prior experiences of mastery in the kinds of tasks that are being confronted. Children's general assessment of their ability in any area (e.g., mathematics, writing, or gymnastics) is based on their past accomplishments in that area (Skaalvik & Hagtvet, 1990). Successful experiences increase their perceived self-efficacy, whereas repeated failures diminish it. Failure experiences are especially detrimental when they occur early in the process of trying to master a task. Many boys and girls are diverted from mastering such sports as tennis and baseball because they have made mistakes early in their participation. They develop doubts about their abilities, which then prevent them from persisting in the task.

The second source of information is **vicarious experience.** Seeing a person similar to oneself perform a task successfully may raise one's sense of self-efficacy; seeing a person similar to oneself fail at a task may lower it (Brown & Inouye, 1978).

Verbal persuasion is the third source. Children can be encouraged to believe in themselves and try a new task. Persuasion is likely to be most effective with children who already have confidence in their abilities and helps boost their performance level.

The fourth source is **physical state.** People monitor their body states in making judgments about whether or not they can do well. When children feel too anxious or frightened, they are likely to anticipate failure. In contrast, children who are excited and interested but not overly tense are more likely to perceive themselves as capable of succeeding.

As Lee and Ben watch their friend Lindsey, they seem to be identifying with her difficulties. Through vicarious experience, they may begin to have some doubts about whether they will be able to hit the ball.

Self-efficacy judgments are related to children's perceptions of their likelihood of success. These judgments also determine the factors to which children attribute their success or failure (McAuley et al., 1989; Pajares, 1996). In the face of difficulty or failure, children who have confidence in their abilities and high self-efficacy will work harder to master challenges. They will attribute their difficulties to a failure to try hard enough, and they will redouble their efforts. Children who have a low sense of self-efficacy tend to give up in the face of difficulty because they attribute their failure to a basic lack of ability (Bandura & Schunck, 1981). The level of self-efficacy also affects how children prepare to handle new challenges. In their thoughts, emotions, and preparation for action, those who are

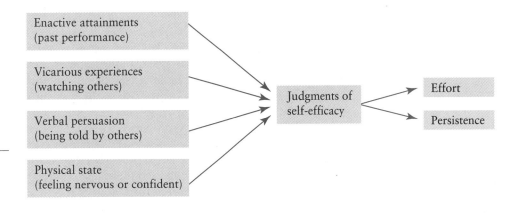

FIGURE 8.3
Four components of self-efficacy

preoccupied by self-doubts differ from those who believe in themselves. The level of self-efficacy also affects how children prepare to handle new challenges. Children with high levels of self-efficacy related to academic achievement are likely to set challenging goals for themselves. They are also likely to regulate their learning behaviors by deliberately enlisting a number of strategies including concentrating, organizing their work, finding a good place to study, taking notes in class, and completing their homework assignments so that they have the best chances of reaching their goals (Zimmerman et al., 1992; Bandura et al., 1996).

Social Expectations

In modern, postindustrial societies, it is extremely difficult for children to develop independent, internal criteria by which to judge their abilities. If the skills of the culture were more manual, perhaps it would be easier for children to make such judgments. In learning to plow a field, for example, one can look back over the land and see whether the furrows are deep enough and the rows straight. Many important areas of accomplishment, however, have no clear, objective standards with which children can readily compare their performance. In writing an English composition, how can one judge whether one has done an adequate job? How, indeed, can a child evaluate improvement?

Several theories of the self suggest that the appraisals and expectations of others become incorporated into one's own self-evaluation. Self-esteem is based on the general positive regard and approval of others, and on the specific expectations they have for one's ability and achievement in certain areas of performance (Harter, 1993; Jussim, 1990a). In attempting to assess their own abilities, children rely on many external sources of evaluation, including grades, teachers' comments, parental approval, and peer approval (Crooks, 1988). If feedback from important adults suggests to children that they are cooperative, intelligent, and creative, these attributes are likely to be incorporated into their self-evaluations. Children who see themselves as cooperative and intelligent are likely to approach social and intellectual tasks with optimistic expectations about their performance. Conversely, feedback suggesting lack of competitiveness, intelligence, and creativity can produce a pessimistic or antagonistic approach to the challenges of skill development.

Social expectations also contribute to children's expectations about their own abilities and behavior (Harris & Rosenthal, 1985). Evaluative feedback that is associated with intellectual ability or skill feeds into children's conceptualization of their own competence. Repeated failure information or remarks that imply lack of ability tend to make children less confident of success in subsequent tasks. The pattern of expectations appears to crystallize during the second and third grades. Preschoolers do not make systematic use of success or failure feedback in predicting their next success (Parsons & Ruble, 1977). Even in the first grade, children's expectations about the grades they will receive on their first report cards are not clearly related to their IQs or to parents' or teachers' expectations, nor are they closely related to children's later estimates of their grades. By the end of the first grade, however, children begin to be more accurate predictors of their performance (Entwisle et al., 1987; Alexander & Entwisle, 1988). By fifth grade, children are more aware of their teachers' expectations for their performance, and they are likely to mirror those expectations in their own academic achievement (Weinstein et al., 1987).

Teachers' Expectations: The Self-Fulfilling Prophecy. The feedback students receive from their teachers is not wholly objective. Teachers' expectations about their students' abilities may be based on objective assessments, but they may also be derived from stereotypes about certain types of children or biases based on prior experiences, like having a child's older siblings in class in prior years or hearing unfavorable comments from other teachers. Merton (1948) suggested that problems may arise through a process that he called the **self-fulfilling prophecy.** This concept refers to the idea that false or inaccurate beliefs can produce a personal reality that corresponds with them.

In the original study on the effect of teacher expectations on student performance, teachers were led to believe that certain students were "late bloomers" who would show major gains in IQ later on in the school year. These children, chosen at random from among first- and second-graders, actually did show increases in IQ of 10–15 points in comparison to the control group (Rosenthal & Jacobson, 1968). The effect did not continue into the third and fourth grades, and overall, the correlation between teachers' expectations and students' measured IQ was modest.

Subsequent naturalistic studies of the self-fulfilling prophecy in classroom settings have shown that it has a consistent, but comparatively small, effect on student performance (Rosenthal, 1994; 1995). One way of expressing the size of the effect is that if one could control for actual ability and prior achievement, the teachers' erroneous expectations might lead to increases in performance among about 10% of children who were targets of high expectations and decreases in performance among about 10% of children who were targets of low expectations (Jussim, 1990b). The impact of these erroneous perceptions is likely to be increased when the person making the judgments is especially rigid or highly motivated to maintain and confirm his or her negative views of a certain group. Thus, one might expect a stronger impact of biased perceptions and the self-fulfilling prophecy among teachers who endorse prejudiced views, whether the target of prejudice is race, gender, social class, disability, religion, or some other classification.

Teachers' expectations for a student's performance are influenced by their assessments of both the student's ability and effort. In one study of elementary-school teachers, a relationship was found between the teachers' explanations for students' success and failure and the emotions they felt under the various conditions. It was presumed that these emotional reactions were among the major cues that teachers sent to students about their performances. When teachers believed that students' poor performances were due to a lack of effort, they were likely to feel angry toward the students, particularly if they believed the students were capable of good work. When children of low ability suddenly began putting forth a great deal of effort, teachers were likely to take pride in their own accomplishments, believing they had really helped these children become more motivated. If low-ability students who were trying hard failed, teachers felt a sense of guilt. Teachers were more willing to accept personal responsibility for certain configurations of student success and failure than for others. The students who made teachers the angriest were the bright ones who did not try hard. The research on teacher expectations illustrates how social expectations influence both perceptions of other people and the quality of interpersonal communication (Prawat et al., 1983).

Mrs. Eno believes that Christy wants to do well and is trying, so she gives her a little more encouragement and tries to reassure her that she can solve this problem. How might Mrs. Eno respond if she thought that Christy was very bright but was not really trying?

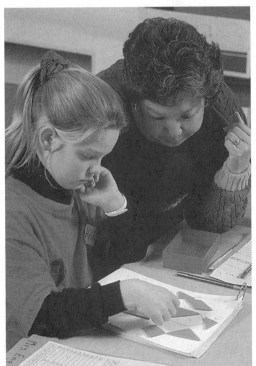

Certain conditions make children more or less vulnerable to internalizing false expectations. Children who are unsure about their abilities and those who are learning something for the first time may be more likely to rely on the information they receive from others to assess their abilities. Being in a new situation, like moving to a new school or changing from elementary to middle school, may increase a child's dependence on social expectations for performance. In middle childhood, when many new domains of skill development are first being introduced, children may be more vulnerable to the effects of biased perceptions and erroneous expectations than are older children (Jussim, 1990b).

In addition, some children appear to monitor their social environment more self-consciously than others (Musser & Browne, 1991). High self-monitoring children are more aware of the emotional and nonverbal behavior of others and make more use of social information to evaluate and regulate their own behavior. These children are more responsive to subtle forms of feedback about their performance, taking in more information about social expectations for their performance than do the children who are comparatively oblivious of the intricacies of the social environment.

Parents' Expectations. Parents' as well as teachers' expectations influence children's perceptions of their abilities. This process was demonstrated in a study of parents' and children's attitudes toward mathematical aptitude (Parsons et al., 1982). Children in Grades 5–11 and their parents were asked about their attitudes toward the children's mathematics achievement. Parents had lower expectations for their daughters' math achievement than for their sons'. They believed that mathematics is more difficult for girls than for boys and requires more effort. Their expectations about their children's aptitude were better predictors of the children's self-assessments than were the children's own past performances in mathematics.

Continuing to focus on the relationship between gender-role bias and the socialization of children's competencies and interests, Eccles (1993) proposed the following model (Figure 8.4):

> The evidence suggests that general (parental) gender-role-beliefs influence perceptions of individual children's competencies and interests, which in turn affect the kinds of experiences parents provide. . . . Essentially, we believe that parents' gender-role stereotypes, in interaction with their children's sex, affect the following mediators: 1) parents' causal attributions for the children's performance; 2) parents' emotional reaction to their children's performance in various activities; 3) the importance parents attach to their children's acquiring various skills; 4) the advice parents provide their children regarding involvement in various skills; and 5) the activities and toys parents provide. In turn, we predict that these subtle and explicit mediators influence the development of the following child outcomes across the various gender-role-stereotyped activity domains: 1) children's confidence in their ability; 2) children's interest in mastering various skills; 3) children's affective reaction to participating in various activities; and as a consequence of these self and task perceptions, 4) the amount of time and type of effort the children end up devoting to mastering and demonstrating various skills. (p. 170)

A number of studies support the underlying dynamics of this model. Independent of actual gender differences in specific domains including math, sports, and English, parents' stereotypes about which gender is more talented in a particular area influence their perceptions of their own child's competence in that area. Parents' perceptions of competence are directly related to their children's perception of competence (Eccles et al., 1990).

Other studies have examined the impact of parents' expectations on the judgments that academically capable children make about their abilities. In a phenomenon de-

FIGURE 8.4

The relationship between parents' gender-role-stereotype beliefs and perceptions to parental actions and behaviors and child outcomes
Source: Adapted from Eccles, J. S., 1993.

Parents' Specific Beliefs and Perceptions

Parents' causal attributions for child

Parents' affective reactions to child's performance and activity choices

Parents' perceptions of child's competence and interests

Parents' expectations for child's success

Parents' perceptions of importance of various activities and skills

Parents' Specific Actions and Behaviors

Parents' advice

Provision of equipment and toys

Provision of specific experiences

Child Outcomes

Child's motivational and psychological characteristics

Child's confidence in his/her ability

Child's interests and subjective task value

Child's affective associations and memories

Child's activity choice

Child's affective reactions

Child's persistence and performance

scribed as the **illusion of incompetence,** some children who perform well on tests of academic achievement (at the 90th percentile or above) perceive themselves as below average in academic ability. These children expect lower levels of success, are less confident, attempt less challenging tasks, and say that their schoolwork is more demanding than peers of similar high ability who have more positive self-evaluations. It appears that parents play a central role in establishing these children's low assessments of themselves. Children who have an illusion of incompetence think that their parents have a low opinion of their abilities and expect little of them. They see their fathers, in particular, as holding to very rigorous standards that they are not expected to meet (Phillips, 1984, 1987). The parent-child dynamics that are likely to underlie this negative assessment were observed in a study involving children with high academic ability and varying levels of perceived academic competence. Children worked with their mothers and fathers on solvable and unsolvable tasks. The fathers of children who had low perceptions of their academic competence were found to interact with their children in more critical or unsupportive ways than did the fathers of children who had high perceptions of their academic competence. Further, the children who had illusions of incompetence were more emotionally upset and dependent when they approached the unsolvable tasks (Wagner & Phillips, 1992).

The discussion of self-evaluation highlights children's sensitivity to their social environment. They become aware of existing roles and norms and of the sanctions for norm violation. Direct experiences with success and failure are important, but they are embedded in a context of social expectations. Messages of reassurance and encouragement from parents and teachers can play a key role in establishing a positive sense of competence and in motivating children to persist in the face of difficult challenges. In addition, parents can advise children that some teachers have prejudiced attitudes and help them identify the signs that such attitudes are operating in the classroom. By the end of middle childhood, children have had enough school experience that they can detect favoritism, bias, and unfair treatment and can devise strategies to protect themselves from the impact of negative biases. The more children are embedded in strong, supportive social relationships, the more confidence they will have in their general worth and the more likely they will be to arrive at accurate assessments of their abilities.

Team Play   During middle childhood, a new dimension is added to the quality of a child's play. Children begin to participate in team sports, and as a result, gain a sense of team success as well as personal success. Team sports are generally more complicated than the kinds of games described as group play in Chapter 7. The rules are so complex that they may require a referee or an umpire if they are to be followed accurately. In these sports, children join together into teams that remain together for the duration of the game. Some children join teams that play together for an entire season, such as Little League. Through participation in team play, one can see a "preworking" of the skills and orientations that will apply to the world of work and to the functioning of the family group. Three significant characteristics of the experience of team membership are relevant to development during this stage: (1) interdependence, (2) the division of labor, and (3) competition.

Interdependence

Team membership carries with it an awareness that one's acts may affect the success or failure of the entire group. There is a definite emphasis on winning and losing, and children may be ostracized or ridiculed if they contribute to a team loss. Although team sports do provide opportunities for individual recognition, it is quite clear that team success casts a halo over even the poorest players and team failure a shadow over even the best. In this sense, participation in team sports is an early lesson in *interdependence.* All of the team members rely on one another, and ideally, it will be to everyone's advantage to assist the weaker members in improving the quality of their play. The best coaches are noted for inspiring this sense of interdependence and mutual support among team members. They urge team members to work together to improve their skills. What often happens, however, is that the poorest players are scorned and scapegoated, particularly if the team loses.

In softball, the division of labor is readily observed. When the team is in the field, each child is assigned a position with a unique function. In order to get the other team out, each player must do his or her job and rely on the other team members to do theirs.

Division of Labor

The **division of labor** as an effective strategy for attaining a goal is experienced through participation with peers on teams. Children learn that each position on a team has a unique function and that the team has the best chance of winning if each player performs a specific function rather than trying to do the work of all the other players. The concept of the team encompasses the variety of activities in which each of the team members actually engages. A complementary concept is cooperation. Team members learn that if the team as a whole is to do its best, the members must help one another. Rather than playing all the roles, a team member tries to help each other member play his or her role as well as possible. Cooperation takes many forms: Members share resources, take time to help other team members improve their skills, plan strategies together, work together on the field, encourage each other, bring out the equipment, or clean up after the game. In many sports, there is a dynamic tension between competition and cooperation. Team members may compete with each other for a more desirable position or for the status of being the top player. At the same time, the team members know that they have to support each other, especially when they play against another team.

The team may well become an experiential model for approaching other complex organizations (Shears & Bower, 1974). Once children learn that certain goals can best be attained when tasks are divided among a group of people, they begin to conceptualize the principles behind the organization of social communities. They recognize that some children are better suited to handling one aspect of the task and others to handling another. Some children enjoy the skill development associated with team play, others enjoy learning the rules and devising strategies, others especially value peer companionship, and still others have a strong inner motive to compete and win (Klint & Weiss, 1987). The distribution of roles to fit the children's individual skills and preferences is a subtle element of the learning that is acquired through team play.

Competition

Finally, team play teaches children about *competition* and the importance of winning. In team sports, both sides cannot win; success for one side must result in failure for the other. If the team experience is a laboratory for learning lessons about the larger social community, this characteristic promotes a view of social situations in competitive terms. Some children come to think of business, politics, popularity, and even interpersonal conflicts as win-lose situations in which the primary goal is to beat one's opponents. The idea of a win-win strategy to resolve conflict is very foreign in this context.

Winning is a great "high." Many young adults have fond memories associated with winning an important game or a big match. They hope to reexperience the energy that occurs as a result of winning as they approach their adult activities. The metaphor of playing on a winning team is deeply interwoven into the world of work, helping to give focus and drive to day-to-day work-related obligations and tasks. When adults look back on their childhood play experiences, many recall the excitement associated with competition and continue to long for this excitement in their daily life. In one study of women in traditional and nontraditional professions, for example, more professional businesswomen and other women in nontraditional fields remembered experiences playing in competitive sports and being on teams with both males and females during their childhood (Coats & Overman, 1992).

In contrast to those who are energized by the challenges of competition, some children are especially sensitive to the pain of failure. The public embarrassment and private shame that accompany failure are powerful emotions. Some children will go to remarkable extremes to avoid failing. In team sports, each game ends with a winning and a losing side. Children who have a low sense of self-esteem are more likely to experience intense anxiety about losing in a competitive situation (Brustad, 1988). Involvement in team sports is guaranteed to bring with it the bitterness of losing and the commitment to avoid it at all costs, experiences that drive some children away from sports and into other domains of competence.

Team play has implications for both intellectual and social development. Children who play team sports learn to see themselves as contributors to a larger effort and learn to anticipate the consequences of their behavior for the group. Games that involve teams are generally so complex that children are called on to learn many rules, make judgments about those rules, plan strategies, and assess the strengths and weaknesses of the other players. All of these characteristics of participation in team sports can stimulate cognitive growth (Smith, 1986). In one study, for example, children were divided into soccer "experts" and soccer "novices" (Schneider & Bjorklund, 1992). The experts had an impressive depth of knowledge about the game of soccer and, when given a memory task involving soccer-related items, were able to use their expertise to perform the task at a high level.

Interest in sports and competitive team play has been used as a motivational "hook" to interest children in other areas of school ability. For example, in Columbus, Ohio, a former Ohio State University football player who also played professional football organized a summer camp for 5th- through 12th-graders. The focus of the camp was to combine sports with math and science education. The curriculum was developed to teach math and science for 2 1/2 hours each day and to spend the remainder of the time in practical applications in the area of sports. For example, the students might learn the principles of physics that account for why a baseball travels faster than a football, and then experiment with these principles on the ball field (Beaulieu, 1992).

In-Group and Out-Group Attitudes

All human societies observe distinctions between in-group and out-group attitudes and behaviors. The **in-group** members share common norms, goals, and values. They also share a common fate; in sports, for example, the team wins or loses as a team. Feelings of cohesiveness with and similarity to members of an in-group prompt behaviors supportive of that group's survival. Typically, individuals tend to distribute resources in such a way that members of their in-group receive more and members of the out-group receive less. However, when in-group norms emphasize fairness and reject discrimination, members are more likely to treat members of the out-group with fairness. Thus, in-group norms can influence the degree to which out-group hostilities are encouraged and expressed or suppressed (Jetten et al., 1996).

The **out-group** is any group whose goals are either in opposition to or inconsistent with the goals of the in-group. Any group may be perceived as an out-group, even though it does not actually pose any physical threat to members of the in-group. For example, students at one university may perceive students at another university as an out-group (i.e., the long-standing football rivalry between Ohio State University vs. The University of Michigan). Students enrolled in one program or major may view students in a similar but competing major as an outgroup (i.e., chemical engineers vs. electrical engineers). In experimental studies, in-groups and out-groups have been formed based simply on wearing a blue or yellow badge, or based on those with blue eyes and those with brown eyes. For sports teams, the out-group's goal of winning is in direct competition with the in-group's similar goal. We learn that moral principles that apply to members of the in-group do not necessarily apply to members of the out-group (Triandis, 1990). In the extreme, adults may justify killing a member of an out-group under conditions of declared war.

As a consequence of team play, children acquire both in-group and out-group attitudes. Children learn to value team goals and contribute to them. Identification with them may require a child to relinquish a personal goal, such as being first at bat, for the good of the team. In exchange, the child receives feedback from the other team members about skills and may improve them with the help of other team members. Children

There are many ways to experience the team concept in middle childhood. These children are in a community music and drama company. Being a member of a choir, acting group, band or orchestra are all ways that children learn to work together as a group toward a common goal.

learn to value their roles as elements in the larger system and to see their interdependence with the other players. They learn that team victories give them great personal satisfaction and that team defeats can be a source of frustration and depression.

The child learns to see the outcome of competition as a win-or-lose situation. The other team is the "enemy," and there is no alternative to trying one's hardest to defeat it. Antagonism toward the out-group is valued in team sports, and any attempt to assist the other team is seen as unethical.

Many older adolescents recall that in-group and out-group attitudes were formed even within their team. Although this may appear contradictory to the concepts of interdependence and group cooperation, it clearly happens. Certain children are "earmarked" as the true athletes of the team, and the others may feel like outsiders. Sometimes, parents who are influential in a community take steps behind the scenes to make sure their children are given special treatment. In these instances, the out-group children may feel that they not only are competing with members of the opposing team but also have to protect themselves from insults, pranks, and other efforts by their own team members to ostracize them.

Children may belong to more than one team, and those who are categorized as members of an out-group may change according to the situation. For example, Ryan and his friend Tom were on the school soccer team together, but they belonged to different summer baseball leagues. During the summer, they had to compete against each other, so it usually turned out that they spent more time together and were closer friends during the school year than they were during the summers.

Team experiences that elaborate in-group and out-group attitudes are socialization experiences that have both positive and negative consequences. Table 8.2 shows the in-group and out-group attitudes that result from experiences in team play. For most children, belonging to a team, making friends, learning new skills, and enjoying the sense of success associated with a collaborative effort are positive experiences of middle

---

TABLE 8.2   In-Group and Out-Group Attitudes that Develop Through Team Play Experiences

In-Group Attitudes	Out-Group Attitudes
The child learns:	The child learns:
1. To value and contribute to team goals.	1. That the outcome of competition is win or lose.
2. To relinquish personal goals for team goals.	2. That the other team is the "enemy."
3. To receive and use feedback and help from team members.	3. That one must try one's hardest to defeat the other team.
4. To value her or his role as an element in a larger system and to perceive interdependence.	4. That there is and should be antagonism between teams.
5. That team victories give personal satisfaction and team defeats bring frustration.	5. That assisting the other team is unethical.

childhood. However, we all know of instances where rivalries escalate into peer hatreds, children from neighboring schools turn against each other, and coaches humiliate and degrade children in order to instill a commitment to the team and a determination to win. Perhaps the question is whether, particularly in team sports, the focal point of the activity is to enhance children's natural impulses for competence and skill elaboration, or whether the team activity becomes a way for adults to vent their own frustrated needs for domination and power.

THE PSYCHOSOCIAL CRISIS: INDUSTRY VERSUS INFERIORITY

According to psychosocial theory (Erikson, 1963), the person's fundamental attitude toward work is established during middle childhood. As children develop skills and acquire personal standards of evaluation, they make an initial assessment of whether or not they will be able to make a contribution to the social community. They also make an inner commitment to strive for success. Some children are keenly motivated to compete against a standard of excellence and achieve success, while others have low expectations about the possibility of success and are not motivated by achievement situations. The strength of a child's need to achieve success is well established by the end of this stage (Atkinson & Birch, 1978).

Industry

Every culture has expectations for skill learning during middle childhood. Here a young boy is learning to polish semi-precious stones that will be used for inlay work. At age 10, he is considered old enough for this work and is proud of what he can accomplish.

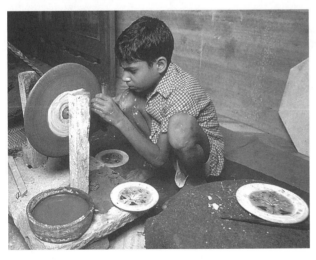

Industry is an eagerness to acquire skills and perform meaningful work. During middle childhood, many aspects of work are intrinsically motivating. The skills are new. They bring the child closer to the capacities of adults. Each new skill allows the child some degree of independence and may even bring new responsibilities that heighten his or her sense of worth. In addition to the self-motivating factors associated with increased competence, external sources of reward promote skill development. Parents and teachers may encourage children to get better grades by giving them material rewards, additional privileges, and praise. Peers also encourage the acquisition of some skills, though they may have some negative input with regard to others. Certain youth organizations, such as scouting and 4-H, make the acquisition of skills a very specific route to success and higher status.

In an effort to develop a measure of industry, Kowaz and Marcia (1991) described the construct as comprising three dimensions:

1. The cognitive component of industry was defined as the acquisition of the basic skills and knowledge valued by the culture.
2. The behavioral component of industry was defined as the ability to apply the skills and knowledge effectively through characteristics such as concentration, perseverance, work habits, and goal directedness.
3. The affective component of industry was defined as a positive emotional orientation toward the acquisition and application of skills and knowledge, such as a general curiosity and desire to know, a pride in one's efforts, and an ability to handle the distresses of failure as well as the joys of success.

Inferiority

Given the internal thrust toward skill building that is generated by motives for competence and external rewards for mastery, it may appear that there should be no real conflict at this stage. One might think that everyone is united in a commitment to the joy and fulfillment that accrue from experiences of competence.

What experiences of middle childhood might generate a sense of **inferiority**? Feelings of worthlessness and inadequacy come from two sources: the self and the social environment. Alfred Adler (1935) directed attention to the central role that organ inferiority may play in shaping a person's perceptions of his or her abilities. **Organ inferiority** is any physical or mental limitation that prevents the acquisition of certain skills. Children who cannot master certain skills experience some feelings of inferiority. Individual differences in aptitude, physical development, and prior experience result in experiences of inadequacy in some domain. No one can do everything well. Children discover that they cannot master every skill they attempt. Even the child who feels quite positive toward work and finds new challenges invigorating will experience some degree of inferiority in a specific skill that he or she cannot master (Box 8.3).

If we assumed that success in one area could compensate for failure in another, we would be safe in minimizing the effect of individual areas of inadequacy on the overall resolution of the psychosocial conflict of industry versus inferiority. However, the social environment does not reinforce success in all areas equally. During middle childhood, success in reading is much more highly rewarded than success in tinkering with broken automobile engines. Likewise, success in team sports is more highly valued than success in operating a ham radio. It is extremely difficult for a child who does not excel in the culturally valued skills to compensate through the mastery of others.

The social environment also generates feelings of inferiority through the process of social comparison. Particularly in the school setting, but even in the home, children are confronted by statements suggesting that they are not as good as some peer, sibling, or cultural subgroup. Children are grouped, graded, and publicly criticized on the basis of how their efforts compare with someone else's. The intrinsic pleasure of engaging in a task for the challenge it presents conflicts with messages that stimulate feelings of self-consciousness, competitiveness, and doubt: "I like playing ball, but I'm not as good as Ted, so I don't think I'll play." Children may refuse to try a new activity because they fear the possibility of being bettered by their peers (Crooks, 1988).

Finally, the social environment stimulates feelings of inferiority through the negative value it places on any kind of failure. Two types of failure messages that may contribute to feelings of inferiority have been described. One type consists of criticisms of the child's motivation. Such criticisms imply that, if the child had really tried, she or he could have avoided failure. The other type refers more specifically to a lack of ability. Here, the implication is that the child does not have the competence to succeed. This

---

BOX 8.3   DISORDERS OF CHILDHOOD THAT INTERFERE WITH SCHOOL SUCCESS

What happens when children have substantial difficulty accomplishing the tasks associated with basic areas of school achievement? The centrality of success in school-based learning for a positive resolution of the psychosocial crisis of industry vs. inferiority brings the problem of childhood disorders to our attention. Three groups of disorders are described here, each one posing significant challenges for academic and social success during middle childhood and beyond (American Psychiatric Association, 1994). Typically, these disorders become more disruptive as children encounter the increasingly complex demands of the school curriculum.

Learning Disorders

Learning disorders are diagnosed when a child's skills and measured abilities in reading, mathematics, or written communication are well below grade level and the level expected for the child's measured I.Q. Learning disorders have been identified in approximately 5% of public school children in the United States. These children are differentiated from others who have low performance because of mental retardation, poor teaching, or cultural factors that interfere with school performance. Typically, learning disorders are linked with deficits in the primary processing system, including speed and accuracy of information processing, attention, and memory. These deficits may be a result of genetic disorders, neurological damage during the prenatal period, or lead poisoning during childhood, but not all children with learning disorders have a history of these conditions. Children who have learning disorders commonly also suffer from low self-esteem and are more likely than other children to drop out of school.

Motor Skills Disorders

Approximately 6% of children in the age range 5 to 11 have a developmental problem in the area of motor skills. They are clumsy and delayed in the typical acquisition of early motor skills such as walking, running, tying their shoes, or using a scissors or knife. In later school years, they have trouble writing with a pencil or pen, are slow to develop skills in putting together puzzles or models, and their athletic skills, such as throwing and catching a ball, are delayed. These children are distinguished from others who have some broader medical diagnosis such as cerebral type of failure message is associated with a pattern of attitudes about the self that has been described as learned helplessness.

Learned helplessness is a belief that one's efforts have little to do with success or failure and that the outcome of attempting tasks is largely outside one's control (Seligman, 1975; Nelson, 1987). In a study of fourth-, fifth-, and sixth-graders, children were asked to verbalize their thoughts as they worked on various tasks. The children's verbalizations following failure showed a clear difference between the mastery-oriented children and the helpless ones. The mastery-oriented children were able to keep a positive attitude, increase their problem-solving efforts, and use their past mistakes to correct their approach. The helpless children began to blame themselves ("I never did have a good memory"). They emphasized the negative aspects of the task or criticized their own abilities and tried to find ways to escape from the situation (Diener & Dweck, 1980). Helpless children tend to discount their successes, and in response to even a few remarks about their lack of ability, generate a self-definition that leads them to take a pessimistic view of their future success (Phillips, 1984; Holloway, 1988).

In middle childhood, children are often shamed for their failure just as toddlers are shamed when they wet their pants. Earlier themes of doubt and guilt are intimately associated with feelings of inferiority. Messages about failure usually suggest that there is an external standard of perfection, an ideal, that the child did not meet. A few failures may generate such strong negative feelings that the child will avoid engaging in new tasks in order to preclude failure.

Failure in school and the public ridicule that it brings have been shown to play a central role in the establishment of a negative self-image. School represents the voice of the larger society. Children who continually fail to meet the standards set by school adults are likely to incorporate a view of themselves as failures. Sometimes, children defend themselves against the threat of failure messages by blaming others for their failures or by bragging to others that they can succeed in other ways. Much as it may appear that these children do not care about school or scorn school goals, the school remains a symbol of cultural authority. Failure in school can easily lead a child to feel locked out of the larger social community.

Extreme cases result in reluctance, self-doubt, and withdrawal of children who feel inferior. The resolution of the crisis in the direction of inferiority suggests that these

---

palsy. The delay in motor skills interferes with academic achievement to the extent that these children struggle with any kind of written assignment and have difficulty completing projects that require manual dexterity. They lack the satisfaction of excelling in physical activities because even simple motor skills such as running or playing catch are sources of frustration.

Communication Disorders

Some children experience a developmental delay in effective social communication. Difficulties may include delays in acquiring new vocabulary, oversimplified grammatical expressions, limited variation in sentence types and structures, problems in sound production such as lisping or omitting certain sounds in spoken speech, stuttering, and problems in understanding certain types of words, expressions, and grammatical constructions. About 3 to 5% of children have some type of developmental communication disorder that is distinct from mental retardation or a hearing impairment that influences speech. These difficulties interfere with academic performance especially since school learning involves ongoing communication of information and ideas. Children who

have communication disorders are also likely to be the target of peer teasing and social ridicule, leading to a pattern of social withdrawal or inappropriate social participation.

Learning disorders, motor skill disorders, and communication disorders are three of the more common childhood disorders among a variety of mental, emotional, and physical disabilities that young children face as they struggle to resolve the crisis of industry versus inferiority. Each of these conditions makes it more difficult for children to succeed in the daily tasks of schooling. Children who experience these disorders may find it difficult to carry out projects or complete assignments that others view as simple. They may also become targets of peer teasing, bullying, or rejection. As a result, they may define themselves as incompetent, inferior, or unable to learn. With appropriate diagnosis and effective intervention, however, children can learn strategies to overcome or compensate for their disabilities. Success in coping with a disability may, in fact, strengthen a child's self-confidence and provide a basis for beliefs of self-efficacy. Many children use the experience of coping with a disability as evidence that they can face and overcome other difficult challenges in their lives.

children cannot conceive of themselves as having the potential to contribute to the welfare of the larger community. This is a serious consequence. It makes the gradual incorporation of the individual into a meaningful social group difficult to achieve. The irony of the crisis at this stage is that the social community, which depends on the individual's motives for mastery for its survival, is itself such a powerful force in negating those motives by communicating messages of inferiority.

The Central Process: Education

Every culture must devise ways of passing on the wisdom and skills of past generations to its young. This is the meaning of education in its broadest sense. Education is different from schooling. The practice of separating formal educational experiences from the direct, intimate hands-on activities of home and community is only about 200 years old. Before the industrial revolution, most children became educated by participating with their parents in the tasks of home life, farming, commerce with neighbors, and participation in religious life (Coleman, 1987). In the case of the nobility, children often had tutors who supervised their education at home.

Today, however, schools bear the primary responsibility for education. Teaching, which began as an extension of the parental role, has become a distinct profession. In our culture, education is not the kind of continuous interplay between the skilled and the unskilled that it is in more traditional cultures. Formal learning takes place in a special building during certain hours of the day. To be sure, the success of that experience in promoting a child's skills and a sense of the self as a learner depends heavily on the ongoing involvement and commitment of family members (Coleman, 1987; Stevenson & Baker, 1987). For today's children, however, school plays a key role in the formation of a personal sense of industry.

During the elementary-school years, the goal of education is to help children develop the basic tools of learning. Central to this process is an introduction to the language of concepts, theories, and relationships that will allow them to organize their experiences (Cole & D'Andrade, 1982). Schools strive to develop verbal and analytic problem solving. Instruction focuses on rules, descriptions, and abstract concepts (Tharp, 1989). Children are exposed to a range of disciplines and to methods of inquiry for dealing with complex problems. Throughout the educational process, children are presented with problems of increasing difficulty. They are given many opportunities to practice their newly developing skills, receiving continuous feedback about their level of competence.

In addition to the acquisition of skills and knowledge, schools emphasize an approach to behavior that can be described as a combination of "citizenship," "social competence," and "study habits." Schools impart a code of conduct that is intended to facilitate the teacher's ability to guide students' attention, help children organize and focus on the tasks at hand, and foster a respectful, cooperative attitude toward adults and peers.

In general, the students' experiences of academic success are a product of the interaction between the teachers' background and ability to relate to students of various

The process of formal education has changed dramatically over the century. The design of the classroom, the roles of teacher and student, and the methods of instruction have all been targets of experimentation and modification. Yet the essential objectives—to impart skills, values, and information from one generation to the next—remain basically the same.

cultural backgrounds and the students' cognitive and noncognitive resources, especially their "citizenship" and "study habit" behaviors (Alexander et al., 1987). In a test of this notion, students' background characteristics, such as gender, ethnicity, and family income, and their basic skills, absenteeism, study habits, and appearance were related to their course work mastery and grades (Farkas et al., 1990). It was clear that teachers' evaluations of course work mastery and actual course grades were significantly related to their assessment of the students' study habits, in addition to their basic skills. In this particular analysis, it was the Asian-American students who benefited most by being rewarded for what teachers perceived to be high levels of class participation, effort, organization, and good-quality homework. As part of the school-based educational process, children are exposed to a combined agenda, focusing both on the elaboration of skills and on the acquisition of behaviors that are associated with success within the school culture.

Going to school results in exposure to adults who provide models for commitment to learning (Rutter, 1983). These adults have skills of their own that give children some sense of how much more there is to learn. Schooling, therefore, provides opportunities not only to gain mastery but also to acquire goals and standards for the development of more advanced skills.

Children are at a stage of cognitive development that permits them to grasp the fundamental principles of the problems that the school poses for them. The art of teaching lies in presenting problems at a level of complexity that is meaningful to each child but a step beyond their present ability level. As a result, learning becomes a tantalizing process in which the problems themselves lure the children into expending effort to solve them. The sense of this process is captured in an adult's reminiscences about his music teacher from high school:

> Beyond anything else, Griff wanted you to love and be as deeply affected by music as he was. His daughter, Ann, recently reminded me that when he was sometimes criticized for the problems students experienced with the difficult music he assigned, Griff would respond: "I don't care what a kid does to music. I care what the music does to the kid." Ever since he first convinced me to take voice lessons and seriously consider a career in music, Griff's visions have been a daily realization, as my life's work has, happily, been devoted to the arts. (Mosel, 1992, p. 12)

However, not all children approach schooling with the same expectations of success or the same trust in adults or in the formal education process. Some groups view education as the means to economic security, intellectual development, and political empowerment. Others are skeptical of teachers, schools, and education. They expect to be alienated from the learning process by a devaluing of their basic language, heritage, and beliefs. They believe that the only way to improve their condition is through major political and economic change. In their view, education per se will not empower them or their children. Children in these groups may conclude that the only way to retain their basic sense of self-confidence is to withdraw from school and try to establish their competence among their peers (Ogbu, 1987; Clark, 1991; Gregory, 1995).

An integral approach to providing a successful educational environment for all children is contextualization of the learning process. To **contextualize** instruction is to carry it out in ways that first draw on a child's existing experiences, previous knowledge, and concepts, and then expand that understanding in new directions. Contextualizing calls for a recognition that the classroom may be organized in a variety of ways: Children may engage in private study and small-group problem solving, for instance, as well as form a large group that listens and responds to the teacher. Contextualization may require the teacher to draw on the heroes and heroines, stories, songs, and myths of a cultural group in order to help children feel comfortable with more abstract concepts. It may also require the acknowledgment of different modes of expression, patterns of social conversation, and language. Finally, contextualizing may call for parents and other important community figures to become involved in the learning process so that the children are not isolated from their social community (Tharp, 1989; Tharp & Gallimore, 1988).

All these efforts may be particularly beneficial to groups who have been alienated from schooling or who approach schooling with mistrust. When the educational process is contextualized, children are strengthened in their own cultural identity. When their strivings for personal and cultural achievement are validated, the conflict that often develops between school professionals and members of minority cultures need not arise. Teachers and school administrators become more confident in the school abilities of children, and children become more willing to persist in order to build competence in school-related tasks (Comer, 1985).

THE PRIME ADAPTIVE EGO QUALITY AND THE CORE PATHOLOGY

Competence

The term **competence** has been used broadly and with diverse meanings in the human development literature. Ford (1985) offered a summary of five distinct uses of this concept:

1. Competence as an outcome measure reflecting one's effectiveness in a specific situation. For example, one might say that a child was competent at solving a specific problem or finding the necessary resources to meet his or her needs.
2. Competence as a personality type. This use of the concept is similar to "resilience," a term used to discuss children who successfully overcome stressful life circumstances and continue to perform well in school (Garmezy & Masten, 1991). Some individuals are described as competent, while others are described as vulnerable or incompetent.
3. Competence as a motivational system. Competence has been used in this sense by Robert White (1959) to describe what he believes is a universal tendency to strive toward higher and higher levels of mastery. According to White, once a child becomes competent at a certain level of functioning, there is an intrinsic push to move to a new, more challenging level. This notion is readily captured in children's fascination with computer games. These games are designed to take the player from one level or domain to the next, each time introducing new dangers, faster speed of play, or a new complexity of movements.
4. Competence as a composite of knowledge, skills, and abilities that permit successful adaptation. For example, one can refer to language competence as a global term encompassing the many different kinds of abilities that come into play in understanding the language of others, expressing one's own thoughts, and adapting to the language demands of specific situations. Each of the developmental tasks might be considered a domain for the development of age-related competence as defined by specific cultural expectations (Masten et al., 1995).
5. Competence as a belief in one's effectiveness. This definition refers to a general belief in one's ability to "get the job done." It is closely related to Bandura's concept of self-efficacy.

This last definition is closest to Erikson's (1982) notion of competence as the prime adaptive ego quality, a belief in one's ability to make sense of and master the demands of a situation.

> Competence, in turn, is the free exercise of dexterity and intelligence in the completion of tasks, unimpaired by infantile inferiority. It is the basis for cooperative participation in technologies, and it relies, in turn, on the logic of tools and skills. (Erikson, 1978, p. 30)

Competence provides the child with a deep confidence in his or her ability to engage new situations and do well. This idea is illustrated in a study that monitored children's perceptions of competence during school transitions from 5th to 6th grade

Lee is demonstrating his competence, not only in producing his invention, but in the confident and enthusiastic way he explains it to his classmates.

and from 6th to 7th grades. The children who had the highest levels of perceived competence also had the strongest positive feelings about how they were doing in school and showed the highest scores on a measure of intrinsic motivation. They wanted to be challenged by their school work, and they liked working independently and figuring things out for themselves. They expressed curiosity about the tasks, saying they would work hard because of their own interest rather than to please the teacher or get good grades (Harter et al., 1992).

Harter (1993) has suggested that there may be two distinct paths of development that emerge during middle childhood: daily monitoring of self-esteem and stable self-esteem. For one group, day-to-day self-esteem is based on current experiences of competence and social approval. For these children, feelings of self-worth vary depending on how people who are important to them treat them that day and on whether the child is comparing his or her accomplishments with someone who is quite a bit better, about the same, or not really as competent. The second group of children tend to have had many positive experiences of approval and competence in the past, which have led to a stable, positive sense of self-worth. As a result, these children are not as dependent upon the changing day-to-day conditions to sustain a positive feeling of worth. They tend to feel good about themselves, and thus enter new situations with a more positive, optimistic expectation of being liked and doing well. Sensing that they are competent, they leave this stage capable of using mastery and the resulting coping strategies to add to their repertoire of adaptive ego qualities—hope, will, and purpose—as they begin to encounter the new demands of early adolescence.

Children who have internalized a sense of competence love to learn and work. They are excited about developing new skills and optimistic about being able to achieve success. These children are the ones who sign up for new activities or start neighborhood clubs, want to be on two or three sports teams, look forward to field trips and school projects, and take pleasure in being asked to help with difficult tasks like planting trees along the highway, building a new playground, or raising money for earthquake victims. In contrast, some children feel a powerful sense of apathy or disinterest, which Erikson referred to as inertia.

Inertia

Inertia is the core pathology of middle childhood.

> The antipathic counterpart of industry, the sense of competent mastery to be experienced in the school age, is that inertia that constantly threatens to paralyze an individual's productive life and is, of course, fatefully related to the inhibition of the preceding age, that of play. (Erikson, 1982, pp. 76–77)

Children who leave early school age with a sense of inhibition fail to participate and engage much during middle childhood. These are not the students who try and fail repeatedly, nor are they the ones whose sense of competence must be reconfirmed daily. Instead, they are students who tend to be passive and withdrawn, never engaging psychologically with the demands of their schools or their communities. Children who leave middle childhood with a sense of inertia are likely to continue to be withdrawn and passive. They will have trouble instigating actions or changing the course of events in their lives. Further, they will not be likely to address challenges or problems by formulating plans of action, evaluating them, and then executing them. Children with a sense of inertia will not believe that they can master the challenges they face, and, thus, they are likely to be swept along by the tide of events.

We all experience periods of inertia, times when we cannot muster the energy, enthusiasm, or confidence to take action. We may become besieged by doubts about our competence and worth—doubts that can produce work blocks, writer's block, waves of fatigue, boredom, procrastination, or aimlessness. Typically, one can survive a few days or even weeks on "automatic pilot," doing the bare minimum to survive. And children may be able to get by for quite a while without exercising much energy or direction, especially if they are being sustained by parents and teachers. However, eventually life brings demands for change and expectations to meet new challenges that have never been faced before. At those times, children who are burdened with a pervasive sense of inertia will be unable to cope.

Applied Topic   ## VIOLENCE IN THE LIVES OF CHILDREN

In recent years, the problem of violence in families, schools, and neighborhoods has threatened to undermine the quality of the psychosocial development and educational attainment for many American children. Each year, an estimated 5 million children are exposed to violence in the form of direct physical abuse, domestic violence between their parents or other members of their household, and exposure to violent crimes in their neighborhood.

Consider the comparison presented in Table 8.3 between the kinds of problems public school teachers worried about in the 1940s and those they worry about today (Toch, 1993). In 1993, an estimated 3 million crimes were committed in or near public school buildings across the United States. In a national survey, 16% of eighth-graders said they feared for their safety when they were at school. Such fears may be stimulated in part by exposure to violence in the media, but they are also associated with real and increased levels of violence among children in schools. The New York City schools reported 5,761 violent incidents in 1992, prompting the mayor to announce a plan to station police officers in all of the city's public schools. Of the nation's eighth-graders, 9% had carried some type of weapon to school in the past month, and one estimate was that about 270,000 guns were in the nation's schools each day.

Many people focus on the availability of guns to children and youth as one source of the problem. But some children feel caught in a cycle of fear: In order to protect themselves from becoming victims, they decide that they need to be armed; on the other hand, the presence of weapons increases the likelihood of violence. Most children, whether inner-city or suburban, say they would have little difficulty obtaining a gun. Stolen guns are available for about $50. Furthermore, the federal government is having trouble restricting access to guns for minors. For example, Congress passed a Gun Free School Zones Act in 1990, but the law was declared unconstitutional. Meanwhile, school systems are spending scarce resources on security systems. In at least 45 urban school districts, children are screened by metal detectors. Some schools are installing bulletproof window glass. Like those in New York City, many school districts are increasing the number of police in and around their schools. In one elementary school in Connecticut, children saw two fellow students gunned down outside the school. The school principal explained, "Kids didn't want to go to class, they couldn't eat or sleep, they burst out crying. . . . We couldn't think about teaching reading, writing and arithmetic until we dealt with these problems (Toch, 1993, p. 34)."

TABLE 8.3 Public School Teachers' Perceptions of Top Disciplinary Problems: 1940 and 1990

1940	1990
Talking out of turn	Drug abuse
Chewing gum	Alcohol abuse
Making noise	Pregnancy
Running in the halls	Suicide
Cutting in line	Rape
Dress-code violations	Robbery
Littering	Assault

SOURCE: Toch, T., 1993.

Consequences of Exposure to Violence

Three consequences of exposure to violence are of especially grave concern. First, large numbers of children and youth are victims of violent crimes, with homicide the third leading cause of death for children ages 5 to 14 and the second leading cause of death for adolescents and young adults ages 15 to 24 in the United States (U.S. Bureau of the Census, 1996). Children who live in poor neighborhoods are especially vulnerable to exposure to violence. In these communities, the loss of an economic base with few people in stable or high-status occupations leads to takeovers by gangs and other organized criminal activities, especially drug traffic. Children are lured into dangerous forms of drug-related transactions, which make them targets of violence on the streets as well as victims of abuse by drug-addicted family members and youth (National Research Council, 1993).

A second consequence of exposure to violence is the increase in the number of children who are themselves aggressive and violent. The number of cases of juvenile violent offenses (criminal homicide, forcible rape, robbery, and aggravated assault) increased from 55,000 in 1983 to 122,000 in 1993 (U.S. Bureau of the Census, 1996). Roughly 28,000 children and adolescents have been identified as murderers (Perry, 1996). In the 1993–94 school year, 50% of public school children reported needing to use some type of strategy to protect themselves from harm from other students in schools. Forty-three percent of teachers in high-poverty schools and 19 percent of teachers in low-poverty schools reported that physical conflict among students was a moderate to serious problem in their schools. In the highest poverty schools, 13% of teachers reported problems involving students' possession of weapons (U.S. Department of Education, 1997).

A third consequence of exposure to violence is the disruption it produces in children's cognitive functioning and mental health (Osofsky, 1995). Children who have been severely abused or exposed to intense violence are now viewed as suffering from symptoms similar to posttraumatic stress disorder (Perry et al., 1995). Evidence suggests that these children preserve sensory and motor memories of the conditions associated with their trauma, which are then released under contemporary conditions of fear. In boys, these symptoms commonly reflect hyperarousal, including startle response, increases in heart rate, sleep disturbance, anxiety, and motor hyperactivity. In girls, the symptoms are more likely to be dissociation, gastrointestinal symptoms, and pain. Under threatening conditions, children who have been traumatized in the past automatically return to these disruptive states, making it difficult to access higher order problem-solving and reasoning skills.

According to the neurobiology of aggression, simple regulatory and impulse functions are governed by the more primitive, reactive areas including the brainstem and the midbrain. More complex functions of language and abstract reasoning develop later and are located largely in the subcortical and cortical areas. The capacity to modify and regulate impulses is a combination of the intensity of the signals emerging from the brainstem and the maturation of the expressive and coping strategies governed by the cortex (Perry, 1994). An overreactive brainstem that produces intense and frequent impulses may result from any one or a combination of factors including fetal exposure to alcohol and drugs, environmental exposure to lead, hormonal abnormalities, head injuries, and exposure to child abuse. When children are reared in a socialization environment of chaos, violence, parental aggression, and harsh and

The increase in violence in or near schools has led to new preventive steps. A teacher gives instructions as children participate in a playground drill to protect themselves in the case of random shooting.

abusive discipline, they lack the opportunity to develop empathy, self-control, and higher order problem-solving skills that might allow them to modulate their strong impulses (American Psychological Association, 1996). Thus, the emergence of violence in young children is viewed as a product of the interaction between an overly reactive lower brain and an underdeveloped cortex.

Prevention Strategies   The prevention of violence in society and reduction in exposure to violence among children have become significant public health issues (Dorfman et al., 1997). This perspective emphasizes a more detailed understanding of the contexts of violence from which strategies for prevention can be devised and evaluated. Rather than focusing solely on the criminal justice definitions and strategies for deterrence, a public health perspective invites collaboration in identifying many layers of prevention. We must learn more about what predisposes young children to respond with violence. And we must try to determine what kinds of socialization environments can counteract or help children control their aggressiveness. Furthermore, we must discover strategies to reduce violence in neighborhoods, schools, and in the media (Sampson et al., 1997). Several directions for prevention have been identified and require coordination:

1. Prevent prenatal and perinatal conditions that cause neurological damage and increase the biological vulnerability for violent behaviors.
2. Develop effective techniques for educating parents and teachers about socialization practices that help develop self-control, empathy, and perspective taking.
3. Develop effective techniques for teaching children how to handle and respond to insults, threats, and frustration.
4. Devise educational experiences that help children reframe cognitions and beliefs that lead them to interpret the behaviors of others as threatening.
5. Reduce exposure to televised violence.
6. Decrease children's access to guns.
7. Increase the sense of social control and cohesion in neighborhoods so that mutual trust is higher, people help one another more, and people are more willing to take steps to intervene when children are acting destructively.

Chapter Summary

During middle childhood, cognitive and social skills develop that are crucial to later life stages. A remarkable synergy occurs across the cognitive domains, bringing new levels of skill development, expanded information, and elaborate cognitive strategies for approaching and solving problems. Children apply their cognitive abilities not only in the academic, school-related domains, but also in an increased capacity for social cooperation, self-evaluation, and peer-group participation. As a result of the combination of cognitive and social skill development, children are able to make significant contributions to the social groups to which they belong. They are also likely to seek approval and acceptance from these groups.

Industry, as we have discussed, focuses primarily on building competence. It is quite clear that the family, peer group, and school all play their part in support of feelings of mastery or failure. However, in our society, school is the environment in which continuous attention is given to the child's success or failure in basic skill areas. The child's emerging sense of industry is closely interwoven with the quality of the school environment and the extent to which the child encounters experiences that both foster enthusiasm for new learning and provide objective feedback about levels of mastery. An understanding of skill development must combine an appreciation of the child's intellectual maturity with a sense of the significant motives that may influence his or her willingness to learn.

Although earlier psychological theories have not considered middle childhood influential in the process of psychological development, the events of this stage play an extremely important part in the psychology of the person. Issues of industry, mastery, achievement, success, social skills, cooperativeness, and interpersonal sensitivity are all salient themes during this stage. A person's orientation to friendship and work, two essential aspects of adult life, begin to take shape.

The applied topic illustrates the psychosocial context of violence. Children can be exposed to prenatal and perinatal risks that disrupt their neurological development. They may be embedded in a family system in which abusive or disorganized parenting reduces their ability to cope with threats or stress. Violence in the neighborhood, media, and school strengthen impulsive, reactive responses and make it increasingly difficult for children to draw upon their higher order reasoning skills to reinterpret or interrupt their sense of anger and threat. Access to weapons, especially guns, leads to new heights of destructive expression for these children.

End of Chapter Case

Irene is a Native American of the Menominee tribe who grew up on a reservation in northern Wisconsin. She recalls her experience of being sent to the mission boarding school and then the government boarding school.

I was in a day school at the reservation for awhile, and then the government had a habit of picking up kids and deciding who was going to the mission boarding schools and who was going to the government boarding schools. Parents really didn't have too much choice. First, I was sent to a mission school and my grandmother didn't like it. She felt the devil about it. My grandmother had no transportation and it was far away so I didn't see her often. Even if your parents brought your clothing you might not get a chance to wear it except when they came. You had to wear the school uniform all the time.

My grandmother knew they were going to whitewash us. She knew the methods they employ and she knew that we were going to have to learn to speak nothing but English because they were not going to let us speak our own language, and they would try to take our religion away. She said, "You have to keep our religion inside of you, in your heart." They wouldn't let us practice our religion because to the government employees we were just a bunch of pagans, uncivilized savages. So I had to keep within me all that I had learned from her.

We were so homesick at the schools. We'd sit and look out the windows at night and listen to the trains going by and just wish we were on those trains. Sometimes kids got sick from loneliness and were sent home. A lot of them couldn't hack it. Also, a lot of kids ran away. Sometimes they were caught; sometimes they

weren't. But if they were caught and brought back they were always punished with severe whippings. Sometimes the boys had their heads shaved. They'd cut all of our hair. None of us had long hair in the government school.

There were probably some pleasurable things, but I just don't remember too many of the pleasant things. I remember that they did waste an awful lot of Holy Water on me because it seemed like I was getting in trouble all the time. They tried to embarrass us girls or humiliate us if we were committing what they thought a wrongful act. Then the nuns would call the priest who would take us over to the boys' building. Then the priest had the pleasure of pouring Holy Water over our head in front of the entire male student body. Well, that got to be a habit for me. In fact, it was the only way I got to see some of my own relatives and my cousins. It got to be a pleasure. I had a chance to see the boys because the boys and girls were always kept separated.

Source: Buss, F.L., 1985.

Thought Questions

1. How does the case illustrate the interaction of cognitive, emotional, and social factors in the educational process?

2. How might Irene's grandmother and her own personality have buffered her from the negative experiences of being sent to boarding school during her middle childhood?

3. How might these experiences have influenced Irene's outlook on education and academic achievement?

4. What do you think may have been the outcome of the crisis of industry vs. inferiority for Irene?

5. What ideas does this case raise about the concept of contextualizing education?

Chapter 9

*R*apid physical changes, self-consciousness,
and a need for peer approval are all
characteristics of early adolescence. Here,
Picasso shows us the delicacy of youth, the
boy taking on a contemplative pose and
emerging, almost as a work of art, into
young manhood.

Early Adolescence (12–18 Years)

Chapter Objectives

- To describe the patterns of physical maturation during puberty for females and males, including an analysis of the impact of early and late maturing on self-concept and social relationships.
- To introduce the basic features of formal operational thought, highlighting the new conceptual skills that emerge and factors that promote the development of formal operational thought.
- To examine patterns of emotional development in early adolescence, including three examples of emotional disorders: eating disorders, delinquency, and depression.
- To describe the further evolution of peer relations in early adolescence, especially the formation of cliques and crowds, and to contrast the impact of parents and peers during this stage.
- To characterize the development of sexuality with a special focus on the transition to coitus, the formation of a sexual orientation, and a detailed review of the factors associated with pregnancy and parenthood in adolescence.
- To describe the psychosocial crisis of early adolescence—group identity versus alienation—the central process through which the crisis is resolved, peer pressure, the prime adaptive ego quality of fidelity to others, and the core pathology—isolation.
- To review the patterns of adolescent alcohol and drug use and the factors associated with their use and abuse within a psychosocial framework.

At this point in our discussion of life stages, we depart again from Erikson's conceptualization. His psychosocial theory views adolescence as a single stage unified by the resolution of the central conflict of identity versus identity confusion. Erikson's approach attempts to address the tasks and needs of children and youth ranging in age from about 11 to 21 within one developmental stage. From our own research on adolescents and our assessment of the research literature, however, we have come to the conclusion that two distinct periods of psychosocial development occur during these years: early adolescence (12–18 years) and later adolescence (18–24 years). This chapter discusses the stage of early adolescence, and Chapter 10 discusses later adolescence.

Early adolescence begins with the onset of puberty and ends with graduation from high school (or roughly age 18). This stage is characterized by rapid physical changes, significant cognitive and emotional maturation, sexual awakening, and a heightened sensitivity to peer relations. We have called the psychosocial crisis of this stage group identity versus alienation. Later adolescence begins at approximately age 18 and continues for about 6 years. This stage is characterized by new advances in the establishment of autonomy from the family and the development of a personal identity. The psychosocial crisis of this period is individual identity versus identity confusion. ❖

DEVELOPMENTAL TASKS

Physical Maturation

The onset of early adolescence is marked by rapid physical changes. These changes—a "height spurt," the maturation of the reproductive system, the appearance of secondary sex characteristics, and the redistribution of body weight—generally begin at age 11 in females and at age 13 in males. Variability in the rate of development is well documented (Brooks-Gunn & Reiter, 1990; Tanner, 1978/1990). The time from the appearance of breast buds to full maturity may range from 1 to 6 years for girls; the

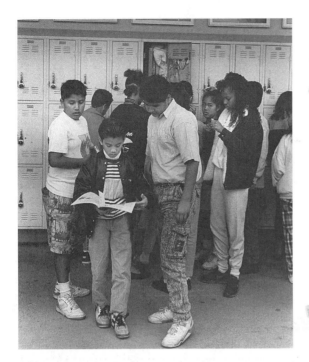

By 8th grade, the physical diversity of the peer group is quite noticeable. Differences in height, weight, and body shape have implications for popularity, leadership, and self-confidence.

male genitalia may take from 2 to 5 years to reach adult size. These individual differences in maturation suggest that during early adolescence, the chronological peer group is biologically far more diverse than it was during early and middle childhood.

Pubertal development influences psychological and social development in at least three ways. First, physical growth alters a person's actual *ability to perform tasks*. Early adolescents are taller and stronger than younger children and have greater coordination and endurance. Second, physical growth can alter how *one is perceived by others*. For example, early adolescents may be viewed as less cuddly or more threatening than younger children. Third, physical growth influences *how adolescents perceive themselves*. The physical changes may be positive, making them feel more like adults or, if the results are disappointing, may make adulthood harder to accept. The direction of influence depends largely on how the changes of puberty are viewed and marked by the society.

The degree to which one's body matches the desired or socially valued body build of the culture influences social acceptance by peers and adults. This match between body shape and cultural values also influences the future course of psychosocial development. Our culture gives special self-esteem advantages to muscular, well-developed males and petite, shapely females. In contrast, it detracts from the self-esteem of thin, gangling boys, underdeveloped girls, and overweight boys and girls.

Physical Changes in Girls

For girls, the onset of puberty occurs at approximately age 11—almost two years sooner than the parallel experience for boys (Table 9.1). The height spurt is usually one of the earliest of the pubertal changes. Initially, the increase in height may be embar-

---

TABLE 9.1 The Development of Primary and Secondary Sex Characteristics for Females and Males

Females	Average Age of Occurrence	Males
Onset of growth spurt	10–11	
Increased activity of oil and sweat glands (acne can result from clogged glands)	11	Increased activity of oil and sweat glands (acne can result from clogged glands)
Initial breast development	11–12	Onset of growth spurt
Development of pubic hair	12	
Onset of menarche (age range is 9–17) Development of underarm hair	12–13	**Growth of testes** Development of pubic hair **Growth of penis**
Earliest normal pregnancy	14	Deepening of the voice
Completion of breast development (age range is 13–18)	15–16	**Production of mature spermatozoa** **Nocturnal emissions** Development of underarm and facial hair
Maturation of skeletal system	17–18	Maturation of skeletal system Development of chest hair

Note: Primary sex characteristics are boldface type.

The primary sex characteristics relate to the development of genitalia and reproductive organs.

Secondary sex characteristics are other physical changes associated with puberty, such as body hair or breast development.

SOURCE: Adapted from Turner, J. S., & Rubinson, L., 1993.

rassing when a girl finds herself towering above her male classmates. To compensate, girls often slouch.

The greatest concern adolescent girls express about their bodies is the perception that they are too fat. In a national survey of adolescents' health concerns, 85% of adolescents said they thought that girls cared a lot about controlling their weight. In contrast, only 30% thought that boys cared a lot about controlling their weight. Despite the strong interest expressed in controlling weight, less than 10% of adolescents thought that their peers cared a lot about eating healthy foods. Among girls, strong concern about controlling weight was more likely to be linked to cigarette and drug use than to healthy eating patterns (Evans et al., 1995). In an attempt to ward off what they perceive as a tendency toward obesity, many early adolescent girls begin a process of strict and often faddish dieting. This strategy is ill-timed since their bodies require well-balanced diets and increased caloric intake during the period of rapid growth.

Concern about being overweight is culturally linked. For example, studies have found that girls who have strong religious backgrounds have a heavier real and ideal weight than less religious girls. African-American girls view a slightly heavier body image as ideal in comparison to white girls. Within African-American youths, one does not see the relationship of obesity and low-self esteem that is often observed in studies of white adolescents (Flynn & Fitzgibbon, 1996; Abell & Richards, 1996; Martin et al., 1988).

Obesity is related to activity level. For girls, one of the compounding factors in obesity is that they tend to reduce their activity level with age. In an ethnically diverse sample of over 550 girls in Grades 5–12, only 36% met the national goal for strenuous activity: 15 minutes of strenuous activity at least three times per week (Wolf et al., 1993). The amount of overall activity and strenuous activity decreased with age, and obesity was negatively correlated with activity. The study also revealed differences in exercise patterns across ethnic groups. Hispanic and Asian-American girls had significantly lower scores on activity level than African-American and white girls. Two cultural hypotheses were formulated to explain this pattern, but neither one has been tested. First, it is possible that strenuous physical activity is viewed as especially unfeminine by Asian-Americans and Hispanics. Second, it is possible that the slender body type is not seen as desirable by these ethnic groups; thus, there is less motivation to do strenuous exercise.

For girls, two of the most noticeable events of puberty are the development of breast buds and the onset of the menstrual cycle (menarche). To the average girl, the development of breast buds is a welcome sign of her growing maturity and femininity (Brooks-Gunn & Warren, 1988). Some girls begin to wear brassieres early in puberty in anticipation of the onset of breast development. Most girls are prepared by their mothers for menstruation. However, menstruation is often handled as a matter of hygiene rather than as a sexual transition (Logan, 1980). Many girls do not understand the relation of menstruation to reproduction. They simply accept their monthly periods as another sign of their femininity.

At the age when most girls begin to menstruate (approximately 12), their male peers may still be ignorant of this phenomenon. The girl is often put in a position of having to explain or hide the facts of her growth. Girls rarely tell their male peers or their fathers about the onset of menarche, but they do discuss it with their female friends and their mothers. The discrepancy in the onset of puberty in boys and girls and the uneven dissemination of information about it may make it difficult for a girl to fully accept the changes she is experiencing. The memoirs of Simone de Beauvoir (1959) reflect this ambivalence:

> We were staying with friends. . . . I awoke horror-stricken one morning: I had soiled my nightdress. I washed it and got dressed: again I soiled my underclothes. I had forgotten Madeleine's vague prophecies, and I wondered what shameful malady I was suffering from. Worried and feeling somehow guilty, I had to take my mother into my confidence: she explained to me that I had now become "a big girl," and bundled me up in a very inconvenient manner. I felt a strong sense of relief when I learned that it had happened through no fault of my own; and as always when something important happened to me, I even felt my heart swell with a sort of pride. (p. 101)

Most girls seem to react to menstruation with a mix of positive and negative feelings. The positive feelings reflect a pride in maturing and in the confirmation of their womanliness. The negative feelings reflect the inconvenience, some unpleasant symptoms, and the possible embarrassment of menstruation (Brooks-Gunn & Reiter, 1990). Negative feelings are especially likely if a girl matures early, at age 9 or 10.

Generally, girls are more dissatisfied than boys with their physical appearance and their overall body image. For girls, self-consciousness and dissatisfaction with their appearance reach their peak between the ages of 13 and 15. By 18, the more satisfied a young woman is with her body image, the more likely she is to have a positive outlook on social relationships with her family, her peers, and people in general (Petersen et al., 1984; Rauste-von Wright, 1989).

Physical Changes in Boys

Boys generally welcome the changes involving increased height and muscle mass that bring them one step closer to adult maturity. On the one hand, a mature physique usually brings well-developed physical skills that are highly valued by peers and adults alike. On the other hand, the period of rapid growth may leave a boy feeling awkward and uncoordinated for a time. This awkwardness results because growth does not take place at the same rate in all parts of the body. One particular discrepancy is the time lag between the height spurt and the increase in muscle strength. For boys, the increase in the rate of growth in height starts at about 12½ years and reaches a peak at around age 14. The peak increase in muscle strength, however, usually occurs about 12–14 months after the peak height spurt (Brierley, 1993). This time lag results in a temporary period during which a boy simply cannot accomplish what he might expect, given his height. Psychologically, this awkward period poses challenges to the boy's self-esteem. He simply looks funny and out of shape, and he may be easily embarrassed. He cannot fully accept his new body image at first, and doubts whether others can.

The onset of the growth of the testes and the penis also poses important challenges for early adolescent males. Testicular growth is one of the first signs of puberty in boys,

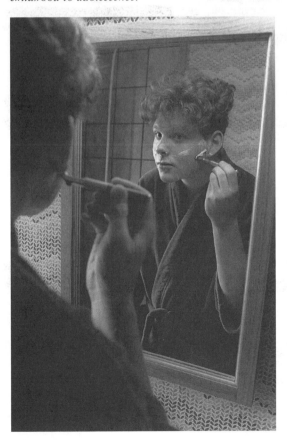

Shaving is one of the positive rituals marking a boy's transition from childhood to adolescence.

but they are generally not well prepared by their parents with information on the maturation of their reproductive organs (Bolton & MacEachron, 1988). Specifically, they are not taught about spontaneous ejaculation and may be surprised, scared, or embarrassed by it. The sexual connotation of the event may make it difficult for boys to seek an explanation from their parents. They are left to gain information from friends and reading material or to worry in private about its meaning. For many boys, spontaneous ejaculation provides an important clue to the way in which physical adult sexuality and reproduction are accomplished. The pleasure of the ejaculation and the positive value of the new information that it provides are counterbalanced by a mild anxiety (Gaddis & Brooks-Gunn, 1985; Marsiglio, 1988; Adegoke, 1993). This is only one of the developments that arouse ambivalence in many boys during early adolescence.

A third area of physical development that has psychological and social meaning for the boy is the development of secondary sex characteristics, particularly the growth of facial and body hair. In many societies, the equipment and the ritual behaviors associated with shaving are closely linked to the masculine sex role. Most boys are eager to express their identification with this role, and they use the slightest evidence of facial hair as an excuse to take razor in hand. The ritual of shaving not only provides some affirmation of the boy's masculinity but it also allows him an acceptable outlet for his narcissism. As he shaves, it is legitimate for him to gaze at and admire his changing image. In some societies, the ability to grow a mustache or a beard is a sign of one's masculinity. In these cultures, boys cultivate and admire their mustaches and/or beards as evidence of their enhanced male status.

The Secular Trend

Along with the genetic influence on growth and sexual maturation, the environment plays an important role in the eventual attainment of one's growth potential. A **secular growth trend** is a decrease over time in the average age at which physical maturation takes place (Van Wieringen, 1978). Changes in hygiene, nutrition, and health care have contributed to an earlier growth spurt over the past century. Children aged 10–14 increased in height by an average of 2 to 3 centimeters every decade from 1900 to 1960. Adult height is not necessarily greater due to this increase; it is simply attained at an earlier age.

Other evidence of a secular trend is the shift in age at menarche. There is some controversy about the extent of this shift. Data reported by Tanner (1978/1990) showed a decrease in the average age at menarche from the 1950s' average age (13.5 to 14) to the 1970s' average age (12.5 to 13). At present, the mean age at menarche is 12.3, but the range is from 9 to 17. Age at menarche varies among countries and even among socioeconomic groups within a country. Historical records based on Roman, Islamic, and medieval writings suggest that females have matured in the age range of 12–14 for many centuries (Bullough, 1981). Lack of precise records and the confounding of health and social class with age at menarche make it difficult to confirm long-term historical trends. Lower age at the onset of menarche is associated with an improved standard of living, including health, diet, and social class (Tanner, 1981). The secular trend has been documented across ethnic group samples that have had comparable access to adequate nutrition (Brooks-Gunn & Reiter, 1990).

What is the relevance of the secular trend for understanding the development of contemporary adolescents in postindustrialized societies? Reproductive capacity and physical adult stature occur at a younger age than at the turn of the century, but full engagement in the adult society requires more training, education, and complex preparation than in the past. Thus, adolescence is prolonged, with more time to experience the risks of unwanted pregnancy, the sense of being in a marginal social status, and the disruptions in the transition from childhood to adulthood. The concept of the secular trend alerts us to the importance of the psychosocial context of physical development. Not only are peers experiencing diverse patterns of growth, but parents and grandparents may also be reacting to a discrepancy between their children's development and their own timetable for growth. What is more, because the period of reproductive capacity starts earlier than it did 50 years ago, young people must cope with special challenges in the expression and regulation of their sexual impulses. One consequence of the earlier onset of puberty is that adolescents may find themselves in potentially high-risk situations at a relatively young age. Given the kinds of risks inherent in a technological society, it is no wonder that adolescent exposure to risk behaviors is a major contemporary health concern (Box 9.1).

Individual Differences in Maturation Rate

The onset of puberty and the rate of change in physical maturation vary. Early and late maturing have psychological and social consequences for both boys and girls. Boys who mature later than their age-mates may experience psychological stress and develop a negative self-image (Clausen, 1975; Mussen & Jones, 1957). Late-maturing boys are treated as if they were younger than they really are. They may become isolated from their peers and may behave in a silly, childish manner in order to gain attention.

On the other hand, boys who mature earlier than their age-mates tend to have an advantage. They develop a positive self-image, in part because they are likely to be given increased responsibility by their parents and teachers. They are generally more satisfied with their bodies, feel more positive about being boys, and are likely to be more involved in school activities by the 10th grade than are late-maturing boys (Blyth et al., 1981). Fifth- and sixth-grade boys who are more physically mature report more

BOX 9.1   SAFETY AND RISK BEHAVIORS IN ADOLESCENCE

One of the stereotypes of adolescence is that it is a time of risk taking. Of course, not all youth expose themselves to risks, and youth are not alone in taking risks. However, some disturbing data suggest that contemporary youth are experiencing high rates of preventable injuries. For instance, the leading cause of death among U.S. adolescents is accidents, especially motor vehicle accidents, and the second is homicides (U.S. Bureau of the Census, 1996). In fact, the death rate due to homicides is higher for adolescents than for any other age group.

In addition to risk behaviors that are associated with mortality, adolescents are known for their rejection of safety precautions. The age range 16–18 is the peak period for the initiation of smoking, drinking, and the use of illicit drugs. One study estimated that one in seven adolescents in the United States has a sexually transmitted disease; 47% of American youth are sexually active and they or their partner do not always use a contraceptive. About 26% of eighth-graders and 38% of tenth-graders reported riding in a car with a driver who was intoxicated or using drugs (Quadrel et al., 1993; Benson, 1992).

Weapon-carrying has also increased dramatically since the middle 1980s. A study of weapon-carrying in two junior high schools in Washington, D.C. found that, among males, 47% had carried knives and 25% had carried guns over the prior two weeks. Among females, 37% had carried knives and 4% had carried guns (Webster et al., 1993). This problem has become so serious that reducing weapon-carrying among adolescents has been formally included as one of the national health objectives for the year 2000.

Adolescents appear to engage in to a wider range of high-risk behaviors between the ages of 12 and 17 and use fewer safety precautions. In a study of over 2000 junior-high and high-school students in rural and urban areas of Iowa, four areas of safety behavior were assessed. The percentage of adolescents who used a safety belt while riding in the front or back seat of a car, or who used any type of helmet while riding a bicycle, moped, skateboard, or snowmobile decreased with age. Similarly, safety strategies associated with swimming, such as checking the depth of the water before diving or always swimming with a partner, decreased with age. At the same time, the percentage who drove a car while drunk or high on drugs increased with age, even when opportunities to drive, which normally increase with age, were taken into account (Schootman et al., 1993).

It's hard to believe that these two fifth grade girls are the same age. Carla has had an early growth spurt. In comparison, Andrea still looks quite childlike. Girls enter puberty at age 10 or 11, but the rate of change is highly variable.

positive daily emotions, better attention, more feelings of being strong, and some greater awareness of states of tension (Richards & Larson, 1993). In general, early-maturing boys experience the kinds of positive mood and sense of centeredness that are reflected in the social qualities of leadership and personal confidence.

Both early- and late-maturing girls experience some tension with regard to their physical development. Since girls mature about two years earlier than boys, the early-maturing girl stands out among all her male and female age-mates. Her stature and breast development violate the cultural equation of femininity with petiteness. Early onset of menstruation is especially stressful, resulting in heightened self-consciousness and anxiety (Hill, 1988). Early maturers are less likely to have been prepared for the onset of menstruation, and they are less likely to have close friends with whom they can discuss it. Early pubertal maturation may result in feelings of social isolation for girls.

Several studies suggest that early pubertal onset is a source of stress for girls (Kornfield, 1990; Caspi & Moffitt, 1991). They experience higher levels of conflict with their parents and are more likely to report depression and anxiety (Wierson et al., 1993). There is some evidence that early-maturing girls earn lower grades and lower scores on academic achievement tests. They are also more likely to be identified as behavior problems in school (Blyth et al., 1981). Early-maturing girls start dating earlier and perceive themselves as more popular with boys than do late-maturing girls. Some studies report that early-maturing girls are more likely to engage in high-risk, promiscuous sexual behavior. In general, however, the timing of the transition to puberty in and of itself is not a strong predictor of a girl's emotional well-being. Rather, timing interacts with other events, such as school transition, family conflict, or peer acceptance, to influence how a girl will construct the meaning of this physical transition (Brooks-Gunn & Reiter, 1990; Richards & Larson, 1993).

Formal Operations

As the body undergoes significant changes during puberty, so too does mental activity. Early adolescents begin to think about the world in new ways, as thoughts become more abstract. Young people are able to think about several dimensions at once rather than focusing on just one domain or issue at a time. Thinking becomes more reflective, and adolescents are increasingly aware of their own thoughts as well as the accuracy or inaccuracy of their knowledge. Adolescents are able to generate hypotheses about events that they have never perceived (Keating, 1990). These complex cognitive capacities have been described by Jean Piaget as **formal operations** (Inhelder & Piaget, 1958; Piaget, 1970, 1972; Chapman, 1988).

Studies of the physical maturation of the brain suggest that two distinct phases of new development occur in adolescence: one is linked with the visuoauditory, visuospatial, and somatic systems from about 13 to 17 and the other with the frontal executive functions from about age 17 to 21. Figure 9.1 highlights the peaks in cortical development during childhood and adolescence, pointing out the new mental abilities that are associated with each new phase of development.

Piaget's Theory of Formal Operational Thought

Piaget proposed a qualitative shift in thinking during adolescence from concrete to formal operational thought. In the period of concrete operational thought, children use mental operations to explain changes in tangible objects and events. In the period of formal operational thought, young people use operations to manipulate and modify thoughts and other mental operations (Piaget, 1972). A central feature of formal operational reasoning is the ability to consider all the possible combinations of propositions and their interrelations. For example, in thinking about trying to get a part-time job, adolescents may consider the number of hours they want to work, their access to transportation, the kind of work they want to do, and the kind of work they think they are qualified for before they start filling out applications. They are able to create different scenarios about working, based partly on what they want and partly on what they know, and then modify their plan based on new information they get about available jobs.

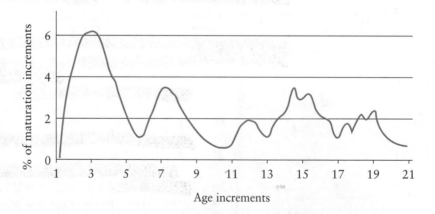

Age increments

Peak 1. Ages 1–6. Rapid brain growth across several areas. Associated with ability to form images, use words, place things in serial order, development of problem-solving tactics.

Peak 2. Ages 6–10. Peak growth in the sensory-motor regions. Associated with operational functions such as determining weight and reasoning about mathematical problems.

Peak 3. Ages 10 $^1/_2$–13. New growth in the visual and auditory regions of the brain. New abilities to perform calculations and to perceive new meanings and functions for familiar objects.

Peak 4. Ages 13–17. New growth in the visuoauditory, visuospatial, and somatic systems of the brain. New ability to review mental operations, find flaws in their reasoning, and use information to revise their problem-solving strategies.

Peak 5. Ages 17–21. New growth in the frontal executive region. New capacities to question and evaluate information, form new and original hypotheses integrating their own experiences with information taken from other sources.

FIGURE 9.1

Peak periods of cerebral maturation
Source: Allison, M., 1992, October/November.

An important characteristic of formal operational thought is the ability to raise hypotheses to explain an event, and then to follow the logic that a particular hypothesis implies. One of the classic experiments that Piaget and Inhelder designed to demonstrate the development of hypotheticodeductive reasoning involves the explanation of the swing of a pendulum. The task is to find out what variable, or combination of variables, controls the speed of the swing. Four factors can be varied: the mass of the object, the height from which the pendulum is pushed, the force with which it is pushed, and the length of the string. To investigate this problem, it is necessary to begin by isolating the separate factors and then varying only one factor at a time while keeping the others constant. As it happens, only the length of the string influences the speed of the pendulum. The challenge then is to demonstrate that the length of the string accounts for the speed and that the other factors do not. Children in the stage of concrete operational thought have difficulty coordinating the interaction among four separate variables and may lose track of what is being varied and what is held constant. After trying one or two strategies, they may simply give up. In contrast, being able to use formal operational thought, a child can create a matrix of variables and test each factor separately to evaluate its contribution (Inhelder & Piaget, 1958; Flavell, 1963).

Six Characteristics of Formal Operational Thought

Six new conceptual skills emerge during the stage of formal operations (Table 9.2) (Neimark, 1982; Demetriou & Efklides, 1985). Each one has implications for how adolescents approach interpersonal relationships and the formulation of personal plans and goals as well as for how they analyze scientific and mathematical information. First, adolescents are able to manipulate mentally more than two categories of variables at the same time; for example, they can consider the relationship of speed, distance, and time in planning a trip (Acredolo et al., 1984). They can draw upon many variables to explain their behavior as well as that of others. Second, they are able to think about things changing in the future. They can realize, for instance, that their current friendships may not remain the same in the years ahead.

Third, adolescents are able to hypothesize about a logical sequence of possible events. For example, they are able to predict college and occupational options that may be open to them, depending on how well they do in certain academic course work in high school. Fourth, they are able to anticipate consequences of their actions. For instance, they realize that if they drop out of school, certain career possibilities will be closed to them.

Fifth, they have the capacity to detect the logical consistency or inconsistency in a set of statements. They can test the truth of a statement by finding evidence that supports or disproves it. They are troubled, for example, by the apparent contradictions between statements such as "All people are equal before the law" and the reality that people who have more money can afford better legal representation and are likely to have different experiences with the legal system than those who are poor.

Sixth, adolescents are able to think in a relativistic way about themselves, other individuals, and their world. They know that they are expected to act in a particular way because of the norms of their community and culture. Adolescents also know that in other families, communities, and cultures different norms may govern the same be-

---

TABLE 9.2   New Conceptual Skills that Emerge During the Stage of Formal Operational Thought

1. Ability to manipulate mentally more than two categories of variables simultaneously.
2. Ability to think about the changes that come with time.
3. Ability to hypothesize logical sequences of events.
4. Ability to foresee consequences of actions.
5. Ability to detect logical consistency or inconsistency in a set of statements.
6. Ability to think in relativistic ways about self, others, and the world.

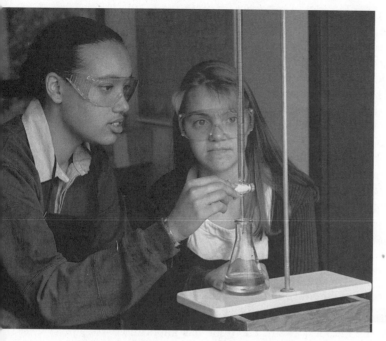

The opportunity to manipulate variables in an experimental situation stimulates formal operational thought. At the same time, the capacity for hypothesis testing makes it possible for students to evaluate the results of their experiments. How might you design chemistry experiments so that they are most likely to foster formal operational reasoning?

havior. As a result, the decision to behave in a culturally accepted manner becomes a more conscious commitment to the society. At the same time, it is easier for them to accept members of other cultures, because they realize that these people are the products of societies with different sets of rules and norms (O'Mahoney, 1989).

These qualities of thought reflect what is possible for adolescents rather than what is typical. Most adolescents and older adults approach problem solving in a practical, concrete way in their common, daily functioning. However, under the most supportive conditions, more abstract, systematic, and self-reflective qualities of thought can be observed and bring a new perspective to the way adolescents approach the analysis of information and the acquisition of knowledge (Fischer, 1980; Eckstein & Shemesh, 1992; Fischer et al., 1993).

Egocentrism

The term *egocentrism* refers to the child's limited perspective at the beginning of each new phase of cognitive development (Piaget, 1926; Inhelder & Piaget, 1958). In the sensorimotor phase, egocentrism appears as an inability to separate one's actions from their effects on specific objects or people. As the scheme for causality is developed, the first process of **decentering** occurs. Infants recognize that certain actions have predictable consequences and that novel situations call for new, relevant behaviors. For example, one cannot turn the light on by turning the knob on the radio. At each developmental stage, decentering is a process that allows the person to approach situations from a more objective, analytic point of view.

In the phase of preoperational thought, egocentrism is manifested in an ability to separate one's own perspective from that of the listener. When a 4-year-old girl tells you about something that happened to her at the zoo, she may explain events as if you had seen them too. When a 3-year-old boy is explaining something to his grandmother over the phone, he may point to objects in the room, unaware that his grandmother cannot *see* over the phone lines.

The third phase of heightened egocentrism occurs in the transition from concrete to formal operational thought. As children develop the capacity to formulate hypothetical systems, they begin to generate assumptions about their own and others' behavior that will fit into these systems. For example, an early adolescent boy may insist that cooperation is a more desirable mode of interaction than competition. He argues that cooperation ought to benefit each participant and provide more resources for the group as a whole. This boy may become angry or disillusioned to discover that teachers, parents, and even peers seek competitive experiences and appear to enjoy them. He may think, "If the cooperative system is so superior, why do people persist in their illogical joy in triumphing over an opponent?" This kind of egocentrism reflects an inability to recognize that others may not share one's own hypothetical system.

In early adolescence, decentering requires an ability to realize that one's ideals are not shared by all others. We live in a pluralistic society in which each person is likely to have distinct goals and aspirations. Early adolescents gradually discover that their neat, logical life plans must be constantly adapted to the expectations and needs of relevant others. As they develop the flexibility of thought that accompanies formal operational perspective taking, their egocentrism usually declines.

Early adolescent egocentrism has two characteristics that may affect adolescents' social interactions as well as their problem solving: preoccupation with their own thoughts and a belief that others are also preoccupied with their thoughts. Early adolescents may become somewhat withdrawn and isolated as the domain of their consciousness expands. Thoughts about the possible and the probable, the near and the distant future, and the logical extension of contemporary events to future consequences all flood their minds. David Elkind (1967) described one aspect of this process as the formation of a **personal fable,** an intense investment in one's own thoughts and feelings, and a belief that these thoughts are unique. Adolescents may conclude that they alone are having certain insights or difficulties and that no one else could understand or sympathize with their thoughts. This tendency to withdraw into their own speculations may cut off access to new information or ideas and inhibit social interaction.

Second, early adolescents may assume that they are the center of interest of others' thoughts and attentions. Elkind (1967) referred to this as an **imaginary audience.** Instead of considering that everyone is equally wrapped up in his or her own concerns and plans, early adolescents envision their own thoughts as being the focus of other people's attention. This subjectivity generates an uncomfortable self-consciousness that makes interaction awkward. There is some question about the cognitive processes involved in this heightened self-consciousness. On the one hand, a preoccupation with the idea that others are watching your every move may be an important element in decentering, directing attention to others and how you may be viewed in their eyes. Thus, self-consciousness stimulates cognitive perspective-taking. On the other hand, an increased ability to consider the point of view of others and their expectations for your behavior may increase self-consciousness.

Egocentrism is a problem not only during the adolescent years. At each new phase of expanding awareness, people tend to rely heavily on their own experiences and perceptions in order to minimize the anxiety associated with uncertainty. Part of the progress of formal thought implies a reliance on reason over experience. Further, we have more confidence in what we know than in what we can see or hear. Thus, we can find ourselves trapped in an egocentric perspective. We may interpret new experiences as examples of familiar concepts rather than as novel events. Further, we may reject evidence for an argument because it does not support an already carefully developed explanation. The business of casting around for new evidence and explanations is a lifelong challenge. It is much easier to rely on earlier assumptions than to continually question one's perspective.

Factors that Promote Formal Operational Thought

Several environmental conditions facilitate the development of formal operational thought and reduce egocentrism. First, early adolescents begin to function in a variety of role relationships that place both compatible and conflicting demands on them. Among these role relationships are son or daughter, worker, student, friend, dating partner, religious believer, and citizen. Early adolescents experience firsthand the pressures of multiple expectations for behavior. At times, for example, expectations for the student role may be at odds with those for the child or the friend role. Ongoing interactions with parents provide a powerful stimulus for cognitive development, especially when parents encourage children to examine their assumptions, to find evidence to support their arguments, and to evaluate the sources of information as they approach problems in daily life (Dunham et al., 1988). Participating in a variety of roles also facilitates relativistic thinking by demonstrating that what is acceptable and valued in one situation may not be in another (Chandler & Boyes, 1982).

Conversations with parents often force adolescents to rethink their assumptions or come up with support for their decisions. Although this is not always pleasant, these kinds of interactions are an important stimulus for more advanced reasoning.

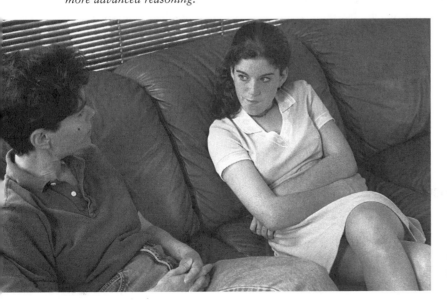

A second environmental factor is the adolescent's participation in a more heterogeneous peer group (Looft, 1971). When children move from their community elementary school to a more centralized junior high and high school, they are likely to become acquainted with other students whose family backgrounds and social class are different from their own. In working and playing with these friends, they realize the extent to which their expectations for the future differ from those of their new acquaintances and their present values are shaped by the families and neighborhood from which they come.

The use of formal operational skills can be observed in adolescent discussions of peer-related issues and in the formation of intimate/romantic relationships, a domain that is new and requires a wide range of hypothesis raising and testing. We have observed our own children as they communicate with friends in person, over the phone, and through notes, helping each other answer questions and generate multiple explanations for a given situation. They may use these explanations to put themselves in a more favorable or desirable position, to gain a person's confidence, to soothe or comfort a distressed friend, or to wiggle out of an uncomfortable circumstance. An example of a conversation between a 15-year-old girl and her best friend follows:

> Cindy: I'm so frustrated I can't stand it. Before Sean and I started to date, he was nice to me. I enjoyed being with him. He said hello to me in the halls; we'd walk along together. We talked about all kinds of things. Now that we're going out, he seems rude and uncaring. When we're with other people, he jumps in when I start to talk and his eyes say "be quiet." He breezes by me in the halls sometimes and when we talk about things (if we talk) he acts as if he is always right. I don't think he cares about me anymore. What's going on?
>
> Donna: I know he likes you because he tells me. Maybe you should talk to him and tell him what he does and how it makes you feel.
>
> Cindy: No, if I do that he'll get mad and he won't like me anymore. Why don't you talk to him?
>
> Donna: No, that wouldn't do any good because then he would know you talked to me about this and he would not like it or he would just say what he thinks would make him look good.

This conversation goes on and on. . . . During the conversation, many possible scenarios are proposed about why this behavior is occurring and many hypotheses are raised about what could be done. The girls project likely outcomes of each set of possible actions and attempt to evaluate the results of each. Finally, a tentative conclusion is reached: Boys treat girls differently when they are involved in a boyfriend/girlfriend relationship than when they are not. In the "just friends" situation, there is a tendency to treat the girl as an equal, but in the boyfriend/girlfriend situation there is a tendency for the boy to expect that he should dominate the girl. A solution is derived: Cindy must shape up Sean. Because she still likes him so much and wants to go out with him, she must try to tell him how she feels and hope he will change his behavior so that it is supportive and comfortable for her. She must be the one to do this. And since Sean really does like her and may not realize how his behavior is affecting her, chances are good that he will respond to Cindy's approach rather than lose her as a girlfriend.

The context of friendship between Cindy and Donna allows Cindy to trust discussing her problem with Donna so that they can examine it fully. It also allows Donna to disagree with Cindy without terminating the conversation. Thus, Cindy can get a somewhat different point of view on her situation and the two friends together can explore a personal problem on a more objective, rational basis than Cindy probably could have done on her own.

The third condition that fosters the development of the cognitive skills of early adolescence is the content of the high school curriculum. Courses in science, mathematics, and language formally expose the student to the logical relationships inherent in the world and introduce them to the hypotheticodeductive style of reasoning. The fine arts and the humanities foster conceptions of ways in which the world has been or might be. They expand the repertoire of representational thought. According to Gardner's model of multiple intelligences discussed in Chapter 8, the visual arts provide a means of integrating and innovating spatial intelligence with interpersonal intelligence. The more complex and differentiated academic environment of the high school can bring substantial gains in conceptual skills for those students who become actively engaged in its academic programs (Kuhn et al., 1988; Linn et al., 1989; Adey & Shayer, 1993).

Although schooling can be a vehicle that promotes formal operational reasoning, not all school experiences are equally effective in promoting abstract, hypothetical reasoning. Keating (1990) described the following characteristics that are important in creating a cognitively stimulating school experience:

> Students need to be engaged with meaningful material; training of thinking skills must be embedded in a knowledge of subject matter, for acquisition of isolated content knowledge is likely to be unproductive; serious engagement with real problems has to occur in depth and over time; students need experiences that lead to placing a high value on critical thinking, to acquiring it as a disposition, not just as a skill; and many of these factors occur most readily, and perhaps exclusively, when students have the opportunity for real, ongoing discourse with teachers who have reasonably expert command of the material to be taught. (p. 77)

The truth is that the key factors that are necessary in order to stimulate abstract reasoning and critical thinking may not be present in much of what students encounter in the high school classroom.

One does not expect to see a mature scientist or a profound philosopher by the end of early adolescence. A young person's formal operational reasoning awaits further encounters with a specific discipline and its full range of significant problems. However, the opportunity for cognitive growth during this period is extensive. Adolescents are able to generate novel solutions and apply them to current life challenges. They also are able to be increasingly objective about the problem-solving process and to gain insight into their own mental activity.

Criticisms of the Concept of Formal Operations

In Piaget's theory of cognitive development, formal operational reasoning is viewed as the final stage in the development of logical thought. A number of scholars have pointed to limitations in this construction. First, questions have been raised about the extent to which there is a qualitative, stagelike consolidation in the use of formal reasoning. Although most scholars would agree that formal operational thinking exists and does characterize the nature of mature, scientific reasoning, many studies show that adolescents and adults typically do not function at the formal operational level, and that their use of formal reasoning is inconsistent across problem areas. For example, Neimark (1975) followed changes in the problem-solving strategies of adolescents over a 3½-year period. Even the oldest subjects in her study, who were 15, did not apply formal operational strategies across all problems. Although performance across problems was not consistent, there did appear to be a progression through levels of problem-solving approaches during the years from 11 to 15. Neimark (1982) described these levels as: (1) no rule, (2) limited rules, (3) collection of rules or unelaborated principles, and (4) general principles. Research has not been able to confirm Piaget's claims that thinking becomes consistently more propositional across problem areas or that formal operational reasoning is a universal characteristic of adolescent reasoning in a variety of cultures (Keating, 1990). Even Piaget speculated that people were most likely to use formal operational reasoning primarily in the area of their greatest expertise.

A second criticism of formal reasoning as a construct is that it is not broad enough to encompass the many dimensions along which cognitive functioning matures. In the model of the developing mind presented in Chapter 8, there are three domains in which growth takes place—the information processing system, the hypercognitive system, and the five specialized structural systems. Increases in speed, efficiency, and capacity of information storage have been documented during the period from ages 11 to 14 (Thatcher et al., 1987). It is likely that improvements in logical reasoning are in part a result of being able to handle greater quantities of information more quickly and efficiently. In addition to development in basic processing, there are gains in knowledge about a number of topics, both as a result of schooling and increased mastery in specific areas of expertise. One consequence of the combination of greater information processing capacity and a broader knowledge base is that hypercognitive processing improves. Adolescents can hold a problem in mind and approach it from several different angles, assessing which domain offers the most promising avenue for a solution (Keating, 1990). Knowledge in each specialized system expands, bringing not only increases in logic but increases in the understanding of the procedures or strategies that are most likely to work for a given problem (Mayer, 1992). Since there are such wide variations in the use of formal operational thought, other information processing approaches have been proposed that help account for how individuals use, modify, or elaborate existing information to generate, select, and critically evaluate solutions to new problems (Wood et al., 1995).

Finally, some scholars claim that formal operational thought does not represent the apex or end point of adult thought and reasoning. As adults mature, they face many problems in which abstract logical-mathematical reasoning must be integrated with the special emotional and social demands of the circumstances. The problem may need to be reframed to suit the situation. The solution may need to be evaluated for its impact on many interrelated parties. The cognitive processes associated with psychotherapy, diplomacy, and spiritual leadership are all examples of what might be considered postformal reasoning (Torbert, 1994; Richards & Commons, 1990).

Emotional Development

Descriptions of adolescence often refer to new levels of emotional variability, moodiness, and emotional outbursts. Clearly, adolescents are more aware than younger children of gradations in their emotional states and are able to attribute them to a wider range of causes. However, some researchers have questioned whether adolescence really brings the peaks and valleys of emotional intensity that are stereotypically linked to this time of life.

In an attempt to assess this question, researchers gave an electronic paging device to children and adolescents aged 9–15 and asked them to describe their emotional state every time they were paged (Larson & Lampman-Petraitis, 1989). Over one week, each participant responded about 37 times. The variability of emotions was not found to increase with age. However, both the boys and the girls in the older group expressed fewer extremely positive emotions and more mildly negative emotions than did the children in the younger group. In a subsequent study using similar methods, daily emotions were monitored in relation to children's pubertal status (Richards & Larson, 1993). Both boys and girls with a more mature body shape at each age reported more frequent thoughts and feelings about love. Pubertal development was slightly related to increased feelings of anger in girls, but in general, physical maturation was not closely linked to patterns of specific emotions in girls. In boys, the relationships between pubertal development and emotions were much stronger. Those boys who were

Adolescents become aware of a new variety of emotions. Girls are likely to turn inward, experiencing feelings of self-doubt, guilt, or depression. Boys are more likely to experience irritability and anger. What might account for these differences?

more mature reported more experiences of feeling frustrated, tense, and "hyper." They also reported a more positive mood, a greater ability to focus their attention, and more feelings of strength. Thus, in boys, pubertal changes were associated with both positive moods and a restless irritability.

Adolescents are aware of a more differentiated palette of emotions than they have experienced before. Among the more troublesome of these emotions are anxiety, shame, embarrassment, guilt, shyness, depression, and anger (Adelson & Doehrman, 1980). Adolescent girls are likely to have a heightened awareness of new levels of negative emotions that focus inward, such as shame, guilt, and depression; boys, in contrast, are likely to have a heightened awareness of new levels of negative emotions that focus on others, such as contempt and aggression (Stapley & Haviland, 1989; Ostrov et al., 1989).

Given the likelihood of a more differentiated range of emotions during adolescence, a major task during this time is to gain a tolerance of one's emotionality. This means accepting one's feelings and not interpreting them as a sign of "going crazy" or "being strange." Adolescents who are highly sensitive to social expectations or overly controlled about expressing or accepting their feelings probably experience a sense of shame about their emotional states. Attempts to rigidly control or defend oneself against feelings are likely to result in social alienation or maladaptive behaviors.

In a study of the coping style of adolescents, Moriarty and Toussieng (1976) summarized the basic orientation to emotions that is achieved during this life stage. The subjects were described as either **sensers** or **censors**. The sensers were willing to be influenced by new experiences. They preferred to seek out new activities, engage people, and question inconsistencies. They accepted their emotions and sought out experiences that would modify their values. The censors, on the other hand, preferred to limit their sensory experiences. They tried to clarify their parents' values by discovering what was acceptable in society. They had limited peer interaction and were uninvolved in school. The censors rejected experiences or ideas that did not confirm their traditional views. Both sensers and censors are normal, healthy adolescents whose coping styles will work in our society. However, the two orientations reflect rather distinct solutions to the challenge of integrating emotional experiences into the self-concept.

Many of the problems of early adolescence are linked to the overly controlled or impulsive expression of emotions. Three topics considered here are eating disorders, delinquency, and depression.

Eating Disorders

Roughly 5 million Americans suffer from eating disorders, 90% of whom are women (DeAngelis, 1997). The two most common are anorexia nervosa and bulimia. **Anorexia** is characterized by a fear of gaining weight, refusal to maintain a minimally normal body weight, and perceptions of one's body as overweight in general or in specific areas (Yates, 1989). Weight loss is viewed as an important accomplishment, and is accompanied by increased self-esteem. Anorexia is found primarily in girls, with the symptoms beginning either shortly after the weight spurt that accompanies puberty or at about age 18. Adolescents with this condition focus their behavior on weight loss. They take an obsessive, determined position in rejecting most foods, accompanied by dieting, fasting, and/or excessive exercise. In addition, they tend to have a distorted perception of their body image, seeing themselves as much fatter than they really are. The outcome of this condition is a potentially life-threatening loss of key body functions as a result of starvation (Millstein & Litt, 1990).

Bulimia involves spurts of binging and overeating followed by the use of different strategies to prevent the absorption of food, such as induced vomiting, the use of laxatives, or strenuous exercise. Bulimia has an incidence of between 1 to 3% in the female adolescent population and is experienced somewhat more commonly by males than is anorexia. Individuals who suffer from bulimia are usually ashamed of their eating and often eat in secret. Their eating is often experienced as a frenzy or an intense loss of control, followed by self-criticism and depression (American Psychiatric Association, 1994).

The origins of eating disorders are not fully understood. Many authors implicate the cultural infatuation with thinness as a stimulus of this condition. A recent public policy initiative is focusing on creating a more positive acceptance of people of various body types and shapes, with less focus on thinness. In addition, advertisers are being urged to regulate ads promoting weight loss programs and products to children and adolescents, as well as to disclose more accurately the amount of weight that can be lost. Physicians are being urged to rely less heavily on height-weight tables that do not take into account body type and the wide range of individual differences in healthy weight (DeAngelis, 1997).

In addition, a preoccupation with body appearance may be provoked by the relatively rapid physical changes associated with puberty. The psychoanalytic view is that eating disorders link back to fear of sexual maturity and are an unconscious strategy to delay entry into adulthood. The family system perspective emphasizes the child's control or overcontrol by parents. Eating disorders, in this view, are a way for the child to exert control or power over one key arena in a context where little power is permitted. In addition to these theories, some clinicians describe the adolescents who suffer from anorexia as having difficulty accepting and expressing their emotions. Compared with adolescents who have other types of emotional disorders, anorexics show less emotional expressivity, greater timidity, and more submissiveness. Anorexics have been described as "duty bound, rigidly disciplined, and moralistic with underlying doubts and anxious hesitancy" (Strober, 1981, pp. 289–290).

Studies of long-term outcomes following diagnosis of anorexia find that appropriate treatment can restore normal body weight. However, a large number of young people who suffered from anorexia as adolescents continue to have social and emotional difficulties, especially problems in empathy, difficulty recognizing and identifying their emotions, obsessive-compulsive disorders, and anxiety (Herpertz-Dahlmann et al., 1996; Hsu, 1996). Over a 10-year period, typically 5.6% of anorexics die from the disorder (DeAngelis, 1997).

Delinquency

In contrast to adolescents whose overcontrol of emotions causes problems, others are impulsive and react strongly to any emotionally arousing environmental stimulus. They seem to be unable to modify the intensity of their reactions. One consequence of this impulsiveness committed by juveniles is involvement in delinquent acts. Delinquent offenses are actions for which an adult could be prosecuted. In addition, there are offenses such as truancy, running away, or under-age drinking, which can involve adolescents with the legal system. Many adolescents commit some type of delinquent act that goes undetected. For most young people, the fear and guilt that follow a delinquent act are usually enough punishment to prevent further violations.

In some adolescents, however, committing several delinquent acts weakens the ability to impose social constraints on such behavior, and the involvement in delinquency intensifies. In 1994, roughly 19% of the total arrests in the United States involved people aged 15–18, but this age group accounted for 31% of the serious crimes, such as motor vehicle thefts, arson, burglary, and murder (U.S. Bureau of the Census, 1996). One national survey categorized about 30% of males and 10% of females as serious violent offenders. These adolescents had committed three or more violent crimes in a one-year period sometime before their 18th birthday. The boys committed more crimes than the girls, and their crimes tended to be more serious (McCord, 1990; Elliott et al., 1989). In a longitudinal study of over 4500 high school seniors and high school dropouts in California and Oregon, over half the sample reported being involved in some type of violent behavior, 65% of the males and 41% of the females. Those youth who were persistently involved in violent acts were also significantly more likely to be involved in other high-risk delinquent behaviors such as selling drugs, committing felonies, and using alcohol, marijuana, and/or other drugs. These extremely violent youth were also more likely to drop out of school and to have other mental health problems. The findings of this study suggest that efforts to curb youth violence must pursue a differentiated approach. In addition to focusing on the serious offenders who have multiple problems and are likely to come to the attention of school and law enforcement authorities, our society needs to find ways to reach the large number of youth who express periodic violence in family and peer contexts (Ellickson et al., 1997).

Since many young people now carry some type of weapon with them, especially knives and guns, questions are raised about the emotional correlates of this type of behavior. Are children who carry weapons primarily preoccupied with fear and motivated by self-defense, or are the weapons an extension of their aggressive motives? In one analysis, teens who carried guns were found to differ from those who carried

In an effort to protect students and staff, many schools have installed metal detectors or security guards at the entrance to the school. What might be some positive and some negative consequences of this kind of monitoring?

knives (Webster et al., 1993). For females, the more people she knew who had been victims of violence, the more likely she was to carry a knife. For males, the two strong predictors of carrying a knife were: having been threatened with a knife and having been frequently involved in fights, although not usually being the one who started them. It appears from these findings that carrying a knife is linked to self-protective motives. Too few females carried guns for the researchers to identify predictors for that group. For the males, however, correlates of carrying a gun included having been arrested before, having been involved in many fights and being one of the people who started them, and believing that shooting people was justifiable in certain circumstances. Gun carrying was linked to a much more violent, aggressive orientation and could not really be construed as a strategy for self-protection.

Depression

One of the emotions that has received considerable attention in the recent literature is depression (Garrison et al., 1989; Robertson & Simons, 1989). **Depression** is used in at least three different contexts (Petersen et al., 1993). First, one can speak of **depressed mood,** which refers to feelings of sadness, a loss of hope, a sense of being overwhelmed by the demands of the world, and general unhappiness. Almost everyone experiences depression at some time or another, describing it as the "blues," feeling "down in the dumps," or feeling "low." People who suffer from depression may experience other symptoms, including worrying, moodiness, crying, loss of appetite, difficulty sleeping, tiredness, loss of interest in or enjoyment of activities, and difficulty concentrating. Depression may range from mild, short-lived periods of feeling sad and discouraged to severe feelings of guilt and worthlessness. A depressed mood may be predictive of more serious emotional disorders, but it is not in itself a clinical diagnosis. One estimate is that about 35% of adolescents, a higher percentage for girls than for boys, have experienced a depressed mood in the previous six months.

The second use of the concept of depression is the notion of a **depressive syndrome.** This term refers to a constellation of behaviors and emotions that occur together. The syndrome usually includes complaints about feeling depressed, anxious, fearful, worried, guilty, and worthless. Roughly 5% of the normal population experiences this syndrome.

The third use of the concept of depression is its central role in clinical diagnosis. For a diagnosis of **major depressive disorder,** the adolescent will have experienced five or more of the following symptoms for at least two weeks:

> Depressed mood or irritable mood most of the day; decreased interest in pleasurable activities; changes in weight or perhaps failure to make necessary weight gains in adolescence; sleep problems; psychomotor agitation or retardation; fatigue or loss of energy; feelings of worthlessness or abnormal amounts of guilt; reduced concentration and decision-making ability; and repeated suicidal ideation, attempts, or plans of suicide. (Petersen et al., 1993, p. 156)

Factors Associated with Adolescent Depression. Adolescents face a number of challenges that make them vulnerable to depression. At present, no single theory is accepted as the explanation for depression. Some research points to genetic factors associated with the clinical diagnosis of depression. However, in recalling the research on the interaction between depressed mothers and their infants discussed in Chapter 5, it is hard to separate genetic and environmental factors in the etiology of clinical depression.

Parental loss or rejection has been found to increase an adolescent's vulnerability to depression (Robertson & Simons, 1989). In one longitudinal study of the consequences of economic pressures on families, a connection was shown between the family's economic stresses and increased parental depression, which produced heightened marital conflict, increased hostility and less nurturance toward the children, and subsequent adjustment problems in adolescent daughters, especially problems with hostility and depression (Conger et al., 1993).

In addition, adolescence is a time of life when one is likely to encounter loss, failure, and rejection as well as an accumulation of negative events and hassles. Even though scholars no longer view adolescence as a unique period of emotional turmoil, it is fairly clear that adolescents are often exposed to more negative events than are younger children. They are more aware of what other people are experiencing and since more is expected of them, there is more to worry about. Adolescents have a wider circle of relationships than younger children, through which they are exposed to more problems, expectations, and disappointments. They report experiencing hassles in the following domains: social alienation (disagreements with teachers, disliking other students); excessive demands (not enough time to meet responsibilities, not enough time for sleep); romantic concerns (dissatisfaction in a romantic relationship); decisions about one's personal future (important decisions about a future career); loneliness and unpopularity (being ignored); assorted annoyances and concerns (money problems, disagreement with a boyfriend or girlfriend); social mistreatment (being taken advantage of, having one's trust betrayed); and academic challenge (struggling to meet other people's standards of performance at school) (Kohn & Milrose, 1993). Within this list, peer relations, including boyfriend-girlfriend relations and the many elements of interpersonal experience that are part of being a member of a friendship group, play a central role. Poor peer relationships in early adolescence are a significant risk factor for depression (Petersen et al., 1991).

Adolescents are relatively inexperienced in coping with these kinds of stressors. They may not have developed strategies for interrupting or reducing the feelings of grief or discouragement that are likely to accompany stressful life events. The combination of pressures on parents, especially marital conflicts and economic pressures, plus exposure to their own failures, disappointments, and loss of relationships with peers and in school, are clearly linked to a negative mood in adolescents, especially sadness and depression (Larson & Ham, 1993). Feelings of depression may also be intensified by accompanying hormonal changes (Susman et al., 1991). Young people may become convinced of their worthlessness, and this distortion of thought may lead them toward social withdrawal or self-destructive actions.

Gender Differences in Depression. Experiences of depression appear to be more common in adolescent girls than boys. This gender difference has been found in comparisons of the depression scores of Anglo, African-American, and Mexican-American and other Hispanic adolescents (Roberts & Sobhan, 1992). In addition, Mexican-American adolescents appear to have a higher incidence of depression than the other ethnic groups. Evidence of a greater risk for depression among females continues to be found in studies of adults (Jones-Webb & Snowden, 1993).

Although prepubescent boys are somewhat more likely to show signs of depression than prepubescent girls, this pattern reverses during adolescence (Nolen-Hoeksema et al., 1991; Petersen et al., 1991). Several ideas have been offered to explain this reversal. First, at puberty, girls become critical of their bodies, especially in their concerns about being overweight and unattractive. This attitude may lead to prolonged feelings of dissatisfaction with the self and a consequent depression. Second, girls tend to look within for explanations of their failures and problems, blaming them on their own lack of ability, whereas boys tend to focus on factors outside the self, blaming other people or unfair conditions for their failures.

Third, although girls tend to receive strong social support from their parents and friends, they are also somewhat more sensitive to the problems that people in their support network are having. Girls who have higher levels of caring and are likely to become involved in the problems of their close friends are more vulnerable to depression (Gore et al., 1993). The negative experiences that a girl's best friend or members of her

Ironically, the fact that girls are likely to try to comfort and support their friends during periods of emotional turmoil makes them more vulnerable to negative moods and depression. How might adolescent girls protect themselves from this negative consequence of close friendships?

friendship group are going through tend to add to her own negative mood. Fourth, girls tend to persist in trying to account for negative events or to explain them, so that these events have more time to disturb them. Boys tend to distract themselves with other thoughts or just to "put them out of their mind" (Nolen-Hoeksema, 1987). Fifth, in adolescence, girls may begin to experience numerous microaggressions spawned by the sexist views of teachers, male peers, and even their parents. These negative messages create a picture of a world in which the adolescent girl is viewed as less important, less competent, and less entitled to her own independent views than her male peers. The result is increased feelings of insecurity, lack of confidence, and new feelings of worthlessness.

Depressed mood is of special concern during early adolescence for several reasons (Maag et al., 1988; Brooks-Gunn & Petersen, 1991). First, it is associated with adolescent suicide (Box 9.2). Although depression is not always a precursor to suicide, there is a link between depression and suicidal thoughts. Second, depression is linked to alcohol and drug abuse. Adolescents who are struggling with strong feelings of depression may turn to alcohol or other drugs to try to alleviate or escape from these feelings. Third, adolescents who are depressed may be unable to participate effectively in the classroom, so that their academic performance deteriorates. Finally, depression during adolescence may be a forerunner of severe depression later in adulthood.

Membership in the Peer Group

The importance of peer interaction for psychosocial development was pointed out in Chapters 7 and 8. During early adolescence, the peer group becomes more structured and organized than it was previously (Newman, 1982). The implications of the indi-

---

BOX 9.2   SUICIDE IN ADOLESCENCE

Suicide at any age is deeply troubling, but adolescent suicide is cause for special anguish and soul searching. Why would a young person, with all of his or her adult life ahead with its endless possibilities and opportunities, choose death? Is it possible that the prospect of becoming an adult is becoming so threatening and terrifying that some young people would rather die than grow up?

Public concern over adolescent suicide has been increasing in response to the change in the suicide rate among adolescents since the early 1960s. Suicide, which is the third leading cause of death among adolescents aged 15–19, rose from 3.6 per 100,000 in 1960 to 11 per 100,000 in 1993 (Garland & Zigler, 1993; U. S Bureau of the Census, 1996). Over this period, the suicide rate for the total population stayed relatively constant. In a comparison of racial and ethnic groups, Native Americans had the highest rate, especially among Apaches (Berlin, 1987). Also, white males were more likely to commit suicide than were African-Americans. Some claim that the rate of 11 per 100,000 is an underestimate, since there is a social stigma to reporting a death as suicide and there are financial consequences to identifying a death as a suicide rather than as an accident. It is suspected that a significant number of adolescent deaths involving automobile accidents were actually suicides.

Although the number of successful suicides among adolescents is still relatively small, an additionally large number of adolescents have attempted suicide. One estimate suggests that there are 50 suicide attempts for every suicide-related death (Sells & Blum, 1996). Statistics show that males are four times as likely as females to complete a suicide, but females are three times as likely to attempt

suicide. National surveys find that from 6 to 13% of adolescents say they have attempted suicide at least once; however, few have actually received any medical treatment or mental health care following the attempt (Garland & Zigler, 1993). And beside actual suicide attempts, a national Gallup survey found that 15% of adolescents had considered suicide (Ackerman, 1993). Instances of suicides prompted by widely publicized suicides, copycat suicides, and clusters of friends who commit suicide as part of a pact suggest that suicidal ideation can be triggered by a variety of external events as well as by internal depression or as a reaction to humiliation or loss.

In attempting to understand the causes of suicide, primary risk factors have been identified (Garland & Zigler, 1993). These factors were reconstructed by studying the lives of adolescents who committed suicide. However, they may not be very useful in predicting whether a particular individual will commit or attempt suicide. These risk factors include:

Drug and alcohol abuse
A prior suicide attempt
A history of psychiatric illness
A history of antisocial, aggressive behavior
A family history of suicidal behavior
The availability of a firearm

In addition to these factors, there is usually some precipitating event. A shameful or humiliating experience, a notable failure, and rejection by a parent or a romantic partner are all examples. Use of drugs that alter cognitive functioning and decrease inhibitions, coupled with easy access to a gun, suggest one likely path from suicidal ideation to suicidal action.

vidual's relation to the peer group become more clearly defined. Before the adolescent period, it is important to have friends but not so important to be a member of a definable group. The child's friends are often found in the neighborhood, local clubs and sports teams, community centers, or classrooms. Before adolescence, friendship groups are homogeneous. They are the product of informal associations, residential area, and convenience. In early adolescence, young people spend more time away from home. Dyadic friendships become an increasingly important source of social support, and the quality of these friendships changes (Levitt et al., 1993).

Cliques and Crowds

crew

In addition to changes in friendships and in the quality and functions associated with close friends, new layers of peer relationships, sometimes known as the clique and the crowd, begin to take shape. **Cliques** are small friendship groups of five to 10 friends (Ennett & Bauman, 1996). Usually these groups provide the framework for frequent interactions both within school and in the neighborhood. Adolescents usually do not refer to their group of friends as a clique, but the term is used to connote a certain "tightness" among the members. They hang out together, know about each others' families, plan activities together, and stay in touch with each other from day to day. Within cliques, intimate information is exchanged and, therefore, a high degree of loyalty is expected. In the transition from middle school or junior high school to the larger, more heterogeneous environment of the high school, there is a reordering of students according to a variety of abilities and a corresponding reordering of friendship groups. It may take some time for adolescents to find their clique, the members of which may change from time to time over the first year or two of high school.

Possess posse

Crowd refers to a large group that is usually recognized by a few predominant characteristics, such as their orientation toward academics, involvement in athletics, use of drugs, or involvement in deviant behavior. When the "leading crowd" of a particular neighborhood elementary or middle school goes off to a more centralized high school, the members of that group find that they are, to some degree, competing with the "leading crowds" of the other neighborhood schools from which the high school draws its students. After some contact at the high school, the several "leading crowds" are reordered into a single "leading crowd." Some students find that their social positions have been maintained or enhanced, whereas others find them to have deteriorated somewhat as a result of a reevaluation of their abilities, skills, or traits.

Popularity and acceptance into a peer group at the high school may be based on one or more of the following characteristics: good looks; athletic ability; social class; academic performance; future goals; affiliation with a religious, racial, or ethnic group; special talents; involvement with drugs or deviant behavior; or general alienation from school. Although the criteria for membership may not be publicly articulated, the groups tend to include or exclude members according to consistent standards. Furthermore, physical attractiveness continues to be a powerful force in determining popularity. For particularly attractive and unattractive adolescents, physical appearance may be a primary determinant of social acceptance or rejection, respectively (Brown, 1990).

Some of the well-known crowds present in American high schools today are called *populars, gangstas* or *hoods, brains, jocks, druggies,* and *dorks or nerds*. A group called the *mods* or *progressives* expressly rejects this traditional social stratification. The progressives emphasize individuality and the value of forming a personal identity. In setting themselves apart from the other groups, however, they form a new one (Stevenson et al., 1987). In racially diverse schools, it is not uncommon for students to identify peer groups based specifically on ethnic categories, such as the Asian group, the Mexican-Americans, and the African-Americans. The crowds can be identified within a school setting by their dress, their language, the activities in which they participate, and the school settings in which they are most likely to congregate. The peer culture in any high school is determined largely by the nature of the peer groups that exist and their characteristic patterns of interaction (Youniss et al., 1994). These large, visible groups provide an array of prototypical identities. Although many adolescents resist being labeled as part of one crowd or another, they usually recognize that these categories of students exist in their school.

In one analysis of over 3000 students in Grades 9–12 drawn from nine high schools in two different states, nine crowd types were identified with a high degree of regularity across the schools. These crowds were labeled by the students as jocks, populars, popular nice, average-normal, brains, partyers, druggies, loners, and nerds (Durbin et al., 1993). These crowds had distinct profiles with respect to their school grades, use of alcohol and drugs, involvement in delinquent acts, involvement in fights and carrying weapons to school, and perceptions of how involved they were in the social life at the school. Thus, the youth culture, as it is sometimes called, actually comprises a number of subcultures, each endorsing somewhat different attitudes toward adults and other authority figures, school and academic goals, and drugs and deviant behavior, and expressing different orientations toward partying and social life (Brown et al., 1993).

Peer groups have boundaries. Membership in cliques is relatively stable, but always vulnerable to change. One description suggests that these groups have some central members who serve as leaders, others who are regularly included in clique activities, and still others who are on the periphery. At the same time, there are the "wannabes," who would like to be part of the clique but for one reason or another are never fully included (Hansell, 1985). Some students try to push their way into a certain group, while others may fall out of a group. Dating someone who is a member of a clique or getting involved in a school activity (such as athletics or cheerleading) may be a way of moving into a new peer group. A more likely scenario is that through gossip, refusal to adhere to group norms, or failure in heterosexual relationships, individuals may slip outside the boundaries of their clique. Changing one's crowd identity may be even more difficult than changing from one clique to another. When the school population is relatively stable, it is difficult to lose the reputational identity one has already established.

Important skills that are learned by becoming a member of a peer group are the assessment of group structure and the selection of the particular group or groups with which one would like to affiliate. As one begins to develop a focused peer-group affiliation, one becomes aware of that group's internal structure and norms (Dunphy, 1963). In adolescence, the structure may include patterns of dominance, dating, and relationships with others outside the group. Associated with each of these dimensions of social structure are sets of norms or expectations for the behavior of the peer-group members. As adolescents discover their positions in the dominance hierarchy of the group, they learn how they may advance within it and what behaviors are expected at various levels. On the basis of all this information, they must decide whether their personal growth is compatible with the peer-group affiliation they have made.

There is some evidence that being a member of a peer group is linked to well-being. The peer group serves as a source of social support and helps to buffer stress. As time goes along, however, many 11th- and 12th-graders perceive the close connections with a single clique as less important or central to their social life. By that time, close dyadic friendships and love relationships begin to play a greater role, and especially for girls, the time and energy that used to be focused on preserving the friendship group is redirected to these more intimate relationships (Smith, 1987).

We suggest that membership in an adolescent peer group is a forerunner of membership in an adult social group. Adolescent peer groups are somewhat less organized than their adult counterparts, but they are considerably more structured than childhood friendship groups. Through peer-group membership, adolescents begin to learn techniques for assessing the organization of social groups and their own position within them. They develop aspirations for advancing their own social standing. In addition, adolescents gain some in-

Peer groups can be influential in reinforcing high risk behaviors like smoking and alcohol use; but they can also support positive social values like teamwork, generosity, and community spirit.

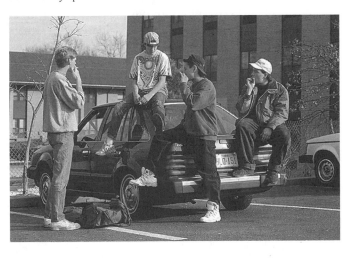

sight into the rewards and costs of extensive group identification. Although the actual friends made during adolescence may change as one grows older, the social skills learned at this time provide a long-lasting basis for functioning in a mature social group.

Parents and Peers

How does involvement with peers during early adolescence relate to closeness to family members? Do adolescents abandon family interactions and values for peer interactions and values? Can closeness to peers compensate for a lack of closeness to parents, or does the intimacy achieved with parents extend outward to a circle of friends? To what extent do parents continue to have an influence on adolescent peer relationships?

In the transition from childhood to adolescence, the child's radius of significant relationships changes. One study looked at the structure and function of social support among African-American, Anglo, and Hispanic children in three age groups: 7, 10, and 14 (Levitt et al., 1993). It concluded that in the transition from ages 7 to 10, extended-family members become increasingly important to children as a source of support. This pattern was found in all three ethnic groups, but the African-American and Hispanic children were more likely to identify extended-family members as sources of support than were the Anglo children. From ages 10 to 14, friends become an increasingly important source of support. In addition, the number of people mentioned as friends increased notably from age 7 to 14. However, at all three ages and in all three ethnic groups, family members continue to be mentioned as the most central in these children's lives, "the people who are the most close and important to you—people you love the most and who love you the most" (Levitt et al., 1993). What is more, at each age, support from the close, inner circle made up largely of family members was an important correlate of well-being and sociability.

As one considers the increasingly important role of peer relationships in early adolescence, keep in mind that under optimal conditions this process takes place against a background of continuing close, supportive relationships with family members. Adolescents describe a variety of overt signs of independence from their families: They may make decisions about clothes, dating, and so on; they may drive cars; they may stay out late; and they may earn their own money. However, they continue to maintain an emotional attachment to their families and to family values.

What is the nature of parent-adolescent interaction? How do differences in its quality influence the adolescent's well-being? Time spent at home in positive interactions with adults appears to have positive consequences for adolescents. In a study of eighth-graders, time spent at home was positively related to perceptions of the family environment as intellectually and culturally stimulating. Also, there was a strong relationship between time spent at home in leisure and recreational activity and a sense of well-being (McMillan & Hiltonsmith, 1982). At the opposite end of the continuum, experiences of parental rejection or neglect were found to be closely linked to low self-esteem and depression (Robertson & Simons, 1989; Rosenberg et al., 1989).

Time spent in public with adults appeared to be more conflictual, however. Adolescents who reported a high level of parental companionship outside the home also reported feeling self-conscious about and preoccupied with the evaluations of others (Adams & Jones, 1982). Although adolescents may feel good about being affectionate with and close to their parents, they are also sensitive to perceived expectations that they should not be too chummy with their parents. Although frequent open communication between adolescents and their parents contributes to a positive relationship, it is misleading to assume that these interactions are consistently positive in tone. It is hard work for parents and adolescents to keep the channels of communication open.

As adolescents go through puberty, conflicts with their parents increase. Conversations are marked by new levels of assertiveness on both sides (Papini & Sebby, 1988; Papini et al., 1988). These conflicts tend to be about rather mundane issues like household chores, how money will be spent, whether the child is spending enough time on schoolwork, or curfews, rather than on basic value issues like political ideology or religious beliefs (Montemayor, 1983; Steinberg, 1990). Resolutions of these family conflicts lead to the establishment of a new balance of power or control within the family (Feldman & Gehring, 1988). This balance appears to be negotiated somewhat differently by males and females.

Steinberg (1981) described parent-child interactions among boys aged 11–14 and their parents. As boys go through puberty, their parents increasingly interrupt them and they in turn increasingly interrupt their mothers. The parents' explanations decline, and family interactions become more rigid. After the period of rapid pubertal growth, however, adolescent-parent conflicts subside somewhat. Mothers interrupt their sons less, and sons become increasingly deferential to their fathers.

The pattern for girls is a bit different (Hill, 1988). In the months following menarche, parents interrupt their daughters more during conversations. Girls are more likely to yield to the interruptions of their mothers, but not to their fathers. Daughters assert themselves with their mothers through a high frequency of interruptions and with their fathers by an unwillingness to yield the conversation when their fathers interrupt them. Over time, parents notably increase their explanations when their opinions differ from their daughter's, suggesting a new respect for her independent views and a new definition of her power in the family. A consequence of frequent, reasonable interactions and a family norm that allows the expression of conflict is that parents can be more effective in communicating their expectations and learning about their child's point of view.

The quality of the home environment, especially the parenting practices, has implications for the adolescent's peer relationships as well as for the quality of parent-child interactions. Recall from the discussion in Chapter 8 that high levels of power assertion by parents are associated with a greater likelihood of peer rejection during middle childhood. Studies of the relationship of parenting practices to adolescent peer-group membership are extending this analysis. A model was proposed to examine the relationship of parenting practices to adolescent behaviors and ultimately to crowd affiliation (Figure 9.2) (Brown et al., 1993; Durbin et al., 1993). Parenting practices, listed in the left-hand column of Figure 9.2, were operationally defined as: the extent to which parents emphasized academic achievement, parental monitoring of adolescent behaviors, and the degree to which parents involved adolescents in decision-making. Three adolescent behaviors, listed in the center column, were measured: the students' grade-point averages, drug use, and self-reliance. Finally, the students were identified as members of one of six crowds: popular, jocks, brains, normals, druggies, or outcasts.

Parenting Practices	Adolescent Behaviors	Crowd Membership
Parental emphasis on achievement	Grade-point average	Popular
		Jock
Parent monitoring	Drug use	Brain
		Normal
Joint decision making	Self-reliance	Druggie
		Outcast

FIGURE 9.2

A model of relationships among parenting practices, adolescent behaviors, and peer group membership SOURCE: Brown et al., 1993.

Parenting practices were significantly linked to the children's behavior, which in turn was a strong predictor of their crowd affiliation. Parenting practices had both direct and indirect impacts on adolescents' crowd memberships. For example, parents who emphasized academic achievement were more likely to have children who were members of the popular or jock crowds and less likely to be druggies. In addition, parents who emphasized academic achievement were likely to have adolescents who had high grades and who were self-reliant, factors that also predicted being popular, and not being members of the druggie or outcast groups. Low parental monitoring and little joint decision making were associated with drug use, low self-reliance, and membership in the "druggie" crowd. Even though adolescents may perceive their involvement with their peers as a domain separate and distinct from their family life, this research suggests that parental socialization practices and their consequences for adolescent behavior continue to influence peer relations.

Sexual Relationships

During adolescence, peer relationships are modified by the introduction of sexual interests and behavior. This increased interest in sexuality is linked in part to the biological changes associated with puberty. However, considerable evidence implicates the social, cultural, and historical contexts as sources of stimulation for sexual fantasy and behavior.

First Intercourse

In many cultures, the act of first intercourse is a significant marker of the transition from adolescence to adulthood. In U.S. society, the norms for engaging in sexual activity differ by ethnic group and gender. In general, sexual activity has been disconnected from marriage and childbearing. Many adolescents and adults do not believe, nor do they behave as if sex ought to be reserved for married couples; but in some subcultures, this is still held as the ideal. And although males and females are becoming more alike in their patterns of sexual activity, most subcultures continue to endorse a pattern that promotes earlier entry into sexual activity for males and a more restrained, reluctant posture regarding sexual activity for females.

The sexual transition may take place in very different contexts for adolescents. It may be a planned event or an unplanned impulse, often combined with alcohol use or a drug high. The sexual encounter may be viewed as a marker of independence or as an act of rebellion against and defiance of the family. It may take place in the context of an on-

As adolescents mature, their sexual activity is more likely to take place in the context of deepening emotional commitment.

going close relationship or as part of a casual encounter. Usually, the earlier the entry into sexual activity and intercourse, the more likely the act is to be part of a profile of high-risk behaviors, including alcohol use, drug use, and delinquent activity. The later the entry, the more likely it is to be seen as a marker of the transition into adulthood or as a planned aspect of the deepening commitment in an ongoing relationship (Flannery et al., 1993; Ketterlinus et al., 1992).

Udry and Billy (1987) devised a model to explain the transition to coitus in early adolescence (Figure 9.3). In that model, three basic dimensions account for the adolescent's initiation of sexual activity: motivation, social controls, and attractiveness. Motivation can be accounted for by biological factors, especially new levels of hormone production; a new level of desire to achieve independence and engage in adult behaviors; and certain internalized norms and attitudes that may either encourage or reduce the motivation for sexual activity. The social controls provide the normative environment within which sexual activity is embedded. According to the model, these controls are a product of parental socialization and practices, school achievement and educational aspirations, and the attitudes and sexual experiences of friends. We want to add to the model's list of social controls the importance of the influence of religious beliefs and values. The third dimension, attractiveness, influences the availability of partners. Attractiveness is defined in part by pubertal maturation, social acceptance or popularity, and also by whether one is judged to be pretty or handsome.

In an effort to assess this model, the researchers found that the transition to sexual intercourse for white boys was most strongly predicted by hormonal levels and by popularity with the opposite sex. Other studies confirm that hormone levels are related to boys' sexual behavior (Udry, 1988; Susman et al., 1985). The norms and expectations encouraging the transition to sexual activity may be so clear for males that it is difficult to find many factors other than pubertal maturation that can account for it.

In contrast, there is no clear relationship between hormone levels or pubertal maturation and girls' sexual activity (Udry et al., 1985; Katchadourian, 1990). For girls, various social controls, including parents, school achievement, friends' attitudes and behaviors, and religious values, all play an important part in predicting sexual intercourse. Girls must reach some level of pubertal maturation before the decision about

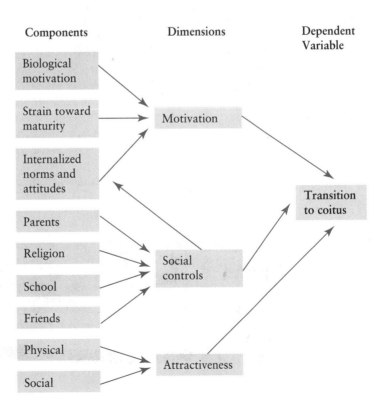

FIGURE 9.3

A model of transition to first coitus in early adolescence

voluntary entry into sexual activity becomes an issue. Beyond that point, however, a girl's decision to become sexually active is influenced by her own self-esteem, personal aspirations, her parents' values, her educational expectations, the capacity of her parents to exercise appropriate control over her social and school activities, and the norms of her peer group (Brooks-Gunn & Furstenberg, 1989; Newcomer & Udry, 1987; Hanson et al., 1987).

One of the clearest cultural influences on adolescent sexual behavior is religious participation. Adolescents who attend religious services and church-related activities frequently and who value religion as an important aspect of their lives have less permissive attitudes toward premarital sex. This finding applies equally to Catholic, Protestant, and Jewish young people. The relationship is accentuated in adolescents who describe themselves as Fundamentalist Protestant or Baptist. However, an adolescent's attitudes toward premarital sex are shaped by many other factors. By the time young people are making independent decisions about religious participation, they also have opinions on premarital sex. Thus, those young people who have more permissive views on sex are less likely to attend religious services and find less satisfaction in religious participation (Thornton & Camburn, 1989).

Dating relationships during early adolescence provide the initial context for sexual activity. Pubertal changes may increase a young person's interest in sexual ideation, but the timing of dating per se depends heavily on the norms of the peer group and the community (Garguilo et al., 1987). One of the strongest predictors of early sexual activity is dating at an early age. Adolescents who "go steady" are much more likely to be sexually active than are those who do not (Hanson et al., 1987).

In the United States, the historical trend has been toward earlier involvement in sexual intercourse for both boys and girls, and greater sexual activity for girls (Dreyer, 1982). The percentage of boys and girls at the high school level reporting sexual intercourse increased consistently after 1925. Recent studies suggest that "by age 15, about 17% of boys and 6% of girls are no longer virgins; at age 18, 67% of boys and 44% of girls are sexually experienced; by age 20, the figures go up to 80% for males and 70% for females" (Katchadourian, 1990, p. 336).

Within ethnic groups, different family and community factors are associated with early or later age of sexual transition (Day, 1992). For example, for Chicano males and females, having a biological father in the home was associated with a later age of sexual intercourse. For Latino females, having a stepfather in the home increased the likelihood of an early entry into sexual activity. For both Chicana and Latina females, low self-esteem was associated with an earlier age of sexual activity. Among African-American females, living in a rural community was associated with earlier entry into sexual activity. For African-American males, especially those under age 18, attending a predominantly African-American high school was associated with earlier entry into sexual activity. However, conservative family values tended to delay sexual activity for African-American males. Among white females, a strong occupational desire and parents' higher levels of education were associated with delayed sexual activity. In this group, high self-esteem was associated with sexual activity at a younger age. All these intergroup differences illustrate that the sexual transition is embedded in a complex psychosocial context and that generalizations about adolescent sexual behavior are likely to miss the mark when differences in gender, ethnicity, and community values are not taken into consideration.

Data regarding entry into sexual activity and age at first intercourse must be interpreted with caution. First, the data reported by ethnicity are often confounded by social class. Second, the differences between rural and urban communities, such as those noted by Day in the study discussed above, are not often included in the analyses. Third, the reporting is retrospective (asking adolescents to think back to when they first engaged in sexual activities) and is vulnerable to inconsistencies and memory errors (Alexander et al., 1993).

Of course, sexual relationships do not necessarily involve intercourse. Many levels of sexual activity, from autoerotic sexual fantasies and masturbation to dyadic behaviors that may include handholding, kissing and hugging, and heavy petting, are involved in becoming a sexual adult. What is more, initial experiences with sexual intercourse do not necessarily result in frequent sexual activity. For example, boys who experience an early-pubertal sexual initiation may not have another sexual experience for a year or more (Brooks-Gunn & Furstenberg, 1989).

Sexual Orientation

Most young people are involved in a variety of romantic relationships during adolescence (Levesque, 1993). Components of both gender identity and sexual orientation are formulated during this period of life. Some early adolescents are sexually permissive and are regularly active in sex play, from petting to intercourse. Other early adolescents are much less sexually active. Some may remain relatively uninterested in sexual relationships, while others think about sexual relationships a good deal. The manner in which early adolescents think about sexual relationships varies. Some are preoccupied by thoughts of very romantic, beautiful relationships. They can become infatuated with rock stars, athletes, movie stars, or other sex symbols. Others manifest rather perverse obsessions with sexual material. Whatever the resulting adult sexual orientation, it can be assumed that the early adolescent's sexual awakenings represent a system that is just being started up and tested out. As a result of sexual experiences, adolescents begin to think of themselves as sexual, develop scripts and schemes for how to act sexually with others, and begin to formulate ideas about the kinds of people they find sexually attractive.

Although one might assume that sexual orientation—heterosexual, homosexual, or bisexual—begins to take shape in early adolescence, the research literature on this point is sparse. Many adolescents report some kind of homosexual experience, such as arousal at the sight of a member of the same sex or a transient infatuation with a same-sex peer. Many adult homosexuals recall that their sexual orientation took shape in adolescence, but exactly how sexual encounters that take place in early adolescence contribute to a homosexual orientation is not well-understood.

The paths to a gay sexual identity vary widely. In one study of a volunteer sample of 77 gay males, most recalled having an awareness of gay feelings as early as middle school or early adolescence but did not label themselves gay until later adolescence (D'Augelli, 1991). The majority (75%) knew they were gay *before* their first sexual experience. And once they had labeled themselves gay, they waited an average of eight

Events like the Gay Pride march serve as a source of support for young people as they try to understand their sexual orientation. These events provide a public forum to celebrate the diversity and strengths of the gay community.

years to disclose their homosexuality to someone else. The reports of adolescents who are openly gay suggest that this is a very stressful realization, one that is commonly accompanied by negative reactions from parents and friends, and by acts of open hostility from school peers (Remafedi, 1987). Anticipating the strong social censure attached to an unconventional sexual orientation, adolescents are likely to deny it to or mask it by functioning as heterosexuals during this period of life.

> I feared not being liked and being alienated. I was president of various school clubs and once I beat up a guy for being a faggot. I was adamant that fags should be booted out of the Boy Scouts. Other kids asked me why I was so rough on them. I did not say. No one suspected me because I did sports and had several girlfriends. (Savin-Williams, 1996, p. 169)

The process of labeling oneself as gay, lesbian, or bisexual is distinct from the process of disclosing it to others (Savin-Williams, 1996). Many young people have an early sense of distinctiveness or alienation from their peers, which consolidates into a gay, lesbian, or bisexual identification during early or late adolescence. However, without support from the homosexual community or trusted homosexual adults and peers, they may resist disclosing this realization, especially to their family members.

Problems and Conflicts Associated with Sexuality

The sexual system is one of the most problematic components of psychosocial development for young people in the United States. Most parents do not feel comfortable discussing sexuality with their children. In addition to private thoughts, impulses, and fantasies, which may result in feelings of guilt or confusion, young people confront conflicting messages about sexual behavior from their peers, the mass media, and the religious community. New risks of sexually transmitted diseases, especially AIDS, introduce anxiety about the expression of sexual impulses. In a sample of over 1000 students from 13 urban and rural California high schools, only 20% of the students thought they had some chance of getting AIDS. However, among those who claimed to be sexually active, 60% had done something to try to avoid exposure to AIDS, most commonly using a condom or having their boyfriend use a condom and having fewer sex partners (Leland & Barth, 1993). The threat of exposure to AIDS is clearly having an impact on how young people think about sexual activity and its associated risks.

A major focus of AIDS and HIV education has been directed toward adolescents. Although adolescents believe that they have a strong understanding of AIDS as a disease, including its transmission and prevention, studies have shown that their knowledge is often confused or incorrect. At the same time, adolescents express little interest in learning more about AIDS. Many young people overestimate how well they understand this health problem. Others are cynical about getting the specific information they need from typical school-based sex-education courses. These courses are often unable to provide the practical information that is needed to resolve questions about contraception, sexual intimacy, and specific patterns of physical contact that might lead to transmission of the disease (Buysse, 1996).

Young people see numerous examples of sexual intimacy on television and in films, suggesting that sexual gratification ought to be more immediate and more satisfying than it is likely to be in real life. Often, they do not find the emotional closeness and understanding they may seek in a sexually intimate relationship. What is more, many adolescents, especially females, are exposed to unwanted sexual activity. In a sample of 7th-, 9th-, and 11th-grade girls, 21% reported unwanted sexual contact, ranging from unwanted touching and fondling to unwanted or forced intercourse (Small & Kerns, 1993). In many of these instances, unwanted sexual intercourse occurred on the first date or in a dating relationship. This pattern illustrates the problematic nature of sexual contact in early adolescence. The boundaries around acceptable sexual contact are unclear, the sexual agenda for males and females is likely to be very different, and other risk-taking behaviors, including alcohol and drug use, may create an unwanted sexual encounter.

In an effort to learn more about adolescents' reactions following their involvement in sexual intercourse, Australian researchers surveyed students in secondary schools in seven of the eight Australian states and territories (Donald et al., 1995). Students were asked about the context of their most recent sexual experience and how they felt about it. The majority of males and females said they felt good about their most recent sexual experience, with older students (16 and 17) more likely to be positive about it than the younger students (15 and under). For girls, five factors were significantly associated with feeling good about their most recent sexual experience: believing that there was a low risk for contracting a sexually transmitted disease; having a "steady" relationship with the partner; having talked with their partner about avoiding pregnancy; having talked with their partner about ways of having sexual pleasure without having intercourse; and not being drunk or high. For boys, two factors were significantly associated with feeling good about their most recent sexual experience: having sex with a "steady" partner and not being drunk or high. Larger percentages of girls than boys were likely to say they felt used or bad after their most recent sexual experience, and the younger girls were more likely than older girls to say they felt bad or used. About equal percentages of girls and boys said they felt guilty after their most recent sexual experience.

The lack of supervision and monitoring by adults as well as the lack of opportunity to talk about sexuality with them can place adolescents at risk for early sexual experiences that are abusive or associated with negative feelings. The sex-linked problems that many people encounter—unintended pregnancy, marital infidelity, rape and other forms of unwanted sexual contact, child sexual abuse, pornography, sexually transmitted diseases—are evidence that the socialization process including efforts by parents, teachers, and religious leaders is failing to promote mature sexuality in significant numbers of adolescents and adults in the United States.

Parenthood in Early Adolescence

One of the consequences of early entry into sexual activity is adolescent pregnancy. To get a sense of the magnitude of this issue, consider the following data. In 1994, 505,000 live infants were born to women aged 19 or younger. The birthrate (the number of births to women per 100,000 women in the age group) for mothers aged 10–14 increased from 1.1 in 1980 to 1.4 in 1989 and has remained at that level through 1994. For adolescents aged 15–19, however, the rate increased from 53 in 1980 to 62 in 1991, and has decreased slightly over the last few years to 59 in 1994 (U.S. Bureau of the Census, 1997).

Social policies advocating the prevention of early pregnancy and public programs for family planning and abortion tend to emphasize the negative consequences of pregnancy for adolescent girls and their babies. However, studies of pregnant adolescents generally find that these girls do not differ much in attitudes, mental health, or cognitive abilities from those who are sexually active but did not become pregnant. Society must be careful not to label a group of adolescent girls as deviant simply because they are pregnant.

Contraception. A critical factor in explaining the high rate of adolescent pregnancy is the ambivalence of American parents, teachers, and teens toward contraception. In comparison with adolescents in many European countries, the majority of American adolescents do not integrate contraception into their view of natural sexual activity. American adolescents are largely uninformed about the variety of methods of contraception and their relation to the biological factors that prevent pregnancy (Morrison, 1985).

The use of contraceptives is associated with religious beliefs, family attitudes and behaviors, and peer norms. For example, low-income African-American female adolescents have more negative attitudes toward birth control than do white female adolescents, and they value fertility more. Thus, African-American females who are sexually active are less likely to use contraceptives (Edelman & Pittman, 1986; Pete & DeSantis, 1990; Zabin et al., 1993). However, African-American adolescent males tend to be more consistent in their use of condoms than other groups (Pleck et al., 1991).

An adolescent's adjustment to teen parenting rests heavily on the social, instrumental, and emotional support she receives from her family. Parents have to find the midpoint between taking over by giving too much advice and help, and abandoning their daughter to figure out everything on her own.

About 40% of adolescent girls believe contraception is the responsibility of the male, but most males are ineffective or inconsistent in their use of contraceptives (Franklin, 1988). In one national survey of adolescent males aged 15–19, 30% reported using condoms all the time, including with their recent partners and with their last partner, and 57% reported using a condom in their last intercourse. These rates are higher than those observed in the early 1980s (Pleck et al., 1991). However, this still leaves 70% of adolescent males who are inconsistent in their use of condoms or who do not use them at all. The view that males have a responsibility to prevent pregnancy, concern about the partner's wishes, and concern about AIDS were all positively related to adolescent males' consistent condom use. On the other hand, concerns about reduced sexual pleasure and the embarrassment of using a condom, coupled with the pattern of having a number of sexual partners, were related to inconsistent condom use. Variations in attitudes about the costs and benefits of it, religious beliefs about it, and lack of concrete knowledge about how to use contraceptives help explain why the technology of contraception is not as successful among sexually active American youth as it could be.

Consequences of Teenage Pregnancy. The phenomenon of teenage parenthood is complex, touching the lives of the adolescent mother and father, the child or children born to them, their parents, and the schools, counseling services, and family-planning services that have been created to help young parents cope with parenthood (Franklin, 1988; Caldas, 1993). The consequences of teenage pregnancy and parenthood for the young mother and her infant depend on the psychosocial context of the pregnancy. Within the time period of early adolescence, there is a big difference between becoming a mother at 14 or at 18. There is also a strong correlation between age at first birth and one's family income at age 27 (Moore et al., 1993). This effect is mediated through a number of other personal and family factors that appear to unfold following the first birth, such as continuing in school, chances of getting married, the kind of work one does and one's personal earnings, and the earning capacity of other family members. For African-American females, the poverty level is high regardless of age at first birth. However, the earlier African-American females begin childbearing, the more children they are likely to have, a factor that increases the level of poverty. For Hispanic females, delaying childbearing resulted in higher educational attainment, a factor that predicts higher personal income by age 27. For white females, delaying the age of childbearing was associated with older age at first marriage, fewer children, and higher personal earnings. For all three ethnic groups, but especially for whites and Hispanics, each year of delayed childbearing had a substantial impact on reducing the chances of ending up in poverty by age 27.

One of the great paradoxes of adolescent parenthood is the contrast between young girls' aspirations about mothering and the actual experience of child-rearing. These are the comments of two young mothers:

Ann (14): When I got pregnant, my parents wanted me to have an abortion, but I'm an only child, and it's a lonely feeling when you're an only child. I just said, "Well, I'm going to keep the baby because now I'll have somebody I'll feel close to, instead of being lonely all the time." (Fosburgh, 1977, p. 34)

Mary (17): It was great, 'cause now I got him and nobody can take him away from me. He's mine, I made him, he's great. Something real can give me happiness. He can make me laugh and he can make me cry and he can make me mad. (Konopka, 1976, p. 39)

Many adolescents do not have the emotional, social, or financial resources to sustain the kind of caring relationship they envision with their children. They may be unable to anticipate that their own needs must often be sacrificed to their babies' needs. One outcome of this discrepancy between aspirations and reality is an outpouring of the young mother's hostility toward her baby. The risk of child abuse is great in families with teen parents, especially when the factors of poverty and single-parent family structure converge with early childbearing (Gelles, 1989; Zuravin, 1988).

Complications during labor and delivery may be devastating to the newborn's health. Are young mothers more likely than older ones to experience such complications? Mothers under 19 are less likely than older mothers to initiate prenatal care during the first trimester of pregnancy. Infants born to mothers under 17 are at greater risk than those born to women in their 20s and 30s. They have a higher risk of dying during the first year, of being born prematurely or at a low birth weight, and of suffering neurological damage as a result of complications associated with delivery (McCarthy & Hardy, 1993). Thus, young parents are more likely to have to cope with the special needs of a developmentally handicapped child. However, these risks arise from converging socioeconomic factors rather than from biological inadequacies of being young. Studies involving large numbers of births at urban hospitals tend to find that younger mothers in general (those under 20) are actually *less likely* to experience complications of pregnancy and negative birth outcomes than older mothers, particularly when factors associated with poverty are taken into account (Roosa, 1984; McCarthy & Hardy, 1993).

Is a pregnant adolescent who marries better off than one who does not? Adolescent pregnancy and adolescent marriage have separate consequences for future educational attainment, occupational achievement, and marital stability. Having a baby in adolescence is associated with lower educational and occupational levels, whether or not the young woman gets married. Getting married in adolescence is associated with a greater chance of divorce or separation than getting married at age 20 or older. Somewhat surprisingly, however, adolescent marriage without children is somewhat more likely to be associated with later marital instability than is adolescent marriage accompanied by adolescent childbirth (Teti & Lamb, 1989). With respect to financial resources, adolescents who are married at the time of their first birth have a higher household income than do those who are single at that time (Astone, 1993).

In an attempt to discover the factors that lead to certain sexual decisions, including the decision to have a child, Pete and DeSantis (1990) conducted a case study of five African-American girls who were pregnant or had recently delivered a child. However, one must be cautious about generalizing these observations to all African-American adolescent mothers or to adolescent mothers as a whole. All five were 14 years old and in the eighth grade. They were from low-income families in Miami, Florida. Despite the small sample size, the focus of this study is especially relevant because it considers the point of view of a critical group.

Several factors that emerged from the interviews with these young mothers challenge some of our beliefs about adolescent pregnancy and confirm others. First, the girls had all declined other opportunities to become sexually active. They said that they had waited to become sexually active until they had established a relationship that they believed was based on trust and love. They had not delayed sexual activity in order to avoid pregnancy, and they had assumed that the person with whom they had sex would not abandon them.

Second, they had not used contraceptives for a variety of reasons. Some had believed that they could not get pregnant ("I thought I was too young to get pregnant"). Some had relied on their boyfriends to use contraception, but the methods used had been inconsistent or nonexistent. Most of the girls were confused about the use of contraceptives or lacked the means to obtain them.

Third, the girls all described a daily life in which they had a large amount of unsupervised free time. They all lived with adults who did not or were not able to supervise their behaviors effectively. One girl had moved out of the house when her mother became hooked on crack. Another girl lived with her grandmother, who could never talk with her about sex or her social life. Although the girls all said they felt close to their parent or guardian, these adults did not monitor their social lives or talk about sexual decisions.

Fourth, the girls had denied that they were pregnant as long as they could:

> However, even though Deb had missed several periods, was sick every morning, and had fainted several times, she vehemently denied she was pregnant for seven months. . . . As Deb so clearly put it, "as long as I did not tell anyone I was pregnant, as far as I was concerned, I wasn't pregnant." (Pete & DeSantis, 1990, p. 151)

Finally, the girls all believed that once a woman became pregnant, it was her responsibility to have and keep the baby. Since they had waited so long to admit the pregnancy, abortion was out of the question. Adoption was also never considered. None of the parents or guardians thought the girls should get married because they thought the girls were too young. All the fathers continued to maintain contact with the mother and baby were involved in the baby's care and provided some financial support. Three of the fathers even took their babies to their homes every other weekend. Even though the girls' parents or guardians were disappointed by the pregnancy, they had not rejected these young mothers. Several had even accepted some responsibility themselves for the pregnancy. Thus, the pregnancy and childbirth had not resulted in a deterioration of the girls' support systems.

Adolescent Fathers. Although the focus on adolescent pregnancy has been on girls, there is growing concern about adolescent fathers. It is difficult, though, to determine the number of teenage fathers. Many young mothers will not reveal the name of their baby's father, many of whom are not adolescents but older men. For example, in 1992 there were 518,000 U. S. women under the age of 20 who gave birth, but only 129,000 men under age 20 were named as fathers (U.S. Bureau of the Census, 1996).

Most studies of adolescent pregnancy find that, contrary to the stereotype, many of the fathers remain in contact with the mother and the child. Some adolescent fathers marry the mothers; others live with them for a while. It is less common for African-American adolescent fathers to live with their child shortly after the infant's birth than it is for white and Hispanic fathers (Marsiglio, 1987). Often, the couple continue to date. In some instances, they actually marry several years after the child is born. In many cases, the father contributes financial support to the mother and child, even when the couple do not marry. Many fathers, however, have little education and are minimally employed, so the material support they can provide is very limited (Robinson, 1988; Hardy & Duggan, 1988).

William Marsiglio (1989) compared African-American and white male adolescents' preferences about pregnancy resolution and family formation. These data were gathered from responses to the hypothetical statement: "Please imagine that you have been dating the same girl who is about your age for the past year and that she told you last week that she was 2 months pregnant with your child. For the purpose of this survey assume that your girlfriend wants you to live with her and your child." Beginning with this premise, the boys in the survey were asked about how likely they would be to live with the child, their attitudes about it, their evaluation of what might be the positive and negative consequences of this decision, and their overall preference of how they would like to see the pregnancy resolved if it were entirely their decision.

African-American adolescents were significantly less likely to endorse abortion as the solution to this situation. This was true even when the adolescent's parents' education was taken into account. For example, none of the African-American males whose parents were college graduates selected abortion as a solution, while 40% of the white males whose parents were college graduates would have preferred abortion. African-American and white males were about equally likely to endorse the idea of living with the child and the baby's mother (45% of both groups selected this option). African-American males were more likely than white males to see an advantage to living with the baby as providing a chance to care for the baby's daily physical needs and to enable them to assume greater financial responsibility for the situation. In other respects, African-American and white males viewed the positive consequences of the situation similarly. White males were more likely than African-American males to see the situation as reducing their chances of pursuing further education and limiting their chances to spend time with their friends. In other respects, African-American and white males evaluated the negative consequences of the situation similarly. African-American males were more likely to agree that living with the child and the mother would require having a steady job.

The study illustrates that African-American adolescent males have a positive attitude toward continuing their relationship with the baby and the baby's mother. However, the patterns of real-life behavior do not provide evidence of this intention, perhaps because African-American males are younger when they father their first child and are therefore less likely to be able to leave their own homes. It may be that African-American adolescents have less chance to find steady job, so they do not have the resources to support their baby. Another explanation may be that in the African-American community, the mother's family is more willing to have her and the baby live with them, so there is no real place for or urgent need of the unwed father.

Fathering a child is bound to stimulate conflicting feelings of pride, guilt, and anxiety in the adolescent boy. He must struggle with the fact that his sexual adventures have resulted in a pregnancy that may bring conflict and pain to someone for whom he cares. Also, he must confront the choices he and his girlfriend have in coping with an unplanned pregnancy. In addition, he may feel excluded from the birth of a child he has fathered. Feeling obligated to provide financial support for his girlfriend and child may lead him to drop out of school and enter the labor market even though he can only hope to be minimally employed (Hendricks & Fullilove, 1983).

Not much is known about the impact of teen fathering on a boy's psychosocial development. What factors might influence whether the boy becomes committed to nurturing and supporting his child or leaves the parenting entirely to the mother and her family?

Little systematic research has been done on the attitudes, knowledge, or behaviors of adolescent fathers or the impact of fatherhood on a teenage boy's subsequent development (Marsiglio, 1993; Meyer, 1991). Researchers who have studied the problem of unwed fathers argue that much stronger emphasis should be placed on the father's responsibility, not only for financial support of the mother and child but also for his continued interaction with his child. Efforts to include young fathers in family-planning programs, parent education, and employment-training initiatives would help strengthen the social context for the young mother and her child and would contribute to the young father's psychosocial development.

For both girls and boys, a key to the prevention of early pregnancy requires building greater confidence in and commitment to the consistent use of contraception as part of any sexual relationship. For girls, fostering a sense of self-efficacy and investment in academic goals leading to postsecondary education and/or professional training is an especially important area for intervention (Plotnick, 1992; Ohannessian & Crockett, 1993). For boys, building greater social expectations and commitment to assuming the financial and social responsibilities associated with fatherhood, including sending clearer messages from family and community that boys have responsibilities in these areas and devising specific opportunities for them to enact these responsibilities, seem promising directions for future intervention (National Urban League, 1987; Olds et al., 1988).

THE PSYCHOSOCIAL CRISIS: GROUP IDENTITY VERSUS ALIENATION

Throughout life, tensions arise between desires for individuality and for connection. Certain cultures emphasize connection over individuality, while others put individuality ahead of connection. However, all societies must deal with both aspects of the ego, the **I** as agent, originator, and executive of one's individual thoughts and actions and the **WE** as agent, originator, and executive of collective, cooperative enterprises that preserve and further the survival of the group (Triandis, 1990). During the early years of adolescence, one confronts a new psychosocial conflict in which pressures to ally oneself with specific groups and to learn to be comfortable functioning as a member of a group are major preoccupations. This conflict is called **group identity versus alienation.**

Group Identity   Group identity refers to the aspect of an individual's self-theory that focuses on membership and connection with social groups. It is an extension of the ego system's sense of WE, which originates in the first attachment relationship of infancy. It is an elaboration of the early sense of trust, in which an infant establishes a foundation of social connection through which both self and other are defined. The WE includes those elements of the mind pertaining to the deep desire to be connected to others and with the underlying belief that one is connected to them. The WE can be compared to the I, which includes those elements of the mind pertaining to the deep desire to be an independent individual with an underlying sense that one's life has meaning and value. The WE and the I are complementary aspects of the ego system, although at times they may be in conflict.

Early adolescents experience a search for membership, an internal questioning about the groups of which they are most naturally a part. They ask themselves, "Who am I, and with whom do I belong?" Although membership in a peer group may be the most pressing concern, questions about other group identifications also arise. Adolescents may seek commitments to religious organizations, evaluate the nature of their ties to immediate or extended family members, and begin to understand the unique characteristics of their racial, ethnic, or cultural identity. Research confirms that in the most positive pattern, peer-group membership does not replace attachment to parents or closeness with family. Rather, the adolescent's network of supportive relations is anchored in the family and expands into the domain of meaningful peer relationships. Typically, adolescents who show strong signs of mental health and adaptive coping strategies can be described as having positive communication and trusting relationships with parents or other close family members as well as strong feelings of trust and security among friends (Raja et al., 1992; Levitt et al., 1993).

In the process of seeking group affiliation, the adolescent is confronted by the fit or lack of fit between personal needs and values and the values held by relevant social groups in the environment. The process of self-evaluation takes place within the context of the meaningful groups that are available for identification. Individual needs for social approval, affiliation, leadership, power, and status are expressed in the kinds of group identifications that are made and rejected during early adolescence (Box 9.3).

A positive resolution of the conflict of group identity versus alienation is one in which adolescents perceive an existing group that meets their social needs and provides them with a sense of group belonging. In one attempt to measure this concept, Luhtanen and Crocker (1992) devised a measure of **collective self-esteem,** defined as the relatively stable evaluation of the value of one's group membership. In this approach, they included several dimensions of group belonging: the enactment of the roles prescribed by the group; one's feelings of comfort and belonging with other group members; one's appraisal of the groups' status in the eyes of others; and the salience of the group in one's life. All four dimensions contribute to the formation of a positive group identification. In order to experience group identification, the person must be engaged in activities associated with it. In addition, the group must be evaluated positively in the person's eyes because of the central role it plays in providing meaning and structure to the person's life and also as a result of the positive meaning that group membership brings through reflection in the assessments of others.

Alienation   *Alienation* refers to a sense of social estrangement, an absence of social support or meaningful social connection (Mau, 1992). The adolescent who experiences alienation does not have a sense of belonging to a group; rather, he or she is continually uneasy in the presence of peers. A negative resolution of the conflict, which leaves the adolescent with a pervasive sense of alienation from peers, may result from at least three different circumstances. First, it may be brought about if parents press the adolescent to

BOX 9.3 GANGS

In the late 1920s and 1930s, the study of delinquency included an analysis of the role of gangs. Early on, it was understood that delinquent behavior was typically group behavior, involving two or more boys in some type of criminal activity. Gangs were viewed as social groups not unlike the kinds of groups that boys in more stable, prosperous neighborhoods create. The motives for joining a gang, "desires for recognition, approbation, and esteem of his fellows, for stimulation, thrill, and excitement, for intimate companionship, and for security and protection" (Burgess & Bogue, 1967, p. 300) do not differ much from the motives that adolescents have for joining any number of social groups and clubs. However, the focus of these groups developed a delinquent emphasis and tradition that was passed from one generation of gang members to the next in a neighborhood. The ethical standards and values of these groups were often contrary to conventional values. In fact, actions that might bring a nondelinquent boy dishonor or shame, such as being arrested, appearing in juvenile court, or being sent to a correctional institution, would be viewed as a source of pride and distinction to a gang member (Burgess & Bogue, 1967).

This analysis of the nature of gangs has not changed much over the years. Gangs continue to thrive in communities all across the United States. They actively recruit new members, engage in violent acts of initiation, and are becoming increasingly associated with drug trafficking and violent crime. Experts say that what drives young people to gangs are poverty, the desire to belong, and the desire to be loved and recognized (Nawojcyk cited by Howell, 1994).

One teenager told Nawojczyk that his mother was hooked on crack cocaine.

He joined the gang looking for love. Another one had an eye that was a little crossed.

He said some people at school made fun of him, 'but my gang don't make fun of me.' (Howell, 1994)

Young people seek love, money, protection, and prestige from gang membership. Adolescents who join gangs are often unsuccessful in school, and may have been suspended or expelled. School failure leads to periods of unsupervised time in the community and an inability to find work. Modern gang activities are supported by a growing and spreading drug trade, easy access to guns, and the communication technology of beepers, cell phones, and voice mail, which allow gang members to coordinate their activities and preserve control over a wider area with increased mobility.

The concept of gangs is closely linked to the theme of group identity. Although gangs have a violent, criminal, and antisocial value system, they provide a highly organized social group for identification. Gangs have clothing, colors, symbols, and signs that provide recognition across settings. Young people are recruited into gangs, making them feel valued and protected by older gang members. Despite the great risks associated with gang activities, the growth in gang membership suggests that gangs address a number of unmet needs of today's youth—needs that are not being met by communities, schools, and families.

---

restrict association to a particular peer group that in turn does not offer the adolescent membership. Second, alienation may result if the adolescent surveys the existing groups and does not find one that really meets his or her personal needs. In this case, the adolescent may never become a member of a peer group. A third basis for the negative outcome occurs when no peer group will offer acceptance or friendship, in which case the adolescent is gradually shut out of all the existing groups in the social environment. For example, some young people ascribe too avidly to adult values and norms. Their peers see them as goody-goodies or nerds and do not welcome them into the peer culture (Allen et al., 1989). Other adolescents have poor social skills—they are either overly aggressive and domineering, or overly withdrawn and socially inept. It is not unusual for adolescents to identify such students in their high school as "loners" or "outcasts" (Brown et al., 1993).

During early adolescence, it is common for young people to become preoccupied with their own feelings and thoughts. They may withdraw from social interactions, unwilling to share the vulnerability and confusion that accompany physical, intellectual, and social growth. In this sense, most adolescents feel some of the loneliness and isolation that are implied by the term *alienation*. They feel they must exercise caution in sharing their most troublesome concerns for fear of peer rejection or ridicule. The maintenance of an interpersonal "cool"—a desire to be perceived as someone who is competent rather than vulnerable—may stand in the way of building strong bonds of commitment to social groups.

The tension between expectations for group affiliation and barriers to group commitment is a product of the self-consciousness and egocentrism typical of this life stage as well as the possibility of rejection by existing groups. The lack of peer social support that may result from a negative resolution of this crisis during adolescence can have significant implications for adjustment in school, self-esteem, and subsequent psychosocial development. Chronic conflict about one's integration into a meaningful social support system can lead to lifelong difficulties in areas of personal health, work, and the formation of intimate family bonds (East et al., 1987; Spencer, 1982, 1988).

THE CENTRAL PROCESS: PEER PRESSURE

Adolescents' family backgrounds, their interests, and styles of dress quickly link them to subgroups of peers who lend continuity and meaning to life within the context of their neighborhoods or schools. The peer-group social structure is usually well-established in most high schools, and members of that structure exert pressure on newcomers to join one peer group or another. **Peer pressure** refers to demands for conformity to group norms and a demonstration of commitment and loyalty to group members. At the same time, young people outside the groups form expectations that reinforce adolescents' connections to specific peer groups and prohibit their movement to others. Likewise, an individual who becomes a member of a group is more acceptable to the social system than one who tries to remain unaffiliated and aloof.

The Role of School Adults in Peer-Group Structuring

School adults appear to accept the peer-group structure as it exists. They make almost no effort to alter this structure of peer organization, which they may even remember from their own high school days. Explicitly, school adults rely on members of specific peer groups to perform certain functions and to act along particular lines. Teachers as well as students appear to expect that individuals who dress in a certain way will be members of one peer group and that students who have a particular level of intellectual skill will belong to another. School adults often rely on the leaders of the various peer groups to convey and enforce school norms for acceptable behavior within the peer groups. Thus, the peer-group structure becomes an important vehicle for the maintenance of order and predictability in the school. Far from challenging this arrangement, school adults count on it to facilitate their work.

Affiliating with a Peer Group

The process of affiliating with a peer group requires an adolescent to accept the pressure and social influence imposed by it. This process provides the context within which the crisis of group identity versus alienation is resolved. Adolescents are at the point in their intellectual development when they are able to conceptualize themselves as objects of expectations. They may perceive these expectations as forces urging them to be more than they think they are—braver, more outgoing, more confident, and so forth. These expectations help define the zone of proximal development for group skills and social competencies. Peer pressure may have a positive effect on the adolescent's self-image and self-esteem, serving as a motive for group identification. Those dimensions of the self that are valued by one's own peer group become especially salient in each young person's self-assessment (Hoge & McCarthy, 1984).

As members of peer groups, adolescents have more influence than they would have as single individuals, they begin to understand the value of collective enterprise. In offering membership, peer groups expand adolescents' feelings of connection and protect them from loneliness. When family conflicts develop, adolescents can seek comfort and intimacy among peers. For adolescents to benefit in these ways from affiliation with a peer group, they must be willing to suppress some of their individuality and find pleasure in focusing on the attributes they share with those peers.

Peer Pressure in Specific Areas

Peer pressure may be exercised in a variety of areas including: involvement with peers, school, and family; drug use; engaging in misconduct; sexual activity; and conformity to patterns of preference in dress, music, or entertainment. Within a particular group, pressures may be strong in one or two areas but not in others. For example, in a comparison of three crowds—the jock-populars, the druggie-toughs, and the loners—the druggie-toughs perceived the strongest peer pressure toward misconduct. Jock-populars perceived greater pressure toward school involvement than the druggie-toughs. However, pressure toward peer involvement (spending free time with peers) was equally high in all three groups (Clasen & Brown, 1985).

Norms for cigarette smoking have been studied as another example of a voluntary behavior that may be influenced through peer pressure. For example, in one study of sources of peer influence on cigarette smoking, the crowd identified as the "burnouts" (combination of druggies, radicals, and punks) smoked four times as many cigarettes per week as the average students and ten times as many cigarettes as the jock/preps (Urberg, 1992). One might expect that the pressure to conform to this behavior would be exceedingly strong within the burnouts crowd, whereas there might be much more variability around norms related to smoking in the other groups.

Conformity and a Sense of Belonging

Peer groups do not command total conformity. In fact, most peer groups depend on the unique characteristics of their members to lend definition and vigor to the roles that emerge within them. However, the peer group places considerable importance on some level of conformity in order to bolster its structure and strengthen its effectiveness in satisfying members' needs. Indeed, most adolescents find some security in peer-group demands to conform. The few well-defined characteristics of the group lend stability and substance to adolescents' views of themselves. In complying with group pressure, adolescents have an opportunity to state unambiguously that they are someone and that they belong somewhere.

Conflict, Tension, and Alienation

Adolescents may also find that some peer expectations conflict with their personal values or needs. For example, they may feel that intellectual skills are devalued by the peer group, that they are expected to participate in social functions they do not enjoy, or that they are encouraged to be more independent from their families than they prefer to be. In most cases, adolescents' personal values are altered and shaped by peer-group pressure to increase their similarity with the other group members. If, however, the peer group's expectations are too distant from adolescents' own values, establishing a satisfying group identification will become much more difficult. As a result, adolescents experience tension and conflict as they try to balance the allure of peer-group membership with the cost of abandoning personal beliefs.

Susceptibility to peer pressure seems to peak at about ages 13 or 14, when adolescents are most sensitive to peer approval and make the initial transition toward new levels of behavioral autonomy and emotional independence from parents (Urberg et al., 1990; Lamborn & Steinberg, 1993). During the years from 14 to 16, adolescents become more adept at resisting peer pressure. Through encounters with peer pressure and opportunities to see how it feels to conform or resist, they develop a growing appreciation for the content of their personal values against the backdrop of peer expectations. However, if the emotional costs of identifying with the peer group become too great, adolescents may not open themselves up to group pressures. Therefore, they will be unable to establish the sense of group identity that is so central to psychosocial growth. An inability to reduce the tension and conflict between group pressure and personal values produces a state of alienation in which the individual is unable either to identify with social groups or to develop personal friendships.

Almost all adolescents experience times when they feel like outsiders. But for some, alienation is the dominant theme; they never enjoy the unconflicted sense of group belonging.

Ethnic-Group Identity

One of the most challenging aspects of establishing group identity facing minority adolescents is the formation of an **ethnic-group identity** (Spencer & Markstrom-Adams, 1990). Ethnic identity is not merely knowing that one is a member of a certain ethnic group, but recognizing that some aspects of one's thoughts, feelings, and actions are influenced by one's ethnic identity. One's ethnic group becomes a significant reference group whose values, outlook, and goals are taken into account as one makes important life choices. Ethnic identity varies across ethnic groups and among individuals within groups. For example, some young people have had more exposure to the cultural norms and values of their ethnic group than other young people. Some have had more guided parental socialization about the existence of prejudice and ways of coping with discrimination. Thus, ethnic identity is more aptly viewed as a psychosocial rather than a demographic variable (Phinney, 1996).

In the United States, a history of negative imagery, violence, discrimination, and invisibility has been linked to African-Americans, Native Americans, Asian-Americans, and Hispanics. Young people in each of these groups encounter conflicting values as they consider the larger society and their own ethnic identity. They must struggle with the negative or ambivalent feelings that are linked with their own ethnic group because of the cultural stereotypes that have been conveyed to them through the media and the schools, and because of the absence of role models from their own group who are in positions of leadership and authority.

Issues of ethnic-group identity may not become salient until early adolescence. As minority children grow up, they tend to incorporate many of the ideals and values of the Anglo culture. Suddenly in adolescence, however, they may find themselves excluded from it. At that time, peer groups become more structured. Sanctions against cross-race friendships and dating relationships become more intense. Minority adolescents may encounter more overt rejection and failure in academic achievement, employment, and school leadership. They may find that their family and ethnic-group values are actually in conflict with the values of the majority culture. These minority adolescents may also feel that they have to choose between their ethnic-group identity and membership in a nonminority group. In some cases, commitment to an ethnic-group identity takes the place of membership in some other peer group. In other instances, minority youths are rejected by their Anglo peers. They may then flounder, not having established a clear ethnic identity, and may struggle through a period of bitter rejection.

Peer group membership may not be as salient for minority youth as it has been described for white adolescents. In one study of family and peer relations, after controlling for social class, African-American adolescents reported both higher levels of parental control and higher levels of family intimacy than did white adolescents (Giordano, et al., 1993). In addition, African-American adolescents reported that they perceived less peer pressure, less need for peer approval, and somewhat lower levels of intimacy in their friendships. One ought not interpret this pattern as indication that friendship relationships are unimportant for African-American adolescents. Rather, friendships may be less intense for African-American adolescents than for whites. African-American adolescents may be socialized to function more independently, to be more flexible in accepting their friends but less dependent on them than on family for feelings of self-worth and emotional security.

In the transition from early to late adolescence, most minority youth experience some critical evaluation of the values and beliefs of the dominant culture and how they conflict with the values and beliefs of their ethnic group. The more fully emersed young children are in the values and traditions of their ethnic heritage, the more likely it is that they will experience a dual or multiple identity; for example, seeing themselves as both American and African-American or American and Asian-American (Phinney, 1997). Over time, and with the benefit of exposure to reading, conversations, and interactions with people from other subgroups, young people begin to synthesize a sense of how their ethnic identity fits into their overall personal identity and how it will influence the quality of their relationships with members of their own and other ethnic groups (Cross, 1991; Phinney, 1996).

THE PRIME ADAPTIVE EGO QUALITY AND THE CORE PATHOLOGY

Fidelity to Others   A positive resolution of the psychosocial crisis of group identity versus alienation results in the achievement of the prime adaptive ego quality referred to as **fidelity to others**—a capacity to freely pledge one's loyalty to a group and to sustain one's faithfulness to the promises and commitments one makes to others. Fidelity to others produces the sentiments that are necessary to preserve small groups and larger communities: dedication to family, civic pride, and patriotism.

Looking ahead to subsequent life stages, one can anticipate the significant role that this ego quality plays in pledging long-term faithfulness to friends, marital partners, children, one's aging parents, and other groups. Research on factors that buffer the effects of stress often cite the contribution of social support to the long-term abilities of individuals to cope with change and to adapt positively to life challenges. Social support implies a capacity for fidelity. People who function as sources of support have the ability to remain compassionately connected to others during periods of hardship and loss as well as during periods of success and prosperity. When one thinks of a true friend, one pictures someone who stands by you even when it is not especially advantageous to do so. A true friend is someone who cares about you and supports you during moments of adversity as well as in times of joy.

Fidelity to others becomes a source of family solidarity as members age and adults are called upon to meet the needs of their own aging parents, a topic we will cover in Chapter 12. The role one plays in caring for one's aging parents is largely voluntary. It is based on one's own definition of **filial obligation,** a sense of duty and responsibility for one's parents. Surely the way adults enact this role reflects their capacity for fidelity to others.

Dissociation   **Dissociation** refers to a sense of separateness, withdrawal from others, and an inability to experience the bond of mutual commitment. It does not mean a preference for being by oneself, but rather a tendency toward social distancing and a reluctance to make the kinds of commitments to others that are required for the establishment and maintenance of enduring friendships. Sometimes this occurs as a result of rejection. Adolescents who experience dissociation are likely to mistrust their peers and may even develop an attitude of hostile resentment toward the amiability and companionship they observe in others. Over time, dissociation results in the formulation of a mental world that is not well coordinated with social reality. A young person who experiences dissociation is likely to feel misunderstood and to lack confidence in his or her ability to communicate with or connect to others.

At a basic level, any sense of "we-ness" requires shared understandings between at least two people and a recognition that they experience some bond of investment in or identification with a common reality. This common reality could involve facing a common enemy, encountering a common crisis, or embracing a common goal. The core pathology of dissociation occurs when the young person is unable to experience the level of mutual understanding or symbolic connection that creates such bonds of "we-ness."

Applied Topic   ## ADOLESCENT ALCOHOL AND DRUG USE

American high-school-age youth have a higher level of illicit drug use than those of any other industrialized nation. By their senior year in high school, 52% of American high school students have tried an illegal drug—whether marijuana, amphetamines, heroin or other opiates, cocaine, or barbiturates. According to a 1996 study, roughly 12% of seniors had smoked marijuana daily for at least one month, and 6% had tried cocaine. In recent years, the increase in marijuana use has been accompanied by a younger age of first use, with close to 15% of 8th-graders saying that they first began to smoke marijuana in 7th grade (Johnston et al., 1996). Figure 9.4 provides an historical overview of the lifetime prevalence of illicit drug use for 12th-graders from 1975 to 1995. Following a period of decline in drug use from 1981 through 1990, drug use among adolescents increased over the first part of the 1990s.

Alcohol use has remained at a stable and relatively high level since 1975. In 1995, 55% of 8th-graders had tried alcohol, 25% said that they have been drunk at least

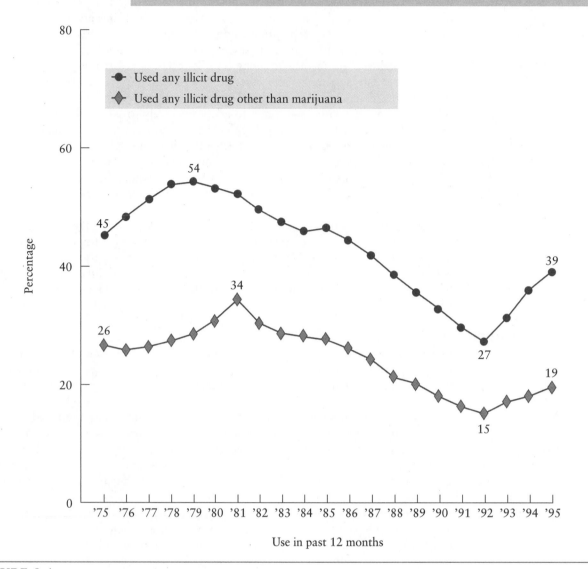

FIGURE 9.4

Historical trends in illegal drug use by U.S 12th-graders, 1975–1995

once in their lives, and 8% said that the first time they got drunk they were in 6th grade. In a rural sample of 7th-graders, about 60% had used alcohol in the past year, and about 8% had used it four or five times a month (Sarvela & McClendon, 1988). The prevalence of binge drinking, consuming five or more drinks in a row, was 30% for high school seniors and 47% for male college students (Johnston et al., 1996).

Factors Associated with Alcohol Use

Let us look at some of the factors associated with the use of alcohol and the part it plays in the adolescent's life. We are especially concerned about understanding the relationship between alcohol use and the major themes of early adolescence: physical development, cognitive development, peer relations, and parent-child relationships.

Physical Effects of Alcohol

Alcohol depresses the central nervous system. Although many people think that alcohol makes one "high," at its greatest levels of concentration in the body it can cause death by suppressing breathing. Although this outcome is extremely rare, it may occur after "chugging" large quantities of alcohol, a practice that is sometimes included in certain adolescent initiation rites and demonstrations of manliness. Recent deaths associated with fraternity initiation activities on college campuses have brought the practice of chugging to heightened attention (Columbus Dispatch, 1997).

There are two other situations in which alcohol use has potentially lethal consequences. One is the use of alcohol in combination with other drugs, especially barbiturates. The other is its use in combination with driving. One study of 10th-, 11th-, and 12th-graders found that 57% had driven while intoxicated and 78% had ridden in a car while the driver was drinking alcohol (DiBlasio, 1986).

The physical development accompanying puberty leads to a heightened awareness of body sensations. In small quantities, alcohol has a relaxing effect that may accentuate pleasurable bodily sensations. Adolescents may use alcohol in an attempt to increase their sense of physical arousal, reduce sexual inhibitions, and minimize the self-consciousness that is a barrier to social interactions. In larger quantities, alcohol may alter reality in such a way that adolescents are willing to take risks or ignore certain physical limitations. When adolescents are intoxicated, the barriers of physical appearance, height, weight, or sexual immaturity may be minimized. Thus, dissatisfaction with one's body image may contribute to an inclination to drink heavily in social situations.

Assessment of Risk

Growth in cognitive development during adolescence suggests that young people are increasingly able to anticipate the consequences of their actions. They can hypothesize about events that have not yet occurred and reason about their possible outcomes. Adolescents should be able to manipulate several variables at one time in order to solve a problem or make a decision. These skills suggest that they can use information about the impact or risk of alcohol to guide their drinking behavior. However, many adolescents do not view alcohol consumption as especially risky. In a national survey, only 25% of high school seniors saw daily drinking as involving great risk, and 45% of high school seniors saw binge drinking (five or more drinks once or twice over a weekend) as involving great risk (Johnston et al., 1996). Students who drink alcohol frequently are less likely to view drinking as risky, while those who drink little or not at all are more likely to see it as involving risk (Small et al., 1993). This pattern suggests cognitive consistency; in other words, adolescents who view a certain level of drinking behavior as highly risky are less likely to engage in it.

In addition to the assessment of risk, some adolescents can be characterized by high levels of sensation seeking. This characteristic includes thrill-seeking, adventure-seeking, disinhibition, and susceptibility to boredom. Youth who have a great need for novel, complex sensory experiences may be willing to take physical risks in order to satisfy this need (Tang et al., 1996).

Reference Groups

The two **reference groups** that influence the acceptability of drinking and the manner in which alcohol is consumed are the family and the peer group. There appear to be many similarities between the ways in which students and adults in a community think about and use alcohol. Barnes (1981) surveyed students and adults in the same community to assess the similarity in their respective patterns of use. The survey results showed similar patterns of use of beer, wine, and other liquors. The adults and students described similar patterns of alcohol use in the home on special occasions or at mealtimes. Three basic reasons for drinking were described by the two groups: conforming functions ("So I won't be different from my friends"); social, festive functions ("It's a good way to celebrate"); and personal effects ("It helps relieve pressure"). The first reason was somewhat more important to adolescents than to adults. The second was most important to both groups. The third was somewhat more important to adolescents than to adults. Neither the first nor the third reason helps to predict if a person will be a heavy drinker, whether student or adult. Barnes concluded that the drinking patterns of students and adults are extremely similar. The adult members of a community set the attitudinal and behavioral tone for alcohol use, and adolescents are socialized to internalize that position.

A somewhat different view is discovered if one asks adolescents about parental approval of drinking patterns. Adolescents perceive their parents as disapproving of almost any drug use. With respect to alcohol use, over 90% perceive their parents to be disapproving of having one or two drinks a day; however, they said their parents had a somewhat more flexible view of binge drinking, with 85% of high school seniors saying their parents would disapprove (Johnston et al., 1996).

The impact of parental sanctions against alcohol use depends heavily on the quality of the parent-child relationship:

> Compared to users, nonusers feel closer to both parents, consider it important to get along well with them, and want to be like them when they grow up. Nonusers' parents more typically provide praise and encouragement, develop feelings of interpersonal trust, and help with personal problems. Perceived as stricter, nonusers' parents more typically have rules about homework, television, curfew, and drugs and alcohol. Yet, they are not more punitive. Instead, parental control is enhanced by praise and encouragement and by an emotionally close relationship that encourages youngsters to seek parental advice and guidance. Young people who feel loved and trusted by parents want to emulate them, not bring embarrassment by inappropriate behavior. (Coombs & Landsverk, 1988, p. 480)

The peer group also contributes to the patterns of alcohol and drug use in adolescence, and helps explain potential inconsistencies in alcohol use. The majority (54%) of high school seniors say that they are around peers who use alcohol to get high, and close to 30% say they are around friends who get drunk at least once a week (Johnston et al., 1996). Even among eighth-graders, about 75% say they are around friends who drink.

Most adolescents do not drink every day. However, many engage in binge drinking, which they perceive as risky but as somehow acceptable within the peer context. Binge drinking is more frequent among boys than among girls and more frequent among the noncollege-bound than among the college-bound. Although adolescents say they perceive greater risk in binge drinking than in taking one or two drinks every day, they are less likely to disapprove of it than of daily drinking. Further, adolescents perceive their peers' attitudes as being much more similar to their own and much less disapproving of binge drinking than the attitudes of their parents (Johnston et al., 1996). Binge drinking and its role in college life are discussed further in Chapter 10.

Alcohol is a part of the life experience of most adolescents. Drinking is something they can do that symbolizes celebration, adult status, and some degree of behavioral independence from parents. Since most adults also drink alcohol, young people may readily perceive their disapproval of adolescent drinking as hypocritical. In this way, drinking may become an avenue for testing the limits of adult authority or for expressing behavioral autonomy from parental control.

From our knowledge of the central role of the peer group during this stage of life, we must assume that alcohol and drug use are influenced largely by peer pressure to conform to a group norm coupled with an adolescent's vulnerability to this pressure (Webster et al., 1994). Peer-group leaders who experiment with alcohol and drugs at a young age or who approve of binge drinking, alcohol, and maruijuana use at parties, or driving while intoxicated are highly influential in encouraging other group members to share these experiences. Peer expectations for drug use may become one criterion for peer-group acceptance. On the other hand, if peer norms reject drug use, the peer group may serve to shield its members from drugs and deny membership to those who use or abuse them. The social reference group's support of drug use during adolescence has long-term effects.

Early Entry into Alcohol and Drug Use

Several studies have attempted to assess the risk factors that influence early entry into alcohol and other drug use (Newcomb & Bentler, 1989). In one study of fourth- and fifth-graders, 15% reported alcohol use without their parents' knowledge (Iannotti & Bush, 1992). Both peer and family variables were significant predictors of the use of alcohol without parents' knowledge. Children who perceived that many of their friends had been drinking and experienced peer pressure to drink were more likely to drink. In addition, children who were in classrooms where a larger number of children reported drinking were also at greater risk of drinking. Perceptions of the amount of drinking that occurred in the family were also an important predictor of early alcohol use. Another study of alcohol and drug use among seventh-graders confirmed the importance of peer and family influences (Farrell et al., 1992).

Significant predictors of alcohol use included several peer factors: friends' approving of alcohol and drugs; feeling pressure to use alcohol and drugs; and knowing friends who had an alcohol and drug problem. There were also two family-related factors: being home alone 20 or more times in the past 30 days after school, and reporting that half or more of the adults the adolescents knew had an alcohol or drug problem.

The risk factors associated with early alcohol and drug use are linked to social class and culture. Control over the sale of alcohol to minors, its cost, and the efforts of parents and other adults, including school officials and the police, to monitor its use among adolescents are all community factors that influence the use of alcohol in early adolescence. In addition, alcohol plays a somewhat different role in various ethnic, cultural, and religious groups. For example, a comparative analysis of African-American, Cuban, non-Cuban Hispanic, and non-Hispanic white sixth- and seventh-grade males in Dade County, Florida, found different rates of alcohol use and different patterns of risk factors that predicted early use in the four groups (Vega et al., 1993). In this particular study, non-Hispanic whites had the highest percentage of early alcohol users (48%), Cubans the next highest (41%), non-Cuban Hispanics the next highest (31%), and African-Americans the lowest (25%). In all groups, low family pride and the adolescent's willingness to participate in delinquent behavior or to break the law were significant predictors of early alcohol use.

We have tried to point out how alcohol and drug use may become a part of the life of normal adolescents during the high school years. Experimentation with alcohol is relatively easy to understand in the context of the adolescent's psychosocial needs and the modeling of alcohol use in the family, peer group, and community. Although alcohol and drug use may be considered a normative "rite of passage" for most adolescents, it appears that children who begin to drink and/or use drugs early in adolescence—that is, before ninth grade—are especially vulnerable to more serious involvement with alcohol and drug use later (Murray, 1997). They experience some combination of family, peer, and psychosocial pressures that increase their willingness to engage in deviant behavior and to ignore or minimize the risks.

Chapter Summary

In the use of alcohol and drugs by high school students, we see all the central themes of early adolescence. First, the physical sensations associated with a drug high point to the adolescent's general sensitivity to sensuality and preoccupation with body changes. Second, the issue of perceived risks suggests the adolescent's growing cognitive capacities. The adolescent is capable of relating to a hypothetical situation as well as to a factual one. Third, the use of alcohol suggests the significance of the peer group and identification with it. Alcohol use is only one behavior that may be motivated primarily by a need for peer acceptance and a desire to conform to peer-group norms. At the same time, family bonds and a sense of family support continue to play a role in strengthening adolescents' ability to resist peer pressures and sustain an underlying sense of their personal worth.

The crisis of group identity versus alienation involves a potential tension between individual and family values and the peer pressures to violate them. In many cases, no deep contradiction exists. Adolescent resistance to parental values may be more realistically interpreted as a demonstration of personal independence rather than as a declaration of guerrilla warfare. On the other hand, the threat of peer rejection may push those adolescents who lack confidence in their own worth to violate essential values in the pursuit of acceptance. Teenage pregnancy, drug addiction, drunken driving, and serious delinquent behavior all reflect adolescents' capacity to engage in high-risk behaviors that have a great potential for modifying the life course and exposing them to new and serious physical and emotional hazards. The cultural climate in which adolescents work out peer-group relationships is of critical importance to success in this stage. Existing social expectations, stereotypical roles, and value orientations may either strengthen or undercut the adolescent's efforts to achieve personal satisfaction in the context of the peer group.

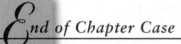

End of Chapter Case

At age 22, Mitja Che recalls a turbulent family life that directly affected his childhood and adolescence.

At 22 I can look back and see that my stepfather may have had good intentions, but he failed miserably as my stepfather. From the age of 5 until I moved out from my mom's house at 14, my stepfather was only a terror in my life. He was very possessive: there was his TV chair, his work space corner of the living room, his personal towel, his special fork, his cooking knives and Teflon pans, his stereo. And the rules were not to be broken. I recollect actually being hit three times, but the constant threats, chases around the house, and raised fists were much more intimidating. My mom repeatedly sent me to a therapist (actually, about five therapists in total) and each therapist would begin by asking me if I resented my stepfather because he was taking the place of my father. I would always respond, "No, he's an asshole." After a few sessions, my mom would be asked to come, and then my stepfather would be asked to join in as well. And then, every time, I was told by the therapist, "Mitja , you don't need to come in next week; I'd like to meet with your mom and stepfather for a session or two." And that was the end of therapy. After years of threats from someone whose drinking only amplified the meanness already there, I moved out of my mom's house into my dad's apartment. The saying, "Out of the frying pan and into the fire," applies nicely here.

Until I moved in full-time with my dad, we had a pretty good arrangement. My brother and I would eat meals with him and go out sometimes, but the remaining free time my brother and I spent without rules such as curfews or mandatory studying time. My father was dating a lot and was not around very often anyway. By this time, I was in high school and was failing many of my classes. I would skip classes to hang out with friends in cafes. I don't think that this bothered my dad too much, but my mother calling him, concerned about my lack of progress, bugged the hell out of him. My father was also an alcoholic, and our household had a lot of irrational arguments: I have always had a sharp tongue and do not back down from confrontations. My brother, on the other hand, always managed to be the baby of the family and would be lurking somewhere in the background, watching the fireworks and occasionally snickering at the ridiculousness of it all. . . . I moved out when the following two things happened: he hit me on two separate occasions, and I once came home to find all of my belongings gone. My brother, alone when I came home one evening, said, "I don't know what you've done, but Franz is pissed, and you'd better get out of here. All of your stuff is with him in the Toyota." My father had threatened before to throw everything of mine off of the local pier, and although I found out later that he didn't actually carry out the threat, I didn't wait around at the time to find out. I called two friends of mine, a wonderful couple in their early 30s, and moved in with them at the age of 15 and stayed with their family for almost three years before renting my own room in another household.

Source: Nestor, H., 1992.

Thought Questions

1. How are the developmental tasks of early adolescence reflected in this case?
2. How might instability in the family have influenced peer group relations for Mitja?
3. How might normative changes of adolescence have contributed to the conflicts Mitja experienced with his stepfather and his biological father?
4. How does Mitja's family situation provide a context for high-risk behavior?
5. What psychosocial resources do you think helped Mitja cope with his situation?
6. Looking ahead, how might the experiences of Mitja's early adolescence influence his ability to cope with the challenges of personal identity formation and intimacy in later stages?

Chapter 10

Engaged in the active resolution of the identity crisis, young people make commitments that will shape the structure of their adult lives. In this portrait, Picasso suggests the balance, focus, and purposefulness of a young woman who has achieved a sense of personal identity.

Later Adolescence (18–24 Years)

Chapter Objectives

- To examine the concept of autonomy from parents and the conditions under which it is likely to be achieved.
- To trace the development of gender identity in later adolescence, including a discussion of how the components of gender role identification that were relevant during the early-school-age period are revised and expanded.
- To describe the maturation of morality in later adolescence with special focus on the role of new cognitive capacities that influence moral judgments and the various value orientations that underlie moral reasoning.
- To analyze the process of career choice, with attention to education and gender-role socialization as two major influential factors.
- To describe the psychosocial crisis of later adolescence—individual identity versus identity confusion—the central process through which this crisis is resolved, role experimentation, the prime adaptive ego quality of fidelity to values and ideals, and the core pathology of repudiation.
- To examine some of the challenges of social life in later adolescence that may result in high-risk behaviors.

The years from 18 to 24 are characterized by heightened sensitivity to the process of identity development. Personal identity is developed as an individual struggles to answer the questions: What is the meaning of my life? Who am I? And where am I headed? Most young people are cognitively complex enough to conjure up alternative scenarios about their own future, including possible kinds of work and various meaningful relationships. They struggle with the uncertainty of having to choose many of their own life's directions. This period is often characterized by a high level of anxiety. Even though most young people are energetic and capable, they are also troubled by the lack of certainty about their future. Some may worry about whether they will be able to succeed in a chosen direction; others may be anxious because they do not even know what direction they wish to take.

Identity development during this period is a cornerstone of the unique individuality of adulthood. With the increase in life choices and life roles in contemporary society, it is probably more important today than it was in the past for young people to embrace particular values, goals, and life commitments as being central to their identity. What is more, they must recognize that the process of clarifying and evaluating their values and goals will continue to be a challenge. Identity is not firm or fixed for life. Rather, it is an orienting framework, a blueprint that helps shape decision making.

Throughout adulthood, there are many opportunities to revisit the identity commitments of later

adolescence. Still, the vision you create for yourself during this period remains salient later in life. People can recall these images as they evaluate their life in middle and later adulthood. They think back to what they may have hoped for or what they may have predicted for their future when they were 18 to 24. Adults may be surprised by how much more they have actually accomplished or how much more pleasure they have experienced in certain roles than they thought they might at that age. Or they may be discouraged and disappointed to realize that some of the hopes, dreams, and goals they had for themselves turned out to be unattainable. Across the span of adulthood, the identity formulations of later adolescence must be reworked and extended.

Although the theme of identity development is often conceptualized within the framework of the college experience, this process is critical for all those in the 18- to 24-year-old range who are making the transition from adolescence into adulthood. In the United States in 1994, 62% of recent high school graduates were enrolled in college (U.S. Bureau of the Census, 1996). This compares to about 45% who went to college after graduating from high school in 1960. Thus, over the past 35 years, it has become normative to continue some form of postsecondary schooling. The other 40% of young people go directly to work, join the military, or enter technical training programs after high school.

Unfortunately, most research on later adolescence has been limited to college students, who are a captive target for scholars of human development.

However, in this chapter we will find ways to illustrate how the construct of personal identity and the related themes of one's relationship with parents, the formulation of a moral ideology, a gender identity, and a set of behaviors and goals related to work are subjects of psychological activity for those later adolescents who do not attend college. ❖

DEVELOPMENTAL TASKS

Autonomy from Parents

Achieving a psychological sense of autonomy from one's parents must be understood as a multidimensional task that is accomplished gradually over the course of later adolescence and early adulthood. **Autonomy** is an ability to regulate one's own behavior and to select and guide one's own decisions and actions without undue control from or dependence on one's parents (Steinberg, 1990). It is not the same as rejection, alienation, or physical separation from parents. Rather, it is an independent psychological status in which parents and children accept each others' individuality. Many areas of similarity between parents and children may provide bonds for a continued close, supportive relationship into adulthood. However, those bonds are discovered through a process of self-definition. Adolescents who achieve autonomy can recognize and accept both the similarities and differences between themselves and their parents, while still feeling a sense of love, understanding, and connection with them.

Autonomy requires independence of thoughts, emotions, and actions. Much of the psychosocial development that has occurred before this stage can be understood as preparing the individual for independence from his or her parents. Such skills as dressing oneself, handling money, cooking, driving a car, reading, and writing have been mastered. Although it is easy to take these skills for granted, they are essential for someone who is living independently. The physical maturation that has taken place also contributes to the possibility of autonomy. Daily survival requires a certain amount of physical strength, coordination, and endurance, qualities that arrive with the physical maturity of adolescence.

Beyond these physical requirements, autonomy involves a psychological sense of confidence about one's unique point of view and an ability to express opinions and beliefs that may differ from those of one's parents (Herman et al., 1997). In early school age, the process of identification and the accompanying internalization of parental values allow the young child to function with a sense of what is appropriate behavior. In early adolescence, the child's ability to emerge from the intimacy of the family may also be promoted by a growing involvement with the peer group. As peer relations become more reciprocal, they satisfy many of the needs for closeness and support that were initially satisfied only within the boundaries of the family. Gradually, the young person's cognitive maturity provides a fund of information, a level of problem-solving ability, and a capacity to plan for the future that help sustain independent living.

The concept of family system **differentiation** has been associated with psychosocial maturity and a healthy emergence of individuality in adolescence. It is typically viewed as the extent to which a social system encourages intimacy while supporting the expression of differences (Bomar & Sabatelli, 1996). Within the family context, identity exploration is facilitated by an open exchange of ideas and a certain level of challenge. Adolescents must have opportunities to express their separateness within the boundaries of the family. They must feel that their parents accept and understand their need to have distinct opinions and views. This takes place as parents encourage their children to express new ideas and differing points of view without making them feel guilty when they disagree (Best et al., 1997). Adolescents who experience high levels of parental control and frequent exposure to parental conflict are likely to have difficulties achieving a comfortable sense of autonomy (Taylor & Oskay, 1995). Separateness is most readily achieved within a context of mutual caring and emotional support. A

Moving into a college residence hall or a new apartment marks a new stage in achieving autonomy from parents. With it come the many tasks and responsibilities of self-sufficiency.

secure attachment to parents, based on a perception of them as committed to their child's well-being, is essential for growth toward independence (Perosa et al., 1996; Palladino-Schultheiss & Blustein, 1994).

Autonomy and Leaving Home

Many later adolescents live outside their parents' homes. Living away from one's parents' household has become a symbol of independence, not only in our society but in some other cultures as well (Mitchell et al., 1989; DeVos, 1989). Whether young people leave home to go to college, join the military, get married, or take a job in another community, they and their parents see this step as a critical transition to adulthood. Before about 1960, marriage was the most traditional reason for moving to a new residence, other than leaving temporarily for college or the military. Since that time, however, it has become increasingly common for adolescents and young adults in the United States to expect to live in a separate residence for some time before marriage.

Parents and adolescent children have different views about the age at which children are expected to leave home. Parents tend to expect children to leave home at an older age, more closely tied to the expected age of marriage, than do adolescent children. Those with more resources are likely to accept an earlier age of leaving home than are low-income families. In addition, parents expect daughters to live at home longer than sons, but these differences are not reflected in the expectations of the adolescents themselves. Thus, this issue is a potential source of family conflict. In stepfamilies, neither parents nor children are likely to expect leaving home to be related to the age of marriage. Children in these families are more likely to view leaving home as a way of becoming independent of a family environment that is not entirely comfortable (Goldscheider & Goldscheider, 1989).

Economic factors and social norms play a significant role in the timing of leaving home. In 1970, 47% of those aged 18–24 were living as the child of a householder, including students who were living in college housing during most of the year but identified their permanent residence as that of their parents, while 38% were married and living in their own household. In 1995, 53% of this age group were living as the child of a householder (including students living at college), and only 21% were married and living in their own household. In both years, a greater percentage of females than males were married and in their own households, while a greater percentage of males than females were living with their parents (U.S. Bureau of the Census, 1996). As norms for age at marriage change, and as the costs of living independently increase, the age for establishing an independent household rises. As a result, the transition from later adolescence to early adulthood will have to be worked out in the context of living in one's parents' household. Young people in the age range 18 to 24 are also creating new household arrangements—living with friends or moving from one set of friends and family to another without a permanent address.

Autonomy and the College Experience

Going away to college is an intermediate move between living at home and establishing a permanent residence before marriage. The mere act of going to college does not in itself bring a sense of leaving home or of psychological autonomy from parents. In fact, most students do not go far from home when they enter college as freshmen; 80% attend college in their home state (U. S. Department of Education, 1997). In addition, many students continue to live at home while they attend college, and most still request and receive both emotional and instrumental support from their parents (Valery et al., 1997).

College freshmen express a variety of attitudes that suggest different views about their desire to be independent from their family. For students entering college in the fall of 1996, 17% said that an important reason for deciding to go to college was to get away from home, while 38% were going to college because their parents wanted them to go. When asked about reasons that were important in selecting the college that they ended up attending, 22% said they wanted to live near home (*Chronicle of Higher Education*, 1997). In fact, as they enter college, students differ markedly in how much work they have already done toward achieving autonomy from their parents, how much they desire it, and what evidence they use to determine whether they have achieved autonomy.

When asked to tell how they knew when they had left home, college students generated eight categories of explanations (Moore & Hotch, 1981), including physical separation (moved to an apartment), emotional separation (don't feel close to the family), and personal control (make own decisions). Some students viewed leaving home as a positive experience and tied it to a sense of increased personal control. Others linked leaving home to negative feelings of emotional separation or homesickness. For most adolescents, whether they are at college or not, the process of achieving a psychological sense of independence from home includes working through feelings of separation and the loss of emotional closeness that was characteristic of an earlier period of childhood, resolving uncertainties about economic independence, facing the challenges of independent decision-making, and taking responsibility for those decisions and their consequences.

The experience of entering college focuses new attention on one's attachment relationships. An area of special interest has been the changing quality of the attachment relationship between college students and their parents as the students leave home (Bloom, 1987). Students who live at college are more likely to rely on the mental representations of their attachment figures, whereas students who live with their parents continue to be involved daily with concrete interactions. Issues of autonomy and control, establishing new guidelines and limits related to participation in family life, involvement in relationships with peers, and management of time and money are resolved in the absence of direct input from parents for most students who live at college, but continue to involve parental input for students who live at home.

For students who live on campus, preoccupation with thoughts and concerns about their parents tends to diminish over the course of the first semester, while new relationships form and a new confidence in their independent decision making builds. The attachment scheme or representation rather than actual interactions with parents is what becomes modified. Many students who attend college away from home begin to have more positive thoughts and feelings about their parents. At the same time, they begin to detect a new level of confidence and respect from their parents, who appreciate that their children are managing to take on new responsibilities and to make good decisions on their own. On the other hand, students who live at home while attending college tend to continue to be preoccupied by concerns and thoughts about their parents based on actual daily interactions, and the quality of their relationships is viewed as more conflictual (Sullivan & Sullivan, 1980; Berman & Sperling, 1991).

In addition to overall patterns of change that are characteristic of students who live at home and those who live on campus, there is evidence of individual differences in the salience of attachment issues. For example, Berman and Sperling (1991) found that college-age females tended to have higher levels of concern about their parents and were more preoccupied by thoughts of them than were college-age males. However, those males who showed an especially high level of concern and preoccupation with thoughts of their parents at the beginning of their freshman year were most likely to be experiencing strong feelings of depression by the end of the term. For females, high levels of attachment to parents were not linked to depression. Perhaps the male students had not fully realized the extent to which their sense of independence was sustained or supported by their parents. Upon separation, they discovered that they had relied more upon their parents for affection and support during the high school years than they had realized. Based on many observations of college-age students, it is clear that some are much less ready than others to embrace the demands for new levels of independence and responsibility.

Gender Identity

Gender is a biologically based and socially defined category. In later adolescence, new and important revisions and elaborations of the child's earlier work on gender-role identification are taking place (see Chapter 7). The developmental task of forming one's gender identity reflects the need to integrate and synthesize the three basic components of gender—its biological, psychological, and social meanings—into a view of oneself as a man or a woman entering into the complex social world of adult life. The formulation of **gender identity** refers to the acquisition of a set of beliefs, attitudes, and values about oneself as a man or a woman in many areas of social life, including intimate relations, family, work, community, and religion (Giele, 1988).

The Role of Culture

The social system exists outside the person and operates independently. As discussed in Chapter 3, according to the *social role theory*, roles are basic building blocks of social organizations. Every organization, including a family, a workplace, a community, and a culture, can be described by its roles. Individuals learn the roles of their social system throughout their lives. Through the socialization process, people internalize the expectations associated with many life roles and apply the socially shared norms and standards linked to them to their own behaviors. This process occurs with respect to gender-related roles as well as to kinship, age, occupation, and other socially constructed roles. For example, when a person becomes a parent, a male is called a father and a female is called a mother. Both are parenting roles, but gender is identified and each role is associated with somewhat different expectations.

All cultures construct gender-differentiated roles, and people expect one another to behave in certain ways because they are male or female. Perhaps more important, they form expectations of how men and women ought to act when they are together so that the distinctions between the genders are demarcated (Freud, 1994). These expectations are taught and learned, beginning early in life.

In the United States, many people argue that gender-based role distinctions are inappropriate, at least as part of public life. They believe that men and women should be considered equal and treated identically in all public matters. But in many cultures, there are extreme, agreed-upon norms prescribing differences between males and females. Often these norms establish specific power differences as part of the gender distinctions. Typically, men have more power than women but this is not always the case.

Others argue that men and women should be considered equal, but that they should be treated in ways that take into account differences in their needs and capacities. For example, a bill introduced in Congress required that all public places such as auditoriums, stadiums, and theaters have twice as many public bathroom facilities for women as for men to take into account the physiological and social differences in women's elimination practices.

In the United States, and in many other industrialized nations, people are engaged in a wide-ranging dialogue about the scientific, legal, and sociohistorical bases of gender roles that is leading to a revision, perhaps even a revolution, in how gender serves as an organizing social structure. While this dialogue takes place across many groups and in many contexts, there is still powerful pressure on young people to achieve their own personal gender identity. Although they may be influenced by certain voices and views in the larger society, later adolescents must decide for themselves about the meaning they will make of their own designation as a male or a female.

Cultures construct gender-differentiated roles. In the U.S., the traditional attire of the bride and groom create an ideal image of feminine beauty and masculine respectability to which many young people aspire.

Gender-Linked Expectations

In later adolescence, biological, psychological, and social systems produce heightened activity in the area of gender identity formulations. The person is learning about bodily feelings and psychological states that are relevant to sexual activity.

Psychologically, a person wrestles with how to meet cultural and ethnic-group expectations related to gender. The knowledge base regarding the implications and consequences of gender for each individual broadens as new understanding about adult roles is acquired. The person's specific social system or social convoy operates to engage the individual by making demands for various degrees and amounts of gender-linked behavior. For example, in a national survey of college freshmen, students were asked to respond to a number of questions about attitudes and values such as, "Activities of married women are best confined to home and family." In 1970, 48% of freshmen agreed with that statement; in 1996 only 24% of freshmen agreed (U. S. Bureau of the Census, 1996; *Chronicle of Higher Education*, 1997). Historical trends modify the outlook of both men and women on their appropriate and "normative" roles. Gender-role expectations exist at the cultural, institutional, interpersonal, and individual levels. As later adolescents learn about these expectations, they must integrate and synthesize them with their assessments of their personal needs and goals.

A Reevaluation of Gender Constancy

Each of the components of sex-role identification discussed in Chapter 7 undergoes some transformation as work on gender identity continues. Later adolescents can appreciate that the use of gender labels is a social convention and that, apart from the genital basis of this label, there are wide individual differences within gender groups in most traits and abilities. What is more, information about genetic anomalies as well as medical technologies may lead later adolescents to realize that it is possible to have a conflict between one's genetic gender and one's external genitalia. Transsexuals develop a gender identity that is opposite to their biological sex. They feel certain of their gender, and at odds with their genital features. In these cases, the possibility of a sex-change operation provides an alternative to the notion of gender constancy (Crooks & Baur, 1996). In other words, later adolescents may realize that gender is not quite as fixed and constant as they may have believed when they were children.

Learning New Sex-Role Standards and Reevaluating Old Ones

The content of sex-role standards—that is, the cultural and subcultural expectations concerning the appropriate behavior of males and females—is different for later adolescents than for young children. The content changes as a result of changing age-related expectations and also of social change. For a 6- or 7-year-old boy, it may have been important to learn to be independent, to stand up for himself, and not to hit girls. For a later adolescent male, the sex-role expectations may include holding a steady job, demonstrating sexual prowess, or being competitive. For a 6- or 7-year-old girl, on the other hand, the emphasis may have been on taking turns, not being too bossy, and staying clean. For a later adolescent female, sex-role expectations may focus on being a caring, supportive friend; expressing maternal, nurturant behavior; or having an attractive figure and knowing how to dress well.

In later adolescence, both males and females begin to develop an analysis of what it takes to "get ahead" in their social world, whether success is defined as finding a mate, getting a good job, being a good parent, or being popular. They may learn to be more flexible in their interpersonal behavior, modifying their strategy to suit their goals. They discover that such traits as assertiveness, goal-directed behavior, competitiveness, being a good communication partner, personal disclosure, and negotiation are all required in social situations, and they learn to develop and apply them as required. In previous generations, some of the traits mentioned above were considered masculine and some feminine. Today, however, they are perceived as helpful to both men and women to be able to succeed in work and family life.

Sex-role standards may change over the 10-year period from a person's early-school-age years to later adolescence. For example, mothers of daughters who were born in the 1970s may have emphasized early autonomy training and encouraged self-reliance, believing that their daughters were more likely to remain single longer and enter nontraditional careers in which they would need to compete effectively with men. However, these girls are entering adulthood in the 1990s, a period when many of the "traditionally feminine" qualities, such as good interpersonal skills, the capacity for empathy, and the ability to build bonds of connection with others, are making a fashionable comeback not just at home but in industry and global affairs, and not just for women but for men as well.

As later adolescents engage in a process of ethnic identity clarification, they may also review and revisit the sex-role standards and stereotypes of their ethnic group (Rotheram-Borus & Wyche, 1994). For example, for Latinas there is a strong cultural emphasis on the role of women as mothers who are nurturant, virtuous, and devoted to their husbands and children. This sex-role standard places pressure on them to restrict their occupational aspirations and to remain close to their family of origin, particularly when it comes to thinking about going to college or planning for a career (Chilman, 1993). In later adolescence, Latinas must review these expectations, weighing the benefits they have had from this kind of close, attentive mothering with their own changing desire for higher levels of educational and occupational attainment.

As one considers the current context of sex-role expectations, it appears that the culture is moving toward more flexible standards. Today, it is recognized that it benefits both men and women to be appropriately assertive and to be sensitive communicators. Former rigid expectations have been relaxed and replaced by a greater diversity of behavior that is considered acceptable for both men and women in our society. The greatest impact of this revision is on the later adolescent population as they formulate their gender identities. There are more options, choices, and goals, and fewer obstacles to expressing personal preferences.

Revising One's Childhood Identifications

The component of parental identifications that contributes to gender identity is also reviewed and revised in later adolescence. During this time, young people begin to encounter a wide range of possible targets for identification. Within the college environment, students meet teachers, residence-hall counselors, and older students whose views and values may differ widely from those of their parents. Outside the college environment, workers meet supervisors, other workers, and social companions whose views and values may differ widely from those of their parents. In addition, later adolescents may admire public figures, such as religious leaders, political leaders, artists, or scholars whose work and ideas are especially inspiring. In the process, later adolescents revisit the content of their parental identifications. They analyze those beliefs, attitudes, and values that they may have "swallowed whole" as children, evaluating which of them are still relevant to their own personal vision of themselves functioning as a man or a woman in their current situation. They try to determine whether the lessons they learned as children about how husbands and wives, fathers and mothers, men and women, treat each other and think about each other remain applicable.

Adding a Sexual Dimension to Gender Identity

In addition to revisions in parental identifications, later adolescents must add a sexual dimension to their gender identity that did not play much of a role in their childhood gender-role identifications. The biological changes of puberty must be incorporated into one's gender identity; adolescents must integrate an adult body into their self-concept. They become aware of their bodies as they experience changes in body shape, height, weight, and strength.

The changes associated with physical maturity for women, especially the development of breasts and the onset of menstruation, introduce new and compelling thoughts about the childbearing role and its place in the young woman's sense of self. These changes do not necessarily compel a young woman to accept the role of mother. However, they present a concrete reminder of her maternal potential and force her to con-

The crystallization of gender identity requires the integration of one's sexuality, including physical appearance, primary and secondary sex characteristics, sexual drives, and fantasies. One's sexual identity is as much a mental representation as a physical reality.

front her intentions about pregnancy and mothering as she integrates her physical self into a gender identity (Zilbach, 1993).

Notions of physical attractiveness become more salient during this time. Adolescents are aware that first impressions are based on physical appearance. Satisfaction with one's physical appearance provides an important basis for approaching social relations with a positive, optimistic outlook (Abell & Richards, 1996). Furthermore, it may influence one's attractiveness or initial desirability as a sexual partner. In contrast, dissatisfaction with one's physical appearance as integrated into the self-concept, may interfere with the formation of positive social relationships, causing the person to approach interpersonal contacts with self-consciousness and a pessimistic expectation that he or she will be rejected.

The hormonal changes of puberty bring new sexual impulses as well as the capacity for reproduction. Hormonal changes stimulate changes in the basis of relationships. These changes call attention to new emotions, such as jealousy, love, depression over loss of love, sexual arousal, and passion. Individual differences in hormone levels are linked to sex-role characteristics. In particular, high levels of testosterone production are associated with aggressiveness in males, with strong needs for achievement and independence in females, and with high levels of sexual energy in both males and females. Women who have high levels of testosterone describe themselves as robust, resourceful, impulsive, and unconventional (Baucom et al., 1985). Maturation of the hormonal system, which influences emotional arousal as well as sexual urges, contributes to the development of one's gender identity.

Research on sexual orientation suggests that later adolescence is a common time for the emergence of a homosexual identity. During this time, young people begin a more active process of integrating their sexual fantasies, their experiences of sexual arousal, and their understanding about sexual behavior into a sexual identity (Herold & Marshall, 1996). Later adolescents, who may have struggled with acknowledging and accepting their homosexual orientation during the high-school period, are likely to resolve these inner conflicts and disclose their sexual orientation to others. This process is fostered by support from at least one close person and by increasing involvement in the gay community. Although disclosure has its risks, failure to disclose or trying to continue to "pass" as heterosexual is typically associated with strong feelings of isolation and self-repudiation (Troiden, 1993).

Finalizing Gender-Role Preference

During later adolescence, new work is done in the area of gender-role preference. Preference is based on an assessment of two factors: how well one can meet the cultural and social expectations associated with one's gender and how positively one views the status associated with it. If later adolescents become aware that their gender prevents them from having access to resources, influence, and decision-making authority, they are likely to experience a decline in their gender-role preference. This could happen to males as well as females, depending on the paths they choose to pursue and the gender biases they encounter. For example, in general we tend to think of career aspirations as being stifled for women as a result of attitudes on the part of men who think that women are simply not suited to a certain type of work. However, the reverse situation may apply to men who are interested in fields such as early-childhood education or nursing.

If later adolescents perceive that, apart from real differences in ability, one gender group is treated with greater respect, given more opportunities, and responded to with more attention or greater rewards, then their gender-role preferences are likely to be recalibrated. Based on our own experiences, it appears that college students do not see much of this type of gender discrimination or preference. They tend to view the college environment as providing plenty of opportunities and equal access to resources for both males and females. What is more, both males and females feel equally oppressed by the stressors of college life and the uncertainties associated with the decisions they are trying to make. Typically, it is not until they enter the world of adult employment that they begin to experience the power differential that continues to operate to the benefit of white men in U.S. society.

Later adolescents who enter the world of work at the end of high school are confronted by the power differential immediately and may experience intimidation that forces them to accept it. For example, a woman who makes two dollars per hour less than a male counterpart may be afraid to say anything because she needs the job. She will have to integrate the reality of what she experiences into the formulation of her gender identity. One strategy is to accept that this is the way things should be according to gender-role norms and that women should defer to men, and their contributions should be treated as less worthwhile. Another strategy may be to look for a different kind of work in a setting where women and men are treated equally. The college population tends to set social trends by according more variety and less rigidity to gender-linked role expectations. On the other hand, the noncollege population tends to set employment trends by breaking down barriers in many male-dominated areas of work, such as construction, trucking, and public safety.

In the United States, there are currently wide variations in attitudes about gender-linked roles, and later adolescents are likely to encounter conflicting expectations regarding gender-role standards. The more diverse the community, the more likely a young person is to encounter contrasting views about what adult men and women ought to be like. The gender-linked expectations one experiences in face-to-face interactions provide a good deal of the content of sex-role standards. For later adolescents, a larger number of friends are available to help work out the conflicts related to sexual behavior and other gender issues (Levitt et al., 1993). Individuals can shape and strengthen the nature of their gender identity by spending time with other people who support their views and values about how men and women ought to behave toward one another and what life paths are most desirable for them. Most studies find that, during the college years, students become more flexible in their gender-role attitudes and more egalitarian in their views about how men and women ought to function in school, work, family, and community life (Pascarella & Terenzini, 1991).

Internalized Morality

The development of morality was introduced in Chapter 7, "Early School Age." At that stage, morality consists primarily of internalizing parental standards and values, recognizing the difference between right and wrong, and learning to control one's behavior in anticipation of its moral consequences. As young people achieve new levels of autonomy from their parents and encounter new situations, they discover that some of the moral principles they learned as 6- or 7-year-olds neither apply to the new situations nor provide much of a rationale for why they should behave one way and not another. Later adolescents explore the distinction between social conventions and moral issues. Behaviors that may have been viewed as moral issues during childhood may be reevaluated as social conventions. Some aspects of one's childhood morality must be dissolved and restructured to meet the impending demands of adulthood. Within the overall process of formulating a personal identity, later adolescents begin to see themselves as moral beings whose actions have implications for the well-being of others. They begin to make moral commitments and to judge their behavior as well as the behavior of others according to new moral standards (Damon, 1996).

New Cognitive Capacities

Later adolescents bring new cognitive capacities to the arena of moral decision-making. They are more aware than younger children of the actual and possible consequences of their actions, both for themselves and for others. They are also able to consider the multiple perspectives that are possible in a moral situation. In addition, they are increasingly aware of the rights and needs of others, and they are able to step outside the situation in order to examine how an action may satisfy their own needs but harm others. Later adolescents are concerned about how principles of social responsibility, human rights, and justice can be preserved in a moral decision.

Stages of Moral Reasoning

Lawrence Kohlberg (1964, 1969; Colby & Kohlberg, 1987) suggested that a qualitative change in a person's ability to identify moral issues and decide about moral behavior is expected from early school age to later adolescence. His theory of the development of moral thought includes three levels of moral reasoning divided into six substages (see Chapter 7, Table 7.3).

At Stage I, called the preconventional level, from about ages 4 to 10, the child is concerned about the external consequences of behavior and about the power of authority figures. Stage II, called the conventional level, from about ages 10 to 18, represents a concern about the maintenance of the existing rule structure and a respect for authority. Stage III, called the postconventional level of moral reasoning, from about age 18 into adulthood, includes an awareness of the social conventions that result in the formulation of rules and laws. From this perspective one can appreciate the cultural relativism of values and a commitment to either a personal or universal set of moral principles, including greater concern about matters of justice. The proportion of people who reach this level of moral reasoning is small, but it increases during early and middle adulthood.

Longitudinal data provide strong evidence of the sequential nature of these stages during childhood and adolescence (Nisan & Kohlberg, 1982; Colby et al., 1983; Snarey et al., 1985; Colby & Kohlberg, 1987). The sequence of stages proposed by Kohlberg is noted in a variety of cultures outside the United States. Research confirming this has been done in Israel, Turkey, the Bahamas, Honduras, Mexico, India, Kenya, Nigeria, and Taiwan. Participants in these studies used forms of reasoning similar to those used by U.S. samples. The adults and adolescents in every culture used levels of reasoning that were higher than those used by the children (Nisan & Kohlberg, 1982; Rest, 1983; Snarey et al., 1985; Colby & Kohlberg, 1987).

Experiences that Promote Moral Reasoning

Although the sequence of stages appears to be well established, the level of moral reasoning that an individual actually attains depends on the kinds of moral challenges and situations encountered. For college students, like the one in the following example, the academic curriculum itself often creates a degree of cognitive disequilibrium that promotes a revision in moral reasoning:

> I was taking a theology class as a freshman in college and was presented with 'bold' alternatives to understand and interpret the creation story—primarily to understand it as a myth. My life up to that point was characterized by asking many questions but arriving at few answers. To those in my fundamentalist background, those questions were annoyances but not unsurmountable problems. In my shift to some answers to those questions, I moved away from fundamentalism to a more broadly based and responsible manner of critical thinking. [What happened?] The professor was very bright and responsible, yet in a sophisticated way he was somewhat irreverent. I was troubled by the dilemmas that this posed for me in terms of my belief structures, but something about the information and the self-assurance of the professor encouraged me to embrace this new way of thinking. (Chickering & Reisser, 1993, p. 240)

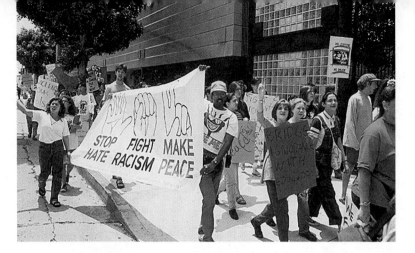

In Los Angeles, a student coalition marched in protest against racism. Through participation in dialogue and social activism, young people clarify their values and formulate their moral code.

Through participation in thought-provoking discussions or challenging life experiences, moral reasoning can advance to the next higher level. Social and educational experiences tend to promote moral reasoning when they draw on existing constructs and also challenge those constructs by making their inadequacies clear (Gfellner, 1986). During later adolescence, young people are exposed to a broader social context at work, in their college courses, or through greater involvement in community and national affairs. Many young people participate in community service, such as volunteering at a soup kitchen or tutoring younger children in reading or math. These experiences can stimulate discussions about differing points of view and a more complex analysis of the many interdependent factors that contribute to the social order. In fact, some communities have established delinquency prevention programs that involve adolescents in community service. As a result, a growing number of young people are likely to have new insights into moral situations (Mason & Gibbs, 1993; Yates & Youniss, 1996).

Exposure to a diversity of information, relationships, and worldviews stimulates moral reasoning. The change from conventional to postconventional morality that begins during adolescence involves a rethinking of traditional moral principles. During this period, there may be a loosening of ties to the family of origin and an increase in encounters with an expanding network of friends, students, and co-workers. Through interactions with diverse reference groups, there is an increasing recognition of the subcultural relativity of one's moral code. There may also be a degree of conflict over which moral values have personal meaning.

Challenges to Kohlberg's View of Moral Reasoning

Kohlberg's view of moral development has been challenged on a number of fronts. One criticism is that his picture of moral reasoning is based on a specific method, one in which individuals are asked to reach judgments about a particular type of moral dilemma. The dilemmas involve a **prohibitive moral judgment,** a decision about violating a law or breaking a promise in order to achieve some other goal. A typical example is the case of Heinz, a man who is placed in the dilemma of having to steal a drug from a pharmacist if he is to save his wife's life. **Prosocial moral judgments** involve a conflict between doing something helpful for someone else and meeting one's own needs. An example would be stopping to help a person whose car has stalled on the highway at the risk of being late for a very important job interview. People seem to be able to think more flexibly about a prosocial dilemma than about a prohibitive one. Moral decisions that draw on empathy and concern for the well-being of another person tend to evoke a higher level of moral reasoning than those that would require breaking a law (Kurdek, 1981; Eisenberg & Strayer, 1987).

Others point out that the level of moral reasoning is influenced largely by the situational context in which the dilemma is posed (Carpendale & Krebs, 1992). An ethical response depends on the norms, demands, short-term and long-term consequences of the situation. Mature moral reasoning takes into account the situational framework in which the dilemma is posed as well as the range of justifications available for taking one stance or another.

Justice versus Caring. A third controversy in the field of moral reasoning focuses on whether women and men approach ethical decision-making differently. Carol Gilligan (1977, 1982/1993, 1988) challenged Kohlberg's perspective, arguing that his description of the developmental course of reasoning about moral dilemmas is incomplete because it is based largely on the reasoning of male subjects about hypothetical rather than real-life situations. She claimed that men and women have distinct orientations toward moral dilemmas. According to Gilligan, women approach moral decisions with greater sensitivity to the context of the problem and a strong sense of caring, focusing on one's responsibility for others and feelings of connection to them. She asserts that men, in contrast, emphasize abstract principles, rules and laws, and the conflicts between the rights of the parties involved in the conflict. A woman, for example, might ask which outcome of a moral dilemma would result in the least harm for all concerned; whereas a man might ask whether one person has the right to infringe on the rights of others (Friedman, et al., 1987). These differences, according to Gilligan, are the product of different socialization patterns and result in different orientations to values, family life, and the basis of self-worth.

Several investigators have examined the claims of consistent differences between men and women in moral orientation. The literature is inconclusive regarding the strength and consistency with which they differ in their use of what have come to be called the *justice orientation* and the *caring orientation.* It appears that experiential and situational issues, as well as concerns about interpersonal obligations and caring, are more dominant in open-ended responses from both men and women than are issues of justice and individual rights (Walker, et al., 1987; Galotti, 1989; Colby & Damon, 1994).

In a cross-sectional study of 8th-graders, 11th-graders, and college sophomores, students were asked to describe their moral reasoning strategies (Galotti, et al., 1991). The instructions were as follows: When faced with a moral dilemma, what issues or concerns influence your decision? In this context, a moral dilemma was defined as "a situation in which different things that you value come into conflict." Eleven themes were identified from these essays (Table 10.1). Reasoning based on moral themes typically associated with a caring orientation was consistently more common than reasoning based on the themes associated with noncontextual, abstract reasoning at all ages, but with age, both males and females added more autonomous, justice-oriented reasoning to their repertoire.

Later adolescents must evolve an integrated value system with which to guide their behavior, particularly in the face of strong pressures to violate their moral beliefs. Young people encounter situations that they have never faced before—situations that require moral evaluation, judgment, and decisions about action. College students may be asked to lend a paper that they have written so another student can turn it in as his

---

TABLE 10.1 Themes that Guide Moral Decisions

Title and Description of Theme

What Others Would Think/Feel: Whether subject (S) consults others, or imagines others in a similar situation, to make a decision.

Effect on Others: Whether S considers the possible benefit or harm to other people in making the decision.

Situation Specifics: Whether S makes explicit references to the decision "depending on the situation."

Effect on Self: Whether S considers the possible benefit or harm to himself or herself in making the decision, including personal guilt and social reaction.

What I Feel: Whether S mentions "intuition" or "gut feeling" in making a decision or mentions "how I would feel." Emphasis on feeling.

Religious Teachings: Whether S considers formal religious teachings (e.g., the Bible, the Talmud) or reasons from experience in an organized religion (to be distinguished from "conscience" or "personal sense of right and wrong").

Greater Societal Good: Whether S refers explicitly to the concerns of society in general or to the "greatest good."

Legal Issues: Whether S refers to local, state, or federal laws.

Personal Code of Ethics: Whether S makes explicit references to a personal set of moral values or ethics, to a personal sense of right and wrong, or to specific principles that are valued most highly; the values of the issues to S; the principles by which S was raised.

Systematic Reasoning: Whether S describes trying to reason logically and systematically without being affected by mood or emotion. If S uses some of the following phrases: "weigh the pros and cons," "gathered all the facts," "think it through," and "look at all the possibilities."

Rights of Others: Whether S explicitly mentions the (legal, personal, or moral) rights of other people (to be distinguished from the benefits or harm to people; see "Effect on Others," above).

As you review this list, try to fit each theme into the three stages of Kohlberg's theory: preconventional reasons, conventional reasons, and postconventional reasons. Then review the list again, trying to make a distinction between the caring and the justice orientation to morality. Which themes most reflect the caring orientation? Which themes reflect the justice orientation? Are there some themes that do not fit into either system?

Source: Galotti et al., 1991.

or her own work. Dilemmas about using illegal drugs, stealing books and journals from the library, or maintaining religious traditions and practices may confront a young person who is away from home for the first time. In these situations, the young person has the opportunity to envision the self as a moral actor and take a course of action most congruent with other facets of her or his personal identity.

Career Choice

The choice of occupation sets the tone for one's early adult lifestyle. The world of work determines one's daily routine, including the time one wakes up, daily activities, expenditures of physical and mental energy, and conditions for both immediate and long-term rewards. Occupation confers social status and provides varying opportunities for advancement. Finally, it represents a direct or indirect expression of one's value system. In subsequent chapters, we will discuss socialization in the work setting and the management of a career. Here we focus on the process of career choice and its impact on development during later adolescence.

Work Experiences in Early Adolescence

Many adolescents hold part-time jobs while they attend high school. In 1995, over half of 16- to 19-year-olds were in the labor force (U.S. Bureau of the Census, 1996). By the time they have graduated from high school, only about 7% of high school seniors say they have never worked for pay (Bachman et al., 1987).

There is some controversy about the benefits of working during high school and the extent to which these work experiences actually make a positive contribution to the occupational component of identity development. Some find that adolescents who work long hours in stressful jobs are more likely to evidence increased cigarette smoking, marijuana and alcohol use, truancy, and poor academic performance in school (Steinberg & Dornbusch, 1991; Manning, 1990; Bachman et al., 1986). Students who work long hours have less time for school activities, socialization with friends, or the development of other areas of interest. The kinds of work opportunities that are available to adolescents are usually minimally skilled jobs with high turnover, low pay, little decision-making responsibility, and little stimulation of skill development. These kinds of jobs are likely to produce depression and low self-esteem, and may contribute to feelings of alienation from the school environment. For some adolescents, time spent in these kinds of work settings is associated with the development of cynical attitudes toward work and greater acceptance of unethical practices by workers.

Other researchers emphasize the diversity of work experiences and the potential benefits of certain kinds of work. Students who are able to find and keep a good job may feel more confident about themselves and their promise for future employment (Bachman et al., 1986). When the work does not involve too many hours, and when it involves skill development that young people see as related to their future career direction, the experience is likely to be associated with higher levels of well-being and less involvement in problem behaviors. For girls, the perception of continuity between school and work, feeling that work improves one's school performance, had an especially positive relationship with mental health and well-being (Mortimer et al., 1992).

Factors Influencing Career Choice

As Figure 10.1 suggests, the process of career decision making is influenced by six major factors: individual, psychosocial-emotional, socioeconomic, societal, familial, and situational (O'Neil et al., 1980). These same factors contribute to sex-role socialization. It is important to see the interrelationship of these two domains for young people in our culture. Sex-role socialization creates a powerful filter through which choices related to career development are made (Eccles, 1987).

Of the six types of factors described in Figure 10.1, high school and college students reported that the individual factors, such as abilities, achievement needs, attitudes, and self-expectancies, most strongly affected their career decision making. They perceived familial, societal, and socioeconomic factors as having little or no impact (O'Neil et al., 1980). This is contrary to social science research, which provides extensive evidence that family factors play a key role in shaping educational aspira-

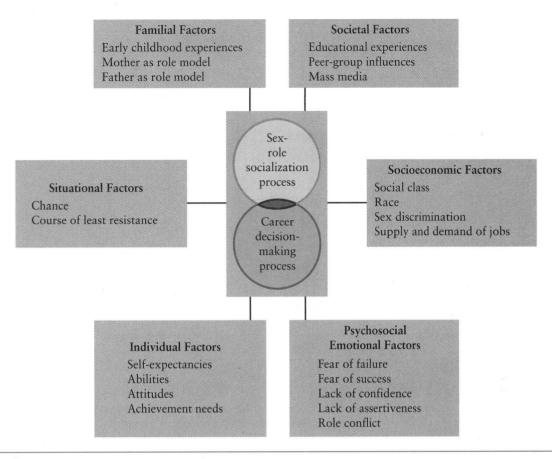

Familial Factors
Early childhood experiences
Mother as role model
Father as role model

Societal Factors
Educational experiences
Peer-group influences
Mass media

Situational Factors
Chance
Course of least resistance

Sex-role socialization process

Career decision-making process

Socioeconomic Factors
Social class
Race
Sex discrimination
Supply and demand of jobs

Individual Factors
Self-expectancies
Abilities
Attitudes
Achievement needs

Psychosocial Emotional Factors
Fear of failure
Fear of success
Lack of confidence
Lack of assertiveness
Role conflict

FIGURE 10.1

Factors affecting the sex-role socialization and career decision-making process
SOURCE: O'Neil, Ohlde, Barke, Prosser-Gelwick, & Garfield, 1980.

tions and occupational goals, while societal and socioeconomic conditions are major factors influencing the job market and the chances of both employment and advancement.

Family Background and Career Opportunities. Family background characteristics are associated with educational opportunities and aspirations from the youngest ages. In the period of early adolescence, children from low-income families and from those in which the parents did not graduate from high school are more likely to drop out of high school and less likely to be enrolled in postsecondary education. Of the seniors graduating from high school in 1992, 49% of those in the lowest socioeconomic group enrolled in a 2- or 4-year postsecondary program, while 91% of those in the highest socioeconomic group enrolled. More of those adolescents in the lowest socioeconomic group enrolled in 2-year programs, while more of those in the middle- and high-income groups enrolled in 4-year college programs (National Center for Education Statistics, 1997). Thus, differences in family resources result in diverging educational backgrounds, which have direct implications for the kinds of careers one is prepared to enter.

Education and Career Choice. One of the major factors influencing career opportunities is education. It is well documented that career advancement and associated earnings are closely linked to levels of educational attainment. Table 10.2 shows the median earned income on the basis of educational level for men and women who were 25 years old or older in 1993. There is no question that continued education beyond high school is a key element in the career development process. As the data indicate, however, educational achievement does not result in the same economic advantages for men and women. Women with one to three years of college earned less than men who had only a high school diploma.

TABLE 10.2	Median Annual Income of Men and Women 25 Years and Older, 1993, by Level of School Completed and Sex.	
	Median Annual Income ($)	
Education	Men	Women
9th to 12th grade, no diploma	21,752	15,386
High school graduate	27,370	19,963
Some college, no degree	32,077	23,056
Bachelor's degree	42,757	31,197

Source: National Center for Education Statistics, 1995.

For youths who leave high school or who graduate but do not go on to college, the job market has several unattractive features.

> Most of the jobs available at this level of educational attainment are routine, menial, temporary, more likely to be part time and to provide reduced monetary and nonmaterial rewards compared with jobs held by older workers. . . . Moreover, jobs within this sector are unusually unstable and may be supervised by rigid, autocratic employers, many of whom, particularly in the fast food industry, are not much older than the novice worker. (Borman & Hopkins, 1987, p. 136)

The impact of school experiences on subsequent career development goes beyond whether or not one plans to attend college. Vocational coursework of a specific nature, such as agricultural training, an emphasis on math and science courses, and frequent conversations with teachers about one's work-related decisions, are all associated with higher income and more stable work records after high school (Hubner-Funk, 1983; Griffin & Alexander, 1978).

For those who do not go on to college, career development appears to have two phases (Freeman & Wise, 1982; West & Newton, 1983). Given the kinds of jobs that are available and the outlook on work that was developed during high school, many young people start out with a rather cavalier approach to work. They take whatever job is available, work without much intention of long-term commitment, and exhibit erratic work behavior. For example, in a survey carried out by the Junior Achievement program, employers found that most high school graduates working for their companies were unprepared to meet their high-priority workplace skills including punctuality, dependability, and completing work assignments on time (*Columbus Dispatch*, 1998). Since most of these jobs do not require much training, one might infer that young workers are simply not motivated to approach them with high levels of conscientiousness. They are likely to quit these jobs when they have earned enough money to pay for the things they want and then remain unemployed for a while until they need more money.

During their 20s, the second phase of career development begins as young adults become more serious about their work. They try to find a good job, become more conscientious about their work performance, and stay with the job for a longer period. This new seriousness about work is likely to be associated with other commitments, especially marriage, and is usually seen as a positive step in the transition to adulthood.

In modern, postindustrialized societies, the path toward occupational attainment is inti-

In many communities, high school graduates begin employment in local factories. The work may be routine, but the pay is steady.

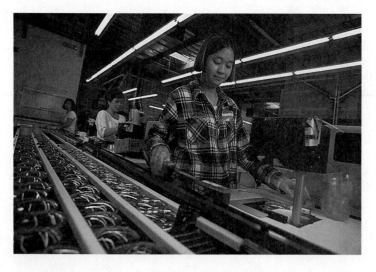

mately linked to educational aspirations and achievements expressed in high school. In a longitudinal study of students who were high school seniors in 1980, 36% of those who said they hoped to earn a bachelor's degree had done so by 1986. In comparison, only 7% of those who expected to attend less than four years of college had earned a bachelor's degree by 1986 (National Center for Education Statistics, 1995). In a more detailed longitudinal study of Swedish females, a similar pattern was found (Gustafson et al., 1992). One group of young women, about 41% of the sample, had high educational motivation at age 15. After completing their compulsory secondary schooling, they attended 2 to 5 years of advanced education leading to a career, and had no children by age 26. The other large group, 28% of the sample, had low educational motivation at age 15, did not go on to advanced education, and had children by age 26. These groups did not differ by parental socioeconomic status or by measured IQ. The authors concluded that, even though women may say that they endorse the idea of combining work and family roles, most women begin to develop aspirations and attitudes during early adolescence that lead to the crystallization of a "homemaker" or "career" orientation that is followed through in young adulthood.

Gender-Role Socialization and Career Choice. Gender-role socialization shapes career decisions through two significant psychological factors. First, as a result of socialization, men and women are likely to form different expectations about their ability to succeed in various career-related skills. Second, as a result of socialization, women and men are likely to establish different value hierarchies, reflecting different views of long-range life goals and their relative importance to one another (Eccles, 1987; McGowen & Hart, 1990).

Self-expectancies about the ability to fulfill the educational requirements and the job duties of specific careers are a major factor in determining career choices (Bridges, 1988; Long, 1989). In studies of career choice or career aspirations among women, those with a strong sense of their own goals, an awareness of their personal needs, and an ability to cope realistically with stress have been more likely to adopt a nontraditional career choice (Nevill & Schlecker, 1988; Long, 1989). In one study, college students were asked to evaluate their ability to complete the educational requirements and fulfill the job duties of ten traditionally male occupations and ten traditionally female occupations (Betz & Hackett, 1981). Males reported higher self-efficacy on five "male" occupations: accountant, draftsman, engineer, highway patrol officer, and mathematician. Females reported higher self-efficacy on five "female" occupations: dental hygienist, elementary-school teacher, home economist, physical therapist, and secretary. Males thought that the most difficult job duties of the 20 occupations listed were those of art teacher. Females thought the most difficult duties were those of engineer. These differences in expectations about the ability to succeed were not paralleled by differences in the students' ability tests in math or English, which might have made certain career choices unrealistic. These data suggest that in the process of career decision making, strong sex-typed conceptualizations of the job demands of specific careers intervene to screen out some alternatives and highlight others.

Gender identity influences attitudes and values that determine one's career goals and related choices. In a study of the educational and occupational attainment of low-income, rural Appalachian females, the importance of family socialization influences was highlighted (Wilson et al., 1993). The families tend to have strong family ties and high levels of consensus about norms for appropriate behaviors. They tend to endorse what have been called traditional gender roles, in which the men are the dominant decision-makers and the women are expected to be homemakers and also hold down low-paying jobs to help support the family. Educational and occupational aspirations are generally higher for male than for female children in these families, but both are encouraged to restrict their aspirations to career options that will keep them close to their childhood homes.

The consequences of gender-role socialization for career choice can be seen in the objectives that freshmen entering college in 1996 said were essential or very important in their lives (Table 10.3). Although men and women shared many common objectives, about 9% more women than men endorsed social values, 17% more women empha-

TABLE 10.3	Life Objectives Considered Essential or Very Important by College Freshmen, 1996	
Objective	Men (%)	Women (%)
Becoming accomplished in a performing art	11.9	12.5
Becoming an authority in own field	66.2	62.3
Obtaining recognition from colleagues for contributions to field	53.1	52.0
Influencing the political structure	20.6	15.4
Influencing social values	34.1	42.9
Raising a family	72.3	72.1
Having administrative responsibility for the work of others	40.0	37.3
Being very well off financially	76.4	72.2
Helping others who are in difficulty	53.4	69.8
Making a theoretical contribution to science	19.4	15.2
Writing original works	14.4	13.7
Creating artistic work	13.3	13.5
Becoming successful in own business	45.8	34.2
Becoming involved in programs to clean up environment	20.4	21.0
Developing a meaningful philosophy of life	42.1	42.1
Participating in a community-action program	20.0	26.6
Helping to promote racial understanding	30.9	37.8
Keeping up to date with political affairs	33.1	26.5
Being a community leader	33.5	30.9

SOURCE: Adapted from *Chronicle of Higher Education,* 1997, Almanac, p. 20.

sized helping others who were in difficulty, and 7% more women than men expressed concern about helping to promote racial understanding. About 12% more men than women valued becoming successful in their own business (*Chronicle of Higher Education,* 1997). Values are likely to direct students toward majors and future careers that will help them experience a sense of personal integrity, a balance between what they say is important and what they do.

Career Decision Making

The idea of career decision making must be evaluated in light of rapid changes in the nature of work, the pervasiveness of the two-earner family lifestyle, the increased likelihood of multiple job and career changes over the life course, and the constant reconfiguration of the job market, especially the current trends toward "downsizing," "work force reductions," and "retraining" (Church, 1993). The idea of occupational choice should not be confused with choice about labor-market participation. Although they may have a wide choice in the kind of work they will do, most people in the United States do not have a choice about whether or not to work (Herring & Wilson-Sadberry, 1993). In fact, almost 7% of young people in the age range of 20–24 have more than one job (U.S. Bureau of the Census, 1997).

Career choice itself reflects a central component of the person's emerging identity. For some young people, occupational choice is a reflection of continued identification with their parents. They may select the same job or career as that of one of their parents, or they may select a career

Many women enter professions that emphasize helping others. What might account for this trend?

because it reflects their parents' aspirations for them. Little personal choice is involved. For some, primarily women, there continues to be a path of primary identification with the roles of wife and mother, with only secondary investment in the labor market. Many of these women, especially those who marry and have children after high school, return to school or to technical training in their 30s and 40s in order to pick up the thread of career development, either as a result of divorce or when their children get older. Increasing numbers of men realize that their occupational career will need to be coordinated and integrated with that of their spouse, so that there are new expectations for flexibility, contributions to household tasks, and active participation in child-rearing. These changes require new thinking by young men about their own commitments to work and family life, as well as a new realization that they, too, need to screen their career aspirations through the lens of family values, just as women have done since the late 1960s.

Studies conducted in the United States, Canada, and Australia all confirm that concerns about future educational and career decisions constitute a major source of worry for adolescents (Violato & Holden, 1988). Seventy-seven percent of students entering college as freshmen in 1996 said that an important reason for going to college was to be able to get a better job (*Chronicle of Higher Education*, 1997). Many people assume that the younger a person is when he or she makes a career choice, the better. Perhaps that is why so many high school students worry about their career choices.

Most career development professionals, however, advise that a decision about a career be delayed until later adolescence or early adulthood (Osipow, 1986). A person who delays the decision has a clearer sense of his or her adult interests and goals. And by delaying the career decision, one has more opportunities to explore alternative work scenarios and to understand more about the labor market. Nonetheless, high schools, colleges, and various industries urge young people to make these decisions as early as possible. Thus, some of the tension that later adolescents experience in connection with a choice of career is a product of the lack of fit between socialization pressures and their own developmental timetable. With the increased likelihood of living to be 75 or 80 years old, there is no great rush to decide on a career by age 20. What is more, if one is likely to change careers two or three times over the life course, then selecting the first career ought to be viewed in a different light. This is not a decision that has to last a lifetime.

Career decision making is linked to other aspects of identity development. In particular, later adolescents worry about the extent to which commitment to a career may conflict with other commitments to family roles or values (Kram, 1985). Some young people struggle with the idea that success in a career may require them to sacrifice intimacy in family life. A young woman summarized this conflict when she described the advice she had received from her parents about her occupational future. Her mother had assured her that it was possible to combine work and family life, and that there are no greater satisfactions in life than those that come from raising a family. Her father, on the other hand, had advised her that, if she hoped to compete and succeed in the world of work, she would have to devote herself entirely to that goal and should give up the idea of having a family (Eccles, 1987). This example illustrates the interconnections between work in career decision-making and the commitment to values in other important areas of life.

Phases of Career Decision Making. Once a person begins to accept certain elements of her or his self-concept as they relate to the occupational aspect of identity, the process of career decision making begins. Tiedeman (Tiedeman & O'Hara, 1963; Miller & Tiedeman, 1972) has developed a model of phases of career decision-making. It illustrates how making career-related decisions helps to clarify one's occupational identity and, at the same time, uses the context of work to promote new learning about other aspects of the self (Figure 10.2). A career decision depends on the outcomes of several tasks during adolescence and early adulthood. With effective problem solving, the person gains increased control over life events and is better prepared to meet the challenges of the next phase of decision making. Tiedeman posits seven phases: the first four emphasize planning and clarification, the last three emphasize implementation.

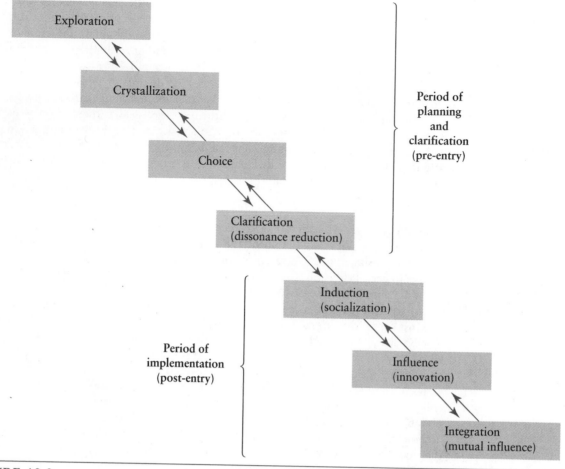

FIGURE 10.2
Seven phases of career decision making
Source: Based on Tiedeman & O'Hara, 1963.

In the **exploration phase,** the person realizes that a career decision must be made and therefore begins to learn more about those aspects of the self and the occupational world that are relevant to the impending decision. The person begins to generate alternatives for action. Uncertainty about the future and the many possible alternatives is accompanied by feelings of anxiety.

In the **crystallization phase,** the person becomes more aware of the alternatives for action and their consequences. Conflicts among alternatives are recognized and some are discarded. The person develops a strategy for making the decision, in part by weighing the costs and benefits of each alternative.

In the **choice phase,** the person decides which action alternative to follow. The decision is solidified in the person's mind as he or she elaborates the reasons why the decision is beneficial. There is a sense of relief and optimism as the person develops a commitment to executing the decision.

In the **clarification phase,** the person more fully understands the consequences of commitment to the decision that has been made. He or she plans definite steps to take and may actually take them or may delay them until a more appropriate time. The self-image is prepared to be modified by the decision.

During the **induction phase,** the person encounters the new environment for the first time. He or she wants to be accepted and looks to others for cues about how to behave. The person identifies with the new group and seeks recognition for his or her unique characteristics. Gradually, the self-image is modified as the person begins to believe in the values and goals of the new group.

In the **influence phase,** the person is very much involved with the new group. He or she becomes more assertive in asking that the group perform better. The person also

With changing technologies, new careers are continually emerging. Dr. Dower loads DNA samples into a gene sequencing machine. How might young people best prepare themselves for the adaptive flexibility required in our changing career environment?

tries to influence the group to accommodate some of his or her values. The self is strongly committed to group goals. During this phase, the group's values and goals may be modified to include the orientation of the new member.

Finally, in the **integration phase,** group members react against the new member's attempts to influence them. The new member then compromises. In the process, he or she attains a more objective understanding of the self and the group. A true collaboration between the new member and the group is achieved. The new member feels satisfied and is evaluated as successful by the self and others.

This model emphasizes continuous interaction between the individual and the work context. At first, interaction is necessary to clarify the person's talents and choice of career. Later, it is necessary to achieve a satisfactory level of adaptation to the work environment. At each juncture, whether the decision relates to college major, occupation, job change, or career redirection, effective decision-making involves all seven phases.

Characteristics of the contemporary labor market may be contributing to new difficulties that later adolescents encounter as they attempt to move through the first four phases of Tiedeman's model:

• The increasing number of jobs and careers available make the *exploration* phase difficult.
• As a result of changes in technology as well as in organizational structure, some skills become obsolete and some job markets dry up. With the advent of desk-top publishing and computer composition, for example, jobs for typesetters are disappearing. A career may become obsolete in the time it takes a young person to prepare for it.
• As established firms lose their identities in corporate mergers, identification with a particular company ceases to be appropriate.
• As most large companies go through restructuring and downsizing, the people who are left are asked to do more tasks of a greater variety. In addition to one's special area of training, it is important to develop support skills, such as word processing, data management, literature search skills, and verbal as well as written communication skills.
• New careers emerge at a rapid pace. From the time one enters the *choice* phase to the time one enters the *influence* phase, new kinds of work roles may become available.
• Career paths are less clear than they once were. Young people are being advised to expect three or four career changes in their lifetime. They may end up moving from the private to the nonprofit sector, from business to education, from service provider to entrepreneur.
• The cost of living, especially the costs of housing, health care, and education, introduces concerns about the amount of money that will be needed to live comfortably. Worries about making money may interfere with effective career decision making.

As a result of the anxiety and complexity that attends career decision making, career counseling has become a significant new career (Box 10.1).

Ideally, one's choice of occupation is the result of personal experimentation, introspection, self-evaluation, fact finding, and intuition. If so, this process becomes intimately interwoven with one's psychological development. In order to make a career choice, people may first choose to pose difficult questions to themselves about their skills, temperament, values, and goals. When they make a decision based on this kind of personal evaluation, they are likely to see their careers as a well-integrated part of their personal identities rather than as activities from which they are alienated or by which they are dominated.

BOX 10.1   ADVICE FROM CAREER COUNSELORS ON CAREER DECISION MAKING

Six suggestions from the career-counseling literature are helpful in developing an effective career decision-making process in later adolescence (Church, 1993; Pollan & Levine, 1997):

1. *Gather information about various careers.* A career decision should be approached at least as systematically as the decision to buy a car. Know enough about your own interests, abilities, and values to select several appropriate occupations. Then find out as much as possible about the educational and training requirements, the future job market, the career ladder, and the various organizations where this kind of work is available.

2. *Engage in work-related tasks in which you experience success.* Success experiences are a critical element in judgments of self-efficacy. If you are to believe that you can succeed in a certain career, it is important to have experiences of success in demanding tasks that either approximate or are directly connected to the career in question.

3. *Recognize the needs relevant to each phase of career decision making.* A person in the crystallization phase may need more specific information about the trade-offs of certain career paths. A person in the choice phase may need to develop a more personal relationship with someone in a particular career.

4. *Seek a variety of sources of information.* Teachers may have one view of a career, managers and supervisors quite another. Talk to people who might be co-workers as well as those who would be bosses. Parents who have their children's long-range welfare at heart may be an important source of help in career decision making. Friends are another important source, especially if they can engage in flexible fantasies about alternative futures.

5. *Build bridges between the abstract and the concrete.* Find opportunities to apply what you learn in the classroom to the work setting and to analyze observations from the work setting by reading, reflecting, and forming general principles about them. Ideally, one's career decisions will be a product of experiences and informed reflection about them.

6. Corporations do not make long-term commitments to their employees, so *do not make a long-term emotional commitment to your employer.* "Your work is not your life. Your work is what you do to have a life" (Pollan & Levine, 1997). So be ready to move, take on new jobs, and always be on the lookout for new positions where you can either make more money, learn new skills, or enjoy benefits that will contribute to your quality of life.

THE PSYCHOSOCIAL CRISIS: INDIVIDUAL IDENTITY VERSUS IDENTITY CONFUSION

Erik Erikson provided a comprehensive treatment of the meaning and functions of individual identity, from his inclusion of this concept in the theory of psychosocial development in 1950 to his analysis of American identity in 1974. His notion of identity involves the merging of past identifications, future aspirations, and contemporary cultural issues. The major works in which he discussed identity are the article, "The Problem of Ego Identity" (1959) and the book, *Identity: Youth and Crisis* (1968). Our presentation of this concept is based on these works.

Later adolescents are preoccupied with questions about their essential character in much the same way that early-school-age children are preoccupied with questions about their origins. In their efforts to define themselves, later adolescents must take into account the bonds that have been built between them and others in the past as well as the direction they hope to take in the future. Identity serves as an anchor point, providing the person an essential experience of continuity in social relationships.

"The young individual must learn to be most himself where he means the most to others—those others, to be sure, who have come to mean most to him. The term *identity* expresses such a mutual relation in that it connotes both a persistent sameness within oneself (self-sameness) and a persistent sharing of some kind of essential character with others." (Erikson, 1959, p. 102)

The Content Component of Identity

The structure of identity has two components: content and evaluation (Breakwell, 1986; Whitbourne, 1986). The *content*, what one thinks about, values, and believes in and the traits or characteristics by which one is recognized and known by others, may be further divided into the inner or private self and the public self. The **private self,** often described as a *sense of self,* refers to one's inner uniqueness and unity, a subjective experience of being the originator of one's thoughts and actions and of

This image captures a contemporary sense of the search for individual identity—a young woman with a broad-rimmed hat, hair flowing, one eye looking outward to the world, and one turned inward on the self.

being self-reflective. Through the private self, one recognizes the range of values and beliefs to which one is committed, and one can assess the extent to which certain thoughts and actions are consistent with those beliefs. The private, subjective sense of self, which develops over the course of the life span, includes four basic elements:

A sense of agency—being the originator of thoughts and actions.

A sense of unity—sensing that one is the same basic self from one moment or one situation to the next.

A sense of otherness—recognizing the boundaries between the self and others.

A sense of decentering or distancing—reflecting on oneself so that one can recognize and own one's thoughts and actions (Blasi, 1991; Glodis & Blasi, 1993).

The elements of the **public self** include the many roles one plays and the expectations of others. As young people move through the stage of later adolescence, they find that social reference groups, including family members, neighbors, teachers, friends, religious groups, ethnic groups, and even national leaders, have expectations of their behavior. A young person may be expected to work, attend college, marry, serve the country in the military, attend religious services, vote, and provide economic support for family members. Persistent demands by meaningful others result in certain decisions that might have been made differently or not made at all if the individual were surrounded by a different configuration of social reference groups. In the process of achieving personal identity, one must synthesize the private sense of self with the public self derived from the many roles and relationships in which one is embedded.

The Evaluation Component of Identity

The second structural component of identity, *evaluation*, refers to the significance one places on various aspects of the identity content. Even though most people play many of the same roles, their identities differ, in part because they place different values on some of these roles. Some people are single-minded, placing great value on success in one domain, such as their vocational goals, and little value in the others. Other people strive to maintain a balance in the roles they play; they consider themselves successful if they can find enjoyment in a variety of relationships and activities.

This assessment of the importance of certain content areas in relation to others influences the use of resources, the direction of certain decisions, and the kinds of experiences that may be perceived as most personally rewarding or threatening. College students, for example, may differ in whether their academic success or interpersonal success is most central to their sense of identity. Students who are more concerned about academic success take a different approach to the college environment, become involved in different kinds of activities, and have a different reaction to academic failure than do students who are more concerned about interpersonal success (Reischl & Hirsch, 1989).

Both the content and evaluation components of identity may change over the life course. In later adolescence, the focus is on integrating the various sources of content and determining which elements have the greatest salience. This is a major accomplishment that requires self-awareness, introspection, and the active exploration of a variety of roles and relationships. However, the individual identity that is formulated at the end of this period is often very abstract because later adolescents have not yet encountered many of the responsibilities, pressures, and conflicts of adult life. The ideological framework of identity has not yet been forged in the flames of reality.

Identity Status

The basic conflict of the psychosocial crisis of later adolescence is individual identity formation versus identity confusion. It results from the enormous difficulty of pulling together the many components of the self, including changing perspectives on one's inner sense of beliefs and values as well as new and changing social demands, into a unified image that can propel the person toward positive, meaningful action. The process of identity formation is confounded by distractions of all sorts. Many young people find it difficult to sort out what they want to be from what their parents have urged them to become. Others have received little encouragement to become a separate person with independent feelings and views. Still others are so beleaguered by feelings of inferiority and alienation that they do not have the optimism necessary to create a positive vision of their future. Some later adolescents find many paths appealing and have difficulty making a commitment to only one.

Identity formation is a dynamic process that unfolds as young people assess their competencies and aspirations within a changing social context of expectations, demands, and resources. A variety of potential resolutions of the psychosocial crisis of individual identity versus identity confusion have been described. At the positive pole is **identity achievement,** at the negative pole is **identity confusion.** Also included are a premature resolution, **identity foreclosure,** a postponement of resolution, **psychosocial moratorium,** and a **negative identity** (Kroger, 1993).

One of the most widely used conceptual frameworks for assessing identity status was devised by James Marcia (1980; Waterman, 1982). Using Erikson's concepts, Marcia assessed identity status on the basis of two criteria: crisis and commitment. **Crisis** consists of a period of role experimentation and active decision-making among alternative choices. **Commitment** consists of a demonstration of personal involvement in the areas of occupational choice, religion, and political ideology. On the basis of Marcia's interview, the status of subjects' identity development is assessed (Table 10.4). People who are classified as *identity-achieved* have already experienced a crisis time and have made occupational and ideological commitments. On the other hand, people who are classified as **identity-foreclosed** have not experienced a crisis but demonstrate strong occupational and ideological commitments. Their occupational and ideological beliefs appear to be close to those of their parents. The foreclosed identity is deceptive. A young person of 18 or 19 who can say exactly what he or she wants in life and who has selected an occupational goal may appear to be mature. This kind of clarity of vision may impress peers and adults as evidence of a high level of self-insight. However, if this solution has been formulated through the wholesale adoption of a script that was devised by the young person's family, it may not actually reflect much depth of self-understanding.

People who are classified as being in a state of *psychosocial moratorium* are involved in an ongoing crisis. Their commitments are diffuse. Finally, people who are classified as **identity-confused** may or may not have experienced a crisis, and they demonstrate a complete lack of commitment. Marcia described the identity-confused group as having a rather cavalier, "party" attitude that allows members to cope with the college environment. He suggested that the more seriously confused persons (such as those described by

TABLE 10.4 Relationship of Identity Status, Crisis, and Commitment		
	Crisis	Commitment
Identity achievement	+	+
Foreclosure	−	+
Moratorium	+	−
Identity confusion	+ / −	−

Some youth develop a negative identity around hate, violence, and racial superiority. This group of skinheads is demonstrating against the observance of Martin Luther King, Jr. Day.

Erikson, 1959) may not appear in his sample because they are unable to cope with college.

Sometimes, cultural expectations and demands provide the young person with a clearly defined self-image that is completely contrary to the cultural values of the community. This is called a *negative identity* (Erikson, 1959). *Failure, good-for-nothing, juvenile delinquent, hood, gangster,* and *loser* are some of the labels that the adult society commonly applies to certain adolescents. In the absence of any indication of the possibilities of success or contribution to the society, the young person accepts such negative labels as a self-definition and proceeds to validate this identity by continuing to behave in ways that will strengthen it. Some young people grow up admiring people who have become very successful by following antisocial or criminal paths. Drug lords; gang leaders; leaders of groups that advocate hate, violence, and vengeance; and people who use elected political positions for personal gain are all examples of possible role models around which a negative identity may be formed.

A negative identity may also emerge as a result of a strong identification with someone who is devalued by the family or the community. A loving uncle who is an alcoholic or a clever, creative parent who commits suicide may stimulate a crystallization within the adolescent as one who may share these undesirable characteristics. Linda, for example, established the negative identity of a person going crazy:

> Her father was an alcoholic, physically abusive man, who terrified her when she was a child. . . . Linda, herself a bright child, became by turns the standard bearer for her father's proud aspirations and the target of his jealousy. Midway through grade school she began flunking all her courses and retreating to a private world of daydreams. . . . "I always expected hallucinations, being locked up, down the road coming toward me. . . . I always resisted seeing myself as an adult. I was afraid that at the point I stopped the tape [the years of wild experimentation] I'd become my parents. . . . My father was the closest person I knew to crazy." (Ochberg, 1986, pp. 296–297)

The foreclosed identity and the negative identity both resolve the identity crisis in ways that fall short of the goal of a positive personal identity. Yet both provide the person with a concrete identity. The more maladaptive resolution of the crisis is **identity confusion.** Young people in this state are unable to make a commitment to any single view of themselves. They may be unable to integrate the various roles they play. In addition, they may be confronted by opposing value systems or by a lack of confidence in their ability to make meaningful decisions. Within the private, subjective self, some young people may reach later adolescence having difficulty accepting or establishing clear ego boundaries, or they may not experience feelings of agency. At an unconscious level, they may have incorporated two or more conflicting ideas about the self—for example, an abusive, harsh, rejecting powerful father and a wise, loving, nurturant, powerful grandmother—that stand in opposition to each other. Under any of these conditions, the demands for integration and synthesis of a personal identity arouse anxiety, apathy, and hostility toward the existing roles, none of which they can successfully adopt.

In comparison to the moratorium group, young people in the confused status are less conscientious, more likely to experience negative emotions, and more disagreeable (Clancy & Dollinger, 1993). They are generally not outgoing; rather, they describe themselves as self-conscious and likely to feel depressed. Several studies have found that young people who are characterized as identity-confused have had a history of early and frequent involvement with drug use and abuse (Jones, 1992). One might speculate that difficulties in resolving earlier psychosocial crises, especially conflicts related to autonomy versus shame and doubt and initiative versus guilt, leave some young people with deficits in ego formation that interfere with the kind of energy and playful self-assertiveness that are necessary in the process of identity achievement.

Dolores, an unemployed college dropout, describes the feeling of meaningless drifting that is associated with identity confusion:

> I have two sisters, and my father always told me I was the smartest of all, that I was smarter than he was, and that I could do anything I wanted to do . . . but somehow, I don't really know why, everything I turned to came to nothing. . . . I had every opportunity to find out what I really wanted to do. But . . . nothing I did satisfied me, and I would just stop. . . . Or turn away. . . . Or go on a trip. I worked for a big company for a while. . . . Then my parents went to Paris and I just went with them. . . . I came back . . . went to school . . . was a researcher at Time-Life . . . drifted . . . got married . . . divorced . . . drifted. [Her voice grew more halting.] I feel my life is such a waste. I'd like to write, I really would; but I don't know. I just can't get going." (Gornick, 1971)

The theoretical construct of identity status assumes a developmental progression. Identity confusion reflects the least defined status. Movement from confusion to foreclosure, moratorium, or achievement reflects a developmental progression. Movement from any other status to confusion suggests regression. A person who has achieved identity at one period may conceivably return to a crisis period of moratorium. However, those who are in a moratorium or achieved status can never be accurately described as foreclosed, since by definition they have already experienced some degree of crisis (Waterman, 1982; Meeus, 1996).

In the process of evolving an individual identity, everyone experiences temporary periods of confusion and depression. The task of bringing together the many elements of one's experience into a coordinated, clear self-definition is difficult and time-consuming. Adolescents are likely to experience moments of self-preoccupation, isolation, and discouragement as the diverse pieces of the puzzle are shifted and reordered into the total picture. Thus, even the eventual positive identity formation will be the result of some degree of identity confusion. The negative outcome of identity confusion, however, suggests that the person is never able to formulate a satisfying identity that will provide for the convergence of multiple identifications, aspirations, and roles. Such individuals have the persistent fear that they are losing their hold on themselves and on their future.

Identity Formation for Males and Females

Questions have been raised about the process of identity formation and its outcome for young men and women in our society. Some investigators have argued that the concept of identity as it has been formulated is a reflection of a male-oriented culture that focuses heavily on occupation and ideology rather than on interpersonal commitments. These criticisms also suggest that the construct of personal identity places greater value on self-sufficiency and autonomy to the exclusion of relationships and connection to the group. From this point of view, identity development ignores the fact that many women tend to be socialized to look to others to define their identity rather than to assume a proactive stance with respect to identity formation. All of these ideas reflect the impact of traditional distinctions in the male and female gender roles on identity formation (Archer, 1992).

As part of the identity process, young people often challenge themselves to take on new levels of achievement and test their resolve.

Other researchers point out that Erikson's construct of personal identity is embedded in a relational context. The process of identity formation requires a reexamination of earlier identifications and a selective internalization of the views and voices of significant others. The interpersonal and ideological commitments around which identity is forged result in a closer bond between the young person and the society (Marcia, 1993; Horst, 1995).

What is more, the kinds of ego strengths associated with identity achievement are equally important to the adaptive functioning of men and women (Ginsburg & Orlofsky, 1981). From this point of view, one might expect to find differences between males and females in the content of identity-related commitments and in the value placed on these content areas, but not in the process of crisis and commitment that leads to achieved identity. Few sex differences in identity status have been discovered (Waterman, 1982). For both sexes, identity achievement is associated with positive ego qualities. "Identity achieved youths generally exhibit higher levels of self-esteem, greater cognitive and ego complexity, postconventional levels of moral reasoning, and a strong capacity for inner-directed behavior" (Craig-Bray et al. 1988, p. 175).

In one analysis of the way older adolescents think about commitments, young people were asked to define the concept of commitment (Galotti & Kozberg, 1987). Few gender differences were found in these definitions, except that women were more likely than men to mention the importance of keeping a promise or their word of honor. Other themes—mutual trust, expression of one's values, a social contract, ordering of priorities, perseverance, obligation, and dedication—were referred to equally often by men and women.

There is evidence that men and women handle the *process* of role experimentation and identity achievement somewhat differently. The uncertainty of the identity crisis is often accompanied by greater anxiety in women than in men (Ollech & McCarthy, 1997). This anxiety may be linked to concerns about achievement strivings. Many women experience conflict between their image of femininity and their desire to set ambitious personal goals (Ginsburg & Orlofsky, 1981). Anxiety may also be a product of the general distress that women feel when they focus on their own agendas rather than on facilitating the agendas of others, as the society seems to expect them to do. The family context is especially important for young women who need to experience continued attachment with parents in the process of individuation (Schultheiss & Blustein, 1994). In this context, the moratorium status, which is considered a positive interlude on the path toward achievement, has been found to be linked to higher levels of self-doubt in women than in men. This finding may result from the strong feelings of guilt women experience when they attempt to assert their self-sufficiency or when they try to disconnect from demanding relationships in order to focus on their own ideas and needs.

Other evidence of gender differences has been found in the *content* of the identity. Erikson's (1968, 1982) work suggests that ideological and vocational commitments are central to identity formation. Gilligan (1982/1993) criticized this orientation, arguing that the interpersonal commitment may be more central for women, and that its clarification opens the way for more advanced exploration of vocations and ideology. Research findings lend support to this concept (Mellor, 1989; Bilsker et al., 1988; Schiedel & Marcia, 1985). The quality of interpersonal relations and the establishment of satisfying social commitments are more relevant to the development of a woman's identity than to the development of a man's. Measures of identity status that distinguish between interpersonal and ideological aspects of identity find that women score higher on interpersonal identity achievement than men (Benson et al., 1992).

THE CENTRAL PROCESS: ROLE EXPERIMENTATION

Later adolescents experiment with roles that represent the many possibilities for their future identities. They may think of themselves in a variety of careers in an effort to anticipate what it would be like to be members of specific occupational groups. They may take a variety of summer jobs, change their college major, read extensively, and daydream about success in several occupations. They consider whether or not to marry, and begin to define the ideal qualities they are looking for in a long-term intimate partner. Dating is one form of role experimentation; it allows for a different self-presentation with each new date. Friendship is another important context within which young people begin to clarify their interpersonal commitments. In addition, later adolescents may evaluate their commitment to their religion, consider religious conversion, or experiment with different rationales for moral behavior. They may examine a variety of political theories, join groups that work for political causes, or campaign for candidates.

During later adolescence, people have few social obligations that require long-term role commitments. They are free to start and stop or to join and quit without serious repercussions to their reputations. As long as no laws are broken in the process of experimenting, young people have the opportunity to play as many roles as they wish in order to prepare themselves for the resolution of the identity crisis without risking serious social censure.

Psychosocial Moratorium

The process of **role experimentation** takes many forms. Erikson (1959) used the term **psychosocial moratorium** to describe a period of free experimentation before a final identity is achieved. Ideally, the moratorium allows individuals freedom from the daily expectations for role performance. Their experimentation with new roles, values, and belief systems results in a personal conception of how they can fit into society so as to maximize their personal strengths and gain positive recognition from the community. The idea of being able to disconnect from daily demands and experiment with new roles may be more difficult for some later adolescents than for others. For example, young people who marry early and who go into the labor force right after high school may not have the luxury of a moratorium.

The concept of the psychosocial moratorium has been partially incorporated into some college programs that permit students to enroll in pass-fail courses before they select a major. The concern is to eliminate the problems of external evaluation during the decision-making process. Some high school students take a year off for work, travel, or volunteer service before deciding about college or a career. College students often express a need for a moratorium by leaving school for a while (Ochberg, 1986), disrupting the expected path of educational and career development. They assert their autonomy by imposing their own timetable and agenda on a socially prescribed sequence. Travel abroad is another strategy for experiencing moratorium. The time spent in another culture can give students an opportunity to demonstrate their self-sufficiency, examine many of their assumptions about values and goals, express their individuality, and break out of whatever social environment they may feel is constraining or overshadowing their sense of self. The moratorium offers temporary relief from external demands and an opportunity to establish their identity.

As parents observe the process of role experimentation, they may become concerned because an adolescent son or daughter appears to be abandoning the traditional family value orientation or lifestyle. The adolescent talks of changing religions, remaining single, or selecting a low-status career. The more vehemently the family responds to these propositions, the more likely the young person is to become locked into a position in order to demonstrate autonomy rather than being allowed to continue the experimentation until a more suitable personal alternative is discovered. Many adolescents seem to want to take a "shocking" stand or to question the "unquestionable" so that they have a feeling of control—a feeling that they have chosen their own path rather than simply followed the one carved out for them by their family, culture, and time in history. Parents are well advised to understand role experimentation as an expression of an appropriate developmental process in which a young person is trying on various roles, beliefs, and philosophies to see "how they fit." If at all possible, parents need to trust in this process, giving their opinions and reactions when appropriate, but encouraging the young person to find the combination of roles, values, goals, and commitments that bring the later adolescent the greatest feelings of enthusiasm and optimism about his or her own future (Box 10.2).

Not all young people approach the process of role experimentation with the same degree of openness to new experiences and new information. Recall from the discussion of emotional style in Chapter 9 the two types of individuals described: the sensers and the censors. Extending this idea further, Michael Berzonsky (1989, 1993; Berzonsky & Sullivan, 1992) hypothe-

How might time spent traveling abroad or living in another culture contribute to role experimentation and enhance the identity development process?

BOX 10.2 ATTACHMENT AND IDENTITY FORMATION

Identity formation is usually viewed as a process that requires young people to distance themselves from the strong expectations and definitions imposed by parents and other family members. To achieve an individual identity, one must create a vision of the self that is authentic, a sense of having taken hold of one's destiny in an effort to reach goals that are personally meaningful. Yet recent research has demonstrated that the quality of family relationships contributes significantly to the young person's ability to achieve a personal identity (Kroger & Haslett, 1988; Kamptner, 1988; Papini et al., 1989).

The relationship can be compared with the contribution of secure attachments in infancy to a subsequent willingness to explore the environment. Later adolescents who have a secure relationship with their parents and who are comfortable in loosening these ties can begin to explore the ideological, occupational, and interpersonal alternatives that will become their own identities. In particular, college students, both males and females, who have a positive attachment to their mothers are more likely to have an achieved identity and are less likely to be in the moratorium or identity-confused status than are students who have in-

secure, mistrustful relationships with their mothers. On the other hand, those who are still emotionally dependent on their parents and require constant reassurance of their affection show a greater tendency to experience identity confusion (Benson et al., 1992).

By the time young people reach later adolescence, those who are securely attached to their parents are confident about their affection and support. At the same time, they trust in their own worth, and in their ability to make decisions (Blain et al., 1993). A sense of family security fosters identity formation in the following ways:

- It fosters confidence in the exploration of social relationships, ideologies, and settings.
- It establishes positive expectations in regard to interpersonal experiences outside the family.
- It fosters the formation of group identities apart from the family, thus providing a transitional context for work on individual identity.
- It provides a basic layer of self-acceptance, permitting the young person to approach the process of identity formation with optimism.

---

sized that in later adolescence individuals differ in how they select, process, and apply self-relevant information. Three types of approaches to identity-information processing were described, each with a somewhat different implication for the place of role experimentation in the resolution of the identity search. The **informational** types "actively seek out and evaluate self-diagnostic information when negotiating identity issues and making decisions" (Berzonsky, 1993, p. 289). The **normative** types are "relatively more defensive and closed to feedback that may threaten hard core areas of the self" (Berzonsky, 1993, p. 290). The **diffuse-avoidant** types "procrastinate and delay dealing with self-relevant issues as long as possible. When push comes to shove, they tend to be influenced by immediate rewards and operate in a situation-sensitive fashion" (Berzonsky, 1993, p. 290). The implication is that the informational types are most likely to initiate role experimentation as a means of clarifying existing beliefs and values. The normative types have to process contradictions among the demands and expectations of the varying roles they play, but if possible they will probably avoid novel experiences that would challenge their views. The diffuse-avoidant types may engage in role experimentation if it is viewed as "cool" or is positively regarded among others in their peer group, but they probably would not take the initiative to seek out new experiences as a conscious, proactive strategy. Figure 10.3 on the following page, shows the relationship between the three information-seeking styles and the four identity statuses described earlier. In that model, exploration or seeking information is associated with both the moratorium and the achieved statuses (White et al., 1998).

Role Experimentation and Ethnic Identity In Chapter 9, we introduced the idea that group identity precedes individual identity. One component of group identity is an orientation toward one's ethnic group. Efforts to understand one's ethnic identity and to clarify one's commitment to a particular ethnic subculture lead to self-definition that facilitates work on personal identity as well. Part of forming a clear sense of personal identity requires an understanding of one's ancestry, especially the cultural and ethnic heritage and the values, beliefs, and traditions that may have shaped one's child-rearing environment as well as one's vision of the future. Ethnic group identity typically involves the incorporation of certain ideals, values, and beliefs that are specific to that ethnic group; a sense of how this ethnic group is regarded by outsiders; and the way in which one orients oneself with respect

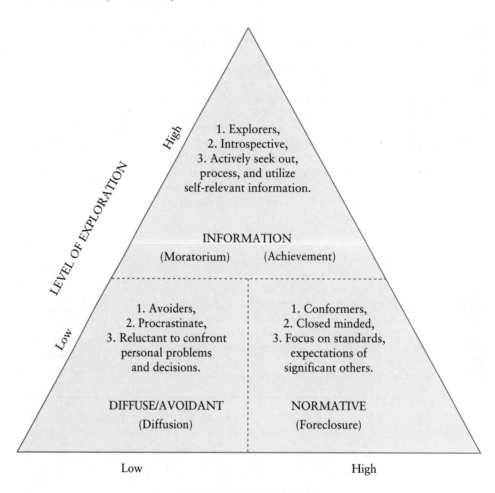

FIGURE 10.3
*Identity status, level of
exploration, and level of
commitment*
Source: White, Wampler,
& Winn, 1998, p. 226.

to this group—that is, whether one seeks out other members of the group, feels proud
of one's membership in it, and has positive attitudes about it (Cross, 1991).

As you might imagine, young people make the transition from early to later adolescence having done different amounts of work in exploring their ethnic group identity.
One theory of ethnic minority identity development offers a five-stage model
(Atkinson et al., 1983):

1. *Conformity.* Identification with the values, beliefs, and practices of the dominant
   culture.
2. *Dissonance.* Recognition and confusion about areas of conflict between the values,
   beliefs, and practices of the dominant culture and those of one's own ethnic group.
3. *Resistance and immersion.* Rejection of many elements of the dominant culture; education about and involvement in one's own ethnic group and its beliefs, values,
   and practices.
4. *Introspection.* Critical examination of the values, beliefs, and practices of both the
   dominant culture and one's own ethnic group's views.
5. *Articulation and awareness.* Identification of those values, beliefs, and practices
   from the dominant culture and one's own ethnic group that are combined into a
   unique synthesis that forms a personal, cultural identity.

In this model, one senses the interaction between ethnic identity and personal identity (Rotheram-Borus & Wyche, 1994). Not all young people experience all of these
stages. Some children are raised in families where ethnic socialization begins at a young
age, and they never experience a sense of accepting the dominant culture. In fact, if
they are raised in a racially segregated community, they may not encounter members
of the dominant culture as significant figures during their early childhood years.

The college environment provides an opportunity to learn about the cultural traditions and history of one's ethnic group, as well as the traditions of other groups. UCLA dance majors are performing traditional African dances for the freshman student convocation.

For many people, the stage of articulation and awareness may not occur until sometime later in adulthood. But for many later adolescents, the transitions from Stage 1, conformity, to Stages 2 and 3 are commonly stimulated by the college experience. The student body is usually much more diverse than one's high school. Young people of many racial, ethnic, social-class, regional, and religious backgrounds come together in college and are expected to live together in the residence halls, learn together in the classrooms, and collaborate in college organizations, social activities, sports, and cultural events. Exposure to this diversity often brings experiences of racial and ethnic prejudice, cultural ethnocentrism, and intergroup conflict. At the same time, exposure to the college curriculum offers an intellectual framework for understanding the historical, psychological, and sociological foundations of racism, prejudice, and cultural conflict (Phinney, 1996).

For young people who remain in low-income, urban communities and do not attend college, the interaction of ethnic identity and personal identity can serve as an adaptive process for coping with high-risk environments. Identification with the history, struggles, and heroism of one's people serves as an anchor of dignity and hope in communities that are disrupted by unemployment and violence (Spencer et al., 1995). Through interaction with other members of their ethnic group, young people build competence and a set of strategies for managing the poverty and hostility they face.

THE PRIME ADAPTIVE EGO QUALITY AND THE CORE PATHOLOGY

Fidelity to Values and Ideologies

Fidelity is closely linked with the notion of commitment. In later adolescence, the ego strength of fidelity refers to "the ability to sustain loyalties freely pledged in spite of the inevitable contradictions and confusions of value systems" (Erikson, 1978, p. 28). Fidelity incorporates the trust and hope of infancy and directs it toward a belief in values and ideologies. Fidelity may be fostered by identification with inspirational role models and by participation in meaningful institutions. It is also achieved as a result of the new cognitive capacities of adolescence that permit self-reflection, relativistic thinking, and insight. Fidelity to values and ideals provides evidence of a reflective, thoughtful person who has taken time to struggle with opposing views and to select those that best reflect his or her personal convictions (Waterman, 1992).

The emergence of fidelity provides a channel for strong passions and drives, guiding this energy toward the preservation of certain values and ideals. It strengthens one's ethical resolve, especially in the face of the many pressures and temptations of adult life. It also creates a bond of belongingness with others who share the same loyalties. At the same time, fidelity in the individual strengthens the society by drawing upon the talents and energy of those who share a common set of values to sustain and support basic institutions such as religious organizations, political parties, educational institutions, and social service agencies (Markstrom-Adams et al., 1994).

Repudiation   **Repudiation** refers to a rejection of certain values, beliefs, and roles. In the diverse and pluralistic society in the U.S., some degree of repudiation may be necessary in order to forge an integrated identity. One cannot embrace all ideologies and roles; each commitment brings some boundaries to one's values and limits one's investment to a certain vision of the self continuing into the future. Repudiation can serve as a mechanism for intergenerational change. For example, a young person may decide that he or she will reject the characteristics of an unloving or abusive parent. In this context, he or she will form his or her identity around suppressing certain negative qualities and learning to enact and endorse opposing positive qualities.

In the extreme case, repudiation results in a hostile rejection of all the ideas, values, and groups that do not adhere to one's own beliefs (Erikson, 1982). It fosters a rigid world view that does not admit to the contributions of others' ideas. The roots of militancy, prejudice, and terrorism lie in the formation of the core pathology of repudiation.

Applied Topic   CHALLENGES OF SOCIAL LIFE

During later adolescence, most young people find ways to loosen themselves from the moorings of family, tradition, and convention. We have referred to this process as role experimentation, and have treated it as a positive, healthy dynamic through which young people begin to know themselves more authentically. In the process of forming a personal identity, young people are likely to be surrounded by others like themselves who have not yet settled on a clear vision of themselves and who have not yet found a set of values and beliefs to which they are willing to commit. In this social context, some young people become greedily self-absorbed; others become avidly ideological; yet others become depressed and confused. As our students have discussed the issues of this period of life and reflected on its challenges, they have pointed out some of the risks that accompany this period of uncertainty and experimentation. The following discussion identifies several of these risks: unwanted sexual attention, binge drinking, and sexually transmitted diseases.

Unwanted Sexual   Unwanted sexual attention can range from unwanted teasing, joking, and suggestive
Attention   gestures to rape. A large number of college-age students experience some type of unwanted sexual attention. For example, in one study of over 4,000 students, faculty, and staff at a large university, over 40% indicated that they had experienced at least one type of unwanted sexual attention at least once (Cochran et al., 1997). Within the workplace, there is also growing concern about sexual harassment, with abuses occurring between supervisors and employees and among employees themselves. This kind of experience can have negative consequences for young people, especially if the attention goes on for a long time and there is no way to avoid it. Young people typically try to ignore this kind of attention, but it is more difficult when the person involved is a faculty member or someone in a position of authority. The second most common strategy is to avoid the person by changing classes, avoiding places where the person is known to go, or, in extreme cases, dropping out of school or quitting the job temporarily. Some young people will confront the person, especially if they view the behavior as severe, but generally avoid confrontation if the person is in a position of authority. Few will report the unwanted sexual attention or make a formal complaint. For many young people, the unwanted sexual attention comes from other members of their social group. The ambiguity of the situation and the lack of clear rules about this kind of behavior leave the burden on the target of unwanted sexual attention to alter or modify their own behavior, even if that means disrupting their daily life.

Binge Drinking

Recent deaths on college campuses have raised new concerns about binge drinking (Thompson, 1998). In comparison to high school seniors or non-college-bound youth, students enrolled full time in college are more likely to engage in **binge drinking** (five or more drinks in a row). Recent surveys find that 39% of college students report this kind of heavy "weekend" drinking, with males participating at a somewhat higher rate (47%) than females (33%). Binge drinking is part of college social life. Over 80% of college students say that they have some friends who get drunk at least once a week and 45% say that their friends wouldn't disapprove if they had five or more drinks once or twice each weekend (Johnston et al., 1997). Binge drinking is often part of the initiation into special clubs or a rite of passage at the 21st birthday.

Binge drinking is an expression of autonomy gone awry. The highest rates of binge drinking are among college students who are not living with their parents. Rates are higher among residential colleges than among commuter colleges, and among members of fraternities and sororities (Gfroerer et al., 1997). Young people get together and begin partying and drinking routinely each weekend. They drink if the football team wins or loses; if exams are over or before they begin; to celebrate birthdays, Halloween, or winning a bet; to recover from breaking up; to welcome new friends or say good-bye; to forget the week past and to cheer on the week ahead. And every so often, the drinking turns into chaos. Fires are started, fights break out, cars are overturned, and furniture and windows are smashed. At this point, young people have trouble asserting control over one another.

Sexually Transmitted Diseases

Sexually transmitted diseases (STDs) include a wide range of bacterial, viral, and yeast infections that are transmitted through forms of sexual contact. Approximately 50% of the U. S. population will acquire one or more STDs by the age range 30–35, with the early and later adolescent age groups showing the greatest risk (Centers for Disease Control, 1992). Although much of the recent attention about STDs has focused on HIV and AIDS, in fact, three diseases, chlamydia, herpes, and papilloma infections, which are not even reported on a national basis, are thought to be the most prevalent of the STDs in the U. S. (Yankauer, 1994).

Some basic practices are relevant for preventing all STDs. These include limiting the number of sexual partners, consistent use of condoms during sexual intercourse, and avoiding unprotected contact during any type of genital sexual activity. Some young people who have not experienced vaginal intercourse engage in other types of sexual experiences through which STDs can be spread (Schuster et al., 1996).

What factors have been identified as placing later adolescents, and college students in particular, at risk for STDs? The following list suggests some of the key issues.

1. College students do not perceive themselves to be a high risk group. This may be due in part to the sense of egocentrism and personal fable discussed in Chapter 9. Students may think of themselves as invincible and underestimate their risk. Even if they understand the principles related to the transmission of STDs, they do not define themselves as personally at risk (Serovich & Greene, 1997).

2. Young people in the U. S. are notoriously inconsistent in their use of contraceptives. In one short-term longitudinal study, college females were inconsistent over a six month period in their use of contraceptives. Many who were using oral contraceptives did not continue to use them six months later. Others who were using condoms consistently at the first interview were no longer using them six months later (Kusseling et al., 1995).

3. Inconsistent condom use is associated with other health-related factors. Young people who are more likely to use

Binge drinking has become a socially acceptable activity on many college campuses. Many celebrations and rituals are centered around the performance of unique feats of consumption.

and abuse alcohol and drugs are also likely to be inconsistent in their condom use. Those who follow a more health-promoting lifestyle, including getting regular exercise and eating a balanced diet, are more likely to be consistent in their condom use (Fortenberry et al., 1997).

4. Unprotected sexual activity is often associated with drunkenness, an activity that is frequent on college campuses. When young people get drunk several times a month, they are more likely to have sexual relations with multiple partners.

5. The consistent use of condoms requires open communication between the partners. Adolescents are often reluctant to discuss the use of a condom, and lack the assertive communication skills to insist. In cases where females are less sexually experienced than males, they may lack the confidence to make this a condition of sexual activity (Crooks & Baur, 1996).

The three examples of unwanted sexual attention, binge drinking, and sexually transmitted diseases illustrate common challenges associated with entry into the expanded social world of later adolescence. These problems are linked to the difficulties later adolescents have in imposing structure and norms on the behavior of their peers, as well as acknowledging their own vulnerability. In a period of life characterized by openness to new experiences and experimentation with the limits and boundaries of life's roles, some young people place themselves and others at risk by pushing the boundaries too far.

Chapter Summary

At the close of later adolescence, most young people have made the transition from childhood to adulthood. They are fully capable of surviving on their own in a complex culture. They have achieved a new level of independence from their parents, so that ties of love, trust, and support are expressed within a framework of mutual respect and autonomous decision making. Those who have resolved the psychosocial crisis of this stage have an integrated identity that includes a definition of themselves as sexual, moral, political, and career participants. Identity achievement represents a private sense of unity and confidence in one's beliefs, as well as a more public integration of roles and commitments to specific values.

The strain of this stage is felt in the tension between the person's need to question and experiment and the society's expectations for closure on significant themes, particularly occupation, gender identity, and political ideology. The expansion of roles and relationships exposes many young people to new views that require evaluation. The crisis of individual identity versus identity confusion suggests a new synthesis of earlier identifications, present values, and future goals into a consistent self-concept. This unity of self is achieved only after a period of uncertainty and open questioning. Role experimentation during this time is an essential strategy for coping with new information and new value orientations. Once young people know what they stand for, they can commit themselves more deeply to others.

End of Chapter Case

Houston A. Baker, Jr., a poet and literary scholar, tells of the impact of one of his college professors on his personal identity.

He intrigued us. Slowly puffing on the obligatory pipe, he would chide us for the routineness of our analyses of revered works in the British and American literary canons. He wore—always—a tie and tweed of Ivy provenance, and at the end of the first session of his "World Literature" course at Howard University in the fall of 1963, I had but one response—I wanted to be exactly like him.

The task was to prove myself worthy. I labored furiously at the beginning assignment—an effort devoted to Marvellian Coy mistresses and pounding parodies thereof. The result was a D and the comment: "This is a perfunctory effort. You have refused to be creative. There are worlds on worlds rolling ever. Try to make contact with them." I was more than annoyed; I was livid. Who did he think he was? I'd show him. My next essay would reveal (cleverly, of course) that I didn't give a tinker's dam for his grade or his comments. "Creative"—indeed!

My second essay might properly have been entitled: Love's labor loosed on William Blake. I strained to see every nuance of the *Songs of Innocence*. I combed the poems for every mad hint that would help forward my own mad argument. I never turned my eyes from the text as I sought to construct the most infuriating (yet plausible) analysis imaginable. I felt my feet dancing to Muhammed Ali rhythms as I slaved away, darting logical jabs at Professor C. Watkins who would (I was certain) be utterly undone when I threw my irreverent straight right. The paper came back with the comment: "This is a maverick argument, but stubbornly logical—A-." Bingo! The grade in itself gave me almost enough courage to seek him out during office hours—but not quite. I corralled a friend to make the pilgrimage with me.

He was extraordinarily gracious on the mid-autumn afternoon when we had our first long talk. "Come in, Mr. Baker—Miss Pierce. How are you?" His tie was loose; he was reared back in his desk chair. There was a clutter of papers and blue books, and they provided a friendly setting for a two-hour conversation. . . . We were thrilled that he considered us (potentially) enough like him to invite us to visit him and his wife two weeks hence—for dessert.

The evening surprisingly took on (in my youthful imagination) the cast of Greenwich Village "Beats" and verboten revelations. The greatest stimulation, however, came when he played the Library of Congress recording of T. S. Eliot reading "The Wasteland." In that moment, I became, willy-nilly, a party to "modernism" in its prototypical form. I was surprised and delighted. I had heard nothing like it before. The Eliotian reading initiated my habit of "listening" for poems rather than "looking" for them. . . . I stepped into a late fall evening with an entirely new sense of myself and of "worlds on worlds" rolling ever.

Source: Baker, H.A., Jr., 1991.

Thought Questions:

1. What elements of the identity process are evident in this case?

2. What are some of the characteristics of Professor Watkins that may have made him a target for identification for Houston Baker?

3. What aspects of the college environment are likely to stimulate the identity process?

4. Have you ever had an intellectual experience that gave you a "new sense of yourself?" What combination of factors come together to permit that to happen?

Chapter 11

The major themes of early adulthood—work, intimacy, marriage, and parenting—are all captured in this image of the Young Harlequin Family. The challenges of adulthood often emerge in efforts to balance and integrate diverse life roles.

Early Adulthood (24–34 Years)

Chapter Objectives

- To identify and define selected concepts that are especially relevant for understanding development during adulthood including life roles, the social clock, the life course, functional autonomy of motives, and tendencies toward growth.
- To analyze the process of forming intimate relationships, including identifying and committing to a long-term relationship, the role of cohabitation in forming close relationships, and the challenges one faces in adjusting to the early years of marriage.
- To describe the factors associated with the decision to have children, the impact of childbearing on the intimate, parental relationship, and the contribution of childbearing to growth in adulthood.
- To explore the concept of work as a stimulus for psychological development in early adulthood with special focus on the technical skills, authority relations, demands and hazards, and interpersonal relations in the work environment.
- To examine the concept of lifestyle as the expression of individual identity, with consideration of single lifestyles.
- To define and describe the psychosocial crisis of early adulthood—intimacy versus isolation; the central process through which the crisis is resolved—mutuality among peers; the prime adaptive ego quality of love; and the core pathology of exclusivity.
- To analyze divorce as a life stressor in early adulthood, including factors contributing to it and the coping process.

Welcome to the study of adulthood. All that has gone before can be seen as preparation; all that follows can be viewed as actualization. We have considered psychosocial development through seven preparatory stages of life encompassing approximately 24 years. During these stages, an individual undergoes rapid physical, cognitive, social, and emotional development. In the United States, *life expectancy is currently about 76 years. Thus, approximately 50 years remain after the seven preparatory stages. In our conceptual scheme, four stages of psychosocial development unfold during these latter 50 years. Let us briefly examine some of the concepts that are important to our discussion of adulthood.* ❖

MAJOR CONCEPTS IN THE STUDY OF ADULTHOOD

Social Roles   Social role is one of the concepts most frequently used for understanding adulthood (Brim, 1966, 1968; Parsons, 1955). The major concepts of social role theory, which were introduced in Chapter 3, are summarized in Table 11.1. We considered this concept in Chapter 7 when we discussed gender-role identification, and again in Chapter 10 when we examined individual identity versus identity confusion. Clearly, roles are learned and enacted during childhood. In adulthood, however, people assume multiple roles that expand their opportunities for self-expression and bring them into contact with a great variety of social demands. Adulthood can be seen as a series of increasingly differentiated and complex roles that the individual plays for substantial lengths of time. The salient roles of adulthood, such as worker, spouse, friend, parent, teacher, mentor, or community leader, give structure to adult identity and meaning to life. Role changes provide opportunities for growth and redefinition (Thoits, 1986).

Involvement in multiple roles allows adults to help socialize younger generations. Only in adulthood do individuals experience the behavioral requirements of many of their roles, which in turn provide a basis on which to train their children for the demands of adulthood (Kite, 1996).

TABLE 11.1	**Major Concepts of Social Role Theory**
Social role	Parts or identities a person assumes that are also social positions: kinship roles, age roles, sex roles, occupational roles
Role enactment	Patterned characteristics of social behavior generated by a social role
Role expectations	Scripts or shared expectations for behavior that are linked to each role
Role gain	Addition of roles
Role strain	Stress caused by too many expectations within a role
Role conflict	Conflict caused by competing demands of different roles
Role loss	Ending of a role; may result in stress and disorientation
Dimensions of life roles that vary from person to person	Number of roles
	Intensity of involvement in roles
	Time demands of each role
	Structure or flexibility of the role

The expectations associated with adult roles provide a frame of reference within which individuals make their own personal decisions. For example, a man may know what is expected of him in the worker role, but he may choose to ignore those expectations and strive for greater responsibilities, more power, or more autonomy. People can either conform to role expectations, revise them, or reject them altogether. In addition to the tensions produced by role conflicts and role strain, some of the stresses of adulthood result from the need to redefine certain role expectations in order to preserve one's sense of self.

Social Clock　Bernice Neugarten and her colleagues (Neugarten et al., 1965) proposed the concept of the **social clock** as a way of understanding adulthood. This term refers to "age norms and age expectations [that] operate as prods and brakes upon behavior, in some instances hastening behavior and in some instances delaying it" (p. 710). Neugarten and her associates suggested that social class groups tend to agree on the appropriate age for significant life events, such as marriage, child-rearing, and retirement. This consensus exerts social pressure on individuals, pushing them to assume a particular role at an expected age. Age norms may also suppress behaviors that are considered inap-

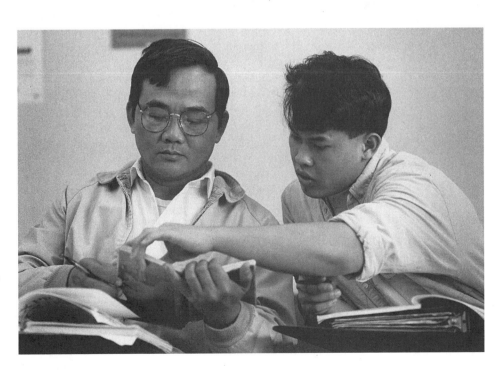

Many adults who did not go to college right after high school are returning to complete their college education in midlife. "Off-time" students are often in the position of receiving help and instruction from students and teachers who are younger than they.

propriate for one's age. Adults are aware of existing norms regarding the timing of certain behaviors and evaluate their own behaviors as being "on time" or "too soon" or "too late." The social clock is constantly being reset as people confront the challenges, demands, and new structures of modern society.

The social clock concept has been elaborated to include norms for the sequencing as well as the timing of transitions in social roles (Rindfuss et al., 1987). Earlier in the century, there was much more agreement about both the ideal timing of most transitions and the normative order. For example, if one thinks of the coordination of the occupational and family careers, then a normative path might have been to finish school, enter the labor market, get married, and have children. However, beginning with adult cohorts surveyed in the 1970s, there is much less consensus about the best age to make these transitions and considerable diversity in patterns of change (Rosenfeld & Stark, 1987). For example, in these more recent cohorts many men start a full-time job before they graduate from high school. Also, many women return to school after marriage. Increasingly, young men and women who are not married have children. As a result of divorce, both men and women enter and then leave their marital role, and of course, this change influences the school, work, and parenting transitions as well.

Life Course

Life course refers to the integration and sequencing of phases of work and family life. Glen Elder (1985), who has been a leader in the elaboration of the life course perspective, describes the two central themes: trajectories and transitions. A **trajectory** is the path of one's life experiences in a specific domain, particularly work and family life. The family trajectory might include marriage, parenthood, grandparenthood, and widowhood. A **transition** is the beginning or close of an event or role relationship. In the work trajectory, for example, transitions might be getting one's first job, being laid off, and going back to school for an advanced degree. Transitions are the events that make up a lifelong trajectory.

The life course concept can be applied to the content of individual life histories as they are expressed in a social and historical time period. Each person's life course can be thought of as a pattern of the adaptations that he or she has made to the configuration of cultural expectations, resources, and barriers experienced during a particular time period.

Figure 11.1 provides a view of the age-linked changes in occupational and family careers. The figure allows you to map the convergence of transitions across the occupational and family trajectories, illustrating periods of potential harmony and conflict between the demands in the two trajectories. In considering adult lives in the 1990s, one can see that this is but one possible map of the interconnections between work and family life in the course of a life. The occupational and family careers look quite different for the following: a woman who extends her educational preparation to include a professional degree, works before marriage, and delays childbearing into her middle to late 30s; a woman who remains single and dedicates her energy to excellence in a career; and a woman who marries right after high school, begins having children at 18, works during her childbearing years out of economic necessity, and then retires at 55 to enjoy her grandchildren and her personal freedom.

The pattern of the life course is influenced by the historical era. The life course of a person who was born in 1900 and died in 1975 might have looked quite different if that person's life had run from 1920 to 1995 instead. The person would have gone through the same chronological phases, but during different periods of history with different opportunities, expectations, and challenges.

The group of people who are roughly the same age during a particular historical period are referred to as a **cohort**. Differences in the occupational opportunities, educational resources, and number of people in the cohort are three factors that may affect the pattern of life events. In addition, major crises, such as war, famine, and political unrest, may alter a trajectory by introducing unanticipated transitions—for example, closing off certain activities, as when young men interrupt their education to go to war, and opening up new opportunities, as when women enter the labor market because many of the men are in the military (Elder et al., 1986; Elder, 1986).

FIGURE 11.1

A hypothetical life course
SOURCE: Adapted from
Atchley, 1975.

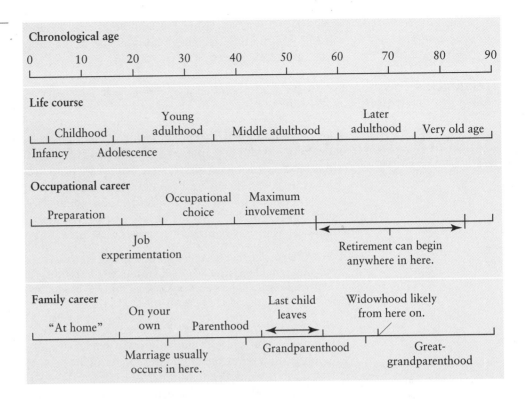

In studying the life course, we are interested not only in the sequencing of events but in the psychological growth that occurs as adults strive to adjust to changing and sometimes conflicting role demands. At different ages, people bring a distinct perspective to these events. For example, a crisis such as widespread unemployment may have a direct impact on the work trajectory of an adult, and also on the family environment or educational opportunities of a child. The developmental level of the person and the particular developmental tasks and psychosocial crises that are most salient at the time will determine how a specific event will influence the life course (Stewart & Healy, 1989).

**Functional
Autonomy of
Motives**

Accounting for the ability to make life choices and create life experiences in adulthood requires a concept that allows us to understand how the mind's energy is freed to recognize and develop new motives, skills, and interests, and create new goals. Gordon Allport's (1961) conceptualization of the **functional autonomy of motives** is helpful in explaining adult motivation. In his view, an individual's motive base is flexible and open to change. A behavior is initially performed because of some need. The individual holds a job, for example, in order to earn enough money to support a family. Over time, the behavior itself may become pleasurable and valued independent of its link to the original need. The person may begin to enjoy the work and value it for its own sake. The valued behaviors—in this case, work behaviors—become functionally autonomous. The person engages in work because of the satisfactions it brings. The person may refuse a higher-paying job because the current work activities are so satisfying. This situation may also be reversed. The person works because of a need for money to support a family. He or she becomes good at making money and finds the process pleasurable. The pursuit of wealth becomes a functionally autonomous motive. Over time, the specific work becomes less valued than opportunities to earn money. The person may readily change jobs in order to receive a higher salary. He or she may begin to ignore their family in order to direct their time and energy toward this newly established goal of accumulating wealth.

The concept of the functional autonomy of motives helps explain how the same behavior may be perpetuated by different motives in two individuals. On the other hand, it also illustrates how similar motives can perpetuate different kinds of behavior. One implication of this concept is that adulthood must be understood not only in terms of role learning and role change, but also in light of the variety of individual motives that direct and sustain behavior.

Tendencies Toward Growth

Robert W. White (1966, pp. 374–405) identified five tendencies toward growth in adulthood: (1) stabilizing of ego identity, (2) freeing of personal relationships, (3) deepening of interests, (4) humanizing of values, and (5) expansion of caring. From his work on adult personality development, White found these to be the basic gains made during adulthood. They appear to be a mixture of the psychosocial crises of early and middle adulthood, suggesting a movement away from preoccupation with the self and an increasing investment in meaningful social relationships. Directions for change in personality development during adulthood are summarized in Table 11.2.

Erikson (1974) described the progression of developmental gains during adulthood in the following way (Notice the parallel to White's approach.):

> In youth you find out what you *care to do* and who you *care to be*—even in changing roles. In young adulthood you learn whom you *care to be with*—at work and in private life, not only exchanging intimacies, but sharing intimacy. In adulthood, however, you learn to know what and whom you can *take care of.* (p. 124)

In summary, the concepts of life roles, the social clock, the life course, functionally autonomous motives, and human growth tendencies all extend an understanding of psychological development in adulthood. Childhood is over. One addresses life with great expectations and exhilaration. After the initial excitement of the period subsides, one comes to realize that there is serious work to be done. Young adults are learning to engage in intense and meaningful relationships in marriage or with intimate partners, friends, and co-workers. At the same time, they are putting into action practices that express the values and beliefs to which they became committed at the close of later adolescence.

We have identified age 24 as the beginning of early adulthood, advancing this from age 22 in earlier editions of this book. From a psychosocial perspective, the time of entry into a new stage is based on a convergence of experiences including: the accomplishments of the previous stage, the resolution of the prior psychosocial crisis, and the beginning efforts to achieve the tasks of the new stage rather than on chronological age. In contemporary society, one begins to experience adulthood as several roles emerge, typically those of worker, committed partner, and parent. As the age of entry

Maya Angelou exemplifies the achievements suggested in Robert White's theory of adult development. Through her poetry she expresses a clear sense of self, her humanistic values, and her deepening commitment to sustaining and nurturing the well-being of future generations.

TABLE 11.2   Tendencies for Change During Adulthood (based on Robert W. White's theory of adult maturity)

Tendency	Definition	Direction of Growth	Growth Trends	Situations that Produce Growth
Stabilizing of ego identity	The self or the person one feels oneself to be	Increase of stability, sharper, clearer, more consistent, and free from transient influences; increasing independence from the daily impact of social judgments and experiences of success and failure	Placement in social roles; preferences for emphasis in role enactment; interests and initiatives the person brings to social roles; individuality; personal integration; sense of competence	Choices: Any incident that serves to heighten the efficacy of accumulated personal experiences as against new outside judgments; fresh experiences of success and failure; new objects of possible identification
Freeing of personal relationships	Responding to people in their own right as individuals	Human relationships that are increasingly responsive to the other person's real nature	Relationships with people who are important and with whom one has frequent and significant contact	Situations in which the other person behaves unexpectedly, thus disrupting one's habituated way of behaving; decreasing defensiveness against anxiety, allowing the person to observe and respond to others' behavior more openly
Deepening of interests	Interest always connected with an activity that wholly engages a person; progressive mastery of knowledge and skills relevant to a sphere of interest	Increasing identification of one's own satisfaction with development of objects of interest so that the inherent nature and possibilities for development of these interests increasingly guide the person's activity and become part of the satisfaction	Living and acting more fully on interests, thus increasing both one's knowledge and capacity to influence what pertains to those interests	Action is undertaken and favorable consequences result; discovery; encouraging the interests of an older or younger person
Humanizing of values	Moral judgments	The person increasingly discovers the human meaning of values and their relation to the achievement of social purposes; increasingly brings to bear his or her own experiences and motives in affirming and promoting a value system	Values, whatever their content, become increasingly a reflection of one's own experiences and purposes	Situations in which existing values become a source of conflict; sudden empathic identification with some new aspect of value conflict
Expansion of caring	Transcendence of egocentrism; such deep concern for the welfare of someone or something that the meaning of one's own life is identified with the wellbeing of the object of care	Increased caring for the welfare of other persons and human concerns	Falling in love; taking care of the young; caring for cultural products and institutions	Situations that evoke the caring necessary to maintain civilized institutions and an environment suitable for raising the next generation; situations that evoke nurturant feelings and that offer an opportunity for nurture to be bestowed

into marriage has advanced over the past twenty years, the majority of young people in the United States are unmarried in the age range of 20 to 24. Later age at marriage is associated with an older age for first childbearing. Students take an average of 5 or 6 years to complete college, and young people seem to be involved in a longer period of job experimentation before settling into their occupational career. All of these factors argue for advancing the approximate age of entry into adulthood. At the same time, one must keep in mind the diversity of life stories that bring some young people into significant role responsibilities, autonomy from family, and self-sufficiency at relatively early ages, and others to delay the typical commitments of adulthood well into their thirties.

DEVELOPMENTAL TASKS

The most important social factors contributing to the creation of a lifestyle are whether one establishes a permanent, intimate relationship with a partner, the characteristics of one's partner, whether one has children and the characteristics of those children, and one's work. The extent to which one has a choice about each of these factors depends on cultural values and restrictions, societal norms and barriers, and socioeconomic factors, especially educational attainment. Each factor interacts with personality, interests, and life goals to shape a lifestyle.

Exploring Intimate Relationships

The period of early adulthood is a time when men and women explore the possibility of forming relationships that combine emotional closeness, shared interests and a shared vision of the future, and sexual intimacy. The nature of these relationships differ. Some young people engage in a form of "serial monogamy," a sequence of dyadic pairings with no commitment to marriage. Others find a same-sex partner with whom they make a long-term commitment even though formal marriage is not possible. However, most young people hope to marry and become involved in dating relationships or friendship relationships, one of which is eventually transformed into a more serious pattern of courtship and marriage.

Marriage is usually the central context within which work on intimate social relationships takes place. In 1996, only 14% of men and 10% of women ages 40–44 had never been married. Among those 65–74 years old in 1996, 4% of men and women had never been married (Figure 11.2) (U.S. Bureau of the Census, 1997). This pattern remained relatively constant from 1900 through the 1990s. Even though people today are more accepting of those who choose to remain single than they were in the 1960s, the number of young people who intend to remain single themselves has changed little (Thornton, 1989). Roughly 100 years of social science research has established that satisfaction in the relationship of marriage contributes significantly to psychological well-being, including a greater sense of social integration and protection from other life stressors. For most adults, happiness in life depends more on having a satisfying marriage than on any other domain of adult life, including work, friendships, hobbies, and community activities. In a longitudinal study of young adults who either remained single or got married and remained married over a 7-year period, those who were married had higher levels of well-being and fewer mental health problems (Horwitz et al., 1996).

The main change in the marriage pattern has been that more young adults postpone marriage until the end of their 20s. The percentage of single never-married women between the ages of 20 and 24 rose from 28% in 1960 to 68.5% in 1996. The comparable increase for single men was from 53% in 1960 to 81% in 1996 (U.S. Bureau of the Census, 1976, 1997; Stengel, 1985). Thus, in the United States, it is now normative for both men and women to be single during the years from 20 to 24.

Delaying the age at marriage is related to several other social trends, including having children at a later age, smaller projected family size, and therefore fewer years devoted to child-rearing. Delaying age at marriage is also related to changing norms regarding sexual experimentation as a single person. The 1980s brought the uncou-

FIGURE 11.2

Never-married persons, by age and sex, 1996

SOURCE: Based on Statistical Abstract of the United States, 1997.

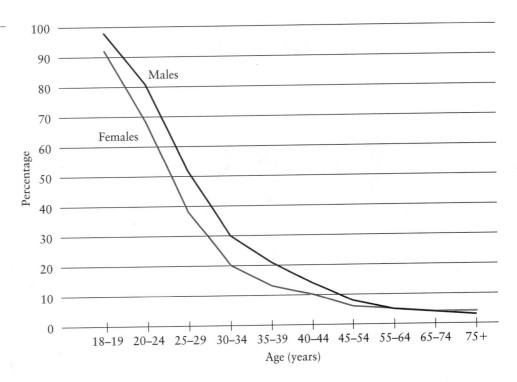

pling of sexual activity, marriage, and childbearing not only for adolescent girls, but for young adult women as well. Younger age at entry into sexual activity and increases in rates of cohabitation and affairs between married men and single women suggest that even though many young women do not marry they become involved in intimate relationships during their 20s (Richardson, 1986). In the future, it seems probable that an increasing proportion of men and women will remain single throughout their 20s, giving the domains of school and work greater influence in the early formulation of a lifestyle.

Readiness to Marry

What determines whether or not the dating relationship will end in matrimony? A basic factor is the person's underlying desire to marry. In a national sample of unmarried people aged 19–25, the mean score on a 5-point scale (where 1 = strongly disagree, and 5 = strongly agree) to the statement "I would like to get married some day," was 4.3 (South, 1993). Only 12.6% of the respondents indicated that they did not want to marry. This analysis revealed some differences among white, African-American, and Hispanic men and women. Given that all the groups held positive attitudes about marriage, the Hispanic men were the most enthusiastic about getting married and the African-American men were the least enthusiastic. Differences among the three ethnic groups of women were small and insignificant when factors of age, education, and employment were taken into account. Within racial groups, the African-American men and women differed more than did the men and women in the other two groups.

Beyond the desire to marry, an important factor is the readiness of the two individuals for a long-term commitment. Work on identity must be far enough along so that the possibility of a deep, emotional involvement with another person will be regarded as exciting rather than frightening. In studies of college students, a relationship has been found between identity status and the quality of intimacy. Those students who had achieved identity reported the most genuine intimate relationships. In contrast, those who were characterized as identity-confused were the least intimate and the most isolated (Orlofsky et al., 1973; Kacerguis & Adams, 1980; Craig-Bray, et al., 1988).

For most of today's college students, commitments to marriage and parenting are postponed until after graduation and the establishment of a career.

For some young adults, readiness for marriage is a response to the social clock. Each social class has its own expectations about the best age for marriage. Thus, a group's ideal age at marriage is a good predictor of the actual age at which individuals in the group will marry (Teachman et al., 1987). For working-class groups, the ideal age for marriage is between 18 and 22. Adolescents who are dating seriously during high school are likely to marry soon after graduation. If working-class adults are still single after the age of 23 or 24, they find that the pool of eligible partners has been reduced significantly, and their anxiety about finding a mate increases. In contrast, young people who attend college tend to have a later timetable for marriage. Advanced education tends to delay marriage more frequently for women than for men, perhaps because women who have had more years of education have alternative means to secure economic resources (Teachman et al., 1987).

Readiness for marriage for some young adults may be determined by a personal agenda, such as completing work for an advanced degree, completing military service, or earning a certain income. In each case, the person with this kind of commitment is less receptive to expressions of love than he or she will be once the goal is achieved. In the U.S. culture, individuals have a great deal of freedom to choose their time of marriage and their marriage partner. Although expectations that one will marry are strong, young adults have the freedom to follow their own timetables.

Selection of a Partner

In the U.S. and other individualistic cultures, most people believe that romantic love is the central reason for choosing a marriage partner. In societies with a more collectivist orientation, however, love is not necessarily relevant to the selection of a marriage partner. In these cultures, the choice may be made by family members, based on religious, financial, or family background factors believed to contribute to a good match, not only for the person but also for the extended family system (Dion & Dion, 1993).

Studies of the process of mate selection in the United States reveal that once a person is ready to consider marriage, the choice of partner and the decision to marry are influenced by a process of deepening attraction and commitment. Figure 11.3 provides a theoretical model of four phases of increasing involvement in the mate-selection process (Adams, 1986). At each phase, the relationship may be terminated if the key issues produce undesirable information or evaluation. Also, the relationship may end if an alternative attraction becomes so strong that it reduces investment in the first relationship. The alternative attraction may be another person, a job, school, or the desire to achieve a personal goal. In contrast, investment in the relationship may increase if no attractive or acceptable alternatives are available (Bui et al., 1996).

In Phase I, partners are selected from among those who are available for interaction. Many of the choices one makes during adolescence and young adulthood, such as where to go to college, where to work, which activities and social functions to attend, and where to take a vacation, determine whom one meets. Once two people meet, the question arises about what factors support their continued involvement.

One's style of interaction—for example, whether one is shy and withdrawn or expressive and outgoing—influences the number and kinds of interactions one has with others. In the most general sense, the choice of a partner depends on the network of interactions in which one is involved. Among those people one encounters, some attract attention and others do not. Physical appearance is an important element in this initial attraction. In addition, people who behave in an admirable, effective manner may be viewed as attractive or desirable. People seek others who will support their goals, who can be encouraging and positive, and who appear to be able to collaborate

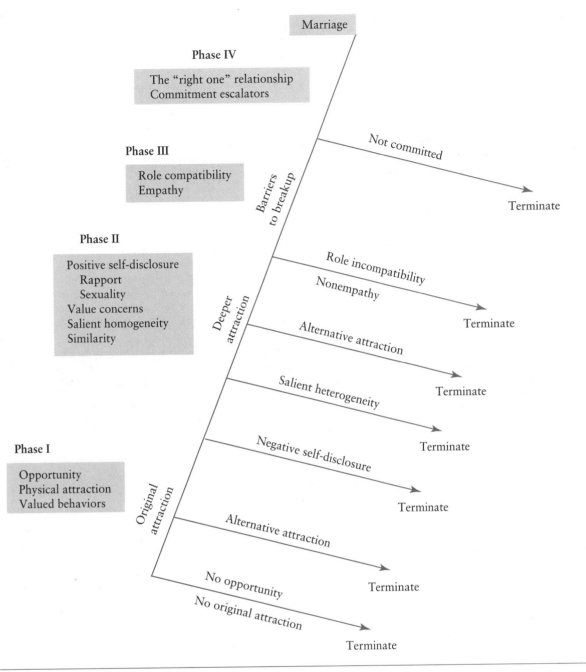

FIGURE 11.3
The mate-selection process in the United States
SOURCE: Based on Adams, 1986.

effectively in shared experiences (Sanders, 1997). Finally, the nature of one's attachment orientation influences the ability to form new intimate relationships (Box 11.1).

In addition to psychological factors that make it possible to engage in a mutually satisfying relationship, demographic realities influence the possibility of meeting suitable partners. In each community, for each age group of women, for example, the number of suitable available partners may differ, depending on such characteristics as the educational level, employment opportunities, and racial composition of the men in that community (South & Lloyd, 1992). The number and characteristics of potential marriage partners differ if one lives in a metropolitan or a more rural community. In one analysis, the sex ratio of men to women was 119 unmarried men for every 100 un-

BOX 11.1   ATTACHMENT STYLE AND RELATIONSHIP FORMATION

Attachment theory has become an important construct in understanding the process of relationship formation. One's attachment style, established in infancy, provides a template for orienting toward intimate relationships in adulthood. Anxiety over abandonment, comfort or discomfort with closeness or emotional disclosure, and the level of self-esteem associated with a secure or insecure attachment can all contribute to the type of partner one seeks and one's ability to sustain an intimate relationship (Brennan & Shaver, 1995; Jones & Cunningham, 1996; Brennan & Morris, 1997).

Bartholomew (1990) developed an attachment typology based on one's attachment experiences in infancy and toddlerhood. One can have a positive or negative assessment of the self, and a positive or a negative assessment of other (Table 11.3). Secure individuals have a positive model of themselves and others. Preoccupied individuals have a positive model of others, but a negative model of the self. Dismissing avoidant individuals have a positive model of self, but a negative model of others. Fearful avoidant individuals have a negative model of both self and others. The secure and the dismissing individuals have high self-esteem, however, they differ markedly in their value of intimacy and their interpersonal style. Secure individuals value relationships and are viewed as warm and nurturing. On the other hand, dismissing individuals minimize relationships in favor of self-reliance, and are viewed as cold or competitive. The fearful avoidant and the preoccupied individuals lack the self-esteem of the secure or dismissing groups. However, the fearful avoid social contact, whereas the preoccupied individuals tend to try hard to engage in relationships. Interestingly, individuals seek out partners with similar attachment styles. Not everyone is looking for a partner with a secure attachment. Fearful, avoidant individuals, for example, prefer other anxious partners over dismissing or secure ones, perhaps because they are better able to interpret and predict the relationship behaviors of those who have a similar attachment orientation (Frazier et al., 1996).

TABLE 11.3   The Attachment Typology

		Working Model of Others	
		POSITIVE	NEGATIVE
Working Model of the Self	POSITIVE	Secure	Dismissing
	NEGATIVE	Preoccupied	Fearful AVOIDANT

Source: Based on Bartholomew, 1990.

married women in rural communities and 106 unmarried men for every 100 unmarried women in metropolitan communities. Thus, later age at marriage for women in urban communities may be explained in part by a lower availability of male partners (McLaughlin et al., 1993).

Recent changes in the marriage patterns of African-Americans appear to be closely linked to the decline in the availability of appropriate African-American male partners. Single, never-married African-American women increased from 17% of the total African-American female population in 1970 to 36.8% in 1996 (U.S. Bureau of the Census, 1997). This pattern is related in part to the high mortality rates of African-American men and in part to their economic marginality. The decline in employment opportunities from 1970 to 1990 in the manufacturing industries where African-American men had made earlier gains coupled with increased crime and drug use in the urban communities contribute to the decline in the pool of "marriageable" men (Raley, 1996; Taylor et al., 1990).

Phase I, original attraction, moves on to Phase II as the partners begin to disclose information about themselves and interact in ways that deepen the relationship. In Phase II, the discovery of basic similarities and a feeling of rapport are central to continuing the relationship. Each person has key values and background characteristics that serve as a filter for assessing whether the other person is an eligible partner. Of course, eligibility is defined differently by different people. For some, any person who is conscious is eligible. Others have criteria that limit the choice of a marriage partner to someone of a certain age range, religion, race, educational background, and family history. For example, some adults would not consider marriage to someone who does not share their religious faith. For these people, only members of their own religious group are perceived as eligible partners. Looking at trends in the United States from the 1920s to the 1980s, religion appeared to play a lesser role and educational level played a greater role in limiting one's choice of a potential marriage partner. Young adults who were raised as Protestants and Catholics are more likely to marry one another today than in the past, whereas those whose highest educational level is a high school diploma and those who have attended college are less likely to intermarry (Kalmijn, 1991).

Many individuals may not even be aware of their own criteria for the eligibility of potential partners. For example, most women expect to marry men who are a few years older than they. Although they do not deliberately state this as a criterion for marriage, they simply do not interact with or feel drawn to a partner who is "too young" or "too old."

Similarity contributes to attractiveness. Most people seek marriage partners who will understand them and provide a sense of emotional support. They do not find attractive those who hold opposing views, come from quite different family backgrounds, or have temperamental qualities unlike their own. People of similar age and economic, religious, racial, and educational backgrounds marry each other in far greater proportions than would be expected by chance alone (Eshelman, 1985; Schoen & Wooldredge, 1989). For example, in 1996, only 0.6% of all married couples were made up of one African-American and one white partner (U.S. Bureau of the Census, 1997).

There are many dimensions along which two people may recognize similarities or differences. They may seem quite different on some dimensions, such as religion and social class, yet discover that they are quite similar on others, such as life goals and political ideology. The more aware individuals are of the themes that are central to their own sense of personal identity, the better they can recognize the dimensions of similarity and difference in other people that will contribute to intimate relationships.

The relationship is likely to proceed from Phase II to Phase III if the partners extend the domains in which self-disclosure occurs, including sexual needs, personal fears, and fantasies. With each new risk taken, the discovery of a positive, supportive reaction in the partner deepens the level of trust in the relationship. Negative reactions following disclosures or the revelation of information that is viewed as undesirable may lead to the termination of the relationship. For instance, premarital conflict about sex and problems in achieving sexual satisfaction in a relationship are likely to be associated with subsequent problems in the relationship, including higher levels of conflict in general and lower levels of relationship satisfaction (Long et al., 1996).

In Phase III, the discovery of role compatibility and empathy begins to give the relationship a life of its own. **Role compatibility** is a sense that the two partners approach a situation in ways that work well together. Whether it is a visit to a relative's home, an office party, a casual evening with friends, or running out of gas on the highway, the two people discover that they like the way each behaves and that their combined behavior is effective. Empathy builds through these observations, enabling each partner to know how the other responds and to anticipate the other's needs.

One aspect of this new level of intimacy is the special way romantic partners interact with one another. In affectionate and playful exchanges, partners often use "baby talk," a type of gentle, high-pitched register in which features of words are altered and new vocabulary may be created. Partners may give one another affectionate nicknames, and create unique signals for communication. The establishment of this intimate communication system acts as another bond

As role compatibility and empathy grow, the relationship takes on a new degree of intimacy and the couple begins to conceptualize a future together.

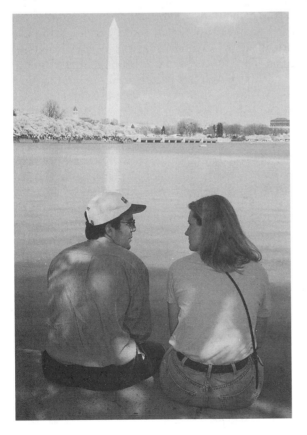

between the couple, creating a personal environment that is not shared with, and often not even known to, others (Bombar & Littig, 1996).

At some point in Phase III, partners may begin to think that they are in love. They may even tell each other, "I love you." The intensity of romantic love has been documented in studies by Keith Davis (1985) on the differences between romantic love and friendship. Lovers describe their relationships as characterized by *fascination, exclusiveness,* and *sexual desire:* "I would go to bed thinking about what we would do together, dream about it, and wake up ready to be with him again" (p. 24). They also express more intense caring for their loved ones than for friends. This caring includes giving their utmost, even to the point of self-sacrifice. The intensity of these characteristics accounts for some of the specialness and unsettling euphoria associated with being in love. It may also explain the relative instability of love relationships—intense emotion is difficult to sustain.

Once the partners enjoy role compatibility and empathy, they move on to Phase IV, the "right one" relationship. In this phase, barriers to breaking up help consolidate the relationship. First, the partners have disclosed and taken risks with each other that they probably have not taken with others. Second, they have achieved comfortable feelings of predictability and empathy that make them more certain about each other than about possible alternative attractions. Third, through frequent role enactment together, they have been identified by others as a couple. Subsequently, there is usually social support for them to remain together. At this point, the costs of breaking up begin to be quite high, including loss of a confidant, a companion, and the social network in which the couple is embedded.

Cohabitation. In contemporary society, cohabitation rather than marriage may be the outcome of this process. In 1996, there were 3.9 million unmarried couple households, an increase from 1.6 million such households in 1980 (U.S. Bureau of the Census, 1997). The probability of women entering a cohabiting relationship before marriage or before reaching the age of 35 increased from 2% for those born between 1928 and 1932 to 32% for those born between 1953 and 1957 (Schoen, 1992). In the youngest cohort, 63% married their first cohabitation partner before age 35.

The views expressed in the popular literature and among many couples are that cohabitation is a way of increasing marital stability by testing couple compatibility before marriage. However, the research literature shows that those couples who have cohabited before marriage are more likely to divorce than those who have not (DeMaris & Rao, 1992). This pattern has been observed in studies in the United States, Sweden, and Canada. The exception to this pattern has been shown only in the most recent U.S. cohorts (those born 1948–1952 and 1953–1957). In these groups, couples who have married after cohabitation and those who never cohabited before marriage are equally stable or, perhaps one might say, equally unstable (Schoen, 1992).

A number of explanations have been offered to account for the greater instability of marriages following cohabitation. Because cohabitation has been comparatively nontraditional in the United States in the past, it has been suggested that people who cohabit have certain characteristics that may contribute to the formation of unstable marriages (Thomson & Colella, 1992). They may be more unconventional, adapting less well to some of the traditional role demands of marriage and holding to a more individualistic view of married life. People who cohabit may have less commitment to the institution of marriage as a lifelong relationship. They may engage in more open conflict, leading to more negativity and hostility in the relationship over time. Although some of these hypotheses have received support, the changing social context of cohabitation and marriage makes it difficult to pin down a satisfactory explanation.

One of the questions being raised about cohabitation is, What type of relationship is it? Is it an informal alternative to marriage, or is it more like singlehood, except that it involves a bond of connection with a partner? In a comparison of women who have cohabited with those who have not, a significantly larger proportion of the cohabiting women want to get married. For these women, cohabitation is not a substitute for marriage but more like an element in the courtship process (Tanfer, 1987). In a 14-year longitudinal analysis of the white high school seniors of the class of 1972, adults who were cohabiting were compared with those who were in a first marriage and those who were single (Rindfuss & VandenHeuvel, 1990). In this analysis, cohabiting couples appeared to be more like singles than like married couples. The vast majority did not define themselves as married. They had employment and educational activities more similar to the single than to the married respondents. And they were more like the singles in saying that they did not plan to have children in the next two years. In this view, cohabitation is described as an "intimate relationship that maximizes individuation" (Landale & Fennelly, 1992).

However, in other samples, cohabitation had a different meaning. In a study of Puerto Rican women who lived on the mainland, primarily in New York, the nature of informal unions was studied (Landale & Fennelly, 1992). The sample ranged in age from 15 through 49. In the group aged 20–29, 16.5% said they were in an informal marriage, but only 8% described their relationship as cohabitation. **Consensual unions** without a civil or religious marriage has been practiced in Latin America for centuries and is regarded as a form of marital union. The practice is becoming less common on the island of Puerto Rico itself, but it is regarded as legitimate among mainland Puerto Rican women. Women who had a child within such a relationship were more likely to describe it as informal marriage than as cohabitation. Women who had been married before were also more likely to describe their current relationship as informal marriage rather than cohabitation. In this sample, it appears that the informal unions were perceived by women to be more like marriage than like singlehood. This literature suggests that cohabitation embraces a continuum of meaning from short-term relationships to long-term commitments. In some subcultures, consensual unions without the formal rites of marriage are perceived as a satisfactory, stable framework for personal and family relationships.

Relationships Between Partners of the Same Sex. The research on gay and lesbian couples is incomplete. What we present here is derived from research based on self-selected volunteer samples. Gay men and lesbians who would not volunteer to participate in research may be different in their outlook or adjustment from those who are comfortable enough to discuss the quality of their relationships. In addition, much of the literature is based on white middle-class participants. Gay men and lesbians are a diverse group with respect to their interests, talents, educational backgrounds, family backgrounds, careers, and other important aspects of adult roles. Thus, the description of gay and lesbian relationships that can be derived from the existing research misses much of the diversity that one would expect to uncover as this form of intimate relationship is studied in greater detail (Macklin, 1987).

> Annette E. Brenner remembers joking when her oldest son was 4 that she'd approve his marrying outside the family's faith as long as he married a woman. When he "came out" to her and her husband at 17, one of her first reactions was to try to "negotiate" him out of his gayness. She offered him a car, a house, if only he would wait and try marriage. He was at boarding school in Connecticut at the time, and she was convinced it was "just a stage." She remembers thinking, "Sure, this week you're a homosexual. Enjoy the experiment, have fun. Next week you'll be a Hare Krishna." Then she became enraged. "What is this kid doing to me?" she'd ask herself. "What was he doing to his grandparents, his brother and sister?" (Gelman, 1992, p. 50)

Homosexual relationships are often established within a climate of secrecy and social stigma, especially fears about parental rejection. Gay and lesbian couples often perceive less social support from family members and seek other members of the gay or lesbian community to validate and encourage their relationship (Hickson et al., 1992). Even when they are in committed relationships, gay and lesbian young adults are likely to manage the negative impact of family rejection by keeping the nature of their homosexual relationship a secret from family members. In a national study of lesbians, 19% reported being "out" to no family members, and only 27% reported being "out" to all family members (Bradford et al., 1994). Although this image management might seem to place a strain on intimate relationships, research shows no significant relationship between the couples' satisfaction in their relationship and the extent to which they are "out" to family members (Green et al., 1995).

The decision to adopt a child emerged as a result of the stability and intimacy of this lesbian couple's committed relationship.

Lesbian relationships are likely to emerge out of close same-sex friendships. Lesbians are somewhat more likely to be able to establish long-term relationships than gay men. Most lesbians describe their relationships as stable, sexually exclusive, and extremely close. They also describe their relationships as closer and more flexible than do gay men or heterosexual couples (Green et al., 1995). Greater levels of satisfaction in the relationship are associated with greater levels of equality and shared decision-making. Equality in the relationship depends on equal resources and commitment to the relationship (Eldridge & Gilbert, 1990). In comparison with heterosexual wives, women in lesbian relationships are more likely to describe greater satisfaction in their sexual activity and greater dissatisfaction with inequalities in the relationship. These women place a strong value on companionship and confiding in one another, but they also expect to experience high levels of autonomy within their relationships.

Gay men are also interested in long-term relationships. However, they are less likely than lesbians to be sexually exclusive, and there is less consensus among them about the importance of sexual exclusiveness (Hary, 1983). In comparison to lesbian relationships, gay men often find partners in the context of a more active, competitive social scene that involves multiple short-term relationships. Among homosexual couples who are in a long-term relationship, there are few other differences between male and female couples with respect to the values they place on their relationship (Lewis et al., 1981). Gay couples report higher levels of closeness and much higher levels of flexibility than do heterosexual couples. What is more, the combination of flexibility and closeness is strongly associated with couple satisfaction (Green et al., 1995). In a comparison of married couples, gay couples, lesbian couples, and cohabiting heterosexual couples, the cohabiting heterosexual couples had lower relationship satisfaction than the other three types of partners, who did not differ significantly from one another (Kurdek & Schmitt, 1986).

Research suggests that many of the same factors are associated with relationship quality across all types of couples: valuing security, permanence, and closeness; expressiveness; perceived rewards for being in the relationship; trust in the partner; good problem-solving and conflict resolution skills; egalitarian decision-making; openness to the expression of differences; and perceived social support (Kurdek, 1995).

Adjustment During the Early Years of Marriage

Once the choice has been made and the thrill of courtship has passed, the first few years of marriage involve a process of mutual adaptation. They can be extremely difficult, particularly because the newly married couple does not anticipate the strains. The partners may be quite distressed to find their "love nest" riddled with the tensions that are a normal part of carving out a life together. In fact, data suggest that the probability of divorce is highest during the first years of marriage, peaking between two and four years. The median duration of marriage is about seven years, a pattern that has been stable since the mid-1970s (U.S. Bureau of the Census, 1997).

There are many sources of tension in a new marriage. If the partners do not have similar religious, educational, or social-class backgrounds, they will have to compromise on many value decisions. Assuming a shared value orientation, certain lifestyle decisions can generate tension. The couple must establish a mutually satisfying sexual relationship. They must also work out an agreement about spending and saving money. They must also respond to each other's sleep patterns, food preferences, work patterns, and toilet habits. The couple may find the demands of their parents and in-laws to be an additional source of conflict. Usually it is the number of demands rather than any single one that makes the adjustment process so difficult.

As part of the adjustment to marriage, the partners must achieve a sense of psychological commitment to each other. The marriage ceremony is intended to make that commitment public and binding. It is safe to say that most people probably do not fully accept the reality of their marriage vows until they have tested the relationship later. There is a period of testing in every marriage, during which each partner is likely to put strain on the relationship to see how strong it really is. The question of trust may be posed as, Will you still love me even if I do. . . ? or Am I still free to do what I did before we were married? Every marriage relationship is different. The partners must discover the limits that their particular relationship can tolerate. But both partners must feel that they still have a degree of freedom within the marriage parameters. They must also believe that the limits on their freedom are balanced by the love they gain in return. As each test is successfully passed, the partners grow closer. They trust each other more and become increasingly sensitive to each other's feelings. Eventually, the tests diminish in number as the question of trust is resolved.

Communication and Marital Adjustment. It is reasonable to expect that intimacy and a high level of marital satisfaction require effective communication and the capacity to cope effectively with conflict. Conflict can be a product of the interaction of two well-developed identities, each with a distinct temperament, values, and goals. It can also be a product of the uneven distribution of power or resources. Conflict can further result from the simple day-to-day need to make decisions, which the couple has never made before. Finally, it can be a product of the failure of a partner or the relationship to meet critical expectations. Whatever the source, marital stability and satisfaction are closely tied to how couples manage conflict (Filsinger & Thoma, 1988).

Three dimensions of conflict seem especially important in differentiating happy and distressed marital relationships. First, the amount of negative communication, especially nonverbal negative expressions and hostile put-downs, are more frequent in distressed than in happy couples. Second, distressed couples show a pattern of **coercive escalation**, a style of interaction in

Distressed couples are more likely to escalate negative interactions, so that one angry remark leads to a chain of hostile responses. How might intimacy continue to thrive for couples who like to argue a lot?

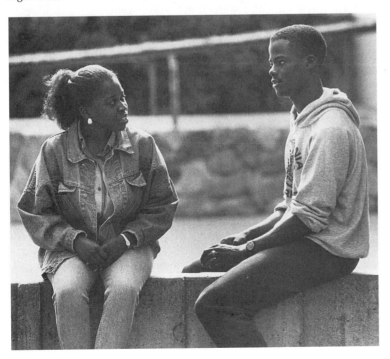

which the probability that a negative remark will be followed by another negative remark increases as the chain of communication gets longer and longer (Gottman & Levenson, 1986). This pattern has been observed at the behavioral level by coding the verbal and nonverbal characteristics of an interaction and at the physiological level by monitoring heart rate, blood pressure, and release of stress hormones during communication (Markman & Notarius, 1987; Schrof, 1994). As the communication becomes increasingly negative, the partners become so physiologically disorganized that they lose access to their more rational ego functions. Over repeated instances, they become sensitive to this physiological state, reaching it sooner. In comparison, happy couples become more effective in soothing each other and in finding ways of preventing conflicts. Third, distressed couples have different perceptions of the approach their partners are taking to resolve a conflict. For example, one partner may think he or she is acting in a constructive way to find a solution, but the other partner may view as patronizing or minimizing the importance of the issue. Congruence between the partners in how they think they and their partners are approaching the resolution of conflict is significantly related to marital satisfaction (Acitelli et al., 1997).

Apart from how they perceive and handle conflict, happy couples enjoy being together. They value the companionship aspects of their marriage, such as spending time together with friends or having dinner together (Kamo, 1993). In a comparison of American and Japanese couples, the latter were significantly less likely to share time together in these ways. However, for both the American and the Japanese couples, those who spent more leisure time together had higher levels of marital satisfaction. The causal nature of this relationship is not fully understood. One might assume that happy couples choose to spend more time together, but it may also be that couples who have opportunities to spend more time together come to feel more positive about their marriage as a result.

Partners who have a high level of marital satisfaction report frequent, pleasurable interaction and a high degree of disclosure (Jorgensen & Gaudy, 1980; Robinson & Price, 1980). Emotional expressiveness, especially by husbands, and a lack of ambivalence about expressing one's feelings are important elements in this communication process, particularly among white middle-class U.S. families (King, 1993). In contrast, a decline in pleasurable interactions and an absence of communication of any kind— even conflicts—are associated with a high probability of divorce (Noller, 1980).

A growing body of literature emphasizes the notion that men and women communicate differently and have different perceptions of the process. This idea has mixed empirical support. In many ways, men and women are alike. For example, both perceive the value of affective or emotional skills in promoting and sustaining friendships and romantic relationships. They both expect close friends, and especially romantic partners, to be able to have the ability to encourage, soothe, reassure, and validate one another (Burleson et al., 1996). When faced with upsetting problems, both women and men are most likely to try to offer suggestions for how to solve the problem or take some action, rather than to simply empathize and identify with the person's problem (Goldsmith & Dun, 1997). When asked about their preferred mode or style of interaction as a couple, husbands and wives both prefer interactions that are **contactful,** that is, open to the other person's point of view and that also clearly express the speaker's own position. They least prefer **controlling** interactions in which one person expresses his or her point of view and does not take the other person's point of view into consideration (Hawkins et al., 1980). These similarities are important indications that men and women approach the process of establishing intimate relationships with many common skills and values.

On the other hand, there are some distinctions in the ways men and women approach communication that have implications for the quality of an intimate relationship. The socialization of both sexes in U.S. culture is still sufficiently distinct to result in differences in expectations and competencies. For example, when faced with a problem, men are more likely to want to deny it or to spend time analyzing and defining it in comparison with women (Goldsmith & Dun, 1997). Similarly, men tend to value the skills of being a good conversationalist or storyteller, and being able to laugh and joke as well as to argue and defend a position somewhat more than do women (Burleson et al., 1996). They tend to be more ambivalent than women about expressing emotions and withdraw to avoid escalating conflict. Women, on the other hand, tend to want to "talk things out" so that everyone feels comfortable with the situation. In conflicts, these styles can become incompatible, especially if the woman is trying to reach consensus and the man withdraws. In general, women expect and desire a degree of closeness that is often not reciprocated. Men, on the other hand, are more likely to be satisfied with the degree of intimacy that they find in marriage and have fewer expectations of or less desire for greater closeness (Dindia & Allen, 1992).

Adjustment in Dual-Earner Marriages

One of the greatest changes in U.S. families in recent years has been the increase in the number of married women who are employed. It is now normative for married women, including those with young children, to be in the labor market. The percentage of employed, married women whose husbands are present rose from 32% in 1960 to 61% in 1996. The number of women with young children who work outside the home has also grown substantially. In 1996, 60.5% of married women with children under 3 years old were in the labor force, compared with 33% in 1975 (U.S. Bureau of the Census, 1997). Rather than drop out of the labor force and return to work after their children are grown, the majority of women now remain in the labor force throughout the early years of parenthood.

There is no question that the involvement of both husband and wife in the labor market requires a redefinition of traditional family roles and the division of labor. Uncertainty about the expectations and behaviors of the spousal roles must be worked out between the partners. Sometimes this uncertainty helps to produce greater intimacy by generating interactions that lead to greater self-disclosure by each partner. Personal preferences and habits must be examined if the partners are to arrive at a successful division of labor that is mutually satisfying. Sometimes, however, this process is threatening. The partners may not really be aware of their expectations of themselves or of the other person until they are married. For example, it is not until some weeks have gone by and no one has done the laundry that it becomes evident that the couple must decide either who will do this task or how to share it.

One analysis of the potential conflicts for dual-earner couples focuses on the relative balance of power and demands for household labor for the two partners (Rosenfeld, 1992). In the traditional male-breadwinner, female-homemaker family model, the husband has more power as a result of his access to financial resources and participates little in the low-status household tasks. The wife, in contrast, has little power and the majority of responsibility for the household tasks. As women have entered the labor market, their access to financial resources has increased. To the extent that their husbands also help in sharing the household tasks, their well-being and mental health improve. For men, especially in families where there is a relatively high family income, as their wives' income matches or surpasses their own and they have to take on a greater role in domestic tasks, their well-being declines and their mental health suffers. Those men who feel demeaned or threatened by demands to participate in household labor are likely to experience depressive symptoms similar to the reactions that women have when they try to carry the full responsibility of household tasks while also participating in the labor market. Finding the balance of power and of household responsibilities that preserves a comfortable feeling of mutual respect and support is a major challenge in the early years of the marriage and has to be fine-tuned and renegotiated throughout the marriage.

Not only has the number of two-worker families increased but also the number of families in which both partners pursue high-powered professional, technical, or administrative careers has risen steadily. A considerable amount of research has been done on these dual-career marriages. The main variables studied and the major findings about these marriages are summarized in Table 11.4.

There are indications that highly educated women who are employed in demanding work roles are less inclined to remain in a marriage relationship that is not emotion-

TABLE 11.4   Major Findings on Dual-Career Marriages

Variable Studied	Findings
Degree of marital satisfaction	Satisfaction related to degree of fit between husband's and wife's attitudes and aspirations. Couples with more traditional sex-role attitudes tend to experience more stress.
Early socialization experiences	Many women in dual-career marriages experienced: 1. Early adjustment to high levels of stress. 2. Little reinforcement for conventional values. 3. A close relationship with parents who supported their career aspirations.
Effects of having husband and wife in the same career field	Wives in the same field as their husbands tend to produce more than those not married to fellow professionals but are less productive and less professionally satisfied than their husbands.
Consequences of status differences between husbands and wives	Degree of stress is related to the extent to which the status difference is congruent with the gender-role identities and expectations of the partners.
Effect of dual careers on family task sharing	Partners tend to do more sharing of traditionally female tasks than do single-career or career/earner couples.
Impact of work world on dual-career family	Negative impact of traditional business, which operates on the assumption that career takes precedence over family and that the employee has a full-time support system at home.
Effects of geographic mobility	Mobility has a negative impact on the wife's career; her needs do not tend to be the determining factor in the decision to move.
Effect of particular structural variations	Couples who share less than two full-time equivalent positions favor a continuation of the arrangement, devote more time to their work, and are more productive than the average full-time employee, yet employers tend to view such an arrangement with reservation.

SOURCE: Based on Macklin, 1987.

ally satisfying. Economic independence allows women to choose or reject marriage, a freedom that many women of earlier historical periods did not enjoy. At the same time, the literature confirms the continuation of a traditional, male-dominated career orientation in these successful dual-career marriages, where both partners agree to let the husband's career take priority over the wife's as long as he also agrees to preserve time for companionate interactions, supports his wife emotionally, and participates at an acceptable level in household and family tasks.

In conclusion, positive adjustment and marital satisfaction in the early years of marriage are a function of the identity status of each partner; the desire for intimacy, open communication, and closeness; participation in pleasurable, companionate time together; the resources available to both and how they are shared; the way power is shared or struggled for; the way conflicts are expressed, avoided, or resolved; and the congruence or lack of it between the husband's and wife's perceptions of their ideal and actual role enactment.

Childbearing   Little has been written about the psychological growth stimulated by the decision to bear children. It is a unique and significant life choice that is made in various ways. During early adulthood, the issue of reproduction is confronted many times. Adults make choices to delay parenting, have another child, wait before having another child, or stop having children altogether. As discussed in Chapter 4, many couples undergo difficult and expensive procedures to conceive a child. Even unplanned pregnancies are products of some kind of decision-making, whether it is a decision to have sexual relations knowing that pregnancy was possible, to avoid using effective means of birth control, to abort the pregnancy, or to carry the child to term (Lydon et al., 1996). In

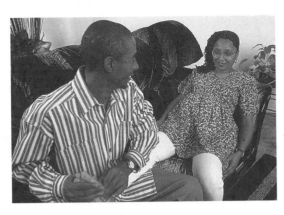

This couple's affection for and commitment to each other is expanding to include love for their unborn child. How might the quality of the parent's relationship influence the experience of pregnancy?

all of these decisions, many powerful themes are reflected: one's sense of fulfilling a masculine or feminine life purpose by having children; one's childhood socialization and identification with parental figures; or religious beliefs about sexuality, contraception, or abortion. Reproduction is the means by which the species perpetuates itself. Regardless of the decisions one reaches, this issue cannot help but heighten one's sense of being and belief that the decisions of adulthood make a difference.

In the United States, women 18 to 20 years old expect to have 2.2 children (U. S. Bureau of the Census, 1997). Usually, the decision to have children is made within the context of a stable partner relationship, and is reached jointly. However, judging from the rate of abortions to married women, one might estimate that as many as 25 to 30% of pregnancies of married couples are unplanned.

In contemporary society, couples typically view the timing for childbearing as a decision they make together in the context of other personal and family goals and commitments. Factors such as religious beliefs, career aspirations, ideals about family life, and social expectations in the family and culture all contribute to a couple's commitment to bearing children and the timing of first and subsequent pregnancies. In a comparison of Dutch and Flemish couples, religious commitment and educational attainment were both associated with the timing of the first pregnancy. For the Flemish couples, who tend to endorse more traditional gender roles, a woman's religious commitment and educational attainment were more predictive of the timing of the first pregnancy than they were of the man. The implication is that for Flemish couples, child-rearing is largely the woman's domain, so they have a greater say in childbearing decisions. Dutch couples, whose family values tend to be more egalitarian, have a later age at first pregnancy. In these couples, the high educational attainment of either partner led to a delay in childbearing. With regard to religious commitment, the couples in which the male had a strong religious commitment had children much earlier than those in which the male did not. Thus, the factors contributing to the timing of childbearing were not governed solely by the female and her preferences (Corijn et al., 1996).

A national survey of U. S. married men and women who were currently childless but of childbearing age measured their attitudes toward wanting to have children and the considerations associated with the desire to have children (Seccombe, 1991). Men in the sample were more supportive than women of the view that it is better to have a child than to be childless. The results suggest distinct patterns for men and women on their orientation toward having children. In the past, men have not had to choose between having a career and having children. It appears that they continue to endorse a view of adulthood in which fatherhood will play an important role. Women, on the other hand, are becoming increasingly sensitive to the difficulties of combining career ambitions and motherhood. Many women perceive that they have to make a choice about whether to have children or to direct their efforts and energy into professional development and career attainment.

In the Seccombe (1991) survey, the benefits the respondents associated with having children included having someone to love, giving their parents grandchildren, having a sibling for another child, having someone to care for them when they were old, and giving them something to do. Women were more likely to endorse the benefit of having someone to care for them when they were old, but for all the other benefits, men and women agreed on their importance. The most important benefit mentioned was having someone to love.

Although the great majority of married couples intend to have children, the timing of their entry into parenthood varies. The notion of the social clock comes into play in this decision. Couples who wait a long time to begin their families may be pressured by parents who are eager to become grandparents or by friends who have already experienced the lifestyle changes that accompany the birth of the first child. In recent years, couples have begun to postpone having children until after the first years of their marriage. This decision is related to several other aspects of adult life. Couples who have a dual-earner marriage have to consider the effect of children on their family income. They may try to anticipate the best timing for childbearing in relation to job security or career advancement. Some couples set certain material goals for themselves as a prerequisite to having children. For example, they may decide to wait until they can buy a home, purchase some furniture, or travel together before they have children. Given the high divorce rate, couples are likely to want to feel confident that their relationship is strong before deciding to have children.

Delayed entry into parenthood has typically been studied in relation to the characteristics of the woman. It has been found to be related to a woman's level of education, her career commitment, and the family's income. In a study of the timing of entry into fatherhood, men who were characterized as late-entry (30 years old or over) were more involved with their children and had more positive feelings about them than did the on-time or early fathers (Cooney et al., 1993). Older fathers may feel that they have less conflict between commitments to work and to family. They may feel that they have already demonstrated their ability to succeed in the "breadwinner" role, and therefore can approach parenthood with more confidence and a greater sense of self-efficacy. Older fathers may have more emotional resources to bring to their marriage and their parenting relationship.

The Impact of Childbearing on the Intimate Relationship

In contrast to the elation that usually accompanies the anticipation of and preparation for the newborn, the arrival of the first child often brings a period of stress to the relationship. In studies of married couples, the transition to parenthood is associated with lower marital satisfaction and happiness (Glenn & McLanahan, 1982; Belsky & Pensky, 1988). However, ratings of marital satisfaction do not usually drop dramatically from very satisfied to very unsatisfied. Couples continue to be satisfied with their marriage after their children are born, but the level of satisfaction is somewhat lower.

Looking more closely at this pattern, Belsky and Rovine (1990) found clear evidence of individual differences among couples. In their longitudinal study of 128 families, they observed four patterns of change in the assessment of marital quality. Some couples showed a rapid decline in marital quality after the first baby was born. Others showed a slow, steady decline. A third group showed no significant change, and a fourth group showed slight increases in marital quality. These findings caution us not to overgeneralize group trends to individual cases.

The decline in relationship satisfaction that may accompany the transition to parenthood can be accounted for in several ways. For the first months after a child is born, both parents are exhausted by lack of sleep. They are generally unskilled in the care of a newborn baby, and both have new responsibilities and a new schedule. Many parents feel inadequate to care for their babies, and turn to their parents, neighbors, pediatricians, and books for advice. This lack of self-confidence creates tension between the marriage partners.

The baby's presence brings out areas of potential conflict between the partners about philosophies of child-rearing or beliefs regarding appropriate child-care practices. Feelings of jealousy, competition, and abandonment may arise in the first months after the child is born. The exclusiveness of the husband-wife relationship is interrupted by the repeated demands of the new baby, and there is less time for the couple to be alone together. Feelings of resentment may be stronger when a couple's sex-role attitudes conflict with the actual activities they end up carrying out after a child is born (Belsky et al., 1986). For example, those men and women who endorse highly traditional views of sex roles after the transition to parenthood and who end up having to function in a more egalitarian mode, both sharing actively in tasks of child care and household, express lower levels of marital satisfaction (MacDermid et al., 1990).

It is not surprising that one's experiences as a child influence how one reacts to the parent role. But it may be somewhat more surprising to learn that recollections of one's child-rearing environment are related to the level of marital satisfaction experienced after the birth of the first child. One study reported a more pronounced decline in marital adjustment after the birth of the first child when either the husband or the wife recalled his or her own parents as cold, rejecting, and involved in a conflictual marriage. In addition, negative child-rearing experiences were related to greater discrepancies between husbands' and wives' assessments of the quality of their marriage after their children were born (Belsky & Isabella, 1985). One interpretation of these observations is that memories of negative childhood experiences are reawakened in the parents after the child's birth and stimulate increased defensiveness. Another interpretation is that adults whose parents were cold and rejecting may not have developed adequate parenting skills themselves. They encounter increased conflict with their spouses when they become parents because they are less competent in this new role.

In an attempt to clarify the effects of many of these factors on marital satisfaction during the transition to parenthood, researchers compared marital activities and evaluations of the marriage by parents and nonparents who had been married the same number of years (MacDermid et al., 1990). They found that over the first three years of marriage, couples' ratings of love and satisfaction declined somewhat. There were no differences in the magnitude of the decline for parents and nonparents. And having children did not account for a greater drop in love or satisfaction than appears to occur as a result of adjusting to marriage in general. This is an important observation that provides new insight into much of the earlier research on marital satisfaction and the transition to parenthood.

However, having children did have a clear impact on marital companionship. The percentage of leisure activities shared by the husband and wife dropped sharply after the baby was born, but it declined only slightly for the couples without children. During the third year of marriage, parents had a greater number of shared activities per day than nonparents, but few when the child was not present. Figure 11.4 shows the number of minutes of joint leisure per day without the child for two groups of parents in comparison with joint leisure for nonparents in the first, second, and third years of marriage. After the birth of their child, couples have only about one-third as many minutes together alone as they had when they were childless. The nature of companionship in marriage thus changes to incorporate a baby and therefore may become less intimate.

Coping with the early months of child-rearing may strengthen the bond between the man and the woman. The partners begin to respect each other's competence in caring for their child. They also begin to conceptualize their roles as parents and to view the increasing complexity of their family structure as a challenge rather than a burden. The new baby adds a degree of energy to the family through expressions of satisfaction, pleasure, and affection.

As the roles of mother and father are added to the adults' repertoire of role relationships, their own expectations (as well as those of others) concerning the raising of a child are aroused. The daily demands of the child helps the parents define their own roles more realistically. Instead of wondering what parents should do, they are occupied with the actual demands of parenting. Through this experiential learning, young adults formulate their own definitions of parental roles. Assuming that the early experiences are successful and parents are able to meet their child's needs, they gradually achieve a new level of self-efficacy in the parenting role, gaining new confidence in their ability to provide a nurturing environment for their child.

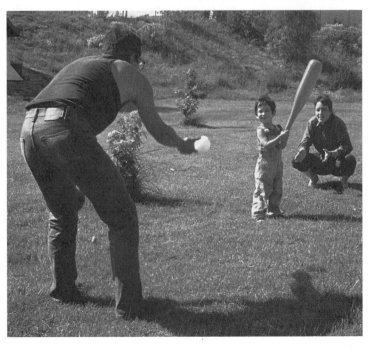

Couples with children find new ways to spend time together that includes their child. Rather than a quiet picnic with music and a bottle of wine, a day at the park becomes a chance for batting practice.

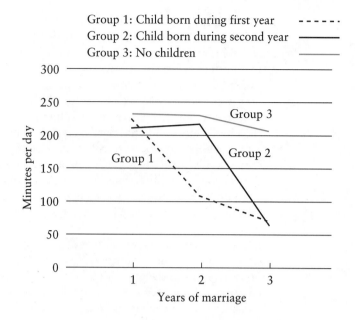

FIGURE 11.4
Duration of joint husband-wife leisure without child, for parents and nonparents
Source: Based on MacDermid, Huston, & McHale, 1990.

The process of social attachment and its impact on the infant was discussed in Chapter 5. The theme of mutuality as the central process for the establishment of trust was stressed. This same mutuality also has an impact on parents. Infants actively engage their parents, evoke unique responses, and, through their differential behaviors, begin to shape parenting behaviors. Infants respond to their parents with shrieks of delight, elaborate smiles, and the active pursuit of them. They are unrestrained in their loving. They mouth, bite, grab, laugh, smile, squeal, and coo in response to pleasure. Through their open demonstrations of affection, infants teach adults about the expression of love and increase their parents' ability to demonstrate it. As parents and children begin to engage in playful interactions, the capacity to establish and maintain reciprocal interactions expands. Children learn how to initiate a play sequence by bringing a toy or making a playful gesture. Parents then learn how to respond by complying to the request for play, sitting down on the floor, bringing out the box of favorite play materials, or tickling and tumbling. As children and parents experience mutual, congruent playful interactions, the bond of affection is strengthened and communication is enhanced (Lindsey et al., 1997).

Parenting is a unique experience of adulthood. There may be some developmental antecedents to parenting, such as baby-sitting, caring for younger siblings, or working with children as a camp counselor or a teacher. However, none of these roles involves the emotional investment and complete responsibility of parenthood. As a parent, an adult has an opportunity to discover new aspects of his or her personality. The parent role has new demands that are distinct from the role of spouse. As a parent, one must respond to a person who cannot fully reciprocate the generosity or caring expressed. In this role, the parent discovers the qualities of nurturance, playfulness, and authoritativeness. As a parent interacts with his or her children, memories of childhood are often revived. Conflicts in one's relationship with one's parents, feelings of sibling jealousy, and recollections of school days, peer relations, fears, and secret dreams are all reviewed as one strives to respond to and guide one's children. In all of this, there is a new opportunity to put old ghosts to rest, reinterpret past events, and achieve a new sense of adult maturity.

The Decision Not to Have Children

Not all couples choose to have children. In 1992, 9.3% of women aged 18–34 expected to have no children during their lifetime. The percentage was lower for Hispanic women (5.7%) than for white and African-American women. More women with a graduate or professional degree expected to be childfree (12%) than women who had graduated from high school (9%) (U.S. Bureau of the Census, 1997). Much like attitudes toward remaining single, attitudes toward a lifestyle in which a couple chooses not to have children are becoming more accepting. This shift is evidenced in part by a change in the sociological jargon from the term "childlessness" to the newer term "voluntarily childfree." The decision not to have children is becoming increasingly common, not only in the United States but also in other industrialized nations, especially as women's educational attainment and occupational commitments are reaching new levels.

Couples who choose not to have children continue to experience social pressures to have children and are aware of negative stereotypes attributed to them by family members. They may be viewed as selfish, less well adjusted, less nurturant, and likely to have a less fulfilling life than couples with children (Somers, 1993). Resisting social expectations that married women ought to bear children requires a high level of personal autonomy and less need for social support from a wide range of reference groups. Voluntarily childfree men have been described as more independent, less tied to tradition, and more flexible than those who are fathers. Similarly, voluntarily childfree women have been described as more self-reliant, assertive, and concerned with personal freedom than women who are mothers (Silka & Kiesler, 1977). In general, couples who decide not to have children have been described as follows: "well educated, live in urban areas, have little or no religious affiliation, and hold nontraditional sex roles" (Somers, 1993, p. 643). They are able to disregard the negative social pressures, and they tend to find support from one another and from a small number of significant family members or close friends (Houseknecht, 1987).

Work Work provides a major structural factor in the establishment of one's lifestyle. It is the primary means of accumulating financial resources. In addition, one's work determines in large part the activities, social relationships, challenges, satisfactions, and hassles or frustrations of daily life. Finally, work is the context within which many adults experience a sense of personal value and social status. In combination with intimate relationships and parenting, efforts to coordinate work and family life produce some of the greatest challenges of adult life.

The concept of work is complex. The following analysis provides a framework for the consideration of work as a psychological variable, looking at global characteristics of work and their potential impact on one's cognitive, social, and emotional development and on one's sense of self in adulthood. This type of analysis is necessary because there is such a wide variety of occupational roles in U.S. society. Each job role places the individual in a somewhat different psychological context, exerting unique psychological demands.

The nature of the workplace is changing rapidly as the close of the 20th century approaches. Many factors, including the shift in emphasis from agriculture and manufacturing to service industries, the increasingly global nature of business, the higher educational standards for entry into many careers, and the rapid evolution and extinction of specific types of work, have introduced new levels of uncertainty into the process of choosing a career, finding work, and staying employed. There is a broad consensus that American workers need to enhance their efficiency and productivity in order to remain competitive in the global economic environment (Coordinating Committee for the Human Capital Initiative, 1993).

The first important distinction concerning occupations has to do with the training and post-training periods. Much of the career development research focuses on preparing a person to enter the labor market (Keller et al., 1991). The early phases of career decision making presented in Tiedeman's model in Chapter 10 focus on self-understanding; career exploration; identifying a good match between personal interests, skills, and values and particular careers; and learning as much as possible about the specific job opportunities within a career domain. However, because of the wide variety of possible occupational choices and associated work settings, one can make only limited progress in preparing to enact a specific occupational role. Even though many employers consider educational attainment a selection criterion, they often use it more as an element in determining one's eligibility for the job rather than as a detailed assessment of

During the training period, new workers learn technical skills as well as strategies for fitting into the social environment with co-workers.

whether one has the background and skills to perform it. In other words, educational attainment is usually viewed as a gross indication of whether one will get into the pool of people who are going to be considered for a position (Miller, 1988). Most jobs require a period of training for the novice employee, which varies from a few weeks in the case of an assembly-line worker to 10 years in the case of a physician. For some people, the stage of young adulthood is over before the training experience is completed.

In addition to the transmission of information about specific skills, the training period often involves the socialization of the worker. Through this process, the novice learns about the technical skills, interpersonal behaviors, work-related attitudes, and authority relations that are valued by the work group. The training period also acquaints the novice with the specific demands and hazards of the particular occupation. This is the induction phase in Tiedeman's model. During the occupational search and training periods, the individual must evaluate the match between personal characteristics and four central components of the work situation: (1) technical skills, (2) authority relations, (3) unique demands and hazards, and (4) interpersonal relations with co-workers. These are the major arenas for new learning in early adulthood.

Technical Skills

Most jobs require a certain degree of technical expertise, which varies greatly from one occupation to another. Individuals must evaluate whether the particular skills required are within their range of competence. They must also determine whether they have the potential to improve their skills, and evaluate whether they derive pleasure and satisfaction from demonstrating these abilities. The job-training phase involves learning new skills. Thus, the success of individuals in learning and applying new skills determines to some extent whether they will remain in the occupation.

Authority Relations

Each job role specifies status and decision-making relationships among people. One aspect of job training is learning which people evaluate one's work, the criteria they use, and the limits of one's autonomy in the job. New workers must respond to both the authority structure and the people who occupy positions in it. In addition, they must assess the channels for decision making and the ways in which they can influence decisions. With respect to the people who occupy positions of authority, new workers must be able to deal with a variety of personalities in positions of higher and lower status. Having a good relationship with one's supervisor is a key element in job satisfaction.

Demands and Hazards

Each job has unique occupational demands, including norms for self-preservation, productivity, and availability. In some work settings, there are expectations for a high level of personal commitment. Leisure time, family activities, and political or community roles are all influenced by one's participation in the work role. In other work settings, however, workers may become alienated, feeling little sense of personal contribution to their employers' overall objectives. The norms vary greatly from one occupation to another. It is the task of individuals to assess how well they fit and how strongly they wish to do so with the unique characteristics of a particular occupational role.

Occupational hazards include a broad range of potential physical and psychological risks associated with the workplace, including exposure to toxins, work-related injuries, and exposure to diseases, reproductive hazards, and working conditions that have negative psychological consequences, such as noise or shift work (Baker, 1989).

Settings differ in the kinds of pressures or hazards they impose on workers. Similarly, individuals differ in their vulnerability to these pressures and hazards, their willingness to risk certain potential dangers, and their evaluation of the payoff for enduring some degree of stress. The individual must ultimately decide whether the particular vulnerabilities are tolerable in light of the rewards.

Interpersonal Relationships with Co-Workers

The final area of learning during the period of occupational search and training involves one's interpersonal relationships with co-workers. Although the potential for friendships in the work setting is usually not advertised as a central component of job satisfaction, it is clearly a dominant feature in the decision to be committed to a particular work setting. The need for friends with whom one can share the anxieties of learning the new job provide strong motives for seeking comradeship on the job. The presence of congenial co-workers who can relax together and share feelings of accomplishment greatly enhances any work setting. In fact, the spirit of friendship on the job may compensate for many stressful situational demands.

Some work settings stress competition among co-workers; incentives are arranged to stimulate competition rather than cooperation. In such settings, new workers must shoulder the strains of their new learning independently. They must learn the game of one-upmanship, taking credit for successes and blaming others for failures. A competitive orientation is more likely to be fostered when workers are organized into teams or units. Intergroup relations tend to be more distrustful and more supportive of the group's self-interest, whereas individual relations tend to be more trusting and cooperative (Pemberton et al., 1996).

Career Opportunities

A number of factors limit the range of occupations open to a given person during the work search phase. Among the most obvious limiting factors are educational attainment, talent, and location. In addition, discrimination on the basis of race and gender continues to thwart the full participation of women and minorities in the work force.

Recent policy changes in the welfare system in the U. S. have led to a renewed interest in the process of supporting the transition from welfare to work. Analyses of programs that try to prepare individuals and families for self-sufficiency show that they typically emphasize some combination of basic education, job skills training, and adaptive work orientation with supports such as child-care subsidies and medical benefits. Some programs put more time and resources into improving the conditions of the jobs as well as fostering employee skills (Friedlander & Burtless, 1994; Kirby, 1996).

The biggest challenge facing individuals in this transition is the lack of jobs that will provide the salary and benefits necessary to raise workers out of the poverty level. Since the 1970s, manufacturing jobs have been replaced by service jobs. Although there are high-level management positions within the service sector, many of the new jobs that have been created are characterized by low wages, limited benefits, and little opportunity for career advancement. These positions may provide a short-term reduction in welfare participation, but for many, especially single mothers who have to cover the costs of child-care arrangements and medical coverage for their children, they do not hold the promise of moving the family out of poverty (Bowen et al., 1995). Experts predict that it will be hard to sustain motivation if people who work cannot cover their basic needs, including child care, and do not feel the enhanced sense of personal worth that is typically associated with working.

In an attempt to synthesize career and individual development, Kathy Kram (1985) proposed a developmental model of career issues (Table 11.5). In it, careers are delineated in three phases: early career, middle career, and late career, which correspond roughly to the phases of career exploration, career establishment and advancement, and career maintenance and disengagement (Osipow, 1986; McAuliffe, 1997). In each phase, career development reflects *concerns about self,* including questions of compe-

---

TABLE 11.5   Characteristic Developmental Tasks at Successive Career Stages

	Early Career	Middle Career	Late Career
Concerns about self	*Competence:* Can I be effective in the managerial/professional role? Can I be effective in the role of spouse and/or parent?	*Competence:* How do I compare with my peers, with my subordinates, and with my own standards and expectations?	*Competence:* Can I be effective in a more consultative and less central role, still having influence as the time to leave the organization gets closer?
	Identity: Who am I as a manager/professional? What are my skills and aspirations?	*Identity:* Who am I now that I am no longer a novice? What does it mean to be a "senior" adult?	*Identity:* What will I leave behind of value that will symbolize my contributions during my career? Who am I apart from a manager/professional, and how will it feel to be without the role?
Concerns about career	*Commitment:* How involved and committed to the organization do I want to become? Do I want to seriously explore other options?	*Commitment:* Do I still want to invest as heavily in my career as I did in previous years? What can I commit myself to if the goal of advancement no longer exists?	*Commitment:* What can I commit myself to outside of my career that will provide meaning and a sense of involvement? How can I let go of my involvement in my work role after so many years?
	Advancement: Do I want to advance? Can I advance without compromising important values?	*Advancement:* Will I have the opportunity to advance? How can I feel productive if I am not going to advance further?	*Advancement:* Given that my next move is likely to be out of the organization, how do I feel about my final level of advancement? Am I satisfied with what I have achieved?
	Relationships: How can I establish effective relationships with peers and supervisors? As I advance, how can I prove my competence and worth to others?	*Relationships:* How can I work effectively with peers with whom I am in direct competition? How can I work effectively with subordinates who may surpass me?	*Relationships:* How can I maintain positive relationships with my boss, peers, and subordinates as I get ready to disengage from this setting? Can I continue to mentor and sponsor as my career comes to an end? What will happen to significant work relationships when I leave?
Concerns about family	*Family role definition:* How can I establish a satisfying personal life? What kind of lifestyle do I want to establish?	*Family role definition:* What is my role in the family now that my children are grown?	*Family role definition:* What will my role in the family be when I am no longer involved in a career? How will my significant relationships with spouse and/or children change?
	Work/family conflict: How can I effectively balance work and family commitments? How can I spend time with my family without jeopardizing my career advancement?	*Work/family conflict:* How can I make up for the time away from my family when I was launching my career as a novice?	*Work/family conflict:* Will family and leisure activities suffice, or will I want to begin a new career?

Source: Kram, 1985.

tence and identity; *concerns about career,* including questions of occupational commitment, advancement, and the quality of relationships in the work setting; and *concerns about family,* especially family role definition and possible conflicts between work and family life. Typical issues facing the person at each phase are suggested in Table 11.5.

Issues of greatest concern during the early career phase reflect the need to demonstrate competence and also to establish a satisfying lifestyle. Career development is never a completely rational process. As organizational loyalty gives way to a "free agent" orientation to career development, individuals have to take a more assertive, risk-taking approach to their career development. In this process, one confronts many myths and uncertainties about the meaning of work, worries about financial self-sufficiency, and conflicts between work and other spheres of life, especially intimate relations and family responsibilities. Fears of the unknown, of taking on new responsibilities, of discovering the limits to one's abilities, and of disappointing important people in one's life must all be faced and reframed if one is to achieve the adaptive flexibility necessary in today's world of work (Patterson, 1997; Stroh & Reilly, 1997).

Lifestyle

The "Bathers" gives us a glimpse into the leisure side of the idea of lifestyle. For many young adults, spending time with friends on the weekends, relaxing at the beach, enjoying the out-of-doors, or getting away for a brief vacation are important elements that add quality to life.

During the course of early adulthood, one experiments with and gradually develops a lifestyle. **Lifestyle** is a social psychological construction that integrates personality characteristics, goals, convictions, and inner conflicts with social opportunities and resources into an organizing pattern of actions and choices (Lombardi et al., 1996; Slavick, 1995). Central components of the lifestyle include the tempo or pace of activities, the balance between work and leisure, the focus of time and energy in specific arenas, and the establishment of social relationships at varying degrees of intimacy. One's lifestyle guides decisions about how to organize one's time and prioritize the use of resources (Englis & Solomon, 1997). One can think of lifestyle as the first translation of the values and commitments of individual identity into action through the devotion of time and energy to certain tasks and relationships and the development of domains of competence. The following discussion illustrates some ways in which the developmental tasks of early adulthood—intimate relationships, childbearing, and career—interact to organize characteristics of the lifestyle.

Pace of Life

The work setting largely determines the structure of time, including when one goes to work and returns, what one feels energetic enough to do after work, how much time to allot for vacations, and what kinds of preparation must be made during nonworking hours for one's daily occupation (Small & Riley, 1990). Activity level, or the pace of life, is influenced in part by one's temperament, health, and fitness. To some extent, it is also influenced by the climate and community. In northern climates, for example, there may be fewer social events away from home during the winter, and life may therefore revolve primarily around the home. In spring and summer, neighborhood activities become a more important stimulus for social life as people emerge from their "caves" and renew their friendships.

The balance of work and leisure is a result of one's disposition toward them and the demands of the work setting. For some people, time with the family is more important than time at work. They highly value the time they have at home with their families and make it a priority when they choose a career. For other people, advancement in work through the expenditure of large amounts of time supersedes commitments to home and leisure. For them, the lifestyles of partners may evolve somewhat separately, since the amount of leisure time they share may be limited. Couples who are able to enjoy leisure activities together that provide opportunities for relaxed, open conversation find that these contribute substantially to the strength and satisfaction in their intimate relationship (Holman & Jacquart, 1988).

Investment in Work

The more involved one is in the competitive demands of work, the less likely one is to feel comfortable about spending time away from it. Conversely, the more engrossed one is in a variety of activities away from work, including hobbies and family events, the more time one will find for leisure. In some occupations, the time schedule leaves little room for personal choice. In others, the income from a single job may not suffice to support the family. Time that might be spent in leisure must be spent in earning additional income through extra work. During later adulthood, following retirement, the balance of work and leisure time has to be revised. Adults who have spent most of their time at work may find themselves poorly prepared for a successful adjustment to the increased leisure of retirement.

Social Network

During early adulthood, the partners in a committed relationship become acquainted with individuals and other couples, forming their social network. They form friendships in the neighborhood and at work. These partners may become involved in the social life of their religious community as well. If they have young children, the parents of other young children at the day-care center or preschool may become important sources of social support. The orientation of the nuclear family toward outsiders is developed during this stage. An important factor in the establishment of adult friendships is the degree of intimacy shared with nonfamily members. Some couples have only a few close friends, while others have a large circle of relatively distant acquaintances. This difference in orientation toward friendship determines one's involvement in social activities, reputation in the community, and the extent to which one depends on the family to meet individual needs for intimacy, approval, and companionship. One potential source of tension in close relationships is a difference between the partners in their orientation toward friendships. If one partner seeks close friendship with other adults but the other partner prefers more distant acquaintances, they may be in continuing conflict about involvement in social activities.

Competing Role Demands

Another source of tension in early adulthood is the competition of role demands. One part of role learning involves a widening circle of competencies and relationships. Another part involves balancing the conflicting expectations of simultaneous role responsibilities. Adults struggle with the conflict between the demands of the work setting and the demands of building an intimate relationship; with the tension between the desire to have children and the desire to achieve in the workplace (Parcel & Menaghan, 1994; Gilbert, 1993). For both men and women, the world of work is likely to provide the most rigorous test of commitment and the greatest pressures for productivity during the early adult years. Pressure in the work setting competes directly with needs for intimacy and also with the time and energy needed for parenting.

In an analysis of the role demands of dual-earner families, Crouter and Manke (1997) identified three distinct dual-earner lifestyles—high status, low stress, and main-secondary—each with its own pattern of role relationships, costs, and benefits. In the *high-status* couples, both partners had high-prestige careers, earned comparatively high salaries, and were involved in their work. In these couples, the division of household work was more equal than in the other two types. They experienced the greatest amount of role overload, had lower levels of love and marital satisfaction, and more marital conflict than the other two groups.

The *low-stress* couples worked about the same amount of hours as the high-status couples, but the jobs were in lower prestige categories. Examples were a mechanic and a secretary, and a salesman and a substitute teacher. Although the couples had levels of involvement similar to the high-status group, they had the lowest amount of role overload. This group had the highest scores in marital satisfaction and love for their spouse, and the lowest scores in marital conflict. In addition, these couples monitored their children more closely and seemed to be more accurate in describing their children's daily activities.

The *main-secondary* couples reflected a lifestyle in which husbands were the primary workers, with higher occupational prestige, more hours worked, and more work involvement than their wives, who typically worked part-time. Women in these relationships had less education and tended to have more household responsibilities. A sex-typed division of labor was reflected in the pattern for girls, who performed more household tasks than girls in the other family types, whereas boys in these families performed fewer household tasks than boys in the other family types.

Health and Fitness

The contemporary emphasis on health and fitness indicates the importance of lifestyle decisions for illness prevention and longevity. Research on health and health-related risks has begun to identify characteristics of a healthy lifestyle (Hofer & Katz, 1996; Nattiv & Puffer, 1991). This usually includes such practices as the use of preventive health services, regular exercise, eating a well-balanced diet high in fruits and vegetables and low in fat, avoiding smoking, limiting the number of sexual partners, and using contraceptives. The concept of encouraging young adults to adopt a lifestyle that promotes health is becoming a focus for preventive health care. (Studies of people who have lived to an old age are discussed in detail in Chapters 13 and 14.) Much of that research suggests that lifestyle patterns established in early and middle adulthood, including one's diet, activity level, exercise, encounters with challenging and intellectually stimulating tasks, and involvement with cigarette smoking and alcohol, all influence health and vitality in later life.

The Single Lifestyle

In addition to the young adults who choose to create lifestyles within a stable, intimate relationship, many others choose to remain single. As cited earlier in the chapter, the trend is for young adults to remain single during their 20s, and most young adults view this choice positively. Of course, the census data disguise the fact that many of the never-married young adults are actually in some form of committed relationship. Some are gay and lesbian couples who cannot legally marry; others are in a long-term cohabiting relationship. For example, R and T have been living together for five years. He is in law school and she is planning to go to medical school. They are committed to one another, but are also supportive of each other's career development. They do not want to impose marriage commitments that might constrain the other partner in her or his career development decisions.

Several stereotypes of the single lifestyle have been examined empirically. One is that singles are lonely. Another is that singles experience a greater variety of sexual partners and have a more exciting sex life than those who are married. Comparisons of single and married adults suggest that neither of these stereotypes is totally accurate. First, many singles do not live alone—they live with family members, significant partners, or roommates. Those who have already been married and divorced are most likely to suffer loneliness because of the absence of companions or confidants. The most isolated unmarried people are women who are single parents living with their children. They have the most restricted opportunities for social interaction. Many unmarried adults who live alone actually have compensated for their limited contacts at home by having a large number of relationships at work or in the community. Living alone is not necessarily associated with lower satisfaction with one's life; in fact, it is often a preferred arrangement (Alwin, 1984). Second, singles who have never been married are not likely to have many sexual partners and are somewhat less likely than married couples to experience frequent sexual intercourse—that is, three or more times per week (Cargan, 1981).

This neigborhood micro brewery provides an easy setting for singles to find company on the weekends. One of the challenges of the single lifestyle is to find comfortable places to meet other singles.

The profile of the single lifestyle is somewhat different for men and women. Highly educated women who value self-determination and career achievement are likely to see distinct advantages in the single lifestyle. Many choose to remain single while they complete their education and establish their career. They may view this period of singlehood as a chance to make important identity-related commitments before they are in a relationship in which they may be expected to negotiate or compromise their occupational goals. These women may also view this period of becoming established in an occupation as "insurance" against the possibility of having to be fully self-supporting at some later time should their marriages fail or their husbands die. Women who remain single experience more rapid advancement in both educational and occupational attainment (Houseknecht et al., 1987). Men, on the other hand, have not historically been subjected to social pressure to choose between career and marriage. Those who remain single into their 30s are likely to be less well educated, less successful in the world of work, and therefore less desirable as partners.

Relatively little systematic research has been done on the meaning of being single. Especially critical to this picture is the path along which singlehood is established. As the previous discussion implies, singles comprise a diverse group. It makes sense to see decisions about remaining single as linked to the broader theme of identity development. In his analysis of singlehood, Stein (1989) suggested a typology of singlehood along two dimensions: stability of the single status and choice of the single status. Within this framework, two groups are single by choice: those who intend to marry but are not ready yet *(ambivalents)* and those who do not intend to marry *(resolved singles)*. One might expect the resolved singles to be satisfied about the quality of their lifestyle and effective in forming relationships that support their choice. In contrast, the *wishful singles* are actively seeking a mate but have not found one yet. The *regretful singles* are becoming resigned to their singlehood, but would have preferred to be married. They may be more depressed about their situation and more dissatisfied with the quality of their lifestyle. Generalizations about adjustment or well-being among singles often fail to consider these kinds of distinctions (Shostak, 1987).

In a study of unmarried adults over the age of 30, researchers found that divorced adults were more satisfied with their single marital status and had higher levels of life satisfaction than those who had never married. Men had a stronger desire to be married than women, while divorced women had the least desire to be married. These differences were mediated by the fact that women had a stronger social support network than men, which probably operated to protect them from experiences of social isolation (Frazier et al., 1996). In this study, participants were asked to give explanations for why they were not married. The most common response was, "I haven't met the right person yet." The next most common was that the person chose to be single, "Marriage is an out-dated, archaic institution rooted in male dominance." These responses illustrate the variety of views about the meaning of singlehood.

In the past, one of the reasons that young people married was the desire to have children. Today, singlehood and parenthood are more commonly combined. In addition to the large number of adolescents who become parents before marriage, reproductive technologies permit women who are single to bear children, and the courts have been increasingly willing to award custody to single men who want to have a family. Thus, through psychosocial evolution, opportunities for parenting have been separated from the need to have an intimate, adult heterosexual relationship.

Lifestyle is an umbrella concept for the variety of patterns of activities, commitments, and satisfactions that make up adult experience. Lifestyles are enormously diverse. Some siblings share households, and roughly 12% of young adult children aged 25 to 34 live with their parents. Same-sex adults live together in committed, intimate relationships, while many adults live alone. In addition, couples may cohabit without any plans to marry. In all of these arrangements, a sense of intimacy may flourish, or a feeling of isolation may grow. Nevertheless, the cultural expectations for marriage, childbearing, and work are confronted, evaluated, and accepted or rejected during these early adult years. In the process of deciding about each of these life tasks, the person begins to crystallize a life pattern that reflects his or her personal response to the array of cultural and social expectations within the context of contemporary resources and opportunities.

THE PSYCHOSOCIAL CRISIS: INTIMACY VERSUS ISOLATION

Intimacy   **Intimacy** is defined as the ability to experience an open, supportive, tender relationship with another person without fear of losing one's own identity in the process. An intimate relationship has both cognitive and affective components. The partners are able to understand each other's point of view. They usually experience a sense of confidence and mutual regard that reflects their respect as well as their affection for each other. Intimacy in a relationship supports independent judgments by each partner. It also permits the disclosure of personal feelings as well as the sharing and developing of ideas and plans.

There is a sense of mutual enrichment in intimate interactions. Each person perceives enhancement of his or her well-being through affectionate or intellectually stimulating interactions with the other (Erikson, 1963, 1980). Coming as it does after the establishment of personal identity, the possibility of establishing intimacy depends on individuals' perceptions of themselves as valuable, competent, and meaningful people.

It is not difficult to understand that a person would be on intimate terms with parents and siblings. The family is clearly a central context for sharing confidences, expressing love, and revealing weaknesses and areas of dependence. The unique task of young adulthood is to establish an intimate relationship with someone outside of one's family. In fact, two people who eventually establish intimacy may begin as complete strangers who have very few, if any, common cultural bonds. Although an extreme degree of difference is unusual, it represents the greatest challenge that may confront two people.

Although intimacy is generally established within the context of the marriage relationship, marriage itself does not automatically produce intimacy. The previous discussion of the early years of marriage indicated several forces potentially disruptive of the establishment of intimacy: (1) the early period of mutual adjustment, (2) the birth of the first child, and (3) the social expectations of members of the extended family.

In addition, differences in interaction styles between men and women suggest that many marriages can survive under conditions of low levels of intimacy. Consistent evidence finds that men interact less intimately than women (Reis et al., 1985; Carli,

1989). They generally demonstrate more competitiveness, less agreement, and lower levels of self-disclosure than women. However, levels of self-disclosure are not related to loneliness for men as they are for women. It appears that men have the same capacity for intimate interaction as women, but they do not choose to exercise it with other men. Whereas women consider intimacy appropriate for both same-sex and opposite-sex relationships, men tend to restrict their intimate interactions to women.

In a large national sample of over 2500 adults, men's and women's relationships were compared (Umberson et al., 1996). Women were shown to have more support from friends, they experienced higher levels of social integration (involvement in personally meaningful relationships), and they were more likely to report having a confidante than were men. Married women received more support from their adult children than did men, whereas men received more support from their spouses than did women. In fact, almost 50% of men said that their confidante was their wife, whereas only 20% of women said their confidant was their husband.

In general, husbands are more likely than wives to be satisfied with the amount of empathy and companionship in their marriages (Scanzoni & Scanzoni, 1981). There are several explanations for this finding. Perhaps men expect less empathic understanding in marriage than women; or perhaps the socialization of girls makes women better than men at providing empathy and understanding. The discussion of all-male and all-female friendship groups presented in Chapter 8 suggests that the kinds of interactive skills that girls develop within their friendship groups, including negotiating, supporting, and cooperating, are better suited to the establishment of intimacy in dyadic and family groups than are the interactive skills developed by boys, including bids for dominance, teasing, and roughhousing.

Another common context for the establishment of intimacy is the work setting. Affiliation and close friendship are likely to develop among co-workers. Workers may express devotion to an older leader or teacher. Through conversations, correspondence, conferences, or informal interaction on the golf course or at the bowling alley, co-workers can achieve an affectionate, playful, and enriching relationship. This kind of intimacy is demonstrated in a conversation reported by Kram (1985):

> Alan was very influential. I respected him as being pretty sharp and pretty astute. He had a lot of guts to tackle the problems that existed in the area and that was the union-management business. I was really identifying with him in terms of what and how you run something, how you manage something. You would sit down and talk about or debate how you do certain things, what should we do in this kind of situation. We would be right in line. I think it was the way I came at a problem; it might be similar to the way he would come at a problem. (p. 33)

The increased presence of men and women as co-workers in the work setting has introduced new difficulties in the establishment of intimacy among co-workers. Problems with sex discrimination and sexual harassment at work are evidence that many men and women have not developed mature strategies for forming mutually respectful, close relationships with adults of the opposite sex. Often, men and women find it difficult to establish an egalitarian relationship at work. They have a hard time engaging in the kinds of informal interactions that bring a sense of closeness to same-sex co-workers, like going to lunch together, stopping for a drink at the end of the day, or going to the gym to work out. Many men find it difficult to establish a style of interaction with women that is forthright but not sexual in tone. And many women find it difficult to be adequately assertive with men so that their ideas are taken seriously and their views are given full consideration.

Whether they are established in the context of marriage, friendship, or work, intimate relationships are often characterized by an atmosphere of romantic illusions such as, "Together we can conquer the world." The romance of an intimate relationship is a reflection of the energy and sense of well-being that come from the support and understanding that are shared within it (Murray et al., 1996). There may also be a degree of jealousy in the relationship. The devotion and commitment of intimate partners are vulnerable to threats of competing alliances (Sharpsteen & Kirkpatrick, 1997). There is a deep sense that intimate relationships are not replaceable.

Isolation

The negative pole of the crisis of early adulthood is **isolation**. As social beings, people have a deep need for a sense of connection and belonging. Isolation, and the accompanying feeling of being unable to experience intersubjectivity or shared meaning, is a major source of psychological distress (Jordan, 1997). As with the other negative poles, most people experience some periods of this extreme. The more fully developed the ego becomes, the more it is characterized by clear boundaries. One by-product of individuality and independence is a heightened sense of separateness from others.

The obstacles to attainment of an intimate relationship are many. Some arise from childhood experiences of shame, guilt, inferiority, or alienation, which undermine the achievement of personal identity. Others result from incompatibility between partners. The number of adjustments that intimacy requires may overwhelm some young adults. Obstacles to intimacy derive from environmental circumstances that may erode the person's feelings of self-worth or interfere with the evolution of a sense of mutuality. Finally, these obstacles may be embedded in the socialization process as children learn distinct gender roles that introduce antagonism between males and females and foster interpersonal styles that stand in the way of forming open, caring interpersonal relationships. Seven themes discussed in the next section illustrate experiences of isolation—loneliness, depression, fragile identity, sexual disorders, situational factors, divergent spheres of interest, and enmeshment.

Even though most people desire intimacy, there are many obstacles to its attainment. Lack of social skills, obsessive self-doubts, fears of social rejection, and chronic depression all contribute to a sense of isolation. How might issues in the workplace contribute to a sense of isolation?

Loneliness

Feelings of loneliness can be separated into three categories: transient, situational, and chronic (Meer, 1985). *Transient loneliness* lasts a short time and passes, as when you hear a song or an expression that reminds you of someone you love who is far away. *Situational loneliness* accompanies a sudden loss or a move to a new city. *Chronic loneliness* lasts a long time and cannot be linked to a specific stressor. Chronically lonely people may have an average number of social contacts, but they do not achieve the desired level of intimacy in these interactions (Berg & Peplau, 1982). Many chronically lonely people are highly anxious about all types of social activities. They believe that

success in social relationships is important, but expect social encounters to be difficult and to end poorly. People who have high levels of social anxiety tend to use interpersonal strategies that place barriers in the way of intimacy. They are likely to be self-deprecating and obsessed by the possibilities of negative outcomes of social interactions. These people tend to let others establish the direction and purpose of interpersonal activities (Langston & Cantor, 1989). Thus, there appears to be a strong relationship between social skills and loneliness. People who have higher levels of social skills, including friendliness, communication skills, appropriate nonverbal behavior, and appropriate responses to others, have more adequate social support systems and lower levels of loneliness (Sarason et al., 1985).

Depression

Isolation may be a cause as well as a consequence of depression. For some women, clinical depression appears to be linked to an orientation toward intimacy in which the self is systematically inhibited and devalued (Jack & Dill, 1992). They have a rigid view of how they should act in an intimate relationship, which is characterized by four major themes: (1) They judge themselves by external standards, feeling that they never quite measure up to what other people expect of them. (2) They believe that they should build a close relationship with a man by putting his needs ahead of their own, and that to do otherwise is selfish. (3) They try to maintain a relationship by avoiding conflict and repressing their own views, if they think those views may lead to disagreement. (4) They perceive themselves as presenting a false front, in which they appear happy and satisfied on the outside although they are angry or resentful inside. Over time, women who endorse this outlook lose contact with their authentic self, and even if the relationship remains stable, they become increasingly depressed.

Fragile Identity

For some people, the possibility of closeness with another person seriously threatens the sense of self. They imagine intimate relationships to be a blurring of the boundaries of their own identities and thus cannot let themselves engage in them. People who experience isolation must continually erect barriers between themselves and others in order to keep their sense of self intact. Their fragile sense of self results from accumulated experiences of childhood that have fostered the development of personal identities that are rigid and brittle or else totally confused. Such a tenuous sense of identity requires that individuals constantly remind themselves who they are. They may not allow their identities to stand on their own strength while they lose themselves, even momentarily, in others. They are so busy maintaining their identities or struggling to make sense out of confusion that they cannot attain intimacy.

Sexual Disorders

Isolation may be linked to sexual disorders. Two widely cited "desire disorders" are **hypoactive sexual desire,** a decrease or absence of interest in sexual activity, and **compulsive sexual behavior,** a compulsive need to relieve anxiety through sex (Rosellini, 1992). A loss of sexual desire is usually accompanied by physical withdrawal from the partner, as well as feelings of guilt and dread about losing intimacy. At the same time, the unafflicted partner often feels angry and guilty about imposing his or her sexual needs on an unresponsive and uninterested partner, as in the following example:

> At first it was fun: feverish kisses in his red Chevy, giggly nights of passion in the apartment. But then came marriage, two kids, and suddenly her husband's hands on her flesh felt like tentacles, and the sight of him approaching made her body stiffen with revulsion. Then the disagreements began, hurtful scenes ending with each of them lying wedged against opposite sides of the bed, praying for sleep. (p. 62)

In the case of compulsive sexual behavior as in the following anecdote, sex is disconnected from pleasure or intimacy:

> Gary's pattern was always the same: first, the unbearable anxiety, never feeling good enough to handle the latest stress at his architect's job. Then, the familiar response—a furtive scanning of newspaper ads, a drive to a strip show, two straight Scotches to catch a buzz, and finally a massage parlor. . . . Afterward, he'd sit naked on the edge of the bed, his thought roiling in disgust: "I must be sick . . . I can't change." But a few days later, the anxiety would begin again and he'd pore over the ads. (p. 64)

Some psychologists view compulsive sexual behavior as an anxiety-based disorder like other compulsions. Others argue that it is an addiction, like alcoholism. Both agree, though, that those who suffer from this disorder are not able to integrate sexual behavior as a meaningful component of an intimate relationship.

Situational Factors

Isolation can also result from situational factors. The young man who goes off to war and returns to find that the "eligible" women in his town are married or the young woman who rejects marriage in order to attend medical school may both find themselves in situations in which their desires for intimacy cannot be met. Although it is logical to suggest that the lonely person should try harder to meet new people or develop new social skills, it is possible that the sense of isolation interferes with more active coping strategies (Peplau et al., 1977).

Divergent Spheres of Interest

Isolation can also be a product of diverging spheres of interest and activity. In a traditional marriage, for example, the husband and wife may participate in distinct roles and activities. Marriages characterized by such a division of life spheres are sometimes referred to as *his-and-her* marriages (Bernard, 1972). The wife stays home most of the day, interacting with the children and the other wives in the neighborhood. The husband is away from home all day, interacting with his co-workers. When the partners have leisure time, they pursue different interests: For instance, the woman likes to play cards and the man likes to hunt. Over the years, the partners have less and less in common. Isolation is reflected in their lack of mutual understanding and lack of support for each other's life goals and needs.

Enmeshment

Although Erikson tended to cast the construct of intimacy in tension with the construct of isolation, some family therapists offer another tension between healthy intimacy and enmeshment (Minuchin, 1978). Within this framework, a family is viewed as a structured system that contains individuals grouped into subsystems linked by patterns of communication, boundaries, alliances, and rules. As individual family members change and grow, the adaptive family experiences transitions that alter the structure. Families are characterized along a continuum from disengaged to enmeshed. The **disengaged** relationships are characterized by infrequent contact and a sense that the members of the family do not really seem to care about one another. This pattern may be viewed as similar to Erikson's concept of isolation within a family group. The **enmeshed** relationships, in contrast, are characterized by over-involvement in one another's lives, to the extent that any change in one family member is met by strong resistance by the others; individuality is viewed as a threat to the relationship. Individuals in an enmeshed relationship may fear isolation to such a degree that they prevent one another from any movement toward autonomy.

THE CENTRAL PROCESS: MUTUALITY AMONG PEERS

The central process through which intimacy is acquired is **mutuality** among peers. Mutuality refers to empathic awareness of one another, understanding of self and other, and the ability and willingness to regulate one's needs in order to respond to the needs of one's partner (Skerrett, 1996). One must be able to give and receive pleasure within the intimate context (Jeffries, 1993). The two young adults must bring equal strengths and resources to the relationship. Their intimacy is built on their ability to meet each other's needs and accept each other's weaknesses. When one partner needs to be dependent, the other is strong and supportive; at other times, the roles may be reversed. Each partner understands that the other is capable of many kinds of relationships. Mutuality facilitates the couple's ability to meet each other's needs in different ways over time rather than producing a static, unitary relationship. In fact, mutuality should enhance both individual and couple development. In the process of supporting each other, both partners perform in ways that they might not have adopted had they been alone.

The concept of mutuality has been used in previous chapters to describe the development of a sense of basic trust during infancy. In that context, the distribution of resources, experience, and strength is quite uneven. Mutuality is possible only because the caregiver is committed to the infant's well-being. Through the consistent efforts of caregivers, children eventually learn to regulate their needs to fit the family pattern. However, children at this stage are not expected to be sophisticated enough to assess and meet their caregivers' needs. In young adulthood, the partners are responsible for fulfilling each other's needs. In most cases, there is no benevolent, superordinate caregiver. Just as the infant learns to trust the caregiver's ability to meet personal needs, each adult partner learns to trust the other's ability to anticipate and satisfy his or her needs. By expressing trust and commitment to one another, each partner strengthens the other partner's ability to believe in and invest in the relationship (Avery, 1989). The partners may also realize that they depend on each other to solve problems that they face as a couple.

Mutuality is strengthened as the two individuals learn to rely on each other and as they discover that their combined efforts are more effective than their individual efforts would be. Mutuality, like attachment, is a characteristic of the dyadic relationship rather than of the individual members in it (Rusbult & Arriaga, 1997) It is formed as two individuals, each of whom has a well-defined identity, discover that they can have open, direct communication, hold each other in high regard, and respond effectively to each other.

THE PRIME ADAPTIVE EGO QUALITY AND THE CORE PATHOLOGY

Love   For thousands of years the nature of love and the qualities of a loving relationship have been described in songs and stories. In the resolution of the crisis of intimacy versus isolation in early adulthood, the ego quality of love emerges as the capacity for mutuality and devotion that transcends the secure attachment of infancy. Robert Sternberg (1988) has described love as a set of feelings, thoughts, and motives that contribute to communication, sharing, and support. According to his theory, almost all types of love may be viewed as a combination of three dimensions: *intimacy,* the emotional investment in a relationship that promotes closeness and connection; *passion,* the expression of physical and psychological needs and desires in the relationship; and *commitment,* the cognitive decision to remain in the relationship. Each of these dimensions is stronger in relationships that are perceived to be exclusive and that have a good chance of enduring than they are in more casual, temporary dating relationships (Whitely, 1993).

Conceptions of love usually include four aspects: ideas about the beloved, feelings that are associated with love, thoughts associated with love, and actions that are likely to occur between the lover and the beloved (Beall & Sternberg, 1995). The exact content of these feelings, beliefs, and actions differs from culture to culture, based on the culture's ideals about human nature, relationships, and cultural roles, especially courtship, marriage, childrearing, and religion.

Within Western cultures, 10 components of a loving relationship have been identified:

1. Promoting the welfare of the loved one
2. Experiencing happiness with the loved one
3. High regard for the loved one
4. Being able to count on the loved one in time of need
5. Mutual understanding of the loved one
6. Sharing oneself and one's possessions with the loved one
7. Receiving emotional support from the loved one
8. Giving emotional support to the loved one
9. Intimate communication with the loved one
10. Valuing the loved one in one's own life

These ten dimensions are present in relationships with parents, siblings, friends, and lovers. The weighting of the 10 components, however, may vary. In addition, some love relationships include a dimension of sexual attraction and others do not.

Exclusivity   The core pathology of this period is **exclusivity**, a shutting out of others. To some extent, exclusivity is a natural element in intimate relations. For example, sexual exclusivity tends to be valued in monogamous, sexual relationships. As a characteristic of a close personal relationship, sexual exclusivity tends to be valued somewhat more by women than by men, and somewhat more by heterosexual men than by homosexual men (Perusse, D. 1994; Masuda, 1994; Hickson et al., 1992). At some level, however, exclusivity can become destructive to one's ability to have relationships. Exclusivity of this type is characterized by intense jealousy, a rivalrous orientation toward anyone who shows an interest in one's friend or loved one, and preoccupation with intense feelings of anger and resentment, both toward the loved one and others (de Silva & Marks, 1994). The person has to expend tremendous energy monitoring the activities of the loved one. As a result, the person is cut off from relationships and ends up excluding himself or herself. Ideally, the experiences of intimacy and love should broaden one's sense of connection and social integration. Through exclusivity, however, one's social support network is limited.

Exclusivity may be extended to the overestimation of one's family, religious group, and national group. As a result of a belief about one's superiority, individuals become unwilling to seek out new people or new experiences. In addition, it may limit one's willingness to entertain new ideas. In order to preserve the belief in the value of one's exclusive world, one has to distort reality, limit access to new information, and restrict movement in the social environment. Thus, exclusivity becomes a substantial impediment to coping.

Applied Topic   ## DIVORCE

Americans have one of the highest rates of marriage among the modern industrial societies. Almost everyone in the U.S. wants to get married, and does. However, the divorce rate is extremely high. You may have read that the divorce rate in the U.S. is one out of every three or every two marriages. However, this rate is really not an accurate measurement of the frequency of divorce. It is based on the number of divorces decreed and the number of marriages performed in a given year. Most divorces, in reality, are not an outcome of marriages performed in the same year. There are many more marriages that may end in divorce during a single year than there are people planning to marry. The divorce-to-marriage ratio inflates our picture of the frequency of divorce.

A more stable index of the frequency of divorce is the ratio of the total number of divorces to the number of married couples in the population. This ratio is plotted in Figure 11.5 for the 128-year period from 1860 to 1988. The divorce rate peaked rapidly after World War II and then fell, after which it rose from 1965 to 1980 (Raschke, 1987). About 45% of all marriages performed during 1988 involved at least one previously married partner. The slight decrease in the divorce ratio from 1982 to 1988 suggests that the divorce rate may be leveling off (U.S. Bureau of the Census, 1997).

The focus of the following section is on the experiences of adults who are going through divorce rather than on the impact of divorce on children. Since the average age at first marriage is about 24 for women and 26 for men, and the median length of marriage is 7 years, one can expect that many individuals experience the divorce process during their early adulthood.

Factors Contributing to Divorce

A large number of variables have been examined as correlates or predictors of divorce. The scope of these analyses encompasses cross-national studies, historical cohort analyses, multi-county comparisons, and cross-sectional comparisons of couples (White, 1990). At the societal level, countries where there are fewer women than men and where women marry at a later age have lower divorce rates. Two other societal factors show

FIGURE 11.5

Number of divorces as a percentage of number of married couples, United States, 1860–1988
SOURCE: Rashke, 1987

For couples in a distressed marriage, hostility and resentment that have been characteristic of their relationship in the past are likely to escalate in the divorce process. Despite the presence of the attorneys, the divorce negotiations are often riddled with angry exchanges.

a curvilinear relationship: the socioeconomic development of the country and women's participation in the labor force. With respect to both of these variables, the divorce rate is lower in the mid-range than at either extreme (Trent & South, 1989).

In a comparison of divorce rates across more than 3000 counties in the United States, another important construct was identified—**social integration,** or the degree to which "people are tied or connected to one another, shared values being an important element in such integration" (Breault & Kposowa, 19187, p. 556). Characteristics of a community influence this sense of connectedness. Among the most significant of these characteristics are *population change,* the number of people who move in or out of a community each year; *religious integration,* the percentage of the population that belongs to a religious organization; and *urbanity,* the percentage of people within each county who live in an urban area. Divorce rates are significantly linked to each of these characteristics. They are higher in counties with high population change, low religious integration, and high urbanity. These findings suggest that the difficulties individual couples experience in their marriages may be aggravated by the community context. Or on the positive side, marriages may be buffered and supported by a critical sense of community identity and shared destiny.

At the level of couple-to-couple comparisons, four variables have been associated with the likelihood of divorce: age at marriage, socioeconomic level, differences in socioemotional development, and the family's history of divorce. In the United States, the incidence of divorce is especially high for couples who marry before the age of 20. These couples are about twice as likely to divorce as couples who marry in their early or mid-20s. Marital instability is also greater for couples who marry in their late 20s or later than it is for those who marry in their early to mid-20s (Booth & Edwards, 1985). Such couples may have been single for a long time. Having coped successfully with single life, they may be less willing to remain in an unsatisfying marriage. They may also be more firmly entrenched in behaviors and habits that are not readily modifiable.

Both for couples who marry young and for those who marry at an older age, dissatisfaction with role performance is a significant factor in marital instability. For young couples, dissatisfaction centers on sexual infidelity and jealousy. For older couples, it focuses on interpersonal conflict, a domineering style, and lack of companionship. Age at marriage is associated with different developmental needs and varying threats to marital stability. Of course, age at marriage is not a single explanatory dimension. For those who marry young, there is also a greater incidence of premarital pregnancy, dropping out of school, and lower-paying employment—all of which contribute to the likelihood of divorce.

The concept of **socioeconomic level** is complex. It may be thought of as a combination of education, occupation, and income. Each of these components is uniquely related to the divorce rate (Glenn & Supancic, 1984). Men with more education have lower divorce rates. Women with more education also have lower divorce rates, except that those with five or more years of college are somewhat more likely to divorce than those who have had only four years (that is, have graduated from college). Within this overall pattern, there is also evidence of the **Glick effect**. Both men and women who have dropped out of high school or college have higher divorce rates than those who have completed high school or college. Further, those who have graduated from high school have a lower divorce rate than those who have had one to three years of college. Glick (1957) explained this pattern as evidence of lack of persistence. Those who are not committed to completing a unit of schooling may also lack the commitment to work at resolving the problems they encounter in marriage.

Many people believe that divorce is a privilege of the rich, but the evidence suggests that the opposite is true: The divorce and separation rates are generally higher among couples with minimal education and low incomes (Reiss, 1980). Total family income is related to marital stability in some distinct ways. First, an erratic income and a high level of indebtedness are more strongly associated with marital disruption than a low, steady income. Second, the relationship between income and marital instability is different for men and women. For men, higher income is associated with low divorce rates. For women, there is no clear relationship between income and marital instability. A critical factor appears to be whether a woman is earning more or less than her husband. Divorces are more likely among the former than the latter (Raschke, 1987).

Socioemotional development is reflected in such dimensions as the partners' self-acceptance, autonomy, and expressiveness. Personality factors associated with emotionality and constraint have been linked with the risk of divorce. Both positive and negative emotionality increase the risk of divorce, while constraint decreases it. The genetic basis of these personality factors and the study of the link between personality factors and marital history among twins has led some researchers to argue that genetic factors play a role in the risk of divorce (Jockin et al., 1996).

Problems in communication are frequently cited by men and women as a major cause of divorce. Couples who are characterized as conflicted in their relationship during the premarital period, who have frequent disagreements and different perceptions of how to resolve arguments, are more likely to be separated or divorced three years after marriage (Fowers et al., 1996). In the past, women have experienced more stress and reported more problems in adjusting to marriage than have men (Veroff et al., 1981). They tend to be more dissatisfied with the level of intimacy in their marriage than are men. These factors were examined earlier in the discussion of adjustment to marriage. Mutual satisfaction in marriage depends heavily on the husband's qualities. The stability of the husband's masculine identity, the happiness of his parents' marriage, his educational level, his social status, and his ability to be comfortable in the expression of emotions all affect marital happiness. Many husbands, however, enter marriage with a deep need to be nurtured and to continue the pattern of care that they received in childhood. The stability of a marriage depends on both partners' achieving a sense of their own identity. This achievement helps to establish the balance in power and mutual respect that are so central to emotional and intellectual intimacy.

The family's history of divorce is yet another factor that contributes to marital instability. Children of divorced parents are more likely to get divorced themselves than are children of intact marriages (Glenn & Kramer, 1987; Keith & Finlay, 1988). One interpretation of this finding that has received some empirical support is that children of divorce hold more favorable attitudes toward

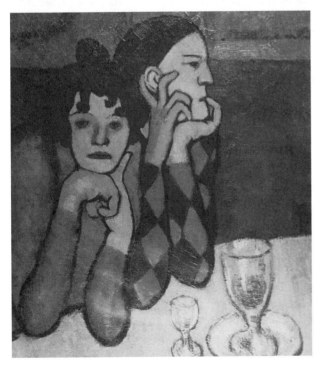

To sustain a marriage, the partners must be able to interact even during periods of conflict. Withdrawal, rejection, and distancing are common reactions to conflict. These strategies may be effective during a brief cooling-off period, but they do replace direct communication for exploring or resolving differences.

divorce as a reasonable strategy for resolving marital conflict (Greenberg & Nay, 1982). Another explanation is that they are likely to marry at an earlier age than children of intact marriages (Keith & Finlay, 1988). The available evidence suggests, however, that the attitudes of children of divorced parents toward marriage and family life are as positive as those of children of intact families. As young adults, however, they may have more reservations and ambivalence about getting married, and a less idealized view of marriage than young adults from intact families. As a result, they may enter marriage with strong expectations of a negative outcome. This expectation may inhibit achieving the level of commitment and self-disclosure characteristic of a mutually intimate relationship (Glenn & Kramer, 1987; Amato, 1988; Wallerstein & Corbin, 1989).

Coping with Divorce   It is an understatement to say that divorce is stressful. Divorce is associated with numerous losses, including the loss of financial resources, emotional support, one's marital and/or parental role, and social support (Kitson & Morgan, 1990). Loss of income may result in other kinds of material loss. For example, a divorced woman and her children may have to move to less expensive housing, sell some of their possessions, and leave the community where they have established a network of friends and social support.

Divorce can also bring role loss and social isolation. Even when a divorce is viewed as a desirable solution, the period from the suggestion of divorce to its conclusion involves a variety of decisions and conflicts that may be painful. Divorced partners may lose contact with family and friends as each person's social support system "takes sides" in the split (Kunz & Kunz, 1995). Many people who experience divorce go through a time of intense self-analysis. They must try to integrate the failure of their marriage with their personal definition of masculinity or femininity, competence as loving people, and long-held aspirations to enact the role of husband or wife, father or mother.

The process of leaving a marriage is different for the partner who initiates the divorce than for the partner who is being left. The initiators view the process as more voluntary, and tend to be more aware of support services and feel more in control even if they experience some sentiments of self-doubt and redefinition. On the other hand, those who do not initiate the divorce are more likely to experience a period of shock and disbelief. They, too, must go through a process of identity redefinition, which often takes longer and may be associated with stronger feelings of emotional turmoil (Duran-Aydintug, 1995; Vannoy, 1995).

The stress-related correlates of divorce are increased health problems, a higher incidence of suicide, and the over-representation of divorced adults in all forms of psychiatric settings (Stack, 1990). One analysis of 80 divorced adults who had children identified six specific stressors: contacts with the former spouse, parent-child interactions, interpersonal relations, loneliness, practical problems such as cooking and cleaning, and financial problems. Of these stressors, problems involving interpersonal relations with peers were most closely tied to lower life satisfaction and a depressed, anxious mood (Berman & Turk, 1981).

Evidence of the impact of divorce on adjustment is provided in a comparison of divorced adults with those who are remarried and those who are in first marriages and have never experienced divorce (Weingarten, 1985). Divorced people had lower morale than those who had remarried. They recalled the past as having been much happier than the present and were more likely to say they were not happy at present. However, they did not have lower self-esteem, more anxiety, or more physical symptoms of stress than did remarried adults. In comparison with married people who have never divorced, the divorced had loweer feelings of satisfaction, less zest for life, and greater anxiety. Even after remarriage, the experience of divorce had a lingering influence on adjustment. Remarried people said they had experienced a lot of difficult life events, were more likely to have used professional help in dealing with personal problems, and were more likely to suffer from stress-related physical sumptoms than married people who had never divorced. The remarried were no different from the never-divorced in personal happiness, self-esteem, or optimism about the future. Reentering the marital state appears to boost morale, but it does not remove the strains of having encountered divorce.

A parish Christmas party provides divorced parents and their children a time to enjoy the social support of their community. Holidays, especially Thanksgiving and Christmas, are difficult times when divorced adults need to use their coping skills to reduce feelings of isolation.

One problem in coping with divorce is that many divorced people retain a strong attachment to their former spouse. Grief in divorce has been compared to bereavement in widowhood. In both cases, there is a loss and a need to adjust to it. Although the loss due to death may be more intense, especially if it was sudden, the loss due to divorce may be more bitter. If an affectionate bond has been established, there is certain to be ambivalence about losing it even when the divorce is desired. Attachment to a former spouse may be positive or negative (one may wish for a reconciliation or blame the spouse, respectively) or both.

In a study of over 200 divorced people, 42% expressed moderate or strong attachment to their former spouse. Some people wondered what their former spouse was doing, spent a lot of time thinking about her or him, expressed disbelief that the divorce had really taken place, and felt that they would never get over it. The attachment was stronger for those who had not initiated the divorce. The lingering feelings of attachment were associated with greater difficulties in adjustment to divorce, especially problems of loneliness and doubt about being able to cope with single life (Kitson, 1982). The stronger the positive or negative post-divorce attachment, the more difficult the adjustment in the years following the divorce (Tschann et al., 1989).

The fact that divorce is stressful does not mean that it is undesirable. Even among the attached spouses described by Kitson, many said that they felt a sense of relief about it. Many divorced parents report that, despite the difficulties of single parenting, life is more manageable than it was in the midst of the continuing arguments and hostility that preceded the divorce.

Most people who experience divorce are determined to cope with the stresses it brings. Unfortunately, many adults do not anticipate the specific kinds of stressors that they will encounter. Of course, they have different coping strategies, some of which may not be effective for the special demands of divorce. Berman and Turk (1981) asked divorced adults to judge the efficacy of 53 strategies for coping with their own stress. Six groups of coping strategies were identified: (1) *social activities,* such as dating or developing new friendships; (2) *learning,* including going back to school or talking to a counselor; (3) *personal understanding,* such as understanding what went wrong; (4) *expressing feelings;* (5) *autonomy*—for example, becoming more independent or taking a job; and (6) *home and family activities,* especially taking care of the house and doing more things with the children. Of these six strategies, social activities, autonomy, and home and family activities were most strongly related to post-divorce life satisfaction. Social activities and autonomy were also linked to fewer perceived problems in the areas of loneliness and interpersonal relations.

The process of coping with divorce requires strategies devised to deal with the aspects of it that are perceived as most troublesome. Further, each of these coping strategies is in an area that lends itself to intervention. Evidence suggests many avenues through which service professionals can be effective in helping adults develop coping skills for resolving some of the stresses of divorce.

Chapter Summary

In early adulthood, individuals begin to apply to themselves all the information they have acquired about adult roles. They may marry or make a commitment to an intimate partner, have children, and choose work roles. Gradually they evolve a style of life. In this process, their commitment to social institutions and to significant others expands. Their worldview becomes more diverse, and their appreciation of the interdependence of systems increases. One of the major sources of stress in this life stage is competition among roles.

In the discussion of occupational training, it was suggested that many new areas of intellectual awareness are stimulated during the apprenticeship period. Self-understanding is integrated with social expectations and historical opportunities as men and women embark on their career paths. One of the most challenging aspects of career development in this early phase is the coordination of work with the establishment of meaningful intimate relationships.

The crisis of intimacy versus isolation emphasizes the evolution of adult sexuality into an interpersonal commitment. This crisis requires that needs for personal gratification be subordinated to needs for mutual satisfaction. Success is comparatively difficult to achieve in our culture because of the basic tension between the norm of independence and the desire for closeness. The research on marriage suggests that willingness to make a personal commitment to another adult is no guarantee of success. But one of the important elements in a marriage relationship is the ability to engage in and resolve conflict.

The theme of intimacy highlights the management of emotion during adulthood. Coping with the challenges of early adulthood requires the integration of cognitive capacities, emotional openness, and effective interpersonal relationships. In the process of coping with divorce, there is a clear need for daily problem solving and emotional expression to manage the grief, loss, and role transitions that accompany this crisis.

*E*nd of Chapter Case

Gail and Dick talk about how love entered into their relationship as they made the transition from living together to deciding to get married.

Dick: We never mentioned love in our relationship. And that's for at least three years. We never committed ourselves to loving each other until well into the fourth year, although I don't know *why*. We'd ask each other if we like each other and placed a great deal of significance on that, but just as significantly we avoided the word "love," and all I remember about the first time we did mention love was that it was kind of a trauma.

Gail: I can remember everything. I think we were arguing about us. And Dick was trying to tell me, without telling me, that he was leaving me. You know, saying there's this problem and that it's stale and it's . . . and so on. And I'm all ready to change and work it out and then he just got frustrated and he said, "But I love you and I really care for you," and then he walked out. That I really couldn't understand. You told me you loved me and walked out and left me! I thought, "Well, that's crazy." I thought that was just the nuttiest thing I ever heard. I thought, "Well, does he feel guilty about hurting me and is that why he's saying it? And if he is all that crazy about me, he wouldn't have been walking out to somebody else!" And he didn't tell me, you know, he never told me he had another girlfriend, which bugged me a lot because I thought he could at least do that. And I had to go

through this whole painful thing of finding out, when somebody said they saw Dick with this little blonde. And I thought, "Well, if that's true, he's probably at her house," and so I went over there and there they were and Dick was mortified. I was bitchy and I wouldn't go away. I just sat there making small talk—and I know now that I loved every minute of it. And so I really didn't believe it.

Dick: You mean you didn't believe it when I said I loved you . . .

Gail: Yeah. But I guess I sort of had it in the back of my mind that we would get back together.

Dick: I was very dissatisfied with this other girl after a very short period of time, and it was interesting, because she outwardly seemed to have everything. I could, you know, I could list off consciously what I wanted and she had it, but it wasn't enough. I think one thing that I was very impressed about was that in comparing the two girls, this girl seemed not to have an independent life of her own. She seemed to be tied to whoever she was with. When we'd be talking with somebody else, she'd voice *my* opinions, and Gail doesn't do that hardly at all. She forms her own opinions and sticks to them. And I found that this really takes a great burden off me in a relationship. And I don't have to be carrying the emotional stability, or the opinions, for two people. It's really like having a burden lifted off yourself when you're not living with a mirror image of yourself but actually another person. At that point I realized that for me Gail was another individual whom I did care for. . . ."

Source: Carl R. Rogers, 1972.

Thought Questions

1. What does love mean for Dick and Gail; in what ways might love be different from liking?
2. How is the relationship between Dick and Gail transformed when love is mentioned?
3. What are the qualities of an intimate relationship that you see illustrated in the case of Dick and Gail? What elements of an intimate relationship appear to be missing in this relationship?
4. Based on this dialogue, what challenges do you imagine Dick and Gail might face in the first few years of marriage? What resources might help them cope with these challenges?

Chapter 12

*P*icasso drew many sketches of the dove, a symbol of peace, hope, and renewal. It captures the essence of generativity, the cornerstone of growth in middle adulthood, as one turns one's resources and creative energy toward the welfare of future generations.

Middle Adulthood (34–60 Years)

*C*hapter Objectives

- To examine the world of work as a context for development, focusing on interpersonal demands, authority relations, and demands for the acquisition of new skills, considering the interaction of work and family life, and examining the impact of joblessness in middle adulthood.
- To examine the process of maintaining a vital intimate relationship in middle adulthood, especially a commitment to growth, effective communication, and creative use of conflict.
- To describe the expansion of caring in middle adulthood as it applies to two specific roles: that of parent and that of an adult child caring for one's aging parents.
- To analyze the broad range of tasks required for the effective management of the household for their impact on the cognitive, social, and emotional development of family members.
- To explain the psychosocial crisis of generativity versus stagnation and the central process through which the crisis is resolved: person-environment interaction and creativity. To define the primary adaptive ego strength of care and the core pathology of rejectivity.
- To apply a psychosocial analysis to the issue of discrimination in the workplace with special focus on the cost to society as well as to the individual when discrimination operates to restrict career access and advancement.

*M*iddle adulthood lasts from about age 34 to 60. According to psychosocial theory, a new reorganization of personality occurs during middle adulthood that focuses on the achievement of a sense of generativity. This new stage integrates the skills and perspectives of the preceding life stages with a commitment of energy to the future. During this period, individual and societal development are critically interwoven. In order for societies to thrive and grow, adults must dedicate their energy and resources to preserving the quality of life for future generations. Therefore, in order for individuals to continue to thrive and grow, societies must provide opportunities for adults to express and fulfill their generative strivings.

Because middle adulthood covers a relatively long period, there are opportunities to review and revise one's values and goals along the way. During middle adulthood, individuals strive to find a balance between their values and actions. Most people discover that this balance is delicate and must be constantly recalibrated. The authors have been impressed, for example, by narratives told by students about their fathers, who regretted that they had not given more time and attention to parenting their children when they were young. As a result, these men now find ways to modify the demands of work life so that they can spend more time with their families. Others told of parents who endured years of long, tedious work hours when they were holding down several jobs in order to achieve a degree of financial security, knowing that they had let their marriage relationships drift. Looking back, they said that they realized it was only temporary and that they would live through the tough times knowing they would be there for each other. Over the course of adulthood, many situations call for decisions that have no single correct answer. Several alternatives may be possible, and one must rely on one's values to determine which choice is best. ❖

DEVELOPMENTAL TASKS

Each adult typically engages in all of the developmental tasks discussed below: managing a career, nurturing an intimate relationship, expanding caring relationships, and managing the household. Through their roles in the family, at work, and in the community, middle adults have broad responsibilities for the nurturance, education, and care of children, adolescents, young adults, and older adults (Lachman & James,

1997). The strains of middle adulthood result largely from difficulties in balancing many roles and managing to navigate through predictable as well as sudden role transitions (Elder et al., 1996). The emotional well-being of the society as a whole rests largely on the capacity of middle adults to succeed in the developmental tasks of their life stage.

Managing a Career

Work is a major context for adult development. Every person who enters the labor market has an occupational career. This career, though, may not appear to be orderly and progressive. It may involve changes in the kind of work performed entry and exit from the labor market due to unemployment or family responsibilities, and periodic return to school for new training. However, one can argue that as long as a person is involved in an effort to make use of her or his skills and talents, there will be significant transactions between the world of work and the person's individual development.

There is a reciprocity between work experiences and individual growth. We expect that people with certain kinds of experiences, abilities, and values will enter certain kinds of work roles (Holland, 1997). Once those roles have been entered, however, the work environment and the kinds of activities that the person performs also influence his or her intellectual, social, and value orientation. One's lifelong occupational career is a fluid structure of changing activities, ambitions, and sources of satisfaction. As people move through middle adulthood, the management of their occupational career becomes a task of central importance to their sense of personal effectiveness and identity and to social integration. Four aspects of the management of a career are discussed for their contribution to adaptation and individual development: achieving new levels of competence; midlife career changes; work and family life; and the impact of joblessness.

Achieving New Levels of Competence in the World of Work

Middle adulthood brings new challenges, a reformulation of ambitions and goals, and new levels of competence in the workplace. Three areas are emphasized here as they relate to the interpersonal and cognitive components of career development: understanding and managing leadership and authority relationships; expanding interpersonal skills; and meeting new skill demands by achieving new levels of mastery in critical skill areas.

Understanding and Managing Leadership and Authority. Authority relations encompass all the hierarchical relationships that give people decision-making authority and supervisory control over others. In the induction phase of career development, one must identify the authority structure operating in the work setting and begin to establish a position in it. In the reformation phase, which typically occurs in middle adulthood, advancement in a career inevitably involves increased responsibility and power to make decisions. Career advancement means assuming leadership in some areas, while in other areas recognizing and cooperating with the leadership of others.

What is leadership? Most people can recognize leadership, but cannot define it accurately. Current views suggest that leadership is not a personality quality as much as it is a relationship among people. Woyach (1991) defines leadership as "the process of helping a group shape a vision of its purpose and goals and of getting people, both inside and outside the group, to commit and recommit themselves to accomplishing that vision." (p. 7).

This definition embodies three basic assumptions. The first assumption is that leadership is a relationship among people. One person alone cannot be a leader; leadership implies a group. What is more, simply because a person is given a title or a position of authority does not mean that others will accept her or him as a leader. A person is a leader to the degree to which others accept that person's ideas and agree to focus their energy in a common direction. Thus, as workers reach new levels of seniority they may emerge as formal or informal leaders because others look to them for guidance and expertise.

The second assumption is that leaders provide a sense of vision or direction. Typically, leaders help groups articulate a common sense of purpose and make a commitment to pursue this purpose. Effective leaders help group members express their own

In middle adulthood, new workplace expectations focus on decision making skills, effective leadership, and the ability to recognize when change is needed.

individual visions, and then integrate them into a common vision. In middle adulthood, the clarification of one's values and goals strengthens one's capacity to lead.

The third assumption is that leaders have an impact on getting the group to work toward achieving its vision. It is not enough to have a shared vision. Workers must be motivated to take action and focus their time, energy, and other resources on accomplishing their goals. Leaders play a role in motivating and encouraging individuals, and helping people work together as a team or group.

Building on this view of leadership, Woyach (1991) argued that leaders try to balance the good of the group with their own self-interest. They try to take into account the best interests of individuals, groups, and communities while they also participate and lead. In addition, groups may benefit from having many members who have leadership qualities. This should not result in constant competition for authority and recognition, but in tremendous energy produced as a result of combining the contributions and positive spirit of each participant.

The requirements of leadership may change as the group develops and members become more aware of others' abilities (Clark & Clark, 1994). As levels of trust and confidence among members increase, a group may take on more complex tasks and, therefore, draw upon the leadership skills of various group members. Groups may go through phases when everyone is overloaded and distracted. During those times, leaders help the group return to its mission and recommit to working together. At other times, the group members may understand their roles and tasks so clearly that the primary acts of leadership involve delegating responsibilities and removing obstacles to the group's success. Thus, understanding leadership and authority relations typically involves the ability to assume authority, respond to higher authorities, and collaborate as a member of a team.

New competitive pressures on corporations are leading to a more flexible, less hierarchical authority structure (Kanter, 1989). With a reduction in the size of many bureaucracies, companies are asking workers to relate to one another in new ways. Leaders need to develop adaptive expertise to accompany their technical expertise (Smith et al., 1997). This involves mobilizing and guiding the direction of innovation, coordinating people and projects, communicating, and managing one's own time and effort (Evers & Rush, 1996). Leaders need to be able to understand the underlying dynamics of their work situation and motivate others to respond to new and changing conditions.

Expanding Interpersonal Relationships. Most occupations place a great deal of emphasis on the development and use of interpersonal skills, especially the ability to interact well with customers and co-workers, and the ability to communicate effectively as underlying criteria in the selection and promotion process (Moss & Tilly, 1996). Even though these skills are not mentioned explicitly in the job description, success in career management requires the ability to influence others, appear credible, develop a fluent conversational style, and learn to work effectively in groups or teams.

The interpersonal values held by the leaders in a work group influence the work environment. Leaders who place a high priority on task performance tend to have a negative attitude toward those workers whom they perceive as interfering with successful task accomplishment. They try to establish an ordered, highly structured work environment in which they can exercise their authority. Leaders who give high priority to interpersonal relationships, on the other hand, are more accepting of workers who may interfere with task accomplishment. They try to establish an environment that will foster full participation of the workers. In one analysis of professional expertise, co-workers were asked to nominate individuals whom they thought were excellent computer software professionals. The nominees had high technical knowledge, broad-based experience, and a high level of social skills (Sonnentag, 1995). Thus, even in a field that might be described as very product oriented and highly competitive, the most admired professionals were more frequently involved in a review and feedback process, consultation with others, and the facilitation of group problem solving.

Meeting New Skill Demands. The characteristics of the occupation and the work setting determine what kinds of work-related skills will dominate the adult's energies. It makes sense to expect that the actual tasks a person does from day to day will influence his or her intellectual development. The *Dictionary of Occupational Titles* (U.S. Department of Labor, Employment & Training Administration, 1993) uses 44 characteristics to describe the unique blend of aptitudes and temperaments required for each type of work. These variables have been condensed to six basic factors: substantive complexity, motor skills, physical demands, management, interpersonal skills, and undesirable working conditions (Cain & Treiman, 1981). Each of these dimensions has the potential to contribute to workers' adaptation to their work life. Further, it is likely that in the process of adapting to these dimensions, the adult will carry over aspects of work-related competence to family and community roles.

Melvin Kohn (1980; Miller et al., 1979) examined the relationship between occupational demands and psychological development. One of the strongest relationships he identified is between the substantive complexity of the job and intellectual flexibility. **Substantive complexity** is the degree to which the work requires thought, independent judgment, and frequent decision making. **Intellectual flexibility** refers to a person's ability to handle conflicting information, grasp several perspectives on a problem, and reflect on his or her own values and solutions.

The substantive complexity of a person's job is directly related to his or her intellectual flexibility. This is true even when one takes into account the level of intellectual flexibility that was shown at the time of job entry. In a 10-year longitudinal study, it was found that the level of intellectual flexibility shown 10 years earlier was strongly related to the degree of substantive complexity present in the job 10 years later. Thus, there appears to be a reciprocal effect between these two dimensions. A substantively complex work setting promotes intellectual flexibility, while at the same time, a high level of intellectual flexibility appears to lead one to increasingly challenging, complex work.

One of the most frequently cited areas of skill development in the contemporary labor market is creative problem solving (Hunt, 1995). The combination of increasingly complex technology, instant international communication, and continuing reorganization of the network of interrelated businesses results in the emergence of a new and changing array of problems. These problems may relate to the need to: recruit and train the work force, bring together changing teams of workers depending on the task, find new strategies for the manufacture and delivery of products, or integrate technologies. The concept of **managerial resourcefulness** is sometimes used to capture the nature of this problem solving (Kanungo & Misra, 1992). It exemplifies what we referred to in Chapter 9 as an example of post-formal reasoning. By middle adulthood, individuals have accumulated a deep knowledge of the specific tasks and routines associated with their work. At the same time, they have either tried or observed a variety of problem-solving strategies. Thus, the challenge for the middle adult worker is to synthesize these two bodies of knowledge to create a flexible approach to emerging problems. Successful development in this area requires resisting the temptation to approach new problems from the same conceptual framework. It means recognizing when conditions have changed or past solutions will not be adequate. At the same time, it requires confidence in one's ability to find new solutions and remain creative under stressful conditions.

Midlife Career Changes

Management of a career does not necessarily mean remaining within the same occupational structure throughout adult life. Work activities or work-related goals may change for at least five reasons.

First, some careers end during middle adulthood. One example is the career of the professional athlete whose strength, speed of reaction time, and endurance decline to the point where he or she can no longer compete.

Second, some adults cannot resolve conflicts between job demands and personal goals. Much has been written about successful business executives who turn to farming and about public relations experts who withdraw to rural areas to sell real estate. During middle adulthood, some workers recognize that the kinds of contributions they thought they could make are simply not possible within their chosen work structure. Others find that they do not have the temperament to be successful in their first career.

A third explanation for midlife career change is the realization that one has succeeded as much as possible a given career. Adults may realize that they will not be promoted further or that changing technology has made their expertise obsolete. Consequently, they may decide to retrain for new kinds of work or return to school to move in new career directions.

Fourth, some women decide to make a greater commitment to career once their children are in high school or college. Many have chosen to withdraw from the labor market for a time in order to fulfill parenting roles. As they return to work, women may continue to expect to combine responsibilities as homemakers with career goals. However, their life course has an anticipated midlife career change built in as they shift their primary involvement from the home to the labor market. Other women who have never worked before marriage face the labor market as novices. These women, sometimes referred to as **displaced homemakers,** may enter the job market as a consequence of divorce or early widowhood, facing extreme economic pressures and competing with younger workers for entry-level positions.

In the broadest sense, John Glenn's career has always been about public service. But his career took a dramatic shift in middle adulthood when he changed from astronaut to U.S. senator.

Fifth, with the restructuring of the work force, some workers are laid off and cannot be rehired in the same field. They have to retrain for a new line of work or for similar work in a new industry.

One must be cautious not to idealize midlife career change. Patterson (1997) outlined some of the fears that may be associated with making a career transition: fear of making an unfavorable discovery about one's abilities as a result of the change; fear of failing to satisfy the expectations of important others; fear of taking on new responsibilities; and fear of giving up a known present for an unknown future. Although this type of change is increasingly common as a result of the changing characteristics of the labor market, the ease or difficulty of making such a change depends in part on the extent to which workers perceive that they have control over the conditions of the change. For example, it is not uncommon for executives of large corporations to become disillusioned or displaced as a result of reorganization. In a study of executives who started up their own businesses after working for a Fortune 500 company, those who were successful in their next endeavor were able to see the change as an opportunity for achievement of new goals, they had significant expertise to bring to the new career, and they drew upon important environmental support in the transition (Eggers, 1995).

Work and Family Life

Almost everyone manages a career while juggling commitments to spouse, children, parents, other household members, and friends. A decision to assume more authority, work longer hours, accept an offer with another company, quit a job, or accept a transfer to a new location will touch the lives of other household and family members. For many people, one of the most draining aspects of career management is the effort to meet the conflicting expectations of marital, parental, and work roles.

In thinking about the interaction between work and family life, it is useful to consider three interrelated concepts: role overload, role conflict, and spillover (Nickols, 1994). **Role overload** occurs as a result of too many demands and expectations to handle in the time allowed. For example, a parent with three children ages 8, 11, and 15 may find that the demands of getting the children ready for school, attending functions at three different schools, picking children up and dropping them off at various places and trying to be emotionally available for the "problem of the day" is exhausting. Role overload can be experienced in family and work roles, or in both.

Role conflict refers to ways that the demands and expectations of various roles conflict with each other. For example, a person might be expected to be an assertive decision-maker at work and a facilitative collaborator at home. Roles can conflict when the demands of one role compete with the demands of another. For example, role conflict occurs when a worker is expected to stay late at the job to finish a project, but that same night is a spouse's birthday or a child's performance.

Spillover occurs when the demands or preoccupations about one role interfere with the ability to carry out another role. For example, a person may be disrupted at work by worries about an ill parent or a child who is having trouble at school. Similarly, a person may be psychologically unavailable at home because of worries about possible layoffs at work.

The combination of role overload, role conflict, and spillover can lead to reduced satisfaction at work and in family roles, and in a decline in the person's sense of well-being (Beale, 1997). On the other hand, spousal support for the partner's involvement in work can increase work satisfaction, and feelings of success and pride in one's accomplishments at work can contribute to marital satisfaction (Dreman, 1997).

Areas of conflict that arise in dual-earner couples often focus on the management of household tasks and child care. Even when both partners are equally involved in the labor force, most couples tend to see child care and certain household maintenance tasks as primarily the wife's domain. This outlook is as common in other countries, such as Canada, Sweden, and Norway, as it is in the United States (Kalleberg & Rosenfeld, 1990). When both husband and wife are working, the wife may experience considerable strain in trying to meet her work commitments while allowing adequate time for nurturance and recreational activities with her children, intimacy with her husband, and maintenance of the emotional climate and physical environment of the home.

Studies of professional couples carried out in the 1970s found that wives were more likely than husbands to assume greater responsibility for the home and family, and to put their spouse's careers ahead of their own (Heckman et al., 1977). Research reported in the late 1980s and early 1990s, when married women's involvement in the labor force had become much more widespread, found the same pattern (Pina & Bengtson, 1993). Most parents in dual-earner families experience a sense of role overload. However, the strain of this overload seems to be greater for women than for men. Husbands and wives continue to agree that women have the primary responsibility for making sure that child-rearing and household tasks are taken care of (Duxbury & Higgins, 1994). This perception has led to the description of working women as performing a "second shift" (Hochschild, 1989). They have demanding work responsibilities at their job, their "first shift," and then come home to additional home-related work responsibilities, their "second shift."

Research on the strategies women use to balance work and family life suggests a variety of patterns (Denmark et al., 1996). Some women resolve the conflict between career aspirations and family commitment by limiting their competitive, achievement-oriented strivings. For them, the dual-earner relationship is a matter of negotiation with their spouse, who is regarded as giving them permission to go to work and who sets the limits on their involvement in work. In contrast, other women find that their workplace sets limits on their achievement through sex-stereotyped assumptions about the woman's commitment to her family role. In these settings, women do not tend to be promoted to high-level administrative or managerial positions in which work demands would begin to invade family commitments. As an example, some companies are reluctant to put women in positions in which they may have to be transferred for fear that their husbands will refuse to make the move. Sometimes women who request flexible or part-time work schedules are labeled as not serious enough about their career (Rodgers & Rodgers, 1989). Finally, other women create a salient professional identity and look for a partner who will support their ambitions.

What is the impact of the dual-career arrangement on men? The emphasis in the literature on the difficulties women face in combining work and family life has created a perception that men are singly devoted to the world of work and are indifferent to or uninvested in home and family life. This is clearly not the case. Studies consistently find that men's happiness in their family roles is a stronger predictor of psychological well-being than adjustment at work (Pleck, 1985). Most men find personal meaning and emotional support in their roles as husband and father. For many men, the positive quality of their marital and parental roles helps them cope more effectively with the stresses of work (Barnett et al., 1992). In many instances, specific lessons from home, including the patience and communication necessary to be an effective parent, the willingness to plan and work out alternative strategies for managing daily tasks with his wife, and the admiration he has for his wife in her paid labor-force activities, actually help a man function more effectively at work.

Perhaps because of the centrality of the quality of home life to men's well-being, many men are sensitive to the possibility that their wife's involvement in the labor force may interfere with the emotional comfort and stability they seek at home. A wife's success in the world of work may reduce a husband's sense of power or importance in the marital relationship. Many men are especially uncomfortable if their wives earn more money than they do. In addition, some men find themselves ill prepared to assume the more direct responsibilities of child-rearing in order to support their wives' involvement in the labor market. However, among dual-career couples, marital harmony is sustained when husbands support their wives' involvement in the world of work and do not feel competitive with them (Wright et al., 1994).

Adaptations to the dual-career marriage are not simple. One cannot say that the women always benefit or that the men always suffer. In fact, there are many dual-career arrangements, each involving the negotiation of roles and responsibilities to meet the convergence of work and family needs. However, a major issue in coping with the dual-career pattern seems to be each partner's capacity to revise basic gender-role expectations for their own and their spouse's behavior. This is not a simple task. It touches on deep emotional commitments to one's view of oneself as a man or a woman, a husband or a wife, and a mother or a father. It also affects the enactment of one's values about being a breadwinner, and making significant work-related accomplishments.

The Impact of Joblessness

Even though the workplace can be a major source of stress, joblessness can be even more disruptive to personal mental health and family functioning. Some people are alienated from work—they find little satisfaction in the work setting and few opportunities for meaningful labor. Others are "downsized" out of work. In 1996, the unemployment rate was 5.4% for men and women. Table 12.1 summarizes the unemployment rates by race, age, and sex for two age groups in middle adulthood. From the statistics, one can see that African-Americans and Hispanics are more likely to be unemployed than are whites. Many of these adults experience chronic unemployment.

Chronically unemployed men have few opportunities to develop competence within the context of work. Because of the cultural emphasis on productive work, they are likely to experience guilt about being unemployed. In addition, unemployment disrupts the self-concept of the traditional definition of the adult male role as breadwinner for the family. As a result of guilt, shame, and anger, these men may find it hard to direct their energy toward creative solutions to life problems. Thus, the inability to work can be expected to become a serious hurdle to the resolution of the psychosocial conflict of generativity versus stagnation (Hopper, 1990).

Currently, unemployment rates are low. At the same time, as a result of the restructuring of the labor market, plant closings and workforce reorganizations have resulted in job losses for many middle adults who have had a history of steady employment, including increased responsibility and advancement. Unemployment in middle adulthood has a major psychological impact on an individual's sense of self-worth and hope for the future. Among middle adult workers, job loss is associated with material deprivation, disruption in family life, and increases in marital conflict. Children and spouses are commonly acutely involved in the effects of job loss on a middle adult parent, and often the entire family experiences new feelings of alienation from social institutions as a result of the experience (Lobo & Watkins, 1995; Perrucci et al., 1997).

Job loss has been associated with both physical and psychological consequences, such as self-doubt, passivity, and social withdraw. Depression is a common consequence and the associated family strains may also lead to new levels of conflict and family violence. In some instances, adjustments that families make to a husband's unemployment result in a further reduction of his sense of importance and accentuate the decline in his

---

TABLE 12.1   Unemployment Rates* by Race, Age, and Sex, 1996

	Male %	Female %
White		
35–44	3.5	3.8
45–54	3.1	3.1
Black		
35–44	7.8	6.9
45–54	6.3	3.8
Hispanic		
35–44	6.3	8.7
45–54	5.1	7.2

*According to the U.S. Bureau of the Census, an unemployed person is anyone who "had no employment during the reference week, who made specific efforts to find a job within the previous 4 weeks . . . and who was available for work during that week." (pp. 394)
Source: U.S. Bureau of the Census, 1997.

The possibility of job loss brings people to the streets. Congressional initiatives to increase the tax on cigarettes brings out strong response from a large group of tobacco workers who see their jobs and way of life threatened.

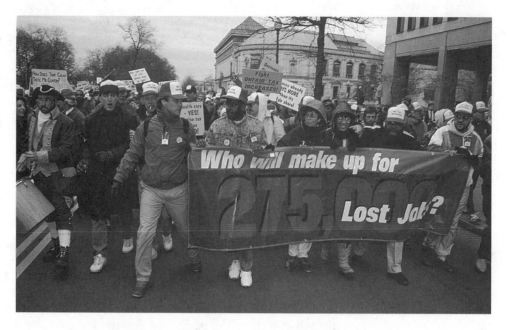

self-respect (Piotrkowski et al., 1987). Social support, especially family strengths and marital satisfaction, are important buffers for the negative effects of unemployment (Vosler & Page-Adams, 1996). In a study of 300 unemployed men, social support from among the person's close relationships played two distinct roles (Vinokur et al., 1987). First, when a significant person reaffirmed the unemployed man's beliefs that looking for a new job was worthwhile and gave him hopeful encouragement, he was more likely to engage in active job-seeking efforts. In addition to this specific support for job seeking, social support provided an important sense of worth and caring that was especially important when job-seeking efforts were not successful. The authors warn that efforts to encourage intensive job seeking may backfire when a highly motivated person meets with repeated failure. Under these conditions, it is especially important for the person to be embedded in social relationships that provide global, unconditional acceptance in order to prevent a process of demoralization and self-destructive behavior.

The threats of job loss can increase stress for those who remain employed as well as for those who become unemployed. For example, in a study of employment conditions on job-related distress, workers in industries that were experiencing high levels of unemployment had a higher incidence of depression than did workers in industries where unemployment was low. Similarly, studies have shown that workers who are "spared" during downsizing and mergers show signs of anxiety and depression. These observations highlight the salience that work has in middle adulthood, especially for those involved in professions that are personally as well as financially rewarding (Reynolds, 1997; Locker, 1997).

Nurturing an Intimate Relationship

Marriage and other long-term intimate bonds are dynamic relationships. They change as the partners mature, as the family constellation changes, and in response to changing events, including family crises and historical events. Focus and effort are required to keep these relationships healthy and vital.

What is a vital marriage? Hof and Miller (1981) described it as:

. . . a relationship in which there is a strong commitment to an enduring marital dyad in which each person experiences increases in fulfillment and satisfaction. There is a strong emphasis on developing effective interpersonal relationships and on establishing and maintaining an open communication system. The ability to give and receive affection in an unconditional way, to accept the full range of feelings toward each other, to appreciate common interests and differences and accept and affirm each other's uniqueness, and to see the other as having equal status in the relationship. (p. 9)

There are at least three requirements for maintaining vitality in an intimate relationship over the period of middle adulthood: a commitment to growth, effective communication, and the creative use of conflict (Mace, 1982). With these three resources, couples learn to work toward change in areas where it is possible, and to accept one another and the characteristics of the relationship in areas where change cannot be accomplished. By expanding their tolerance for differences and admiration for their strengths, new levels of intimacy can be achieved (Jacobson & Christensen, 1996).

A Commitment to Growth

The partners must be committed to growth both as individuals and as a couple. This means they must accept the idea that they will change in important ways and that the relationship, too, will change. Caring and acceptance of each other must deepen. Each person must also be willing to permit changes in attitudes, needs, and interests in the other (Levinger, 1983; Marks, 1989). Within any enduring marriage, each person experiences a dynamic tension between pressures and desires for personal growth on the one hand, and the pressures and demands to preserve the relationship on the other. Both of these forces have the potential to overwhelm or dominate the sense of mutuality. As a result, a vital marriage requires both partners to be open to the need to be themselves (as they continue to discover new things) and an energizing, interpersonal chemistry that is resilient even in the face of the harshest challenges.

One common example of the need to permit individual growth within a marriage occurs when a woman who has been primarily responsible for child care and household management expresses an interest in joining or returning to the paid labor force. Annette, who had worked as a nurse before she married, decided that it was time to go back to work. Her three children were in elementary and middle school, and her husband had a full-time job, so that she was by herself for long hours during the day. She began to feel depressed and jealous of everyone else's active lives, so she took a position at a local hospital, working three afternoons and on Saturday each week. At first, her husband, Gary, fussed and resisted. Why did she need to go to work? he asked. They didn't really need the money, and Gary liked to know that she would be at home when he came back from work. He wasn't used to having to take the kids to their activities after school. Plus, Saturday used to be his day to hang out with his friends from work. The kids fussed at being asked to get dinner ready. But Annette insisted that she had to get back to work—her mental health and happiness depended on it. The first months were terrible. Annette wondered if she were doing the right thing, and Gary used every trick in the book to lure her back to the house. But there was no denying the value of this new job for Annette's self-confidence, her renewed feeling of personal identity, and her ability to return to the home with new energy and enthusiasm for her husband, children, and family life. Gary began to get a bit more involved in the children's lives and actually looked forward to the Saturdays they spent together. Soon the children began to see their mother in a new light, as a professional who took care of other people as well as them. They also felt a new surge of independence in being able to handle the dinner meal on their own. Gary and Annette felt closer to each other as a result of Annette's new independence and Gary's new level of involvement in the lives of the children.

Effective Communication

The couple must develop an effective communication system. This means there must be opportunities for interaction. If competing life roles, including work and parenting, dramatically reduce opportunities for interaction, the couple will risk drifting apart. They will have increasingly fewer shared experiences and will be less readily influenced by each other's observations and reactions. Studies of the correlates of marital happiness find that there is a reciprocal relationship between interaction and happiness. In a longitudinal study, couples who were happier early in their marriage showed higher levels of interaction in later years (Zuo, 1992). After a number of years of marriage, the two variables were strong predictors of each other: Those who were happy were involved in more frequent interactions, and similarly, those who were involved in frequent interactions were happier.

For many couples who do not have an effective communication system, resentments accumulate with no opportunity to resolve them. A common experience is that the wife wants to talk things over, but the husband does not see what good this will do. *Harmonious, satisfied couples* listen to and consider each other's problems. They validate each other's concerns by expressing understanding, even if they cannot offer solutions. *Dissatisfied couples,* on the other hand, avoid problems or counterattack. Instead of validating the spouse's concern, the partner raises his or her own complaints and criticisms. Over the years, levels of complaining and negativism escalate, and each partner becomes increasingly disenchanted with the other (McGonagle et al., 1993). In the early years of marriage, it appears that negativity in the marriage is disruptive to marital stability. Later in marriage, however, couples seem to learn how to weather some of the more difficult arguments, but the frequency of disagreements continues to be a strong predictor of marital disruption.

One way of thinking about the differences between harmonious and dissatisfied couples is to view the role of communication in the ability to establish and maintain effective feedback loops (see the discussion of systems theory in Chapter 3). **Feedback loops** are mechanisms that identify and respond to change in the environment. In the context of communication within a couple, feedback loops serve to continue, modify, or interrupt a certain interaction. A woman may smile and laugh to encourage her husband's telling of a recent family incident. Or she may frown, look at her watch, and try to interrupt if she thinks the story is too embarrassing.

In harmonious couples, partners accurately interpret the intent of one another's communications and predict the impact of their communications on the other person (Denton et al., 1994). Harmonious couples develop and redevelop the feedback loops needed to maintain understanding. In contrast, dissatisfied couples may not have had effective feedback loops to begin with, and the interaction pattern tends to be disruptive. The lack of internal feedback loops reduces the capacity of the system to achieve equilibrium and to adjust to changes in the partners or to changing conditions that affect the marriage. Marriages tend to thrive when communication is a central mechanism for adapting to change and promoting development.

Creative Use of Conflict

A vital marriage is sustained through *the couple's ability to make creative use of conflict.* In relationships where the partners have equal status and appreciate each other's individuality, there are bound to be conflicts. Although high levels of negativity and discord are disruptive to a marriage, some amount of conflict must be permitted in order to sustain the sense of individuality that is central to a vital marriage. The partners must understand conflict, concur that it is acceptable to disagree, and develop strategies for resolving conflict (Cole & Cole, 1985; Sher & Weiss, 1991). Even though satisfied couples cannot always resolve their conflicts, they are able to prevent conflicts from escalating into intense hostility. Many times their disagreements are left at a stalemate (Vuchinich, 1987). If one partner expresses a complaint or acts unpleasantly, the other does not retaliate with another negative action. Rather, negative comments on the part of one person are likely to provoke the partner's sympathy or acceptance (Roberts & Krokoff, 1990; Halford et al., 1990). When satisfied couples disagree, they try to remain calm during the interaction and search for a resolution that is satisfactory to both partners. As a rule, levels of conflict and hostility are greater within the family than they are at the workplace or in the community. Among satisfied couples, however, the impact of anger is minimized, and the goal remains to achieve a mutual level of understanding.

Nurturing vitality in an intimate relationship is a long-term task. The challenge is for the partners to create continued interest, nurturance, and appreciation for each other even after they have achieved high levels of security, trust, and empathy, so that the components of a loving relationship operate continuously in the relationship. The significance of this task is relevant for the ongoing nature of the relationship and the social support it provides as the couple enters later life. In addition, the quality of the marital relationship during middle adulthood provides the context for

Vern and Linda treasure the time they have together. Their marriage is energized by their diverse interests coupled with the enjoyment they take in each other's company.

the children's emerging understanding of intimacy and marital roles. As children mature into middle childhood and early adolescence, they pay attention to and try to make sense of the quality of their parents' interactions with each other. As children observe their parents, they acquire a sense of how they function as husband and wife. Of course, children do not perfectly replicate their parents' marriages. However, the degree of egalitarianism, conflict style, and expression of affection that children observe can influence their ideas about the kind of partner they seek and how they will enact the marital role (VanLear, 1992).

Expanding Caring Relationships

Middle adults have opportunities to express caring in many roles. This section focuses on two roles: parenting and the care of one's own aging parents. Both domains offer numerous challenges to the intellectual, emotional, and physical resources of the adult caregiver.

Parenting

Being a parent is a difficult, demanding task that requires a great deal of learning. Because children are constantly changing and are often unpredictable, adults must be sensitive and flexible in new situations in order to cope successfully with their demands. Each period of the child's development calls for new and innovative parenting strategies. Child-rearing experiences are different with each child, and the changing family constellation brings new demands for flexibility and learning. With each successive child, however, there seems to be less anxiety about parenting skills. Children help adults learn about parenting through their responses to their parents' efforts and their own persistence in following the path of development.

Developmental Stages of the Family. At each stage of a child's life, the demands on parents change. Infants require constant care and attention. Preschoolers require educational toys and interaction with peers. They can spend a great deal of time in independent play, but they require mindful supervision. Early and middle school-age children require parental reassurance about their skills, talents, and fears. The early adolescent requires little in the way of physical care but continuing emotional support and guidance, new financial demands, and help in facilitating participation in athletics, after-school activities, and social life.

Several models of family development have been proposed by family researchers. These schemes, especially the ones described by Duvall (1977), Hill (1965), and Spanier, Sauer, and Larzelere (1979), emphasize changes in the family that are tied to changes in the developmental levels of children. The implication is that the changing needs, competence, and social interactions of the children stimulate changing interactions, activities, and values among family members.

There are criticisms, though, of this view of family development. First, the length of the marriage and the ages of the parents are confounded with the ages or stages of the children. It is possible that the parents' ages as much as the children's ages or some combination of the two account for changes in family emphasis (Nock, 1979; Spanier et al., 1979). Second, this view does not explain the growth of families that do not have children or that are a product of remarriage in which the marital relationship has a shorter history than the parental one. Third, from a psychosocial perspective, the influence of parents and children is regarded as reciprocal. Children's developmental changes have the potential to influence the quality of their interactions with parents and vice versa. Further, from a systems perspective, each family member can prompt conflict, change, or growth in every other member. The affectional bonds that family members share, as well as the need to protect one another from external threats, contribute to a dynamic interdependence. To some degree, each family member is vulnerable to the influence of every other member.

For the purposes of this discussion of parenting, we have chosen to consider the potential influences of phases of family development on adult development. This approach has the advantage of showing the reciprocity of psychosocial themes across the generations. It highlights the processes through which development may prompt new growth among parents. Although middle adults might be parenting children at any age range, we will focus on the four periods below. These periods correspond to the most likely transitions that take place as parents age from 34 to 60.

1. The years when children are in early and middle childhood
2. The years when children are adolescents
3. The years when no children are living at home
4. Grandparenthood

The years when children are in early and middle childhood. School-age children tap parents' resources for ideas about things to do, places to go, and friends to meet. They seek new experiences in order to expand their competence and investigate the larger world outside the home. Parents become active as chauffeurs, secretaries, and buffers between their children and the rest of the community. During this time, parents have many opportunities to function as educators for their children. They actively contribute to their children's academic success through such activities as reading with them, helping them with homework, praising them for school success, and talking with teachers, visiting the school, and participating in school projects. Research on academic success makes it clear that parents' aspirations for their children, their overall parenting skills, and their involvement in their children's education make a substantial contribution to their children's progress (Jenkins, 1989; Eccles, 1993). Parents who combine appropriate challenges with warmth and support have children who are highly motivated and want to do well in school.

Parenting during this period has the potential for boosting an adult's sense of pride in skills and knowledge already accumulated. Parents are gatekeepers to the resources of the community. They come to see themselves through their children's eyes, as people who know about the world—its rewards, treasures, secrets, and dangers.

During this phase of parenthood, adults are likely to be active in school-related organizations. They find themselves reacting to events that occur in school, planning activities to take place at school, or working with other parents to provide some service, opportunity, or facility for their children that does not currently exist. Through efforts to further their own children's development, parents begin to evolve an attitude toward—even a philosophy of—education that will have implications for a whole community of children. When parents are forced to protect, defend, or reprimand their own children because of events that have taken place in school, they develop a stance toward school and its function in the community. For some parents, school seems like a hostile place. They did not do well in school themselves and do not have much confidence in their own academic abilities. These parents may find it difficult to retain a

The Carlsons have taken lots of family trips. Now that the boys are adolescents, they enjoy reminiscing about past adventures and planning new ones. It's getting harder to reach agreement, however, because the boys push harder for their own preferences and Mom and Dad have less power over the final decision.

sense of self-worth if their children become overly involved in school. Out of their own defensiveness, they may even introduce barriers to their children's academic success.

The years when children are adolescents. Parents tend to view the years of their children's adolescence as extremely trying. Adolescents are likely to have a great deal of behavioral independence. They spend most of the day away from home and apart from adult supervision. As adolescents gain in physical stature and cognitive skills, they are likely to challenge parental authority.

During this time, the principles that parents have emphasized as important for responsible, moral behavior are frequently tested. Children are exposed to many voices, including the media, popular heroes and heroines, peers, and school adults, that suggest the idea that there may be more than one ideal way to behave and more than one definition of success. On the one hand, parents must allow their children freedom to permit them to exercise their own judgment. On the other, they must be ready to give support when the children fail to meet adult expectations or when they show poor judgment. Parents must be able to maintain a degree of authority about standards or limits that continue to operate for young adolescents. Parents of adolescents, therefore, attempt to balance freedom, support, and limit setting in the needed proportions so that their children can grow increasingly independent while still being able to rely on an atmosphere of family reassurance (Newman, 1989; Ryan & Lynch, 1989).

Adolescent children are the front line of each new generation. The questions they raise and the choices they make reflect not only what they have learned but also what they are experiencing in the present and what they anticipate in the future. Parents of adolescents are likely to feel persistent pressure to reevaluate their own socialization as well as their effectiveness as parents. Questions are raised about their preparation for their own future as well as their children's. The ego boost parents experienced from being viewed as wise and resourceful is likely to be replaced by doubt as they and their children face an uncertain future. Parents who can respond to their adolescents in an open, supportive way can benefit by finding an opportunity to clarify their own values. They can begin building new parent-child relationships that will carry them and their emerging adult children into later adulthood.

The years when no children are living at home. The period during which adult children leave home has been designated developmentally as the **launching period** (Mattessich & Hill, 1987). For families with few children, this period may last only a few years. In larger families, though, the transition may take 10–15 years. Alternative patterns are clearly evident in current U.S. families. Thirty percent of parents with children in their 20s have one or more of them living at home (Aquilino, 1990). By the time adult children marry, they are almost always ready to leave the parental home.

Roles change during this time. Most women enter menopause during this period, bringing a close to the couple's natural childbearing years (Box 12.1). The relationship between the husband and the wife also changes as parenting activities diminish. Some couples become closer—closer than they have been since they first fell in love. However, divorces also occur after the children leave home. Parents are likely to begin a review and evaluation of their performance as parents as they see the kinds of lives their children have established for themselves. Erikson (Erikson et al., 1986) found that during this period, many parents continue to build their identities on the accomplishments of their children. Parents also begin to find new targets for energy and commitment that they had previously directed toward the care of their children.

The transitional period during which children leave home does not seem to be a negative time for adults. A woman who was anticipating her children leaving home described her feelings this way:

> "From the day the kids are born, if it's not one thing, it's another. After all these years of being responsible for them, you finally get to the point where you want to scream, 'Fall out of the nest already, you guys, will you? It's time.' It's as if I want to take myself back after all these years—to give me back to me, if you know what I mean. Of course, that's providing there's any 'me' left." (Rubin, 1980, p. 313)

There is evidence of greater cohesiveness and affection in the marriage relationship after the children leave home, especially in marriages that had been satisfactory before (Houseknecht & Macke, 1981; Mullan, 1981). Parents are usually pleased as they follow their children's accomplishments. Further, children's independence may permit parents to use their financial resources to enhance their own lifestyle.

Of course, adults maintain certain parental functions during this stage. Many children remain financially dependent on their parents, even after leaving home. If the children are in college or in postgraduate study, the parents may experience greater financial demands than at any earlier period in their parenting history. In many families, parents take on extra labor-market activities and additional loans to meet the fi-

---

BOX 12.1   MENOPAUSE

At some time during their late 40s or 50s, most women experience the **climacteric,** or the involution and atrophy of the reproductive organs. Many physiological changes accompany the close of fertility, including: the cessation of menstruation (menopause), gradual diminution in the production of estrogen, atrophy of the breasts and genital tissues, and shrinkage of the uterus (Morokoff, 1988). Controversy exists about whether menopause affects women at a psychological level because of either its symbolic meaning or the physiological changes it produces. Let us consider the research on menopause—and the entire experience of the climacteric—within the context of its meaning for the woman who is engaged in the task of developing a sense of generativity.

The most commonly reported symptom is a frequent "hot flash," a sudden onset of warmth in the face and neck that lasts several minutes. Sometimes it is accompanied by dizziness, nausea, sweating, or headaches. About 75%–85% of women going through natural menopause report this symptom. Other physiological symptoms are related to the reduction of vaginal fluid and loss of elasticity (Huerta et al., 1995). The symptoms appear to be closely related to a

drastic drop in the production of estrogen. Postmenopausal women produce only one-sixth as much estrogen as do women who regularly menstruate. Several studies on the use of estrogen treatment have found that the administration of this hormone to menopausal women alleviates or even prevents menopausal symptoms.

It is fairly well established, then, that menopause causes recognizable physical changes that the adult woman may or may not view as unpleasant. The severity of symptoms is determined in part by the attitude of the culture toward the infertile older woman. In cultures that reward women for reaching the end of the fertile period, menopause is associated with few physiological symptoms. The following study describing the reaction of women in India found that menopause was associated with increased social status:

> The absence of menstrual flow signaled an incredible elevation of stature for these women. Women were released from a veiled, secluded life in a compound to talk and socialize (even drink) with menfolk. They then became revered as models of wisdom and experience by the younger generation (Gillespie, 1989, p. 46).

nancial requirements of their children's college and professional education. Children who have left home may not have resolved decisions about occupation and marriage. For them, their parents remain a source of advice and support as they go through periods of identity and intimacy formation and consolidation. Parents begin to feel the pressure of challenges to their value orientation as their children experiment with new roles and lifestyles. During this stage, parents may serve as sounding boards, as sources of stability, or as jousting partners in young people's attempts to conceptualize their own lifestyle. Middle adults may begin to feel free to alter their roles and redirect their energies. However, some parents experience resistance from their children, who expect their parents to remain the same as they themselves change and grow. Young adult children take many different paths in leaving the parental home, and in many cases they return for intervals when they look for a new job, find a new roommate, recover from a love relationship that has ended, return from military service, or drop out of college (Thornton et al., 1993). Throughout these transitions, young adults look to their parents as a source of stability and to their home as a "safe harbor" while they try to establish their own life structure.

One of the major events that occurs during this period is the child's decision to marry. Parents may be expected to accept a new person into their family—their child's husband or wife. Along with this new relationship comes a connection to an entirely new, and often totally unknown, group of in-laws. In the U.S., parents are usually at the mercy of their child's decision in this matter. They may find themselves associated through marriage with a family that differs significantly from their own or one that shares many of their own family's beliefs and values.

The first few years of marriage, as discussed in Chapter 11, are somewhat precarious. Parents may have to reintegrate an adult child into the family at this stage if his or her marriage is not successful. It can be assumed that a child who leaves a marriage needs some temporary parental reassurance and support in order to regain confidence in his or her ability to form an intimate relationship. Thus, at times of crisis, middle adults may need to practice parenting skills they have not used for a while and develop new skills in helping their children deal with new challenges.

Similarly, a woman's own attitudes toward aging and her involvement in adult roles influence the ease or difficulty with which she experiences menopause. In U.S. society, for example, a woman who is going through menopause at age 50 may also be experiencing the severe illness or death of her parents and the marriage of her youngest child. Menopausal status is not a good predictor of a woman's health or her psychological well-being. Role strain and prior health are more accurate predictors (McKinlay et al., 1987).

The majority of publications dealing with menopause focus on issues of treatment for symptoms, and the pros and cons of hormone replacement therapy. Comparatively few focus on its social and psychological correlates. The tendency is to treat menopause as an illness or a deficit, the loss of reproductive capacity, rather than as a normative transition into a new phase of adult life (Rostosky & Travis, 1996). This contrast is illustrated in a study which compared the concerns regarding menopause and related health care needs of Uruguayan women and the perceptions that gynecologists had of these concerns. Gynecologists thought women were more concerned about hormone replacement therapy, surgery, physical symptoms, and sexual functioning than the women actually were. The women were more concerned about future opportunities for self-development and opportunities for increased independence and a changed lifestyle than the physicians realized (Defey et al., 1996). Other studies support the view that women view menopause as both a limited physiological experience and a more general marker of entry into a new period of life (Jones, 1997).

With a life expectancy of 80 years or more, one might see menopause as the transition to the second half of life. For women who have failed to develop a sense of generativity, who continue to view their children as a path to self-fulfillment, or who are frightened by the prospect of growing old, menopause may be accompanied by a sense of stagnation. On the other hand, for women who have developed a sense of personal achievement and whose early adulthood goals have been accomplished, menopause signifies the beginning of a period in which new energy may be directed to broader, community-oriented tasks. These women are likely to feel more energetic as they uncover new facets of their personality and new avenues for their creative ambitions and goals.

Grandparents often take the role of teaching their grandchildren new skills. These Japanese grandparents, who are avid baseball fans, are very proud of what their grandson can accomplish.

Grandparenthood. Grandparenthood, the time when an adult witnesses the birth of a new generation, might be considered the beginning of an additional stage in family development. But the transition to it is outside one's own control. Whenever one's children have children of their own, the grandparent becomes alerted to a new sense of ancestry, lineage, and membership in an expanding kinship network. With grandparenthood, adults begin to observe their children as parents. As people reflect on their own roles 20–30 years earlier, they may attribute some of their children's successes to their own parenting techniques and may take responsibility for some of the failures, too (Erikson et al., 1986). In Chapter 13, we consider in greater detail the role of grandparenthood and its significance to the adult. Suffice it to say that as grandparents, adults have the opportunity to relate to small children as an expression of the continuity of their lives into the future. Of course, not all grandparents relate to their grandchildren from this philosophical point of view. However, the attainment of the grandparent role has the potential for bringing with it a new perspective on time, purpose, and the meaning of life that may serve as a source of reassurance during later adulthood.

Adults differ in how they define the role of grandparent. They may see themselves as carriers of the family traditions and dispensers of wisdom, as needed experts in child care, as convenient and trusted baby-sitters, or as admirers from afar. As grandparents, adults are asked to reinvest energy in small children. The quality of the relationship that develops between grandparents and grandchildren depends not so much on the fact that they are relatives as on the kinds of experiences the two generations share. Grandparents may also find that the quality of their relationship with their grandchildren is mediated by the child's parents. Especially when the grandchildren are little, the amount of time they spend with their grandparents and the way the grandparents view them are filtered through the quality of the adult relationship that their parents have with their own parents, the grandparents (Brubaker, 1990).

A Psychosocial Analysis of Contributions of Parenting to Adult Development. During the process of parenting, adults have an opportunity to review their own development through the experiences they share with their children. They may recall their own thrill at watching a firefly light up or trepidation the night before high school graduation. Parenthood helps adults realize how far they have come in their own efforts at self-definition. At each phase of family development, adults consolidate the gains made in their own growth while learning the skills needed to facilitate the development of their children.

The parent role may stimulate further cognitive and emotional development when parents view the role as both positive and desirable (Newman & Newman, 1988). Of course, not all parents regard their role that way. Some turn against their children or drop to new low levels of functioning. Yet this important role has growth-promoting possibilities. Given the critical importance of parenting for species survival and for psychosocial evolution, it is highly unlikely that the enactment of the parent role will prove detrimental to most adults. On the contrary, parenting may bring new levels of insight, intellectual flexibility, and social commitment.

The attachment process is central to human relationships. A person's attachment structure may change over the life course. In some respects, the bond that ties children to their parents is the same as the bond that ties parents to their children. But in other ways, the attachment of parents to their children is unique. It is normally characterized by a strong sense of responsibility and an uneven distribution of resources and authority. As a consequence of this deep and enduring attachment, parents are likely to be highly receptive to the range of new information, experiences, and thoughts that are evoked as they observe and interact with their children.

Parents are continually thrown into cognitive disequilibrium. Discrepancies between the competence and expectations a parent has and the realities encountered with each child provide a stimulus for cognitive growth. Parents face numerous discrepancies and are usually highly motivated to resolve them. As a result, parenting may be viewed as having potential influence on at least six aspects of cognitive development during adulthood. First, parenting requires a more probabilistic view of the future and an accompanying contingency approach to planning. Second, parenting promotes the formulation of a philosophy of life in which the rules and limits that parents impose on their children are related to central values and goals.

Third, parenting supports a greater appreciation of individual differences and a more highly differentiated view of individual strengths, weaknesses, and potential. Fourth, parenting requires and promotes the capacity to hold two or more opposing ideas in the mind at the same time. Fifth, the need to protect and nurture children requires the development of greater skill in anticipating the future. Finally, parenting has the potential consequence of expanding the realm of consciousness. Through parenting, adults become increasingly aware of themselves and others; increasingly capable of conceptualizing past, present, and future; and able to function at varying levels of abstraction in order to be effective with children at different developmental levels.

Parenting contributes to the expansion of caring. Seven aspects of emotional development can be identified as potential consequences of parenting. First, parenting brings a depth of commitment that is tied to the responsibility for the survival of a child. The depth of commitment is strengthened through the reinforcing nature of the child's responses to attempts to meet his or her needs. Second, parenting brings adults into contact with new channels for expressing affection. Third, it requires that adults achieve a balance between meeting their own needs and those of others. Fourth, parenting enhances adults' feelings of value and well-being through the significant role they play in the child's life. Fifth, parents achieve a degree of empathy for their child that widens the array of their emotional experiences. Sixth, parents may experience new levels of emotional intensity in reaction to their child's behavior. Lastly, many parents learn to help their children express and understand emotions. By playing a therapeutic role for their children, parents may become more effective in accepting and expressing their own emotions.

Parenting is stressful. It is full of conflicts and challenges, demanding time that the partners might otherwise spend with each other or in pursuit of their own interests and ambitions. We argue, however, that parenting generates the kind of conflict that promises an enormous potential for personal growth. By providing a meaningful, responsive context for children, parents have the opportunity to articulate their own value systems and observe the consequences of their efforts in the continuous development of their children. Psychosocial growth requires a willingness to engage in tasks that may temporarily increase stress, uncertainty, and complexity. Thus, it does not mean turning away from or minimizing tension. It frequently means choosing the challenge that is noticeably difficult or intriguingly complex in hopes of growing while struggling to meet it.

Caring for One's Aging Parents

People tend to regard middle adulthood as a time devoted to future generations. However, another test of one's capacity for generativity comes in the form of commitment to one's aging parents. One of the significant challenges of middle adulthood is the struggle to respond effectively to one's parents as well as one's children and grandchildren. As one ages from 30 to 50, one's parents may age from 60 to 80. The number of adults over the age of 65 increased from over 25 million in 1980 to almost 34 million in 1996. Further, the number of adults over the age of 85 was 3.8 million, an increase of over 100% since 1970 (U.S. Bureau of the Census, 1997). It is becoming increasingly likely that most middle adults will confront the challenge of meeting the needs of their own aging parents. Similarly, it is also increasingly possible that their aging parents will survive through a period of vigorous and independent later adulthood into a period of frail and vulnerable old age.

What is the nature of filial obligation as it is viewed from the perspectives of adult children and their aging parents? Who provides what kinds of help? What characterizes optimal parent-child relationships during this phase of life?

What Is Filial Obligation? What can aging parents expect of their adult children? How do adult children define their responsibilities for their parents? In an analysis of three generations of women, it was clear that each cohort perceived a strong sense of **filial obligation,** a feeling of responsibility to care for their aging parents (Brody et al., 1984; Roff & Klemmack, 1986). In one study of filial obligation, 144 elderly parents and their adult children were asked to respond to 16 items that could be viewed as elements of filial obligation. The items are listed in Table 12.2, along with the percentage of each group that endorsed them. Parents and adult children clearly agree on the top three items: helping to understand resources, giving emotional support, and talking over matters of importance. They also agree that children should not be expected to live near the parent, or write or visit weekly. Items that are starred indicate a significant difference in endorsement by the two groups.

Based on the results of this study, children have a greater sense of obligation than their parents expect of them. Parents do not seem to be comfortable with some forms of help, such as accepting financial assistance, having their children revise their work schedules in order to provide help, and living in a child's home (Hamon & Blieszner, 1990). In fact, it is more likely that an adult child will live in the household of an older parent than the reverse. And studies of intergenerational economic transfers find that older adults, those 65 and over, give more in cash and gifts than they receive from younger generations (Aquilino, 1990).

Who Provides Help? The evidence suggests that daughters assume much more of the responsibility for their aging parents than do sons (Finley, 1989). This involvement is one element of the basic "kinkeeping" tasks that have traditionally been incorporated into women's socialization. Daughters are more likely than sons to provide care for their aging parents even when the daughters are employed. In addition, the daughters provide more direct care, such as bathing or dressing a parent, as well as emotional

TABLE 12.2 Perceptions of Filial Responsibility by Adult Children and Their Parents (Percentages)

Item	Children	Parents
Help understand resources	99.3	97.2
Give emotional support	97.2	95.7
Talk over matters of importance	96.5	98.6
Make room in home in emergency*	94.4	73.0
Sacrifice personal freedom*	93.7	81.0
Care when sick*	92.4	64.3
Be together on special occasions	86.0	86.7
Give financial help*	84.6	41.1
Give parents advice	84.0	88.7
Adjust family schedule to help*	80.6	57.4
Feel responsible for parent**	78.2	66.4
Adjust work schedule to help*	63.2	42.1
Parent should live with child*	60.8	36.7
Visit once a week	51.4	55.6
Live close to parent	32.2	25.7
Write once a week	30.8	39.4

Note: Ranking reflects percentage of respondents who "strongly agreed" or "agreed" with each item.
*Fisher's Exact Test indicated significant differences in proportion of endorsement for children and parents at *p < .001 or **p < .05.
Source: Hamon & Blieszner, 1990.

It is quite common for an adult daughter to have responsibility for her aging mother. The closer the two women were during the daughter's childhood, the easier it is for the two to preserve a positive relationship as the aging mother becomes more dependent on the daughter's help.

support, such as listening to a parent's concerns or helping her or him feel important and loved. However, both sons and daughters are about equally likely to assist in some of the tasks involving relations with health and human service organizations, scheduling medical checkups, and reviewing insurance and other financial matters. Research shows that aging adults who have three or more children, whether they are sons or daughters, are more likely to end up living with one of them than are adults with fewer than three children. However, for other forms of support, such as receiving telephone calls, visiting, and helping in daily tasks, older adults who have one daughter receive more support than those who have one or more sons (Spitze & Logan, 1990).

What Factors Promote an Optimal Relationship Between Adults and Their Aging Parents? The nature of the continuing relationship between adult children and their aging parents is not focused solely on caregiving. The norms of independence and self-sufficiency are strong among the current aging population, many of whom state that they do not need assistance from their adult children. However, when asked whom they view as their preferred source of assistance should they need it, aging parents mention their children first, before friends, siblings, or other relatives (Hogan et al., 1993). Likewise, adult children view themselves as being primarily responsible for meeting their parents' needs; however, most do not expect to have to meet a variety of such needs.

In adulthood, the ongoing parent-child relationship is one of choice. Children feel a moral obligation to reciprocate the care and devotion their parents extended to them when they were young. In addition, a moral obligation to "honor thy father and thy mother" may have been incorporated into the children's religious training. However, the goal of child-rearing in this society generally includes the value of promoting the offspring's independence. This means that children are encouraged to leave home, establish residences of their own, and be economically self-sufficient. Nevertheless, most families continue to live relatively close to one another, with 80% of adults reporting that at least one child is less than an hour's drive away. In addition, over 75% of older adults talk to their children at least once a week. Even under conditions of geographic distance, many children say they feel close to their parents and share a positive sense of connection (Hooyman & Kiyak, 1993).

Adult children are often in a position of trying to supplement the care and support they provide their parents by coordinating social services and interacting with various public agencies. However, many feel unprepared for this aspect of the caring relationship (Zarit & Eggebeen, 1995). They are not comfortable dealing with hospitals, insurance agencies, social service agencies, or residential treatment facilities. However, when older adults require the services of these organizations, their adult children typically know their parents' unique needs and are among the best people to interpret them for service providers. In addition, through such contacts, middle adults have the opportunity to modify and improve the services offered by these agencies, making them more effective for future generations of aging adults.

Despite some difficulties in achieving a satisfying adult child-aging parent relationship, there are important possibilities for expressing generativity in this relationship. The manner in which adults respond to their parents provides a model for their own children. By dealing in a sensitive, caring way with their aging parents, adult children provide a pattern of responsiveness that may be a guide to their own children as the parents reach later adulthood.

Caring for aging parents brings middle adults face to face with the eventuality of their own aging and death. For many adults, this may be anxiety provoking since they are not ready to die. They are in the midst of complex role demands, and many people depend on their strength and competence. However, through interaction with their aging parents, they can perceive a time in life when they will be more prepared to accept death. By making a commitment to their aging parents, they may have less fear about feeling abandoned or being a burden in their own later years.

Managing the Household

People tend to live in groups. According to the U.S. Bureau of the Census (1997), all the people who live in a house or other "housing unit," such as an apartment, a single room, or any space designated as separate living quarters, are part of a **household.** In the United States, the Census Bureau records all individuals as living either in households or in group quarters, such as emergency shelters, juvenile detention centers, mental hospitals, prisons, military barracks, or college dormitories. In 1996, there were 99,627,000 households in the United States. The average household size was 2.65 people, and 70% were defined as **family households** involving two or more individuals related by birth, marriage, or adoption.

Households are much more than a convenient way of counting people. *Household* is a term that describes the entity that is created by people for a particular style of living. Households are bounded units that pool their resources, earn and spend money, interact with the labor market, and engage in social interaction with their neighbors (Wallerstein & Smith, 1991). Management of the household refers to all the planning, problem solving, and activities adults must engage in order to take care of themselves and others who are entrusted to their care.

The household system has the potential for providing an environment that facilitates human growth and mental health. Learning to create such an environment is a developmental task of the middle adult years. Households have the potential for much greater variety and flexibility than most work settings. Besides a given number of tasks that must be done each day, the members of a household may designate any kind of work as an appropriate task. The adult's challenge is to create an environment that will enhance the potential of each household member and thereby benefit the entire family unit. The significance of the household can be appreciated by thinking about the consequences of its absence, especially in the case of homeless individuals and families (Box 12.2)

BOX 12.2 HOMELESSNESS

The household provides a basic life structure for most people in all cultures. The demands and tasks of household management call forth responses that stimulate cognitive, social, and personal development during adulthood. The household is not only a physical setting, but also a shared psychological context for a group of people. In nomadic tribal groups, for example, the continuity of the household is preserved by the group of people and their shared belongings even though the location of the household changes. The capacity to maintain a household and to nurture household members reflect the leadership skills, creativity, and self-reliance that are characteristics of maturity in middle adulthood.

The term *homeless* refers to people who live on the streets or in public shelters. They have no permanent resting place and no private space (Lindsey, 1994). In 1990, the U.S. census identified roughly 50,000 people who were homeless and 190,000 who lived in emergency shelters for the homeless (U.S. Bureau of the Census, 1992). Many of these people are mentally ill and have been released from mental institutions. Some are drug and alcohol abusers, others are runaway youths.

The fastest growing segment of the homeless population, families with children, constitutes approximately 40% of people who become homeless, while on any given night, an estimated 20% of the homeless population are families (Shinn and Weitzman, 1996). A survey of 29 U.S. cities found that in 1996, children accounted for 27% of the homeless population (Waxman and Hinderliter, 1996). These proportions are likely to be higher in rural areas.

A combination of the reduction in the buying power of social welfare benefits and shortages in low-income housing have contributed to the increase in the number of families with children who live on the streets or in emergency shelters. Paths toward homelessness for families are diverse. Some of the most common precursors are job loss, domestic violence, substance abuse, mental illness, and divorce (Koblinsky & Anderson, 1993). Although some homeless individuals are in a sudden crisis, many have stumbled from one temporary living situation to the next, and others have never been able to establish a permanent home. Some of these people are singularly alone and unable to develop minimal social relationships. This is an unusual phenomenon, since most people have some ability to have meaningful social relationships. Among homeless mothers, for example, many have no friends or family. They lack a family social support system or a sense of social connection, often as a result of some form of victimization earlier in their

Management of the household, much like the workplace, requires leadership in order to set priorities and goals, manage resources, and operationalize plans. The scarcer the resources, the greater the pressure on the adult to make careful decisions and to find creative solutions to the daily challenges of meeting the household's physical and psychological needs.

Leadership begins in the family, as adults model the process of shared decision-making and children learn to participate in family problem solving. Family members discover ways to work together to achieve a shared vision of the future (Woyach, 1991; Blanchard, 1996). The family environment is the first place where children discover that they can have a voice. Parents can create a family atmosphere in which the spirit of democracy comes alive through a careful balance of freedom and responsibility, respect for individuality, and commitment to the welfare of others.

Building Coalitions

One of the most difficult and subtle kinds of new learning that occurs during middle adulthood is the development of an understanding of how the structures of other organizations affect one's life and the lives of family members. These other groupings may include: (1) individuals, (2) members of the extended family (for example, one's in-laws), (3) other families, (4) business or work-related associations, (5) religious groups, (6) educational groups, and (7) community groups. This concept was introduced briefly in Chapter 3 in describing Bronfenbrenner's (1979) model of the mesosystem. The family is interconnected with other social systems that can expand its resources. Its contact with social groups must include the maintenance of goodwill and some evidence of group identification and commitment. Social groups also generate norms that may make demands on the family. Hence, adults must be able to protect the family from excessive external demands while retaining valuable and satisfying external relationships.

Most adults are not astute at recognizing how they are influenced by the institutions in which they participate. How do hiring practices at one's workplace influence the kinds of co-workers one is likely to meet? How do the voting patterns of the city or

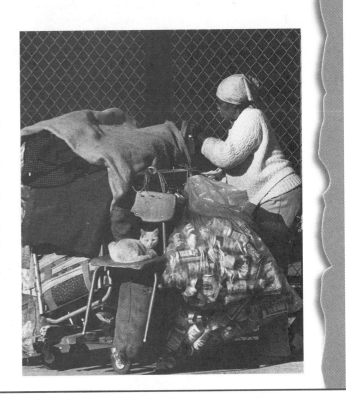

lives. These women commonly suffer from some degree of emotional dysfunction, possibly as a result of an earlier crisis, which is often exacerbated by the use of alcohol and drugs (Grigsby et al., 1990; Wright & Devine, 1993).

In homelessness, society confronts a painful example of psychosocial stagnation—the inability of mature adults to meet their basic needs for shelter, food, and clothing—combined with its own failure to prevent their condition from reaching this degree of vulnerability. In the face of the cultural value placed on independence, self-sufficiency, and hard work, U.S. society has difficulty making effective public responses. Policies and programs to assist homeless families have typically focused on short-term emergency intervention without a coordinated effort to address the complex needs, including living arrangements, employment, mental health services, drug or alcohol treatment, the building of a network of support, and gradual integration into a sense of community (Weinreb & Buckner, 1993).

Louise earns a bit of money by redeeming aluminum cans. Because of her cat, she cannot be admitted to a shelter, so she keeps her belongings close by in her cart and sleeps outdoors.

state one lives in influence how funds are allocated to schools, social welfare programs, or transportation resources that directly influence the quality of family life? These and other questions suggest that there are many possible contacts between organizational structures and one's ability to guide and control the household environment.

Families differ in their investment in relationships outside the family unit. In some households, the nuclear family is more important than any other group. Such households expend little energy outside the family boundaries. At the other extreme are families who are involved in a number of community groups and who incorporate their extended families into frequent group activities. In some families, each person is encouraged to establish a group of close friends. In others, each person's friends are screened or evaluated by the other family members. The adult's task is to define the family's preferred stance toward other social groups and to create opportunities to build desired relationships.

The family's relations with the **extended family** are a delicate matter. This is the realm of family politics. Courtesies, obligations, insults, and slights within the boundaries of family units are among the most stressful and challenging experiences with which most individuals have to deal. When children decide to marry, they bring two family networks together that may or may not get along. Parents may or may not convey support to their child's partner or spouse; sisters and brothers have partners who may or may not support each other. Likewise, parents may divorce and remarry, bringing one family system into contact with another. All these transitions introduce challenges in sustaining valued coalitions and protecting the family from disruptive forces (Whitbeck et al., 1994).

The value of the many tasks required to establish and maintain a supportive household environment is difficult to assess. However, in recent, high-profile divorce cases, corporate spouses expected to share equally the assets their partners had accumulated during the years of their marriage. In one case, Lorna Wendt wanted half the $100 million in assets she said her husband, Gary Wendt, the CEO of a major corporation, was worth. The court agreed to a $20 million settlement, half of Gary Wendt's "hard assets." The rationale for this type of settlement is based on the following ideas:

> A lot of work that's done in the home is invisible: cooking, cleaning, marketing, clerical work. Plus there's emotional work, which is particularly invisible—whether it's childrearing, dealing with problems at school, providing support to your spouse. . . . These corporate (spouses) perform other kinds of work which is more business-related. They move frequently, so there's the challenge of finding houses, buying new houses, fixing them up, settling children into new schools. They're also directly involved in the business in terms of entertaining, meeting clients, being a confidante, helping their (partners) make hiring decisions, knowing the business. (Cohn, 1998, p. 14.)

At present, the society's ability to recognize and value the accomplishments linked to management of the household are poorly developed. At the same time, more emphasis is being placed on the centrality of the home environment in fostering intellectual development, social competence, health, and emotional well-being.

One-Parent Families

In 1995, about 31% of all family groups with children under the age of 18 were one-parent families, 26% were headed by women and 5% were headed by men (U.S. Bureau of the Census, 1997). Among African-American families, the proportion of female-headed families with children under 18 rose from 31% in 1970 to 58% in 1995. Among white families, the proportion of one-parent families rose from 8% in 1970 to almost 21% in 1995. Among Hispanic families, about 31% were headed by a mother in 1995.

The greatest stress on the single mother is the lack of financial resources. In 1990, 44% of all families comprising single mothers and children had a family income below the poverty level (U.S. Bureau of the Census, 1992). Poverty in these families is a result of a number of factors: single mothers tend to have a lower earning capacity, they work fewer hours, and even when they receive some child support, they bear a substantial portion of their children's expenses.

In addition to stresses associated with poverty, single parents may suffer from social isolation, continuous pressure to meet the needs of their children, and experiencing overload in trying to combine work, parenting, and household decision-making without a partner (Alwin, 1984; Gongla & Thompson, 1987). Social isolation may result from the need to move to a new residence or to change jobs frequently. Multiple demands on a single parent's time may leave little opportunity for participation in the social network of the community. Single parents also worry that they place too many responsibilities on their children and that they cannot give their children the needed time and attention. Thus, role overload is often combined with emotional strain, which results in feelings of being chronically on the edge of crisis (McLanahan & Adams, 1987).

Kin support may be an important resource that buffers many single-parent families from the negative consequences of poverty and role overload. Data from the National Survey of Black Americans was used to better understand the nature of kin-based support for African-American mothers (Jayakody et al., 1993). Families in African-American communities benefit from the assistance provided by immediate and extended-family members. Much of this assistance is in the form of child care, financial help, and emotional support (McAdoo, 1980). In this particular study, special attention was given to differences in the nature of kin support for married, divorced or separated, widowed, and never-married mothers. The majority of these women lived close to their families—in the same city, neighborhood, or house—and interacted frequently with them. Over half of the never-married mothers said they interacted with family members nearly every day; most of the women said they felt close to their families.

The results of this study illustrate several important aspects of the challenges that face single African-American mothers. First, they appear to be embedded in close, satisfying networks of family relationships. Second, although expressions of satisfaction and closeness to family were high in this group, actual support to single mothers from their kin varied from 80% who received emotional support, to 25% who received financial support, and slightly less than 20% who received support in the form of child care. Third, patterns of kin support vary according to regional subcultural customs, the age and need of the mother, and the mother's proximity to her kin. Thus, the instrumental needs of single African-American mothers, especially financial and child-care needs, are not and probably cannot be met fully through their kin network.

How well can single mothers manage their parenting role in the face of their many role demands? Some studies emphasize the deficit perspective; for example, identifying factors that place children or adolescents from single-parent families at risk for antisocial behavior and delinquency (Bank et al., 1993). Other studies focus on adaptation and coping within the single-parent structure, addressing factors that help sustain a positive parent-child relationship (Simons et al., 1993). Retrospective studies show that many children who are identified as having psychological problems, especially temper tantrums, bullying, cheating, stealing, and fighting, are from divorced, single-mother families. However, prospective studies, those that look at child-rearing practices and subsequent child outcomes, show that poor parenting practices, especially emotional unavailability, ineffective discipline, minimal supervision, and a dominating, hostile style of interaction, produce these negative child outcomes in both single-parent and two-parent families (Patterson, 1992). Thus, while single-parent families face many additional problems, it is clearly inaccurate to label all of them "problem families."

In the African-American community, kin support goes across generations and reaches over wide geographic boundaries. Four generations of the Williams family come together to celebrate Natalie's birthday.

People Who Live Alone

In the discussion of household management, we have assumed that the household consists of two or more people whose lives are intertwined. Questions about decision-making, consensus, and shared responsibilities are all raised in the context of a group of people living together. However, in 1996, about 25 million people in the U. S. lived alone. These one-person households more frequently consist of men in the younger age groups (under 35) and women in the older age groups (55 and over) (U.S. Bureau of the Census, 1997). Single-person households include people who have never married, are divorced or separated, and are widowed. The reasons for living alone and the backgrounds for this life pattern vary considerably.

Little is known about the differences in psychosocial development between adults who live alone and those who live with others. Some of the aspects of household management, including organizing time, planning for the future, making decisions, and establishing relationships with other social groups, pose challenges to the person living alone. On the other hand, assigning responsibility and establishing a pattern for group decision making clearly are not required. People who live alone may not feel the need to engage in elaborate planning and evaluation when they are the only ones who will be immediately affected by their choices. Therefore, they may be freer to decide spontaneously as each opportunity presents itself.

Most people who live alone compensate for the few contacts they have within their household by maintaining a relatively large number of outside friends. They may spend less time overall in the company of others, but they are more deliberate in identifying confidants who can meet their social needs. Particularly in the area of establishing relationships with other social structures, the situation of living alone appears to promote social integration (Alwin et al., 1985).

In summary, the developmental task of household management draws upon many leadership skills in order to build a home environment that is comfortable, adaptive to changing demands, and responsive to the needs and goals of those who live together. The realm of the household is unique because it allows adults to perform with maximum flexibility, creativity, and adaptability in response to the daily needs and long-term goals of the household members.

THE PSYCHOSOCIAL CRISIS: GENERATIVITY VERSUS STAGNATION

Generativity   A new capacity for directing the course of action in one's own life and in the lives of others emerges during middle adulthood. The psychosocial crisis of **generativity** versus **stagnation** can be understood as a pressure on the adult to be committed to improving the life conditions of future generations (Erikson, 1963). "Generativity . . . encompasses *procreativity, productivity,* and *creativity,* and thus the generation of new beings, as well as of new products and new ideas, including a kind of self-generation concerned with further identity development" (Erikson, 1982, p. 67). According to Erikson's observations (Erikson et al., 1986), generativity is formed as a result of experiences of maintaining the world, nurturing and being concerned, and caring.

It is worth pausing to consider what it means to *generate.* A basic dictionary definition is "to bring into existence." Through generativity, adults may change the world by introducing new things, ideas, beings, or bonds of relationship—all of which had not existed before. Although Erikson emphasizes the salience of generativity in middle adulthood, it makes sense to view this critical capacity as emerging over the life course. Stewart and Vandewater (1998) suggest that generativity emerges through three phases: generative desire or motivation, a belief in one's capacity for generative action, and a subjective sense of generative accomplishment. In later adolescence and early adulthood, many individuals experience a desire to be generative, to have an impact on the world. This motive might be expressed in a person's goals. For example, young people who want to promote better interracial understanding or to improve the educational experiences of young children might be said to have generative motives. Next, one begins to realize opportunities for generative action and a growing confidence in one's capacity to have an impact. Generativity may be expressed through a wide variety of actions including procreation, parenting, invention, teaching, expanding the knowledge base, improving the physical or social environment, and artistic creation (Kotre, 1998). Generativity may be expressed by making a success of a remarriage involving children who have been neglected in their early childhood. It may also mean innovating in the workplace; in the scientist's lab; in poetry, art, music, or literature; or in creating some splendid form of recreation like a theme park or a refreshing new food like frozen yogurt. Finally, in looking back on one's life, one can assess these actions and make a judgment about whether one's generative aspirations or motives have been realized.

Generativity is critical to the survival of any society. At some point, adult members of the society must begin to feel an obligation to contribute their resources, skills, and creativity to improving the quality of life for the young. To some degree, this motive is aroused as one recognizes the inevitability of mortality—one will not be around forever to direct the course of events. Therefore, one must make contributions to the society, on both personal and public levels, that will stand some chance of continuing after one's death.

Measuring Generativity

The importance of generativity for understanding the positive, prosocial aspects of adult behavior has led to efforts to create measures of it for adult populations. The meaning of generativity is being clarified and elaborated through attempts to operationalize it. One line of research provided a cross-sectional comparison of dimensions of generativity among subjects in early (22–27), middle (37–42), and later (67–72) adulthood (McAdams et al., 1993). Four aspects of generativity were measured: generative concern, a sense that one is making a difference in the lives of others; generative commitments, personal strivings or goals that have a generative nature; generative actions, a checklist of actions that the person has performed in the past two months that involved creating, maintaining, or offering; and generative narratives, autobiographical recollections coded for generative meaning.

Across all age groups, generative concern was significantly correlated with happiness and life satisfaction. When all four measures of generativity were combined, the middle adults scored higher than the young or older age groups. The measures of generative commitment and generative narration were higher for the middle adult group. The pattern of responses showed significant differences between the middle adult and

Volunteering one's time to share knowlege and skills with young children is clearly an expression of caring. How might generativity and volunteering be related?

the younger adult groups, but the middle adults and the older adults were not significantly different. The implication is that once the generative orientation emerges, it appears to endure in the life goals and activities of a person into later adulthood. A similar example is found in the psychosocial crisis of identity. Once the identity orientation emerges, it, too, appears to endure as a recurring theme to be revised and reworked in later stages.

Peterson and Stewart (1993) measured generativity by scoring the following themes in narrative writing samples: productivity, caring, and general generativity. *Productivity* focuses on "developing or growing through the generation of tangible products or ideas. . . . Feelings of stagnation are also scored . . . whenever a person mentions frustration at not being able to contribute something tangible to society." *Caring* involves all expressions of caring for, taking care of, and doing something for, as well as taking care not to do any thing harmful. *General generativity* is a global expression "about making a lasting contribution, especially to future generations." Peterson and Stewart's sample was made up primarily of people in the stage of early adulthood. Their findings confirm Erikson's prediction that there are foreshadowings of psychosocial themes in earlier life stages. Peterson and Stewart found that expressions of generativity were especially notable among young adults who had become parents.

The theme of generativity versus stagnation permeates the psychological dynamics of adult life. In the following section, we discuss the negative pole, stagnation, and its expression in narcissistic self-preoccupation and depression. Since the mid-1980s, the severity of problems related to depression in adulthood have been documented, and several different patterns have been described. Although much is written about the negative side of adult life, including people who commit crimes or betray their families, it is important to recognize that the positive forces of generativity are equally dominant in guiding the lives of most adults and that they produce acts of creative leadership and caring.

Stagnation

Stagnation suggests a lack of psychological movement or growth. Adults who devote their energy and skills to the sole end of self-aggrandizement and personal satisfaction are likely to have difficulty looking beyond their own needs or experiencing satisfaction in taking care of others. Those unable to cope with managing a household, raising children, or managing their career are likely to feel psychological stagnation at the end of middle adulthood.

The experience of stagnation may differ for the narcissistic adult and the depressed adult. *Narcissistic people* are self-absorbed. They expend energy accumulating wealth and material possessions. They relate to others in terms of how people can serve them. Narcissistic people can exist quite happily until the physical and psychological consequences of aging begin to make their impact. At that point, and continuing toward old age, self-satisfaction is easily undermined by anxieties related to death. It is not uncommon for such persons to undergo some form of religious or humanitarian "conversion" after a serious illness or an emotional crisis forces them to acknowledge the limitations of a totally self-involved lifestyle.

Chronically depressed people do not feel a sense of accomplishment during middle adulthood—they think of themselves as worthless. They are unable to perceive themselves as having sufficient resources to make any contribution to their society. These people are likely to have low self-esteem, doubt opportunities for future improvement, and are therefore unwilling to invest energy in conceptualizing future progress.

One of the most commonly noted sources of stagnation in middle adulthood is role stagnation associated with employment. People who have been in their job a long time may be threatened by younger workers, stuck in a routine, or passed over for recognition and leadership. Rather than taking up the challenge to mentor new employees or to invent new approaches to their work, they become resentful, avoidant, and withdrawn, and may develop physical or emotional symptoms associated with the stress of their frustration (Raskas & Hambrick, 1992; Yerushalmi, 1993).

In an analysis of men at midlife, Farrell and Rosenberg (1981) provided some insight into stagnation. The case of Tony Williams illustrates how a life of unresolved stresses and disappointments coupled with a defensive denial results in a picture of increasing bankruptcy of personal and interpersonal meaning:

> A number of midlife stresses have hit Tony in the past five years. They began with the death of his mother when Tony was 40. Tony tells of the death with the same apparent stoicism he showed throughout the evening. "When your time is up, you gotta go," he says. But he says that his father went into a prolonged depression, moping around watching television, having no energy for family activities.
>
> Then two friends from childhood died within a year. Tony says, "Better them than me." He doesn't seem to overtly mourn their loss, but he does appear to exaggerate his fatalistic willingness to accept fate as he reports on this period, insisting that he does not fear death.
>
> Over the years Tony had become active in the Knights of Columbus. He helped organize an annual Christmas party for retarded children, and told of how good it felt to stand by as the kids came up to sit on Santa's knee and receive their gifts. But during the past few years he has pulled away from this activity, claiming that younger men coming in are "messing up" what he helped to build. His final break with them came last year, when he ruptured a disc in his back while lifting a heavy barrel at work. He had to spend three weeks in the hospital and none of his friends came to visit him.
>
> This back injury marked a sharp turning point, evoking all the bitterness and depressive symptomatology kept in check after earlier life reversals and his mother's death. His medical treatment required that he stay home a month after returning from the hospital, but that was seven months ago. Tony's doctor tells him he is fine, but Tony has not returned to work because he ostensibly is trying to obtain workman's compensation for the injury and lost work time. His lawyer is still working on the case, and Tony fears that if he goes back to work he'll lose his case. So he stays at home, takes occasional walks, listens to police calls on a police radio, and watches television. His children have grown increasingly annoyed with him. "All he does is pick," says Mary. "He won't let Mom sit down to do a crossword puzzle. He won't let me sew because it interferes with his radio. And if you stay around the house, he starts reading stories out of the newspaper to you. So me and my brother, we leave the house."

Middle adulthood extends over many years. During this stage, people encounter many complex challenges for which they may not be fully prepared. Promotion to an administrative position, the need to care for an aging parent, and the negotiation of a divorce are examples. Brim (1992) argues that both success and failure bring people face to face with redefining and reexamining their goals. At many points, adults doubt their ability to move ahead, achieve their goals, or make meaningful contributions. Feelings of stagnation surge temporarily. People may recognize that unless they redefine their situation or take some new risks, the quality of their lives will deteriorate. They face the possibility of feeling outdated by new technology, outmoded by new lifestyles, overburdened by role demands, or alienated from meaningful social contacts. At these moments of crisis, adults may become entangled in a process of self-protection and withdrawal that results in permanent stagnation. However, they may also be able to muster new resources and see things from a new perspective that will permit continuing growth and the expansion of generativity.

THE CENTRAL PROCESS: PERSON-ENVIRONMENT INTERACTION AND CREATIVITY

Two aspects of the central process that lead to the development of generativity in middle adulthood are person-environment interaction and creativity. The first is the facilitative interaction between the individual and the social environment, which includes the family, work setting, neighborhood, and larger political community. To a great extent, this environment provides a person's basis of experience. Day-to-day interactions, the expectations for behavior, the available resources, and the social supports that are necessary to the growth of self-confidence are elements of the social environment.

Person-Environment Interaction

Successful personality growth depends on the interaction between a person's needs, skills, and interpersonal style and the demands of the environments in which he or she is embedded. The concept of interaction suggests a potential for reciprocal influence between individuals and settings. Consequently, the structure and demands of settings may alter a person's behavior, values, goals, and sense of self-worth. However, people also have an impact on the settings in which they participate. Adults do more than maintain or respond to their environments, they shape it (Endler, 1983). People play roles to express their individual styles. They define their roles for themselves as well as having their roles defined by others. For instance, parents as well as office workers live within structures of expectations. In their own ways of interpreting, denying, or otherwise responding to these expectations, adults present an increasingly independent and authentic "me" if they are moving toward the stabilization of ego identity. If not, they may be more responsive to the expectations of others than is healthy for the continued emergence of a stable identity.

Most people have some degree of choice about their social environment. They can, for example, decide whom they will marry, whether or not to have children, which occupation they will follow, and where they will live. To the degree that they have a choice in these matters, they are able to influence the kinds of transactions that occur between their personality and their social milieu. Making good decisions about social settings requires that they understand themselves, the nature of other people, and the social institutions that are part of their social environment.

Many people have trouble conceptualizing how they are shaped by the demands of their social settings. This kind of analysis requires a complex understanding of social settings and some idea of the types of demands that such environments are likely to make. It also requires the ability to speculate about how things may change in the future. For instance, it is one thing to fall in love with someone and decide to marry. It is quite another to try to foresee what it would be like to live with that person for 20 or more years.

Although participation in some settings is a matter of choice, many others are the result of chance. Some settings can be abandoned or altered if they do not meet the individual's need; other settings are permanent and difficult to alter. If one is in an unsuitable setting, one must be willing to leave it if possible or discover a way to influence it so that it meets one's needs more adequately. Some people, however, find themselves in social settings that can be neither abandoned nor altered. For example, a group of workers in Michigan were trained for employment in an automotive plant. When the economy slumped, they were laid off. These workers did not have enough money saved to move to another town, there were no new jobs, and they did not have the resources or the incentive to retrain for other types of employment. When one is forced to remain in social settings that are contrary to one's needs, the possibility of developing generativity is seriously diminished. Further, if one is unable to experience a personal sense of effectiveness at home, at work, or in the community, then one is unlikely to feel capable of contributing to future growth in these spheres.

Fortunately, the social environment is so multifaceted that individuals are likely to experience satisfaction in their participation in at least one setting even if they are dissatisfied in others. Under these conditions, individuals can compensate for their inability to be creative in some settings by placing increased effort and investment in those in which they can more easily attain satisfaction. This may require that individuals reorder their priorities. If there is little opportunity to find satisfaction in work, for example, one must begin to reevaluate the importance of contributions to one's family, religion, or community.

Creativity

The second part of the central process in the establishment of generativity is personal creativity. Although **creativity** has been defined in many ways, for our purposes we will consider it the willingness to abandon old forms or patterns of doing things in favor of new ways. This requires the generation, evaluation, and implementation of new ideas. Within this definition, one can include creative acts that touch the lives of many people as well as individual acts that touch the lives of a few. The importance of a creative response, no matter how small, is that it redefines the world and opens the door to new possibilities (Taylor, 1975; Arieti, 1976). Creativity provides an outlet for caring for something that has not yet been defined or experienced.

Through creative effort, adults impose a new perspective on the organization, expression, or formulation of ideas. Creative adults are not dominated by social forces

Creativity brings a new way of seeing and understanding the familiar. Picasso, whose life was an outpouring of creativity, shows us the human form in an impossible but completely harmonious arrangement.

but are able to direct the course of events themselves. They are at a point in their development at which their own creative responses can become a source of influence on others. Through the process of creative problem solving, adults may help reshape the social environment in order to meet both personal and social needs more satisfactorily. Throughout middle adulthood, adults are faced with situations in family, child-rearing, and work settings that provide stimuli for creative problem solving. In their efforts to take into account the requirements of the social setting and to be productive in it, people must develop creative plans. They must also attempt to carry out those plans, a task that itself may require further creativity. The essence of creative problem solving is the formulation of a new plan and the ability to translate it into reality.

Fostering creativity during middle adulthood requires deliberate attention. Given one's embeddedness in many demanding social roles, it is often difficult to step aside and view one's situation from a fresh perspective. Arieti (1976) recommended nine conditions that foster creativity, which are listed in Table 12.3. This list reveals the need to engage in somewhat opposing processes, such as inactivity and alertness. One must strive to be open to the flood of inner and outer experiences and to step away from trying to maintain control over all aspects of the environment. At the same time,

TABLE 12.3	Conditions that Foster Creativity
Aloneness	Being alone allows the person to make contact with the self and to be open to new kinds of inspiration.
Inactivity	Periods of time are needed to focus on inner resources and to be removed from the constraints of routine activities.
Daydreaming	Allows exploration of one's fantasy life and venturing into new avenues of growth.
Free thinking	Allows the mind to wander in any direction without restriction and permits the similarities among remote topics or concepts to emerge.
State of readiness to catch similarities	One must practice recognizing similarities and resemblances across perceptual or cognitive domains.
Gullibility	A willingness to suspend judgment allows one to be open to possibilities without treating them as nonsense.
Remembering and replaying past traumatic conflicts	Conflict may be transformed into more stable creative products.
Alertness	A state of awareness that permits the person to grasp the relevance of seemingly insignificant similarities.
Discipline	A devotion to the techniques, logic, and repetition that permit creative ideas to be realized.

Source: Based on Arieti, 1976.

one must be alert to insights into the relevance of certain experiences and willing to transform them into action.

From the outset, the creative process involves frustrations and risk. In order to try new things, people must give up some old, reliable ways of doing things. In this process, people must anticipate the possibility that their efforts will fail. They may flounder for a seemingly long period, unable to identify the solution that will allow for forward movement. For some, the anxiety associated with prolonged uncertainty and possible failure may be so great that creative solutions are never realized (Sapp, 1992). Their sense of generativity is blocked by a fear of the unknown or by an inability to violate conventional norms of behavior.

For those who are not inhibited by the fear of failure, the repeated efforts to generate creative solutions eventually result in the formulation of a philosophy of life. This philosophy incorporates the psychological needs of people, the ideals toward which individuals and groups strive, and the impact of social settings on the functioning of individuals, as well as the direction of human development into the future. Through risk taking, occasional failure, and a predominance of successful creative efforts, adults achieve a sense of what they believe in and what gives meaning to life. With this remarkable integration of experience and information, people enter later adulthood.

There is an old story about three men who were observed laying bricks for the wall of a church. When asked what they were doing, the first man said he was laying bricks, the second said he was building a wall, and the third said he was building a church. During middle adulthood, one must arrive at a philosophy of life that will impart significance to daily activities. One part of generativity lies in the actual attainment of creative goals. The other part lies in the perspective one brings to one's lifework.

Erikson suggested that the outcome of the crisis of generativity versus stagnation has implications for adults at the next life stage in the form of **grand-generativity**:

> The reconciling of generativity and stagnation involves the elder in expressing a "grand-generativity" that is somehow beyond middle age's direct responsibility for maintaining the world. The roles of aging parent, grandparent, old friend, consultant, adviser, and mentor all provide the aging adult with essential social opportunities to experience grand-generativity in current relationships with people of all ages. In these relationships, the individual seeks to integrate outward-looking care for others with inward-looking concern for self. As a complement to caring for others, the elder is also challenged to accept from others that caring which is required, and to do so in a way that is itself caring. In the context of the generational cycle, it is incumbent upon the aged to enhance feelings of generativity in their caregivers from the younger generations. (Erikson et al., 1986, pp. 74–75)

THE PRIME ADAPTIVE EGO QUALITY AND THE CORE PATHOLOGY

Care The ego strength associated with the achievement of generativity is **care.**

> Care, is a widening commitment *to take care of* the persons, the products, and the ideas one has learned *to care for.* All the strengths arising from earlier developments in the ascending order from infancy to young adulthood (hope and will, purpose and skill, fidelity and love) now prove, on closer study, to be essential to the generative task of cultivating strength in the next generation, for this is indeed the "store" of human life. (Erikson, 1982, p. 67)

The psychosocial achievement of middle adulthood is to identify the domains in which one has opportunities to influence the quality of the social environment so that it becomes more hospitable, humane, nurturant, or supportive of one's own visions for the future. Caring expands in different domains for different people, but always leads to having the welfare of people and enduring things (including ideas) deeply at heart. There is an action component to caring, in that people work to care for what they can. As the crisis of generativity versus stagnation is resolved in a positive direction, adults find new energy and innovative ways to express their capacity for care.

Rejectivity Caring strongly for certain people, products, and ideas can cause people to reject any person or group that appears to threaten them. **Rejectivity** refers to an unwillingness to embrace certain individuals, groups, or ideas in one's circle of care, and, at an extreme level, to view these threats as appropriate targets for hostility, even annihilation. Ironically, one may exhibit great courage and dedication to protect the objects of one's care by directing intense aggression toward those one rejects.

Erikson (1982) refers to this process as "pseudospeciation," through which one defines another group as different, dangerous, and potentially less human than one's own. Under the rubric of pseudospeciation, family members can become scapegoats, neighboring communities can establish intense rivalries, racial or religious groups can terrorize others, and regions or countries can go to war. Thus, rejectivity goes beyond an intellectual selectivity of certain ideas and groups as more central to one's identity than others, taking on an aggressive energy, drawn from the power and authority of one's status in middle adulthood. The risk of rejectivity for the society is that certain groups will become so powerful that they can cause the extermination or domination of other groups. As each subgroup falls out of the circle of caring, the society as a whole reaches a new level of stagnation.

Applied Topic ## DISCRIMINATION IN THE WORKPLACE

> "The U.S.A. is just a horrible place to try to raise a family and have a career. . . . When I was working in the U.S.A., it was a struggle to find decent day care . . . and if I missed a half-day of work [because] my kid had a temperature of 104, I was lectured on how this let down the [department]. In Israel there is 3 months paid maternity leave, day-care centers on every block, and if you *don't* take off from work for your kid's birthday party the department chairman will lecture you on how important these things are to kids and how he never missed one while his kids were little." (Astrophysicist Sara Beck, currently a tenured professor at Tel Aviv University, quoted in Barinaga, 1994, p. 1472)

> "A big-city police officer once shared with me his frustration at waiting nineteen years to make detective. In those days before affirmative action, he had watched, one year after another, as less qualified whites were promoted over him. Each year he had swallowed his disappointment, twisted his face into a smile, and congratulated his white friends as he hid his rage—so determined was he to avoid being categorized as a race-obsessed troublemaker. . . . Even though he made detective years ago, and even though, on the side (and on his own time), he managed to become a successful businessman and an exemplary member of the upwardly striving middle class, he says the anger still simmers within him. He worries that someday it will come pouring out, that some luckless white person will tick him off and he will explode, with tragic results." (quoted in Cose, 1993, p. 61)

The United States has been characterized as an "achieving society." As a cultural group, we value individual achievement, usually expressed through accomplishments in the world of work. Thus, in the United States, for men and increasingly for women, the mark of successful adulthood is frequently equated with success in the labor market, which is typically attributed to personal characteristics of ability, intelligence, and motivation. Conversely, a lack of success in the labor market is attributed to deficiencies in personal characteristics: lack of ability, low intelligence, and poor motivation. Individuals are unlikely to attribute their successes to conditions of the workplace, vagaries in the economy, luck, or conditions of society that give them a special advantage and others an unfair disadvantage. Yet, many Americans face serious and persistent disadvantages in the workplace that are linked to being different from the white, male, Protestant, middle-class norm (Jones, 1988).

In the past, women and minority workers in the U.S. have been restricted to low-paying jobs in the agricultural, service, or factory sectors. In 1964, the Civil Rights Act made it illegal to refuse to hire a person or discriminate in compensation, firing practices, or any other employment benefits based on race, color, religion, sex, or national origin. This act made the practice of restricting access to employment opportunities illegal and opened up many arenas for professional development that had previously been denied (Hodson & Sullivan, 1995). Nonetheless, barriers to full involvement of women and minorities in the labor market continue.

The continuation of discrimination in the workplace is an exceedingly costly problem for the society as a whole. Discriminatory practices that lead to the disaffection of individuals from the world of work is costly in economic terms—in lower levels of productivity, high turnover, high levels of irritability and conflict among workers, lawsuits, and less identification with the company and its goals. It is costly in personal terms as well. Feelings of frustration about not being recognized for one's competence or being passed over for promotion by less competent workers interfere with the development of a generative orientation. These experiences may lead to a more self-serving orientation, focusing exclusively on "protecting me and mine," or to a pervasive sense of futility about the future.

Disparities in Income and the Occupational Structure

In 1994, the median income of year-round, full-time workers was $23,894 for white females and $32,440 for white males; $20,628 for African-American females and $24,405 for African-American males; and $18,418 for Hispanic females and $20,525 for Hispanic males. Females with bachelor's degrees had monthly salaries that were 53% of those of men with the same degrees. In 1994, 14.5% of the population had incomes below the poverty level—12% of whites, 31% of African-Americans, and 31% of Hispanics. Unemployment patterns showed that African-Americans were twice as likely as whites to be unemployed (U.S. Bureau of the Census, 1996).

One explanation for racial, ethnic, and gender differences in salary, rates of poverty, and rates of unemployment is that workers from different groups are distributed unevenly in the occupational structure. Jobs continue to be gender-stereotyped, with women being socialized and encouraged to work in vocations that involve helping and serving others. For example, women comprised 46% of those employed in 1996. However, they made up 64% of those working in technical, sales, and administrative support, and 60% of those in service occupations such as child care, food preparation, and service. Similarly, women comprise a small segment of the skilled trades where strong unions can protect salary scale and benefits. In the federal civil service sector women comprise roughly 75% of those in the lowest grades, earning $10,000 to $24,000, and only 9% of the jobs at the highest grades, earning $70,000 to $80,000.

Group differences in occupational position resulting in different salary structures and risks of layoffs are not necessarily evidence of discrimination. Discrimination exists when two people doing the same job are paid substantially different wages. It occurs when factors other than merit prevent a person from being hired, promoted, or rewarded through various forms of compensation or increase a person's risk of being fired. Specifically, discrimination occurs when a person is evaluated on the basis of group membership rather than individual performance. In the workplace, this process operates as an in-group—out-group dynamic in which members of the in-group view members of the out-group as deficient and, at some level, possibly threatening to their continued success and well-being.

How Discrimination Perpetuates Itself

Employers, supervisors, and others in positions of power typically establish a normative profile for their employees and judge each new one against it. This profile may include deeply held beliefs and values on the part of men about women. Men may wonder whether women can perform the same kinds of jobs, and effectively assume responsibility to supervise men, whether clients will place their trust in women executives, or whether women will be dedicated to their work when conflicts between work and family arise. In the same vein, this profile may include deeply held beliefs and values on the part of whites about nonwhites, especially beliefs that they are superior to nonwhites in ability and that the cultural characteristics of nonwhites will be disruptive or damaging to productivity in the workplace (Jones, 1988). In addition, because of the historical and continued separation of neighborhoods, schools, and churches on the basis of race, few white adults have firsthand, personal relationships with persons of color. Decisions about promotions or assignments to positions of increased responsibility are often made in situations where senior employees, mostly white, choose other white candidates with whom they feel more comfortable.

Consider the following situation. At Monsanto, the chemical company based in St. Louis, in 1990 an aggressive recruitment effort resulted in 17% minority nonunion new hires and 21% female nonunion new hires. The company was serious about increasing the presence of minorities and women in its chemical subsidiaries and had taken efforts to do so since the 1970s. However, in 1990, of those who quit the company voluntarily, 26% were women and 20% were minorities. Through the use of exit interviews, the company discovered the following important discriminatory aspects of the work environment:

> Fully 100% of the minorities who had left said they wanted more job responsibility and that they had experienced difficulty in dealing with their supervisors. Also, 30% more departed minorities than whites felt that Monsanto needs to give employees more help in adjusting to their jobs. Furthermore, they felt treatment by their bosses seemed arbitrary and unfair. . . . Twenty percent more women than men said they were treated unfairly concerning pay and promotion decisions. And of the 40% of the women who had new jobs, a huge 70% said their new employers offered greater opportunities for career advancement. (Ellis, 1991, pp. 60–61)

In many work settings, a small group of white men make the major decisions. Since women and minorities are not present, their points of view are not represented, and potentially stereotyped beliefs are never challenged.

Psychosocial Analysis: Discrimination and Coping

In general, in discussing psychosocial development, one examines the outcome for the individual in achieving a positive resolution of the psychosocial crisis. But when considering discrimination in the workplace, one must also look at the consequences for a society. Discrimination in the workplace is one expression of societal stagnation. It is a defensive posture in which those in power try to protect their status, profits, and power by preventing members of less powerful groups from gaining a foothold. Rather than treating diversity as a factor that can improve the overall flexibility and resources of the work setting, discrimination operates to reduce it. Over time, the fate of individuals who have been discriminated against becomes a great cost to the society at large. Some give up and become chronically unemployed or underemployed, resulting in a loss of human capital. Others remain in a discriminatory workplace, trying to "get by," not making trouble, and yet operating behind a veil of caution. African-American middle-class adults tell the same stories repeatedly about how much effort and energy they spend trying to help white people feel comfortable with them (Whitaker, 1993). Over time, this expenditure is both exhausting and deeply frustrating. One outcome of the various forms of discrimination is the development of an unspoken resentment of work that may be communicated in some form to their children, thus transmitting a cross-generational, cynical outlook on work.

However, the history of the U.S. is also filled with many tales of individuals who succeed against the odds. These adults recognize the risks of staying in a setting that does not fit well with their healthy desire to create, produce, and care. They may strike out on their own by setting up their own companies, they may challenge unfair practices through the courts, and they may mentor younger workers to help them cope with the conflicts they face in the workplace. The responsibility for coping with discrimination does not rest entirely on the victims. There are also examples of work settings that have taken active steps to challenge their own practices. Companies have been cited for their policies to support the hiring and promotion of women into senior positions, and for their innovations in weaving new levels of understanding about diversity into all aspects of employee development (Konrad, 1990; Gleckman et al., 1991).

The future of the American work force of the 21st century is already upon us. Women and ethnic minorities are the fastest-growing groups of new employees. By the year 2000, racial and ethnic minorities are expected to comprise one-third of the school-age children (American Council on Education, 1988). Their preparation for and participation in the labor market will be a determining factor in the quality and productivity of the U.S. economy in the 21st century. The psychosocial approach, which highlights the interdependence of the individual and the society, is most dramatically illustrated in the connection between contemporary workplace policies and practices and their implications for the maturation of a sense of industry among school-age children.

Chapter Summary

During the middle adult years, people have an opportunity to make significant contributions to their culture. Through work, home, and child-rearing, people express their own value orientations, moral codes, personalities, and talents. They grow more sensitive to the multiple needs of those around them and more skillful in influencing the social environment.

The developmental tasks of middle adulthood are extremely complex and require long-term persistence. During middle adulthood, people gauge their self-worth largely in relation to their contributions to complex social units, especially work, family, and community. Each task calls for a new level of conceptualization of the interaction of the self with immediate and more remote social systems and an increased ability to balance one's individual needs with system goals. Nurturing, managing, caring, and the attainment of new levels of skill are fostered as one engages in the primary tasks of middle adulthood. These competencies provide a foundation for establishing the emotional and social support for oneself and others that is central to collaborative efforts in the workplace, mentoring younger workers, maintaining and expanding intimate relationships, and preserving optimal functioning for older adults. The well-being of the community as a whole rests largely on the effectiveness of people in middle adulthood in reaching new levels of psychosocial maturity.

The psychosocial crisis of the middle adult years is really a moral crisis of commitment to a better way of life. The society must encourage adults to care for others besides themselves. The egocentrism of toddlerhood, early school age, and adolescence must eventually come to an end if the social group is to survive. In the same way that intimacy (giving oneself to another) requires identity, generativity (giving oneself to the next generation) requires love of specific others. The interpersonal sources of satisfaction that exist during middle adulthood are the primary forces propelling people toward a generative approach to society as a whole.

In the applied topic of discrimination in the workplace, there is evidence of societal stagnation. Often it is middle adults in leadership positions who, by deliberate practice or informal example, set a tone that promotes the exclusion of certain workers on the basis of age, gender, racial or ethnic group, or other group characteristics. At the same time, others in middle adulthood suffer from discriminatory policies and are unable to reach the levels of achievement and contribution that their talents merit. Social policies and practices that interfere with a person's ability to perform meaningful work, or to achieve recognition and respect for their work, pose a hazard to individual psychosocial development and to the future of the social group. These practices, born from the core pathology of rejectivity, act in opposition to the fundamental needs of a society to care about its members and foster the most optimistic ambitions and goals possible in younger generations.

End of Chapter Case

Joseph, an athletic, active adult has been married to his wife, Connie, for 40 years. His daughter, Patricia, who graduated from college with a degree in nursing, is a senior administrator for a state health agency. Joseph reflects on Patricia, and his role in her development.

"Oh, looking back, I guess what I wanted most for her, physically, was to have a good leg (laughs).* Otherwise, to be what she is today—happy doing her thing. My main goal for her was for her to be *happy,* to do her own thing.

I think she did well, this far. She saw something that she wanted to do, and she's doing it. She has her own head screwed on right. She's a self-made, motivated person.

I wouldn't have chosen that she become a nurse. But there's nothing wrong with it. If that's what they want, go to it.

I encouraged her to be the registrar of the board of nursing. "Keep your finger in with all the medical changes and everything." Which she has. She writes the books now. People have the exams and so forth, while she just looks them over and approves them. I probably encouraged her to take this job because it would be easier for her, physically. Lifting people up on a bed, rolling over, it's tough. She's only what? A hundred pounds?

She's a politician. I influenced her there. I was involved in politics myself, and she saw that. Actually she's a better politician than me, I would say. She learned very well.

Once she sets her mind on something, a goal or an objective, she goes after it. I'd say that I've

done that many times myself. That was probably one of the traits that she picked up from me. You know, save for tomorrow, maybe, more than, say, the other children but, as I said before, every one of them is different. And I would say that Pat plans probably more for the future, probably appreciates the things she has. She enjoys the good life, too, you know.

I place a lot of value on happiness. I tried to see that my children were happy. If they're happy, that's the important thing. You can't buy happiness; you have to make it, despite the inevitable ups and downs. Like I tried to tell them, you never win. You may think you win, but it is never over.

I still would say that it is important to always be available. I'm available, for whatever they want. Whether it be support or money or whatever. Even now, even though they don't need anything like financial support anymore, I am here and Connie's here, and we just try to make a family that they can rely on when they want and need it."

Source: Snarey, J., 1993.

Thought Questions

1. How is the idea of generativity reflected in this case?
2. What are Joseph's parenting values? How might they be expressed in action?
3. What conflicts do Joseph's remarks suggest about his own self-concept and his father role?
4. What do you think might be Patricia's view of her father? How might Joseph's enactment of the father role have influenced Patricia's development in work and family?
5. How might Joseph's role as a father have influenced his roles as worker and spouse?

* Patricia suffered from pseudoarthrosis at the age of five. Her leg curved in, she had to wear a special brace, and when her leg broke, she had to go through a long period of treatments.

Chapter 13

The integrating theme of later adulthood is a search for personal meaning. The old man gently cradling a sheep reflects Picasso's preoccupation with the search for peace in the trouble-torn years of his later adulthood.

Later Adulthood (60–75 Years)

Chapter Objectives

- To describe factors that promote intellectual vigor during later adulthood with a focus on the areas of cognitive functioning that have been studied including productivity in the workplace, memory, Piagetian-type tasks, and practical problem solving.
- To examine the process of redirecting energy to new roles and activities with special focus on role gain, such as grandparenthood; role loss, such as widowhood; and new opportunities for leisure.
- To explore the construct of life satisfaction in later adulthood and factors associated with subjective well-being.
- To describe the development of a point of view about death as a major psychological task of later adulthood.
- To explain the psychosocial crisis of integrity versus despair, the central process of introspection, the prime adaptive ego quality of wisdom, and the core pathology of disdain.
- To apply theory and research to understanding the process of adjustment to retirement in later adulthood.

In this chapter and Chapter 14, we consider the challenges, changes, and new avenues for development in later life. Psychosocial theory assumes that new opportunities for growth emerge at each life stage. In strong contrast to the stereotype of aging as an undesirable process associated with accumulated deficits and decline, these chapters highlight continuous coping and adaptation. Like each of the preceding stages, later adulthood is marked by stressors, risks, and forces that can disrupt growth. However, the epigenetic principle implies that one cannot understand the full unfolding of human life without appreciating the beliefs, practices, and social relationships of those in later adulthood and old age. What is more, the interdependence of the stages in a human life story suggests that the ways that older adults function and are treated will have immediate impact on the psychosocial development of individuals in all the earlier periods of life. The courage and vitality of older adults are sources of inspiration that motivate children and younger adults to continue facing the challenges of their daily lives with optimism.

The integrating theme of later adulthood is a search for personal meaning. On entering this stage, adults begin to assert the competence and creativity attained during middle adulthood. As life progresses, motivation for achievement and power may give way to a desire for understanding, reminiscent of the toddler's need to know why and the

later adolescent's need to challenge and experiment with life roles. The individual continues to be confronted with essential problems of definition and explanation during later adulthood. At this stage, adults apply the wealth of their life course experiences, perspective on time, and adaptation to life crises to a personally satisfying answer to the question of life's meaning.

Physical, social, and intellectual development are intricately interrelated during later life. The more research that is carried out on aspects of aging, the greater the appreciation for the sense that patterns of aging are neither universal nor irreversible. For example, although many older adults become more sedentary and lose aerobic capacity, there are societies in which older adults continue to perform strenuous labor and remain free from heart disease and respiratory difficulties. Many life conditions, especially poverty, malnutrition, poor sanitation, and limited health care, can advance the aging process. On the other hand, access to a stimulating social environment, program of physical activity, and well-balanced diet can increase physical and intellectual functioning (Rowe & Kahn, 1998). Due to the extremes in intellectual competence, social involvement, and independence that differentiate healthy older people from those who are seriously ill, it is essential to keep in mind individual differences in physical and mental health when thinking about patterns of growth in later adulthood. ❖

DEVELOPMENTAL TASKS

The life histories of older adults are enormously varied. Depending on life experiences, health, resources, education, family support, and cultural and religious orientation, later adulthood is perceived and enacted differently by each person. The idea of developmental tasks that reflect similar themes for all older adults is bound to miss the vivid and complex reality of each person's experiences. Nevertheless, the tasks discussed here reflect major themes that are likely to be confronted in the later years. These themes suggest new barriers to adaptation as well as new opportunities. Changes in memory and speed of neural processing may make the accomplishment of daily tasks a greater challenge. Role loss and the death of loved ones introduce needs for new kinds of support and changes in daily lifestyle. They also convey a concrete message that a transition to a new period of the life span is under way.

Promoting Intellectual Vigor

Memory, reasoning, information processing, problem-solving abilities, and mental rigidity or fluidity all influence the adult's capacity to introspect, assess his or her personal past history, and plan for the future. These intellectual capacities also influence the adult's ability to remain involved in productive work, advise and guide others, and invent new solutions to the problems of daily life. How can one understand cognitive functioning and change in later life? The study of intelligence and cognition in later adulthood is plagued by practical and theoretical challenges that make it difficult to make broad generalizations. In the following sections, we review some of the problems associated with the study of intelligence and aging. Specific issues are then discussed, including productivity in the workplace as evidence of intellectual capacity, memory, the ability to solve Piagetian tasks, and practical problem solving. This discussion ends with an overview of changes in various mental abilities. The focus then shifts to an analysis of the impact of heredity and environment on intelligence, and factors that help to sustain high levels of intellectual functioning in later life.

Problems in Defining and Studying Intelligence in Later Adulthood

Four problems are raised in evaluating the research on intelligence in later life (Stuart-Hamilton, 1996). First, one must differentiate between age differences and age changes. Let us say that in a cross-sectional study conducted in 1996, 70-year-olds performed less well than 40-year-olds. The difference may be clear, but it may not be a result of age alone. The 70-year-olds would have been born in the 1920s, and the 40-year-olds in the 1950s. Differences in performance may well be a product of different educational opportunities, varying experiences with standardized tests, or other **cohort** factors. For example, only 9% of those aged 65–74 in 1996 had completed a bachelor's degree; whereas twice as many adults aged 35–44 had attained that level of education. Educational opportunities have increased markedly during the 20th century, so that younger cohorts are much more likely to have benefited from formal schooling at both the high school and college levels (U.S. Bureau of the Census, 1997). In cross-sectional studies of cognitive functioning, it is important to recognize the contribution of historical factors as well as possible developmental or aging factors that may contribute to observed differences in performance. Even in longitudinal studies that follow change over time, if only one cohort is sampled, it is impossible to tell whether changes from one period to the next are products of age and development or of particular resources and deficits characterizing that particular generation.

A second problem is the definition of abilities. **Cognitive functioning** is a broad term that encompasses such varied abilities as vocabulary, problem solving, and short-term memory. It is possible that the pattern of change in abilities with age depends on which are tested. Some abilities are frequently used and have been developed to a high level of efficiency. For example, an architect is more likely to retain abilities in spatial relations and reasoning than is someone whose lifework is not intimately connected with the construction and organization of spatial dimensions.

A third and related problem is the level of abstraction and the relevance of the tasks used to measure adult cognitive functioning. The definition of intelligence that is used in the design and application of most intelligence tests refers to capacities that are predictive of school-related success. The criteria for assessing adult intelligence are necessarily more heterogeneous than the ability to succeed in the school curriculum. As people move through adulthood, their approach to the use of information and problem solving becomes modified by the contexts in which they are most often involved. As a result, cognitive problem solving is adapted based on the resources available and the time frame required for task performance. As an example, a senior administrator may expect that certain information will be provided by other offices and reviewed by staff before it reaches her. Thus, skills that she may have developed in the past are not used as often, and new skills are used in anticipating the impact of her decision on other units or translating the information into action (Dixon, 1992).

Finally, factors associated with health are always intertwined with the functioning of older adults, although they are often not directly measured. In a longitudinal study of intelligence, Riegel and Riegel (1972) found that there were clear declines in performance among subjects who died before the next testing period. Vocabulary skills, which normally remain high or continue to show increases with age, are especially likely to decline in older subjects who will die within the coming few years (White & Cunningham, 1988). In related work, research has shown that adults who are in the early stages of dementia are often included in samples described as normal or normative. This inclusion lowers the mean of the total group and overestimates the negative association of age and intelligence (Sliwinski et al., 1996). At each older age, the inclusion of adults who are in an early phase of a progressive illness lowers the average performance of the group as a whole.

Productivity in the Work Setting

In attempting to define intelligence in adulthood, several researchers have looked at the pattern of productivity in the work setting. Special attention has been given to the relationship between creative achievement and age. The pattern that has been described is one of a fairly rapid rise to a peak in mid-career, followed by a gradual decline (Simonton, 1988). However, it is clear that opportunities for creative contribution persist throughout the career. What is more, as adults perceive that they may be approaching the end of their career, they may be especially inspired to make a distinctive statement. Thus, last works or career "swan songs" are often marked by a profound simplicity and originality that set them apart from earlier work and illustrate a special facet of the person's creative potential (Simonton, 1989).

Research carried out in the 1950s and 1960s found that people were at their most productive during their 40s. Productivity in the humanities was found to remain high until later adulthood, whereas productivity in the creative arts declined rapidly after age 40 (Dennis, 1966). The applicability of this profile for current workers is questionable, though. Today, people live in good health through a considerably longer period. The opportunity for occupational contributions can extend across many decades, leading to new expressions of creativity. People are remaining in the labor market longer and exploring new avenues for productive work at older ages than in the past (Quinn, 1998).

The role of older scholars and scientists is influenced by cultural values. For example, China has a shortage of scientists. Although the retirement age in China is 60, scientists who hold the title of professor can work in their laboratories until age 70. And those who have made unusual contributions may work after age 70, depending on their health. At the same time, there is an active attempt to advance the 45- to 55-year-old scientists by promoting them to leadership (Guangzhao, 1985). This climate encourages productivity throughout later adulthood. A review of research on aging and the U. S. workplace echoes the importance of considering the interaction between the nature of the job, the occupational climate, and the productivity and well-being of older workers (Hansson et al., 1997).

Memory

Several aspects of cognitive functioning including reaction time, visual-motor flexibility (the translation of visual information into new motor responses), and memory show

In his 70's, after years in prison, Nelson Mandela emerged as a vigorous leader in South Africa. His career suggests the potential that people have for remarkable social contributions and active leadership in later adulthood.

evidence of decline with age. The exact nature of changes in memory with age are a topic of active and ongoing research (Giambra et al., 1995). A common model of memory functions breaks memory into three forms: the sensory register, short-term memory, and long-term memory. In this model, the **sensory register** is the neurological processing activity that is required to take in visual, auditory, tactile, and olfactory information. **Short-term memory** is the working capacity to encode and retrieve 5 to 9 bits of information in the span of a minute or two. This is the scratch pad of memory, if you will, that is used when someone tells you a telephone number or gives you his or her address. **Long-term memory** is a complex network of information, concepts, and schemes related by associations, knowledge, and use. It is a storehouse of a lifetime of information. Remembering something for more than a few minutes involves moving the information from short-term to long-term memory, storing it in relation to other associated knowledge, and being able to recognize, retrieve, or reconstruct it at a later time (Hultsch & Dixon, 1990).

The memory functions that are most relevant to an understanding of cognitive ability in aging have to do with the ability to transfer information from short to long-term memory and then retrieve it. Studies that compare the short-term memory abilities of older and younger adults find that age is not associated directly with capacity for short-term memory, but with the ability to transfer newly learned information to long-term memory and then retrieve it upon demand. Older adults are just as effective as younger adults in recognizing information that was learned in the past, but they have difficulty summoning up a specific name or number when they want to find it (Rowe & Kahn, 1998).

Furthermore, older adults find that their memory functions are especially likely to be disrupted under conditions in which information is presented rapidly and contextual cues are absent. In a memory task involving the recall of five- and eight-word strings, older adults (65–73) retained fewer words than younger adults (18–22) when the word strings were presented at high speed and were not arranged in a meaningful sentence. However, speed of presentation did not significantly reduce recall when the words were arranged in a normal semantic order (Wingfield et al., 1985).

Recent research has focused on the relationship of intelligence and context to performance on memory tasks. These studies find that age alone continues to be an important predictor of performance on many memory tasks (West et al., 1992). In addition, contemporary intelligence, especially verbal intelligence, is an equally strong predictor of performance on many tasks. However, several contextual factors, especially satisfaction with social support; education; the personality characteristic of introversion; illness; and intellectual activity, are important predictors of contemporary intelligence (Arbuckle et al., 1992). Normative patterns showing declines in memory do not tell the whole story. The actual pattern of change with age varies, depending on significant contemporary circumstances.

In addition to actual declines in some kinds of memory performance, about 50% of older adults complain of memory problems. It is interesting that even after participating in programs designed to improve memory performance, these complaints persist (Scogin et al., 1985). Anxiety and frustration over memory loss nag many older adults, even those whose memory performance has not dramatically declined. However, memory complaints may reflect the person's accurate subjective assessment of a slowing in the retrieval process (Jonker et al., 1996).

Piagetian Tasks

Some research has focused on the ability of older adults to perform various Piagetian tasks, such as classification, conservation, and formal operational problem solving. In many areas, older adults perform less well than middle or young adults. They have been described as performing classification and problem-solving tasks in a more egocentric, idiosyncratic way than younger adults (Denney, 1982). Older adults have a particular point of view that may not make sense to others but that they insist in applying since it has worked for them in the past. In the area of conservation, however, the evidence is mixed. Some studies have found that older adults do not handle the conservation of volume task as well as younger subjects but do perform other conservation tasks quite well. Other studies report no differences in conservation between younger and older subjects (Selzer & Denney, 1980). In one comparison, academic background rather than age was related to the performance of formal operational problem solving. College-age men and women did as well as college-educated men and women aged 63–75 on tests of formal thought. However, those who had majored in the natural or physical sciences while in college did better than those with social science and humanities backgrounds (Blackburn, 1984).

Research based on the standard Piagetian tasks has been criticized for its lack of relevance and familiarity to older subjects. In an attempt to control for the relevance of the task, Poon and Fozard (1978) studied the effect of the familiarity and datedness of objects on the time it took for subjects to name them. Some objects were clearly dated from the early 1900s; others were contemporary items used in the 1960s and 1970s. Subjects 60–70 years old named the dated objects faster than did the younger subjects, while the younger subjects aged 18–20 named the contemporary objects faster than did the older subjects. The implication of this research is that the performance of older adults may be partly a product of their familiarity with the materials provided.

Practical Problem Solving

In another approach to problem solving, 10 older adults participated in constructing a set of practical problem-solving questions in order to help ensure their relevance to an older sample (Denney & Pearce, 1989). One problem they posed was, "An elderly woman can drive her car to run errands except in the winter when the weather is bad. What should she do about getting groceries and other necessities when the weather is bad?" Answers to this and other questions were rated on a scale of 1 to 4, depending on the number of safe and effective solutions offered. Subjects in their 40s performed best. Subjects in their 50s, 60s, and 70s scored about the same, but slightly less well than those in their 30s and 40s, and about as well as those in their 20s. One could not conclude, however, that problem-solving abilities showed a pattern of deterioration since this was not a longitudinal study. One might conclude that, even when the problems are authentic, older adults are not as likely to try to generate multiple solutions as they are to identify one or two solutions that have a good chance of succeeding.

Patterns of Change in Different Mental Abilities

John Horn (1979) proposed that the course of mental abilities across the life span is not uniform. Some areas are strengthened and others decline. Horn made an especially strong case for differentiating **crystallized intelligence** (Gc) and **fluid intelligence** (Gf). Gc is the ability to bring knowledge accumulated through past learning into play in appropriate situations. Gf, on the other hand, is the ability to impose organization on information and generate new hypotheses. Both kinds of intelligence are required for optimal human functioning.

Gc and Gf can be identified as integrated structures in both early and later adulthood (Hayslip & Brookshire, 1985). However, Horn argued that the two kinds of thinking draw on somewhat different neurological and experiential sources. Gc reflects the consequences of life experiences within a society. Socialization in the family, exposure to the media, and participation in school, work, and community settings all emphasize the use and improvement of Gc. It increases with age, experience, and physical maturation, and remains at a high level of functioning throughout adulthood.

Gf is characteristic of what is meant by the expression that someone has a "good head on his or her shoulders." Finding a general relationship and applying it without having been schooled in that problem-solving area is an example of Gf, as is being able

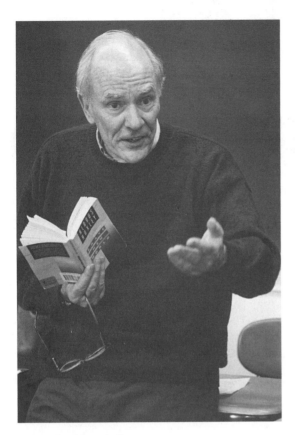

Senior faculty at colleges and universities draw upon both crystallized and fluid intelligence. They have accumulated a reservoir of knowledge and experience. At the same time, they must respond flexibly to new issues, unexpected questions, and new technologies in order to remain effective scholars.

to approach new problems logically and systematically. Older adults do not spontaneously impose organization on new information. They are less likely than younger persons to attend to the incidental information or process-level learning that contributes to Gf. Horn also hypothesized that Gf depends more on the specific number of neurons available for its functioning than does Gc. Thus, neurological loss would be more damaging to Gf than to Gc. Subsequent research has supported the notion that neural efficiency, often recognized through changes in sensory functioning and speed of response, is closely related to fluid intelligence and shows an age-related decline, independent of disease (Baltes & Lindenberger, 1997).

K. Warner Schaie (1994; Schaie & Hertzog, 1983; Hertzog & Schaie, 1988) reported on the results of a 35-year cohort sequential study of adult intellectual development. Six mental abilities were measured: inductive reasoning, spatial orientation, perceptual speed, numeric ability, verbal ability, and verbal memory. The youngest participants had an average age of 25, the oldest an average age of 88. In general, the longitudinal data showed less decrement with age than did the cross-sectional data (Figure 13.1). Verbal ability showed no decline between age 25 and 88. Perceptual speed and numeric ability showed the greatest declines. The rate of decline in performance was modest but consistent when participants were in their late 60s and more substantial in their 80s. However, once factors associated with slowing of processing and response time were taken into account, the degree of decline with advanced age was notably smaller. The variation within age groups in the sample remained stable over time. In other words, even though measured intelligence changed over time, the position of one person in relation to another in the same age group remained about the same.

The Interaction of Heredity and Environment on Mental Functioning

For years it was assumed that the environment played an increasingly major role in intellectual functioning over time. The accumulation of life experiences, education, and socialization were expected to introduce new bases of knowledge and problem-solving structures. However, recent work suggests that the construct of the **reaction range** introduced in Chapter 4 continues to provide an appropriate framework for understanding intelligence in adulthood. Research on identical and fraternal twins who were 80 years old or older found that heritability for general cognitive ability was about 60% (McClearn et al., 1997). In other words, genetic factors substantially contribute to the stability of cognitive capacities over the life span.

Given the strong contribution of heredity to cognitive ability, its expression in observable behavior depends on the nature of the environment. Roughly 30% of the variability between twins was accounted for by their environment—both the shared environment reflected in growing up in the same family and community and the non-shared environment, including the different interactions they had with their parents, other siblings and friends, and their participation in different types of educational and social settings. The stimulating or stifling nature of the environment, including access to social support, the quality of health care, exposure to disease, and opportunities for continuing involvement in challenging work, transforms the genotype into an observed phenotype (Gottesman, 1997).

B. F. Skinner (1983) described some possible environmental qualities that fail to reinforce systematic thinking or new ideas in aging people. Many people who live alone, for example, lack the diversity of social interaction that produces cognitive discrepancy and new concepts. Older people may be reinforced for talking about the past. Their recollections of early memories are interesting to students and younger colleagues.

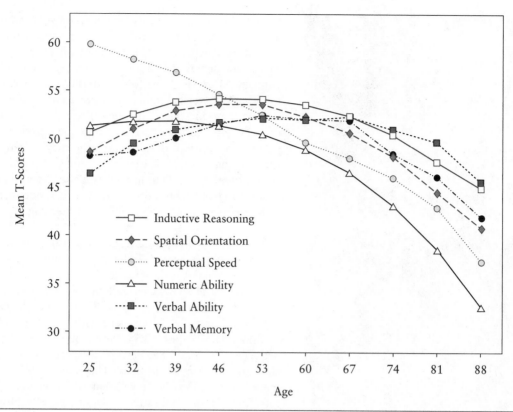

FIGURE 13.1
Longitudinal estimates of mean factor scores for the six ability constructs
SOURCE: Schaie, 1994.

However, preoccupation with these reminiscences does not encourage thinking in new directions. Skinner claimed that one is more likely to repeat oneself as one ages. He suggested that it may be important for older adults to move into new areas of work in order to prevent repetition of old ideas. Skinner believed that it is possible to analyze how the quality of one's thinking is influenced by the circumstances of aging and also to identify interventions that will prevent the deterioration of cognitive abilities. These interventions included attempts to be sensitive to the signs of fatigue, planning for regular opportunities for stimulating verbal interactions with others, making careful outlines of written work to avoid distraction, and acting on ideas as they come to one's mind rather than counting on remembering them later.

Cognitive functioning in later adulthood is neither unidimensional nor stable. There are substantial differences among individuals as well as differences among cognitive domains within the same person (Hoyer & Rybash, 1994). Recalling the model of the developing mind presented in Chapter 8, one can recognize that adults experience tremendous growth in domain-specific areas of knowledge. Within these domains, many complex networks of information, strategies, and frameworks of meaning are elaborated that result in high-level, flexible functioning. The overall level of functioning is subject to environmental influences that promote particular specialization and cognitive organization based on the demands of the situation, the stresses and challenges of daily life, and the opportunities for mastery in particular areas of competence. At the same time, certain aspects of the processing base that are dependent on neural functioning may decline with age. The decline, though, is not always great, and studies have shown that capacities described as elements of fluid intelligence, such as speed of response, inductive reasoning, and spatial orientation, can benefit from targeted interventions (Schaie, 1994; Van Boxtel et al., 1997).

On the basis of extensive longitudinal research, Schaie (1994) identified seven factors that are associated with retaining a high level of cognitive functioning in later adulthood:

Absence of cardiovascular and other chronic diseases
Favorable environment linked to high socioeconomic status
Involvement in a complex and intellectually stimulating environment
Flexible personality style at midlife
High cognitive functioning of spouse
Maintenance of a high level of perceptual processing speed
Rating oneself as being satisfied with life accomplishments in midlife

In this list there is evidence of the interplay of the biological, psychological, and social systems that contribute to cognitive functioning in the later years.

Redirecting Energy to New Roles and Activities

Role transition, role gain, and role loss are present in every period of the life span. In later adulthood, however, a convergence of role transitions is likely to lead to a revision of major life functions. Roles are lost through widowhood, retirement, and the death of friends. At the same time, new roles such as grandparent, senior adviser, or community leader require the formation of new patterns of behavior and relationships.

Grandparenthood

Within the course of family development, the role of grandparent may require a renewal of skills that have been stored away along with the bottle sterilizer and potty chair. Grandparents begin to renew their acquaintance with the delights of childhood, including diapering the baby, telling fairy tales, taking trips to the zoo, and having the pleasure of small helping hands with baking, gardening, or carpentry. A person's skills, patience, and knowledge may be more in demand in the grandparent role than they were in the parent role.

People differ in the meaning they place on the grandparent role and in the way they enact it. In one of the first empirical studies of grandparenthood, Neugarten and Weinstein (1964) interviewed the grandparents in 70 middle-class families. The following five grandparenting styles were identified, each expressing a distinct interpretation of the role:

1. *Formal.* This type of grandparent was interested in the grandchildren but careful not to become involved in parenting them other than by occasional baby-sitting.
2. *Funseeker.* This type of grandparent had informal, playful interactions with the grandchildren, enjoying mutually self-indulgent fun with them.
3. *Surrogate parent.* This style was especially likely for grandmothers who assumed major child-care responsibilities when the mother worked outside the home.
4. *Reservoir of family wisdom.* This style was an authoritarian relationship in which a grandparent, usually the grandfather, dispensed skills and resources. Parents as well as grandchildren were subordinate to this older authority figure.
5. *Distant figure.* This type of grandparent appeared on birthdays and holidays but generally had little contact with the grandchildren.

It is clear from this list of grandparenting styles that the role prescriptions for the grandparent are ambiguous enough to permit wide differences in their enactment.

Cherlin and Furstenberg (1986/1992) conducted telephone interviews with a national sample of 510 grandparents. They classified their sample into three groups: remote, companionate, and involved. The *remote grandparents* (29% of the sample) had seen their grandchildren less than once every two or three months in the past year. Most of them lived far away from their grandchildren, but in some cases, the lack of contact was a result of emotional rather than physical distance.

The *companionate grandparents* (55% of the sample) had seen their grandchildren at least once every two or three months in the past year, but there were low levels of exchange of services or resources with the child's family and very little "parentlike" be-

Increasingly, more grandparents fall into the "involved" category, taking on parenting responsibilities for their grandchildren on a daily basis.

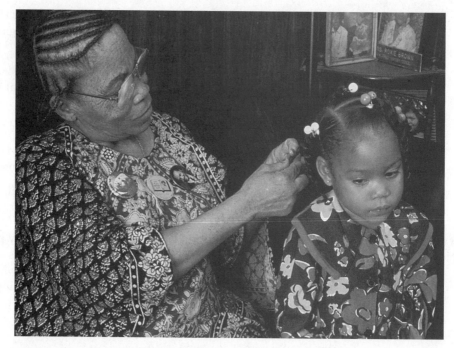

havior toward the child. These grandparents were likely to characterize their relationship as one in which they could have fun with their grandchildren and then send them home. They observed a "norm of noninterference" when it came to the conflicts a child was having with his or her parents, or any concerns about the child's behavior or the parents' child-rearing strategies.

The *involved grandparents* (16% of the sample) saw their grandchildren at least once every two to three months and showed both high levels of exchanges in services and resources and in "parentlike" behaviors. In fact, most of these involved grandparents had frequent interactions with their grandchildren, especially while they were young. Almost all grandparents noted that they had had less time together with their teenage grandchildren because they had become involved in more activities on their own. But the involved grandparents were more likely to take direct action by contacting their adolescent grandchildren and making plans to spend time together.

Most older adults take great pride in their grandchildren. Grandparenthood has a variety of personal meanings that contribute to the grandparent's overall sense of purpose and worth (Kivnick, 1983; 1985). Grandchildren symbolize an extension of personal influence that will most assuredly persist well beyond the grandparent's death. To this extent, grandchildren help older adults feel more comfortable about their own death. Older adults see concrete evidence that some thread of their lives will persist into the future, giving a dimension of immortality to themselves and to the family ancestry that they represent.

In an analysis of the sources of vitality in later life, Erikson, Erikson, and Kivnick (1986) found that relationships with grandchildren played the following critical role:

> The major involvement that uniformly makes life worth living is the thought of and participation in their relationships with children and grandchildren. Their pride in their own achievement in having brought up their young, through thick and thin, and their satisfaction in the way these young have developed gives them, for the most part, deep gratification. With the arrival of grandchildren, they may identify themselves as ancestors, graduated to venerability. Listen to their voices as they trace their own ancestry and that of their children's traits: "She has her mother's fire, that first girl of ours. She has more energy and more projects than anyone. Come to think of it, my mother had that fire, too. And my wife's two grandmothers." "My son is a perfectionist, like me." "The kids are innately smart, like their father." (p. 326)

Grandchildren also stimulate older adults' thoughts about time, the changing of cultural norms across generations, and the patterning of history. In relating to grandchildren as they grow up, grandparents discover elements of the culture that remain stable.

Some familiar stories and songs retain their appeal from generation to generation. Certain toys, games, and preoccupations of children of the current generation are remembered by grandparents from their own childhood. Grandparents may also become aware of changes in the culture that are reflected in new child-rearing practices; new equipment, toys, and games; and new expectations for children's behavior at each life stage. The communication that adults maintain with their grandchildren allows them to keep abreast of the continuities and changes in their culture that are reflected in the experiences of childhood. Through their grandchildren, adults avoid a sense of alienation from the contemporary world (Gutmann, 1985). The more involved grandparents are in the daily care and routines of their grandchildren, the more central they become to a young child's sense of security and well-being. This kind of importance is a benefit not only to the child but also to the older adult's assessment of his or her personal worth (Tomlin & Passman, 1989).

Some adults interpret the role of grandparent as an opportunity to pass on to grandchildren the wisdom and cultural heritage of their ancestry. In the process of fulfilling this role, older adults must try to find meaning in their experiences and communicate it in meaningful ways to their grandchildren. Grandparents select many avenues to educate their grandchildren, influencing their thoughts and fantasies. Storytelling, special trips, long walks, attending religious services, and working on special projects are all activities that allow grandparents some moments of intimacy with their grandchildren. Educating one's grandchildren involves a deep sense of investment in experiences and ideals that one believes to be central to a fruitful life.

The many ways in which grandchildren can contribute to an adult's feelings of well-being have been replicated in studies conducted in European countries (Smith, 1991). A German grandmother addressed the meaning that her grandson gave to her life, stating:

> "Yes, he is the most important thing in my life, because I have nothing else at the moment. They all say I spoil him. I don't know. Mama is a little bit strict, and so I always am careful not to spoil him too much. And it is actually Carsten this and Carsten that; he means so much to me. Since I am a pensioner, I have time for him." (Sticker, 1991, p. 39)

Grandparent Caregivers. Although the majority of middle-class grandparents claim that they assume a philosophy of noninterference, evidence suggests that grandparents are taking an increasing role in their grandchildren's care. In a national survey of families and households, 1 in 10 grandparents was found to have a custodial or primary role in the care of their grandchild for a minimum of 6 months. In most cases, the care was far longer (Fuller-Thomson et al., 1997; Triffon, 1997).

Grandparents play an especially important role in supporting the development of their grandchildren during times of family stress (Werner, 1991). In contemporary American society, one can view grandparents as a potential resource that is called into active duty when certain difficulties arise for parents. In cases of parental divorce, grandparents often assume a more central role in the lives of young children. Some custodial mothers move back home with their parents. In addition, grandparents often assume more child-care responsibilities during this time. Following divorces in which the mother has primary custody of the children, the grandchild's relationships with his or her maternal grandparents are more likely to be enhanced, whereas the relationships with the paternal grandparents are likely to decline. Several studies have shown that having positive ongoing relationships with grandparents during the years following parents' divorce is associated with a child's ability to manage school demands, maintain positive relationships with peers and teachers, and have fewer behavior problems (Heatherington et al., 1985; Heatherington et al., 1989).

Grandparents also play a key role when their young, unmarried daughters become pregnant. The pattern of unmarried teen mothers living with parents is especially common in African-American families. Roughly 30% of African-American children live in an extended family (Tolson & Wilson, 1990). African-American grandmothers are likely to perceive themselves and to be perceived by their daughters as actively involved in child-rearing (Werner, 1991). Among young adult, African-American parents, the grandmother is most often viewed as the person to count on for child-care assistance, advice, and emotional support (Hunter, 1997). These grandmothers may be young themselves, just entering middle adulthood, when they assume the grandparent role.

The presence of grandmothers appears to affect the family atmosphere as well as the child-rearing environment in African-American families. In one study of 64 African-American families, the presence of a grandmother was associated with a high level of moral-religious orientation in the family (Tolson & Wilson, 1990). Having a grandmother in the home allows the mother to be more flexible and able to manage daily demands without having to be strict in planning and arranging for daily tasks; thus, there is a reduction in much of the stress that characterizes single-parent families.

Maternal employment is a third condition in which grandparents are likely to give direct support. In a national sample of 796 mothers who had children under age 5 and who were employed, 24% said their mother, or the child's grandmother, was the principal child-care provider (Presser, 1989). These grandmothers provided an average of 27 hours per week of child care, and almost 40 hours per week if the mothers were employed full time. Clearly, these grandmothers were intimately involved in the lives of their grandchildren and were directing significant energy, talent, and time to this role.

Loss of Grandparent-Grandchild Contact. In contrast to the picture of an increasing role for grandparents in caring for their grandchildren, a growing number of grandparents are losing contact with their grandchildren as a result of parental divorce, conflict between the parents, death of an adult child, or adoption of a grandchild after remarriage. Disruption in the grandparent-grandchild relationship is especially great when the grandparent's adult child is not named as the custodial parent after a divorce. This loss of contact is a profound stressor, and grandparents are taking actions to find legal remedies to guarantee continued visitation with their grandchildren (Kruk, 1995).

Widowhood

Among those 65 to 74 years old, 10% of men and 33% of women are widowed (U.S. Bureau of the Census, 1997). For many adults, the psychosocial consequences of widowhood include intense emotional grief, loss of social and emotional support, and loss of material and instrumental support. Most older widowers remarry, whereas the vast majority of widows live alone.

Widows. Widows must learn to function socially and in their own households without the presence of a marriage partner. Adaptation to this role requires resilience, creative problem solving, and a strong belief in one's personal worth. A woman who is widowed at age 60 has an expected 23 more years of life in which to create a new, single head-of-household lifestyle.

In addition to the bereavement itself, a number of stressors challenge the coping resources of widows. Studies of economic changes among widows show that many continue to experience marked fluctuations in their financial resources for years following widowhood (Zick & Smith, 1991; Bound et al., 1991). Women who have never participated in the labor market during their married years may have no marketable skills and feel insecure about entering the labor force. In addition, they may be uninformed or uneasy about using social service agencies to meet their needs. For most women, the loss of their husband is most keenly felt as a loss of emotional support, as expressed in the following: "He is most apt to be mentioned as the person the widow most enjoyed being with, who made her feel important and secure" (Lopata, 1978, p. 221). The transition to widowhood may be especially difficult for those who have been caring for an ill partner, emotionally hoping for recovery yet observing constant decline (Bass & Bowman, 1990).

Despite the extreme pain and prolonged grief that accompany widowhood, most people cope with it successfully. In a study of women aged 60 through 98 who had recently become widows, there was a high degree of self-sufficiency (O'Bryant & Morgan, 1990). The majority of respondents said they performed a variety of daily tasks, including transportation, housekeeping, shopping, preparing meals, personal care and hygiene, financial and other decisions, and providing financial support without help from others. Over 30% said they managed their own home repairs, yard

In widowhood, children and siblings are primary sources of immediate social support. They play an especially important role when they can accept the widow's grief and give her opportunities to talk about her husband and their life together.

work, and legal questions without help. From this study, a picture emerges of older, widowed women functioning at a high level of independence and autonomy and benefiting from assistance from others, especially their children, in specific domains, depending on where help is needed.

Widows are likely to find support from their siblings, children, and friends. Over time, a widow's siblings, especially her sisters, may become a key source of emotional support as well as direct, instrumental assistance with home repairs and shopping (O'Bryant, 1988). In an exploratory analysis of the responses of widows in a support group discussion, comments about the positive and negative contributions of their social support network were analyzed (Morgan, 1989). The widows described their nonfamily, reciprocal friendship relationships as somewhat more positive than their family relationships. In many cases, widows found that as a result of their own sense of family obligation, they were drawn into negative events occurring in their families, especially divorce, illness, and the death of other family members. These negative events added to their distress and prevented them from receiving the support they felt they needed at the time of their own loss.

The analysis also concluded that the most positive form of immediate support from family, especially children, was a willingness to accept the widow's feelings of grief and to talk openly about their father. Social support from friends included a similar willingness to allow the widow to take her time in finding a new identity. These women did not want to be forced to "get over it" too quickly or to be told how "strong" they were and how well they were handling their grief: "'The fact that you're using the strength that you have, just to cope, and to stay alive (another voice: 'to survive') is a big job and they don't recognize that, you know it makes you angry'" (Morgan, 1989, p. 105). The widows wanted to have their anger, grief, and the disruption in their lives acknowledged and accepted by their friends. In this way, they felt they could begin to come to terms with their loss and build a new life.

Widowers. Widowers are more likely than widows to suffer intense depression following the loss of their spouses (Umberson et al., 1992). Perhaps because men in traditional marriages rely heavily on their wives for both the instrumental support of managing daily household tasks and the emotional/social support of companionship and social activity, their lives are more intensely disrupted when their wives die. This may result in an immediate search for a new marriage partner. In a two-year follow-up study of dating and remarriage after widowhood, 61% of men and 19% of women had remarried or were in a new romantic relationship by 25 months after the death of their spouses. For men, a higher monthly income and level of education were the best predictors of being remarried. For both men and women, involvement in a new relationship was positively associated with psychological well-being and was interpreted as a positive coping strategy (Schnieder et al., 1996).

Widowhood also results in increased death rates among surviving spouses. In a longitudinal study of over 1.5 million married Finnish adults, the rates of mortality after the death of a spouse were calculated. For all causes of death that were monitored in this study, mortality rates were higher for widowed persons than for those persons still married. In addition, higher mortality rates were especially notable for the men in the study, particularly in the first six months after death. The process of bereavement seems to accelerate the course of preexisting diseases, and leads to increased rates of suicides, accidents, and alcohol-related deaths (Martikainen & Valkonen, 1996).

Leisure Activities

Older adults commonly find that as the role responsibilities of parenthood and employment decrease, they have more time and resources to devote to leisure activities. Involvement in leisure activities is associated with higher levels of well-being and lower stress. In a study of adaptation to widowhood, such activities were most commonly social activities with family and friends. Recent widows and widowers who were more involved in leisure activities had lower levels of stress than those who did not participate. This does not mean that they were less bereaved, but perhaps social activities helped them to feel less isolated and gave them a sense of continuing social value (Patterson, 1996).

Different types of leisure activities are available that meet a variety of psychosocial needs. In a study of the benefits of leisure activities, men and women aged 56 and over were asked to describe the sources of satisfaction found in their primary leisure activities (Tinsley et al., 1985). From the study, six clusters of leisure activities and their primary benefits were described, which are listed in Table 13.1. The table suggests that different clusters of activities meet different needs. It also provides some psychologically equivalent activities for adults who may be unable to continue one activity or who may be uninterested in it but are willing to try a new one.

The area of **volunteerism** is a growing interest for older adults. Among adults aged 65 to 74, 45% are involved in volunteer activities averaging about 4 hours per week (U.S. Bureau of the Census, 1997). Especially in the year or two following retirement,

---

TABLE 13.1   Clusters of Leisure Activities and their Psychological Benefits

Cluster	Primary Benefit
1. Playing cards Playing bingo Bowling Dancing	Companionship
2. Picnicking	Experiencing something new and unusual
3. Watching sports (not on TV) Watching television	Escape from the pressure of dealing with others
4. Raising houseplants Collecting photographs Collecting antiques Reading	Solitude and security
5. Knitting or crocheting Woodworking Ceramics	Expressiveness and recognition, but in a solitary context
6. Volunteer service Volunteer professional activities Attending meetings of social groups Attending meetings of religious groups	Intellectual stimulation, self-expression, and service

SOURCE: Based on Tinsley, Teaff, Colbs, & Kaufman, 1985.

individuals who are not already involved in volunteer service are especially open to considering it (Caro & Bass, 1997). Volunteering provides a meaningful structure to daily life, especially when other significant work and family roles are becoming less demanding. At the same time, certain types of volunteer work have been shown to have a positive impact on cognitive complexity and memory functions. The opportunity to assume new responsibilities and learn new skills are two of the rewards of volunteering in later adulthood (Newman et al., 1995).

One area not included in Table 13.1 is physical exercise. It is becoming a focus of leisure activity for increasing numbers of older adults, since benefits are linked to better health, positive self-esteem, and a new zest for life. Research suggests a relationship between physical fitness, especially a regular pattern of aerobic exercise, and the improvement of certain visual-spatial cognitive abilities that typically decline with age (Shay & Roth, 1992). In the past, professionals were reluctant to encourage vigorous activity for older adults. They believed that a person who was unaccustomed to active physical exercise might be harmed by it. However, research on exercise in adulthood suggests that not only can adults profit from a program of exercise, but some of the negative consequences of a sedentary lifestyle can be reversed. For example, Hopkins and her associates (1990) described a program in which women aged 57–77 participated in a low-impact aerobic dance class 3 times a week for 12 weeks. The program included stretching, walking, dance movements, large arm movements, and major leg muscle movement. After 12 weeks, the group showed improvement in cardiorespiratory endurance (walking half a mile as fast as possible), flexibility, muscle strength, body agility, and balance. A comparison group of women who did not participate showed stability or decline in all of these areas.

Physical exercise has been identified as a component of optimal aging. It is associated with increased muscle tone, strength, and endurance, which build confidence about one's body movement, coordination, and stamina. Exercise also increases perceptions of self-control and self-efficacy in meeting one's own needs. As a result, people who exercise tend to have a generally more positive self-evaluation and higher levels of self-confidence than their inactive peers (Fontane, 1996).

Redirection of energy to new roles in later adulthood requires a degree of flexibility and resilience that often goes unnoticed in observations of older adults. Try to imagine what life might be like for you 30 or 40 years from now. Will you be prepared to embrace the technology, lifestyle, or age-role expectations that you will encounter during your own later adulthood? We are impressed by how readily most older adults adapt to new roles, especially those of retiree and widow, for which there is little early preparation or social reward.

Accepting One's Life

For people in the U.S. who were 60 years old in 1995, the average life expectancy was 21 more years, 19 for males, and 23 for females (U.S. Bureau of the Census, 1997). Major improvements in hygiene, nutrition, and medical technology have allowed more people to experience a vigorous later adulthood today than was true 70 years ago. Thus, one of the significant challenges of aging is learning to accept the reality of one's life and formulate a vision of this new phase of later adulthood.

> Weren't you ever afraid to grow old, I asked?
> "Mitch, I *embrace* aging."
> Embrace it?
> "It's very simple. As you grow, you learn more. If you stayed at twenty-two, you'd always be as ignorant as you were at twenty-two. Aging is not just decay, you know. It's growth. It's more than the negative that you're going to die, it's also the positive that you *understand* you're going to die, and that you live a better life because of it." (Albom, 1997, p. 118)

Illness and Health

The ability to experience a sense of well-being and acceptance of one's life is associated with physical health. In addition to an increase in vulnerability to **acute** illnesses, such as influenza, over 80% of people over the age of 65 have at least one **chronic** condition such as arthritis, hypertension, or diabetes. Chronic illnesses are long-lasting, and

In his later life, Renoir suffered from severe arthritis. He coped with his illness by binding brushes to his hands so he could continue to paint.

can be characterized by periods of intense illness followed by periods of remission or by progressive decline. Table 13.2 shows the rate (persons per 1000 in the age group) of some chronic conditions among persons aged 65–74 and those aged 75 and older (U.S. Bureau of the Census, 1997).

From Table 13.2, it is evident that heart disease is still the leading cause of death for men and women in the United States. However, it begins about 10 years earlier for men than for women. After menopause, however, women are at a greater risk for heart disease than men. What is more, women are less likely than men to be accurately diagnosed as suffering from a heart attack, are less likely to recover from it, and are more likely to suffer the complications of stroke. The lifestyle factors associated with heart disease are about the same for men and women. However, men are more likely to be at risk because they do not get the physical activity they need; they eat more meat and fat and less fruit and fiber than women; they are less likely to go to the doctor for regular check-ups; and they are generally more likely to deny being sick (Guttman, 1998).

Life Satisfaction

By later adulthood, evidence about one's successes and failures in the major tasks of middle adulthood—marriage, child-rearing, and work—has begun to accumulate. Data by which to judge one's adequacy in these areas are abundant. As involvement in the child-rearing role decreases, adults have an opportunity to increase their focus on the degree of harmony in their marriage relationship. They can assess whether they have successfully responded to the changes in their relationship or whether their marriage has deteriorated with the departure of their children. In viewing their own children as mature adults, parents are able to determine whether they have helped them meet the challenges of intimacy, work, and child-rearing with creativity and morality. In the work role, older adults can begin to estimate the degree to which their productivity has matched their abilities and the extent to which they have met their private goals for occupational accomplishment.

Robert Peck (1968) expanded Erikson's concept of psychosocial crises of adulthood by defining new crises of middle adulthood and old age. His ideas about the crises of old age emphasize the ability of the ego to transcend the role loss and physical disabilities associated with aging, and to find satisfaction in new activities, new pleasures, and a new sense of one's contribution to the lives of others (See Table 13.3). The process of accepting one's past life as it has been may be a difficult personal challenge. One must be able to incorporate certain areas of failure, crisis, or disappointment into one's self-image without being overburdened by a sense of inadequacy. Individuals also must be able to take pride in areas of achievement even when those accomplishments fall short of personal expectations. At the same time, older adults face the challenge of defining new goals for the future.

Brim (1992) described an adaptive process of matching one's desire for growth and mastery with one's current abilities through the example of his father's approach to aging. Brim's father, who lived to be 103, had been raised on a farm in Ohio. However, he left the farm to attend Harvard and then Columbia to get his Ph.D. He was a university professor until he retired. Then Brim's father and his wife bought a farm, remodeled the farmhouse, and settled into farming. In the early years of retirement, he cleared and thinned the trees on the hills and mountains of his farm. After awhile, he stopped working the hillsides and planted a large vegetable and flower garden. Brim's father tilled the garden with a power tiller. When he was 90, he bought a riding trac-

TABLE 13.2   Prevalence of Selected Chronic Conditions by Age and Sex, 1994

Chronic Condition	Conditions (1,000)	Rate[1]			
		Male		Female	
		65 to 74 years old	75 years old and over	65 to 74 years old	75 years old and over
Arthritis..........................	33,446	430.8	424.9	513.6	604.4
Dermatitis, including eczema...........	9,192	25.3	[2]17.6	38.8	40.2
Trouble with—					
Dry (itching) skin.................	6,166	36.6	46.7	30.8	40.5
Ingrown nails....................	5,987	40.9	38.8	52.9	61.4
Corns and calluses...............	4,356	21.0	[2]17.8	46.5	58.1
Visual impairments	8,601	78.4	113.7	48.0	110.7
Cataracts	6,473	79.0	214.7	140.0	259.2
Hearing impairments	22,400	298.8	447.1	183.3	307.8
Tinnitus.........................	7,033	118.1	106.6	67.7	79.9
Deformities or orthopedic impairments ...	31,068	144.4	169.3	161.8	189.9
Ulcer	4,447	27.1	[2]30.9	42.8	22.3
Hernia of abdominal cavity...........	4,778	54.7	55.6	70.0	72.3
Frequent indigestion................	6,957	44.6	51.5	41.0	45.3
Frequent constipation...............	4,040	[2]13.8	60.2	47.3	102.2
Diabetes........................	7,766	102.4	115.6	101.0	91.8
Migraine	11,256	[2]17.1	[2]5.2	29.9	26.2
Heart conditions	22,279	319.3	429.9	250.8	361.4
High blood pressure (Hypertension)......	28,236	307.7	339.2	378.7	417.5
Varicose veins of lower extremities.......	7,260	32.5	58.5	109.0	83.8
Hemorrhoids.....................	9,321	51.0	66.6	70.2	58.6
Chronic bronchitis	14,021	41.7	68.0	79.0	51.7
Asthma.........................	14,562	39.3	70.3	62.8	34.1
Hay fever, allergic rhinitis without asthma ..	26,146	79.6	58.6	92.2	78.8
Chronic sinusitis	34,902	118.2	113.9	175.5	176.1

[1]Conditions per 1,000 persons.

[2]Figure does not meet standards of reliability or precision.

SOURCE: U.S. Bureau of the Census, 1997.

TABLE 13.3   Robert Peck's Psychosocial Crises for Old Age

Ego Differentiation Versus Work-role Preoccupation	The ability to develop a set of valued activities and attributes separate from the primary roles of worker or parent.
Body Transcendence Versus Body Preoccupation	The emphasis is on finding pleasure and satisfaction in social interactions and intellectual activities that are not hindered by the discomforts of aging and illness.
Ego Transcendence Versus Ego Preoccupation	The capacity to find satisfaction in contributing to the lives of others so that one's own death feels less important, less a final close to one's impact.

Adapted from Peck, 1968.

tor. After awhile, he could no longer manage the large garden, so he focused on a small border garden and four large window boxes that he planted with flowers. As his eyesight became more impaired, he shifted from reading to listening to "talking books," and when he had to give up actually planting the window boxes, he enjoyed watering them and looking at the flowers. Brim's father approached each new challenge of physical decline by investing in a new project and taking pride in his achievements within that domain.

Subjective Age and Satisfaction. A number of investigators have raised questions about sources of life satisfaction and stress in later adulthood and their relation to perceptions of well-being. One especially intriguing question is whether people in their 60s and 70s feel "old" and just what that means. Most older adults do not perceive themselves as elderly (Kahana et al., 1980). However, those who do view themselves as old tend to have more difficulty adjusting to life than those who perceive themselves as middle-aged. Identification with the label *old* is associated with several life stresses, including poor health, reduced activity, widowhood, and reduced income level (Ward, 1977). The fear of growing old is also linked to lower levels of life satisfaction. Adults over 55 who are worried about encountering illness, loneliness, social rejection, and poverty when they are old are also significantly less satisfied with the current quality of their lives (Klemmack & Roff, 1984). They may be chronic worriers.

Although it may not be adaptive for later adults to view themselves as old, it appears that it is also a sign of frustration to view oneself as much younger than one's real age. Montepare and Lachman (1989) asked people ranging in age from the teens to the 80s to describe the age that corresponded to the way they felt (the **subjective age**) and the type of person whose interests and activities were most like theirs. Figure 13.2 shows the subjective age identities (dotted lines) in comparison with the actual ages of the male and female subjects. Younger subjects were likely to have a somewhat *older* subjective age identity. Conversely, older subjects were likely to have a *younger* subjective age identity, and the discrepancy was most noticeable among the oldest women. For younger men and women, having an older subjective age identity was associated with higher life satisfaction. For the oldest men, there was no relationship between subjective age and life satisfaction, but among the oldest women, those with the youngest subjective age had lower life satisfaction. At advanced ages, those with the least discrepancy between their real and subjective ages had the greatest satisfaction. Although it appears to be common for older adults to identify themselves as younger than they are, a major discrepancy between real and subjective age may reflect significant frustration over one's actual age and its constraints.

Life Goals and Satisfaction. The majority of older adults express a generally high level of life satisfaction. Nonetheless, they continue to aspire to new goals and strive for new levels of optimal functioning. A person's life goals and needs may change over the course of later adulthood, depending on life circumstances. Rather than viewing satisfaction in later adulthood solely in terms of wrapping things up and facing a roleless, undifferentiated future, older adults continue to formulate personal goals and assess

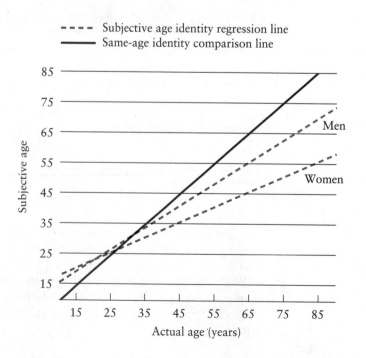

FIGURE 13.2
Subjective age identity and actual age
SOURCE: Montepare & Lachman, 1989.

their current life satisfaction in light of how well they are able to achieve those goals. In a study of older adult volunteers, participants were asked to describe the personal goals that were most important to their life satisfaction (Rapkin & Fischer, 1992a, 1992b). The 10 groups of life goals identified are listed in Table 13.4. These goals were grouped into five clusters: (1) a high-demand group of people who had many goals that were seen as important or vital to their life satisfaction; (2) an age-prescribed group that was concerned with safety, security, and increased dependence on services, and that showed a preference for disengagement from activities and social relationships; (3) a self-focused group that was especially concerned about having an easy life with little regard for safety, security, or independence; (4) a socially engaged group that had strong concerns about independence and maintaining their social roles and relationships; and (5) a low-demand group that had few goals except for reducing activity and disengaging. In a comparison of these five groups, the socially engaged group had significantly lower scores in depression than the other four. They had the highest score in self-esteem, whereas the self-focused group had the lowest score.

An important observation of this research was that each group had its own pattern of predictors of satisfaction. For example, age was not related to satisfaction in the group as a whole, but within the age-prescribed cluster, the older subjects had higher satisfaction than the younger subjects. Gender was also not related to satisfaction in the group as a whole, but women in the high-demand group had higher levels of satisfaction, as did men in the socially engaged group. One must conclude that an understanding of life satisfaction must be based on the way each person frames his or her contemporary situation and his or her view of the future. Individual differences in satisfaction are due in part to how well people are able to achieve what they perceive as most possible and desirable as they face the challenges of aging.

Demographic variables do not predict perceived life satisfaction adequately. A person's satisfaction with life remains fairly stable over the years despite losses of important roles and some decline in health (Costa et al., 1987). For older women, staying healthy, especially in terms of being able to remain independent and not become a burden on others, is so central to feelings of well-being that other hopes and concerns seem to be minimized. A 69-year-old woman described her situation as follows, "God's been good to me. My health is good. I can cut grass, climb ladders, and can paint. If you can do that at 69, that's pretty good, isn't it?" (Bearon, 1989, p. 774). Other factors that women

---

TABLE 13.4   Personal Goals of Older Adults

Goal	Definition
Active improvement	To actively improve or increase involvement in many domains of life
Maintenance of social values and relationships	To maintain reciprocal social relationships and community ties, to uphold religious beliefs, and to be financially self-sufficient
Disengagement	To reduce social and community obligations, to increase religious involvement, and to remain independent from social services for the aged
Energetic lifestyle	To be romantically involved and physically attractive, to be energetic and healthy, to get around independently, and to improve one's living situation
Safety and security	To worry about safety and security in the neighborhood and in getting around, avoiding health hazards and financial problems
Stability	To worry about stability in the neighborhood and predictability in the health-care system
Increased reliance on services	Not to be troubled with having to solve problems and wanting to be able to rely on services to meet one's needs
Easy life	To be able to be impulsive, do what one wants, stay independent from family, live in comfort, and have plenty of leisure time
Reduced activity	To reduce volunteer activities because of poor health
Independence in living	To live independently and to have privacy

SOURCE: Based on Rapkin & Fischer, 1992.

mention as significant contributors to their life satisfaction over the years are their education, religiosity, positive attitude, volunteerism, and family (Glass & Jolly, 1997).

In an analysis of subjective well-being and life satisfaction among older African-Americans, the most important predictors of well-being in this sample were subjective assessments of health, a low number of stressful life events, a sense of personal efficacy, and self-esteem (Tran et al., 1991). In addition, marital status and age were positively associated with well-being. Neither educational level nor income were direct predictors of well-being; however, education and income were linked to factors that did predict well-being. Those with less education tended to have more chronic health conditions, which were associated with poorer perceived health and a lower sense of well-being. Similarly, lower income was associated with lower feelings of self-esteem, which itself was linked to lower feelings of well-being.

Personality and Well-Being. We all know people who have lived difficult lives yet appear to be full of zest and enthusiasm. We also know people who appear to have had the benefits of many of life's resources yet are continually complaining about problems. In response to this reality, some researchers have looked to personality factors to predict subjective life satisfaction (Costa & McCrae, 1980; McCrae & Costa, 1983). Three personality characteristics that have been linked with life satisfaction in later life are extroversion, usefulness/competence, and trust. **Extroversion** includes such qualities as sociability, vigor, sensation seeking, and positive emotions. A personality dimension described as **neuroticism** is consistently associated with discouragement, unhappiness, and hopelessness. It is characterized by anxiety, hostility, and impulsiveness. The implication is that real-life events are screened and interpreted through the filter of personality. Whether specific events will contribute to feelings of satisfaction or dismay depends on how they are interpreted. Some people are more likely to be grumblers, while others are more likely to be celebrants of life. Another personality factor associated with well-being and high self-esteem in older adults is usefulness/competence. This quality is associated with informal volunteer work, higher levels of involvement with others, and a greater sense of purpose and structure in the use of time (Ranzijn et al., 1998).

Erikson et al. (1986) highlighted the importance of trust in the acceptance of one's life:

> The life cycle, however, does more than extend itself into the next generation. It curves back on the life of the individual, allowing, as we have indicated, a reexperiencing of earlier stages in a new form. This retracing might be described as a growth toward death, if that did not ring false as a metaphor. Maples and aspens every October bear flamboyant witness to this possibility of a final spurt of growth. Nature unfortunately has not ordained that mortals put on such a fine show.
>
> As aging continues, in fact, human bodies begin to deteriorate and physical and psychosocial capacities diminish in a seeming reversal of the course their development takes. When physical frailty demands assistance, one must accept again an appropriate dependence without the loss of trust and hope. The old, of course, are not endowed with the endearing survival skills of the infant. Old bodies are more difficult to care for, and the task itself is less satisfying to the caretaker than that of caring for infants. Such skills as elders possess have been hard won and are maintained only with determined grace. Only a lifetime of slowly developing trust is adequate to meet this situation, which so naturally elicits despair and disgust at one's own helplessness. Of how many elders could one say, "He surrendered every vestige of his old life with a sort of courteous, half humorous gentleness"? (p. 327)

Developing a Point of View about Death

During later adulthood, it is inevitable that serious, possibly frightening, preoccupations about death will fill the individual's thoughts. In middle adulthood, most people experience the death of their parents. During later adulthood, one's peers, including spouses, die. These deaths are sources of psychological stress and require the emotional process of grief and mourning as well as the cognitive strain of trying to accept or understand them. At the same time, these deaths stimulate a more immediate recognition of one's own mortality.

Changing Perspectives about Death

The development of a perspective on death is a continuous process that begins in childhood and is not fully resolved until later adulthood. The earliest concern with death, which occurs during toddlerhood, reflects an inability to conceive of an irreversible state of lifelessness. Toddlers are likely to think that a person may be dead at one moment and "undeaded" the next. By middle school age, children have a rather realistic concept of death but are unlikely to relate that concept to themselves or to others close to them (Anthony, 1972). Thoughts about one's death and the formulation of a conceptualization of death become increasingly well articulated from early through later adolescence (Noppe & Noppe, 1997). In the process of forming a personal identity, young people ask new questions about mortality, the meaning of life, and the possibility of life after death.

During middle adulthood, people recognize that they have already lived over half of their lives. There is more time in the past than in the future. The issue of death becomes increasingly concrete as parents and older relatives die. At the same time, adults begin to have a larger impact on their families and communities. Increased feelings of effectiveness and vitality lessen the threat of death (Feifel & Branscomb, 1973; Fried-Cassorla, 1977). The degree to which individuals gain satisfaction from their own contributions to future generations determines the extent of their anxiety about death during this stage. Achievement of a sense of generativity usually allows adults to accept that their impact will continue to be felt even after death.

Ideally, during later adulthood, ego concerns about death decrease. Individuals come to accept their own lives as they have lived them and begin to see death as a natural part of the life span. Death no longer poses a threat to personal value, the potential for accomplishment, or the desire to influence the lives of others. As a result of having accepted one's life, one can accept its end without discouragement. This implies not a willingness to die but an acceptance of the fact of death. It takes great courage to face the fact of one's own death and, at the same time, to live out the days of one's life with optimism and enthusiasm. Older adults who achieve this degree of acceptance of their death appreciate that the usefulness of their contributions does not necessarily depend on their physical presence (Kübler-Ross, 1969, 1972).

The notion that one's understanding of the concept of death changes with development is complemented by the idea that people go through a process in coming to terms with their own death. In the 1960s, Elisabeth Kübler-Ross engaged in groundbreaking work to understand the thoughts, feelings, and needs of patients who were dying. Through her interviews with over 400 patients, she began to clarify a process of coping with one's death. She identified five stages that are likely to occur between the awareness of a terminal illness and ultimate acceptance of one's death: denial; anger and resentment; bargaining for a reprieve; depression and mourning one's death; and acceptance or a willingness to face the reality of one's death. She also discovered how eager most people were to have someone who would listen to their thoughts and how grateful they were to interact with someone about their death rather than have it treated as a taboo or unmentionable topic (Kübler-Ross, 1969; 1981).

Subsequent research has suggested that there is no single, typical path in the dying process. Some people alternate between accepting and denying their death. They understand their situation, yet fall into periods of disbelief. Some people are able to bring what they view as an acceptable close to their life, saying goodbye to family and friends, finding comfort in the support of others. Others die while still in a state of fear or denial (Kasterbaum, 1981; 1985). Kübler-Ross's stages are not a fixed sequence, but a useful model for considering the dynamic ego processes that are engaged as one faces death. The capacity to confront the reality of death can be seen as a profound occasion for new insight (Kübler-Ross, 1981).

The evolution of a point of view about death requires the capacity to absorb the loss of one's close relatives and friends as well as to accept one's own death. The former task may be even more difficult than the latter, in that the death of peers begins to destroy one's social group. Losing one's friends and relatives means losing daily companionship, a shared world of memories and plans, and a source of support for values and social norms. The circumstances surrounding the deaths of others may also be very frightening. Older adults observe peers suffering through long illnesses, dying abruptly

At the age of 91, a year before his death, Picasso painted this amazing self-portrait. He faces his death with eyes wide open. No pretenses, some fear, some wonder.

in the midst of a thriving and vigorous life, or dying in absurd, meaningless accidents. After each death, the surviving adults must ask themselves about the value of each of these lives and subsequently about the value of their own life.

Death Anxiety

Several researchers have considered the sources of personal anxiety about death and the changes in preoccupation with death at various ages. Although older adults seem to think about death more frequently than do young adults, they do not appear to feel more threatened by it. In a survey of over 400 adults in early, middle, and later adulthood, death was a more salient issue for the oldest (over 60) age group (Kalish & Reynolds, 1976). They felt that they were more likely to die in the near future. They knew more people who had died and were more likely than younger subjects to have visited a cemetery or attended a funeral. The oldest adults were more likely to have made some specific arrangements related to their death, including purchasing cemetery space, writing a will, and making funeral arrangements. Yet fear of death was lowest in this age group, and the percentage who said that they were unafraid of death or even eager for it was highest.

Fear of personal death is natural and normal. Death may be feared for a variety of reasons, some of which relate to the actual process of dying and others to the consequences of it. Concerns about the process of dying include fears of being alone, being in pain, having others see one suffering, or losing control of one's mind and body. Concerns about the consequences of dying include fears of the unknown, loss of identity ("People will forget about me"), the grief others will feel, the decomposition of the body, and punishment or pain in the hereafter (Florian & Kravetz, 1983; Conte et al., 1982).

Death does not seem to be as frightening to older adults as it is to younger people. Table 13.5 shows the responses of three age groups of adults to the following question, "Some people say they are afraid to die and others say they are not. How do you feel?" Admission of fear decreased with age, and lack of fear or even eagerness to die increased. In another study of over 1200 adults, a similar pattern was observed (Bengston et al., 1977). Expressed fear decreased with age. The group aged 45–49 had the greatest fear of death, while the group aged 70–74 had the lowest.

There are at least three explanations for this finding. First, older people tend to be more religious and may find comfort in the concept of life after death. Second, older

---

TABLE 13.5   Fear of Death (Percentages)

	Age		
	20–39	40–59	60+
Afraid/terrified	40	26	10
Neither afraid nor unafraid	21	20	17
Unafraid/eager	36	52	71
Depends	3	3	2

Source: Based on Kalish & Reynolds, 1976.

people may feel more accepting of their lives and the decisions they have made than younger people. This view is supported by the responses of subjects in the Kalish and Reynolds study (1976) to the following question, "If you were told that you had a terminal disease and that you had six months to live, how would you want to spend your time?" Older adults were more likely to concentrate on their inner lives or to continue their lives as they were. Young-adult and middle-aged subjects expressed more concern about their relationships with loved ones. The youngest subjects were most likely to want new experiences. The idea of death was viewed as less tragic and disruptive by the older subjects than by the younger ones. A third explanation is that older people are more familiar with death. They have had more opportunities to experience the deaths of others, and have made more preparations for their own deaths. Realistically, they expect death in the near future. Death is less an uncertainty. Many people who were over 60 in the mid-1970s never anticipated the healthy old age that they were enjoying. The years after 65 were seen as an unexpected bonus that their parents and grandparents had not enjoyed.

Grief and Bereavement

Grief refers to the cognitive and emotional reactions that follow the death of a loved one. It can vary in duration and intensity, and it can fade and reappear at unexpected moments. In a study of family members who were responsible for caring for a person suffering from later-life dementia, after the person had died five aspects of grief were identified: preoccupation with thoughts of the deceased person, longing for the person, painful emotions, feelings of dissociation—feeling disconnected from reality, and sensory illusions that led to the impression that the deceased person was still present (Aneshensel et al., 1995). Of these five aspects of grief, preoccupation was the most common and lasted the longest after the person's death.

Bereavement is the long-term process of adjustment to the death of a loved one, and is more all-encompassing than grief. It is commonly accompanied by physical symptoms, role loss, and a variety of intense emotions, including anger, sorrow, anxiety, and depression. The stress of bereavement increases the likelihood of illness and even death among survivors.

In the face of bereavement, there is a need to "work through" the reality of the loss as well as the feelings that accompany it. The experience of the bereaved person is not that different from the experience of the person who is coping with his or her own death. Psychiatrist Erich Lindemann (1944) worked with many of the people whose relatives had died in the Coconut Grove fire in Boston. His writings continue to provide a basis of understanding the bereavement process. Lindemann described the normal grief reaction as involving three phases. First, the person must achieve "emancipation from bondage to the deceased." This "bondage" may include feelings of guilt about ways he or she had criticized or even harmed the person who had died. Second, the person must make an adjustment to all the aspects of the environment from which the deceased is missing. Third, the person must begin to form new relationships. Lindemann found that one major obstacle to working through this loss is a desire to avoid the accompanying emotions and intense physical distress. According to his analysis, the strategy of avoiding grief only prolongs the survivor's physical, mental, and emotional preoccupation with the dead person.

The depression and confusion accompanying grieving may decrease the survivors' sensitivity to their own physical health and pose risks to their mental health as well. People in deep mourning may have feelings of uselessness or emptiness that prevent them from seeking help for their own physical or emotional health problems. Some people try to cope with their grief by increasing their use of medication, alcohol, or tranquilizers, which may threaten their physical health. Loss of appetite and lack of sleep are other symptoms of grief that contribute to the pattern of increased vulnerability during this time.

Among people who have lost a spouse, intense depression is experienced by those who described their marriage as positive and vital. It is clear that this loss strikes at the

Death-related rituals help the bereaved to cope with their loss as well as with the painful realization of their own mortality. In Columbia, a group of boys bring flowers to the cemetery where their friend is buried.

core of an older adult's sense of attachment, social integration, and personal worth (Futterman et al., 1990). In a comparison study of older widows and widowers with adults who were not experiencing bereavement, the widowed adults showed greater signs of depression, psychopathology, and grief at 2 months after the loss (Thompson et al., 1991). At 12 and 30 months after the loss, the two groups were comparable in levels of depression and psychopathology, but the bereaved group continued to experience higher levels of grief than the nonbereaved group. The research, confirmed by other observations, suggests that, among older adults, one may not expect a full resolution of the grief work associated with the death of a spouse. Rather, older adults come to accept a certain empty place in their hearts for their deceased partner and learn to find appropriate times to experience their profound sense of loss.

Death-Related Rituals

The American culture's rituals surrounding death of a loved one permit adults to cope with death-related anxiety. The elaborate arrangements for a burial service—viewing the body; the selection of a coffin or urn, gravestone, or burial site; and provision for care of the grave—allow adults to work through the reality of their own death by focusing on aspects of it over which they can exercise some control. The details of a funeral and burial may not bring adults closer to an emotional acceptance of death, but they do impart some feeling of certainty about the events immediately following their own death. In fact, some people think of their funeral as a last social statement. All of the plans surrounding a death are designed to heighten the perception of the individual's social status and moral virtue. The event of death is a direct contradiction of the cultural values of activity, productivity, and individuality. In order to disguise the view of death as a final failure, individuals may attempt to maintain an illusion of competence by planning the circumstances of their own funeral.

A Cultural Comparison. To appreciate how people cope with death, it is helpful to consider the cultural rituals that have emerged for structuring the response to death. Box 13.1, which describes the Amish way of death, illustrates how death is openly incorporated into every aspect of life. The service and ritual are expressions of the belief in a spiritual immortality and a simultaneous recognition of separation. Families customarily care for their aging parents within their own homes. Dying persons are surrounded by their families, who provide reassurance of generational continuity. The bereaved family members receive help and care from community members for at least

BOX 13.1   THE AMISH WAY OF DEATH

The importance that the Amish place on their funeral ceremonies is reflected not only in familiarity with death but also in an intensified awareness of community. As an Amish man reported in a family interview, "The funeral is not for the one who dies, you know; it is for the family."

The Amish community takes care of all aspects of the funeral occasion, with the exception of the embalming procedure, the coffin, and the horse-drawn wagon. These matters are taken care of by a non-Amish funeral director who provides the type of service that the Amish desire.

The embalmed body is returned to the home within a day of the death. Family members dress the body in white garments in accordance with the biblical injunction found in Revelation 3:5. For a man, this consists of white trousers, a white shirt, and a white vest. For a woman, the usual clothing is a white cape and apron that she wore at both her baptism and her marriage. At baptism, a black dress is worn with the white cape and apron; at marriage, a purple or blue dress is worn with the white cape and apron. It is only at her death that an Amish woman wears a white dress with the cape and apron that she put away for the occasion of her death. This is an example of the lifelong preparation for death as sanctioned by Amish society. The wearing of white clothes signifies the high ceremonial emphasis on the death event as the final rite of passage into a new and better life.

Several Amish women stated that making their parents', husbands', or children's funeral garments was a labor of love that represented the last thing they could do for their loved ones. One Amish woman related that each month her aged grandmother carefully washed, starched, and ironed her own funeral clothing so that it would be in readiness for her death. This act appears to have reinforced for herself and her family her lifelong acceptance of death and to have contributed to laying the foundation for effective grief work for herself and her family. This can be seen as an example of the technique of preventive intervention called *anticipatory guidance* (Caplan, 1964), which focuses on helping individuals to cope with impending loss through open discussion and problem solving before the actual death.

After the body is dressed, it is placed in a plain wooden coffin that is made to specifications handed down through the centuries. The coffin is placed in a room that has been emptied of all furnishings, in order to accommodate the several hundred relatives, friends, and neighbors who will begin arriving as soon as the body is prepared for viewing. The coffin is placed in a central position in the house, both for practical considerations of seating and to underscore the importance of the death ceremonial.

The funeral service is held in the barn in the warmer months and in the house during the colder seasons. The service is conducted in German and lasts 12 hours, with the same order of service for every funeral. The guests view the body when they arrive and again when they leave to take their places in the single-file procession of the carriages the burial place.

Source: Bryer, 1979.

---

the first year after a family death. In one study, Amish families found six conditions especially helpful for coping with death:

> (a) The continued presence of the family, both during the course of the illness and at the moment of death; (b) open communication about the process of dying and its impact on the family; (c) the maintenance of a normal life-style by the family during the course of the illness; (d) commitment to as much independence of the dying person as possible; (e) the opportunity to plan and organize one's own death; (f) continued support for the bereaved for at least a year following the funeral, with long-term support given to those who do not remarry. (Bryer, 1979, p. 260)

The Right to Die

The transition from illness to death in contemporary society is becoming increasingly complex. As a result of growing knowledge and medical technology, it is possible to sustain life and explore a variety of treatment strategies for those who suffer from terminal illnesses. Under conditions of coma or loss of the capacity to make an informed decision, questions arise about the continuation or withdrawal of treatment. Both physicians and patients are sometimes viewed as victims of technology that can sustain life beyond the person's will to live. At the same time, efforts to legalize physician-assisted suicide have raised serious concerns about the possibility of practices that would place pressure on older adults to end their lives in order to save family members or insurance companies the cost of extended treatment and care (Palermo, 1995; Dubler & Sabatino, 1991).

An emerging concern focuses on a person's right to die and, perhaps even more, on the right to a "good" end of life. Typically, people view a "good" death as one in which pain is minimal, open communication about it is possible, and the dying person's own values and choices are respected (Zuckerman, 1997). In order to achieve these objectives, increasing numbers of families are seeking care in a hospice environment. **Hospice** is an integrated system of medicine, nursing, counseling, and spiritual care for the dying person and his or her family. Its goal is to achieve the highest possible quality of life for the dying person and the family, alleviating physical and emotional pain to the degree possible, while supporting family strengths to cope with the process of dying, loss of the loved one, and long-term bereavement (Smith, 1997).

THE PSYCHOSOCIAL CRISIS: INTEGRITY VERSUS DESPAIR

The conflict of integrity versus despair is resolved through a dynamic process of life review and self-evaluation. Contemporary factors such as health, family relationships, and role loss or role transition are integrated with an assessment of one's past aspirations and accomplishments. Thoughts of the past may be fleeting or a constant obsession. Memories may be altered to fit contemporary events, or contemporary events may be reinterpreted to fit memories. The achievement of integrity is the culmination of a life of psychosocial growth. Psychologically speaking, it is the peak of the pyramid in that it addresses the ultimate question: How do I find meaning in life given the ultimate reality of death? Achievement of integrity in later adulthood inspires younger age groups to continue to struggle with the challenges of their own life stages.

Integrity   The term **Integrity,** as used in Erikson's theory, refers to the ability to accept the facts of one's life and face death without great fear. The attainment of it is ultimately a result of the balance of all the psychosocial crises that have come earlier, accompanied by all the ego strengths and core pathologies that have accumulated along the way. Integrity comes only after some considerable thought about the meaning of one's life. Older adults who have achieved a sense of integrity view their past in an existential light. They appreciate that their lives and individuality are due to an accumulation of personal satisfactions and crises. Integrity is not so much a quality of honesty and trustworthiness, as the term is used in daily speech, as it is an ability to integrate one's past history with one's present circumstances and to feel content with the outcome.

Despair   The opposite pole of integrity is *despair.* It is much more likely that adults will resolve the crisis of integrity versus despair in the negative direction than that infants will resolve the crisis of trust versus mistrust in the negative direction. For infants to experience trust, they must depend on the benevolence of a responsible caregiver who will meet their essential needs. In most cases, this caregiver is present, and the infant learns to rely on him or her. In order to experience integrity, however, older adults must incorporate into their self-image a lifelong record of conflicts, failures, and disappointments, along with accomplishments. They must confront what is sometimes referred to as the "death of dreams," a realization that some of their most cherished hopes for themselves or their children cannot be accomplished in their lifetime (Oates, 1997).

In addition, older adults must face some degree of devaluation and even hostility from the social community. The negative attitudes expressed by family members, colleagues, and younger people toward the perceived lack of competence, dependence, or old-fashioned ways of older people may lead many of them to feel discouraged about their self-worth. The gradual deterioration or loss of certain physical capacities, particularly hearing, vision, and motor agility, contribute to an older person's frustration and discouragement. Older adults recognize that they cannot perform certain tasks as well as they did in the past or that their domains of independent functioning and mastery have diminished.

Furthermore, there is a general cultural sentiment that the death of an older person—in contrast, for example, with that of a child or youth—while sad, is not a great loss to society since that person had already contributed what she or he was likely to contribute. Thus, older adults may perceive that society is already letting go of them, even before they are ready to let go of life (Jecker & Schneiderman, 1994).

All of these factors are likely to create a feeling of regret about one's past and a continuous, haunting desire to be able to do things differently, or of bitterness over how one's life has turned out. People who resolve the crisis of later adulthood in the direction of despair cannot resist speculating about how things might have been or about what actions might have been taken if conditions had only been different. They are preoccupied with the "if only's" of their past, disrupting a calm acceptance of death. Despairing individuals either seek death as a way of ending a miserable existence or desperately fear death because it makes impossible any hope of compensating for past failures.

Depression

The theme of depression has been treated in several sections of this text, especially as a concern in early adolescence, in the mother-infant relationship, and as it is linked with life stressors such as unemployment and divorce. Given the close link between the concepts of depression and despair, it should come as no surprise that depression has been a topic of research in the study of adulthood and aging. A number of cross-sectional studies have documented a U-shaped pattern in the presence of depressive symptoms with age. These symptoms are especially evident in early adulthood, between the ages of 25 and 30; they decline in middle adulthood; and increase again in those over age 70 (Kessler et al., 1992). The same factors that are associated with depression in younger age groups are also associated with depression in older age groups. Even though the risk of depression increases in later life, it cannot be attributed to the aging process itself. The negative physiological changes associated with aging, such as high blood pressure, reduced breathing capacity, reduced muscle strength, slowed reaction time, memory loss, and loss of visual or auditory acuity, are not associated in and of themselves with depression (Lewinsohn et al., 1991). Thus, depression as a complex affective and cognitive syndrome does not automatically "come with the territory" of aging but occurs in a subset of older adults, especially those who have experienced a decreased activity level; reduced access to a significant close, confiding relationship; and have accumulated physical health problems that limit independence and dampen the sense of enthusiasm for pleasant activities (Lewinsohn et al., 1991).

THE CENTRAL PROCESS: INTROSPECTION

In order to achieve a sense of integrity, the individual must engage in deliberate self-evaluation and private thought. The final achievement of a sense of integrity requires the ability to **introspect** about the gradual evolution of life events and to appreciate their significance in the formation of the adult personality (Walasky et al., 1983–84). This state can be reached only through individual effort. It may even require temporary isolation, shutting out the influences of potentially competitive or resentful associates.

One mode for engaging in self-evaluation is reminiscence. **Reminiscence** has been defined as the recollection of "long-term memories of events in which the reminiscer is either a participant or an observer" (Ross, 1989, p. 341). This process of nostalgic remembering allows adults to recapture some of the memorable events in their life histories. Reminiscence may be a playful recalling of a life adventure or a painful review of some personal or family crisis. The process of simple reminiscence has been described as comprising four elements: the selection of an event or "story" to retell or review; immersion in the details of the story, including the strong emotions linked to the event; withdrawal from the past by distancing oneself from the event or comparing past and present; and bringing closure to the memory by summing up, finding some lesson, or making a general observation. Through this kind of process, a person builds a mental and emotional bridge between the past and the present (Meacham, 1995).

Reminiscence is linked to positive adjustment in later life, especially better health, a more positive outlook, and a better ability to cope with the challenges of daily life. However, not all forms of reminiscence are of equal benefit. In particular, reminiscences of the integrative or instrumental type tend to be associated with high levels of

Through reminiscence and introspection, older adults piece together the meaning and direction of their lives. Although friends and family can help sustain a positive outlook, much of the psychological work required to achieve integrity must be done alone.

well-being, whereas obsessive reminiscences are not. **Integrative reminiscence** involves reviewing one's past in order to find meaning or to reconcile one's current and prior feelings about certain life events. **Instrumental reminiscence** focuses on the past—on accomplishments, efforts to overcome difficulties, and experiences to help cope with current difficulties. **Obsessive reminiscences** suggest an inability to resolve or accept certain past events and a persistent guilt or despair over them (Wong & Watt, 1991). Contrast the following two narratives:

"When I was a teenager, my parents broke up and both remarried. I was very resentful because they did not seem to care about my feelings or needs. But as I grow older and look back, I understand that they were really not compatible with each other. They had suffered for many years before their divorce." [Integrative reminiscence] "My husband died when I was away for two days visiting my friends in the West. He fell in the bathtub and eventually died because there was no one there to help him. It has been years now, but I still cannot forgive myself for leaving him home alone for two days." [Obsessive reminiscence] (Wong & Watt, 1991, p. 276)

Reminiscence appears to lend continuity to older adults' self-concepts. They can trace the path of their own development through time and identify moments that were of central importance in the crystallization of their personal philosophies. Through reminiscence, older adults can revise the meaning of past events by using current wisdom to understand or accept what took place in the past. The focus of reminiscence depends on personality, the specific nature of stressful life events, and the degree to which the older person is searching for new levels of self-understanding (Quackenbush & Barnett, 1995). For example, reminiscence was encouraged in a group of veterans who had been involved in the Normandy invasion at the end of World War II. The veterans retold their experiences of loss, grief, and shock, and how those experiences influenced their lives over the subsequent 50-year period. Formulating their experiences in a storylike format and retelling their stories to others provided a means of coping with the stressors of this past experience (Harvey et al., 1995).

Reminiscence serves as an integrating process that has positive value in an eventual attainment of integrity. In excess, however, it can dominate reality, taking over the time and energy that might be directed toward more appropriate active social involvement. Some adults tend to dwell on sad events and allow earlier disappointments to preoccupy their current thoughts. In that case, their past lives take precedence over current circumstances. No new events can compete successfully with past memories for their attention.

Of course, the process of introspection is affected by the selectivity of memory, dominant value orientation, and general quality of supportiveness or destructiveness in the social milieu. Given these contaminants of purely objective self-assessment, individuals must engage in repeated soul searching to sort out their lives and come to terms with some of the discordant events that have inevitably been part of their history. They must determine whether the essential nature of their personal identity has survived through time. Individuals must evaluate the quality of their close relationships and determine the degree to which they are able to meet the needs of others. They must identify those contributions that have represented a serious effort to improve the quality of others' lives. Finally, older adults must determine the extent to which their philosophy of life has been accurately translated into significant actions.

Ryff and Heincke (1983) used a psychosocial model to test the possible changes in personality configurations in later adulthood. Early, middle, and later adults were asked to respond to a variety of statements from three time perspectives; as they applied in the present, in the past during an earlier life stage, and in the future in a later life stage. Generativity was perceived by all age groups as being highest during middle adulthood, regardless of the respondents' ages. Similarly, integrity was perceived as being highest in later adulthood. Older adults rated themselves as being higher in integrity at present than in the past. Young and middle-aged adults expected to be higher in integrity in the future than they were at present. This research suggests that people not only experience changes in the directions that psychosocial theory would predict but also anticipate changes in those directions at various life stages. These expectations influence how one prepares for future life stages and evaluates them once they arrive.

THE PRIME ADAPTIVE EGO QUALITY AND THE CORE PATHOLOGY

Wisdom

The well-being of society rests in part on the capacity of older adults to attain wisdom. We look to those with experience and knowledge to help us face life's challenges. Professor Donald Cram, a Nobel Prize winning organic chemist, has continued to teach for 45 years, inspiring students and encouraging them to pursue complex scientific questions.

When people are asked about the positive goals of later life, they frequently mention wisdom, which they expect to emerge in later adulthood and to grow with increasing age (Heckhausen et al., 1989; Sternberg, 1990). **Wisdom** has been defined as the "fundamental pragmatics of life," a type of expert knowledge that reflects sound judgment and good advice about important life issues that usually involve high levels of uncertainty (Baltes et al., 1992). Erikson identified wisdom as the prime adaptive ego quality of later adulthood in that it reflects a detached concern for life and a desire to learn and communicate essential lessons from experience in the face of impending death (Erikson et al., 1986).

Wisdom has been characterized by five basic features (Baltes et al., 1992, p. 272):

1. *Factual knowledge* about fundamental life matters such as general knowledge about the human condition and specific knowledge about life events, their age-related occurrence and their expected and unexpected course.
2. *Procedural knowledge,* including strategies and ways of approaching the management and interpretation of life matters, including linking past, present, and future.
3. *Life span contextualism,* approaching problems with the realization that events are embedded in a multidimensional context, including age-related, culturally defined, role-related, and sociohistorical frameworks, and that they take their meaning from certain distinct domains, especially family, work, and leisure.
4. *Relativism of values and life goals,* allowing the person to appreciate differences among individuals and societies with respect to the priorities they place on certain values, as well as the ability to preserve a certain core of universal values.
5. *Recognition and management of uncertainty,* incorporating the realization that the future cannot be totally predicted, and that many aspects of the past and present are not fully known, plus an ability to manage and cope with this uncertainty.

Using this approach to defining wisdom, researchers coded the narratives of younger and older adults who were analyzing the life course of a fictitious character. Older adults had equally high levels of wisdom as younger adults and higher levels under some circumstances (Baltes et al., 1992). Of course, not all people who live to old age function at a high level of wisdom. More research is needed to determine what factors foster wisdom among older adults. Three dimensions that have been hypothesized to promote wisdom are opportunities to experience a wide variety of life situations and circumstances; encouragement by a mentor or guide to expand one's capacity for thinking about problems from a multidimensional, psychohistorical perspective; and a strong generative orientation or a desire to continue to gain insight into how people meet the challenges of life (Baltes & Smith, 1990).

Disdain   Wisdom reflects flexibility of thought, openness to new interpretations, and a willingness to accept the complexity of life. In contrast, **disdain** conveys rejection of ideas and persons, and an arrogance that implies that one's own opinions and views are superior. It can be understood as a defensive response to the repulsion one feels for one's physical self and failed past. Rather than becoming more patient, more compassionate, and less critical in their later life, older adults who develop disdain are more likely to express contempt for others and detach from the world around them (Erikson et al., 1986).

Applied Topic   RETIREMENT

One definition of retirement is that the person works less than full time year round and receives income from a retirement pension earned during earlier periods of employment (Atchley, 1977). Some people define retirement as the time at which people begin to receive social security or other pension benefits. However, retirement also refers to a psychosocial transition—a predictable, normative change that involves preparation, redefinition of roles and role behaviors, and ongoing psychological adjustment as the structure and significance of paid employment are replaced by other activities (Floyd et al., 1992).

Of course, some people never retire, some die before they reach retirement age, and others continue to work on a part-time schedule. Some people of retirement age leave their primary job and take another full-time or part-time job in a related field or a totally different one. Many adults who are self-employed or whose work involves creative skills, such as acting, music, painting, or writing, simply continue to work into their late adulthood (Herzog et al., 1991). In fact, from an historical perspective, retirement is a relatively new concept. At the turn of the century, almost 70% of men over the age of 65 were in the paid labor force, compared to 17% in 1996 (U.S. Senate, Special Committee on Aging, 1986; U.S. Bureau of the Census, 1997). Men now spend about 20% of their lives in retirement. As the period of healthy later adulthood expands for them, this percentage will increase as well.

Adjustment to Retirement   Adjustment during the retirement transition is an individual process. Retirement can be viewed as a combination of benefits and losses. Although most older adults cope effectively with the changes associated with it, approximately one-third of adults report significant difficulty during this process (Fletcher & Hansson, 1991). Weiss (1997) described a longitudinal study of men and women who were over age 63 and intended to retire in the coming year or had recently retired. Most anticipated that retirement would bring a reduction in stress, especially coping with the challenges and crises of the workplace. Workplace conditions such as lack of challenge, reorganization, and downsizing (with its accompanying increased demands on remaining employees) are stressors that workers are glad to leave behind when they retire (Henkens & Tazelaar, 1997). Three factors that seem to influence retirement adjustment include planning for it, perceptions of it, and the extent of income loss (Newman & Newman, 1983; Mutran et al., 1997).

Planning for Retirement

Preparation for retirement involves a willingness to anticipate and address the changes that may occur in finances, family roles, daily activity, and social interactions. In a national survey of men aged 60–74, fewer than 4% had participated in retirement preparation programs. Workers who might benefit most from these programs, especially those with lower retirement income, are less likely to learn about or participate in them (Beck, 1984; Ferraro, 1990).

Perceptions of Retirement

Perceptions of retirement involve a person's relief or resentment about it. Jahoda (1982) argued that in addition to the manifest or obvious functions of paid employment, especially income and possibly status, there are a number of latent functions that provide important psychological benefits. She identified the following functions: providing a structure for the use of time; a context for social contact; a content for self-identity; regular, predictable activities; and a sense of participation in a collective effort. Retirement may be perceived as resulting in deprivation in each of these areas and therefore as presenting a threat to psychological well-being.

Several measures have been devised to assess the stresses associated with retirement and the anxiety people feel as they anticipate it. Sharpley (1997) found that when retirees reflected on factors that caused them stress in everyday living, three areas emerged: missing work, problems with personal health, and relationship issues. Fletcher and Hansson (1991) constructed a measure of retirement anxiety that captures some of the apprehensions that adults have as they anticipate retirement. It illustrates how people come to rely on work as a primary social structure and highlights the difficulties they face as they confront the transition to retirement. In particular, Fletcher and Hansson found that for those who suffer from retirement anxiety, two factors were especially troubling. First, people who had high levels of retirement anxiety worried about the loss of structured social involvement and connection. This concern was linked to worry about losing friendships, being lonely, and having little in common with former co-workers after retirement. Second, people worried about having to be assertive or proactive in finding new relationships and activities that would meet their needs. This concern was linked to a general difficulty in handling life transitions, a high level of uncertainty about the future, and a general feeling of loss of identity. Although one might think that people who have high levels of retirement anxiety would utilize services that help people plan for retirement, this was not the case. They may try to deny this transition by avoiding planning and counseling sessions.

In addition to worries about being unable to meet one's social needs following retirement, some adults find the transition difficult because they feel a lack of control. When people perceive that they are working or not working by their own choice and that they determine how much work to do, they have higher levels of health and well-being. However, when they perceive that their involvement or lack of involvement in work is being decided by someone else and they have little say in it, they are likely to have more difficulty adjusting to retirement, more health problems, and a greater incidence of depression (Gall et al., 1997).

People whose work has brought them little satisfaction and those who are ready to become involved in new activities may feel more effective and independent after they retire (Floyd et al., 1992). They are likely to find new sources of enjoyment, new opportunities to spend time with family and friends, a sense of relief at not having to deal with the stressors of their job, and a new feeling of freedom to develop their interests or to exert more control over their daily life, as the following account makes clear:

> "This widowed man lives alone in a cabin in a sparsely populated, rural area. Throughout his working career, he held a variety of low-paying jobs that, in retrospect, neither required nor permitted real discipline or enterprise. He did not particularly like his jobs, and he was never viewed as performing them with particular success. For this man, retirement seems to signify not the loss of valuable structure, but his release from a series of rigid, repetitive demands that in and of themselves precluded inventiveness and enthusiasm. Retirement presents him with a new opportunity to reexperience the initiative that he now recalls as having characterized him until his mid-teens.
>
> This man has always enjoyed music. He has always loved listening to the radio and playing records. As an adolescent, he tinkered with radio equipment until the advent of transistors and integrated circuits. Over the years he has accumulated a collection of some two to three thousand 78 rpm records. Recognizing that plastic record disks are likely to warp or break, he has recently begun to copy them onto cassettes. He has removed his tape deck and large loudspeakers from their cabinet and strapped them to a mover's dolly, onto which he has built ap-

A retired farmer, Robert taught himself how to weave caning material. He repairs worn-out chair seats. It gives him pleasure to restore something worth saving, and the activity keeps him connected to his community. His services are in high demand.

propriate shelves. Each day, when he goes to the senior center for lunch, he wheels his movable entertainment center out to his pickup truck and brings his friends their favorite songs.

This man has also begun to make his own TV dinners, using the partitioned trays on which his "meals on wheels" are delivered. He cooks large quantities of meat and vegetables and freezes them in these single-meal trays for easy access. The quality of this man's products is far from professional. In fact, his entertainment center looks rather slapdash, and the contents of his frozen meals do not always retain their flavor or texture when reheated. What is striking, instead, is the enthusiasm, the delight, and the pride with which he has devised his various projects. In each case he perceived a problem, combined his own ingenuity with the resources at hand to devise a solution that is satisfactory for his own needs, and created something that is usable, gives him pleasure, and remains a real source of personal pride." (Erikson et al., 1986, pp. 181–182)

Adjustment to retirement is expected to change with time. Atchley (1976) proposed three phases of adjustment: a honeymoon period, which is busy and positive; a let-down phase, in which the meaning and structure of work are missed; and a reorientation phase, in which a stable life routine is established. In an attempt to assess this model, one study grouped retired men into six 6-month intervals from the date of retirement. Men in the period of 13–18 months after retirement were significantly more dissatisfied with life and had lower levels of physical activity than did those in the first 6 months after retirement. Later periods showed lower levels of satisfaction than the first 6 months but not the marked depression of the 13- to 18-month period (Ekerdt et al., 1985). These findings support the idea of an early euphoria phase as well as a later letdown phase. The pattern and degree of recovery are not as clearly described in this research.

Income Loss

Finally, adjustment to retirement is especially difficult when it is associated with a dramatic reduction in income. There is about a 25%–30% reduction in income after retirement, which is somewhat greater for those who retire before age 65 (Palmore et al., 1984). Although work-related expenses, taxes, and child-care expenses may decrease, health and recreational expenses may increase.

Older householders' annual income is derived from social security (37%), earnings (25%), property (23%), and pensions (13%). About 14% of all retired households receive income from at least three sources: social security, private pensions, and other assets (Kart et al., 1989). In 1995, the median income for families headed by someone 65 years old or over was $28,301; about 10.5% of those individuals 65 years old and over had incomes below the poverty level. Poverty is greater for older minorities and those who live alone (U.S. Bureau of the Census, 1997).

A Look Toward the Future of Retirement

The ongoing dialogue among older workers, retirees, and organizations is likely to result in the formulation of more varied, flexible alternatives to full retirement. An increasing number of businesses are eliminating a mandatory retirement age. At the same time, movements toward reducing the work force seem to include the development of early retirement plans, including phased retirement, part-time work, and reduced or redefined job expectations. Exploration in retirement options seems to be taking two directions at the same time: how to retain older workers in meaningful work roles and how to permit more flexible earlier retirement programs (Herzog et al., 1991).

Several long-range concerns suggest a need to reexamine the "right-to-retirement" concept. First, prospects for a longer, healthier adulthood mean that a large proportion of the population will be out of the labor force for nearly one-third of their adult lives. With a reduced fertility rate, there may not be enough younger workers available to support this large nonworking population. In addition, it is becoming increasingly difficult to see how one can earn enough income during the 40 or so years of employment to pay for 20 or more years of retirement. Second, many older adults who are well educated and have enjoyed working want to continue some of the positive experiences through constructive work. They do not want to retire, and with the lifting of the mandatory retirement age, they do not have to. There is a developing resistance to retirement evident in the attitudes of professionals in their 50s and 60s. In-depth interviews with university professors, physicians, lawyers, business professionals, and social service professionals, revealed that over 35% were negative about retiring and another 20% were ambivalent. One of those who was quite negative expressed it this way:

> "I'd probably try to get part-time teaching jobs, writing or editing, or research somewhere until I fall over. I mean really, I just can't imagine [retirement]. . . . This teaching is a rewarding activity. I don't hanker to retire to the sun belt and sit around and contemplate my navel. I just couldn't do that." (Karp, 1989, p. 752)

Third, people who reenter the labor force during midlife or make major career changes then will want to persist in these new activities in order to fulfill both personal and societal expectations of achievement. Many women who delayed entry into the labor market or achieved a professional degree after their spouse had completed his degree want to extend their work life into their late 60s and 70s (Carp, 1997). The recent generation of older workers who are now in their 50s and 60s have become used to a more fluctuating work history, moving from one company or employer to another. They are more accustomed to taking charge of their occupational career, rather than relying on the built-in career ladder of a single occupation or employer. Thus, just as the past few generations have begun to grow accustomed to retirement, new generations of older adults are finding ways to prolong their productive work lives, negotiating new and innovative ways of making transitions in and out of the paid labor force.

Chapter Summary

Variability in the patterns of adjustment during later adulthood results from the interaction between the individual's personality characteristics, health, coping strategies, and ego strengths and the range of circumstances that may befall him or her. Certain regularities can be anticipated in the termination of old roles and the establishment of new ones. Consolidation of attitudes toward one's life and the reality of one's death brings about a new perspective on life and leads to a more universal moral orientation.

The tasks of later adulthood—promoting intellectual vigor, redirecting energy to new roles and activities, accepting one's life, and developing a point of view about death—require a balance among investments in past, present, and future. There is an expectation that energy will be spent in the evaluative process of reviewing and accepting one's past achievements. However, this focus on the past must be complemented by the enactment of new roles, the resolution of new problems, and efforts to find new, engaging challenges in the present.

The psychosocial crisis of integrity versus despair captures the courage and creative synthesis required in later adulthood. In the face of an increasingly evident mortality, experienced in physical changes, role loss, and the death of peers, most older adults are able to define and articulate the thread of meaning in their lives. They are able to look back with satisfaction at past achievements and acceptance of past failures. In this process, they find a certain practical wisdom that is shared with others and becomes their legacy for the future.

The role transitions that accompany retirement illustrate the challenge of later adulthood. Retirement usually results in leaving a major life structure, one that provided social status, focus, purpose, and economic resources. The potential loss of daily stimulation poses threats to both cognitive and social functioning. Because so much of one's social status is linked to one's occupational attainment, leaving one's work role is almost like giving up one's social identity. Older adults face numerous adjustments after retirement, including role loss. They must restructure their lives so that they continue to feel pride in past achievements without dwelling in the past, and so that they seek new and realistic opportunities for making use of their talents in the present.

It is critical to be sensitive to the image that children, adolescents, young and middle-aged adults, and older adults themselves have of later adulthood. One should not underestimate the impact that one's perceptions of later life have on well-being and optimism at every earlier life stage. If the later years hold no promise, all earlier stages will be tinted with a sense of desperation. On the other hand, if the later years can be anticipated with optimism, people will be free at each earlier stage to experience life in a more confident, accepting manner.

End of Chapter Case

Mitch Albom, in his forties, rediscovers his former college professor, Morrie Schwartz, who is dying from amyotrophic lateral sclerosis (ALS), a progressive neurological disease that attacks body muscles and leaves one increasingly paralyzed. Mitch and Morrie meet every Tuesday for the last four months of Morrie's life.

"Everyone knows they're going to die," he said again, "but nobody believes it. If we did, we would do things differently."

So we kid ourselves about death," I said.

"Yes. But there's a better approach. To know you're going to die, and to be *prepared* for it at any time. That's better. That way you can actually be *more* involved in your life while you're living."

How can you ever be prepared to die?

"Do what the Buddhists do. Every day, have a little bird on your shoulder that asks, 'Is today the day? Am I ready? Am I doing all I need to do? Am I being the person I want to be?'"

He turned his head to his shoulder as if the bird were there now.

"Is today the day I die?" he said. . . .

"The truth is, Mitch," he said, "once you learn how to die, you learn how to live." I nodded.

"I'm going to say it again," he said. "Once you learn how to die, you learn how to live." He smiled, and I realized what he was doing. He was making sure I absorbed this point, without embarrassing me by asking. It was part of what made him a good teacher.

Did you think much about death before you got sick, I asked.

"No." Morrie smiled. "I was like everyone else. I once told a friend of mine, in a moment of exuberance, 'I'm gonna be the healthiest old man you ever met!'"

How old were you?

"In my sixties."

So you were optimistic.

"Why not? Like I said, no one really believes they're going to die."

But everyone knows someone who has died, I said. Why is it so hard to think about dying?

"Because," Morrie continued, "most of us all walk around as if we're sleepwalking. We really don't experience the world fully, because we're half-asleep, doing things we automatically think we have to do." . . . .

"Mitch. Can I tell you something?

Of course, I said.

"You might not like it."

Why not?

"Well, the truth is, if you really listen to that bird on your shoulder, *if you accept that you can die at any time*—then you might not be as ambitious as you are."

I forced a small grin.

"The things you spend so much time on—all the work you do—might not seem as important. You might have to make room for some more spiritual things."

Spiritual things?

"You hate that word, don't you? 'Spiritual.' You think it's touchy-feely stuff."

Well, I said.

He tried to wink, a bad try, and I broke down and laughed.

"Mitch," he said, laughing along, "even I don't know what 'spiritual development' really means. But I do know we're deficient in some way. We are too involved in materialistic things, and they don't satisfy us. The loving relationships we have, the universe around us, we take these things for granted."

He nodded toward the window with the sunshine streaming in. "You see that?" You can go out there, outside, anytime. You can run up and down the block and go crazy. I can't do that. I can't go out. I can't run. I can't be out there without fear of getting sick. But you know what? I *appreciate* that window more than you do."

Source: Albom, M., 1997.

Thought Questions

1. What is the point of view about life and death that Morrie is developing?

2. Why is it difficult for most people to have an open conversation about death?

3. What does this conversation suggest about Morrie's psychosocial development? To what extent are issues of intimacy, generativity, and integrity reflected in this dialogue?

4. How might the conditions of Morrie's illness influence his outlook on death?

5. What kinds of issues would you want to discuss if you had a mentor like Morrie who was willing to help you learn about living and dying?

Chapter 14

*F*ather Christmas is a perfect representative of the very old. He has all the benefits of extreme old age, but he is ever young in spirit; in fact he is immortal.

Very Old Age (75 Until Death)

Chapter Objectives

- To identify very old age as a unique developmental period for those of unusual longevity; a stage with its own developmental tasks and psychosocial crisis.
- To describe some of the physical changes associated with aging, including changes in fitness, behavioral slowing, sensory changes, and vulnerability to illness, and the challenges these changes pose for continued psychosocial well-being.
- To develop the concept of an altered perspective on time and history that emerges among the long-lived.
- To explore elements of the lifestyle structure for the very old, especially living arrangements and gender role behaviors.
- To identify and describe the psychosocial crisis of immortality versus extinction, the central process of social support, the prime adaptive ego quality of confidence, and the core pathology of diffidence.
- To apply research and theory to concerns about meeting the needs of the frail elderly.

*P*ablo Picasso, whose works illustrate this book, lived to be 91 years old. When he was 79 he married Jacqueline Roque, with whom he enjoyed 12 years of married life. During the last 20 years of his life, he remained productive and energetic, persistently experimenting with new art forms and ideas.

Other examples of people who achieved major accomplishments after age 80 (Wallechinsky et al., 1977; Wallechinsky & Wallace, 1993) include:

At 100, Grandma Moses was still painting.

At 99, twin sisters Kin Narita and Gin Kanie recorded a hit CD single in Japan and starred in a television commercial.

At 94, George Burns, who won an Oscar at age 80 for his role in The Sunshine Boys, performed at Proctor's Theater in Schenectady, New York, 63 years after he had first played there.

At 93, George Bernard Shaw wrote the play Far-fetched Fables.

At 91, Eamon de Valera served as president of Ireland.

At 91, Hulda Crooks climbed Mount Whitney, the highest mountain in the continental United States.

At 89, Arthur Rubenstein gave one of his greatest piano recitals in New York's Carnegie Hall.

At 88, Konrad Adenauer was chancellor of Germany.

At 87, Mary Baker Eddy founded the Christian Science Monitor.

At 81, Benjamin Franklin effected the compromise that led to the adoption of the U.S. Constitution. ❖

THE LONGEVITY REVOLUTION

We are entering a period of human experience in which increasing numbers of people are living into old age. In 1996, 5.7% of the U.S. population was 75 and over, and this age group is expected to make up 10% of the population in 50 years. In 1980, over 2 million people were 85 and over; by 1996, this group had grown to 3.8 million. Of these, 57,000 were 100 years old and over. The 85-and-over population, which is the fastest-growing age group in the United States, is expected to triple in size from 1980 to 2020 (U.S. Bureau of the Census, 1989a, 1997; U.S. Senate, Special Committee on Aging, 1986). Every morning on television, weather forecaster Willard Scott wishes happy birthday to men and women who are 100 years old or more. In 1997, Jeanne Clament, the world's officially longest living person, died at the age of 122. In an interview the year before her death, Ms. Clament was quoted as saying, "I've never had but one wrinkle and I'm sitting on it." In 1996, she recorded a rap CD as a document of her love of life (*Time*, August 18, 1997).

Jeanne Clament, who died in 1997 at the age of 122, was the world's longest living person whose birth date could be verified. Ms. Clament liked chocolates, smoked cigarettes, and had a wonderful sense of humor. Here she displays her Guinness certificate acknowledging her record-winning longevity.

As more and more people live to be 75 and over, questions continue to be raised regarding the upper limit of the human life span. Meyers and Manton (1984) demonstrated that the most enduring members of each new generation of aging adults appear to be living longer. **Life endurance** is the age to which 1 person in 100,000 can be expected to survive. Between 1900 and 1980, the age of the most enduring adults in the U.S. population increased from 105 to 111 for men and from 105 to 114 for women.

The 20th century is unique in human history in the large percentage of people who live well beyond their reproductive and childrearing years into later adulthood and very old age. This new facet of life raises questions about the pattern of mortality after achieving reproductive success, and what, if any, limit there might be to the human life span. Current demographic extrapolations suggest that the average life expectancy at birth is predicted to be 85 by the year 2050 (Wilmoth, 1998). Genetically based diseases that emerge only in the second half of life, such as breast and colon cancer or adult-onset diabetes, become more common as larger numbers of people reach advanced age. At the same time, medical and technological interventions hold the promise of reducing mortality in later life. Life expectancy is most influenced by interventions that prevent infants and children from dying, insuring that more people will reach advanced ages of 70 or over. Interventions that influence the life expectancy at ages 70 and over, however, will only increase overall life expectancy by a few years. Nonetheless, significant discoveries that might prevent death from cancers and/or cardiovascular diseases could affect large populations and continue to extend human longevity.

From an evolutionary perspective, the human species is a highly complex organism, designed to survive over a relatively long period in order to find a mate, reproduce, and rear and nurture their young until they are old enough to reproduce. The adaptive value of life after this sequence is not well understood. At the same time, it is clear that there is a genetic basis to longevity suggesting that for some subgroups, being long-lived has proven adaptive (Olshansky et al., 1998). The more knowledge that is gained about the biological processes of aging and the genetic basis of diseases that emerge in later life, the more likely it is that human longevity can be extended.

Each new cohort of the very old will benefit from the information and technology that have been developed during this century. Those adults in the United States who will be over 75 in the year 2000 are quite likely to be high school graduates, to have benefited from many of the educational and health-related innovations of the mid-20th century, and to be even more vigorous than our current older population.

In an attempt to learn the secrets of longevity, Jim Heynen (1990) interviewed 100 people who were 100 years or older. He found wide variations in their lifestyles and philosophical perspectives. Some of the advice they offered on how to live a long life follows:

"Mind your own business, have a good cigar, and take a shot of brandy." *Brother Adelard Beaudet, Harrisville, Rhode Island*

"I've lived long because I was so mean." *Pearl Rombach, Melbourne, Florida*

"I always walked several miles a day. I'd talk to the flowers." *Mary Frances Annand, Pasadena, California*

"Don't smoke before noon. Don't drink or smoke after midnight. The body needs 12 hours of the day to clear itself." *Harry Wander, Boise, Idaho*

"I've been a tofu eater all my life; a mild, gentle man, never a worrier." *Frank Morimitsu, Chicago, Illinois*

"I picked my ancestors carefully." *Stella H. Harris, Manhattan, Kansas*

"Regular hours, taking it easy, smiling, whistling at the women when they walk by." *John Hilton, Fort Lauderdale, Florida*

**A New
Psychosocial
Stage: Very Old
Age**

The fact that an increasing number of people are reaching advanced years and that they share several characteristics leads us to hypothesize a new stage of psychosocial development that emerges at the upper end of the life span, after one has exceeded the life expectancy for one's birth cohort. We call this stage *very old age*. Though it was not specifically identified in Erikson's original formulation of life stages, in his book *Vital Involvement in Old Age* (Erikson et al., 1986), Erikson began to characterize the dynamics of psychosocial adaptation in this period of life. We have formulated a psychosocial analysis of development for the very old, based on research literature, firsthand reports, and personal observations of the very old, to describe the developmental tasks, psychosocial crisis, central process, prime adaptive ego quality, and core pathology of this stage. We approach this formulation of a new stage realizing that in many domains, especially physical functioning, reaction time, memory, and fluid intelligence, variability increases significantly with age (Morse, 1993). The following are some of the many reasons that an increasing number of individual differences can be noted during later life:

> The combined effects of individuals' unique experiences over more years would produce increasing differences among them; genetically based differences would have more time to be expressed and to cause individuals to diverge; and older people, somewhat freer of societal constraints, would be more likely to choose their own courses of action. (Morse, 1993, p. 156)

The concept of reaction range offers a framework for understanding the enormous variability in vitality and functioning during very old age. Genetic factors influence longevity, vulnerability to illnesses, intelligence, and personality factors that contribute to coping. Conditions of poverty, discrimination, social alienation, and lack of social support are likely to be linked to lower levels of functioning in relation to one's potential and to greater vulnerability to the restrictive impact of illness in later life. On the other hand, adequate finances, social integration, social support, and access to appropriate services are likely to be linked to higher levels of functioning in relation to one's potential and to greater resilience in the face of illness.

The variations in life experiences and outlook among the very old are great; chronological age becomes less useful as an indicator of aging. Neugarten (1981) found it useful to distinguish between two groups of the very old: the old-old and the young-old. The old-old have "suffered major physical or mental decrements," which increase their dependence on health and social services. This group will grow as the number of adults over 75 increases. Currently, it forms a minority of the very old. The majority of people over 75 can be described as the young-old. They are competent, vigorous, and relatively healthy. They live in their own households and participate in activities in their communities.

Our intention is to discuss some of the most salient characteristics of life after 75 and to articulate what appears to be a psychosocial crisis peculiar to this period. We attempt to find evidence of common challenges and successful strategies for coping with them amid the great diversity of individual experiences.

**The Gender Gap
Among The Very
Old**

A discussion of aging in the U.S. must acknowledge the shifting sex composition of the population at older ages. In 1996, 54% of those 65–69 years old were women; 56% of those 70–74 years old were women; and 72% of those 85 years old and over were women. This gender difference in longevity is observed in virtually all countries of the world, but the differences are accentuated in the developed countries (U.S. Bureau of the Census, 1997). The imbalance in the sex composition is much more noticeable today than it was 50 years ago, when there were about as many men as women in the over-65 category (U.S. Bureau of the Census, 1983). Because those currently in the stage of very old age are predominantly women, many of the social issues of aging, especially poverty, health care, the future of social security, and housing, are also viewed as "women's issues."

DEVELOPMENTAL TASKS

Despite the wide variability in capacities, lifestyles, and world views in later life, three themes characterize the challenges that face individuals in very old age. First, they must adapt to the pattern of physical changes, monitoring their health and modifying their lifestyle to accommodate these changes. Second, they must conceptualize their lives within a new time frame, realigning thoughts about past, present, and future in a way that helps older adults stay connected to the present in a meaningful way. Third, they must develop new life structures, especially living arrangements and social relationships, that provide comfort, interest, and appropriate levels of care.

Coping with the Physical Changes of Aging

There is no way to avoid the realization that one's body is not what it used to be:

> With aging, as the overall tonus of the body begins to sag and innumerable inner parts call attention to themselves through their malfunction, the aging body is forced into a new sense of invalidness. Some problems may be fairly petty, like the almost inevitable appearance of wrinkles. Others are painful, debilitating, and shaming. Whatever the severity of these ailments, the elder is obliged to turn attention from more interesting aspects of life to the demanding requirements of the body. This can be frustrating and depressing. (Erikson et al., 1986, p. 309)

The theme of physical changes of aging can be approached much like its counterpart in early adolescence. Although the rate of change may be slower, older adults notice changes in a wide range of areas including appearance, body shape, strength and stamina, and the accumulation of chronic illnesses. This section will identify major areas of physical change. However, the more important issues are the meaning adults attribute to their physical condition and coping strategies they invent to adapt to these changes.

The patterns of change described below are usual or average trends; they do not occur at the same rate in every person, nor does every person experience all of them. For instance, older adults are more diverse in their sensory acuity than are young adults.

Most of us know older adults who are more vigorous and zestful than we are. On the other hand, we also know older adults who are painfully limited in their ability to function because of physical disabilities. Many factors influence the progression of physical changes associated with aging, not the least of which is the level of fitness that was established and maintained during early and middle adulthood.

Fitness

There is a great deal of variation in fitness among people after age 70 as patterns of activity or inactivity, endurance or frailty, and illness or health take their toll. What is described here might be thought of as usual patterns of aging. However, these changes are not inevitable and, in many instances, are reversible or modifiable with appropriate intervention (Rowe & Kahn, 1998). Decline in physical health and fitness begins to be noticed by most people in their late 20s and early 30s. As those who love baseball are likely to claim, "the legs are the first to go." On a more positive note, most people's strength and capacity for moderate effort are about the same at age 70 as they were at age 40 (Stevens-Long & Commons, 1992). However, older people are less resilient after a period of prolonged exertion. Their respiratory and circulatory systems usually degenerate to some extent, and are less capable of providing the heart and muscle tissue with oxygenated blood as quickly as they once could. One result is that sudden changes in posture can cause an older person to feel lightheaded. In order to adapt successfully to this kind of bodily change, the older person may find it necessary to move more slowly and to change positions more deliberately. This observable change in the tempo of movement may be incorrectly interpreted as fatigue or weakness, when in fact it is often a purposeful strategy for preventing dizziness.

Slowed metabolism reduces the need for calories, but there is a new risk. Reduction in food intake—particularly the elimination of foods such as milk—may result in the lack of essential vitamins and minerals in an older person's

Many of the physical signs of aging are obvious in this close-up of Mrs. Brent—wrinkles, sagging skin, receding gums, thinning hair, stooping shoulders. But age didn't rob her of twinkling eyes or a playful smile.

diet. The resulting malnutrition may then contribute to feelings of weakness and a lack of resilience. These effects may mistakenly be attributed to the aging process itself. In order to cope successfully with a diminished appetite, the very old person must become more conscientious in selecting foods that will provide the nutritional elements necessary for healthy functioning.

An increasing number of factors make it difficult to maintain a high level of physical fitness in later life. Figure 14.1 illustrates patterns of the loss of bodily functions associated with age in six areas. For each body area, the level of functioning at age 30 is taken as 100%, and the losses are plotted in comparison with this level. Most of the bodily changes begin in middle adulthood, but the rate of change appears to increase after age 60. As you can see, maximum breathing capacity decreases the most and brain weight changes the least. The consequences of an inactive life, especially obesity and degeneration in muscle strength, contribute to an even greater decline in physical capacity, particularly after age 60.

Commitment to physical fitness is important for adults in order to face the later years in the best possible physical condition. Maintenance of optimal physical condition in very old age depends on being active in earlier periods of adulthood. Overweight adults, as well as those of normal or below-normal weight, need to commit themselves to a program of moderate physical activity that can be continued throughout life.

With advancing age, some people tend to become more sedentary and lose interest in physical activity. In order to maintain optimal functioning and to retard the degenerative effects of aging, very old adults must continue to have frequent and regular opportunities for physical activity. A regular program of walking or other aerobic exercise for example can enhance cardiovascular functioning and reverse some of the effects of a sedentary adult lifestyle. It also increases muscle strength, balance, and, as

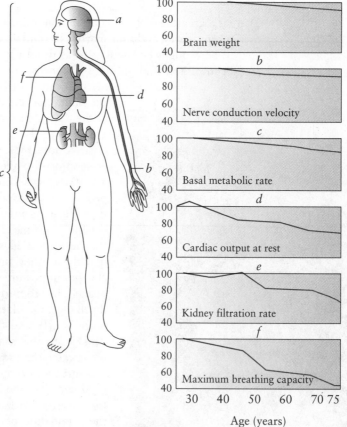

FIGURE 14.1

Loss of bodily functions with increasing age.
SOURCE: Leaf, 1973.

a result, general motor coordination. At the same time, exercise increases self-confidence. Research on weight, or resistance, training shows that even among the very old, a steady program of exercise builds muscle strength, which contributes to agility and an overall sense of well-being (Ades et al., 1996). Experimental studies of the effects of exercise on cognitive functioning show that it also leads to improvements in various central nervous system functions. These benefits of exercise are attributed to higher levels of oxygen, which improve the metabolism of glucose and neurotransmitters in the brain, as well as to increased levels of arousal, which increase response speed (Dustman et al., 1989; Birren & Fisher, 1992).

Behavioral Slowing

One of the most commonly noted markers of aging is a gradual slowing in response to stimuli. Such **behavioral slowing** is observed in motor responses, reaction time, problem-solving abilities, memory skills, and information processing (Salthouse, 1985; Bashore et al., 1989; Birren & Fisher, 1992). The speed of behavior is a composite outcome of the time it takes to perceive a stimulus, retrieve related information from memory, integrate it with other relevant stored information, reason as necessary about the required action, and then take action, whether that means simply pressing a button or performing a surgical procedure. Age-related slowing is more readily observable in complex tasks requiring mental processing than in routine tasks. The more complex the task, the greater the **processing load,** that is, the more domains of information are called into play and the more work is necessary to select response strategies (Cerella, 1994). Meta-analyses that combine the results of a variety of studies over a wide range of tasks find that the response time for older subjects (60–75 years old) is a linear function of the response time of younger subjects (16–25 years old). The greater the processing load, the longer it takes younger subjects to respond. In turn, the response time of older subjects increases in a linear relationship to the response time of younger subjects (Perfect, 1994).

As a result of behavioral slowing, it takes longer for older adults to perform daily tasks. When Ben takes his trip to the grocery, it takes him more time than it did 10 years ago to walk through the aisles, read the labels, decide on his purchases, and count his change.

Biological, learned, and motivational factors have been identified to account for behavioral slowing. At the biological level of analysis, there is evidence of the slowing of neural firing in certain brain areas, which may result in slower speed of information processing. The extent of this slowing depends on the kinds of tasks and the specific cognitive processes involved (Bashore et al., 1997).

Slowing of response may also be a product of learned cautiousness. With experience, people learn to respond slowly in order to avoid making mistakes. Finally, it also may be a product of a low level of motivation to perform a task. In experiments in which reaction time is being tested, adult subjects may be uninterested in the task and thus unwilling to try to achieve a high level of functioning.

The implications of the consequences of behavioral slowing are currently being examined. Some researchers argue that even the slightest reduction in the speed of neural firing may result in reduced sensory and information-processing capacities. Further, it may reduce a person's chances of survival if a situation arises in which a sudden evasive action or an immediate response is required. Others suggest that if a moment of thought is required before an action is taken, slowness may increase a person's chances of survival.

A more common consequence of slowing is its impact on cognitive functioning. If the nervous system functions at a slowed rate, it takes more time to scan and perceive information, to search long-term memory, to integrate information from various knowledge domains, and to make a response. With increased input each year, it is possible that the time needed for processing information increases. In the face of complex cognitive tasks, information may be lost or distractions may intervene if the process takes too long (Birren & Fisher, 1992). For example, Hertzog (1989) examined the relationship of age and speed of performance in a variety of mental abilities among people ranging in age from 43 to 89. He found that the speed-of-performance measure was a better predictor of mental abilities than was age. Other research looked at crystallized and fluid intelligence (Horn, 1982). Recall from Chapter 13 that crystallized intelligence tends to increase with age, whereas fluid intelligence declines. When the factor of speed of responding was removed from the tests of fluid intelligence, the decline with age was significantly less. These studies support the claim that changes in speed of responding account for much, although probably not all, of the documented evidence of declines in intellectual performance with age. The debate continues, however, about whether this slowing is general, influencing all types of cognitive activity, or specific to certain domains. Further, there is considerable evidence that contemporary circumstances, especially physical fitness and health, as well as the kinds of medications one is taking and the presence of immediate stressors in one's life, influence speed of responding (Willis et al., 1990).

Since slowing occurs gradually, most adults compensate for it by making their environments more convenient or by changing their lifestyles. However, it becomes more hazardous in situations that require the older adult to keep pace with a tempo that cannot be modified. For instance, some older people encounter problems because of the amount of time given to cross a street at a green light. For them and others with physical impairments, the amount of time the light stays green is insufficient to permit them to get to the other side of the street safely.

As older people recognize some situations in which they have trouble responding quickly, they must review the tempo of their day. The very old need to become more selective in their choice of activities so that they can allocate enough time for the tasks most important to them and perform them satisfactorily. This means exercising greater control over their time and being less concerned about whether they are in harmony with the tempo of others.

Sensory Changes

Every sense modality—vision, hearing, taste, touch, and smell—is vulnerable to age-related changes. With age, greater intensity of stimulation is required to make the same impact on the sensory system that was once achieved with lower levels of stimulation. Some of the changes in vision, hearing, taste, and smell are given in Table 14.1. These changes begin in early adulthood and their effects increase throughout the remainder of life (Kline & Scialfa, 1997).

Vision. **Visual adaptation** involves the ability to adjust to changes in the level of illumination. Pupil size decreases with age, so that less light reaches the retina. Thus, older adults need higher levels of illumination to see clearly. In addition, it takes them longer

TABLE 14.1   Changes in Sensory Systems after Age 20

Age Group	Vision	Hearing	Taste and Smell
20–35	Constant decline in accommodation as lenses begin to harden at about age 20	Pitch discrimination for high-frequency tones begins to decline	No documented changes
35–65	Sharp decline in acuity after 40; delayed adjustment to shifts in light and dark	Continued gradual loss in pitch discrimination to age 50	Loss of taste buds begins
65 +	Sensitivity to glare; increased problems with daily visual tasks; increases in diseases of the eye that produce partial or total blindness	Sharp loss in pitch discrimination after 70; sound must be more intense to be heard	Higher thresholds for detecting sour, salt, and bitter tastes; higher threshold for detecting smells, and errors in identifying odors

Source: Based on Newman & Newman, 1983.

to adjust from dark to light and from light to dark. Many older adults are increasingly sensitive to glare, and may draw the shades in their rooms to prevent bright light from striking their eyes. Slower adaptation time and sensitivity to glare interfere with night driving. Some of the visual problems of people over 75 are difficulty with tasks that require speed of visual performance, such as reading signs in a moving vehicle; a decline in near vision, which interferes with reading and daily tasks; and difficulties in searching for or tracking visual information (Kosnik et al., 1988; Kline, 1994).

Several physiological conditions seriously impair vision and can result in partial or total blindness in old age. These conditions include cataracts, which are a clouding of the lenses, making them less penetrable by light; deterioration or detachment of the retina; and glaucoma, which is an increase in pressure from the fluid in the eyeball. Note in Table 13.2 in Chapter 13 that the incidence of visual impairments, especially cataracts, increases dramatically from later adulthood (65 to 74) to very old age (over 75). By very old age, 12% of men and 26% of women experience problems with cataracts. Recent medical innovations have made cataract surgery much less complicated than it was in the past. In many cases, the lens is removed and replaced with an artificial one. In other cases, the person is fitted with contact lenses. Recovery of normal vision is now possible as long as the eyes are healthy in other respects (Clayman, 1989).

Loss of vision poses serious challenges to adaptation—it has the effect of separating people from contact with the world. Such impairment is especially linked with feelings of helplessness. Most older adults are not ready to cope with the challenge of learning to function in their daily world without being able to see. For them, the loss of vision reduces their activity level, autonomy, and willingness to leave a familiar setting. For many older adults, impaired vision results in the decision to give up driving altogether or night driving, causing a significant loss of independence. However, this loss can be minimized by the availability of inexpensive, flexible public transportation.

Hearing. Hearing loss increases with age. About 45% of men and 31% of women age 75 and over have some hearing impairment (U.S. Bureau of the Census, 1997). The most common effects of hearing loss are a reduced sensitivity to both high-frequency (high-pitched) and low-intensity (quiet) sounds, and a somewhat decreased ability to understand spoken messages. Certain environmental factors, including exposure to loud, unpredictable noise and injuries, such as damage to the bones in the middle ear, influence the extent of hearing loss.

Loss of hearing interferes with a basic mode of human connectedness—the ability to participate in conversation. Hearing impairment may be linked to increased feelings of isolation or suspiciousness. Further, a person may hear things imperfectly, miss parts of conversations, or perceive conversations as occurring in whispers rather than in ordinary tones (Wallace et al., 1994).

The very old adult who is aware of these facts may be able to compensate intellectually for diminished auditory sensitivity. Knowing the people one is with and believing that one is valued by them can help reassure a person about the nature of conversations and allay suspicions. Self-esteem plays an important part in this process. The older person with high self-esteem is likely to be able to make the intellectual adjustment needed to interpret interactions and to request clarification when necessary. Such requests may even serve to stimulate greater interaction and produce greater clarity in communication. Older people with a hearing loss and high self-esteem tend to insist that people who want to communicate with them should face them when they speak.

In contrast, older people who have low self-esteem are likely to be more vulnerable to suspicions about the behavior of others because they doubt their own worth. They are more likely to perceive inaudible comments as attempts to ridicule or exclude them. These experiences contribute to feelings of rejection, and can produce irritability and social withdrawal.

Taste and Smell. There are wide variations in the density of taste receptors among adult humans. With age, the number of taste buds decreases. Older adults have a higher threshold than young adults for detecting sweet, sour, bitter, and salty tastes. Some of

Irene still relies on her sense of smell to select the ripest fruit and the juiciest tomatoes.

this reduced sensitivity may be related to the impact of certain medications or poor oral hygiene (Receputo et al., 1996a). An especially important implication of insensitivity to salt is that older adults may add salt to their food and thereby aggravate hypertension. Older adults also require greater intensity to detect odors and are more likely to misidentify them (Receputo et al., 1996b). Changes in the senses of smell and taste may result in a loss of appetite or a disruption of normal eating habits. Loss of appetite (which may accompany illness and new medications), pain due to dental problems, and changes in the digestive system all contribute to malnutrition among the elderly.

As a result of the various patterns of aging among the very old, it is impossible to prescribe an ideal pattern of coping. What one hopes to achieve is a balance between

---

BOX 14.1   ORGANIC BRAIN SYNDROMES: DEMENTIA

Organic brain syndromes are a major cause of institutionalization among the elderly. These disorders can involve loss of memory for recent and past events; confusion or disorientation, causing the person to be unaware of the day of the week, season of the year, or city in which he or she lives; a loss of control over daily functions such as toileting, feeding, and dressing; and an inability to focus attention.

In acute brain syndromes, the onset of confusion is relatively sudden. Often this pattern is associated with a severe illness, such as heart failure, alcoholism, or extreme malnutrition. In these cases, the symptoms of the brain syndrome can often be reversed if the accompanying illness can be treated. Supportive counseling, attention to diet, and skill training to reestablish control of daily functions may restore the person's previous level of adaptive behavior.

Chronic brain syndrome, on the other hand, produces a more gradual loss of memory reduced intellectual functioning, and an increase of mood disturbances, especially hostility and depression. Whereas a number of conditions can cause acute brain syndrome, a smaller number of diseases are linked to chronic brain syndrome. Alzheimer's disease is the most common form of this syndrome, accounting for about 50% of the dementias among the elderly. The incidence of this disease increases with age, with fewer than 2% of people below age 60 affected by it, while an estimated

30% to 50% of those aged 85 to 100 experience some symptoms (Hooyman & Kiyak, 1993; Rowe & Kahn, 1998).

The person with Alzheimer's disease experiences gradual brain failure over a period of seven to 10 years. Symptoms include severe problems in cognitive functioning, especially increased memory impairment; problems with self-care; and behavioral problems such as wandering, asking the same questions repeatedly, and becoming suddenly angry or stubborn (O'Leary et al., 1993). Currently, there is no treatment that will reverse Alzheimer's disease. Treatments address specific symptoms, especially mood and memory problems, and attempt to slow its progress.

As the number of older adults with Alzheimer's disease and related disorders has grown, the plight of their caregivers has aroused increasing concern (Weiler et al., 1994). Most Alzheimer's patients are cared for at home, often by their adult children. The caregiving process is ongoing, with an accumulation of stressors and periodic transitions in the patient's condition that require a restructuring of personal, work, and family life for the caregiver. Caregivers often experience high levels of stress and depression as they attempt to cope with their responsibilities and as they assess the effectiveness or ineffectiveness of their efforts. The care of an older person with some form of dementia is fraught with problems and frustrations, but it also provides some opportuniself-sufficiency and a willingness to accept help, preserving as much as possible of the person's dignity and optimizing day-to-day mobility. This is described in the following excerpt:

> Appropriate dependence can be accommodated and accepted by elders when they realistically appraise their own physical capacities. One of our more practical elders simply states, "Of course, you're still interested in everything. But you don't expect yourself to do everything, the way you used to. Some things you just have to let go." However, inappropriate restriction can be, in its way, insulting and belittling. In describing his current life, one widowed man expresses both his refusal to accept restriction and his willingness to rely on appropriate assistance: "I can stay up here in the woods because I know if I really need help, my son will be here inside of three hours. Now, this deal with fixing my own water pipes, I'd have never tried that without my son so nearby, and I didn't even need him. (Erikson et al., 1986, pp. 309–310)

Health, Illness, and Functional Independence

A mild but persistent decline in the immune system is observed as a correlate of aging. As a result, older adults are more susceptible to infections and take a longer time to heal. In addition, substantial numbers of older adults are afflicted with one or more chronic conditions such as arthritis, diabetes, or high blood pressure, which may require medication and interfere with daily functioning (See Table 13.2, Chapter 13). Questions are currently being raised about the extent to which these illnesses can be prevented and the degree to which they prohibit older adults from retaining independent functioning in activities of daily life (Box 14.1) (Rowe & Kahn, 1998).

Do people generally experience a rapid, general decline in health after age 65 or 70? A longitudinal study of older adults helped to answer this question (Palmore et al., 1985). A group of older men and women who were studied in 1972 were interviewed again between 1980 and 1983. The average age of the group at the time of follow-up was 81. Five areas were evaluated: social functioning, economic stability, mental health, physical health, and the ability to perform the activities of daily living.

ties for satisfactions and feelings of encouragement (Aneshensel et al., 1995) The "uplifts" and "hassles" frequently reported by caregivers give some insight into the typical day-to-day experience of caring for a person who is suffering from Alzheimer's disease (Kinney & Stephens, 1989). The uplifts include:

Seeing care recipient calm.
Pleasant interactions between care recipient and family. Seeing care recipient responsive.
Care recipient showing affection.
Friends showing understanding about caregiving.
Family showing understanding about caregiving.
Care recipient recognizing familiar people.
Care recipient being cooperative.
Leaving care recipient with others at home.
Care recipient smiling/winking.
Being in care recipient's presence.
Receiving caregiving help from family. (Kinney & Stephens, p. 404)

Some of the hassles include:

Care recipient being confused/not making sense.
Care recipient's forgetfulness.
Care recipient's agitation.
Care recipient declining mentally.
Care recipient not cooperating.
Care recipient's bowel/bladder accidents.
Seeing care recipient withdrawn/unresponsive.
Dressing care recipient.
Bathing care recipient.
Assisting with care recipient's toileting.
Care recipient declining physically.
Care recipient not showing interest in things.
Care recipient not sleeping through the night.
Care recipient asking repetitive questions. (Kinney & Stephens, p. 403)

Two of the symptoms most difficult to manage are sleep disturbances and wandering. As cognitive functioning declines, the pattern of sleep deteriorates. A person with Alzheimer's disease sleeps for only short periods, napping on and off during the day and night. Often the napping is accompanied by wakeful periods at night, during which the person is confused, upset, and likely to wander. Caregivers must therefore be continuously alert, night and day. Their own sleep is disturbed as they try to remain alert to the person's whereabouts. When the disease reaches this level, family caregivers are most likely to find it necessary to institutionalize the family member (Aneshensel et al., 1995).

Aerobic exercise is highly recommended to maintain physical health, stamina, and a sense of well-being in later life. What strategies might be effective for encouraging sedentary older adults to participate in exercise classes?

The group as a whole experienced no significant decline in social functioning or economic stability over the 10-year period. There were moderate declines in mental and physical health and in the ability to perform the activities of daily living. For example, for the activities of daily living, the average rating on a 6-point scale dropped from 5.1 ("Can perform all the usual instrumental and physical activities but at times this becomes a strain for the person, and he/she would welcome intermittent assistance with some of these") to 4.1 ("Can perform the usual instrumental and physical activities around home under usual circumstances, but requires assistance when additional or extraordinary demands are made such as for long distance travel, major shopping trips, large financial transactions, or during a crisis situation") (Palmore et al., 1985, p. 247).

There was also an impressive range in the ability to function among the people in this sample. Some adults showed marked declines in functioning over the 10-year period, while others actually showed improvements. Some factors assessed in the first period predicted the level of functioning in the second. Women and African-Americans had lower levels of functioning after 10 years. The adults whose mental health scores were high in 1972 also had higher social functioning 10 years later. In addition, those who were married maintained higher levels of functioning in most areas.

The very oldest adults showed the most marked declines in all areas, a finding suggesting that deterioration may accelerate with increasing age. This pattern of rapid decline may be a result of the greater interrelatedness of functioning among those over 80. In those who are very old, when one area of functioning declines, difficulties in many others do, too. For example, loss of a spouse may result in social withdrawal, loss of appetite, sleep disturbance, loss of energy, unwillingness to take medication, and decline in physical activity. All of these changes can produce a rapid deterioration of the respiratory, circulatory, and metabolic systems.

Guralnik and Kaplan (1989) described the predictive factors of middle adulthood that were linked to healthy aging. Data collected in 1974, 1982, and 1984 were reported for a sample of people born between 1895 and 1919. Those who were in the top 20% of healthy functioning in later adulthood had average weight, higher family income, and no symptoms of hypertension, arthritis, or back pain; they did not smoke; and they consumed an average amount of alcohol. Physical activity, including any sports, exercise, walking, swimming, vigorous aerobic exercise, or calisthenics or stretching, could not be evaluated as a predictor in this study since it was included as a selection variable that differentiated the top group of older adults from the others.

Despite some negative stereotypes of the very old, the level of independent functioning among adults 80 years old and older is high. Figure 14.2 shows the percentages of men and women in a sample of over 1700 noninstitutionalized white adults 80 years old and older who could perform each of four functional indicators of physical ability. About one-third of the total sample was characterized as physically able—they reported no difficulty with any of the four tasks. The absence of cardiovascular disease and arthritis were important predictors of remaining physically able after age 80.

Research of this type must be repeated with various samples and different measures in order to clarify these patterns. One can conclude from the data that needs for assistance in daily living and mental or physical health care change gradually during the 70s and accelerate during the 80s and afterward.

Developing a Psychohistorical Perspective

Development in very old age includes gains as well as losses. Through encounters with diverse experiences, decision making, parenting and other forms of tutoring or mentoring of younger generations, and efforts to formulate a personal philosophy, adults reach new levels of conscious thought. Very old adults are more aware of alternatives; they can look deeply into both the past and the future and can recognize that opposing forces can exist side by side (Riegel, 1973). Through a process of creative coping, very old adults in each generation blend the salient events of their past histories with the demands of current reality. The product of this integration of past, present, and future is the formation of a **psychohistorical perspective.**

Think about what it means to have lived for 75 or more years. Those adults who were 80 years old in 1990 had lived through two world wars and the Great Depression by the time they were 35. They had experienced the political leadership of 16 presidents. During their lives, they had adapted to dramatic technological innovations in communication, transportation, manufacturing, economics, food production, leisure activities, and health care. They had also experienced striking changes in cultural and political values.

One consequence of a long life is the accumulation of experiences. Another is the realization that change is a basic element of all life at the individual and social levels (Clayton & Birren, 1980). Sometimes these changes appear cyclical; at other times they appear to bring real progress. Within the framework of an extended life, very old adults have opportunities to gain a special perspective on conditions of continuity and change within their culture. In the process of developing a psychohistorical perspective, very old adults develop a personal understanding of stability and change, the effects of history on individual lives, and one's place in the chain of events.

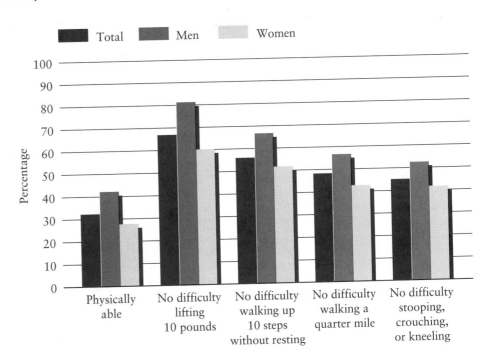

FIGURE 14.2

Physical ability of noninstitutionalized white persons aged 80 and older, 1984.

SOURCE: Harris, Kovar, Suzman, Kleinman & Feldman, 1989.

The very old provide a wealth of knowledge about skills, arts, and events from the past. Ilias Kementeides received the National Endowment of the Arts folk art award for his mastery in making and playing the Greek lyre. He is preserving the tradition for his grandchildren.

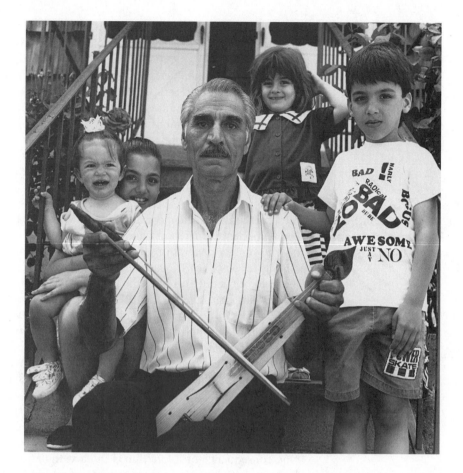

We are all part of the process of psychosocial evolution. Each generation adds to the existing knowledge base and reinterprets the norms of society for succeeding generations. The very old are likely to be parents, grandparents, and great-grandparents. Many are seeing their lines of descent continue into the fourth generation, which will dominate the 21st century. The opportunity to see several generations of offspring brings a new degree of continuity to life, linking memories of one's own grandparents to observations of one's great grandchildren (Wentowski, 1985). We can expect the value of the oral tradition of history and storytelling to take on new meaning as the very old help their great grandchildren feel connected to the distant past. We can also expect a greater investment in the future as the very old see in their great grandchildren the concrete extension of their ancestry three generations into the future.

As society becomes more accustomed to having a significant group of very old adults functioning in the community, some scholars anticipate that a culture of aging will emerge in technological societies. This culture is likely to provide more opportunities for the expression of the pragmatic wisdom accumulated over a long life time through theater, music, the arts, and critical commentary. At the same time, new roles will evolve for "successful agers" as mentors and advisors to the young (Baltes & Staudinger, 1993; Keith, 1994).

Erikson (Erikson et al., 1986) identified the emergence of these tendencies in the very old in the following:

> The elder has a reservoir of strength in the wellsprings of history and storytelling. As collectors of time and preservers of memory, those healthy elders who have survived into a reasonably fit old age have time on their side—time that is to be dispensed wisely and creatively, usually in the form of stories, to those younger ones who will one day follow in their footsteps. Telling these stories, and telling them well, marks a certain capacity for one generation to entrust itself to the next, by passing on a certain shared and collective identity to the survivors of the next generation: the future. (p. 331)

Traveling Uncharted Territory: Life Structures of the Very Old

How should very old people behave? What norms exist to guide their social relationships or the structure of their daily lives? What does a healthy 85-year-old woman consider appropriate behavior, and what expectations do others have of her? When we talk about traveling uncharted territory, we are assuming that very old age is a time of life for which there are few age-specific social norms. The very old are creating their own definitions of this life stage (Keith, 1982). You may have heard the expression "life begins at 80." One interpretation of this adage is that because there are so few norms for behavior and so few responsibilities when one reaches very old age, one can do whatever one wants.

The MacArthur Foundation Research Network on Successful Aging (Rowe & Kahn, 1998) has offered a new, interdisciplinary perspective on the distinction between *usual* and *successful* aging. Those characterized by usual aging may be functioning well but are at high risk for disease, disability, and reduced capacity for functional independence. In contrast, the successful agers are characterized by three interdependent features (Figure 14.3). They have a "low risk of disease and disease-related disabilities; high mental and physical function; and active engagement with life" (p. 38).

Consider this life plan written by an older woman for her college alumnae magazine:

> I feel more like 17, but I am 85½, the aged parent of four loving, busy children in four distant states, children I hope will stay loving by my being as little nuisance to them as possible.
>
> To reduce my nuisance to the earth also, I have tried to limit my travel, pets and housing. I do, though, like having more than one room, so that when one space becomes fouled with work, escape to another is possible.
>
> Soon I expect to move to a Quaker retirement place, one chosen because from it I can walk to an open stacks college library, college swimming pool, and to a Quaker meeting. One chosen, also, because in its possibly ultimate nursing wing, the patients look bright-eyed, not as if they were doped, as in so many such places.
>
> Because bit by bit I see my memory disappearing, I have asked the child who is my successor trustee and executor to record the final names and numbers of my life. I have also been gradually unloading property I don't need, but keeping a few beautiful objects. Finally, I have arranged for a medical school to get my body, and then, at last, to have my ashes cremated and thrown into the sea. No need for a memorial service.
>
> With all these necessary details seen to, despite a certain bodily unsteadiness and a right knee that seems to lock up on me, I am looking forward to, indeed I expect—or anyway hope for a decade or more of interest, possibly a little usefulness, and, if all goes well—a reasonable amount of plain, good fun. (Stone, 1998, p. 4)

In an effort to describe the norms that older adults use to guide their conduct, researchers asked older adults from New York City and Savannah, Georgia to respond to six pictures similar to the two drawings in Figure 14.4 (Offenbacher & Poster,

FIGURE 14.3
Components of successful aging.
SOURCE: Rowe & Kahn, 1998, p. 39.

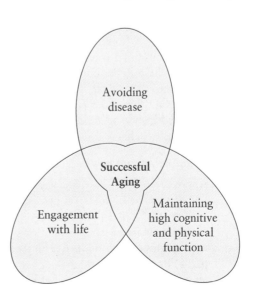

FIGURE 14.4
Typical drawings that researchers might use to establish social norms of the very old.
SOURCE: Drawings based on Offenbacher & Poster, 1985.

1985). The responses to the following two questions were used to construct a code of conduct: "How do you think that people who know this person, such as family or friends, feel about him/her?" and "How do you feel about this person?"

Four normative principles were found in the responses:

1. Don't be sorry for yourself.
2. Try to be independent.
3. Don't just sit there; do something.
4. Above all, be sociable.

This code of conduct suggests that older people believe that being sociable, active, and independent constitute successful living in later life. Of course, older adults are not alone in valuing these qualities. However, these norms are important as sources of self-esteem for this age group. They promote a sense of vigor and a shield against depression or discouragement.

The themes "Don't be sorry for yourself" and "Don't just sit there" suggest that the very old continue to see their lives as precious resources not to be wasted in self-pity and passivity. The emphasis on activity as opposed to meditation reflects the Western cultural value of a sense of agency—thinking is not as highly valued as action. In contrast, doing things, having an impact, and receiving the feedback that action stimulates provide the keys to successful living. Although the results of this research cannot be taken as the final word on the norms that govern the behavior of all very old adults, they are an important step in understanding the structure that very old people impose on their lives. Subsequent studies support the idea that finding meaning in one's existence, continuing to experience a sense of social competence, and perceptions of self-efficacy help older adults maintain a sense of well-being (Baltes & Baltes, 1990; Coleman, 1992; Ryff, 1995).

The fact that older adults must carve out new patterns of adapting to later life is illustrated in two specific areas of functioning: living arrangements and gender-role definitions, which are discussed below.

Living Arrangements

Approximately 75% of U.S. adults aged 75 and over own their own homes. However, the pattern of living arrangements for most people changes noticeably after age 75 (Figure 14.5). Before then, the majority of older adults live in family households, mostly as married couples. Among adults aged 75 and older, however, only 41% live with a spouse and 44% live in nonfamily households; that is, they either live alone (42%) or with a nonrelative (2%). The percentage of older women who live alone after age 75 has been increasing steadily, so that it is now normative. The statistics re-

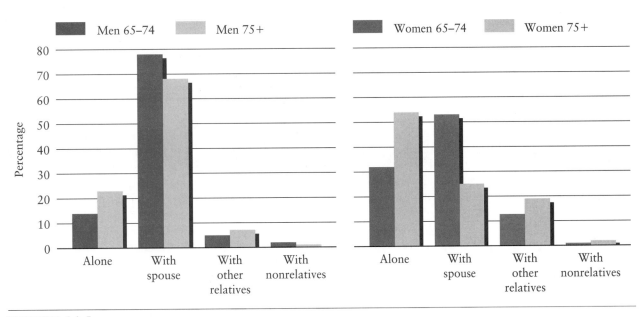

FIGURE 14.5

Living arrangements for older adults by age and sex, 1995 [percentages].
Source: Based on U.S. Bureau of the Census. 1996. Table No. 64.

Most older women who live alone tend to adapt well to this independent life style. Ruth lives in her home in the country, but she keeps in touch with her friends and family by phone. The grocery and pharmacy deliver, and Ruth can always get a ride into town with a neighbor. What factors might force Ruth to give up her independence?

veal that in 1965, 30% of women over 75 lived alone, while in 1995, 54% did (U.S. Bureau of the Census, 1996). Older women are less likely to live with other family members after the death of their spouse than they were in the past. Further, feelings of subjective well-being appear to be high among older widows who live alone (Alwin, 1984).

One implication of these trends in living arrangements is that increasing numbers of very old women are establishing a new single lifestyle in which they function as heads of households. While still in need of social interaction and support services, they are often relieved of the responsibilities of caring for spouses who were ill. Depending on their own health, these women may be freer to direct their time and interests toward their friends, grandchildren, hobbies, and activities than they have been at any other time in their lives.

The pattern of elderly women living alone is similar in Canada, the United Kingdom, and the United States, but is not common in Japan, where less than 10% of women aged 65 and over live alone. Most of these women live with relatives in three-generation households. Among those 85 and over, only 5–6% of Japanese women live alone. In most developing countries, families provide housing and care for the very old. Although people in these countries may not experience the same degree of longevity as in the U.S., there is a clear pattern of elderly widows living with their sons or daughters (U.S. Bureau of the Census, 1987).

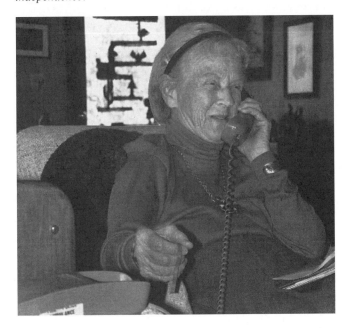

In the United States, living arrangements for older women differ by race and ethnic group (Choi, 1991). Older unmarried Asian-American women, for example, are much more likely to live with other family members than to live alone, in comparison to white women of similar economic and educational backgrounds. Within the Asian-American ethnic groups, acculturation appears to increase the likelihood of choosing to live alone. Those who immigrated to the United States before 1965 or were born in the United States are more likely to live alone than the more recent immigrants. And in a comparison among the Asian-American cultures, older Japanese women were more likely to live alone than the Chinese, Filipino, and Korean women. Consistent with patterns for white women, the more children these Asian-American women had, the less likely they were to be institutionalized (Burr & Mutchler, 1993).

The majority of very old men—about 70%—are married and live with their spouses; only 23% are widowed. In contrast, 27% of very old women are married and 64% are widowed (U.S. Bureau of the Census, 1997). Widowed men are much more likely to remarry, which they tend to do quickly. However, remarriage among the very old is still a new frontier. Sexual and social stereotypes inhibit some older people from considering remarriage. In addition, potential financial consequences may make remarriage undesirable. For instance, a widow may lose her husband's pension or her social security benefits if she remarries. However, some older couples cope with this problem by living together instead of marrying. In fact in 1996, there were 221,000 households consisting of unmarried couples 65 years old and over (U.S. Bureau of the Census, 1997). On the other hand, those who do remarry usually view the new relationship quite positively. One older woman described her new marriage as follows, "We're like a couple of kids. We fool around—have fun. We go to dances and socialize a lot with our families. We enjoy life together. When you're with someone, you're happy" (Rosenfeld, 1978, p. 56).

Interstate Migration. Although most older adults remain in their home communities, the trend toward interstate migration has increased since the mid-1960s (Flynn et al., 1985). Over the past five years, roughly 135,000 older adults ages 75 and over moved to a new residence across state lines each year (U.S. Bureau of the Census, 1997). Further, many of these older interstate migrants will live out their lives in communities in which they did not grow up, work, or raise their children. They are pioneers, establishing new friendships, community involvements, and lifestyles. Another significantly large group of older adults return to their birth state, especially after one spouse dies or in the case of serious disability, in order to be close to family caregivers. In addition to these permanent moves, many older adults participate in seasonal migration—residents from southern states go north for the summer, and residents of northern states go south for the winter. Over time, some of these seasonal migrants decide to establish a permanent residence in the state they visit. This is especially likely for northern residents who establish permanent residence in the South (Hogan & Steinnes, 1998).

Housing Options. Differences in lifestyle, health, interest, ability to perform daily activities, marital status, and income enter into the very old person's preference for housing arrangements. Housing for the elderly—sometimes referred to as *retirement housing*—has expanded dramatically, and developers have experimented with a great variety of housing configurations that are intended to meet the special needs of particular aging populations. These options range from inner-city hotels for those with minimal incomes to sprawling luxury villages with apartments, medical clinics, and sponsored activities. The majority of older adults live in urban areas, and 31% of them live in inner-city neighborhoods. As a result, any economic factors that affect the housing options within urban communities have a significant impact on the living arrangements of older adults (Box 14.2). Since older adults tend to have a limited income and depend on the quality of community resources and social support for the their well-being, moving can be an especially difficult life event, adversely affecting their overall well-being (Singelakis, 1990; Ryff & Essex, 1992).

Institutional Care. On any given day, about 5% of adults over 65 live in nursing homes and other group-care settings. The rate of institutionalization increases with age, from about 2% of those 65–74 years old to 23% of those 85 and over. These rates, based on one moment in time, underestimate the risk of having to spend some time in a nursing home during one's later life. The lifetime probability of an older adult spending some time in a nursing home is estimated to be between 25% and 50%, depending on the technique used to make this projection. About 75% of people in nursing homes do not have spouses. In addition, the likelihood of a person living in a nursing home increases when there is no family member who can help manage his or her daily living needs (U.S. Senate, Special Committee on Aging, 1986).

BOX 14.2 THE IMPACT OF GENTRIFICATION ON THE VERY OLD

Gentrification refers to a pattern of real-estate change in which a higher-income group buys property and develops residential and commercial projects in an area that has previously been serving a lower-income group. Usually the result is that the nearby neighborhoods attract wealthier residents, housing and rental prices increase, and the lower-income residents are forced to move out. Since older adults tend to remain in their homes for a long time, they are likely to live in neighborhoods that become a target for gentrification—urban areas that may have deteriorated over the years of their residence, but where social supports and services continue to remain available and readily accessible.

Several consequences of gentrification have a negative impact on the housing options of older adults (Singelakis, 1990). First, apartments are converted to condominiums, which older adults cannot afford. Second, in areas where there is no rent control, the rent rises above the rate the older person is able to pay. Where there is rent regulation, some landlords use harassment to force out the original residents. Third, properties that have been used as single-room-occupancy hotels are demolished, and new structures are built. Single-room-occupancy hotels provide low-cost housing as well as social support to many older adults who live alone. From 1970 to 1982, over half the single-room-occupancy units in the country were lost to various urban gentrification projects (Hopper & Hamberg, 1986).

In a survey of 115 older adults living on the Upper West Side of Manhattan, 79% had incomes of less than $10,000 in 1989 (Singelakis, 1990). The mean age of this group was 75. Of this group, 99% rented, 68% lived alone, and 74% paid less than $300 per month for rent. In this community, 52% of the single-room units had become unavailable over the past seven years. These older adults reported that gentrification had resulted in having to walk farther to find affordable shopping. They knew that if they were forced to leave their current apartment because of increased rent, they could not afford to live in the same neighborhood. And if they were forced to leave, 64% did not know where they could live. Fewer than 8% of the sample felt that they could live with a friend or a family member if their apartment was no longer available.

People tend to think that once older adults are admitted to a nursing home, they stay there until they die. In fact, there is actually a high annual turnover among nursing-home residents. Often a person enters a nursing home for a period of convalescence after hospitalization and then returns home. Nursing homes and housing for the very old have adapted to these changing needs of their clients since the mid-1970s. Many nursing homes are part of a *continuing-care retirement community*, a residential setting offering housing and medical, preventive health, and social services to residents who are well at the time they enter the community. Once admitted, they are guaranteed nursing care if they become ill or disabled (Cohen et al., 1988). In an analysis of nursing-home use among residents in continuing-care retirement communities, the risk of being transferred to the nursing-home facility appeared to be greater than the rate for older adults in the local community, but the length of stay per admission was shorter (Cohen et al., 1989). The nursing home may be used for recuperative purposes rather than having patients stay in the hospital for a longer period.

At 97 years of age, Stella has had to move into a nursing home because she can no longer walk. Periodic visits from her great-grandson keep her in good spirits. He plays, and she is a most appreciative audience.

This practice may reduce overall medical costs and provide a better recovery environment than being discharged to one's home before one can fully manage all the demands of self-care.

In trying to cope with a spouse who had Alzheimer's disease, Mr. G. decided to move to a continuing-care retirement community. He lived in the minimal-care residential part of the community, and his wife lived in a full-service unit. With this arrangement, he could remain close to his wife without having the full responsibility for her care. This solution relieved Mr. G. of many of the financial burdens he had encountered in trying to care for his wife at home. The move also prevented him from becoming socially isolated, a concern of many very old adults who are caring for their spouses.

The fastest growing component of the Medicare program is community-based long-term health care, which provides medical and social services to those who are chronically ill and are eligible for institutionalization but who, nevertheless, live in the community. At their best, these programs are designed to function around and support the informal care-giving, supplementing and providing relief for family members and friends who are trying to care for the very old. They bring comfort to the very old clients who prefer to remain in their homes. These programs also offer flexibility by providing needed services and modifying them as a person's condition changes. Long-term home health-care programs evolve in response to the pattern of need that emerge in a community and the quality of the services available. As the programs develop, their emphasis tends to shift from providing services to those who would otherwise be institutionalized to preventing institutionalization among a high-risk population (Kaye, 1995; Kasper, 1997).

The benefits of remaining in one's home, despite serious limitations in functional independence, are: preserving the person's sense of autonomy and dignity, reducing expenses, and sustaining relationships with family and friends. In contrast, the move to a nursing home tends to be associated with higher levels of dependence and greater emphasis on "going along with the program," rather than on initiating one's own plans and projects. In a comparison of older women living in their homes and those living in a nursing care facility, the researchers were interested in how the living arrangements might influence cognitive problem solving. The former group became more engaged in the hypothetical problems, their solutions suggested a greater sense of perceived control over the solutions, and they approached the problems in a more abstract, relativistic manner (Collins et al., 1997). The results of this work suggest that the nursing home environment may operate to undermine cognitive functioning by reducing the need for independent problem-solving activity.

Gender-Role Definitions

The way in which very old adults view masculinity and femininity is yet another aspect of traveling uncharted territory. How do the very old define gender roles? How does gender influence behavior? Do very old adults make the same distinctions as college-age populations about the behaviors appropriate or desirable for men and women? These questions remain to be answered.

Evaluating the Concept of Sex-Role Convergence. Some researchers have reported a transformation of sex-role orientation during midlife. Men become more nurturant and more concerned with social relationships, while women become more assertive and concerned with independence and achievement as they get older. Thus, some scholars argue that men and women become more androgynous and, in that sense, more similar in gender orientation during later life (Gutmann, 1987).

The extent to which men and women become more similar in outlook and behavior in later adulthood and very old age is a subject of controversy. Unfortunately, few data from longitudinal or cohort sequential studies are available to address this topic. Cross-sectional data collected from men and women across a wide age span from early adulthood to very old age have focused on men's and women's endorsement of affiliative and instrumental values. Men and women appear to be similar in their **affiliative values,** that is the amount of time they spend and the degree of satisfaction they feel in helping or pleasing others. At each age, men appear to be more invested in **instrumental values** than women—that is, in the amount of time they spend and the degree of satisfaction they feel in doing things that are challenging. However, the youngest age groups appear to value instrumentality more highly and devote more time to it than the oldest age group. Thus, gender differences persist in instrumentality, but the opportunities and centrality of instrumentality become somewhat less prominent for both older men and women, while affiliative behavior is equally important for both men and women and at both ages (Fultz & Herzog, 1991).

The stereotypes that are applied to aging men and women reflect similar patterns. College students and older adults (with a mean age of 70) were asked to generate characteristics in response to one of four target stimuli: a 35-year-old man, a 35-year-old woman, a 65-year-old man, and a 65-year-old woman (Kite et al., 1991). Age stereotypes were more prevalent than gender stereotypes. The attributes that were used to characterize older men and women were similar and distinct from the attributes used to characterize younger men and women. In general, the older target subjects were evaluated more negatively by the younger subjects, but not as negatively by the older subjects. These negative qualities included unattractive physical qualities as well as irritable and depressed personality qualities. What is more, younger subjects were more likely to characterize both male and female older subjects as lacking in instrumental traits, such as achievement orientation and self-confidence. However, they did not view older subjects as lacking in affiliative traits, such as caring about others or being kind or generous. One implication of this study is that the gender convergence that has been hypothesized as taking place with advanced age may be more a construction of a younger generation applying its stereotypes to older adults than it is actually a perception of the very old themselves.

Sex-role changes, where they are observed, may be due to changing circumstances rather than to a normative pattern of development in later life. For example, many older women experience a transition from living with their husbands to living alone after age 75. This change is linked to new demands for independence, self-reliance, and agency. Women who are able to meet these challenges by developing independent living skills, making effective use of social supports and community resources, and initiating new relationships are likely to experience a heightened sense of well-being.

For many older married couples, the physical effects of aging bring new needs for assistance in some of the tasks of daily living. Since men usually marry younger women, they are more likely to require the assistance of their wives in the later years of marriage, thus shifting the balance of power and increasing their sense of dependency. This may be especially true when husbands retire while their wives continue to work; when husbands can no longer drive and must depend on their wives for transportation; or when husbands are restricted from performing the types of household tasks that once were their domain, such as mowing the grass, shoveling snow, repairing the home, or other tasks requiring muscle strength and endurance.

Romance and Sexuality. Older men and women tend to be tied to many of the sex-role standards of their historical cohort. For example, older women are likely to believe that the only kinds of relationships that are possible between men and women are romantic or courtship relationships (Adams, 1985). Few very old women have friendships with very old men, partly because few older men are available but also because most older women have no models for independent friendship relationships with men. During their early and middle adult years, their friendships with men were formed while they were part of a couple or were mediated by some other situation, such as a work setting.

Today's very old adults are also likely to be uncomfortable about sexuality and dating. Current research on sexuality in later life confirms that older adults have sexual needs, benefit from sexual expression, and are able to be sexually active (Hodson & Skeen, 1994). Nonetheless, most older women do not readily integrate sexuality into their single lifestyle. They are members of a generation that did not feel comfortable about open sexuality outside the marriage relationship. After widowhood or latelife divorce, they find it difficult to become involved in a sexual relationship.

Many men among the current cohort of the very old also behave in accordance with the sex-role standards of their young adulthood. Although women far outnumber men at advanced ages, men still seem to prefer to remarry rather than play the field, although they have become a scarce and valuable commodity. The norm of serial monogamy guides these men's behavior. They are probably motivated to remarry by a desire to continue to be taken care of as well as to satisfy their sexual needs.

A study of romantic involvement among elderly African-Americans illustrates the differences in outlook of older men and women (Tucker et al., 1993). Among this group, there are only 68 men for every 100 women aged 65 and over. This ratio declines even more dramatically for those 75 and older. Among the sample studied, 52% of the men over 75 were married and 9% of the women were married. What is more, among those men over 75 who were not married, 21% said they were romantically involved and 40% of those not romantically involved said they would like to be. In contrast, among the unmarried women over 75, only 2% said they were romantically involved and 5% said they would like to be. Among the oldest African-American men, desire for romantic involvement remained strong, but among the women, it declined dramatically. Older African-American women regarded the prospect of romantic involvement as costly, seeing older men as being interested in them because they had money and because the men needed to be taken care of. This outlook is exemplified in the following:

> I wouldn't want a third man. I had two and I'm afraid that the first thing that would come between us is how much money I got. I ain't got none to give them what I work hard for. Men want someone to wait on them, to be a servant, just take care of them. (Tucker et al., 1993, p. S128)

It appears that African-American men continue to seek romantic involvements because they benefit greatly from these relationships both financially and in terms of physical and emotional support. In contrast, African-American women see these relationships as a risk or a burden. They find social support and emotional connection with family members, especially sisters, neighbors, and in-laws.

Sexuality, intimacy, and romance remain important among older married couples. The majority of couples who have enjoyed a close, sexually active relationship report little change in satisfaction from age 60 to 85 (Bretschneider & McCoy, 1988). Some couples explore different ways of experiencing sexual pleasure in later life, and others report a more relaxed, sexually satisfying quality in their lovemaking. Most research on the topic confirms that older married adults continue to experience sexual desires and find satisfaction in sexual intimacy (Turner & Rubinson, 1993).

Older adults continue to face negative ageist social attitudes about sexual activity that may inhibit their sexual behavior. These include assumptions that very old adults do not have sexual desires, they cannot have intercourse because of sexual dysfunction, that sex may be dangerous to their health, that they are physically and sexually unattractive, and that it is morally wrong or "sick" for older adults to be sexually active (Turner & Rubinson, 1993). Current cohorts of very old adults have little knowledge about sexuality and aging. A number of studies have demonstrated that increasing knowledge through various types of sex-education programs can increase permissive attitudes about sexuality among older adults (Hillman & Stricker, 1994). These interventions have involved the elderly themselves, nursing students, college students, nursing-home staff, and adult children of aging parents. However, increased knowledge does

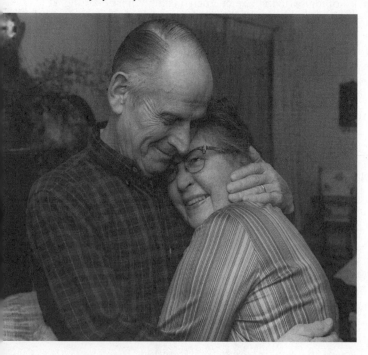

For Karl and Jean, the tenderness in their relationship has grown over the years. Having lived such a long life together, they are more appreciative of each other now, and are able to give each other great comfort as well as physical pleasure.

not always result in more permissive attitudes. Especially among health-care staff in institutional settings, the institutional regulations, personal moral values, and the practical problems of permitting sexual activity among patients may combine to promote a more negative attitude even with advanced information about sexuality and aging.

Cohort factors may change the current societal attitudes toward sexuality among the very old. Because so many more adult women are in the workplace, they have more experience with male colleagues. Also, changing sexual norms have already led many more adults to experience nonmarital sexual relationships. A growing openness about homosexual relationships may reduce some of the stigma against forming same-sex bonds in later life. Acceptance of new sexual relationships in later life is more likely because many adults will have experienced a larger number of sexual relationships in their earlier years of adulthood. The high divorce rate since the mid-1970s means that in the future, many more older women will have had the experience of developing a single lifestyle that includes a network of both male and female friends. As the value of intimacy for health and well-being is more fully recognized, we may expect future groups of older adults to be more comfortable about forming homosexual as well as heterosexual intimate relationships.

THE PSYCHOSOCIAL CRISIS: IMMORTALITY VERSUS EXTINCTION

By the end of later adulthood, most people have developed a point of view about death. Although they may continue to experience anxiety about their impending death, they have found the courage to confront their fears and overcome them. If older adults have achieved integrity, they believe that their life has made sense. This brings a sense of personal dignity about the choices they have made and the goals they have achieved without despair over the failures, missed opportunities, or misfortunes that may have occurred. Thus armed, the very old can accept the end of life and view it as a natural part of the life span. They are capable of distilling wisdom from the events of their lives, including their successes and mistakes.

However, the very old are faced with a new challenge–a conflict between the acceptance of death and the intensifying hope for immortality. Thus, the very old struggle to find meaning in their survival. All of us struggle with a certain disbelief about our own mortality. Even though we know that death is a certainty, an element of human thought prevents us from facing the full realization of death and makes us continue to hope for immortality. This quality may be adaptive in that people who have a sense of hope cope with the reality of death better than those who do not.

BOX 14.3 ERIKSON ON AGING

The Eriksons' advice (Erickson et al., 1986) on aging suggests the achievement of experiential transcendence:

With aging, there are inevitably constant losses—losses of those very close, and friends near and far. Those who have been rich in intimacy also have the most to lose. Recollection is one form of adaptation, but the effort skillfully to form new relationships is adaptive and more rewarding. Old age is necessarily a time of relinquishing—of giving up old friends, old roles, earlier work that was once meaningful, and even possessions that belong to a previous stage of life and are now an impediment to the resiliency and freedom that seem to be requisite for adapting to the unknown challenges that determine the final stage of life.

Trust in interdependence. Give and accept help when it is needed. Old Oedipus well knew that the aged sometimes need three legs; pride can be an asset but not a cane.

When frailty takes over, dependence is appropriate, and one has no choice but to trust in the compassion of others and be consistently surprised at how faithful some caretakers can be.

Much living, however, can teach us only how little is known. Accept that essential "not-knowingness" of childhood and with it also that playful curiosity. Growing old can be an interesting adventure and is certainly full of surprises.

One is reminded here of the image Hindu philosophy uses to describe the final letting go—that of merely being. The mother cat picks up in her mouth the kitten, which completely collapses every tension and hangs limp and infinitely trusting in the maternal benevolence. The kitten responds instinctively. We human beings require at least a whole lifetime of practice to do this. (pp. 332–333)

Immortality   We have argued that the very old have a unique appreciation of change. They begin to serve themselves as links in a long, fluid chain of historical and biological growth and change. The positive pole of this crisis is a confidence in the continuity of life, a transcendence of death through the development of a symbolic sense of immortality.

A psychosocial sense of **immortality** may be achieved and expressed in many ways (Lifton, 1973). Here we explore five possible paths toward immortality. First, one may live on through one's children, sensing a connection and attachment to the future through one's life the lives of one's offspring. This type of immortality can be extended to include devotion to one's country, social organizations or groups, or humankind.

Second, one may believe in an afterlife or in a spiritual plane of existence that extends beyond one's biological life. Most religions espouse the concept of a state of harmony with natural forces so that after death, one endures beyond this earthly life.

Third, one may achieve a sense of immortality through one's creative achievements and impact on others. Many people find great comfort in believing that they are part of a chain of positive influences on the lives of others. This sense of immortality is clearly tied to the achievement of generativity in middle adulthood. Adults who have made a strong commitment to improving the quality of life for future generations during middle adulthood are likely to see evidence of this effort by the time they reach very old age. In this sense of immortality, the bond between an individual and his or her community makes death less terrifying. An African proverb advises that you live as long as someone knows your name. Thus, the more embedded you are in your community and the more lives you have touched, the greater will be your sense of continuity or transcendence.

The conflict between immortality and extinction is captured in this etching. Picasso, the tiny, aging infant, is dwarfed by the powerful imagery of his art. Here he assembles all the forces that are ebbing in his old age—sexuality, heroism, power, risk, and magic. And yet, through art, these images will always be alive just as he created them.

Fourth, one may develop the notion of participation in the chain of nature. In death, one's body returns to the earth and one's energy is brought forth in a new form.

Fifth, one may achieve a sense of immortality through what Lifton (1973) described as **experiential transcendence:**

> This state is characterized by extraordinary psychic unity and perceptual intensity. But there also occurs . . . a process of symbolic reordering. . . . Experiential transcendence includes a feeling of . . . "continuous present" that can be equated with eternity or with "mythical time." This continuous present is perceived as not only "here and now" but as inseparable from past and future. (p. 10)

This concept of immortality is independent of religion, offspring, or achievement. It is an insight derived from moments of rapture or ecstasy in which all that one senses is the power of the moment. In these experiences, life and death dissolve, and all that remains is continuous being (Box 14.3).

Extinction   The negative pole of this crisis is a sense of being bound by the limits of one's own life history. In place of a belief in continuous existence and transformation, one views the end of life as an end to motion, attachment, and change. Instead of faith in the ideas of connection and continuity, one experiences a great fear of **extinction**—a fear that death brings nothingness.

The following quotations from a study of very old men suggest the range in sentiment about immortality and extinction (Rosenfeld, 1978, p. 10). About 28% of the adults in the study were described as having low morale and made statements such as the following, "I feel I'm a forgotten man. I don't exist anymore. . . . I don't feel old . . . I'm just living out my life." About 25% were stoic but not very positive about their condition: "You know you're getting old. You have to put your mind to it and take it as it comes. You can't get out of it. Take it gracefully." Almost half found their lives full and rewarding: "I go home with my cup overflowing. There are so many opportunities to do things for people. These are the happiest days of my life."

THE CENTRAL PROCESS: SOCIAL SUPPORT

Social support has been defined as the social experiences that lead people to believe that they are cared for and loved, esteemed and valued, and belong to a network of communication and mutual obligation (Cobb, 1979). **Social support** is a broad term that includes the quantity and interconnectedness or web of social relationships in which a person is embedded, the strength of those ties, the frequency of contact, and the extent to which the support system is perceived as helpful and caring (Bergeman et al., 1990). It is commonly divided into two different but complementary categories: *socioemotional support,* which refers to expressions of affection, respect, and esteem, and *instrumental support,* which refers to direct assistance including help with chores, medical care, or transportation. Both types of social support, but especially emotional support, contribute to maintaining well-being and fostering the possibility of transcending the physical limitations that accompany aging (Rowe & Kahn, 1998).

Benefits of Social Support

Social support plays a direct role in promoting health and well-being, even when a person is not facing a specific stressful situation. First, because social support involves meaningful social relationships, it reduces isolation. People who have intimate companions in later life have higher levels of life satisfaction. They feel valued and valuable. This kind of support is likely to be most appreciated when it comes from friends and neighbors, members of the community who are not bound by familial obligation to care about the person but who do so anyway. Second, the presence of caring, familiar people provides a flow of affection, information, and advice; transportation, and assistance with meals and daily activities, finances, and health care—all critical resources (Stephens & Bernstein, 1984). In addition, the presence of a support system tends to reduce the impact of stressors and protect people from some of their negative consequences, especially serious illnesses and depression (Murrell & Norris, 1991). The health benefits of social support are especially notable for older men (Seeman et al., 1994).

Third, social integration and membership in a meaningful social support network are associated with increased longevity. Five different longitudinal studies have demonstrated that a high level of social integration is associated with lower mortality rates (Rowe & Kahn, 1997). The support system often serves to encourage an older person to maintain health-care practices and to seek medical attention when it is needed. Members of the immediate family as well as close relatives and friends provide direct care during times of grave illness or loss and encourage the older person to cope with difficulties and to remain hopeful (Russell & Cutrona, 1991).

The Dynamics of Social Support

Very old people are likely to experience declines in physical stamina. They may also have limited financial resources. In order for the very old to transcend the limitations of their daily living situations, they must be convinced that they are embedded in a network of social relationships in which they are valued. But their value cannot be based solely on a physical exchange of goods and services. Rather, it must be founded on an appreciation of the person's dignity and a history of reciprocal caring.

The value of reciprocity in both emotional and instrumental support is strong in our culture. People want and expect to be able to give about the same as or more than they receive. It follows then that most older adults continue to see themselves as involved in a reciprocal, supportive relationship with their friends. Feelings of usefulness and competence continue to be important correlates of well-being in later life. Older adults are especially likely to experience positive feelings of life satisfaction when they are able to provide assistance to others at times of significant life transition or need, such as the unemployment or divorce of a child (Davey & Eggebeen, 1998).

Older adults may expect to receive more care from their children when they are ill than they can provide in exchange. By shifting to a life-span perspective, however, they can retain a sense of balance by seeing the help they receive now as comparable to the help they gave at earlier life stages (Ingersoll-Dayton & Antonucci, 1988). When very old people are highly valued, it is not as important that they reciprocate in the exchange of tangible resources. Wisdom, affection, joie de vivre, and a positive model of surviving into old age are intangible resources that are highly valued by members of the very old person's social support network. Being valued may also mean that the person's advice and conversation are adequate exchange for some of the services and assistance provided by family and friends.

Of course, being an integral part of a social system does not begin in later life. It has its origins in infancy with the formation of a mutual relationship with a caregiver. Social support systems are extended in childhood and early adolescence through identification with a peer group and in early and middle adulthood through marriage, child-rearing, and relationships with co-workers and adult friends. In later life, family members are usually the primary sources of social support, especially one's spouse, children, and siblings. The quality of the relationship between an adult child and an aging parent has a long history. Clearly, the nature of the support that an aging parent is able to receive or that an adult child is willing to provide is influenced by the feelings of closeness and connection that were fashioned during the child-rearing process and also by the child's relationship to the parents during early adulthood years.

For very old people, especially women, the likelihood of living alone is high. After the death of a spouse, men and women must realign their social support systems from among relationships that include their adult children, friends, relatives, neighbors, and new acquaintances in order to satisfy their needs for interaction and companionship. Very old adults who are childless and those who have no surviving children or siblings are especially vulnerable to ending their lives in isolation (Hays, 1984). In contrast, those who are able to preserve a diverse network are more likely to be the healthiest, to make the most use of appropriate community services, and to experience the highest levels of well-being (Litwin, 1997; Bosworth & Schaie, 1997).

These four women have been playing bridge together almost every week for 20 years. Movement of one of them to a retirement community has not disrupted the game. The continuity of social support is a mainstay of their emotional and physical well-being.

For many older adults, religious participation provides an additional source of social support. Older adults are more likely than younger adults to describe themselves as religious in their beliefs and their behavior. Mary, who at age 80 has experienced the deaths of three brothers, her husband, and her daughter-in-law, gives and receives emotional support through her faith:

> I always have a lot of faith. The good Lord has always given me the strength to go on. I was raised to believe and pray when I have problems I go to Mass every Sunday, and we have other special days when we go to Mass. I'm a eucharistic minister. God makes me do things to feel better—I serve people and God. I go to buildings to give communion to people who can't get out. (Rowe & Kahn, 1998, p. 164)

The place of religion in the lives of the very old is especially significant for African-Americans, who are more likely than whites to attend religious services regularly, even at advanced ages. They are also more likely to describe themselves as very religious, a characterization that reflects the frequency of their private prayer, of their strong emotional commitment, and of their reading of religious material. Religious involvement among elderly African-Americans is not predicted by income or education, however (Taylor, 1986). In one study of older African-American residents of an urban area, church membership was significantly related to well-being, particularly as a result of the perceived support they received from other church members (Walls & Zarit, 1991).

Ethnic identity itself may also become an important vehicle for social support in later life (Cool, 1987). It can provide a variety of sources of nonfamilial support, from a loose network of associations to membership in formal clubs and organizations. Members of an ethnic group may feel a strong sense of community as a result of their shared exposure to past discrimination, realization of common concerns, and sense of responsibility to preserve some of the authenticity of their ethnic identity for future generations. Participation in such a support network may be another vehicle for contributing wisdom gained through life experiences to those who will follow. Insofar as members of ethnic groups have felt somewhat marginal in the larger society in the past, their mutual support in later life may protect them from some of the negative stereotypes that the society imposes on the very old.

Involvement in a social support system can be viewed as an essential ingredient in the achievement of a sense of immortality. The social support system confirms the value of very old people, providing direct evidence of their positive impact on others and a sense of embeddedness within their social communities. The social support system of the very old usually includes adult children. Positive interactions with them contributes to the sense of living on through one's offspring and their descendants. Interactions with members of the social support system, especially those marked by feelings of warmth, caring, and celebration, may be moments of experiential transcendence for very old people. They feel the fullness and joy of existence that transcend physical and material barriers.

THE PRIME ADAPTIVE EGO QUALITY AND THE CORE PATHOLOGY

Confidence   In this discussion, **confidence** refers to a conscious trust in oneself and an assurance about the meaningfulness of life. In this definition, one finds an integration of the earliest psychosocial crisis of trust versus mistrust, with the crisis of integrity versus despair. In very old age, after a lifetime of facing challenges and experiencing losses and gains, one has a new belief in the validity of one's intuition, a trust in one's world view, and a continued belief in one's capacity to participate in the world on one's own terms. Confidence is sustained by a stable, supportive social network (Lang et al., 1997). Older adults who feel they are able to engage in the activities they enjoy and interact with people they value are also more likely to believe that they can adapt to the challenges they face. As a result of their confidence, they are less disrupted by stressful events and more hopeful about being able to find successful solutions in the face of negative events (Pushkar et al., 1997).

Physical health and age, per se, are not the best predictors of confidence. One's perceptions of physical health problems and how one sees oneself in comparison to others may be more important predictors of confidence than an objective measure of health status. Some people view themselves as more impaired and dependent than they actually are, while others, who may be suffering from serious illnesses, continue to view their situation with optimism (Ryff, 1995). Similarly, one's perception of the adequacy of social support and its appropriateness in response to one's needs is more important to the sense of confidence than the financial value of resources exchanged (Davey & Eggebeen, 1998).

Over the course of the lifespan, psychosocial theory predicts that each individual will confront issues related to the negative poles of the psychosocial crisis of each stage. We argue that finding ways to integrate the negative pole of each stage into an overall positive world view strengthens and humanizes one's character. Encounters with each negative pole provide a deeper sense of empathy for the suffering of others and a more profound appreciation for the courage that it takes to live out one's life with an open, generous, hopeful outlook. We suggest that confidence emerges not because of a life of one success after the next, but out of a sequence of struggles in which creative energy is required to find a positive balance between positive and negative forces (J. Erikson, 1988).

Diffidence   **Diffidence** refers to an inability to act because of overwhelming self-doubt. It is considered one of the basic factors underlying personality disorders (Livesley et al., 1992). Diffidence is evidenced by an unusual amount of difficulty in making daily decisions without advice and reassurance from others; great reluctance in undertaking projects or becoming involved in activities because of lack of confidence; and fears of being unable to care for oneself, which result in the fear of being alone (APA, 1994).

Diffidence is likely associated with hopelessness. Among the elderly, hopelessness is experienced as a negative expectancy about the future and a sense of futility about having an impact on impending events. The combination of hopelessness and depression are strongly associated with suicidal ideation among the elderly (Uncapher et al., 1998). Feelings of diffidence can result from increased dependency and loss of control due to physical illness, loss of social support, or marked reduction in the quality of life. Or they can be a product of a continuous process of ego pathology, building on the negative resolutions of earlier psychosocial crises. It is clear that in later life, the courage and energy required to remain flexible and adaptive to change must be derived from the well of ego resources established over the life course. For some of the very old, this precious resource is missing, and they face the end of life in a state of passivity and doubt.

Applied Topic   ## MEETING THE NEEDS OF THE FRAIL ELDERLY

In thinking about the frail elderly, it is helpful to distinguish between optimal ability and actual ability levels (Denney, 1982; Gottesman et al., 1973). **Optimal ability** is what a person is capable of doing when he or she is motivated and well prepared. **Actual ability** is how the person usually performs. At every period of life, there is a gap between these two abilities. However, there may also be some limits to the optimal level of performance. For example, one might observe that a middle-school-age boy is not as strong as he might be if he exercised more and used his muscles in a more concentrated effort. However, even after exercise and training, his optimal strength would still be less than that of an adolescent who has experienced the increase in muscle mass that accompanies puberty.

Does aging itself impose limits on the optimal performance level of the very old or is it the environment and the expectations of others that reduce effective functioning? In tests of hearing, for example, older adults often show reduced sensitivity to high-frequency and low-intensity sounds. However, the hearing tests themselves create a barrier to performance. Since older people are cautious about making errors, they tend to say they have heard a tone only if they are absolutely certain that they have. In one study, older subjects were instructed to take a chance and respond even if they were not completely sure about having heard the tone. Their hearing tests showed significant improvement over normal testing conditions (Reese & Botwinick, 1971).

The goal of providing services or community resources to the frail elderly should be to enhance a realistic level of performance. On the one hand, one should not try to encourage 80-year-olds to live the lives of teenagers or people in their 50s. On the other hand, one should not hold such minimal expectations for the elderly that they are robbed of their autonomy and ability to meet challenges or to strive toward achievable goals. One of the current issues that has become a focus of research and policy debate is the extent to which physical frailty in very old age is treatable or preventable, and how to reduce dependency, especially long-term nursing care (Hadley et al., 1993).

Defining Frailty   Frailty has typically been operationalized in terms of **dependency**. One common approach is to list difficulties in the activities of daily living (ADLs), including bathing, dressing, transferring from the bed to a chair, using the toilet, and eating. Sometimes these assessments include walking a short distance, since this degree of motor ability is usually required to function independently. Beyond these basic types of self-care, an expanded notion of dependency refers to difficulties in managing instrumental activities of daily living (IADLs), such as shopping, preparing meals, doing light housework, using transportation, or using the telephone. These tasks, while clearly more complex than the ADLs, are essential to maintaining one's daily life without dependence on informal or formal community support services (Guralnik & Simonsick, 1993). Figure 14.6 shows the numbers of adults who receive different types of care in relation to the extent of their dependency—that is, the number of activities of daily living with which they need assistance. The largest group requires help with one or two ADLs, the vast majority of assistance coming from informal community resources, especially family and friends.

Dependency or difficulty in managing activities of daily living increases markedly after age 85. Many factors combine to produce this dependency. In most postindustrial societies, later adulthood is characterized by a sedentary lifestyle. Estimates suggest that only about 10% of older adults are active enough to sustain appropriate levels of muscle strength and cardiovascular capacity (Fiatarone & Evans, 1993). Weakness resulting from disuse combines with certain biological changes, diseases, medications, and malnutrition to produce muscle atrophy, risk of falling, reduced arousal and cognitive capacity, and a gradual decline in confidence in being able to cope with even moderate types of physical exertion.

On the other hand, measures of functional limitations often fail to differentiate between what a person says he might be able to do in a hypothetical context (when completing a survey), and what he actually does in his day-to-day life. For example, some people may respond to a questionnaire saying that they are able to walk half a mile without help, but they do not actually ever walk that much. Others may respond that they cannot walk half a mile without help, but in fact they walk several blocks on most days to go to the store near their home. When observed in their natural setting, many older adults use compensatory strategies to overcome some physical impairment or integrate the support of others so that they can enact certain functions even though

FIGURE 14.6

Levels of dependency and types of care Note: Number of persons who receive nursing-home care and informal and formal care in the community according to level of disability. Community-dwelling persons represented in this figure actually receive help for one or more activities of daily living (ADLs) or instrumental activities of daily living (IADLs) ADLs include bathing, dressing, eating, transferring, using the toilet, and continence. IADLs include preparing meals, shopping, managing money, doing light housework, doing heavy housework, and getting outside.

SOURCE: Based on Hing & Bloom, 1990.

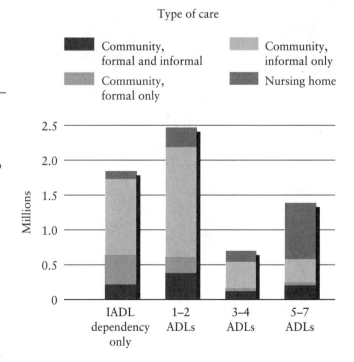

Type of care

■ Community, formal and informal
▨ Community, informal only
▨ Community, formal only
▨ Nursing home

they are seriously disabled. For example, in a sample of women who needed assistance in more than three areas of daily living, over one-fourth still managed to get to church services once a week or more. They did not allow their physical limitations to restrict their role involvement (Idler, 1987; Glass, 1998).

For many older adults, problems with remaining independent change from time to time. In the winter, when streets are icy and the weather is cold, a person may need more help because it is difficult to walk outside or wait for the bus. In the event of an acute illness requiring a period of hospitalization, the person may temporarily need support during the posthospital recovery but does not require long-term institutionalization. Full recovery from a week or two of being bedridden may require additional physical therapy, rebuilding muscle tone and endurance, and rebuilding confidence in being able to manage daily tasks. The outcome for the older person depends on the patient, caregiver, and health-care system—all sharing expectations for recovery and rehabilitation rather than viewing the person as permanently weakened and destined for prolonged dependency (Schulz & Williamson, 1993).

Supporting Optimal Functioning

To support optimal functioning of the elderly, one must accurately assess their limitations. One does not want to take away the supports that help very old adults sustain their independence or overreact to their physical or intellectual limitations. This tendency, however, is observed in the responses of some adult children to their aging parents. Once the children realize that their parents are not functioning at the same high level of competence that they enjoyed previously, the children move toward a **role reversal**. The children may infantilize or dominate their parents, insisting on taking over all financial matters or attempting to relocate their parents to a more protective housing arrangement. Gradually, some take away all their parents' decision-making responsibilities.

Although children may view such actions as being in the parents' best interests, they may fail to take their parents' preferences into account. For example, adult children tend to overemphasize the importance of health and financial considerations for their parents and to overlook the significance of familiar housing in preserving the companionship and daily support that are critical to their parents' sense of well-being (Kahana, 1982). Adult children may also fail to realize how important decision-making tasks and responsibility for personal care are to the maintenance of their parents' personality structure. In mutually satisfying relationships between adult daughters and their aging mothers, the daughters made sure that their mothers were consistently involved in decisions that affected their lives, even when the mothers were heavily dependent on their daughters for daily care (Pratt et al., 1989).

In many nursing homes, there is a similar tendency to reduce or eliminate expectations of autonomy by failing to give residents responsibilities for planning or performing the activities of daily life. Routine chores such as cooking, cleaning, shopping for groceries, doing laundry, planning meals, answering the phone, paying bills, and writing letters all give older adults the sense that life is going along as usual. Replacing these responsibilities with unstructured time may subject very old people to more stress than continuing to expect some forms of regular contribution to daily life. Thus, paid work assignments and struc-

Certain modifications of the physical environment help promote optimal functioning. At WalMart, wheelchairs are equipped with baskets to allow older adults to enjoy shopping even if they are physically challenged.

tured daily responsibilities are activities that an institutional setting can provide to help maintain a high level of social and intellectual functioning among the residents.

Supporting the optimal functioning of frail elderly people requires an individualized approach. Each person has a unique profile of competencies and limitations. For some, the physical environment presents the greatest barriers to optimal functioning. A person who cannot walk without fear of falling, cannot see well, or cannot grasp objects because of arthritis may need to have modifications in the home that will compensate for these limitations. Many creative strategies have been introduced that permit people with serious physical disabilities to retain an optimal level of autonomy in their homes.

The Role of the Community

For some very old adults, the quality of the neighborhood presents the greatest barrier to optimal functioning. Older people may be afraid of vandalism, theft, or other forms of neighborhood crime. They may need transportation, emergency medical services, and convenient social settings. The availability of meals-on-wheels, transportation services, and home maintenance services within a community can sustain independent living and promote a high level of self-efficacy among older adults. Table 14.2 summarizes the results of a study of the importance and critical distance of neighborhood services for the very old. The *critical distance* is the limit beyond which a very old person would find the service inaccessible (Newcomer, 1976). Of course, one must keep in mind that the critical distance may vary with the topography. Climbing two blocks up a steep hill may be more difficult for a very old person than four blocks of flat walking. Interventions at the community level may be necessary to meet the safety, health, and social needs of some older adults who want to remain in their communities.

For other very old adults, the absence of meaningful interpersonal relationships is the greatest barrier to optimal functioning. The role of the informal social support system cannot be underestimated in meeting the needs of the frail elderly. Children,

---

TABLE 14.2   Critical Distances of Neighborhood Services for the Elderly

Service	Critical Distance	Maximum Recommended Distance
Bus stop	On site to 3 blocks	1 block
Outdoor area	On site to 3 blocks	3 blocks
Laundromat	On site	On site
Grocery store	1–10 blocks	6 blocks
Supermarket	1–10 blocks	6 blocks
Bank	1–10 blocks	6 blocks
Post office	1–3 blocks	3 blocks
Department store	1–3 blocks	3 blocks
Cleaners	1–11 blocks	6 blocks
Senior center	On site	On site
Beauty shop or barber	On site to 10 blocks	10 blocks
Physician	1–10 blocks	10 blocks
Butcher shop	1–10 blocks	6 blocks
Snack bar	1–10 blocks	10 blocks
Public library	On site to 10 blocks	10 blocks
Dentist	1–10 blocks	10 blocks
Eye doctor	1–10 blocks	10 blocks
Foot doctor	Indeterminate	10 blocks
Center (for all ages)	Used as senior center	On site
Movie	Indeterminate[1]	10 blocks
Church or synagogue	Indeterminate[1]	Indeterminate[1]
Bar	No importance	No importance

[1]Distance indeterminate because of high percentage of persons who do not use and only small number who do use.

Source: Based on Newcomer, 1976.

spouses, other relatives, and neighbors are all important sources of help. Within communities, very old people are themselves likely to provide significant help to age-mates who may be ill, bereaved, or impaired in some way. Most older adults prefer not to have to ask for help. However, they are much better off if they have someone to turn to than if they have no one.

In one community intervention service in New Haven, Connecticut called LIFE (Learning Informally from the Elderly), community professionals charged with providing services to the frail elderly organized interviews and community meetings with them to learn what challenges they were facing in trying to remain as independent as possible in their neighborhood (Pallett-Hehn & Lucas, 1994). The professionals were surprised to find that the older adults brought safety concerns to the fore as a primary issue and that health and service concerns were secondary. In order to preserve and continue the dialogue, the professionals fostered the creation of Elder Forums, neighborhood groups where older adults discuss their mutual concerns and possible solutions. Each month, representatives from the Elder Forums come together in an assembly with professionals and policy makers to raise concerns that had been dis-

At her 100th birthday, life for Fern is still filled with joy and surprises.

cussed in the Elder Forum and to identify communitywide resources or changes in policy and procedures for addressing the concern.

The Role of Creative Action

People can do a lot for themselves to promote a fulfilling later life. Through instruments such as a **living will, durable power of attorney,** and the **psychiatric will** people can declare what kinds of assistance they are and are not willing to accept in their very old age. Both the living will and the designation of someone as having a durable power of attorney for health-care decisions allow adults who are unable to give reasoned, informed consent to medical treatment a vehicle for expressing their preferences about it. Through these advance statements, older adults can express their position on receiving psychiatric treatment, on conditions under which they would accept institutionalization, and on various types of life-extending medical interventions. Despite these options, relatively few adults have formalized their wishes in this way (Zweibel & Cassel, 1989; Jehle, 1994).

Very old adults can alter the structure of their environment to enhance their sense of well-being. They may move to a warmer climate, to homogeneous-age communities, or to more modest homes or apartments that entail fewer maintenance responsibilities. They may participate in exercise classes or other guided physical activity to improve their strength, endurance, and flexibility. Very old adults may select some family and friendship relationships that they sustain through frequent interaction, mutual help giving, and shared activities. They may participate in activities in community settings, including churches, senior centers, libraries, and volunteer organizations, through which they retain a sense of purpose and social connection. As at earlier ages, very old people make certain choices that direct the course of their lives and influence their overall level of adjustment.

In summary, the quality of life for the frail elderly depends on four factors: (1) the specific nature and timing of the health-related limitations that accompany aging; (2) the availability of appropriate resources within the home, family, and community to help compensate for or minimize those limitations; (3) the selective emphasis that the person gives to some life experiences over others as being central to well-being; and (4) the person's motivational orientation to continue to find creative strategies to adapt to change.

Chapter Summary

In attempting to describe the psychosocial development of the very old, we are drawn to concepts that have a strong non-Western philosophical flavor. We have introduced such concepts as psychohistorical perspective, experiential transcendence, immortality, and social support—themes that reflect the need to assume a long-range perspective on life and its meaning. The concept of time changes with advanced age so that the continuity of past, present, and future becomes clearer. With the attainment of a deep confidence in being meaningfully integrated into an effective social system, the very old can find pleasure in the natural flow of events without concern about the accumulation of material goods or the need to exercise power.

The actual quality of daily life for the very old is influenced to a great extent by their health. For many of them, daily activities are restricted by one or more chronic diseases. Nevertheless, the majority of the very old continue to live in their own households and perform tasks of daily living independently. A key to their independence lies in whether or not they are integrated into effective social support networks. Social support provides help, resources, meaningful social interaction, and a psychological sense of being valued. The very old who survive within a support system can transcend the real limitations of their health, finding comfort and continuity in their participation in a continuing chain of loving relationships. Those who are isolated, however, are more likely to face the end of their lives bound to the tedium of struggling with physical limitations and resenting their survival.

End of Chapter Case

The following case illustrates the importance of psychological attitudes in allowing a person with serious physical problems to play a meaningful role in a social setting for the frail elderly. Mr. Z.'s outlook helps him maintain his vitality and express his love of life:

Mr. M.L.Z. is an 89-year-old white male of Eastern European origin. He lives in a midsized nursing home in the Middle West. Many of his daily activities revolve around his circulating among the facility's residents, chatting, playing cards, reading to them, and "fetching things." Most important, Mr. Z. carries his old battered violin about with him and at the drop of a hat will play a tune or break into song in a surprisingly strong, clear, melodic voice. He claims to be able to sing songs in any one of seven languages, and with the least encouragement will try out several for anyone who will listen.

Mr. Z. is small (5′3″), frail-looking, and completely bald. He has facial scars and wears extremely thick-lensed glasses. He seems to be known and well liked by practically all residents and staff of the facility in which he resides, and by many visitors there as well.

He recalls a colorful history. He "escaped" his homeland at the tender age of 15½ to avoid compulsory military service and fled to Russia. There he was inducted into the army, and was subsequently sent off to duty in Siberia, where he lived for about six years. After another tour of duty in a border patrol he deserted, made his way across Europe, and eventually came to the United States. Here he took odd jobs, educated himself, and in time "got into show business"; he became a vaudeville prompter. In time his contacts in entertainment took him around the world. Yet time took its toll.

He tells of marrying a woman with whom he lived for "almost 40 years." They had no children and she died some 15 years ago. Following her death, he began to experience a series of physical difficulties. An operation for cataracts left him with the need for very thick glasses. At one time he had a toupee made, which he has not worn for some time. One leg was amputated because of a diabetic condition and he now wears a prosthetic leg. In addition, he wears a hearing aid, false teeth, and, for the last year, a heart pacer. Several years ago he experienced what he calls a "small stroke," which left him "mixed up" for a few days. But he "worked this out," he reports, by "walking a lot," an activity in which he engages frequently.

Mr. Z. says he has never smoked and drinks only on "occasions" or holidays, and then only to a limited degree. He scorns food fads, and eats "mostly" fresh fruits and "lots of vegetables"; he loves fish and drinks lots of tea.

Despite all his troubles, Mr. Z. maintains what is apparently a cheerful, optimistic view of life and circumstances, while he pursues his "hobby" of energetically helping his fellow residents keep their spirits up and their interests high.

He is very highly regarded and seen as filling a very important role in his nursing home as a teller and entertainer.

Source: Schwartz, A. N., Snyder, C. L., & Peterson, J. A., 1984.

Thought Questions

1. Imagine that you were having lunch with Mr. Z. What questions would you want to ask him?
2. What are the physical challenges of aging with which Mr. Z. must cope?
3. Why might Mr. Z. be living in a nursing home?
4. How would you describe Mr. Z.'s psychohistorical perspective?
5. What are the unique, creative adaptations that characterize Mr. Z.'s story?
6. Think of your own life at age 89. What will it be like? What can you do now and in the years to come to be a successful ager in your 80s and 90s?

Appendix:
Variations in Life Expectancy

The four tables in this appendix contain information about variations in life expectancy. In Table 1, information about the average remaining lifetime for persons aged 65, 75, and 80 in eight birth cohorts indicates the likelihood of reaching very old age for males and females by race.

Table 2 compares the average lifetimes of men and women in the 50 states. Numerous regional factors are associated with longevity, including variations by state in financial and health care resources, education, exposure to environmental hazards, and lifestyle. The data may also reflect genetic patterns in members of regional subgroups.

In Tables 3 and 4 we provide international data on longevity. In Table 3 consistent patterns in gender differences are indicated in 16 developed countries. In Table 4 the impact of economic and educational development on longevity is viewed from a global perspective.

TABLE 1 Average Remaining Lifetime at Various Ages by Sex and Race, 1900 to 1994

Exact Age, Race, and Sex	1994	1989	1978	1968	1954	1939–1941	1929–1931	1900–1902
All Classes								
At birth	75.7	75.3	73.3	70.2	69.6	63.6	59.3	49.2
65 years	17.4	17.2	16.3	14.6	14.4	12.8	12.3	11.9
75 years	11.0	10.9	10.4	9.1	9.0	7.6	7.3	7.1
80 years	8.3	8.3	8.1	6.8	6.9	5.7	5.4	5.3
White								
Male:								
At birth	73.3	72.2	70.2	67.5	67.4	62.8	59.1	48.2
65 years	15.6	15.2	14.0	12.8	13.1	12.1	11.8	11.5
75 years	9.6	9.4	8.6	8.1	8.2	7.2	7.0	6.8
80 years	7.2	7.1	6.7	6.2	6.3	5.4	5.3	5.1
Female:								
At birth	79.6	79.2	77.8	74.9	73.6	67.3	62.7	51.1
65 years	19.1	19.0	18.4	16.4	15.7	13.6	12.8	12.2
75 years	12.0	11.9	11.5	9.8	9.4	7.9	7.6	7.3
80 years	9.0	8.9	8.8	7.0	7.0	5.9	5.6	5.5
Black and Other Races†								
Male:								
At birth	64.9	64.8	65.0	60.1	61.0	52.3	47.6	32.5
65 years	13.6	13.6	14.1	12.1	13.5	12.2	10.9	10.4
75 years	8.9	8.8	9.8	9.9	10.4	8.2	7.0	6.6
80 years	6.8	6.9	8.8	8.7	9.1	6.6	5.4	5.1
Female:								
At birth	73.9	73.5	73.6	67.5	65.8	55.6	49.5	35.0
65 years	17.2	17.0	18.0	15.1	15.7	13.9	12.2	11.4
75 years	11.2	11.0	12.5	11.5	12.0	9.8	8.6	7.9
80 years	8.6	8.5	11.5	9.3	10.1	8.0	6.9	6.5

†Black only for 1994, 1989, 1929–1931, and 1900–1902.
Source: U.S. Bureau of the Census, 1984, 1992, 1997.

TABLE 2 Average Lifetime in Years, by Sex and States: 1989-1991

State	Both Sexes Number	Both Sexes Rank[1]	Male	Female	State	Both Sexes Number	Both Sexes Rank	Male	Female	State	Both Sexes Number	Both Sexes Rank	Male	Female
U.S.	75.37	(x)	71.83	78.81										
AL	73.64	46	69.59	77.61	KS	76.76	13	73.40	79.99	ND	77.62	4	74.35	80.99
AK	74.83	36	71.60	78.60	KY	74.37	41	70.72	77.97	OH	75.32	29	71.99	78.45
AZ	76.10	22	72.66	79.58	LA	73.05	49	69.10	76.93	OK	75.10	33	71.63	78.49
AR	74.33	42	70.54	78.13	ME	76.35	19	72.98	79.61	OR	76.44	18	73.21	79.67
CA	75.86	23	72.53	79.19	MD	74.79	37	71.31	78.13	PA	75.38	28	71.91	78.66
CO	76.96	6	73.79	80.01	MA	76.72	14	73.32	79.80	RI	76.54	16	73.00	79.77
CT	76.91	8	73.62	79.97	MI	75.04	34	71.71	78.28	SC	73.51	48	69.59	77.34
DE	74.76	38	71.63	77.74	MN	77.76	2	74.53	80.85	SD	76.91	8	73.17	80.77
DC	67.99	51	61.97	74.23	MS	73.03	50	68.90	77.10	TN	74.32	43	70.38	78.18
FL	75.84	24	72.10	79.60	MO	75.25	30	71.54	78.82	TX	75.14	32	71.41	78.87
GA	73.61	47	69.65	77.46	MT	76.23	20	73.05	79.49	UT	77.70	3	74.93	80.38
HI	78.21	1	75.37	81.26	NE	76.92	7	73.57	80.17	VT	76.54	16	73.29	79.68
ID	76.88	10	73.88	79.93	NV	74.18	45	70.96	77.76	VA	75.22	31	71.77	78.56
IL	74.90	35	71.34	78.31	NH	76.72	14	73.52	79.77	WA	76.82	12	73.84	79.74
IN	75.39	27	71.99	78.62	NJ	75.42	26	72.16	78.49	WI	76.87	11	73.61	80.03
IA	77.29	5	73.89	80.54	NM	75.74	25	72.20	79.33	WV	74.26	44	70.53	77.93
					NY	74.68	39	70.86	78.32	WY	76.21	21	73.16	79.29
					NC	74.48	40	70.58	78.27					

(x) Not applicable.

Source: National Center for Health Statistics, 1998.

[1] Massachusetts and New Hampshire share the rank of 14; Rhode Island and Vermont share the rank of 16. Therefore ranks 15 & 17 are omitted.

TABLE 3   Life Expectancy at Birth and at Age 65, by Sex, for Various Countries: Data Sources from 1993–95

	Males		Females	
	At Birth	At Age 65	At Birth	At Age 65
Austria	73.5	15.2	80.1	18.8
Canada	75.2	16.1	81.2	20.1
Czech Republic	69.7	12.7	76.7	16.1
Denmark	72.8	14.1	78.1	17.8
England and Wales	74.3	14.7	79.6	18.5
Finland	72.8	14.5	80.3	18.7
France	74.2	16.6	82.6	21.4
Germany	73.3	14.7	79.8	18.6
Hungary	65.3	12.1	74.6	15.8
Israel	75.3	15.8	79.3	17.8
Italy	74.4	15.5	80.8	19.4
Netherlands	74.6	14.7	80.4	19.1
Norway	74.9	15.2	80.7	19.3
Russian Federation	58.3	11.0	72.9	15.5
Sweden	76.2	16.0	81.6	19.8
United States	72.3	15.5	78.4	18.7

Source: WHO, 1998.

TABLE 4   Life Expectancy at Birth by Continent or Region: 1994

Continent and Region	1994 Life Expectancy (Years)
World total	**62**
More developed regions	74
Less developed regions	61
Africa	53
Asia, excluding Near East	62
Near East	67
Latin America and the Caribbean	68
North America	76
Europe	76
(Former) Soviet Union	69
Oceania	70

Source: U.S. Bureau of the Census, 1994.

Glossary

abortion Termination of a pregnancy before the fetus is capable of surviving outside the uterus.

accommodation (a) In Piaget's theory of cognitive development, the process of changing existing schema in order to account for novel elements in the object or the event. (b) In vision, changes in the curvature of the lens in response to the distance of the stimulus.

achievement motivation Internal state of arousal that leads to vigorous, persistent, goal-directed behavior when an individual is asked to perform a task in relation to some standard of excellence and when performance will be evaluated in terms of success and failure.

actual ability How we usually perform, as compared to optimal ability, how we perform at our best.

acquired immunodeficiency syndrome (AIDS) A deficiency of the immune system due to infection with the human immunodeficiency virus.

acute illness Illness that begins suddenly and lasts a brief time, such as a cold.

adaptation The total process of change in response to environmental conditions.

adaptive self-organization The process by which an open system retains its essential identity when confronted with new and constant environmental conditions. It creates new substructures, revises the relationships among components, and establishes new, higher levels of organization that coordinate existing substructures.

adaptive self-regulation Adjustments made by an operating system in which feedback mechanisms identify and respond to environmental changes in order to maintain and enhance the functioning of the system.

advocate A person who pleads another's cause.

affect Emotion, feeling, or mood.

affiliative behavior Actions intended to form positive, affectionate bonds with others.

affiliative values The amount of time spent and the degree of satisfaction achieved in helping or pleasing others.

age-graded expectation An assumption that someone should do something because of how old he or she is.

agency Viewing the self as the originator of action.

aggressive-rejected children A path to peer rejection in which children are aggressive and attribute hostile intentions to others.

aggressive-withdrawn children A path to peer rejection in which children are both aggressive and self-conscious.

alienation Withdrawal or separation of people or their affections from an object or position of former attachment.

allele The alternate state of a gene at a given locus.

alliances Bonds or connections between families, groups, or individuals.

Alzheimer's disease The most common form of chronic brain syndrome involving gradual brain failure over a period of 7 to 10 years.

amniocentesis The surgical insertion of a hollow needle through the abdominal wall and into the uterus of a pregnant woman to obtain fluid for the determination of sex or chromosomal abnormality of the fetus.

amniotic sac A thin membrane forming a closed sac around the embryo and containing a fluid in which the embryo is immersed.

anal stage In Freud's psychosexual theory, the second life stage, during which the anus is a primary source of sexual satisfaction. Issues of willfulness and order are central to this stage.

androgeny The capacity to express both masculine and feminine characteristics as the situation demands.

anesthetic A substance that produces loss of sensation with or without loss of consciousness.

anomaly Irregularity, something that is inconsistent with the normal condition; abnormality.

anorexia nervosa An emotional disorder in which the person loses the ability to regulate eating behavior; the person is obsessed with a fear of being overweight and avoids food or becomes nauseous after eating.

anxiety A painful or apprehensive uneasiness of mind, usually over an impending or anticipated problem.

anxious-avoidant attachment Infants avoid contact with their mothers after separation or ignore their efforts to interact. They show less distress at being alone than other babies.

anxious-resistant attachment Infants are very cautious in the presence of the stranger. Their exploratory behavior is noticeably disrupted by the caregiver's departure. When the caregiver returns, the infants appear to want to be close to the caregiver, but they are also angry, so that they are very hard to soothe or comfort.

Apgar scoring method Assessment of the newborn based on heart rate, respiration, muscle tone, response to stimulation, and skin color.

aptitude Potential for learning and future performance of a skill.

articulation and awareness Identification of those values, beliefs, and practices from the dominant culture and one's own ethnic group that are combined into a unique synthesis that forms a personal, cultural identity.

artificial insemination Injection of donor sperm into a woman's vagina to promote conception.

assimilation   In Piaget's theory of cognitive development, the process of incorporating objects or events into existing schema.

assumption   A fact, statement, or premise that is considered true and that guides the underlying logic of a theory.

attachment   The tendency to remain close to a familiar individual who is ready and willing to give care, comfort, and aid in time of need.

attachment behavioral system   A complex set of reflexes and signaling behaviors that inspire caregiving and protective responses in adults; these responses shape a baby's expectations and help create an image of the parent in the child's mind.

auditory acuity   The ability to recognize sounds of varying pitch and loudness.

auditory system   The body parts and neural connections related to hearing.

authoritarian   A style of decision making in which the leader assumes total responsibility for making decisions and assigning responsibility. The authoritarian leader or parent expects obedience from everyone in a lower status position.

authority   A person who has power and influence and who is seen by others as the legitimate decision maker.

authority relations   All the hierarchical relationships that give one person decision-making authority and supervisory control over another.

authority structure   An influence and decision-making system of relationships in business, government, education, and families.

autonomous morality   A more mature moral perspective in which rules are viewed as a product of cooperative agreements.

autonomy   The ability to behave independently, to do things on one's own.

autosomal   A chromosome other than a sex chromosome.

avoidance conditioning   A kind of learning in which specific stimuli are identified as painful or unpleasant and are therefore avoided.

babbling   Consonant-vowel sounds repeated over and over, which begin at about 4 months.

Babinski reflex   A response in which toes extend and fan out when the sole of the foot is gently stroked. This reflex is a sign of an immature nervous system. Eventually, a stroke on the sole of the foot makes one's toes curl down.

bar mitzvah   In the Jewish religion, a ceremony celebrated at age 13 to mark a boy's entry into adult status (*bat mitzvah* for girls).

behavioral slowing   Age-related delay in the speed of response to stimuli.

bereavement   The emotional suffering that follows the death of a loved one.

bilingualism   The ability to speak two languages fluently.

binge drinking   Five or more drinks in a row.

biological adaptation   A process whereby species evolve that have characteristics most suitable to the conditions of the environment.

biological system   Includes all those processes necessary for the physical functioning of the organism. Sensory capacities, motor responses, and the workings of the respiratory, endocrine, and circulatory systems are all biological processes.

boundaries   In family systems theory, what determines who is considered to be a family member and who is an outsider. They influence the way information, support, and validation of the family unit are sought and the way new members are admitted into the family. Some families have very strict rules that maintain a narrow boundary around the family. Few sources of information or contact are admitted. Other families extend the sense of belonging to a wide range of people who bring ideas and resources to the family system.

bulimia   A habitual disturbance in eating behavior mostly affecting young women of normal weight, characterized by frequent episodes of grossly excessive food intake followed by self-induced vomiting to prevent weight gain.

care   The commitment to be concerned.

career   Occupation(s) or profession(s) followed as a lifework.

care giving   In Bowlby's theory, the nurturing responses of the caregiver that comprise a corresponding behavioral system that we often refer to as parenting.

case study   A research method consisting of an in-depth description and analysis of a single person, family, or group.

categorization   The process of arranging, classifying, or describing by labeling or naming.

causal agent   A person or object that makes something happen.

causality   The relation between a cause and an effect.

cell differentiation   A process whereby cells take on specialized structures related to their function.

cell nucleus   The part of the cell that contains the material essential to reproduction and protein synthesis.

censors   In a study by Moriarty and Toussieng these were participants who preferred to limit their sensory experiences. They tried to clarify their parents' values by discovering what was acceptable in society. They had limited peer interaction and were uninvolved in school. They rejected experiences or ideas that did not confirm their traditional views.

central process   The dominant context or mechanism through which the psychosocial crisis is resolved.

cephalocaudal   The direction of development that follows from the head to the feet.

cerebellum   A part of the brain located in the back; the area that coordinates muscle activity and equilibrium.

cerebral cortex   The layer of gray matter in the brain that serves to coordinate central nervous system functions.

cerebrum   The upper part of the brain; the seat of conscious mental processes.

cervix   The narrow lower end of the uterus, which forms the beginning of the birth canal.

cesarian section   Delivering a newborn by lifting it out through an incision in the uterine wall.

choice phase   In Tiedeman's model, this is the phase when the person decides which action alternative to follow. The decision is solidified in the person's mind as he or she elaborates the reasons why the decision is beneficial. There is a sense of relief and optimism as the person develops a commitment to executing the decision.

chromosome   One of the rodlike bodies of a cell nucleus that contain genetic material and that divide when the cell divides. In humans there are 23 pairs of chromosomes.

chronic illness   Illness that lasts a long time. It may begin suddenly and recur or become progressively more serious.

chronological age   The number of years and months since birth.

circular reaction   In cognitive development, the infant's use of familiar actions to achieve familiar results.

circumcision   Removing the foreskin that covers the glans of the penis.

clarification phase   In Tiedeman's model, in this phase the person more fully understands the consequences of commitment to the decision that has been made. He or she plans definite steps to take and may actually take them in this phase or may delay them until a more appropriate time. The self-image is prepared to be modified by the decision.

classical conditioning   A form of learning in which a formerly neutral stimulus is repeatedly presented with a stimulus that evokes a specific reflexive response. After repeated pairings, the neutral stimulus elicits a response similar to the reflexive response.

classification   The action of grouping objects according to some specific characteristics they have in common, including all objects that show the characteristic and none that do not.

climacteric   The period of menopause for women and a parallel period of reduced reproductive competence for men.

clinical studies   Research conducted on populations who are or have been treated for a problem, or who are waiting to be treated.

clique   A small friendship group of five to ten people.

codominance   A condition in which both genes at a specific allele contribute to the characteristic that is expressed, as in AB blood type.

coercive escalation   A style of interaction in which the probability that a negative remark will be followed by another negative remark increases as the chain of communication gets longer and longer.

cognition   The capacity for knowing, organizing perceptions, and problem solving.

cognitive behaviorism   The study of those cognitive dimensions related to understanding a person's ability to learn and perform tasks.

cognitive competencies   A person's knowledge, skills, and abilities.

cognitive differentiation   The act of adding additional units of information, which increases the complexity of a concept.

cognitive functioning   A very broad term that encompasses the range of cognitive abilities.

cognitive map   An internal mental representation of the environment.

cognitive representation   Scheme, mental image.

cognitive style   A characteristic way of analyzing problems and organizing events.

cognitive theory   An analysis of the quality of thought and changes in thought at various stages of development.

cognitive unconscious   The range of mental structures and processes that operate outside awareness but play a significant role in conscious thought and action.

cohabitation   A relationship in which a man and woman live together but are not married.

cohort   (a) In research design, a group of subjects who are studied during the same time period; (b) In life course analysis, a group of people who are roughly the same age during a particular historical period.

cohort sequential study   A research design that combines cross-sectional and longitudinal methods. Cohorts consist of participants in a certain age group. Different cohorts are studied at different times. New cohorts of younger groups are added in successive data collections to replace those who have grown older. This design allows the analysis of age differences, changes over time, and the effects of social and historical factors.

collective self-esteem   Defined as the relatively stable evaluation of the value of one's group membership.

combinatorial skills   The ability to perform mathematical operations, including addition, subtraction, and multiplication. These skills are acquired during the stage of concrete operational thought.

commitment   Consists of a demonstration of personal involvement in the areas of occupational choice, religion, and political ideology.

communication disorders   Delay in the capacity to participate in effective social communication, including delays in acquiring new vocabulary, oversimplified grammatical expressions, limited variation in sentence types and structures, problems in sound production such as lisping or omitting certain sounds in spoken speech, stuttering, and problems in understanding certain types of words, expressions, and grammatical constructions.

communication repairs   Periods of recovery in normal mother-infant interactions which follow periods of mismatch so that infants and mothers cycle again through points of coordination in their interactions.

comparative assessments   Self-understanding that relies on comparisons of oneself with social norms and standards or of oneself with specific other people.

competence   The exercise of skill and intelligence in the completion of tasks.

competence (sense of)   The sense that one is capable of exercising mastery over one's environment.

competence motivation   The desire to exercise mastery by effectively manipulating objects or social interactions.

competition   A contest between rivals.

compulsions   Repetitive ritualized actions that serve as mechanisms for controlling anxiety.

compulsive sexual behavior   A compulsive need to relieve anxiety through sex.

concrete operational thought   In Piaget's theory, a stage of cognitive development in which rules of logic can be applied to observable or manipulatable physical relations.

conditioned response   A response that is evoked by a stimulus as a result of repeated, systematic association.

conditioned stimulus   A stimulus that evokes a response as a result of repeated, systematic association.

confidence   A conscious trust in oneself and in the meaningfulness of life.

conformity   Behavior in accordance with some specified standard or expectation.

congenital   Existing from the time of birth.

conscious   The kind of mental activity of which one is aware.

consensual union   Without civil or religious marriage ceremonies but regarded as a form of marital union.

conservation   The concept that physical changes do not alter the mass, weight, number, or volume of matter. This concept is acquired during the concrete operational stage of cognitive development.

constructivist perspective   Suggests that gender differences are a product of particular interactions that have a certain socially agreed-upon, gender-related meaning. In this view, the specific behaviors that are described as masculine or feminine depend largely on the situation, including expectations that people will behave in gender-appropriate ways.

contactful interactions   Open to the other's point of view, and clearly expressing the speaker's point of view.

contextual dissonance   Discrepancy between a characteristic of the individual and norms related to that characteristic within the community, for example being one of few poor children in a middle-class school.

contextual dissonance   The difference between characteristics of the primary childrearing and home environment, and other environments in which the child participates.

contextualist   A person who argues that behavior takes its meaning from the situation or circumstances in which it occurs.

contextualization of learning   Offering instruction in ways that first draw upon a child's existing experiences, knowledge, and concepts and then expand them in new directions.

contraception   The deliberate prevention of conception or impregnation by any of various drugs, techniques, or devices.

contraceptive   A method of preventing conception or impregnation.

contractions   Tightening of the uterine muscles during childbirth.

control   The key to successful experimentation. The experimenter must exercise control in selecting the children or families who participate in a study. The participants must be able to bring equivalent competencies to the situation. If this condition is not met, one cannot assume that differences in behavior between groups are due to the treatment.

control group   The subjects in an experiment who do not experience the manipulation or treatment and whose responses or reactions are compared with those of subjects who are treated actively to determine the effects of the manipulation.

controlling interactions   One person expresses his or her point of view and doesn't take the other person's point of view into consideration.

conventional morality   A stage of moral reasoning described by Kohlberg in which right and wrong are closely associated with the rules created by legitimate authorities, including parents, teachers, or political leaders.

cooperation   Working or acting together for a common purpose or benefit.

coordination   Refers to two related characteristics of interaction, matching and synchrony.

coping   Active efforts to respond to stress. Coping includes gathering new information, maintaining control over one's emotions, and preserving freedom of movement.

core pathologies   Destructive forces that result from severe, negative resolutions of the psychosocial crises.

correlation   A measure of the strength and direction of the relationship among variables.

correlation coefficient   A numeric index of the strength of relationship between variables. It is a number which can range from values of +1.0 to -1.0.

creativity   The willingness to abandon old forms or patterns of doing things and to think in new ways.

crisis   A dramatic emotional or circumstantial upheaval in a person's life. In psychosocial theory, this often refers to a normal set of stresses and strains rather than to an extraordinary set of events and consists of a period of role experimentation and active decision-making among alternative choices.

critical period   A time of maximum sensitivity to or readiness for the development of a particular skill or behavior pattern.

crossing-over   Interchange of genes or chromosome segments.

cross-sectional study   A research design in which the behavior of subjects of different ages, social backgrounds, or environmental settings is measured once to acquire information about the effects of these differences.

crowd   A large group that is usually recognized by a few predominant characteristics, such as the preppies, the jocks, or the druggies.

crystallization phase   In Tiedeman's model, this is the phase when the person becomes more aware of the alternatives for action and their consequences. Conflicts among alternatives are recognized and some alternatives are discarded. The person develops a strategy for making the decision, in part by weighing the costs and benefits of each alternative.

crystallized intelligence   Skills and information that are acquired through education and socialization.

cultural continuity   A smooth transition from the role expectations of childhood through adolescence and adulthood.

cultural determinism The theoretical concept that culture shapes individual experience.

cultural discontinuity Discrete expectations associated with each stage or period of life.

cultural norms Shared expectations held by members of society for one another's behavior.

cultural relativism A premise of cultural anthropology that the meaning of a specific ritual or norm must be interpreted in light of the values and goals of the culture.

culture The concepts, habits, skills, arts, technology, religion, and government of a group of people during a specific period.

cumulative relation In heredity, when the allelic states in a single pair of genes combine to influence a trait.

curriculum The courses offered by an educational institution.

day care A variety of programs and settings designed to care for infants and young children on a daily basis.

decentering Gaining some objectivity over one's own point of view; reducing the dominance of one's subjective perspective in the interpretation of events.

defense mechanism A technique, usually unconscious, that attempts to alleviate the anxiety caused by the conflicting desires of the id and the superego in relation to impulses (e.g., repression, denial, projection).

delinquency Wrongful, illegal, or antisocial behavior.

dementia Disorders, either acute or chronic, that have various causes and results, some reversible and some irreversible, and that involve serious impairment or loss of intellectual capacities, control of bodily functions, and personality integration.

democratic A style of decision making in which the leader involves all group members in reaching a decision. The democratic leader expects all members to share responsibility for decisions that are made.

dependency In the study of aging, an assessment of difficulties in the activities of daily living usually required to function independently. Beyond very basic types of self-care, an expanded notion of dependency refers to difficulties in managing instrumental activities of daily living.

dependent variable A factor that is defined by a subject's responses or reactions, and that may or may not be affected by the experimenter's manipulation of the independent variable.

depressed mood Refers to feelings of sadness, a loss of hope, a sense of being overwhelmed by the demands of the world, and general unhappiness.

depression A state of feeling sad, often accompanied by feelings of low personal worth and withdrawal from relations with others.

depressive syndrome This term refers to a constellation of behaviors and emotions that occur together. The syndrome usually includes complaints about feeling depressed, anxious, fearful, worried, guilty, and worthless.

deprivation The state of being without something one needs.

despair Feeling a loss of all hope and confidence.

developmental stage A period of life dominated by a particular quality of thinking or a particular mode of social relationships. The notion of stages suggests qualitative changes in competence at each phase of development.

developmental tasks Skills and competences that are acquired at each stage of development.

developmental viability When the fetus is regarded as having a good chance of surviving outside the uterus.

dialect A form of language that differs from the standard in pronunciation, grammar, and word meaning.

differentiation The extent to which a social system encourages intimacy while supporting the expression of differences.

diffidence The inability to act, due to overwhelming self-doubt.

diffuse-avoidant types People who procrastinate and delay dealing with self-relevant issues as long as possible. They tend to be influenced by immediate rewards and operate in a situation-sensitive fashion.

dilatation Condition of being stretched open beyond normal limits.

discipline A strategy for punishing or changing behavior.

disdain A feeling of scorn for the weakness and frailty of oneself or others.

disengaged relationships Infrequent contact and a sense that the members of the family do not really seem to care about one another.

disorganized attachment Babies' responses are particularly notable in the reunion sequence. In the other three attachment patterns, infants appear to use a coherent strategy for managing the stress of the situation. The disorganized babies have no consistent strategy. They behave in contradictory, unpredictable ways that seem to convey feelings of extreme fear or utter confusion.

displaced homemakers Women in middle adulthood who enter the labor market for the first time. Many of these women enter the job market as a consequence of divorce or early widowhood, face extreme economic pressures, and must compete with much younger workers for entry-level positions.

dissociation Dissolving the ties, no longer associating together.

dissonance Recognition and confusion about areas of conflict between the values, beliefs, and practices of the dominant culture and those of one's own ethnic group.

division of labor Splitting the activities needed to accomplish a task between participants.

dizygotic twins Developed from two fertilized ova; fraternal twins.

DNA Deoxyribonucleic acid. DNA molecules are the chemical building blocks of chromosomes found in the cell nucleus.

dominance hierarchy A social ordering with the most controlling and assertive people at the top and the more submissive people at the bottom.

dominance If one allele is present, its characteristic is always observed whether or not the other allele of the allelic pair is the same.

dominant gene   A form of a gene that is always expressed in the phenotype when the gene is present, as in the example of Rr for tongue rolling.

doubt   A sense of uncertainty about one's abilities and one's worth.

Down syndrome   A chromosomal irregularity in which the child has an extra chromosome 21. The condition results in mental retardation.

dramatic role playing   Taking on a role in fantasy play.

dual-career marriage   A marriage in which both partners have high-powered professional, technical, or administrative careers.

dual-earner marriage   A marriage in which both partners work to earn money.

durable power of attorney   An advanced statement allowing adults who are unable to give reasoned, informed consent to medical treatment a vehicle for expressing their preferences about treatment by designating someone to make decisions for them.

dyadic relationship   A two-person relationship.

early adolescence   The period of psychosocial development that begins with the onset of puberty and ends around 18 years of age, usually with graduation from high school.

early adulthood   The period of psychosocial development that begins in the early 20s and ends in the early 30s.

early school age   The period of psychosocial development that begins when the child enters school around the age of five and ends around the age of seven.

effacement   The shortening of the cervical canal.

efficacy   The power to produce effects.

egalitarian   Marked by the treatment of others as peers and equals out of a belief in human equality.

ego   In psychosexual theory, the mental structure that experiences and interprets reality. The ego includes most cognitive capacities, including perception, memory, reasoning, and problem solving.

egocentric speech   In Piaget's observation, toddlers use this to control and direct their behavior. The speech is considered egocentric because it is not intended to communicate with anyone else and often doesn't make sense to anyone else. Vygotsky suggested that egocentric speech is a component of the problem-solving function.

egocentrism   The perception of oneself at the center of the world; the view that others and events base their behavior on or occur as a result of one's own perceptions.

ego ideal   A set of positive standards, ideals, and ambitions that represent the way a person would like to be.

ego processes   All processes necessary for thinking and reasoning; for example, memory.

ego satisfaction   Sources of satisfaction that bring a sense of personal accomplishment, pride, or power, or meet other inner motives and goals.

ego strength   The soundness of the individual's personality.

Electra conflict   In Freud's psychosexual theory, the central conflict of the phallic stage for a girl, when she desires intimacy with her father and expresses hostility toward her mother.

electronic fetal heart rate monitoring   Continuous monitoring of fetal heart rate using an electronic amplification device.

embryo   The developing human individual from the time of implantation to the end of the eighth week after conception.

embryology   A branch of biology that studies the nature and development of embryos.

emotional regulation   Strategies for coping with intense emotions, both positive and negative. Caregiver behavior and observation are important factors in the development of emotional regulation.

emotions   States of feeling.

empathy   The capacity to recognize and experience the emotional state of another person.

empty nest   The time when children leave the home.

enactive attainment   Personal experiences of mastery.

enmeshed relationships   Characterized by over-involvement in one another to the extent that any change in one family member is met by strong resistance by the others; individuality is viewed as a threat to the relationship.

enzymers   Complex proteins produced by living cells that act as catalysts for biochemical reactions.

epigenetic principle   A biological plan for growth such that each function emerges in a systematic sequence until the fully functioning organism has developed.

equilibration   Efforts to reconcile new perspectives and ideas about basic moral concepts, such as justice, intentionality, and social responsibility, with existing views about what is right and wrong when a stage change occurs.

equilibrium   In Piaget's theory, the balance every organism strives to attain in which organized structures (sensory, motor, or cognitive) provide effective ways of interacting with the environment.

equivalence   In cognitive theory, the concept that two objects of the same size and shape remain the same in quantity even though the shape of one of them is changed.

estrogen   The major female sex hormone.

ethics   Principles of conduct founded upon a society's moral code.

ethnic group identity   Knowing that one is a member of a certain ethnic group; recognizing that aspects of one's thoughts, feelings, and actions are influenced by ethnic membership; and taking the ethnic group values, outlook, and goals into account when making life choices.

ethnicity   Traits, background, allegiance, or association that are associated with an ethnic group.

ethnic subculture   The cultural values and behavioral patterns characteristic of a particular group in a society that shares a common ancestry; memories of a shared historical past; and a cultural focus on symbolic elements that distinguish the group from others.

ethology   The comparative investigation of the biological bases of behavior from an evolutionary perspective, to determine the proximal causes of behavioral acts, the relative contribution of inheritance and learning to these acts, and the adaptive significance and evolutionary history of different patterns of behavior within and across species.

Eurocentric   Considering Europe and Europeans as focal to world culture, history, economics, philosophy, morality, and so on.

evaluation   A determination of the worth of one's skill in a particular behavior.

evolution   A theory that accounts for the changes from one species to another as well as modifications within species over time.

exclusivity   A shutting out of others for elitist reasons.

exosystem   One or more settings that do not involve the developing person as an active participant, but in which events occur that affect, or are affected by, what happens in the setting containing the developing person.

expansion   Elaborating on a child's expression by adding more words.

expectancies   Expectations about one's ability to perform, the consequences of one's behavior, and the meaning of events in one's environment.

expectations   Views held by oneself or by others about what would be appropriate behavior in a given situation or at a given stage of development.

experiential transcendence   A way of experiencing immortality through achieving a sense of continuous presence.

experimental group   The subjects who experience the manipulation or treatment in an experiment.

experimentation   A method of research that is conducted under repeatable and highly controlled conditions, in which some variable or group of variables is systematically manipulated while others are held constant; used to assess cause-and-effect relationships.

exploration phase   In Tiedeman's model, this is the phase when a person realizes that a career decision must be made and therefore begins to learn more about those aspects of the self and the occupational world that are relevant to the impending decision. The person begins to generate alternatives for action. Uncertainty about the future and the many alternatives is accompanied by feelings of anxiety.

extended family   The family group that includes family members other than the nucleus of parents and children.

extinction   (a) In classical conditioning, the reduction of an association when the unconditioned stimulus is not presented. (b) The negative pole of the psychosocial crisis of very old age in which it is feared that the end of life is the end of all continuity.

extroversion   Personality dimension that includes such qualities as sociability, vigor, sensation seeking, and positive emotions.

fallopian tube   The tube, extending from the uterus to the ovary, in which fertilization takes place.

false labor   Uterine contractions that do not indicate the start of the birth process.

family constellation   The many variables that describe a family group, including the presence or absence of mother and father, sibling number, spacing, sex, and the presence or absence of extended family members in the household.

family day care   A child-care arrangement in which a person cares for several children in his or her own home, often along with the person's own children.

family household   Two or more individuals living together who are related by birth, marriage, or adoption.

family of origin   The family to which one is born.

family of procreation   The family one begins as an adult.

fantasy   A form of symbolic thought that is not restrained by the limits of reality.

fast mapping   Forming a rapid, initial, partial understanding of the meaning of a word by relating it to the known vocabulary and restructuring the known-word storage space and its related conceptual categories.

fear of loss of love   A motive for parental identification in which the child tries to be like the parent in order to preserve a sense of closeness with the loved parent.

feedback   Information about how a particular activity is being carried out that returns to a central control mechanism. Feedback may be automatic information from muscles about a physical activity or evaluative information from a teacher about academic performance.

fertility   The capacity to reproduce.

fertilization   The penetration of an egg by a sperm.

fetal alcohol syndrome   A condition of the fetus involving central nervous system disorders, low birth weight, and malformations of the face; the condition is associated with heavy use of alcohol by mothers, especially during the last trimester of pregnancy.

fetoscopy   Examination of the fetus through the use of a fiberoptic lens.

fetus   The unborn infant. Usually the term *fetus* refers to infants between 8 weeks of gestational age and birth.

fidelity (I)   The ability to freely pledge and sustain loyalties to others.

fidelity (II)   The ability to freely pledge and sustain loyalties to values and ideologies.

filial obligation   The responsibilities of adult children for their aging parents.

fitness   The genetic contribution of an individual to the next generation's gene pool relative to the average for the population, usually measured by the number of offspring or close kin that survive to reproductive age.

fitness   Patterns of activity or inactivity, endurance or frailty, and illness or health that influence the ability to manage tasks of independent daily living.

fixation   In psychoanalysis, a preoccupation with the issues and tasks of a particular stage of development; an inability to progress to more mature stages.

fixed action pattern   A genetically guided sequence of complex highly patterned behavior, such as nest building or mating, that is characteristic of a particular species and is prompted or triggered by a specific stimulus pattern that signals or releases the innate behavior pattern.

fluid intelligence   The ability to impose organization on information and to generate new hypotheses.

formal operational thought   In Piaget's theory, the final stage of cognitive development characterized by reasoning, hypothesis generating, and hypothesis testing.

frail elderly   Older people who may have delicate health, one or more inactivating chronic conditions, and possibly some form of dementia.

fraternal twins   Children born at the same time who developed from two different ova.

full-term baby   A baby who has developed in utero for the complete gestational period of 9 months or approximately 36 weeks.

functional autonomy of motives   In Allport's theory, the notion that behaviors may initially be performed because of specific motives, but may continue because the person enjoys them and/or finds them useful in new ways.

gamete   A mature germ cell involved in reproduction.

gender   The sex of the person.

gender identification   A person's incorporation into their self-concept of the valued characteristics of male or female that become integrated into an early scheme for thinking of oneself as male or female.

gender identity   A set of beliefs, attitudes, and values about oneself as a man or woman in many areas of social life including intimate relations, family, work, community, and religion.

gender label   Words that identify one's gender, as boy, girl, man, or woman.

gender preference   The development of a personal preference for the kinds of activities and attitudes associated with the masculine or feminine sex role.

gender schema   A personal theory about cultural expectations and stereotypes related to gender.

gene   The fundamental physical unit of heredity. A gene is a linear sequence of nucleotides along a segment of DNA that carries the coded instructions for synthesis of RNA, which, when translated into protein, leads to hereditary character.

gene pool   Genetic information contained in the genes of the population or culture that provides the ancestry for an individual.

generativity   The capacity to contribute to the quality of life for future generations. A sense of generativity is attained toward the end of middle adulthood.

genetic anomalies   Neurological or physical abnormalities that have a genetic cause.

genetic counseling   Recent discoveries make it possible to identify genes responsible for certain forms of disease and genetic anomalies. Couples who have reason to believe that they may carry genes for one of these can be tested and advised about the probability of having children who may be afflicted.

genetic engineering   The development and application of scientific methods, procedures, and technologies that allow direct manipulation of genetic material in order to alter the hereditary traits of a cell, organism, or population.

genetics   The study of heredity.

gene transfer   The insertion of copies of a gene into living cells in order to induce synthesis of the gene's product; the desired gene may be microinjected into the cell directly, or it may be inserted into the core of a virus by gene splicing and the virus allowed to infect the cell to replicate the gene in the cell's DNA.

genitalia   The reproductive organs, especially the external ones.

genital stage   In Freud's psychosexual theory, the final life stage, during which the genitals are the primary source of sexual satisfaction and in which sexual impulses are directed toward members of the opposite sex.

genome   A full set of chromosomes that carries all the inheritable traits of an organism.

genotype   The hereditary information contained in the cells. Genotype may or may not be observable in the phenotype (see phenotype).

gentrification   A pattern of real-estate change in which a higher-income group buys property and develops residential and commercial projects in an area that has previously been serving a lower-income group.

gestation   The period from conception to birth.

gestational age   The age of the fetus from the time of conception.

Glick effect   Statistical evidence of lack of persistence that relates dropping out of high school or college with a high probability of divorce.

global empathy   Distress experienced and expressed as a result of witnessing someone else in distress.

grammar   Rules for the arrangement of words and phrases in a sentence and for the inflections that convey gender, tense, and number.

grasp reflex   An automatic involuntary movement present at birth that disappears as the nervous system matures. Any object placed in the infant's palm will be firmly grasped.

grief   Deep sorrow resulting from a loss.

group identity   The positive pole of the psychosocial crisis of early adolescence in which the person finds membership in and value convergence with a peer group.

group play   An early form of game, such as Ring Around the Rosie or London Bridge, in which winning or losing is not as important as the ritualized behavior.

growth rate   The amount of growth that occurs during a given period of time.

guilt   An emotion associated with doing something wrong or anticipating doing something wrong.

habituation   A form of adaptation in which the child no longer responds to a stimulus that has been repeatedly presented.

hemophiliac   A person who lacks a specific blood protein that causes blood to clot after a wound.

hemophilia   A sex-linked hereditary disease in which blood clots very slowly.

heredity   The qualities and potential transmitted genetically from one generation to the next.

heterogeneous   Having different qualities.

heteronomous morality   A child's moral perspective, in which rules are viewed as fixed and unchangeable.

heterosexual relationships   Associations and friendships with members of the opposite sex.

heterozygous   Characterized by the presence of different alleles of a particular gene at the same locus.

holophrase   A word functioning as a phrase or sentence.

homeostasis   A relatively stable state of equilibrium.

homozygous   Characterized by the presence of matched alleles of a particular gene at the same locus.

hope   An enduring belief that one can attain one's essential wishes.

hormones   A group of chemicals, each of which is released into the bloodstream by a particular gland or tissue and has a specific effect on tissues elsewhere in the body.

household   All persons who occupy a housing unit, including related family members and all unrelated persons.

hue   The property of light by which the color of an object is classified as red, blue, green, or yellow in reference to the spectrum.

human genome   The full set of chromosomes that carries all the inheritable traits of the human organism.

human immunodeficiency virus (HIV)   The cause of AIDS, it gains access to the body through the bloodstream and attacks the brain, sometimes causing damage and dementia.

hypercognitive system   Within the model of the mind, all the functions that make meaning of something. The hypercognitive system tries to interpret a particular task or problem, evaluate what is required to solve it, and then assign the problem to the one or more specialized systems that are best equipped to solve it.

hypothesis   A tentative proposition that can provide a basis for further inquiry.

hypoactive sexual desire   A decrease or absence of interest in sexual activity.

hypothetico-deductive reasoning   A method of reasoning in which a hypothetical model based on observations is first proposed and then tested by deducing consequences from the model.

id   In psychoanalytic theory, the mental structure that expresses impulses and wishes. Much of the content of the id is unconscious.

ideal self   A view of the self as one would wish it to be.

identical twins   Children born at the same time who developed from the same ovum.

identification   The process through which one person incorporates the values and beliefs of a valued other such as a parent.

identification with the aggressor   This motive is aroused when children experience some degree of fear of their parents. In order to protect themselves from harm, they perform behaviors that are similar to those they fear. This kind of identification may give children a magical feeling of power as well as decrease the parents' tendency to aggress against them.

identity   In cognitive theory, the concept that an object is still the same object even though its shape or location has been changed.

identity achievement   Individual identity status in which, after crisis, a sense of commitment to family, work, political, and religious values is established.

identity confusion   The negative pole of the psychosocial crisis of later adolescence in which there is confusion about who one is and what one's resources and talents are. Also, there is a lack of commitment to family, work, political, and religious values.

identity crisis   A sudden disintegration or deterioration of the framework of values and goals that a person relies on to give meaning and purpose to daily life.

identity confusion   The negative pole of psychosocial crisis of later adolescence, in which a person is unable to integrate various roles or make commitments.

identity foreclosure   Individual identity status in which a commitment to family, work, politics, and religious values is established prematurely, without crisis.

illusion of incompetence   Expressed by children who perform well in academic achievement tests yet perceive themselves as below average in academic ability and behave in accordance with this perception.

imaginary audience   The preoccupation with what you believe other people are thinking about you.

imaginary companion   A fantasized character created by a child's symbolic capacities.

imitation   Repetition of another person's words, gestures, or behaviors.

immortality   The positive pole of the psychosocial crisis of very old age, in which the person transcends death through a sense of symbolic continuity.

imprinting   A process whereby an animal comes to follow a large object, usually its mother, at some point after birth.

impulse   Internal psychological drive for certain types of behavior such as aggressive or sexual impulses.

impulse control   Control of internal psychological drives for particular types of behavior.

incentive   Something that motivates one to act, such as a reward for succeeding.

incest   Sexual relations between people so closely related that they are forbidden by law to marry.

independence   Self-government; a state of not being subject to the control of others or not relying on others for support.

independent variable   A factor that is manipulated in an experiment, and the effects of the manipulation measured.

individual identity   The commitment to a personal integration of values, goals, and abilities that occurs as personal choices are made in response to anticipated or actual environmental demands at the end of adolescence.

individuation   The process of becoming a unique and distinct person.

induction   A form of discipline that points out the consequences of a child's actions for others.

induction phase   In Tiedeman's model, in this phase the person encounters the new work environment for the first time. He or she wants to be accepted and looks to others for cues about how to behave. The person identifies with the new group and seeks recognition for his or her unique characteristics. Gradually the self-image is modified as the person begins to believe in the values and goals of the work group.

industry   A sense of pride and pleasure in acquiring culturally valued competences. The sense of industry is usually acquired by the end of the middle childhood years.

inertia   A paralysis of thought and action that prevents productive work.

infancy   The period of psychosocial development that begins when the child is born and ends when the child is approximately 2 years old.

infant mortality rate   The number of infants who die during the first year of life per 1000 live births throughout that year.

inferiority   A sense of incompetence and failure that is built on negative evaluation and lack of skill.

infertility   Inability to conceive or carry a fetus through the gestational period.

inflections   Word endings that indicate tense and number.

influence phase   In Tiedeman's model, in this phase the person is very much involved with the new group. He or she becomes more assertive in asking that the group perform better. The person also tries to influence the group to accommodate some of his or her values. The self is strongly committed to group goals. During this phase, the group's values and goals may be modified to include the orientation of the new member.

informational types   People who actively seek out and evaluate self-diagnostic information when negotiating identity issues and making decisions.

in-group   A group of which one is a member; contrasted with out-group.

inhibition   A psychological restraint that prevents freedom of thought, expression, and activity.

inhibitory control   An ability to slow down one's actions upon request, to suppress a movement in response to instructions, and to override the tendency to respond to a global display and pay close attention to the details in a stimulus. Inhibitory control in toddlerhood provides a basis for the formation of conscience and moral development in the early school age period. It allows the young child to respond more easily to parental requests and to interrupt or suppress undesirable behavior.

initiative   The ability to offer new solutions, to begin new projects, or to seek new social encounters; active investigation of the environment.

innate   Present at birth.

insight   In Piaget's theory of cognitive development, the last phase of sensorimotor intelligence, in which children solve problems by thinking over the possible solutions and selecting the correct one to try.

instinct   An inherited and largely unalterable tendency of an organism to make a complex specific response to environmental stimuli.

instrumental   Guiding behavior toward solving problems and accomplishing tasks.

instrumental values   The amount of time spent and the degree of satisfaction achieved in doing things that are challenging.

instrumental conditioning   A form of associational learning in which the behaving organism emits responses that are shaped into the desired response by reinforcement. Once the desired response occurs it is strengthened by continued reinforcement.

instrumental reminiscence   Emphasizes past accomplishments, past efforts to overcome difficulties, and the use of past experiences to approach current difficulties.

integration phase   In Tiedeman's model, in this phase group members react against the new member's attempts to influence them. The new member then compromises. In the process, he or she attains a more objective understanding of the self and the group. A true collaboration between the new member and the group is achieved. The new member feels satisfied and is evaluated as successful by the self and others.

integrative reminiscence   Involves reviewing one's past in order to find meaning or to reconcile one's current and prior feelings about certain life events.

integrity   The ability to accept the facts of one's life and to face death without great fear. The sense of integrity is usually acquired toward the end of later adulthood.

intellectual flexibility   A person's ability to handle conflicting information, to take several perspectives on a problem, and to reflect on personal values in solving ethical problems.

interdependence   (a) Marked by all the elements in a system relying on one another for their continued growth. (b) Systems that depend on each other.

intermittent reinforcement   A schedule of reinforcement that varies the amount of time or the number of trials between reinforcements.

internalization   A process in which the values, beliefs, and norms of the culture become the values, beliefs, and norms of the individual.

inter-observer reliability   Typically two or more observers' codings of the same situation are compared to determine whether different observers rated the same event in the same way. When inter-observer reliability is high, one has confidence that all the observers are describing or coding the events in the same way. When inter-observer reliability is low, the researchers must determine why and correct the differences in observation techniques.

intersubjectivity   A shared repertoire of emotions that enables infants and their caregivers to understand each other and create shared meanings; they can engage in reciprocal, rhythmic interactions, appreciate state changes in one another, and modify their actions in response to emotional information about one another.

interview   A research method in which subjects are questioned about various aspects of their lives, including their feelings and thoughts.

intimacy   The ability to experience an open, supportive, tender relationship with another person without fear of losing one's own identity in the process of growing close. The sense of intimacy is usually acquired toward the end of early adulthood.

intrapsychic   Occurring within the psyche, mind, or personality of an individual.

intrinsic motivation   A drive to behave in a certain way that comes from within the person.

introspection   Deliberate self-evaluation and examination of private thoughts and feelings.

in utero   In the uterus.

in vitro   In an artificial environment.

in vivo   Biological processes occurring or caused to occur within the living body of a plant or animal.

irregular verbs   Verbs that do not conform to the usual pattern of inflection; for example, sell, sold; see, saw.

irritability   The ease with which stimuli cause disruption or pain.

isolation   (a) A crisis resolution in which situational factors or a fragile sense of self leads a person to remain psychologically distant from others. (b) The state of being alone.

kibbutz   An Israeli community in which members share the ownership of all property and the profits from production. Children are reared communally.

labor   The period of involuntary contractions of the uterine muscles that occurs prior to giving birth.

lactation   Presence and secretion of milk that automatically occurs in the breasts of the mother of a newborn infant.

language perception   The ability to recognize sounds and differentiate among sound combinations before the meanings of these sounds are understood.

language production   The generation of language material by an individual. One of the first significant events is the naming of objects.

latency stage   In Freud's psychosexual theory, the fourth life stage, during which no significant conflicts or impulses are assumed to rise. Superego development proceeds during this period.

later adolescence   The period of psychosocial development that begins around the time of graduation from high school and ends in the early 20s.

later adulthood   The period of psychosocial development that begins in the early 50s and ends with death.

launching period   The time in family life during which children leave home.

learned helplessness   A belief that one's efforts have little to do with success or failure and that the outcome of task situations is largely outside one's control.

learning   Any relatively permanent change in thought and/or behavior that is the consequence of experience.

learning disorders   Disorders identified when a child's skills and measured abilities in reading, mathematics, or written communication are well below grade level and below the level expected for the child's measured I.Q. Learning disorders are linked with deficits in the primary processing system, including speed and accuracy of information processing, attention, and memory.

learning theory   A set of principles that account for changes in behavior at every stage of life, usually focusing on ways in which controlled changes in the environment produce predictable changes in behavior.

life careers   Activities in particular domains that last for a significant amount of time during one's life, such as the parenting career.

life course   Refers to the integration and sequencing of phases of work and family life.

life crisis   An unusual level of stress and tension that occurs during one's life, including psychosocial crises and events in one's life that cause tension, such as the death of a parent.

life endurance   The age to which one person in 100,000 can be expected to survive.

life expectancy   The average number of years from birth to death as based on statistical analyses of the length of life for people born in a particular period.

life review   A process of recalling significant life events, accomplishments, and difficulties from earliest memories up to the present.

life span   The length of an individual's existence.

lifestyle   A relatively permanent structure of activity and experience, including the tempo of activity, the balance between work and leisure, and patterns of family and social relationships.

linguistic system   Combination of vocabulary, grammar, phonetics, and language customs.

literacy   The state of being able to read and write.

living will   An advanced statement through which a person can express his or her position on receiving psychiatric treatment, on conditions under which they would accept institutionalization, and on various types of life-extending medical interventions.

loneliness   A feeling of sadness related to being alone; failing to meet one's needs for companionship.

longitudinal study   A research design in which repeated observations of the same subjects are made at different times, in order to examine change over time.

long-term memory   A complex network of information, concepts, and schemes related by associations, knowledge, and use. It is a storehouse of a lifetime of information.

love   An emotion characterized by a capacity for mutuality that transcends childhood dependency.

love withdrawal   A form of discipline in which parents express disappointment or disapproval and become emotionally cold or distant.

low-birth-weight babies   Infants who weigh less than 2,500 grams (about 5 pounds, 8 ounces) at birth. This may be a result of being born before the full period of gestation or it may result from the mother's inadequate diet, smoking, or use of drugs.

macrosystem   Refers to consistencies in the form and content of lower-order systems (micro-, meso-, and exo-) that exist, or could exist, at the level of the subculture or the culture as a whole, along with any belief systems of ideology underlying such consistencies.

major depressive disorder   Person will have experienced five or more symptoms for at least two weeks: depressed mood or irritable mood most of the day; decreased interest in pleasurable activities; changes in weight or perhaps failure to make necessary weight gains in adolescence; sleep problems; psychomotor agitation or retardation; fatigue or loss of energy; feelings of worthlessness or abnormal amounts of guilt; reduced concentration and decision-making ability; and repeated suicidal ideation, attempts, or plans of suicide.

malnutrition   A condition of ill health that results from faulty or inadequate food intake.

managerial resourcefulness   Flexible, creative problem solving in the workplace, particularly when facing new problems and changing conditions.

mastery   Competence or skill.

mastery (sense of)   A self-conceptualization that one has acquired certain competence, skill, or control over one's environment.

matched groups sampling   Two or more groups of subjects who are similar on many dimensions are selected as the sample for an experiment. The effects of different treatments or manipulations are determined by comparing the behavior of these groups.

matching   The infant and the caregiver are involved in similar behaviors or states at the same time.

maternal deprivation   Lack of opportunities for interaction with a mother or primary caregiver.

maturation rate   The rate at which certain personal, biological, and behavioral characteristics emerge and develop in an individual through the process of growth.

means-end relationship   A sensorimotor scheme for the causal connection between certain actions and certain consequences.

meiosis   An aspect of cell division resulting in the number of chromosomes in gamete-producing cells being reduced to one half.

memory   The power and process of recalling and reproducing what has been learned or experienced. It can be exercised as short-term memory and long-term memory.

menarche   The beginning of regular menstrual periods.

menopause   The ending of regular menstrual periods.

mental age   One's age as measured by an intelligence test. Usually, mental age is determined by the level of difficulty of the questions the person can answer correctly.

mental image   A form of representational thought that involves the ability to hold the picture of a person, object, or event in one's mind even in the absence of the stimulus itself.

mental operations   A transformation, carried out in thought rather than action, that modifies an object, event, or idea.

mentor   A trusted counselor or guide.

mesosystem   The interrelations among two or more settings in which the developing person actively participates (such as, for a child, the relations among home, school, and neighborhood peer group; for an adult, among family, work, and social life).

metabolism   A collective term for all the chemical processes that take place in the body: In some (catabolic), a complex substance is broken down into simpler ones, usually with the release of energy; in others (anabolic), a complex substance is built up from simpler ones, usually with the consumption of energy.

metacognition   Thinking about one's own thinking, including what individuals understand about their reasoning capacities and about how information is organized, how knowledge develops, how reality is distinguished from belief or opinion, how to achieve a sense of certainty about what is known, and how to improve understanding.

methodology   Particular techniques used to conduct a research investigation.

microsystem   A pattern of activities, roles, and interpersonal relations experienced by the developing person in a given setting with specific physical and material characteristics.

middle adulthood   The period of psychosocial development that begins in the early 30s and ends in the early 50s.

middle childhood   The period of psychosocial development that begins at about age 6 and ends when the child enters puberty.

middle school   A school containing grades 6 through 8.

mistrust   A sense of unpredictability in the environment and suspicion about one's own worth. Experiences with mistrust are most critical during infancy.

mitochondrial DNA   DNA from mitochondria, rich in proteins, fats, and enzymes, which are found outside the nucleus of a cell and which produce energy for the cell through cellular respiration. The DNA is passed on solely through the mother and can be used to trace genetic lineage.

model   In social learning theory, the one who is imitated.

modeling   Demonstrating behaviors that can be imitated by others.

monozygotic twins   Twins who develop from a single fertilized egg. These twins have identical genetic characteristics.

moral judgments   Cognitive decisions about right or wrong behavior that involve an underlying rationale.

moral prescriptions   Positive rules for valued behavior.

moral prohibitions   Rules to suppress negatively valued behavior.

moral development   The acquisition of the principles or rules of right conduct and the distinction between right and wrong.

moral script   The culture's expectations about valued and devalued behaviors for children of each age and in each social context.

mortality (infant)   The number of deaths per 100,000 live births.

motherese   The simplified, redundant style of speaking used by adults and older children so that they are more likely to be understood by a child who is learning language.

motor skills disorders   Developmental problems in the area of motor skills including delays in early motor skills such as walking, running, tying shoes, or using a scissors or knife. Later motor skills disorders may be reflected in trouble writing with a pencil or pen, putting together puzzles or models, and difficulties such as throwing and catching a ball.

motive   Something that causes a person to act.

motor functions   Bodily movement of both voluntary and reflexive types.

multipara   A woman who has borne two or more children or who is pregnant for the second time.

mutuality   Ability of two people to meet each other's needs and share each other's concerns and feelings.

myelination   The formation of a soft, white, fatty material called myelin around certain nerve axons, to serve as an electrical insulator that speeds nerve impulses to muscles and other effectors.

narcissistic   Extremely self-absorbed and self-loving.

naturalistic observation   A research method in which subjects' behavior is observed and described as it occurs in its natural setting without experimental intervention.

natural selection   A process whereby those individuals best suited to the characteristics of the immediate environment are most likely to survive and reproduce.

need   Physical or psychological requirement for well-being.

negative identity   A clearly defined self-image that is completely contrary to the cultural values of the community.

negative reinforcer   In operant conditioning, a stimulus such as electric shock that increases the rate of response when removed.

negativism   Refusal to comply with others' requests.

neighborhood   The physical area and the residents of the area where one lives.

neonatal   Affecting the newborn, especially during the first month of life.

neural tube   The tube formed during the early embryonic period that later develops into the brain, spinal cord, nerves, and ganglia.

neurological development   Growth of the nervous system.

neuron   A nerve cell with specialized processes that is the fundamental functional unit of nervous tissue.

neuroticism   A personality dimension consistently associated with discouragement, unhappiness, and hopelessness. Neuroticism includes such qualities as anxiety, hostility, and impulsiveness.

neutral stimulus   In classical conditioning, this is a stimulus that initially illicits a response of interest or attention, but nothing more, but after being paired with the unconditioned stimulus for a number of trials, it comes to illicit the response on its own and comes to be known as the conditioned stimulus.

normative   Conforming to an average pattern.

normative types   People who are relatively more defensive and closed to feedback that may threaten hard core areas of the self.

norms   Collective expectations, or rules for behavior, held by members of a group or society.

nuclear family   A household grouping that includes the mother, father, and their children.

nurturance   The tendency to attempt to care for and further the growth and development of another.

obesity   A condition characterized by being excessively fat.

objective   Based on facts and not influenced by personal feelings, interpretations, or prejudices.

object permanence   A scheme acquired during the sensorimotor stage of development, in which children become aware that an object continues to exist even when it is hidden or moved from place to place.

object relations   The component of ego development that is concerned with the self, self-understanding, and self-other relationships.

observation   A research method in which behavior is watched and recorded.

observational learning   Changes in thought or behavior that result from watching others.

obsessions   Persistent repetitive thoughts that serve as mechanisms for controlling anxiety.

obsessive reminiscences   Suggests an inability to resolve or accept certain past events and a persistent guilt or despair over these events.

occupational career   The pattern of participation in the labor market.

occupational status   A hierarchy of status among large groups of occupations that reflects their relative power, influence, and respect among members of the society.

Oedipal conflict   In Freud's psychosexual theory, the central conflict of the phallic stage, in which the boy has strong desires for the mother, strong aggressive feelings toward his father, and strong fears of castration by the father.

old-old   Among the very old, those who have suffered major physical or mental decrements.

open system   Structure that maintains its organization even though its parts constantly change.

operant conditioning   A form of learning in which new responses are strengthened by the presentation of reinforcements.

operational definition   In research, the way an abstract concept is defined in terms of how it will be measured.

operationalize   To translate an abstract concept into something that can be observed and measured.

optimal ability   The level of performance of which one is capable at the highest levels of motivation and preparation.

oral stage   In Freud's psychosexual theory, the first life stage, during which the mouth is the primary source of sexual satisfaction. Issues of self-concept and personal worth are important at this stage.

organic brain syndromes   Disorders involving memory loss, confusion, loss of ability to manage daily functions, and loss of ability to focus attention.

organ inferiority   In Adler's theory, a strong sense that some organ of one's body is weak and inferior. The person becomes preoccupied with thoughts of this weakness.

out-group   A group that competes with one's own group; contrasted with in-group.

overregularize   In language acquisition, the tendency to utilize a rule for the formation of the past tense of regular verbs when one can not remember the past tense of an irregular verb. As a child's vocabulary grows, the need to apply the rule to unfamiliar verbs declines.

ovum   An egg; the female germ cell.

parenting   The rearing of children.

peer   A person belonging to the same group, often on the basis of age or grade.

peer pressure   Expectations to conform and commit to the norms of one's peer group.

perception   The recognition and organization of sensory experiences.

personal fable   An intense investment in one's own thoughts and feelings and a belief that these thoughts are unique.

personal history   The life events that occur during an individual's development.

person-environment fit   The fit between the person's needs, skills, and interpersonal style and the characteristics of the environments in which the person participates.

perspective taking   The ability to consider a situation from a point of view other than one's own.

phallic stage In Freud's psychosexual theory, the third stage of development, during which the Oedipal and Electra conflicts occur.

phenotype Observable characteristics that result from a particular genotype and a particular environment.

phenylketonuria (PKU) A genetic disease that restricts intellectual development if it is not treated.

phobia An intense, irrational fear.

phonetics The sound system of a language.

physical culture Encompasses the objects, technologies, structures, tools and other artifacts of a culture.

physical state Within self-efficacy theory, the state of arousal or excitement that provides information as one makes a judgment of whether one is likely to succeed or fail in a certain task.

placenta The vascular organ that connects the fetus to the maternal uterus and mediates metabolic exchanges.

plasticity The capability of being molded.

polygamy A family organization in which a spouse may have more than one mate.

polygynous family One in which a man has more that one wife.

population All units for potential observation.

positive reinforcer In operant conditioning, a stimulus such as food or a smile that increases the rate of response when present.

postconventional morality In Kohlberg's stages of moral reasoning, the most mature form of moral judgments. Moral decisions are based on an appreciation of the social contract that binds members of a social system and on personal values.

postpartum depression A period of sadness that may be experienced by the mother after giving birth, which appears to be related to hormonal activity.

power assertion A discipline technique involving physical force, harsh language, or control of resources.

preconscious Absent from but capable of being readily brought into consciousness.

preconventional morality In Kohlberg's stages of moral reasoning, the most immature form of moral judgments. Moral decisions are based on whether the act has positive or negative consequences, or whether it is rewarded or punished.

prediction Declaration in advance usually with precision of calculation.

preoperational thought In Piaget's theory of cognitive development, the stage in which representational skills are acquired.

preterm baby A baby who is born before the full gestational period.

primary process The seemingly unorganized mental activity, characteristic of the id and the unconscious, that occurs in dreams, fantasies, and related processes. It is characterized by an absence of negatives, a here-and-now focus, and symbolic flexibility.

prime adaptive ego qualities Mental states that form a basic orientation toward the interpretation of life experiences; new ego qualities emerge in the positive resolution of each psychosocial crisis.

primipara A woman who has borne one child or who is pregnant for the first time.

primitive causality An understanding of cause and effect acquired by infants that is based solely on sensory and motor experience, not symbolic logic.

private self Refers to one's inner uniqueness and unity, a subjective experience of being the originator of one's thoughts and actions and of being self-reflective.

processing system Within a model of the mind, the elements of thinking that enter into every form of intellectual endeavor including the speed of processing information, the control of processing information, and the storage and retrieval of information.

processing load In problem solving, the number of domains of information called into play and the amount of work necessary to select response strategies.

prohibitive moral judgment In Kohlberg's research, a decision about violating a law or breaking a promise in order to achieve some other goal.

prompting Urging a child to say more about an incomplete expression.

prosocial behavior Positive social behavior such as helping another person.

prosocial moral judgments In Kohlberg's research, these involve a conflict between doing something helpful for someone else and meeting one's own needs.

psychiatric will An advanced statement that explains the kinds of psychiatric treatment a person is or is not willing to accept when they are no longer able to make an informed decision.

psychohistorical perspective An integration of past, present, and future time with respect to personal and societal continuity and change.

psycholinguistics The study of language as it is affected by psychological factors.

psychological system Includes those mental processes central to the person's ability to make meaning of experiences and take action. Emotion, memory and perception, problem solving, language, symbolic abilities, and our orientation to the future all require the use of psychological processes. The psychological system provides the resources for processing information and navigating reality.

psychosexual theory Freud's theory of psychological development, which proposes that cognitive, emotional, and social growth are associated with predictable changes in sexual sensitivity during childhood. This theory is sometimes called psychoanalytic theory.

psychosocial Of or pertaining to the interaction between social and psychological factors.

psychosocial approach Highlights the continuous interaction of the individual and the social environment. At each period of life, people spend much of their time mastering a unique group of psychological tasks that are essential for social adaptation within their society. Each life stage brings a normative crisis, which can be viewed as a tension between one's competencies and the new demands of society. The resolution of each crisis provides a new set of social abilities that influences the person's general orientation to the next stage and the succeeding stages.

psychosocial crisis   A predictable life tension that arises as people experience some conflict between their own competences and the expectations of their society.

psychosocial environment   The influence of culture, values, resources, demands, competences, and motives that are embedded in the structure of the social and physical environment.

psychosocial evolution   The contribution of each generation to the knowledge and norms of society.

psychosocial moratorium   A period of free experimentation before a final identity is achieved.

psychosocial theory   A theory of psychological development that proposes that cognitive, emotional, and social growth are the result of the interaction between social expectations at each life stage and the competences that people bring to each life challenge.

psychotemporal perspective   Sense of time as it is affected by psychological factors.

puberty   The period of physical development at the onset of adolescence when the reproductive system matures.

public self   Includes the many roles one plays and the expectations of others.

punishment   A penalty or negative experience imposed on a person for improper behavior.

purpose   The ability to imagine and pursue valued goals.

quasi-experimental study   The assignment of participants to treatment was not controlled by the experimenter but was a result of some pattern of life events.

quickening   Sensations of fetal movement, usually during the second trimester of fetal growth.

radius of significant relationships   The groups of important people in one's life; the breadth and complexity of these groups change over the life span.

random sampling   A method for choosing the sample for a study in which each member of the population under investigation has an equal chance of being included.

range of applicability   The behavior a theory is intended to explain.

rapport   Harmony and understanding in a relationship.

reaction range   The range of possible responses to environmental conditions that is established through genetic influences.

readiness   A time when a child's physical, cognitive, social, and emotional maturation is at a level to undertake new learning or to engage in a more complex, demanding type of activity or relationship.

reality principle   The motivating force or mechanism by which the ego protects the person by preventing id impulses from being gratified until a socially acceptable form of expression can be found.

receptive language   The ability to understand words.

recessive gene   A form of a gene that is expressed in the phenotype only when a similar allele is present. In combination with a dominant gene the characteristics associated with the recessive gene are masked.

reciprocal interactions   Interactions in which the behavior of each participant influences the responses of the others.

reciprocal roles   Roles such as student and teacher that are linked. Each role is partly defined by the other roles that support it. The function of the role is determined by its relation to the surrounding role groups to which it is allied.

reciprocity   A scheme describing the interdependence of related dimensions, such as height and width or time and speed.

reference group   A group with which an individual identifies and whose values the individual accepts as guiding principles.

reflex   An involuntary motor response to a simple stimulus.

reinforcement   In operant conditioning, the positive consequence that follows a given behavior.

reinforcement schedules   The frequency and timing with which reinforcements are presented.

rejectivity   The unwillingness to include certain others or groups of others in one's generative concerns.

reliability   The consistency of a test in measuring something.

reminiscence   Process of thinking and/or telling about past experiences.

repeatable   In research, it is important that others carry out a similar investigation and observe the same results as the original investigator. In order for this to occur, the original investigator must carefully define all the procedures and equipment used, describe all the essential characteristics of the participants (such as age, sex, and social class background), and describe the setting or situation where the observations were made.

representational skill   Skills learned in the preoperational stage, including mental imagery, symbolic play, symbolic drawing, imitation, and language, that permit the child to represent experiences or feelings in a symbolic form.

repudiation   Rejection of roles and values that are viewed as alien to oneself.

research design   A plan for conducting research that includes the method for gathering data, the sample selected to participate in the study, the frequency with which data are to be gathered, and the statistical techniques that are to be used in analyzing the data.

resilience   The capacity to recover from stress.

resistance and immersion   Rejection of many elements of the dominant culture; education about and involvement in one's own ethnic group and its beliefs, values, and practices.

response   A behavior that follows a particular stimulus event.

response repertoire   The range of behaviors that a person or animal is capable of performing.

responsiveness   Reacting readily to another's request or need.

retina   The light-sensitive membrane lining the back of the eye on which images are cast by the cornea and lens.

retrospective study   A research design in which subjects are asked to report on experiences they had earlier in their lives.

reversibility   A scheme describing the ability to undo an action and return to the original state.

reward   A positive consequence that follows desired behavior.

reward structure The pattern of positive consequences that occurs within an institution, a classroom, or a family group to encourage particular behaviors.

risk To expose to danger with a possibility of loss or injury.

rite of passage A ritual associated with a crisis or a change of status (for example, marriage for an individual).

ritual A formal and customarily repeated act or series of acts.

RNA Ribonucleic acid; a compound that conveys the information in the DNA strands to the cytoplasm in order to stimulate the production of specific amino acids.

role A set of behaviors that have some socially agreed-upon functions and for which there exists an accepted code of norms, such as the role of teacher, child, or minister.

role conflict Refers to the state of tension that occurs when the demands and expectations of various roles conflict with each other.

role compatibility Partners in a relationship approach situations in a manner that works well; their behaviors and responses complement one another.

role diffusion The negative pole of the psychosocial crisis of later adolescence in which the person cannot make a commitment to any unified vision of the self.

role enactment Patterned characteristics of social behavior that one performs as a result of being in a specific role.

role expectations Shared expectations for behavior that are linked to a social role.

role experimentation The central process for the resolution of the psychosocial crisis of later adolescence, which involves participation in a variety of roles before any final commitments are made.

role overload Refers to the state of tension that occurs when there are too many demands and expectations to handle in the time allowed.

role prescription The specific behaviors and norms associated with a particular role.

role reversal Assuming the behaviors of a person in a reciprocal role, as when a child acts toward his or her parent as a parent.

role spillover The state of tension that occurs when the demands or preoccupations about one role interfere with the ability to carry out another role.

role strain The conflict and competing demands made by several roles that the person holds simultaneously.

role-taking abilities Skills related to understanding and enacting the roles of others.

rooting An infant reflex in which the baby's head turns toward the direction of the cheek that is stimulated.

rule Principle or regulation governing conduct, action, procedure, ritual.

saline solution A solution containing salt.

sample The group of people who have been selected to participate as subjects in a research project.

sampling A method of choosing subjects in a study.

scaffolding A process through which a child and an adult attempt to arrive at a shared understanding about a communication, at which point the adult interacts so as to expand or enrich the child's communicative competence.

schedules of reinforcement The frequency and regularity with which reinforcements are given.

scheme In Piaget's theory, the organization of actions into a unified whole, a mental construct.

school phobia A strong, irrational fear of some aspect of the school situation, interpreted in psychoanalytic theory as an expression of a child's reluctance to leave the mother.

scientific observation Acts or instances of viewing or noting facts or occurrences for scientific purposes that are objective, repeatable, and systematic.

scientific process A process for building a body of knowledge involving observation, theory construction, operationalizing the theory, testing the theory, and evaluating and revising the theory.

secondary process The conscious mental activity and logical thinking controlled by the ego and influenced by environmental demands.

secondary sex characteristics The physical characteristics other than genitals that indicate sexual maturity, such as body hair, breasts, and deepened voice.

secular growth trend A tendency observed since approximately 1900 for more rapid physical maturation from one generation to the next, probably as a result of favorable nutrition, increased mobility, and greater protection from childhood diseases.

secure attachment Infants actively explore their environment and interact with strangers while their mothers are present. After separation, the babies actively greet their mothers or seek interaction. If the babies were distressed during separation, the mothers' return reduces their distress and the babies return to exploration of the environment.

self-concept The characteristics and attributes one applies to oneself.

self-control The ability to control impulses and to achieve intended outcomes.

self-efficacy A sense of confidence that one can perform the behaviors that are demanded in a specific situation.

self-encodings Evaluations and concepts related to information about oneself.

self-esteem The evaluative dimension of the self that includes feelings of worthiness, pride, and discouragement.

self-fulfilling prophecy False or inaccurate beliefs can produce a reality that corresponds with these beliefs.

self-theory An organized set of ideas about the self, the world, and the meaning of interactions between the self and the environment.

semiotic thinking The understanding that one thing can stand for another.

senescence The process of becoming old.

sensers In a study by Moriarty and Toussieng, these were participants who were willing to be influenced by new experiences. They preferred to seek out new activities, engage people, and question inconsistencies. They accepted their emotions and sought out experiences that would modify their values.

sensitive period A span of time during which a particular skill or behavior is most likely to develop.

sensitivity (of caregiver)   Attentiveness to an infant's state, accurate interpretation of the infant's signals, and well-timed responses that promote mutually rewarding interactions.

sensorimotor adaptation   Infants use their reflexes to explore their world, and they gradually alter their reflexive responses to take into account the unique properties of objects around them. This provides the basis for sensorimotor intelligence.

sensorimotor intelligence   In Piaget's theory of development, the first stage of cognitive growth during which schema are built on sensory and motor experiences.

sensorimotor play   Sensory exploration and motoric manipulation that produce pleasure.

sensory functions   The responses of the body and nervous system to a variety of stimuli; vision, hearing, taste, smell, and touch.

sensory receptors   Millions of microscopic structures throughout the body that collect information about the external environment or the body's internal state. Receptors are attuned to particular stimuli, and fire when excited.

sensory register   The neurological processing activity that is required to take in visual, auditory, tactile, and olfactory information.

sensory stimulation   Events that have an impact on any of the sense receptors, including sounds, sights, tastes, smells, or tactile stimuli.

separation anxiety   Feelings of fear or sadness associated with the departure of the object of attachment.

serial monogamy   Having one intimate relationship at a time as opposed to having several at once.

sex-linked characteristics   Characteristics for which the allele is found on the sex chromosomes.

sex-role identification   The integration of knowledge about one's gender, awareness of cultural expectations associated with each sex, identification with the like-sex parent, and preference for one's sex role.

sex-role preference   A positive value for the expectations and norms held for a specific gender group.

sex-role standards   Attributes held by the culture for males and females. These attributes can include both precepts and sanctions.

sexual orientation   Sexual attraction to one's own sex (homosexual) or the other sex (heterosexual).

sexually transmitted diseases   STDs include a wide range of bacterial, viral, and yeast infections that are transmitted through forms of sexual contact.

shame   An intense emotional reaction to being ridiculed or to a negative self-assessment.

shaping   In behavior modification, altering behavior by reinforcing progressively closer approximations of the desired behavior.

short-term memory   The working capacity to encode and retrieve five to nine bits of information in the span of a minute or two. This is the scratch pad of memory, if you will, that is used when someone tells you a telephone number or gives you his or her address.

sibling   Brother or sister.

sign   Something that represents something else, usually in an abstract, arbitrary way; for example, a word for an object.

social attachment   A strong, affectionate bond that develops between infants and their caregivers.

social clock   Expectations for orderly and sequential changes that occur with passage of time as individuals move through life.

social cognition   Concepts related to understanding interpersonal behavior and the point of view of others.

social competence   The skills involved in making friends, maintaining friendships, and enjoying the benefits of close peer relations.

social convention   Socially accepted norms and regulations that guide behavior.

social culture   Encompasses the norms, roles, beliefs, values, rites, and customs of a culture.

social desirability   The quality of a person's responding or behaving in ways that are viewed as valuable, acceptable, or proper by others.

social integration   Being comfortably involved in meaningful interpersonal associations and friendship relations.

socialization   The process of teaching and enforcing group norms and values to the new group members.

social learning theory   A theory of learning that emphasizes the ability to learn new responses through observation and imitation of others.

social milieu   The environment, especially the people, the norms, and the cultural expectations in one's surroundings.

social perspective taking   The capacity to recognize the point of view held by others, especially when it differs from one's own.

social play   Children join with other children in some activity.

social pretend play   Children coordinate their pretense. They establish a fantasy structure, take roles, agree on the make-believe meaning of props, and solve pretend problems.

social referencing   The process by which infants use facial features and verbal expressions as clues to the emotional responses of another person, often the mother, and as information about how to approach an unfamiliar, ambiguous situation.

social role   A set of behaviors that have some socially agreed-upon functions and for which there exists an accepted code of norms, such as the role of teacher, child, or minister.

social role theory   The theory that emphasizes participation in varied and more complex roles as a major factor in human development.

social support   Information leading people to believe that they are cared for and loved, that they are esteemed and valued, and that they belong to a network of communication and mutual obligation.

societal processes   All those processes through which a person becomes integrated into society; for example, cultural rituals.

societal system   Includes those processes through which a person becomes integrated into society. Societal influences include social roles, rituals, cultural myths, social expectations, leadership styles, communication patterns, family organization, ethnic and subcultural influences, political and religious ideologies, patterns of economic prosperity or poverty and war or peace, and exposure to racism, sexism, and other forms of discrimination, intolerance, or intergroup hostility. The impact of the societal system on psychosocial development results largely from interpersonal relationships, often relationships with close or significant others.

sociobiology   The scientific study of the biological basis of social behavior that focuses on practices within populations that increase the likelihood of certain genes surviving in subsequent generations of offspring.

socioeconomic level   One's ranking based on a number of social and financial indicators, including years of education, occupation, and income.

solicitude   Attentive care and protectiveness.

solitary pretense   Children are involved in their own fantasy activities, such as pretending that they are driving a car or giving a baby a bath.

soothability   The ability to regain a calm state following irritation or pain.

specialized structural systems   Within the model of the mind, the cognitive capacities best suited to particular familiies of problems and associated with a unique profile of mental abilities. They include: qualitative-analytic, quantitative-relational, causal-experimental, verbal-propositional, and spatial-imaginal.

sperm   The male germ cell.

stagnation   A lack of psychological movement or growth during middle adulthood that may result from self-aggrandizement or from the inability to cope with developmental tasks.

statisically significant   Pertaining to observations that are unlikely to occur by chance and that therefore indicate a systemmatic cause.

status   Relative social prestige or rank.

stimulus   Any change in the energy of the environment that has the potential to influence a perceiver.

stimulus generalization   The capacity for similar stimuli to evoke the same response.

stranger anxiety   Feelings of fear or apprehension in the presence of unfamiliar people, especially during infancy.

strange situation   A standard laboratory procedure designed to describe patterns of attachment behavior. A child is exposed during a 20-minute period to a series of events that are likely to stimulate the attachment system. Child and caregiver enter an unfamiliar laboratory setting; a stranger enters; the caregiver leaves briefly; and the caregiver and infant have opportunities for reunion while researchers observe child, caregiver, and their interactions.

stratified sampling   A method for choosing the sample for a research study in which subjects are selected from a variety of levels or types of people in the population.

subjective age identity   The age one feels oneself to be, based on perceived similarity to people of this age.

substantive complexity   The degree to which one's work requires thought, independent judgment, and frequent decision making.

superego   In psychoanalytic theory, the mental function that embodies moral precepts and moral sanctions. The superego includes the ego ideal, or the goals toward which one strives, as well as the punishing conscience.

surrogate mother   Woman who conceives and bears a child for an infertile couple.

survey   A research method in which carefully worded questions are asked of a large number of respondents, either orally or in writing.

swaddling   The practice of wrapping a baby snugly in a soft blanket which is a common technique for soothing a newborn in many cultures.

symbol   An object, image, or word that represents something. A symbol can be a word that represents an object, as chair, or an object that represents a concept, as a dove.

symbolic drawing   Drawing that represents a specific thought.

symbolic play   Imaginative or pretend activities that express emotions, problems, or roles.

synchronize   To coincide or agree in time.

synchrony   Infant and caregiver move from one state to the next in a fluid manner. Interactions of the infant and caregiver are rhythmic, well-timed, and mutually rewarding.

syntax   The rules for ordering words in a specific language.

system   A combination of things or parts, forming a complex or unitary whole and functioning as a unit.

systematic   In a careful, orderly way. Scientists have a framework of questions that they strive to answer based on what is already known and what theories predict. They approach research by having clear objectives, carefully defining the purpose of their work, and describing the specific methods they will use.

systems theories   Take the position that the whole is more than the sum of its parts. Any system, whether it is a cell, an organ, an individual, a family, or a corporation, is composed of interdependent elements that share some common goals, interrelated functions, boundaries, and an identity. The system cannot be wholly understood by identifying each of the component parts. The processes and relationships of those parts make for a larger coherent entity.

taboo   Proscribed by society as improper or unacceptable.

tactile stimulation   Any stimuli that evoke a response from the sensory receptors in the skin. Touching, tickling, pinching, and rubbing are examples.

talent   Areas of skill or competence.

teachable moments   The times when a person is maturationally most ready to learn a new skill.

technology   A technical method of achieving a practical purpose.

telegraphic speech   Two-word sentences, used by children, that omit many parts of speech but convey meaning.

temperament   Innate characteristics that determine the person's sensitivity to various sense experiences and his or her responsiveness to patterns of social interaction.

teratogens   Agents that produce malformations during the formation of organs and tissues.

test   Groups of questions or problems that usually indicate and measure abilities, potentials, or psychological characteristics.

testis-determining factor   The gene or genes on the Y-chromosome that is responsible for setting into motion the differentiation of the testes during embryonic development.

testosterone   A hormone that fosters the development of male sex characteristics and growth.

theory   A logically interrelated system of concepts and statements that provides a framework for organizing, interpreting, and understanding observations, with the goal of explaining and predicting behavior.

toddlerhood   The period of psychosocial development that begins around the age of two and ends around the time the child enters kindergarten.

treatment group   In some experiments, one group of participants has a certain set of experiences or receives information, usually referred to as a treatment, that is not provided to another group.

trimester   A period of three months during the nine months of pregnancy.

trust   An emotional sense that both the environment and oneself are reliable and capable of satisfying basic needs.

ultrasound   A technique for producing visual images of the fetus in utero through a pattern of deflected sound waves.

unconditioned response   A response that is evoked by a stimulus prior to opportunities for learning; sometimes described as a reflexive response.

unconditioned stimulus   A stimulus that evokes a response prior to opportunities for learning.

unconscious   In Freud's psychosexual theory, a reservoir of wishes, needs, and fantasies that influence behavior but of which we are not normally aware.

uterus   In the female reproductive system, the hollow muscular organ in which the fertilized ovum normally becomes embedded and in which the developing embryo and fetus is nourished and grows.

validity   The extent to which a test measures what it is supposed to measure.

value   A principle or quality that is intrinsically desirable.

variability   Within evolutionary theory, genetically based variations within a species that contribute to species survival under conditions of dramatic environmental changes.

variables   Dimensions that can have a number of different values.

verbal persuasion   Encouragement from others.

vicarious   An experience achieved through the imagined participation in events that happen to another person.

vicarious reinforcement   Through observing others, a person can learn a behavior and also acquire the motivation to perform the behavior or resist performing that behavior depending on what is observed about the consequences of that behavior.

visual acuity   The ability to detect visual stimuli under various levels of illumination.

visual adaptation   The ability to adapt to changes in the level of illumination.

visual tracking   Following an object's movement with one's eyes.

vocabulary   A list of the words a person uses and understands.

vocalizations   Any sounds or utterances a person makes.

volunteerism   Involved in some form of volunteer service.

volunteer sampling   In which subjects for a study are selected from volunteers.

will   The determination to exercise free choice and self-control.

willfulness   Wanting to have your own way.

wisdom   The detached yet active concern with life itself in the face of death.

withdrawal   General orientation of wariness toward people and objects.

withdrawn children   A path to peer rejection in which children are shy and self-conscious.

worldview   A way of making meaning of the relationships, situations, and objects encountered in daily life in a culture.

work clock   Timetable of expectations for the progression of work life.

young-old   Among the very old, those who remain healthy, vigorous, and competent.

zone of proximal development   The emergent developmental capacity that is just ahead of the level at which the person is currently functioning.

zygote   The developing individual formed from two gametes.

References

Abel, E. L. (1984). *Fetal alcohol syndrome and fetal alcohol effects*. New York: Plenum.

Abell, S. C., & Richards, M. H. (1996). The relationship between body shape and satisfaction and self-esteem: An investigation of gender and class differences. *Journal of Youth and Adolescence, 25,* 691–703.

Acitelli, L. K., Douvan, E., & Veroff, J. (1997). The changing influence of interpersonal perceptions on marital well-being among black and white couples. *Journal of Social and Personal Relationships, 14,* 291–304.

Ackerman, G. L. (1993). A congressional view of youth suicide. *American Psychologist, 48,* 183–184.

Acredolo, C., Adams, A., & Schmid, J. (1984). On the understanding of the relationships between speed, duration, and distance. *Child Development, 55,* 2151–2159.

Adams, B. N. (1986). *The family: A sociological interpretation* (4th ed.). San Diego: Harcourt Brace Jovanovich.

Adams, G. R., & Jones, R. M. (1982). Adolescent egocentrism: Exploration into possible contributions of parent-child relations. *Journal of Youth and Adolescence, 11,* 25–31.

Adams, R. G. (1985). People would talk: Normative barriers to cross-sex friendships for elderly women. *Gerontologist, 25,* 605–611.

Adegoke, A. A. (1993). The experience of spermarche (the age of onset of sperm emission) among selected boys in Nigeria. *Journal of Youth and Adolescence, 22,* 201–209.

Adelson, J., & Doehrman, M. J. (1980). The psychodynamic approach to adolescence. In J. Adelson (Ed.), *Handbook of adolescent psychology* (pp. 99–116). New York: Wiley.

Ades, P. A., Ballor, D. L., Ashikaga, T., Utton, J. L., & Nair, K. S. (1996). Weight training improves walking endurance in healthy elderly persons. *Annals of Internal Medicine, 124,* 568–572.

Adey, P., & Shayer, M. (1993). An exploration of long-term far-transfer effects following an extended intervention program in the high school science curriculum. *Cognition & Instruction, 11,* 1–29.

Adler, A. (1935). The fundamental views of individual psychology. *International Journal of Individual Psychology. 1,* 5–8.

Adler, N. E., David, H. P., Major, B. N., Roth, S. H., Russo, N. F., & Wyatt, G. (1990). Psychological responses after abortion. *Science, 248,* 41–44.

Ainsworth, M. D. S. (1973). The development of infant-mother attachment. In B. M. Caldwell & H. N. Ricciuti (Eds.), *Review of child development research* (Vol. 3). Chicago: University of Chicago Press.

Ainsworth, M. D. S. (1979). Infant-mother attachment. *American Psychologist, 34,* 932–937.

Ainsworth, M. D. S. (1985). Patterns of infant-mother attachments: Antecedents and effects on development. *Bulletin of the New York Academy of Medicine, 61,* 771–791.

Ainsworth, M. D. S. (1989). Attachments beyond infancy. *American Psychologist, 44,* 709–716.

Ainsworth, M. D. S., Bell, S. M. V., & Stayton, D. J. (1971). Individual differences in strange-situational behavior of one-year-olds. In H. A. Schaffer (Ed.), *The origins of human social relations*. London: Academic Press.

Ainsworth, M. D. S., Blehar, M. C., Waters, E., & Wall, S. (1978). *Patterns of attachment: A psychological study of the strange situation*. Hillsdale, NJ: Erlbaum.

Albert, S., Amgott, T., Krakow, M., & Marcus, H. (1977). *Children's bedtime rituals as a prototype rite of safe passage*. Paper presented at the annual convention of the American Psychological Association, San Francisco, CA.

Albom, M. (1997). *Tuesdays with Morrie: An old man, a young man, and life's greatest lesson*. New York: Doubleday.

Alessandri, S. M. (1992). Mother-child interactional correlates of maltreated and nonmaltreated children's play behavior. *Development and Psychopathology, 4,* 257–270.

Alexander, B. H., Checkoway, H., van Netten, C., Muller, C. H., Ewers, T. G., Kaufman, J. D., Mueller, B. A., Vaughn, T. L., & Faustman, E. M. (1996). Semen quality of men employed at a lead smelter. *Occupational & Environmental Medicine, 53,* 411–416.

Alexander, K. L., & Entwisle, D. R. (1988). Achievement in the first two years of school: Patterns of processes. *Monographs of the Society for Research in Child Development, 53*(2, Serial No. 218).

Alexander, K. L., Entwisle, D. R., & Thompson, M. S. (1987). School performance, status relations, and the structure of sentiment: Bringing the teacher back in. *American Sociological Review, 52,* 655–682.

Alexander, C. S., Somerfield, M. R., Ensminger, M. E., Johnson, K. E., & Kim, Y. J. (1993). Consistency of adolescents' self-report of sexual behavior in a longitudinal study. *Journal of Youth and Adolescence, 22,* 455–473.

Allen, J. P., Weissberg, R. P., & Hawkins, J. A. (1989). The relation between values and social competence in early adolescence. *Developmental Psychology, 25,* 458–464.

Allison, M. (1992, October/November). The effects of neurologic injury on the maturing brain. *Headlines, 2–6, 9–10.*

Allport, G. (1961). *Pattern and growth in personality*. New York: Holt, Rinehart & Winston.

Alter, R. C. (1984). Abortion outcome as a function of sex-role identification. *Psychology of Women Quarterly, 8,* 211–233.

Alwin, D. (1984). Living alone. *ISR Newsletter, 12,* 3–4.

Alwin, D. F., Converse, P. E., & Martin, S. S. (1985). Living arrangements and social integration. *Journal of Marriage and the Family, 47,* 319–334.

Amato, P. R. (1988). Parental divorce and attitudes toward marriage and family. *Journal of Marriage and the Family, 50*, 453–462.

American Council on Education. (1988). *One-third of a nation*. Washington, DC: Author.

Aquilino, W. S. (1990). Likelihood of parent-adult child coresidence. *Journal of Marriage and the Family, 52*, 405–419.

Ambrose, J. A. (1963). The concept of a critical period in the development of social responsiveness. In B. M. Foss (Ed.), *Determinants of infant behavior* (Vol. 2). New York: Wiley.

American Academy of Pediatrics. (1995). The inappropriate use of school "readiness" tests. *Pediatrics, 95*, 437–438.

American Psychiatric Association. (1993). *DSM-IV Draft Criteria*. Washington, DC. APA.

American Psychiatric Association. (1994). *Diagnostic and statistical manual of mental disorders*. (4th ed.). Washington, DC: Author.

American Psychiatric Association. (1994). *Diagnostic and statistical manual of mental disorders*. (4th ed.). Washington, DC: APA.

American Psychiatric Association. (1994). *Diagnostic and statistical manual of mental disorders, DSM-IV* (4th ed.) Washington, DC: Author.

American Psychological Association. (1982). *Ethical principles in the conduct of research with human participants*. Washington, DC: Author.

American Psychological Association. (1992). Ethical principles of psychologists and code of conduct. *American Psychologist, 47*, 1597–1611.

American Psychological Association. (1996). *Reducing violence: A research agenda*. Washington, DC. Author.

Anderson, R. C., Wilson, P. T., & Fielding, L. G. (1988). Growth in reading and how children spend their time outside of school. *Reading Research Quarterly, 23*, 285–303.

Anderson, W. F. (1992). Human gene therapy. *Science, 256*, 808–813.

Andersson, B. (1989). Effects of public day care: A longitiudinal study. *Child Development, 60*, 857–866.

Andersson, B. (1992). Effects of day-care on cognitive and socioemotional competence of thirteen-year-old Swedish schoolchildren. *Child Development, 63*, 20–63.

Aneshensel, C. S., Pearlin, L. I., Mullan, J. T., Zarit, S. H., & Whitlatch, C. J. (1995). *Profiles in caregiving: The unexpected career*. San Diego, CA: Academic Press.

Anglin, J. M. (1993). Vocabulary development: A morphological analysis. *Monographs of the Society for Research in Child Development, 58*.

Anthony, S. (1972). *The discovery of death in childhood and after*. New York: Basic Books.

Aoki, C., & Siekevitz, P. (1988). Plasticity in brain development. *Scientific American, 259*, 56–64.

Apgar, V. (1953). Proposal for a new method of evaluating the newborn infant. *Anesthesia and Analgesia, 32*, 260–267.

Arbuckle, T. Y., Gold, D. P., Andres, D., Schwartzman, A., & Chaikelson, J. (1992). The role of psychosocial context, age, and intelligence in memory performance of older men. *Psychology and Aging, 7*, 25–36.

Archer, J. (1991). Human sociobiology: Basic concepts and limitations. *Journal of Social Issues, 47*, 11–26.

Archer, S. L. (1992). A feminist's approach to identity research. In G. R. Adams, T. P. Gullotta, & R. Montemayor (Eds.), *Adolescent identity formation: Advances in adolescent development* (pp. 25–49). Newbury Park, CA: Sage.

Arieti, S. (1976). *Creativity: The magic synthesis*. New York: Basic Books.

Armstrong, B. G., McDonald, A. D., & Sloan, M. (1992). Cigarette, alcohol, and coffee consumption and spontaneous abortion. *American Journal of Public Health, 82*, 85–87.

Associated Press. (1993, August 15). Baby on the way through new technique. *Columbus Dispatch* p. 5A.

Aronfreed, J. (1969). The concept of internalization. In D. A. Goslin (Ed.), *Handbook of socialization theory and research*. Chicago: Rand McNally.

Arsenio, W. F., & Kramer, R. (1992). Victimizers and their victims: Children's conceptions of the mixed emotional consequences of moral transgressions. *Child Development, 63*, 915–927.

Asher, S. R., Hymel, S., & Renshaw, P. D. (1984). Loneliness in children. *Child Development, 55*, 1456–1464.

Aslin, R. N. (1987). Visual and auditory development in infancy. In J. D. Osofsky (Ed.), *Handbook of infant development* (2nd ed., pp. 5–97). New York: John Wiley & Sons.

Astone, N. M. (1993). Are adolescent mothers just single mothers? *Journal of Research on Adolescence, 3*, 353–372.

Atchley, R. C. (1975). The life course, age grading, and age-linked demands for decision making. In N. Datan & L. H. Ginsberg (Eds.), *Life-span developmental psychology: Normative life crises*. New York: Academic Press.

Atchley, R. C. (1976). *The sociology of retirement*. New York: Halsted.

Atchley, R. C. (1977). *The social forces of later life*. Belmont, CA: Wadsworth.

Atkinson, J. W., & Birch, D. (1978). *Introduction to motivation* (2nd ed.). New York: Van Nostrand.

Atkinson, D. R., Morten, G., & Sue, D. W. (1983). *Counseling American minorities: A cross-cultural perspective.* (2nd ed.). Dubuque, IA: William C. Brown.

Au, T. K., Sidle, A. L., & Rollins, K. B. (1993). Developing an intuitive understanding of conservation: Invisible particles as a plausible mechanism. *Developmental Psychology, 29*, 286–299.

Avery, C. S. (1989). How do you build intimacy in an age of divorce? *Psychology Today, 23*(5), 21–31.

Azar, B. (1997). It may cause anxiety, but day care can benefit kids. *APA Monitor, 28*, 13.

Bachman, J. G., Bare, D. E., & Frankie, E. I. (1986). *Correlates of employment among high school seniors* (Monitoring the Future Occasional Paper 20). Ann Arbor, MI: Institute for Social Research.

Bachman, J. G., Johnston, L. D., & O'Malley, P. M. (1987). *Monitoring the future: Questionnaire responses from the nation's high school seniors, 1986*. Ann Arbor, MI: Survey Research Center, Institute for Social Research.

Bailey, J. M., Bobrow, D., Wolfe, M., & Mikach, S. (1995). Sexual orientation of adult sons of gay fathers. *Developmental Psychology, 31*, 124–129.

Bailey, J. M., & Pillard, R. (1991). A genetic study of male sexual orientation. *Archives of General Psychiatry, 48*, 1089–1096.

Bailey, J. M., & Pillard, R. (1994). The innateness of homosexuality. *The Harvard Mental Health Letter, 10*, 4–6.

Baillargeon, R. (1987). Object permanence in $3^1/_2$ and $4^1/_2$-month-old infants. *Developmental Psychology, 23*, 655–664.

Baillargeon, R., & DeVos, J. (1991). Object permanence in young infants: Further evidence. *Child Development, 62*, 1227–1246.

Baillargeon, R., & Graber, M. (1988). Evidence of location memory in 8-month-old infants in a nonsearch AB task. *Developmental Psychology, 24,* 502–511.

Baker, E. L. (1989). Surveillance in occupational health and safety. *American Journal of Public Health, 79,* 9–11.

Baker, H. A., Jr. (1991). From An apple for my teacher: Twelve writers tell about teachers who made all the difference. In H. L. Gates, Jr. (Ed.), Bearing witness: selections from African-American Autobiography in the twentieth century. New York: Pantheon Books, pp. 317–319.

Baltes, P. B., Baltes, M. M. (1990). *Successful aging: perspectives from the behavioral sciences.* Cambridge, MA: Cambridge University Press.

Baltes, P. B., & Staudinger, U. M. (1993). The search for a psychology of wisdom. *Current Directions in Psychological Science, 2,* 75–80.

Baltes, P. B., & Lindenberger, U. (1997). Emergence of a powerful connection between sensory and cognitive functions across the adult life span. A new window to the study of cognitive aging? *Psychology and Aging, 12,* 12–21.

Baltes, P. B., & Smith, J. (1990). The psychology of wisdom and its ontogenesis. In R. J. Sternberg (Ed.), *Wisdom: Its nature, origins and development* (pp. 87–120). New York: Cambridge University Press.

Baltes, P. B., Smith, J., & Staudinger, U. M. (1992). Wisdom and successful aging. In T. B. Sonderegger (Ed.). *Psychology and aging.* (pp. 123–168). Lincoln NE: University of Nebraska Press.

Bandura, A. (Ed.). (1971). *Psychological modeling.* Chicago: Aldine-Atherton.

Bandura, A. (1973). *Aggression: A social learning analysis.* Englewood Cliffs, NJ: Prentice-Hall.

Bandura, A. (1977). *Social learning theory.* Englewood Cliffs, NJ: Prentice-Hall.

Bandura, A. (1982). Self-efficacy mechanism in human agency. *American Psychologist, 37,* 122–147.

Bandura, A. (1986). *Social foundations of thought and action.* Englewood Cliffs, NJ: Prentice-Hall.

Bandura, A. (1986). *Social foundations of thought and action: A social cognitive theory.* Englewood Cliffs, NJ: Prentice-Hall.

Bandura, A. (1989). Regulation of cognitive processes through perceived self-efficacy. *Developmental Psychology, 25,* 729–735.

Bandura, A. (1989). Social cognitive theory. *Annals of Child Development, 6,* 1–60.

Bandura, A. (1991). Social cognitive theory of moral thought and action. In W. M. Kurtines & J. L. Gewirtz (Eds.), *Handbook of moral behavior and development: Vol. 1. Theory* (pp. 45–103). Hillsdale, NJ: Erlbaum.

Bandura, A. (1991). Social cognitive theory of moral thought and action. In W. M. Kurtines & J. L. Gewirtz (Eds.), *Handbook of moral behavior and development: Theory, research and applications* (Vol. 1, pp. 71–129). Hillsdale, NJ: Erlbaum.

Bandura, A., Barbaranelli, C., Caprara, G. V., & Pastorelli, C. (1996). Multifaceted impact of self-efficacy beliefs on academic functioning. *Child Development, 67,* 1206–1222.

Bandura, A., & Schunck, D. H. (1981). Cultivating competence, self-efficacy, and intrinsic interest through proximal self-motivation. *Journal of Personality and Social Psychology, 41,* 586–598.

Bandura, A., & Walters, R. H. (1963). *Social learning and personality development.* New York: Holt, Rinehart & Winston.

Bank, L., Forgatch, M. S., Patterson, G. R., & Fetrow, R. A. (1993). Parenting practices of single mothers: Mediators of negative contextual factors. *Journal of Marriage and the Family, 55,* 371–384.

Bankart, B. (1989). Japanese perceptions of motherhood. *Psychology of Women Quarterly, 13,* 59–76.

Banks, M. S., & Dannemiller, J. L. (1987). Infant visual psychophysics. In P. Salapatek & L. Cohen (Eds.), *Handbook of infant perception* (Vol. 1). Orlando, FL: Academic Press.

Barinaga, M. (1991). How long is the human life-span? *Science, 254,* 936–938.

Barinaga, M. (1994). Surprise across the cultural divide. *Science, 263,* 1468–1472.

Barnes, G. M. (1981). Drinking among adolescents: A subcultural phenomenon or a model of adult behaviors? *Adolescence, 16,* 211–229.

Barnett, R. C., Marshall, N. L., & Pleck, J. H. (1992). Men's multiple roles and their relationship to men's psychological distress. *Journal of Marriage and the Family, 54,* 358–367.

Barrett, C. J. (1981). Intimacy in widowhood. *Psychology of Women Quarterly, 5,* 473–487.

Bartholomew, K. (1990). Avoidance of intimacy: An attachment perspective. *Journal of Social and Personal Relationships, 7,* 147–178.

Bartz, K. W., & Levine, E. S. (1978, November). Child rearing by black parents: A description and comparison to Anglo and Chicano parents. *Journal of Marriage and the Family, 40,* 709–719.

Bashore, T. R., Osman, A., & Heffley, E. F., III. (1989). Mental slowing in elderly persons: A cognitive psychophysiological analysis. *Psychology and Aging, 4,* 235–244.

Bashore, T. R., van der Molen, M. W., Ridderinkhof, K. R., & Wylie, S. A. (1997). Is the age-complexity effect mediated by reductions in a general processing resource? *Biological Psychology, 45,* 263–282.

Bass, D. M., & Bowman, K. (1990). The transition from caregiving to bereavement: The relationship of care-related strain and adjustment to death. *Gerontologist, 30,* 35–42.

Bassuk, E. L. (1991). Homeless families. *Scientific American, 265,* 66–74.

Bates, E., O'Connell, B., & Shore, C. (1987). Language and communication in infancy. In J. Osofsky (Ed.), *Handbook of infant development* (2nd ed., pp. 149–203). New York: Wiley.

Bates, G. W. (1981). On the nature of the hot flash. *Clinical Obstetrics and Gynecology, 24,* 231.

Bates, J. E. (1987). Temperament in infancy. In J. D. Osofsky (Ed.), *Handbook of infant development* (2nd ed., pp. 1101–1149). New York: John Wiley & Sons.

Batson, C. D., Polycarpou, M. P., Harmon-Jones, E., Imhoff, H. J., Mitchener, E. C., Bednar, L. L., Klein, T. R., & Highberger, L. (1997). Empathy and attitudes: Can feeling for a member of a stigmatized group improve feelings toward the group? *Journal of Personality and Social Psychology, 72,* 105–118.

Baucom, D. H., Besch, P. K., & Callahan, S. (1985). Relation between testosterone concentrations, sex-role identity, and personality among females. *Journal of Personality and Social Psychology, 48,* 1218–1226.

Bauer, P. J. (1993). Memory for gender-consistent and gender-inconsistent event sequences by twenty-five-month-old children. *Child Development, 64,* 285–297.

Baulieu, E. (1989). Contragestion and other clinical applications of RU486, an antiprogesterone at the receptor. *Science, 245,* 1351–1357.

Baumgardner, A. H. (1990). To know oneself is to like oneself: Self-certainty and self-affect. *Journal of Personality and Social Psychology, 58,* 1062–1072.

Baumrind, D. (1995). Commentary on sexual orientation: Research and social policy implications. *Developmental Psychology, 31,* 130–136.

Bayley, N. (1970). Development of mental abilities. In P. H. Mussen (Ed.), *Carmichael's manual of child psychology.* (3rd ed., Vol. 1). New York: Wiley.

Beale, R. L. (1997). Multiple familial-worker role strain and psychological well-being: Moderating effects of coping resources among Black American parents. In R. J. Taylor, J. S. Jackson, & L. M. Chatters (Eds.), *Family life in Black America* (pp. 132–145). Thousand Oaks, CA: Sage.

Beall, A. E., & Sternberg, R. J. (1995). The social construction of love. *Journal of Social and Personal Relationships, 12,* 417–438.

Beardsley, T. (1996). Vital data. *Scientific American, 274,* 100–105.

Bearon, L. G. (1989). No great expectations: The underpinnings of life satisfaction for older women. *Gerontologist, 29,* 772–778.

Beaulieu, L. (1992, June 28). Teaching more than just sports. *Columbus Dispatch,* p. 6D.

Beauvoir, S. de. (1959). *Memoirs of a dutiful daughter.* New York: World.

Beck, S. H. (1984). Retirement preparation programs: Differentials in opportunity and use. *Journal of Gerontology, 39,* 596–602.

Beere, C. A. (1990). *Gender roles: A handbook of tests and measures.* New York: Greenwood.

Begley, S. (1995, September 2). The baby myth. *Newsweek,* pp. 38–41.

Beit-Hallahmi, B. (1987). Critical periods in psychoanalytic theories of personality development. In M. H. Bornstein (Ed.), *Sensitive periods in development: Interdisciplinary perspectives* (pp. 211–221). Hillsdale, NJ: Erlbaum.

Bell, S. M., & Ainsworth, M. D. S. (1972). Infant crying and maternal responsiveness. *Child Development, 43,* 1171–1190.

Belsky, J. (1996). Parent, infant, and social-contextual antecedents of father-son attachment security. *Development Psychology, 32,* 905–913.

Belsky, J., Campbell, S. B., Cohn, J. F., & Moore, G. (1996). Instability of infant-parent attachment security. *Developmental Psychology, 32,* 921–924.

Belsky, J., Fish, M., & Isabella, R. 1991. Continuity and discontinuity in infant negative and positive emotionality: Family antecedents and attachment consequences. *Developmental Psychology, 27,* 421–431.

Belsky, J., Gilstrap, B., & Rovine, M. (1984). The Pennsylvania infant and family development project: Vol. 1. Stability and change in mother-infant and father-infant interaction in a family setting at one, three, and nine months. *Child Development, 55,* 692–705.

Belsky, J., & Isabella, R. A. (1985). Marital and parent-child relationships in family of origin and marital change following the birth of a baby: A retrospective analysis. *Child Development, 56,* 342–349.

Belseky, J., Lang, M., & Huston, T. L. (1986). Sex typing and division of labor as determinants of marital change across the transition to parenthood. *Journal of Personality and Social Psychology. 50,* 517–522.

Belsky, J., & Pensky, E. (1988). Marital change across the transition to parenthood. *Marriage and the Family Review, 12,* 133–156.

Belsky, J., & Rovine, M. (1990). Patterns of marital change across the transition to parenthood. *Journal of Marriage and the Family, 52,* 5–20.

Bem, S. L. (1981). Gender schema theory: A cognitive account of sex-typing. *Psychological Review, 88,* 354–364.

Bem, S. L. (1989). Genital knowledge and gender constancy in preschool children. *Child Development, 60,* 649–662.

Benedict, R. (1934/1950). *Patterns of culture,* New York: New American Library.

Benenson, J. F. (1993). Greater preference among females than males for dyadic interaction in early childhood. *Child Development, 64,* 544–555.

Bengston, V. L., Cuellar, J. B., & Ragan, P. K. (1977). Stratum contrasts and similarities in attitudes toward death. *Journal of Gerontology, 32,* 76–88.

Benson, J. B., & Uzgiris, I. C. (1985). Effect of self-initiated locomotion on infant search activity. *Developmental Psychology, 21,* 923–931.

Benson, M. J., Harris, P. B., & Rogers, C. S. (1992). Identity consequences of attachment to mothers and fathers among late adolescents. *Journal of Research on Adolescence, 2,* 187–204.

Benson, P. L. (1992). *The troubled journey: A profile of American youth.* Minneapolis: RespecTeen/Lutheran Brotherhood.

Berg, J. H., & Peplau, L. A. (1982). Loneliness: The relationship of self-disclosure and androgyny. *Personality and Social Psychology Bulletin, 8,* 624–630.

Bergeman, C. S., Plomin, R., Pedersen, N. L., McClearn, G. E., & Nesselroade, J. R. (1990). Genetic and environmental influences on social support: The Swedish adoption/twin study of aging. *Journal of Gerontology: Psychological Sciences, 45,* 101–106.

Berk, L. E. (1993). *Infancy, childhood, and adolescence.* Boston: Allyn & Bacon.

Berkowitz, L. (1973). Control of aggression. In B. M. Caldwell & H. N. Ricciuti (Eds.), *Review of child development research* (Vol. 3). Chicago: University of Chicago Press.

Berkowitz, L. (1984). Some effects of thoughts on anti- and prosocial influences of media events: A cognitive-neoassociation analysis. *Psychological Bulletin, 95,* 419–427.

Berkowitz, L. (1986). Situational influences on reactions to observed violence. *Journal of Social Issues, 42,* 93–103.

Berlin, I. N. (1987). Suicide among American Indian adolescents: An overview. *Suicide and Life-Threatening Behavior, 17,* 218–232.

Berman, W. H., & Sperling, M. B. (1991). Parental attachment and emotional distress in the transition to college. *Journal of Youth and Adolescence, 20,* 427–440.

Berman, W. H., & Turk, D. C. (1981). Adaptation to divorce: Problems and coping strategies. *Journal of Marriage and the Family, 43,* 179–189.

Bernard, J. (1972). *The future of marriage.* New York: World.

Berndt, T. J. (1979). Development changes in conformity to peers and *parents. Developmental Psychology, 15,* 608–616.

Berndt, T. J. (1981). Relations between social cognition, nonsocial cognition, and social behavior: The case of friendship. In J. H. Flavell & L. D. Ross (Eds.), *Social cognitive development: Frontiers and possible futures.* Cambridge: Cambridge University Press.

Berrueta-Clement, J. R., Schweinhart, L. J., Barnett, W. S., Epstein, A. S., & Weikart, D. P. (1984). *Changed lives: The effects of the Perry Preschool Program on youths through age 19.* Ypsilanti, MI: High/Scope Press.

Bertalanffy, L. von (1950). The theory of open systems in physics and biology. *Science, 111,* 23–28.

Bertalanffy, L. von (1968). *General systems theory* (Rev. ed.). New York: Braziller.

Bertenthal, B. I., & Fischer, K. W. (1983). The development of representation in search: A social-cognitive analysis. *Child Development, 54,* 846–857.

Berzonsky, M. D. (1989). Identity style: Conceptualization and measurement. *Journal of Adolescent Research, 4,* 267–281.

Berzonsky, M. D. (1993). Identity style, gender, and social-cognitive reasoning. *Journal of Adolescent Research, 8,* 289–296.

Berzonsky, M. D., & Sullivan, C. (1992). Social-cognitive aspects of identity style: Need for cognition, experiential openness, and introspection. *Journal of Adolescent Research, 7,* 140–155.

Best, K. M., Hauser, S. T., & Allen, J. P. (1997). Predicting young adult competencies: Adolescent era parent and individual influences. *Journal of Adolescent Research, 12,* 90–112.

Betancourt, H., & Lopez, S. R. (1993). The study of culture, ethnicity, and race in American psychology. *American Psychologist, 48,* 629–637.

Betz, N. E., & Hackett, G. (1981). The relationship of career-related self-efficacy expectations to perceived career options in college women and men. *Journal of Counseling Psychology, 28,* 399–410.

Biddle, B. J. (1979). *Role theory: Expectations, identities, and behaviors.* New York: Academic Press.

Biddle, B. J. (1986). Recent developments in role theory. In R. H. Turner & S. F. Short, Jr. (Eds.), *Annual Review of Sociology, 12,* 67–92.

Biddle, B. J., & Thomas, E. J. (1966). *Role theory: Concepts and research.* New York: Wiley.

Bigler, R. S., & Liben, L. S. (1992). Cognitive mechanisms in children's gender stereotyping: Theoretical and educational implications of a cognitive based intervention. *Child Development, 63,* 1351–1363.

Bijstra, J., Van Geert, P., & Jackson, S. (1989). Conservation and the appearance-reality distinction: What do children really know and what do they answer? *British Journal of Developmental Psychology, 7,* 43–53.

Bilsker, D., Schiedel, D., & Marcia, J. (1988). Sex differences in identity status. *Sex Roles, 18,* 231–236.

Biringen, Z., Emde, R. N., Campos, J. J., & Appelbaum, M. I. (1995). Affective reorganization in the infant, the mother, and the dyad: The role of upright locomotion and its timing. *Child Development, 66,* 499–514.

Birren, J. E., & Fisher, L. M. (1992). Aging and slowing of behavior: Consequences for cognition and survival. In T. B. Sonderegger (Ed.), *Psychology and aging.* Lincoln: University of Nebraska Press.

Blackburn, J. A. (1984). The influence of personality, curriculum, and memory correlates on formal reasoning in young adults and elderly persons. *Journal of Gerontology, 39,* 207–209.

Blain, M. D., Thompson, J. M., & Whiffen, V. E. (1993). Attachment and perceived social support in late adolescence: The interaction between working models of self and others. *Journal of Adolescent Research, 8,* 226–241.

Blanchard, K. H. (1996). *Empowerment takes more than a minute.* San Francisco: Berrett-Koehler Pub.

Blasi, A. (1991). The self as subject in the study of personality. In D. Ozer, J. Healy, & A. Stewart (Eds.), *Perspectives in personality* (Vol. 3, Part A, pp. 19–37). London: Kingsley.

Blass, E. M., & Ciaramitaro, V. (1994). A new look at some old mechanisms in human newborns: Taste and tactile determinants of state, affect, and action. *Monographs of the Society for Research in Child Development, 59,* (Serial No. 1).

Blass, E. M., & Hoffmeyer, L. B. (1991). Sucrose as an analgesic for newborn infants. *Pediatrics, 87,* 215–218.

Bloom, L. (1993, Winter). World learning. *Society for Research in Child Development Newsletter,* pp. 1, 9, 13.

Bloom, M. V. (1987). Leaving home: A family transition. In J. Bloom-Feshbach & S. Bloom-Feshbach (Eds.), *The psychology of separation and loss.* San Francisco: Jossey-Bass.

Blos, P. (1979). *The adolescent passage.* New York: International Universities Press.

Blyth, D. A., Bulcroft, R., & Simmons, R. G. (1981). *The impact of puberty on adolescents: A longitudinal study.* Paper presented at the annual convention of the American Psychological Association, Los Angeles, CA.

Bohan, J. S. (1993). Regarding gender. *Psychology of Women Quarterly, 17,* 5–21.

Bolton, F. G., Jr., & MacEachron, A. E. (1988). Adolescent male sexuality: A developmental perspective. *Journal of Adolescent Research, 3,* 259–273.

Bomar, J. A., & Sabatelli, R. M. (1996). Family system dynamics, gender, and psychosocial maturity in late adolescence. *Journal of Adolescent Research, 11,* 421–439.

Bombar, M. L., & Littig, L. W. (1996). Babytalk as a communication of intimate attachment: An initial study in adult romances and friendships. *Personal Relationships, 3,* 137–158.

Booth, A., & Edwards, J. N. (1985). Age at marriage and marital instability. *Journal of Marriage and the Family, 47,* 67–75.

Borke, H. (1973). The development of empathy in Chinese and American children between 3 and 6 years of age: A cross-cultural study. *Developmental Psychology, 9,* 102–108.

Borman, K. M., & Hopkins, M. (1987). Leaving school for work. *Research in the Sociology of Education and Socialization, 7,* 131–159.

Bornstein, M. H. (1995). Parenting infants. In M. H. Bornstein (Ed.), *Handbook of parenting: Vol. 1. Children and parenting.* pp. 3–39), Mahwah, NJ: Lawrence Erlbaum.

Bornstein, M. H. (1985). How infant and mother jointly contribute to developing cognitive competence in the child. *Proceedings of the National Academy of Science, USA, 82,* 7470–7473.

Bornstein, M. H. (1992). Perception across the life cycle. In M. H. Bornstein & M. E. Lamb (Eds.), *Developmental psychology: An advanced textbook* (3rd ed., pp. 155–209), Hillsdale, NJ: Erlbaum.

Bornstein, M. H. (1995). Parenting infants. In M. H. Bornstein (Ed.), *Handbook of parenting. Volume I: Children and parenting* (pp. 3–41). Mahwah, NJ: Erlbaum.

Bornstein, M. H., Kessen, W., & Weiskopf, S. (1976). The categories of hue in infancy. *Science, 191,* 201–202.

Bosworth, H. B., & Schaie, K. W. (1997). The relationship of social environment, social networks, and health outcomes in the Seattle longitudinal study: Two analytical approaches. *Journals of Gerontology, Series B, Psychological Sciences & Social Sciences, 52B,* P197–P205.

Bound, J., Duncan, G. J., Laren, D. S., & Oleinick, L. (1991). Poverty dynamics in widowhood. *Journal of Gerontology, 46,* S115–S124.

Bowen, G. L., Desimone, L. M., & McKay, J. K. (1995). Poverty and the single mother family: A macroeconomic perspective. *Marriage and Family Review, 20,* 115–142.

Bowen, M. (1978). *Family therapy and clinical practice.* New York: Aronson.

Bower, T. G. R. (1987). *Development in infancy* (2nd ed.). New York: W. H. Freeman.

Bower, T. G. R. (1989). *The rational infant: Learning in infancy.* New York: W. H. Freeman.

Bowlby, J. (1960). Separation anxiety. *International Journal of Psychoanalysis, 41,* 69–113.

Bowlby, J. (1980). *Attachment and loss (vol. 3). Loss, sadness, and depression.* New York: Basic Books.

Bowlby, J. (1988). *A secure base: Parent-child attachment and healthy human development.* New York: Basic Books.

Boyatzis, C. J., & Watson, M. W. (1993). Preschool children's symbolic representation of objects through gestures. *Child Development, 64,* 729–735.

Bradford, J., Ryan, C., & Rothblum, E. D. (1994). National lesbian health survey: Implications for mental health care. *Journal of Consulting and Clinical Psychology, 62,* 228–242.

Bradley, R. H., Caldwell, B. M., & Rock, S. L. (1988). Home environment and school performance. A ten-year follow-up and examination of three models of environmental action. *Child Development, 59,* 852–867.

Bradley, R. H., Whiteside, L., Mundfrom, D. J., Casey, P. H., Kelleher, K. J., & Pope, S. K. (1994). Early indications of resilience and their relation to experiences in the home environments of low birthweight, premature children living in poverty. *Child Development, 65,* 346–360.

Braine, M. D. S. (1976). *Children's first word combinations. Monographs of the Society for Research in Child Development, 41*(1).

Brainerd, C. J. (1977). Cognitive development and concept learning: An interpretive review. *Psychological Bulletin, 84,* 919–939.

Braungart, J. M., Plomin, R., Defries, J. C., & Fulker, D. W. (1992). Genetic influence on tester-rated infant temperament as assessed by Bayley's Infant Behavior Record: Nonadoptive and adoptive siblings and twins. *Developmental Psychology, 28,* (1), 40–47.

Brazelton, T. B. (1977). Implications of infant development among the Mayan Indians of Mexico. In P. H. Leiderman, S. T. Tulkin, & A. Rosenfeld (Eds.), *Culture and infancy: Variations in the human experience* (pp. 151–187). New York: Academic Press.

Brazelton, T. B. (1987). Behavioral competence of the newborn infant. In G. B. Avery (Ed.), *neonatology: Pathophysiology and management of the newborn* (pp. 379–399). Philadelphia: Lippincott.

Brazelton, T. B. (1987). *What every baby knows* (pp. 11–13). Reading, MA: Addison Wesley.

Brazelton, T. B., Koslowski, B., & Main, M. (1974). The origins of reciprocity: The early mother-infant interaction. In M. Lewis & L. A. Rosenblum (Eds.), *The effect of the infant on its caregiver* (pp. 49–76). New York: Wiley-Interscience.

Brazelton, T. B., Nugent, J. K., & Lester, B. M. (1987). Neonatal behavioral assessment scale. In J. D. Osofsky (Ed.), *Handbook of infant development* (2nd ed., pp. 780–817). New York: John Wiley & Sons.

Breakwell, G. M. (1986). *Coping with threatened identities.* London: Methuen.

Breault, K. D., & Kposowa, A. J. (1987). Explaining divorce in the United States, 1980. *Journal of Marriage and the Family, 49,* 549–558.

Brennan, K. A., & Morris, K. A. (1997). Attachment styles, self-esteem, and patterns of seeking feedback from romantic partners. *Personality and Social Psychology Bulletin, 23,* 23–31.

Brennan, K. A., & Shaver, P. R. (1995). Dimensions of adult attachment, affect regulation, and romantic relationship functioning. *Personality and Social Psychology Bulletin, 21,* 267–283.

Bretherton, I. (1985). Attachment theory: Retrospect and prospect. In I. Bretherton & E. Everett (Eds.), *Growing points of attachment theory and research* (pp. 3–35). *Monographs of the Society for Research in Child Development, 50* (1–2, Serial No. 209).

Bretherton, I. (1990). Open communication and internal working models: Their role in the development of attachment relationships. In R. Dienstbier & R. A. Thompson (Eds.), *Nebraska Symposium on Motivation 1988: Vol. 36. Socioemotional Development* (pp. 57–113). Lincoln, NE: University of Nebraska Press.

Bretschneider, J. G., & McCoy, N. L. (1988). Sexual interest and behavior in healthy 80- to 102-year-olds. *Archives of Sexual Behavior, 17,* 109–129.

Bridges, J. S. (1988). Sex differences in occupational performance expectations. *Psychology of Women Quarterly, 12,* 75–90.

Bridges, L. J., Connell, J. P., & Belsky, J. (1988). Similarities and differences in infant-mother and infant-father interaction in the strange situation: A component process analysis. *Developmental Psychology, 24,* 92–100.

Brierley, J. (1993). *Growth in children.* London: Cassell Educational Limited.

Brim, G. (1992). *Ambition: How we manage success and failure throughout our lives.* New York: Basic Books.

Brim, G. (1992). *Ambition.* New York: Basic Books.

Brim, O. G., Jr. (1966). Socialization through the life cycle. In O. G. Brim, Jr. & S. Wheeler (Eds.), *Socialization after childhood.* New York: Wiley.

Brim, O. G., Jr. (1966). Socialization through the life cycle. In O. G. Brim & S. Wheeler (Eds.), *Socialization after childhood: Two essays*. New York: Wiley.

Brim, O. G., Jr. (1968). Adult socialization. In J. Clausen (Ed.), *Socialization and society*. Boston: Little, Brown.

Brockner, J. (1984). Low self-esteem and behavioral plasticity. In L. Wheeler (Ed.), *Review of personality and social psychology* (Vol. 4, pp. 237–271). Beverly Hills, CA: Sage.

Broderick, C. B. (1993). *Understanding family process: Basics of family systems theory*. Newbury Park, CA: Sage.

Brody, E. M., Johnsen, P. T., & Fulcomer, M. C. (1984). What should adult children do for elderly parents? Opinions and preferences of three generations of women. *Journal of Gerontology, 39,* 736–746.

Bronfenbrenner, U. (1979). *The ecology of human development*. Cambridge, MA: Harvard University Press.

Bronson, G. (1979, February 9). Issue of fetal damage stirs women workers at chemical plants. *Wall Street Journal*.

Bronson, G. W. (1973). Infants' reactions to an unfamiliar person. In L. J. Stone, H. T. Smith, & L. B. Murphy (Eds.), *The competent infant*. New York: Basic Books.

Brooks-Gunn, J., & Furstenberg, F. F., Jr. (1989). Adolescent sexual behavior. *American Psychologist, 44,* 249–257.

Brooks-Gunn, J., Klebanov, P. K., Liaw, F., & Spiker, D. (1993). Enhancing the development of low-birth-weight, premature infants: Changes in cognition and behavior over the first three years. *Child Development, 64,* 736–753.

Brooks-Gunn, J., & Petersen, A. C. (1991). Studying the emergence of depression and depressive symptoms during adolescence. *Journal of Youth and Adolescence, 20,* 115–120.

Brooks-Gunn, J., & Reiter, E. O. (1990). The role of pubertal processes. In S. S. Feldman & G. R. Elliott (Eds.), *At the threshold: The developing adolescent* (pp. 16–53). Cambridge: Harvard University Press.

Brooks-Gunn, J., & Warren, M. P. (1988). The psychological significance of secondary sexual characteristics in 9- to 11-year-old girls. *Child Development, 59,* 161–169.

Brown, B. B. (1990). Peer groups and peer cultures. In S. S. Feldman & G. R. Elliott (Eds.), *At the threshold: The developing adolescent* (pp. 171–196). Cambridge: Harvard University Press.

Brown, B. B., Mounts, N., Lamborn, S. D., & Steinberg, L. (1993). Parenting practices and peer group affiliation in adolescence. *Child Development, 64,* 467–482.

Brown, I., Jr., & Inouye, D. K. (1978). Learned helplessness through modeling: The role of perceived similarity in competence. *Journal of Personality and Social Psychology, 36,* 900–908.

Brown, J. D., & Gallagher, F. M. (1992). Coming to terms with failure: Private self-enhancement and public self-effacement. *Journal of Experimental Social Psychology, 28,* 3–22.

Brown, J. D., & Mankowski, T. A. (1993). Self-esteem, mood, and self-evaluation: Changes in mood and the way you see you. *Journal of Personality and Social Psychology, 64,* 421–430.

Brown, J. D., & Smart, S. A. (1991). The self and social conduct: Linking self-representation to prosocial behavior. *Journal of Personality and Social Psychology, 60,* 368–375.

Brown, J. L., & Pollitt, E. (1996). Malnutrition, poverty, and intellectual development. *Scientific American, 274,* 38–43.

Brown, J. R., & Dunn, J. (1992). Talk with your mother or your sibling? Developmental changes in early family conversations about feelings. *Child Development, 63,* 336–349.

Brown, R. (1973). *A first language: The early stages*. Cambridge: Harvard University Press.

Brown, R. (1965). *Social psychology*. New York: Free Press.

Brubaker, T. H. (1990). Families in later life: A burgeoning research area. *Journal of Marriage and the Family, 52,* 959–981.

Brustad, R. J. (1988). Affective outcomes in competitive youth sport: The influence of intrapersonal and socialization factors. *Journal of Sport and Exercise Psychology, 10,* 307–321.

Bryant, J., Carveth, R. A., & Brown, D. (1981). Television viewing and anxiety: An experimental examination. *Journal of Communication, 31,* 106–119.

Bryer, K. B. (1979). The Amish way of death: A study of family support systems. *American Psychologist, 34,* 255–261.

Buescher, P. A., Roth, M. S., Williams, D., & Goforth, C. M. (1991). An evaluation of the impact of maternity care coordination on Medicaid birth outcomes in North Carolina. *American Journal of Public Health, 81,* 1625–1629.

Bui, K-V. T., Peplau, L. A., & Hill, C. T. (1996). Testing the Rusbult model of relationship commitment and stability in a 15-year study of heterosexual couples. *Personality and Social Psychology Bulletin, 22,* 1244–1257.

Bukowski, W. M., Gauze, C., Hoza, B., & Newcomb, A. F. (1993). Differences and consistency between same-sex and other-sex peer relationships during early adolescence. *Developmental Psychology, 29,* 255–263.

Bullock, M., & Lutkenhaus, P. (1988). The development of volitional behavior in the toddler years. *Child Development, 59,* 664–674.

Bullough, V. L. (1981). Age at menarche: A misunderstanding. *Science, 213,* 365–366.

Burchinal, M., Lee, M., & Ramey, C. (1989). Type of day-care and preschool intellectual development in disadvantaged children. *Child Development, 60,* 128–137.

Burgess, E. W., & Bogue, D. J. (1967). The delinquency research of Clifford R. Shaw and Henry D. McKay and Associates. In E. W. Burgess & D. J. Bogue (Eds.), *Urban Sociology* (pp. 293–317). Chicago: University of Chicago Press.

Burke, B. (1987). The role of playfulness in developing thinking skills: A review with implementation strategies. In S. Moore & K. Kolb (Eds.), *Reviews of research for practitioners and parents* (No. 3, pp. 3–8). Minneapolis: Center for Early Education and Development.

Burleson, B. R., Kunkel, A. W., Samter, W., & Werking, K. J. (1996). Men's and women's evaluations of communication skills in personal relationships: When sex differences make a difference—and when they don't. *Journal of Social and Personal Relationships, 13,* 201–224.

Burr, J. A., & Mutchler, J. E. (1993). Nativity, acculturation, and economic statues: Explanation of Asian American living arrangements in later life. *The Journals of Gerontology, 48,* S55–S63.

Burr, W. R., & Christensen, C. (1992). Undesirable side effects of enhancing self-esteem. *Family Relations, 41,* 480–484.

Burt, R. D., Vaughan, T. L., & Daling, J. R. (1988). Evaluating the risks of cesarean section: Low Apgar score in repeat C-section and vaginal deliveries. *American Journal of Public Health, 78,* 1312–1314.

Bus, A. G., vanIzendoorn, M. H., & Pellegrini, A. D. (1995). Joint book reading makes for success in learning to read: A meta-analysis on intergenerational transmission of literacy. *Review of Educational Research, 65*, 1–21.

Buss, A. H., & Plomin, R. (1984). *Temperament: Early developing personality traits*. Hillsdale, NJ: Erlbaum.

Buss, A. H., & Plomin, R. (1986). The EAS approach to temperament. In R. Plomin & J. Dunn (Eds.), *The study of temperament: Changes, continuities, and challenges*. Hillsdale, NJ: Erlbaum.

Buss, F. L. (1985). *Dignity: Lower income women tell of their lives and struggles* (pp. 153–154). Ann Arbor, MI: University of Michigan Press.

Butler, R. (1989). Mastery versus ability appraisal: A developmental study of children's observations of peers' work. *Child Development, 60*, 1350–1361.

Butler, R. (1990). The effects of mastery and competitive conditions on self-assessment at different ages. *Child Development, 61*, 201–210.

Butler, R., & Ruzany, N. (1993). Age and socialization effects on the development of social comparison motives and normative ability assessment in kibbutz and urban children. *Child Development, 64*, 532–543.

Butterfield, E. C., Nelson, T. O., & Peck, V. (1988). Developmental aspects of the feeling of knowing. *Developmental Psychology, 24*, 654–663.

Buysse, A. (1996). Adolescents, young adults, and AIDS: A study of actual knowledge vs. perceived need for additional information. *Journal of Youth and Adolescence, 25*, 259–271.

Byrne, G. (1988). Artificial insemination report prompts call for regulation. *Science, 241*, 895.

Cain, P. S., & Treiman, D. J. (1981). The DOT as a source of occupational data. *American Sociological Review, 46*, 253–278.

Caldas, S. J. (1993). Current theoretical perspectives on adolescent pregnancy and childbearing in the United States. *Journal of Adolescent Research, 8*, 4–20.

Caldera, Y. M., Huston, A. C., & O'Brien, M. (1989). Social interactions and play patterns of parents and toddlers with feminine, masculine, and neutral toys. *Child Development, 60*, 70–76.

Calkins, S. D., & Fox, N. A. (1992). The relations among infant temperament, security of attachment, and behavioral inhibition at twenty-four months. *Child Development, 63*, 1456–1472.

Campbell, J. (1990). Self-esteem and clarity of the self-concept. *Journal of Personality and Social Psychology, 59*, 538–549.

Campos, R. G. (1989). Soothing pain-elicited distress in infants with swaddling and pacifiers. *Child Development, 60*, 781–792.

Campos, J. J., & Barrett, K. C. (1984). Toward a new understanding of emotions and their development. In C. E. Izard, J. Kagan, & R. B. Zajonc (Eds.), *Emotions, cognition, and behavior* (pp. 229–263). Cambridge: Cambridge University Press.

Campos, J. J., Campos, R. G., & Barrett, K. C. (1989). Emergent themes in the study of emotional development and emotion regulation. *Developmental Psychology, 25*, 394–402.

Camras, L. A., Malatesta, C., & Izard, C. E. (1991). The development of facial expression in infancy. In R. Feldman & B. Rime (Eds.), *Fundamentals of nonverbal behavior* (pp. 73–105). New York: Cambridge University Press.

Canfield, R. L., & Haith, M. M. (1991). Young infants' visual expectations for symmetric and asymmetric stimulus sequences. *Developmental Psychology, 27*, 198–208.

Caplan, G. (1964). *Principles of preventive psychiatry*. New York: Basic Books.

Carey, S. (1978). The child as word learner. In M. Halle, G. Miller, & J. Bresnan (Eds.), *Linguistic theory and psychological reality* (pp. 264–293). Cambridge: MIT Press.

Cargan, L. (1981). Singles: An examination of two stereotypes. *Family Relations, 30*, 377–385.

Carli, L. L. (1989). Gender differences in interaction style and influence. *Journal of Personality and Social Psychology, 56*, 565–576.

Carlo, G., Knight, G. P., Eisenberg, N., & Rotenberg, K. J. (1991). Cognitive processes and prosocial behaviors among children: The role of affective attributions and reconciliations. *Developmental Psychology, 27*, 456–461.

Carlson, V., Cicchetti, D., Barnett, D., & Braunwold, K. (1989). Finding order in disorganization. Lessons from research on maltreated infants' attachment to their caregivers. In D. Cicchetti & V. Carlson (Eds.), *Child maltreatment: Theory and research on the causes and consequences of maltreatment* (pp. 494–528). New York: Cambridge University Press.

Caro, F. G., & Bass, S. A. (1997). Receptivity to volunteering in the immediate postretirement period. *Journal of Applied Gerontology, 16*, 427–441.

Caron, A. J., Caron, R. F., & MacLean, D. J. (1988). Infant discrimination of naturalistic emotional expressions: The role of face and voice. *Child Development, 59*, 604–616.

Carp, F. M. (1997). Retirement and women. In J. M. Coyle (Ed.), *Handbook of women and aging* (pp. 112–128). Westport, CT: Greenwood Press.

Carpendale, J. I. M., & Krebs, D. L. (1992). Situational variation in moral judgment: In a stage or on a stage? *Journal of Youth and Adolescence, 21*, 203–224.

Carper, J. (1995). *Stop aging now: the ultimate plan for staying young and reversing the aging process*. New York: HarperCollins Publishers.

Carr, M., Kurtz, B. E., Schneider, W., Turner, L. A., & Borkowski, J. G. (1989). Strategy acquisition and transfer among American and German children: Environmental influences on metacognitive development. *Developmental Psychology, 25*, 765–771.

Carroll, D. W. (1986). *Psychology of language*. Pacific Grove, CA: Brooks/Cole.

Carroll, J. L., & Rest, J. R. (1982). Moral development. In B. B. Wolman (Ed.), *Handbook of developmental psychology*, (pp. 434–451). Englewood Cliffs, NJ: Prentice-Hall.

Caspi, A., & Moffitt, T. E. (1991). Individual differences are accentuated during periods of social change: The sample case of girls at puberty. *Journal of Personality and Social Psychology, 61*, 157–168.

Cassady, G., & Strange, M. (1987). The small-for-gestational-age (SGA) infant. In G. B. Avery (Ed.), *Neonatology: Pathophysiology and management of the newborn* (pp. 299–331). Philadelphia: Lippincott.

Cassidy, J., & Asher, S. R. (1992). Loneliness and peer relations in young children. *Child Development, 63*, 350–365.

Centers for Disease Control. (1992). Sexual behavior among high school students. *Morbidity and Mortality Weekly Report, 40,* 885–888.

Cerella, J. (1994). Generalized slowing in Brinley Plots. *The Journals of Gerontology, 49,* P65–P71.

Cernoch, J. M., & Porter, R. H. (1985). Recognition of maternal axillary odors by infants. *Child Development, 56,* 1593–1598.

Chalmers, J. B., & Townsend, M. A. R. (1990). The effects of training in social perspective taking on socially maladjusted girls. *Child Development, 61,* 178–190.

Chandler, M., & Boyes, M. (1982). Social cognitive development. In B. B. Wolman (Ed.), *Handbook of developmental psychology* (pp. 387–402). Englewood Cliffs, NJ: Prentice-Hall.

Chapman, M. (1988). *Constructive evolution: Origin and development of Piaget's thought.* New York: Cambridge University Press.

Chapman, M., & McBride, M. L. (1992). Beyond competence and performance. Children's class inclusion strategies, superordinate class cues, and verbal justifications. *Developmental Psychology, 28,* 319–327.

Charlesworth, W. R. (1992). Darwin and developmental psychology: Past and present. *Developmental Psychology, 28,* 5–16.

Chase-Lansdale, P. L. (1993). The impact of poverty on family process. *The Child, Youth, and Family Services Quarterly, 16,* 5–8.

Chase-Lansdale, P. L., & Owen, M. T. (1987). Maternal employment in a family context: Effects on infant-mother and infant-father attachments. *Child Development, 58,* 1505–1512.

Chasnoff, I. J. (1988). *Drugs, alcohol, pregnancy, and parenting.* Hingham, MA: Kluwer.

Chazan, S. E. (1981). Development of object permanence as a correlate of dimensions of maternal care. *Developmental Psychology, 17,* 79–81.

Cherlin, A. J., & Furstenberg, F. F. (1986/1992). *The new American grandparent: A place in the family, a life apart.* Cambridge: Harvard University Press.

Chickering, A. W., & Reisser, L. (1993). *Education and identity* (2nd ed.). San Francisco: Jossey-Bass.

Chilman, C. S. (1993). Hispanic families in the United States: Research perspective. In H. P. McAdoo (Ed.), *Family ethnicity: Strength in diversity* (pp. 141–163). Newbury Park, CA: Sage.

Chronicle of Higher Education. (1997, August 29). *Almanac: Facts about the U.S., each of the 50 states, and D.C., 44,* Washington, DC: Author.

Choi, N. G. (1991). Racial differences in the determinants of living arrangements of widowed and divorced elderly women. *Gerontologist, 4,* 496–504.

Church, G. J. (1993, November 22). Jobs in an age of insecurity. *Time, 142(22),* 32–39.

Church, J. (1966). *Three babies: Biographies of cognitive development.* New York: Random House.

Cicchetti, D., & Schneider-Rosen, K. (1984). Theoretical and empirical considerations in the investigation of the relationship between affect and cognition in atypical populations of infants. In C. E. Izard, J. Kagan, & R. B. Zajonc (Eds.), *Emotions, cognition, and behavior* (pp. 366–408). Cambridge: Cambridge University Press.

Clancy, S. M., & Dollinger, S. J. (1993). Identity, self, and personality: 1. Identity status and the five-factor model of personality. *Journal of Research on Adolescence, 3,* 227–246.

Clark, A. L., & Howland, R. I. (1978). The American Samoan. In A. L. Clark (Ed.), *Culture, childbearing, and the health professionals,* (pp. 154–172). Philadelphia: F. A. Davis.

Clark, J. E., & Phillips, S. J. (1993). A longitudinal study of intralimb coordination in the first year of independent walking: A dynamical systems analysis. *Child Development, 64,* 1143–1157.

Clark, J. E., Phillips, S. J., & Petersen, R. (1989). Developmental stability in jumping. *Developmental Psychology, 25,* 929–935.

Clarke-Stewart, K. A. (1989). Infant day care: Maligned or malignant? *American Psychologist, 44,* 266–273.

Clarke-Stewart, K. A., & Fein, G. G. (1983). Early childhood programs. In P. H. Mussen (Ed.), *Handbook of child psychology: Vol. 2. Infancy and developmental psycho-biology* (pp. 917–1000). New York: Wiley.

Clark, K. E., & Clark, M. B. (1994). *Choosing to lead.* Charlotte, NC: Leadership Press Ltd.

Clark, M. L. (1991). Social identity, peer relations, and academic competence of African-American adolescents. *Education and Urban Society, 24,* 41–52.

Clark, M. L., & Ayers, M. (1988). The role of reciprocity and proximity in junior high school friendships. *Journal of Youth and Adolescence, 17,* 403–411.

Clasen, D. R., & Brown, B. B. (1985). The multidimensionality of peer pressure in adolescence. *Journal of Youth and Adolescence, 14,* 451–468.

Clausen, J. A. (1975). The social meaning of differential physical and sexual maturation. In S. E. Dragastin & G. H. Elder (Eds.), *Adolescence in the life cycle: Psychological change and social context.* Washington, DC: Hemisphere.

Clayman, C. B. (1989). *The American Medical Association encyclopedia of medicine.* New York: Random House.

Clayton, V. P., & Birren, J. E. (1980). The development of wisdom across the life span: A reexamination of an ancient topic. In P. B. Baltes & O. G. Brim, Jr. (Eds.), *Life-span development and behavior* (Vol. 3, pp. 104–135). New York: Academic Press.

Clifton, R., Perris, E., & Bullinger, A. (1991). Infants' perception of auditory space. *Developmental Psychology, 27,* 187–197.

Coats, P. B., & Overman, S. J. (1992). Childhood play experiences of women in traditional and nontraditional professions. *Sex Roles, 26,* 261–271.

Cobb, S. (1979). Social support and health through the life course. In M. W. Riley (Ed.), *Aging from birth to death.* Boulder, CO: Westview.

Cochran, C. C., Frazier, P. A., & Olson, A. W. (1997). Predictors of responses to unwanted sexual attention. *Psychology of Women Quarterly, 21,* 207–226.

Cohen, M. A., Tell, E. J., Bishop, C. E., Wallack, S. S., & Branch, L. G. (1989). Patterns of nursing home use in a prepaid managed care system: The continuing care retirement community. *Gerontologist, 29,* 74–80.

Cohen, M. A., Tell, E. J., & Wallack, S. S. (1988). The risk factors of nursing home entry among residents of six continuing care retirement communities. *Journal of Gerontology: Social Sciences, 43,* S15–S21.

Cohn, B. (1998). What a wife's worth. *Stanford,* March/April, 14–15.

Coie, J. D., & Krehbiel, G. (1984). Effects of academic tutoring on the social status of low-achieving, socially rejected children. *Child Development, 55,* 1465–1478.

Colby, A., & Damon, W. (1994). Listening to a different voice: A review of Gilligan's "In a Different Voice." In B. Puka (Ed.), *Caring voices and women's moral frames: Gilligan's view. Moral development: A compendium,* Vol. 6 (pp. 275–283). New York: Garland Publishing.

Colby, A., & Kohlberg, L. (1987). *The measurement of moral judgment: Vol. 1. Theoretical foundations and research validation.* Cambridge: Cambridge University Press.

Colby, A., Kohlberg, L., Gibbs, J., & Lieberman, M. (1983). A longitudinal study of moral judgment. *Monographs of the Society for Research in Child Development, 48*(1, Serial No. 200).

Cole, C. L., & Cole, A. L. (1985). Husbands and wives should have an equal share in making the marriage work. In H. Feldman & M. Feldman (Eds.), *Current controversies in marriage and family* (pp. 131–141). Newbury Park, CA: Sage.

Cole, D., & La Voie, J. C. (1985). Fantasy play and related cognitive development in 2 to 6 year olds. *Developmental Psychology, 21,* 233–240.

Cole, M., & D'Andrade, R. (1982). The influence of schooling on concept formation: Some preliminary conclusions. *Quarterly Newsletter of the Laboratory of Comparative Cognition, 4,* 19–26.

Coleman, J. S. (1987). Families and schools. *Educational Researcher, 16,* 32–38.

Coleman, P. G. (1992). Personal adjustment in late life: Successful aging. *Reviews in Clinical Gerontology, 2,* 67–78.

Coll, C. T. G. (1990). Developmental outcome of minority infants: A process-oriented look into our beginnings. *Child Development, 61,* 270–289.

Collins, F. S. (1992). Cystic fibrosis: Molecular biology and therapeutic implications. *Science, 256,* 774–779.

Collins, K., Luszcz, M., Lawson, M., & Keeves, J. (1997). Everyday problem solving in elderly women: Contributions of residence, perceived control and age. *Gerontologist, 37,* 293–302.

Colombo, J., Mitchell, D. W., Coldren, J. T., & Freeseman, L. J. (1991). Individual differences in infant visual attention: Are short lookers faster processors or feature processors? *Child Development, 62,* 1247–1257.

Comer, J. P. (1985). Empowering black children's educational environments. In H. P. McAdoo & J. L. McAdoo (Eds.), *Black children: Social, educational, and parental environments* (pp. 123–138). Newbury Park, CA: Sage.

Comstock, G. A. (with Haejung Paik). (1991). *Television and the American child.* San Diego: Academic Press.

Conger, R. D., Conger, K. J., Elder, G. H., Lorenz, F. O., Simons, R. L., & Whitbeck, L. B. (1993). Family economic stress and adjustment of early adolescent girls. *Developmental Psychology, 29,* 206–219.

Connolly, K., & Dalgleish, M. (1989). The emergence of a tool-using skill in infancy. *Developmental Psychology, 25,* 894–912.

Constantinople, A. (1969). An Eriksonian measure of personality development in college students. *Developmental Psychology, 1,* 357–372.

Conte, H. R., Weiner, M. B., & Plutchik, R. (1982). Measuring death anxiety: Conceptual, psychometric, and factor-analytic aspects. *Journal of Personality and Social Psychology, 43,* 775–785.

Cool, L. E. (1987). The effects of social class and ethnicity on the aging process. In P. Silverman (Ed.), *The elderly as modern pioneers.* Bloomington: Indiana University Press.

Coombs, R. H., & Landsverk, J. (1988). Parenting styles and substance use in childhood and adolescence. *Journal of Marriage and the Family, 50,* 473–482.

Cooney, T. M., Pedersen, F. A., Indelicato, S., & Palkovitz, R. (1993). Timing of fatherhood: Is "on-time" optimal? *Journal of Marriage and the Family, 55,* 205–215.

Coordinating Committee for the Human Capital Initiative. (1993, October). Report of the committee on the changing nature of work. *APS Observer,* pp. 9–24.

Corcoran, M. E., & Chaudry, A. (1997). The dynamics of childhood poverty. *The Future of Children, 7.*

Corijn, M., Liefbroer, A. C., & Gierveld, J. De J. (1996). It takes two to tango, doesn't it? The influence of couple characteristics on the timing of the birth of the first child. *Journal of Marriage and the Family, 58,* 117–126.

Corina, D. P., Vaid, J., & Bellugi, U. (1992). The linguistic basis of left hemisphere specialization, *Science, 255,* 1258–1260.

Cose, E. (1993, November 15). Rage of the privileged. *Newsweek,* pp. 56–63.

Costa, P. T., & McCrae, R. R. (1980). The influence of extroversion and neuroticism on subjective well-being: Happy and unhappy people. *Journal of Personality and Social Psychology, 38,* 668–678.

Costa, P. T., Zonderman, A. B., McCrae, R. R., Coroni-Huntley, J., Locke, B. Z., & Barbano, H. E. (1987). Longitudinal analyses of psychological well-being in a national sample: Stability of mean levels. *Journal of Gerontology, 42*(1), 50–55.

Coursin, D. B. (1974). Overview of the problem. In M. Winick (Ed.), *Nutrition and fetal development.* New York: Wiley.

Cowan, C. P., & Cowan, P. A. (1988). Who does what when partners become parents: Implications for men, women, and marriage. In R. Palkovitz & M. B. Sussman (Eds.), *Transitions to parenthood* (pp. 105–132). New York: Hawthorn Press.

Cowley, G. (1997, June 30). How to live to 100. *Newsweek,* 56–67.

Cox, M. J., Owen, M. T., Lewis, J. M., & Henderson, V. K. (1989). Marriage, adult adjustment, and early parenting. *Child Development, 60,* 1015–1024.

Cox, M. J., Owen, M. T., Henderson, V. K., & Margand, N. A. (1992). Prediction of infant-father and infant-mother attachment. *Developmental Psychology, 28,* 474–483.

Crack-using woman admits guilt in the death of her fetus. (1997, December 3) *New York Times,* Sec. A. p. 33.

Craig-Bray, L., Adams, G. R., & Dobson, W. R. (1988). Identity formation and social relations during late adolescence. *Journal of Youth and Adolescence, 17,* 173–188.

Crain, W. C. (1985). *Theories of development: Concepts and applications* (2nd ed.). Englewood Cliffs, NJ: Prentice-Hall.

Crain-Thoreson, C., & Dale, P. S. (1992). Do early talkers become early readers? Linguistic precocity, preschool language, and emergent literacy. *Developmental Psychology, 28,* 421–429.

Creswell, J. W. (1994). *Research design: Qualitative and quantitative approaches.* Thousand Oaks, CA: Sage.

Crick, N. R., & Ladd, G. W. (1993). Children's perceptions of their peer experiences: Attributions, loneliness, social anxiety, and social avoidance. *Developmental Psychology, 29,* 244–254.

Crittenden, P. M. (1985). Maltreated infants: Vulnerability and resilience. *Journal of Child Psychology and Psychiatry, 26,* 85–96.

Cronin-Golomb, A. (1995). Semantic networks in the divided cerebral hemispheres. *Psychological Science, 6,* 212–218.

Crooks, R., & Baur, K. (1996). *Our sexuality* (6th ed.) Pacific Grove, CA: Brooks/Cole.

Crooks, T. J. (1988). The impact of classroom evaluation practices on students. *Review of Educational Research, 58,* 438–481.

Cross, D. R., & Paris, S. G. (1988). Developmental and instructional analyses of children's metacognition and reading comprehension. *Journal of Educational Psychology, 80,* 131–142.

Cross, W. E., Jr. (1991). *Shades of black: Diversity in African-American identity.* Philadelphia: Temple University Press.

Crouter, A. C., & Manke, B. (1997). Development of a typology of dual-earner families: A window into differences between and within families in relationships, roles, and activities. *Journal of Family Psychology, 11,* 62–75.

Crystal, R. G. (1995). Transfer of genes to humans: Early lessons and obstacles to success. *Science, 270,* 404–410.

Cummings, E. M., Greene, A-L., & Karraker, K. H. (Eds.). (1991). *Lifespan perspectives on stress and coping.* Hillsdale, NJ: Erlbaum.

Cummings, E. M., Iannotti, R. J., & Zahn-Waxler, C. (1989). Aggression between peers in early childhood: Individual continuity and developmental change. *Child Development, 60,* 887–895.

Cunningham, F. G., MacDonald, P. C., Gant, N. F., Leveno, K. J., Gilstrap, L. C. III, Hankins, G. D. V., & Clark, S. L. (1997). *Williams' obstetrics* (20th ed.). Stamford, CT: Appleton & Lange.

Cummings, J. S., Pellegrini, D. S., Notarius, C. I., & Cummings, E. M. (1989). Children's responses to angry adult behavior as a function of marital distress and history of interparent hostility. *Child Development, 60,* 1035–1043.

Damon, W. (1996). The lifelong transformation of moral goals through social influence. In P. B. Baltes & V. M. Staudinger (Eds.), *Interactive minds: Life-span perspectives on the social foundation of cognition* (pp. 198–220). New York: Cambridge University Press.

Damon, W. (1980). Patterns of change in children's social reasoning: A two-year longitudinal study. *Child Development, 51,* 1010–1017.

Damon, W., & Hart, D. (1988). *Self-understanding in childhood and adolescence.* New York: Cambridge University Press.

Darney, P. D., Myhra, W., Atkinson, E. S., & Meier, J. (1989). Sero survey of human immunodeficiency virus infection in women at a family planning clinic: Absence of infection in an indigent population in San Francisco. *American Journal of Public Health, 79,* 883–885.

Darwin, C. (1859/1979). *The illustrated "Origin of species."* Abridged and introduced by Richard E. Leakey. New York: Hill & Wang.

D'Augelli, A. R. (1991). Gay men in college: Identity processes and adaptation. *Journal of College Student Development, 32,* 140–146.

Davey, A., & Eggebeen, D. J. (1998). Patterns of intergenerational exchange and mental health. *Journal of Gerontology, Series B, Psychological Sciences, 53B,* P86–P95.

Davey, G., & Cullen, C. (1988). *Human operant conditioning and behavior modification.* New York: Wiley.

Daveydov, V. V. (1995). The influence of L. S. Vygotsky on education theory, research, and practice. *Educational Researcher, 24,* 12–21. (Translated by Stephen T. Kerr)

Davis, A. (1995). The experimental method in psychology. In G. Breakwell, S. Hammond, & C. Fyfe-Schaw (Eds.), *Research methods in psychology.* Thousand Oaks, CA: Sage.

Davis, K. E. (1985, February). Near and dear: Friendship and love compared. *Psychology Today, 19,* 22–30.

Davison, M. L., King, P. M., Kitchener, K. S., & Parker, C. A. (1980). The stage sequence concept in cognitive and social development. *Developmental Psychology, 16,* 121–131.

Day, D. (1992). The transition to first intercourse among racially and culturally diverse youth. *Journal of Marriage and the Family, 54,* 749–763.

DeAngelis, T. (1997). APA co-sponsors briefing on anorexia. *APA Monitor, 28,* p. 51.

DeAngelis, T. (1997). When children don't bond with parents. *APA Monitor, 28,* 10–12.

De Casper, A., & Fifer, W. (1980). Of human bonding: Newborns prefer their mothers' voices. *Science, 208,* 1174–1176.

DeCasper, A. J., & Spence, M. J. (1986). Prenatal maternal speech influences newborns' perceptions of speech sounds. *Infant Behavior and Development, 9,* 133–150.

Defey, D., Storch, E., Cardozo, S., & Diaz, O. (1996). The menopause: Women's psychology and health. *Critical Science and Medicine, 47,* 1447–1456.

DeMaris, A., & Rao, K. V. (1992). Premarital cohabitation and subsequent marital stability in the United States: A reassessment. *Journal of Marriage and the Family, 54,* 178–190.

Demetriou, A., & Efklides, A. (1985). Structure and sequence of formal and postformal thought: General patterns and individual differences. *Child Development, 56,* 1062–1091.

Demetriou, A., Efklides, A., & Platsidou, M. (1993). The architecture and dynamics of developing mind: Experiential structuralism as a frame for unifying cognitive developmental theories. *Monographs of the Society for Research in Child Development, 58* (5–6, Serial No. 234).

Demi, A., Bakeman, R., Moneyham, L., Sowell, R., & Seals, B. (1997). Effects of resources and stressors on burden and depression of family members who provide care to an HIV-infected woman. *Journal of Family Psychology, 11,* 35–48.

Demo, D. H., & Ganong, L. H. (1994). Divorce. In P. C. McKenry & S. J. Price (Eds.), *Families and change: Coping with stressful events* (197–218). Thousand Oaks, CA: Sage.

Denmark, F. L., Novick, K., & Pinto, A. (1996). Women, work, and family: Mental health issues. In J. A. Sechzer, S. M. Pfafflin, F. L. Denmar, A. Griffin, & S. J. Blumenthal (Eds.), *Women and mental health. Annals of the New York Academy of Sciences,* (Vol 789, pp. 101–117).

Denney, N. W. (1982). Aging and cognitive changes. In B. B. Wolman (Ed.), *Handbook of developmental psychology* (pp. 807–827). Englewood Cliffs, NJ: Prentice-Hall.

Denney, N. W. (1982). Aging and cognitive changes. In B. B. Wolman (Ed.), *Handbook of developmental psychology* (pp. 807–827). Englewood Cliffs, NJ: Prentice-Hall.

Denney, N. W., & Pearce, K. A. (1989). A developmental study of practical problem solving in adults. *Psychology and Aging, 4,* 438–442.

Dennis, W. (1966). Creative productivity between the ages of twenty and eighty years. *Journal of Gerontology, 21,* 1–8.

Denton, W. H., Burleson, B. R., & Sprenkle, D. H. (1994). Motivation in marital communication: Comparison of distressed and nondistressed husbands and wives. *American Journal of Family Therapy, 22,* 17–26.

DeSilva, P., & Marks, M. (1994). Jealousy as a clinical problem: Practical issues of assessment and treatment. *Journal of Mental Health, 3,* 195–204.

DeVos, S. (1989). Leaving the parental home in six Latin American countries. *Journal of Marriage and the Family, 51,* 615–626.

Diaz, R. M. (1983). Thought and two languages: The impact of bilingualism on cognitive development. *Review of Research in Education, 10,* 23–54.

DiBlasio, F. A. (1986). Drinking adolescents on the roads. *Journal of Youth and Adolescence, 15,* 173–188.

Dickstein, S., & Parke, R. D. (1988). Social referencing in infancy: A glance at fathers and marriage. *Child Development, 59,* 506–511.

Diener, C. I., & Dweck, C. S. (1980). An analysis of learned helplessness: 2. The processing of success. *Journal of Personality and Social Psychology, 39,* 940–952.

Dindia, K., & Allen, M. (1992). Sex differences in self-disclosure: A meta-analysis. *Psychological Bulletin, 112,* 106–124.

Dinges, D. F., Davis, M. M., & Glass, P. (1980). Fetal exposure to narcotics: Neonatal sleep as a measure of nervous system disturbance. *Science, 209,* 619–621.

Dion, K. K., & Dion, K. L. (1993). Individualistic and collectivistic perspectives on gender and the cultural context of love and intimacy. *Journal of Social Issues, 49,* 53–69.

DiPietro, J. A., Porges, S. W., & Uhly, B. (1992). Reactivity and developmental competence in preterm and full-term infants. *Developmental Psychology, 28,* 831–841.

Dishion, T. J., Patterson, G. R., Stoolmiller, M., & Skinner, M. L. (1991). Family, school, and behavioral antecedents to early adolescent involvement with antisocial peers. *Developmental Psychology, 27,* 172–180.

Dixon, R. A. (1992). Contextual approaches to adult intellectual development. In R. J. Sternberg & C. A. Berg (Eds.), *Intellectual development* (pp. 350–380). New York: Cambridge University Press.

Dodge, K. A. (1989). Coordinating responses to aversive stimuli: Introduction to a special section on the development of emotion regulation. *Developmental Psychology, 25,* 339–342.

Dodge, K. A., Pettit, G. S., McClaskey, C. L., Brown, M. M. (1986). Social competence in children. *Monographs of the Society for Research in Child Development, 51* (2, Serial No. 213).

Donald, M., Lucke, J., Dunne, M., & Raphael, B. (1995). Gender differences associated with young people's emotional reactions to sexual intercourse. *Journal of Youth and Adolescence, 24,* 453–464.

Donovan, W. L., & Leavitt, L. A. (1989). Maternal self-efficacy and infant attachment: Integrating physiology, perceptions, and behavior. *Child Development, 60,* 460–472.

Dorfman, L., Woodruff, K., Chavez, V., & Wallack, L. (1997). Youth and violence on local television news in California. *American Journal of Public Health, 87,* 1311–1316.

Dormody, T. J., Seevers, B. S., & Clason, D. L. (1993). *The Youth Leadership Life Skills Development Scale: An Evaluation and Research Tool for Youth Organizations* (Research Report 672). LasCruces, New Mexico: New Mexico State University Agricultural Experimentation.

Downey, G., & Walker, E. (1989). Social cognition and adjustment in children at risk for psychopathology. *Developmental Psychology, 25,* 835–845.

Dreman, S. (1997). *The family on the threshold of the 21st century: Trends and implications.* Mahwah, NJ: Lawrence Erlbaum.

Dreyer, P. H. (1982). Sexuality during adolescence. In B. B. Wolman (Ed.), *Handbook of developmental psychology* (pp. 559–601). Englewood Cliffs, NJ: Prentice-Hall.

Dryfoos, J. G. (1994). *Full service schools: A revolution in health and social services for children, youth and families.* San Francisco: Jossey-Bass.

Dubler, N. N., & Sabatino, C. P. (1991). Age-based rationing and the law: An exploration. In R. H. Binstock & S. G. Post (Eds.), *Too old for health care? Controversies in medicine, law, economics, and ethics* (pp. 92–119). Baltimore, MD: Johns Hopkins University.

Duncan, G. J., Brooks-Gunn, J., & Klebanov, P. K. (1994). Economic deprivation and early childhood development. *Child Development, 65,* 296–318.

Dunham, R. M., Kidwell, J. S., & Portes, P. R. (1988). Effects of parent-adolescent interaction on the continuity of cognitive development from early childhood to early adolescence. *Journal of Early Adolescence, 8,* 297–310.

Dunn, J., Brown, J., & Beardsall, L. (1991). Family talk about feeling states and children's later understanding of others' emotions. *Developmental Psychology, 27,* 448–455.

Dunphy, D. C. (1963). The social structure of urban adolescent peer groups. *Sociometry, 26,* 230–246.

Duran-Aydintug, C. (1995). Former spouses exiting role-identities. *Journal of Divorce and Remarriage, 24,* 23–40.

Durbin, D. L., Darling, N., Steinberg, L., & Brown, B. B. (1993). Parenting style and peer group membership among European-American adolescents. *Journal of Research on Adolescence, 3,* 87–100.

Dustman, R., Emmerson, R., Ruhling, R., Shearer, D., Steinhaus, L., Johnson, S., Bonekat, H., & Shigeoka, J. (1989). Age and fitness effects on EEG, ERP's, visual sensitivity and cognition. *Neurobiology of Aging, 10,* 2–15.

Duvall, E. M. (1977). *Family development* (5th ed.). Philadelphia: Lippincott.

Duxbury, L., & Higgins, C. (1994). Interference between work and family: A status report on dual-career and dual-earner mothers and fathers. *Employee Assistance Quarterly, 9,* 55–80.

Dweck, C. S. (1992). The study of goals in psychology. *Psychological Science, 3,* 165–167.

Eagly, A. H. (1987). *Sex differences in social behavior: A social-role analysis.* Hillsdale, NJ: Erlbaum.

East, P. L., Hess, L. E., & Lerner, R. M. (1987). Peer social support and adjustment of early adolescent peer groups. *Journal of Early Adolescence, 7,* 153–163.

East, P. L., & Rook, K. S. (1992). Compensatory patterns of support among children's peer relationships: A test using school friends, nonschool friends, and siblings. *Developmental Psychology, 28,* 163–172.

Easterbrooks, M. A. (1989). Quality of attachment to mother and to father. Effects of perinatal risk status. *Child Development, 60,* 825–830.

Eccles, J., Wigfield, A., Harold, R. D., & Blumenfeld, P. (1993). Age and gender differences in children's self- and task perceptions during elementary school. *Child Development, 64,* 830–847.

Eccles, J. S. (1993). School and family effects on the ontogeny of children's interests, self-perceptions, and activity choices. In J. E. Jacobs (Ed.), *Developmental perspectives on Motivation: Nebraska Symposium on Motivation, 1992* (pp. 145–208). Lincoln, NE: University of Nebraska Press.

Eccles, J. S. (1987). Gender roles and women's achievement-related decisions. *Psychology of Women Quarterly, 11,* 135–171.

Eccles, J. S., Jacobs, J. E., & Harold, R. D. (1990). Gender-role stereotypes, expectancy effects, and parents' role in the socialization of gender differences in self perceptions and skill acquisition. *Journal of Social Issues, 46,* 182–201.

Eckerman, C. O., Davis, C. C., & Didow, S. M. (1989). Toddlers' emerging ways of achieving social coordinations with a peer. *Child Development, 60,* 440–453.

Eckerman, C. O., & Didow, S. M. (1989). Toddlers' social coordinations: Changing responses to another's invitation to play. *Developmental Psychology, 25,* 794–804.

Eckerman, C. O., & Didow, S. M. (1996). Nonverbal imitation and toddlers' mastery of verbal means of achieving coordinated action. *Developmental Psychology, 32,* 141–152.

Eckstein, S., & Shemesh, M. (1992). The rate of acquisition of formal operational schemata in adolescence: A secondary analysis. *Journal of Research in Science Teaching, 29,* 441–451.

Edelman, M. W., & Pittman, K. J. (1986). Adolescent pregnancy: Black and white. *Journal of Community Health, 11,* 63–69.

Eder, R. A. (1989). The emergent personologist: The structure and content of 3$\frac{1}{2}$-, 5$\frac{1}{2}$-, and 7$\frac{1}{2}$-year-olds' concepts of themselves and other persons. *Child Development, 60,* 1218–1228.

Eder, R. A., Gerlach, S. G., & Perlmutter, M. (1987). In search of children's selves: Development of the specific and general components of the self-concept. *Child Development, 58,* 1044–1050.

Edwards, C. P. (1995). Parenting toddlers. In M. H. Bornstein (Ed.), *Handbook of parenting: Vol. 1. Children and parenting* (pp. 41–63). Mahwah, NJ, Erlbaum.

Edwards, C. P., Gandini, L., & Giovannini, D. (in press). The contrasting developmental timetables of parents and preschool teachers in two cultural communities. In S. Harkness & C. Super (Eds.), *Parental cultural beliefs systems.* New York: Guilford.

Edwards, C. P., & Whiting, B. B. (1988). *Children of different worlds.* Cambridge: Harvard University Press.

Egeland, B., Jacobvitz, D., & Sroufe, L. A. (1988). Breaking the cycle of abuse. *Child Development, 59,* 1080–1088.

Egeland, B., & Sroufe, L. A. (1981). Attachment and early maltreatment. *Child Development, 52,* 44–52.

Eggers, J. H. (1995). Developing entrepreneurs: Skills for the "wanna be," "gonna be," and "gotta be better" employees. In M. London (Ed.), *Employees, careers, and job creation.* San Francisco: Jossey-Bass.

Eisenberg, N., & Strayer, J. (1987). Critical issues in the study of empathy. In N. Eisenberg & J. Strayer (Eds.), *Empathy and its development* (pp. 3–13). Cambridge: Cambridge University Press.

Eisenberg, N., & Strayer, J. (1987). *Empathy and its development* (pp. 3–13). Cambridge: Cambridge University Press.

Ekerdt, D. J., Bosse, R., & Levkoff, S. (1985). An empirical test for phases of retirement: Findings from the normative aging study. *Journal of Gerontology, 40,* 95–101.

Elias, M. (1998). Study: Most don't regret abortions. *USA Today: Health* http//www.usatoday.com/life/health/women/abortion/1hwab009.htm.

Elias, M. J., Beier, J. J., & Gara, M. A. (1989). Children's responses to interpersonal obstacles as a predictor of social competence. *Journal of Youth and Adolescence, 18,* 451–465.

Elder, G. H. (1975). Age differentiation and the life course. *Annual Review of Sociology, 1,* 165–190.

Elder, G. H. (1985). *Life course dynamics: Trajectories and transitions, 1968–1980.* Ithaca, NY: Cornell University Press.

Elder, G. H. (1986). Military times and turning points in men's lives. *Developmental Psychology, 22,* 233–245.

Elder, G. H., Caspi, A., & van Nguyen, T. (1986). Resourceful and vulnerable children: Family influences in hard times. In R. K. Silbereisen et al. (Eds.), *Development as action in context* (pp. 167–186). Berlin: Springer-Verlag.

Elder, G. H. Jr., George, L. K., & Shanahan, M. J. (1996). Psychosocial stress over the life course. In H. B. Kaplan (Ed.) *Psychosocial Stress: Perspectives on structure, theory, life course, and methods.* Orlando, FL: Academic Press, 247–291.

Eldridge, N. S., & Gilbert, L. S. (1990). Correlates of relationship satisfaction in lesbian couples. *Psychology of Women Quarterly, 14,* 43–62.

Elkind, D. (1967). Egocentrism in adolescence. *Child Development, 38,* 1025–1034.

Ellickson, P., Saner, H., & McGuigan, K. A. (1997). Profiles of violent youth: Substance use and other concurrent problems. *American Journal of Public Health, 87,* 985–991.

Elliott, D. S., Huizinga, D., & Menard, S. (1989). *Multiple problem youth: Delinquency, substance use, and mental health problems.* New York: Springer-Verlag.

Ellis, J. E. (1991, July 8). Monsanto's new challenge: Keeping minority workers. *Newsweek,* pp. 60–61.

Ellsworth, C. P., Muir, C. P., & Hains, S. M. J. (1993). Social competence and person-object differentiation: An analysis of the still-face effect. *Developmental Psychology, 29,* 63–73.

Elmer-Dewitt, P. (1991). Making babies. *Time, 138,* 56–63.

Emde, R. N., Biringen, Z., Clyman, R. B., & Oppenheim, D. (1991). The moral self of infancy: Affective core and procedural knowledge. *Developmental Review, 11,* 51–270.

Emde, R. N., & Buchsbaum, H. K. (1990). "Didn't you hear my mommy?" Autonomy *with* connectedness in moral self-emergence. In D. Cicchetti & M. Beeghly (Eds.), *The self in transition: Infancy to childhood* (pp. 35–60). Chicago: University of Chicago Press.

Emde, R. N., Johnson, W. F., & Easterbrooks, A. (1987). The dos and donts of early moral development: Psychoanalytic tradition and current research. In J. Kagan & S. Lamb (Eds.), *The emergence of morality in young children* (pp. 245–276). Chicago: University of Chicago Press.

Emery, A. E. H., & Mueller, R. F. (1992). *Elements of medical genetics* (8th ed.) Edinburgh: Churchill Livingstone.

Endler, N. S. (1983). Interactionism: A personality model but not yet a theory. In M. M. Page (Ed.), *Nebraska Symposium on Motivation, 1982* (pp. 155–200). Lincoln, NE: University of Nebraska Press.

Englis, B. G., & Solomon, M. R. (1997). Where perception meets reality: The social construction of lifestyles. In L. R. Kahle & L. Chiagouris (Eds.), *Values, lifestyles, and psychographics: Advertising and consumer psychology* (pp. 25–44). Nahwah, NJ: Erlbaum.

Ennett, S. T., & Bauman, K. E. (1996). Adolescent social networks: School, demographic and longitudinal considerations. *Journal of Adolescent Research, 11,* 194–215.

Entwisle, D. R., & Alexander, K. L. (1990). Summer setback: Race, poverty, school composition, and achievement. *American Sociological Review, 57,* 72–84.

Entwisle, D. R., & Alexander, K. L. (1987). Long-term effects of cesarean delivery on parents' beliefs and children's schooling. *Developmental Psychology, 23,* 676–682.

Entwisle, D. R., Alexander, K. L., Pallas, A. M., & Cadigan, D. (1987). The emergent academic self-image of first-graders: Its response to social structure. *Child Development, 58,* 1190–1206.

Epstein, S. (1973). The self-concept revisited; or, a theory of a theory. *American Psychologist, 28,* 404–416.

Epstein, S. (1991). Cognitive-experiential self-theory: An integrative theory of personality. In R. Cutis (Ed.), *The self with others: Convergences in psychoanalytic, social, and personality psychology* (pp. 111–137). New York: Guilford.

Epstein, S., Lipson, A., Holstein, C., & Huh, E. (1993). Irrational reactions to negative outcomes: Evidence for two conceptual systems. *Journal of Personality and Social Psychology, 62,* 328–339.

Erikson, E. H., Erikson, J. M., & Kivnick, H. Q. (1986). *Vital involvement in old age.* New York: Norton.

Erikson, E. H. (1959). The problem of ego identity. *Psychological Issues, 1,* 101–164.

Erikson, E. H. (1963). *Childhood and society* (2nd ed.). New York: Norton.

Erikson, E. H. (1968). *Identity: Youth and crisis.* New York: Norton.

Erikson, E. H. (1969). *Gandhi's truth: On the origins of militant nonviolence.* New York: Norton.

Erikson, E. H. (1972). Play and actuality. In M. W. Piers (Ed.), *Play and development* (pp. 127–167). New York: Norton.

Erikson, E. H. (1974). *Dimensions of a new identity.* New York: Norton.

Erikson, E. H. (1975). "Identity crisis" in autobiographic per-

spective. In E. H. Erikson (Ed.), *Life history and the historical moment* (pp. 17–47). New York: W. W. Norton.

Erikson, E. H. (1977). *Toys and reasons.* New York: W. W. Norton.

Erikson, E. H. (1978). Reflections on Dr. Borg's life cycle. In E. H. Erikson (Ed.), *Adulthood* (pp. 1–31). New York: Norton.

Erikson, E. H. (1980). Themes of adulthood in the Freud-Jung correspondence. In N. J. Smelser & E. H. Erikson (Eds.), *Themes of work and love in adulthood* (pp. 43–74). Cambridge: Harvard University Press.

Erikson, E. H. (1982). *The life cycle completed: A review.* New York: Norton.

Erikson, J. M. (1988). *Wisdom and the senses: The way of creativity.* New York: Norton.

Escalona, S. K. (1968). *The roots of individuality.* Chicago: Aldine.

Eshelman, J. R. (1985). One should marry a person of the same religion, race, ethnicity, and social class. In H. Feldman & M. Feldman (Eds.), *Current controversies in marriage and family* (pp. 57–66). Newbury Park, CA: Sage.

Etzioni, A. (1976, November). The husband's rights in abortion. *Trial.*

Evans, N., Gilpin, E., Farkas, A. J., Shenassa, E., & Pierce, J. P. (1995). Adolescents' perceptions of their peers' health norms. *American Journal of Public Health, 85,* 1064–1069.

Evers, F. T., & Rush, J. C. (1996). The bases of competence: Skill development during the transition from university to work. *Management Learning, 27,* 275–299.

Fabes, R. A., Eisenberg, N., McCormick, S. E., & Wilson, M. S. (1988). Preschoolers' attributions of the situational determinants of others' naturally occurring emotions. *Developmental Psychology, 24,* 376–385.

Fabes, R. A., Eisenberg, N., Nyman, M., & Michealieu, Q. (1991). Young children's appraisals of others' spontaneous emotional reactions. *Developmental Psychology, 27,* 858–866.

Fagot, B. I., & Leinbach, M. D. (1989). The young child's gender schema: Environmental input, internal organization. *Child Development, 60,* 663–672.

Farkas, G., Grobe, R. P., Sheehan, D., & Shuan, Y. (1990). Cultural resources and school success: Gender, ethnicity, and poverty groups. *American Sociological Review, 55,* 127–142.

Farmer, T. W., & Rodkin, P. C. (1996). Antisocial and prosocial correlates of classroom social positions: The social network centrality perspective. *Social Development, 5,* 174–188.

Farrar, M. J., Raney, G. E., & Boyer, M. E. (1992). Knowledge, concepts, and inferences in childhood. *Child Development, 63,* 673–691.

Farrell, A. D., Danish, S. J., & Howard, C. W. (1992). Risk factors for drug use in urban adolescents: Identification and cross-validation. *American Journal of Community Psychology, 20,* 263–286.

Farrell, M. P., & Rosenberg, S. D. (1981). *Men at midlife.* Boston: Auburn House.

Feifel, H., & Branscomb, A. (1973). Who's afraid of death? *Journal of Abnormal Psychology, 81,* 282–288.

Feinman, C. F. (1992). *The criminalization of a woman's body.* Binghamton, NY: Hawthorn Press.

Feinman, S., & Lewis, M. (1983). Social referencing at ten months: A second-order effect on infants' responses to strangers. *Child Development, 54,* 878–887.

Feldman, H., & Feldman, M. (1975). The family life cycle: Some suggestions for recycling. *Journal of Marriage and the Family, 37,* 277–284.

Feldman, S. S., & Gehring, T. M. (1988). Changing perceptions of family cohesion and power across adolescence. *Child Development, 59,* 1034–1045.

Fenson, L., Dale, P. S., Reznick, J. S., Bates, E., Thal, D. J., & Pethick, S. J. (1994). Variability in early communicative development. *Monographs of the Society for Research in Child Development, 59* (Serial No. 5).

Fenster, L., Eskenazi, B., Windham, G. C., & Swan, S. H. (1991). Caffeine consumption during pregnancy and fetal growth. *American Journal of Public Health, 81,* 458–461.

Fentress, J. C., & McLeod, P. J. (1986). Motor patterns in development. In E. M. Blass (Ed.), *Handbook of behavioral neurobiology: Vol. 8. Developmental psychobiology and developmental neurobiology.* New York: Plenum.

Ferraro, K. F. (1990). Cohort analysis of retirement preparation, 1974–1981. *Journal of Gerontology, 45,* S25.

Ferster, C. B., & Culbertson, S. A. (1982). *Behavior principles* (3rd ed.). Englewood Cliffs, NJ: Prentice-Hall.

Fiatarone, M. A., & Evans, W. J. (1993). The etiology and reversibility of muscle dysfunctions in the aged. *The Journals of Gerontology, 48,* 77–83.

Field, D. (1981). Can preschool children really learn to conserve? *Child Development, 52,* 326–334.

Field, T., Healy, B., Goldstein, S., Perry, S., Bendell, D., Schanberg, S., Zimmerman, E. A., & Kuhn, C. (1988). Infants of depressed mothers show "depressed" behavior even with nondepressed adults. *Child Development, 59,* 1569–1579.

Field, T. M. (1991). Young children's adaptations to repeated separations from their mothers. *Child Development, 62,* 539–547.

Field, T. M., Cohen, D., Garcia, R., & Greenberg, R. (1984). Mother-stranger face discrimination by the newborn. *Infant Behavior and Development, 7,* 19–25.

Field, T. M., Healy, B., Goldstein, S., & Guthertz, M. (1990). Behavior-state matching and synchrony in mother-infant interaction of nondepressed versus depressed dyads. *Developmental Psychology, 26,* 7–14.

Field, T. M., Sandberg, D., Garcia, R., Vega-Lahr, N., Goldstein, S., & Guy, L. (1985). Pregnancy problems, postpartum depression, and early mother-infant interactions. *Developmental Psychology, 21,* 1152–1156.

Field, T. M., Woodson, R. W., Greenberg, R., & Cohen, C. (1982). Discrimination and imitation of facial expressions by neonates. *Science, 218,* 179–181.

Filsinger, E. E., & Thomas, S. J. (1988). Behavioral antecedents of relationship stability and adjustment. *Journal of Marriage and the Family, 50,* 785–795.

Fincham, F., & Jaspars, J. (1979). Attribution of responsibility to the self and other in children and adults. *Journal of Personality and Social Psychology, 37,* 1589–1602.

Finley, N. J. (1989). Gender differences in caregiving for elderly parents. *Journal of Marriage and the Family, 51,* 79–86.

Fischer, K. W. (1980). A theory of cognitive development: The control and construction of hierarchies of skills. *Psychological Review, 87,* 477–531.

Fischer, K. W., & Bidell, T. R. (1992, Winter). Ever younger ages: Constructive use of nativist findings about early development. *Newsletter of the Society for Research in Child Development,* pp. 1, 10, 11, 14.

Fischer, K. W., Bullock, D., Rotenberg, E. J., & Raya, P. (1993). The dynamics of competence: How context contributes directly to skill. In R. Wozniak & K. Fischer (Eds.), *Development in context: Acting and thinking in specific environments* (JPS Series on Knowledge and Development, Vol. 1, pp. 93–117). Hillsdale, NJ: Erlbaum.

Fischer, K. W., & Rose, S. P. (1994). Dynamic development of coordination of components of brain and behavior: A framework for theory and research. In G. Dawson & K. W. Fischer (Eds.), *Human behavior and the developing brain* (pp. 3–66). New York: Guilford.

Fischer, K. W., & Silvern, L. (1985). Stages and individual differences in cognitive development. *Annual Review of Psychology, 36,* 613–648.

Flaks, D. K., Ficher, I., Masterpasqua, F., & Joseph, G. (1995). Lesbians choosing motherhood: A comparative study of lesbian and heterosexual parents and their children. *Developmental Psychology, 31,* 105–114.

Flannery, D. J., Rowe, D. C., & Gulley, B. L. (1993). Impact of pubertal status, timing, and age on adolescent sexual experience and delinquency. *Journal of Adolescent Research, 8,* 21–40.

Flavell, J. H. (1963). *The developmental psychology of Jean Piaget.* Princeton, NJ: Van Nostrand.

Flavell, J. H. (1974). The development of inferences about others. In W. Mischel (Ed.), *Understanding other persons.* Oxford: Blackwell, Basil & Mott.

Flavell, J. H. (1982). On cognitive development. *Child Development, 53,* 1–10.

Flavell, J. H. (1982). Structures, stages, and sequences in cognitive development. In W. A. Collins (Ed.), *The concept of development* (pp. 1–28). Hillsdale, NJ: Erlbaum.

Flavell, J. H., Flavell, E. R., & Green, F. L. (1987). Young children's knowledge about the apparent-real and pretend-real distinctions. *Developmental Psychology, 23,* 816–822.

Fleming, A. S., Ruble, D. N., Flett, G. L., & Shaul, D. L. (1988). Postpartum adjustment in first-time mothers: Relations between mood, maternal attitudes, and mother-infant interactions. *Developmental Psychology, 24,* 71–81.

Fletcher, W. L., & Hansson, R. O. (1991). Assessing the social components of retirement anxiety. *Psychology and Aging, 6,* 76–85.

Florian, V., & Kravetz, S. (1983). Fear of personal death: Attribution structure and relation to religious belief. *Journal of Personality and Social Psychology, 44,* 600–607.

Floyd, F. J., Haynes, S. N., Doll, E. R., Winemiller, D., Lemsky, C., Burgy, T. M., Werle, M., & Heilman, N. (1992). Assessing retirement satisfaction and perceptions of retirement experiences. *Psychology and Aging, 7,* 609–621.

Flynn, C. B, Longino, C. F., Jr., Wiseman, R. F., & Biggar, J. C. (1985). The redistribution of America's older population: Major national migration patterns for three census decades, 1960–1980. *Gerontologist, 25,* 292–296.

Flynn, K., & Fitzgibbon, M. (1996). Body image ideals of low-income African American mothers and their preadolescent daughters. *Journal of Youth and Adolescence, 25,* 615–630.

Fonagy, P., Steele, H., & Steele, M. (1991). Maternal representations of attachment during pregnancy predict the organization of infant-mother attachment at one year of age. *Child Development, 62,* 891–905.

Fontane, P. E. (1996). Exercise, fitness, feeling well. *American Behavioral Scientist, 39,* 288–305.

Foote, D. (1986, February). And baby makes one. *Newsweek, 68*, 70.

Ford, C. S. (1945). *A comparative study of human reproduction.* New Haven, CT: Yale University Publications in Anthropology, No. 32.

Ford, M. E. (1985). The concept of competence. Themes and variations. In H. A. Marlowe & R. A. Weinberg (Eds.), *Competence development. Theory and practice in special populations.* Springfield IL: Charles C. Thomas.

Ford, M. R., & Lowery, C. R. (1986). Gender differences in moral reasoning: A comparison of the use of justice and care orientations. *Journal of Personality and Social Psychology, 50*, 777–783.

Forehand, R., Roberts, M. W., Doleys, D. M., Hobbs, S. A., & Resick, P. A. (1976). An examination of disciplinary procedures with children. *Journal of Experimental Child Psychology, 21*, 109–120.

Fortenberry, J. D., Costa, F. M., Jessor, R., & Donovan, J. E. (1997). Contraceptive behavior and adolescent lifestyles: A structural modeling approach. *Journal of Research on Adolescence, 7*, 307–329.

Fosburgh, L. (1977, August 7). The make-believe world of teen-age maturity. *New York Times Magazine* pp. 29–34.

Fowers, B. J., Montel, K. H., & Olson, D. H. (1996). Predicting marital success for premarital couple types based on PREPARE. *Journal of Marital and Family Therapy, 22*, 103–119.

Fowler, F. L., Jr. (1993). *Survey research methods* (2nd ed.). Thousand Oaks, CA: Sage.

Fox, N. A., & Davidson, R. J. (1984). Hemispheric substrates of affect: A developmental model. In N. A. Fox & R. J. Davidson (Eds.), *The psychobiology of affective development* (pp. 353–381). Hillsdale, NJ: Erlbaum.

Fox, N. A., & Davidson, R. J. (1987). Electroencephalogram asymmetry in response to the approach of a stranger and maternal separation in 10-month-old infants. *Developmental Psychology, 23*, 233–240.

Fox, N. A., Kimmerly, N. L., & Schafer, W. D. (1991). Attachment to mother/attachment to father. *Child Development, 62*, 210–225.

Francis, P. L., Self, P. A., & Horowitz, F. D. (1987). The behavioral assessment of the neonate: An overview. In J. D. Osofsky (Ed.), *Handbook of infant development* (2nd ed., pp. 723–779). New York: John Wiley & Sons.

Frankenberg, W. K., & Dodds, J. B. (1967). The Denver Developmental Screening Test. *Journal of Pediatrics, 71*, 181–191.

Franklin, D. L. (1988). Race, class, and adolescent pregnancy: An ecological analysis. *American Journal of Orthopsychiatry, 58*, 339–355.

Frazier, P., Byer, A. L., Fischer, A. R., Wright, D. M., & DeBord, K. A. (1996). Adult attachment style and partner choice: Correlational and experimental findings. *Personal Relationships, 3*, 117–136.

Frazier, P., Arikian, N., Benson, S., Losoff, A., & Maurer, S. (1996). Desire for marriage and life satisfaction among unmarried heterosexual adults. *Journal of Social and Personal Relationships, 13*, 225–239.

Freeman, R. B., & Wise, D. A. (1982). *The youth labor market: Problems in the United States.* Chicago: University of Chicago Press.

French, D. C. (1984). Children's knowledge of the social functions of younger, older and same-age peers. *Child Development, 55*, 1429–1433.

French, D. C. (1988). Heterogeneity of peer-rejected boys: Aggressive and nonaggressive subtypes. *Child Development, 59*, 976–985.

French, D. C. (1990). Heterogeneity of peer-rejected girls. *Child Development, 61*, 2028–2031.

Freud, A. (1936). *The ego and mechanisms of defense.* New York: International Universities Press.

Freud, A., & Dann, S. (1951). An experiment in group upbringing. In R. Eissler, A. Freud, H. Hartmann, & E. Kris (Eds.), *The psychoanalytic study of the child* (Vol. 6). New York: International Universities Press.

Freud, S. (1955). An analysis of a phobia in a 5-year-old boy. In J. Strachey (Ed.), *The standard edition of the complete psychological works of Sigmund Freud* (Vol. 10). London: Hogarth. (First German edition, 1909).

Freud, S. (1905/1953). Three essays on the theory of sexuality. In J. Strachey (Ed.), *The standard edition of the complete psychological works of Sigmund Freud* (Vol. 7). London: Hogarth Press.

Freud, S. (1925/1961). Some psychical consequences of the anatomical distinction between the sexes. In J. Strachey (Ed.), *The standard edition of the complete psychological works of Sigmund Freud* (Vol. 19). London: Hogarth Press.

Freud, S. (1933/1964). New introductory lectures on psychoanalysis. In J. Strachey (Ed.), *The standard edition of the complete psychological works of Sigmund Freud* (Vol. 22). London: Hogarth Press.

Freud, S. (1994). The social construction of gender. *Journal of Adult Development, 1*, 37–46.

Frey, K. S., & Ruble, D. N. (1987). What children say about classroom performance: Sex and grade differences in perceived competence. *Child Development, 58*, 1066–1078.

Fried, P. A., Watkinson, B., Dillon, R. F., & Dulberg, C. S. (1987). Neonatal neurological status in a low-risk population after prenatal exposure to cigarettes, marijuana, and alcohol. *Journal of Developmental and Behavioral Pediatrics, 8*, 318–326.

Fried-Cassorla, M. (1977). *Death anxiety and disengagement.* Paper presented at the annual convention of the American Psychological Association, San Francisco, CA.

Friedlander, D., & Burtless, G. (1994). *Five years after: The long-term effects of welfare-to-work programs.* New York: Russell Sage Foundation.

Friedman, W. J., Robinson, A. B., & Friedman, B. L. (1987). Sex differences in moral judgments? A test of Gilligan's theory. *Psychology of Women Quarterly, 11*, 37–46.

Froming, W. J., Allen, L., & Jensen, R. (1985). Altruism, role-taking, and self-awareness: The acquisition of norms governing altruistic behavior. *Child Development, 56*, 1123–1228.

Fuller-Thomson, E., Minkler, M., & Driver, D. (1997). A profile of grandparents raising grandchildren in the United States. *Gerontologist, 37*, 406–411.

Fultz, N. H., & Herzog, A. R. (1991). Gender differences in affiliation and instrumentality across adulthood. *Psychology and Aging, 6*, 579–586.

Futterman, A., Gallagher, D., Thompson, L. W., Lovett, S., & Gilewski, M. (1990). Retrospective assessment of marital adjustment and depression during the first two years of spousal bereavement. *Psychology and Aging, 5*, 277–283.

Gaddis, A., & Brooks-Gunn, J. (1985). The male experience of pubertal change. *Journal of Youth and Adolescence, 14*, 61–69.

Gall, T. L., Evans, D. R., & Howard, J. (1997). The retirement adjustment process: changes in the well-being of male retirees across time. *Journals of Gerontology, Series B-Psychological Sciences and Social Sciences, 52B,* P110–P117.

Galotti, K. M. (1989). Gender differences in self-reported moral reasoning: A review of new evidence. *Journal of Youth and Adolescence, 18,* 475–488.

Galotti, K. M., & Kozberg, S. F. (1987). Older adolescents' thinking about academic/vocational and interpersonal commitments. *Journal of Youth and Adolescence, 15,* 147–163.

Galotti, K. M., Kozberg, S. F., & Farmer, M. C. (1991). Gender and developmental differences in adolescents' conceptions of moral reasoning. *Journal of Youth and Adolescence, 20,* 13–30.

Gardner, H. (1983). *Frames of mind: The theory of multiple intelligences.* New York: Basic Books.

Gardner, H., Kornhaber, M. L., & Wake, W. K. (1996). *Intelligence: Multiple perspectives.* Ft. Worth, TX: Harcourt Brace.

Garguilo, J., Attie, I., Brooks-Gunn, J., & Warren, M. P. (1987). Dating in middle school girls: Effects of social context, maturation, and grade. *Developmental Psychology, 23,* 730–737.

Garland, A. F., & Zigler, E. (1993). Adolescent suicide prevention: Current research and social policy implications. *American Psychologist, 48,* 169–182.

Garmezy, N. (1991). Resilience in children's adaptation to negative life events and stressed environments. *Pediatric Annals, 20,* 459–466.

Garmezy, N., & Masten, A. S. (1991). The protective role of competence indicators in children at risk. In E. M. Cummings, A. L. Greene, and K. H. Karraker (Eds.), *Lifespan developmental psychology: Perspectives on stress and coping* (pp. 151–174). Hillsdale, NJ: Erlbaum.

Garrison, C. Z., Schluchter, M. D., Schoenbach, V. J., & Kaplan, B. K. (1989). Epidemiology of depressive symptoms in young adolescents. *Journal of the American Academy of Child and Adolescent Psychiatry, 28,* 343–351.

Garrod, A. (1993). *Approaches to moral development: New research and emerging themes.* New York: Teachers College Press.

Garton, A. F. (1992). *Social interaction and the development of language and cognition.* Hillsdale, NJ: Erlbaum.

Garvey, C. (1977). *Play.* Cambridge: Harvard University Press.

Gavin, L. A., & Furman, W. (1989). Age differences in adolescents' perceptions of their peer groups. *Developmental Psychology, 25,* 827–834.

Geary, D. C., & Brown, S. C. (1991). Cognitive addition: Strategy choice and speed of processing differences in gifted, normal, and mathematically disabled children. *Developmental Psychology, 27,* 398–406.

Geary, D. C., Brown, S. C., & Samaranayake, V. A. (1991). Cognitive addition: A short longitudinal study of strategy choice and speed-of-processing differences in normal and mathematically disabled children. *Developmental Psychology, 27,* 787–797.

Gelles, R. J. (1989). Child abuse and violence in single-parent families: Parent absence and economic deprivation. *American Journal of Orthopsychiatry, 59,* 492–501.

Gelman, D. (1992, February 24). Born or bred: The origins of homosexuality. *Newsweek,* pp. 46–53.

Gerbner, G., Gross, L., Morgan, M., & Signorelli, N. (1980). The "mainstreaming" of America: Violence profile no. 11. *Journal of Communication, 30,* 10–29.

Getchell, N., & Robertson, M. A. (1989). Whole body stiffness as a function of developmental level in children's hopping. *Developmental Psychology, 25,* 920–928.

Gfellner, B. M. (1986). Ego development and moral development in relation to age and grade level during adolescence. *Journal of Youth and Adolescence, 15,* 147–163.

Gfroerer, J. C., Greenblatt, J. C., & Wright, D. A. (1997). Substance use in the U.S. college-age population: Differences according to educational status and living arrangement. *American Journal of Public Health, 87,* 62–65.

Giambra, L. M., Arenberg, D., Zonderman, A. B., & Kawas, C. (1995). Adult life span changes in immediate visual memory and verbal intelligence. *Psychology and Aging, 10,* 123–139.

Gibbs, J. C. (1979). Kohlberg's moral stage theory: A Piagetian revision. *Human Development, 22,* 89–112.

Gibson, E. J., & Walker, A. S. (1984). Development of knowledge of visual-tactual affordances of substance. *Child Development, 55,* 453–460.

Gibson, J. J. (1962). Observations on active touch. *Psychological Review, 69,* 477–491.

Giele, J. Z. (1988). Gender and sex roles. In N. J. Smelser (Ed.), *Handbook of sociology* (pp. 291–326). Newbury Park, CA: Sage.

Gilbert, L. A. (1993). *Two careers/one family.* Newbury Park, CA: Sage.

Gillespie, C. (1989). *Hormones, hot flashes, and mood swings.* New York: Harper & Row.

Gillies, P. (1989). A longitudinal study of the hopes and worries of adolescents. *Journal of Adolescence, 12,* 69–81.

Gilligan, C. (1977). In a different voice: Women's conceptions of self and morality. *Harvard Educational Review, 47,* 481–517.

Gilligan, C. (1982). *In a different voice.* Cambridge: Harvard University Press.

Gilligan, C. (1982/1993). *In a different voice: Psychological theory and women's development.* Cambridge: Harvard University Press.

Gilligan, C., (1988). *Mapping the moral domain: A contribution of women's thinking to psychological theory and education.* Cambridge, MA: Harvard University Press.

Gilligan, C., & Attanucci, J. (1988). Two moral orientations. In C. Gilligan, J. V. Ward, J. M. Taylor, & B. Bardige (Eds.), *Mapping the moral domain.* Cambridge: MA: Harvard University Press.

Ginsburg, S. D., & Orlofsky, J. L. (1981). Ego identity status, ego development, and focus of control in college women. *Journal of Youth and Adolescence, 10,* 297–307.

Giordano, P. C., Cernkovich, S. A., & DeMaris, A. (1993). The family and peer relations of black adolescents. *Journal of Marriage and the Family, 55,* 277–287.

Gittler, J., & McPherson, M. (1991). Drugs and drug abuse. In *Information Please Almanac,* 1992 (45th ed.). Boston: Houghton Mifflin.

Glass, J. C., Jr., & Jolly, G. R. (1997). Satisfaction in later life among women 60 or over. *Educational Gerontology, 23,* 297–314.

Glass, T. A. (1998). Conjugating the "tenses" of function: Discordance among hypothetical, experimental, and enacted function in older adults. *Gerontologist, 38,* 101–112.

Gleckman H., Smart, T., Dwyer, P., Segal, T., & Weber, J. (1991, July 8). Race in the workplace. *Business Week,* pp. 50–62.

Glenn, N. D., & Kramer, K. B. (1987). Marriages and divorces of children of divorce. *Journal of Marriage and the Family, 49,* 811–826.

Glenn, N. D., & McLanahan, S. (1982). Children and marital happiness. A further specification of the relationship. *Journal of Marriage and the Family, 44,* 63–72.

Glenn, N. D., & Supancic, M. (1984). The social and demographic correlates of divorce and separation in the United States: An update and reconsideration. *Journal of Marriage and the Family, 46,* 563–575.

Glick, P. C. (1957). *American families.* New York: Wiley.

Glodis, K. A., & Blasi, A. (1993). The sense of self and identity among adolescents and adults. *Journal of Adolescent Research, 8,* 356–380.

Gold, M., & Petronio, R. J. (1980). Delinquent behavior in adolescence. In J. Adelson (Ed.), *Handbook of adolescent psychology* (pp. 495–535). New York: Wiley.

Goldberg, S. (1977). Infant development and mother-infant interaction in urban Zambia. In P. H. Leiderman, S. R. Tulkin, & A. Rosenfeld (Eds.), *Culture and infancy: Variations in the human experience* (pp. 211–244). New York: Academic Press.

Goldberg, S., & DiVitto, B. (1995). Parenting children born preterm. In M. H. Bornstein (Eds.), *Handbook of parenting, Volume 1: Children and parenting.* (pp. 209–232). Mahwah, NJ: Erlbaum.

Goldenberg, C. N. (1989). Parents' effects on academic grouping for reading: Three case studies. *American Educational Research Journal, 26,* 329–352.

Goldfield, E. C. (1989). Transition from rocking to crawling: Postural constraints on infant movement. *Developmental Psychology, 25,* 913–919.

Goldscheider, F. K., & Goldscheider, C. (1989). Family structure and conflict: Nest leaving expectations of young adults and their parents. *Journal of Marriage and the Family, 51,* 87–97.

Goldsmith, D. J., & Dun, S. A. (1997). Sex differences and similarities in the communication of social support. *Journal of Social and Personal Relationships, 14,* 317–337.

Goldsmith, H. H., Buss, A. H., Plomin, R., Rothbart, M. K., Thomas, A., Chess, S., Hinde, R. A., & McCall, R. B. (1987). Roundtable: What is temperament? Four approaches. *Child Development, 58,* 505–529.

Goldsmith, H. H., & Campos, J. J. (1986). Fundamental issues in the study of early development: The Denver twin temperament study. In M. E. Lamb & A. Brown (Eds.), *Advances in developmental psychology* (pp. 231–283). Hillsdale, NJ: Erlbaum.

Golinkoff, R. M., Hirsh-Pasek, K., Bailey, L. M., & Wenger, N. R. (1992). Young children and adults use lexical principles to learn new nouns. *Developmental Psychology, 28,* 99–108.

Golombok, S., Cook, R., Bish, A. & Murray, C. (1995). Families created by the new reproductive technologies: Quality of parenting and social and emotional development of the children. *Child Development, 66,* 285–298.

Gongla, P. A., & Thompson, E. H. (1987). Single-parent families. In M. B. Sussman & S. K. Steinmetz (Eds.), *Handbook of marriage and the family* (pp. 397–418). New York: Plenum.

Gopnik, A., & Meltzoff, A. (1987). The development of categorization in the second year and its relation to other cognitive and linguistic developments. *Child Development, 58,* 1523–1531.

Gopnik, A., & Meltzoff, A. N. (1992). Categorization and naming: Basic-level sorting in eighteen-month-olds and its relation to language. *Child Development, 63,* 1091–1103.

Gopnick, A., & Meltzoff, A. N. (1997). *Words, thoughts, and theories.* Cambridge, MA: MIT Press.

Gore, S., Aseltine, R. H., & Colten, M. E. (1993). Gender, social-relational involvement, and depression. *Journal of Research on Adolescence, 3,* 101–126.

Gorer, G. (1938). *Himalayan village: An account of the Lepchas of Sikkim.* London: Michael Joseph.

Gorman, C. (1997, March 31). What about the kids? *Time,* pp. 68–69.

Gornick, V. (1971, January 10). Consciousness. *New York Times Magazine.*

Gottesman, I. I. (1997). Twins: En route to QTLs for cognition. *Science, 276,* 1522–1523.

Gottesman, L. E., Quarterman, C. E., & Cohn, G. M. (1973). Psychosocial treatment of the aged. In C. Eisdorfer & M. P. Lawton (Eds.), *The psychology of adult development and aging.* Washington, DC: American Psychological Association.

Gottman, J. M., & Levenson, R. W. (1986). Assessing the role of emotion in marriage. *Behavioral Assessment, 8,* 31–48.

Grandquist, H. (1950). *Child problems among the Arabs.* Helsinki: Soderstrom.

Gratch, G., & Schatz, J. A. (1987). Cognitive development: The relevance of Piaget's infancy books. In J. D. Osofsky (Ed.), *Handbook of infant development* (2nd ed., pp. 204–237). New York: John Wiley & Sons.

Gray, P. (1996). Incorporating evolutionary theory into the teaching of psychology. *Teaching of Psychology, 29,* 207–209.

Green, R. J., Bettinger, M., & Zacks, E. (1995). Are lesbian couples fused and gay male couples disengaged? Questioning gender straightjackets. In J. Laird & R-J. Green (Eds.), *Lesbians and gays in couples and families* (pp. 185–230). San Francisco: Jossey-Bass.

Greenberg, E. F., & Nay, W. R. (1982). The intergenerational transmission of marital instability reconsidered. *Journal of Marriage and the Family, 44,* 335–347.

Greenhouse, L. (1992, June 30). Surprising decision: Majority issues warning on White House effort to overturn Roe. *The New York Times* pp. A1 & A7.

Greenwald, J. (1993, November 22). Bellboys with B.A.s. *Time, 142*(22), 36–37.

Gregory, L. W. (1995). The "turnaround" process: Factors influencing the school success of urban youth. *Journal of Adolescent Research, 10,* 136–154.

Griffin, L. J., & Alexander, K. L. (1978). Schooling and socioeconomic attainments: High school and college influences. *American Journal of Sociology, 84,* 319–347.

Grigsby, C., Baumann, D., Gregorich, S. E., & Roberts-Gray, C. (1990). Disaffiliation to entrenchment: A model for understanding homelessness. *Journal of Social Issues, 46,* 141–156.

Grolnick, W. S., Bridges, L. J., & Connell, J. P. (1996). Emotion regulation in two-year-olds: Strategies and emotional expression in four contexts. *Child Development, 67,* 928–941.

Grossman, F. K., Eichler, L. S., & Winickoff, S. A. (1980). *Pregnancy, birth, and parenthood*. San Francisco: Jossey-Bass.

Grusec, J. E. (1992). Social learning theory and developmental psychology: The legacies of Robert Sears and Albert Bandura. *Developmental Psychology, 28,* 776–786.

Grusec, J. E., & Abramovitch, R. (1982). Imitation of peers and adults in a natural setting: A functional analysis. *Child Development, 53,* 636–642.

Grych, J. H., & Fincham, F. D. (1990). Marital conflict and children's adjustment: A cognitive-contextual framework. *Psychological Bulletin, 108,* 267–290.

Guangzhao, Z. (1985). Retirement age for Chinese scientists. *Science, 230,* 738.

Gulko, J., Doyle, A., Serbin, L. A., & White, D. R. (1988). Conservation skills: A replicated study of order of acquisition across tasks. *Journal of Genetic Psychology, 149,* 425–439.

Gunnar, M. R., Larson, M. C., Hertsgaard, L., Harris, M. L., & Brodersen, L. (1992). The stressfulness of separation among 9-month-old infants: Effects of social context variables and infant temperament. *Child Development, 63,* 290–303.

Gunnar, M. R., Mangelsdorf, S., Larson, M., & Hertsgaard, L. (1989). Attachment, temperament, and adrenocortical activity in infancy: A study of psychoendocrine regulation. *Developmental Psychology, 25,* 355–363.

Guralnik, J. M., & Kaplan, G. A. (1989). Predictors of healthy aging: Prospective evidence from the Alameda County study. *American Journal of Public Health, 79,* 703–708.

Guralnik, J. M., & Simonsick, E. M. (1993). Physical disability in older Americans. *The Journals of Gerontology, 48,* 3–10.

Gustafson, S. B., Stattin, H., & Magnusson, D. (1992). Aspects of development of a career vs. homemaking orientation among females: The longitudinal influence of educational motivation and peers. *Journal of Research on Adolescence, 2,* 241–259.

Gutmann, D. (1987). *Reclaimed powers: Toward a new psychology of men and women in later life*. New York: Basic Books.

Gutmann, D. L. (1985). Deculturation and the American grandparent. In V. L. Bengtson & J. F. Robertson (Eds.), *Grandparenthood* (pp. 173–181). Newbury Park, CA: Sage.

Guttmann, B. (1932). *Die Stammeslehvender des Chagga* (Vol. 1). Munich: C. H. Beck.

Guttman, M. (1998, January 2–4). Who's healthier: Men or women? *USA Weekend,* p. 4–13.

Habicht, J. P., Yarbrough, C., Lechtig, A., & Klein, R. E. (1974). Relation of maternal supplementary feeding during pregnancy to birth weight and other sociological factors. In M. Winick (Ed.), *Nutrition and fetal development*. New York: Wiley.

Hadley, E. C., Ory, M. G., Suzman, R., & Weindruch, R. (1993). Foreword. *The Journals of Gerontology, 48,* vii–viii.

Hahn, R. A., & Muecke, M. A. (1987). The anthropology of birth in five U.S. ethnic populations: Implications for obstetrical practice. *Current Problems in Obstetrics, Gynecology, and Fertility, 10,* 133–171.

Hakuta, K., & Garcia, E. E. (1989). Bilingualism and education. *American Psychologist, 44,* 374–379.

Halford, G. S., & Boyle, F. M. (1985). Do young children understand conservation of number? *Child Development, 56,* 165–176.

Halford, W. K., Hahlweg, K., & Dunne, M. (1990). Cross-cultural study of marital communication and marital distress. *Journal of Marriage and the Family, 52,* 487–500.

Hall, W. S. (1989). Reading comprehension. *American Psychologist, 44,* 157–161.

Haller, E., & Waterman, M. (1985). The criteria of reading group assignments. *Reading Teacher, 38,* 772–782.

Hamon, R. R., & Blieszner, R. (1990). Filial responsibility expectations among adult child–older parent pairs. *Journal of Gerontology: Psychological Sciences, 45,* P110–P112.

Hans, S. L. (1987). Maternal drug addiction and young children. *Division of Child, Youth, and Family Services Newsletter, 10,* 5, 15.

Hansell, S. (1985). Adolescent friendship networks and distress in school. *Social Forces, 63,* 698–715.

Hanson, S. L., Myers, D. R., & Ginsburg, A. L. (1987). The role of responsibility and knowledge in reducing teenage out-of-wedlock childbearing. *Journal of Marriage and the Family, 49,* 241–256.

Hansson, R. O., DeKoekkoek, P. D., Neece, W. M., & Patterson, D. W. (1997). Successful aging at work: Annual review, 1992–1996: The older worker and transitions to retirement. *Journal of Vocational Behavior, 51,* 202–233.

Hardy, J. B., & Duggan, A. K. (1988). Teenage fathers and the fathers of infants of urban teenage mothers. *American Journal of Public Health, 78,* 919–922.

Harris, M. (1992). *Language experience and early language development: From input to uptake*. Hillsdale, NJ: Erlbaum.

Harris, M. J., & Rosenthal, R. (1985). Mediation of interpersonal expectancy effects: 31 meta-analyses. *Psychological Bulletin, 97,* 363–386.

Harris, P. (1975). Development of search and object permanence during infancy. *Psychological Bulletin, 82,* 332–334.

Harris, P. L., & Kavanaugh, R. D. (1993). *Young children's understanding of pretense. Monographs of the Society for Research in Child Development, 58*(1).

Harris, T., Kovar, M. G., Suzman, R., Kleinman, J. C., & Feldman, J. J. (1989). Longitudinal study of physical ability in the oldest old. *American Journal of Public Health, 79,* 700.

Hart, B., & Risley, T. R. (1992). American parenting of language-learning children: Persisting differences in family-child interactions observed in natural home environments. *Developmental Psychology, 28,* 1096–1105.

Hart, C. H., Ladd, G. W., Burleson, B. R. (1990). Children's expectations of the outcomes of social strategies: Relations with sociometric status and maternal disciplinary styles. *Child Development, 61,* 127–137.

Harter, S. (1982). The perceived competence scale for children. *Child Development, 53,* 87–97.

Harter, S. (1985). Competence as a dimension of self-evaluation: Towards a comprehensive model of self-worth. In R. Leahy (Ed.), *The development of the self* (pp. 55–121). New York: Academic Press.

Harter, S. (1985). *The self-perception profile for children.* (Manual). Denver, CO: University of Denver Press.

Harter, S. (1993). Visions of self: Beyond the me in the mirror. In J. E. Jacobs (Ed.), *Nebraska Symposium on Motivation: 1992* (Vol. 40, pp. 99–144). Lincoln: University of Nebraska Press.

Harter, S., Whitesell, N. R., & Kowalski, P. (1992). Individual differences in the effects of educational transitions on young adolescents' perceptions of competence and motivational orientation. *American Educational Research Journal, 29,* 777–807.

Hartup, W. W. (1989). Social relationships and their developmental significance. *American Psychologist, 44,* 120–126.

Harvey, J. H., Stein, S. K., & Scott, P. K. (1995). Fifty years of grief: Accounts and reported psychological reactions of Normandy invasion veterans. *Journal of Narrative & Life History, 5,* 315–332.

Hary, J. (1983). Gay male and lesbian relationships. In E. D. Macklin & R. Rubin (Eds.), *Contemporary family forms and alternative lifestyles: Handbook on research and theory.* Newbury Park, CA: Sage.

Haskett, M. E., & Kistner, J. A. (1991). Social interactions and peer perceptions of young physically abused children. *Child Development, 62,* 979–990.

Haskins, R. (1989). Beyond metaphor: The efficacy of early childhood education. *American Psychologist, 44,* 274–282.

Havighurst, R. J. (1972). *Developmental tasks and education* (3rd ed.). New York: David McKay.

Hawkins, J. L., Weisberg, C., & Ray, D. W. (1980). Spouse differences in communication style preference, perception, behavior. *Journal of Marriage and the Family, 42,* 585–593.

Hawley, G. A. (1988). *Measures of psychosocial development: (MPD).* Odessa, FL: PAR.

Hay, D. F. (1980). Multiple functions of proximity seeking in infancy. *Child Development, 52,* 636–645.

Hays, J. A. (1984). Aging and family resources: Availability and proximity of kin. *Gerontologist, 24,* 149–153.

Hayslip, B., Jr., & Brookshire, R. G. (1985). Relationships among abilities in elderly adults: A time lag analysis. *Journal of Gerontology, 40,* 748–750.

Healthy People 2000: National Health Promotion and Disease Prevention Objectives. (1990). Washington, DC: U.S. Department of Health and Human Services, Public Health Service, DHHS publication PHS 91-50212.

Hearold, S. (1986). A synthesis of 1043 effects of television on social behavior. In G. Comstock (Ed.), *Public communications and behavior* (Vol. 1, pp. 65–133). New York: Academic Press.

Heath, S. B. (1989). Oral and literate traditions among black Americans living in poverty. *American Psychologist, 44,* 367–372.

Heatherington, E. M., Cox, M., & Cox, R. (1985). Long-term effects of divorce and remarriage on the adjustment of children. *Journal of the American Academy of Psychiatry, 24,* 518–530.

Heatherington, E. M., Stanley-Hagan, M., & Anderson, E. R. (1989). Marital transitions: A child's perspective. *American Psychologist, 44,* 303–312.

Heckhausen, J. (1987). Balancing for weaknesses and challenging developmental potential: A longitudinal study of mother-infant dyads in apprenticeship interactions. *Developmental Psychology, 23,* 762–770.

Heckhausen, J., Dixon, R. A., & Baltes, P. B. (1989). Gains and losses in development throughout adulthood as perceived by different adult age groups. *Developmental Psychology, 25,* 109–121.

Heckman, N. A., Bryson, R., & Bryson, J. B. (1977). Problems of professional couples: A content analysis. *Journal of Marriage and the Family, 39,* 323–330.

Heinicke, C. M. (1995). Determinants of the transition to parenting. In M. H. Bornstein (Ed.), *Handbook of parenting, Vol 3: Status and social conditions of parenting.* Mahwah, NJ: Erlbaum, 277–303.

Heinicke, C. M., & Guthrie, D. (1992). Stability and change in husband-wife adaptation and the development of positive parent-child relationships. *Infant and Behavior Development, 15,* 109–127.

Heitlinger, A. (1989). Current medical, legal, and demographic perspectives on artificial reproduction in Czechoslovakia. *American Journal of Public Health, 79,* 57–61.

Helman, C. G. (1990). *Culture, health, and illness* (2nd ed.). London: Wright.

Hendricks, L. E., & Fullilove, R. E. (1983). Locus of control and use of contraception among unmarried black adolescent fathers and their controls: A preliminary report. *Journal of Youth and Adolescence, 12,* 225–233.

Henkens, K., & Tazelaar, F. (1997). Explaining retirement decisions of civil servants in the Netherlands: Intentions, behavior, and the discrepancy between the two. *Research on Aging, 19,* 139–173.

Herbert, W. (1996). The moral child. *U.S. News & World Report, 120,* 52–59.

Herkovits, M. (1948). *Man and his works.* New York: Knopf.

Huxley, J. (1942). *Evolution: The magic synthesis.* New York: Harper.

Herman, M. R., Dornbusch, S. M., Herron, M. C., & Herting, J. R. (1997). The influence of family regulation, connection, and psychological autonomy on six measures of adolescent functioning. *Journal of Adolescent Research, 12,* 34–67.

Hernandez, D. J. (1993). Childhood poverty: Trends, causes, and policies. *The Child, Youth, and Family Services Quarterly, 16,* 3–4.

Herpertz-Dahlmann, B., Wewetzer, C., Hennighausen, K., & Remschmidt, H. (1996). Outcome, psychosocial functioning, and prognostic factors in adolescent anorexia nervosa as determined by prospective follow-up assessment. *Journal of Youth and Adolescence, 25,* 455–472.

Herold, E. S., & Marshall, S. K. (1996). Adolescent sexual development. In G. R. Adams, R. Montemayor, & T. P. Gullotta (Eds.), *Psychosocial development during adolescence: Advances in adolescent development* (Vol. 8, pp. 62–94). Thousand Oaks, CA: Sage.

Herring, C., & Wilson-Sadberry, K. R. (1993). Preference or necessity? Changing work roles of black and white women, 1973–1990. *Journal of Marriage and the Family, 55,* 315–325.

Hertzog, C. (1989). Influences of cognitive slowing on age differences in intelligence. *Developmental Psychology, 25,* 636–651.

Hertzog, D., & Schaie, K. W. (1988). Stability and change in adult intelligence: 2. Simultaneous analysis of longitudinal means and covariance structures. *Psychology and Aging, 3,* 122–130.

Herzog, A. R., House, J. S., & Morgan, J. N. (1991). Relation of work and retirement to health and well-being in older age. *Psychology and Aging, 6,* 202–211.

Hess, R., & Holloway, S. (1984). Family and school as educational institutions. *Review of Child Development Research: Vol. 7. The Family* (pp. 179–222). Chicago: University of Chicago Press.

Hetherington, E. M. (1967). The effects of familial variables on sex typing, on parent-child similarity, and on imitation in children. In J. P. Hill (Ed.), *Minnesota Symposium on Child Psychology* (Vol. 1, pp. 82–107). Minneapolis: University of Minnesota Press.

Hetherington, E. M. (1989). Coping with family transitions: Winners, losers, and survivors. *Child Development, 60,* 1–14.

Heynen, J. (1990). *One hundred over 100: Moments with one hundred North American Centenarians.* Golden Co: Fulcrum Publishing.

Hickey, T. L., & Peduzzi, J. D. (1987). Structure and development of the visual system. In P. Salapatek & L. Cohen (Eds.), *Handbook of infant perception* (Vol. 1). Orlando, FL; Academic Press.

Hickson, F. C., Davies, P. M., Hunt, A. J., & Weatherburn, P. (1992). Maintenance of open gay relationships: Some strategies for protection against HIV. *AIDS Care, 4,* 409–419.

Hill, J. P. (1988). Adapting to menarche: Familial control and conflict. In M. R. Gunnar & W. A. Collins (Eds.), *Development during the transition to adolescence. Minnesota Symposium on Child Psychology* (Vol. 21, pp. 43–77). Hillsdale, NJ: Erlbaum.

Hill, R. (1965). Decision making and the family life cycle. In E. Shanas & G. Streib (Eds.), *Social structure and the family: Generational relations.* Englewood Cliffs, NJ: Prentice-Hall.

Hillman, J. L., & Stricker, G. (1994). A linkage of knowledge and attitudes toward elderly sexuality: Not necessarily a uniform relationship. *Gerontologist, 34,* 256–260.

Hing, E., & Bloom, B. (1990). Long-term care for the functionally dependent elderly. *Vital Health Statistics, 13,* No. 104.

Hodges, J., & Tizard, B. (1989). Social and family relationships of ex-institutional adolescents. *Journal of Child Psychology and Psychiatry, 30,* 77–97.

Hodson, D. S., & Skeen, P. (1994). Sexuality and aging: The hammerlock of myths. *Journal of Applied Gerontology, 13,* 219–235.

Hof, L., & Miller, W. R. (1981). *Marriage enrichment: Philosophy, process, and program.* Bowie, MD: R. J. Brady.

Hofer, T. P., & Katz, S. J. (1996). Healthy behaviors among women in the United States and Ontario: The effect on use of preventive care. *American Journal of Public Health, 86,* 1755–1759.

Hoffman, M. L. (1970). Moral development. In P. H. Mussen (Ed.), *Carmichael's manual of child psychology* (3rd ed., Vol. 2). New York: Wiley.

Hoffman, M. L. (1977). Moral internalization: Current theory and research. In L. Berkowitz (Ed.), *Advances in experimental social psychology* (Vol. 10). New York: Academic Press.

Hoffman, M. L. (1982). Development of prosocial motivation: Empathy and guilt. In N. Eisenberg (Ed.), *The development of prosocial behavior* (pp. 281–313). New York: Academic Press.

Hoffman, M. L. (1987). The contribution of empathy to justice and moral judgment. In N. Eisenberg & J. Strayer (Eds.), *Empathy and its development* (pp. 47–80). Cambridge: Cambridge University Press.

Hoffman, S. J. (1985). Play and the acquisition of literacy. *Quarterly Newsletter of the Laboratory of Comparative Human Cognition, 7,* 89–95.

Hoffner, C., & Badzinski, D. M. (1989). Children's integration of facial and situational cues to emotion. *Child Development, 60,* 411–422.

Hogan, D. P., Eggebeen, D. J., & Clogg, C. C. (1993). The structure of intergenerational exchanges in American families. *American Journal of Sociology, 98,* 1428–1458.

Hogan, T. D., & Steinnes, D. N. (1998). A logistic model of the seasonal migration decision for elderly households in Arizona and Minnesota. *Gerontologist, 38,* 152–158.

Hoge, D. R., & McCarthy, J. D. (1984). Influence of individual and group identity salience in the global self-esteem of youth. *Journal of Personality and Social Psychology, 47,* 403–414.

Holahan, C. K., Sears, R. R., & Cronbach, L. J. (1995). *The gifted group in later maturity.* Stanford, CA: Stanford University Press.

Holden, C. (1987). The genetics of personality. *Science, 237,* 598–601.

Holden, C. (1989). Koop finds abortion evidence "inconclusive." *Science, 243,* 730–731.

Holland, J. L. (1997). *Making vocational choices: A theory of vocational personalities and work environments.* (3rd ed.). Odessa, FL: Psychological Assessment Resources.

Holloway, S. D. (1988). Concepts of ability and effort in Japan and the United States. *Review of Educational Research, 58,* 327–345.

Holloway, S. D., & Fuller, B. (1992). The great child-care experiment: What are the lessons for school improvement? *Educational Researcher, 21,* 12–19.

Holman, T. B., & Jacquart, M. (1988). Leisure-activity patterns and marital satisfaction. *Journal of Marriage and the Family, 50,* 69–78.

Holmes, T. H., & Rahe, R. H. (1967). The social readjustment rating scale. *Journal of Psychosomatic Research, 11,* 213–218.

Holstein, J. A., & Gubrium, J. F. (1995). *The active interview.* Thousand Oaks, CA: Sage.

Holzman, C., & Paveth, N. (1998). Preterm birth. From prediction to prevention. *American Journal of Public Health, 88,* 183–184.

Hooyman, N. R., & Kiyak, H. A. (1993). *Social gerontology* (3rd ed.). Boston: Allyn and Bacon.

Hopkins, B., & Westra, T. (1990). Motor development, maternal expectation, and the role of handling. *Infant Behavior and Development, 13,* 117–122.

Hopkins, D. R., Murrah, B., Hoeger, W. W. K., & Rhodes, R. C. (1990). Effect of low-impact aerobic dance on the functional fitness of elderly women. *Gerontologist, 30,* 189–192.

Hopper, K. (1990). Public shelter as "a hybrid institution": Homeless men in historical perspective. *Journal of Social Issues, 46,* 13–29.

Hopper, K., & Hamberg, L. (1986). The making of America's homeless: From skid row to new poor, 1945–1984. In R. Bratt, C. Harman, & A. Meyerson (Eds.), *Critical per-*

spectives on housing. Philadelphia: Temple University Press.

Horn, J. L. (1979). The rise and fall of human abilities. *Journal of Research and Development in Education, 12*, 59–78.

Horn, J. L. (1982). The aging of human abilities. In B. B. Wolman (Ed.), *Handbook of developmental psychology* (pp. 847–870). Englewood Cliffs, NJ: Prentice-Hall.

Hornblower, M. (1996). It takes a school. *Time, 147*, 36–38.

Hornik, R., & Gunnar, M. R. (1988). A descriptive analysis of infant social referencing. *Child Development, 59*, 626–634.

Hornik, R., Risenhoover, N., & Gunnar, M. (1987). The effects of maternal positive, neutral, and negative affective communications on infant responses to new toys. *Child Development, 58*, 937–944.

Horobin, K., & Acredolo, C. (1989). The impact of probability judgments on reasoning about multiple possibilities. *Child Development, 60*(1), 183–200.

Horst, E. A. (1995). Reexamining gender issues in Erikson's stages of identity and intimacy. *Journal of Counseling and Development, 73*, 271–278.

Horwitz, A. V., White, H. R., & Howell-White, S. (1996). Becoming married and mental health: A longitudinal study of a cohort of young adults. *Journal of Marriage and the Family, 58*, 895–907.

Hochschild, A. (1989). *The second shift*. New York: Avon.

Hodson, R., & Sullivan, T. A. (1995). *The social organization of work*. Belmont, CA: Wadsworth.

House, J. S. (1985, Winter). Social support. *LSA, 8*, 5–8.

Houseknecht, S. K. (1987). Voluntary childlessness. In M. B. Sussman & S. K. Steinmetz (Eds.), *Handbook of marriage and the family* (pp. 369–396). New York: Plenum.

Houseknecht, S. K., & Macke, A. S. (1981). Combining marriage and career: The marital adjustment of professional women. *Journal of Marriage and the Family, 43*, 651–661.

Houseknecht, S. K., Vaughan, S., & Statham, A. (1987). Singlehood and the careers of professional women. *Journal of Marriage and the Family, 49*, 353–366.

Howell, C. (1994). Coroner delivers primer to directors. *Arkansas-Democrat Gazette*, Wed. Feb. 2.

Howes, C. (1987). Peer interaction of young children. *Monographs of the Society for Research in Child Development, 53*(1, Serial No. 217).

Howes, C., & Phillipsen, L. (1992). Gender and friendship: Relationships within peer groups of young children. *Social Development, 1*, 230–242.

Howes, C., & Stewart, P. (1987). Child's play with adults, toys, and peers: An examination of family and child-care influences. *Developmental Psychology, 23*, 423–430.

Howes, C., Unger, O., & Seidner, L. B. (1989). Social pretend play in toddlers: Parallels with social play and with solitary pretend. *Child Development, 60*, 77–84.

Howes, P., & Markman, H. J. (1989). Marital quality and child functioning: A longitudinal investigation. *Child Development, 60*, 1044–1051.

Hoyer, W. J., & Rybash, J. M. (1994). Characterizing adult cognitive development. *Journal of Adult Development, 1*, 7–12.

Hsu, L. K. G. (1996). Outcome of early onset anorexia nervosa: What do we know? *Journal of Youth and Adolescence, 25*, 563–568.

Huber, J. (1990). Macro-micro links in gender stratification. *American Sociological Review, 55*, 1–10.

Hubert, N. C., Wachs, T. D., Peters-Martin, P., & Gandour, M. J. (1982). The study of early temperament: Measurement and conceptual issues. *Child Development, 53*, 571–600.

Hubner-Funk, S. (1983). Transition into occupational life: Environmental and sex differences regarding the status passage from school to work. *Adolescence, 18*, 709–723.

Huerta, R., Mena, A., Malacara, J., & Diaz, J. (1995). Symptoms at perimenopausal period: Its association with attitudes toward sexuality, life-style, family function, and FSH levels. *Psychoneuroendocrinology, 20*, 135–148.

Huesmann, L. R., & Eron, L. D. (1986). *Television and the aggressive child: A cross-national comparison*. Hillsdale, NJ: Erlbaum.

Huesmann, L. R., & Malamuth, N. M. (1986). Media violence and antisocial behavior: An overview. *Journal of Social Issues, 42*, 1–6.

Hultsch, D. P. & Vixon, R. A. (1990). Learning and memory in aging. In J. E. Birren & K. W. Schaie (Eds.) *Handbook of the psychology of aging*. San Diego: Academic Press.

Hunt, E. B. (1995). *Will we be smart enough? A cognitive analysis of the coming workforce*. New York: Russell Sage.

Hunter, A. G. (1997). Counting on grandmothers: Black mothers' and fathers' reliance on grandmothers for parenting support. *Journal of Family Issues, 18*, 251–269.

Huston, A. C., Donnerstein, E., Fairchild, H., Feshbach, N. D., Katz, P. A., Murray, J. P., Rubinstein, E. A., Wilcox, B. L., & Zuckerman, D. (1992). *Big world, small screen: The role of television in American society*. Lincoln: University of Nebraska Press.

Huston, A. C., McLoyd, V. C., & Coll, C. G. (1994). Children and poverty: Issues in contemporary research. *Child Development, 65*, 275–282.

Hutt, S. J., Tyler, S., Hutt, C., & Foy, H. (1988). *Play exploration and learning: A natural history of the preschool*. New York: Routledge.

Huxley, J. (1941). *The uniqueness of man*. London: Chatto & Windus.

Huxley, J. (1942). *Evolution: The magic synthesis*. New York: Harper.

Hymel, S., Bowker, A., & Woody, E. (1993). Aggressive versus withdrawn unpopular children: Variations in peer and self-perceptions of multiple domains. *Child Development, 64*, 879–896.

Hymel, S., Rubin, K. H., Rowden, L., & LeMare, L. (1990). Children's peer relationships: Longitudinal predictions of internalizing and externalizing problems from middle to late childhood. *Child Development, 61*, 2004–2021.

Iannotti, R. J. (1985). Naturalistic and structured assessments of prosocial behavior in preschool children: The influence of empathy and perspective taking. *Developmental Psychology, 21*, 46–55.

Iannotti, R. J., & Bush, P. J. (1992). Perceived versus actual friends' use of alcohol, cigarettes, marijuana, and cocaine: Which has the most influence? *Journal of Youth and Adolescence, 21*, 375–389.

Idler, E. L. (1987). Religious involvement and the health of the elderly: some hypotheses and an initial test. *Social Forces, 66*, 226–238.

Ingersoll-Dayton, B., & Antonucci, T. C. (1988). Reciprocal and nonreciprocal social support: Contrasting sides of intimate relationships. *Gerontology, 43*, S65–S73.

Inhelder, B., & Piaget, J. (1958). *The growth of logical thinking from childhood to adolescence.* New York: Basic Books.

Isabella, R. A., & Belsky, J. (1991). Interactional synchrony and the origins of infant-mother attachment: A replication study. *Child Development, 62*, 373–384.

Isabella, R. A., Belsky, J., & von Eye, A. (1989). Origins of infant-mother attachment: An examination of interactional synchrony during the infant's first year. *Developmental Psychology, 19*, 418–426.

Izard, C. E. (1977). *Human emotion.* New York: Plenum.

Izard, C. E., Haynes, O. M., Chisholm, G., & Baak, K. (1991). Emotional determinants of infant-mother attachment. *Child Development, 62*, 906–917.

Jack, D. C., & Dill, D. (1992). The silencing the self scale: The schemas of intimacy associated with depression in women. *Psychology of Women Quarterly, 16*, 97–106.

Jacklin, C. N., & Maccoby, E. E. (1978). Social behavior at 33 months in same-sex and mixed-sex dyads. *Child Development, 49*, 557–569.

Jacobson, E. (1964). *The self and the object world.* New York: International Universities Press.

Jacobson, N. S. & Christensen, A. (1996). *Integrative couple therapy: Promoting acceptance and change.* New York: W. W. Norton.

Jacobson, S. W., Fein, G. G., Jacobson, J. L., Schwartz, P. M., & Dowler, J. K. (1985). The effect of intrauterine PCB exposure on visual recognition memory. *Child Development, 56*, 853–860.

Jacobson, S. W., & Frye, K. F. (1991). Effect of maternal social support on attachment: Experimental evidence. *Child Development, 62*, 572–582.

Jacobson, S. W., Jacobson, J. L., O'Neill, J. M., Padgett, R. J., Frankowski, J. J., & Bihun, J. T. (1992). Visual expectation and dimensions of infant information processing. *Child Development, 63*, 711–724.

Jahoda, M. (1982). *Employment and unemployment.* Cambridge, England: Cambridge University Press.

James, W. (1892/1961). *Psychology: The briefer course.* New York: Harper & Row.

Jarboe, P. J. (1986). A comparison study of distress and marital adjustment in infertile and expectant couples. Unpublished doctoral dissertation, Ohio State University.

Jayakody, R., Chatters, L. M., & Taylor, R. J. (1993). Family support to single and married African-American mothers: The provision of financial, emotional, and child care assistance. *Journal of Marriage and the Family, 55*, 261–276.

Jecker, N. S., & Schneiderman, L. J. (1994). Is dying young worse than dying old? *Gerontologist, 34*, 66–72.

Jeffries, V. (1993). Virtue and attraction: Validation of measure of love. *Journal of Social and Personal Relationships, 10*, 99–118.

Jehle, F. F. (1994). *The complete and easy guide to social security and medicare: 1994.* Peterborough, NH: Fraser-Vance Publishing.

Jenkins, L. E. (1989). The black family and academic achievement. In G. L. Berry & J. K. Asamen (Eds.), *Black students* (pp. 138–152). Newbury Park, CA: Sage.

Jetten, J., Spears, R., & Manstead, A. S. R. (1996). Intergroup norms and intergroup discrimination: distinctive self-categorization and social identity effects. *Journal of Personality and Social Psychology, 71*, 1222–1233.

Jewett, S. (1973). Longevity and the longevity syndrome. *Gerontologist, 13*, 91–99.

Jockin, V., McGue, M., & Lykken, D. T. (1996). Personality and divorce: A genetic analysis. *Journal of Personality and Social Psychology, 71*, 288–299.

Johnston, L. D., O'Malley, P. M., & Bachman, J. G. (1997). *National survey results on drug use from The Monitoring the Future Study, 1975–1995. Vol. II: College students and young adults.* Washington, DC: National Institutes of Health.

Johnston, L. D., O'Malley, P. M., & Bachman, J. D. G. (1996). *National survey results on drug use from Monitoring the Future Study, 1975–1995: Vol. 1. Secondary school students.* Rockville, MD: National Institute on Drug Abuse.

Jones, J. B. (1997). Representations of menopause and their health care implications: A qualitative study. *American Journal of Preventive Medicine, 13*, 58–65.

Jones, J. M. (1988). Racism in black and white: A bicultural model of reaction and evolution. In P. A. Katz, & D. A. Taylor (Eds.), *Eliminating racism* (pp. 117–136). New York: Plenum.

Jones, J. T., & Cunningham, J. D. (1996). Attachment styles and other predictors of relationship satisfaction in dating couples. *Personal Relationships, 3*, 387–399.

Jones, R. M. (1992). Ego identity and adolescent problem behavior. In G. R. Adams, T. P. Gullota, & R. Montemayor (Eds.), *Adolescent identity formation* (pp. 216–233). Newbury Park, CA: Sage.

Jones, S. S., Smith, L. B., & Landau, B. (1991). Object properties and knowledge in early lexical learning. *Child Development 62*, 499–516.

Jones-Webb, R. J., & Snowden, L. R. (1993). Symptoms of depression among blacks and whites. *American Journal of Public Health, 83*, 240–244.

Jonker, C., Launer, L. J., Hooijer, C., & Lindeboom, J. (1996). Memory complaints and memory impairment in older individuals. *Journal of the American Geriatrics Society, 44*, 44–49.

Jordan, B. (1983). *Birth in four cultures: A crosscultural investigation of childbirth in Yucatan, Holland, Sweden and the United States* (3rd ed.). Montreal: Eden Press.

Jordan, J. V. (1997). Relational development through mutual empathy. In A. C. Bohart & L. S. Greenberg (Eds.), *Empathy reconsidered: New directions in psychotherapy.* Washington, DC: American Psychological Association.

Jordan, N. C., Huttenlocher, J., & Levine, S. C. (1992). Differential calculation abilities in young children from middle- and low-income families. *Developmental Psychology, 28*, 644–653.

Jorgensen, S. R., & Gaudy, J. C. (1980). Self-disclosure and satisfaction in marriage: The relation examined. *Family Relations, 29*, 281–287.

Josephson, W. L. (1987). Television violence and children's aggression: Testing the priming, social script, and disinhibition predictions. *Journal of Personality and Social Psychology, 53*, 882–890.

Josselson, R. (1987). *Finding herself: Pathways to identity development in women.* San Francisco: Jossey-Bass.

Judson, F. N. (1989). What do we really know about AIDS control? *American Journal of Public Health, 79,* 878–882.

Jussim, L. (1990a). Expectancies and social issues: Introduction: *Journal of Social Issues, 46,* 1–8.

Jussim, L. (1990b). Social realities and social problems: The role of expectancies. *Journal of Social Issues, 46,* 9–34.

Kacerguis, M. A., & Adams, G. R. (1980). Erikson stage resolution: The relationship between identity and intimacy. *Journal of Youth and Adolescence, 9,* 117–126.

Kagan, J. (1958). The concept of identification. *Psychological Review, 65,* 296–305.

Kagan, J. (1984). The idea of emotion in human development. In C. E. Izard, J. Kagan, & R. B. Zajonc (Eds.), *Emotions, cognition, and behavior* (pp. 38–72). Cambridge: Cambridge University Press.

Kagan, S. L. (1990). Readiness 2000: Rethinking rhetoric and responsibility. *Phi Delta Kappan, 1,* 21–23.

Kagitcibasi, C. (1990). Family and socialization in cross-cultural perspective: A model of change. In J. J. Berman (Ed.), *Nebraska Symposium on Motivation, 1989: Cross-cultural perspectives.* Lincoln, NE: University of Nebraska Press.

Kahana, B. (1982). Social behavior and aging. In B. B. Wolman (Ed.), *Handbook of developmental psychology* (pp. 871–889). Englewood Cliffs, NJ: Prentice-Hall.

Kahana, B., Kahana, E., & McLenigan, P. (1980). The adventurous aged: Voluntary relocation in the later years. Paper presented at the meeting of the American Orthopsychiatric Association, Toronto, Canada.

Kalb, C. (1997 May 5). How old is too old? *Newsweek,* p. 64.

Kalish, C. W., & Gelman, S. A. (1992). On wooden pillows: Multiple classification and children's category-based inductions. *Child Development, 63,* 1536–1557.

Kalish, R. A., & Reynolds, D. K. (1976). *Death and ethnicity: A psychocultural study.* Los Angeles, CA: University of Southern California Press.

Kalleberg, A. L., & Rosenfeld, R. A. (1990). Work in the family and in the labor market. *Journal of Marriage and the Family, 52,* 331–346.

Kalmijn, M. (1991). Shifting boundaries: Trends in religious and educational homogamy. *American Sociological Review, 56,* 786–800.

Kalverboer, A. F., Hopkins, B., & Geuze, R. (1993). *Motor development in early and later childhood: Longitudinal approaches.* New York: Cambridge University Press.

Kamo, Y. (1993). Determinants of marital satisfaction: A comparison of the United States and Japan. *Journal of Social and Personal Relationships, 10,* 551–568.

Kamptner, N. L. (1988). Identity development in late adolescence: Causal modeling of social and familial influences. *Journal of Youth and Adolescence, 17,* 493–514.

Kanter, R. M. (1989). The new managerial work. *Harvard Business Review, 67,* 85–92.

Kanungo, R. N., & Misra, S. (1992). Managerial resourcefulness: A reconceptualization of management skills. *Human Relations, 45,* 1311–1332.

Kaplan, B. J. (1986). A psychobiological review of depression during pregnancy. *Psychology of Women Quarterly, 10,* 35–48.

Karmel, M. (1983). *Thank you, Dr. Lamaze.* Philadelphia: Lippincott.

Karp, D. A. (1989). The social construction of retirement among professionals 50–60 years old. *Gerontologist, 29,* 750–760.

Kart, C. S., Longino, C. F., & Ullmann, S. G. (1989). Comparing the economically advantaged and the pension elite: 1980 census profiles. *Gerontologist, 29,* 745–749.

Kasper, J. D. (1997). Long-term care moves into the mainstream. *Gerontologist, 37,* 274–276.

Kastenbaum, R. (1981). *Death, society and human experience* (2nd ed.) Palo Alto, CA: Mayfield.

Kastenbaum, R. (1985). Dying and death: A life-span approach. In J. Birren and K. W. Schaie (Eds.), *Handbook of the psychology of aging.* New York: Van Nostrand Reinhold.

Katchadourian, H. (1990). Sexuality. In S. S. Feldman & G. R. Elliott (Eds.), *At the threshold: The developing adolescent* (pp. 330–351). Cambridge: Harvard University Press.

Katz, D., & Kahn, R. L. (1966). *The social psychology of organizations.* New York: Wiley.

Katz, P. A., & Walsh, P. V. (1991). Modification of children's gender-stereotyped behavior. *Child Development, 62,* 338–351.

Kaufman, G. (1989). *The psychology of shame.* New York: Springer.

Kaye, L. W. (1995). *New developments in home care services for the elderly: Innovations in policy, program, and practice.* Binghampton, NY: The Haworth Press.

Keating, D. P. (1990). Adolescent thinking. In S. S. Feldman & G. R. Elliott (Eds.), *At the threshold: The developing adolescent* (pp. 54–90). Cambridge: Harvard University Press.

Kegan, R. (1982). *The evolving self: Problems and process in human development.* Cambridge: Harvard University Press.

Keil, P. F. (1975). *The development of the young child's ability to anticipate the outcome of simple causal events.* Paper presented at the meeting of the Society for Research in Child Development, Denver, CO.

Keith, J. (1982). *Old people as people: Social and cultural influences on aging and old age.* Boston: Little, Brown.

Keith, J. (1994). Old age and age integration: An anthropological perspective. In M. W. Riley, R. L. Kahn, A. Foner, & K. A. Mack (Eds.), *Age and structural lag: Society's failure to provide meaningful opportunities in work, family, and leisure* (pp. 197–216). New York: John Wiley & Sons.

Keith, V. M., & Finlay, B. (1988). Parental divorce and children's education, marriage, and divorce. *Journal of Marriage and the Family, 50,* 797–810.

Keller, J. W., Pitrowski, C., & McLeod, C. R. (1991). The development of a career development program. *Education, 112,* 470–473.

Kelly, M. L., Power, T. G., & Wimbush, D. D. (1992). Determinants of disciplinary practices in low-income black mothers. *Child Development, 63,* 573–582.

Keltenbach, K., Weinraub, M., & Fullard, W. (1980). Infant wariness toward strangers reconsidered: Infants' and mothers' reactions to unfamiliar persons. *Child Development, 51,* 1197–1202.

Kermoian, R., & Campos, J. J. (1988). Locomotor experience: A facilitator of spatial cognitive development. *Child Development, 59,* 908–917.

Kessen, W. (1965). *The child.* New York: Wiley.

Kessler, R. C., Foster, C., Webster, P. S., & House, J. S. (1992). The relationship between age and depressive symptoms in two national surveys. *Psychology and Aging, 7,* 119–126.

Ketterlinus, R. D., Lamb, M. E., Nitz, K., & Elster, A. B. (1992). Adolescent nonsexual and sex-related problem behaviors. *Journal of Adolescent Research, 7,* 431–456.

Kimura, D. (1992). Sex differences in the brain. *Scientific American, 267,* 119–125.

Kindermann, T. A. (1996). Strategies for the study of individual development within naturally-existing peer groups. *Social Development, 5,* 158–173.

King, L. A. (1993). Emotional expression, ambivalence over expression, and marital satisfaction. *Journal of Social and Personal Relationships, 10,* 601–607.

Kinney, J. M., & Stephens, M. A. P. (1989). Hassles and uplifts of giving care to a family member with dementia. *Psychology and Aging, 4,* 402–408.

Kirby, J. J. (1996). Welfare to work transition. *Human Development Bulletin, 1,* 1–5.

Kite, M. E. (1996). Age, gender, and occupational label: A test of social role theory. *Psychology of Women Quarterly, 20,* 361–374.

Kite, M. E., Deaux, K., & Miele, M. (1991). Stereotypes of young and old: Does age outweigh gender? *Psychology and Aging, 6,* 19–27.

Kitson, G. C. (1982). Attachment to the spouse in divorce: A scale and its application. *Journal of Marriage and the Family, 44,* 379–393.

Kitson, G. C., & Morgan, L. A. (1990). Consequences of divorce. *Journal of Marriage and the Family, 52,* 913–924.

Kitzinger, S. (1982). The social context of birth: Some comparisons between childbirth in Jamaica and Britain. In C. P. MacCormack (Ed.), *Ethnography of fertility and birth* (pp. 181–203). London: Academic Press.

Kivnick, H. Q. (1983). Dimensions of grandparenthood meaning: Deductive conceptualization and empirical derivation. *Journal of Personality and Social Psychology, 44,* 1056–1068.

Kivnick, H. Q. (1985). Grandparenthood and mental health: Meaning, behavior, and satisfaction. In V. L. Bengtson & J. F. Robertson (Eds.), *Grandparenthood* (pp. 151–158). Newbury Park, CA: Sage.

Klemmack, D. L., & Roff, L. L. (1984). Fear of personal aging and subjective well-being in later life. *Journal of Gerontology, 39,* 756–758.

Kline, D. W. (1994). Optimizing the visibility of displays for older observers. *Experimental Aging Research, 20,* 11–23.

Kline, D. W., & Scialfa, C. T. (1997). Sensory and perceptual functioning: Basic research and human factors implications. In A. D. Fisk & W. A. Rogers (Eds.), *Handbook of human factors and the older adult* (pp. 27–54). San Diego, CA: Academic Press.

Klinnert, M. D., Emde, R. N., Butterfield, P., & Campos, J. J. (1986). Social referencing: The infant's use of emotional signals from a friendly adult with mother present. *Developmental Psychology, 22,* 427–432.

Klint, K. A., & Weiss, M. R. (1987). Perceived competence and motives for participating in youth sports: A test of Harter's competence motivation theory. *Journal of Sport Psychology, 9,* 55–65.

Kluger, J. (1997, March 10). Will we follow the sheep? *Time,* 67–72.

Knight, C. C., & Fischer, K. W. (1992). Learning to read words: Individual differences in developmental sequences. *Journal of Applied Developmental Psychology, 13,* 377–404.

Koblinsky, S. A., & Anderson, E. A. (1993, Spring-Summer). Studying homeless children and their families: Issues and challenges. *Division 7 Newsletter,* pp. 1–3.

Kochanska, G. (1997). Multiple pathways to conscience for children with different temperaments: From toddlerhood to age 5. *Developmental Psychology, 33,* 228–240.

Kochanska, G., Aksan, N., & Koenig, A. L. (1995). A longitudinal study of the roots of preschoolers' conscience: Committed compliance and emerging internalization. *Child Development, 66,* 1752–1769.

Kochanska, G., Kuczynski, L., & Radke-Yarrow, M. (1989). Correspondence between mothers' self-reported and observed child-rearing practices. *Child Development, 60*(1), 56–63.

Kochanska, G., Murray, K., & Coy, K. C. (1997). Inhibitory control as a contributor to conscience in childhood: From toddler to early school age. *Child Development, 68,* 263–277.

Kochanska, G., & Radke-Yarrow, M. (1992). Inhibition in toddlerhood and the dynamics of the child's interactions with an unfamiliar peer at age 5. *Child Development, 63,* 325–335.

Kohlberg, L. (1964). Development of moral character and moral ideology. In M. L. Hoffman & L. W. Hoffman (Eds.), *Review of child development research* (Vol. 1). New York: Sage.

Kohlberg, L. (1966). A cognitive-developmental analysis of children's sex-role concepts and attitudes. In E. E. Maccoby (Ed.), *The development of sex differences.* Stanford, CA: Stanford University Press.

Kohlberg, L. (1969). Stage and sequence: The cognitive-developmental approach to socialization. In D. A. Goslin (Ed.), *Handbook of socialization theory and research.* Chicago: Rand McNally.

Kohlberg, L. (1976). Moral stages and moralization: The cognitive-developmental approach. In T. Lickona (Ed.), *Moral development and behavior.* New York: Holt, Rinehart & Winston.

Kohn, M. L. (1980). Job complexity and adult personality. In N. J. Smelser & E. H. Erikson (Eds.), *Themes of work and love in adulthood* (pp. 193–210). Cambridge: Harvard University Press.

Kohn, P. M., & Milrose, J. A. (1993). The inventory of high-school students' recent life experiences: A decontaminated measure of adolescents' life hassles. *Journal of Youth and Adolescence, 22,* 43–55.

Kohut, H. (1971). *The analysis of the self.* New York: International Universities Press.

Konopka, G. (1976). *Young girls: A portrait of adolescence.* Englewood Cliffs, NJ: Prentice-Hall.

Konrad, P. (1990, August 6). Welcome to the woman-friendly company. *Business Week,* pp. 48–55.

Kopp, C. B. (1982). Antecedents of self-regulation: A developmental perspective. *Developmental Psychology, 18,* 199–214.

Kopp, C. B. (1989). Regulation of distress and negative emotions: A developmental view. *Developmental Psychology, 25,* 343–354.

Kornfield, S. (1990). *Impact of parental marital status, gender, and pubertal development on adolescent.* Unpublished manuscript, University of Georgia.

Kosnik, W., Winslow, L., Kline, D., Rasinski, K., & Sekuler, R. (1988). Visual changes in daily life throughout adulthood. *Gerontology, 43,* P63–P70.

Kotre, J., & Kotre, K. B. (1998). Intergenerational buffers: The damage stops here. In McAdams, D. P., & de St. Auburn E. (Eds.). Generativity and adult development: Psychosocial perspectives on caring for and contributing to the next generation. Washington, DC: *American Psychological Association,* 367–389.

Kotre, J. (1995). Generative outcome. *Journal of Aging Studies, 9,* 33–41.

Kotre, J. N. (1995). *White gloves: How we create ourselves through memory.* New York: Free Press.

Kowaz, A. M., & Marcia, J. E. (1991). Development and validation of a measure of Eriksonian industry. *Journal of Personality and Social Psychology, 60,* 390–397.

Kram, K. E. (1985). *Mentoring at work: Developmental relationships in organizational life.* Glenview, IL: Scott, Foresman.

Krannich, R. S. (1980). Abortion in the United States: Past, present, and future trends. *Family Relations, 29,* 365–374.

Kroger, J. (1993). *Discussions on ego identity.* Hillsdale, NJ: Erlbaum.

Kroger, J., & Haslett, S. J. (1988). Separation-individuation and ego identity status in late adolescence: A two-year longitudinal study. *Journal of Youth and Adolescence, 17,* 59–80.

Kropp, J. P., & Haynes, O. M. (1987). Abusive and nonabusive mothers' ability to identify general and specific emotion signals of infants. *Child Development, 58,* 187–190.

Kruk, E. (1995). Grandparent-grandchild contact loss: Findings from a study of "grandparents rights" members. *Canadian Journal on Aging, 14,* 737–754.

Kübler-Ross, E. (1969). *On death and dying.* New York: Macmillan.

Kübler-Ross, E. (1972, February). On death and dying. *Journal of the American Medical Association, 219,* 10–15.

Kübler-Ross, E. (1981). *Living with dying.* New York: Macmillan.

Kuczynski, L., Zahn-Waxler, C., & Radke-Yarrow, M. (1987). Development and content of imitation in the second and third years of life: A socialization perspective. *Developmental Psychology, 23,* 276–282.

Kuhl, P. K. (1987). Perception of speech and sound in early infancy. In P. Salapatek & L. Cohen (Eds.), *Handbook of infant perception* (Vol. 1). Orlando, FL: Academic Press.

Kuhn, D., Amsel, E., & O'Loughlin, M. (1988). *The development of scientific thinking skills.* New York: Academic Press.

Kuhn, D., Garcia-Mila, M., Zohar, A., & Andersen, C. (1995). Strategies of knowledge acquisition. *Monographs of the Society for Research in Child Development, 60,* (4, Serial No. 245).

Kunz, J., & Kunz, P. R. (1995). Social support during the process of divorce: It does make a difference. *Journal of Divorce and Remarriage, 24,* 111–119.

Kurdek, L. A. (1981). Young adults' moral reasoning about prohibitive and prosocial dilemmas. *Journal of Youth and Adolescence, 10,* 263–272.

Kurdek, L. A. (1995). Lesbian and gay couples. In A. R. D'Augelli & C. J. Patterson (Eds.), *Lesbian, gay, and bisexual identities over the lifespan: Psychological per-*

spectives (pp. 243–261). New York: Oxford University Press.

Kurdek, L. A., & Schmitt, J. P. (1986). Relationship quality of partners in heterosexual married, heterosexual cohabiting, and gay and lesbian relationships. *Journal of Personality and Social Psychology, 51,* 711–720.

Lacayo, R. (1988). Baby M. meets Solomon's sword. *Time,* p. 97.

Lacayo, R. (1996). Law and order. *Time, 147,* 48–56.

Lachman, M. E., & James, J. B. (1997). *Multiple paths of midlife development.* Chicago: The University of Chicago Press.

Ladd, G. W., Price, J. M., & Hart, C. H. (1988). Predicting preschooler's peer status from their playground behaviors. *Child Development, 59,* 986–992.

Lamb, M. E. (1976). Twelve-month-olds and their parents: Interaction in a laboratory playroom. *Developmental Psychology, 12,* 237–244.

Lamb, M. E., & Elster, A. B. (1985). Adolescent mother-infant-father relationships. *Developmental Psychology, 21,* 768–773.

Lamborn, S. D., & Steinberg, L. D. (1993). Emotional autonomy redux: Revisiting Ryan and Lynch. *Child Development, 64,* 483–499.

Lang, F. R., Featherman, D. L., & Nesselroade, J. R. (1997). Social self-efficacy and short-term variability in social relationships: The MacArthur successful aging study. *Psychology and Aging, 12,* 657–666.

Langston, C. A., & Cantor, N. (1989). Social anxiety and social constraint: When making friends is hard. *Journal of Personality and Social Psychology, 56,* 649–661.

Landale, N. S., & Fennelly, K. S. (1992). Informal unions among mainland Puerto Ricans: Cohabitation or an alternative to legal marriage. *Journal of Marriage and the Family, 54,* 269–280.

Lanza, E. (1992). Can bilingual two-year-olds code-switch? *Journal of Child Language, 19,* 633–658.

Larson, M. C., Gunnar, M. R., & Hertsgaard, L. (1991). The effects of morning naps, car trips, and maternal separation on adrenocortical activity in human infants. *Child Development, 62,* 362–372.

Larson, R., & Ham, M. (1993). Stress and "Storm and Stress" in early adolescence: The relationship of negative events with dysphoric affect. *Developmental Psychology, 29,* 130–140.

Larson, R., & Lampman-Petraitis, C. (1989). Daily emotional states as reported by children and adolescents. *Child Development, 60,* 1250–1260.

Lawn, R. M., & Vehar, G. A. (1986). The molecular genetics of hemophilia. *Scientific American, 254,* 48–56.

Laszlo, E. (1972). *Introduction to systems philosophy: Toward a new paradigm of contemporary thought.* New York: Harper & Row.

Leaf, A. (1973). Growing old. *Scientific American, 229,* 52.

Lee, L. C. (1975). Toward a cognitive theory of interpersonal development: Importance of peers. In M. Lewis & L. A. Rosenblum (Eds.), *Friendship and peer relations.* New York: Wiley.

Leinbach, M. D., & Fagot, B. I. (1986). Acquisition of gender labels: A test for toddlers. *Sex Roles, 15,* 655–667.

Leland, N. L., & Barth, R. P. (1993). Characteristics of adolescents who have attempted to avoid HIV and who have communicated with parents about sex. *Journal of Adolescent Research, 8,* 58–77.

Lemkau, J. R. (1988). Emotional sequelae of abortion: Implications for clinical practice. *Psychology of Women Quarterly, 12,* 461–472.

Lemonick, M. D. (1997, December 1). The new revolution in making babies. *Time,* 40–46.

Lenneberg, E. H. (1967). *Biological foundations of language.* New York: Wiley.

Lerner, H. G. (1989). *The dance of intimacy.* New York: Harper & Row.

Lerner, J. V., & Lerner, R. M. (1983). Temperament and adaptation across life: Theoretical and empirical issues. In P. B. Baltes & O. G. Brim (Eds.), *Life span development and behavior, 5,* (pp. 197–231). New York: Academic Press.

LeVay, S. (1991). A difference in hypothalamic structure between heterosexual and homosexual men. *Science, 253,* 1034–1037.

Levesque, R. P. (1993). The romantic experience of adolescents in satisfying love relationships. *Journal of Youth and Adolescence, 22,* 219–252.

Levin, I. (1986). *Stage and structure: Reopening the debate.* Norwood, NJ: Ablex.

LeVine, R. A. (1977). Child rearing as cultural adaptation. In P. H. Leiderman, S. R. Tulkin, & A. Rosenfeld (Eds.), *Culture and infancy: Variations in the human experience* (pp. 15–28). New York: Academic Press.

Levinger, G. (1983). Development and change. In H. H. Kelley, et al. (Eds.), *Close relationships* (pp. 315–359). New York: W. H. Freeman.

Levitt, M. J., Guacci-Franco, N., & Levitt, J. L. (1993). Convoys of social support in childhood and early adolescence: Structure and function. *Developmental Psychology, 29,* 811–818.

Levitt, M. J., Weber, R. A., & Clark, M. C. (1986). Social network relationships as sources of maternal support and well-being. *Developmental Psychology, 22,* 310–316.

Levitt, M. J., Weber, R. A., & Guacci, N. (1993). Convoys of social support: An intergenerational analysis. *Psychology and Aging, 8,* 323–326.

Levy, G. D., & Carter, D. B. (1989). Gender schema, gender constancy, and gender-role knowledge: The roles of cognitive factors in preschoolers' gender-role stereotype attributions. *Developmental Psychology, 25,* 444–449.

Levy-Shiff, R., Sharur, H., & Mogilner, M. B. (1989). Mother- and father-preterm infant relationship in the hospital preterm nursery. *Child Development, 60,* 93–102.

Lewinsohn, P. H., Rohde, P., & Crozier, L. C. (1991). Age and depression: Unique and shared effects. *Psychology and Aging, 6,* 247–260.

Lewis, H. B. (1987). Shame and the narcissistic personality. In D. L. Nathanson (Ed.), *The many faces of shame* (pp. 93–132). New York: Guilford Press.

Lewis, R. A., Kozac, E. B., Milardo, R. M., & Grosnick, W. A. (1981). Commitment in same-sex love relationships. *Alternative Lifestyles, 4,* 22–42.

Lewit, E. M., & Baker, L. S. (1995). School readiness. *The Future of Children, 5,* 128–139.

Liben, L. S., & Signorella, M. L. (1993). Gender-schematic processing in children: The role of initial interpretations of stimuli. *Developmental Psychology, 29,* 141–149.

Lieberman, A. F., Weston, D. R., & Pawl, J. H. (1991). Preventive intervention and outcome with anxiously attached dyads. *Child Development, 62,* 199–209.

Liebert, R. M., & Sprafkin, J. (1988). *The early window: Effects of television on children and youth* (3rd ed.). New York: Pergamon Press.

Lifton, R. J. (1973). The sense of immortality: On death and the continuity of life. *American Journal of Psychoanalysis, 33,* 3–15.

Lindblad, B. S. (1987). *Perinatal nutrition.* San Diego: Academic Press.

Lindbohm, M., Hemminki, K., Bonhomme, M. G., Anttila, A., Rantala, K., Heikkilä, P., & Rosenberg, M. J. (1991). Effects of paternal occupational exposure on spontaneous abortions. *American Journal of Public Health, 81,* 1029–1033.

Lindemann, E. (1944). Symptomology and management of acute grief. *American Journal of Psychiatry, 101,* 141–148.

Lindsey, E. W. (1994). Homelessness. In P. C. McKenry & S. J. Price (Eds.), *Families and change: Coping with stressful events* (pp. 281–302). Thousand Oaks, CA: Sage.

Lindsey, E. W., Mize, J., & Pettit, G. S. (1997). Mutuality in parent-child play: Consequences for children's peer competence. *Journal of Social and Personal Relationships, 14,* 523–538.

Linn, M. C., Clement, C., Pulos, S., & Sullivan, P. (1989). Scientific reasoning during adolescence: The influence of instruction in science knowledge and reasoning strategies. *Journal of Research in Science Teaching, 26,* 171–187.

Litwin, H. (1997). Support network type and health service utilization. *Research on Aging, 19,* 274–299.

Livesley, W. J., Jackson, D. N., & Schroeder, M. L. (1992). Factorial structure of traits delineating personality disorders in clinical and general population samples, *Journal of Abnormal Psychology, 101,* 432–440.

Lobel, T. E., & Menashri, J. (1993). Relations of conceptions of gender-role transgressions and gender constancy to gender-typed toy preferences. *Developmental Psychology, 29,* 150–155.

Lobo, F., & Watkins, G. (1995). Late career unemployment in the 1990s: Its impact on the family. *Journal of Family Studies, 1,* 103–113.

Locker, B. Z. (1997). Job loss and organizational change: Psychological perspectives. In A. J. Pickman (Ed.), *Special challenges in career management: Counselor perspectives.* Mahwah, NJ: Lawrence Erlbaum.

Loehlin, J. C. (1992). *Genes and environment in personality development,* Thousand Oaks, CA: Sage.

Loftus, E. F. (1993). The reality of repressed memories. *American Psychologist, 48,* 518–537.

Logan, D. D. (1980). The menarche experience in 23 foreign countries. *Adolescence, 15,* 247–256.

Lombardi, D. N., Melchior, E. J., Murphy, J. G., & Brinkerhoff, A. L. (1996). The ubiquity of life-style. *Individual Psychology: Journal of Adlerian Theory, Research & Practice, 52,* 31–41.

Long, B. C. (1989). Sex-role orientation, coping strategies, and self-efficacy of women in traditional and nontraditional occupations. *Psychology of Women Quarterly, 13,* 307–324.

Long, E. C. J., Cate, R. M., Fehsenfeld, D. A., & Williams, K. M. (1996). A longitudinal assessment of a measure of premarital sexual conflict. *Family Relations, 45,* 302–308.

Looft, W. R. (1971). Egocentrism and social interaction in adolescence. *Adolescence, 12,* 485–495.

Lopata, H. Z. (1978). Widowhood: Social norms and social integration. In H. Z. Lopata (Ed.), *Family factbook*. Chicago: Marquis Academic Media.

Lopez, A., Gelman, S. A., Gutheil, G., & Smith, E. (1992). The development of category-based inductions. *Child Development, 63,* 1070–1090.

Lorenz, K. F. (1935). Der Kumpan in der Urwelt des Vogels. *Journal Ornithologie, 83,* 137.

Lorenz, K. F. (1937/1961). Imprinting. In R. C. Birney & R. C. Teevan (Eds.), *Instinct*. Princeton, NJ: Van Nostrand.

Lucariello, J. (1987). Spinning fantasy: Themes, structure, and the knowledge base. *Child Development, 58,* 434–442.

Ludemann, P. M. (1991). Generalized discrimination of positive facial expressions by seven- and ten-month-old infants. *Child Development, 62,* 55–67.

Ludemann, P. M., & Nelson, C. A. (1988). Categorical-representation of facial expressions by 7-month-old infants. *Developmental Psychology, 24,* 492–501.

Luhtanen, R., & Crocker, J. (1992). A collective self-esteem scale: Self-evaluation of one's social identity. *Personality and Social Psychology Bulletin, 18,* 302–318.

Lydon, J., Dunkel-Schetter, C., Cohan, C. L., & Pierce, T. (1996). Pregnancy decision making as a significant life event: A commitment approach. *Journal of Personality and Social Psychology, 71,* 141–151.

Lyons-Ruth, K., Connell, D. B., Zoll, D., & Stahl, J. (1987). Infants at social risk: Relations among infant maltreatment, maternal behavior, and infant attachment behavior. *Developmental Psychology, 23,* 223–232.

Maag, J. W., Rutherford, R. B., Jr., & Parks, B. T. (1988). Secondary school professionals' ability to identify depression in adolescents. *Adolescence, 23,* 73–82.

McAdams, D. P., Diamond, A., de St. Aubin, E., & Mansfield, E. D. (1997). Stories of commitment: the psychosocial construction of generative lives. *Journal of Personality and Social Psychology, 72,* 678–694.

McAdams, D. P., St. Aubin, E., & Logan, R. L. (1993). Generativity among young, midlife, and older adults. *Psychology and Aging, 8,* 221–230.

McAdoo, H. P. (1980). Black mothers and the extended family support network. In L. F. Rodgers-Rose (Ed.), *The black woman*. Beverly Hills, CA: Sage.

McAdoo, H. P. (1985). Racial attitude and self-concept of young black children over time. In H. P. McAdoo & J. L. McAdoo (Eds.), *Black children: Social, educational, and parental environments* (pp. 213–242). Newbury Park, CA: Sage.

McAuley, E., Duncan, T. E., & McElroy, M. (1989). Self-efficacy cognitions and causal attributions for children's motor performance: An exploratory investigation. *Journal of Genetic Psychology, 150,* 65–73.

McAuliffe, G. (1997). A constructive developmental perspective on career counseling. In *The Hatherleigh guide to vocational and career counseling* (pp. 1–16). New York: Hatherleigh Press.

McCabe, A. E., Siegel, L. S., Spence, I., & Wilkinson, A. (1982). Class-inclusion reasoning: Patterns of performance from three to eight years. *Child Development, 53,* 780–785.

McCarthy, J., & Hardy, J. (1993). Age at first birth and birth outcomes. *Journal of Research on Adolescence, 3,* 373–392.

McClearn, G. E., Johansson, B., Berg, S., Pedersen, N. L., Ahern, F., Petrill, S. A., & Plomin, R. (1997). Substantial genetic influence on cognitive abilities in twins 80 or more years old. *Science, 276,* 1560–1563.

McClelland, J. L., & Rumelhart, D. E. (1986). *Parallel distributed processing* (Vol. 2). Cambridge, MA: MIT Press.

Maccoby, E. E. (1992). The role of parents in the socialization of children: An historical overview. *Developmental Psychology, 28,* 1006–1017.

Maccoby, E. E., & Jacklin, C. N. (1987). Gender segregation in childhood. In E. H. Reese (Ed.), *Advances in child development and behavior* (Vol. 20, pp. 239–287). New York: Academic Press.

Maccoby, E. E. (1988). Gender as a social category. *Developmental Psychology, 24,* 755–765.

Maccoby, E. E. (1990). Gender and relationships: A developmental account. *American Psychologist, 45,* 513–520.

McCord, J. (1990). Problem behaviors. In S. S. Feldman & G. R. Elliott (Eds.), *At the threshold: The developing adolescent* (pp. 414–430). Cambridge: Harvard University Press.

McCrae, R. R., & Costa, P. T. (1983). Psychological maturity and subjective well-being: Toward a new synthesis. *Developmental Psychology, 19,* 243–248.

MacDermid, S. M., Huston, T. L., & McHale, S. M. (1990). Changes in marriage associated with transition to parenthood. *Journal of Marriage and the Family, 52,* 475–486.

McDonald, A. D., Armstrong, B. G., & Sloan, M. (1992). Cigarette, alcohol, and coffee consumption and prematurity. *American Journal of Public Health, 82,* 87–90.

Mace, D. R. (1982). *Close companions*. New York: Continuum.

MacFarlane, J. A. (1975). Olfaction in the development of social preferences in the human neonate. In *Parent-infant interaction*. Ciba Foundation Symposium, 33, 103–113.

McGonagle, K. A., Kessler, R. C., & Gotlib, I. H. (1993). The effects of marital disagreement style, frequency, and outcome on marital disruption. *Journal of Social and Personal Relationships, 10,* 385–404.

McGowen, K. R., & Hart, L. E. (1990). Still different after all these years: Gender differences in professional identity formation. *Professional Psychology—Research & Practice, 21,* 118–123.

McKinlay, J. B., McKinlay, S. M., & Brambilla, D. J. (1987). Health status and utilization behavior associated with menopause. *American Journal of Epidemiology, 125,* 110–121.

Macklin, E. (1987). Non-traditional family forms. In M. B. Sussman & S. K. Steinmetz (Eds.), *Handbook of marriage and the family* (pp. 317–353). New York: Plenum.

McLanahan, S., & Adams, J. (1987). Parenthood and psychological well-being. In R. Turner & J. Short (Eds.), *Annual review of sociology* (Vol. 13). Palo Alto, CA: Annual Reviews.

McLaughlin, D. K., Lichter, D. T., & Johnston, G. M. (1993). Some women marry young: Transitions to first marriage in metropolitan and nonmetropolitan areas. *Journal of Marriage and the Family, 55,* 827–838.

MacLean, D. J., & Schuler, M. (1989). Conceptual development in infancy: The understanding of containment. *Child Development, 60,* 1126–1137.

McLeod, J. D., & Shanahan, M. J. (1993). Poverty, parenting, and children's mental health. *American Sociological Review, 58,* 351–366.

McLoyd, V. C. (1990). The impact of economic hardship on black families and children: Psychological distress, parenting, and socioemotional development. *Child Development, 61,* 311–346.

McMillan, D. W., & Hiltonsmith, R. W. (1982). Adolescents at home: An exploratory study of the relationship between perception of family social climate, general well-being, and actual behavior in the home setting. *Journal of Youth and Adolescence, 11,* 301–315.

MacTurk, R. H., McCarthy, M. E., Vietze, P. M., & Yarrow, L. J. (1987). Sequential analysis of mastery behavior in 6- and 12-month-old infants. *Developmental Psychology, 23,* 199–203.

Madden, N. A., Slavin, R. E., Karweit, N. L., Doaln, L. J., & Wasik, B. A. (1993). Success for All: Longitudinal effects of a restructuring program for inner-city elementary schools. *American Educational Research Journal, 30,* 123–148.

Mahler, M., Pine, F., & Bergman, A. (1975). *The psychological birth of the human infant.* New York: Basic Books.

Mahler, M. S. (1963). Thoughts about development and individuation. *Psychoanalytic Study of the Child, 18,* 307–324.

Main, N., Kaplan, N., & Cassidy, J. (1985). Security in infancy, childhood, and adulthood: A move to the level of representation. In I. Bretherton & E. Everett (Eds.), *Growing points of attachment theory and research* (pp. 60–104). *Monographs of the Society for Research in Child Development, 50* (1–2, Serial No. 209).

Malatesta, C. A., & Izard, C. E. (1984). The ontogenesis of human social signals: From biological imperative to symbol utilization. In N. A. Fox & R. J. Davidson (Eds.), *The psychobiology of affective development* (pp. 161–206). Hillsdale, NJ: Erlbaum.

Malle, B. F., & Horowitz, L. M. (1995). The puzzled of negative self-views: An explanation using the schema concept. *Journal of Personality and Social Psychology, 68,* 470–484.

Mandel, D. R., Jusczyk, P. W., & Pisoni, D. B. (1995). Infants' recognition of the sound patterns of their own names. *Psychological Science, 6,* 314–317.

Mandel, J. L., Monaco, A. P., Nelson, D. L., Schlessinger, D., & Willard, H. (1992). Genome analysis and the human X chromosome. *Science, 258,* 103–109.

Mangelsdorf, S. C., Plunkett, J. W., Dedrick, C. F., Berlin, M., Meisels, S. J., McHale, J. L., & Dichtellmiller, M. (1996). Attachment security in very low birth weight infants. *Developmental Psychology, 32,* 914–920.

Manning, W. D. (1990). Parenting employed teenagers. *Youth and Society, 22,* 184–200.

Marcia, J. E. (1980). Identity in adolescence. In J. Adelson (Ed.), *Handbook of adolescent psychology* (pp. 159–187). New York: Wiley.

Marcia, J. E. (1993). The relational roots of identity. In J. Kroger (Ed.), *Discussions on ego identity* (pp. 101–120). Hillsdale, NJ: Erlbaum.

Marcus, G. F. (1996). Why do children say "Breaked"? *Current Directions in Psychological Science, 5,* 81–85.

Markman, H. I., & Notarius, C. I. (1987). Coding marital and family interaction: Current status. In T. Jacob (Ed.), *Family interaction and psychopathology* (pp. 329–390). New York: Plenum.

Marks, S. R. (1989). Toward a systems theory of marital quality. *Journal of Marriage and the Family, 51,* 15–26.

Markstrom-Adams, C., Hofstra, G., & Dougher, K. (1994). The ego-virtue of fidelity: A case for the study of religion and identity formation in adolescence. *Journal of Youth and Adolescence, 23,* 453–469.

Marshall, W. A. (1973). The body. In R. R. Sears & S. Feldman (Eds.), *The seven ages of man.* Los Altos, CA: William Kaufman.

Marsiglio, W. (1987). Adolescent fathers in the United States: Their initial arrangements, marital experience, and educational outcomes. *Family Planning Perspectives, 19,* 240–251.

Marsiglio, W. (1988). Adolescent male sexuality and heterosexual masculinity: A conceptual model and review. *Journal of Adolescent Research, 3,* 285–303.

Marsiglio, W. (1989). Adolescent males' pregnancy resolution preferences and family formation intentions: Does family background make a difference for blacks and whites? *Journal of Adolescent Research, 4,* 214–237.

Marsiglio, W. (1993). Adolescent males' orientation toward paternity and contraception. *Family Planning Perspectives, 25,* 22–31.

Martikainen, P., & Valkonen, T. (1996). Mortality after the death of a spouse: Rates and causes of death in a large Finnish cohort. *American Journal of Public Health, 86,* 1087–1093.

Martin, C. L. (1989). Children's use of gender-related information in making social judgments. *Developmental Psychology, 25,* 80–88.

Martin, C. L., Eisenbud, L., & Rose, H. (1995). Children's gender-based reasoning about toys. *Child Development, 66,* 1453–1471.

Martin, C. L., & Halverson, C. F. (1987). The roles of cognition in sex roles acquisition. In D. B. Carter (Ed.), *Current conceptions of sex roles and sex typing: Theory and research* (pp. 123–137). New York: Praeger.

Martin, C. L., Wood, C. H., & Little, J. K. (1990). The development of gender stereotype components. *Child Development, 61,* 1891–1904.

Martin, G. B., & Clark, R. D., III. (1982). Distress crying in neonates: Species and peer specificity. *Developmental Psychology, 18,* 3–9.

Martin, S., Houseley, K., McCoy, H., Greenhouse, P., Stigger, F., Kenney, M. A., Shoffner, S., Fu, V., Korslund, M., Ercanli-Huffman, F. G., Carter, E., Chopin, L., Hegsted, M., Clark, A. J., Disney, G., Moak, S., Wakefield, T., & Stallings, S. (1988). Self-esteem of adolescent girls as related to weight. *Perceptual and Motor Skills, 67,* 879–884.

Marx, J. (1988). Are aging and death programmed in our genes? *Science, 242,* 33.

Mason, M. G., & Gibbs, J. C. (1993). Social perspective taking and moral judgment among college students. *Journal of Adolescent Research, 8,* 109–123.

Masten, A. S., Coatsworth, J. D., Neemann, J., Gest, S. D., Tellegen, A., & Garmezy, N. (1995). The structure and coherence of competence from childhood through adolescence. *Child Development, 66,* 1635–1659.

Masuda, M. (1994). Exclusivity in heterosexual romantic relationships. *Japanese Journal of Experimental Social Psychology, 34,* 164–182.

Mattessich, P., & Hill, R. (1987). Life cycle and family development. In M. B. Sussman & S. K. Steinmetz (Eds.), *Handbook of marriage and the family* (pp. 437–469). New York: Plenum.

Mau, R. Y. (1992). The validity and devolution of a concept: Student alienation. *Adolescence, 27,* 731–741.

May, R. B., & Norton, J. M. (1981). Training-task orders and transfer in conservation. *Child Development, 52,* 904–913.

Mayer, R. (1992). *Thinking, problem solving, and cognition* (2nd ed.). New York: W. H. Freeman.

Meacham, J. A. (1995). Reminiscing as a process of social construction. In B. K. Haight & J. D. Webster (Eds.), *The art and science of reminiscing: Theory, research, methods, and applications* (pp. 37–48). Philadelphia, PA: Taylor & Francis.

Mead, M. (1935). *Sex and temperament in three primitive societies.* New York: Morrow.

Mead, M. (1928/1950). *Coming of age in Samoa.* New York: New American Library.

Mead, M. (1949/1955). *Male and female: A study of the sexes in a changing world.* New York: Mentor.

Mead, M., & Newton, N. (1967). Cultural patterning of perinatal behavior. In S. A. Richardson & A. F. Guttmacher (Eds.), *Childbearing—its social and psychological aspects.* Baltimore: Williams & Wilkins.

Meer, J. (1985, July). Loneliness. *Psychology Today, 19,* 28–33.

Meeus, W. (1996). Studies on identity development in adolescence: An overview of research and some new data. *Journal of Youth and Adolescence, 25,* 569–598.

Mellor, S. (1989). Gender differences in identity formation as a function of self-other relationships. *Journal of Youth and Adolescence, 18,* 361–375.

Meltzoff, A. N., & Borton, R. W. (1979). Intermodal matching by human neonates. *Nature, 282,* 403–404.

Mendel, G. (1866). Experiments with plant hybrids. *Proceedings of the Brunn Natural History Society.*

Merton, R. K. (1948). The self-fulfilling prophecy. *Antioch Review, 8,* 193–210.

Messer, D. J., Rachford, D., McCarthy, M. E., & Yarrow, L. J. (1987). Assessment of mastery behavior at 30 months: Analysis of task-directed activities. *Developmental Psychology, 23,* 771–781.

Messick, S. (1989). Meaning and values in test validation: The science and ethics of assessment. *Educational Researcher, 18,* 5–11.

Meyer, V. (1991). A critique of adolescent pregnancy prevention research: The invisible white male. *Adolescence, 26,* 217–222.

Meyers, G. C., & Manton, K. G. (1984). Compression of mortality: Myth or reality? *Gerontologist, 24,* 346–353.

Miller, A. L., & Tiedeman, D. V. (1972). Decision making for the 70s: The cubing of the Tiedeman paradigm and its application in career education. *Focus on Guidance, 5.*

Miller, D. C. (1991). *Handbook of research design and social measurement* (5th ed.). Newbury Park, CA: Sage.

Miller, G. A., & Gildea, P. M. (1987). How children learn words. *Scientific American, 257,* 94–99.

Miller, J. (1988). Jobs and work. In N. J. Smelser (Ed.), *Handbook of sociology* (pp. 327–359). Newbury Park, CA: Sage.

Miller, J., Schooler, C., Kohn, M. L., & Miller, K. A. (1979). Women and work: The psychological effects of occupational conditions. *American Journal of Sociology, 85,* 66–94.

Miller, N. B., Cowan, P. A., Cowan, C. P., Hetherington, E. M., & Clingempeel, W. G. (1993). Externalizing in preschoolers and early adolescents: A cross-study replication of a family model. *Developmental Psychology, 29,* 3–18.

Miller, P. H. (1993). *Theories of developmental psychology* (3rd ed.). New York: W. H. Freeman.

Miller, P. J., & Sperry, L. L. (1987). The socialization of anger and aggression. *Merrill-Palmer Quarterly, 34,* 217–222.

Miller, W. B. (1992). An empirical study of the psychological antecedents and consequences of induced abortion. *Journal of Social Issues, 48,* 67–93.

Millstein, S. G., & Litt, I. F. (1990). Adolescent health. In S. S. Feldman & G. R. Elliott (Eds.), *At the threshold: The developing adolescent* (pp. 431–456). Cambridge: Harvard University Press.

Min, Y. I., Correa-Villasenor, A., & Stewart, P. A. (1996). Parental occupational lead exposure and low birth weight. *American Journal of Industrial Medicine, 30,* 569–578.

Minuchin, S. (1978). Structural family therapy: Activating alternatives within a therapeutic system. In I. Zwerling (Ed.), *The American family.* Philadelphia: Smith, Kline & French.

Mischel, W. (1973). Toward a cognitive social learning reconceptualization of personality. *Psychological Review, 80,* 252–283.

Mischel, W. (1979). On the interface of cognition and personality: Beyond the person-situation debate. *American Psychologist, 34,* 740–754.

Mischel, W., Shoda, Y., & Rodriguez, M. L. (1989). Delay of gratification in children. *Science, 244,* 933–938.

Mistretta, C. M., & Bradley, R. M. (1977). Taste in utero: Theoretical considerations. In J. M. Weiffenbach (Ed.), *Taste and development* (pp. 279–291). DHEW Publication no. NIH 77-1068. Bethesda, MD: U.S. Department of Health, Education, and Welfare.

Mitchell, B. A., Wister, A. V., & Burch, T. K. (1989). The family environment and leaving the parental home. *Journal of Marriage and the Family, 51,* 605–614.

Miyake, K., Campos, J., Kagan, J., & Bradshaw, D. (1986). Issues in socioemotional development in Japan. In H. Azuma, I. Hakuta, & H. Stevenson (Eds.), *Kodomo: Child development and education in Japan* (pp. 239–261). New York: W. H. Freeman.

Molfese, D. L., Molfese, V. J., & Carrell, P. L. (1982). Early language development. In B. B. Wolman (Ed.), *Handbook of developmental psychology* (pp. 301–322). Englewood Cliffs, NJ: Prentice-Hall.

Montemayor, R. (1983). Parents and adolescents in conflict: All families some of the time and some families most of the time. *Journal of Early Adolescence, 3,* 83–103.

Montepare, J. M., & Lachman, M. E. (1989). "You're only as old as you feel": Self-perceptions of age, fears of aging, and life satisfaction from adolescence to old age. *Psychology and Aging, 4,* 73–78.

Montgomery, D. E. (1993). Young children's understanding of interpretive diversity between different-age listeners. *Developmental Psychology, 29,* 337–345.

Moore, D., & Hotch, D. F. (1981). Late adolescents' conceptualizations of home-leaving. *Journal of Youth and Adolescence, 10,* 1–10.

Moore, K. L. (1993). *The developing human: Clinically oriented embryology* (5th ed.). Philadelphia: Saunders.

Moore, K. A., Myers, D. E., Morrison, D. R., Nord, C. W., Brown, B., & Edmonston, B. (1993). Age at first childbirth and later poverty. *Journal of Research on Adolescence, 3,* 393–422.

Morgan, D. M. (1989). Adjusting to widowhood: Do social networks really make it easier? *Gerontologist, 29,* 101–107.

Moriarty, A. E., & Toussieng, P. W. (1976). *Adolescent coping.* New York: Grune & Stratton.

Morokoff, P. J. (1988). Sexuality in perimenopausal and postmenopausal women. *Psychology of Women Quarterly, 12,* 489–511.

Morrison, A. P. (1989). *Shame: The underside of narcissism.* Hillsdale, NJ: Analytic Press.

Morrison, D. M. (1985). Adolescent contraceptive behavior: A review. *Psychological Bulletin, 98,* 538–568.

Morse, C. K. (1993). Does variability increase with age? An archival study of cognitive measures. *Psychology and Aging, 8,* 156–164.

Mortimer, J. T., Finch, M., Shanahan, M., & Ryu, S. (1992). Work experience, mental health, and behavioral adjustment in adolescence. *Journal of Research on Adolescence, 2,* 25–57.

Mosel, S. (1992, Fall). Remembering great teachers at Parker: Chauncey Griffith. *Parker Magazine,* p. 12.

Moss, P., & Tilly, C. (1996). "Soft" skills and race: an investigation of Black men's employment problems. *Work & Occupations, 23,* 252–276.

Mullan, J. (1981). *Parental distress and marital happiness: The transition to the empty nest.* Unpublished doctor dissertation, University of Chicago.

Murdock, G. P. (1934). *Our primitive contemporaries.* New York: Macmillan.

Murdock, G. P., & White, D. R. (1969). Standard cross-cultural sample: *Ethnology, 8,* 329–369.

Murphy, L. (1956). *Personality in young children: Vol. 2. Colin, a normal child.* New York: Basic Books.

Murphy, L. B. (1972). *Infant's play and cognitive development* (pp. 99–126). New York: Norton.

Murray, B. (1997). Why aren't antidrug programs working? *APA Monitor, 28,* p. 30.

Murray, S. L., Homes, J. G., & Griffin, D. W. (1996). The self-fulfilling nature of positive illusions in romantic relationships: Love is not blind, but prescient. *Journal of Personality and Social Psychology, 71,* 1155–1180.

Murrell, S. A., & Norris, F. H. (1991). Differential social support and life change as contributors to the social class-distress relationship in older adults. *Psychology and Aging, 6,* 223–231.

Mussen, P. H., & Jones, M. C. (1957). Self-conceptions, motivations, and interpersonal attitudes of late and early maturing boys. *Child Development, 28,* 243–256.

Musser, L. M., & Browne, B. A. (1991). Self-monitoring in middle childhood: Personality and social correlates. *Developmental Psychology, 27,* 994–999.

Mutran, E. J., Reitzes, D. C., & Fernandez, M. E. (1997). Factors that influence attitudes toward retirement. *Research on Aging, 19,* 251–273.

Nash, J. M. (1997). Fertile minds. *Time,* 48–56.

Nathanielsz, P. W. (1996). The timing of birth. *American Scientist, 84,* 562–569.

National Center for Education Statistics. (1994). *National household education survey of 1993: School readiness data file user's manual.* NCES 94-193. Washington, DC: U.S. Department of Education.

National Center for Education Statistics. (1995). *Digest of education statitics: 1995.* Washington, DC: U.S. Government Printing Office.

National Center for Education Statistics. (1997). *The condition of education: 1997.* Washington, DC: U.S. Government Printing Office.

National Center for Health Statistics. (1998). U.S. Decennial life tables for 1989-91, Vol. II, State life tables no. 1, Alabama. Hyattsville, MD: National Center for Health Statistics.

National Commission on Children. (1993). *Just the facts: A summary of recent information on America's children and their families.* Washington, DC: Author.

National Research Council (1993). *Losing generations: Adolescents in high risk settings.* Washington, DC: National Academic Press.

National Urban League. (1987). *Adolescent male responsibility, pregnancy prevention, and parenting program: A program development guide.* New York: Author.

Nattiv, A., & Puffer, J. C. (1991). Lifestyles and health risks of collegiate athletes. *Journal of Family Practice, 33,* 585–590.

Naulty, J. S. (1987). Obstetric anesthesia. In G. B. Avery (Ed.), *Neonatology: Pathophysiology and management of the newborn.* Philadelphia: Lippincott.

Newsweek. (1989, July 17). The future of abortion, pp. 14–26.

Neckerman, H. J. (1996). The stability of social groups in childhood and adolescence: The role of the classroom social environment. *Social Development, 5,* 131–145.

Neimark, E. D. (1975). Longitudinal development of formal operations thought. *Genetic Psychology Monographs, 91,* 171–225.

Neimark, E. D. (1982). Adolescent thought: Transition to formal operations. In B. B. Wolman (Ed.), *Handbook of developmental psychology* (pp. 486–499). Englewood Cliffs, NJ: Prentice-Hall.

Neisser, U., Boodoo, G., Bouchard, T. J., Jr., Bodkin, A. W., Brody, N., Ceci, S. J., Halpern, D. F., Loehlin, J. C., Perloff, R., Sternberg, R. J., & Urbana, S. (1996). Intelligence: Knowns and unknowns. *American Psychologist, 51,* 77–101.

Nelson, C. A. (1987). The recognition of facial expressions in the first two years of life: Mechanisms of development. *Child Development, 58,* 889–909.

Nelson, E. (1987). Learned helplessness and children's achievement. In S. Moore & K. Kolb (Eds.), *Reviews of research for practitioners and parents* (No. 3, pp. 11–22). Minneapolis: Center for Early Education and Development.

Nelson, K. (1973). Structure and strategy in learning to talk. *Monographs of the Society for Research in Child Development, 38*(1–2).

Nelson, K. (1981). Individual differences in language development: Implications for development and language. *Developmental Psychology, 17,* 170–187.

Nestor, H. (1992). *Family portraits in changing times.* Portland, OR: New Vision Press.

Neugarten, B., & Weinstein, R. (1964). The changing American grandparent. *Journal of Marriage and the Family, 26,* 199–204.

Neugarten, B. L. (1981). Growing old in 2020: How will it be different? *National Forum, 61*(3), 28–30.

Neugarten, B. L., Moore, J. W., & Lowe, J. C. (1965). Age norms, age constraints, and adult socialization. *American Journal of Sociology, 70,* 710–717.

Nevill, D. D., & Schlecker, D. I. (1988). The relation of self-efficacy and assertiveness to willingness to engage in traditional/nontraditional career activities. *Psychology of Women Quarterly, 12,* 91–98.

Newcomb, M. D., & Bentler, P. M. (1989). Substance use and abuse among children and teenagers. *American Psychologist, 44,* 242–248.

Newcomer, R. (1976). An evaluation of neighborhood service convenience for elderly housing project residents. In P. Suedfeld & J. Russell (Eds.), *The behavioral basis of design.* New York: McGraw-Hill.

Newcomer, S., & Udry, J. R. (1987). Parental marital status effects on adolescent sexual behavior. *Journal of Marriage and the Family, 49,* 235–240.

Newman, B. M. (1989). The changing nature of the parent-adolescent relationship from early to late adolescence. *Adolescence, 24,* 916–924.

Newman, B. M., & Newman, P. R. (1983). *Understanding adulthood.* New York: Holt, Rinehart & Winston.

Newman, J. L., Roberts, L. R., & Syre, C. R. (1993). Concepts of family among children and adolescents: Effect of cognitive level, gender, and family structure. *Developmental Psychology, 29,* 951–962.

Newman, P. R. (1982). The peer group. In B. B. Wolman (Ed.), *Handbook of developmental psychology* (pp. 526–535). Englewood Cliffs, NJ: Prentice-Hall.

Newman, P. R., & Newman, B. M. (1988). Parenthood and adult development. In R. Palkovitz & M. B. Sussman (Eds.), *Transitions to Parenthood, Marriage and Family Review, 12,* 313–337.

Newman, S., Karip, E., & Faux, R. B. (1995). Everyday memory function of older adults: The impact of intergenerational school volunteer programs. *Educational Gerontology, 21,* 569–580.

Nickols, S. Y. (1994). Work/family stresses. In P. C. McKenry & S. J. Price (Eds.), *Families and change: Coping with stressful events* (pp. 66–87). Thousand Oaks, CA: Sage.

NIH/CEPH Collaborative Mapping Group. (1992). A comprehensive genetic linkage map of the human genome. *Science, 258,* 67–86.

Ninio, A., & Rinott, N. (1988). Fathers' involvement in the care of their infants and their attributions of cognitive competence to infants. *Child Development, 59,* 652–663.

Nisan, M., & Kohlberg, L. (1982). Universality and variation in moral judgment: A longitudinal and cross-sectional study in Turkey. *Child Development, 53,* 865–876.

Nock, S. L. (1979). The family life cycle: Empirical or conceptual tool? *Journal of Marriage and the Family, 41,* 15–26.

Nolen-Hoeksema, S. (1987). Sex differences in unipolar depression: Evidence and theory. *Psychological Bulletin, 101,* 259–282.

Nolen-Hoeksema, S., Girgus, J. S., & Seligman, M. E. P. (1991). Sex differences in depression and explanatory style in children. *Journal of Youth and Adolescence, 20,* 233–246.

Noller, P. (1980). Misunderstandings in marital communication: A study of couples' nonverbal communication. *Journal of Personality and Social Psychology, 39,* 1135–1148.

Noppe, I. C., & Noppe, L. D. (1997). Evolving meanings of death during early, middle, and later adolescence. *Death Studies, 21,* 253–275.

Norem, J. K., & Cantor, N. (1988). Capturing the "flavor" of behavior: Cognition, affect, and integration. In A. Isen & B. Moore (Eds.), *Affect and social behavior.* New York: Academic Press.

Nsamenang, A. B. (1992). *Human development in cultural context: A Third World perspective.* Cross-cultural research and methodology series (Vol. 16). Newbury Park, CA: Sage.

Oates, W. E. (1997). Reconciling with unfulfilled dreams at the end of life. T. D. Hargrave & S. M. Hanna (Eds.), *The aging family: New visions in theory, practice, and reality.* New York: Brunner/Mazel, pp. 259–269.

O'Bryant, S. (1988). Sibling support and older widows' well-being. *Journal of Marriage and the Family, 50,* 173–183.

O'Bryant, S. L., & Morgan, L. A. (1990). Recent widows' kin support and orientations to self-sufficiency. *Gerontologist, 30,* 391–398.

O'Campo, P. Gielen, A. C., Faden, R. R., Xue, X., Kass, N., & Wang, M. (1995). Violence by male partners against women during the childbearing year: A contextual analysis. *American Journal of Public Health, 85,* 1092–1097.

Ochberg, R. L. (1986). College dropouts: The developmental logic of psychosocial moratoria. *Journal of Youth and Adolescence, 15,* 287–302.

Offenbacher, D. I., & Poster, C. H. (1985). Aging and the baseline code: An alternative to the "normless elderly." *Gerontologist, 25,* 526–531.

Ogbu, J. U. (1987). Variability in minority school performance: A problem in search of an explanation. *Anthropology and Education Quarterly, 18,* 312–334.

Okagaki, L., & Sternberg, R. J. (1993). Parental beliefs and children's school performance. *Child Development, 64,* 36–56.

Ohannessian, C. M., & Crockett, L. J. (1993). A longitudinal investigation of the relationship between educational investment and adolescent sexual activity. *Journal of Adolescent Research, 8,* 167–182.

Olds, D. L., Henderson, C. R., Jr., Tatelbaum, R., & Chamberlin, R. (1988). Improving the life-course development of socially disadvantaged mothers: A randomized trial of nurse home visitation. *American Journal of Public Health, 78,* 1436–1445.

O'Leary, P. A., Haley, W. E., & Paul, P. B. (1993). Behavioral assessment in Alzheimer's disease: Use of a 24-hr log. *Psychology and Aging, 8,* 139–143.

O'Leary, S. (1995). Parental discipline mistakes. *Current Directions in Psychological Science, 4,* 11–13.

Ollech, D., & McCarthy, J. (1997). Impediments to identity formation in female adolescents. *Psychoanalytic Psychology, 14,* 65–80.

Olshansky, S. J., Carnes, B. A., & Cassel, C. (1990). In search of Methuselah: Estimating the upper limits to human longevity. *Science, 250,* 634–640.

Olshansky, S. J., Carnes, B. A., & Grahn, D. (1998). Confronting the boundaries of human longevity. *American Scientist, 86*, 52–61.

Olweus, D. (1993). *Bullying at school: What we know and what we can do.* Cambridge, MA: Blackwell Press.

Olweus, D. (1995). Bullying or peer abuse at school: Facts and intervention. *Current Directions in Psychological Science, 4*, 196–200.

O'Mahoney, J. F. (1989). Development of thinking about things and people: Social and nonsocial cognition during adolescence. *Journal of Genetic Psychology, 150*, 217–224.

O'Neill, D. K., & Gopnik, A. (1991). Young children's ability to identify the sources of their beliefs. *Developmental Psychology, 27*, 390–397.

O'Neil, J. M., Ohlde, C., Tollefson, N., Barke, C., Piggott, T., & Watts, D. (1980). Factors, correlates, and problem areas affecting career decision making of a cross-sectional sample of students. *Journal of Counseling Psychology, 27*, 571–580.

Oosterwegel, A., & Oppenheimer, L. (1993). *The self-system: Developmental changes between and within self-concepts.* Hillsdale, NJ: Erlbaum.

Oppenheim, D., Sagi, A., & Lamb, M. E. (1988). Infant-adult attachments on the kibbutz and their relation to socioemotional development four years later. *Development Psychology, 24*, 427–433.

Orlofsky, J. L., Marcia, J. E., & Lesser, I. M. (1973). Ego identity status and intimacy versus isolation crisis of young adulthood. *Journal of Personality and Social Psychology, 27*, 211–219.

Osipow, S. H. (1986). Career issues through the life span. In M. S. Pallak & R. Perloff (Eds.), *Psychology and work: Productivity, change, and employment* (pp. 137–168). Washington, DC: American Psychological Association.

Osofsky, J. D. (1995). The effect of exposure to violence on young children. *American Psychologist, 50*, 782–788.

Oster, H., Hegley, D., & Nagel, L. (1992). Adult judgments and fine-grained analysis of infant facial expressions: Testing the validity of a priori coding formulas. *Developmental Psychology, 28*, 1115–1131.

Ostrov, E., Offer, D., & Howard, K. I. (1989). Gender differences in adolescent symptomatology: A normative study. *Journal of the American Academy of Child and Adolescent Psychiatry, 28*, 394–398.

Owen, M. T. (1997). *Mother-child interaction and cognitive outcomes associated with early child care: Results of the NICHD study.* Symposium presented at the Biennial Meeting of the Society for Research in Child Development, Symposium #2-210.

Padawer, J. A., Fagan, C., Janoff-Bulman, R., Strickland, B. R., & Chorowski, M. (1988). Women's psychological adjustment following emergency cesarean versus vaginal delivery. *Psychology of Women Quarterly, 12*, 25–34.

Paikoff, R. L., Parfenoff, S. H., Williams, S. A., McCormick, A., Greenwood, G. L., & Holmbeck, G. N. (1997). Parenting, parent-child relationships, and sexual possibility situations among urban African American preadolescents: Preliminary findings and implications for HIV prevention. *Journal of Family Psychology, 10*, 11–22.

Pajares, F. (1996). Self-efficacy beliefs in academic settings. *Review of Educational Researcher, 66*, 543–578.

Palermo, G. B. (1995). Should physician-assisted suicide be legalized? A challenge for the 21st century. *International Journal of Offender Therapy & Comparative Criminology, 39*, 367–376.

Palkovitz, R. (1985). Fathers' attendance, early contact, and extended care with their newborns: A critical review. *Child Development, 56*, 392–406.

Palladino-Schultheiss, D., & Blustein, D. (1994). Contributions of family relationship factors to the identity formation process. *Journal of Counseling Development, 73*, 159–166.

Pallett-Hehn, P., & Lucas, M. (1994). LIFE: Learning informally from elders. *Gerontologist, 34*, 267–271.

Palm, G. F., & Palkovitz, R. (1988). The challenge of working with new fathers: Implications for support providers. In R. Palkovitz & M. B. Sussman (Eds.), *Transitions to parenthood* (pp. 357–376). New York: Haworth.

Palmer, C. F. (1989). The discriminating nature of infants' exploratory actions. *Developmental Psychology, 25*, 885–893.

Palmore, E. B., Fillenbaum, G. G., & George, L. K. (1984). Consequences of retirement. *Journal of Gerontology, 39*, 109–116.

Palmore, E. B., Nowlin, J. B., & Wang, H. S. (1985). Predictors of function among the old-old: A 10-year follow-up. *Journal of Gerontology, 40*, 244–250.

Papini, D. R., Datan, N., & McCluskey-Fawcett, K. A. (1988). An observational study of affective and assertive family interactions during adolescence. *Journal of Youth and Adolescence, 17*, 477–492.

Papini, D. R., & Sebby, R. A. (1988). Variations in conflictual family issues by adolescent pubertal status, gender, and family member. *Journal of Early Adolescence, 8*, 1–15.

Papini, D. R., Sebby, R. A., & Clark, S. (1989). Affective quality of family relations and adolescent identity exploration. *Adolescence, 24*, 457–466.

Papousek, H., & Bernstein, P. (1969). The functioning of conditioning stimulation in human neonates and infants. In A. Ambrose (Ed.), *Stimulation in early infancy.* London: Academic Press.

Parcel, T. L., & Menaghan, E. G. (1994). *Parents' jobs and children's lives.* New York: Aldine de Gruyter.

Parents should talk to college students about alcohol. (1997, October 12). *Columbus Dispatch*, p. 7H.

Park, K. A., Lay, K., & Ramsay, L. (1993). Individual differences and developmental changes in preschoolers' friendships. *Developmental Psychology, 29*, 264–270.

Park, K. A., & Waters, E. (1989). Security of attachment and preschool friendships. *Child Development, 60*, 1076–1081.

Park, S-Y., Belsky, J., Putnam, S., & Crnic, K. (1997). Infant emotionality, parenting, and 3-year inhibition: Exploring stability and lawful discontinuity in a male sample. *Developmental Psychology, 33*, 218–227.

Parker, J. G., & Asher, S. R. (1993). Friendship and friendship quality in middle childhood: Links with peer group acceptance and feelings of loneliness and social dissatisfaction. *Developmental Psychology, 29*, 611–621.

Parkhurst, J. T., & Asher, S. R. (1992). Peer rejection in middle school: Subgroup differences in behavior, loneliness, and interpersonal concerns. *Developmental Psychology, 28*, 231–241.

Parsons, J. E., Adler, T. F., & Kaczala, C. M. (1982). Socialization of achievement attitudes and beliefs: Parental influences. *Child Development, 53*, 310–321.

Parsons, J. E., & Ruble, D. N. (1977). The development of achievement-related expectancies. *Child Development, 48,* 1075–1079.

Parsons, T. (1955). Family structure and the socialization of the child. In T. Parsons & R. F. Bales (Eds.), *Family, socialization, and interaction process.* Glencoe, IL: Free Press.

Parsons, T., & Bales, R. F. (Eds.). (1955). *Family socialization and interaction process.* New York: Free Press.

Pascarella, E. T., & Terenzini, P. T. (1991). *How college affects students: Findings and insights from twenty years of research.* San Francisco: Jossey-Bass.

Passman, R. H., & Longeway, K. P. (1982). The role of vision in maternal attachment: Giving 2-year-olds a photograph of their mother during separation. *Developmental Psychology, 18,* 530–533.

Patterson, C. J. (1992). Children of lesbian and gay parents. *Child Development, 63,* 1025–1042.

Patterson, C. J. (1995). Families of the lesbian baby boom: Parents' division of labor and children's adjustment. *Developmental Psychology, 31,* 115–123.

Patterson, D. (1987). The causes of Down's syndrome. *Scientific American, 257*(2), 52–61.

Patterson, G. R. (1982). *Coercive family processes.* Eugene, OR: Castalia.

Patterson, G. R. (1992). Developmental changes in antisocial behavior. In R. D. Peters, R. J. McMahon, & V. L. Quignsey (Eds.), *Aggression and violence throughout the lifespan.* Newbury Park, CA: Sage.

Patterson, I. (1996). Participation in leisure activities by older adults after a stressful life event: The loss of a spouse. *International Journal of Aging and Human Development, 42,* 123–142.

Patterson, L. E. (1997). Client resistance to career counseling. In *The Hatherleigh guide to vocational and career counseling* (pp. 17–33). New York: Hatherleigh Press.

Pavlov, I. P. (1927/1960). *Conditioned reflexes.* New York: Dover Press.

Peck, R. C. (1968). Psychological developments in the second half of life. In B. L. Nevgarten (Ed). *Middle age and aging.* Chicago: University of Chicago Press, pp. 88.

Pelham, B. W. (1991). On the benefits of misery: Self-serving biases in the depressive self-concept. *Journal of Personality and Social Psychology, 61,* 670–681.

Pelham, B. W., & Swann, W. B., Jr. (1989). From self-conceptions to self-worth: On the sources and structure of global self-esteem. *Journal of Personality and Social Psychology, 57,* 672–680.

Pellegrini, D. S. (1985). Social cognition and competence in middle childhood. *Child Development, 56,* 253–264.

Pemberton, M. B., Insko, C. A., & Schopler, J. (1996). Memory for and experience of differential competitive behavior of individuals and groups. *Journal of Personality and Social Psychology, 71,* 953–966.

Peplau, L. A., Russell, D., & Heim, M. (1977). An attributional analysis of loneliness. In I. Frieze, D. Bar-Tal, & J. Carroll (Eds.), *Attribution theory: Applications to social problems.* San Francisco: Jossey-Bass.

Perfect, T. J. (1994). What can Brinley Plots tell us about cognitive aging? *The Journals of Gerontology, 49,* P60–P64.

Perosa, L. M., Perosa, S. L., & Tam, H. P. (1996). The contribution of family structure and differentiation to identity development in females. *Journal of Youth and Adolescence, 25,* 817–837.

Perret-Clermont, A., Perret, J., & Bell, N. (1991). The social construction of meaning and cognitive activity in elementary school children. In L. B. Resnick, J. M. Levine, & S. D. Teasley (Eds.), *Perspectives on socially shared cognition* (pp. 41–62). Washington, DC: American Psychological Association.

Perrucci, C. C., Perrucci, R., & Targ, D. B. (1997). Gender differences in the economic, psychological and social effects of plant closings in an expanding economy. *Social Science Journal, 34,* 217–233.

Perry, B. D. (1994). Neurobiological sequelae of childhood trauma: PTSD in children:. In M. M. Murburg (Ed.), *Catecholamine function in posttraumatic stress disorder: Emerging concepts.* Washington, DC: American Psychiatric Press, 233–255.

Perry, B. D. (1996). Aggression and violence: the neurobiology of experience. *The Develop Mentor,* http://www.bcm.tmc.edu/civitas

Perry, B. D., Pollard, R., Blakley, T., Baker, W., & Vigilante, D. (1995). Childhood trauma, the neurobiology of adaptation and "use-dependent" development of the brain: How states become traits. *Infant Mental Health Journal, 16,* 271–291.

Perusse, D. (1994). Mate choice in modern societies: Testing evolutionary hypotheses with behavioral data. *Human Nature, 5,* 255–278.

Pete, J. M., & DeSantis, L. (1990). Sexual decision making in young black adolescent females. *Adolescence, 25,* 145–154.

Petersen, A. C., Compas, B. E., Brooks-Gunn, J., Stemmler, M., Ey, S., & Grant, K. E. (1993). Depression in adolescence. *American Psychologist, 48,* 155–168.

Petersen, A. C., Sarigiani, P. A., & Kennedy, R. E. (1991). Adolescent depression: Why more girls? *Journal of Youth and Adolescence, 20,* 247–272.

Petersen, A. C., Schulenberg, J. E., Abramowitz, R. H., Offer, D., & Jarcho, H. D. (1984). A self-image questionnaire for young adolescents (SIQYA): Reliability and validity studies. *Journal of Youth and Adolescence, 13,* 93–111.

Peterson, B. E., & Stewart, A. J. (1993). Generativity and social motives in young adults. *Journal of Personality and Social Psychology, 65,* 186–198.

Pettit, G. S., Dodge, K. A., & Brown, M. M. (1988). Early family experience, social problem-solving patterns, and children's social competence. *Child Development, 59,* 107–120.

Phillips, D. A. (1984). The illusion of incompetence among academically competent children. *Child Development, 55,* 2000–2016.

Phillips, D. A. (1987). Socialization of perceived academic competence among highly competent children. *Child Development, 58,* 1308–1320.

Phinney, J. S. (1996). Understanding ethnic diversity: The role of ethnic identity. *American Behavioral Scientist, 40,* 143–152.

Phinney, J. S. (1996). When we talk about American ethnic groups, what do we mean? *American Psychologist, 51,* 918–927.

Phinney, J. S. (1997). Variations in bicultural identification among African American and Mexican American adolescents. *Journal of Research on Adolescence, 7,* 3–32.

Piaget, J. (1926). *The language and thought of the child.* New York: Harcourt, Brace.

Piaget, J. (1952). *The language and thought of the child.* London: Routledge & Kegan Paul.

Piaget, J. (1929). *The child's conception of physical causality.* New York: Harcourt, Brace. (Originally published in French 1926)

Piaget, J. (1932/1948). *The moral judgment of the child.* Glencoe, IL: Free Press.

Piaget, J. (1951). *Play, dreams, and imitation in childhood.* New York: Norton.

Piaget, J. (1962). *Play, dreams, and imitation in childhood.* New York: Norton.

Piaget, J. (1941/1952). *The child's conception of number.* London: Kegan Paul, Trench & Trubner.

Piaget, J. (1936/1952). *The origins of intelligence in children.* New York: International Universities Press.

Piaget, J. (1954). *The construction of reality in the child.* New York: Basic Books.

Piaget, J. (1963). The attainment of invariants and reversible operations in the development of thinking. *Social Research, 30,* 283–299.

Piaget, J., & Inhelder, B. (1969). *The psychology of the child.* New York: Basic Books.

Piaget, J. (1970). Piaget's theory. In P. H. Mussen (Ed.), *Carmichael's manual of child psychology* (3rd ed., Vol. 1). New York: Wiley.

Piaget, J. (1972). Intellectual evolution from adolescence to adulthood. *Human Development, 15,* 1–12.

Piaget, J. (1972b). *The psychology of intelligence.* Totowa, NJ: Littlefield Adams.

Piaget, J. (1978/1985). *The equilibration of cognitive structures.* Chicago: University of Chicago Press.

Pick, H. L. (1989). Motor development: The control of action. *Developmental Psychology, 25,* 867–870.

Piers, M. W., & Landau, G. M. (1980). *The gift of play.* New York: Walker.

Pillow, B. H. (1991). Children's understanding of biased social cognition. *Developmental Psychology, 27,* 539–551.

Pina, D. L., & Bengtson, V. L. (1993). The division of household labor and wives' happiness: Ideology, employment, and perceptions of support. *Journal of Marriage and the Family, 55,* 901–912.

Piotrkowski, C. S., Rapoport, R. N., & Rapoport, R. (1987). Families and work. In M. B. Sussman & S. K. Steinmetz (Eds), *Handbook of marriage and the family* (pp. 251–283). New York: Plenum.

Pleck, J. H. (1985). *Working wives, working husbands.* New York: Sage.

Pleck, J. H., Sonenstein, F. L., & Ku, L. C. (1991). Adolescent males' condom use: Relationships between perceived cost-benefits and consistency. *Journal of Marriage and the Family, 53,* 733–746.

Plomin, R. (1987). Developmental behavioral genetics and infancy. In J. D. Osofsky (Ed.), *Handbook of infant development,* (2nd ed., pp. 363–414). New York: John Wiley & Sons.

Plomin R. (1990). *Nature and nurture: An introduction to human behavioral genetics.* Pacific Grove, CA: Brooks/Cole.

Plomin, R. (1994). *Genetics and experience.* Thousand Oaks, CA: Sage.

Plomin, R. (Ed.). (1994). *Individual differences and development* (Vol. 6). Thousand Oaks, CA: Sage.

Plomin, R., & McClearn, G. E. (1993). *Nature, nurture, and psychology.* Hyattsville, MD: American Psychological Association.

Plotnick, R. D. (1992). The effects of attitudes on teenage premarital pregnancy and its resolution. *American Sociological Review, 57,* 800–811.

Polednak, A. P. (1991). Black-white differences in infant mortality in 38 standard metropolitan statistical areas. *American Journal of Public Health, 81,* 1480–1482.

Pollan, S. M., & Levine, M. (1997). *Die broke: A radical, four-part financial plan.* New York: HarperCollins.

Pollitt, E. (1994). Poverty and child development: relevance of research in developing countries to the United States. *Child Development, 65,* 283–295.

Poon, L. W., & Fozard, J. L. (1978). Speed in retrieval from long-term memory in relation to age, familiarity, and datedness of information. *Journal of Gerontology, 33,* 711–717.

Porter, R. H., Balogh, R. D., & Makin, J. W. (1988). Olfactory influences on mother-infant interactions. In C. Rovee-Collier & L. Lipsitt (Eds.), *Advances in infancy research* (Vol. 5, pp. 39–68). Norwood, NJ: Albex.

Posada, G., Gao, Y., Wu, F., Posada, R., Tascon, M., Schoelmerich, A., Sagi, A., Kondo-Ikemura, K., Haaland, W., & Synnevaag, B. (1995). The secure-base phenomenon across cultures: Children's behavior, mothers' preferences, and experts' concepts. *Monographs of the Society for Research in Child Development, 60,* 27–48.

Power, T. G. (1985). Mother- and father-infant play: A developmental analysis. *Child Development, 56,* 1514–1524.

Pratt, C. C., Jones, L. L., Shin, H., & Walker, A. J. (1989). Autonomy and decision making between single older women and their caregiving daughters. *Gerontologist, 29,* 792–797.

Prawat, R. S., Byers, J. L., & Anderson, A. H. (1983). An attributional analysis of teachers' affective reactions to student success and failure. *American Educational Research Journal, 20,* 137–152.

Presser, H. B. (1989). Some economic complexities of child care provided by grandmothers. *Journal of Marriage and the Family, 51,* 581–591.

Pushkar, D., Arbuckle, T., Conway, M., Chaikelson, J., & Maag, U. (1997). Everyday activity parameters and competence in older adults. *Psychology and Aging, 12,* 600–609.

Putallaz, M. (1987). Maternal behavior and children's sociometric status. *Child Development, 58,* 324–340.

Pye, C. (1986). Quiché Mayan speech to children. *Journal of Child Language, 13,* 85–100.

Quadrel, M. J., Fischhoff, B., & Davis, W. (1993). Adolescent (in)vulnerability. *American Psychologist, 48,* 102–116.

Quakenbush, S. W., & Barnett, M. A. (1995). Correlates of reminiscence activity among elderly individuals. *International Journal of Aging & Human Development, 41,* 169–181.

Quiggle, N. L., Garber, J., Panak, W. F., & Dodge, K. A. (1992). Social information processing in aggressive and depressed children. *Child Development, 63,* 1305–1320.

Quinn, J. B. (1988, February 15). A crisis in child care. *Newsweek,* p. 57.

Quinn, J. F. (1988). Employment and the elderly. *The Gerontologist, 38,* 254–259.

Radke-Yarrow, M., Cummings, E. M., Kuczynski, L., & Chipman, M. (1985). Patterns of attachment in two- and three-year-olds in normal families and families with parental depression. *Child Development, 56,* 591–615.

Ragan, P. K. (1980). *Work and retirement: Policy issues.* Los Angeles: University of Southern California Press.

Raja, S. N., McGee, R., & Stanton, W. R. (1992). Perceived attachment to parents and peers and psychological well-being in adolescence. *Journal of Youth and Adolescence, 21,* 471–486.

Raley, R. K. (1996). A shortage of marriageable men? A note on the role of cohabitation in Black-White differences in marriage rates. *American Sociological Review, 61,* 973–983.

Ranzijn, R., Keeves, J., Luszcz, M., & Feather, N. T. (1998). The role of self-perceived usefulness and competence in the self-esteem of elderly adults: Confirmatory factor analyses of the Bachman revision of Rosenberg's self-esteem scale. *Journal of Gerontology: Psychological Sciences, 53B,* P96–P104.

Rapkin, B. D., & Fischer, K. (1992a). Framing the construct of life satisfaction in terms of older adults' personal goals. *Psychology and Aging, 7,* 138–149.

Rapkin, B. D., & Fischer, K. (1992b). Personal goals of older adults: Issues in assessment and prediction. *Psychology and Aging, 7,* 127–137.

Raschke, H. J. (1987). Divorce. In M. B. Sussman & S. K. Steinmetz (Eds.), *Handbook of marriage and the family* (pp. 597–624). New York: Plenum.

Raskas, D. F., & Hambrick, D. C. (1992). Multifunctional managerial development: A framework for evaluating the options. *Organizational Dynamics, 21,* 5–17.

Rauste-von Wright, M. (1989). Body image satisfaction in adolescent girls and boys: A longitudinal study. *Journal of Youth and Adolescence, 18,* 71–83.

Raver, C. C. (1996). Relations between social contingency in mother-child interaction and 2-year-olds' social competence. *Developmental Psychology, 32,* 850–859.

Receputo, G., Mazzoleni, G., DiFazio, I., & Alessandria, I. (1996b). Study on the sense of taste in a group of Sicilian centenarians. *Archives of Gerontology & Geriatrics,* Suppl. 5, 411–414.

Receputo, G., Mazzoleni, G., Rapisarda, R., & Di Fazio, I. (1996a). Sense of smell in centenarians from eastern Sicily. *Archives of Gerontology & Geriatrics,* Suppl. 5, 407–410.

Reese, J. N., & Botwinick, J. (1971). Detection and decision factors in auditory behavior of the elderly. *Journal of Gerontology, 26,* 133–136.

Reinisch, J. M., & Karow, W. G. (1977). Prenatal exposure to synthetic progestins and estrogens: Effects on human development. *Archives of Sexual Behavior, 6,* 257–288.

Reinisch, J. M., & Sanders, S. A. (1984). Prenatal gonadal steroidal influences on gender-related behavior. In G. D. DeVries, J. P. C. DeBruin, H. B. M. Uylings, & M. A. Corher (Eds.), *Sex differences in the brain: The relation between structure and function: Vol. 61. Progress in Brain Research.* Amsterdam: Elsevier.

Reis, H. T., Senchak, M., & Solomon, B. (1985). Sex differences in the intimacy of social interaction: Further examination of potential explanations. *Journal of Personality and Social Psychology, 48,* 1204–1217.

Reischl, T. M., & Hirsch, B. J. (1989). Identity commitments and coping with a difficult developmental transition. *Journal of Youth and Adolescence, 18,* 55–70.

Reiss, I. L. (1980). *Family systems in America* (3rd ed.). New York: Holt, Rinehart & Winston.

Remafedi, G. (1987). Adolescent sexuality: Psychosocial and medical implications. *Pediatrics, 79,* 326–330.

Rempel, J. K., Holmes, J. G., & Zanna, M. P. (1985). Trust in close relationships. *Journal of Personality and Social Psychology, 49,* 95–112.

Renshaw, P. D., & Brown, P. J. (1993). Loneliness in middle childhood: Concurrent and longitudinal predictors. *Child Development, 64,* 1271–1284.

Rest, J. R. (1983). Morality. In P. H. Mussen (General Ed.), *Handbook of child psychology: Vol. 3. Cognitive development* (J. H. Flavell & E. M. Markman, Eds.). New York: Wiley.

Reynolds, J. R. (1997). The effects of industrial employment conditions on job-related distress. *Journal of Health & Social Behavior, 38,* 105–116.

Rice, M. L. (1989). Children's language acquisition. *American Psychologist, 44,* 149–156.

Richards, F., & Commons, M. L. (1990). Postformal cognitive-developmental theory and research: A review of its current status. In C. N. Alexander & E. J. Langer (Eds.), *Higher stages of human development: Perspectives on adult growth* (pp. 229–257). New York: Oxford University Press.

Richards, M. H., & Larson, R. (1993). Pubertal development and the daily subjective states of young adolescents. *Journal of Research on Adolescence, 3,* 145–169.

Richardson, L. (1986, February). Another world. *Psychology Today, 20,* 22–27.

Ricks, M. H. (1985). The social transmission of parental behavior: Attachment across generations. In I. Bretherton & E. Waters (Eds.), *Growing points of attachment: Theory and research* (pp. 211–227). *Monographs of the Society for Research in Child Development, 50* (1–2, Serial No. 209).

Ridenour, M. V. (Ed.). (1978). *Motor development: Issues and applications.* Princeton, NJ: Princeton Books.

Rindfuss, R. R., Swicegood, C. G., & Rosenfeld, R. A. (1987). Disorder in the life course: How common and does it matter? *American Sociological Review, 52,* 785–801.

Rindfuss, R. R., & VandenHeuvel, A. (1990). Cohabitation: Precursor to marriage or alternative to being single? *Population and Development Review, 16,* 703–726.

Riegel, K. F. (1973). Dialectic operations: The final period of cognitive development. *Human Development, 16,* 346–370.

Riegel, K. F., & Riegel, R. M. (1972). Development, drop, and death. *Developmental Psychology, 6,* 306–319.

Riley, T., Adams, G. R., & Nielsen, E. (1984). Adolescent egocentrism: The association among imaginary audience behavior, cognitive development, and parental support and rejection. *Journal of Youth and Adolescence, 13,* 401–417.

Roberts, L. J., & Krokoff, L. J. (1990). Withdrawal, hostility, and displeasure in marriage. *Journal of Marriage and the Family, 52,* 95–105.

Roberts, R. E., & Sobhan, M. (1992). Symptoms of depression in adolescents: A comparison of Anglo, African, and Hispanic Americans. *Journal of Youth and Adolescence, 21,* 639–652.

Robertson, J., & Robertson, J. (1989). *Separation and the very young*. New York: Free Association Books.

Robertson, J. F., & Simons, R. L. (1989). Family factors, self-esteem, and adolescent depression. *Journal of Marriage and the Family, 51*, 125–138.

Robin, D. J., Berthier, N. E., & Clifton, R. K. (1996). Infants' predictive reaching for moving objects in the dark. *Developmental Psychology, 32*, 824–835.

Robinson, E. A., & Price, M. G. (1980). Pleasurable behavior in marital interaction: An observational study. *Journal of Consulting and Clinical Psychology, 48*, 117–118.

Rochat, P. (1989). Object manipulation and exploration in 2- to 5-month-old infants. *Developmental Psychology, 25*, 871–884.

Rodgers, F. A., & Rodgers, C. (1989). Business and the facts of family life. *Harvard Business Review, 67*, 121–129.

Roff, L. L., & Klemmack, D. L. (1986). Norms for employed daughters' and sons' behavior toward frail older parents. *Sex Roles, 14*, 363–368.

Rogers, C. R. (1972). *Becoming partners: Marriage and its alternatives*. New York: Delacorte Press.

Rogoff, B., Mistry, J., Goncu, A., & Mosier, C. (1993). Guided participation in cultural activity by toddlers and caregivers. *Monograph of the Society for Research in Child Development, 58*, (8 Serial No. 236).

Rogoff, B., & Morelli, G. (1989). Perspectives on children's development from cultural psychology. *American Psychologist, 44*, 343–348.

Rohner, R. P. (1984). Toward a conception of culture for cross-cultural psychology. *Journal of Cross-cultural Psychology, 15*, 111–138.

Roosa, M. W. (1984). Maternal age, social class, and the obstetric performance of teenagers. *Journal of Youth and Adolescence, 13*, 365–374.

Rosch, E. (1978). Principles of categorization. In E. Rosch & B. Lloyd (Eds.), *Cognition and categorization* (pp. 27–48). Hillsdale, NJ: Erlbaum.

Rose, S. A., Feldman, J. F., & Wallace, I. F. (1992). Infant information processing in relation to six-year cognitive outcomes. *Child Development, 63*, 1126–1141.

Rose, S. A., & Ruff, H. A. (1987). Cross-modal abilities in human infants. In J. D. Osofsky (Ed.), *Handbook of infant development* (2nd ed., pp. 318–362). New York: John Wiley & Sons.

Rosellini, L. (1992, July 6). Sexual desire. *U.S. News & World Report, 113(1)*, 60–66.

Rosen, A. B., & Rozin, P. (1993). Now you see it, now you don't: The preschool child's conception of invisible particles in the context of dissolving. *Developmental Psychology, 29*, 300–311.

Rosen, K. S., & Rothbaum, F. (1993). Quality of parental caregiving and security of attachment. *Developmental Psychology, 29*, 358–367.

Rosen, W. D., Adamson, L. B., & Bakeman, R. (1992). An experimental investigation of infant social referencing: Mothers' messages and gender differences. *Developmental Psychology, 28*, 1172–1178.

Rosenblatt, R. A., Mattis, R., & Hart, L. G. (1995). Abortions in rural Idaho: Physicians' attitudes and practices. *American Journal of Public Health, 85*, 1423–1425.

Rosenberg, M. (1979). *Conceiving the self*. New York: Basic Books.

Rosenberg, M., Schooler, C., & Schoenbach, C. (1989). Self-esteem and adolescent problems: Modeling reciprocal effects. *American Sociological Review, 54*, 1004–1018.

Rosenfeld, A., & Stark, E. (1987). The prime of our lives. *Psychology Today, 21*, 62–72.

Rosenfeld, A. H. (1978). *New views on older lives*. Rockville, MD: National Institute of Mental Health.

Rosenfeld, S. (1992). The costs of sharing: Wives' employment and husbands' mental health. *Journal of Health and Social Behavior, 33*, 213–225.

Rosenthal, R. (1994). Interpersonal expectancy effects: A 30-year perspective. *Current Directions in Psychological Science, 3*, 176–179.

Rosenthal, R. (1995). Critiquing *Pygmalion*: A 25-year perspective. *Current Directions in Psychological Science, 4*, 171–172.

Rosenthal, R., & Jacobson, L. (1968). *Pygmalion in the classroom: Teacher expectations and student intellectual development*. New York: Holt, Rinehart & Winston.

Ross, G., Kagan, J., Zelazo, P., & Kotelchuck, M. (1975). Separation protest in infants in home and laboratory. *Developmental Psychology, 11*, 256–257.

Ross, M. (1989). Relation of implicit theories to the construction of personal histories. *Psychological Review, 96*, 341–357.

Rostosky, S. S., & Travis, C. B. (1996). Menopause research and the dominance of the biomedical model 1984–1994. *Psychology of Women Quarterly, 20*, 285–312.

Roth, W. E. (1953). Precautions during pregnancy in New Guinea. In M. Mead & N. Calas (Eds.), *Primitive heritage*. New York: Random House.

Rotheram-Borus, M. J., & Wyche, K. F. (1994). Ethnic differences in identity development in the United States. In S. L. Archer (Ed.), *Interventions for adolescent identity development* (pp. 62–83). Thousand Oaks, CA: Sage.

Rovee, C. K., & Rovee, D. T. (1969). Conjugate reinforcement of infant exploratory behavior. *Journal of Experimental Child Psychology, 8*, 33–39.

Rovee-Collier, C. (1987). Learning and memory in infancy. In J. D. Osofsky (Ed.), *Handbook of infant development* (2nd ed., pp. 98–148). New York: John Wiley & Sons.

Rovee-Collier, C., Schechter, A., Shyi, G. C. W., & Shields, P. (1992). Perceptual identification of contextual attributes and infant memory retrieval. *Developmental Psychology, 28*, 307–318.

Rowe, J. W., & Kahn, R. L. (1997). Successful aging. *Gerontologist, 37*, 433–440.

Rowe, J. W., & Kahn, R. L. (1998). *Successful aging*. New York: Pantheon Books.

Rubin, K. H. (1980). Fantasy play: Its role in the development of social skills and social cognition. *New Directions in Child Development, 9*, 69–84.

Rubin, K. H., LeMare, L. J., & Lollis, S. (1990). Social withdrawal in children: Developmental pathways to peer rejection. In S. R. Asher & J. D. Coie (Eds.), *Peer rejection in childhood* (pp. 217–252). Cambridge: Cambridge University Press.

Rubin, L. B. (1980). The empty nest: Beginning or ending? In L. A. Bond & J. C. Rosen (Eds.), *Competence and coping during adulthood* (pp. 309–331). Hanover, NH: University Press of New England.

Ruff, H. A. (1984). Infants' manipulative exploration of objects: The effects of age and object characteristics. *Developmental Psychology, 20,* 9–20.

Ruff, H. A., Saltarelli, L. M., Capozzoli, M., & Dubiner, K. (1992). The differentiation of activity in infants' exploration of objects. *Developmental Psychology, 28,* 851–861.

Rumelhart, D. E., & McClelland, J. L. (1986). *Parallel distributed processing* (Vol. 1). Cambridge, MA: MIT Press.

Runyan, W. M. (1982). *Life histories and psychobiography: Explorations in theory and method.* New York: Oxford University Press.

Rusbult, C. E., & Arriaga, X. B. (1997). Interdependence theory. In S. Duck (Ed.), *Handbook of personal relationships: Theory, research and interventions* (2nd ed., pp. 221–250). Chichester, England: John Wiley & Sons.

Russell, D. W., & Cutrona, C. E. (1991). Social support, stress, and depressive symptoms among the elderly: Test of a process model. *Psychology and Aging, 6,* 190–201.

Rusting, R. L. (1992). Why do we age? *Scientific American, 267,* 130.

Rutter, M. (1983). School effects on pupil progress: Research findings and policy implications. *Child Development, 54,* 1–29.

Rutter, M. (1990). Commentary: Some focus and process considerations regarding effects of parental depression on children. *Developmental Psychology, 26,* 60–67.

Rutter, M. (1995). Maternal deprivation. In M. H. Bornstein (Ed.), *Handbook of parenting: Vol. 4: Applied and practical parenting* (pp. 3–31). Hillsdale, NJ: Erlbaum.

Ryan, R. M., & Lynch, J. H. (1989). Emotional autonomy versus detachment: Revisiting the vicissitudes of adolescence and young adulthood. *Child Development, 60,* 340–356.

Ryff, C. D. (1995). Psychological well-being in adult life. *Current Directions in Psychological Science, 4,* 99–104.

Ryff, C. D., & Essex, M. J. (1992). The interpretation of life experiences and well-being: The sample case of relocation. *Psychology and Aging, 7,* 507–517.

Ryff, C. D., & Heincke, S. G. (1983). Subjective organization of personality in adulthood and aging. *Journal of Personality and Social Psychology, 44,* 807–816.

Sabatelli, R. M., Meth, R. L., & Gavazzi, S. M. (1988). Factors mediating the adjustment to involuntary childlessness. *Family Relations, 37,* 338–343.

Sagi, A., & Hoffman, M. L. (1976). Empathetic distress in the newborn. *Developmental Psychology, 12,* 175–176.

Sagi, A., Lamb, M. E., Lewkowicz, K. S., Shoham, R., Dvir, R., & Estes, D. (1985). Security of infant-mother, -father, and -metapelet attachments among kibbutz-reared Israeli children. In I. Bretherton & E. Everett (Eds.), *Growing points of attachment theory and research* (pp. 257–275). *Monographs of the Society for Research in Child Development, 50* (1–2, Serial No. 209).

Salthouse, T. A. (1985). Speed of behavior and its implications for cognition. In J. W. Birren & K. W. Shaie (Eds.), *Handbook of the psychology of aging* (pp. 400–426). New York: Van Nostrand Reinhold.

Saltz, R., & Saltz, E. (1986). Pretend play training and its outcomes. In G. Fein & M. Rivkin (Eds.), *The young child at play: Reviews of research* (Vol. 4, pp. 155–173). Washington, DC: National Association for the Education of Young Children.

Salzinger, S., Feldman, R. S., Hammer, M., & Rosario, M. (1993). The effects of physical abuse on children's social relationships. *Child Development, 64,* 168–187.

Sameroff, A. J. (1982). Development and the dialectic: The need for a systems approach. In W. A. Collins (Ed.), *The concept of development: The Minnesota Symposia on Child Psychology* (Vol. 15). Hillsdale, NJ: Erlbaum.

Sameroff, A. J. (1987). Psychologic needs of the parent in infant development. In G. B. Avery (Ed.), *Neonatology: Pathophysiology and management of the newborn* (pp. 358–378). Philadelphia: Lippincott.

Sameroff, A. J., & Chandler, M. J. (1975). Reproductive risk and the continuum of caretaking casualty. In F. D. Horowitz, M., Hetherington, S. Scarr-Salapetek, & G. Siegel (Eds.), *Review of child development research* (Vol. 4). Chicago: University of Chicago Press.

Sampson, R. J., Raudenbush, S. W., & Earls, F. (1997). Neighborhoods and violent crime: A multilevel study of collective efficacy. *Science, 277,* 918–924.

Sanders, R. E. (1997). Find your partner and do-si-do: The formation of personal relationship between social beings. *Journal of Social and Personal Relationships, 14,* 387–415.

Sandler, J., Holder, A., & Meers, P. M. (1963). The ego ideal and the ideal self. *Psychoanalytic Study of the Child, 18,* 139–158.

Sansavini, A., Bertoncini, J., & Giovanelli, G. (1997). Newborns discriminate the rhythm of multisyllabic stressed words. *Developmental Psychology, 33,* 3–11.

Sapp, D. D. (1992). The point of creative frustration and the creative process: A new look at an old model. *Journal of Creative Behavior, 26,* 21–28.

Sarason, B. R., Sarason, I. G., Hacker, T. A., & Basham, R. B. (1985). Concomitants of social support: Social skills, physical attractiveness, and gender. *Journal of Personality and Social Psychology, 49,* 469–480.

Sarvela, P. D., & McClendon, E. J. (1988). Indicators of rural youth drug use. *Journal of Youth and Adolescence, 17,* 335–348.

Savin-Williams, R. (1996). Self-labeling and disclosure among gay, lesbian, and bisexual youths. In J. Laird & R-J Green (Eds.), *Lesbians and gays in couples and families: A Handbook for therapists* (pp. 153–182). San Francisco: Jossey-Bass.

Scanzoni, L. D., & Scanzoni, J. (1981). *Men, women, and change: A sociology of marriage and family* (2nd ed.). New York: McGraw-Hill.

Scarr, S. (1992). Developmental theories for the 1990s: Development and individual differences. *Child Development, 63,* 1–19.

Schaffer, H. R., & Emerson, P. E. (1964). *The development of social attachments in infancy. Monographs of the Society for Research in Child Development, 29,* (whole No. 94).

Schatz, M. (1983). Communication. In J. H. Flavell & E. M. Markman (Eds.), *Handbook of child psychology* (Vol. 3, pp. 841–889). New York: Wiley.

Schaie, K. W. (1965). A general model for the study of developmental problems. *Psychological Bulletin, 64,* 92–107.

Schaie, K. W. (1992). The impact of methodological changes in gerontology. *International Journal of Aging and Human Development, 35,* 19–29.

Schaie, K. W. (1994). The course of adult intellectual development. *American Psychologist, 49,* 304–313.

Schaie, K. W. (1996). Intellectual development in adulthood. In J. E. Birren, K. W. Schaie, R. P. Abeles, M. Gatz, & T. A. Salthouse (Eds.), *Handbook of the psychology of aging.* (4th ed., pp. 226–286). San Diego, CA: Academic Press.

Schaie, K. E., & Hertzog, C. (1983). Fourteen-year cohort-sequential analyses of adult intellectual development. *Developmental Psychology, 19,* 531–543.

Schickedanz, J. A. (1986). *More than the ABCs: The early stages of reading and writing.* Washington, DC: National Association for the Education of Young People.

Schneider, W., & Bjorklund, D. F. (1992). Expertise, aptitude, and strategic remembering. *Child Development, 63,* 461–473.

Schiedel, D. G., & Marcia, J. E. (1985). Ego identity, intimacy, sex-role orientation, and gender. *Developmental Psychology, 21,* 149–160.

Schneider, D. S., Sledge, P. A., Shuchter, S. R., & Zisook, S. (1996). Dating and remarriage over the first two years of widowhood. *Annals of Clinical Psychiatry, 8,* 51–57.

Schoen, R. (1992). First unions and the stability of first marriages. *Journal of Marriage and the Family, 54,* 281–284.

Schoen, R., & Wooldredge, J. (1989). Marriage choices in North Carolina and Virginia, 1969–71 and 1979–81. *Journal of Marriage and the Family, 51,* 465–482.

Scholnick, E. K. (1995, Fall). Direction I: Knowing and constructing plans. *SRCD Newsletter* 1–2.

Schootman, M., Fuortes, L. J., Zwerling, C., Albanese, M. A., & Watson, C. A. (1993). Safety behavior among Iowa junior high and high school students. *American Journal of Public Health, 83,* 1628–1629.

Schrof, J. M. (1994). A lens on maternity. *U.S. News & World Report, 116,* 66–69.

Schultheiss, D. P., & Blustein, D. L. (1994). Contributions of family relationship factors to the identity formation process. *Journal of Counseling and Development, 73,* 159–166.

Schulz, R., & Willamson, G. M. (1993). Psychosocial and behavioral dimensions of physical frailty. *The Journals of Gerontology, 48,* 39–43.

Schuster, C. S. (1986). Intrauterine development. In C. S. Schuster & S. S. Ashburn (Eds.), *The process of human development* (pp. 67–94). Boston: Little, Brown.

Schuster, M. A., Bell, R. M., & Kanouse, D. E. (1996). The sexual practices of adolescent virgins: Genital sexual activities of high school students who have never had vaginal intercourse. *American Journal of Public Health, 86,* 1570–1576.

Schwartz, A. N., Snyder, C. L., & Peterson, J. A. (1984). *Aging and life: An introduction to gerontology* (2nd ed.). New York: Holt, Rinehart & Winston.

Schweinhart, L. J., & Weikart, D. P. (1988). The High/Scope Perry Preschool Program. In R. H. Price, E. L. Cowen, R. P. Lorion, & J. Ramos-McKay (Eds.), *Fourteen ounces of prevention* (pp. 53–66). Washington, DC: American Psychological Association.

Scogin, F., Storandt, M., & Lott, L. (1985). Memory-skills training, memory complaints, and depression in older adults. *Journal of Gerontology, 40,* 562–568.

Scott, J. P. (1987). Critical periods in processes of social organization. In M. H. Bornstein (Ed.), *Sensitive periods in development: Interdisciplinary perspectives* (pp. 247–268). Hillsdale, NJ: Erlbaum.

Sears, P. S., & Barbee, A. H. (1978). Career and life satisfaction among Terman's gifted women. In J. Stanley, W. George, & C. Solano (Eds.), *The gifted and the creative: Fifty year perspective.* Baltimore: Johns Hopkins University Press.

Seccombe, K. (1991). Assessing the costs and benefits of children: Gender comparisons among childfree husbands and wives. *Journal of Marriage and the Family, 53,* 191–202.

Seeman, T. E., Berkman, L. F., Blazer, D., & Rowe, J. W. (1994). Social ties and support and neuroendocrine function: The MacArthur studies of successful aging. *Annals of Behavioral Medicine, 16,* 95–106.

Segal, L. B., Oster, H., Cohen, M., Caspi, B., Myers, M., & Brown D. (1995). Smiling and fussing in seven-month-old preterm and full-term Black infants in the still-face situation. *Child Development, 66,* 1829–1843.

Seligman, M. E. P. (1975). *Helplessness.* San Francisco: W. H. Freeman.

Sells, C. W., & Blum, R. W. (1996). Morbidity and mortality among U.S. adolescents: An overview of data and trends. *American Journal of Public Health, 86,* 513–519.

Selman, R. L. (1971). Taking another's perspective: Role-taking development in early childhood. *Child Development, 42,* 1721–1734.

Selman, R. L. (1980). *The growth of interpersonal understanding: Developmental and clinical analysis.* New York: Academic Press.

Selman, R. L. (1994). The relation of role taking to the development of moral judgment in children. In B. Puka (Ed.), *Fundamental research in moral development. Moral development: A compendium,* Vol. 2. (pp. 87–99). New York: Garland.

Selzer, S. C., & Denney, N. W. (1980). Conservation abilities among middle-aged and elderly adults. *Aging and Human Development, 11,* 135–146.

Sera, M. D., Troyer, D., & Smith, L. B. (1988). What do two-year-olds know about the sizes of things? *Child Development, 59,* 1489–1496.

Serbin, L. A., Powlishta, K. K., & Gulko, J. (1993). The development of sex typing in middle childhood. *Monographs of the Society for Research in Child Development, 58* (Whole No. 232).

Serovich, J. M., & Greene, K. (1997). Predictors of adolescent sexual risk taking behaviors which put them at risk for contracting HIV. *Journal of Youth and Adolescence, 26,* 429–444.

Setterlund, M. B., & Niedenthal, P. M. (1993). "Who am I? Why am I here?": Self-esteem, self-clarity, and prototype matching. *Journal of Personality and Social Psychology, 65,* 769–780.

Share, D. L., McGee, R., & Silva, P. A. (1989). IQ and reading progress: A test of the capacity notion of IQ. *Journal of the American Academy of Child and Adolescent Psychiatry, 28,* 97–100.

Sharpley, C. F. (1997). Psychometric properties of the Self-perceived Stress in Retirement Scale. *Psychological Reports, 81,* 319–322.

Sharpsteen, D. J., & Kirkpatrick, L. A. (1997). Romantic jealousy and adult romantic attachment. *Journal of Personality and Social Psychology, 72,* 627–640.

Shay, K. A., & Roth, D. L. (1992). Association between aerobic fitness and visuospatial performance in healthy older adults. *Psychology and Aging, 7,* 15–24.

Shears, L. M., & Bower, E. M. (1974). *Games in education and development.* Springfield, IL: Charles C. Thomas.

Shepard, L. A., & Smith, M. L. (1986). Synthesis of research on school readiness and kindergarten retention. *Educational Leadership, 44,* 78–86.

Sher, T. G., & Weiss, R. L. (1991). Negativity in marital communication? Where's the beef? Special Issue: Negative communication in marital interaction: A misnomer? *Behavioral Assessment, 13,* 1–5.

Shinn, M., & Weitzman, B. (1996). Homeless families are different. In *Homelessness in America.* Washington, DC: National Coalition for the Homeless.

Shostak, A., & McLouth, G. (1985). *Men and abortion.* New York: Praeger.

Shostak, A. B. (1987). Singlehood. In M. B. Sussman & S. K. Steinmetz (Eds.), *Handbook of marriage and the family* (pp. 355–368). New York: Plenum.

Siegel, B. (1996). Is the emperor wearing clothes? Social policy and the empirical support for full inclusion of children with disabilities in the preschool and early elementary grades. *Social Policy Report, X,* 2–17.

Silka, L., & Kiesler, S. (1977). Couples who choose to remain childless. *Family Planning Perspectives, 9,* 16–25.

Silver, M. (1995). Sex and violence on TV. *U.S. News & World Report, 119,* 62–68.

Silverman, P. R. (1989). Deconstructing motherhood. *Readings: A Journal of Reviews and Commentary in Mental Health, 4,* 14–18.

Silverstein, A. B., Pearson, L. B., Aguinaldo, N. E., Friedman, S. L., Tokayama, D. L., & Weiss, Z. T. (1982). Identity conservation and equivalence conservation: A question of developmental priority. *Child Development, 53,* 819–821.

Simonton, D. K. (1988). Age and outstanding achievement: What do we know after a century of research? *Psychological Bulletin, 104,* 251–267.

Simonton, D. K. (1989). The swan-song phenomenon: Last-works effects for 172 classical composers. *Psychology and Aging, 4,* 42–47.

Simons, R. L., Beaman, J., Conger, R. D., & Chao, W. (1993). Stress, support and antisocial behavior trait as determinants of emotional well-being and parenting practices among single mothers. *Journal of Marriage and the Family, 55,* 385–398.

Simons, R. L., Lorenz, F. O., Wu, C., & Conger, R. D. (1993). Social network and marital support as mediators and moderators of the impact of stress and depression on parental behaviors. *Developmental Psychology, 29,* 368–381.

Singelakis, A. T. (1990). Real estate market trends and the displacement of the aged: Examination of the linkages in Manhattan. *Gerontologist, 30,* 658–666.

Singer, D. G., & Singer, J. L. (1990). *The house of make-believe: Children's play and developing imagination.* Cambridge: Harvard University Press.

Singer, J. L. (1975). *The inner world of daydreaming.* New York: Colophon Books.

Singer, L. T., Davillier, M., Bruening, P., Hawkins, S., & Yamashita, T. S. (1996). Social support, psychological distress, and parenting strains in mothers of very low birth weight infants. *Family Relations, 45,* 343–350.

Singer, W. (1995). Development and plasticity of cortical processing architectures. *Science, 270,* 758–764.

Skaalvik, E. M., & Hagtvet, K. A. (1990). Academic achievement and self-concept: An analysis of causal predominance in a developmental perspective. *Journal of Personality and Social Psychology, 58,* 292–307.

Skerrett, K. (1996). From isolation to mutuality: A feminist collaborative model of couples therapy. *Women and Therapy, 19,* 93–106.

Skinner, B. F. (1938). *The behavior of organisms.* New York: Appleton-Century-Crofts.

Skinner, B. F. (1983). Intellectual self-management in old age. *American Psychologist, 38,* 239–244.

Skinner, B. F. (1987). Whatever happened to psychology as the science of behavior? *American Psychologist, 42,* 780–786.

Slade, A. (1987). A longitudinal study of maternal involvement and symbolic play during the toddler period. *Child Development, 58,* 367–375.

Slavik, S. (1995). Presenting social interest to different lifestyles. Special Issue: Counseling homosexuals and bisexuals. *Individual Psychology: Journal of Adlerian Theory, Research & Practice, 51,* 166–177.

Slavin, R. E. (1987). Grouping for instruction in the elementary school. *Educational Psychologist, 22,* 109–127.

Sliwinski, M., Lipton, R. B., Buschke, H., & Stewart, W. (1996). The effects of preclinical dementia on estimates of normal cognitive functioning in aging. *Journals of Gerontology Series B-Psychological Sciences & Social Sciences, 51B,* P217–P225.

Slobin, D. I. (1985). *The cross-linguistic study of language acquisition* (Vols. 1, 2). Hillsdale, NJ: Erlbaum.

Small, S. A., & Kerns, D. (1993). Unwanted sexual activity among peers during early and middle adolescence: Incidence and risk factors. *Journal of Marriage and the Family, 55,* 941–952.

Small, S. A., & Riley, D. (1990). Assessment of work spillover into family life. *Journal of Marriage and the Family, 52,* 51–62.

Small, S. A., Silverberg, S. B., & Kerns, D. (1993). Adolescents' perceptions of the costs and benefits of engaging in health-compromising behaviors. *Journal of Youth and Adolescence, 22,* 73–88.

Smetana, J. G. (1985). Preschool children's conceptions of transgressions: Effects of varying moral and conventional domain-related attributes. *Developmental Psychology, 21,* 18–29.

Smetana, J. G. (1986). Preschool children's conceptions of sex-role transgressions. *Child Development, 57,* 862–871.

Smetana, J. G., Schlagman, N., & Adams, P. W. (1993). Preschool children's judgments about hypothetical and actual transgressions. *Child Development, 64,* 202–214.

Smith, B. A., & Blass, E. M. (1996). Taste-mediated claiming in premature, preterm, and full-term human infants. *Developmental Psychology, 32,* 1084–1089.

Smith, D. C. (1997). *Caregiving: Hospice-proven techniques for healing body and soul.* New York: Macmillan Publishing.

Smith, D. M. (1987). Peers, subcultures, and schools. In D. Marsland (Ed.), *Education and youth* (pp. 41–64). London: Falmer Press.

Smith, E. M., Ford, J. K., & Kozlowski, S. W. J. (1997). Building adaptive expertise: Implications for training design strategies. In M. S. Quinones & A. Ehrenstein (Eds.), *Training for a rapidly changing workplace: Applications of psychological research.* Washington, DC: American Psychological Association.

Smith, L. B., Jones, S. S., & Landau, B. (1992). Count nouns, adjectives, and perceptual properties in children's novel word interpretations. *Developmental Psychology, 28,* 273–286.

Smith, P. K. (Ed.). (1991). *The psychology of grandparenthood: An international perspective.* London: Routledge.

Smith, P. K., Hunter, T., Carvalho, A. M. A., & Costabile, A. (1992). Children's perceptions of playfighting, playchasing and real fighting: A cross-national interview study. *Social Development, 1,* 211–221.

Smith, T. L. (1986). Self-concepts of youth sport participants and nonparticipants in grades 3 and 6. *Perceptual and Motor Skills, 62,* 863–866.

Snarey, J. (1993). *How fathers care for the next generation: A four-decade study.* Cambridge, MA: Harvard University Press.

Snarey, J. R., Reimer, J., & Kohlberg, L. (1985). Development of social-moral reasoning among kibbutz adolescents: A longitudinal cross-sectional study. *Developmental Psychology, 21,* 3–17.

Snow, C. E. (1984). Parent-child interaction and the development of communicative ability. In R. L. Schiefelbusch & J. Pickar (Eds.), *Communicative competence: Acquisition and intervention* (pp. 69–108). Baltimore: University Park Press.

Snow, C. E. (1987). Beyond conversation: Second language learners' acquisition of description and explanation. In J. P. Lantolf & A. Labarca (Eds.), *Research in second language learning: Focus on the classroom* (pp. 3–16). Norwood, NJ: Ablex.

Snyder, C. R. (1994). *The psychology of hope: You can get there from here.* New York: Free Press.

Snyder, C. R., Harris, C., Anderson, J. R., Holleran, S. A., Irving, L. M., Sigmon, S. T., Yoshinobu, L., Gibb, J., Langelle, C., & Harney, P. (1991). The will and the ways: Development and validation of an individual-differences measure of hope. *Journal of Personality and Social Psychology, 60,* 570–585.

Smolowe, J. (1997). A battle against biology; a victory in adoption. *Time, 150,* p. 46.

Somerson, M. D. (1997, April 20). Gazing into genetics' crystal ball. *The Columbus Dispatch,* p. 1A–2A.

Somers, M. D. (1993). A comparison of voluntarily childfree adults and parents. *Journal of Marriage and the Family, 55,* 643–650.

Sonnentag, S. (1995). Excellent software professionals: Experience, work activities, and perception by peers. *Behavior & Information Technology, 14,* 289–299.

Sophian, C. (1988). Limitations on preschool children's knowledge about counting: Using counting to compare two sets. *Developmental Psychology, 24,* 634–640.

Sophian, C., & Yengo, L. (1985). Infants' understanding of visible displacements. *Developmental Psychology, 21,* 932–941.

Sosa, R., Kennell, J., Klaus, M., Robertson, S., & Urrutia, J. (1980). The effect of a supportive companion on perinatal problems, length of labor, and mother-infant interaction. *New England Journal of Medicine, 303,* 597–600.

South, S. J. (1993). Racial and ethnic differences in the desire to marry. *Journal of Marriage and the Family, 55,* 357–370.

South, S. J., & Lloyd, K. M. (1992). Marriage opportunities and family formation: Further implications of imbalanced sex ratios. *Journal of Marriage and the Family, 54,* 440–451.

Spanier, G. B., Sauer, W., & Larzelere, R. (1979). An empirical evaluation of the family life cycle. *Journal of Marriage and the Family, 41,* 27–38.

Spearman, C. (1927). *The abilities of man.* New York: Macmillan.

Speckhard, A. C., & Rue, V. M. (1992). Post-abortion syndrome: An emerging public health concern. *Journal of Social Issues, 48,* 95–119.

Spelke, E. S., von Hofsten, C., & Kestenbaum, R. (1989). Object perception in infancy: Interaction of spatial and kinetic information for object boundaries. *Developmental Psychology, 25,* 185–186.

Spence, M. J., & DeCasper, A. J. (1987). Prenatal experience with low-frequency maternal-voice sounds influence neonatal perception of maternal voice samples. *Infant Behavior and Development, 10,* 133–142.

Spencer, M. B. (1982). Personal and group identity of black children: An alternative synthesis. *Genetic Psychology Monographs, 103,* 59–84.

Spencer, M. B. (1988). Self-concept development. In D. T. Slaughter (Ed.), *Black children in poverty: Developmental perspectives* (pp. 59–72). San Francisco: Jossey-Bass.

Spencer, M. B., Cunningham, M., & Swanson, D. P. (1995). Identity as coping: Adolescent African-American males' adaptive responses to high-risk environments. In H. W. Harris, H. C. Blue, & E. E. H. Griffith (Eds.), *Racial and ethnic identity: Psychological development and creative expression* (pp. 31–52). New York: Routledge.

Spencer, M. B., & Markstrom-Adams, C. (1990). Identity processes among racial and ethnic minority children in America. *Child Development, 61,* 290–310.

Sperling, D. (1989, March 10). Success rate for in vitro is only 9%. *USA Today,* p. 1D.

Spitz, R. A. (1945). Hospitalism: An inquiry into the genesis of psychiatric conditions in early childhood. *Psychoanalytic Study of the Child, 1,* 113–117.

Spitz, R. A. (1946). Anaclitic depression. *Psychoanalytic Study of the Child, 2,* 313–342.

Spitze, G., & Logan, J. (1990). Sons, daughters, and intergenerational social support. *Journal of Marriage and the Family, 52,* 420–430.

Sprunger, L. W., Boyce, W. T., & Gaines, J. A. (1985). Family-infant congruence: Routines and rhythmicity in family adaptations to a young infant. *Child Development, 56,* 564–572.

Sroufe, L. A. (1979). Socioemotional development. In J. D. Osofsky (Ed.), *Handbook of infant development* (pp. 462–516). New York: Wiley.

Sroufe, L. A., & Fleeson, J. (1986). Attachment and the construction of relationships. In W. W. Hartup & Z. Rubin (Eds.), *Relationships and development* (pp. 51–72). Hillsdale, NJ: Erlbaum.

Sroufe, L. A., Schork, E., Motti, F., Lawroski, N., & La Freniere, P. (1984). The role of affect in social competence. In C. E. Izard, J. Kagan, & R. B. Zajonc (Eds.), *Emotions, cognition, and behavior* (pp. 38–72). Cambridge: Cambridge University Press.

Stack, D. M., & Muir, D. W. (1992). Adult tactile stimulation during face-to-face interactions modulates five-month-olds' affect and attention. *Child Development, 63,* 1509–1525.

Stack, S. (1990). The impact of divorce on suicide, 1959–1980. *Journal of Marriage and the Family, 52,* 119–128.

Stallings, J. A. (1995). Ensuring teaching and learning in the 21st century. *Educational Researcher, 24,* 4–8.

Standley, K., Soule, B., & Copans, S. A. (1979). Dimensions of prenatal anxiety and their influence on pregnancy outcome. *American Journal of Obstetrics and Gynecology, 135,* 22–26.

Stapley, J. C., & Haviland, J. M. (1989). Beyond depression: Gender differences in normal adolescents' emotional experiences. *Sex Roles, 20,* 295–308.

Stattin, H., & Klackenberg-Larsson, I. (1991). The short- and long-term implications for parent-child relations of parents' prenatal preferences for their child's gender. *Developmental Psychology, 27,* 141–147.

Stechler, G., & Halton, A. (1982). Prenatal influences on human development. In B. B. Wolman (Ed.), *Handbook of developmental psychology* (pp. 175–189). Englewood Cliffs, NJ: Prentice-Hall.

Stein, P. J. (1989). The diverse world of the single adult. In J. M. Henslin (Ed.), *Marriage and family in a changing society* (3rd ed.). New York: Free Press.

Steinberg, L. (1990). Autonomy, conflict, and harmony in the family relationship. In S. S. Feldman & G. R. Elliott (Eds.), *At the threshold: The developing adolescent* (pp. 255–277). Cambridge: Harvard University Press.

Steinberg, L., & Dornbusch, S. M. (1991). Negative correlates of part-time employment during adolescence: Replication and elaboration. *Developmental Psychology, 27,* 304–313.

Steinberg, L. D. (1981). Transformations in family relations at puberty. *Developmental Psychology, 17,* 833–840.

Stengel, R. S. (1985, September 2). Snapshot of a changing America. *Time,* pp. 16–18.

Stephens, M. A. P., & Bernstein, M. D. (1984). Social support and well-being among residents of planned housing. *Gerontologist, 24,* 144–148.

Sternberg, R. J. (1985). *Beyond IQ: A triarchic theory of human intelligence.* Cambridge: Cambridge University Press.

Sternberg, R. J. (1988). *The triangle of love.* New York: Basic Books.

Sternberg, R. J. (1990). *Wisdom: Its nature, origins and development.* New York: Cambridge University Press.

Stevens, J. H., Jr. (1988). Social support, locus of control, and parenting in three low-income groups of mothers: Black teenagers, black adults, and white adults. *Child Development, 59,* 635–642.

Stevens, J. H., Jr. & Bakeman, R. (1985). A factor analytic study of the HOME scale for infants. *Developmental Psychology, 21,* 1196–1203.

Stevens-Long, J., & Commons, M. L. (1992). *Adult life: Developmental processes.* (4th ed.). Mountain View, CA: Mayfield Publishing.

Stevenson, B. W., Roscoe, B., Brooks II, R. H., & Kelsey, T. (1987). Profiles of mod revivalists: A case study of a reemerging adolescent group. *Adolescence, 22,* 393–404.

Stevenson, D. L., & Baker, D. P. (1987). The family-school relation and the child's school performance. *Child Development, 58,* 1348–1357.

Stevenson, H. W. (1992, December). Learning from Asian schools. *Scientific American, 267(6),* 70–77.

Stevenson, H. W., Chen, C., & Lee, S. (1993). Mathematics achievement of Chinese, Japanese, and American children: Ten years later. *Science, 259,* 53–58.

Stewart, A. J., & Healy, J. M. (1989). Linking individual development and social changes. *American Psychologist, 44,* 30–42.

Stewart, A. J., & Vandewater, E. A. (1998). The course of generativity. In D. P. McAdams & E. De St. Aubin (Eds.), *Generativity and adult development* (pp. 75–100). Washington, DC: American Psychological Association.

Sticker, E. J. (1991). The importance of grandparenthood during the life cycle in Germany. In P. K. Smith (Ed.), *The psychology of grandparenthood: An international perspective* (pp. 32–49). London: Routledge.

Stipek, D., Recchia, S., & McClintic, S. (1992). Self-evaluation in young children. *Monographs of the Society for Research in Child Development, 57(1,* Serial No. 226).

Stone, B. K. (1998). I feel more like 17. *Bryn Mawr Alumnae Bulletin,* Summer, p. 4.

Streissguth, A. P., Barr, H. M., Sampson, P. D., Darby, B. L., & Martin, D. C. (1989). IQ at age 4 in relation to maternal alcohol use and smoking during pregnancy. *Developmental Psychology, 25,* 3–11.

Stringfellow, L. (1978). The Vietnamese. In A. L. Clark (Ed.), *Culture, childbearing, and the health professionals* (pp. 174–182). Philadelphia: F. A. Davis.

Strober, M. (1981). A comparative analysis of personality organization in juvenile anorexia nervosa. *Journal of Youth and Adolescence, 10,* 285–295.

Stroh, L. K., & Reilly, A. H. (1997). Rekindling organizational loyalty: The role of career mobility. *Journal of Career Development, 24,* 39–54.

Stuart-Hamilton, I. (1996). Intellectual changes in late life. In R. T. Woods (Ed), *Handbook of the clinical psychology of aging* (pp. 23–41). Chichester, England: John Wiley & Sons.

Students, employers disagree on seniors' job readiness, survey shows. (1998, January 23). *Columbus Dispatch,* Employment '98 supplement, p. 9.

Sullivan, H. S. (1949). *The collected works of Harry Stack Sullivan* (Vols. 1, 2). New York: Norton.

Sullivan, K., & Sullivan, A. (1980). Adolescent-parent separation. *Developmental Psychology, 16,* 93–104.

Sullivan, M. W., Lewis, M., & Allesandri, S. M. (1992). Cross-age stability in emotional expressions during learning and extinction. *Developmental Psychology, 28,* 58–63.

Super, C. M., Kagan, J., Morrison, F. J., Haith, M. M., & Weiffenbach, J. (1972). Discrepancy and attention in the five-month infant. *Genetic Psychology Monographs, 85,* 305–331.

Susman, E. J., Dorn, L. D., & Chrousos, G. P. (1991). Negative hormones and affect levels in young adolescents: Concurrent and predictive perspectives. *Journal of Youth and Adolescence, 20,* 167–190.

Susman, E. J., Nottelmann, E. D., Inoff, G. E., Dorn, L. D., Cutler, G. B., Jr., Loriaux, D. L., & Chrousos, G. P. (1985). The relationship of relative hormone levels and physical development and social-emotional behavior in young adolescents. *Journal of Youth and Adolescence, 14,* 245–264.

Sutton-Smith, B. A. (1972). Syntax for play and games. In R. E. Herron & B. Sutton-Smith (Eds.), *Child's play*. New York: Wiley.

Swann, W. B., Jr. (1990). To be known or be adored? The interplay of self-enhancement and self-verification. In E. T. Higgins & R. M. Sorrentino (Eds.), *Handbook of motivation and cognition: Foundations of social behavior* (pp. 404–448). New York: Guilford.

Swyer, P. R. (1987). The organization of perinatal care with particular reference to the newborn. In G. B. Avery (Ed.), *Neonatology: Pathophysiology and management of the newborn* (pp. 13–44). Philadelphia: Lippincott.

Tanfer, K. (1987). Premarital cohabitation among never-married women. *Journal of Marriage and the Family, 49,* 483–497.

Tang, C. S. K., Wong, C. S. Y., & Schwarzer, R. (1996). Psychosocial differences between occasional and regular adolescent users of marijuana and heroin. *Journal of Youth and Adolescence, 25,* 219–239.

Tangney, J. P. (1991). Moral affect: The good, the bad, and the ugly. *Journal of Personality and Social Psychology, 61,* 598–607.

Tangney, J. P., Wagner, P., Fletcher, C., & Gramzow, R. (1992). Shamed into anger? The relation of shame and guilt to anger and self-reported aggression. *Journal of Personality and Social Psychology, 62,* 669–675.

Tanner, J. M. (1981). *A history of the study of human growth*. Cambridge, England: Cambridge University Press.

Tanner, J. M. (1990). *Foetus into man: Physical growth from conception to maturity* (Rev. ed.). Cambridge: Harvard University Press.

Taylor, I. A. (1975). An emerging view of creative actions. In I. A. Taylor & J. W. Getzels (Eds.), *Perspectives in creativity*. Chicago: Aldine-Atherton.

Taylor, M., Cartwright, B. S., & Carlson, S. M. (1993). A developmental investigation of children's imaginary companions. *Developmental Psychology, 29,* 276–285.

Taylor, R. D., & Oskay, G. (1995). Identity formation in Turkish and American late adolescents. *Journal of Cross-Cultural Psychology, 26,* 8–22.

Taylor, R. J. (1986). Religious participation among elderly blacks. *Gerontologist, 26,* 630–636.

Taylor, R. J., Chatters, L. M., Tucker, M. B., & Lewis, E. (1990). Black families. *Journal of Marriage and the Family, 52,* 993–1014.

Teachman, J. D., Polonko, K. A., & Scanzoni, J. (1987). Demography of the family. In M. B. Sussman & S. K. Steinmetz (Eds.), *Handbook of marriage and the family* (pp. 3–57). New York: Plenum.

Tedesco, L. A., & Gaier, E. L. (1988). Friendship bonds in adolescence. *Adolescence, 23,* 127–136.

Teller, D. Y., & Bornstein, J. H. (1987). Infant color vision and color perception. In P. Salapatek & L. Cohen (Eds.), *Handbook of infant perception* (Vol. 1). Orlando, FL: Academic Press.

Terman, L. M. (1925). *Genetic studies of genius*. Stanford, CA: Stanford University Press.

Terman, L. M., & Oden, M. H. (1947). *The gifted child grows up: Twenty-five years' follow-up of a superior group*. Stanford, CA: Stanford University Press.

Terman, L. M., & Oden, M. H. (1959). *The gifted group at mid-life: Thirty-five years' follow-up of a superior group*. Stanford, CA: Stanford University Press.

Terman, L. M., & Oden, M. H. (1959). The gifted group at mid-life: *Thirty-five years; follow-up of the superior child*. Stanford, CA: Stanford University Press.

Teti, D. M., & Lamb, M. E. (1989). Outcomes of adolescent marriage and adolescent childbirth. *Journal of Marriage and the Family, 51,* 203–212.

Teti, D. M., Nakagawa, M., Das, R., & Wirth, O. (1991). Security of attachment between preschoolers and their mothers: Relations among social interaction, parenting stress, and mothers' sorts of the attachment Q-set. *Developmental Psychology, 27,* 440–447.

Tharp, R. G. (1989). Psychocultural variables and constants: Effects on teaching and learning in schools. *American Psychologist, 44,* 349–359.

Tharp, R. G., & Gallimore, R. (1988). *Rousing minds to life: Teaching, learning, and schooling in social context*. Cambridge: Cambridge University Press.

Thatcher, R. W., Walker, R. A., & Giudice, S. (1987). Human cerebral hemispheres develop at different rates and ages. *Science, 236,* 1110–1113.

Thelen, E. (1995). Motor development: A new synthesis. *American Psychologist, 50,* 79–95.

Thoits, P. A. (1986). Multiple identities: Examining gender and marital status differences in distress. *American Sociological Review, 51,* 259–272.

Thomas, A., & Chess, S. (1977). *Temperament and development*. New York: Bruner/Mazel.

Thomas, A., & Chess, S. (1980). *The dynamics of psychological development*. New York: Bruner/Mazel.

Thomas, A., & Chess, S. (1986). The New York longitudinal study: From infancy to early adult life. In R. Plomin & J. Dunn (Eds.), *The study of temperament: Changes, continuities, and challenges*. Hillsdale, NJ: Erlbaum.

Thomas, A., Chess, S., & Birch, H. (1970). The origin of personality. *Scientific American, 223,* 102–109.

Thomas, M. H., & Drabman, R. S. (1977). *Effects of television violence on expectations of others' aggression*. Paper presented at the annual convention of the American Psychological Association, San Francisco, CA.

Thompson, J. J. (1998). Plugging the Kegs. *U.S. News and World Report, 124,* 63–67.

Thompson, L. (1993). Conceptualizing gender in marriage: The case of marital care. *Journal of Marriage and the Family, 55,* 557–569.

Thompson, L. W., Gallagher-Thompson, D., Futterman, A., Gilewski, M. J., & Peterson, J. (1991). The effects of late-life spousal bereavement over a 30-month interval. *Psychology and Aging, 6,* 434–441.

Thompson, M. W., McInnes, R. R., & Willard, H. F. (1991). *Genetics in medicine* (5th ed.). Philadelphia: Saunders.

Thompson, R. A. (1990). Emotion and self-regulation. In R. A. Thompson (Ed.), *Nebraska Symposium on Motivation, 1988* (Vol. 36, pp. 367–467). Lincoln: University of Nebraska Press.

Thompson, R. A., Connell, J. P., & Bridges, L. J. (1988). Temperament, emotion, and social interactive behavior in the strange situation: A component process analysis of attachment system functioning. *Child Development, 59,* 1102–1110.

Thompson, S. K. (1975). Gender labels and early sex role development. *Child Development, 46,* 339–347.

Thomson, E., & Colella, U. (1992). Cohabitation and marital stability: Quality or commitment? *Journal of Marriage and the Family, 54,* 259–267.

Thornton, A. (1989). Changing attitudes toward family issues in the United States. *Journal of Marriage and the Family, 51,* 873–893.

Thornton, A., & Camburn, D. (1989). Religious participation and adolescent sexual behavior. *Journal of Marriage and the Family, 51,* 641–654.

Thornton, A., Young-DeMarco, L., & Goldscheider, F. (1993). Leaving the parental nest: The experience of a young wife cohort in the 1980s. *Journal of Marriage and the Family, 55,* 216–229.

Tichauer, R. (1963). The Aymara children of Bolivia. *Journal of Pediatrics, 62,* 399–412.

Tiedeman, D. V., & O'Hara, R. P. (1963). *Career development: Choice and adjustment.* New York: College Entrance Examination Board.

Time. (1993, March 22). Alas, slavery lives: A new report details a world still plagued by human bondage, p. 26.

Time. (August 18, 1997). *Milestones:* Died. Jeanne Calment. p. 19.

Tinsley, H. E. A., Teaff, J. D., Colbs, S. L., & Kaufman, N. (1985). System of classifying leisure activities in terms of the psychological benefits of participation reported by older persons. *Journal of Gerontology, 40,* 172–178.

Tinsley, V. S., & Waters, H. S. (1982). The development of verbal control over motor behavior: A replication and extension of Luria's findings. *Child Development, 53,* 746–753.

Tolson, T. F. J., & Wilson, M. N. (1990). The impact of two- and three-generational black family structure on perceived family climate. *Child Development, 61,* 416–428.

Tolman, E. C. (1932/1967). *Purposive behavior in rats and men.* New York: Appleton-Century-Crofts.

Tolman, E. C. (1948). Cognitive maps in rats and men. *Psychological Review, 55,* 189–208.

Tomlin, A. M., & Passman, R. H. (1989). Grandmothers' responsibility in raising 2-year-olds facilitates their grandchildren's adaptive behavior. A preliminary intrafamilial investigation of mothers' and maternal grandmothers' effects. *Psychology and Aging, 4,* 119–121.

Tomlin, A. M., & Passman, R. H. (1991). Grandmothers' advice about disciplining grandchildren: Is it accepted by mothers, and does its rejection influence grandmothers' subsequent guidance? *Psychology and Aging, 6,* 182–189.

Torbert, W. R. (1994). Cultivating postformal adult development: Higher stages and contrasting interventions. In M. E. Miller & S. R. Cook-Greuter (Eds.), *Transcendence and mature thought in adulthood: The further reaches of adult development* (pp. 181–203). Lanham, MD: Rowman & Littlefield.

Tracy, R. L., & Ainsworth, M. D. S. (1981). Maternal affectionate behavior and infant-mother attachment patterns. *Child Development, 52,* 1341–1343.

Tran, T. V., Wright, R., & Chatters, L. (1991). Health, stress, psychological resources, and subjective well-being among older blacks. *Psychology and Aging, 6,* 100–108.

Trawick-Smith, J. (1988). "Let's say you're the baby, OK?": Play leadership and following behavior of young children. *Young Children, 43,* 51–59.

Trent, K., & South, S. J. (1989). Structural determinants of the divorce rate. *Journal of Marriage and the Family, 51,* 391–404.

Trethowan, W. (1972). The couvade syndrome. In J. Howells (Ed.), *Modern perspectives in psycho-obstetrics.* New York: Brunner/Mazel.

Triandis, H., Lambert, W., Berry, J., Lonner, W., Heron, A., Brislin, R., & Draguns, J. (Eds.). (1980). *Handbook of cross-cultural psychology: Vols. 1-6.* Boston: Allyn & Bacon.

Triandis, H. C. (1990). Cross-cultural studies of individualism and collectivism. In J. J. Berman (Ed.), *Nebraska Symposium on Motivation: 1989* (Vol. 37, pp. 41–134). Lincoln: University of Nebraska Press.

Triffon, B. J. (1997). Grandparents: Parenting again. *Columbus Parent, 9,* 17.

Troiden, R. R. (1993). The formation of homosexual identities. In L. D. Garnets & D. C. Kimmel (Eds.), *Psychological perspectives on lesbian and gay male experiences. Between men—between women* (pp. 191–217). New York: Columbia University Press.

Tronick, E. Z. (1989). Emotions and emotional communication in infants. *American Psychologist, 44,* 112–119.

Tronick, E. Z., Als, H., & Brazelton, R. B. (1979). Early development of neonatal and infant behavior. In F. Falkner & J. M. Tanner (Eds.), *Human growth,* Vol. 3, *Neurobiology and nutrition* (pp. 305–328). New York: Plenum.

Tronick, E. Z., & Cohn, J. F. (1989). Infants-mother face-to-face interaction: Age and gender differences in coordination and the occurrence of miscoordination. *Child Development, 60,* 85–92.

Tschann, J. M., Johnston, J. R், & Wallerstein, J. S. (1989). Factors in adults' adjustment after divorce. *Journal of Marriage and the Family, 51,* 1033–1046.

Tucker, M. B., Taylor, R. J., & Mitchell-Kernan, C. (1993). Marriage and romantic involvement among aged African Americans. *The Journals of Gerontology, 48,* S123–S132.

Tudge, J. R. H. (1992). Processes and consequences of peer collaboration: A Vygotskian analysis. *Child Development, 63,* 1364–1379.

Tudge, J. R. H., & Winterhoff, P. A. (1993). Vygotsky, Piaget, and Bandura: Perspectives on the relations between the social world and cognitive development. *Human Development, 36,* 61–81.

Turiel, E. (1983). *The development of social knowledge: Morality and convention.* Cambridge: Cambridge University Press.

Turner, J. S., & Rubinson, L. (1993). *Contemporary human sexuality.* Englewood Cliffs, NJ: Prentice-Hall.

Turner, P. J., & Gervai, J. (1995). A multidimensional study of gender typing in preschool children and their parents: Personality, attitudes, preferences, behavior, and cultural differrences. *Developmental Psychology, 31,* 759–772.

Udry, J. (1988). Biological predispositions and social control in adolescent sexual behavior. *American Sociological Review, 53,* 709–722.

Udry, J. R., & Billy, J. O. G. (1987). Initiation of coitus in early adolescence. *American Sociological Review, 52,* 841–855.

Udry, J. R., Billy, J. O., Morris, N. M., Groff, T. R, & Raj, M. S. (1985). Serum androgenic hormones motivate sexual behavior in adolescent boys. *Fertility and Sterility, 43,* 90–94.

Umbel, V. M., Pearson, B. Z., Fernandez, M. C., & Oller, D. K. (1992). Measuring bilingual children's receptive vocabularies. *Child Development, 63,* 1012–1020.

Umberson, D., Chen, M. D., House, J. S., Hopkins, K., & Slaten, E. (1996). The effect of social relationships on psychological well-being: Are men and women really so different? *American Sociological Review, 61,* 837–857.

Umberson, D., Wortman, C. B., & Kessler, R. C. (1992). Widowhood and depression: Explaining long-term gender differences in vulnerability. *Journal of Health and Social Behavior, 33,* 10–24.

Uncapher, H., Gallagher-Thompson, D., Osgood, N. J., & Bongar, B. (1998). Hopelessness and suicidal ideation in older adults. *Gerontologist, 38,* 62–70.

Urberg, K. A. (1992). Locus of peer influence: Social crowd and best friend. *Journal of Youth and Adolescence, 21,* 439–450.

Urberg, K. A., Shyu, S. J., & Liang, J. (1990). Peer influence in adolescent cigarette smoking. *Addictive Behavior, 115,* 247–255.

U.S. Bureau of the Census. (1983). *American in transition: An aging society.* Current Population Reports (Ser. P-23, No. 128). Washington, DC: U.S. Government Printing Office.

U.S. Bureau of the Census. (1987). *An aging world.* International Population Reports (Ser. P-95, No. 78). Washington, DC: U.S. Government Printing Office.

U.S. Bureau of the Census. (1976). *Population profile of the United States, 1975.* Current Population Reports (Ser. P-20, No. 292). Washington, DC: U.S. Government Printing Office.

U.S. Bureau of the Census. (1989). *Population profile of the United States, 1989.* [Current Population Reports (Ser. P-23, No. 159)]. Washington, DC: U.S. Government Printing Office.

U.S. Bureau of the Census. (1989a). *Population profile of the United States, 1989.* Current Population Reports (Ser. P-23, No. 159). Washington, DC: U.S. Government Printing Office.

U.S. Bureau of the Census. (1991). *Statistical abstract of the United States: 1991* (111th ed.). Washington, DC: U.S. Government Printing Office.

U.S. Bureau of the Census. (1992). *Statistical abstract of the United States, 1992* (112th ed). Washington, DC: U.S. Government Printing Office.

U.S. Bureau of the Census. (1995). *Statistical abstract of the United States: 1995.* (115th ed.). Washington, DC: U.S. Government Printing Office.

U.S. Bureau of the Census. (1996). *Statistical abstract of the United States, 1996* (116th ed.). Washington, DC: U.S. Government Printing Office.

U.S. Bureau of the Census. (1997). *Statistical abstract of the United States, 1997* (117th ed.). Washington, DC: U.S. Government Printing Office.

U.S. Bureau of the Census. (1989). *The black population in the United States, March, 1988.* Current Population Reports (Ser. P-20, No. 442). Washington, DC: U.S. Government Printing Office.

U.S. Department of Education. (1995). *Digest of education statistics: 1995.* Washington, DC: U.S. Government Printing Office.

U.S. Department of Education. (1997). *The condition of education: 1997.* Washington, DC: U.S. Government Printing Office.

U.S. Department of Health, Education, and Welfare. (1979). *Smoking and health: A report of the surgeon general.* Washington, DC: U.S. Government Printing Office.

U.S. Department of Labor, Employment & Training Administration. (1993). *Selected characteristics of occupations defined in the revised dictionary of occupational titles.* Washington, DC: U.S. Government Printing Office.

U.S. News & World Report. (1996). Fewer pregnancies, fewer abortions. April 1, 1996.

U.S. News & World Report. (1997). How RU-486 works. March 3, 1997.

U.S. Senate, Special Committee on Aging. (1986). *Aging America–Trends and projections.* Washington, DC: U.S. Government Printing Office.

Usher, R. (1987). Extreme prematurity. In G. B. Avery (Ed.), *Neonatology: Pathophysiology and management of the newborn* (3rd ed., pp. 264–298). Philadelphia: Lippincott.

Valdez-Menchaca, M. S., & Whitehurst, G. J. (1992). Accelerating language development through picture book reading: A systematic extension to Mexican day care. *Developmental Psychology, 28,* 1106–1114.

Valery, J. H., O'Connor, P., & Jennings, S. (1997). The nature and amount of support college-age adolescents request and receive from parents. *Adolescence, 32,* 323–337.

Van Boxtel, M. P. J., Paas, F. G. W. C., Houx, P. J., & Adam, J. J. 1997). Aerobic capacity and cognitive performance in a cross-sectional aging study. *Medicine & Science in Sports & Exercise, 29,* 1357–1365.

Vandell, D. L., Henderson, V. K., & Wilson, K. S. (1988). A longitudinal study of children with day-care experiences of varying quality. *Child Development, 59,* 1286–1292.

van Ijzendoorn, M. H., Goldberg, S., Kroonenberg, P. M., & Frenkel, O. J. (1992). The relative effects of maternal and child problems on the quality of attachment: A meta-analysis of attachment in clinical samples. *Child Development, 63,* 840–858.

van Ijzendoorn, M. H., & Kroonenberg, P. M. (1988). Cross-cultural patterns of attachment: A meta-analysis of the strange situation. *Child Development, 59,* 147–156.

VanLear, C. A. (1992). Marital communication across the generations: Learning and rebellion, continuity and change. *Journal of Social and Personal Relationships, 9,* 103–123.

Vannoy, D. (1995). A paradigm of roles in the divorce process: Implications for divorce adjustment, future commitments, and personal growth. *Journal of Divorce and Remarriage, 24,* 71–87.

Van Wieringen, J. C. (1978). Secular growth changes. In F. Falkner & J. M. Tanner (Eds.), *Human growth* (Vol. 2, pp. 445–473). New York: Plenum.

Vanzetti, N., & Duck, S. (1996). *A lifetime of relationships.* Pacific Grove, CA: Brooks/Cole.

Vaughn, B., Egeland, B., Sroufe, L. A., & Waters, E. (1979). Individual differences in infant-mother attachment at 12 and 18 months: Stability and change in families under stress. *Child Development, 50,* 971–975.

Vaughn, B. E., Bradley, C. F., Joffe, L. S., Seifer, R., & Barglow, P. (1987). Maternal characteristics measured prenatally are predictive of ratings of temperamental "difficulty" on the Carey Infant Temperament Questionnaire. *Developmental Psychology, 23,* 152–161.

Vaughn, B. E., Lefever, G. B., Seifer, R., & Barglow, P. (1989). Attachment behavior, attachment security, and temperament during infancy. *Child Development, 60,* 728–737.

Vega, W. A., Zimmerman, R. S., Warheit, G. J., Apospori, E., & Gil, A. G. (1993). Risk factors for adolescent drug use in four ethnic and racial groups. *American Journal of Public Health, 83,* 185–189.

Veroff, J., Douvan, E., & Kulka, R. A. (1981). *The inner American: A self-portrait from 1957 to 1976.* New York: Basic Books.

Vinokur, A., Caplan, R. D., & Williams, C. C. (1987). Effects of recent and past stress on mental health: Coping with unemployment among Vietnam veterans and nonveterans. *Journal of Applied Social Psychology, 17,* 708–728.

Violato, C., & Holden, W. B. (1988). A confirmatory factor analysis of a four-factor model of adolescent concerns. *Journal of Youth and Adolescence, 17,* 101–113.

Vizziello, G. F., Antonioloi, M. E., Cocci, V., & Invernizzi, R. (1993). From pregnancy to motherhood: the structure of representative and narrative change. *Infant Mental Health Journal, 14,* 4–16.

Volling, B. L., Youngblade, L. M., & Belsky, J. (1997). Young children's social relationships with siblings and friends. *American Journal of Orthopsychiatry, 67,* 102–111.

Vorhees, C. V., & Mollnow, E. (1987). Behavioral teratogenesis: Long-term influences on behavior from early exposure to environmental agents. In J. D. Osofsky (Ed.), *Handbook of infant development* (pp. 913–971). New York: Wiley.

Vosler, N. R., & Page-Adams, D. (1996). Predictors of depression among workers at the time of a plant closing. *Journal of Sociology & Social Welfare, 23,* 25–42.

Vuchinich, S. (1987). Starting and stopping spontaneous family conflicts. *Journal of Marriage and the Family, 49,* 591–601.

Vygotsky, L. S. (1978). *Mind in society.* Cambridge, MA: Harvard University Press.

Vygotsky, L. S. (1962). *Thought and language.* Cambridge, MA: MIT Press.

Waas, G. A. (1988). Social attributional biases of peer-rejected and aggressive children. *Child Development, 59,* 969–975.

Wagner, B. M., & Phillips, D. A. (1992). Beyond beliefs: Parent and child behaviors and children's perceived academic competence. *Child Development, 63,* 1380–1391.

Walasky, M., Whitbourne, S. K., & Nehrke, M. F. (1983–84). Construction and validation of an ego integrity status interview. *International Journal of Aging & Human Development, 18,* 61–72.

Walden, T. A., & Ogan, T. A. (1988). The development of social referencing. *Child Development, 59,* 1230–1240.

Waldman, I. R. (1996). Aggressive boys' hostile perceptual and response biases: the role of attention and impulsivity. *Child Development, 67,* 1015–1033.

Walford, R. L. (1990). The clinical promise of diet restriction. *Geriatrics, 45,* 81–83, 86–87.

Walker, A. (1991). Beauty: When the other dancer is the self. In H. L. Gates, Jr. (Ed.), *Bearing witness: Selections from African-American autobiography in the twentieth century.* New York: Pantheon Books, pp. 257–258.

Walker, L. J. (1988). The development of moral reasoning. *Annals of Child Development, 5,* 33–78.

Walker, L. J. (1989). A longitudinal study of moral reasoning. *Child Development, 60,* 157–166.

Walker, L. J., de Vries, B., & Trevethan, S. D. (1987). Moral stages and moral orientations in real-life and hypothetical dilemmas. *Child Development, 58,* 842–858.

Walker, L. J., & Taylor, J. H. (1991a). Family interactions and the development of moral reasoning. *Child Development, 62,* 262–283.

Walker-Andrews, A. S. (1986). Intermodal perception of expressive behaviors: Relation of eye and voice? *Developmental Psychology, 22,* 373–377.

Walker-Andrews, A. S., & Harris, P. L. (1993). Young children's comprehension of pretend causal sequences. *Developmental Psychology, 29,* 915–921.

Wallace, E., Hayes, D., & Jerger, J. (1994). Neurotology of aging: The auditory system. In M. L. Albert & J. E. Knoefel (Eds.), *Clinical neurology of aging* (2nd ed., pp. 448–464). New York: Oxford University Press.

Wallechinsky, D., & Wallace, A. (1993). *The book of lists.* New York: Little, Brown.

Wallechinsky, D., Wallace, I., & Wallace, A. (1977). *The book of lists.* New York: Morrow.

Wallerstein, I., & Smith, J. (1991). Households as an institution of the world-economy. In R. L. Blumberg (Ed.), *Gender, family, and economy: The triple overlap* (pp. 225–242). Newbury Park, CA: Sage.

Wallerstein, J. S., & Corbin, S. B. (1989). Daughters of divorce: Report from a 10-year follow-up. *American Journal of Orthopsychiatry, 59,* 593–604.

Walls, C. T., & Zarit, S. H. (1991). Informal support from black churches and the well-being of elderly blacks. *Gerontologist, 31,* 490–495.

Ward, R. A. (1977). The impact of subjective age and stigma on older persons. *Journal of Gerontology, 32,* 227–232.

Waterman, A. (1992). Identity as an aspect of optimal psychological functioning. In G. Adams, T. P. Gullotta, & R. Montemayor (Eds.), *Adolescent identity formation: Advances in adolescent development* (Vol. 4., pp. 50–72). Newbury Park, CA: Sage.

Waterman, A. S. (1982). Identity development from adolescence to adulthood: An extension of theory and a review of research. *Developmental Psychology, 18,* 341–358.

Waterman, A. S., & Whitbourne, S. K. (1981). The inventory of psychosocial development. *Journal Supplement Abstract Service: Catalog of Selected Documents in Psychology, 11,* (Ms. No. 2179).

Watson, J. S. (1970). *Smiling, cooing, and "the game."* Paper presented at the annual meeting of the American Psychological Association, Miami Beach, FL.

Waxman, L., & Hinderliter, S. (1996). *A status report on hunger and homelessness in America's cities: 1996.* Washington, DC: U.S. Conference of Mayors.

Webster, R. A., Hunter, M., & Keats, J. A. (1994). Peer and parental influences on adolescents' substance use: A path analysis. *International Journal of Addiction, 29,* 647–657.

Webster, D. W., Gainer, P. S., & Champion, H. R. (1993). Weapon carrying among inner-city junior high school students: Defensive behavior vs. aggressive delinquency. *American Journal of Public Health, 83,* 1604–1608.

Weiler, P. G., Chiriboga, D. A., & Black, S. A. (1994). Comparison of mental status tests: Implications for Alzheimer's patients and their caregivers. *The Journals of Gerontology, 49,* S44–51.

Weinberg, R. A. (1989). Intelligence and IQ: Landmark issues and great debates. [Special issue]. *American Psychologist, 44*(2), 98–104.

Weingarten, H. R. (1985). Marital status and well-being: A national study comparing first-married, currently divorced, and remarried adults. *Journal of Marriage and the Family, 47,* 653–662.

Weinraub, M., Clemens, L. P., Sockloff, A., Ethridge, T., Gracely, E., & Meyers, B. (1984). The development of sex role stereotypes in the third year: Relationship to gender labeling, identity, sex-typed toy preference, and family characteristics. *Child Development, 55,* 1493–1503.

Weinreb, L., & Buckner, J. C. (1993). Homeless families: Program responses and public policies. *American Journal of Orthopsychiatry, 63,* 400–409.

Weinstein, R. S., Marshall, H. H., Sharp, L., & Botkin, M. (1987). Pygmalion and the student: Age and classroom differences in children's awareness of teacher expectations. *Child Development, 58,* 1079–1093.

Weiss, B., Dodge, K. A., Bates, J. E., & Petit. G. S. (1992). Some consequences of early harsh discipline: Child aggression and a maladaptive social information processing style. *Child Development, 63,* 1321–1335.

Weiss, R. S. (1997). Adaptation to retirement. In I. H. Gotlib & B. Wheaton (Eds), Stress and Adversity over the Life Course: Trajectories and Turning Points. New York: Cambridge University Press, 232–245.

Wellman, H. M. (1990). *The child's theory of mind.* Cambridge: MIT Press.

Wellman, H. M., Cross, D., & Bartsch, K. (1986). Infant search and object permanence: A meta-analysis of the A-not-B error; *Monographs of the Society for Research in Child Development, 51* (3, Serial No. 214 whole).

Wenar, C. (1982). On negativism. *Human Development, 25,* 1–23.

Wentowski, G. J. (1985). Older women's perceptions of great-grandmotherhood: A research note. *Gerontologist, 25,* 593–596.

Wentworth, N., & Haith, M. M. (1992). Event-specific expectations of 2- and 3-month-old infants. *Developmental Psychology, 28,* 842–850.

Werker, J. F. (1989). Becoming a native listener. *American Scientist, 77,* 54–59.

Werner, E. E. (1991). Grandparent-grandchild relationships amongst U.S. ethnic groups. In P. K. Smith (Ed.), *The psychology of grandparenthood: An international perspective* (pp. 68–82). London: Routledge.

West, J. R. (1986). *Alcohol and brain development.* London: Oxford University Press.

West, M., & Newton, P. (1983). *The transition from school to work.* London: Croom Helm.

West, R. L., Crook, T. H., & Barron, K. L. (1992). Everyday memory performance across the life span: Effects of age and noncognitive individual differences. *Psychology and Aging, 7,* 72–82.

Whitaker, M. (1993). White and black lies. *Newsweek, Nov. 15, 122,* 52–54.

Whitall, J., & Getchell, N. (1995). From walking to running: Applying a dynamical systems approach to the development of locomotor skills. *Child Development, 66,* 1541–1553.

Whitbeck, L., Hoyt, D. R., & Huck, S. M. (1994). Early family relationships, intergenerational solidarity, and support

provided to parents by their adult children. *Journal of Gerontology, 49,* S85–S94.

Whitbourne, S. K. (1986). *The me I know: A study of adult identity.* New York: Springer-Verlag.

Whitbourne, S. K., Zuschlag, M. K., Elliot, L. B., & Waterman, A. S. (1992). Psychosocial development in adulthood: A 22-year sequential study. *Journal of Personality and Social Psychology, 63,* 260–271.

White, B. L., Kaban, B. T., & Attanucci, J. S. (1979). *The origins of human competence.* Lexington, MA: D. C. Heath.

White, J. M., Wampler, R. S., & Winn, K. I. (1998). The identity style inventory: A revision with a sixth grade reading level (ISI-6G). *Journal of Adolescent Research, 13,* 223–245.

White, L. K. (1990). Determinants of divorce: A review of research in the eighties. *Journal of Marriage and the Family, 52,* 904–912.

White, R. W. (1966). *Lives in progress* (2nd ed.). New York: Holt, Rinehart & Winston.

White, N., & Cunningham, W. R. (1988). Is terminal drop pervasive or specific? *Journal of Gerontology: Psychological Sciences, 43,* P141–P144.

White, R. W. (1959). Motivation reconsidered. The concept of competence. *Psychological Review, 66,* 297–333.

White, R. W. (1960). Competence and the psychosexual stages of development. In M. R. Jones (Ed.), *Nebraska Symposium on Motivation* (Vol. 8). Lincoln: University of Nebraska Press.

White, R. W. (1974). Strategies of adaptation: An attempt at systematic description. In G. V. Coelho, D. A. Hamburg, & J. E. Adams (Eds.), *Coping and adaptation* (pp. 47–68). New York: Basic Books.

Whitely, B. E., Jr. (1993). Reliability and aspects of the construct validity of Sternberg's triangular love scale. *Journal of Social and Personal Relationships, 10,* 475–480.

Wierson, M., Long, P. J., & Forehand, R. L. (1993). Toward a new understanding of early menarche: The role of environmental stress in pubertal timing. *Adolescence, 28,* 912–924.

Wilcox, A. J., & Skjoerven, R. (1992). Birth weight and perinatal mortality. The effect of gestational age. *American Journal of Public Health, 82,* 378–382.

Williams, C., & Bybee, J. (1994). What do children feel guilty about? Development and gender differences. *Developmental Psychology, 30,* 617–623.

Willis, S., Diehl, M., Gruber-Baldini, A., Marsiske, M., & Haessler, S. (1990, March). Correlates and predictors of intellectual performance and intellectual change in older adults. Paper presented at the Third Cognitive Aging Conference, Atlanta, GA.

Willwerth, J. (1991, May 13). Should we take away their kids? *Time,* pp. 62–63.

Wilmoth, G. H. (1992). Abortion, public health policy, and informed consent legislation. *Journal of Social Issues, 48,* 1–17.

Wilmoth, J. R. (1998). The future of human longevity: A demographer's perspective. *Science, 280,* 395–397.

Wilson, E. O. (1978). *On human nature.* Cambridge, MA: Harvard University Press.

Wilson, R. S., & Matheny, A. P., Jr. (1986). Behavior genetics research in infant temperament: The Louisville twin study. In R. Plomin & J. Dunn (Eds.), *The study of temperament:*

Changes, continuities, and challenges. Hillsdale, NJ: Erlbaum.

Wilson, S. (1995). Quasi-experimental designs. In G. Breakwell, S. Hammond, & C. Fyfe-Schaw (Eds.), *Research methods in psychology*. Thousand Oaks, CA: Sage.

Wilson, S. M., Peterson, G. W., & Wilson, P. (1993). The process of educational and occupational attainment of adolescent females from low-income, rural families. *Journal of Marriage and the Family, 55*, 158–175.

Wingfield, A., Poon, L. W., Lombardi, L., & Lowe, D. (1985). Speed of processing in normal aging: Effects of speech rate, linguistic structure, and processing time. *Journal of Gerontology, 40*, 579–585.

Winston, R. M. L., & Handyside, A. H. (1993). New challenges in human in vitro fertilization. *Science, 260*, 932–936.

Wolf, A. M., Gortmaker, S. L., Cheung, L., Gray, H. M., Herzog, D. B., & Colditz, G. A. (1993). Activity, inactivity, and obesity: Racial, ethnic, and age differences among schoolgirls. *American Journal of Public Health, 83*, 1625–1627.

Wolff, P. H. (1963). Observations on the early development of smiling. In B. M. Foss (Ed.), *Determinants of infant behavior* (Vol. 2). New York: Wiley.

Wolff, P. H. (1966). Causes, controls, and organization of behavior in the neonate. *Psychological Issues, 5* (1, whole No. 17).

Wolff, P. H. (1987). *The development of behavioral states and the expression of emotions in early infancy*. Chicago: University of Chicago Press.

Wong, P. T. P., & Watt, L. M. (1991). What types of reminiscence are associated with successful aging? *Psychology and Aging, 6*, 272–279.

Wood, W., Rhodes, N., & Biek, M. (1995). Working knowledge and attitude strength: An information-processing analysis. In K. E. Petty & J. A. Krosnick (Eds.), *Attitude strength: Antecedents and consequences* (pp. 283–313). Mahwah, NJ: Lawrence Erlbaum.

Woodward, K. L. (1997, March 10). Today the sheep . . . *Newsweek*, 60.

Woolley, J. D., & Wellman, H. M. (1993). Origin and truth: Young children's understanding of imaginary mental representations. *Child Development, 64*, 1–17.

World Health Organization. (1998). World health statistics annual, 1996. Geneva, Switzerland; World Health Organization.

Woyach, R. B. (1991). *Preparing for leadership: A young adult's guide to leadership skills in a global age*. Columbus, OH: The Mershon Center, The Ohio State University.

Wright, D. W., Nelson, B. S., & Georgen, K. E. (1994). Marital problems. In P. C. McKenry & S. J. Price (Eds.), *Families and change: Coping with stressful events* (pp. 40–65). Thousand Oaks, CA: Sage.

Wright, J. D., & Devine, J. A. (1993). Family backgrounds and the substance-abusive homeless: The New Orleans experience. *The Community Psychologist, 26*, 35–37.

Yalom, I. D., Green, R., & Fisk, N. (1973). Prenatal exposure to female hormones. *Archives of General Psychiatry, 28*, 554–561.

Yang, R. K., Zweig, A. R., Douthitt, T. C., & Federman, E. J. (1976). Successive relationships between maternal attitudes during pregnancy, analgesic medication during labor and delivery, and newborn behavior. *Developmental Psychology, 12*, 6–14.

Yankauer, A. (1994). Sexually transmitted diseases: A neglected public health priority. *American Journal of Public Health, 84*, 1894–1897.

Yarrow, L. J. (1963). Research in dimensions of early maternal care. *Merrill-Palmer Quarterly, 9*, 101–114.

Yarrow, L. J. (1964). Separation from parents in early childhood. In M. L. Hoffman & L. W. Hoffman (Eds.), *Review of child development research* (Vol. 1). New York: Sage.

Yarrow, L. J. (1970). The development of focused relationships during infancy. In J. Hellmuth (Ed.), *Exceptional infant* (Vol. 1). New York: Brunner/Mazel.

Yarrow, L. J., McQuiston, S., MacTurk, R. H., McCarthy, M. E., Klein, R. P., & Vietze, P. M. (1983). The assessment of mastery motivation during the first year of life. *Developmental Psychology, 19*, 159–171.

Yates, A. (1989). Current perspectives on the eating disorders: 1. History, psychological, and biological aspects. *Journal of the American Academy of Child and Adolescent Psychiatry, 28*, 813–828.

Yates, M., & Youniss, J. (1996). Community service and political-moral identity in adolescents. *Journal of Research on Adolescence, 6*, 271–284.

Yerushalmi, H. (1993). Stagnation in supervision as a result of developmental problems in the middle-aged supervisor. *Clinical Supervisor, 11*, 63–81.

Yin, R. K. (1994). *Case study research: Design and methods*. Thousand Oaks, CA: Sage.

Youngblade, L. M., & Belsky, J. (1992). Parent-child antecedents of 5-year-olds' close friendships: A longitudinal analysis. *Developmental Psychology, 28*, 700–713.

Youngblade, L. M., & Dunn, J. (1995). Individual differences in young children's pretend play with mother and sibling: Links to relationships and understanding of other people's feelings and beliefs. *Child Development, 66*, 1472–1492.

Younger, B. (1992). Developmental change in infant categorization: The perception of correlations among facial features. *Child Development, 63*, 1526–1535.

Youniss, J. (1980). *Parents and peers in social development: A Sullivan-Piaget perspective*. Chicago: University of Chicago Press.

Youniss, J., McLellan, J. A., & Strouse, D. (1994). "We're popular, but we're not snobs.": Adolescents describe their crowds. In R. Montemeyor, G. R., Adams, & T. P. Gwllotta (Eds.), *Personal relationships during adolescence. Advances in adolescent development*. Vol. 6 (pp. 101–122). Thousand Oaks, CA: Sage.

Yurdakok, K., Yavuz, T., & Taylor, C. E. (1990). Swaddling and acute respiratory infections. *American Journal of Public Health, 80*, 873–875.

Zabin, L. C., Astone, N. M., & Emerson, M. R. (1993). Do adolescents want babies? The relationship between attitudes and behavior. *Journal of Research on Adolescence, 3*, 67–86.

Zahn-Waxler, C., & Kochanska, G. (1990). The origins of guilt. In R. A. Thompson (Ed.), *Nebraska Symposium on Motivation, 1988* (Vol. 36, pp. 183–258). Lincoln: University of Nebraska Press.

Zahn-Waxler, C., Kochanska, G., Krupnick, J., & McKnew, D. (1990). Patterns of guilt in children of depressed and well mothers. *Developmental Psychology, 26*, 51–59.

Zahn-Waxler, C., Radke-Yarrow, M., & King, R. A. (1977). *The impact of the affective environment on young children.* Paper presented at the biennial meeting of the Society for Research in Child Development, New Orleans, LA.

Zahn-Waxler, C., Radke-Yarrow, M., Wagner, E., & Chapman M. (1992). Development of concern for others. *Developmental Psychology, 28,* 126–136.

Zahn-Waxler, C., Robinson, J. L., & Emde, R. N. (1992). The development of empathy in twins. *Developmental Psychology, 28,* 1038–1047.

Zakriski, A. L., & Coie, J. D. (1996). A comparison of aggressive-rejected and nonaggressive-rejected children's interpretations of self-directed and other-directed rejection. *Child Development, 67,* 1048–1070.

Zarit, S. H., & Eggebeen, D. J. (1995). Parent-child relationships in adulthood and old age. In M. Bornstein (Ed.), *Handbook of parenting: Vol. 1 Children and parenting* (pp. 119–140). Mahwah, NJ: Lawrence Erlbaum.

Zelnik, M., & Kantner, J. F. (1980). Sexual activity, contraceptive use, and pregnancy among metropolitan area teenagers: 1971–1979. *Family Planning Perspectives, 12,* 230–237.

Zeskind, P. S. (1983). Cross-cultural differences in maternal perceptions of cries of low- and high-risk infants. *Child Development, 54,* 1119–1128.

Zeskind, P. S., Klein, L., & Marshall, T. R. (1992). Adult's perceptions of experimental modifications of durations of pauses and expiratory sounds in infant crying. *Developmental Psychology, 28,* 1153–1162.

Zick, C. D., & Smith, K. R. (1991). Patterns of economic change surrounding the death of a spouse. *Journal of Gerontology, 46,* S310–S320.

Zigler, E. (1993). *Head Start and beyond: A national plan for extended childhood intervention.* New Haven, CT: Yale University Press.

Zigler, E. F., Kagan, S. L., & Hall, N. W. (1996). *Children, families, and government: Preparing for the twenty-first century.* Cambridge: Cambridge University Press.

Zilbach, J. J. (1993). Female adolescence: Toward a separate line of female development. In M. Sugar (Ed.), *Female adolescent development* (2nd ed., pp. 45–61). New York: Bruner/Mazel.

Zimmerman, B. J., Bandura, A., & Martinez-Pons, M. (1992). Self-motivation for academic attainment: The role of self-efficacy beliefs and personal goal setting. *American Educational Research Journal, 29,* 663–676.

Zimmerman, M. A., Salem, D. A., & Maton, K. I. (1995). Family structure and psychosocial correlates among urban African-American adolescent males. *Child Development, 66,* 1598–1613.

Zucker, K. J. (1985). The infant's construction of his parents in the first six months of life. In T. M. Field & N. A. Fox (Eds.), *Social perception in infants.* Norwood, NJ: Ablex.

Zuckerman, B., Frank, D. A., & Hingson, R. (1989). Effects of maternal marijuana and cocaine use on fetal growth. *New England Journal of Medicine, 320,* 762–768.

Zuckerman, C. (1997). Issues concerning end-of-life care. *Journal of Long Term Home Health Care, 16,* 26–34.

Zuo, J. (1992). The reciprocal relationship between marital interaction and marital happiness: A three-wave study. *Journal of Marriage and the Family, 54,* 870–878.

Zuravin, S. J. (1988). Child maltreatment and teenage first births: A relationship mediated by chronic sociodemographic stress? *American Journal of Orthopsychiatry, 58,* 91–103.

Zweibel, N. R., & Cassel, C. K. (1989). Treatment choices at the end of life: A comparison of decisions by older patients and their physician-selected proxies. *Gerontologist, 29,* 615–621.

Credits

Chapter 1: xii, Scala/Art Resource, NY/ © 1999 Estate of Pablo Picasso/Artists Rights Society (ARS), New York; 3, (left), © David Young-Wolff/PhotoEdit; 3, (right), © David Young-Wolff/PhotoEdit; 6, © Timothy Ross/The Image Works; 8, (left), © Cassy Cohen/PhotoEdit; 8, (top right), © Michael Dwyer/Stock Boston; 8, (bottom right), © Bill Bachman/PhotoEdit; 12, © Bruce Roberts/Photo Researchers; 13, ©N. R. Rowan/The Image Works; 14, © David Young-Wolff/PhotoEdit; 16, Agence France Press/Corbis- Bettmann; 17, © Elizabeth Crews/The Image Works; 20, © Lawrence Migdale; 24, Copyright 1965 by Stanley Milgram. From the film OBEDIENCE, distributed by the Pennsylvania State University, Audio Visual Services; 26, © Miro Vintoniv/Stock Boston; 28, Rachel Newman.

Chapter 2: 30, Pushkin Museum, Moscow, Russia/ Bridgeman Art Library, London/New York/ © 1999 Estate of Pablo Picasso/Artists Rights Society (ARS), New York; 34, © Bob Daemmrich/Stock Boston; 39, © Lawrence Migdale/Photo Researchers; 40, © Karen Preuss/The Image Works; 42, © Margaret Miller/Photo Researchers; 44, © Stuart Rosner/Stock Boston; 45, © Fritz Hoffmann/The Image Works; 46, A. K. G., Berlin/Superstock/ © 1999 Estate of Pablo Picasso/Artists Rights Society (ARS), New York; 49, © Bill Bachman/Photo Researchers; 50, © David H. Wells/The Image Works; 53, © Bob Daemmrich/The Image Works; 58, UPI/Corbis - Bettmann.

Chapter 3: 60, Pushkin Museum of Fine Arts, Moscow, Russia/Bridgeman Art Library, London; Superstock/ © 1999 Estate of Pablo Picasso/Artists Rights Society (ARS), New York; 63, (left), © Michael Tweedie/Photo Researchers; 63, (right), © Michael Tweedie/Photo Researchers; 64, © Tom Stack and Associates; 65, Stock Montage; 66, ARS/NY/ SPADEM; 67, © 1999 Estate of Pablo Picasso/Artists Rights Society (ARS), New York; 70, © Elizabeth Crews; 71, © Bob Daemmrich/The Image Works; 75, © Elizabeth Crews/Stock Boston; 76, © Elizabeth Crews; 80, © 1999 Estate of Pablo Picasso/Artists Rights Society (ARS), New York; 81, (top), © Kathy McLaughlin/The Image Works; 81, (bottom left), © Michael Newman/PhotoEdit; 81, bottom (right), © A. Ramsey/PhotoEdit; 86, top, © Ulrike Welsch/Photo Researchers; 86, bottom, © Rob Crandall/ Stock Boston.

Chapter 4: 90, Superstock/ © 1999 Estate of Pablo Picasso/ Artists Rights Society (ARS), New York; 94, (left), © Biophoto Associates/SPL/Photo Researchers; 94, (right), © CNRI/SPL/Photo Researchers; 95, © Charles Gupton/ Stock Boston; 98, Pablo Picasso, Three Musicians, 1921. Philadelphia Museum of Art: A. E. Gallatin Collection/ © 1999 Estate of Pablo Picasso/Artists Rights Society (ARS), New York; 100, Agence France Presse/Corbis-Bettmann; 101, © Paul Conklin/PhotoEdit; 102, (bottom right), © Tim Davis/Photo Researchers; 102, (bottom left), © Christopher Brown/Stock Boston; 103, © Lennart Nilsson/Albert Bonniers Förlag, A CHILD IS BORN, Dell Publishing Company; 107, (left), © Lennart Nilsson/Albert Bonniers Förlag, A CHILD IS BORN, Dell Publishing Company; 107, (right), © Lennart Nilsson/Albert Bonniers Förlag, A CHILD IS BORN, Dell Publishing Company; 108, © Lennart Nilsson/Albert Bonniers Förlag, A CHILD IS BORN, Dell Publishing Company; 110, © Lennart Nilsson/Albert Bonniers Förlag, A CHILD IS BORN, Dell Publishing Company; 111, © Guigoz/Petit Format/Photo Researchers; 113, top, © Lennart Nilsson/Albert Bonniers Förlag, A CHILD IS BORN, Dell Publishing Company; 113, (bottom), Courtesy of Stanford Hospital; 115, © John Eastcott/Yva Mumatiuk/Stock Boston; 119, © Patrick Zachmann/Magnum Photos; 120, © Suzanne Arms/The Image Works; 123, © John Griffin/The Image Works; 131, © A. Ramey/Stock Boston.

Chapter 5: 136, Pablo Picasso, Spanish, 1881-1973, Untitled, gouache on illustration board, 1904, 41.6 x 29.9 cm, Bequest of Kate L. Brewster, 1950. 128, photograph © 1994, The Art Institute of Chicago. All rights reserved. © 1999 Estate of Pablo Picasso/Artists Rights Society (ARS), New York; 140, © Mel Rosenthal/The Image Works; 143, © Robert Brenner/PhotoEdit; 144, Diane Rosenstein and Helen Oster (1988); 145, © 1999 Estate of Pablo Picasso/Artists Rights Society (ARS), New York; 152, © Alan Carey/The Image Works; 157, © Frank Siteman/ Stock Boston; 158, © Mark Richard/PhotoEdit; 165, (left), © Elizabeth Crews; 165, (right), © Elizabeth Crews; 166, © George Bellerose/Stock Boston; 167, Philip R. Newman; 169, © Gale Zucker/Stock Boston; 171, © Nina Leen/Life Magazine; 174, © Laura Dwight/ PhotoEdit; 175, © Felicia Martinez/PhotoEdit; 178, © Jeffry Myers/Stock Boston

Chapter 6: 182, A. K. G., Berlin/Superstock / © 1999 Estate of Pablo Picasso/Artists Rights Society (ARS), New York; 185, © Elizabeth Crews; 187, © Tony Freeman/PhotoEdit; 189, © Elizabeth Crews; 192, © David Young-Wolff/ PhotoEdit; 195, © Elizabeth Crews; 198, © Elizabeth Crews; 200, © Elizabeth Crews; 203, © Elizabeth Crews; 205, © Elliott Erwitt/Magnum Photos; 208, © Myrleen Ferguson/PhotoEdit; 210, © David Young-Wolff/PhotoEdit;

212, © Margaret Miller/Photo Researchers; 214, © Robert Brenner/PhotoEdit; 216, © George Gardner/Stock Boston; 219, © Elizabeth Crews/Stock Boston; 220, © Elizabeth Crews.

Chapter 7: 224, © 1999 Estate of Pablo Picasso/Artists Rights Society (ARS), New York; 227, © K. Rosenthal/Stock Boston; 229, © Elizabeth Crews/The Image Works; 231, © Ken Lax/Photo Researchers; 233, © Tony Freeman/PhotoEdit; 235, © Michael Siluk/The Image Works; 237, © Christopher S. Johnson/Stock Boston; 239, © Elizabeth Crews/The Image Works; 242, © Michael Weisbrot/Stock Boston; 246, © Elizabeth Crews; 248, © Elena Rooraid/PhotoEdit; 250, © Elizabeth Crews; 253, © Laura Dwight/PhotoEdit; 254, © Michael Newman/PhotoEdit; 255, © Dwayne Newton/PhotoEdit; 257, © Elizabeth Crews.

Chapter 8: 262, Christie's Images, New York/ © 1999 Estate of Pablo Picasso/Artists Rights Society (ARS), New York; 266, P. R. Newman; 268, © Michael Siluk/The Image Works; 271, © Elizabeth Crews/Stock Boston; 273, © Dwayne Newton/PhotoEdit; 276, © Blair Seitz/Photo Researchers; 278, © Elizabeth Crews/The Image Works; 281, © David Strickler/The Image Works; 283, © Michael Newman/PhotoEdit; 285, © Russell D. Curtis/Photo Researchers; 288, © David Young-Wolff/PhotoEdit; 290, P. R. Newman; 291, © Cameramann/The Image Works; 294, (left), © Topham/The Image Works; 294, (right), © Elizabeth Crews/The Image Works; 296, © Karen Preuss/The Image Works; 299, © Mark Richards/PhotoEdit.

Chapter 9: 302, John Hay Whitney Collection, New York/Bridgeman Art Library, London/Superstock ©1994 ARS, New York, SPADEM, Paris; 305, © Spencer Grant/Stock Boston; 307, © Michael Weisbrot/Stock Boston; 309, © Bob Daemmrich/Stock Boston; 312, © John Eastcott/Yva Momatiuk/The Image Works; 313, © Elizabeth Crews; 316, © Nancy Richmond/The Image Works; 319, © Michael Newman/PhotoEdit; 320, © David Young-Wolff/PhotoEdit; 323, © Rob Crandall/The Image Works; 326, © Nancy Durrell McKenna/Photo Researchers; 329, © Michael A. Dwyer/Stock Boston; 332, © Bill Aron/PhotoEdit; 335, © Katherine McGlynn/The Image Works; 339, © Michael Newman/PhotoEdit.

Chapter 10: 348, Index/Bridgeman Art Library/ © 1999 Estate of Pablo Picasso/Artists Rights Society (ARS), New York; 352, © Dana White/PhotoEdit; 354, © David Roth, 1998; 357, Museum of Modern Art, New York/A.K.G./Superstock/ © 1999 Estate of Pablo Picasso/Artists Rights Society (ARS), New York; 360, © David Young-Wolff/PhotoEdit; 364, © Mark Richards/PhotoEdit; 366, © Bob Daemmrich/Stock Boston; 369, © John Nordall/The Image Works; 371, Phillips, The International Fine Art Auctioneers/Bridgeman Art Library, London/New York/ © 1999 Estate of Pablo Picasso/Artists Rights Society (ARS), New York; 373, © Steve Rubin/The Image Works; 374, © Robert Ginn/PhotoEdit; 376, © David Simson/Stock Boston; 379, © Gregg Mancuso/Stock Boston; 381, © Lichtenstein/The Image Works.

Chapter 11: 384, Scala/Art Resource; 387, © Jean-Claude Lejeune/Stock Boston; 390, © Jean-Claude Lejeune/Stock Boston; 394, © Elena Rooraid/PhotoEdit; 397, P. R. Newman; 400, © Hella Hammid/Photo Researchers; 401, © Spencer Grant/Stock Boston; 405, © Michael Newman/PhotoEdit; 407, © Elizabeth Crews/The Image Works; 410, © Rhoda Sidney/Stock Boston; 413, Art Resource, NY/ © 1999 Estate of Pablo Picasso/Artists Rights Society (ARS), New York; 416, © Spencer Grant/Photo Researchers; 419, Pablo Picasso, Spanish, 1881-1973, Untitled, gouache on illustration board, 1904. 41.6 x 29.9 cm Bequest of Kate L. Brewer, 1950, 128. Photograph by the Art Institute of Chicago. All rights reserved./ © 1999 Estate of Pablo Picasso/Artists Rights Society (ARS), New York; 424, © Michael Newman/PhotoEdit; 425, National Gallery of Art, Washington, D. C./ Superstock/ © 1999 Estate of Pablo Picasso/Artists Rights Society (ARS), New York; 427, © Myrleen Ferguson/PhotoEdit.

Chapter 12: 430, Private Collection/Bridgeman Art Library, London/New York/ © 1999 Estate of Pablo Picasso/Artists Rights Society (ARS), New York; 434, © Billy E. Barnes/PhotoEdit; 436, © Liss/Gamma Liaison; 440, © Paul Conklin/PhotoEdit; 443, © Kathy Sloane/Photo Researchers; 445, © Elizabeth Crews/The Image Works; 448, © David Young-Wolff/PhotoEdit; 451, © 1999 Estate of Pablo Picasso/Artists Rights Society (ARS), New York; 453, © Spencer Grant/Photo Researchers; 455, © Bill Bachmann/PhotoEdit; 457, © Richard Hutchings/PhotoEdit; 461, Bridgeman Art Library/ © 1999 Estate of Pablo Picasso/Artists Rights Society (ARS), New York; 465, © Bill Bachmann/The Image Works.

Chapter 13: 468, Giraudon/Art Resource, NY/ © 1999 Estate of Pablo Picasso/Artists Rights Society (ARS), New York; 473, © Louise Gubb/The Image Works; 475, © Lionel Delevingne/Stock Boston; 478, © Michael Newman/PhotoEdit; 481, © Alan Oddie/PhotoEdit; 484, Giraudon/Art Resource, NY/ © 1999 Estate of Pablo Picasso/Artists Rights Society (ARS), New York; 490, © 1999 Estate of Pablo Picasso/Artists Rights Society (ARS), New York; 492, © Timothy Ross/The Image Works; 496, © Monique Manceau/Photo Researchers; 497, © Gregg Mancuso/Stock Boston; 500, © Gary Walts/The Image Works.

Chapter 14: 504, © 1999 Estate of Pablo Picasso/Artists Rights Society (ARS), New York; 507, © Robert Ricci/Gamma Liaison; 509, © Karen Preuss/The Image Works; 511, © Skjold/The Image Works; 514, © Carl Glassman/The Image Works; 516, © Spencer Grant/PhotoEdit; 518, © Gale Zucker/Stock Boston; 521, © P. Davidson/The Image Works; 523, © Susan Woog Wagner/Photo Researchers; 526, © Jim Whitmer/Stock Boston; 528, © 1999 Estate of Pablo Picasso/Artists Rights Society (ARS), New York; 530, © Karen Preuss/The Image Works; 534, © Bonnie Kamin/PhotoEdit; 536, © Alan Carey/The Image Works.

Figures, Tables, and Excerpts

Chapter 1: 27: Table 1.4 from *NEWSWEEK* - Michael F. Roizen, M.D. © 1977, Newsweek, Inc. All rights reserved. Reprinted by permission. 29: Excerpt from *One Hundred Over 100: Moments with One Hundred North American Centenarians,* by J. Heynen. Copyright © 1990 Fulcrum Publishing. Reprinted by permission.

Chapter 2: 58-59: Excerpt from *Life History and the Historical Moment,* by Erik H.Erikson. Copyright © 1975 by Erik H. Erikson. Reprinted by permission of W.W. Norton & Company, Inc.

Chapter 3: 84: Excerpt reprinted by permission of the publisher from *The Ecology of Human Development,* by Urie Bronfenbrenner, Cambridge, Mass.: Harvard University Press. Copyright © 1979 by the President and Fellows of Harvard College. 88-89: Excerpt from *Family Portraits in Changing Times,* by H. Nestor, pp. 100-103. Portland, OR: New Vision Press.

Chapter 4: 96: Figure 4.4 from "The Molecular Genetics of Hemophilia," by R. M. Lawn and G. A. Vehar, *Scientific American,* 1986, 254, 50. Copyright © 1986. All rights reserved. 101: Figure 4.5 adapted from "Genetic Aspects of Intelligent Behavior," by I. Gottesman. In N. Ellis (Ed.), *Handbook of Mental Deficiency,* p. 255. Copyright © 1963 McGraw-Hill. Reprinted by permission of the author. 102: Figure 4.6 from "Familial Studies of Intelligence: A Review," by T. J. Bouchard and M. McGue, *Science,* 1981, 212, 1055-1059. Copyright © 1981 AAAS. Reprinted with permission. 104: Quote from "Success rate for an in vitro is only 9%," by D. Sperling, USA TODAY, 1989, March 10, p. 1D. Copyright 1989. *USA TODAY.* Reprinted with permission. 104: Quote from "A battle against biology: A victory in adoption," by J. Smolowe, *TIME,* 1977, 150, p. 46. Reprinted by permission. 109: Figure 4.7 from *The Developing Human: Clinically Oriented Embryology,* 4th Ed., by K. L. Moore. Copyright © 1993 W. B. Saunders. Reprinted with permission. 114: Figure 4.8 from Clarke-Stewart, A. & Koch, J. B. (1983). *Children: Development through adolescence.* New York: John Wiley & Sons, p. 65. 135: Excerpt from "Intergenerational buffers: The damage stops here," by J. Kotre and K. B. Kotre, pp. 367-389. In McAdams, D. P., and E. de St. Aubin (eds.), *Generativity and adult development: Psychosocial perspectives on caring for and contributing to the next generation.* Copyright 1998 American Psychological Association. Reprinted by permission.

Chapter 5: 147: Figure 5.1 based on W. K. Frankenberg and J. B. Dodds (1967). *The Denver Developmental Screening Test.* Journal of Pediatrics, 71, 181-191. 149: Table 5.3 from "The Origin of Personality," by A. Thomas, S. Chess and H. Birch, *Scientific American,* 1970, 223, 102-109. 151: Table 5.1 based on Ainsworth, 1973, 1985. 154: Table 5.5 from "Open communication and internal working models: Their roles in the development of attachment relationships," by I. Bretherton. In R. Dienstbier & R. A. Thompson (eds.), *Nebraska Symposium on Motivation, 1988: Socioemotional Development,* 36, 60-61. Copyright © 1990 by University of

Nebraska Press. Reprinted by permission of University of Nebraska Press. 162: Figure 5.4 from "Object permanence in young infants: Further evidence," by R. Baillargeon & J. DeVos, *Child Development,* 1991, 62, 1237. Copyright © 1991 Society for Research in Child Development. Reprinted by permission. 165: Table 5.7 from "Socioemotional development," by L. A. Sroufe. In J. D. Osofsky (ed.), *Handbook of Infant Development,* pp. 462-516. Copyright © 1979 John Wiley & Sons, Inc. Reprinted by permission of John Wiley & Sons, Inc. 180-181: Excerpt from *What Every Baby Knows,* by T. B. Brazelton, pp. 11-13. Copyright © 1987 Addison-Wesley. Reprinted by permission.

Chapter 6: 186: Table 6.1 from *Infants, Children, and Adolescents,* by L. E. Berk, p. 299. Copyright © 1993 by Allyn & Bacon. Reprinted with permission. 194: Figure 6.1 from "Variability in early communicative development," by L. Fenson, et al, *Monographs of the Society for Research in Child Development,* 1994, 59(5), 38. Copyright © 1994 The Society for Research in Child Development, Inc. Reprinted with permission. 203-204: Excerpt from "Play and the Acquisition of Literacy," by S. J. Hoffman, *Quarterly Newsletter of the Laboratory of Comparative Human Cognition,* 7, 89-95. Reprinted with permission. 222-223: Excerpt from "Beauty: When the other dancer is the self," by A. Walker, pp. 257-258. In H. L. Gates, Jr. (ed.), *Bearing Witness: Selections from African-American Autobiography in the Twentieth Century.* Copyright © 1991 Pantheon Books. Reprinted with permission.

Chapter 7: 245: Figure 7.2 from *Self-understanding in Childhood and Adolescence,* by W. Damon & D. Hart, p. 56. Copyright © 1988 by Cambridge University Press. Reprinted with permission of Cambridge University Press. 258: Figure 7.3 from U. S. Department of Education. *Readiness for kindergarten: Parent and teacher beliefs.* NCES 93-257. Washington, D.C.: National Center for Education Statistics, Office of Educational Research and Improvement, 1993; National Center for Education Statistics. Public School kindergarten teachers: Views on children's readiness for school. Statistical analysis report. Washington, D.C.: U.S. Department of Education, 1993. 261: Excerpt from *Dignity: Lower Income Women Tell of Their Lives and Struggles,* by F. L. Buss, pp. 172-173. Copyright © 1985 University of Michigan Press. Reprinted by permission.

Chapter 8: 279: Figure 8.2 from "The Architecture and Dynamics of Developing Minds," by A. Demetriou, A. Efklides, & M. Platsidou, *Monographs of the Society for Research in Child Development,* 1993, 58, p. 124. Copyright © 1993 by University of Nebraska Press. Reprinted by permission of University of Nebraska Press. 286: Figure 8.4 and excerpt adapted from "School and Family Effects on the Ontogeny of Children's Interests, Self-perceptions, and Activity Choices," by J. S. Eccles. In J. E. Jacobs (ed.), *Nebraska Symposium on Motivation,* 1992. Copyright © 1993 by University of Nebraska Press. Reprinted by permission of University of Nebraska Press. 298: Table 8.3 from "Violence in Schools: When Killers

Name Index

Subject Index